CW01209004

About the International Institute for Strategic Studies

The IISS, founded in 1958 and now celebrating its 50th anniversary, is the primary source of accurate, objective information on international strategic issues for politicians, diplomats, foreign affairs analysts, international business executives, economists, the military, defence commentators, journalists, academics and the informed public.

The Institute is independent, owing no allegiance to any government or any political or other organisation. The IISS stresses rigorous research with a forward-looking policy orientation and places particular emphasis on bringing new perspective to the strategic debate.

The Institute's individual and corporate membership is drawn from nearly 100 countries, and its staff and governance are international in perspective and character.

The Institute's work is grounded in an appreciation of political, economic and social problems that cause instability and conflict, as well as the factors that can lead to international cooperation. Through its 'paradiplomatic' activity, including the annual Shangri-La and Manama Dialogues, it provides oil that eases the friction of international affairs. The IISS has unique convening power, frequently bringing together defence ministers, foreign ministers, national security advisers, top military officers and academics to discuss pressing issues.

IISS publications provide authoritative analysis of world events, military affairs and conflict. They are read by key decision-makers and business people, as well as professionals concerned with foreign policy worldwide.

Alastair Buchan, the first director (1958–69) of the
Institute for Strategic Studies

Image reproduced by kind permission of the artist, David Poole

The Evolution of Strategic Thought
Classic Adelphi Papers

Routledge
Taylor & Francis Group
LONDON AND NEW YORK

IISS

First published 2008
by Routledge
2 Park Square, Milton Park, Abingdon, Oxon, OX14 4RN

Simultaneously published in the USA and Canada
by Routledge
270 Madison Ave., New York, NY 10016

In association with the International Institute for Strategic Studies
Arundel House, 13–15 Arundel Street, Temple Place,
London WC2R 3DX, UK
www.iiss.org

Routledge is an imprint of the Taylor & Francis Group, an informa business

© 2008 The International Institute for Strategic Studies

DIRECTOR-GENERAL AND CHIEF EXECUTIVE John Chipman
DESIGN John Buck
EDITORIAL Katharine Fletcher, Dr Ayse Abdullah

Typeset in Garamond by
RefineCatch Limited, Bungay, Suffolk
Printed and bound in Great Britain by
Antony Rowe Ltd, Chippenham, Wiltshire

All rights reserved. No part of this book may be reprinted or
reproduced or utilised in any form or by any electronic,
mechanical, or other means, now known or hereafter
invented, including photocopying and recording, or in any
information storage or retrieval system, without permission in
writing from the publishers.

The views expressed in the papers collected in this volume are the
authors' own and should not be taken to represent the views of the
Institute or its members.

British Library Cataloguing in Publication Data
A catalogue record for this book is available from the British Library

Library of Congress Cataloging in Publication Data
A catalog record for this book has been requested

ISBN10: 0-415-45961-3 (hbk)
ISBN10: 0-203-92831-8 (ebk)

ISBN13: 978-0-415-45961-7 (hbk)
ISBN13: 978-0-203-92831-8 (ebk)

Contents

Introduction   1
PATRICK M. CRONIN

1 The Evolution of NATO   31
Adelphi Paper 1, 1961
ALASTAIR BUCHAN

2 Controlled Response and Strategic Warfare   73
Adelphi Paper 19, 1965
T. C. SCHELLING

3 The Control of Proliferation: Three Views   85
Adelphi Paper 29, 1966
SOLLY ZUCKERMAN, ALVA MYRDAL AND LESTER B. PEARSON

4 Israel and the Arab World: The Crisis of 1967   121
Adelphi Paper 41, 1967
MICHAEL HOWARD AND ROBERT HUNTER

5 The Asian Balance of Power: A Comparison with European Precedents   195
Adelphi Paper 44, 1968
CORAL BELL

6 Change and Security in Europe: Part II: In Search of a System   214
Adelphi Paper 49, 1968
PIERRE HASSNER

7 Urban Guerrilla Warfare   265
Adelphi Paper 79, 1971
ROBERT MOSS

Contents

8 Oil and Influence: The Oil Weapon Examined   328
   Adelphi Paper 117, 1975
   HANNS MAULL

9 The Spread of Nuclear Weapons: More May Be Better   383
   Adelphi Paper 171, 1981
   KENNETH N. WALTZ

10 Intervention and Regional Security   429
   Adelphi Paper 196, 1985
   NEIL MACFARLANE

11 Humanitarian Action in War: Aid, Protection and
   Impartiality in a Policy Vacuum   520
   Adelphi Paper 305, 1996
   ADAM ROBERTS

12 The Transformation of Strategic Affairs   595
   Adelphi Paper 379, 2006
   LAWRENCE FREEDMAN

Index   679

Introduction

For half a century, the International Institute for Strategic Studies (IISS) has helped to define the field of global security and strategic studies through a series of influential monographs called the Adelphi Papers, which have appeared on an average of eight times per year since the early 1960s. The IISS – or the ISS, as it was known during its first decade, before it added another 'I' to reflect its international nature – inaugurated what would become a staple of strategic studies: carefully researched, scholarly studies which today fill the pigeonholes, inboxes and bookshelves of professors, journalists, *éminences grises* and policymakers around the world.

The meaning behind the name of the series remains something of a mystery. The Institute's original quarters at 18 Adam Street were located in an area of central London known as Adelphi (from *adelphoi*, Greek for 'brothers'), so named because buildings in the area had been developed by four brothers – James, John, Robert and William Adam. But the series title may also have been chosen for a less immediately obvious reason. In contrast to the obscurity of 'Adelphi', the title of the Institute's journal, *Survival*, was an overt – and apocalyptic – reference to the issue that had catalysed the organisation into existence: the fear that mounting Soviet military power might provoke nuclear war. Both publications were intended to widen the circle of well-informed men and women who might be in a position to make intelligent policy in the parlous Cold War era. Thus it might be supposed that the name 'Adelphi' was chosen to suggest the need to create a transatlantic, and eventually a global, fraternity or network of knowledgeable and influential thinkers to help preserve peace and security.

A single volume – even one as generously thick as the present one – cannot possibly do justice to the depth of insight contained in and breadth of issues covered by nearly 400 monographs published over five decades. In selecting chapters for this book, I have been forced to thrust aside papers that were hugely influential at the time of writing, produced by scholars who achieved (and, in many cases, are still achieving) well-deserved accolades for their research. All the same, this necessarily subjective, even idiosyncratic, selection offers a splendid promenade down 50 years of strategic thought from the middle of the twentieth century to the present. While some of the chapters in

2   *Patrick M. Cronin*

this volume illustrate the limits of what can be understood and foreseen at any given time (it is worth bearing in mind that the typical Adelphi Paper is written to remain current for about five years), others show impressive prescience, and all shed some kind of light on contemporary security challenges.

The book is partly inspired by the example of an edited volume that stimulated a generation of strategists, compiled during the Second World War by Edward Mead Earle, Princeton professor and pioneer of the American school of strategic studies, with the intention of providing Americans with an introduction to *The Makers of Modern Strategy*. Professor Sir Michael Howard, a founder and president emeritus of the IISS, upon becoming a professor at King's College, London in the 1950s, reflected on the importance and the uniqueness of that volume: 'Gradually it became clear what a huge and fertile field I had been set to cultivate and how very little had as yet been tilled.'[1]

The field of strategic studies was flourishing in the United States at this time; indeed the 1950s would be remembered as 'the golden age of strategy'.[2] Michael Howard recalls the challenge of establishing the ISS in the United Kingdom in this period:

> A flood of literature had been pouring out of the USA . . . by writers such as [Bernard] Brodie . . . Herman Kahn, William Kaufmann, Henry Kissinger, Klaus Knorr, Oskar Morgenstern, Paul Nitze, Robert Osgood, Thomas Schelling, Jacob Viner and Albert Wohlstetter. We saw one of our first tasks at the ISS as being to familiarise ourselves and our members with what these pundits were thinking.[3]

The Institute's first director, Alastair Buchan, persuaded leading thinkers to participate in a conference at Oxford in the summer of 1959 to aid this process.

Buchan was a shrewd choice to head the new European-based think tank. Born in 1918, he was no stranger to the tragedy of war, which no doubt influenced his thinking on matters of militaries and defence. Alastair Francis Buchan was the son of John Buchan, first Baron Tweedsmuir of Elsfield, Scottish historian, governor general of Canada, commander-in-chief of the Dominion of Canada, from 1915 a war correspondent for *The Times*, and author of *The Thirty-Nine Steps*, among over a hundred books. Alastair's paternal uncle and namesake was killed in action in the First World War in 1917 leading the Royal Scots Fusiliers.

Buchan, a lifelong committed Atlanticist,[4] soon built a reputation of his own as a gifted journalist. From 1948 to 1951 he was assistant editor of the *Economist*,[5] then from 1951 to 1955 the Washington correspondent of the *Observer*. After returning to London, he served as the *Observer's* diplomatic and defence correspondent until 1958. In that year, Buchan won the first Atlantic Community Award for the best journalistic appraisal of the North Atlantic Treaty Organisation (NATO). He went on to serve as director of the ISS for nearly 12 years, leaving to become commandant of the Royal College of

Defence Studies, London, and then Montague Burton Professor of International Relations at the University of Oxford, a post he held until his death in February 1976. Long after he had left the Institute, Professor Buchan would relish inviting his best students to join the IISS.

This accomplished man from a remarkable family restricted himself to the humble role of rapporteur at the Institute's first conference in 1959. But his notes and musings on the event were to be thoroughly ventilated: his report of the conference was to be the Institute's first publication, a book entitled *NATO in the 1960s*, and many of its ideas were echoed in the Institute's 1961 inaugural Adelphi Paper, *The Evolution of NATO*, incorporated in this anthology.

The original monograph was as modest as the musty, Dickensian Adam Street office itself, typed in plain text on plain parchment with numbered, rather than titled sections. Members of the Institute received the paper for free, with additional copies made available at a cost of five shillings, or 80 cents, per copy. The content, equally unadorned, set a standard for coherent strategic analysis at a time when there was a growing need for informed assessments that reached beyond the daily headlines. Although the author claimed Adelphi Paper 1 was 'concerned primarily with the central machinery and institutions of NATO', it in fact captured far more important verities about alliances and transatlantic relations. Above all else, Buchan grasped the overriding necessity of East–West strategic nuclear parity. His insights were no doubt aided by the illustrious cast of scholars and practitioners who reviewed the paper, including Albert Wohlstetter, Michael Howard, Sir John Slessor, Sir Anthony Buzzard, Raymond Aron and Helmut Schmidt.

Alastair Buchan's Atlanticism earned him trust on both sides of the ocean. He was appreciated in the United States because he articulated a rationale for NATO and called on Europeans to shoulder greater burdens and responsibilities, both individually and collectively. He underlined the need for a recovering Europe to spend more on conventional arms and to establish a European nuclear deterrent. At the same time, Buchan represented British and European interests. He recognised that only properly informed and engaged European elites could steer an abruptly ascendant American superpower away from the precipice of nuclear war. Alastair Buchan was, like his father, a fine writer, but his scholarly task was a difficult one, and it had the urgency of being undertaken against the backdrop of the Berlin Crisis – not the easiest climate in which to convince a broad network of people to be reflective and take a strategic and long-term view. But despite these difficulties, Buchan managed nevertheless to communicate a persuasive vision.

Adelphi Paper 1 picked up where *NATO in the 1960s* left off, with an appreciation of the fact that any large multilateral institution, and especially an alliance of democracies, was bound to face difficulties 'for the simple reason that it is much harder to initiate and pursue a constructive debate between sovereign nations than within them'.[6] NATO has always had its critics and those who question its relevance. Though Buchan genuinely believed in the value of the Alliance, he never flinched from airing opposing points of view. He realised that, to some, 'the organisation creates a distasteful image of a largely military organisation of severely limited usefulness, membership of which tends to embarrass the more liberal Atlantic powers in their relations with the uncommitted world'.[7] But Buchan was convinced that the world, lacking a supranational enforcement agency, needed the Atlantic alliance to build durable and practical institutions to withstand muscular Soviet coercion in Europe and the centrifugal forces of decolonisation, or what he called 'disimperialism'.[8]

As with so many Adelphi Papers that would follow, the Institute's first paper seemed to anticipate the future, arguably even presaging the Cuban missile crisis the following year: 'the alliance is going to have to withstand severe pressures in the years immediately ahead, even if it does not actually have to fight a war'.[9] If NATO were to withstand future crises, it was vital that the machinery of the Alliance be built on shared aims and common liberal Western values. Buchan observed that the Kennedy administration wanted Allies to contribute more to 'upholding the free world'. This contribution, Buchan noted, would have material, military and human aspects. In addition, it also had:

> a moral aspect, the development of a sense of common identity between American policy and [that] of her leading European allies, so that the diplomatic and political onus of confronting the Soviet bloc or representing the interests of the free world is not born solely by the United States.[10]

Contemporary arguments that America concentrates too much on hard power, and leaves Europe to be a normative superpower focused on the rule of law, illustrate the enduring relevance of Buchan's concerns about the common values and objectives of the transatlantic alliance.

For Buchan, the fact that US–Soviet nuclear parity made nuclear war unwinnable meant that changes needed to be made to the Alliance's strategic calculus. He found particularly myopic the mid 1950s US policy of placing a decisive emphasis on firepower over manpower, and persuading NATO Allies to rely on low-yield nuclear weapons and medium-range missiles to defend Europe. He argued that to prevent fatal mistakes, and to reverse the trend towards the proliferation of battlefield and tactical nuclear weapons in Europe, the European pillar of the Atlantic Alliance would need to be buttressed. It was necessary not only for Europe to counter Soviet power, but also to create a counterweight to American power. For if the United States exercised all of the power at its disposal, 'she [ran] two grave risks. The first [was] incurring the concealed resentment of European governments and public opinion . . . Second, [the US exercising all of its power] multiplies the effect of mistakes in American policy and increases the difficulty of correcting them.'[11] Something like the first problem can be seen coming to pass in recent episodes such as the divisions over the US-led invasion of Iraq in 2003. The second is a succinct explanation of why a powerful Cold War America was such a double-edged sword for its European allies: American military might, which could deter conflict, was also capable of precipitating it.

In this first paper, Buchan also lays out a *raison d'être* for the Institute and the Adelphi Papers, making the case that Europe can and should use the 'force of ideas', not only 'the idea of forces' – although he thought more forces could be useful, too. Europeans, he wrote, 'could make a vital contribution in the realm of ideas, but only if they were adequately informed'. Buchan worried that Washington had been 'largely tone deaf to the views of its allies during the mid-fifties' and he wondered whether 'the fact that the worst mistakes in American strategic policy – the decision to over-emphasise nuclear firepower, to distribute low-yield weapons to the allies, to continue primary reliance on the manned bomber – were made during that period, was not perhaps mere chance'.[12]

Buchan's legacy endures in his contribution to effective institutions aimed at keeping the peace. After his death, the IISS established a lecture in his name, to be given annually by a distinguished statesman or intellectual. In the 2005 lecture, given by the director general of the International Atomic Energy Agency, Mohamed ElBaradei, Buchan was praised for using such institutions to educate and engage the public and civil society in the critical issues of security, including proliferation.

Buchan's contributions to NATO itself were also noteworthy. He hewed to the conviction that alliances were means to larger ends; helping to define NATO's common ends so that the Atlantic community might cohere for the purpose of providing 'a better system of security and stability' he viewed as his lifelong challenge. As Henry Kissinger observed in the first Alastair Buchan Lecture in 1976, Buchan was a champion of the importance of what he saw as the inevitable bond between North America and Europe. 'Beneath the sceptical air', said the US secretary of state, 'was a passionate commitment to the values and traditions we cherish as Western civilisation.' Buchan's focus, added Kissinger, 'was not simply the structure of global politics and the roots of war; it was the central role of the West in preserving peace and giving it moral purpose. This Institute is a monument to his quest.'[13]

In June 1965, the Institute published, at nine pages, the shortest paper in the Adelphi series. Future Nobel Prize winner Thomas Schelling produced the pithy essay, entitled *Controlled Response and Strategic Warfare*, having spent the first half of 1965 in residence at the Institute as a visiting research associate. The then professor of economics at Harvard University had already published a widely acclaimed volume, *The Strategy of Conflict*, as well as another valuable study, *Strategy and Arms Control*, which he co-authored with fellow Adelphi Paper author[14] and future US government official, Morton Halperin.

In the late 1950s, Schelling had worked on game theory, particularly in relation to nuclear weapons and deterrence. In 1958, he came with his family to London, where he met influential scholars and former military officers interested in theories of deterrence and limited war. One of those influential men was Alastair Buchan, who was in the early years of establishing the Institute and who invited Schelling to spend time there to think and write.

Schelling's Adelphi Paper reflected on the cardinal security issue occupying Washington at the time. American presidents, first John F. Kennedy and then Lyndon Johnson, favoured responding to a number of military contingencies with flexible or 'controlled' options over employing an 'all-or-none' approach. Schelling observed that this was nothing new – in 1957, British politician and IISS founding council member Denis Healey had been among those advocating 'graduated deterrence', a sequence of threatened responses to aggression that was 'everything that "massive retaliation" was not'. The rationale of a flexible response policy was that it avoided reliance on military responses 'too big to be credible or too big to be wise'. In the context of 'general war', a showdown between the US and the Soviet Union, however, Schelling observed, the notion of graduated deterrence raised profound questions about 'the character of war itself':[15] *Could* escalation in fact be limited in conflicts between nuclear powers? Was war in the nuclear age even winnable?

US Secretary of Defense Robert McNamara had introduced the idea of a 'controlled nuclear war' doctrine in a speech in Ann Arbor, Michigan, in June 1962. He had proposed that, even in 'general war', destruction should not be unconfined, but instead deterrence should continue, discrimination should be attempted and options should be kept open. 'We usually think of deterrence as having failed if a major war ever occurs. And so it has', Schelling wrote, 'but it could fail worse if no effort were made to extend deterrence into war itself.'[16]

For an economist, Schelling had a keen appreciation for history. The son of a naval officer, he referred the new thinking on controlled responses and nuclear 'hostage-taking' back to Thucydides's account of the tactics of King Archidamus of Sparta. In his paper, he quotes the king speaking in Thucydides:

> When they see our actual strength . . . they will be more inclined to give way, since their land will still be untouched and, in making up their minds, they will be thinking of advantages which they still possess and which have not yet been destroyed. For you must think of their land as though it was a hostage in your possession.[17]

While acknowledging that the issue warranted further study, Schelling underscored the problematic nature of 'counter-value' or 'counter-city' strategic targeting, as opposed to counterforce targeting of military installations:

> One might pretend, in order to make war as fearsome as possible, that the obvious way to fight a war if we cannot successfully destroy military

forces is to destroy the enemy's cities, while he does the same to us with the weapons that we are powerless to stop. But, once the war started, that would be a witless way to behave, about as astute as head-on collision to preserve the right of way.[18]

Always one to use evocative analogies to elucidate complex strategic concepts, Schelling explains the concept of nuclear escalation in terms of kidnapping:

> If I [waylay] your children after school, and you kidnap mine, and each of us intends to use his hostages to guarantee the safety of his own children and possibly to settle some other disputes as well, there is no straightforward analysis that tells us what form the bargaining takes, which children in our respective possessions get hurt, who expects the other to yield – and how it all comes out.[19]

After spending a year at RAND in California, Schelling settled at Harvard, dividing his time between the economics department and the Center for International Affairs. One of the ideas he formulated while at Harvard, the notion that, in the absence of communication with others, a person will tend to make a choice on the basis of their idea of what is obvious or natural, was so influential that it crept into mainstream nuclear policy and doctrine as what is sometimes referred to as the 'Schelling Point'. Schelling was awarded the Nobel Peace Prize in 2005 for enhancing 'our understanding of conflict and co-operation through game-theory analysis'.

If the first five years of the Institute was focused on coming to terms with strategic nuclear parity, the mid 1960s saw attention turn to the dangers of onward nuclear proliferation. The Nuclear Non-Proliferation Treaty (NPT) would be signed in 1968, and in the run-up to that cornerstone of the non-proliferation regime, the Institute co-sponsored a conference on the issue at the Guild Inn hotel near Toronto from 23–26 June 1966.[20] Three of the most noteworthy speeches – by Sir Solly Zuckerman, Swedish Ambassador Alva Myrdal and Canadian Prime Minister Lester B. Pearson – were subsequently published as Adelphi Paper 29, *The Control of Proliferation: Three Views*.

Though he would later become famous for his work on non-proliferation and his contributions as a public servant, Sir Solly Zuckerman began his career as a zoologist at the London Zoological Society in 1928. He had, unusually, distinguished himself as a zoological researcher and professor of anatomy before he entered the debate on nuclear proliferation. During the Second World War, Zuckerman spent time looking at the impact of strategic bombing; it is likely that this work shaped his beliefs on proliferation and the exploitation of peaceful nuclear energy. His experience in the field undoubtedly informed his opposition to the nuclear-arms race, and added authority to his argument that it is important not to deny a peaceful world the benefits of nuclear energy. In 1960, Zuckerman was made chief scientific adviser to the

UK Ministry of Defence, and he subsequently became chief scientific adviser to the British government, a post he held from 1964 to 1971.

As a scientist, Zuckerman focused on the impact of the NPT on the peaceful exploitation of nuclear energy – a timely subject in 2008, given the renaissance of interest in nuclear power as a 'green', or at least non-hydrocarbon, source of fuel. He judged that 'the growth of world population means that conventional sources of energy will ultimately become scarce, and correspondingly more expensive than nuclear power'. Furthermore, he believed that it was a lesson of the history of the industrial age 'that no technological "benefit" can ever be stifled'. Developing societies had every right to 'harness technology as the basis of their new industries'. Ensuring security and survival must be coupled with promoting industry and prosperity: 'Whatever steps are taken – in the interests of survival – to inhibit the first [nuclear technology for military purposes] should clearly not shut the door to the second [nuclear technology in a world at peace].'[21]

At the same time, Zuckerman drew attention to 'the risk of opening the door to military exploitation'. Since 1945, a new nuclear power had emerged on average every five years, and proliferation, however gradual, would increasingly necessitate a variety of flexible safeguards; both passive and active restraints. Nuclear weapons were 'a hideous danger for mankind, at the same time as there are endless useful potentialities for nuclear energy in the civil field'.[22] The tensions between the dual uses of nuclear energy meant that trade-offs would be needed. While his colleagues on the dais at the Guild Inn stressed urgency, Zuckerman counselled balance: 'In our efforts to prevent the proliferation of weapons, we should not ... drive ourselves into the paradoxical situation that we deny a peaceful world the benefits of nuclear energy.' Though difficult, taking steps towards both disarmament and the effective monitoring of fissile material was important: 'The smallest steps forward in either field mean progress',[23] he concluded. Zuckerman formally retired as a governmental adviser in 1969, but he remained influential until his death in 1993.

Ambassador Alva Myrdal began her career promoting social welfare in Sweden during the Great Depression. Like Solly Zuckerman, she appears to have moved into the field of security studies in response to the horrendous experience of the Second World War. One of the first women to distinguish herself in international security in the twentieth century, she also helped to establish one of Europe's leading think tanks, the Stockholm International Peace Research Institute (SIPRI).

Her Adelphi Paper contribution begins by noting the paradox that, in the mid 1960s, both arms racing and arms control were thriving activities. This, she observed, illustrated the profound challenge of achieving nuclear disarmament. Her realism was passionate: 'The salvation of the world is not anticipated as coming about by some sudden stroke of redemption. It must be achieved, if achieved it can be, by laborious construction, using as foundations the hard facts of the military and political realities as they exist.'[24]

Myrdal sought to look beyond simple treaty-based approaches to arms control. Her thinking had something in common with that of the George W. Bush administration when it created the Proliferation Security Initiative (PSI), the ad hoc global coalition to check proliferation on the high seas. Like the devisers of the PSI, Myrdal favoured an instrumental over a classic approach to arms control: rather than waiting for a non-proliferation regime to work, she championed the wider adoption of the Swedish practice of 'verification by challenge', and was very much taken with the concept of creating regional nuclear-free zones, beginning in Europe.

While optimistic about non-proliferation in the short term, she warned that with China gaining in confidence and strength, and potentially unstable developing countries aligned against the West beginning to acquire nuclear weapons, the long-term challenges to non-proliferation were substantial. Ambassador Myrdal concluded by saying that 'Disarmament is no subject for small-scale accommodation, still less for technical or legalistic gimmicks. Disarmament measures must be as real as are arms and missiles.' In her view, there were two paths humanity could take, and only that of disarmament offered 'the chance to open up a widening path away from the horror world that man is conjuring up for himself'.[25]

Alva Myrdal went on to play a key role in the disarmament debate, winning the Nobel Peace Prize with Alfonso García Robles in 1982, and writing and speaking frequently until her death in 1986.

Lester Pearson, prime minister of Canada from 1963 until 1968, enjoyed a distinguished career in politics and international security that culminated in his being awarded the Nobel Peace Prize in 1957 for his efforts in defusing the Suez crisis through the United Nations. Widely considered in his home country to be the 'father of the concept of peacekeeping', Pearson played a pivotal role in strengthening both NATO and the United Nations, and in so doing carved out a distinctive niche for Canada in international negotiations as an honest broker adept at finding common ground. His work had a profound impact on Canada's approach to international security. Pearson's own ability to disarm opposing viewpoints could be seen in his Guild Inn speech when he quipped, 'the offensiveness or defensiveness of a weapon depended on whether you were in front of it or behind it'.[26]

His capstone address completes Adelphi Paper 29. His speech, entitled 'The Broader View', is redolent of the contemporary concepts of globalisation and interdependence. In it, Pearson states that nuclear weapons have created a convergence between national and international interests because 'the destructive capacity of nuclear weapons' means that 'it is the common *national* objective of all peoples and governments to remove the possibility that these weapons will ever be used'.[27] He warns that 'a further spread of these weapons . . . left unchecked . . . will one day destroy our civilization'.[28] Like Myrdal, Pearson felt that immediate action was needed.

The field of strategic studies underwent a growth spurt in the 1960s. The rise of the security think tank came about in no small part thanks to

American charitable foundations, the Ford Foundation in particular, which provided generous financial support to several research organisations, including the IISS. New security research institutions that were founded and expanded in this period include the Strategic and Defence Studies Centre at the Australian National University, the Canadian Institute of International Affairs, the Institut International d'Etudes Stratégiques in France, the Deutsche Gesellschaft für Auswärtige Politik in Germany, the Institute for Defence Studies and Analyses in New Delhi, the Graduate Institute of International Studies in Switzerland and the Atlantic Institute in the United States, to name just a few among a burgeoning wave.

If a West–East axis served as the principal analytic model for the IISS in its early years, the Institute also always showed a dedication to understanding military affairs in the round. This was a particular aim of historian Michael Howard, who was instrumental in establishing strategic studies in Britain; helping to create not only the IISS, but also a War Studies Department at King's College, London. Four months after the Third Arab–Israeli War of June 1967, Howard (then working at King's) and Dr Robert Hunter (then lecturer at the London School of Economics and later US Ambassador to NATO) wrote a penetrating analysis that placed that conflict in context.

In Adelphi Paper 41, *Israel and the Arab World: The Crisis of 1967*, both authors were at pains to apologise for the paper's alleged shortcomings, in particular regarding documentation and available sources. But they made 'no apology ... for attempting an interpretive history rather than – if such a thing is ever possible – a dispassionate chronicle'.

They began by observing that there had from the start been indicators that war could break out in Israel–Palestine, but that for some time, the situation had remained uncertain. 'This conflict between Jews – a nation without a State – and Arabs – a nation divided into too many States – was evident to some experts from the beginning', Howard and Hunter wrote. 'But it was slow to acquire international significance.'[29] By the mid 1930s, some two decades after Britain had assured its support for a 'National Home for the Jewish People' in the Balfour Declaration, 'the British had realised the full difficulty of the task they had taken on. Unless there was to be continual warfare in Palestine, the Arabs had somehow to be reconciled to the new arrivals.'[30] Thirty years later, 'the whole Arab world exploded into wrathful activity and the Great Powers suddenly realised that they had on their hands a crisis of major proportions; an imminent conflict between client states to whose survival their own prestige and power were deeply committed.'[31]

The 'central mystery' of the crisis, according to the authors, was what had driven Egyptian President Gamal Abdel Nasser to cross obvious red lines by sending forces into the Sinai Peninsula to occupy Sharm el-Sheikh and close the Straits of Tiran in May 1967 as, in his words, an 'affirmation of our rights and our sovereignty over the Gulf of Aqaba'.[32] Clearly, Israel would react with overwhelming force. 'The knowledge that Israel was likely to take action on her own unless something was done for her was certainly a major factor in the calculations of Washington and London.' Engulfed in Vietnam, the Pentagon could only look upon another war with 'undiluted dismay'.[33] But the United States felt obligated to defend Israel and thus, on 23 May, President Johnson announced that the straits were international waters and the blockade was illegal.

When Israel mobilised in spite of the intervention, regional opprobrium was unleashed. Many years before the era of Arab satellite television and al-Jazeera, Arab radio stations broadcast 'a stream of hatred, threats, and vilification. One after another the States of the Arab League fell into line and mobilized forces for the explicit purpose of [Israeli troops'] destruction.'[34] An issue of straits became an issue of survival.

If few foresaw the timing of the war, fewer still predicted its rapidity. It began at 7:45 am on Monday 5 June, when the Israeli air force struck Egyptian airfields. Israel occupied the Sinai Peninsula and the West Bank in less than a week. The Six-Day War ended on 10 June, but not before killing some 18,000 combatants.

The authors of Adelphi Paper 41 correctly predicted that, for military reasons alone, the Six-Day War would be found worthy of study by military staff colleges. 'Like the campaigns of the younger Napoleon, the performance of the Israeli Defence Force provided a text-book illustration for all the classical Principles of War: speed, surprise, concentration, security, information, the offensive, above all training and morale.'[35]

But beyond military effectiveness, the authors stressed that what was most impressive about the Israeli campaign was the acute political awareness it showed. Israel had 'observed a principle which appears in few military textbooks but which armed forces neglect at their peril: the Clausewitzian principle of Political Context, which the British ignored so disastrously in 1956'. Israeli officials knew that their political environment meant that fighting prolonged beyond a few days would not be tolerated: 'The Israeli High Command ... worked on the assumption that it would have three days to complete its task before outside pressures compelled a cease-fire.'[36] In the end, it got away with six, but Europeans and Americans had been unhappy when Israel disregarded a UN demand for a ceasefire and launched its offensive against Syria. In the face of international condemnation, Israel knew time was not on its side, and it needed to wrap things up fast.

In the Cold War context, in which every regional war had the potential to escalate into an East–West struggle, Howard and Hunter believed that 'tacit agreement between the super-powers to co-operate in preventing overt conflicts which threaten international peace and security' would be the principal check on unbridled regional wars, keeping conflicts contained and brief as in the case of the Six-Day War. However, neither power would be particularly eager to risk a second conflict to undo the results of any initial war, even in the event that one side had succeeded in its immediate aims. 'The lesson is a sombre one', they wrote, because, in this situation, 'a premium [is placed] on adventurism and pre-emption.'[37]

Sir Michael Howard has retired from the University of Oxford, where he taught from 1968 to 1987, but he continues to write and lecture. Robert Hunter, who would test his Middle East experience in a variety of future roles, including as special adviser on Lebanon to the Speaker of the US House of Representatives and as a member of the US negotiating team for talks on the West Bank and Gaza, is now a senior adviser at RAND and vice-president of the Atlantic Treaty Association.

In writing on the Six-Day War when they did, Howard and Hunter were providing almost instant analysis. From their vantage point, the impressive speed of the Israeli military victory was one of the war's most striking features. Perhaps this rapid victory, rather than the prospect of enduring Arab–Israeli tensions, was at the forefront of their minds when they concluded:

> Wars, it used to be said, settle nothing. Unfortunately the statement was untrue: they can settle many problems, and are sometimes, regrettably, the only way of settling them. But they also create new ones, sometimes so grave that one may look back to the old almost with nostalgia.[38]

In hindsight, these lessons could be open to challenge: this editor will allow readers to make their own analysis. But it is surely difficult not to see parallels between the Six-Day War and more recent conflicts, including both Gulf Wars and the current tensions amongst Palestinians (Hamas and Fatah) and Israel, in which military actions and the failure to achieve reconciliation have bred yet further grievances and problems.

The Howard and Hunter paper was focused on a particular region and a particular war, albeit a region and a war especially critical to international security. Many Adelphi Papers over the past five decades have offered similarly trenchant regional analyses. The constraints on a single volume preclude publishing across the breadth of this detailed national and regional expertise, but the following Adelphi Paper authors and contributors warrant a mention for their outstanding regional analyses. On Europe, the work of Philip Windsor, Curt Gasteyger, Christoph Bertram, Hans-Joachim Spanger, Edward Mortimer, Philip Gordon, Ivo Daalder, Uwe Nerlich, David Yost, Stephen Larrabee and John Chipman, who today is director-general and chief executive of the IISS, has been particularly illuminating. On Russia and the Soviet Union, Malcolm Mackintosh, Marshall Shulman, David Holloway, Helmut Sonnenfeldt, Roy Allison, Harry Gelman, Hannes Adomeit, Kurt Campbell and Eugene Rumer have all offered special insights; likewise on the greater Middle East, Geoffrey Kemp, Shahram Chubin, Claire Spencer, Efraim Karsh, Mark Heller, Adeed Dawisha, Yair Evron, Ali Ansari and Olivier Roy have made valuable contributions. Gerald Segal, Paul Dibb, Carlyle Thayer, Michael Leifer, Yukio Satoh, Rosemary Foot, Amitav Acharya and Evelyn Goh have written insightfully on East Asia; as have Raju Thomas,

Sir Hilary Synnott and Shekhar Gupta on South Asia; Ali Mazrui, Jeffrey Herbst, Ken Menkhaus and Robert Jaster on Africa; and Jack Davis and Gregory Treverton on Latin America.

A good example of an Adelphi Paper that combines an understanding of a particular region with broader strategic analysis is Australian scholar Coral Bell's *The Asian Balance of Power: A Comparison with European Precedents*, a cogent analysis of shifting power arrangements that retains relevance today.

Bell, who began her career in the Australian diplomatic service before distinguishing herself as an academic at the London School of Economics and elsewhere, boldly attempts in Adelphi Paper 44 the 'dangerous and delicate task' of applying balance-of-power concepts to a dynamic Asia.[39] Writing in the middle of the Vietnam War, Coral Bell was concerned about America's future ability and will to play a major role in regional order. Both the war and the wider project of trying to contain rising Chinese power carried, she observed, a 'very high cost'. Referring to the hotly disputed justifications for the Vietnam War, she added that 'the objectives of policy will have to remain swaddled in a certain amount of protective verbal flannel'.[40]

Today it might be argued that, while China's People's Liberation Army is enamoured of high technology, and no longer favours strategies designed to drag its opponents down in a struggle against long-haul insurgencies, as it did when sponsoring the 'people's wars' of the 1960s, the US by contrast is now keen to rediscover classic concepts of counter-insurgency of the kind that it employed in the 1960s against just those 'people's wars', albeit for use in different theatres. In 1968, Bell was worrying that America, crucial to Southeast Asia's balance of power, was at risk of becoming increasingly embroiled in a revolutionary war, as it succumbed to the attrition tactics of its insurgent opponents. 'The theory of people's war is for Chinese decision-makers essentially a theory about the *absorption of the adversary's resources*.' Insurgency offered 'a blueprint for Chinese victory by military proxy' by ' "destroying the enemy by drawing him in deeper to drown in the sea of people's war" '.[41] Reading Bell's paper 40 years on, one might have the sense that, if history is not quite repeating itself, there is nevertheless a certain symmetry between the events of the two eras.

Bell was also thinking about the challenge posed by a rising China long before that concern became fashionable. She pointed out that the integration of China into the emerging regional order would require Chinese acquiescence. She was not pessimistic about China's ability to evolve into a responsible global power, and saw as an encouraging sign the fact that the United States had, in her view, adapted remarkably quickly to its newfound post-war responsibilities for maintaining global order: 'one is struck by the transformation which a few years' experience of the burdens of the dominant power can produce.'[42] Alongside this optimism, however, was concern about the damaging divisions over Asia in Washington's policy circles: 'The reason why America's Asian policy has presented a rather dishevelled and disoriented image, like the feathers of a bird caught in passing in a brisk game of

14 *Patrick M. Cronin*

shuttlecock, is that the forces between whom the Asian policy options are batted about in Washington have been unfortunately well matched in skill and moral zeal.'[43]

Moving our focus westward, Adelphi Papers 45 and 49 on *Change and Security in Europe* were written by Pierre Hassner, who was at the time of writing a research associate at the Centre d'Etudes des Relations Internationales (CERI) in Paris. It is perhaps unsurprising that Hassner, who received his education in France, should have developed an interest in issues of European security, an interest that he pursued through his time as a research associate at the IISS in the summer of 1966 and which eventually led to his appointment as emeritus research director at CERI. Part I of *Change and Security in Europe*, Adelphi Paper 45, gives the background to issues of European security, while Part II, published in July 1968 and reprinted in this volume, examines the problems presented by various possible European security systems.

Hassner began by asking whether the future security system for Europe would be designed *for* or *by* Europeans. He went on to consider the boundaries of Europe, the definition of 'security' and the structure of an integrated European system – issues he viewed as vital, and which had been hotly debated in Europe ever since the time of the founding of the ISS.

Two points in particular strike a reader of these papers: how clearly Hassner writes about strategic choices, and how uncertain the future direction of Europe appeared just four decades ago. For Hassner, settling the 'German question' had been the decisive factor shaping Europe in the first half of the twentieth century; in the latter half the key issue was the outcome of the East–West contest. Thus, the future might variously hold a continuation of a bipolar Europe, the disengagement of the outside powers, a Europe of loosely united states, or a truly integrated Europe.[44]

If Europeanisation through integration were to prevail, Hassner added, it would need to happen in two stages: first within the Eastern and Western blocs, and then between them. He counselled a sober approach to the process of integration:

> The two basic principles, as enunciated by Stanley Hoffmann, would be to act neither as if tomorrow was already here, nor as if it would never come. A third principle is to be prepared to be surprised and disappointed by the actual settlement, if and when our efforts succeed.[45]

Hassner is an important representative of the erudite French school of security. Over the decades, a remarkable contribution to the IISS has been made by such intellectuals as François de Rose, Raymond Aron, André Beaufre, Pierre Lellouche, Thierry de Montbrial, Jean-Louis Gergorin, Thérèse Delpech, Olivier Debouzy and former IISS director and current council chairman François Heisbourg. Collectively, they constitute a vital element in a re-emergent, recovered European security voice; independent while caring deeply about preserving transatlantic bonds.

Introduction 15

Whether one is thinking about al-Qaeda or the insurgency in Iraq today, Adelphi Paper 79 by Robert Moss on *Urban Guerrilla Warfare* has many insights relevant to the contemporary security world. In contrast to Hassner's intellectually wide-ranging, but necessarily Cold War-era-tinted paper, Moss, who had taught history at the Australian National University and written on Latin America and Asia for the *Economist*, produced in 1971 an Adelphi Paper that speaks truths about terrorism and political violence that are echoed by the front pages of today's newspapers. Its relevance survives the contrast between the political movements and goals of its period with the transcendental and millenarian aura of the al-Qaeda movement.

At the time of Moss's writing, insurgency, in the form of the Maoist people's wars taking place in the countryside of many developing countries, was bleeding into revolutionary violence and terrorism, and migrating from the countryside to the city. Moss pointed to a recent upsurge in revolutionary violence, much of it concentrated on the urban environment: 'In Latin America, the heirs of Che Guevara have made the city their target; and Maoist groups in India have launched a terrorist campaign in New Delhi and Calcutta.' This urban political violence would continue, Moss predicted glumly: 'The kidnapping of ambassadors, the hijacking of aircraft and the bombing of company offices are likely to continue to be familiar hazards of life in the 1970s.'[46] Urban terrorists did not seek

> control of territory, but control of men's minds. They are essentially political partisans, for whom success or failure will hinge less on what happens on the battleground than on their capacity to get their message across, to erode the morale of the forces of order, and to induce a general 'climate of collapse'.[47]

Moss identifies urban terrorism as a subset of a wider phenomenon of urban militancy: 'The terrorist has a political tool; the urban guerrilla has a strategy for revolution (however utopian it may seem).' He includes as a long appendix to his paper a 'minimanual' for the urban guerrilla written by Brazilian rebel leader Carlos Marighella, who was shot dead in a police ambush in São Paulo at the end of 1969. Moss quotes Marighella on this guerrilla strategy:

> It is necessary to turn political crisis into armed conflict by performing violent actions that will force those in power to transform the political situation of the country into a military situation. That will alienate the masses who, from then on, will revolt against the army and the police and thus blame them for this state of things.[48]

Moss detected three main contemporary forms of urban guerrilla warfare: '(i) "Technological terrorism" in the industrial cities; (ii) Ghetto revolts and separatist uprisings; and (iii) Urban violence in the pre-industrial cities (notably Latin America).'[49] He makes three general observations in the paper about the patterns of political violence in both developed and underdeveloped cities. Firstly, he notes the importance of the disruptive effects of population movements and internal migration: 'The cities of the third world are like sponges, sucking in the surplus rural populations faster than they can absorb them.' Secondly, he discusses the sense of relative deprivation – what today is often classified as a 'root cause': 'Men do not rebel because they are deprived, but because they are conscious that they are deprived.' But, thirdly, Moss also notes that there are limits at least to terroristic urban violence, given the character of its perpetrators. Terrorism, he says, is the work of 'a tiny self-styled revolutionary elite', who suffer from 'the corrupting effect of the systematic use of political violence, and its reinforcement of the totalitarian impulse'.[50] It is difficult for a popular movement to survive as such if its leaders' arrogance leads them to disregard the demands of the people they purport to represent.

Although Moss never attempted to forecast the future, he certainly made observations about political violence and terrorism that are highly germane to today. For instance, among the terrorist methods he identified were the use of propaganda and the subversion of security forces – both tactics witnessed in insurgencies today. He also underscored the vulnerability of modern democracies to terrorism:

> Terrorism may prove to have the most dangerous effects in Western industrial societies ... ghetto revolts in the United States could disrupt the most powerful economy in the world and impose severe constraint on America's capacity to act as a great power. A sustained campaign of urban terrorism in Europe might undermine popular faith in the democratic system and raise the prospect of a more repressive form of government.[51]

Here a moral element to strategy is suggested, as Moss highlights a key vulnerability: the temptation to stray from their own liberal Western values that modern states can experience when subjected to campaigns of political violence.

In the 1970s, the focus of strategic thought was migrating from the threat of nuclear war, through 'hot' conventional war in the Middle East, to revolutionary political violence and terrorism. But another new theme also entered the arena of international security following the 1973 Middle East war: what German international relations scholar Hanns Maull in his 1975 Adelphi Paper entitled *Oil and Influence* dubbed 'the oil weapon'.

Maull, who was born in 1947 and studied in Munich and London, was a researcher at the IISS from 1973–74, and later served as European director of the Trilateral Commission. Since 1991, he has held the Chair of Foreign Policy and International Relations at the University of Trier.

In Adelphi Paper 117, Maull defines the 'oil weapon' as 'any manipulation of the price and/or supply of oil by exporting nations with the intention of changing the political behaviour of the consumer nations'. Such a weapon of course remains available today, not only to Middle Eastern oil producers, but also to countries as diverse as Russia and Venezuela. In the final analysis, wrote Maull, 'oil power is the power which stems from the dependence of the consumer nations on oil'.[52] He observed that, despite the risks associated with a high degree of dependence on oil imports, especially imports from the Middle East, as the immediate oil shock of 1973 was short lived, Western complacency about energy dependence soon returned and expanded.

The successful wielding of the oil weapon in 1973–74 was not the first time petroleum had been used to attempt to force policy changes from other states. Previous Middle Eastern conflicts had also triggered the weapon: in the 1956 Suez crisis, the Canal and the Iraq Petroleum Company pipeline from the Iraqi oilfields to the Mediterranean were closed and about two-thirds of Middle Eastern exports to Europe had to be re-routed or were cut off. During the Six-Day War in 1967, the Suez Canal was again closed, this time for a much longer period, and Kuwait, Libya, Iraq and Saudi Arabia stopped production following the outbreak of war.[53] Yet in neither of these instances did an oil crisis result. Maull's Adelphi Paper systematically addresses why the oil weapon scored such a remarkable success in 1973, when only six years earlier it had failed, and he contemplates what role it might play in future international relations.

While producer nations would always have to grapple with the problem of finding a common political objective that would enable them to act together, they had in their favour the rising dependence of Europe, Japan and the United States on Middle Eastern oil. Between 1956 and 1973, US oil imports had increased from around 57 million tons to around 300 million tons annually, with the percentage of the country's annual energy supply that was imported rising from around 6% in 1956 to around 17% in 1973. Dependence on Arab oil imports expressed as a percentage of total energy supply in 1973, while far greater in Western Europe (45%) and Japan (33%), had also increased quickly in the United States, to 5% from 1.3% in 1956.[54]

Despite this growing dependence, Maull drew a relatively optimistic, if very tentative conclusion about the future of the oil weapon. Oil power would continue because of the imbalanced trade relationship between producer and consumer nations. However, 'it may well have reached its peak and could lessen in the medium term. The only real qualitative increase which might come about in the future would be the possibility of being able to use the oil weapon selectively.' The 1973 shock notwithstanding, 'oil power is not unlimited except in the sense that it could trigger a vicious circle of growing and uncontrollable damage'.[55] Precisely because the consequences of using the oil weapon were potentially so great, and universal, while a future Arab–Israeli war remained the most likely context in which oil would again be used in this way, Maull reasoned that the rationality brought about by interdependence ought to help deter any such usage. A 'cataclysmic oil war cannot totally be ruled out', Maull wrote, but 'so long as the oil producers continue to supply the world with a vital share of its energy supply, the result would be a suicidal spiral of escalation and destruction on a world-wide scale'.[56]

Maull highlighted a fundamental paradox: namely, that the use of oil as a weapon was severely circumscribed and could well become more so, yet, at the same time, it was also likely to become increasingly powerful and important:

> This paradox is explained by the fact that the oil weapon, which is simply the ultimate sanction of oil power, is a sanction that will not be lightly resorted to but will nevertheless, by its very existence, constitute an omnipresent factor in international relations. Oil diplomacy will replace the actual use of the oil weapon because, while the latter is a relatively awkward and costly political instrument of last resort, oil diplomacy can make full use of all dimensions of oil power and the forms of power derived from it: threats, symbolic sanctions (embargoes without cut-backs, stoppages), wealth, military power and, finally, economic power.[57]

Maull also identified the trend of emerging economic powers in the developing world exerting greater influence in the international system. 'The net result of the oil crisis in 1973–74 was a fundamental change in the international political system. A new group of actors has achieved prominence and begun to exert its influence in world politics.' Although the rise of producer-country power would not be fast or apply to all oil-rich nations, Maull did nevertheless correctly observe the emergence of a new pole, if that was what it was, in world politics. 'These powers will assume a mediating position between the highly developed countries and the majority of the Third World', he wrote:

> They will in many aspects still be dependent on their great-power ally and their economic partners among developed countries, but their economic leverage will allow them to build a considerable and diversified power base, attracting surrounding states and areas which will then serve as raw material suppliers, markets and receivers of capital investment.[58]

Some 15 years after the signing of the NPT, nuclear weapons continued to proliferate, albeit gradually, more or less as predicted by Sir Solly Zuckerman. In this context, a leading realist theorist, Kenneth N. Waltz, offered up one of the more provocative theses published in the Adelphi Paper series. Adelphi Paper 171, published in 1981, was called *The Spread of Nuclear Weapons: More May Be Better*, and it challenged the conventional wisdom about the inherent security benefits of non-proliferation:

> Someday the world will be populated by ten or twelve or eighteen nuclear-weapon states. . . . What the further spread of nuclear weapons will do to the world is therefore a compelling question.

> Most people believe that the world will become a more dangerous one as nuclear weapons spread. The chances that nuclear weapons will be fired in anger or accidentally exploded in a way that prompts a nuclear exchange are finite, though unknown. Those chances increase as the number of nuclear states increase. More is therefore worse. Most people also believe that the chances that nuclear weapons will be used vary with the character of the new nuclear states – their sense of responsibility, inclination toward peace, devotion to the status quo, political stability, and administrative competence ... If nuclear weapons are acquired by countries whose governments totter and frequently fall, should we not worry more about the world's destruction than we do now? And if nuclear weapons are acquired by two states that are traditional and bitter rivals, should that not also foster our concern?[59]

Waltz challenged such beliefs because they dealt with imagined dangers rather than with carefully calculated likelihoods. 'We want to know both the likelihood that new dangers will manifest themselves and what the possibilities of their mitigation may be. We want to be able to see the future world, so to speak, rather than merely imagining ways in which it may be a better or a worse one.'[60] To this end, he proposed making deductions about this future world from the structure of the international political system, and inferences from the historical record.

The system and the historical record both suggested to Waltz that nuclear weapons could actually slow down rather than speed up arms races, that nuclear arms have in the past and would in the future be likely only to spread gradually, and that even a weak state with a nuclear weapon would be unlikely to launch such a weapon in anger. The dangers from further proliferation were nevertheless real and they included the risk – of which Israel's 1981 raid on Iraq's nuclear reactor at Osirak was a reminder – 'that each new nuclear state may tempt an old one to strike preventively in order to destroy an embryonic nuclear capability before it can become militarily effective'.[61]

Waltz was critical of applying different standards to different powers. Furthermore, he believed that the United States and others should provide security assurances to those countries developing nuclear weapons. He concluded that:

> The gradual spread of nuclear weapons is better than no spread and better than rapid spread. We do not face a set of happy choices. We may prefer that countries have conventional weapons only, do not run arms races, and do not fight. Yet the alternative to nuclear weapons for some countries may be ruinous arms races with high risk of their becoming engaged in debilitating conventional wars.[62]

In short, Waltz wrote, 'the spread of nuclear weapons is something that we have worried too much about and tried too hard to stop'.[63]

As we move into the 1980s, a concern with great-power military interventions in the developing world gains in prominence. Dr Neil Macfarlane, author of Adelphi Paper 196, *Intervention and Regional Security*, is a Canadian scholar who wrote his doctoral dissertation under the tutelage of Hedley Bull, the brilliant Australian thinker who took up the Montague Burton International Relations Professorship after the death of Alastair Buchan. On completing his dissertation, which focused on Soviet-supported wars of national liberation and Soviet interventions in the developing world, Macfarlane took up a research associate posting to the IISS, which he held from 1981–82. A manuscript begun during this tenure was subsequently finished while Macfarlane was teaching at the University of Virginia, and *Intervention and Regional Security* was eventually published in the spring of 1985.

The paper examines cases of intervention in developing-world conflicts and seeks to determine their causes and consequences, and the patterns they display. This was a timely issue when the paper was published because of three developments on the international stage: the increased capacity of the USSR to project force throughout the developing world; the diffusion of power, especially in the form of arms, throughout the world; and a growing dependence in the Western world on resources from Asia, Africa and Latin America – precisely those regions where today China is noted for its investment activity. The paper's case studies are Angola 1975–76, the Horn of Africa 1977–78, Chad 1980–82 and Afghanistan 1979 to the time of writing.

Macfarlane, like many Adelphi Paper authors, was apt to interrogate and clarify complex terminology; challenging ambiguous and subjective meanings for the benefit of his readers. He observed for instance that a definition of intervention, as a coercive military intrusion into the internal affairs of another state' failed to distinguish between action on behalf of governments, action against governments, and action taken in instances where no governmental authority exists.[64]

There were, in Macfarlane's view, several factors that seemed to make intervention more rather than less likely. In particular, he argued that countries fragmented along ethnic, religious, class and ideological lines tended to be the most susceptible to intervention. Not all weak states mirrored Angola's division among three major ethnic groups (the Ovimbundu, the Mbundu and the Bakongo), but 'societies which ultimately experience military intervention are generally lacking in political integration and chronically unstable, and their populations have little if any commitment to central political authority'.[65] The paper examines the ways in which the absence of legitimacy and popular consent makes weak states prone to outside intervention.

Macfarlane was ahead of the curve in thinking about the problem of weak and failed states. The IISS Armed Conflict Database tracks some 70 conflicts that are ongoing or simmering, and there appeared in 2007 to be at least two dozen or more very weak states in the developing world. Although some analysts have noted a decline in developing-world conflicts – following a sharp rise immediately after the Cold War — the fact remains that there are plenty of weak states that are riven with sectarianism. Afghanistan, Iraq and Sudan are perhaps the three most discussed today.

According to Macfarlane, the motivations of external actors for intervening vary. He identifies several not mutually exclusive motivators, including ideological commitment, the quest for influence, considerations of status and prestige, strategic and security concerns, and economic gain. Although the Cold War may have supplied more ideological justifications for interventions than does the current world order, even then the defence of national or regional security was a primary motive. For instance, Macfarlane concludes that the Soviet invasion of Afghanistan was probably mainly propelled by concerns about basic security:

> Growing instability along the USSR's southern fringe, and the Islamic fundamentalism which was in part its cause, provoked concern in Moscow. This was aggravated by the ethnic and religious affinities between the population in Afghanistan and the inhabitants of Soviet Central Asia, and by longer-term demographic shifts in the USSR itself. These factors encouraged a demonstration of resolve to defend Soviet interests in the region.[66]

Factors constraining intervention include the demands of alliances, domestic considerations and international opinion.

Whatever the catalyst for an intervention, there tends to be a divergence between short-term effects (interventions are often successful on the terms of discrete original goals) and long-term effects (it is far less clear as to whether the broader aims of interventions hold up over time). As Macfarlane writes, 'It is difficult to find . . . an unambiguously successful intervention.'[67]

Macfarlane's basic scepticism about the long-term value of intervention provokes him to an analogy about the right to bear arms in the United States: 'although possessing and using a gun may in specific circumstances protect one from harm as well as contributing to the social good, that does not mean that widespread personal ownership of lethal weapons is constructive or contributes to social order'.[68]

He goes on to ponder the possible future international regulation of military intervention, and in doing so anticipates elements of the vigorous debates over the 'responsibility to protect' and the interventions in Afghanistan and Iraq. He reasons that 'in the longer term, the record would suggest that intervention is likely to be unrewarding. The military instrument may perhaps buy time, but it is too blunt to resolve the political and social conflicts which provoked the intrusion.'[69] Macfarlane, who today holds the Lester B. Pearson Chair of International Relations at the University of Oxford, updated these ideas in a subsequent Adelphi Paper.[70]

By the mid 1990s, it was clear that the end of the Cold War had ushered in what some were calling not 'the end of history', but 'a new world disorder'.

Reading Professor Sir Adam Roberts' Adelphi Paper 305 from December 1996, *Humanitarian Action in War*, can give one a sense — widely felt at the time — that somehow the Cold War had been far simpler.

Civil wars, bad governance, massive economic disruption and natural disasters were of course not new, but the responses to them were. 'War, civil war, dictatorship, earthquake, famine and refugee flows have been familiar phenomena throughout recorded history. In the past, they rarely led to large-scale international effort such as in the early 1990s. Clearly there were some new factors at work.'[71] 'Humanitarian action as a response to war, and to violent crises within states', Roberts wrote, 'has been tried in the 1990s as never before.'[72]

Writing with characteristic clarity, always mindful of precision, and with what one reviewer dubbed 'the sturdy Englishman's distaste for grand prescriptions', Adam Roberts surveyed the contemporary security scene. The US involvement in Somalia had begun as a humanitarian exercise, but ended in the disaster memorialised in the book — and subsequent film — *Black Hawk Down*. The UN response to Bosnia was 'mired in controversy and largely discredited by the fall of Srebrenica in 1995'.[73] And then there were the actions in Liberia, Northern Iraq, Rwanda and Zaire. Roberts notes that 'the pendulum that swung so far towards humanitarian action in the first half of the 1990s has since then been moving in the opposite direction . . . Many countries are showing signs of reluctance to become deeply involved in war-torn countries and regions, even in a humanitarian role.' But for Roberts, 'the key issue is not whether there is a place for humanitarian action in international politics, but what that place is, and what forms such action can usefully take'.[74]

For him, the problem was not the idea of humanitarian intervention in itself but its execution:

> The central argument of this paper is that a failure to develop serious policies regarding the security of humanitarian action, and of affected peoples and areas, has been the principal cause of the setbacks of humanitarian action in the 1990s. Such security issues, the inherent difficulties of which are undeniable, have been handled repeatedly in a short-term and half-hearted manner, often with elements of dishonesty and buck-passing.[75]

One of the thorniest questions in these complex emergencies concerned the role of the military. Roberts writes that:

> The question of defining exactly what the military role should be and how great a commitment it required proved to be difficult and controversial . . . the record of outside military involvement supporting humanitarian action is full of instances of vacillation and retreat, poor coordination,

a reluctance to make serious commitments and take serious risks, and achieving at best only temporary results.[76]

In his systematic dissection of the issues, Roberts asked many salient questions, including which humanitarian actions actually saved lives and which simply prolonged conflict. Can humanitarian intervention, Roberts insists on asking, 'stop the killing as well as the dying?' His paper challenges the notion of a 'right' to engage in 'humanitarian intervention' as presumptuous, if not a slippery slope towards justifying any nation's whim to intervene anywhere. It also challenges policymakers to think more carefully about their ends and means, asking 'Has the increased emphasis of governments on humanitarian action been an abdication from serious policy-making?'[77] Roberts detects excessive short-termism and vagueness of aims:

> In many instances of 'humanitarian intervention' since 1990, the repeated emphasis on the word 'humanitarian' has gone hand-in-hand with the absence of a serious long-term policy with respect to the target country, except in the limited matters of providing food and medical aid, and trying to get rival factions to reach a peace accord.[78]

While Roberts does not object to the new term 'complex emergencies', and accepts both the definition of humanitarian intervention as 'military intervention in a state without the approval of its authorities, and with the purpose of preventing widespread suffering or death', and the fact that, as such, it represents an important exceptional violation of the principle of non-intervention, he does worry that analysts are concealing old problems by using new terms; the new label may have made it easier to intervene, but no easier to actually solve deep-seated problems. He also reflects that the term 'complex emergencies' 'fits, perhaps too easily, the ambition of some within the UN system to tackle simultaneously' a host of problems that are unlikely to be soluble.

For all the problems of humanitarian intervention, and Roberts identifies many in his paper, the demand for 'international humanitarian action in wars and other crises' was unlikely to abate. 'Even if humanitarian action goes through cycles of decline', Roberts concluded, 'it will not disappear; it reflects interests as well as altruism. Decision-makers need to plan for such action, offer assistance, and be aware of its merits and weaknesses.'[79]

Complex humanitarian emergencies proliferated with the end of the Cold War, but by the beginning of the twenty-first century, intervening in them tended to be seen in Washington as largely being a job for America's allies. The higher strategic calling of the world's preponderant military power, particularly after 11 September 2001, was to lead a global fight against terrorism. But if the United States was to be successful in this fight, Professor Sir Lawrence Freedman wrote in 2006, it would have to understand the differences between the period of the 1991 Gulf War, when a 'revolution in military affairs', or RMA, seemed to be having its effect, and those of the interventions in Afghanistan in 2001 and Iraq in 2003. The 'contemporary era', as Freedman calls it in Adelphi Paper 379, might be understood as the time of *The Transformation of Strategic Affairs*. Some eight years earlier, Freedman had written an Adelphi Paper on the RMA, putting the so-called 'revolution in information and technical areas' into a wider context. But during the administration of President George W. Bush, revolution had given way to transformation, although the impact of information technology remained crucial. Now the strategic environment was shaping military technology, rather than the other way around.

Despite the relative ease with which superior US-led military power was able to remove first the Taliban and then Saddam Hussein from power, there followed a longer insurgency in which US military dominance appeared less effective, given the need to control populations on the ground. As Freedman wrote:

> The US would not be the first apparently unbeatable military power to find itself undone by an inability to take seriously or even to comprehend enemies that rely on their ability to emerge out of the shadows of civil society, preferring minor skirmish to major battle, accepting no possibility for decisive victory but instead aiming to unsettle, harass, demoralise, humiliate and eventually to wear down their opponents.[80]

Freedman argued not that 'major regular wars will not occur in the future or that it is pointless to prepare for them', rather that, 'for the moment, the most perplexing problems of security policy surround irregular rather than regular war'.[81]

Adelphi Paper 379 addresses the difficulty that the US armed forces face in shifting their focus from preparing for regular wars, in which combat is separate from civil society, to irregular wars, in which combat is integrated with civil society. It contends that the political context of contemporary irregular wars means that the purpose and practice of Western democratic forces must be governed by liberal values if they are to be sustainable. Freedman also argues that the challenge of irregular warfare becomes easier to meet when military operations are understood to contribute to the development of a compelling narrative about the likely course and consequence of a conflict. Finally, he says that while it is vital that those employed by armed forces remain sensitive at all times to political context and to the role of narratives in shaping this context, a key test of success will always be the defeat of the opposing forces. 'Strategy is about choice', Freedman writes:

> It depends on the ability to understand situations and to appreciate the dangers and opportunities they contain. The most talented strategists are able to look forward, to imagine quite different and more benign situations from those that currently obtain and what must be done to reach

them, as well as more malign situations and how they might best be prevented.[82]

Whereas Alastair Buchan talked about a bipolar arms race and the state fragility brought about by 'disimperialism', Freedman writing 45 years later describes a contemporary system characterised by a much larger and more diffuse state system, and a trend toward the demilitarisation of inter-state relations, particularly among the great powers. The significant trends today are the creation of transnational networks, the supreme influence of culture and the importance of narratives.

The 1991 Gulf War saw the success, Freedman observed, of the kind of manoeuvre warfare in which the enemy was disoriented by means of highly mobile firepower, made possible by technical superiority and the skilful orchestration of professional forces. But if the successful execution of the doctrine of 'AirLand Battle' renewed trust in US military power, the United States was about to find far fewer foes willing to fight superior American military might on its own terms. Freedman cited a school of thought that spoke of 'fourth-generation warfare' (4GW) that, unlike previous generations of warfare (line-and-column, massed firepower and blitzkrieg), occurred on a dispersed battlefield, reducing the importance of centralised logistics and mass, and creating a tendency for victory to come through the implosion of the enemy rather than through physical destruction. 'The essence of 4GW lies in the blurring of boundaries – between war and peace, between civilian and military, between tactics and strategy, between order and chaos. Such war cannot be contained in either time or space.' Instead it spans the spectrum of human activity: 'Unfortunately, whereas the RMA points to a singular form of regular warfare, which because it so suits the US is unlikely to be fought, 4GW points to almost everything else.' 'The methods that are classified as 4GW are those used by the weak against the strong. Those fighting a conventionally superior capability wish to avoid direct battle in order to survive over the long term.'[83]

This new warfare has elevated the importance of what is sometimes called 'hearts-and-minds' strategy, which uses compelling narratives, or storylines, to explain complex events in a way that ensures that networks cohere and stay intact. In the new environment, Freedman writes, 'instead of being geared to eliminating the assets of the enemy, [military operations] might need to be focused on undermining those narratives on which that enemy bases its appeal and which animates and guides its activists'.[84]

Recognition of this new environment means in addition avoiding the temptation of succumbing to a reliance on air power, or believing in the idea that 'air power might work on its own, at least as a coercive instrument'.[85] It also calls for better strategic communications, and necessitates the careful and considered application of hearts-and-minds strategies. It is inadvisable, for instance, to strive to address local security and local grievances while simultaneously attempting state-building.

Of course, what the paper called a 'transformation' was simply the newfound prominence of elements of warfare that had been around for a very long time, and the shift to irregular war was:

> hardly novel. Those who served in the anti-colonial wars of the twentieth century would recognise many of the dilemmas faced by their contemporary counterparts as they try to think of ways to win over sullen populations by offering current security and hope for the future, acquiring reliable intelligence, setting traps while avoiding obvious ambushes, flushing out militants and turning some into informers.[86]

But in fighting on this well-trodden terrain, Western allies needed to follow a narrative based on liberal values:

> President Bush framed the response to 9/11 in terms of national security and it was on this basis that Afghanistan and Iraq were occupied. Within this framework it was accepted that the insidious nature of the threat required measures that could not be guaranteed to accord at all times with liberal values. In light of its experience since 2003 the Bush administration might wish it had handled matters differently. In particular, this experience has pointed to the perils of ignoring questions of legitimacy in the conduct of military operations.[87]

With 400 Adelphi Papers published over the first half-century of the IISS, the field of strategic studies could be forgiven for seeming somewhat well worn. But as we can see from the papers selected for this volume, the constant shifts in the strategic terrain, the breadth of the challenges and the rise of new actors at both state and non-state levels have ensured a consistently high demand for a deeper understanding of international security. As future scholars and policymakers confront the challenges of tomorrow, a good starting point would be to mine the research and analysis represented in these impressive monographs.

As the compiler of this volume on the occasion of the Institute's jubilee anniversary, I feel a privilege akin to that which I enjoyed in my first job after leaving the University of Oxford in 1984, at the Congressional Research Service. There I was granted unfettered access to the stacks at the Library of Congress, which in theory held every book ever published in the English language, or at least since the founding of the Library in 1800. A similar sense of awed discovery has accompanied the process of compiling this volume. I only wish the reader as much pleasure in reading these papers as I have had in selecting them.

Patrick M. Cronin, Editor of the Adelphi Papers, 2007,
IISS Director of Studies, 2005–7

Notes

1. Michael Howard, *Captain Professor: The Memoirs of Sir Michael Howard* (London: Continuum, 2006), p. 145.
2. See Fred Kaplan, *The Wizards of Armageddon* (New York: Simon and Schuster, 1983).
3. Howard, *Captain Professor: The Memoirs of Sir Michael Howard*, p. 163.
4. The last article written by Buchan before his death, which was written on the occasion of America's bicentennial in July 1976 and published in *Foreign Affairs*, was an essay about the deep interpenetration between Britain and America. Alastair Buchan, 'Two Hundred Years of American Policy: Mothers and Daughters (or Greeks and Romans)', *Foreign Affairs*, July 1976.
5. The Institute has always enjoyed an association with the *Economist*. The magazine's diplomatic editor, Edwina Moreton, sits on the IISS Advisory Council, and her late husband, Gerald Segal, served with great distinction as the Research Director of the IISS until his untimely death at the age of 46. Their remarkable daughter, Rachel Segal, assisted with this introduction before returning to Cambridge University.
6. Alastair Buchan, *The Evolution of NATO*, Adelphi Paper 1 (London: ISS, 1961), p. 1, p. 31 in this volume.
7. *Ibid.*, p. 3, p. 33 in this volume.
8. *Ibid.*, p. 5, p. 35 in this volume.
9. *Ibid.*, p. 2, p. 32 in this volume.
10. *Ibid.*, p. 8, p. 38 in this volume.
11. *Ibid.*, p. 27, p. 54 in this volume.
12. *Ibid.*, p. 31, p. 57 in this volume.
13. Henry A. Kissinger, 'The Inaugural Alastair Buchan Memorial Lecture', Institution of Electrical Engineers, Savoy Place, London, 25 June 1976. The lecture is available on the IISS website at http://www.iiss.org/conferences/alastair-buchan/alastair-buchan-lecture-transcripts.
14. See Morton Halperin, *Chinese Nuclear Strategy: The Early Post-Detonation Period*, Adelphi Paper 18 (London: ISS, 1965).
15. T.C. Schelling, *Controlled Response and Strategic Warfare*, Adelphi Paper 19 (London: ISS, 1965), pp. 3–4, pp. 73–4 in this volume.
16. *Ibid.*, p. 4, p. 75 in this volume.
17. *Ibid.*, p. 5, p. 76 in this volume.
18. *Ibid.*, p. 7, p. 79 in this volume.
19. *Ibid.*, p. 9, p. 81 in this volume.
20. The other sponsors were the American Assembly of Columbia University, the Canadian Institute of International Affairs and the Carnegie Endowment for International Peace.
21. Solly Zuckerman, Alva Myrdal and Lester B. Pearson, *The Control of Proliferation: Three Views*, Adelphi Paper 29 (London: ISS, 1966), p. 1, p. 86 in this volume.
22. *Ibid.*, p. 7, p. 95 in this volume.
23. *Ibid.*, p. 8, p. 96 in this volume.
24. *Ibid.*, p. 9, p. 97 in this volume.
25. *Ibid.*, p. 20, p. 112 in this volume.
26. *Ibid.*, p. 21, p. 113 in this volume.
27. *Ibid.*
28. *Ibid.*, p. 26, p. 120 in this volume.
29. Michael Howard and Robert Hunter, *Israel and the Arab World: The Crisis of 1967*, Adelphi Paper 41 (London: ISS, 1967), p. 1, p. 124 in this volume.
30. *Ibid.*, p. 2, p. 125 in this volume.
31. *Ibid.*, p. 15, p. 143 in this volume.

32 *Ibid.*, p. 20, p. 151 in this volume.
33 *Ibid.*, p. 21, p. 152 in this volume.
34 *Ibid.*, p. 25, p. 158 in this volume.
35 *Ibid.*, p. 39, p. 178 in this volume.
36 *Ibid.*, p. 41, p. 178 in this volume.
37 *Ibid.*, p. 41, p. 178 in this volume.
38 *Ibid.*, p. 43, p. 181 in this volume.
39 Coral Bell, *The Asian Balance of Power: A Comparison with European Precedents*, Adelphi Paper 44 (London: ISS, 1968), p. 1, p. 195 in this volume.
40 *Ibid.*, p. 6, p. 202 in this volume.
41 *Ibid.*, p. 8, pp. 204–5 in this volume.
42 *Ibid.*, p. 4, p. 199 in this volume.
43 *Ibid.*, p. 5, p. 201 in this volume.
44 Pierre Hassner, *Change and Security in Europe: Part II: In Search of a System*, Adelphi Paper 49 (London: ISS, 1968), pp. 24–35, pp. 247–61 in this volume.
45 *Ibid.*, p. 35, p. 261 in this volume.
46 Robert Moss, *Urban Guerrilla Warfare*, Adelphi Paper 79 (London: IISS, 1971), p. 1, p. 265 in this volume.
47 *Ibid.*
48 *Ibid.*, p. 3, p. 269 in this volume.
49 *Ibid.*, p. 4, p. 269 in this volume.
50 *Ibid.*, p. 8, p. 275 in this volume.
51 *Ibid.*, p. 16, p. 287 in this volume.
52 Hanns Maull, *Oil and Influence: The Oil Weapon Examined*, Adelphi Paper 117 (London: IISS, 1975), p. 1, p. 328 in this volume.
53 *Ibid.*, p. 2, p. 329 in this volume.
54 *Ibid.*, p. 3, p. 331 in this volume.
55 *Ibid.*, p. 17, p. 351 in this volume.
56 *Ibid.*, p. 36, p. 377 in this volume.
57 *Ibid.*, pp. 35–6, p. 376 in this volume.
58 *Ibid.*, p. 36, p. 376 in this volume.
59 Kenneth N. Waltz, *The Spread of Nuclear Weapons: More May Be Better*, Adelphi Paper 171 (London: IISS, 1981), p. 1, p. 383 in this volume.
60 *Ibid.*, p. 384 in this volume.
61 *Ibid.*, p. 14, p. 401 in this volume.
62 *Ibid.*, p. 28, p. 422 in this volume.
63 *Ibid.*, p. 29, p. 424 in this volume.
64 Neil Macfarlane, *Intervention and Regional Security*, Adelphi Paper 196 (London: IISS, 1985), pp. 1–2, pp. 430–1 in this volume.
65 *Ibid.*, p. 5, p. 435 in this volume.
66 *Ibid.*, p. 14, p. 448 in this volume.
67 *Ibid.*, p. 36, p. 478 in this volume.
68 *Ibid.*, p. 39, p. 482 in this volume.
69 *Ibid.*, p. 55, p. 504 in this volume.
70 S. Neil Macfarlane, *Intervention in Contemporary World Politics*, Adelphi Paper 350 (Oxford: Oxford University Press for the IISS, 2002).
71 Adam Roberts, *Humanitarian Action in War: Aid, protection and impartiality in a policy vacuum*, Adelphi Paper 305 (Oxford: Oxford University Press for the IISS, 1996), p. 10, p. 522 in this volume.
72 *Ibid.*, p. 7, p. 520 in this volume.
73 *Ibid.*
74 *Ibid.*
75 *Ibid.*, p. 9, p. 522 in this volume.
76 *Ibid.*, p. 8, p. 521 in this volume.

77 *Ibid.*, pp. 8–9, p. 521–2 in this volume.
78 *Ibid.*, p. 26, p. 537 in this volume.
79 *Ibid.*, p. 79, pp. 579–80 in this volume.
80 Lawrence Freedman, *The Transformation of Strategic Affairs*, Adelphi Paper 379, (Abingdon: Routledge for the IISS, 2006), pp. 5–6, p. 595 in this volume.
81 *Ibid.*, pp. 6 and 7, pp. 595 and 597 in this volume.
82 *Ibid.*, p. 9, p. 598 in this volume.
83 *Ibid.*, pp. 20–21, pp. 608–9 in this volume.
84 *Ibid.*, p. 26, p. 613 in this volume.
85 *Ibid.*, p. 63, p. 643 in this volume.
86 *Ibid.*, p. 93, p. 668 in this volume.
87 *Ibid.*, p. 48, pp. 631–2 in this volume.

1 The Evolution of NATO
Adelphi Paper 1, 1961

Alastair Buchan

Introduction

I have taken the liberty of introducing our new Adelphi Papers with a paper of my own. It represents purely my own views, but is the fruit of observations and conversations with officials and private citizens on both sides of the Channel and the Atlantic over a number of months. It is offered as a contribution to the forthcoming international debate about the future course and structure of NATO which cannot, despite Berlin, be delayed very much longer.

This paper is concerned primarily with the central machinery and institutions of NATO and only secondarily with the military and political plans that should emerge from them. I have, however, dwelt at some length on the problem of European defence in order to illustrate and emphasise the deficiencies of the existing system of intergovernmental planning and consultation. Readers must therefore excuse me if the paper seems in places somewhat negative in tone, and refers only to certain matters of high policy and controversy rather than exploring them.

A few members of the Institute have been kind enough to read and comment on this paper, and I am particularly grateful for the comments of Albert Wohlstetter, Michael Howard, Sir John Slessor and Sir Anthony Buzzard, as well as for the endorsement of the central ideas which it contains by Raymond Aron, Helmut Schmidt and others.

Alastair Buchan, November 1961

I

It is difficult for a large alliance of democratic countries to alter its objectives, its policy or its *modus operandi*, for the simple reason that it is much harder to initiate and pursue a constructive debate between sovereign nations than within them. The nature of the external challenge is seen from many different perspectives: new ideas are communicated only slowly, are easily misunderstood, and even when accepted must be translated in terms of different national traditions and preoccupations. It is like changing the course of a sailing fleet, beating up against wind and tide in the days before wireless – in this case a fleet in which the leaders of the vanguard can no longer be sure that the adventurous or reluctant captains sailing in company with them will necessarily respond in time to the movements of their helms if they suddenly adopt a new tack to avoid the rocks they see ahead, more especially if they tack in different directions.

The first purpose of this paper is to examine the pressures both external and internal, that appear to necessitate changes in the military and political stance of the North Atlantic Treaty powers, and an extension of the responsibilities of their central organisation, NATO. Its second is to consider pragmatic means by which the co-ordination of national policies could be improved. It is prompted in part by the need to reconsider several of the assumptions and suggestions contained in the first of the Institute's "Studies in International Security"[1], written in 1959, in the light of developments during the last two years. It has been written under the shadow of the Berlin crisis, and of the other dramatic events of 1961, but I have tried to look beyond them to the world of the mid and later sixties, using the clarification of official policies which these events have elicited as one among a number of guideposts.

The alliance is a more healthy and vital system than the number of doctors who are continuously taking its pulse might suggest. Certainly NATO is in no need of any synthetic injection, such as extending the responsibilities of its central institutions to cultural or economic affairs, in order to increase its vitality or its importance. But there can be little disagreement that, in this autumn of 1961, a number of developments have become apparent which makes it urgent to explore the maladies or maladjustments from which it is generally thought to be suffering. The Vienna meeting, the collapse of the nuclear test negotiations, and Mr Khrushchev's subsequent statements and actions on Berlin, suggest that the alliance is going to have to withstand severe pressures in the years immediately ahead, even if it does not actually have to fight a war. Though neither side has yet made an incautious physical move, or closed the door on further negotiations, the atmosphere of East–West relations is clearly deteriorating. At the same time there is a new Administration in Washington which has already signified by its actions that it is prepared to consider important modifications in the relationship of the United States to its European partners. With developments in missiles and satellites the strategic context is altering. Any doubts that still lingered two years ago that France might become at least a nominal nuclear power have now been dispelled. Britain is on the point of recasting her relationship with continental Europe. And a period of unrelenting change has produced many less dramatic developments.

Indeed, the pressures of change, not only in the extent of the political and military challenge to the Atlantic powers, but in the economic sphere as well – the need, for instance, to organise economic aid or to stabilise raw material prices upon the widest possible basis – has led to a revival of interest in the idea of Atlantic Union or federation.

It may well be that at some point in the indeterminate future it will be necessary to think in very wide and radical terms about the creation of an indissoluble political federation among the Atlantic powers. All that one can say for certain is that at this moment neither public opinions nor political leaders in the Atlantic countries are conditioned to think in such terms, or to accept such a proposal if they were in fact confronted with it. NATO is an alliance of sovereign powers, it has no supranational authority like the institutions of EEC and it is extremely doubtful if the Treaty could be amended to provide this without months and probably years of debate, except in the wake of some great disaster. The only responsible course at present, therefore, is to work for the improvement of those central Atlantic institutions that do exist, regarding the creation of truly effective means of intergovernmental planning and co-ordination both as urgent in their own right and as the essential preliminary to a more formal and far reaching pooling of sovereignty at some future date. An alliance has disadvantages as well as advantages for the nations who compose it: it limits their freedom of action, complicates their diplomacy, and exposes them to fresh dangers as well as guarding them from the old ones. If its protective and centralising functions appear to be ineffective or inadequate, the constituent nations could come to feel that they are getting the worst of both worlds.

II

Reconsideration of the functions and functioning of NATO is impeded both by its most ardent supporters and its most active critics. To some people in the West, the strengthening of NATO is synonymous with the cohesion and unity of the democratic world itself, forgetting that NATO cannot and should not attempt to comprise all aspects of the policy of the Atlantic powers towards the rest of the world. To others, the organisation creates a distasteful image of a largely military organisation of severely limited usefulness, membership of which tends to embarrass the more liberal Atlantic powers in their relations with the uncommitted world.

It is perfectly true that NATO has a limited function, and the creation of OECD to handle a different range of aims and interests has fortunately made this quite clear. NATO is concerned with the confrontation of the Soviet challenge to the Atlantic powers, with the "Cold War" and the deterrence of hotter war. Though this comprehends a large and growing area of policy it is not all embracing. But the point that concerns us is that the nature of this function is changing and that it may need a certain reorganisation of priorities and ideas to discharge even this limited responsibility. My preliminary purpose, therefore, is briefly to examine the external changes which require a redefinition of the scope of its responsibilities, and the developments within the Atlantic powers themselves which may call for a reorganisation of its structure and an increase in its authority.

There seem to me to be three developments in the non-Atlantic world which are gradually but profoundly modifying the whole context in which the original purpose of creating NATO, to assure the stability and security of the North Atlantic area, must be considered. The first is the mounting evidence, not of any dramatic change in the objectives of Soviet policy, but of the steady widening of the range of challenges which Moscow now feels able to offer to the West. This challenge was, of course, never a purely military one or confined to Europe alone. But what has become particularly marked in the last two years is the confidence which Mr. Khrushchev now feels that Soviet military policy has given the Soviet Union a new freedom of action, by multiplying the difficulties and dangers of exerting any direct pressure upon Russia itself, to challenge Western interests throughout the world by less dangerous and less obvious means than war.

To a considerable extent this confidence is justified. It is true that American strategic strength still poses a very formidable threat to the Soviet Union. It is also true that the United States has not yet lost the will to implement that threat, and, though there is no more talk of "massive retaliation" for acts of local aggression, the clear intent of American policy is to make the Russians very circumspect for fear of sliding into a nuclear war with the United States. But though the Soviet long range strategic threat to the United States itself is not as large in number of bombs or bombers as the American threat to Russia, her threat to the allies of the United States is very considerable. This fact alone is an asset to Soviet diplomacy for one of the unvarying aims of Soviet policy is the disintegration of NATO itself.

Moreover, with the steady transference of the strategic strength of both sides into increasingly invulnerable forms of retaliatory power, smaller ICBMs in hard or mobile bases, Polaris type submarines and stand off bombs, the ability of each side to maintain a counter force capability – to threaten the destruction of a high proportion of the other's strategic striking power in the event of war – must become a matter of great uncertainty. If, as the sixties progress the prospect of strategic war seems likely to involve, sooner or later, a mutual exchange of blows on great cities and industrial centres, the credibility of the American resort to it, even under extreme provocation, must become very speculative unless all the NATO countries were prepared to undertake programmes of civil defence so vast as to strain the resources of many of them and to create severe tensions between allies of unequal geographic and economic resources. Despite the continuing strategic superiority of the West in its diversity of long range weapons, the ability of the United States to exert direct pressure on the Soviet Union by a credible threat of strategic action, with or even without the consent of its allies, which has been declining steadily throughout the fifties, is now likely to decline still further, and very probably cannot be recovered except by crash programmes so menacing – space weapons for instance – as to be in themselves a likely cause of war.

What this uncertainty does is to dispose of any lingering Western hope of being able to meet Soviet challenges at a quite different level from that at which they are offered, to offset the tactical move by the strategic threat. To some extent this is already apparent. In so far as any move in Soviet policy implies a direct military threat against the NATO area, this can only be offset by the same kind of military forces which it is prepared to use. President Kennedy's statements and actions on Berlin make it very clear that he understands this. Tempting as it may have been for him to accept the view of some of his advisers, that the Berlin situation called for an overwhelming threat of American force, the plain fact is that the state of European and American opinion, plus the real strategic facts of life, would have made such a course irresponsible and disastrous. But Berlin apart, Mr. Khrushchev knows that his freedom to support "movements of colonial liberation" or to exploit the forces of unrest in Asia, Africa or Latin America is in fact increasing unless his agents can be thwarted, not centrally but at the seat of trouble, and generally by non-military means, a policy which he rightly believes it is difficult for the West to pursue. No better illustration of the diminishing cover of the American strategic umbrella could have been provided than the Laos crisis of 1961. Thus, Soviet policy is not only creating a necessity for a much wider range of Western military responses, but imposing the need to co-ordinate non-military policy in a way never envisaged in the earlier years of NATO.

The second external factor, closely allied to the first, of which any reconsideration of NATO's responsibilities must take account, is that the process of disimperialism, which has been set in motion by her own members, is inevitably creating a precarious world order that may take a generation or more to find firmer foundations. With the number of sovereign states increasing almost monthly, so the likelihood of situations if internal chaos or local aggression, a Congo, a Laos, a Kuwait, increase also. This danger has arisen at a time when the peace keeping machinery of the United Nations is still very immature and also is being actively undermined by the Soviet Union. It is one to which none of the NATO powers can be indifferent, since many of them have close ties with the new countries, some of them such as Norway, Denmark and Canada are actively concerned in the existing peace keeping efforts of the United Nations, and all of them would be immediately involved if intervention by other NATO allies were to bring them face to face with the forces of the Soviet Union or its allies. At the same time modern communications are shrinking the world so as to increase the speed and scope of action and reaction however remote the original seat of trouble may be from the Atlantic area.

The third inter-related development concerns the delicacy of the overall strategic balance of power between NATO and the Soviet Union which has been created by the combination of cataclysmic explosive power with very rapid means of delivering it. This has three effects. First, it means that all the military preparations of NATO powers must be considered with an eye to advancing the prospects of reaching at least limited agreements with the Soviet Union to mitigate the worst dangers of the delicate balance:— surprise attack, accidental war, miscalculation: and this in turn requires effective political co-operation in all military *planning*, especially of NATO dispositions in Germany. Second, it increases the importance of civil control over military *action*, and, in a world increasingly dependent on computer-fed intelligence, of interposing political judgement at all levels of military decision and reducing to a minimum the dangers of automatic reaction. This is a problem that affects the Soviet Union just as much as NATO, but is easier for her to solve. Because of the delicacy of the balance and the complexity of the technological environment the alliance can no longer hope to behave as an alliance in times of stress unless it can master the problem of central civil control over the central military command systems it has created, at all times and all levels of response. Finally, it makes urgent the development of a means of providing a unified political responses in swiftly moving diplomatic exchanges such as we have seen over Berlin. The speed of international action and reaction, the increasingly important factors of popular opinion and morale, the significance of the views of the uncommitted spectators of the East and West conflict mean that inter-allied disagreements over diplomatic strategy can undermine the political strength of NATO, in a tense situation, every bit as much as disparities of military power.

III

One reason why NATO has often seemed slow to adjust itself to changes in the external world is that the member governments are naturally averse (except in the wake of a grave crisis such as Suez) to acknowledging and adjusting themselves to changes in the balance of power within the alliances. Yet if the outside world has changed beyond recognition in the twelve years since the North Atlantic Treaty was signed, so also has relationship between the NATO powers themselves. It seems to me that there are three trends which have been discernible for the last year or two which must be taken as fully into account as external developments if the alliance is to develop greater cohesion and strength and its central institution to acquire greater authority.

The first and most important is the gradual change in the politico-strategic relationship of the United States to its European NATO allies and vice versa. Here there seem to be two contrary forces at work on both sides. On the one hand, as the problem of maintaining a credible system of strategic deterrence in the open West becomes more and more complex, the disparity between the strategic resources of the United States and the European allies becomes more marked. As the deterrent forces come to centre increasingly round the nuclear submarine, the mobile or hard based missile, and elaborate satellite or other early warning systems, the dependence of the allies on the United States becomes greater for these are programmes which not only require resources which no single European country, or perhaps all of them collectively could command, but are the product of continuous American programmes of research and development in which European countries have been only partially or fitfully engaged. Even if the European allies as a whole were to decide to compete in this sphere, they could not match the geographic advantages that are becoming of increasing importance in the missile era, which a large and relatively sparsely populated land area and proximity of the two great oceans give to the United States. One cannot avoid the conclusion that the strategic pre-eminence of the United States which was decisive even during the hegemony of the medium bomber is likely to increase whatever the strategic policy of Britain, France or the other European NATO allies, and whatever their leaders may feel or say about the impossibility of being dependent on another country for their ultimate survival.

In the short run this is also true of tactical forces. Because France is still heavily committed in Algeria, because British defence policy has not been readjusted from the disastrous misreading of the future which led her in 1957 to decide to return to a small volunteer army while increasing her nuclear forces, and because the dramatic economic growth of the rest of Europe has led to an acute manpower shortage in many countries, the main burden of increasing the flexibility of Western strategy and diplomacy is likely, for the next year or two, to fall principally on the United States which, for a number of reasons, can expand the size of her conventional forces more easily than her allies. Unless and until European defence policies are adjusted, the dominance of the United States in NATO will continue to extend to every aspect of defence planning. In terms of the kinds of military strength which will be most valuable in the years ahead, Britain, France and even Germany are relatively weak powers. Moreover, American strategic forces (other than her ground forces based in Europe) will become less and less dependent on European bases (except for valuable but not vital facilities such as air refuelling and submarine replenishment) as the main weight of American deterrence becomes concentrated in the Polaris submarines, and the *Minuteman* and the B52 based in the United States. This in turn will attenuate the already tenuous physical control over American strategic policy or decisions which some European governments have considered that they exercise by reason of having American strategic weapons based on their soil.

But in the larger political context, I think most thoughtful Americans would acknowledge that the United States, largely as a result of the external pressures we have examined, is now becoming more dependent on, and more directly affected by, the policies of her European NATO allies. For one thing, as international relations become more complex with the steady increase in the number of sovereign states, as action in one area tends to react more rapidly and forcibly on others, as Soviet and Chinese policy becomes increasingly concerned with discrediting the Atlantic Allies as a whole in the eyes of the uncommitted world, so the United States becomes increasingly affected by the colonial policies of her European allies or their continuing relations with their former colonies. This is particularly true of developments in Africa, the dark continent on which so much light is now focussed. The American attempt, in the earlier days of NATO, to stand as the champion of anti-colonialism while maintaining an intimate political relationship in NATO with Britain, France, Belgium, Holland and Portugal has not only proved unconvincing to the world at large, but has less and less relevance now that the three most important colonial powers are committed to policies of disimperialism which help solve the American dilemma but also create new problems for the United States just as much as her European allies.

For another, the Kennedy Administration has expressed a very understandable desire to shift more of the burden of upholding the free world, on to the shoulders of her increasingly prosperous and dynamic allies. This has a material aspect: it means greater European participation in foreign aid and technical assistance programmes. It has a military aspect: it means greater European participation in the defence of the NATO area, and assistance in the building up of the contingency reserves for possible use outside it. It has a human aspect: it means giving greater weight to European experience and knowledge, particularly of former colonial areas. And it has a moral aspect, the development of a sense of common identity between American policy and those of her leading European allies so that the diplomatic and political onus of confronting the Soviet bloc or representing the interests of the free world is not born solely by the United States.

In the relationship of European allies to the United States it seems to me that these two trends, the increasing military dominance of the United States and her increasing political, economic and tactical dependence on Europe, can be seen in reverse. The European NATO powers, whether they are prepared to acknowledge it or not, become strategically more dependent on American technological prowess all the time. Even Britain, which aspired to a measure of strategic independence must seek at best a wholly interdependent relationship with the United States if her strategic deterrent system is to retain any credibility through the middle and later sixties.[2] By the same token, the attempt to construct a French system of strategic deterrence around a small force of manned bombers by 1965 and around an IRBM by 1968, without American assistance, is now widely questioned, even in French government circles. So fair and well informed an assessor of his country's interests as M. Raymond Aron has recently recorded his own conviction that this objective is impossible of achievement in this decade.[3] In other words the United States is in an even stronger position than in the past to direct, or, if she insists, to dictate, the military policy of the alliance. Most European governments know this, and are beginning to realise that the only way they can ensure a continuing and steadfast American commitment to the security of Europe in the era of nuclear parity is by assisting the United States to develop more flexible forms of military response and defence.

But the group of allies with whom the United States must maintain close political relations are very different societies from those whose governments signed the North Atlantic Treaty twelve years ago. Most of them have recovered, and surpassed, their old economic and social dynamism: and they have restored and extended their own interests and contacts throughout the world. At the same time their confidence in American political leadership which was very high in the early days of NATO, is nowadays qualified; partly because of the mistakes of the Eisenhower years; partly because of the failure of the American policy-making process in Washington to mature and develop at the same pace as the development of American physical powers and responsibilities; partly, in the NATO and cold war context, by reason of a less ideological and more empiric assessment of Soviet political aims and the requirements of co-existence. Indeed, the American school of thought which has in the past been nervous of strengthening or extending the functions of NATO for fear of associating the United States too closely with the old colonial powers, has its counterpart, especially after Cuba, in the fears of many Europeans at being too closely associated with the United States in NATO lest they damage their own relations with the new or uncommitted countries.

It is obviously unwise to attempt any generalisations about an area of such diverse national psychologies and traditions of thought as Europe. What is beyond dispute, in my view, is that the restored pride and dynamism of Europe makes it likely that these countries will tend to play a critical or even obstructive role in the formulation of allied policy, unless a means can be found which gives them full responsibility of playing a constructive role. Moreover there can be no reason to assume that this is not a permanent development or is likely to be less marked when certain grand old men of a passing generation have quit the European scene, for the new Europe is not the creation merely of de Gaulle, Adenauer and Macmillan. Similarly there is no inherent reason why the new Europe should not accept the equity and logic of the Kennedy Administration's desire to share more of the present American burden with Europe, but only if Europe is given a larger voice in determining the policies which it necessitates. The change in the nature of the external challenge makes it as impossible for the United States to use her increasing strategic dominance in the alliance in order to lay down general policies for the West, as in effect she tried to do through a large part of the 1950s, as it is for the European NATO allies to develop or maintain independent systems of strategic deterrence or national defence. This increasing dependence of the two halves of the alliance on each other could be the source of enormous friction or of a better working relationship and more powerful central institutions, depending on the intelligence and candour with which it is confronted.

The second important internal development springs also from the recovery of Europe. The implicit assumptions on which the institutions of NATO, certainly the military machinery, were founded was that the alliance consisted of three powers with worldwide interests and responsibilities, the United States, Britain and France, and nine (later increased to twelve) countries whose primary interest was in their security in their own particular area. This view corresponded closely with reality in the early 1950s when Britain and France were still imperial powers in the old sense, and when the other European countries were still preoccupied with the reconstruction of their domestic economies. But the distinction is now becoming increasingly blurred. The worldwide responsibilities of Britain and France have diminished, though they are still of considerable importance, and Britain is becoming increasingly reluctant to use military means for the defence of her own without the support of allies. Moreover, the interests and influence of the other NATO countries have increased. Italy, for instance, has developed important economic, and to some extent political, relationships of her own with the Middle East and Eastern Europe. Canada is expanding her relationships not only throughout the Commonwealth but in the Far East. Germany not only plays an increasingly important part in the defence of Europe, but is spreading her interests throughout the world. Turkey is vitally involved in the affairs of the Middle East. Norway and Greece are now worldwide shipping powers. The Netherlands has an unfinished chapter in her relations with South East Asia. Belgium and Portugal still have a vital role to play, for good or ill, in Africa, (here it is not so much that their interests have expanded, as that the area in which they are involved is now of greater political importance to the alliance than ten years ago).

No doubt it is possible, on a narrow definition of overseas interests and responsibilities, to make out a case for regarding Britain and France as still "world powers" in a sense that the others are not. The essential point, however, is that the distinction is now too tenuous to be made the basis of an effective formula for allied co-operation and co-ordination of policy in the years ahead. The old one will die hard in France, for the notion of a tripartite directorate of NATO is dear to the heart of President de Gaulle, though many other thoughtful Frenchmen are aware how much the world is changing. But any attempt to implement it would create unceasing friction between the "great", the "middle" and the "small" powers in NATO, and markedly weaken their willingness to accept the risks and strains which membership of NATO involves.

Though President Kennedy appears to have made certain undefined concessions to President de Gaulle's view during his visit to Paris in May, 1961, it is clear that the only long-term solution is to find a way of drawing all thirteen countries (for Iceland does not claim to have more than local interests, though these she claims tenaciously) into closer association with the United States. For between them her thirteen allies have a range of world-wide interests, information, opportunities and commitments equal to her own, whereas no smaller group of NATO powers has. There would be a curious irony in erecting a Troika in Paris at the moment when we are resisting it in Geneva and New York.

The third development within the relationships of the Atlantic powers themselves may provide the incentive to develop such means of strengthening the political authority of NATO. This is the need to develop stronger regional associations on both sides of the Atlantic. The British government has now announced its intention of negotiating membership of the European Economic Community and it seems probably that within the next two years she (together with Denmark and possibly Greece and Portgual) will have become a full member of it. This change in British policy is likely to have certain very important effects within NATO. Quite apart from the recasting of her relationships with the Commonwealth on which so much attention has been focussed, it means that she is tacitly abandoning the attempt, which has dominated her post-war policy, to maintain a special relationship, in political and military matters, with the United States, and has accepted the force of the Kennedy Administration's contention that her influence in Washington will henceforward be commensurate with her influence, in Paris, Bonn and other capitals of continental Europe. This altered perspective in London is likely to have a double effect. In the first place, Britain's decision to give a high priority to her political and economic relations with her European neighbours and to enter an association with them (if she can negotiate the terms of entry) which is not merely consultative but involves a certain cession of sovereignty and a highly co-ordinated system of planning, should do much to allay fears that have long been expressed in France, and to a lesser extent in other European countries, of Anglo-American domination of the alliance, it should thus weaken the demand for tripartism. Secondly, since Britain, of all European NATO countries, is the one least likely to be attracted to the idea of a European "Third Force", the fact that she is quietly having to relinquish her special bilateral relationship with the United States is likely to make her all the more anxious to develop and strengthen the only existing forum of multilateral trans-Atlantic political consultation, the NATO Council. The same is also likely to be true of the smaller recruits to EEC who will be equally loth to sacrific the trans-Atlantic links. EEC may in time acquire some limited responsibility in defence matters, even perhaps come to discharge some of the functions of the abortive EDC, but not if it means precluding European governments from contact with the source of virtually all Western strategic power, the United States. The political and military development of EEC is therefore dependent upon the strengthening of NATO.

By the same token, Canada will almost certainly feel impelled to accept membership of the Organisation of American States. This is a move that is clearly desirable in its own right. But Canada will be loth to become more deeply involved in the affairs of her own hemisphere unless her lines of political communication, not just with Britain but with Europe as a whole, can be kept open and improved.

IV

If one is right in thinking that these six developments – the widening of the Soviet challenge to the West as a consequence of nuclear parity; the growing difficulty of maintaining a stable system of international relations in the age of disimperialism; the importance of civil control over military decision and of unified diplomatic action; the increasing military dependence of Europe on the United States and the growing political dependence of the United States on Europe; the blurring of the old distinction in NATO between powers of greater and lesser interests; and the needs and desire to offset the trend toward regionalism within the alliance – are those which are likely to be most important for, and to have the most far reaching effect upon security and cohesion, then certain conclusions seem to me to follow. The first is that the significance and authority of the political institutions of the alliance must be enhanced. The importance of a resolution of conflicting interests outside the NATO area is now as great as making common cause over those that directly affect the Atlantic area itself. Allied with this is the need to develop entirely new means of interposing political judgement between every step of military planning, long term or emergency. And both problems require an allied solution since a closer working arrangement on political questions merely between the larger powers in NATO no longer meets the needs of the case.

The second is that the defence of Europe, which will remain the central responsibility of NATO, needs reconsideration, not merely in the light of the Berlin crisis, but of changes in the strategic and technological environment, and the altering European-American relationship.

The third derives, perhaps, from the other two, the need to maintain a high degree of internal confidence and external caution and resolution by developing a new relationship between the political institutions of NATO on the one hand, and strategic weapons and the planning that surrounds them on the other.

V

In the early days of NATO the principal emphasis of the allied governments was on the speediest possible development of central military commands. The central political institutions, the NATO Council with its fifteen permanent representatives and the office of the Secretary General and his staff were developed more slowly, and until 1956 or 1957 were considered by the member governments to be less important. The shock of the Suez debacle gave rise to the Committee of Three, Mr. Lester Pearson of Canada, Signor Martino of Italy, and Mr. Halvard Lange of Norway, and on their recommendation the powers of the Secretary-General were enhanced and the Council's terms of reference were widened to include discussion of questions outside the NATO area. But despite these reforms of five years ago neither the Council nor the NATO secretariat wield the authority or are equipped for the responsibilities which the need for a high degree of political co-ordination imposes.

What are these responsibilities? They seem to divide into two categories, those concerned with the direct confrontation of the Soviet Union in Europe, and those deriving from the need to maintain a stable pattern of international relationships in the rest of the world. The third responsibility, of possible control over military decisions, I shall leave for later consideration.

Now it would be absurd to suggest that the NATO Council does not spend a great deal of its time in considering questions of European security and the fact that it does, that the representatives of the smaller or more exposed European powers are in constant touch with American, British or French views and support, partly accounts for the fact that Soviet attempts to apply pressure and blackmail on them in turn has met with only marginal success.

But regular consultation on problems or threats as they arise is one thing, joint planning is quite another. Two points cannot fail to impress the outside observer of the operations of NATO. The first is that the NATO Council in Paris has little authority over the military planning either of the Standing Group and the Military Committee in Washington or of their most dynamic subordinate command, Supreme Headquarters Europe. It is consulted, it is informed, it is advised by the military authorities as occasion serves, but it does not wield any real authority over the work of the international military institutions of the alliance, in any way comparable to that which national cabinets wield over national military planning. The Council thus has little power to determine the military environment in which it may be asked to reach political judgements. As such it can, for the most part, only function as a clearing house of individual national aspirations and anxieties.

In the second place, the permanent NATO Secretariat is not a strong enough body to undertake effective long range planning on behalf of the alliance. Except in certain specialised and technical financial fields, governments have not encouraged the formation of a civil staff of high enough calibre to act as an international policy co-ordination centre, which will earn the respect of governments in the way that the staff of OEEC has done or as the new "Eurocrats" in the central institutions of EEC are earning it.

It may be argued that this is a false analogy, that it is impossible to attempt long range or detailed political planning in the same way in which it has proved both necessary and possible for international staffs to make long range economic forecasts or military plans. (The relative unimportance of the Policy Planning Staff in the State Department can be cited as evidence.) This is true of many aspects of politics and diplomacy but not all. In Europe especially there are certain intractable or endemic problems (made intractable as much by differences between allies as between the alliance and Russia) which call for the kind of continuing concentration which only a high class staff can bring to bear. It was, for instance, a rude shock to discover that virtually no international staff work had been done on the Berlin problem between the ending of the 1958/9 crisis and the recrudescense of the Soviet threat to Berlin in the spring of 1961. We may pay very dearly for this.

A crucial area of policy to which NATO, as an institution, has made virtually no contribution is arms control and those aspects of disarmament policy that would affect Europe. Yet this is as central to the aims and responsibilities of the alliance as military planning, and in many ways much more difficult; because there is no central staff in the NATO secretariat permanently at work on those problems, the plans formulated by national governments, often hastily, have more than once foundered on the hostility of other member governments to them (perhaps because their officials have not devoted consistent attention to the problem) or else on the natural caution of the international military staffs.[4] A great deal of consistent attention is now being devoted to arms control and disarmament policy by the United States government and American universities. But little of this is communicated to other governments in NATO, without whose support the United States is unlikely to make much headway with the Soviet Union or in the United Nations. Certainly as far as the application of American ideas is concerned, one can be quite certain that a common policy cannot be evolved, without the creation of a joint staff to work on it, and NATO is clearly the right place to create such a team.

Yet another field in which the views of NATO, the civil institution, as distinct from SHAPE, the military headquarters, carry little weight is the evaluation of trends in the policy of the Soviet Union or other countries potentially hostile to the alliance. By this I do not mean either purely military intelligence or intelligence gathering which is so delicate a task that it can probably only be conducted by national governments. What I do mean is the evaluation of intentions and broad trends of Soviet and Communist policy by competent experts. So often one hears an official of one NATO government bewailing the fact that another government places quite a different interpretation on Soviet policy and ascribing difficulties in achieving joint action or a common outlook to this cause. Insofar as this can be corrected, NATO is clearly the place in which to make the attempt, not by occasional conferences, but by having an influential international staff continuously considering the evidence. Here the blurring of the old distinction between the "great" and the lesser powers is relevant; the smaller NATO powers with their widening interests now often have important insights to contribute to the views of the larger powers.

On questions of European and Atlantic security, it seems to me that events have demonstrated clearly that intergovernmental consultation alone is no longer adequate to the demands of the Sixties, and that nothing less than the evolution of a system of joint political planning by a strong international staff will give governments the necessary foundation on which to develop a more unified policy. But the problem of dealing with situations outside the NATO area is more complex.

The need is obvious, for, as the world shrinks, the extent to which the unilateral action of one NATO power directly affects the interests and security of the others increases sharply. The events of the post-war years provide direct evidence of this. The failure of Belgium to launch the Congo as a viable sovereign state and the consequent chaos which ensued, not only complicated the task and jeopardised the authority of the UN on whose effective functioning all the members of NATO are dependent (though President de Gaulle may at present think otherwise), but also jeopardised British and French relationships with their Commonwealth and Community associates in Africa. Conversely, the pace of British and French policy in Africa has had a profound effect on the position of Belgium and Portugal. American policy in Latin America – and not just the Cuban debacle – now increasingly affects the interests of her NATO allies there, just as her Asian and African policies interact upon theirs. At one of the focal points of the cold war the failure of France and the United States to co-ordinate their local policies in the successor states of Indo-China during the past seven years has not only harmed those two countries, but the West as a whole.

There is no simple answer here. To suggest, even if it were acceptable to the NATO governments concerned, that the same kind of joint planning should be developed as for questions of European policy would be a mistake. The new countries – most particularly in Africa – are intensely suspicious of any effort to devise a monolithic Western policy towards them. An overt attempt to create "a political general staff", as some American and some Europeans (notably Sir Anthony Eden) have suggested, would do considerably more harm than good. At the same time the hopes that are still nourished in many NATO countries that somehow or other it can be made clear to the uncommitted world that NATO is concerned purely with the confrontation of Russia and that membership of it implies no support for the policies of other allies in other parts of the world, are proving a delusion.

This does not mean that NATO should try and plan a collective policy for action in the non-NATO world. But it does mean that its member governments now have an absolute duty to inform their allies, and to submit, through the NATO Council, their policies and plans for action in other parts of the world to the collective judgement of a group of allies whose interests are more and more closely inter-related. It could be argued that this can be done through the ordinary process of diplomacy. But collective judgements are sometimes more valuable that individual ones. The new Belgian government now wisely takes the line that it would prefer to have its African policy actively criticised in the NATO Council than be heard in polite silence by its allies and then to see them vote against it at the UN. The United States might have been deterred from its Cuban folly if it had over asked its NATO allies to help it assess the balance of risks in the Caribbean (just as the British and French decision to make war on Egypt would never have survived discussion in the NATO Council).

It can also be argued that to accept such a commitment to consult one's allies would lead to inaction and paralysis on the part of the major powers. I find this argument unconvincing. For one thing, there is no virtue in action for its own sake and there is a high premium on avoiding rash action outside the NATO area. For another, in the delicate balance of contemporary international affairs it is unlikely that the acts of the leading NATO powers in Africa, the Middle East or Asia will achieve their purpose unless they have the support of their Atlantic allies.

At this moment Angola presents, in many ways, as difficult a problem for the alliance as Berlin. There may be a justification for Dr Salazar's colonial policy, but it is hard to discern it, and the basic assumptions of Portuguese policy, and the methods used to enforce them, are in flat contradiction with those which govern the aims and actions of the other colonial powers in NATO, and the non-colonial allies who are almost as closely affected. Portugal may have to be persuaded to change the whole foundation of her colonial policy if the word NATO is not to stink in African nostrils, and all the member countries to suffer in greater or lesser degree. Yet where can such a resolution of conflicting views and interests be reached if not in the NATO Council. Unlike the UN its deliberations are private and discreet: it comprises those countries on whose goodwill the security and prosperity of Portugal are wholly dependent: and they can, if they must, wield the ultimate sanction of expulsion, for the military contribution to NATO of Portugal is negligible and her strategic value is now greatly diminished. If the allies cannot persuade Portugal to modify her colonial policy, then world opinion, Communist, non-aligned or even in the NATO countries themselves, can only conclude that the political institutions of the alliance are mere facades.

I do not mean to suggest that consultation on wider problems, or those outside the NATO area, should in any way be given priority over the evolution of a common policy on European questions or those concerned with the military confrontation of the Soviet Union. Any such idea would be absurd. But the one is essential to the other in the sense that the smaller countries in the alliance can only be expected to have a degree of confidence in NATO, to give its interests a high priority in their planning, to accept the risks as well as benefits which membership confers, if it gives them access to the American, British and French policy-making process and an opportunity to exert an influence upon it over a wide range of questions, in a way which the conventional diplomatic intercourse of friendly countries would not. Since their interests are becoming increasingly extended, intimate knowledge of the factors which may decide American policy toward, say, South East Asia or British policy in the Persian Gulf, has a distinct bearing on their readiness to face the strains of a Berlin crisis. Moreover, there are broad questions of national policy to which a proper answer can only be givern after candid discussion in NATO. The most obvious one at present is whether Britain should try to help keep the peace in the Middle East and Far East by maintaining nearly half her forces there at great cost or whether she should concentrate her strength more in Europe. The argument is a finely balanced one in terms of the interests of the allies as much as Britain, but I doubt if it can be satisfactorily solved by national discussion alone.

The third reform of the political machinery of NATO concerns the status of the members of the Council. For the past ten years the NATO countries have for the most part, appointed professional diplomats as their permanent representatives on the Council. The value of the NATO Council is enormous, for it is the only body of Western political representatives which meets regularly every week or more often (in addition to the Spring and December meetings of Foreign Ministers). Important subjects can thus be discussed by men who have a thorough knowledge of oach others' minds and without creating the sense of crisis which special gatherings of Ministers or officials from different capitals tend to cause. But it is doubtful whether, if the

Secretariat is to be strengthened, if the terms of reference of the Council are to be widened, and if it is to acquire certain operational responsibilities which we will discuss later, professional diplomats can carry enough weight with their own governments and public opinions to make the Council the really influential centre of discussion and decision that the course of events now demands. Skilful and experienced as professionals may be in dealing with the agenda of the Council, there seems to me a strong case for appointing men with political standing in their own country, who can speak directly to the heads of governments and, where constitutionally possible, to parliaments. There is no question of abandoning the extremely useful rules of privacy which govern discussion in the Council: the point is to have a man who can convince his own public opinion by direct means that the interests of his country have not been overlooked in reaching a decision which may not be wholly palatable, after full and candid discussion with his peers.

The arrangement would differ according to the constitutional practice of different countries. In those with a parliamentary and cabinet government such as Britain, Canada, or Belgium, Norway and Denmark, it would presumably involve the appointment of a Minister of State or a Minister for North Atlantic Affairs, as the permanent representative on the NATO Council, perhaps with a seat in the Cabinet. In the United States it would mean the appointment of a special representative of the President who would either be a member of the National Security Council in absentia or would report direct to it in the same way the Mr. Adlai Stevenson and his predecessors have reported direct from the United Nations (the appointment of the present American representative to NATO, Mr. Thomas Finletter, who has been an influential political figure at home, goes half way to meet this requirement). In the Fifth Republic and those countries which are governed by one man, it would involve the appointment of someone high in his confidence. This is not a reform that is likely to take place overnight: the point is that if several of the leading NATO countries appoint men of this calibre the others would feel bound to follow suit.

Since the countries of the alliance are not yet prepared to take a step towards creating a federation, there would be no question of giving a revised Council any supranational powers. The point is to enhance its status in the eyes of governments, electorates and adversaries so that its declarations and recommendations have the maximum impact on the course of events. The professional diplomat should remain on the national delegation for his advice will be invaluable if the Council's terms of reference are enlarged, but the chief representative should be a figure of political weight. It is only by this means that NATO can respond swiftly to diplomatic probes, and avert, for instance, the tardy and ragged response which was all the Western powers could make to the closing of the East Berlin frontier on 13th August. In times of high tension it is probably necessary to establish a political operations centre, akin to a military command post, if the inherent disadvantage of a large alliance when facing a single adversary is to be overcome; and, in a democratic alliance,

VI

A future historian may find it strange that, since the Soviet Union became a nuclear power in the same year that the North Atlantic Treaty Organisation was launched, and has been continuously augmenting this form of military strength throughout the whole lifetime of the alliance, it should have taken the NATO powers so long to accept the implications of nuclear parity. He will probably find the explanation to this puzzle in the intense reluctance of Western leaders and their publics to believe that their centuries-old leadership in technology was drawing to an abrupt close – a revolution in accepted ideas, compounded in the last few years by the very real difficulty in assessing the effect on the strategic balance of power of a revolutionary form of striking power, the ballistic missile.

Whatever the cause, I think it is fair to say that only in the last year or so have Western governments really begun to adjust their whole military planning and their conception of the requirements of security and stability in the Atlantic area to the fact that Russia is a strong nuclear, air and missile power, and even so the process of adjustment is proceeding at an uneven pace in different countries. Throughout much of the previous three years, the process of clarification has been muddied by anxious speculation as to whether the nuclear stalemate itself could be maintained or whether the difficulties and confusions which surrounded the early years of the American missile programme, and the problems of offsetting – by technical means in the open West – the relative invulnerability of Soviet striking power which is achieved by political means, might not undermine the strategic balance of power itself.

That anxiety persists but it began to slacken some eighteen months ago when it became clear that the United States was making effective progress towards the re-establishment of a secure and stable system of strategic deterrence, founded on the solid fuelled missile in hard, mobile or underwater bases and in the intercontinental bomber. As this programme advances towards completion, in two to three years time, so the chances of any general attack on the Atlantic area, whether based on calculation or miscalculation, diminishes. The closing of the "missile gap" (if it was ever of real strategic significance), and of the "intelligence" or vulnerability gap, (which is) will have given the United States during the middle and later 1960s the same ability to provide for the overall protection of the area from large scale attack that its hegemony in nuclear striking power afforded in the early days of the alliance. (To look further ahead is unwise at this moment. No-one can claim to assess with any assurance the effects of space weapons or even dependable reconnaissance satellites upon the strategic balance.)

But the new situation is creating a different relationship between the United States and her allies and already imposes a different set of military requirements on the alliance as a whole than those which obtained during the supremacy of the medium bomber and before the Soviet nuclear stockpile attained its present size. It does not mean that the integrity or the effectiveness of the American commitment to the defence of Europe in the event of major attack is weakening, for reasons that have been fully set out in an authoritative article by Albert Wohlstetter "Nuclear sharing : NATO and the Nth country" in the April, 1961 issue of *Foreign Affairs*. It must not be forgotten that the American signature to the North Atlantic Treaty was not an act of disinterested generosity but derived from a well thought decision that the survival of Western Europe was essential to the survival of the United States itself. Nothing has happened to alter that judgement, and now that the protagonists of "agonising reappraisal" have had their day and a clearer vision of the American national interest has been restored in Washington, it is apparent that any talk of American withdrawal from Europe to a Fortress America position was always a hollow bluff. If there were any doubt about it President Kennedy's decision not only to maintain the present level of American forces in Europe, despite the drain on the foreign exchange resources of the United States, and even to reinforce them in a crisis, should finally dispose of any such questionings in the United States, in Europe and in Moscow.

Nevertheless, the advent of nuclear parity has profoundly altered the nature of the American guarantee to Europe. The existence even of an effective, well protected strategic retaliatory force can no longer deter all forms of threat to Europe. As the relative counterforce capability of the United States diminishes with the growth and diversification of Soviet long range striking power, so the deterrent value of the threat of massive nuclear retaliation against anything short of a massive attack on Europe and the United States must diminish with it; in other words, strategic nuclear weapons must become increasingly a deterrent only to the use of their Soviet counterparts. Now that both sides have a continuous spectrum of weapons of mass destruction in their armouries, the kind of limited challenge presented by a crisis over Berlin, or on the line of the Iron Curtain, by a threat to Northern Norway, to the Baltic Straits or to Greece (let alone in South East Asia or the Middle East), can be met only at the level at which it is offered. To rest the defence of Europe on a force which could withstand a military challenge only for a few hours without resorting to nuclear weapons must lead to insecurity and diplomatic paralysis.

One reason it has taken so long for governments and military leaders to accept the logic of events has been the attempt to build around the tactical atomic weapon a doctrine of limited atomic war. NATO governments were all the more ready to engage in such an exercise, partly because of the historic dislike of large standing armies in some countries, partly because of the widely held belief that the disbursement of tactical atomic weapons to the European allies gave them a measure of control over American policy. Moreover, army staffs have seen in this development an opportunity, hitherto reserved for air forces and navies, to graft their tactics on to the most advanced and spectacular developments in military science. The consequence has been that the NATO "shield" forces in the Central Area have been increasingly trained and organised for atomic warfare only, a military posture which is at the worst highly dangerous in terms of miscalculation, and at best irrelevant to the kinds of challenge to Western nerve, morale and clear judgement that are likely to arise.

At the same time, the belief that it would be possible to fight a war in Europe in which nuclear weapons were confined to battlefield targets, without incurring an impossibly high risk of escalation into thermo-nuclear strategic war, even if its aims were limited, is dying a slow but sure death for two reasons which Henry Kissinger, originally one of the chief architects of the theory of limited nuclear war, has candidly and courageously pointed out in his recent book, *The Necessity for Choice*. It has proved impossible to develop an agreed inter-service doctrine on what limitations could be accepted and observed once nuclear weapons had been introduced into the battle. And the development of the medium range missile and the nuclear armed fighter bomber increases the potential depth of the battlefield to a point where both adversaries would find it very difficult to determine whether they were being subjected in, say, Poland or the Low Countries, to interdiction attack or to the first wave of strategic bombing aimed at their heartlands.

The Kennedy Administration deserves great credit for grappling with this problem of the overdependence of NATO's European defences on nuclear weapons so soon after taking office. The President's action in making clear that there would be no reduction in American forces in Europe, and possibly even an increase in times of emergency, should remove any fear that in the American desire to see stronger indigenous conventional forces there is the first step in some American policy of withdrawal within its shell. But it is essential to keep the problem of strengthening the NATO shield in proper perspective. In the first place, no one has suggested, and there seems no valid military requirement for, a dramatic increase in the size of the NATO shield force in the central area. If one accepts the current NATO doctrine, which seems to me sound in this respect, that it is not the role of the NATO ground forces to fight a prolonged battle for the defence of Europe,[5] so much as to hold conflict at the lowest possible level for the longest possible time in order to win a breathing space for a considered political decision by both sides on the implications of mounting to a higher level of warfare, then the figure of thirty divisions stationed in the Central Area in normal times is adequate. By this I mean full strength divisions and not the shadowy skeletons that too often pass muster in the NATO order of battle. If that figure can be reached as it could be with the completion of the German programme and the honouring by Britain and France of their original commitments of four divisions, it represents a numerical superiority of three to two over the Soviet divisions normally stationed in the German Democratic Republic. It is quite true that Mr. Khrushchev has, during the summer of 1961, taken a number of actions designed to convince public opinion in the NATO countries that attempts to improve their conventional strength are worthless since he has only to snap his fingers to summon up much greater reserves. He has arrested the run down of the Soviet ground forces announced in January 1960 (this policy was probably suspended late in 1960 or early in 1961, and possibly for reasons unconnected with the Berlin crisis): and he has suspended demobilisation of the present class of conscripts, thus augmenting the Soviet forces above their 1959 level. But the economic and social pressures which originally made him anxious to reduce Soviet mobilised manpower are as strong as ever, and it is reasonable to assume that his actions are designed to have a short term effect and do not represent a permanent change of Soviet policy.

But, by the same token it is essential in terms of a strong Western diplomacy and morale that the NATO forces in Central Europe can be augmented above the level of thirty divisions and four thousand aircraft, for limited periods of high tension in order to register determination by non-provocative means. And this requires on increase in the strategic reserves of the leading NATO powers, for it is only they who can put a significant number of efficient reserve forces into Europe at relatively short notice. Since in the present state of British and French commitments elsewhere, it is really only the United States who can provide a strategic reserve large enough to have a real diplomatic significance, how does this affect the need, which has been noted earlier, to redistribute the European and American shares of the common burden? The answer, to my mind, lies not so much in terms of quantity as of quality.

The quality of the non-American units in Germany is uneven in terms of equipment, training, mobility and efficiency – discrepancies of which the Russians are keenly aware. The United States would find a readier response if she asked her allies to improve the training, manning and equipment of their conventional forces up to the high standard of her own forces in Europe, using economic resources with which they are now for the most part liberally endowed, rather than markedly to increase their size, at a time when manpower suitable and available for military service is scarcer in Europe than in the United States. (Even so it may require significant changes in the manpower policy of several NATO allies since high quality units inevitably create a demand for technicians and highly qualified men who are now scarce all over Europe.) For it is an irony of the present situation that the United States, with a high wartime birthrate, increasing automation in industry, endemic unemployment and a selective service system, is politically readier to augment her conventional forces than most European countries. However, to ask the United States to station permanently still larger conventional forces in Europe would be disastrous in terms of mutual confidence and respect within the alliance. To ask her to maintain her present commitment and increase her reserve commitment in return for a rapid improvement of the efficiency of the European NATO forces is the more reasonable equation. It would be a double irony if the European partners were unable to meet their half of the equation when one considers that the German, British and French armies were the most efficient in the world at a time when the American army was an ill-paid, socially despised and miniscule force. Moreover, the European countries are also making important advances in conventional weapons such as anti-tank missiles. If the European allies cannot match American forces in terms of quality, then the equitable and psychologically unifying course would be to contribute a greater proportion of the cost of maintaining them in Europe.

In the second place, few responsible people have suggested that NATO can wholly dispense with shorter range nuclear weapons nor contemplate resting the security of Europe on conventional forces alone. Their continued presence in Europe is necessary, first, to deter their use by the Soviet forces in any minor war situation occurring in Europe. And, second, to remove any temptation to the Soviet Union to take a leaf from the pages of German history and present the United States and Britain with the *fait accompli* of a conquered Western Europe by a swift offensive in the manner of May 1940, using her strong tactical air power to reinforce her limited strength on the ground. The essential point is that such weapons as *Honest John, Sergeant, Pershing*, and the nuclear armed fighter-bombers should be regarded as a form of penultimate reserve firepower to be employed only – but only – when it is clear that massive aggression, conventional or nuclear, is under way, and not as part of the resources which divisional or subordinate commanders would expect to have made available to them in the early stages of combat. Since they are purely American weapons, launcher as well as warhead, they should always have been concentrated in special American units[6] under the direct command of the Commanders-in-Chief of the Central and Southern areas (they are not deployed in the Northern area), to be used only on the highest political authority. But the policy of devolving them has gone so far that it will be difficult enough to reverse it, and correct the false premises on which the training of national forces, most particularly the British and German armies, have been proceeding, without immediately carrying the opposite policy to its logical conclusion. One should therefore be content for the present to see Army nuclear support weapons held under the authority of Army commanders but no lower down the chain of command, while insisting that present and future generations of tactical aircraft have a conventional as well as, if need be, a nuclear capability. This is a policy which is now being publicly resisted by the German Defence Minister, Herr Strauss, who said in a recent interview in the *Frankfurter Allgemeine Zeitung* that nuclear weapons should remain integrated in the division in order to increase the effectiveness of the deterrent.[7] The form of political control over the use of these shorter range nuclear weapons will be discussed in the last section.

The tactics of the nuclear and the conventional battlefield are very different and it will not be easy for commanders to re-adapt their training to techniques which give first priority to the latter. It is hard not to feel considerable sympathy with politicians and military commanders – in Germany and elsewhere – who, having originally accepted the necessity of tactical atomic weapons with reluctance, are now being asked to reverse the premises on which their planning and training for the last six or seven years has been based. It might be easier to accept the necessity for such an alteration if greater emphasis were also laid on another major priority of Alliance planning – progress on arms control. Too much of NATO's military planning has proceeded in a political vacuum without reference to the broader requirements of international stability. The need to find ways of checking the upward spiral of arms and forces and eliminating the most likely cause of war, is now very much in the minds of all the political leaders of the NATO powers. At the same time it is becoming evident that the requirements of stability dictate that such restraints should not depend only on the successful outcome of complex or protracted multilateral negotiations with the Soviet Union, but that they may have to be initiated by unilateral action on both sides. It is belatedly coming to be recognised that arms control and military planning are not antithetical, but two facets of the same policy.

In the context of NATO this has two special implications. The first is that as more radical approaches to the problem of arms control run into technical or political objections, so it may prove necessary to make a start with some form of agreed limitation of armaments, particularly of nuclear weapons in Europe, the area which both sides rightly regard as the one where war could most easily erupt. If this is the case, NATO must work towards a military posture which makes it possible to contemplate such a proposal. (This was one of the weaknesses of General Norstad's proposal of last year for an IRBM force in Europe.) The second requirement of arms control is to evolve the clearest and most watertight system of command over nuclear weapons to convince the adversary that we are doing everything that human ingenuity can devise to mitigate the dangers of war through accident, irresponsibility or miscalculation. A declared policy of concentrating the physical control of tactical nuclear weapons in Europe at the highest efficient level of responsibility (as the Russians themselves claim to do) might have a valuable effect in adjusting the distorted Soviet perspective on NATO military planning.[8] Moreover, a greater concern for the place of arms control in military planning would give a constructive, rather than a purely defensive complexion, to the central institutions of the alliance.

VII

The controversy which was in full swing during the spring and early summer (until overtaken by the Berlin crisis) over the proper role of tactical atomic weapons in Europe, clearly illustrates how faulty the system of policy coordination in NATO has become. The statements on the subject made by President Kennedy, the Secretary of Defence and other American officials on this subject, though in my view quite correct, have clearly implied that when the United States changes its policy so does the Alliance. But this is the language of an earlier epoch in NATO, before the European countries had regained strong governments and strong views of their own. The upshot has been dignified but fully public argument between the German and American governments, with the British government, which now privately accepts the validity of the American view but is acutely embarrassed on the question of conventional manpower, trying to keep a foot in both camps. And this on a subject which is at the very heart of NATO's own responsibilities.

Now, as I have suggested earlier, the United States possesses, to an even greater extent than in the early days of NATO, the power to dictate the military policy of the alliance, even in the non-nuclear field. But if she exercises this power to the full she runs two grave risks. The first is that of incurring the concealed resentment of European governments and public opinion. Europeans cannot but admit the prowess of the United States in military technology, but they are not prepared to accord her any hegemony in the realm of ideas, even if their own views are less well informed. And to create such tensions could militate against the true interests of the United States since she is increasingly dependent on the political support of her European partners.

In the second place, it multiplies the effect of mistakes in American policy and increases the difficulty of correcting them. This will, I think, emerge clearly when it is possible to write the inner history of military policy in the alliance during the last five or six years. American policy between 1954 and 1959 placed a decisive emphasis on firepower as compared with manpower, and persuaded its NATO allies of the importance of low yield nuclear weapons and medium range missiles to the defence of Europe. This policy was accepted at first with misgivings by the European allies, but later with enthusiasm as they became aware that this would largely relieve them of the need to increase their mobilised manpower. Then American views began to change, but since the allies had only a very fragmentary picture through occasional briefings of the NATO Council, or the ineffective Military Representatives' Committee in Washington, of the considerations which were causing American policymakers to revise their view, they continued to apply the lesson they had learnt so well. The consequence is that the British, German, Canadian and French staffs are still much more enthusiastic about the use of low yield nuclear weapons as part of their normal fire power than the American army, which is abandoning the pentomic division – and with it the cliché that soldiers cannot be expected to fight with anything but the best weapons, – and is trying to evolve a tactical doctrine that places less emphasis on nuclear weapons.

It seems to me that it is in the interests of the United States to avert this kind of cleavage between herself and her NATO allies (which has been muted but not healed by the Berlin crisis), and to shorten the time lag in conforming to modifications in military concepts, of which she must clearly be the fountain head since technology has so profound an effect upon them. The best way to do this would be to ensure that her allies had continuous access to the inner debate from which American policy emerges, and that they were treated with greater candour concerning American weapon developments. In other words, that all her NATO allies should now be on the same footing, as far as exchange of confidential information and views are concerned, as Britain and Canada have been since before NATO was founded. If the military policy of all the allies for the defence of Europe is to respond to and keep pace with technological development and events in the outside world, there is no alternative to a system of joint international planning in which the United States has a powerful but not overweening influence.

The obvious response is that such a system exists already. All NATO commands, including the two Supreme Commands which play an important part in the planning process, are international though their commanders are American. They report to the Standing Group, that is to the representatives of the United States, British and French Chiefs of Staff in Washington, who in turn report to the Military Committee which consists of the Chiefs of Staffs of the alliance. Their recommendations and modifications to each five year plan then go before the NATO Council for approval. In theory all military planning in NATO is internationally formulated and does not go into effect until it receives the unanimous assent of the highest civil authority in the alliance and the member government which it represents.

But significant differences have developed between theory and practice. For one thing the Standing Group in Washington has become a somewhat shadowy organisation with little influence either in the Pentagon or in the alliance as a whole. SHAPE has become the dynamic centre of military planning and since it is only twelve miles from NATO, while the Standing Group and the representatives of the Military Committee are three thousand, the Supreme Commander Europe has in reality become the Chief of Staff of the alliance. With a man of such remarkable qualities as General Norstad this situation has been, on the whole, acceptable. But even during his five years at SHAPE certain weaknesses have been apparent which are likely to become glaring if a less gifted soldier-diplomat succeeds him.

One is that it imposes a great strain on one man to function as a planner, as a military advisor to an international organisation, and as a potential commander of so vast an area as NATO Europe. Another is that SHAPE as a planning headquarters tends to fall between two stools. It is directed by an American, but as an international commander his views do not necessarily represent those of the US government. When General Norstad made public his views in November, 1960, on the desirability of stationing MRBMs in Europe, he was widely thought, throughout Europe and the rest of the world, to be voicing a new American policy when in fact he was attempting to speak only in his international role. Thus there is a danger that new ideas emanating from the NATO military staffs may be suspect in Europe as looking like American dictation, and equally suspect in Washington because they have not been through the American policy making process.

But there are two more serious defects in the NATO planning process. One is that the formulation of military policy takes place entirely within military channels, and the military and civil channels meet only at the highest level, where it is hard to effect alteration or modification. This is not to cast any doubt upon the ability and integrity of NATO military staffs or military planning as such. But as weapons become more lethal and more costly, as manpower and military budgets rise, and as research and development becomes more complex, so the area of purely military consideration diminishes, while the diplomatic, arms control, or economic aspects of military choices become more important. It is for this reason that foreign offices and treasuries have become so deeply involved in problems which even a decade ago would have been considered within the exclusive competence of Chiefs of Staff. It is also one reason why Ministers of Defence, who are a constitutional innovation of the last twenty years in all the NATO countries, have become such important political figures. To continue to plan through purely military staffs on the international level now contradicts national practice. Since it is far easier to reconcile the sometimes conflicting requirements of political stability and military defence when planning is in its formative stages, the case for a joint civil-military staff or a welding of the stronger secretariat we have envisaged for NATO with the existing military machine, is a strong one.[9]

The other weakness is that American legislation and practice preclude American officials from discussing with their fellow members of international staffs (except the British) any planning considerations that involve the use of nuclear weapons. Every NATO staff has, in effect, an American wing in which a number of highly important papers circulate which may be seen only by American eyes. No one wishes to prejudice security, but the upshot of this has been that other governments have had only a very cloudy impression of American dispositions in Europe in so far as nuclear weapons are concerned, of the purpose they are designed to serve, or the action the United States would take in an emergency. In so far as the British are (by reason of the 1958 amendment to the MacMahon Act) more closely in the American confidence than other countries, this serves to accentuate the sense of division between the Anglo-Saxon and the continental halves of the alliance, and in any case can hardly survive Britain's entry into a closer political relationship with Europe. Bi-lateral agreements, such as have been made between the United States and certain countries to inform them about certain aspects of nuclear technology or tactics with which they may be especially concerned, are not adequate to give this sense of participation in the evolution of NATO policy as a whole which is so clearly needed to increase trans-Atlantic confidence. It is true that security is an important consideration, but in view of the publicity that inevitably attends so much of Western planning and development, it is only one consideration among several to be weighed. The fact that American senior officers in NATO have of late felt it necessary to stretch their instructions to the limit, in order to give their colleagues and associates in NATO a clearer picture of American dispositions and policy, is a recognition of this. The time, however, has come to change the instructions.

To summarise this aspect of the problem: with the demise of the strategy of "massive retaliation" the American conception of the requirements of the defence of Europe has markedly altered. Since American military power, both strategic and tactical, is decisive for the security of Europe, the NATO allies must pay close attention to these changes. But it is politically most unwise for the United States either to assume that when she changes her policies her allies will respond except after long delay and much public friction, or that she can dictate military policy to them, even if the new policy offers them much greater security (as I believe in this case it does). But without better access to the American policy making process, now can the allies keep in close touch with the factors which make it necessary to modify American policy, or justify their own consequential actions to their own publics. The European allies are neither cowardly nor stupid, even if they may be somewhat self-centred, but lacking the grist for the kind of continuous debate in policy which centres on Washington, without large staffs or continuous technological progress of their own, they need a clearer insight than they now get into the considerations which affect American decisions, especially if they must justify costly and unpopular decisions to their own parliaments and publics.

At the same time the existing machinery for the joint planning of European defence has developed certain weaknesses. SHAPE has acquired too important a place in it, which has forced the Supreme Commander into an equivocal role as an international officer and a representative of the US government. The allied military channels of planning and consultation have too little connection with political planning. And the inability of American officials to discuss the considerations that affect nuclear weapons gives European staffs and governments only a hazy conception of American overall policy, which leads to unrealism or archaism in the policies and attitudes of the latter.[10] The Kennedy Administration is reported to be disappointed with the response of its allies to its proposals for strengthening the conventional defences of Europe. But American practice over recent years must bear a large share of the blame.

Nor is this by any means a one way exchange. Not only have the European allies important contributions to make in the field of military technology, as the extent to which British, French and Italian designs and inventions have been accepted by the US forces indicates. They could make a vital contribution in the realm of ideas, but only if they were adequately informed. American policy was largely tone deaf to the views of its allies during the mid-fifties when Mr. Dulles was at the State Department and Admiral Radford was Chairman of the Joint Chiefs of Staff and also when European opinion was extremely ill-informed about the trends of strategy and weapons development. The fact that the worst mistakes in American strategic policy – the decision to over-emphasise nuclear firepower, to distribute low yield weapons to the allies, to continue primary reliance on the manned bomber – were made during that period, was not perhaps mere chance.

VIII

If the considerations which I have outlined are correct, they point in one direction. If the NATO Council is to become a more effective and authoritative centre for the coordinating of national policies, the standing of its individual members should be enhanced and its secretariat must be considerably strengthened. At the same time internal developments within the alliance make it impossible to create any executive committee or political directorate of the nominally or traditionally most influential member governments. If the military policy of the alliance is to be the servant rather than the master of political aims, and a unifying rather than divisive process, there should be closer liaison between political and military planning, and continuous and intimate access on the part of the European allies to the American policy making process.

The time has, therefore, come in my view, to consider a radical overhaul of the institutions and machinery of the alliance broadly along the following lines.

(1) The NATO Council should be retained in its present form with two changes. (a) Its members should be elevated in status from professional diplomats to those with political standing in their own countries. (b) The offices of Secretary-General and Chairman of the Council which have been combined since 1957 should be separated. Chairmanship of a body which operates by the unanimity rule is a full time job, analogous to that of Prime Minister in a Cabinet government. In the case of NATO the task requires a great deal of discreet contact with governments at the highest level and carefully formulated public statements. It must be held by a figure who commands a special degree of public and political confidence throughout the alliance. It is the Chairman of the Council who should be the principal public spokesman of the Alliance.

(2) The post of Secretary-General should be retained but its functions should be transformed. The Secretary-General should be what his name implies, the senior official in the alliance. The best national analogy is that of a Permanent Under-Secretary of a Department in the British civil service system (though he should not, I think, be British). He should be a man of powerful intellect and considerable experience, with a strong control over the official machinery. His task would not be to evolve policy so much as to draw together the threads of official planning and controversy so that his political masters can be presented with clear and intelligible choices. He would be a powerful but not a public figure.

(3) Under the Secretary-General there should be a single unified Secretariat responsible for both political and military planning. Under him should come four Deputy Secretary-Generals: (a) for military planning and arms control, (b) for European affairs, (c) for extra European affairs, including liaison with the other alliances, SEATO, CENTO and ANZUS (which means in effect keeping in close touch with the development of American, British and French policy in the Middle and Far East), (d) for economic affairs, dealing with the industrial and financial problems of infrastructure, burden sharing and support costs, rationalization of national

armaments programmes and related questions. (This department would be concerned with the economics and finance of NATO itself and should not overlap with the functions of OECD.) Each would have an international staff under them.

(4) The Deputy Secretary-General for Military Planning would be a civilian but under him would come a new appointment, the Chief of Staff of NATO, a senior military officer (preferably one who has held the highest military office, Chief of Staff or Chairman of the Chiefs of Staff, in his own country) who would be the apex of the military planning machine. He would have the same privileges as a Chief of Staff in the British or American systems, that is to say, right of access not only to his immediate superior but to the Chairman and the individual members of the Council. He would have a strong international military staff, including three Deputy Chiefs of Staff, one from each service. But, it would be the responsibility of the Deputy Secretary to present the military requirements of the alliance for reconciliation with the political and economic requirements of his fellow Deputy Secretary-Generals.

The Standing Group in Washington could then be disbanded and the Military Representative Committee there would be broken up so that its members became part of national delegations and the military advisers to their representative on the Council. At the same time SHAPE would become an operational rather than a planning headquarters. This would imply no demotion for SACEUR, for in the era of missiles and sensitive early warning systems, operational responsibility for an area stretching from the North Cape to Tabriz and involving the forces of thirteen different countries, is quite enough load for one man to handle, if indeed it is not already too much.

(5) Such a reorganisation would be designed to improve the efficiency of an alliance of governments and the new Secretariat would not have supranational powers. It is therefore necessary to devise means for regular and effective national control of and agreement to, the proposals of this powerful new staff. Otherwise its work and authority will be undermined by national doubts and jealousies. To a large extent this will be met by creating a more authoritative NATO Council but there are still thorny problems of an expert kind which need continuous review and resolution. It has long seemed to me that two short meetings a year of NATO Foreign Ministers (one of which includes Finance and Defence Ministers) is inadequate for this purpose, since there is time only for the most general *tour d'horizon* at each meeting. What seems to be required is (a) A quarterly or half yearly meeting of Defence Ministers, whose increasing importance we have noted, plus their Chiefs of Staff, to review the work of the Military Planning department of the Secretariat. (b) A half yearly meeting of Foreign Ministers to review the work of the two political sections. (c) A yearly or half yearly meeting of Ministers of Finance and Trade (or Industry) to review the work of the economic section. Clearly

these meetings could be made to overlap to give at least one general plenary session.

It is always a rash step for a layman to attempt to draw up even the most general and outline sketch for an official organisation and I can imagine a number of objections to this proposal for a single secretariat under a strengthened Council.

The first is that to obliterate any formal distinction between the various NATO powers, for instance by abolishing the Standing Group, by lessening the importance of SACEUR and by making the NATO Council the effective governing instrument of the Alliance is to obsure the very different size, strength and resources of the various allies. But in fact the shadow would be discarded for the substance, and the differing importance of the allies could be more usefully registered by the distribution of senior appointments in a more powerful working team. The following suggests one reasonable distribution of power and responsibilities.

Chairman of the Council	A smaller European power.
Secretary-General	United States.
Deputy Secretaries General	(a) Military: United Kingdom or France.
	(b) For European Affairs: Canada or Italy.
	(c) For extra European Affairs: France or United Kingdom.
	(d) For Economic Affairs: Germany.

Clearly, the attempt to create a more effective and unified machinery for the coordination of policy would fail if any of these different offices were regarded as the perogative of a particular government, and personalities, personal gifts and personal experience, were to play no part in the choice of the senior officials. However, it would be wise to establish certain fixed principles at the outset if this reorganisation is to fulfil its aim. One is that the Secretary-General, with his revised responsibilities, should be an American (and of course a civilian). It is only by placing an American at a key point in the structure that the alliance can rely upon continuous contact with the working bureaucracy in Washington, a function complementary to that of the American representative on the Council whose job is to act as an interpreter of American policy at the highest level. It is true that the American civil service and administrative system does not breed many men of the type required, but in other international organisations Americans have fulfilled a post of this kind with great success. A second principle is that the Deputy Secretary-General for Military Planning should not be an American. This is not suggested in order to satisfy British or French *amour propre*, but because of the importance in terms of inter-allied confidence of interposing an influential non-American voice in the military planning process of the alliance. The Chief of Staff, however, probably should be an American; with a British, French and German Deputy Chief of Staff under him.

Finally, the question of whether the Supreme Commander Europe should continue to be an American should be determined by the policy of Britain and France. The decision should not be determined by the fact that at present only an American can control the use of nuclear weapons, since as we shall discuss in the last section, this may need modification. But at the moment the United States is making the greatest single contribution, direct and indirect, to the security of Europe. If this should change, if France were to assume a larger share of the burden and the position of French senior officers to become less controversial than at present, the case for a French SACEUR would be a strong one, for the restoration of the conventional defences of Europe is one which France is historically and geographically best suited to undertake.

The second objection to the idea of a combined civil-military secretariat in NATO is that men of the required calibre to make it a really effective centre of international planning would not be forthcoming, would not be made available by national governments. Certainly, if this were true, it would be a grave objection, for nothing would be gained by creating a large second-rate bureaucracy at the heart of the alliance. But this is a problem by no means confined to NATO for it affects the relations of governments in the UN, its specialised agencies and other international organisations. The crucial point (which has been recognised in other spheres) is that the interests of a government may now be much better served by seconding one of its best men to NATO than by retaining him within its own Foreign Office or Ministry of Defence. In considering men for the NATO secretariat, which should be strong rather than large, governments should ask themselves if they can spare X; if the answer is Yes, he should not be appointed: if the answer is No, then he is the right man. There is no doubt that if certain governments took the lead in seconding men of high quality, the others would, in self protection, have to follow suit.

The third objection is that of the military, namely that in a combined organisation of this kind military considerations may tend to get obscured or that military advice may not be presented to the Council and to member governments with the clarity and detachment that is needed. This objection can be met in two ways. One is to acknowledge that it has some force by giving to the Chief of Staff the right of access to the Council. The other is to remind military staffs that the field of pure military planning or considerations is diminishing all the time and cannot be considered, even if it ever could, in a political and economic vacuum without doing grave damage to the general objectives of the alliance. In this sense the reorganisation would merely have the effect of bringing the practice within NATO into line with that of most of its member governments. With the development of Ministries of Defence over the last two decades, the purely military element in the machinery of defence planning has tended to diminish in importance. The evolution of national security policy, which in earlier periods of non-war was largely a matter of trilateral bargaining between the Chief or Chiefs of Staff, the Treasury and the head of the government, to-day involves continuous consultation between civilian and military planners at all levels and embracing many departments. The time is overdue to make the evolution of international security policy follow the same pattern.

Then it can be asked whether a mere reorganisation of the machinery of the alliance would have a significant effect upon the problems which have been discussed earlier. Is not the spirit of the alliance, and the attitude of member governments towards their obligations of much greater importance? Until these change, would not a reorganisation of the central institutions be an attempt to cure the symptoms rather than the causes of division and malaise?

In the case of national governments this is very often the case: the setting up of the Ministry of X or the disbandment of Ministry Y, rarely, though not always, provides a solution to the real problem. But in the case of international organisations this is not true. Structure may have a considerable bearing upon the policy which it adopts, as Mr. Khrushchev clearly acknowledges when he demands a reorganisation of the machinery of the United Nations. Moreover, in an alliance, rather than a world organisation, the adjustment of the central machinery can have a distinct bearing upon the readiness of the member governments to accept and support the decisions and plans of the alliance as a whole, because they are better able to convince their own publics that they themselves have played an important part in the shaping of these decisions. In the case of NATO it is no accident that the governments of some of the smaller countries are unwilling to defend or implement NATO policy, because it is only hazily understood by officials and regarded by public opinion as dictated by the United States. In the same way the uncooperative role of France in NATO in the last few years is connected with the fact that the only senior appointment held by a Frenchman in the central machinery, membership of the Standing Group in Washington, has lost all real power or significance.

Finally, the most cogent objections to the strengthening of the central institution of NATO is that it might tend to bureaucratise the already difficult process of arriving at national or international decisions on policy, slow down the reactions of the leading powers to developments in the external world, and reduce policy decisions merely to inarticulate compromises between different national positions. To a certain extent, this problem is inherent in the existence of the alliance itself, but I would argue that such a reorganisation would minimise it for two reasons. The first is that by giving the smaller allies a more intimate working knowledge of the trends of British and American policy and contingency planning, it would, in fact, give the larger countries a freer hand to take swift action, political or military, in a crisis. The second is that by enhancing the status of the Council *and* creating a strong civil-military secretariat, it would be possible to work at international decisions at the proper level. A more authoritative Council by itself would be insufficient since busy political figures cannot be expected to spend the hours and weeks of discussion which are generally necessary to evolve constructive policies, whereas junior teams of officials can. Without a stronger secretariat, the members of the Council would be apt merely to parrot standard national policies and attitudes instead of having the fruits of intelligent official debate within the Secretariat as the starting point of discussion. Without a stronger Council much of the work of the Secretariat would go to waste, gathering dust in the archives of national government.

This reorganisation, in my view, would have a significant effect upon the cohesion and effectiveness of the Alliance. But most important of all, no solution to the problem of a better relationship between NATO and strategic weapons and planning, which has been exercising governments and thoughtful people throughout the alliance for the last few years, is conceivable without a reshaping of the central institutions. It is for this reason that I have left the consideration of this particular problem until the last.

IX

At the present time, there is less discussion than in recent years in all the countries of the Alliance about the credibility of the American strategic deterrent in the event of war in Europe. The proposition, so keenly debated by American as well as European experts, that, with the advent of full nuclear parity the ability of the United States to take strategic action in face of a threat to her European allies is declining, has for the moment lost some of its force for three reasons. The first is a better and less formalistic appreciation of the realities of the situation of which Albert Wohlstetter's "Nuclear Sharing: NATO and the N+1 Country"[11] is the outstanding example. This demonstrates, among other things, that in the present technological context it would be virtually impossible for the President of the United States to distinguish between a large-scale attack on Europe and the first wave of an attack likely to engulf his own country immediately, even if the former did not also involve the mass slaughter of Americans. The second is the fact that the United States is now well on the way to developing a more effective and secure retaliatory capability than seemed the case even eighteen months ago. The third is the clear statements of President Kennedy that the United States government intends to honour its commitments and is not – for the foreseable future – making any move towards that "nuclear isolationism" which some pessimists had deduced from earlier political and technological trends.

Nevertheless, American strategic nuclear weapons remain a potential source of tension and division between the European allies and the United States. This is not surprising: not only are strategic nuclear weapons terrifying things to contemplate but no system of collective security has been constructed hitherto in which the vast preponderance of strategic power would remain under the unilateral control of one ally while all were equally exposed to the strategic attack by the adversary. It is easy to make two mistakes about the state of European opinion in this context. One is to underrate the degree of

European confidence in the integrity of the American intentions towards Europe — mistaking the clever rationalizations of a small number of military intellectuals for the views of serious and informed Europeans as a whole.[12] The other is to point to the basic ambivalence of the general European attitude, on the one hand fear that the United States will not come to the aid of Europe, and on the other alarm that she may take precipitate action in an emergency — the desire for a finger on the safety catch and on the trigger — as a reason for ignoring it.

The contradiction probably arises from the superimposing of one era of American strategic policy upon the other: alarm at the danger of precipitate American action stems from the earlier years of the Eisenhower regime when the doctrine of "massive retaliation" was official American policy; fear that the United States might not be able to come to Europe's aid grew up during the later Eisenhower years, especially the period of the missile muddle when it appeared that the strategic balance of power might be tilting seriously against the United States. Both fears are largely out of date, but the fact that they exist shows the weakness of the central institution. To eradicate this ambiguous thinking among America's allies requires action on two phases: first, a firm and agreed American strategic policy to meet the needs of the present day: this I think the new Administration, aided by the technical achievements of its predecessor, is now moving towards. The second is to devise means whereby the European allies can acquire some control over their own destiny in return for a greater contribution to the general strength of the Alliance.

Moreover, a new development is making the devising of such means more urgent. The American strategic deterrent is becoming increasingly centred in the Polaris submarine and in missiles and aircraft based on North America itself, and as a result American bases in Europe will become progressively less important. As this happens, the admittedly tenuous control over, or association with, American strategic policy and decisions which some European governments have felt they exercised, by virtue of having these overseas bases on their soil, will also evaporate. And unless some new form of political association takes its place, the sense of frustration, the sense of being powerless over the issue of peace and war which so quickly breeds a sense of defeatism, may increase (as appears to be the case in Italy).[13] In some sections of European public opinion there may be relief that the bases are gone, since the country in question will present a less important target in the event of war: governments, however, are more likely to feel uneasy at losing an important *raison d'entree* in Washington (as well as dollars).

The other source of tension is the existence of the British "independent contribution to the deterrent" in national hands, and France's potential *force de frappe*. The two can not be equated, for the British V-bomber force exists in considerable numbers while the French force is still several years from completion: the operational life of the one is to be continued by means of American assistance which is not likely to be forthcoming for the other. But as purely national forces, their effects are the same. One is to reencourage the diversion of defense resources from efforts in other directions, in ground, anti-submarine and tactical air forces, which the United States, the smaller allies, and even many members of the British and French governments themselves know to be a higher real priority for the security of the Alliance as a whole. The other is to encourage the myth that the road to influence in Washington and prestige in the Alliance lies through the possession of nuclear weapons, and thus to expose Germany, where the debate is still confused to a constant temptation to take the same road. It is true that the danger is less than it was a year or two ago: it has been proved that the British deterrent cannot survive without American assistance: British policy in this respect may be profoundly modified by entry into the Common Market: and the *force de frappe* will be no more than a tactical force when it materialises. Moreover the American Administration has now in its disarmament proposals come out flatly against the transference of control over nuclear weapons to any country not possessing them. But this does not absolve the members of the alliance from taking thought in order to remove the root causes which prompted Britain and France to become nuclear powers in the first place, and to provide a formula whereby scarce resources could be recovered from their programmes with the minimum loss of face in London and Paris.

Before considering how these two sources of malaise, ambivalence about American intentions and the resentments caused by British and French policy, can be alleviated, I feel it important to explain why I no longer consider that one proposal that has been suggested, by myself among others, – the so called "NATO deterrent" – would at present fit the needs of the case. The idea of creating a European based striking force controlled by NATO itself was an attempt, made at a time when no constructive alternative was being considered by governments

(a) To overcome the fears that were generated in Europe during the worst period of the missile muddle and the tail end of the Eisenhower years about the readiness and ability of the United States to continue to deter nuclear attack in Europe.
(b) To obviate the need for a programme of nuclear tests in France.
(c) To mitigate the politically divisive effect of British policy which was fast running down its forces in Germany while preparing to spend £600 million on the *Bluestreak* missile.
(d) To devise a strong central command and control system when it seemed both necessary and possible to construct a system of hard based MRBMs in Europe.

The idea would have been difficult to translate into practice, and it would have needed considerable pragmatism and good will to operate such a system. But the value of the idea itself has been waning over the past year or so. Apart from the greater firmness of American policy, as evidenced by the Kennedy

Administration, based on technology and developments inherited from its predecessor, it became less and less practicable as it became clear that only submarine based missiles provided by the United States would possess sufficient invulnerability over the years to pose a medium range threat to the Soviet Union. This enormously complicated the problems of command and control, eliminated any question of a new programme planned and undertaken by the alliance as a whole, and demolished any idea of multilateral teams controlling the missiles.

The idea may need reconsideration at some point in the future, for instance if all efforts at arms control and disarmament should fail, China should become a serious nuclear power, the United States be forced to direct a large part of its resources to the Pacific and thereby have to ask its European allies to shoulder part of the system of strategic deterrence as well as local defence. If so a much more drastic reconstruction of NATO will be required to make it a confederal system with institutions of supranational power.

But the debates which the idea of a NATO deterrent have generated have at least had the useful effect of illuminating a profound confusion that has existed throughout the alliance concerning the meaning of the key word "control". NATO is a bilingual alliance and it therefore is not surprising that the French word *controle* which means examination, criticism, verification, should have become confused with the English word *control* which in this context means physical grasp of levers and buttons. In terms of NATO *controle* can be roughly equated with access to planning and policy decisions, *control* with influence over operational decisions.

If one examines the reasons which lead Britain and then France to become nuclear powers, it seems to me clear that it was the desire for *controle* rather than *control* which was the dominant motive. Similarly, during all the anxieties of the past few years the main desire in the other European countries, including Germany, has not been to acquire nuclear warheads or means of delivery for their own sake, so much as to gain access to and influence over the formulation of American strategic policy, especially as it affects NATO, which the possession of the actual hardware has given to the British government. The more that European governments can be certain, from intimate contact with the American policy making process, that they know what the President of the United States would do in a given situation of war or crisis, the greater will be their sense of confidence in American policy and the freer will be his hand. The idea of fifteen heads of governments or even their representatives consulting on the grimmest of operational decisions in the very limited time which modern high speed delivery permit, is inconceivable. But to know what the most powerful ally intends to do in an emergency, to be clear what the choices open to him are, is essential to the political cohesion of the alliance.

It is here that a strengthened Council and a powerful civil-military Secretariat would make such a valuable contribution. By creating a strong international planning staff, under an American Secretary-General (who might well be also a US Assistant Secretary of Defence or State, to give him a secure place in Washington's own chain of command) and a non-American Deputy Secretary-General for Military Planning, a long step forward would have been taken to ensure that the Council and their governments were kept fully abreast of the developments and modifications of American policy and weapons month by month. How great the influence of non-American views on American strategic planning would be, it is impossible to forecast: but the system would justify itself merely if European governments were fully clear as to what American policy is and is likely to be. If this could be done, then I see no particular merit, at least for the time being, in schemes such as that outlined by President Kennedy in Ottawa on May 17th, 1961, to create a NATO seaborne missile force of five or more Polaris submarines "truly multi-lateral in ownership and control". The one unit which cannot effectively operate under an international crew is a submarine, and since they are wholly American in design and construction they would be better under American captains, receiving their orders from American control stations. It is *controle* of the plan for the submarines that concerns the allies, far more than control of Polaris missile firing panels.

I can imagine two immediate American objections to such a proposal. The first is that to accord the alliance as a whole the kind of association with American strategic planning which Britain has enjoyed in varying degrees since NATO started, might mean amending the MacMahon Act, and would certainly involve a drastic revision of official American practice and attitudes. But I find it difficult to believe that if the President made it clear to Congress that such a step would increase rather than diminish his freedom of action in an emergency and also ensure that American nuclear weapons remained in American hands, it would fail to grasp his meaning. As to the question of security, it must be candidly pointed out that American security is, or has been until recently, the worst in the alliance. To make the necessary information[14] available on American strategic planning to the allies, would be to ensure that their responsible representatives at all levels were given the information in its proper perspective and setting rather than having to acquire it piecemeal from leaks in the American technical and daily press, and from the distorted statements of American senior officers intent on making a good case for more funds before Congressional Committees or lobbying against the decisions of their civil superiors.

The other objection is harder to meet. It can be argued that the American policy making process is such an untidy one, that policy evolves out of such a violent and prolonged tug-of-war between opposing views, services and interests, between Congress and the White House, between the State Department and the Defense Department, that no one can say with certainty what position has been reached on any given subject at a particular time. To involve the allies too closely in this process might mislead them and create discord rather than harmony within the alliance. This is a real problem[15] but it can be over-stressed. It is true that the American policy making process is very different from that of any European government. But as far as strategic policy is concerned, the lead time involved in modern weapons necessarily makes American planning a long term affair. As far as more general policy is concerned, it is precisely to avoid the kind of charges of vacillation which have been levelled from certain European quarters against the White House over the Berlin question, that it is necessary to develop within NATO a policy coordinating centre where differences can be thrashed out in private at an early stage before they become arguments between governments at the highest level and with the fullest publicity.

To summarise: if NATO can be developed into a powerful centre of policy coordination and planning and treated with full confidence by the United States, there will be less need to contemplate giving NATO operational control over strategic weapons or creating a NATO striking force.

It is vital to maintain this distinction between allied consultation. on planning and national control of operational decisions as far as strategic weapons are concerned. The latter must be taken by the national governments that possess them. To deny the President the power of unfettered action in an emergency would be to rob the Western deterrent of much of its credibility. But just because this is so his allies must know what alternative courses are open to them. Moreover, if the United States is prepared to treat NATO as an essential part of the planning and consultative mechanism for the evolution of her own strategic planning, she will be able to avoid the dilemma of having to hand over control of some of her strategic weapons to her allies, or else of having a number of nervous allied Prime Ministers on the telephone on the steps of the White House in time of crisis. Equally such an initiative would provide a means of reconciling the British, and later the French, nuclear capability with the requirements of the alliance. Clearly the statesmanlike course would be for the United States to put that part of its strategic nuclear forces which are still based on Europe, including the VIth Fleet, under the planning control of a reorganised NATO on condition that the United Kingdom did likewise. Both countries could be protected by provision that in the event of conflict in one of their other treaty areas, SEATO or CENTO, they could withdraw their European based nuclear forces (all British nuclear forces are European based) by agreement with the NATO Council. These forces would remain under national command in peace time, but their deployment and potential employment would cease to be a closed secret between Washington and London, between Bomber Command and SAC, and form part of the whole NATO plan, subject to the *controle* of the Council through the Chief of Staff. If it became clear, as I think it would, that the real channel of British influence in Washington lay through the NATO Council and the appointments held by her representatives in the Secretariat, the incentive to prolong the life of the British independent deterrent as a status symbol, and to preserve her special American connection, would diminish. There would be less need to consider a successor to the present V-Bomber force, and the British nuclear weapons programme could be reduced to a research and development effort, liberating resources for a much needed expansion of the British contribution to the military strength of the alliance in other fields.

It can be argued that no British or American decision at this stage will affect French policy. I am not sure that this is true. What is true is that, at this moment, no such initiative would affect President de Gaulle's views on the development of the *force de frappe*. If, however, his allies can, in the three years before it becomes truly operational, demonstrate that a framework of alliance planning can be created into which such a force can be accepted (it will in reality be a tactical not a strategic force) without any loss of French influence or prestige, then the monetary costs – inevitably higher than the original forecasts – plus the clear demonstration of its insignificant diplomatic value as a purely national force, could well create a change in French policy.

If the wise course is to leave strategic nuclear weapons under national operational control and command, while insisting that the planning that surrounds their use be submitted to the *controle* of a strengthened Council and Secretariat, should the same apply to the shorter range tactical weapons which will remain in Europe, though with a more limited role. Here I think there is a strong case for devolving *control* upon the NATO Council itself. While it is unquestionably right that only the President should have the power to activate SAC, it is not right that the power to order the use of tactical atomic weapons should rest solely with himself and the Supreme Commander Europe. Since they would do immense damage to the territories of the European allies, even if their use did not lead to total war, it would be psychlogically wise and unifying to vest control in the NATO Council. Moreover, if they are to be employed only when it is clear that large scale aggression is under way, the difficulty of reaching a decision on their use is by no means insurmountable given two conditions: that the permanent Council consists of men of considerable authority within their own governments, and that civil-military planning within NATO has a carefully evolved and agreed outline "rules of engagement" to meet the principal contingencies in which such weapons might have to be used.

X

The evolution of a stronger centre for the Alliance or a stronger Alliance are not finite goals for the Atlantic Community, but means to a common end – the avoidance of war, the defence of the legitimate interests of the allies throughout the world, and the construction of a better system of security and stability. At present no better means presents itself, and we shall be neglecting our opportunities if we fail to make what we can of NATO simply because we must acknowledge that its functions are limited and that other agencies have an equally constructive role to play in creating a new world order.

I have tried to outline my own view of the need, the opportunity and the means of creating a more dynamic centre for the Alliance without altering its basic structure. Clearly if such an idea were found acceptable it would need considerable refinement, thought and adjustment before it could take root. In conclusion, I would like to point to the degree of common interest that exists in evolving such a centre in all the countries of the Alliance, for it has too often come to be assumed in recent years that any modification that advantages one ally must disadvantage others.

First, the smaller countries of the Alliance would gain immeasurably. At present, they are tarred with the brush, in Soviet or uncommitted eyes, of alignment with the three Western nuclear powers without really being able to play a constructive or influential role in the formulation of Alliance policy. The reports of their permanent representative on the NATO Council in Paris, or the military Representatives Committee in Washington, are a useful source of diplomatic information but they have not the sense of participating in centrally evolved policies – as Mr. Khrushchev knows very well when he invites these Prime Ministers to the Kremlin. Their contribution might not enable them to many of the most key positions in a new civil-military Secretariat of enlarged responsibilities, but it would enable them to participate in every aspect of its work.

For France, the new system would reject the shadow and often the substance of what President de Gaulle has always required of the Alliance. There would be no French veto on the decisions of the Alliance, but instead an opportunity to exert a strong French influence upon policy in its formative stage. If closer association with the real problems and needs of NATO should convince President de Gaulle that it is the historic role of France to revitalise the defences of a Europe that must inevitably become more dependent on its own resources, rather than standing aloof from what he conceives to be a largely American organisation, the power and influence of France within the Alliance would grow rapidly.

For Germany, where both major parties now attach great importance to NATO and German membership of it, the strengthening of the central institution would help to mitigate that sense of frustration which a divided country is bound to feel. The present German loyalty to NATO and the declared readiness of her government to abide by its decisions could easily wither if NATO proved incapable of taking decisions or at least preparing the ground for them. A more centralised command and control system for short-range nuclear weapons together with a better system of consultation over a wide range of politico-military problems would involve considerably less discrimination against Germany than other suggestions which have been put forward.

For Britain, a decision to submit more of her policy planning to the *controle* of NATO would be to grasp history by the forelock. For reasons that I have suggested earlier, as Britian becomes less a world power and more intimately concerned with Europe, so the importance of NATO must rise. Her aloofness from Europe, the tendency of successive governments to treat her NATO commitments as expendable has diminished British influence in continental Europe at a time when for economic and political reasons she is becoming vitally dependent on it. If national pride can accept the hard fact that the old Anglo-American partnership is dissolving, that henceforth the main road to Washington will lie through Paris, Bonn and Brussels, a strengthened and expanded NATO becomes a vital British interest.

For the United States, such a proposal creates both difficulties and opportunities. It would require great firmness and consistency of policy to accept the role of NATO as an integral part of the American policy-making process. Yet if it be the case that the United States is becoming politically more affected all the time by the policies of her NATO allies, and if she wishes to shift part of her material and political burdens and responsibilities on to their shoulders while she retains control of strategic and nuclear weapons, she has really little alternative but to take the lead in evolving means whereby Canada and her European allies have greater access to her counsels.

Finally, it is worth noting that the great assault which Soviet policy has launched is aimed not at the military forces of the Alliance but at its political cohesion. If NATO can be dismembered politically, then no amount of physical rearmament can redress this defeat. It is to the increase of confidence of ally in ally that these proposals are addressed.

Notes

1 *NATO in The 1960s* by Alastair Buchan, Weidenfeld & Nicolson, 12s. 6d., and Frederick Praeger, $3.00.
2 Principally thought the development of the *Skybolt* air to ground missile to prolong the effective life of the V. Bomber force in face of improving Soviet air defences, but also through the development and deployment of new forms of early warning such as B.M.E.W.S.
3 "La Strategie de l'age thermonucleaire", *Le Figaro*, May 25th 1961.
4 It must be said in justice to the NATO military staffs that they have done their very best to fill the gap left by the weakness of the NATO secretariat and to do some serious work on arms control themselves.
5 Neither side will accept defeat in Europe without recourse to nuclear weapons. Conventional forces there are essentially an arms control device to prevent nuclear war breaking out. This is the point that seems to elude President de Gaulle when he tells his visitors that French troops will only fight to the death under French command and for French soil. A prolonged conventional war in Europe, testing the last ounce of national morale and will is an inconceivable state of affairs.
6 In this connection it is interesting to learn that the German government originally held the same view. Herr Strauss explained recently:
"We asked the Americans years ago whether – in order to avoid the problem of arming the Bundeswehr with these weapons systems, with carriers to be fitted with warheads in emergencies, and still maintain the same firepower along the entire front line – whether they were prepared to incorporate American artillery and rocket battalions into German divisions. Then Germans would not be equipped with atomic weapons." The American reply was that for budgetary and organisational reasons, this was impossible. – A New Army for the New Germany by George Bailey. *The Reporter*, July 20th, 1961.

7 13th May, 1961. Reprinted in *Survival*, July/August, 1961.
8 The command and control system for the NATO forces may have a direct bearing upon the impending Berlin crisis. When Mr Walter Lippmann interviewed Mr. Khrushchev on 17th April, he asked why he considered the German problem so urgent. "Because there must be a German solution before 'Hitler's Generals with their 12 NATO divisions' get atomic weapons from France and the United States". This may be no more than a good excuse to force a solution that protects the existence of the G.D.R. But having discussed the question myself with senior Soviet officials on several occasions during the last year, I find it difficult to overstate the scepticism with which they regard the present "double key" NATO command and control arrangements for nuclear weapons, as long as they are officially integrated in German or other NATO divisions. This scepticism is not confined to Russians.
9 I am aware that there is a great deal of informal interchange of views between the NATO military staffs, the secretariat and the members of the Council. I am no admirer of tidy organisational blue-prints, but such interchanges no longer seem to me adequate to the demands of today.
10 Michael Howard has raised the very relevant question of how such a proposal to bring allied governments and officials more closely within the ambit of American strategic planning, as it affects nuclear weapons, might affect the prospects of arms control agreements, such as proposals to denuclearise the two Germanys, or withold certain types of nuclear weapons from Central Europe. The problem has got to be faced, but, for my own part, I would not consider it impossible to solve. There is no question of US officials disclosing the technical information that would enable a European non-nuclear power to become one, nor indeed any necessity to impart highly classified information such as targets which might filter through the arms control inspectorate into the adversaries' hands. At the same time, I doubt if the German or any other NATO government would accept the discrimination which geographical denuclearisation would involve without having continued and closer access to the overall policy of the alliance and the United States.
11 *Foreign Affairs*, April 1961.
12 Professor Daniel Lerner, Professor of Sociology at MIT, has recently summarised the results of a continuous survey of European leaders of opinion which MIT has been conducting in Britain, France and Germany since 1954. He reports that even in France 68% of those questioned recently expressed their belief that the United States would continue to guarantee the security of Europe, despite its own vulnerability. Lecture at U.C.L.A., February 24th, 1961.
13 It can plausibly be argued that the country where neutralist sentiment is most vocal, namely Britain, is the European ally whose government has the closest access to American strategic policy and planning. However, I think that a close examination of the debate in Britain reveals rather different motives for such neutralist feeling as exists from those which its advocates most commonly put forward. It is inextricably bound up with feelings of an old power towards a young power, and really forms a chapter in the two centuries old Anglo-American debate rather than in the history of the development of the alliance.
14 I do not see any requirement to communicate such deadly secrets as targetting plans, though it would require general discussion of the principles on which the plans to fight war as well as deter it are based.
15 There is a case to be made for moving NATO itself to Washington so that the NATO Council could play an active part in this policy making debate: Washington is after all the geographical centre of the alliance as well as the capital of its most powerful member. However, in view of the fact that a distinctive European consciousness is emerging and that the United States may have to ask Europe to share some of its burdens, Paris still seems the best centre.

2 Controlled Response and Strategic Warfare
Adelphi Paper 19, 1965
T. C. Schelling

I

If any two words characterize the military doctrine of Presidents Kennedy and Johnson and Secretary of Defence McNamara – and two words is about all a doctrine gets these days to describe itself – the leading contender is 'flexible response'. As early as his first defence-budget message in the spring of 1961, President Kennedy spoke of making military force continuously responsive to policy direction, of proportioning any military response to its provocation, and of maintaining effective communications, command, and control throughout any emergency. 'Controlled response' is a favourite synonym; and Secretary McNamara is known for his interest in 'multiple options', in having a choice of response for a variety of contingencies and not having to rely on a unique all-or-none riposte.

As a generic concept, 'flexible response' can be most easily described as everything that 'massive retaliation' was not. And it is nothing new. Several British defence analysts – among them Denis Healey, Britain's present Secretary of State for Defence – were advocating 'graduated deterrence' as early as 1957, meaning a sequence of threatened responses to aggression rather than a commitment to leap into all-out war. Even Secretary of State Dulles, author in 1954 of 'massive retaliation' as the threat to check all mischief, large and small, had begun barely three years afterwards to articulate a policy of graduated response in Europe. He urged downgrading the massive nuclear response so that, 'instead of those who are non-aggressive having to rely upon all-out nuclear retaliatory power for their protection, would-be aggressors will be unable to count on a successful conventional aggression, but must themselves weigh the consequences of invoking nuclear war'. Former Secretary Acheson, writing at the same time, went further and proposed that even the tactical nuclear threshold be pushed upward by acquiring a strong conventional (nonnuclear) military barrier that could make the enemy the one who had to face the hard choice of introducing nuclear weapons, even tactically, with all their uncertainty and risk of the war's getting out of hand.

The general philosophy of flexible response – of avoiding reliance anywhere on a military response too big to be credible or too big to be wise – has to be distinguished from its specific applications. In Europe it has come to be identified almost exclusively with the advocacy of larger non-nuclear capabilities; the American government has sought that particular 'option' with an obstinacy equalled only by its opposition in France and Germany – an opposition that can almost be characterized as an 'inflexible response' to Secretary McNamara. In South-East Asia 'flexible response' has mainly meant searching for techniques to combat insurgency that are less unwieldy than nuclear weapons or even conventional armies; and most recently it has been characterized by limited reprisals, as in the Gulf of Tonkin, or 'controlled escalation' in the bombing of North Vietnamese targets.

But 'flexible response' has also been given a specific meaning in relation to general war and its deterrence. This is the meaning that we shall explore here. By 'general war' is meant a war involving the strategic weapons and homelands of the United States and the Soviet Union. And here the doctrine raises profound questions about the character of war itself.

II

As a doctrine, 'massive retaliation' (or rather, the threat of it) was in decline almost from its enunciation in 1954. But until 1962 its final dethronement had yet to be attempted. All-out, indiscriminate, 'society-destroying' war was still ultimate monarch, even though its prerogative to intervene in small or smallish-medium conflicts had been progressively curtailed. Beyond some threshold, all hell was to be unleashed in a war of attempted extermination, a competition in holocaust, a war without diplomacy and without 'options' yet unused, a war in which the backdrop of ultimate deterrence had collapsed on the contenders – a war that would end when all weapons were spent. But in a speech at Ann Arbor, Michigan, in June 1962 – a speech reportedly similar to an earlier address in the NATO Council – Secretary McNamara proposed that even in 'general war' at the highest level, in a showdown war between the great powers, destruction should not be unconfined. Deterrence should continue, discrimination should be attempted, and 'options' should be kept open for terminating the war by something other than sheer exhaustion.

'The United States has come to the conclusion' said Secretary McNamara, 'that to the extent feasible, basic military strategy in a possible general war should be approached in much the same way that more conventional military operations have been regarded in the past. That is to say, principal military objectives ... should be the destruction of the enemy's military forces, not of his civilian population ... giving the possible opponent the strongest imaginable incentive to refrain from striking our own cities'.

The ideas that Secretary McNamara expressed in June 1962 have been nicknamed the 'counterforce strategy'. They have occasionally been called, as well, the 'no-cities strategy'. As good a name would be the 'cities strategy'. The newer strategy at last recognized the importance of cities – of people and their means of livelihood – and proposed to pay attention to them in the event of major war.

Cities were not merely targets to be destroyed as quickly as possible to weaken the enemy's war effort, to cause anguish to surviving enemy leaders, or to satisfy a desire for vengeance after all efforts at deterrence had failed. Instead, live cities were to be appreciated as assets, as hostages, as a means of influence over the enemy himself. If enemy cities could be destroyed twelve or forty-eight hours later, and if their instant destruction would not make a decisive difference to the enemy's momentary capabilities, destroying *all* of them at once would be to abandon the principal threat by which the enemy might be brought to terms.

We usually think of deterrence as having failed if a major war ever occurs. And so it has; but it could fail worse if no effort were made to extend deterrence into war itself.

Secretary McNamara incurred resistance on just about all sides. The peace movements accused him of trying to make war acceptable; military extremists accused him of weakening deterrence by making war look soft to the Soviets; the French accused him of finding a doctrine designed for its incompatibility with their own 'independent strategic force'; some realists considered it impractical, and some analysts argued that the doctrine made sense only to a superior power, yet relied on reciprocity by an inferior power for which it was illogical. The Soviets joined in some of these denunciations, and have yet to acknowledge that they share the American government's interest in limiting such a war – though their reaction acknowledges receipt of the message.

This was the first explicit public statement by an important official that deterrence should be extended into war itself and even into the largest war, that any war large or small might have the character of 'limited war' and ought to, that (as live captives have often been worth more than enemy dead on the battlefield) live Russians and whole cities together with our unspent weapons might be our most valuable assets, and that this possibility should be taken seriously in war plans and the design of weapons. The idea was not wholly unanticipated in public discussion of strategy; but suggestions by analysts and commentators about limiting even a general war had never reached critical mass. Secretary McNamara's 'new strategy' was one of those rare occurrences, an actual policy innovation or doctrinal change unheralded by widespread public debate.

Debate followed, but it has not much clarified the issues that the Secretary of Defence had raised, nor has Mr. McNamara himself spelled out the strategy in much detail. Indeed, in his most recent testimony on the defence budget, some of his calculations were based on premises that seemed to imply a reluctance to take his own strategy seriously. This could easily have been due to a common difficulty in defence planning: budgets need calculations, and the 'incalculables', however central they are to strategy, get subordinated to 'hard facts', whether or not hardness equals relevance or assumptions are facts.

Some of the Press speculated that Secretary McNamara was abandoning his former interest in flexible response at the highest level of warfare. Examination of his testimony leaves the question unanswered. One conclusion does emerge, though: the new strategy, especially its city-hostage aspect, has yet to make its influence felt in military research and development. The technological implications remain to be explored.

There might appear to be no need to explore them if the Secretary is losing his enchantment with the idea. But ideas, once brought to light, can often live on their merits and not as dependants of the men who brought them to light. These ideas have real merits; there are even signs that the Russians are at last beginning to appreciate them (and enemy appreciation is critically important to any strategy of conditional restraint). We can be sure this is no ephemeral notion. Indeed, it is not altogether new, having been cogently advanced some 2,400 years ago by King Archidamus of Sparta, a man, according to Thucydides, with a reputation for both intelligence and moderation.

'And perhaps', he said, 'when they see that our actual strength is keeping pace with the language that we use, they will be more inclined to give way, since their land will still be untouched and, in making up their minds, they will be thinking of advantages which they still possess and which have not yet been destroyed. For you must think of their land as though it was a hostage in your possession, and all the more valuable the better it is looked after. You should spare it up to the last possible moment, and avoid driving them to a state of desperation in which you will find them much harder to deal with.'[1]

III

There were two components of the strategy that Secretary McNamara sketched. Most comment has implied that they are two sides of the same coin, and whether we call it heads or tails we mean the same. But they are distinct. 'Counterforce' describes one of them; 'cities' (or 'no-cities') describes the other. The two overlap just enough to cause confusion.

Badly expressed they sound alike. In 'counterforce' language the principle is to go for the enemy's military forces, not for his cities (not right away, anyhow). In 'no-cities' language, the principle is to leave the cities alone, at least at the outset, and confine the engagement to military targets. If we were at a shooting gallery, had paid our fee and picked up the rifle and could shoot either the clay pipes or the sitting ducks, 'shoot the pipes' would mean the same as 'don't shoot the ducks'. But we are not talking about a shooting gallery. The reason for going after the enemy's military forces is to destroy them before they can destroy our own cities (or our own military forces). The reason for not destroying the cities is to keep them at our mercy. The two notions are not so complementary that one implies the other: they are separate notions to be judged on their separate merits.

There is of course the simple-minded notion that war is war, and if you are not to hit cities you've got to hit something. But that comes out of the shooting gallery, not military strategy. The idea of using enemy cities as hostages, coercing the enemy with the threat of their destruction, can make sense whether or not the enemy presents military targets worth spending our ammunition on.

It may not make sense; the enemy may be crazy, he may not be equipped to know reliably and quickly what targets we have destroyed, he may not be able to control his own conduct according to the consequences we confront him with. But if it does make sense, or is worth trying at the outset, it makes sense whether or not we can simultaneously conduct an effective campaign to reduce his military capabilities.

The counterforce idea is not simply that one has to shoot something, and if cities are off limits, one seeks 'legitimate' targets in order to go ahead with a noisy war. It is a more serious notion: that a good use of weapons is to spend them in the destruction of enemy weapons, to disarm the enemy by trading our weapons for his. If we can forestall his attack on our cities by a disarming attack on his weapons, we may help to save ourselves and our allies from attack.

The 'counterforce' idea involves the destruction of enemy weapons so that he cannot shoot us even if he wants to. The 'cities' idea is intended to provide him with an incentive not to shoot us even if he has the weapons to do it. (It can also, with no loss of manliness, be recognized as a decent effort to keep from killing tens of millions of people whose guilt, if any, is hardly commensurate with their obliteration.)

The two notions complement each other, of course, in that both are intended to keep the enemy from using his weapons against us, one through forcible disarmament and the other through continued deterrence. There is some incompatibility, though. The city-hostage strategy would work best if the enemy had a good idea of what was happening and what was not happening, if he maintained control over his own forces, if he could perceive the pattern in our action and its implications for his behaviour, or even if he were in direct communication with us sooner or later. The counterforce campaign would be noisy, likely to disrupt the enemy command structure, and somewhat ambiguous in its target selection as far as the enemy could see. It might also impose haste on the enemy, particularly if he had a diminishing capability to threaten our own cities and were desperate to use it before it was taken away from him.

My purpose here is not to choose between the two or to prescribe an appropriate compromise, but to emphasize that these are different strategies that somewhat support each other, somewhat obstruct each other, and somewhat compete for resources. Either alone could make sense. A completely reliable and effective counterforce capability would make it unnecessary to deter the enemy's use of his weapons by keeping his cities conditionally alive; it would simply remove his weapons. And a completely successful threat against his cities would immobilize his weapons and induce capitulation. (In the latter case the 'war' would not look like a big one, in noise and damage, but the sense of commitment and showdown would make it 'all-out' in what was at stake.)

The question is often raised whether a 'counterforce' strategy is not self-contradicting: it depends on a decisive military superiority over the enemy, and yet to succeed it must appeal equally to the enemy, to whom it cannot appeal because he must then have a decisive inferiority. This widespread argument involves a switch between the two meanings, 'counterforce' and 'cities'. A decisive capability to disarm the enemy and still have weapons left over, in a campaign that both sides wage simultaneously, is not something that both sides can exploit. Both may aspire to it; both may think they have it; but it is not possible for both to come out ahead in this contest. (It could be possible for *either* to come out ahead according to who caught the other by surprise. In that case we should say that each had a 'first-strike counterforce capability', superiority attaching not to one side or the other but to whoever initiates the war. This is an important possibility but not one the United States government aspired to in its counterforce strategy.)

It can, however, make sense for both sides to take seriously a 'cities' strategy that recognizes cities as hostages, that exploits the bargaining power of an undischarged capacity for violence, threatening damage but only inflicting it to the extent necessary to make the threat a lively one. In fact, this 'cities' aspect of the so-called 'counterforce' strategy should appeal at least as much to the side with inferior strategic forces. If the inferior side cannot hope to disarm its enemy, it can only survive by sufferance. It can only induce such sufferance by using its capacity for violence in an influential way. This almost surely means not exhausting a capacity for violence in a spendthrift orgy of massacre, but preserving the threat of worse damage yet to come.

Some commentators calculated that the Soviets would merely 'disarm' themselves by directing their weapons at American forces. Since it had been observed that a 'counterforce' campaign made no sense, it was often concluded, on the analogy of the shooting gallery, that the Soviets naturally had to fire all their weapons somewhere else. And where else could that be but cities? A facetious answer that brings out the speciousness of the argument is that the Soviets could just as well fire the missiles at their own cities. By firing all their weapons at American cities, they virtually guarantee the destruction of their own, and historians would not much care whether the Soviet cities were destroyed by weapons produced domestically or abroad. The idea that restraint in warfare, if it favours the United States, could not be in the Soviet interest has about the same compelling appeal as the idea that a Japanese surrender in 1945, if it favoured the United States, could not make sense to the Japanese.

Separating the two components of this strategy is also necessary in dealing with whether a 'counterforce' strategy is of transient or enduring interest. There has been a genuine argument whether the United States can reliably expect a capability to disarm the Soviet Union by an offensive campaign, bolstered by defence of the homeland. By 'genuine', I mean an argument that either side could win, depending on the facts, and that neither can win by sheer logic or casuistry. The outcome is going to depend on technology, costs, and the sizes of budgets; the actual facts may never be reliably clear. By the middle of the 1960s neither side had any clear-cut win in the argument, and testimony of the Defence Department left the question open. But if we distinguish the 'counterforce' from the 'city-threatening' components of the strategy, it is evident that one part of the strategy does, and the other does not, depend on the outcome of this argument. If as a result of technology, budgets, and weapon choices, it is going to turn out that we do not have a capability to disarm the enemy forcibly, then of course a strategy that depends on doing so becomes obsolete – at least until some later time when that capability is available. But there is no reason why that makes the 'cities' strategy obsolete. In fact, it virtually yields front rank to the 'cities' strategy.

One might pretend, in order to make war as fearsome as possible, that the obvious way to fight a war if we cannot successfully destroy military forces is to destroy the enemy's cities, while he does the same to us with the weapons that we are powerless to stop. But, once the war started, that would be a witless way to behave, about as astute as head-on collision to preserve the right of way. And general nuclear war is probably fearsome enough anyway to deter any but a most desperate enemy in an intense crisis; making it somewhat less fearsome would hardly invite efforts to test just how bad the war would be. And in the intense crisis, belief that the war could be controlled if it broke out, and stopped short of cataclysm, might actually help to deter a desperate gamble on pre-emption. So the alleged hard choice between keeping deterrence as harsh as possible and making war, if it should occur, less harsh, may not be the dilemma it pretends to be.

IV

The situation in which either side could hurt the other but not disarm it could arise in two different ways. It could arise through both sides' procuring and deploying forces of such a kind that each force was not vulnerable to disarming attack by the other side. Or it could come about through warfare itself.

Discussions of 'counterforce warfare' often imply that the war involves two stages. In the first, both sides abstain from an orgy of destruction and concentrate on disarming each other, the advantage going to the side that has the bigger or better arsenal, the better target location and reconnaissance, the advantage of speed and readiness, and the better luck. At some point this campaign is over, for one side or both; a country runs out of weapons or runs out of military targets against which its weapons are any good, or reaches the point where it costs so many weapons to destroy enemy weapons that the exchange is unpromising.

At this stage it is possible, but only barely possible, that both sides have disarmed themselves and each other, and are momentarily secure from further attack. But any practical evaluation suggests that each side would have weapons left over by the time it had done all the counterforce damage it could do, or could afford to do, to the other's arsenal. Residual weapons will remain and the war is not over.

Now what happens? The more optimistic explanations of a counterforce strategy imply that at this point the United States has a preponderance of residual weapons, therefore an overwhelming bargaining power, and faces the prospect of an 'all-out' city-destruction war with less to lose than the enemy, whose residual arsenal can do some damage whereas the American one can do damage unlimited. This threatened city war is usually implied to be an all-or-none affair, like full-speed collision on the highway, and the driver who has his whole family in the car is expected to yield to the driver who has only part of his family in the car.

This is unsatisfactory. This counterforce exchange – this first stage in major war – accomplishes partial disarmament on both sides, possibly quite unequally, setting the stage in noisy and confusing fashion for a second stage of dirty war, a stage of nuclear bargaining with cities at stake, a stage of 'violence', of implicit and explicit threats, and probably some competitive destruction of cities themselves to a length that is hard to foretell.

So we have two routes that might lead to this confrontation of violence, one by way of procurement and technology in peacetime, the other by way of a counterforce campaign in war itself. The situation would not be this static, of course. It could be that one side can further disarm the other, in a process that takes time, so that there is pressure on the country with the more vulnerable forces to exploit its capacity for violence before it is taken away by the enemy. And, of course, if this brink is arrived at through counterforce warfare, the situation is one of fright and alarm, noise and confusion, pain and shock, panic or desperation, not just a leisurely confrontation of two countries measuring their capacities for violence. The two 'stages' could overlap – indeed, if counterforce action were unpromising for one side, it might omit that stage altogether and proceed with its campaign of coercion. Indeed it might be forced to accelerate its campaign of terror and negotiation by the prospect of losing part of its bargaining power to the other side's counterforce action.

We know little about this kind of violence on a grand scale. On a small scale it occurs between the Greeks and the Turks in Cyprus, and it occurred between the settlers and the Indians in the Far West. It occurs in gang warfare, sometimes in racial violence and civil wars. Terror is an outstanding mode of conflict in localized primitive wars; and unilateral violence has been used to subdue satellite countries, occupied countries, or dissident groups inside a dictatorship. But *bilateral* violence, as a mode of warfare between two *major* countries, especially nuclear-armed countries, is beyond any experience from which we can draw easy lessons.

There are two respects in which a war of pure violence would differ from the violence in Algeria or Cyprus. One is that insurgency warfare typically involves two actively opposed sides – the authorities and the insurgents – and a third group, a large population subject to coercion and cajolery. Vietnam in the early 1960s was less like a war between two avowed opponents than like gang warfare with two competing gangs selling 'protection' to the population.

There is a second difference. It involves the technology of violence. Most of the violence we are familiar with, whether insurgency in under-developed areas or the blockade and strategic bombing of World Wars I and II, were tests of endurance over time, in the face of violence inflicted over time. There was a limit on how rapidly the violence could be exercised. The dispenser of violence did not have a reservoir of pain and damage that he could unload as he chose, but had some maximum rate of delivery; and the question was who could stand it longest, or who could display that he would ultimately win the contest and so persuade his enemy to yield. Nuclear violence would be more in the nature of a once-for-all capability, to be delivered fast or slow at the discretion of the contestants. Competitive starvation works slowly; and blockade works through slow strangulation. Nuclear violence would involve deliberate withholding and apportionment over time; each would have a stockpile subject to rapid delivery, the total delivery of which would simply use up the reserve (or the useful targets).

If I waylaid your children after school, and you kidnap mine, and each of us intends to use his hostages to guarantee the safety of his own children and possibly to settle some other disputes as well, there is no straightforward analysis that tells us what form the bargaining takes, which children in our respective possessions get hurt, who expects the other to yield – and how it all comes out.

There has been remarkably little analysis of this problem in print. It has sometimes been argued, superficially, that the Soviets might blast an American city to prove they meant business, that the Americans would be obliged to blast two Soviet cities in return, and that the Soviets would feel it incumbent on them to blast three (or four?) cities in return, and so the process would go on, growing in intensity until nothing was left. This is an important possibility, but there is nothing 'natural' about it. It is not necessarily a submissive response to destroy half as much in return rather than twice as much. The appropriate strategy for showing resolve, firmness, endurance, contempt, and righteousness is not an easy one to determine. The cold-blooded *acceptance* of pain might be just as impressive as the cold-blooded infliction of it. Pericles endorsed the principle when he told the people of Athens, in the face of a Spartan ultimatum, 'And if I thought I could persuade you to do it, I would urge you to go out and lay waste your property with your own hands and show the Peloponnesians that it is not for the sake of this that you are likely to give in to them'.

This is a strange and repellent war to contemplate. The alternative once-for-all massive retaliation in which the enemy society is wiped out as nearly as possible in a single salvo is less 'unthinkable' because it does not demand any thinking. A single act of resignation, however awful the consequences, is still a single act, an exit, not only a resignation *to* one's fate but a resignation *of* responsibility. The suspense is over. And it may seem less cruel because it does not have a cruel purpose compared with deliberate, measured violence that carries the threat of more. (It is merely purposeless.) It does not require calculating how to be frightful, how to terrorize an adversary, how to behave in a fearsome way and how to persuade somebody that we are more callous or less civilized than he, and can stand the violence and degradation longer than he can. A pure spasm of massive retaliation, if believed to be sufficiently catastrophic, is more like an act of euthanasia, while a consciously conducted 'cities' strategy has the ugliness of torture. Maybe one of the reasons why thermo-nuclear warfare has been likened to 'mutual suicide' is that suicide is often an attractive escapist solution compared with having to go on living. Still, though a conscious 'cities' strategy may be uglier, it would be more responsible than automated all-out fury.

And it might involve destruction of cities. Some nuclear blows might be exchanged until somebody came to terms. There is no guarantee that the terms would reflect the arithmetic of potential violence. If one side can destroy two-thirds of the other, and only be destroyed one-third itself, this does not guarantee that it wins the bargaining hands down, having its own way altogether just because it is decisively superior. Nor does it mean that it has about 'two-thirds' of the bargaining power, and should expect an outcome with which it is twice as pleased (or half as displeased) as its adversary. There is no simple mathematics of bargaining that tells both sides what to expect so that they can jointly recognize the result as a foregone conclusion.

There is no compelling reason to suppose that one side must unconditionally surrender; nor is there any compelling reason to suppose that one side would not unconditionally surrender. The more 'successful' the nuclear bargaining is for both sides, the more weapons will be left unused at the end. In the absence of unconditional surrender both sides retain some weapons. (This only means that both sides keep some cities.) It is an inconclusive way to terminate a war, but better than some conclusive ways.

A war of that sort would have to be *brought* to a close, consciously and by design. It could not simply run down by exhaustion when all the targets were destroyed or all the ammunition expended; the whole idea is to keep the most precious targets undestroyed and to preserve weapons as bargaining assets. Some kind of cease-fire or pause would have to be reached and phased into an armistice, by a bargaining process that might at the outset have to be largely tacit, based on demonstration more than on words, but that sooner or later would have to become explicit.

Even the crudest cease-fire would have to be monitored against surprise resumption of the war. And a negotiated armistice would raise many of the technical problems we associate with arms control and disarmament – inspection and surveillance, judgements of wilful or inadvertent violation, self-inflicted destruction or assisted demolition of excessive residual weapons – but on the demanding time-schedule of missile and supersonic warfare.

Hopefully, motivations would be strengthened as much as leisure were curtailed. There is no guarantee it could be done, no assurance that stable stopping points could be found. But it is the end that counts; the 'last word' may be as important as the 'first strike'; and the terminal stage deserves the same emphasis in planning as the opening salvo. Planning for the terminal stage could not be left, as it often was in wars of the past, to improvisation after the war had started; both ideas and equipment would have to be developed in advance.

There is no sign that the technological implications of such a war – a war that has to be consciously ended, and its ending policed – have received any emphasis or even been explored. The role of manned aircraft in the present 'missile era' could look quite different if war termination were treated as the culmination, not as an afterthought. The criteria for aircraft design might change; for many purposes of surveillance, endurance might be more important than speed, and 'uncontested reconnaissance' might be as important as armed reconnaissance. The payload for a supersonic transport might be people rather than nuclear warheads – negotiators, inspectors, and demolition crews. The information required for conducting a coercive war – bomb-damage information on both sides, for example – and for processing and interpreting the information, would be different, probably more comprehensive, than that required for a contest in pure destruction. And the role of allied strategic forces – British or French Polaris-type submarines, for example – looks very different when the advantages of preserving weapons are commensurate with the advantages of expending them. Small national forces no longer appear solely as an expensive but minor redundancy, especially if the major combatants deplete their own and each other's forces by counterforce action.

Early expression of this 'controlled-nuclear-war' doctrine, in Secretary McNamara's Ann Arbor speech for example, emphasized the need for the most careful control and co-ordination of military forces in wartime – a matter, certainly, of the utmost importance. But in the context of bitter disputes about European nuclear forces, especially the projected French nuclear force, the doctrine was both used and – even more – interpreted as a case for centralized American control. The alleged incompatibility of the strategy with a separate French force was used by Americans as an argument against that force, and by French as an argument against the strategy.

Since the Americans did not win their argument anyway, it is unfortunate that they launched their strategy newborn into the dispute, there to be discredited with at least certain audiences by its role as a debating point. The strategy deserved a more auspicious *début*. Especially unfortunate was any suggestion that, if the Americans lost the argument on European forces, they lost their new strategy with it. There is no very compelling reason why the French should be less interested than the Americans in the controlled, coercive use of their own nuclear capacity for civilian destruction, or uninterested in the United States' pursuing a sensible strategy.

A comparatively small French force cannot, of course, have a 'counterforce' strategy of its own against the Soviet Union, and may contribute little to a joint counterforce capability with its allies; but, as we have seen, that is only one side of the coin. The all-or-none use of strategic nuclear forces may actually make no more sense for a country with a small force than for a country with a stupendous one, except that the smaller force's life expectancy during war may be too short to permit holding any weapons as a coercive reserve. If, though, the force can be made capable of surviving (and, if not, it can probably not seriously threaten retaliation but only threaten to make the enemy take the initiative), then the one-shot retaliatory strike that spends all weapons, and all bargaining power, in a futile act of heroic vengeance – an act so lacking in purpose as to make even the threat a dubious one – can be abandoned for a more serviceable strategy. The implications of a controlled, coercive response strategy need more exploration on both sides of the Atlantic.

Note

1 Thucydides, *The Peloponnesian War*, trans. Rex Warner (Penguin Books, 1954), pp. 58–59.

3 The Control of Proliferation
Three Views
Adelphi Paper 29, 1966

Sir Solly Zuckerman, Ambassador Alva Myrdal and the Rt Hon Lester B. Pearson

The International Assembly on Nuclear Weapons, at which these three papers were delivered, was held at the Guild Inn, Scarborough, near Toronto, on 23–26 June 1966. The conference was sponsored by the American Assembly of Columbia University, the Canadian Institute of International Affairs, the Carnegie Endowment for International Peace and the Institute for Strategic Studies. Some sixty people, from twenty-five countries, took part – politicians, diplomats, national and international civil servants, scholars, military men and journalists. The Assembly included representatives from all the military nuclear powers (except China) and almost all the civil nuclear powers. Although the deliberations were entirely private, a public address was given by a prominent guest speaker on the evening of each day: on 23 June by Sir Solly Zuckerman, Chief Scientific Adviser to the British Government; on 24 June by Ambassador Alva Myrdal, Leader of the Swedish Delegation to the Eighteen-Nation Disarmament Conference in Geneva; and, in a final session on 25 June, by the Canadian Prime Minister, the Rt Hon Lester B. Pearson.

We reproduce here the texts of these three speeches; a few minor insignificant changes have been made, solely conversions from the spoken word to the written. The text of the Assembly's Final Report appears in the September 1966 issue of *Survival*.

TECHNOLOGICAL ASPECTS OF PROLIFERATION

Sir Solly Zuckerman

The subject which I have been asked to discuss is the impact which a non-proliferation treaty would have on the exploitation of atomic energy for peaceful purposes.

At the outset, I should make it plain that I propose to abide by Lord Chalfont's distinction between the terms proliferation and dissemination: proliferation essentially means that you make 'it' yourself, whatever 'it' may be, while dissemination refers to what you get from someone else. Most people believe that when it comes to nuclear weapons, both proliferation and dissemination are bad for mankind, although, as we all sadly know, they as yet cannot agree about the way to stop the process. But equally they are agreed that it is right to encourage the proliferation and dissemination of nuclear technology because of its promise in economic fields.

The aim of the International Atomic Energy Agency, as agreed in its United Nations statute, is to 'seek to accelerate and enlarge the contribution of atomic energy to peace, health and prosperity throughout the world'. I have therefore to use the terms proliferation and dissemination in the sense spelt out by Lord Chalfont, to apply not only to military but also to civil fields; and not only to hardware but also to technical information. My concern throughout is to draw a distinction between the potential of nuclear technology for military purposes, and its possible significance in a world at peace. Whatever steps are taken – in the interests of survival – to inhibit the first should clearly not shut the door to the second.

When I focus the question I have been set more sharply, two distinct issues become apparent: first, the adequacy of the measures that have so far been proposed in order to control the use of fissile material already available or potentially available, and particularly of the plutonium which is produced in civil reactors, as an assurance that there would be no infringement of a non-proliferation treaty once one had been negotiated; and, second, whether there is a reciprocal relation between reactor technology on the one hand and weapons technology or technology in general on the other. Both questions are highly technical. This, however, is not a scientific meeting, nor is my speciality as a scientist nuclear technology. I shall, therefore, discharge my remit within the limits of the general knowledge I have gained of the subject, and in the framework of a brief review of the part which the exploitation of nuclear physics plays in the whole spectrum of advanced technology today. It would be as well if I first dealt with this general problem before touching on the narrower issue of the relation of military to civil nuclear technology, and on the still narrower one of controls.

General

Nuclear energy is the most recent of the series of technological advances which have critically determined the shape and size of our civilization. Each of these – whether the wheel or fire or steam power – has had a major effect on man's social life, and the pattern of our own lives is now set by the interaction of all. By 'our' I do not, however, mean the entire world. Ever since the Neolithic Age the different elements of our technological armoury have spread unevenly and at a different pace across the globe. There are peoples who have not yet emerged from the Stone Age, in a period when others are launching manned vehicles into space.

In spite of historical anomalies such as these, the web of technology has become more and more closely knit over the past twenty years or so – and more closely knit not only in advanced societies such as our own, but also in emergent countries which are now trying to harness technology as the basis of their new industries. A modern plant, whether it be a power-generating station, a fertilizer factory, an oil well or a coal mine, depends not only on the basic science to which it relates, but also on the systems of control engineering that derive from advanced electronics and from computer technology. As education spreads and as the means of communication improve, we must, therefore, expect that the process whereby the advances of science and technology are incorporated into everyday life will gather strength over the whole world. No emergent country trying to remove itself from its past will wish to retrace the slow stages of the technological and industrial evolution by which Great Britain, France, the United States and Canada were transported from the eighteenth into the twentieth century. Everyone knows that the process can now be short-circuited. Before the Revolution of 1917, the USSR was largely illiterate; from the point of view of education, science, technology and industry, it is in the front rank of nations today. And other countries which may still be largely illiterate — at any rate from the point of view of Western culture — already have their nuclear plants and steel industries.

Another lesson which can be drawn from the history of our industrial civilization is that no technological 'benefit' can ever be stifled. When it was invented by Stephenson 150 years ago, the steam engine was as much opposed as are chemical pesticides today. Even a panel of experts appointed by as distinguished a body as the Royal Society of London reported that 'it was dangerous for trains to exceed 30 miles an hour because air would enter the compartments and passengers would be suffocated'. Many of the more important scientists who were in at the birth of atomic physics — men like Rutherford and Bohr — were of the opinion that nuclear energy could never be exploited. But in spite of their view, atomic energy is now as much a fact of life as coal was the source of energy for the development of the original steam engine, and both have to be seen as major elements in the pattern of the world's present industrial civilization.

While the various aspects of modern technology all tend to interact in our industrial culture, different kinds of new enterprise are obviously related to different measures of scientific competence, at the same time as they in turn promote in varying degree and at varying speed new forms of technical development. It took some fifty years from J. J. Thomson's initial proof that the atom was divisible to the building of a nuclear reactor and the development of a nuclear bomb. It has taken less than twenty to exploit solid-state physics, by way of a variety of servo-mechanisms and computers, to the point that a television camera can be landed with relatively absolute accuracy on a predetermined spot on the moon. The rate of technological development is, of course, dependent on the volume of scientific resources which can be put into different ventures. We usually measure the volume in terms of money. But money essentially means trained scientific man-power and other scarce resources, and we know that what is spent on one thing cannot be spent on another. The accelerating pace of the technological evolution of our society inevitably entails higher costs, and clear decisions about social priorities. What is technically possible may not necessarily be either socially desirable or economically sensible. Apart from the USA and USSR, no one dares try to be in the first league in the exploitation of space technology. It is doubtful whether more than a few countries can afford an advanced modern computer industry.

The proliferation of nuclear technology

When we discuss the problem of proliferation, we have first to ask, therefore, where nuclear technology stands in relation to the whole complex of modern technological development. In attempting an answer, the prime questions that have to be considered are, first, is there a real need for any form of proliferation or dissemination of nuclear technology; second, is nuclear technology a vital band in the whole spectrum of modern technology, in the sense that without it others would also be lacking; and, third, does the exploitation of nuclear technology for civil purposes open the door to its military exploitation?

My own answer to the first question would, for the following main reasons, be 'yes'. First, in spite of the vast but unmeasured resources of oil and natural gas in the world, the growth of world population means that conventional sources of energy will ultimately become scarce, and correspondingly more expensive than nuclear power, which is already a competitive source of energy in the United Kingdom. Second, conventional sources of energy, regarded as primary materials, are unevenly distributed over our globe. Most of the world's coal deposits are north of the Equator; not all countries have oil or gas fields. If it were not for the potentialities of nuclear power, there would, therefore, be no possibility that certain barren parts of the world could ever become habitable. Even today nuclear power is helping support some of the permanent surveying team exploring the icy wastes of Antarctica. Third, nuclear technology and power open the gates to a host of major economic and socially desirable developments: for example, to large-scale desalination of sea water in territories where fresh water is at a premium. And, finally, if the spread of nuclear technology were to be inhibited now, and its exploitation for civil purposes left to the major industrial countries already in the field, the gap between the developed and the underdeveloped peoples would be bound to widen, with a continuation and exacerbation of the world's political problems. The Atoms for Peace Programme was launched in 1955, under the auspices of the United Nations, essentially by the then nuclear powers. It held out to the world the promise that the applications of nuclear physics could help solve many pressing social problems. This remains a real possibility, and it cannot be denied now.

My answer to the second question would be somewhat equivocal. Nuclear technology constitutes a most important band in the spectrum of modern technological knowledge, but it is questionable whether it has as yet had as pervasive an influence on the rest of technology as has, say, the explosive growth of electronics, stemming largely from the invention of the transistor. This is mainly because its development has occurred behind a wall of secrecy, which has prevented, or at least delayed, many of the metallurgical and chemical discoveries and engineering processes that have flowed from it becoming incorporated into other areas of our technological culture. As a result, some industrialized countries which have devoted relatively little effort to its promotion have not suffered economically by desisting, while a few which have devoted a lot have not gained much. On the other hand, there can be no doubt that with the vast effort they have put into the promotion of nuclear technology, both the USA and the USSR, and the UK to a lesser extent, have gained a great deal in general technological and industrial competence, and that the gain would have been even greater if the demands of national security had not prevented a readier and more open flow of nuclear knowledge.

The answer to my third question can only be 'yes'. The exploitation of nuclear technology does open the door to military applications, but with essential qualifications, with which I shall deal later. The exploitation of nuclear energy means in the first instance the building and operation of nuclear reactors, and this in turn means the production of plutonium. There are no secrets any longer about the basic principles which underlie the design of an atomic bomb. In my view, it would, therefore, be unreal to believe that men who are sufficiently competent to build, operate and maintain a nuclear reactor, and then separate the plutonium produced, would not also have the competence to manufacture at least a simple nuclear weapon.

Passive constraints to the spread of nuclear technology

Since the risk of opening the door to military exploitation exists, we need to ask how real it is and where and how it can be actively controlled. It is necessary to say 'actively controlled' because there are also passive constraints which are retarding the spread of nuclear technology.

The first of these is finance. While the nuclear powers are actively competing in selling reactors, most of those at the buying end cannot afford the cost in terms of either money or men. International finance and technological aid thus become the main controlling factors in the spread of nuclear industry to the underdeveloped countries; and this, and neither a lack of technological expertise nor political choice, explains in large part the slow spread of nuclear power for peaceful purposes.

Of the two types of cost, the manpower element is probably the more important. If the advanced nations of the world are to lead the underdeveloped countries to the benefits of nuclear power, they also have to help them educate scientists and technologists. By definition, these men would be trained to a scientific culture alien to the general life of their homelands, where, for a complex of reasons, they would be unlikely to find the kind of environment which would match their trained talents. Frustration at home and possible political unrest, as well as material for the international brain-drain, are thus other possible immediate consequences of, and constraints to, the spread of nuclear technology to underdeveloped countries.

Financial and technical aid, and education, are not the only passive constraints which limit the spread of nuclear power. In addition, there is the major problem of the continuing provision of nuclear fuel and other scarce and expensive industrial materials. The general question of the proliferation or dissemination of nuclear technology is thus far from simple. And it constitutes far more than an attempted assessment of the balance of risk of the spread of nuclear weapons in relation to the civil advantages which nuclear power could confer. What first has to be balanced is the total cost in resources, human and otherwise, which the development of nuclear power would demand in countries which have so far not entered the field, in comparison with the achievement of other social objectives. There are risks of varying magnitude wherever we look. There can be no general answer to the problem of balancing the risks, and each case has to be treated on its own merits.

I find it odd that while many writers have speculated about the dangers of the proliferation of nuclear arsenals, and others have been at pains to point out that since 1945 a new military nuclear power has so far emerged only once every five years, not many have been concerned to ask why there are still so few power or production, as opposed to research, reactors in the world. In my view this is not because of bilateral controls, or international controls, of the use of by-product fissile material; nor is it because of moral scruples about the horrors implied by nuclear weapons – although considerations such as these have certainly played a part. I believe that the passive constraints to which I have referred have played the bigger part in the slow spread of nuclear technology, at the same time as I believe that countries which might have made, say, a few nuclear weapons from what plutonium they produce have desisted for a variety of reasons, of which enlightened self-interest was certainly one.

Active constraints to the manufacture of nuclear weapons

Let me turn now to the question of safeguards to control the military use of nuclear materials, and let me begin by saying that the likelihood is that where it would be relatively simple for a country to undertake the construction and operation of a nuclear reactor, it could prove difficult to control the ultimate use of the fissile material which would be produced; whereas in circumstances where the construction and running of a reactor would prove difficult, that is to say, in countries which do not enjoy a high level of technical competence, the problem of control would be easy. Or, to put it differently, control would be fairly easy in the case of dissemination, whereas the difficulties would be directly proportional to the extent of unaided development in the case of proliferation.

As I have already indicated, the basic principles underlying the design of an atomic bomb have been set out in the open literature. The first and crucial requirement for inhibiting the further proliferation of nuclear weapons is, therefore, to devise an internationally acceptable code of 'nuclear' law which would prevent any significant diversion of fissile and other nuclear materials from civil to military application, at the same time as it would not impose unacceptable limitations to the development and application of nuclear technology for peaceful purposes.

To prevent this happening, bilateral and multilateral systems of controls already exist, or are being developed, through the agency of the IAEA. These normally apply to the utilization of fissile material provided by another power, or to production facilities established with imported equipment, and to successive generations of fissile material allowed for in the original transaction. A start has also been made in applying IAEA safeguards, both in the United States and in the United Kingdom, to fissile material that has been domestically produced. Bradwell, one of the UK's largest nuclear power stations, has just been opened to IAEA inspection. So far, there is little experience in the application of safeguards to large-scale power reactors (i.e. those in excess of 100 MW) and no experience in safeguards at U-235 or plutonium separation plants. Measures for extending safeguards to plants designed to reprocess nuclear material are also now under examination, and the first commercial chemical processing plant now coming into service in the USA will be subject to safeguards.

In all these developments it is important that safeguards should be framed flexibly, and that they should be reviewed and modified as we learn more about the operation and monitoring of nuclear facilities. Otherwise, the IAEA system would be quickly discredited by a failure to apply practical, economic and minimal, but at the same time effective, controls at the key points in the chain of acquisition and usage of nuclear materials. These would include power and research reactors, chemical separation plants where fissile material originates, and isotope separation plants in the case of U-235, as well as fuel fabrication and handling facilities. It would be necessary to establish quantitatively the production of all fissile material and to follow it through to bonded store. How this should be done with the least effort, and without generating irritation and suspicion, is in my view for the technical experts to decide amongst themselves. Control requirements for plutonium would range from reactor records of fuel loaded and discharged, through reactor operating power levels, irradiation history of fuel and estimation of plutonium produced. For U-235, control would include full information about electricity supplies, supported by full information about all material entering and leaving the plant area. There may be other points to be agreed in negotiation, such as the question of resident inspectors, and numbers and sources of inspectors, and there would be other facilities to be considered, including research and development. The issues to which I have referred illustrate what I have in mind.

For an international system of safeguards to be acceptable, however, it seems to me essential that it should neither widen nor appear to widen the gap between the developed and the less developed countries. So far as possible, the same controls should, therefore, apply to both nuclear and non-nuclear military powers who seek to use nuclear technology for peaceful purposes.[1]

Safeguards, cut-off and reduction of stockpiles

In the long run, of course, a system of safeguards which would operate most effectively against those least competent in nuclear technology, and hardly at all upon those able to progress by themselves, could not prove effective. In the short run it might be rejected out of hand. Consequently the more a 'cut-off' agreement designed to prohibit the production of fissile material for weapon purposes is associated with a reduction in nuclear weapon stockpiles, the more would verification measures appropriate to the nuclear-weapon powers approximate to those agreed as necessary for the prevention of proliferation of nuclear weapons and for the control of international trade in reactors for civil purposes.

Were such a system of international safeguards to be accepted and applied – permitting, as it would, the full exploitation of nuclear technology for peaceful purposes, without increasing the danger of military proliferation – there should be an end to the notion that to be a member of the 'nuclear club' one would have to have demonstrated an ability to carry out a nuclear explosion. 'Nuclear status' should be assigned to any country that is able to demonstrate its competence in the exploitation of nuclear energy. This means an effective knowledge of such matters as the associated metallurgical and chemical processes, of the nuclear properties of fuels, of the effects of radiation on materials, as well as an ability to apply at the industrial level standards and techniques once thought only possible in the laboratory. I can cite a well-known illustration of what is meant by these standards. The conventional standard used in the welding of boilers is 'permissible drops a minute'. No more than one drop in five years – not minutes – is permissible in the atomic field. Other engineering standards are every bit as exacting. It is far easier for writers to talk of these things than for scientists and engineers to achieve them.

Nuclear test ban

I have gone into the concept of safeguards at some length because I believe it offers the most promising way of instituting active constraints to the manufacture of nuclear weapons, and so of implementing a non-proliferation treaty. It facilitates a positive rather than a negative approach to the development and control of nuclear energy; it does not stifle its civil applications; and it is capable of effective realization, given the will. With the concept of safeguards, I have associated a cut-off in the production of fissile material for weapon purposes. A cut-off not only would help inhibit the proliferation of nuclear weapons, but would also limit weapon stockpiles among the powers which already produce nuclear weapons. It could also lead to the reduction of stockpiles, given an agreement to transfer to peaceful purposes some of the fissile material at present in nuclear armouries.

A further constraint complementary to both of these concepts would be a comprehensive test ban, although it may be that the importance of this can be overestimated in the context of proliferation.

Underground tests, and the achievement of their objectives, demand a great deal of expertise. The development of even a relatively unsophisticated weapon for purposes of testing would necessitate the use of expensive and sophisticated materials and equipment. This consideration would become increasingly important with increasing sophistication in weapon design.

I find it difficult to see how any country which is poor in technical and economic resources could readily embark on a programme of underground tests, particularly when it is remembered that, even if the weapon itself can be provided, a train of expensive courses must follow to create an effective armoury. Nevertheless, the existence of a comprehensive test ban would be one more vital safeguard in a chain of non-proliferation measures. A ban would in any event be desirable to discourage and possibly prevent a technological breakthrough which could conceivably upset what is usually regarded as an existing nuclear balance between the two major nuclear powers.

There is no need for me to dwell here on the difficulties that have arisen in discussions of underground nuclear tests. As we all know, the point on which there is no agreement is the need for on-site inspection in order to verify some seismic events which may occur and which cannot be identified as earthquakes from instrumental records alone. This is essentially a political matter, and it is for governments to decide where the balance of advantage lies, whether to live with the risk of the present nuclear balance being upset by the applications of the results of some test or tests, or whether to extend the test ban in order to help discourage the proliferation of nuclear weapons. As in the case of safeguards, it may be that on this issue the powers which now dispose of nuclear weapons might have to make what some people would be inclined to regard as a sacrifice in order to achieve effective non-proliferation measures, and so reduce the scale of the perils with which this meeting is concerned.

Adequacy of constraints

As Mrs Myrdal has pointed out in Geneva, almost every step in the development of a capacity to use atomic energy for peaceful purposes could be a step which might eventually allow the production of nuclear weapons. And as she further observed: 'We could, of course, all agree that it is important to block the road to nuclear weapon development as early as possible. But we must be aware that what we are facing is a long ladder with many rungs, and the practical question is: On which of these is it reasonable and feasible to introduce international blocking? The question is interconnected with the one of control: Where is that step located at which clear evidence of preparation [for the manufacture of nuclear weapons] begins to show and at which control can be made effective?'

We cannot ascribe our failure to formalize non-proliferation arrangements for nuclear weapons to the fact that there has been a spread of nuclear technology for peaceful purposes. Nor is the failure due to a lack of ability on the part of scientists to formulate reasonable and feasible means of safeguards. At present it is primarily due, as most of the background papers before this Assembly show, to political disagreements between the East and the West in respect of wider military arrangements. While these exist, scientists have to beware lest by an over-elaboration of possible controls, they not only distort what could be reasonable and feasible measures of control, but also inhibit the whole development of nuclear technology.

The problem of delivery systems

As we all know, constructing nuclear weapons is only one part of the problem of proliferation. There is also the question of buying, building and operating the aircraft and missiles without which nuclear warheads would be regarded as mere status symbols. This issue is a further passive constraint to the proliferation of nuclear weapon development.

Most countries, however, already possess aircraft, and theoretically these could suffice as delivery systems, given they had the range to operate against predetermined enemy targets, and given that the latter lacked the defences with which to deal with relatively unsophisticated intruders. Militarily I find it difficult to believe that this could ever be the case. I can hardly imagine that any country would embark upon a policy in which it would threaten the use of nuclear weapons, however simple, if it did not possess advanced strike aircraft and adequate defences of its own. Control in this respect is clearly in the hands of the greater powers. If the sale or use of such aircraft were properly controlled, this particular aspect of the risk of proliferation would disappear.

Missile development is in another category. First of all, despite advancing space research and satellite communications, it is highly improbable that there would be an international sale of the kind of missiles which might be used as vehicles for nuclear warheads. Secondly, the problem of devising, developing and building missiles which could be used to deliver nuclear warheads accurately is extremely difficult technologically, and very costly, both in materials and in manpower. Few countries are advanced in the field of solid-fuel technology. Guidance systems based upon advanced gyros and servo-mechanisms demand a level of expertise which has not been spread very widely. The miniaturization of circuits in the exploitation of solid-state physics is also a very difficult problem. If we wish to feel absolutely secure about this aspect of the problem of dissemination, the solution would, of course, be to agree on effective safeguards against the dissemination of knowledge in these fields and against the provision of technical or financial aid for work aimed at developing medium- and long-range surface-to-surface missiles. I know the difficulties of achieving this, and I realize that some countries might well feel they were being discriminated against if others, particularly the greater powers, stopped selling components which could be used in the development of missiles. To obtain wide-spread co-operation in such a step, it might therefore be necessary for the nuclear powers to associate with a non-proliferation agreement other measures of arms control or disarmament by which they, too, were bound.

Conclusion

I propose to end, where I began, with the dual proposition that nuclear weapons – if regarded as weapons for use – imply a hideous danger for mankind, at the same time as there are endless useful potentialities for nuclear energy in the civil field. The considerations I have put before you force me to the conclusion that no country would be denied knowledge which would be useful to its economic development if it desisted from the manufacture of atomic weapons. The military and civil exploitations of nuclear technology are not necessarily linked. In our efforts to prevent the proliferation of weapons, we should not, therefore, drive ourselves into the paradoxical situation that we deny a peaceful world the benefits of nuclear energy.

Neither uranium mines, nor plants for the fabrication of reactor fuel elements, nor reactors are in themselves a military danger. They promote no military purpose unless they are coupled with plants for the extraction of fissile material and with facilities for the fabrication of that material into weapons. And it is only the latter which has any exclusively military purpose. Fissile material either in process of production or in use can be safeguarded against any diversion to military application. If all such plants were monitored under some international agreement, most of the dangers of the military exploitation of atomic energy would be averted. There are, in short, no significant technical problems in controlling the use of the fissile material which would be produced in civil reactors.

There can be few governments which are not now aware, at least in general terms, of the relatively enormous price which the military nuclear powers have had to pay in order to achieve that status. Capital costs, running costs, and a never diminishing shortage of scientific manpower are a perpetual reminder of that price, as no doubt they are powerful economic deterrents to such other countries as may sometimes be tempted to believe that political and military power is necessarily associated with the possession of nuclear weapons. This may have been true once; it may still be true in some cases; but experience has shown that it is not necessarily true in all circumstances. Even within the esoteric framework within which these matters are usually discussed, nuclear weapons are hardly ever the same thing, or hardly ever mean the same thing, to different people. The cost of deploying them can be far greater than that of producing them, and there is every shade to the theoretical concept of military nuclear power – from total unreality to total stability.

The consensus of informed opinion is that the proliferation of nuclear weapons – whether by acquisition, if that were possible, or by domestic production – would bring the world into a greater state of peril than the one in which it now stands. The arguments on this subject are fully deployed in the background papers before the Assembly. Either nuclear energy could be the end-all, or it could be the be-all of humanity, depending on how it is used. Our political differences have forced us to consider the problem of proliferation essentially from the former point of view. We are so concerned with the dangers of nuclear bombs that, to offset them, some would even forego the potential benefits of nuclear power. We would, as it were, kill the goose that lays the golden egg because of its hideous quack.

But we cannot run away from the problem like this. Sooner or later, depending on where, man will have to use nuclear energy for his peaceful purposes. Somehow or other we have therefore to overcome the present impasse, and decide whether the reasons for foregoing agreement in the military nuclear field are commensurate with the losses which such a failure entails in the civil field. The dangers of our past industrial milestones – steam power, trains, motor cars, aeroplanes – were exaggerated at the time they were reached. But there can be no question of overestimating the dangers to man of the military exploitation of atomic power. Equally there must be no underestimation of the value to man, indeed of the vital necessity, of harnessing nuclear energy for peaceful ends. If nuclear weapons were to spread far and wide, man might well be destroyed. But if nuclear power for civil purposes were inhibited because of our fear of the proliferation of nuclear weapons, men might well starve when their numbers become twice what they now are – by the year 2000, we are warned, little more than the time that has passed since the first nuclear bomb was exploded.

The negotiations for a non-proliferation treaty, for an extension of the test ban, for any measure of disarmament, are long and arduous. So, too, are the technical efforts to build up an effective and acceptable IAEA scheme of monitoring. But both enterprises are vital, as indeed they are parallel. The smallest steps forward in either field means progress. The politician can rest assured that the scientist is fully aware of this fact, and of the need to achieve agreement in the fields with which negotiations are concerned.

Note

1 It has been argued that, for powers already producing nuclear weapons and already possessing large stockpiles of fissile material, verification of usage of nuclear materials (after a cut-off or cessation in production for weapon purposes) need not be very stringent, since there would be little or no incentive to divert such materials from peaceful activities. In these cases the military significance of small diversions would be negligible. On the other hand, for the non-nuclear-weapon

powers any diversion might be significant, and hence in their case much greater stringency is required in verification of production and usage of nuclear materials.

© *Sir Solly Zuckerman* 1966

POLITICAL ASPECTS OF NON-PROLIFERATION

Ambassador Alva Myrdal

Let me start out by stating how paradoxical is the situation whenever in this period of history we assemble to discuss any aspect of disarmament. On one hand, the race for armaments is being run faster than ever in most nations of the world; on the other, the debate on disarmament is being pursued with more seriousness and in more realistic terms than ever before. The era has long since gone by when disarmament discussions were relegated to the sphere of ideology, moralism and, yes, romanticism.

The negotiations, so persistently continuing, seemingly against all odds, at the Eighteen-Nation Disarmament Conference (ENDC) in Geneva testify to the fact that at the present time international public opinion conceives of the situation as imminently dangerous. And the leading statesmen of the world seem to be serious in a search for remedies which can be translated into political realities. The salvation of the world is not anticipated as coming about by some sudden stroke of redemption. It must be achieved, if achieved it can be, by laborious construction, using as foundations the hard facts of the military and political realities as they exist.

My point of departure will be exactly the same. But speaking in my personal capacity here, I wish to carry the debate beyond what is actually on the agenda in Geneva and ask: What possibilities in terms of regulations of armaments is it realistic to discuss in the setting of the actually prevalent political conditions and trends?

Our duty at conferences such as this one must be to open up perspectives. And the perspectives for reaching agreements on disarmament measures and for neutralizing threatening conflicts seem to me to devolve in some rather definite stages, one after another. The one closest to our point in time calls for a discussion of measures, such as non-proliferation, which are most definitely realizable. The perspective of the next order is also fairly clearly discernible: certain other matters pertaining to disarmament have then to be discussed as opportunities which must be grasped within the next five or at the utmost ten years, lest they be irretrievably lost. The pertinent, most imperative task for that period is, I believe, to create neutralized and nuclear-free zones – i.e. to combine solving political problems in certain regions with sealing them off against nuclear armament – a measure most blatantly needed in Europe. Beyond these stages lies a third, more distant one, perhaps barely thinkable, but predicated on the need to save the world from insanity in the longer run. For that stage we would have to proceed to discuss more definite all-round disarmament, not least in order to make decisive economies available for developing the poverty-stricken regions of the world, a need that will become critical when our young generation comes of age, facing, as they might well do, global catastrophe – and this is no rhetorical exaggeration. I submit that we must study these perspectives together and study them *now*. Because what help is non-proliferation today if we anyway have to face holocaust?

The agenda for today: non-proliferation of nuclear weapons

This whole conference, as well as the negotiators in Geneva, unanimously proceeds on the basic assumption that to stop the spread of nuclear weapons to additional countries is desirable *per se* and that it is urgent. I whole-heartedly agree. But should we not also all agree that the measures tailored to achieve this 'non-proliferation', as I will continue to label it for short, must be so selected that they constitute a *beginning* of the long-run development towards security, or at least that they do not obstruct or retard it?

Let me therefore attempt a bird's eye analysis of our conference topic with these main assumptions in mind. Immediately, we face a choice between two different methods to reach the goal of non-proliferation. One possibility is what I might term the 'classical' approach, which envisages achieving non-proliferation through a treaty-bound political agreement. In reality, this only calls for a solemn pledge by countries which are so far non-nuclear-weapon states to refrain from acquiring such weapons. This approach is the one mainly dealt with by Lord Chalfont in his background paper, and it has also been the main avenue followed in the negotiations in Geneva.

The second method might be called the 'instrumental' or 'operational' one. It would seek to achieve non-proliferation by agreements which make acquisition of nuclear weapons materially impossible, or well-nigh so. It ought to be self-evident that the most direct route to non-proliferation would be to prohibit the very production of fissile material for weapon purposes and to build in operational controls which would guarantee that the agreement be adhered to. Another, only somewhat less decisive way is to prohibit certain steps which are practically necessary preliminaries for production of nuclear weapons. The one outstanding loophole which then has to be closed is that of conducting underground tests.

Standing at this crossroad, our task should be first to compare, in a fair and rational way, the *efficacy* and general merits of these alternative methods just briefly described, and then to compare, also as objectively as we can, their political *acceptability* in the circumstances of our time.

Let me then state bluntly that by far the least effective is the 'classical' method, i.e. a simple treaty purporting to get pledges that the nuclear-weapon-club membership should not be extended beyond its present number of five states. It would not result in any reduction of present nuclear armouries, and it would mean no stop to the nuclear armaments race, which goes on at a speed which really terrifies mankind. Such a treaty might have been of greater avail if the sense of urgency which is now evidenced by the superpowers had led them to work for such an agreement before China and France had 'bombed their way' into the nuclear club. Or even earlier: the most propitious moment that has been registered in our long-drawn-out history of disarmament negotiations was certainly that moment twenty years ago when the Baruch plan offered to internationalize atomic energy. Or, we might daydream still further backwards and surmise that the one auspicious day was before the decision was ever taken to steer research and development in the atomic field towards the making of bombs. But once man has eaten of the tree of knowledge, the fall into sin can hardly be undone.

The fact remains that even if we were to arrive at an agreement on the lines of either of the two draft treaties on non-proliferation, officially proposed by the USA and the USSR, it would not achieve one iota of disarmament. Still, it would have a political value if an agreement could pass the threshold into reality. But here we are confronted not only with the argument of low-grade efficacy from a disarmament point of view but with veritable obstacles of a political order. For the purpose of assessing the probable weight of these obstacles, we have to look at the two distinct elements which constitute a treaty of the kind proposed. On one hand, it contains an element which has been most appropriately described as 'non-dissemination', placing the main responsibility on the present nuclear weapon nations, which should undertake not to 'disseminate' nuclear weapons to other states, while these in a corresponding but passive rôle agree not to accept the favours of such dissemination. On the other hand, it would prohibit what I am treating as the central element, as 'proliferation' proper, namely attempts by hitherto non-nuclear-weapon states to proceed to production of such weapons. How promising in reality are the prospects of success when we size up the political situation in regard to these two issues of non-dissemination and non-proliferation?

On the non-dissemination side, the responsibility rests solely with the present nuclear weapon states. The political situation can be summed up in a couple of sentences. There is no expectation that France or China will enter into any pledge not to 'disseminate' nuclear weapons to other countries, although there is no likelihood either that they will proceed on such a course. Further, there exists a probability verging on certainty that, with or without any treaty, the two superpowers, the United States and the USSR, are bound not to 'disseminate' nuclear weapons to any state that does not already possess them, in the sense of transferring independent control over such weapons to additional countries.

But between the superpowers, so patently joined by a common interest, there has entered a reservation or divergence as to interpretation which has come to constitute a definite stumbling block: the question whether 'nuclear-sharing' can take place within an alliance. The issue has taken on such magnitude that already, on this seemingly very tractable measure of a pledge of 'non-dissemination' on the part of the nuclear weapon powers, the political acceptability seems to be close to nil. In the straightforward language of foreign policy, the hurdle has so far been localized to the NATO alliance, or to be more specific, to the clash of interest as to the rôle of Germany in nuclear affairs. But, as has lately been repeatedly stressed, the problem has longer shadows. If the treaty language as suggested by the United States is to stand, the door would not be closed to nuclear arming of any alliances, existing or future ones, although a veto on the use of such weapons is foreseen as being retained by the present nuclear-weapon powers. Then there would be no definite end to 'dissemination'. Rather, an inducement would perhaps be created for states to abandon non-alignment and neutrality, and 'go nuclear' collectively. This would be an opening to a future fraught with unknowns.

So far, the non-nuclear-weapon countries have not opted for such a course. Their attention has been centred on the proliferation issue proper, i.e. the possibility of stopping them from becoming the sixth or seventh or nth state to produce nuclear weapons of its own. As long, however, as there is no agreement in view between the superpowers on the simpler 'non-dissemination' issue, there has been no political necessity for the potential nuclear-weapon countries to circumscribe their postures. Their concrete defence plans and their ultimate willingness to forego nuclear weapons have not yet been the object of real negotiations. No doubt there is a risk inherent in any delay; the political climate and the military threats in many regions might change appreciably in the course of the time which is now being lost in fruitless debate.

One such risk, for which particularly the non-aligned nations are keeping their eyes wide open, is exactly what is going to happen to the character of alliances: will allied countries in one's neighbourhood get a greater share in the world's nuclear strength? It should not be overlooked that the problems, here described in the euphemistic terms of non-dissemination and non-proliferation, of receiving nuclear arms as a gift or of getting protection from them or of manufacturing them, are diabolically intertwined in many regions, Asia no less than Europe. That is one reason why the issues which I have predicted as belonging to stage two become more and more pressing, namely the connection between alliances and the possibilities of alternatives such as denuclearized zones.

But a more acute question mark as to the political value of a non-proliferation treaty on the 'classical' model is raised in Geneva and the United Nations, particularly by the non-aligned among the non-nuclear-weapon states. It is dictated by what to them is an overriding aim: that steps be taken which bring to a halt and then turn into reverse the present arms race, so costly to our economies and so horrifying to our minds. When an impressive overture was made in Moscow by the agreement of 1963 to stop nuclear testing in all media except underground, the optimism engendered in the world was not least due to the fact that this was a measure making demands on nuclear and non-nuclear-weapon countries in one and the same grasp. There, on the one hand, three nuclear weapon countries, among them the two superpowers, agreed to *cease* testing, thus foregoing certain further developments of arms technology (or so we believed). On the other hand, some hundred non-nuclear-weapon countries, simultaneously agreed *not to start* such testing, thus closing a fairly important option for independent manufacture of nuclear weapons. Psychologically and politically, it meant indicating to their own electorates that they were ready to pursue a non-nuclear-weapons course. It is those latter countries, and more particularly their spokesmen in Geneva, who claim that the next steps in the disarmament field must use the same two-pronged approach, asking of both types of nations a manifestation of their determined will to start to sacrifice nuclear armaments and options.

So far, in the last three years, we have seen precious little of any determination on the part of the nuclear-weapon countries to make a start on a new course leading to reduced armaments and greater world security. No wonder that the have-nots are not inspired to take political decisions of a one-sided character, when the real danger of nuclear war-machines is not being reduced. Of course, they do not threaten to begin production of nuclear weapons as a gesture of spite; they just continue to be reluctant to sign a treaty of the kind presented. This reluctance to sign has a foundation in realistic political consideration of the opinions within their countries.

The non-aligned nations in Geneva, as well as several others, speaking in the UN, strongly believe that disarmament measures should be a matter of mutual renunciation. Therefore, they have refused to subscribe to the judgement that the most urgent disarmament measure in our time is an international treaty merely on non-proliferation, which would leave the present five nuclear weapon nations free to continue to build up their arsenals, to perfect the deadliness of their weapons and to deploy them more widely among allies. Also, they have begun to think that we are wasting time when, for more than a year, the issue of non-proliferation has monopolized the deliberations both in the UN and at Geneva, without any sign of progress. A brave Canadian might say: 'Tant de bruit pour une telle petite omelette!'

Let us rather examine the alternative, or what I have called the 'instrumental' approach to non-proliferation, leaving non-dissemination as the continued concern of the nuclear weapon powers. This approach offers two steps, to be undertaken consecutively or, preferably, simultaneously. They have persistently been advocated as an alternative, or adjunct, to a non-proliferation treaty of the more 'classical' model by representatives of the smaller and particularly the non-aligned nations, who tend to advance somewhat more freely, faster and further than the superpowers and the countries aligned in their blocs. The advantages of these alternatives seem very clear-cut, both from the technical angle of efficacy and from the political angle of acceptability. One is the cutting-off of production of fissile material for weapons purposes, to which I will shortly return; I start with the other one, the prohibition of underground test explosions, which for the sake of convenience had been sidestepped in the Moscow treaty.

The benefits of a treaty prohibiting nuclear tests underground are obvious. They run in both the directions desired, since such a ban would stifle nuclear weapons developments in the 'have' countries, and reduce practically to zero the possibilities for the 'have-not' countries to produce nuclear weapons on their own. This latter aspect is singularly little studied by the superpowers, although everybody has tacitly taken for granted that the great number of states who signed the Moscow treaty would also enter upon these new obligations, if alongside them again went at least three of the nuclear weapon states. The loophole left by the Moscow treaty offers a not insignificant opportunity for potential nuclear-weapon countries to test any nuclear explosives which they might try to evolve deskwise. The other steps, which, consisting in research and development work, are preliminary to production of nuclear weapons, would be practically impossible to control, however important it is considered to be a halt them. Underground test explosions constitute the most tangible or visible, or perhaps one should say audible, preparatory measure in that they can be detected with a fair degree of certainty even from afar.

In this connection, I cannot refrain from mentioning that the possibilities for international co-operation in regard to teleseismological detection are widening. The road is now being paved for informal, voluntary co-operation between national seismological stations, as signified by a recent meeting of a 'club' for detection purposes held in Stockholm. While the interpretation of any data, and particularly the question as to their usefulness for 'identifying' seismic events as either natural or man-made, would be left to authorities within each interested nation, the very existence of opportunities for facilitating indirect, long-distance surveillance methods would make the claims for direct, on-the-spot inspections dwindle. These claims might even be made to disappear. Inspections entail many more difficulties and pitfalls than are usually explicitly admitted by their advocates, such as exactly localizing the epicentre of a suspected event, or rushing in the inspection apparatus in time, or obtaining conclusive evidence by collecting radio-active debris, etc. On the other hand, indications, observable from the outside, are becoming more and more reliable; besides teleseismic signals, there is the evidence of human activity around a suspected test-site, which is observable from satellites, etc. A further fact to ponder is that when great powers have discussed on-site inspections, whether seven or three or none, they seem to have done so from an exclusively 'adversary' position; at least, nobody has explained what would be the rights of the hundred other states, parties to a treaty, to ask for inspections, or to what inspections they would have the duty to submit.

This last observation has pointed up how dangerous it is to allow political factors to obscure what should be straightforward technical considerations of the efficacy of a certain measure. I boldly venture to state that *from a technical, operative point of view a comprehensive test ban would be a highly efficient means to forestall proliferation of nuclear weapons to further countries, and that it would not be too difficult to construct control measures which would give resonable assurances about adherence to the treaty obligations.* One element in a control system is what we from the Swedish side have called verification by challenge, i.e. the pressure upon a suspected party to give all available reassuring information, including possibly an invitation to inspection in order to exculpate itself. But let me not dwell on details; where there is a will, there is always a way.

The obstacles seem to be much more of a political order and concerned with national rather than international interests, be it the risk that what is still called 'the other side' will cheat or the risk that it might spy. I am trying hard not to enter upon the domains of domestic policy in any country. But the very persistence with which the superpowers' policymakers raise objections in relation to a test ban is to me a sign that they have not considered the comprehensive test ban with respect to its merits as a *non-proliferation* measure, closing the option for additional countries to 'go nuclear'.

If due consideration were given to its instrumental value for achieving non-proliferation, it seems to me that the superpowers would be nearer to concluding such an agreement, and that even the issue of control might loose some of its spellbinding power. But of course there is always the possibility that we are mistaken or misled. The arguments so far brought forward against speedy agreement on a comprehensive test ban may not be the real ones. Perhaps it is just shadow-boxing. Perhaps the superpowers have new military reasons for not *wanting* to cease testing.

Many experts could be quoted in support of a mounting suspicion that the recent stepping up of underground nuclear testing is connected with expectations, on the part of both the superpowers, of securing some important technological breakthrough in weapons development, perhaps particularly as regards an anti-ballistic missile system. If this is the case, military reasons for not wanting to stop testing should be presented overtly, instead of letting the negotiations stall on the rather sterile discussions on inspections and the risk of espionage. The effects of new weapon developments, not least in terms of costs and political tension, are highly important in the eyes of smaller nations and might influence our pros and cons for non-proliferation. And, reflected in the looking-glass of reason, they could hardly be reassuring to the great powers themselves. A recent White House report on arms control and disarmament, prepared by a committee headed by Jerome Wiesner, had some ominous words to say about the dangers, particularly the political dangers, of improving the *quality* of nuclear weapons: 'It is, after all, the continuing competition to perfect and deploy new armaments that absorbs quantities of time, energy and resources that no static strategic environment would demand; that exacerbates US and Soviet relations with unreal considerations of strategic advantage or disadvantage; that keeps political leaders in both great powers off-balance and ill-prepared for far-reaching agreements; that fixes the attention of both sides on the most threatening aspects of the opposing posture; and, especially, that provides heightened risks of a violent spasm of procurement – one spurring to new levels of cost, distrust, and the explosive dangers of an unending competition in arms' (p. 14). If such are the designs for the future, we had better be told. I need not spell out that if what is hidden behind the unwillingness to give up underground testing is a new race to perfect the deadliest quality of nuclear weapons, then it will be hard for anybody to place great trust in talks about disarmament.

Restricting myself, however, to the political arguments which lie more open to observation, I can only judge that they would weigh heavily in favour of giving high priority in the Geneva negotiations to a comprehensive test-ban treaty. Like the measure of a 'cut-off', next to be discussed, a test ban would hold out more hope of speedy agreement than the 'classical' non-proliferation treaty, if only because neither measure could become bogged down on the German problem. Judged as a whole, the cost to the superpowers of acceding to a full test-ban treaty would seem small indeed, while to the world at large the gain would be very great.

The tendency to overlook all but 'adversary' postures and interests is even more noticeable in regard to the second measure which constitutes an 'instrumental' approach to non-proliferation, namely a categorical cut-off of the production of fissile material for weapon purposes. As an actual proposal in Geneva, it is embedded in a more complex US package. But the nuclear weapon powers seem hardly to have taken into account that such a measure might be construed as a decisive non-proliferation measure. It would be effective for the haves and the have-notes alike, since it would imply a formal undertaking by perhaps hundreds of nations never to start such production, and at the same time require from the nations who wield nuclear weapons that they just 'freeze' their stockpiles of nuclear war material at the present levels.

To be effective, and trustworthy, such an agreement presupposes effective control measures. They are not as easy to implement, in one sense, as in the case of a test ban, since they cannot to a comparable degree be of the indirect variety. On the other hand, their selection should be easy, since recourse would be taken to IAEA safeguards, elaborated in Vienna through a consensus between East and West, between aligned and non-aligned countries. Important contributions have lately been made towards establishing simplified bench rules for such a system in order to make the control as unobtrusive as possible, and to allay any fears that it might be used for spying either on military installations or on atomic production secrets.

What remains is to reach an agreement on a general outline for the successive implementation of certain steps. This time-table aspect is important, since it will decide when different countries should accept control over the various rungs on the nuclear-production ladder. A kind of rank order suggests itself: the first point of control might be established at sale or other transfer between countries of reactors and fuel elements, extending to *all* countries in the present IAEA system; next, control might be introduced at all *new* installations of plutonium separation plants, even if domestic in origin; and, finally, the control might come to embrace all chemical separation and gas diffusion plants (or these might even become internationalized as Leonard

Beaton has suggested). Some political objections are being heard in relation both to control of transfers between countries and to control of domestic plants for peaceful purposes. But the point is that such objections would be smaller than those that would be raised if IAEA safe-guards under present conditions were applied to all countries; they should even disappear altogether. At present, the nuclear-weapon countries refuse general inspection because some of their plants may be working for military purposes as well as for peaceful uses of atomic energy. But if a cut-off agreement were reached, there would exist, after a certain time-lag, no plants of the former kind to protect from control.

What, then, are the prospects on a larger political scale for such an agreement? On the part of the hitherto non-nuclear-weapon countries, their willingness to accept curtailment of a technical option to produce nuclear weapons would be considerably greater than it has been in regard to the political non-proliferation treaty. They have persistently argued that this measure and the test ban should have priority over the 'naked' non-proliferation treaty. Most decisive would be that the two measures offer the double-pronged approach desired, with sacrifices shared by all kinds of countries and with a definitely constraining effect on the terrifying arms race. The superpowers, on their side, have not proffered any arguments that would make an agreement seem impossible. As a matter of fact, in April 1964 both the USA and the USSR, in a parallel move, announced that they were voluntarily cutting off, to a materially not unimportant extent, their production of enriched uranium and of plutonium for military purposes. To make assurance doubly sure, one may point to their statements, or even boasts, so often repeated, that they possess 'overkill capacity'. The whole world is already at their mercy. *The practical conclusion is that the beneficial effects of an agreement to curtail production of fissile material for weapons purposes as from today would be immeasurably greater than the sacrifices called for* – if anything worthy of the label 'sacrifice' is at all involved.

A practical point to consider, however, is that no issue should be made of what stockpiles the nuclear countries at present possess, or how they measure up to each other, so that there need be no discussion about any balance being upset. The existing balance, not measurable but pragmatically estimated to provide sufficient deterrence, would not be affected by any simple 'freezing' of the situation. Thus, a decision to cut off production of nuclear material for weapon purposes presents such a remarkably well underpinned measure that it would seem to take only a watt of political dynamism to allow it to rise to the stage of implementation. What is requested is just that we should take the consequence of the conviction we all share that the world has enough of nuclear weapons material.

Parenthetically, I may add that this point once reached, the time will certainly come for raising the bid for some true sacrifices, for transferring into energy for peaceful uses more and more of the fissile material intended for weapons. Because, in addition to the other benefits, in terms of non-proliferation and relaxation of political tensions, this measure yields definite material gains. We who are so ruefully concerned with the plight of the under-developed countries should not turn our sight away from the fact recently cited by the IAEA that the total flow of electric energy in the world would be doubled if we could use for peaceful purposes the fissile material that is already produced and stored for weapons purposes, and already paid for on military budgets.

Before concluding this, the major and more professional part of my speech, let me sum up by saying that it is astonishing that we – in Geneva, to be precise – are not immediately proceeding to work out (*a*) a cut-off and (*b*) a test-ban agreement. May I add an *argumentum ad hominem* here: one should not underrate the fact that these are measures which important so-called 'potential' nuclear-weapon countries offer, and that thereby they *do* offer their own renunciation of nuclear weapons, provided, of course, they are in good company. If these two agreements were reached, they might well be crowned by a general non-proliferation treaty. When that has been placed first and so much time lost on it, something has evidently gone wrong with the time-table in our disarmament negotiation. Perhaps too many have been afflicted with a kind of politico-psychological blindness. I cannot help being reminded of the Andersen story 'The Emperor's New Clothes'. The Danish poet had some shrewd psychological insight. Let me quote the passage about when it began to dawn upon the Emperor that the people were right, that he was dressed in simply nothing: 'All the same, he thought to himself, I've got to go through with it as long as the procession lasts'.

The agenda for tomorrow: regional solutions to political and military problems

What I have discussed so far is truly the agenda of today. To achieve a *freeze* or containment of nuclear armaments – with respect to their quantity and quality as well as their further spread – must in a rational light be regarded as feasible today, even if some political side glances, which in this domain are often of a prestige character, have so far hampered progress. Still, so long as we have been dealing with these *ad hoc*, 'collateral' measures, to speak the language of the ENDC – however necessary they may be for beckoning a new course for the world – no real disarming has come into sight nor any solutions of the political problems which keep subdivisions of our globe armed against each other. No nation seems willing to let the level of its armaments effectively recede in the situation of today, with its highly poignant political realities such as Vietnam – which I have hesitated even to mention. But it is difficult to be very hopeful about our ability *to proceed much beyond what I have termed first-order measures in the disarmament field – i.e. the non-proliferation category – if*, pari passu, *some political problems specifically connected with disarmament proposals are not solved.*

When I bring in this political aspect, I am frankly striking out beyond my mandate as Swedish delegate to the ENDC, and I want to underline that I am talking in my personal capacity only. But I hold that it is high time to attempt to block out certain lines of international policy-making for an intermediate stage, after we have – hopefully – succeeded in 'containing' nuclear armaments and before we can be ready to tackle the final objective: truly international regulation of armaments, large-scale disarmament and the establishment of a new international order of peace, law and progress. Of course, this does not mean waiting idly until one set of problems is solved. It only means doing the planning in a prospective way along an axis of time.

To continue this line of thought, my suggestion for this intermediate stage is that we should start to look at both disarmament and internationally disruptive conflicts from *a regional point of view*. Such a review makes it evident that some of the most hotly contended issues in various regions are no longer 'rational' but are aftermaths of old conflicts. It seems unreasonable that we should let these postures jam our efforts permanently, unsettling the whole international situation. This is not least true in regard to certain politico-military arrangements – of alliances or great-power support – which are beginning to have outlived their period of usefulness.

Such specific postures, which I hold are slowing up disarmament progress and 'irrationally' aggravating the international scene because they are outdated, and which consequently we 'ought' to be able to clear out of the way in the not too distant future, are to be found particularly with respect to Latin America, the Middle East and Europe. These three trouble areas, which I want explicitly to mention as ripe for clearing, are also the very ones for which denuclearized zones have been most concretely discussed. The connections with disarmament are much less direct in relation to the two remaining storm centres, which may be briefly indicated as southern Africa and Asia, where conflicts probably also have more deep-seated roots and would call for major reconsiderations of policies, both by the great powers and by those not so great.

The simplest case for bold tackling within the nearest future would seem to refer to Latin America. The states of that region have advanced furthest towards an agreement for a zone free of nuclear weapons. But the negotiations have also pin-pointed what the political stumbling blocks for making the agreement comprehensive are, their names being Cuba, the Panama zone, perhaps Puerto Rico – anyway, questions related to great-power politics. How the path should be cleared is not for me to say. But it cannot be too much emphasized that in an historical perspective these political difficulties *must* be resolved, and soon. The solutions cannot come from the negotiations in Geneva, which are necessarily dealing with programmes in global and fairly schematic terms. Nor would it seem to be much use getting repeated assurances from member states in the UN that they favour the idea of a nuclear-free zone in Latin America, if those who are parties to the political issues involved do not sit down to undo the Gordian knots. I am afraid that we – the rest of the world – are powerless to proceed much further, if the superpowers and the states in the region concerned do not soon come to some new, really constructive agreements about the issues which impede the denuclearization of that region, so full of problems with deep-seated social, economic and political origins, but in reality now so far removed from the risk of any great-power confrontation.

This is very obviously true for Latin America. It should not be much less true for the countries of the Middle East and the larger part of Africa. Again, plans for a denuclearized zone have advanced fairly far on the African side. Again, also, there would be no sense in any build-up for great-power confrontation in that area – no 'rationality' in terms of the vital interests of the states concerned, no 'reasonableness' in terms of the need to preserve world peace. The nettles of prolonged conflicts, centred on Arab–Israel history but threatening a much larger region, must be grasped, studied, uprooted and transformed by some systematically developed growth into peaceful co-operation. This is not sermonizing – far be it from me. But it is no more than *Realpolitik* to state the need for assuagement and accommodation in that region in connection with serious negotiations on disarmament measures, in the first instance for agreements on a denuclearized zone. Progress along one of the lines – tension reduction and/or denuclearization – will greatly increase the chance for realistic, durable solutions. When states in the region of Africa who are also parts of, or neighbouring on, the Middle East have explicitly stated that they want to be saved from a ruinous arms race, and most of all a nuclear arms race, this is a challenge, a pointer to an unfulfilled task in our period of history.

More and more voices are now also heard saying that it is high time to solve, or at least neutralize, those political issues in Europe which stand in the way of international *détente* and regional arrangements in the disarmament field. Again, ingenious plans get presented for denuclearized or even demilitarized zones. We don't need to go back to the Eden plan of more than ten years ago; we can most profitably focus on plans currently being studied in the chancelleries of European states. They are predominantly Polish and Scandinavian in origin. To the first category belong the various versions of the Rapacki, later Gomulka, plan for some form of denuclearization in Central Europe, initially by agreement between Poland, Czechoslovakia, East and West Germany. (Since in the first instance the Gomulka plan calls only for a 'freeze' of the nuclear warheads already deployed in the region, coupled with a system of control to impede further 'import', it might have been included among the first-period measures. Anyway, it might be used as an early starter, a trial period in tension reduction.)

A plan for an agreed nuclear-free zone in Scandinavia – which already exists *de facto* – has been urged by the Finnish President, Kekkonen. In a way, it may be said that a Swedish outline exists for a combination of the Rapacki and Kekkonen plans, originally launched in a more general form by our former Foreign Minister, Undén. The more recent Swedish position announces a willingness 'to accede to a nuclear-free zone of the greatest possible extension in Central and Northern Europe'. This is to be interpreted as an expectation of seeing, first the causes of tensions sufficiently allayed in Central Europe to allow a start to be made for some nuclear disarmament or at least containment, and, thereafter, a readiness to proceed with Scandinavian action. And some such future series of events is exactly what is internationally called for: to get neutralized an area which, seen in the light of history, must be said to be just ready to move out of its position as the main storm centre of the world.

Speaking from the point of view of realistic politics, I believe that the rumblings we now hear from within the alliances which have divided Europe, NATO and the Warsaw Pact, are healthy signs. Perhaps we are closer than has so far been acknowledged to the two alliances signing a non-aggression pact. Perhaps we are even closer than we know to a moment when it will be recognized that the rigid division of Europe in blocs has outlived its function, which was established in a different phase of history. Whatever the forms for agreements or for closer co-operation in Europe are going to be, one thing seems certain, namely that it belongs to the past to use the two blocs in Europe to mark a major confrontation line between world powers and thus to treat Europe as the main centre for the possible conflagration of a world war. It belongs instead to our time to realize that the risks of war are receding from Europe – a statement for which I could quote support from many sources, not only General de Gaulle. The 'cold war' under whose shadow we have lived for twenty years is judged by objective observers to be drawing to a close. Consequently, the problems of Europe which are still outstanding, the tasks of establishing foundations for peace and co-operation all through Europe, is a matter to be settled now, within the nearest period in sight. The world cannot afford to have Europe artificially paralyzed by a construed superpower rivalry. And the world cannot with hope and confidence move into the next period of history, with its prospect of even more harassing issues, with the heritage of Europe unsettled.

This is a 'must' not only if history is interpreted in some kind of teleological way; it is also dictated by the political postures taken by the countries of Europe. Not one of them, at least on the Continent, has declared itself *for*, and all can be assumed to be *against*, any participation if an even colder war is going to settle on the ocean named Pacific, whether that confrontation be called a crusade against Communism or not. To free Europe from the shackles of an outdated 'cold war' is a task that definitely belongs to the next period of history – perhaps we cannot afford to give it more than five years. Parallel to the work for that goal, the foundations for truly important disarmament measures can and should be built up. Of course, the disarmament measures, such as a non-aggression pact or a denuclearized zone, need not wait for the conclusion of political agreements. They might serve as an ignition key, and they would most certainly be elements in a mutual causation process, where political confidence and disarmament measures cumulatively support each other. But one thing seems to me certain: *now* is the time to begin the prospective planning for a Europe that may not be 'united' but that should accommodate itself to a stage when it is not split into two enemy camps, with a few neutrals in between.

The agenda for the day after tomorrow

If we possessed the assurance that we were on the way to solving the problems of the immediate future, here treated under the general rubric of non-proliferation, and if we had reasonable hopes of clearing up the regional undervegetation of big-power problems, involving a certain neutralization of some important zones in the world, only then would there seem to be hopeful grounds for drawing up blue-prints of a world that could tackle also its global problems with reason, I might even say with sanity. To begin with, the whittling away of the present system of alliances – which have shown certain signs of being on their way out, whether as a result of intentional, constructive planning or not – and the disappearance of real or suspected *ad hoc* interventions by great powers would make it possible for the superpowers to come to grips with disarmament projects really worthy of the name. Their mutual deterrence would then be a matter more definitely restricted to their concern with each other, rather than extended to promised protection of allies, and, in consequence, it would not be challenged at a number of danger spots.

I have been speaking like an optimist so far – because I have tried to look at our immediate future in a rational and practical way. It is more difficult to be hopeful about projecting disarmament measures into the more distant future and in a global perspective. But let us nevertheless examine the possibility of whether we could not, for that period, use as a starting key for quite considerable reductions of armaments generally in the world the compromise idea, known as the 'Gromyko umbrella', which envisages a considerable reduction of the mutual deterrence systems but not their total elimination. Such an opportunity might persist for quite some time, i.e. as long as no other state or constellation of states posed a threat of comparable magnitude to that of the two superpowers. A difficulty is that the imagination even of disarmament specialists does not seem to measure up to the real exigencies of planning for a time with a lesser degree of great-power dominance and a greater degree of disarmament. One example may be taken from the debate about a suggestion I made in reference to the 'Gromyko umbrella', namely that we should study it more like algebra and less like a political game. Instead of concentrating on the most proximate steps in arms reduction, we might construct some hypothetical alternatives as to the size and mix of the reduced nuclear deterrents which would be at the disposal of the two superpowers in the last stage of the disarmament process. An objection has often been raised that this would upset 'the balance' because of the preponderance of Soviet armed forces in relation to Europe. But, clearly, a last stage will never be reached if the thinking in terms of blocs has not disappeared; this ultimate deterrent was supposed to operate only between the superpowers as nations, and land-based troops are then not very much in the picture. I mention this in order to prove that we certainly have difficulties with our powers of imagination when we start to deal with problems of peace and disarmament.

An even greater challenge in history has to be met if that long-range period of reduced tensions is ever to materialize, namely that of peaceful co-existence with China. More generally, we must, while there is still time, forge such bonds of converging interest, co-operation and integration within the international community that we can allay that most terrifying apprehension of a war in the future between the richest and the poorest continents – a war which would at the same time be largely a contest between privileged whites and underprivileged non-whites. For that risk is quite real if, instead of planning, we just let history slide on. It would, of course, mean a capitulation – an insane, criminal capitulation to primitivism – since it would mean renouncing the fact that man is, after all, given capacities for rational insight and constructive planning.

If we want to plan for a saner future, there are two sectors of particular importance for which I would ask special attention, as being most closely related to our topic of disarmament. One is the prospective rôle of the United Nations. For brevity's sake, I shall here only state as a dictum that in the plans for progressive and realistic disarmament too little attention has so far been given to how the increasing functions of the UN have to dovetail with the divestment of responsibilities which the great powers have at present taken on themselves for the rest of the world. Obviously, the UN will have to be equipped to deal in a very different way from now with local conflicts which do not, or should not be allowed to, involve great-power intervention and consequently the risk of great-power confrontation.

A second major sector in our combined planning for peace and disarmament must have reference to the economic needs of the underdeveloped regions. It ought to be obvious that they cannot be left to proceed on the present course of – relatively speaking – sliding backwards from the average levels obtained in the world. Prognoses of a sordidly realistic nature spell out destinies that are in terms of famine and catastrophe for them during the next generation rather than in terms of 'development'. In the face of this plight, many benevolent schemes for development aid have been proffered, but, to be honest, all of them are ridiculously inadequate in relation to the needs which should be met. Some persons, or even governments, have advocated that as disarmament proceeds, the savings thus made should be devoted, to a large extent and sometimes at a fixed percentage, to development assistance. Neither I nor my Government has been a great believer in such a piecemeal procedure. The kind of assistance now actively envisaged, which is only to be measured by a hundredth fraction of our national income or by a few billion dollars, can well be accommodated alongside military expenditures in our rich countries, as examples show. No appreciable shifts in the world economic situation will, I believe, be made before we are quite ready to leave what I have called the agenda of today, and even of tomorrow, and face with a resoluteness hitherto unseen the agenda of the world future. Any economies that can be made in the period of freezing nuclear armaments or even in the period of regional disengagement will be fairly insignificant in comparison with what steps towards disarmament and a world order should entail, and equally insignificant measured by actual needs in the underprivileged world.

Because of this conviction, I hold that the economists who were asked by the UN to study the social and economic consequences of disarmament were right to base their calculations on the total military economy. Although it would be naïve to hope for the reduction of military expenditures to zero, the best yardstick to use when trying to find out what portions might be saved is obtained by estimating total costs. I could go on to quote figures of more than a hundred billion dollars spent annually for purposes of the prospective destruction of other human beings. I could perhaps most tellingly use the statement that this outlay for military purposes now nearly equals the aggregated gross national products of all the underdeveloped countries. But I believe that even this vista is not wide enough – because the main asset which might be liberated is one with an untold multiplier effect. It is in the domain of research, planning and construction that we now have the greatest immobilization of development resources for the poorer peoples, because of the drain of brainpower and manpower monopolized for military purposes.

The risk, then, in all our discussions on the non-proliferation of nuclear weapons, is that for sheer lack of imagination and courage we pursue disarmament plans which are too near-sighted, disarmament plans which are overawed by the currently reigning constellation of interests. But, after all, the national interests which we defend so keenly are infinitesimally small in comparison with the world we may be about to lose. Therefore, we must chart the road in such a way that the very first step leads in the right direction. I have tried to make the case, which is the one pleaded by the non-aligned countries quite generally, that the step towards 'non-proliferation' has to go via agreements on a cut-off of the production of fissile material for weapon purposes and via a comprehensive test ban, both with a next to universal application. The great powers must at the very outset demonstrate that they have resolved to enter on a forward course, leading away from collision and towards the goals of relaxation of tensions and reversal of the armaments race. Disarmament is no subject for small-scale accommodation, still less for technical or legalistic gimmicks. Disarmament measures must be as real as are arms and missiles. I was tempted to say that disarmers must be as realistic as generals and admirals, but I sincerely believe we are more realistic. We plan as they do for first steps in a setting of today's reality. But beyond these steps we see two roads: one leads towards more and more tormenting cramps of the political situation and economic frustration in the world; the other offers the chance to open up a widening path away from the horror world that man is conjuring up for himself.

© *Ambassador Alva Myrdal 1966*

THE BROADER VIEW

The Rt Hon Lester B. Pearson

To wind up this discussion of the dangers arising from the threat of the further spread of nuclear weapons, I venture to place before you, briefly and in an oversimplified way, my views on these dangers and on possible measures at least to reduce them. I have no particular qualifications to undertake this task except that I am Prime Minister, and as such I have available the views of all the experts in the Canadian Government service.

My only personal qualification would be that I have been associated in one form or another with disarmament conferences since I first went to the first Geneva Disarmament Conference in the early 1930s as a very junior secretary in the Canadian Delegation. At that time, with junior secretaries from other delegations, we had the answer to all the questions. We often used to meet for dinner after the day's sessions, at a café in Geneva, the Bavaria, where we exchanged views on the follies and misdemeanours of our elder delegates, and how, if we were only given the chance, we could have solved all these matters. I remember one night when we had been sitting during the day in a committee where our seniors had been arguing as to what constituted an offensive weapon and a defensive weapon in connection with naval disarmament: if a gun was 8.4111 calibre it was offensive, and if it was 7.2111 it was defensive. We agreed that this was all pretty silly and that the answer to this particular question was a simple one that could have been discovered within fifteen minutes of the opening of the meeting: namely that the offensiveness or defensiveness of a weapon depended on whether you were in front of it or behind it. There was nothing else to be said about it.

So I was much more of an expert in those days than I am now. Each year, I confess, I find it more difficult to be sure that one has any of the answers to any of the aspects of this problem of disarmament.

In recent years, arms control proposals have foundered on the reef of what is judged to be the national interest, without, I believe, sufficient weight being given by governments to their broader responsibility to the international community as a whole. Yet when the destructive capacity of nuclear weapons makes national interest coincide with international responsibility, surely it is the common *national* objective of all peoples and governments, to remove the possibility that these weapons will ever be used. There is nothing exclusively international about this. It is a national matter.

There is no need for me to dwell on the fantastic and frightening development of military power since the end of World War II. By the early 1960s, however, this development, fortunately for us all, had resulted in a relatively stable, if uneasy, balance of nuclear strength between the United States and the Soviet Union, a balance based on the ability of each to destroy the other, regardless of by whom or where the first attack was launched, a balance of shared capacity for mutual annihilation. The knowledge that rash action by either one which threatened the vital interests of the other might lead to a nuclear exchange fatal to both has up to the present deterred both sides from pushing any such action to a 'show-down'. The sobering realities of this power balance were starkly revealed in the Cuban crisis of 1962, when the escape from a 'show-down' showed how close we were to it.

One result of the reaction to that particular confrontation may well have been the subsequent agreement between Washington, Moscow and London on a Partial Nuclear Test Ban. A short time later, the great powers were able to agree on a United Nations resolution prohibiting the orbiting in outer space of weapons of mass destruction. Following that, it was agreed to install a direct communication link, a radio telephonic axis if you like, between Washington and Moscow.

These measures were important, since they were the first tangible steps towards arms control after continuous debate and negotiation since 1946. But beyond their intrinsic importance, I suggest that they were also of importance because they marked a tacit understanding by the two nuclear superpowers to try to avoid direct confrontations which would threaten the outbreak of nuclear war. In this way, both East and West have acknowledged the danger of disrupting the existing power balance. They have attempted to reduce conflicts of interest even if they have by no means succeeded in eliminating all potentially dangerous situations.

The existence, now, of a *détente* between East and West – even an uneasy one – does provide us with an opportunity to re-examine afresh the need to control the arms race, to question whether we should continue to devote such a tragically large proportion of human and material resources to the development and improvement of weapons whose use in any circumstances, for any reason, would threaten humanity's very survival.

A thorough re-appraisal is particularly appropriate today, when both the major powers face the question of whether or not to take a significant new step in the arms race, whether to produce and to deploy an anti-ballistic missile system. The deployment of such a system would be an enormously costly undertaking, which in the end would probably lead, as the ballistic missile race did, to ever mounting defence budgets without any permanent increase in national security or international stability.

There are those who will argue that it is not just a question of the two major powers agreeing not to deploy ABM systems in relation to each other. They point to the need for protective measures against the looming threat of Communist China, with its potential nuclear capability. But I suggest that the day when North America or Europe should be genuinely concerned about a nuclear attack by China is still many years in the future. Moreover, it is my view that fear of possible ultimate developments should not deter us from a course of action which offers promise of substantial benefits in the immediate future. If the result of the kind of re-assessment I have mentioned were a tacit understanding by the US and USSR to refrain from the development of ABM systems – and so prevent a new dimension of escalation of the arms race – the dividends in terms of reduced tension and enhanced international stability would place us all in a much better position to examine the vital political issues which still divide us and which so largely determine our prospects for reducing armaments. Furthermore, to drop the development of ABM systems would remove a major reason advanced for continuing underground testing, about which I will have something to say a little later.

We accept the inevitability of change in international relationships and institutions. The world does not stand still. So any balance of power which now exists is not permanently assured. The elements of the nuclear equation do not remain constant. New factors emerge, and old ones change. The major powers are continually refining and improving – I apologize for the use of these two words – their nuclear weapons. Within the present decade, two additional nations have emerged as nuclear powers. Other potential candidates are now weighing the advantages and the disadvantages of joining the nuclear club. Moreover, the number of states capable of developing their own nuclear weapons is constantly increasing; my own country could manufacture them without too much difficulty any time it desired to do so. We now face – not as an academic problem but in a very real and urgent form – the dangers of proliferation. These dangers are upon us. Surely the further spread of nuclear weapons will increase the risk of nuclear war and the insecurity of all nations. It could add a new and threatening factor to historical, ethnic and territorial disputes existing between nations. A decision by one country to acquire nuclear weapons would almost certainly generate strong pressure on others to take similar action. International relations would thereby be made more complicated and more dangerous. Agreements on arms control measures would become more difficult to achieve, and any prospect of progress in this field would recede into the far distance. Moreover, there would be a greater risk of nuclear war breaking out as a result of human error flowing from defective control arrangements or through the action of irresponsible elements into whose hands – and there would be more of these hands – the weapons might fall.

I understand that this Assembly's discussions have indicated that further nuclear proliferation is most likely to occur in countries faced with a conventional or nuclear threat but lacking the protection and security afforded by membership in a nuclear alliance. In such circumstances, certain non-aligned countries might be persuaded to create a nuclear arsenal in the vain hope of improving their national security, or in anticipation of a similar development by a hostile neighbour, or in order to enhance their national prestige and their international influence.

The prevention of such nuclear proliferation is important and urgent. In his annual report for 1965, the UN Secretary-General describes this as 'the most urgent question of the present time, which should remain at the very top of the disarmament agenda'. President Johnson has made it clear that a central place in his Administration's policy is the effort to control, to reduce and ultimately to eliminate modern engines of nuclear destruction – to act now to prevent nuclear spread, to halt the nuclear arms race and to reduce nuclear stocks. In his message to the Eighteen-Nation Disarmament Conference of last February 1, Chairman Kosygin said: 'If we do not put an end to the proliferation in the world of nuclear weapons, the threat of the unleashing of nuclear war will be increased many times.' Unfortunately, all the potential nuclear powers have not taken such an unequivocal stand.

The issues involved in this matter are so complex that no single measure is likely to provide a solution. Where considerations of national security and international prestige are closely intertwined, answers must be sought in several directions if we are to succeed in preventing nuclear proliferation. Measures proposed will need to take into account the factors motivating countries to seek nuclear weapons and to make provision for appropriate disincentives. Obviously, too, we must concentrate on those countries capable of achieving nuclear status – not in the more remote future, but over the next decade – and there are many of them.

The discussions at present going on – perhaps I should say dragging on – at the Eighteen-Nation Disarmament Conference for an international treaty to limit the spread of nuclear weapons make little progress, despite the urgency of the matter. The time used for argument on general principles will have been wasted unless it results eventually in an instrument linking both the nuclear and the non-nuclear countries. These discussions have revealed the existence of two different types of problems. The first is the question of multilateral nuclear-sharing. This has its origin in the desire of non-nuclear members of NATO, for instance, for a voice in the planning and management of the nuclear forces on which they feel their own security so largely depends. Clearly, a precise definition of proliferation is required. What exactly does it mean?

On this issue, we in Canada stand on the principles embodied in the Irish resolution adopted by an overwhelming majority at the General Assembly in 1961. We are convinced that proliferation would not occur under the terms of a treaty which required that the present nuclear powers must always retain full control of their nuclear weapons. Perhaps such a treaty, however, should prohibit, clearly and specifically, the transfer of such control to states, groups of states or other entities, requiring that the present nuclear states must at all times maintain the power of veto over deployment and firing of such nuclear weapons. The nuclear-sharing issue is, of course, closely connected with a second and broader question, that of European security, which, in its turn, is concerned with the settlement of important political questions on that continent.

While much of the present lack of progress in efforts to prevent nuclear proliferation derives from difficulties about nuclear-sharing and European security, it still seems to me that in the long run these questions may prove less intractable than the other problem which I have just mentioned, that of the national development of nuclear weapons by states with the technical skill, resources and industrial base which could enable them to produce such weapons, and who may feel that this is necessary for security reasons.

The discussions at this Assembly have shown that, for the non-aligned countries, security assurances to prevent this development raise complex issues affecting their non-aligned status, their relations with the great powers and with their immediate neighbours. In India, for example, which is confronted by a hostile China, these issues are particularly acute and have recently given rise to considerable public discussion. Within the last few weeks the Foreign Minister of India stated in the Indian Parliament that if the nuclear powers wished a non-proliferation treaty, they must be prepared themselves to make some sacrifices. Among other things, he went on to recount the merits of a multilateral international guarantee to reassure the non-nuclear countries against nuclear blackmail.

Security assurances of this kind raise important issues, of course, for the nuclear powers. These powers already have commitments to their allies, and the acceptance of new commitments might tend to strain their military resources and complicate their political relations with other nuclear powers as well as with rivals of countries to whom a guarantee was extended. While the great powers might be prepared to accept responsibilities commensurate with their status, there are of course limits to the responsibilities they can be expected to undertake in this and related fields.

Much attention has been given recently to this whole question of providing the non-aligned countries with adequate assurances about security which at the same time might help to dissuade them from developing their own nuclear weapons. President Johnson made a constructive contribution when he declared in 1964 that 'nations not following the nuclear path will have our strong support against threats of nuclear blackmail'. At the last session of the United Nations General Assembly, US delegates suggested that such assurances might take the form of an Assembly resolution. More recently, Chairman Kosygin has proposed a type of indirect assurance under which the nuclear powers would undertake not to use nuclear weapons against non-nuclear countries which do not have nuclear weapons on their territory. While this proposal has certain attractions, we must recognize the difficulty in establishing as a fact whether nuclear weapons are present in certain areas or not. A United Nations resolution signifying the intention of members to provide or support assistance to non-nuclear states subject to nuclear attack, or threats of such attack, might provide a form of useful collective assurance in no way incompatible with other and more direct arrangements. Perhaps we should explore this possibility.

Mention should be made of another difficult question, that of safeguards. Over the past decade, considerable progress has been made in elaborating the concept and in developing the practical application of the means of preventing nuclear materials which are supplied for peaceful purposes from being diverted to the manufacture of weapons. As a major uranium exporter committed to supplying nuclear materials only for peaceful purposes, Canada will continue to support strongly steps to bring about general acceptance of international safeguards because they must be general, either under the system developed by the International Atomic Energy Agency or through equivalent arrangements of an organization such as Euratom. In the common effort to contain the nuclear threat, we regard safeguards as one of the important instruments which the international community has at its disposal.

Canada has participated actively in the working out of the IAEA safeguards system. Only a few days ago we demonstrated again our support for and confidence in that system, in respect to our agreement with Japan for cooperation in the peaceful uses of atomic energy. We have signed an agreement in Vienna under which the IAEA assumes the responsibility for administering the safeguards incorporated in the Japan-Canada Agreement.

If a non-proliferation treaty is to be effective, to inspire confidence and to endure, it will also require some means of verifying that the obligations undertaken by the signatories are being carried out. This should include a provision to ensure that peaceful nuclear activities and materials are not being used clandestinely for military purposes. If safeguards are to be acceptable and effective, they must be applicable to all states. These recognized systems of safeguards, which are already applied by many countries to transactions, my own country among them, involving transfers of nuclear materials for peaceful purposes should be applied to cover all international transfers. In this way an important step forward would be taken to prevent the development of nuclear weapons by additional countries. We in Canada support the inclusion in any treaty of a provision designed to achieve this objective.

I have suggested that the production of nuclear weapons by non-aligned countries would serve neither their individual national interest nor their collective responsibility to the international community. I think this is true, but I also suggest that it is unreasonable to expect such non-aligned countries to renounce in perpetuity modern methods of defence if the nuclear powers themselves are not prepared to accept some restraints and parallel obligations, such as the extension of the nuclear test ban to underground testing. Such a comprehensive test ban would help to prevent the indigenous development, and hence the further spread, of nuclear weapons. At the same time, it would meet some of the objections of the non-aligned to what they suggest are the one-sided commitments they are being asked to make. Moreover, the political and psychological benefits likely to flow from such an agreement would help create the atmosphere in which it would be possible to make progress on further steps towards arms control. In order to ensure that it would not be clandestinely violated, however, a comprehensive test ban treaty must make provision for adequate verification machinery. We must never lose sight of the importance of verification in agreements which affect the essentials of international security and stability.

There is one further question – that of nuclear-free zones. Negotiations are going on for the establishment of a nuclear-free zone in Latin America. Heads of African states have decided that Africa should be free of nuclear weapons. Again, however, one of the major stumbling blocks is a narrow concept of national interest. In this connection it is well to remember that, in 1959, countries with interests in the continent of Antarctica – both nuclear and non-nuclear states – were able to reconcile their differing viewpoints and to conclude a treaty which, among other things, established the continent of Antarctica as a nuclear-free zone and laid down procedures whereby treaty obligations could be effectively verified in this respect. This required some surrender of immediate national interest in favour of a broader collective responsibility to the international community. I would hope that in such areas as Latin America and Africa, and perhaps eventually the Middle East, the Far East, Europe, the Arctic and other regions where political factors are admittedly far more complex than those obtaining in Antarctica, we shall also see immediate national interest subordinated to the wider but also national interest of stability and peace. All nations should encourage the countries that are now actively engaged in working out arrangements for nuclear-free zones. Should one be successfully established in a populated are, we shall have an important precedent and a model for further arrangements of this kind which would contribute to preventing the spread of nuclear weapons.

I have already mentioned the emergence of China as a nuclear power and as a new factor in the nuclear equation. The Chinese leaders, on the mainland, appear bent on achieving an effective military nuclear capability however long it takes and however much it may cost. To those seeking a peaceful world order, this prospect can only be viewed with deep concern. Yet so long as China remains outside existing international councils, isolating herself from the influence of other governments and world opinion, she is the more likely to remain a recalcitrant and disturbing factor in the world balance of power. You can draw your own conclusions from that.

It is clear that progress towards the peaceful settlement of disputes and effective measures of arms control requires that all the principal world powers – including continental China – be party to international discussions of these questions. Therefore, we should do everything possible to bring China into discussions about disarmament and other great international issues. At least let us not be responsible for her not coming in. Her inclusion may make her more conscious of her responsibilities as a member of the international community. In this endeavour, those who already have direct contact with Peking have a special and important rôle to play.

I have spoken of some of the realistic and, I believe, acceptable measures that could help to solve the problem of proliferation. Any, or all of them, could be incorporated in an eventual non-proliferation treaty, or associated with such a treaty, or indeed agreed upon independently.

Agreed upon in any context, these measures would at least constitute some restraint on the spread of nuclear weapons. They would focus world interest on the fact that the world community is trying to find the answer to this vital life-or-death question; they would reassure a world fearful of nuclear devastation that the world family has at least begun to accept its collective responsibility for limiting a further spread of these weapons, which, left unchecked, will one day destroy our civilization. Surely mankind, in 1966, is capable of giving at the least these indications that our civilization is not only worth saving but also capable of doing what is so desperately wanted in the hearts of all men: preserving true peace and establishing real security.

© *The Rt Hon Lester B. Pearson 1966*

4 Israel and the Arab World
The Crisis of 1967
Adelphi Paper 41, 1967

Michael Howard and Robert Hunter

Preface

We do not attempt in this paper to give a detailed account of the Third Arab–Israeli War of June 1967. We try simply to set the conflict in its historical and political perspective, to examine its immediate origins, to account for the remarkable course which it took, and to discuss its significance for a world which shows fewer signs than ever of abandoning the use of violence as an instrument of policy. For many years to come the war and its antecedents will provide valuable data for analysts both of military and of political affairs. It is for them that this study is primarily intended, rather than for a general public for whom a number of vivid accounts have already been provided by skilled journalists and for whom more detailed histories will no doubt be produced in course of time.

The audience to whom this study is addressed will immediately observe its shortcomings. Apart from anything else, it is not documented; it draws more heavily upon Israeli than upon Arab sources; and it does not attempt the kind of impartiality which can be achieved only by refraining from any interpretation of the events it describes. The lack of documentation is due to the fact that much of the information used has been obtained from participants or observers under seal of confidence. The lack of balance in sources is due less to any lack of co-operation from Arab governments than to the extraordinary helpfulness shown by Israeli officials, soldiers, and politicians at all levels. If as a result our presentation is in any way incomplete or unfair, the responsibility is ours alone.

We make no apology, however, for attempting an interpretive history rather than – if such a thing is ever possible – a dispassionate chronicle. We are aware that our interpretation will be acceptable neither to those who believe that the war was the result of a Soviet attempt to embarrass the United States and gain a bargaining counter for use in the conflict over Vietnam; nor to those – perhaps, unfortunately, still a majority in the Arab world – who see it as the outcome of a plot by the imperialist powers, using Zionism as their cat's-paw, to frustrate the aims of the Arab revolution and reassert their hegemony over the Middle East. We realize also that much information was not available to us, in the time at our disposal, which might have made us reconsider our conclusions. We hope, however, that within its limits this paper will be found of some value to students of international relations, and even to those who are unfortunate enough to have to conduct them.

We wish to thank those many officials, scholars, soldiers, and observers in London, Washington, New York, and the Middle East who have given us such generous assistance. Any errors of fact or judgment, however, are our responsibility alone. But most of all our thanks are due to the Director and Staff of the Institute for Strategic Studies, who accepted with every appearance of cheerful resignation this heavy additional burden on their time.

M.H.
R.H.
September 1967

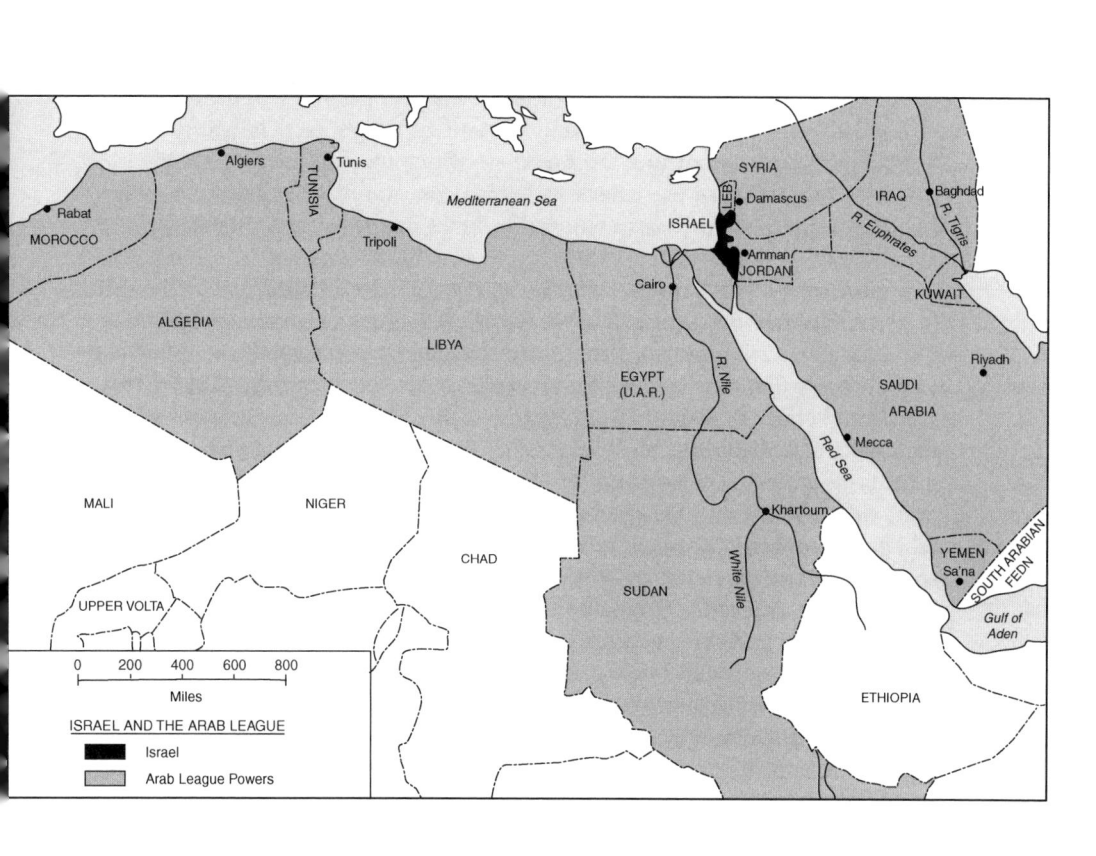

ISRAEL AND THE ARAB LEAGUE
- Israel
- Arab League Powers

I. The conflict

Historians who like to trace the origins of political regimes to such written documents as the Declaration of Independence, Magna Carta, or the Oath of the Tennis Court must accord a similar respect to the 'Balfour Declaration'; that remarkable assurance which the British Government gave to the Zionist Organization in November 1917.

This document, the product as much of political calculation as of generous idealism, ran as follows:

> His Majesty's Government view with favour the establishment in Palestine of a National Home for the Jewish People and will use their best endeavours to facilitate the achievement of this object, it being clearly understood that nothing shall be done which may prejudice the civil and religious rights of existing non-Jewish communities in Palestine or the rights and political status enjoyed by Jews in any other country.

Significant as this promise was to the eventual establishment of a Jewish State, it did not create the Jewish nation. The very existence of a Zionist Organization with ambitions to 'return' to Palestine and sufficient influence to gain the support of one of the greatest powers in the world showed how strong and effective Jewish nationalism had already become in a world where nationalism was rapidly replacing religion as the chief ideological driving force of mankind. The wording of the second part of the Declaration, however, showed that the British Government fully realized that the Palestine which it proposed to 'liberate' from the Ottoman Empire was not a blank space to be freely settled with politically congenial immigrants. It was not only the loosely worded promises which Sir Henry MacMahon, British High Commissioner in Egypt, had made to Hussein, Sharif of Mecca, to 'recognize and support the independence of the Arabs' which had to be reconciled with the Balfour Declaration. Nor were the complications introduced by the Sykes-Picot agreement, dividing the Middle East into European spheres of influence, to create the greatest ultimate difficulties. Little regarded at the time, but eventually to constitute the greatest problem of all, was the reaction in such cities as Cairo, Damascus, and Beirut of men educated according to a European pattern, in nationalism of a European style, who objected strongly to the introduction of an alien element into their community by an equally alien power; and one which had bid for their own sympathies with very similar promises of national self-fulfilment.

This conflict between Jews – a nation without a State – and Arabs – a nation divided into too many States – was evident to some experts from the beginning. But it was slow to acquire international significance.[1] Arab nationalism became more vocal and influential as the economic and political development of the Middle East dissolved its traditional social structure; yet so long as the number of Jews in Palestine did not increase significantly – the total was 80,000 when the British assumed their Mandate from the League of Nations in 1922 – the conflict might have remained latent and Arab objections academic. But the number did increase. In 1924 the imposition by the American Government of quotas on immigration to the United States cut off the Jews of Europe – particularly Eastern Europe – from the haven where most of them would have preferred to find refuge. Even then there was little about the arid lands of Palestine to attract Jews from the European communities where they had lived, precariously but not uncomfortably, for so many centuries; until in 1933 the advent to power in Germany of the Nazi regime, and the development of similar regimes eleswhere in Europe, made their life in those communities grimly intolerable.

Until then, the British authorities in Palestine had little difficulty in restricting immigration, as their policy demanded, to the economic capacity of the country to absorb new arrivals. Now humanitarian considerations led them to increase the immigration quota yearly, until by 1939 the Jewish population stood at 450,000: nearly one-third of the total population of Palestine.[2]

The Arab population reacted naturally and violently to this influx. Rational reflection might have persuaded them – as it might, under not dissimilar circumstances, have persuaded the indigenous inhabitants of North America – that the advent of all these skilled and hard-working immigrants would increase the productivity of the country and provide a better life for all its inhabitants. But they preferred to fight to preserve their land as they knew it. The first serious clashes came in 1929. Thereafter there was a continuing pattern of conflict between Jews and Arabs. In 1936 the Arabs precipitated what the British termed a 'rebellion' but what the Arabs themselves regarded as a war to repel invaders from their native soil. Within three years the conflict was to cost 4,000 lives. The British gave the immigrants what protection they could, but it was not enough. The Jews had to organize the military defence of their own settlements. This was nothing new to many of them: in the ghettos of Eastern Europe they had lived surrounded by populations quite as hostile and often as violent as the Arabs, and had developed techniques of communal defence which were now revived and adapted by their semi-official defence organization, the Haganah. The Jews in Israel in fact had to assume the burden of defending themselves against their enemies ten years before the British abandoned the Mandate and left them on their own.

It was not only the Arabs whom the Haganah learned to fight. By now the British had realized the full difficulty of the task they had taken on. Unless there was to be continual warfare in Palestine the Arabs had somehow to be reconciled to the new arrivals. In 1937 the Peel Commission proposed a straightforward partition of the country – as the United Nations were to do ten years later. Neither party would accept this solution. To impose it by force would have involved a military effort which the British, belatedly arming to meet an even greater menace, had neither the will nor the capacity to make. Instead, in 1939 the British Government adopted a policy set out in a White Paper, which for a whole generation was to be *the* White Paper, in an attempt to meet the Arab objections.[3] This set, as the limit to Jewish immigration, the proportion of one-third of the population of Palestine, which meant in practice that a further 75,000 Jews might immigrate over the next five years. After that, no further immigration would be allowed without Arab consent. The White Paper also declared unequivocally that the British Government did not intend that 'Palestine should become a Jewish State'. Instead it visualized a Palestinian State in which Jews and Arabs would 'share authority in such a way that the essential interests of each are secured'.

The White Paper did little to pacify the Arabs, and it infuriated the Jews. Not only had the Zionist craving for an independent State, as opposed to a 'National Home', increased as the Jewish population of Palestine swelled, but also the prospective check on immigration, at a time when their race was suffering a persecution unparalleled even in their own terrible annals, appeared to them – and not only to them – as a policy of intolerable heartlessness. For five years, however, the question rested in suspense, while British and Jews fought an adversary who threatened the survival of both. But as the war ebbed from the Middle East the conflict re-emerged, and the Jewish extremists, with improved weaponry and military expertise, began to direct their energies against British as well as Arab targets.

As for the Arabs, the war had done nothing to appease their anger, and much to exacerbate it. Their political and social system had been violently disrupted. British occupation forces had been ubiquitous, exigent, and not always tactful. In the Middle East, as elsewhere in the world, the Second World War had shattered the image of placid invincibility which had enabled the British to maintain so vast a suzerainty in the area with so small an expenditure of force. Now Arab nationalism was ready to explode not only against the humiliating foreign domination, but also against the native monarchs and oligarchies who were prepared to sustain it. The British were wise enough not to attempt to impose direct rule, but tried to preserve their influence, in an area which they still regarded as vital to their strategic and economic interests, by collaborating with the native rulers: a policy whose total failure in Egypt was partially balanced by its success in the Hashemite monarchies of Transjordan and Iraq. But friendship with these or any other Arab states could be preserved only by maintaining the White Paper policy on Palestine; and this meant turning back the boatloads of homeless Jews who were flocking from the ruins of post-war Europe, and infuriating their influential sympathizers in the United States.

Britain's first post-war Foreign Secretary, Mr Ernest Bevin, rashly staked his reputation on solving the Palestine problem. He failed. Eighty thousand British troops were pinned down in peace-keeping operations between two peoples whose dislike for themselves they grew heartily to reciprocate, for purposes which not only imposed a financial burden that the over-stretched

British resources could simply not afford but were of doubtful relevance to British interests. It is not surprising that in 1947, thirty years after the ill-fated Balfour Declaration had been issued, the British abandoned responsibility for Palestine to the United Nations and announced their intention of relinquishing the Mandate in May of the following year. Britain, declared her Government, 'was not prepared to undertake the task of imposing a policy on Palestine by force of arms'.

The United Nations Special Committee on Palestine recommended, as the Peel Commission had done ten years earlier, that Palestine should be partitioned into a Jewish and an Arab State, with economic union and an international regime for the city of Jerusalem. The frontiers they proposed looked curious on the map, each State being allotted three separate areas which only touched at two single points. The Jewish State was allotted the north-east, a coastal strip embracing Tel Aviv and Haifa, and a wedge containing Beersheba and the Negev Desert with an outlet on the Gulf of Aqaba. But the frontiers followed the lines of settlement with reasonable accuracy, and the Jews, who were concerned at this stage rather to establish their sovereignty than to extend their lands, declared themselves ready to accept them.[4] The Arabs remained implacable. There now existed, in the Arab League (which had been formed largely under British auspices in 1945), a political mechanism making possible the joint action of all Arab States. In October 1947 the League set up a Military Committee and agreed in principle to establish a joint command.

In principle the Arabs were unanimously hostile to the establishment of a Jewish State. In practice, then as now, their hostility varied in intensity. At one extreme stood Syria, for long the focus of extreme Arab nationalism, and Iraq. The United Nations partition proposals touched off violent riots in Damascus and Aleppo. In Syria, compulsory service was introduced, military appropriations were voted totalling $2 million, and army officers resigned their commissions to serve in an Arab Liberation Army, units of which began to raid Jewish settlements over the border early in 1948.[5] At the other extreme stood Saudi Arabia, less directly interested, more responsive to Western influence, its rulers less subject to pressure from university students and city mobs. Pressure of this kind could be, and was, brought to bear on the Egyptian Government in Cairo; but a military involvement was the last thing its Army Command wanted. Egyptian participation, however, was virtually forced by the serpentine policy of King Abdullah of Transjordan. Abdullah viewed the United Nations proposals with equanimity, for he proposed, with British acquiescence, to annex the Arab territories of Palestine on the West Bank of the Jordan, including Jerusalem itself. The prospect of such gains made it easy for him to accept the creation of a Jewish State in the coastal valley; but the prospect of so great an extension of Jordanian territory and influence was so unwelcome to the Egyptians that they accepted common action in Palestine as the best way to balance it.

When, on the eve of the formal ending of the British Mandate on 15 May

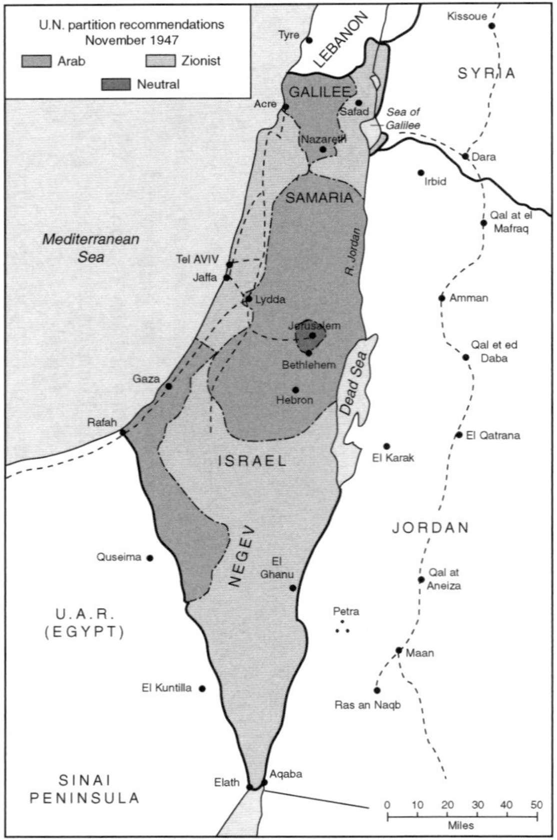
U.N. partition recommendations
November 1947
Arab
Zionist
Neutral
Tyre
LEBANON
Kissoue
SYRIA
GALILEE
Acre
Safad
Sea of
Galilee
Nazareth
Dara
Irbid
SAMARIA
Mediterranean
Sea
R. Jordan
Qal at el
Mafraq
Tel AVIV
Jaffa
Lydda
Amman
Jerusalem
Bethlehem
Qal et ed
Daba
Gaza
Hebron
Dead Sea
Rafah
El Qatrana
El Karak
ISRAEL
JORDAN
NEGEV
Quseima
El
Ghanu
Qal at
Aneiza
Petra
U.A.R.
(EGYPT)
Maan
El Kuntilla
Ras an Naqb
SINAI
PENINSULA
Elath
Aqaba
0 10 20 30 40 50
Miles

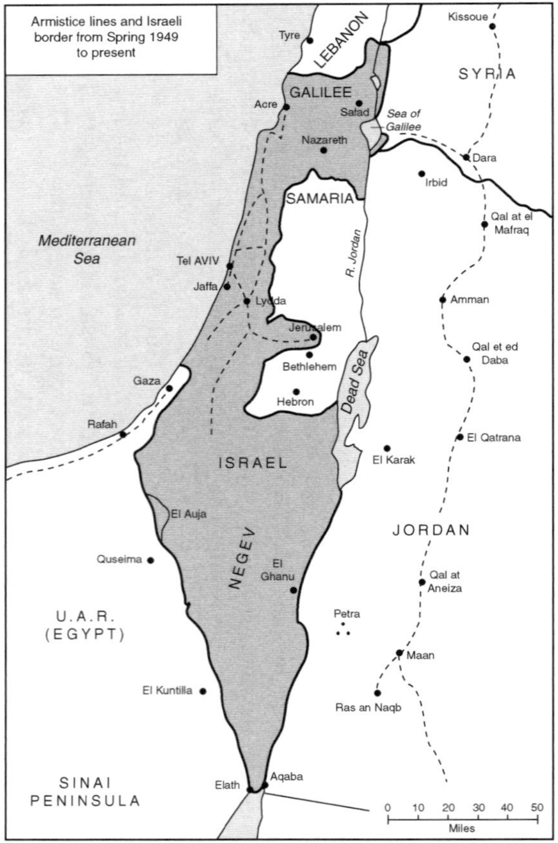
Armistice lines and Israeli
border from Spring 1949
to present
Tyre
LEBANON
Kissoue
SYRIA
GALILEE
Acre
Safad
Sea of
Galilee
Nazareth
Dara
Irbid
SAMARIA
Mediterranean
Sea
R. Jordan
Qal at el
Mafraq
Tel AVIV
Jaffa
Lydda
Amman
Jerusalem
Bethlehem
Qal et ed
Daba
Gaza
Hebron
Dead Sea
Rafah
El Qatrana
El Karak
ISRAEL
El Auja
JORDAN
NEGEV
Quseima
El
Ghanu
Qal at
Aneiza
Petra
U.A.R.
(EGYPT)
Maan
El Kuntilla
Ras an Naqb
SINAI
PENINSULA
Elath
Aqaba
0 10 20 30 40 50
Miles

1948, David Ben-Gurion proclaimed in Tel Aviv 'the establishment of the Jewish State in Palestine, to be called Israel', fighting had already been in progress, and increasing in intensity, for about four months, as the two sides jockeyed for advantage. Now both rushed in to fill the vacuum left by the withdrawing British troops. As at the outset of all civil wars, local success or failure was determined by local circumstances, and often by a hair's breadth. The Haganah, with its spearhead of shock-troops the Palmach, was ready to fight the Palestine Arabs, but it was not prepared either in armament or in organization to deal with the regular forces of Syria, Iraq, Jordan, and Egypt when these began to close in on them from north, east, and south. Courage, ingenuity, and the clumsiness of their opponents enabled the heavily outnumbered Israelis to check the Syrian and Egyptian advance, but they could not prevent the Jordanians from overrunning the West Bank of the Jordan, capturing the Old City and the heights dominating Jerusalem, and severing the road to the coast. The four-week cease-fire imposed by the United Nations on 11 June was accepted with relief by both sides as a necessary breathing space, but no more.

When the truce ended on 9 July the Israelis were in considerably better shape. The old Haganah protective forces were rapidly developing into an army organized for regular warfare, and heavy weapons – mainly paid for by American contributions – were being flown in from Europe, principally from Czechoslavakia. When the Mandate ended in May, the Israeli Army had numbered only 35,000 men and women, with four guns, no heavy mortars, and 1,500 machine guns between them. By October they were 80,000 strong, with 250 guns, 45 heavy mortars, and 7,550 machine guns.[6] But more important still was the growth in their skill, self-confidence, and ruthlessness. In July they conquered the Arab areas of central and northern Galilee, linking up their settlements in the Upper Jordan Valley with the coastal area round Tel Aviv; and by driving the Arabs from Lydda and Ramle they gained a broad corridor to the beleaguered city of Jerusalem. These were areas of unquestionably Arab settlement. Their inhabitants, uprooted from homes they had occupied for centuries, fled east towards Syria and Jordan or south to the protection of the Egyptians at Gaza. In the week from 9 to 18 July, when the United Nations were able to negotiate another cease-fire, Israel transformed itself from a collection of settlements scattered among an alien community into a compact and formidable State.

Still neither side was prepared to accept the new situation as definitive. The Arabs expressed their fury and resentment by repeated breaches of the truce. The Israelis also had unfinished business. In the south of the country round Beersheba, isolated Jewish settlements were still surrounded by Egyptian forces. These were relieved by attacks in October, and in December the whole area of the Upper Negev was cleared.[7] This opened up the Lower Negev, an area of the greatest potential importance to the new State. Its mineral wealth was considerable; it gave access to the Indian Ocean, bypassing the Suez Canal; and it separated Israel's two most dangerous adversaries, Egypt and Jordan. On 10 March 1949 the Israelis established themselves in Eilat, and a month later the Armistice Agreement with Jordan confirmed their frontier to the east.

The frontiers finally established by the Armistice Agreements were far from ideal. In the north the Syrians still held their old frontiers on the heights dominating the Upper Jordan Valley. In the centre the Jordanian positions reached to within twelve miles of the coast, and the salient at Latrun cut the direct road from Jerusalem to Tel Aviv. In the south the Egyptians occupied the coastal strip from Gaza to El Arish, which flanked the southern Israeli settlements and was to become a festering plague-spot of miserable refugees.[8] But in comparison with the position at the beginning of the year the Israelis had much to be thankful for. It is not surprising that their statesmen were quite ready to convert the Armistice Agreements into a definitive peace.

These agreements were reached during the course of 1949, separately negotiated by Israel with each of the principal belligerents: Egypt, Lebanon, Jordan, and Syria.[9] In all of them it was emphasized that they did not constitute a political settlement and that their provisions were 'dictated exclusively by military considerations and [were] valid only for the period of the Armistice'. It was further recognized, in the words of the Egyptian agreement, 'that rights, claims, or interests of a non-military character in the area of Palestine covered by this Agreement [might] be asserted by either Party, and that these, by mutual agreement being excluded from the Armistice negotiations, shall be, at the discretion of the Parties, the subject of later settlement'. In particular it was laid down that the Armistice Demarcation Lines established between the belligerent forces were not to be regarded as political or territorial boundaries – only as lines beyond which the armed forces of the contracting parties were not allowed to move. But the belligerents did agree in equally emphatic terms to keep the peace. They affirmed that they would not resort to military force in settlement of the Palestine question; that there would be no aggressive action 'undertaken, planned, or threatened' by their armed forces against one another; and that each side would respect the right of the other to its security and freedom from attack. Arrangements were made for the peaceful enforcement of the armistice agreements, which we will consider further below.

With the exception of Abdullah of Jordan, whose acquisition of the Old City of Jerusalem and the West Bank of the Jordan left him no less satisfied than the Israelis, the Arabs regarded the armistice as a humiliating defeat imposed on them by *force majeure*; the force, not of Israel alone, but of the Great Powers, who, acting in rare unanimity, had brought the United Nations to recognize the State of Israel and permit her to retain the *de facto* borders established by her military power. For the swelling forces of Arab nationalism, the loss of Palestine to an alien invader was a blow as bitter as the loss of Alsace-Lorraine had been to France: a reverse never to be forgotten and certainly never to be accepted as permanent. The Syrians immediately overturned the government which had led them to defeat; in Egypt a similar movement, primarily among the younger officers, was to operate more slowly but no less drastically to bring about the revolution of 1952, which eventually brought President Nasser to power. As for Jordan, the assassination of the over-subtle Abdullah in July 1951 provided a grim warning to his incompetent son Talal and his formidably competent grandson Hussein when they succeeded him. If the war had brought the Hashemite house territory and prestige, it had also brought some half a million Palestinian refugees who, settled on the West Bank of the Jordan with full rights of citizenship, saw to it that Jordan did not lag behind its neighbours in its imprecations against the common foe.

The existence of these refugees would have ensured, if such insurance had been necessary, that time would do nothing to appease Arab feelings. During the war whole communities had fled from Palestine, encouraged by their leaders and certainly not discouraged by the Jews. Such actions of Jewish extremists as the abominable Deir Yassin massacre were exceptional, but they lost nothing in the telling. In December 1948, after the fighting had died down, the General Assembly of the United Nations resolved that all refugees who so wished be allowed to return to their homes and that those not wishing to do so should be compensated by the Israeli Government. On this and later resolutions Israel constantly prevaricated. How could 700,000 Jews allow the return of nearly a million Arabs to their lands without risking the destruction of the Jewish State? Yet how could they refuse it without inflicting on innocent people an injustice reminiscent of so many which the Jews had themselves suffered throughout their own melancholy history? And why should the Arab governments compound this injustice by persuading the Palestinians to forget their past and find a home in new lands? By 1966 the number of these refugees registered with the United Nations Relief and Works Agency was 1.3 million: 700,000 in Jordan, 300,000 in the Gaza Strip, and 300,000 divided between the Lebanon and Syria. Their presence continued to demonstrate vividly why the State of Israel, however defensive and conciliatory its policy, constituted by its very existence a standing provocation to the whole of the Arab world.[10]

The States of the Arab League, therefore, though accepting the military armistice, refused recognition to Israel, and made war on her with all the economic weapons that lay to hand. A state of belligerency, they insisted, still obtained, and gave them full rights of blockade. Pressure was exerted against firms dealing with Israel, airlines were not allowed to include both Arab States and Israel in the same routes, and ships were not allowed to visit Arab States after touching at Israeli ports. There were regional boycott offices, a Prize Court – in fact all the paraphernalia and regulations of nations at war. After the revolution of 1952 the Egyptian Government sharply increased its pressure until, in October 1955, it imposed a comprehensive prohibition of all commercial and financial dealings with 'the enemy'.

Egypt was in a better position than any other Arab State to do Israel economic harm. From the very beginning she had established a blockade on Israeli shipping through the Suez Canal. This was extended in 1953 to include all goods being shipped to Israel. Israel appealed to the United Nations in vain. In 1951 a United Nations condemnation was ignored by Egypt. In 1954, when the question was raised again, a Soviet veto prevented any effective action being taken on Israel's behalf. As Israel's economy expanded and her volume of international trade grew, these restrictions became increasingly irksome. They might in the long run have been intolerable, if she had not been able to develop an alternative outlet to the south and east from the Negev port of Eilat, at the head of the Gulf of Aqaba. But shipping from the Gulf of Aqaba could only reach the open sea by passing through Egyptian territorial waters at the Straits of Tiran; and that remote passage began to acquire an international importance rivalling that of the Dardanelles.

The legal position respecting these waters has long been a point of contention. The Straits of Tiran certainly lie within Egypt's territorial waters. But are there high seas within the Gulf of Aqaba itself? If so, then right of passage through the Straits cannot be abridged; but if not, then passage through the Straits becomes subject to Egyptian regulation, though not – for merchant vessels at least – prohibition.

On the other hand, if the littoral states could agree among themselves, the Gulf could be closed to all shipping. But is Israel a littoral State? The Arabs deny it every time they deny Israel's right to exist; Israel is strongly supported on this point by her Western friends. Even if Israel's right to exist were granted, the Arabs would still contend that she has no right to a stretch of coastline on the Gulf.[11] Beyond this, Egypt takes her stand on belligerent rights. The Security Council adopted a resolution in September 1951 which asserted in passing that 'the Armistice regime ... is of a permanent character [and] neither party can reasonably assert that it is actively a belligerent or requires to exercise the right of visit, search, and seizure for any legitimate purpose of self-defence'. But Egypt ignored this resolution, and averred that she was under no obligation to convert the Armistice Agreement into a definitive peace. Here the issue rests, though it is conceivable that the international community would not choose to tolerate this claim of belligerency.

For the Israelis the free use of the port of Eilat appeared essential, if not to survival, then certainly to the development of their State; and it is never easy to distinguish between the two. The mineral resources of the Negev, especially its phosphates, its potash, and its methane gas, provided the basis for an industry to balance the agrarian settlements of the centre and north. For David Ben-Gurion and many of his old Zionist followers, the area satisfied a still deeper need, a hinterland where the pioneer spirit could be nourished to balance the thriving cosmopolitan conurbations of the coastal plain. Little could be done to develop Eilat during the first ten years of Israel's existence. In 1957 the port was handling only 41,000 tons of cargo a year. But by 1959 that figure had tripled; in 1965 it had reached 500,000 tons,[12] including 90 per cent of Israel's oil imports; and Israeli planners expected that by 1970 the tonnage would have topped the million mark. Any threat to Eilat was thus seen as a threat to the future of Israel itself – something of which the Arabs were very well aware – and to repel it the Israelis were prepared if necessary to fight.

The first time they found it necessary to do so was in 1956. In 1953 Egypt had begun to restrict Israeli commerce through the Straits, making all shipping subject to inspection by Egyptian coastguards. These measures increased in intensity until, in September 1955, Egypt broadened the blockade and included a ban on overflights by Israeli aircraft. This definitive closing of the Straits led the Israeli Government to order its Chief of Staff, General Moshe Dayan, to prepare contingency plans for capturing the Egyptian positions at Sharm-el-Sheikh, at Ras Nasrani, and on the islands of Tiran and Sinafir, from which the blockade was enforced. The Prime Minister, Mr Ben-Gurion, wanted to strike at once, but was restrained by his colleagues. A full year passed; a year during which raids on Israeli territory by Palestinian Arab *fedayeen* based on the Gaza Strip and the West Bank of the Jordan increased in frequency and provoked massive reprisals. Then the opportunity which Israel needed was provided by the decision of France and Great Britain to respond by force to President Nasser's nationalization of the Suez Canal.

In spite of the reluctance of successive British governments to reveal the full details of this curious episode, the essential facts are now clearly established. On 29 October 1956, with the approval and foreknowledge of both France and Britain, Israeli forces invaded the Sinai Peninsula, ostensibly in response to the *fedayeen* raids. The following day Britain and France sent Egypt and Israel an ultimatum, calling upon both countries to withdraw their forces ten miles from the Suez Canal, and further calling upon Egypt to permit a joint expeditionary force to occupy the Canal Zone. On 31 October, British and French aircraft began air attacks against military targets in Egypt, while Egypt sank ships to block the Canal. The destruction of the Egyptian Air Force, the rapid withdrawal of Egyptian forces, and the failure of Egypt's allies Jordan and Syria to come to her aid must not be allowed to obscure the remarkable achievement of the Israeli Army in overrunning the greater part of the Sinai Peninsula within six days and, on 5 November, hoisting the Israeli flag over the Egyptian fort at Sharm-el-Sheikh.[13] The same day French and British forces began to land near Port Said.

The United Nations General Assembly had called for a cease-fire on 2 November. With British and French vetos preventing any action by the Security Council, the General Assembly seemed faced with the alternative of taking drastic action under the famous 'Uniting for Peace' resolution (which had been introduced by the Western powers in 1950 after the Korean experience) or pursuing the anodyne course of requesting the Secretary-General to negotiate directly with the powers concerned. In the event, a third course of action was adopted; one which was to prove effective in bringing about the withdrawal of foreign troops on Egyptian soil, in fostering eleven years of relative security for Israel, and in preventing a return to a *status quo* that had entailed a long-term threat to Israel's economic development and a pattern of constant border disturbances. This was the establishment of the United Nations Emergency Force. The concept was largely that of Mr Lester Pearson, at the time Canadian Minister for External Affairs. Its successful implementation, however, was due entirely to the pertinacious diplomacy of Mr Dag Hammarskjöld, Secretary-General of the United Nations.

The role of the Force, in Mr Hammarskjöld's words, was simply 'to enter Egyptian territory with the consent of the Egyptian Government, in order to help maintain quiet during and after the withdrawal of non-Egyptian troops and to secure compliance with the other terms established in the [cease-fire] resolution of 2 November 1956'.

Its establishment was finally approved by the General Assembly on 7 November; and on the same day, two days after Israel, Britain and France accepted the cease-fire. On 15 November UNEF landed in Egypt, and the withdrawal of the invading forces began. By 22 January Israeli troops had evacuated all territory beyond the original Armistice Demarcation Lines, with the significant exceptions of the Gaza Strip and the east coast of the Sinai Peninsula down to the Straits of Tiran. There, in spite of constant pressure from the United Nations, they remained. When at length, in March 1957, the Government of Israel consented to withdraw them, it was only on receiving explicit assurances from the United States Government (with which France and Britain were to associate themselves) that no nation had the right to prevent free and innocent passage in the Gulf of Aqaba. 'The United States', declared President Eisenhower on 20 February, 'was prepared to exercise this right itself and to join with others to secure general recognition of this right'.[14]

In different ways, the outcome of the 1956 crisis was satisfactory both for Egypt and for Israel. For the Israelis it ended the *fedayeen* raids from Jordan and the Gaza Strip; and a United Nations presence, backed by guarantees from the principal Western powers, appeared to assure free use of the Gulf of Aqaba. For President Nasser it brought an immense increase in prestige in that he was able to claim victory in repelling the Anglo-French invasion from Egyptian soil. The longer-term effects of the crisis were still more satisfactory for the Arab world. Britain's inept intervention destroyed such influence as she had left in the Middle East. The position of her friends became untenable. Saudi Arabia imposed oil sanctions; Hussein of Jordan denounced the Anglo-Jordanian Treaty of 1946 and renounced his British subsidies in return for a promise of help from Egypt, Syria, and Saudi Arabia; even Nuri-es-Said in Iraq, Britain's oldest client in the Middle East, tried to insure himself – in vain, as it turned out – by demanding Britain's expulsion from the Baghdad Pact. The United States, fearing that the Soviet Union would exploit the situation thus created, tried to take Britain's place. In January 1957 President Eisenhower pledged American help to any Middle East State against aggression by 'States controlled by International Communism'; a label, it would be charitable to assume, intended rather to placate a suspicious Congress than to indicate the State Department's true assessment of the Middle East situation. Thus empowered, he was able to send arms and aid to Jordan, the Lebanon, and Saudi Arabia. The left-wing regime in Syria was beyond wooing by such means and replied to the advent of the Americans by defiantly stressing their links with the Soviet Union. This flirtation with Moscow, alarming as it appeared to the West, was short-lived, and the following year Syria contracted instead her unhappy marriage with Egypt in the United Arab Republic.

But even outside the borders of Syria, American influence and protection was shown to be no more welcome than British. The Lebanese and Jordanian Governments accepted it at the cost of bloody internal strife, which spilt over into Iraq and precipitated, in July 1958, the overthrow of Nuri-es-Said's pro-Western regime. For a moment it looked as though the Lebanese and Jordanian Governments might go the way of Nuri's, and American marines and British paratroops were rushed in to sustain them. But by the end of the year it was clear in both Washington and London that there could no longer be any security for Arab governments which rested on the support of Western bayonets. It was clear also, from the course of events both in Egypt and in Iraq, that the Arab world had its own bulwarks against the Soviet penetration whose prospect had caused the West such acute alarm. And it was clear that, if the Russians had little prospect of dominating the Middle East in the immediate future, the West had even less. The influence which any Great Power could henceforth expect to exercise in the area would depend on its use of the traditional techniques of diplomacy, trade, economic assistance, and cultural influence. The Great Powers might, acting in concert or by mutual consent, set limits to the activities of the Arab States and of Israel; but they could do little positively to direct or control them. This somewhat belated recognition on the part of the outside world marked a new stage in the history of Middle Eastern affairs.[15]

The slackening of the tension which had been created by the Western interventions between 1956 and 1958 meant that Arab politics now fell into natural disarray. During these years when the forces of Arab revolutionary nationalism from the Mahgreb to Syria could plausibly contend that they were being subjected to a concerted counter-attack by a Holy Alliance of Western imperialism, President Nasser provided a focal point for the Arab world, if not precisely a leader behind whom all were prepared to rally. With the ebbing of the alleged imperialist threat – though few Arabs would allow that this ebbing was anything but temporary – old rivalries reappeared, complicated by new clashes of personality. Kessim's Iraq proved to be no more friendly to Egypt than that of Nuri-es-Said, and Kessim's revolutionary credentials were quite as good as Nasser's. Within the United Arab Republic

(UAR) the centralization of authority at Cairo proved as unwelcome to the forces of the Left in Syria as the sweeping measures of socialization which Nasser promulgated in July 1961 were disagreeable to those of the Right. In September 1961 a group of army officers seized power in Damascus, announced Syria's secession from the UAR, and installed a conservative government which annulled most of the socialist measures which Nasser had introduced. It was not long before this regime, and Kessim's, were replaced by others more friendly towards Egypt; but the success of the reactionaries led Nasser to press forward the more ruthlessly with his own revolution in Egypt; to renew his attacks on the monarchist regimes in Jordan and Saudi Arabia; and stridently to demand unity against imperialism, reaction, and Zionism, which 'despite apparent contradictions, have common aims and march in one procession directed by imperialism'.

Nasser in fact was quite happy to play the Mazzini of the Arab Revolution when he could not play the Cavour. Whichever role he played, whether the visionary promoter of the Arab social revolution or the sagacious architect of Arab unity, the theme remained the same: *fuori gli stranieri!* The imperialists might have removed their physical presence, but they had left a bridge-head behind in Israel, sustained by Western capital and Western arms. The more nationalism took on the hue of social revolution the more Israel came to be seen as the spearhead of the Western imperialist conspiracy. In Syria, the home of the Ba'athist Party which formulated these ideas with the greatest violence and precision and where a succession of increasingly extremist regimes displaced that which had broken with Egypt, willingness to attack Israel became the acid test of revolutionary zeal. As a revolutionary, Nasser could not allow himself to be outdistanced by the Ba'athists, whose influence had spread far beyond Syria. And any aspiring architect of Arab unity knew well that the most effective cement for that precarious structure was the hatred of Israel which was felt throughout the Arab world and, even where it was not felt, still had to be professed by every figure in the public eye.

All this must be taken into account if we are to understand why, by the 1960s, hatred of Israel had acquired so self-generating a quality within the Arab world and had become so intrinsic and necessary a part of Arab politics. Even if the fact of Israel's existence might, after fifteen years, have been accepted, the *idea*, and all the implications Arab intellectuals read into it, remained utterly intolerable. But the inconvenience of the fact itself was brought uncompromisingly to the fore when, in late 1963, work neared completion on an Israeli project designed to pump fresh water out of Lake Tiberias to irrigate the Negev Desert.[16]

This question of the Jordan waters would be one of great technical complexity even if it were not confused by bitter political dispute. Briefly, the River Jordan above Lake Tiberias, before it becomes adulterated by the saline affluents farther downstream, was a major source of fresh water for the irrigation schemes both of Israel and of Jordan, and could also be put to valuable use by Syria and the Lebanon. In 1955 Mr Eric Johnston, of the United States, presented a plan which allotted to each State enough water to fulfil its estimated needs. Although his proposals were acceptable to the technical experts of all the countries concerned, the Arab governments continued, for political reasons, to withhold their consent.[17] So the Israelis went ahead on their own, and began to build at Eshed Kinrot on Lake Tiberias a pumping station to raise water from the lake 1,100 feet over the Galilean watershed to flow down through the coastal plain and irrigate the Negev Desert. The Jordanians complained that this action, besides being of doubtful legality, complicated their own irrigation problems, since the reduction of the fresh water content of Lake Tiberias increased the salinity of the southern outflow on which they themselves largely depended. This the Israelis denied. They also maintained that they were drawing off from the Jordan no more than the quota allotted to them under the Johnston scheme; to which the Arabs riposted that the capacity of the irrigation works under construction indicated an intention of exceeding this considerably. In any case the Eshed Kinrot pumping station was due to begin operations early in 1964, and the prospect caused sufficient concern for the Arab States temporarily to suspend their differences and meet to discuss what should be done.

The Israeli action created among the Arabs a degree of unity, however illusory and however impermanent, such as had not been seen since the Western interventions five years before. Nasser-Mazzini once again gave place to Nasser-Cavour. In December 1963, Heads of the Arab States were invited to attend a conference in Cairo the following month. The monarchs of Jordan and Saudi Arabia, those doubtful allies of the Arab social revolution, were treated with unwonted geniality. The Syrian extremists were given stern warnings by a unusually sober and statesmanlike Cairo Press. The shrill demands from Damascus for immediate war against Israel met with the reply, 'The UAR will not let itself be pushed into a battle with Israel before the attainment of unity among all Arab countries'. Nasser himself was even blunter. 'We cannot use force today', he said, 'because circumstances do not allow us'. What circumstances he would have considered auspicious it is difficult to judge. They would certainly have included the acquiescence of the Soviet Union, if not the United States, on whose aid the Egyptian economy was at that stage still very dependent.[18]

The only measures President Nasser was meanwhile prepared to adopt were long-term ones. At the Summit Conference in Cairo in January 1964, the Arab States agreed to reply to the Israeli water-diversion scheme by one of their own which would drastically reduce the amount of water available to Israel. Two of the streams which feed the Upper Jordan originate outside Israeli territory, the Hasbani in Lebanon, the Baniyas in Syria. The Hasbani was to be diverted westward into the Litani River, and irrigate the Lebanon. The Baniyas was to be diverted south-east by a canal through Syrian territory into the River Yarmuk in Jordan. Since the Baniyas rises within a few hundred yards of Israeli territory, and the configuration of the ground would keep the course of the canal close to the frontier for much of its length, the Baniyas scheme would be highly vulnerable to Israeli attack. In order to deter such an attack, military dispositions would have to be made, and an Arab Unified High Command was established under the Egyptian General Ali Ali Amer to plan them.

Finally, the Palestine refugees were enlisted in the struggle. It was after all on their behalf that all these efforts were being made; and the confrontation was likely to enlist more sympathy, especially among the developing countries, if it could be presented not as one between an alliance of Arab powers and the small State of Israel, but as the concern of the native people of Palestine fighting, as the people of Algeria had so successfully fought, to drive out a settlement of alien colonialists. A Palestine 'Entity' was therefore created, and the eloquent M. Ahmed Shukeiry, until recently Saudi Arabia's representative at the United Nations, was appointed its spokesman. Four months later this Entity was accorded a formal unveiling – if that is the *mot juste* – at a great conference in Jerusalem, opened by King Hussein himself.

The programme inaugurated at Cairo in January 1964 was further developed at Summit Conferences in Alexandria in September 1964 and Casablanca in 1965. The practical problems involved, combined with the presence of the conservative Jordanians and Saudi Arabians and the moderate Moroccans and Tunisians, gave these conferences a cautious and pragmatic tone. On the recommendation of the Algerians, it is true, the Palestine Entity was clothed with flesh as the Palestine Liberation Organization, authorized to establish a Liberation Army, and set up headquarters at Gaza on Egyptian-administered territory. But King Hussein, who considered with some reason that M. Shukeiry was as interested in subverting the Hashemite regime as that of the Israelis, refused to permit him to operate from Jordanian territory. No other Arab State was prepared to offer him much in the way of practical help; and his bellicose pronouncements aroused, outside Algeria and Syria, only chilly disapproval. Poor M. Shukeiry was so disillusioned that at the Casablanca Conference he offered his resignation; but his sponsors did not find it convenient to accept it.

Little progress was made in any other direction. The States not immediately concerned in the confrontation (Kuwait, Egypt, Saudi Arabia, Libya, Algeria, Morocco, and the Yemen) set up a fund to provide weapons for those which were (Syria, Lebanon, and Jordan).[19] But General Amer had to report, at Alexandria, that he saw no prospect of his command being ready for action until 1966; and his task was made more difficult by the blank refusal of any of the three States concerned to accept Egyptian forces on her territory. All had good reason to assess the military threat from Israel remote in comparison with the undesirable impact which the presence of such troops would make on the delicate balance of their own internal politics. In any case, the Casablanca Conference concluded hopefully, the problem was not an immediate one. War with Israel was inevitable; but it would not come for some five to ten years.

For two years, therefore, the Arab world was able to put up a remarkable show of unity and moderation; even checking the virulent mutual abuse which had become so familiar a feature of their radio programmes. For this President Nasser deserves much of the credit. His prolonged involvement in the Yemen civil war disinclined him to adventures anywhere else, and so long as the Israel question could be made the common concern of the whole Arab world, the Syrians could be effectively curbed. Cairo was in friendly relations with both Jordan and Iraq, in spite of the severity with which their governments treated President Nasser's more intemperate supporters within their own borders. Egypt and Saudi Arabia appeared to be working amicably together to find a solution to the Yemen civil war. President Nasser seemed to have abandoned the cause of the Arab social revolution in the interests of Arab unity, and the question of Israel was interred in a multiplicity of expert committees.

What happened to reverse this situation over the next eighteen months – and reverse it so totally that in May 1967 President Nasser stood at the head of an Arab world apparently united on a policy of immediate war? Perhaps the most significant factor was the rise in the Arabian firmament of a star rivalling even Nasser in brilliance: King Feisal of Saudi Arabia, who succeeded to the throne of his brother Saud in November 1964. With its feudal economic and social structure, its friendliness towards the West, and the rivalry it posed for control of South Arabia after the British withdrawal, Saudi Arabia was anyhow among the least likely of Arab States to become an obedient satellite to Egypt. Now it began to appear as a formidable rival. In December 1965 Feisal visited his brother monarch the Shah of Iran. The following month he visited Hussein of Jordan. He placed substantial armament orders with Western firms. In January 1966 he floated the idea of an 'Islamic Summit'. Although he blandly denied that this would in any way disrupt the fabric of Arab unity to which he professed unchanging devotion, and stressed that he was concerned only with emphasizing the spiritual ties which bound Islam together, the implications of this move were evident. Feisal had set himself up as a rallying point for all the forces in the Arab world which resented the speed and the direction of the Arab social revolution.

Syria – where a yet more radical regime came into power in February 1966 – at once denounced his manoeuvre and demanded a counter-summit of Egypt, Iraq, Syria, and Algeria to frustrate it. The search for Arab unity was at an end. Nasser did indeed delay taking sides for as long as he could. Not until March did he openly attack Feisal. Thereafter, however, his denunciations become more ferocious until, in July, he publicly abandoned the principle of Arab summits altogether since, as he put it, they were being perverted to reactionary purposes.[20] The refusal of the United States in May to open negotiations for an additional $150 million in economic aid may have done something to confirm him in this change of course. In November he signed a defence pact with Syria, and the following month went on record accusing Feisal, Hussein, and President Bourguiba of Tunisia – whose consistently moderate attitude he must have found both a trial and a menace – of aping the example of Nuri-es-Said and selling out the Arab nation to the forces of imperialism.

In all this it is likely that he was receiving active encouragement from the Soviet Union. The reappearance of a pro-Western bloc in the Middle East, which threatened to embrace Iran, could not have been welcome to Moscow. Mr Kosygin visited Cairo in May 1966, and Soviet interest in Damascus had never entirely disappeared since the flirtation of 1957–58. The least that can be said on the basis of available evidence is that the Soviet Union no doubt viewed the re-establishment of unity between the revolutionary Arab States – Egypt, Syria, Algeria, and Iraq – with at least as much approval as the West had viewed King Feisal's efforts to combat them. How far either was due to the direct action and encouragement of outside powers it is not at present possible to assess. But the turn of events was one which brought war with Israel closer.

For the Syrians with whom Nasser had once more entered into close alliance were, if possible, even more violent in their attitude towards Israel than they had been two years earlier, when he had so successfully diluted the Syrian bitters with the cold water of Arab summitry. It has been suggested indeed that the defence pact of November 1966 was primarily a device to restrain them. The Syrians had not regarded M. Shukeiry's Palestine Liberation Organization, operating – or, rather, not operating – under strict Egyptian control, as any substitute for action on their own part. They had sponsored an organization of their own, *El Fatah* ('Conquest'), whose commando units began in 1965 to attack, usually infiltrating through Lebanese and Jordanian territory to raid northern Israel, much as, ten years earlier, the *fedayeen* of the Gaza Strip and the West Bank had harassed the south. The Israeli reaction was, as usual, one of massive retaliation.[21] In May 1965 their armed forces attacked the Jordanian frontier villages of Qalqiliya, Jenin, and Shuleh, which they suspected of harbouring *El Fatah* units. In October they struck at the Lebanese village of Houlé. Whatever their effect on the Lebanese and Jordanian Governments, these measures did not, apparently, dismay the Syrians. In May 1966 President Al Atassi demanded a war of liberation against the Israelis on the lines of that being fought against the United States in Vietnam. In Damascus a Higher Defence Committee was set up to 'make all arrangements for preparing all sectors of the public and mobilizing them in the battle in face of Israeli threats and aggressive intentions'. A spiral of raid and counter-raid seemed to be opening which was likely to lead, as it had in Gaza ten years before, to a climactic and formal recourse to force.

The situation in the north was the more complicated in that the Syrians had considerable *bona fide* grievances against Israel, arising out of the original armistice agreements of 1949. By these agreements a Demilitarized Zone was established on the Israeli-Syrian borders.[22] The agreement laid it down that these arrangements were 'not to be interpreted as having any relation whatsoever to ultimate territorial arrangements'; but Israel claimed the Demilitarized Zone as part of her national territory. Further, Israel installed fortifications and stationed border police there, to which the Syrians objected as a breach of the demilitarization agreement; and, finally, Israeli farmers had begun to cultivate some of the territory, which seemed to the Syrians to be a deliberate attempt to gain an advantage, in direct contradiction of the principle laid down in the agreement that 'no military or political advantage should be gained under the truce'.

To deal with problems arising out of interpretation and implementation of the Armistice Agreements the United Nations had set up a Truce Supervision Organization (UNTSO), which was assisted in its duties by Mixed Armistice Commissions of the appropriate belligerent powers.[23] The Israelis had attended no regular meetings of the Syrian Commission since 1951, and had shown considerable reluctance to permit UNTSO observers to investigate some of their activities within the Demilitarized Zone. By 1967, however, mutual complaints had reached a level which made both sides regard the Commission as a useful vehicle for their protests. Each had raids and counter-raids to complain of.[24] In addition, in July 1966, the Israelis had attacked, with artillery and aircraft, the works on the Baniyas water-diversion scheme just across their border; while the Syrians had repeatedly fired on Israelis attempting to cultivate land in the Demilitarized Zone. Predictably the Commission broke up, disagreeably and inconclusively, after only three emergency meetings. But meanwhile two incidents occurred which transcended the normal level of border dispute. The first was the Israeli attack on the Jordanian village of Es Samu on 13 November 1966. The second was the air battle on 7 April 1967, when Israeli aircraft, without loss to themselves, shot down six Syrian MiG fighter aircraft. The repercussions of these events were, as we shall see, to be very considerable indeed.

The Samu raid followed the failure of Israel to get any satisfaction after a complaint to the Security Council about mines laid on her territory by *El Fatah* units. The incident was repeated near the Jordanian frontier; so the Israelis took matters into their own hands with a daylight attack by armour, aircraft, and infantry which did considerable damage to the village and killed eighteen Jordanians.[25] Public opinion even in Israel objected to the violence of this blow against the mildest of their adversaries, and Israel was condemned by the Security Council. But in view of the failure of the Council to condemn the activities of the Syrians, she was naturally unimpressed. 'If Hussein has control of the West Bank and failed to prevent terrorism', asked Yigal Allon, her Minister of Labour, 'why is he entitled to our indulgeuce? And if he does not exercise control there, what interest have we in preserving his regime? . . . The action at Samu demonstrated to the Powers that Israel is not willing to submit its security to diplomatic bargaining'. In fact the Samu raid precipitated such angry demonstrations in Jordan that Hussein took stern measures to repress his dissident elements; which were seized on by supporters of the Israeli action as further proof of its effectiveness. It had, they suggested, given Hussein the excuse he needed to show himself master in his own house.

The second incident arose over one of the Israeli attempts to cultivate land in the Demilitarized Zone. Syrian small-arms fire against an Israeli tractor was answered by fire from Israeli forces who somehow happened to be in the neighbourhood. Artillery, tanks, and ultimately aircraft joined in, the Israeli aircraft silencing the Syrian gun positions, shooting down six aircraft of the intercepting fighter patrol sent up to meet them, and sweeping on over Damascus in jubilant demonstration of their victory. Even more than the Samu raid, this demonstrated Israel's ability and willingness to react, indeed to over-react, to provocations of the kind which the Syrians had no intention of discontinuing. And like the Samu raid it showed the disunity that still obtained among Israel's principal enemies. Hussein's purge of his activists infuriated the Syrians, who redoubled their attacks on his regime, both in the Press and over Damascus Radio. The Jordanians retaliated by jubilantly broadcasting details of the Syrian aircraft forced down over Jordanian territory; and both Syria and Jordan complained loudly of the Egyptian failure to do anything to help them, taunting Nasser – significantly in view of later developments – with sheltering behind the United Nations Emergency Force. Considering that Hussein refused to allow Egyptian units on his territory and that Syria refused Egypt's offer to establish an air base on her soil, they really had little cause for complaint. But Nasser could not stand by indefinitely and watch his allies suffer such humiliating reversals; and more important, neither could the Russians. M. Gromyko, Soviet Foreign Minister, visited Cairo in April. It is likely that this question had an important place on his agenda.

Were such humiliations likely to continue? The Israeli Government derived no satisfaction from inflicting them, and fully realized the dangers it incurred in doing so: dangers arising not simply from another war fought, like that of 1948, on three fronts against superior forces, but from antagonizing the Great Powers. The Prime Minister, Mr Levi Eshkol, like David Ben-Gurion before him, believed in the need to retain, almost at any cost, the sympathy of the United States. He was almost as anxious to avoid antagonizing the Soviet Union; and the Soviet Union, he knew, watched with paternal concern over the fortunes of the kaleidoscopic regimes in Damascus.

Yet opinion in Israel would not indefinitely put up with the kind of provocation offered by the *El Fatah* raids.[26] Mr Eshkol's reputation was one for sagacity rather than for decisiveness. He presided over an uneasy coalition delicately responsive to shifts in public opinion – a coalition itself under heavy criticism from the Rafi party founded by Ben-Gurion in 1965, through which such colourful figures as Moshe Dayan, Shimon Peres, and Teddy Kolleck demanded greater drive in government, a more positive foreign policy, and in general a more vigorous and forward-looking 'style'. These demands were attractive to the younger generation of Israelis – 'Sabras', born in Israel, justly proud of their achievements, impatient of the older generation of East European immigrants who still so largely dominated the government, less conscious than that generation of Israel's debt to diplomacy and good fortune as well as to her own energy and military force. The last thing Mr Eshkol and his colleagues wanted was a military adventure which would darken the already gloomy economic situation and complicate relations with the Great Powers. But if the Syrians went on with their raids, how was such an adventure to be avoided?

From September 1966 to May 1967 Mr Eshkol and his colleagues – including a little surprisingly, General Rabin, the Chief of Staff – went on record with a series of increasingly vehement statements threatening Syria with condign punishment if the offensive incidents continued. We have seen how little effect these had as a deterrent to the Syrian Government. They may have been more effective in quietening public opinion in Israel itself. What is beyond question is their contribution to the general sense of uneasiness in the Middle East. They came to a climax on 13 May, when Mr Eshkol declared, both in a press conference and in a live broadcast, that Israel would react in her own fashion to the harassing of her borders – 'at the place, the time, and in the manner we choose. . . . We shall not recognize the limitations they are trying to impose on our reprisals. If they try to disturb our border, then their border will be disturbed'. Furthermore, Israel would react to any attempt to divert the headwaters of the Jordan or to interfere with the freedom of her shipping to the Red Sea. Her armed forces were being overhauled and receiving new equipment, and would be able to fulfil any demands that might be made on them. At the same time General Rabin, speaking to a military audience, was reported as saying that so long as the government continued in power in Damascus the *El Fatah* raids were likely to continue; not an unreasonable appreciation, but one which was seized on by the Arab press and inflated into a threat to overthrow the Ba'athist regime by force.

Mr Eshkol's remarks were unusually strongly-worded, but it is doubtful whether Israeli public opinion would have been satisfied with anything less. It was perhaps his domestic audience that he had in mind when he made them: certainly he can hardly have anticipated their effect abroad. The whole Arab world exploded into wrathful activity and the Great Powers suddenly realized that they had on their hands a crisis of major proportions; an imminent conflict between client states to whose survival their own prestige and power were deeply committed.

II. The crisis

The celebration of the foundation of the State of Israel in the spring of each year always increased tension between Israel and her Arab neighbours.[1] For the Arabs, particularly the Palestinian exiles, it was an occasion for mourning. For the Israelis it was a day of rejoicing and of military parades, the main national celebration being held in each large Israeli town in turn. In 1967, for the first time since 1961, it was the turn of Jerusalem. This always caused trouble. Apart from the natural sensitivity of the Jordanians to any ceremonies in this disputed city, Jerusalem lay within the 'defensive area' as defined by the Armistice Agreement, in which the deployment of armed forces was rigorously limited. In 1961, in defiance of a ruling by the Security Council, Israel had ignored these limitations. This year she intended to be more cautious. The Government hoped to obtain the attendance of the diplomatic corps at an event which so signally marked the status of Jerusalem as an integral part of Israel, and as a bait they reduced the military parade to dimensions compatible with the Armistice Agreement. They did not succeed. Not even the Western powers sent official representatives. The Arabs lodged a protest with the United Nations just the same; and the absence of heavy units gave credibility to the rumours that they were being reserved for action somewhere else. Nonetheless Mr Eshkol came under heavy criticism in the Knesset and the press for making such concessions. Nationalist sentiment in Israel, already irritated at his failure to respond effectively to the *El Fatah* raids, saw this as further evidence of weakness. Should not Independence Day, it was asked, be a moment for national self-assertion rather than diplomatic finesse?

Foreign observers in Tel Aviv considered that pressures of this kind were very largely responsible for the crop of bellicose statements by Mr Eshkol, General Rabin, and their colleagues during the week leading up to Independence Day. Many believed that the Israeli Government was primarily anxious to prevent any further action by Syria which might intensify a demand for retaliation, and that it was to deter such action, as well as to disarm their own critics, that its members spoke as they did. But there is much about the situation that still remains obscure. Rumours of an impending blow against Syria were current in Tel Aviv. These may have been purely self-generating; they may have been deliberately kindled by the Israeli Government as part of their general programme of deterrence; or they may have been rooted in fact (indeed, it is possible that Israeli forces were conducting demonstrations near the frontier for the Syrians' benefit). Whatever the origins of these rumours, they appear to have reached Damascus and Cairo in the form of specific reports of Israeli troop movements indicating that a massive attack was being mounted on Syrian territory. President Nasser was later to be very precise about this. 'On 13 May', he said on 22 May, 'we received accurate information that Israel was concentrating on the Syrian border huge armed forces of about 11–13 brigades. These forces were divided into two fronts, one south of Lake Tiberias and one north of the Lake. The decision made by Israel at the time was to carry out an attack against Syria starting on 17 May. On 14 May we took action, discussed the matter, and contacted our Syrian brothers. The Syrians also had this information'.

They had indeed, and the indications are very strong that they received it from the same source – the Soviet Union. It was natural enough that the Soviet Union should have warned her friends of rumours of an impending attack. To report specific troop movements, however, was more serious. No such movements had been detected by UNTSO observers, according to the Secretary-General's Report of 18 May. A force of the size reported could hardly have been concentrated without extensive mobilization measures which would have been generally observed and discussed by the many foreign visitors to Israel. Besides, a large concentration of this kind was quite alien to the Israel military style. A punitive expedition capable of striking deep into Syrian territory could have been rapidly mounted from the area round Haifa by rapidly assembled forces within a few hours. The Soviet Ambassador was invited by Mr Eshkol to inspect the alleged concentration areas for himself. He refused. The evidence for a concentration of the kind described by President Nasser is at present so tenuous as to be entirely unconvincing. But in discounting it we cannot entirely exclude two hypotheses: first, that an attack of some sort was intended; and, second, that the Israeli Government, for the reasons discussed above, wished such an intention to be generally believed at home and abroad, and encouraged rumours accordingly.

The effectiveness of a threat does not depend only on the credibility of the threatening party. Important also is the vulnerability of the party threatened, and the Syrian Government, the product of the last of an apparently ceaseless succession of *coups d'état*, was very precarious indeed. Another Israeli blow like that of 7 April might easily have caused its overthrow, a further period of instability, and embarrassment both to its Soviet patrons and to its Egyptian friends. But how could such a blow be deterred? The Syrian Army, a political rather than a military force, was in no state to resist serious attack. Relations with Jordan were sulphurous: Jordanian 'reactionism' ranked with Zionism and Imperialism in the diabolical Trinity accused of plotting the downfall of the Arab revolution. And Egypt, with no bases on Syrian soil, could bring at best only indirect help. But President Nasser had already twice failed to assist Arab States against Israeli attack. He could not afford to stand by yet a third time without suffering a serious loss of prestige – and one which his rivals in Jordan and Saudi Arabia would be glad to exploit. All these factors, it may be conjectured, played some part in the Russian decision to issue such categoric warnings to Cairo and Damascus on the basis of such flimsy evidence. They may not have believed an Israeli attack to be quite so imminent as they alleged; but the possibility of one was self-evident, and it was better to be safe than sorry.

If the Russians had any doubts about the reality of the danger, they were not widely shared in Cairo or Damascus. On 13 May the Cairo newspaper *Al-Ahram* wrote that the statements by Mr Eshkol meant that an attack on Syria was imminent. 'If Israel now tries to set the region on fire, then it is definite that Israel herself will be completely destroyed in this fire, which will surround it on all sides, thus bringing about the end of this aggressive racist base'. In Damascus the Foreign Minister informed ambassadors of the States represented on the Security Council of the threatening Israeli aggression. The following day, Sunday 14 May, General Mohammed Fawzy, Chief of Staff of the Egyptian Armed Forces, flew to Damascus to examine the situation and co-ordinate plans with the Syrian Government. On the Monday the Egyptian Army began to move, in an obvious and spectacular fashion. Convoys converged on Cairo from camps farther south, passed through the city for hours, causing major traffic dislocation on their way, and headed out in the direction of Alexandria and Ismailia. Next day, 16 May, a state of emergency was proclaimed for the Egyptian armed forces. 'If Israel attempts to fulfil its foolish threats', quoted Cairo Radio from the newspaper *Al-Akhbar*, 'it will find forces ready to face it, forces specially maintained for this purpose. Measures laid down by the joint Syrian-UAR defence agreement are already being implemented'.

Spectacular as these troop movements were, their scale was not such as to cause the Israelis serious alarm. They were seen as a military demonstration to satisfy Arab public opinion rather than as a preparation for serious attack. General Gavish, Commander of the Sinai front, normally had only a single battalion to observe both the Egyptian and the Jordanian frontiers; the Israeli Army Command quietly increased his strength to two brigades, and awaited events. So far the situation was well under control. A potential threat had been checked by a counter-threat. If Israel had seriously contemplated an attack on Syria she would now know that this would precipitate hostilities with Egypt as well, and would no doubt have been effectively deterred. The Russians had shown themselves wise counsellors, and President Nasser a loyal ally. At this point the matter might have rested, save for two factors. The first was Arab public opinion. The second was the presence of the United Nations Emergency Force.

The Syrian cry for help and the Egyptian military demonstration set off throughout the Arab world a wave of emotion such as could hardly have been predicted and which was to have considerable influence on the course of events. There was hardly an Arab city from Casablanca to Baghdad where demonstrations of some kind did not occur. No Arab government, whatever its political complexion, could afford to be backward in pledging both moral and material support in the battle apparently provoked by aggressive Zionism. Iraq promised help on 15 May. On the 17th both Iraq and Jordan placed their forces in a state of alert. Lebanon called off a courtesy visit by the American Sixth Fleet.[2] On the 18th Kuwait placed its forces under the United Command already established by Egypt and Syria, and three days later Jordan offered to do the same. Libya and the Sudan pledged their support on 22 May. On the 23rd King Feisal of Saudi Arabia declared at the conclusion of his state visit to London that 'any Arab who falters in taking part in this battle, which may mark his destiny, is not worthy to have the name of Arab'. King Hassan of Morocco sent his personal adviser, M. Ahmed Balafrej, to Cairo with promises of support. Algeria declared a state of alert and called for volunteers from the old FLN. Even M. Bourguiba of Tunisia informed the Secretary-General of the Arab League on 25 May that his country was 'bound by obligations taken by it during the first and second Arab Summits . . . concerning the problem of Palestine and the possibility of Israeli aggression against any Arab State'. By 27 May all thirteen members of the Arab League had declared their solidarity in aiding any of their members who had to defend itself against Zionist aggression; and in their van was the Palestine Liberation Organization, whose radio stations in Cairo poured out against Israel an uninterrupted stream of threats and abuse. For the Palestinians this was *Der Tag*, the moment of revenge and return for which they had waited so impatiently. 'The menace and challenge of Israel have persisted for too long', cried the Palestine Service of Cairo Radio on 16 May. 'The very existence of Israel in our usurped land has endured beyond all expectation. An end must be put to the challenge of Israel and to its very existence. . . . Welcome to aggression by Israel, for it will send us into action to destroy it! . . . Welcome to the battle for which we have long waited! The hour of battle is imminent. In fact, this is the hour of battle'.

The views of the unfortunate Palestinian Arabs and the violence of their spokesmen should not be regarded as typical of the whole Arab world. Nevertheless the feeling was clearly general that a crisis was at hand, that the whole question of Palestine was once more reopened, and that an opportunity had arisen to reverse the settlement of 1956, if not indeed that of 1949. It was a feeling that President Nasser himself evidently came quickly to share; but even if he had not, it was too strong to be ignored or suppressed. The Arab world, in appearance at least, was suddenly united and looking to him for action. It is doubtful whether under such circumstances any Arab statesman could have told the demonstrators to go home, politely refused all offers of military help, muzzled M. Shukeiry, and declared that his objectives were now achieved.

This swelling support, the confidence he derived from it, and the realization that if he did not exploit it others would, may do something to explain President Nasser's actions over the next two weeks. And the first which require some explanation are those respecting the United Nations Emergency Force and the Straits of Tiran.

The United Nations Emergency Force, behind whose sheltering skirts the radio stations of Damascus and Amman had been repeatedly accusing Nasser of hiding, consisted by now of 3,378 men. A Yugoslav reconnaissance battalion patrolled most of the international frontier in the Sinai Desert, with a platoon at Sharm-el-Sheikh. The northern end of the frontier and the western part of the demarcation line in the Gaza Strip was the responsibility of a Brazilian infantry battalion, while Indian and Swedish infantry battalions patrolled the eastern part of the line. UNEF Headquarters were in Gaza itself. Its commander, Major-General Rikhye of the Indian Army, was in Gaza on the evening of 16 May when the liaison officer of the United Arab Republic arrived with a message from the Egyptian Chief of Staff, General Fawzy, demanding the withdrawal of all UN forces along Egypt's borders.[3] The officer added, according to General Rikhye's own account, that the posts at El Sabha on the Sinai border and at Sharm-el-Sheikh on the Straits of Tiran must be evacuated immediately, since Egyptian forces would occupy them that night. It is still not clear whether this additional demand, which was to have such major international repercussions, was made on the instructions of General Fawzy alone, or on those of President Nasser himself. In any case, General

Rikhye pointed out that the whole procedure was grossly improper. Any such request must be made to the Secretary-General; whom he at once informed.

Next morning the Yugoslav contingent at El Sabha found its observation posts already occupied and their camp surrounded by Egyptian forces. The situation grew increasingly tense. At midday on the 17th General Rikhye received a further demand for the withdrawal of his forces in Sinai, which he again refused. On the morning of the 18th the Egyptians forced Yugoslav troops out of their positions at El Amr and El Kuntilla, and at noon the commander of the contingent at Sharm-el-Sheikh was given fifteen minutes to withdraw his forces – an ultimatum he rejected. That night, however, instructions reached General Rikhye from the Secretary-General to withdraw UNEF as requested. He at once complied. Israeli and Egyptian forces again confronted each other directly in the Sinai Desert and the Gaza Strip.

The legality of the Secretary-General's action in withdrawing UNEF has never been called into question. The force derived its right to be on Egyptian soil from the Egyptian Government, and once the consent of that government was withdrawn it had no legal basis for remaining. The refusal of the Israelis to accommodate the force – a refusal which their representative at the United Nations repeated on 18 May – well illustrated the rights of sovereign States in the whole question. U Thant's wisdom in complying so rapidly with the Egyptian request, and the propriety of his doing so without referring the matter either to the Security Council or to the General Assembly, was however questioned, immediately and publicly, both by the President of the United States and by the British Foreign Secretary. It has been suggested, not only that U Thant could legitimately have played for time and thus provided the opportunity for passions to ebb, but also that President Nasser expected him to do so, and was as surprised as anyone else by his immediate acquiescence. On this last point many informed observers speak with conviction, but evidence is hard to come by. Certainly the actions of the Egyptians forces on the ground, where they were already forcibly taking over the UN positions on the morning of 17 May, do nothing to bear out this interpretation.

The Secretary-General published on 26 June a comprehensive reply to his critics chronicling and justifying his actions, and in this the difficulties under which he operated are made very clear. The message from General Rikhye showed that rapid action was imperative. A little more than an hour after receiving it U Thant was in conference with M. El Kony, the Permanent Representative of the UAR at the United Nations, who denied all knowledge of his government's request. U Thant stated the position as he saw it. If Egypt made a formal request for the withdrawal of the force, he would be compelled to comply. But the temporary withdrawal of the force from all or part of the demarcation line and the international frontier would be unacceptable 'because the purpose of the United Nations Force in Gaza and Sinai is to prevent a recurrence of fighting, and it cannot be asked to stand aside in order to enable the two sides to resume fighting'. Next day U Thant consulted informally with the representatives of the countries providing contingents for UNEF. The

Canadian representative pointed out forcefully, and, as it proved, accurately, what was likely to happen if the force was withdrawn, and advised delay. The Indians and the Yugoslavs insisted that Egypt was acting within her rights and that they must comply with her request. The forces of these two countries were those immediately involved and their political leaders had long enjoyed particularly friendly relations with President Nasser. Moreover, they were powers of medium size in the uncommitted world, and the importance of asserting the principle of national sovereignty was bound to bulk large in their minds.[4]

It was in the knowledge of this division among the nations directly involved that U Thant had to decide how to act when he received, on the afternoon of 18 May, the formal Egyptian request for UNEF's withdrawl; which was accompanied by the warning that any appeal to President Nasser to rescind it would be rebuffed. He referred the matter to the UNEF Advisory Committee, where the same views were expressed formally as had been informally aired the previous day.[5] The Indian and Yugoslav representatives made it clear that their contingents were likely to be withdrawn as soon as their governments were informed of the situation. Mr Ignatieff of Canada urged consultation with the Security Council powers, but the idea did not find favour. Nobody, apparently, proposed that the Committee should exercise its right of requesting a meeting of the General Assembly. It was accepted that the Secretary-General should comply with the Egyptian request and report his actions to the Security Council and the General Assembly. This he did in appropriately sombre terms.

> It is true [he concluded his report on 18 May] that UNEF has allowed us for ten years to ignore some of the hard realities of the underlying conflict. The Governments concerned, and the United Nations, are now confronted with a brutally realistic and dangerous situation. . . . I do not wish to be alarmist, but I cannot avoid the warning to the Council that in my view the current situation in the Near East is more disturbing, indeed I may say more menacing, than at any time since the fall of 1956.

Could U Thant have acted otherwise? It must be remembered that he was presented on the ground with a virtual *fait accompli*. United Nations forces were already being jostled out of their positions by Egyptian troops. They were dependent for maintenance and supply on Egyptian good will. There was at best only the slenderest legal grounds for delaying their withdrawal, and such delay would have aroused strong objections from a substantial number – perhaps indeed a majority – of member States of the United Nations, including two who were providing a considerable part of the force. Soviet action would certainly have paralyzed the Security Council; the General Assembly would certainly have ended its deliberations in deadlock; the position of the forces on the ground would rapidly have become impossible; but a day or so might have been gained for President Nasser to reflect on all the possible consequences of his actions. Dag Hammarskjöld might have played a lone and perhaps a successful hand.[6] But U Thant had been appointed to his post, and held it successfully for six years, precisely because he was not a Hammarskjöld. His actions were correct, if unimaginative. And it is significant that the criticisms levelled against them in North America and Great Britain have found few echoes in Communist countries or the Third World; to whom, in the United Nations, the Secretary-General owes a responsibility no less than that to the Western powers.

The withdrawal of UNEF brought the crisis into a new and very much graver stage. It was no longer possible to see the Egyptian movements in Sinai as a mere promenade. Israel ordered a limited mobilization of reserves, to which Egypt, on 21 May, replied in kind. But eyes were now fixed, not on Sinai, but on Sharm-el-Sheikh, which UNEF finally evacuated on 23 May.[7] Two days earlier Amman Radio had taunted Nasser, in very typical fashion, with the dilemma he now faced. 'This is the question all Arabs are asking: will Egypt restore its batteries and guns and close its territorial waters in the Tiran Strait to the enemy? Logic, wisdom, and nationalism make it incumbent on Egypt to do so. . . . If she fails to do so, what value would there be in military demonstrations?' The Israelis had given repeated warnings that they would regard such an act as a *casus belli*. They had done so in 1956: the growth of the port of Eilat made it still more probable that they would again in 1967. Such a step would transform the Egyptian actions from a massive deterrent demonstration – and one which had probably served its purpose – into a deliberate challenge to war against an adversary who had twice within the past twenty years defeated them in the field.

By what calculations and by what stages President Nasser decided to take this step is still obscure. Indeed it remains the central mystery of the whole crisis. There is no cause to suppose that the Soviet Union gave him any encouragement. She had at no time endorsed Egypt's case on the Gulf of Aqaba – one which would have disagreeable implications for herself in the Baltic and the Black Sea. Her military advisers knew as much as anyone, and more than most, about the comparative state of armament, training, and morale of the Egyptian, Syrian, and Israeli armed forces. The protection of Syria and the humiliation of Israel was one thing; open war in the Middle East between the protégés of the Communist and Western worlds was quite another. It is generally believed that the Russians were now regarding with alarm the spread of the holocaust which they had so insouciantly touched off. But if the Soviet Ambassador was advising caution, the press of the Arab world was demanding just the opposite. Once Egyptian forces occupied Sharm-el-Sheikh, any action short of restoring the *status quo ante* 1956 would have been painted by Nasser's enemies and rivals as weakness and betrayal. The only way lay forward – a *fuite en avant*, even if necessary into war.

All this must at present remain in the realm of speculation. Whatever his reasoning, President Nasser announced his decision in the course of a visit to his forces in Sinai on the evening of Monday 22 May.

> The armed forces yesterday [he declared] occupied Sharm-el-Sheikh.

> What does this mean? It is affirmation of our rights and our sovereignty
> over the Gulf of Aqaba, which constitutes territorial waters. Under no
> circumstances will we allow the Israeli flag to pass through the Gulf of
> Aqaba. The Jews threaten war. We tell them you are welcome, we are
> ready for war, but under no circumstances will we abandon any of our
> rights. This water is ours.

The army, he said, was ready to defend the rights of the Arab people as a whole. 'They are all behind you, praying for you day and night and believing that you are the pride of their nation, of the Arab nation. This is the feeling of the Arab people in Egypt and outside Egypt. We are confident that you will honour the trust.'

But the Arab unity to which he referred had its limits. President Nasser was still the revolutionary, warning his people against the reactionaries, those running dogs in the imperialist-Zionist plot.

> Reaction casts doubt on everything and so does the Islamic alliance. We
> all know that the Islamic alliance is now represented by three States: the
> Kingdom of Saudi Arabia, the Kingdom of Jordan, and Iran. They are
> saying that the purpose of the Islamic alliance is to unite the Muslim
> against Israel. I would like the Islamic Alliance to solve the Palestine
> question in only one way – by preventing the supply of oil to Israel. . . .
> It is an imperialist alliance, and this means it sides with Zionism
> because Zionism is the main ally of imperialism. . . . They say they want
> to co-ordinate their plans with us. We cannot co-ordinate our plans with
> Islamic alliance members because it would mean giving our plans to the
> Jews and Israel.

It will be seen how large a part 'anti-imperialism' played in President Nasser's declarations, even before the Western powers had made their position in the dispute clear. Already Syrian and Egyptian newspapers were describing the imminent Israeli offensive in terms of an imperialist plot against the revolutionary Arab world. Such assumptions could only accentuate the division between the revolutionary Arab States and those which, however sincere their detestation of Israel, still tried to retain their links with the West. Jordanian offers of military co-operation were cold-shouldered in Cairo. In Damascus, press attacks on the Hashemite Kingdom reached a new peak of intensity. And on 23 May, in consequence of a terrorist bomb explosion in a frontier town in which 14 Jordanians were killed, Jordan broke off diplomatic relations with Syria. Whatever the aspirations of its statesmen and thinkers, Arab unity was still far from being an accomplished fact.

The blockade of the Straits of Tiran, however, was. On 24 May *Al-Ahram* reported that the Straits had been closed not only by guns and patrol-boats but also with mines: a report which Western official circles received with justifiable scepticism. Israeli vessels, it said, would be exposed to fire; others would be asked to stop for inspection of their cargoes. On 25 May the Egyptian Foreign Minister, M. Riad, gave further details. The United Arab Republic would, he declared, consider the entry of an Israeli ship into her territorial waters as an act of aggression which would 'oblige us to take all measures to ensure the integrity of our territory and territorial waters and the safety of our armed forces'. In addition 'any attempt by any nation to use our territorial waters to send strategic materials to Israel would be considered an unfriendly act constituting assistance to the Israeli war effort against the UAR and all Arab countries'. Finally he asserted that the claim of the 'imperialist States' to act as guardians over what they termed an international waterway was prejudicial to the sovereignty of the UAR.

For the imposition of the blockade had brought prompt reaction from Israel and the West. The crisis was now one of international proportions. Israel had withdrawn from the Straits in 1957 only after she had received from the Western powers the most explicit assurances that these powers would guarantee freedom of passage for her ships. Mr Eshkol, speaking in the Knesset on 23 May, now demanded publicly, as Israeli diplomats were doing privately, that those powers should live up to their obligations. 'This is indeed a test for a solemn and clear international commitment on the implementation of which depends the existence of a regime of international security and law. . . . In view of this situation I again call on the Great Powers to act without delay to maintain the right of free access for shipping to our southern port'. And Mr Abba Eban, Israel's Foreign Minister, was despatched to Paris, London, and Washington to secure the necessary assurances.

Mr Eshkol's statement was described in the Israeli press as 'restrained'. Certainly there were those, especially in the senior ranks of the army, who found it inadequate and would have preferred to attack at once before the Egyptian forces in Sinai had time to consolidate. But it was agreed not only by the Cabinet but by opposition leaders – including Mr Begin, General Dayan, and Mr Ben-Gurion – that the intentions of the Western powers should be sounded before Israel risked action on her own.[8] Nevertheless there were, and still remain, strong rumours that an immediate attack was intended and was called off only on the urging of the United States. Here again, as with Israel's intention towards Syria ten days earlier, we can only speculate. The rumours may have been founded on fact – though it is improbable that such an attack could have been launched before 26 May. They may have been totally false. Or they may have received covert official blessing in order to force the hand of the Western powers.

The knowledge that Israel was likely to take action on her own unless something was done for her was certainly a major factor in the calculations of Washington and London. Those calculations were not simple ones. The United States was deeply involved in Vietnam. The Department of Defense could only regard the possibility of another conflict, which would make further demands on their resources, with undiluted dismay. Sympathetic as public opinion was to the cause of Israel, it was doubtful how far that sympathy would stretch in terms of an official commitment which might come to resemble, in its open-ended demands on American blood and treasure, that to the Republic of South Vietnam. In any case, as the Senate Foreign Affairs Committee made clear to the Secretary of State, there could be no question of the United States again assuming such a commitment without effective allies. This time America must not go it alone. For the British the problem was still graver. To support Israel meant antagonizing the entire Arab world, including her traditional allies and the oil-producing States. A withdrawal of Arab sterling balances and an interruption of oil supplies would be blows which her chronically sick economy would find it hard to bear. The disadvantages of such a course were depressingly obvious. The gains were less easy to assess.

Yet unless the Western powers took some action, the Israelis undoubtedly would, and no one could calculate the consequences. On 23 May, when the news of the blockade reached Washington, President Johnson issued a statement to the effect that 'the United States considers the Gulf to be an international waterway and feels that a blockade of Israeli shipping is illegal and potentially disastrous to the cause of peace. The right of free, innocent passage of the international waterway is a vital interest of the international community'. The following day, in the course of an address to a trade union meeting in Margate, Mr Harold Wilson recalled the British declaration of March 1957 that the Straits of Tiran constituted an international waterway, 'through which the vessels of all nations have a right of passage', and that Britain would 'assert this right on behalf of all British shipping and [was] prepared to join with others to secure general recognition of this right'. 'The declaration then made', went on Mr Wilson, 'remains the view and policy of Her Majesty's Government and we shall promote and support international action to uphold this right of free passage'. To this end, he said, the Minister of State at the Foreign Office, Mr George Thomson, was being sent to Washington, and to confer with the United Nations Delegation in New York.

While Mr Thomson flew to America, the Foreign Secretary himself, Mr George Brown, set off on a deferred visit to Moscow. There he held talks which he afterwards described as 'very full, very detailed, exceedingly friendly, and constructive'. 'What we are all concerned with', he told the press on 26 May, 'is seeing that a conflagration does not break out'. Privately he reported signs of dissension within the Soviet Government over the best course to pursue. Similar exchanges were in progress between Moscow and Washington through normal diplomatic contacts, and the West was satisfied that the Soviet Union was urging restraint on the Arabs. The Soviet Ambassador indeed roused President Nasser at 3.30 on the morning of 26 May to advise him to take no rash initiative.[9] Mr Kosygin also sent to Mr Eshkol a note urging him 'emphatically to take all measures to prevent a military conflict which would be fraught with very grave consequences to the cause of peace and international security'.[10] But whatever pressure the Soviet Union may have been applying behind the scenes, she did not vary her public posture of support for the Arab case; and she used it to frustrate all attempts by the Western powers to gain support for their position in the United Nations.

When President Nasser announced the closing of the Straits on the evening of 22 May, U Thant was already on his way to Cairo on a visit which, arranged some time earlier, had now been accelerated. In spite of his absence, Canada and Denmark, the two states who had at the meeting of the UNEF Advisory Committee most strongly opposed UNEF's withdrawal, called for an immediate meeting of the Security Council. When it met on 24 May, with the representatives of Israel and Egypt in attendance without votes, Canada and Denmark put forward a resolution which expressed full support for U Thant's efforts in Cairo to pacify the situation, requested all member States to refrain from steps likely to worsen it, and invited the Secretary-General to report back on his return. M. El Kony, for Egypt, strongly objected to this as an attempt to cut the ground from under U Thant's feet, and attacked Britain and the United States for 'an intensive and brutal policy beyond their boundaries and far away from their territories'. Dr Fedorenko for the Soviet Union took the same line. 'Is there not more of a concealed desire here to interfere in the affairs of someone else rather than a true concern for the peace and security of the Near East'? Even among less implacably hostile States it was difficult for the Western powers, who had already made their attitude to the closing of the Straits so clear, to gain support for a motion even so innocuously worded. They could not obtain the nine votes necessary to secure acceptance of the motion, or even persuade their colleagues to enter into private discussions about it. The representatives of India, Ethiopia, Nigeria, and Mali broadly supported the line taken by Dr Fedorenko. It was clear that the Western powers' claim to impartiality carried little conviction at the United Nations. The declarations already made by their leaders revealed them to be already strongly *parti-pris*.

They could not even speak with a united voice among themselves. General de Gaulle was *a priori* unlikely to toe a line which had been drawn in Washington and London. Israel had been a good customer for French armaments and a useful ally during the days when France, struggling to retain Algeria, saw her principal enemies in the Arab world. But those days were over. France now had no quarrel with the Arabs. She had good reason to hope that intelligent diplomacy and cultural prestige would restore her to the position of influence in the Arab world which she had failed to maintain by force of arms and which was likely to be denied her so long as she was associated with the Anglo-Americans. Early on in the crisis General de Gaulle had proposed consultations among 'The Big Four' to deal with the problem. Britain and the United States had expressed their readiness to try this solution, but the Soviet Union would not co-operate. Thereafter France affirmed her strict neutrality in the dispute. 'France is committed in no sense or on any subject to any one of the States involved', stated President de Gaulle on 2 June. 'The State which uses arms first, whatever that may be, would have neither France's approval nor its support'.[11]

In face of the hostility not only of the Soviet Union but of France, India, and a great part of the Afro-Asian world, there was thus little chance that Britain and the United States could gain a majority in the United Nations for action to secure the opening of the Straits. If the Western powers were to take action, they would have to do so on their own. The British proposed that this should be done by an appeal to all members of 'The International Maritime Community' to issue a Declaration that the Gulf of Aqaba was an international waterway into which and through which all nations should have right of passage, and to assert their intention of maintaining that right on behalf of their own and all other vessels. But there was to be no indication in the Declaration that force would be used, if necessary, to maintain that right: an omission deliberately contrived to secure the greatest number of signatories but one which robbed the document of much of its effectiveness as a guarantee. It was a point which did not escape the attention of the Israeli Foreign Office.

The State Department, however, was considering also a further proposal. An international naval force might be set up if all else failed, to patrol the Gulf and, it was hoped, by its mere presence deter the Egyptians from enforcing the blockade. With this went suggestions for testing the blockade. Israel had already considered doing this and was preparing vessels for the purpose when Mr Eban was despatched to Washington. The support they could expect from the Western powers, in the event of their doing so, was one of the principal questions which Mr Eban had to explore. On 25 May Mr Dean Rusk and officials of the State Department explained to him the proposals which they had in mind. The following day he was received by the President. Mr Johnson, it is reported, was frank about the problems which he faced in persuading Congress to sanction any action which was likely – as had the famous encounter in the Gulf of Tonkin in August 1964 – to involve the United States in war. But he emphatically urged Israel not to take any unilateral action. He gave equally emphatic, if somewhat indefinite, assurances that so long as Israel did not act on her own, she could rely on the support of the United States. He only asked time for diplomacy to work.

With these assurances, for what they were worth, Mr Eban returned home. On 31 May Mr George Brown announced in the House of Commons the project of the Maritime Declaration, and the following day the State Department declared their support for this 'British initiative'. Little support came from anyone else. The French Minister for Information said drily on 2 June that 'it does not noticeably advance matters'. Canada, West Germany, and Italy were reported to be considerably less than enthusiastic. By 4 June positive reactions had been received only from Australia, New Zealand, the Netherlands, and Iceland. From this also the Israeli Government doubtless drew their own conclusions.

Useless as the Maritime Declaration proved as a measure either to restrain or to help Israel, it served to infuriate the Arab States. Since Arab propaganda had from the very outset of the crisis depicted Israeli actions as part of a general 'imperialist plot', it is doubtful whether any action taken by the

Western powers could have convinced the Arab world of their dispassionate desire for a peaceful resolution of the conflict. Now that they had openly aligned themselves with Israel, there was an eruption of fury. 'It is now crystal clear', said Cairo Radio on 3 June, 'that the imperialist, mad, immoral Anglo-American plot is no different from the tripartite aggression against our glorious Egyptian people in 1956. . . . The rulers in London and Washington are dragging the Israeli rulers to annihilation and destruction to protect their exploitation, greed, and insatiable lust for power and dominion'. But the Arabs were in a good position to deter, or if necessary to punish, Israel's Western allies. On 29 May the Iraqi Government announced their intention of imposing a ban on all oil supplies to powers supporting Israeli 'aggression', and invited all other oil-producing States in the region to take similar action. They further summoned a conference of interested States to discuss ways and means, which met at Baghdad on 4 June. In the event, these States were able to take action which certainly damaged the economy of the United Kingdom, if of nobody else; but it had not the slightest effect on the war.

By the end of May a growing air of pensiveness, to use no stronger term, was becoming apparent in both Washington and London. It was pointed out in both capitals – and promptly denied by the Israeli Embassies – that anyhow no merchant vessels flying the Israeli flag had passed through the Straits of Tiran for the past two years. Official circles in Washington were beginning to discuss the cost of subsidizing Israel to enable her to do without the port of Eilat. A number of British newspapers – *The Economist*, *The Observer*, *The Financial Times* – pointed out that a commitment to the continuing existence of the State of Israel was a very different matter from risking a world war to enable Israeli ships to use the Gulf of Aqaba. And on Monday 5 June – a day more memorable for other events – *The Guardian* boldly suggested negotiations with President Nasser. 'Ultimately of course the right of free passage must be asserted. . . . Immediately, however, it might be possible to accept President Nasser's formulation if he on his side were willing to let the case go to the International Court'.

The formulation referred to, which Nasser had outlined to U Thant in Cairo on 24 May, certainly looked moderate enough. President Nasser was reported to have made four points. The Straits of Tiran should be recognized as Egyptian territorial waters; Israel should fully accept the provisions of the 1949 armistice; the United Nations should police all frontiers and demarcation lines; and the Israelis should strictly observe the demilitarized zones. If access to the Gulf of Aqaba was really the only problem to be solved, a compromise solution might have been found. But President Nasser was quite frank in expressing his view that it was not; and his statements gave good ground for assuming that his intention was now to restore the *status quo ante bellum*, not of 1956, but of 1948.

His public announcements in fact contrasted very remarkably with the reasonable tones in which he talked to U Thant and envoys from the West.[12] 'The Arabs insist on their rights', he declared to the Pan-Arab Workers

Federation on 26 May, in a speech repeatedly re-broadcast by Cairo Radio the following day, 'and are determined to regain the rights of the Palestinian people. The Arabs must accomplish this set intention and this aim. . . . If Israel embarks on aggression against Syria or Egypt the battle against Israel will be a general one and . . . our basic objectives will be to destroy Israel.' Two days later he reiterated this view at a large Press Conference. The Straits, he said, was only part of the major problem caused by Israel's aggression in simply existing. 'We do not accept any method for co-existence with Israel'. And the following day he told members of the Egyptian National Assembly, 'We have completed our preparations and are ready to confront Israel. We are ready to reopen the case of Palestine. The question today is not of Aqaba nor is it the Tiran Strait or the UNEF. It is the rights of the people of Palestine'. These pronouncements make it hard to believe that the conflict could have been resolved by a judgment of the International Court about rights of belligerency, innocent passage, or strategic goods. The most that such a judgment, at this stage, could have done would have been to deprive Israel of a clear *casus belli*.

Nevertheless President Nasser had assured U Thant, as he had assured the Soviet Ambassador, that he would not strike the first blow. Such an assurance had limited value. With forces in such close and direct confrontation, escalation from an incident was almost inevitable. For States armed with modern aircraft, the temptation to launch a pre-emptive attack was terrifyingly strong. In any case, Nasser had good reason to hope the Israelis would play into his hands. In a remarkably frank and perceptive article in *Al-Ahram* on 26 May his friend M. Mohammed Hasanein Haikal gave his grounds for supposing that they would.

> The closure of the Gulf of Aqaba . . . [he wrote] means first and last that the Arab nation represented by the UAR has succeeded for the first time, *vis à vis* Israel, in changing by force a *fait accompli* imposed on it by force. . . . To Israel this is the most dangerous aspect of the current situation – who can impose the accomplished fact and who possesses the power to safeguard it. Therefore it is not a matter of the Gulf of Aqaba but of something bigger. It is the whole philosophy of Israeli security. Hence I say that Israel must attack.[13]

This was not an unfair summary of the Israeli predicament. By the end of May the question of Eilat was secondary to the menace presented to Israel by an Arab world mobilized behind Egypt, overtly bent on the destruction of the Jewish State and the restoration of the Palestinians to their lost lands. The Israelis had long before learned to live with the abuse directed at them from Radios Cairo, Damascus, and Amman. They might not have taken even President Nasser's speeches too seriously; it was still widely assumed that his involvement in the Yemen would make him unwilling to precipitate another war. But two developments convinced them that the crisis was at hand.

The first was the build-up of Egyptian forces in Sinai after the closing of the Straits. Within a week seven divisions had been rushed into the area, two of them armoured; and although their positions could indicate a defensive posture, many of them were concentrated too far forward on the frontier to be given the benefit of the doubt; and there was an armoured force poised in central Sinai in a position to strike across the Negev and sever communications with Eilat.[14] And the second, and far more alarming, development was the spectacular *rapprochement* of King Hussein of Jordan and President Nasser on 30 May.

Jordan's position was peculiarly unenviable. Although she posed the greatest strategic threat to Israel by her capacity to cut the country in two, the salient of the West Bank made her by far the most vulnerable of the Arab powers to Israeli attack. Her security lay only in close co-operation with the other Arab powers; but this would almost certainly involve accepting the forces of her Allies on her territory, which King Hussein was profoundly reluctant to do. The presence of Egyptian or Iraqi troops stationed among his Palestinian subjects was likely to cause irreparable damage to his precarious regime. Nevertheless, by the end of May, war seemed so imminent that the price had to be paid. On 30 May King Hussein flew to Cairo, was met and publicly embraced by President Nasser, and signed a defence pact which asserted that each country would react to an attack on the other as if it were an attack on itself. A Defence Council and joint command was set up under General Fawzy. Five days later Iraq joined the pact. On 4 June Iraqi forces moved into Jordan, and General Riad of the Egyptian Army flew into Amman with two Egyptian commando battalions, to take over the new command.

The collapse of Hussein's moderating influence and the triumph of revolutionary-nationalist forces in Jordan had long been considered by the Israeli High Command to be an eventuality which, like the closing of the Straits of Tiran, would compel them to go to war. For the Israelis it came as the climax to the long week of tension which had begun with President Nasser's speech on the evening of 22 May.

We have seen how, on the 23rd, the Cabinet sent Mr Eban to sound out the intentions of the Western powers. It also authorized a general mobilization, which took place on the 24th. Men and vehicles suddenly disappeared from Israeli towns, Within twenty-four hours the army was deployed in full strength along the frontiers: troops trained to take the offensive and now longing for the order to do so. It was an open secret that the whole philosophy of the Israeli armed forces was one of attack: the principle of the offensive was ingrained even in the smallest sub-units. The small extent of Israeli territory, its absence of natural barriers, gave no serious strategic alternative. For men brought up in such a doctrine, the next few days were to be agonizing. From Arab radio stations all round them came a stream of hatred, threats, and vilification. One after another the States of the Arab League fell into line and mobilized forces for the explicit purpose of their destruction. Meanwhile their own government urged moderation, and Mr Eban negotiated in Europe and

North America with distant powers whose will and capacity to bring effective and immediate help was not rated by the men in the Sinai Desert as highly as one might like to believe.

It is not surprising that under the circumstances confidence in Mr Eshkol's government began to ebb. Within the army, senior officers watched with professional apprehension as chances of mounting a successful surprise attack waned with the growth in the size and preparedness of the enemy forces. In the country as a whole – and once the army was mobilized, no valid distinction between country and army was really possible – pressure grew for the return to power of the heroic figures of the Rafi party, the venerable David Ben-Gurion, the spectacular Moshe Dayan. General Dayan, having placed himself at the disposal of the Chief of Staff, was acting as a sort of unofficial Inspector-General, visiting the units of the army in Sinai, discussing their operational roles and raising their morale. His invigorating presence made him increasingly appear as the man of the hour. Even senior officers loyal to the government and with no love for Dayan began to press for his appointment to the post of Minister of Defence.

Mr Eshkol hesitated. To abandon the portfolio of Defence, which since the time of Mr Ben-Gurion had always been held by the Prime Minister, would be a grave constitutional step as well as a humiliating personal sacrifice. If he had to take it, his candidate for the post, it was generally known, would have been his colleague Yigal Allon, a figure whose military achievements in the war of 1948 were at least equal to those of Dayan in 1956, and whose political ambitions he had less reason to mistrust. Moreover, between Dayan and his colleagues in the Rafi party on the one hand, and Mr Eshkol's own colleagues in Mapai on the other, there were bitter personal antagonisms which would make co-operation almost impossible. This disagreeable necessity might be avoided if the external pressure abated, so a decision was delayed until Mr Eban returned from Washington. This he did on the evening of 27 May, and his report was considered at a long Cabinet meeting the following day. Mr Eban conveyed the assurances of support which he had received from President Johnson and also his warnings against Israel taking any initiative of her own. Several of his colleagues found the assurances unconvincing. In any case the question of the Straits, as President Nasser had made clear, was now secondary to that of the survival of Israel: the presence of an Egyptian detachment at Sharm-el-Sheikh was unimportant compared to the seven menacing divisions in Sinai. As for the idea of Israel accepting the closure of Eilat and continuing to exist as a pensioner of the West, it would only have to be raised to be scornfully dismissed. There was still no majority in the Cabinet in favour of taking the plunge into war, with all the uncertainties and horrors which this might involve; but the government was not persuaded that the destinies of the country could be left entirely in American hands.

No decision was reached, but some announcement to the country had to be made. Mr Eshkol broadcast that evening. The whole nation was listening, waiting for a lead: civilians at home and in cafes, the army in their messes or on transistor sets in their tents in the desert. The performance was a disaster. The Prime Minister was tired; he had a bad cold; he lost his place in his script; and he had nothing particular to say. Israel, he said, would try to resolve the crisis by diplomacy, but she would defend herself if necessary. She would remain in a state of readiness, and the army could be relied on to do its duty. No trumpet could have been more uncertain. The worst suspicions of the government's indecisiveness seemed to be confirmed. There were rumours of direct action by army leaders – not a Syrian-type *coup d'état* but a collective resignation by the High Command which would be equally effective in bringing about the fall of the government. Only one thing could now reassure public opinion – the co-option of Moshe Dayan. Further negotiations were brief. On 1 June it was announced that General Dayan and two other opposition leaders, Mr Menaghem Begin and Mr Joseph Saphir, would join the coalition in a Government of National Unity. Dayan would receive the portfolio of Defence.

Dayan's appointment was greeted in Israel with unanimous relief. Abroad, it was widely seen as a sign that the government had resolved on war. This was not quite accurate. The decision for war was taken only gradually. General Dayan brought to the Cabinet an expert knowledge of the military situation which did much to increase their self-confidence, but he proved more moderate in his views than had been generally expected. It was Mr Begin, an old leader of the extremist group Irgun Zwai Leumi, who brought the greatest access of strength to the 'hawks'. In so far as there was a clear-cut debate over the issue, the 'hawks' were able to present an increasingly strong case as the Egyptians moved up their forces in Sinai and as Iraqi troops began to enter Jordan. The arguments for delay rested on Mr Eban's reports from Washington; reports not simply of American assurances of support, but of American displeasure if Israel should be the first to resort to force. At the very least, he insisted, Israel must not seem to have acted 'with improper haste'.

American displeasure was still a powerful deterrent, but by Sunday 4 June it was the only one left. The Israeli High Command was in any case sceptical about it. They had reason to believe that an Israeli initiative would command sufficiently influential sympathy in Washington to counteract any pressure there might be for the imposition of serious sanctions. All depended on the speed and success of the attack, and on this score the military leaders were still confident. They reckoned they could inflict sufficient damage on the enemy forces to remove the threat to Israel's borders before the Great Powers intervened; and they knew that time was likely to be very short indeed.

The Cabinet met again on the morning of 4 June. At this meeting, it is reported, the High Command was able to present its arguments in a fashion which resolved the last doubts. Next morning the war began.

III. The war

The war opened at 7.45 on the morning of Monday 5 June, when the Israeli Air Force struck their first blow at the airfields of the UAR.[1] By the end of the week the Israeli armed forces had occupied the Sinai Peninsula, including the eastern bank of the Suez Canal and the western shores of the Tiran Straits; they had conquered the whole West Bank of the Jordan and with it the entire city of Jerusalem; and they had seized the heights from which the Syrian Army had for so long dominated the Upper Jordan Valley. The armies of Egypt and Jordan had been virtually destroyed, and that of Syria routed. There was nothing to stop Israel, if she so wished, from occupying the Suez Canal area, Amman, and Damascus. Military power had not only once again changed the map of the Middle East: it had transformed the pattern of international relations, with consequences which it is still impossible to foresee.

It was only the rapidity of this victory that surprised military specialists in the West. Most of them had assumed that once the war began, superior Israeli training, intelligence, and morale would compensate for any disadvantage in numbers and in strategic position. The total mobilized strength of the Israeli Army was some 275,000 men – and women – organized into 22 infantry brigades, eight armoured brigades, and one parachute brigade. In the south, they confronted an Egyptian force in the Sinai Peninsula of about 100,000 men; the total mobilized strength of the Egyptian Army was 240,000 men, of whom about 50,000 were in the Yemen. And in the east, Israel confronted a Jordanian force of 55,000; the Syrian Army, numbering 50,000; and an Iraqi division moving up through Jordan. Time did not permit the engagement of forces promised by other members of the Arab League. All these armies had been provided with up-to-date equipment by wealthier powers anxious to maintain their influence in the area and find markets for their armament industries. The Israelis had about 800 tanks, including British *Centurions*, American *Super-Shermans*, and M-48 *Pattons*, and French AMX-13s.[2] The Egyptian total was somewhat larger, with a nucleus of Soviet T-54s and T-55s, and many of the older T-34s. They also had a substantial number of tank destroyers. Jordan's 250 tanks were mainly *Pattons* and *Centurions*; the Syrian 400 (only 200 operational) were provided by the Russians; the Iraqis were equipped with both British and Soviet armour. In the air, Syria and Egypt relied on Russian MiG interceptors and fighter-bombers, of which Syria had about 100 and Egypt 400, Egypt possessing also a force of about 80 Tupolev and Ilyushin medium and light bombers which could have done serious damage to Israeli cities. Jordan had almost two dozen British *Hunter* fighter-bombers. The Israeli Air Force was equipped almost completely by the French aircraft industry: *Mirage* III-C and *Super-Mystere* fighters, *Mystere* IV fighter-bombers (about 140 in all), as well as 50 obsolescent *Ouragan* fighter-bombers, 60 *Magister* training aircraft, which could be – and were – used for ground support, and 25 *Vautour* light bombers. If the belligerent powers had been equal in all other respects, Israel would have been quickly crushed.[3]

But they were not equal. In the first place, the military establishments of Israel and of her adversaries reflected the basic difference in the social and economic structure of their societies. The Arab States were still basically agrarian communities with small political and technical élites. Their officer corps, as is usual in developing countries, contained a large proportion of the best-educated and most politically conscious elements in the nation. Many of the officers were skilled professionals, but there appear to have been many others, especially in the Syrian Army, who regarded political fanaticism as a substitute for military expertise and who were concerned more with the army's role in domestic politics than with national defence. Between the officers and their barely literate soldiers a great gap yawned, betraying the extent to which the Arab revolution remained a middle-class monopoly and showing how little it had as yet affected the peasants from whom the army was still recruited. The Arab soldiers fought with courage but with neither fanaticism nor skill. More important, they had not developed the qualities of intelligence and initiative in their NCOs and junior officers on which the effectiveness of modern armies so largely depends. When plans broke down, as plans invariably do in war, when no orders were available from superior authority, they collapsed; much as the armies of eighteenth-century Europe collapsed before the onslaught of revolutionary France.

Israel, by contrast, was a homogeneous and tightly integrated society, with a high level of general education and a lively realization of the importance of military efficiency to its very survival. It was indeed a garrison State of a kind almost unique in the modern world. Out of a population of 2.75 million, its regular armed forces numbered only some 10,000. The remainder of its standing army, 60,000 strong, consisted of national servicemen who served for two and a half years before being relegated to a reserve from which they were called up for annual training of varying length: two months for officers, five weeks for NCOs, and one month for other ranks. These were minimum periods: the army seldom had difficulty in extending training time if it needed to do so. Not until the age of 45 did this obligation cease, and then the Israeli citizen enrolled in the Civil Defence Force. Service in the technical branches was somewhat longer, and pilots in the Air Force enlisted for a minimum period of five years when they were 18 years old, and were operational after three years' training. Military units were drawn as far as possible from residents of a single neighbourhood, particular members being designated to ensure that mobilization instructions, broadcast in code over the radio, got round to everyone. Test mobilizations were frequent: at any time the reservist might be called out in the middle of the night to report to his unit, and be fully operational by dawn; while vehicles (like horses in Europe before 1914) were as subject to requisition as men.

Finally, the Israeli forces had the great advantage of knowing where they would have to fight. Every yard of their frontiers and the surrounding terrain had been studied from maps, from aerial photographs, and possibly from the reports of clandestine reconnaissance patrols. Terrain conditions were systematically analyzed. Israeli tanks and infantry held exercises over ground as similar as possible to that over which they would have to operate. As a result, when the Sinai campaign began, the Israeli forces showed themselves far more familiar with the conditions of the battlefield than did the Arabs, who had occupied it for so many years.

Full mobilization of the Israeli armed forces produced a quarter of a million men and women: 10 per cent of the total population. The strain which this imposed on the economy was obviously considerable, and during the 1967 crisis many Western experts believed that the impossibility of sustaining it for long would force Israel to seek a rapid settlement, whether by capitulation or by war. They exaggerated, much as their predecessors in 1914 had exaggerated in predicting that the strain of mobilization on the European powers would force them to conclude peace within a few weeks. People become very ingenious in wartime, and Israel's small size gave her mobilization arrangements a remarkable degree of flexibility. It certainly suited Israel's policy to have her friends believe that circumstances would compel her, failing their intervention, to force the issue one way or the other, within a few days. Privately, experts in Tel Aviv suggested that the economy even of a fully mobilized Israel would remain viable until the end of the year.

This pattern of military service was very similar to the model created by Prussia in the early nineteenth century; another small country needing to maximize her military resources against her more powerful neighbours. But whereas the Prussian system had resulted in the militarization of society, the Israeli resulted in the civilianization of the army. Israeli troops went about their work with a complete absence of the barrack-square discipline which the forces of other nations consider essential to the maintenance of disciplined obedience. The Israeli Army could do without it, and regarded it as a waste of time. Its units came together to do a particular job, which was examined, discussed, decided upon, and executed in a workmanlike manner. If they fell down on that job, they knew it would mean the end of Israel. Officers maintained their authority not by orthodox discipline but by personal example. Their function was to lead and if necessary to get killed, as many of them did. But if they did get killed, their men knew what to do – and even if they did not, their training and their *esprit de corps* enabled them to keep the initiative. The morale and efficiency of the Israelis was not the product of military indoctrination; it was rooted in their realization that they had escaped massacre once, and were unlikely to get a second chance.

There was another similarity between Israel and Prussia. States surrounded by openly hostile neighbours are strongly tempted to strike first and eliminate one of them, rather than wait until they choose their time to attack concentrically with superior forces. Such pre-emption is certainly the path of conventional military wisdom, although there may be strong political reasons against it. But Israel's territory was so minute that she could hardly afford to follow the path of political and legal rectitude by allowing her adversaries to strike the first blow and hope to recoup her losses in a counter-attack. Her airfields were too concentrated and vulnerable to a pre-emptive strike. On the ground she could within a few hours lose Eilat and the Upper Jordan Valley and have her country cut in two. No definition of 'aggression' had yet been devised to suit the circumstances of all States. Here it is enough to suggest that Dr Fedorenko's comparison, in the United Nations Security Council, of Israel's offensive in Sinai with Hitler's attack on the Soviet Union, was not one which commanded very wide agreement.

At 7.45 a.m. on 5 June, Israeli military authorities announced that Egypt had opened a land and air attack. Egyptian armoured forces, they contended, had moved at dawn towards the Negev, and Israeli radar had picked up numerous Egyptian aircraft approaching their borders. Later reports spoke of exceptionally heavy shelling of Israeli outposts from the Gaza Strip. One need neither take these reports at their face value nor dismiss them as complete fabrications. Egyptian air patrols probably were seen on Israeli radar screens. There was certainly shelling from the Gaza Strip. The Israeli command was naturally sensitive to the threat which the Egyptian armoured force in Central Sinai posed to Eilat, and its movements that morning may have looked particularly menacing. But it remains very doubtful whether there was anything so unusual about these Egyptian activities as to justify so shattering a riposte. The explanation – and if necessary the justification – for the Israeli offensive must be found in the realm of strategy rather than that of tactics. The decision to launch it was not based entirely on General Gavish's report from Beersheba.

At the moment when the above announcement was being made over Israeli radio stations, Israeli aircraft were opening their attack on nineteen Egyptian airfields in Sinai and the Nile Delta. In the battle to come, complete command of the air was necessary not only to give Israeli forces freedom of movement on the ground – especially in the Sinai Peninsula – but also to free the country of the nagging anxiety about the vulnerability of her cities. The time was well chosen. The Egyptian aircraft had already flown their dawn patrol and were grounded while their pilots had breakfast. They were not lined up in a state of complete unpreparedness wing-to-wing as has sometimes been alleged, but were dispersed at maximum readiness, and sometimes even taxi-ing for take-off. The Israelis did not even give the Egyptians warning by first attacking their radar stations: they sent their aircraft in low over the sea, or sweeping behind the mountains of the Sinai Peninsula. They probably used electronic deception measures as well. The attacks were so timed as to allow each pilot three passes at his allotted target; then he returned to base, refuelled, and attacked again. With intervals of only ten minutes, attacks against the airfields continued uninterruptedly for three hours. By noon the Egyptian Air Force had lost nearly 300 aircraft, and was of little further use as a fighting force.

The success of this blow was due to two factors alone: intelligence and training. Of the first little can be reliably said, but the results speak for themselves. Among the intelligence services of the world, that of Israel has a high reputation. The effectiveness with which it tapped enemy communications was surprisingly revealed a few days later, when it committed a remarkable breach of security by publishing an intercepted radio-telephone conversation between President Nasser and King Hussein. And the Israeli Air Force had carried out sufficient flights over Egyptian territory over the past few days to have a very exact knowledge of its targets. This knowledge was fed to a group of pilots who had received a gruelling course of training involving a weekly briefing on their targets, a major battle practice every four months, and once a year a full-scale exercise. There had never been any doubt in the minds of the Air Staff that their major function would be a pre-emptive strike. In the words of General Ezer Weizmann, the creator of the Air Force and its Chief of Staff until 1966, the only place where Israel could be defended was over Cairo. His successor, Brigadier-General Mordecai Hod, brought Weizmann's preparations to completion. He knew that this time, unlike 1956, he could expect no help from the Royal Air Force: but this was a handicap he saw no reason to regret.

Outsiders found it hard to believe that this astonishing and perhaps decisive success did not have some recondite cause, and they interpreted it in predictable ways. American and British commentators looked for a 'secret weapon' – some kind of air-to-ground homing missile which would explain the accuracy with which the Egyptian aircraft were destroyed on the ground. None existed. The only unexpected weapon the Israelis used, and one probably under development by most air forces, was a bomb fitted with retroactive rockets to give it a vertical descent to ensure maximum destruction of runways; a weapon naturally not used against the forward airfields in Sinai, such as El Arish, which the Israelis expected to capture and use themselves. Indeed one of the principal advantages of the Israeli aircraft lay in their comparative *lack* of sophistication, which simplified maintenance and refuelling, making possible the fast turn-arounds which enabled pilots to fly six or more sorties in a single day.

This capacity of the Israelis to get the utmost out of their machines and men took their adversaries completely by surprise. It was this that led President Nasser to assert on 9 June, 'If we say now that it was a stronger blow than we had expected, we must say at the same time . . . that it was bigger than the potential at his [the enemy's] disposal . . . the enemy was operating with an air force three times stronger than his normal force'. This assessment, combined with memories of 1956 and the *a priori* assumption of an 'imperialist-Zionist plot', predisposed the Arabs to believe in Anglo-American intervention even before King Hussein informed Nasser, early on the morning of 6 June, that a Jordanian radar station had detected approaching from the sea a large flight of aircraft which could only come from British or American carriers. This report was promptly and indignantly denied by both governments concerned. The British had no aircraft carriers nearer than Malta and Aden, a thousand miles from the scene of action. The American Sixth Fleet in the Mediterranean was, fortunately, being closely observed by units of the Soviet fleet, which no doubt reported to Moscow the absence of any unusual activity. Certainly the Soviet Government and press ignored the report. Later, King Hussein himself was to retract it. How it originated – whether in misreading of signals, Israeli spoofing, or the deliberate passing of false information – is still unknown and will probably remain so. But the damage was done. On 6 June Kuwait and Iraq announced the cessation of all oil supplies to the United Kingdom and the United States; Iraq, Syria, and the Sudan broke off diplomatic relations with these Western powers, and Syria and the Lebanon interrupted the flow of oil through the pipelines on their territories. The American and British invitation to the United Nations to send inspectors to their fleets and airfields, reiterated throughout the week, were disregarded. The belief remained that even if American and British aircraft were not taking part in the actual attacks – and the Syrians in fact reported that British aircraft had been identified over their territory – they were maintaining an 'air umbrella' over Israel itself, enabling the Israeli Air Force to exert its full strength in offensive operations.[4] Unfortunately it is likely to be many years before this belief is eradicated from the Arab mind.

In fact the reaction in Washington, London, and Moscow to the outbreak of war was one of unanimous consternation. The British feared for their oil supplies; the Russians and Americans dreaded the prospect of escalation to a greater cataclysm still. Mr Kosygin took the initiative in opening up the 'hot line' from Moscow to Washington with a personal message to President Johnson, in which he is reported as expressing his concern at the turn of events and urging joint action to secure a cease-fire. A cease-fire call from the United Nations was predictable; but in what terms should it be couched? From the beginning the United States and the United Kingdom advocated a cease-fire call without conditions. India, the Soviet Union, and a number of Afro-Asian States held out for a motion condemning Israel and demanding a withdrawal of all her forces to their original positions. They had a case for doing so: the experience of 1948 had shown that cease-fire lines usually harden into frontiers. Had they realized the extent of Israel's initial victories, it is unlikely that they would have prolonged matters as they did; but the delay of the Israeli High Command in issuing a definitive communiqué left them, perhaps designedly, in ignorance. When information about the extent of Egyptian aircraft losses began to leak out during the afternoon of 5 June, the Israeli Army spokesman denounced them as 'premature, unclear, and utterly unauthorized'. Not until two o'clock the following morning did General Hod make a statement, and then it was very precise. The Israeli Air Force had destroyed for certain 286 Egyptian, 52 Syrian, 27 Jordanian, and nine Iraqi aircraft, and claimed a further 34 probabilities. They had lost only twenty aircraft themselves.

Even if these figures did not immediately command the credibility they were later shown to deserve, they made it clear that any prolongation of the fighting was likely to be to the Arabs' disadvantage. At the United Nations the Soviet Union reversed its position. On the afternoon of Tuesday 6 June the Security Council unanimously called upon the governments concerned 'as a first step to take forthwith all measures for an immediate cease-fire and for a cessation of all military activity in the area'.

By that time a great deal had happened in the theatre of war. In their broadcasts the Arabs indicated neither surprise nor resentment at the Israeli attack, but rather relief that the expected battle had begun. 'The decisive moment has come', declared the announcer on Cairo Radio: 'The battle has come and be it welcome'. 'Today is the day of the great revenge', he exhorted the Palestinian Arabs, 'revenge against the criminal gang which violated your blood and freedom. Fight, my brother, with all the hate you have against imperialism and Zionism'. A statement broadcast by the Federation of Arab Oil Workers was remarkably frank. 'The Zionists', it announced, 'fell into the trap and started a treacherous aggression on the forward positions of the Arab armies'. No Arab nation could now ignore the call to the *jihad*, the Holy War. Lebanon, Syria, Iraq, Kuwait, the Sudan, Algeria, the Yemen, and Jordan all declared war on Israel. Morocco announced the despatch of troops to the Middle East; Saudi Arabia announced that its troops were entering Jordan; even in moderate Tunisia mobs attacked the embassies of Britain and the United States. Syrian artillery opened fire on Israeli settlements in the Upper Jordan Valley; Syrian aircraft bombed an airfield at Megiddo, attacked a number of villages near Haifa, and claimed to have left the Haifa oil refineries in flames. Iraq claimed, equally without foundation, that her aircraft had raided Tel Aviv. Jordanian artillery did actually begin a spasmodic long-range bombardment of the suburbs of Tel Aviv. At considerably closer range its guns began, at 8.30 a.m., to shell the Jewish quarter of Jerusalem, and soon firing had broken out at many other points on the Israel-Jordan border. There was now military action on three fronts.

The Israeli Air Force reacted against the Syrian and Iraqi air bases, with the results announced by General Hod early next day. Jordan, however, was given a chance. Syria's hostility was accepted as inevitable in Tel Aviv, but it seemed possible that King Hussein might just be able to keep his country out of war. If he did so Israel would be spared a campaign on a second front against an adversary for whose military capacity she had a certain respect. Soon after the Jordanian shelling began, Mr Eshkol used the UNTSO headquarters in Jerusalem to pass a message to King Hussein assuring him that if Jordan did not open serious hostilities Israel would not retaliate. Shortly afterwards he reiterated this assurance, in more general terms, in a statement to the Knesset. King Hussein ignored it. Even if he had known the extent of the damage the UAR Air Force had suffered, it is doubtful whether he could have done anything else. The ink was hardly dry on his pact with the UAR; an Egyptian general was already in command of his armed forces; and his own army commanders were unlikely to have tolerated any hesitation. The shellfire on Jerusalem intensified and extended to the Israeli enclave at Mount Scopus; Jordanian forces occupied UNTSO Headquarters in the old Government House, a vantage point commanding the entire city of Jerusalem; and Jordanian aircraft raided Natanya and the Israeli air base at Kfar Sirkin.

Israel struck back heavily. By midday her air force had finished with the Egyptian airfields and was able to concentrate on the Jordanian bases at

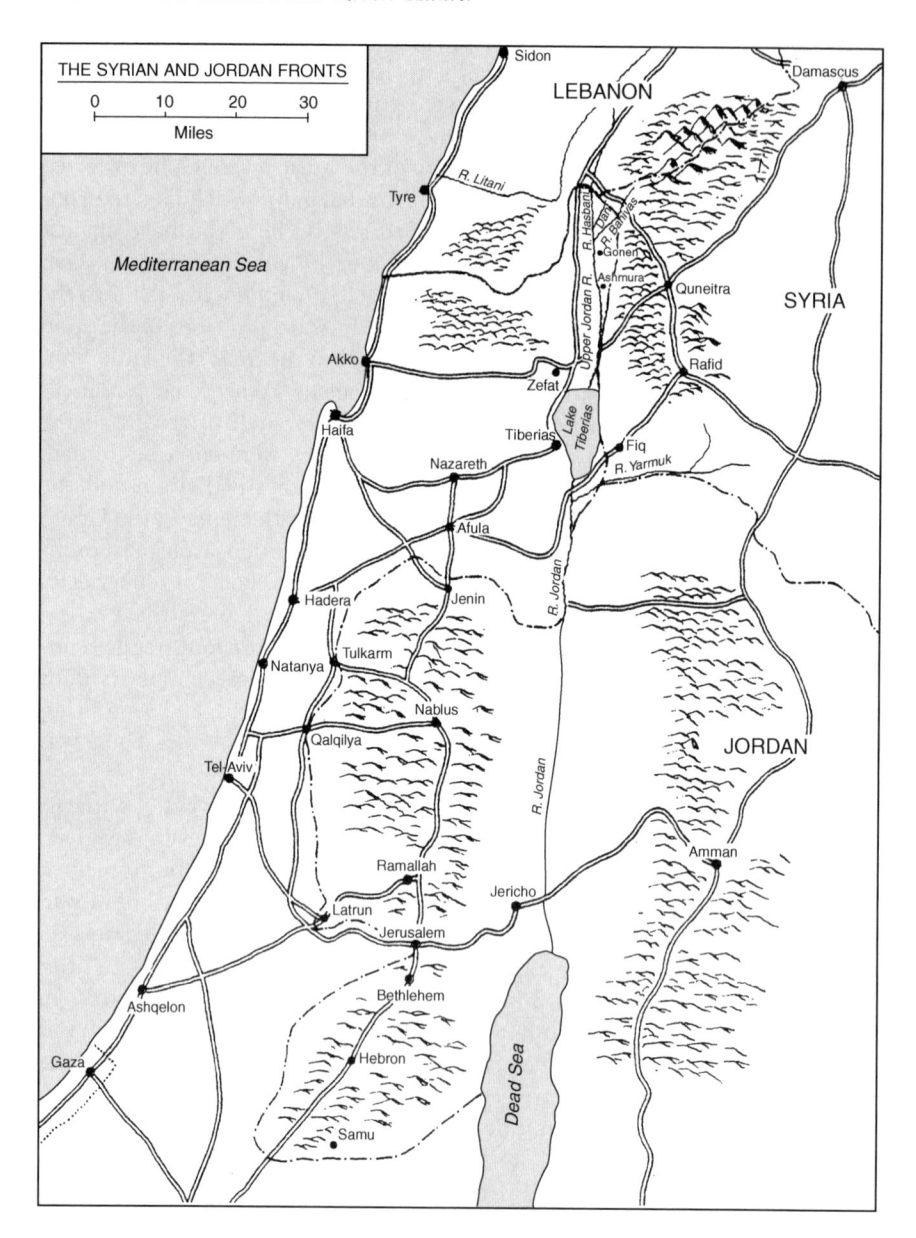

Mafraq and Amman, where all Jordan's first-line aircraft were quickly put out of action. On the ground, also, the Israelis swung over to the attack. With so few troops deployed on this front it was essential at least to 'fix' the Jordanian forces until reinforcements could be made available from the main battle in Sinai, and this could be most effectively done by the most ferocious offensive possible. In the words of a senior Israeli military expert, 'We were too weak to do anything else'. As it was, the Israelis were able, with the one brigade stationed in Jerusalem, an armoured brigade of reservists from the coastal plain, a parachute brigade detached from the southern front, and an armoured force intended for action against Syria, to drive the Jordanians across the Jordan before operations against Egypt were completed. Even the most optimistic planner would have been unwise to stake much on such an outcome. Its explanation lies almost entirely in Israel's command of the air. On the evening and night of 5 June the Jordanians fought stubbornly and well in the close country and suburbs around Jerusalem and Jenin, inflicting heavy casualties on their assailants. But by Tuesday the 6th movement in daylight was impossible. Israeli aircraft wiped out their convoys and repeatedly attacked their static positions. Israeli armoured columns penetrated deeply behind their defences. By the night of the 6th, the Jordanian Army had collapsed.

The Israeli attacks on Jordan were largely improvised. On the Jerusalem front, while Colonel Amitai's brigade attacked south of the Old City during the afternoon of the 5th and recaptured Government House, the area commander, Brigadier-General Narkiss, prepared to attack to the north with infantry and armour. His infantry consisted of Colonel Gur's parachute brigade, which had been rushed up from the southern front and most of whose members had never seen the terrain over which they were to fight. Fighting at night in a closely built-up area, against troops defending positions they had been preparing for years, the parachutists had to force their way through to seize the heights which dominated the Old City, from the Sheikh Jarah quarter in the north to the Augusta Victoria Hospital on the Mount of Olives to the east. It was a bloody soldiers' battle in which the Israelis did not have the advantage of surprise and the forces of the Arab Legion opposed to them fought tenaciously. By daybreak on 6 June the Israeli forces had somehow struggled through to Sheikh Jarah and controlled most of the area to the north of the Old City. Meanwhile, to their left, Colonel Ben-Ari's armoured force had advanced northward to clear the hills between Jerusalem and Ramallah, frontally attacking heavily fortified positions with excellent fields of fire. By the morning of the 6th it had broken the crust of the Jordanian defences. In the west, another unit of the brigade had stormed the town of Latrun, which for eighteen years had blocked the road from Jerusalem to Tel Aviv. Both parts of his command converged on Ramallah, and cleared it that night. Next day, Wednesday the 7th, against purely sporadic opposition, Ben-Ari's armour pushed on to Jericho; and later that morning it was on the banks of the Jordan.

Meanwhile in Jerusalem the parachute brigade, fighting throughout the day and night of Tuesday the 6th, had consolidated its hold on the heights to the north-east, while Colonel Amitai's troops cleared the Abu Tor district south of the city in bitter fighting. By the morning of Wednesday the 7th the two Israeli pincers had almost closed round the Old City, and General Dayan ordered them to seize it before the cease-fire agreement reached at the United Nations the previous evening could come into effect. They attacked at 8.30 a.m.; by 2 p.m. the city was in their hands. Dayan himself, Rabin, and Narkiss made their way to the Wailing Wall of the Temple and gazed in silence. The Jews had returned to Jerusalem, after nineteen hundred years.

Meanwhile the rest of the West Bank had fallen into Israeli hands, as a result of the attack launched from the north by the force detached from Brigadier-General Elazar's northern command. Elazar received the order to attack at noon on 5 June, primarily to silence the heavy Jordanian fire on the Israeli positions. The attack which he actually launched at 5 p.m. was rather more ambitious in scope. His objective was the town of Nablus in the very centre of the West Bank. He launched his principal attack with a mechanized brigade, supported by tanks, against Jenin, where heavy fighting continued throughout the night. He also launched a feint attack in the Jordan Valley down the right bank of the river, which effectively distracted Jordanian forces from the main thrust. Next day all attempts by the Jordanians to move over the mountain roads, forward or backward, were defeated by the Israeli Air Force, which attacked their convoys with a terrible mixture of high explosive and napalm. By the 7th Jordanian resistance was broken. Elazar's forces joined hands at Nablus with a detachment of Ben-Ari's brigade advancing from the south. Israeli forces stood along the length of the Jordan from Dan to the Dead Sea, while over the bridges poured a stream of terrified Arab refugees, some of them going into exile for the second time in their lives. An Arab population of 900,000, however, including 500,000 Palestinian refugees, remained. It remains to be seen how far the superb success of General Elazar's armoured thrust has created for Israel rather more problems than it solved.

While the Israelis were wresting Jerusalem and the West Bank from the Jordanians, the decisive battle of the war was fought in the sands and hills of Sinai. Here the Egyptians had concentrated seven divisions. That in the Gaza Strip, the 20th Division, consisted mainly of the Palestine Liberation Army. The 7th Division lay to the west of it, from the international frontier at Rafah to El Arish. South of the 7th was the 2nd Division, covering the vital road junction at Abu Aweiqila. The 3rd Division was in second line, in the area of Gebel Libni, Bir Hamma, and Bir Hasana. The 6th was stationed in the centre of the peninsula on the route from Suez to Eilat, between Nakhl and El Thamad. The principal armoured division, the 4th, lay well back, between Bir Gifgafa and Bir el Thamada. Another armoured force of something less than divisional strength was said by the Israelis to be moving in Central Sinai in the general direction of Kuntilla – the force which they believed to be threatening the Lower Negev. The 7th and 2nd Divisions were dug into strong positions barring the three roads which led across the Sinai Peninsula to the Canal at El Qantara, Ismailia, and Suez. The Israeli forces had to breach this line and the one behind it held by the 3rd Division, bring the armour to battle, and destroy the fighting force of the Egyptian Army – their first objective. Their second was to seize and hold Sharm-el-Sheikh, where there was a small Egyptian force; and their third, to provide security for that position, was to clear and occupy the Sinai Peninsula. It was at first an open question whether they should press on to that passage of ill-omen, the Suez Canal.

Israel and the Arab World 171

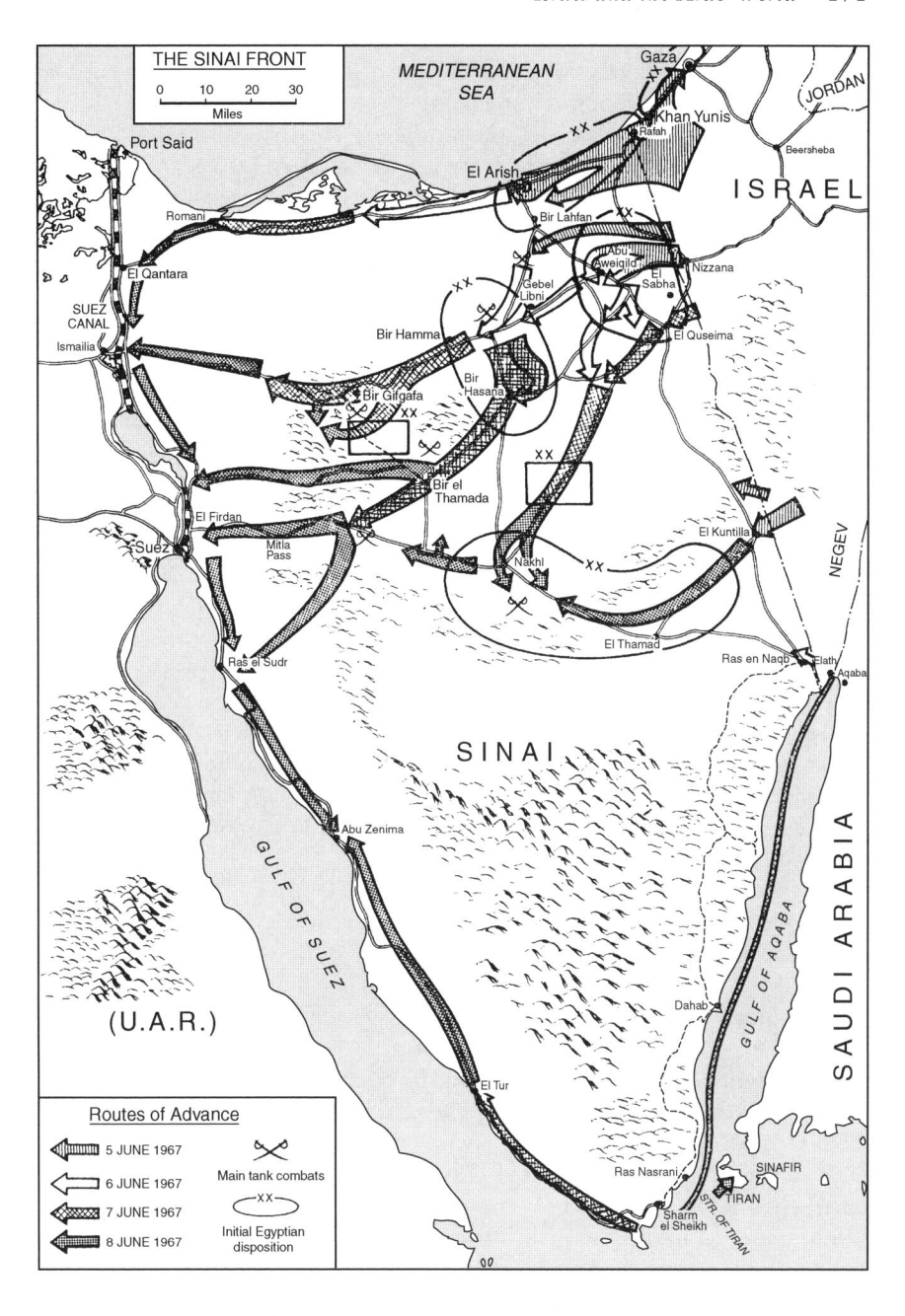

To achieve these objectives General Gavish had three divisional groups, under Brigadier-Generals Tal, Joffe, and Sharon.[5] Though numerically outnumbered, his forces had an armoured strength almost comparable to the Egyptian; and whereas about half the Egyptian tanks were allocated to infantry divisions, the Israeli tank force was concentrated in all-armoured units which packed a very considerable punch. The contrast between the two patterns of organization was interesting. The Israeli was that which had brought the Germans their victories in the early years of the Second World War, and which the British had adopted in the Western Desert and, initially, in Normandy. The Egyptians, under Russian tutelage, modelled themselves on the mixed units which were generally adopted in Europe in the latter years of the war, when all-armoured units had proved highly vulnerable to resolute infantry armed with anti-tank weapons. In close country the advantage overwhelmingly lies with mixed units, but in this desert the older formations again proved their worth. It is anyhow doubtful whether the Russians fully appreciated the problems of desert fighting, which they had themselves never had to face. The Egyptians were not trained for the quicksilver mobility of operations without flanks and virtually without supply lines. They sat in ponderous hedgehogs – not unlike the Eighth Army 'Boxes' in front of Tobruk in summer 1942 – from which they refused to be drawn. Given their standard of training, this may well have been the wisest course for them to follow.

Gavish attacked at 8.15 a.m. on 5 June. Tal struck in the north against the 7th Division. Sharon, based on Nizzana, attacked the 2nd Division before Abu Aweiqila. Joffe, whose force consisted entirely of reservists (he himself in civil life was head of Israel's Nature Conservancy Board), passed between them, threading his way through sand dunes generally held to be impassable, till at about 4 p.m. he reached the road from Abu Aweiqila to El Arish, where he sat intercepting Egyptian forces moving forward to reinforce their front or, next morning, hurrying rearwards in retreat. Farther south a brigade advanced from Kuntilla, more as a feint to draw Egyptian forces southward than as a serious threat.

Tal attacked in broad daylight, but avoided 7th Division's well-mined front. He divided his forces into two. The brigade on the left wing, like Joffe's force, crossed territory which the Israelis had discovered, by careful tests, to be less impassable than the Egyptians had supposed. They took the Egyptians in the flank, achieving complete surprise, and destroyed, after heavy fighting, a force double their strength. The brigade on the right had a harder time. They had little difficulty in breaking through to the coast at Khan Yunis and cutting off the Palestinians in the Gaza Strip; who were then dealt with by a brigade from General Gavish's reserve. But when they turned west to attack Rafah, they encountered strong prepared positions – fortifications, anti-tank guns, entrenched tanks – manned for the most part by extremely resolute troops. No surprise, no indirect approach was possible. The left-wing brigade, with the divisional reserve, had now come up on their right, and the whole division battered its way grimly forward down the road towards El Arish. By now the air force was available to take part in the ground battle, and air strikes helped to overwhelm the strongest positions.[6] A battalion reached El Arish before midnight; but it was dawn before the last Egyptian stronghold was overcome.

At Abu Aweiqila General Sharon also had a very tough nut to crack: an entrenched position protected by minefields and anti-tank guns, held by four battalions of infantry, six regiments of artillery, and about 90 tanks. He attacked by night – the night of 5 June, which also saw Tal's armour break through to El Arish, Narkiss's parachute troops seize the heights of Sheikh Jarah outside Jerusalem, and Elazar's forces battle their way through Jenin. During the afternoon his infantry and armour closed up to the main Egyptian positions, driving in their outposts.

Flanking forces were sent round the position to north and south, cutting the roads to Quseima, Gebel Libni, and El Arish. Tanks established themselves north-west of the position, six artillery regiments on the east, while a parachute battalion was landed by helicopter to attack from the north. At 10.45 p.m. the barrage began, and half an hour later, their objective illuminated by searchlights, the infantry and armour went in to the attack. The battle went on all night. By six o'clock next morning the last resistance had collapsed.

The main Egyptian defences were now shattered. There were still two Egyptian infantry and two armoured divisions intact, whereas the Israelis had only two brigades – one in General Joffe's division, one in the south at Kuntilla – which had not been fighting uninterruptedly for twenty-four hours. But the Egyptians now had to conduct a mobile war, of a kind for which they had not been trained, against an enemy who enjoyed complete command of the air and whose morale, always high, was now raised by victory to a pitch of exhilaration at which physical fatigue was almost forgotten. Only these factors can explain the remarkable achievements of the Israeli Defence Force during the next two days.

Much of Tuesday 6 June had to be devoted to consolidation, mopping up, and planning for the next stage. General Gavish's reserve brigade completed the clearing of the Gaza Strip; General Tal's troops smashed the last Egyptian positions south of El Arish at Bir Lahfan, and while a task force set out along the coast road towards the Suez Canal, the rest of his division turned south to make contact with General Joffe's second brigade, which had come up through Abu Aweiqila and was clearing resistance round Gebel Libni. At Gebel Libni, Tal and Joffe laid their plans for the advance. Large Egyptian forces still lay before them, but those forces depended on two roads: one to Ismailia through Bir Hamma and Bir Gifgafa, one to Suez through Bir el Thamada and the Mitla Pass. By a rapid advance these roads could be blocked and the entire Egyptian Army trapped in the desert. Farther south, a thrust by General Sharon could block the retreat of the Egyptian right wing at Nakhl. Speed was essential before the enemy could recover and regroup, and the Israelis wasted no time. The advance began at once and continued through the night.

By the evening of Wednesday 7 June Joffe's leading brigade under Colonel Iska was in position at the eastern end of the Mitla Pass, barring the road to Suez. Behind them the Pass itself was already blocked by a huge tangle of wrecked vehicles destroyed by the Israeli Air Force. Iska's brigade fought all night against the Egyptian forces bearing down on them, and somehow held their ground until relieved next day by Joffe's second brigade, which forced its way through the wreckage in the Pass to reach the banks of the Canal at 2 a.m. on the morning of Friday 9 June. Tal and Sharon also successfully blocked their roads; but to reach Bir Gifgafa and Nakhl, respectively, they had to pass through the main forces of the enemy armour. For both this involved thirty-six hours of continuous and confused fighting as the armoured forces of both sides streamed in the same direction along the same tracks. Sharon came upon the tanks of an Egyptian armoured brigade abandoned intact by their crews. The commander was taken prisoner and explained to his astonished captors that he had been ordered to withdraw but nothing had been said about taking the tanks with him – and that to blow them up would make too much noise. Both at Nakhl and at Gifgafa the Israeli tanks established ambushes which trapped the retreating Egyptians.

Throughout the three days of Tuesday, Wednesday, and Thursday the Israeli Air Force roved the desert at will, where necessary cooperating in the land battle but mainly seeking out and destroying enemy forces wherever they saw them. By Friday morning, when the cease-fire at last came into effect, hardly an Egyptian unit remained intact. The desert was littered with the debris of thousands of vehicles, including over 700 Russian tanks. Egyptian soldiers in tens of thousands, for the most part abandoned by their officers, had cast away arms, equipment, and boots and were hopelessly making their way across the waterless desert in the direction of home. The *jihad* was over. In the course of it, on 7 June, a small force of patrol boats had sailed down the Gulf of Aqaba and, landing unopposed, hoisted the Israeli flag at the Straits of Tiran.

Meanwhile, in New York, Mr Abba Eban was fighting his country's battles at the Security Council. Although the sympathy of the Western world had not, on the whole, been forfeited by Israel's apparent action in striking the first blow, it was not likely to extend to any blatant violation of a cease-fire resolution by the United Nations. Support from public opinion in the United States, so long as no American involvement was required, was overwhelmingly strong – so strong that Mr Dean Rusk felt it necessary to soften the statement of one of his officials that the United States was 'neutral in thought, word, and deed' by explaining that neutrality was a concept in international law which did not imply indifference. But for Britain, much as she sympathized with the Israeli cause, the prospect of prolonged conflict in the Middle East, with all that this implied for her relations with the Arab world, was intensely disagreeable. The French Government, to the fury of most articulate French public opinion, reaffirmed its position of glacial neutrality; while the Soviet Union could only view the humiliation of her clients in the Arab world with alarm and despondency.

The refusal of the Soviet Union to intervene on their behalf, which must have been made clear to the Arab leaders at the very beginning of the conflict, made it the more necessary for her to sponsor their cause at the United Nations; not only to salvage her own reputation with them but to save them from the consequences of their own folly. Dr Fedorenko found himself in a difficult position. On the one hand, he had to get a cease-fire as quickly as possible. On the other, he had to read into the record the maximum abuse of Israel's aggression and the iniquity of her supporters in the West. Mr Eban and Mr Gideon Raphael, Israel's Permanent Representative at the United Nations, may have consoled themselves for the hours of abuse which they had to endure from Dr Fedorenko and his Communist and Arab colleagues with the reflection that every hour thus spent was being put to good use by the Israeli High Command.

But it was not in the interests of the Western powers to see the Arabs and their Russian sympathizers reduced to complete despair. Besides, the longer the conflict lasted, the greater was the risk of its spreading. An example of how this might happen occurred on the afternoon of Thursday 8 June, when Israeli aircraft attacked the US Navy vessel USS *Liberty* some 14 nautical miles north of El Arish. The circumstances leading up to this attack have not been made public, any more than the real reasons for the presence of this vessel so close to the battle zone; but the Israelis were able to convince the United States Government that the bombing was due to a genuine error of identification, and it seems highly probable that *Liberty*, an electronic intelligence vessel, was monitoring the wireless traffic of both sides. Whatever the facts of the case, this attack led to a reaction in the US Sixth Fleet, whose aircraft flew off to investigate. Realizing that the Russians in their turn might react to this move, a direct explanation was sent over 'the hot line'. The affair in fact was very competently handled; but it must have increased the general anxiety for a cease-fire.

The Security Council, it will be remembered, had already on the afternoon of 6 June called upon the governments concerned 'as a first step to take forthwith all measures for an immediate cease-fire and for a cessation of all military activities in the area'. Mr Abba Eban at once informed the Security Council that his country welcomed the cease-fire appeal, but that its implementation 'depended on the acceptance and co-operation of the other parties'. Syria and Iraq, whose forces were as yet only marginally engaged in the war, rejected the appeal. The UAR remained silent. Only Jordan, whose forces on the West Bank were at their last gasp, responded immediately, but the Israelis were not yet ready to leave her alone. Pointing out that, since the Jordanian Army was under Egyptian command, this decision was of doubtful validity, they continued to fight – in Jerusalem, as we have seen, with redoubled vigour. On 7 June a wrathful Dr Fedorenko sponsored a more strongly worded motion, adopted unanimously by the Security Council, which '*demand*[*ed*] that the Governments concerned should as a first step cease fire and discontinue all military activities at 20.00 hours GMT on 7 June 1967'. This the Israelis accepted. By then the Old City of Jerusalem was securely in their hands.

On the Sinai front, the obstinacy of the UAR Government played straight into the hands of Israel. It was not until the evening of Thursday 8 June that their delegate conveyed to the Security Council their acceptance of the cease-fire. By then General Gavish's forces had completed the rout of the Egyptians in Sinai and had only to close up to the Suez Canal. Only Syria now remained.

Up till now the Israeli forces opposite Syria had remained on the defensive, while the Syrians confined themselves to occasional raids in battalion strength and frequent, heavy shelling of the *kibbutzim* in the Jordan Valley below them. It is not clear at what point the Israeli Government took the decision to attack Syria, but the decision is not likely to have caused much controversy. Israeli public opinion would have found it difficult to understand or forgive a campaign which, having disposed of Egypt and Jordan, left intact the enemy whose hostility to Israel had been most implacable, whose activities had been directly responsible for the war, and whose forces still dominated one of the most fertile stretches of Israeli land. But the problems of launching an attack were considerable. The Syrian heights above the Upper Jordan Valley are a steep escarpment rising 1,000 feet to the bare plateau which stretches eastwards to Damascus and beyond. The Syrian Army had not only constructed positions from which they could dominate the valley, but also fortified the plateau to a depth of some ten miles with a continuous zone of wire, minefields, trenches, gun emplacements, pill-boxes, and tanks. Constructed under Russian direction, it was a masterpiece of defensive fortification, and suitably equipped with artillery, machine-guns, anti-aircraft batteries, and rocket-launchers. Viewing the ground afterwards, it seemed impossible that any army in the world could have taken it, except by a campaign lasting for weeks.

It took the Israelis about twenty-four hours. Their attack was preceded by heavy air attacks which began on the morning of Thursday 8 June and went on all day and all night. There was great pressure to launch the assault that day, before the Syrians could take advantage of the United Nations' demand for a cease-fire, but there were strong reasons against doing so; including the need to bring up forces from other fronts and the value of giving the air barrage time to take effect. As a result the attack was forestalled by a Syrian request for a ceasefire to begin at 3.20 a.m. GMT on Friday 9 June. The Israelis ignored this (as indeed did the Syrian artillery) and attacked at 11.30 that morning. General Elazar struck in the extreme north of the Jordan Valley up the slopes near the Baniyas head waters with a force of infantry, armour, and parachute troops. There was no cover: the way was led by bulldozers carving out tankable tracks under heavy fire. It took three hours and about 700 casualties to gain the crest. At the same time subsidiary attacks were delivered farther down the valley opposite Gonen and Ashmura; and early next morning another mixed force attacked Syria in the far south, tanks and infantry clambering up from the Yarmuk valley, helicopters dropping parachute troops on the escarpment, and moved north-west over the plateau towards Boulmiye and Rafid.

Astonishing as the Israelis' achievement was in getting up on to the escarpment at all, this might have been only the beginning of their task. A considerable part of the Syrian defences still stretched before them. Yet on Saturday 10 June they had little more to do except advance. After the first few hours of resistance the Syrian troops collapsed and fled. This was not due entirely to the efforts of the Israeli forces; the Syrian Government itself took a hand. Early on the Saturday morning Damascus Radio announced the fall of

Qnaitra, Syrian Army headquarters and the only major town between the frontier and Damascus. It did so, it has been suggested, in order to strengthen the hand of their representative at the United Nations, who for the past twenty-four hours had been trying to persuade the Security Council to force Israel into accepting the cease-fire. Hearing that their main base had fallen, the Syrian forces panicked. The Israelis were able to walk over positions which might have held them up for weeks. By 2.30 on the afternoon of 10 June they really were in Qnaitra. Two hours later the cease-fire came into effect.

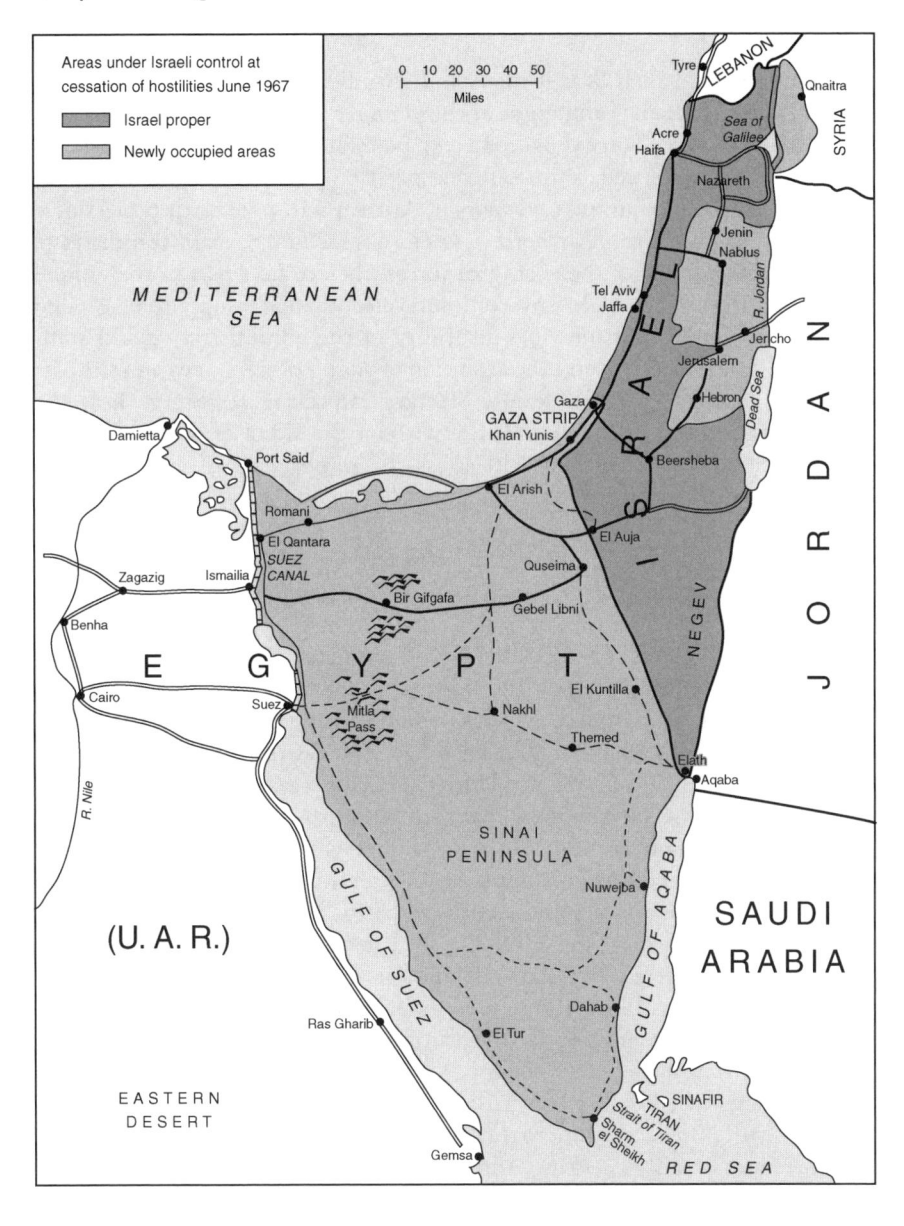

The Third Arab–Israeli War was over. The only prisoners taken by the Israel Defence Force were about 5,500 officers and NCOs. It had inflicted an unknown number of casualties, including perhaps as many as 15,000 killed. It had destroyed or captured 430 combat aircraft and 800 tanks. Its own losses totalled 40 aircraft and just over 3,000 men, of whom 676 were dead. Henceforward there was not likely to be very much difficulty about Israeli rights of passage through the Straits of Tiran.

IV. Conclusion

The Third Arab–Israeli War is likely to be studied in staff colleges for many years to come. Like the campaigns of the younger Napoleon, the performance of the Israeli Defence Force provided a text-book illustration for all the classical Principles of War: speed, surprise, concentration, security, information, the offensive, above all training and morale. Airmen will note with professional approval how the Israeli Air Force was employed, first to gain command of the air by destruction of the enemy air forces, then to take part in the ground battle by interdiction of enemy communications, direct support of ground attacks, and finally pursuit. The flexibility of the administrative and staff-system will be examined, and the attention of young officers drawn to the part played by leadership at all levels. Military radicals will observe how the Israelis attained this peak of excellence without the aid of drill-sergeants and the barrack-square. Tacticians will stress the importance they attached, in this as in previous campaigns, to being able to move and fight by night as effectively as they did by day.

Above all it will be seen how Israel observed a principle which appears in few military text-books but which armed forces neglect at their peril: the Clausewitzian principle of Political Context, which the British ignored so disastrously in 1956. The Israeli High Command knew that it was not operating in a political vacuum. It worked on the assumption that it would have three days to complete its task before outside pressures compelled a cease-fire. In fact it had four, and needed five. The general disapproval even in the West when Israel ignored the United Nations' cease-fire call and opened its offensive against Syria showed how narrow was the margin on which it had to work. The lesson is clear. So long as there remains a tacit agreement between the superpowers to co-operate in preventing overt conflicts which threaten international peace and security, a nation using open force to resolve a political problem must do so rapidly, if it is to succeed at all. Once it *has* succeeded, the reluctance of the Great Powers to countenance a second conflict means that it is likely to preserve its gains. The lesson is a sombre one, placing as it does a premium on adventurism and pre-emption.

Could the war have been prevented? And has it in fact resolved the political problems which led to the military confrontation? The answers to these questions will differ according to the level at which one examines the situation, and there are, broadly speaking, three: the basic hostility between Israel and the Arab World; the closing of the Straits of Tiran; and the immediate threat to Israel's security posed by the Arab political and military measures taken in the last days of May.

It has been widely assumed in the West – and perhaps in the Soviet Union as well – that the first of these situations was one which, even if it could not be peacefully resolved, was decreasingly likely to erupt into open war: that, as with the East–West confrontation, cold war would give place to peaceful co-existence and ultimately to mutual toleration. This confidence in the power of time and enlightened self-interest to solve all problems, doubtfully warranted as it is by past experience, is perhaps the only thing that keeps diplomats from despair; but there was little ground for such confidence in the history of Israeli-Arab relations over the past twenty years. The trauma inflicted on the Arab consciousness by the establishment of Israel and the expulsion of a million native Palestinians was likely to grow more rather than less acute as Arab national self-consciousness increased. What could be taught about the event to generations of Arab schoolboys, except that it was a monstrous and intolerable injustice? The situation might have been more tolerable if the Israelis had not been, in spite of their absorption of many Middle Eastern Jews, so evidently a *Western* people, with Western skills, standards, and affiliations. The Arab and Soviet accusations against Israel of being an outpost of Western imperialism are, at the level at which they are made, self-evidently absurd. Yet they reflect a deeper reality. 'Imperialism' does not necessarily indicate a deliberate intention to conquer and subjugate other peoples. The dominance of Europe over much of the world in the nineteenth century, and of the United States in the twentieth, derived from the ascendancy gained by more energetic, self-confident, and ingenious peoples over less effectively organized and dynamic cultures. The Israelis, more than any indigenous Middle Eastern people, display the qualities of hard work, technical expertise, and self-confidence which historians once mistakenly associated with the Protestant religion and the spirit of capitalism. They may have gone to Palestine, as an earlier generation of refugees from persecution went to New England, to seek sanctuary from the storms of the outside world; but their sanctuary is not, any more than was New England, a quiet and contemplative retreat. The Israelis have pressed relentlessly on their neighbours in the cultivation of land. Plans are on foot for turning the Negev Desert into a great industrial complex by desalination – assisted by nuclear energy. Tel Aviv has become a major conurbation, Haifa a leading Mediterranean port, and Eilat's future is now assured. All this economic expansion the West naturally regards with admiration and approval. The Arabs see it with different eyes. Who, they are bound to ask, is by the end of the twentieth century likely to dominate the Middle East?

Time was not, and is not, likely to assuage the conflict between an Israel waxing in self-confidence, wealth, and economic activity and an Arab world whose political and cultural progress seems to involve the kind of nationalistic self-assertion usually associated with the States of Europe in the nineteenth century. The most that one could ask is that outside powers should do nothing to make the conflict worse; but even this is asking a great deal. Short of a policy of total non-involvement in Middle Eastern affairs, economic, military, cultural, or political, it is difficult to visualize how any party in the area can be helped, however innocently, without increasing its power to harm the others. The apparent callousness with which the Great Powers put arms into the hands of these sworn enemies is only a symptom of the way in which encouraging the development of two antagonistic parties is unlikely to reduce the antagonism. Whether they adopt, like the French Government since 1962, a dispassionate commercial approach, or like the British and Russians openly espouse the cause of specific regimes, the policy of external powers will be simply one factor – and not necessarily a very important one – in a situation which local conditions will ultimately determine. Britain, the United States, and no doubt the Soviet Union have all been through demiurgical phases in which they believed they had the power and the responsibility to mould the Middle East. Their statesmen now are sadder, wiser, and considerably more modest men.

Could external powers have done more to head off or to resolve the crisis which led to this war? The State Department has been criticized for failing to take note of the crisis until it was too late; the unspoken assumption being that it was in the power of the United States, by timely action, to save the situation. This assumption is a considerable one. The crisis was precipitated by local circumstances: primarily the revolutionary fervour of Syria and the political predicament of the UAR, working on the growing pressure of national self-assertiveness within Israel. The Soviet Union did not help matters by its warning of imminent Israeli attacks against Syria, but they were warnings for which the Israelis themselves had, perhaps deliberately, provided enough evidence to alert the Syrians without Soviet aid. Soviet intervention was incidental to the pattern of mutual warnings seen as mutual menaces, leading to explosive armed confrontation. By the time the crisis erupted, the Western powers were firmly classed as adversaries by the revolutionary Arab States. The worst construction was put on all their actions. Any pressure they could bring to bear on President Nasser – and after the withdrawal of American aid this was not considerable – would have been automatically discounted as part of the general imperialist-Zionist-reactionary conspiracy. And even the least paranoic Arab statesmen could hardly regard as impartial powers which, while taking a strong stand on Israeli rights of navigation in the Gulf of Aqaba, had nothing whatever to say about the rights of a million Palestinian Arabs dispossessed of their lands.

From 15 May onwards the initiative was in the hands of President Nasser, and about his decisions, to evict UNEF and close the Straits, much remains to be learned. About the first, the Western powers were in a position to do very little. The United Nations are not an embodiment of abstract International Justice as visualized in London and Washington, but a political body composed of numerous mutually antagonistic members, all of whose views have to be taken into account by the Secretary-General; and over the question of UNEF the Western powers, for a number of reasons, were almost certainly in a minority. Had U Thant appealed on the issue to the General Assembly, he is likely to have received an over-whelming vote of confidence. But the Straits were a different matter. The point at issue here was not one of international law: it was that of the credibility of a solemn and explicit Western guarantee. In reimposing his blockade President Nasser was, whether consciously or not, placing in jeopardy not only the economic future of Israel but also the reliability of the United States and Great Britain as allies. The implications of that for the world as a whole were very grave indeed.

The assurances which the United States and Britain had given to Israel over this issue were so inescapable that failure to implement them would have involved both powers in a humiliation as public as that suffered by France and Britain in 1956 – or indeed in 1938. The Western powers naturally attempted to gain world support by invoking international law and maritime rights, but found little backing anywhere for their position. They faced, therefore, the prospect of a lonely and prolonged confrontation with the Arab world which, whatever the outcome, could only cause them serious economic and political damage and in which they would enjoy very little neutral sympathy. Once President Nasser closed the Straits, in fact, Britain and America no longer had the status of external powers: they were up to their necks in the crisis themselves.

It was their good fortune, paradoxically, that within a few days the crisis had moved on to a graver stage and become a matter, not of Israel's economic future, but of her survival. The massing of Egyptian troops in Sinai, the creation of the United UAR-Jordanian Command, the movement of Iraqi forces into Jordan, created a situation for Israel in which it was immaterial whether the United States guaranteed passage through the Tiran Straits or not. War could now only be prevented by an assurance to Israel by the Western powers that they would react to an attack on Israeli territory as they would to one on their own. The President of the United States was in no position to issue such an assurance, and without the United States Britain could do nothing. The Israelis realized this very well.

Wars, it used to be said, settle nothing. Unfortunately the statement was untrue: they can settle many problems, and are sometimes, regrettably, the only way of settling them. But they also create new ones, sometimes so grave that one may look back to the old almost with nostalgia. Israel's victories have eliminated many of the points in dispute over the past twenty years. Whatever now happens, Syrian guns will not fire down on the Upper Jordan Valley, the City of Jerusalem will not be divided, and the future of Eilat is assured. The anomaly of the Gaza Strip is likely to be eliminated, and wherever the new frontier is drawn between Israel and Jordan, it will not run within twelve miles of the coast. But the Israelis may well look back with regret to the days when Israel was almost as homogeneous a Jewish State as its Zionist founders intended; for it will never be that again. Two and a half million Jews now control territory containing nearly a million and a half Arabs, and whatever settlement is made on the West Bank, Arabs are likely in future to make up at least a quarter of Israel's population. Israel will be confronted with all the problems of a multiracial society, in which the minority group is potentially hostile and sustained by powerful consanguineous supporters beyond the frontier.

On her ability to solve this problem Israel's future security will depend. If the Arab States have learned anything from their defeat, it should be the folly of challenging Israel to the kind of war which only fully developed societies can effectively fight. The re-equipment of their armies and air forces with modern weapons will not restore their military efficiency; it would be like fitting another heavy suit of armour on to a half-grown boy who has already proved unable to bear its weight. But half-grown boys, as the Israelis will recall, can be handy shots with slings and smooth pebbles from the brook. The weapon of revolutionary peoples, as Colonel Boumedienne among others has pointed out, is revolutionary war. There was not much scope for guerrillas in the Sinai Desert; but among a large, discontented Arab population in Israel herself, who knows?

We do not suggest that events in Israel will take the course of those in, for example, southern Africa, Algeria, or Vietnam. The Jewish population will still be in a majority, and a policy of apartheid based on religion is likely to be even less workable than one based on race. The advantages of terrain enjoyed by guerrillas in North Africa and South-East Asia are not to be found in the Sinai Desert or the restricted area of the West Bank, although Jordan, Syria, and the Lebanon could still provide sanctuary for the forces of a new 'Liberation Front'. But a renewal of the kind of inter-communal friction – the sniper at the upper window, the grenade lobbed into the coffee house – that was so common under the Mandate is by no means to be ruled out. If a fourth Arab–Israeli war occurs, this is the shape it is likely to take; and the military brilliance recently displayed by the Israeli nation and its leaders will not be very relevant to its conduct. If Israeli statesmanship does not match up to her military achievements, her victories may, like so many victories in the past, bear very bitter fruit.

Israel thus faces a dilemma to which her military talents provide no solution, and to which even nuclear weapons will be irrelevant. A strategically secure frontier, in the south and the east, will give her a strategically insecure population. There are no doubt hawks in the Cabinet who would gladly see the Arabs expelled again or at least encouraged, by very firm methods, to leave; but they are fortunately unlikely to carry the day. Barring that solution, the Arabs must be absorbed; and however hard the Israelis work to absorb them, Arab nationalist propagandists will work equally hard to inflame their grievances. The Israelis can congratulate themselves on their success in reconciling the small Arab population for twenty years within their borders, but the change in the dimensions of their task is likely to transform its entire nature. It is hard, indeed, to see how it can be accomplished at all, unless the Israelis abandon many of their Zionist ideals and revert to the older concept of a Palestine shared peacefully between Arab and Jew.

Such a policy would certainly make easier the task of moderate statesmen within the Arab world. At present they enjoy a precarious ascendancy. The war so clamorously demanded by the revolutionary nationalists has taken place and ended in disaster. King Hussein's stock stands high. Not only was his policy vindicated by events, but he emerged from a war he did not want with as great credit as any of his allies. But no amount of statesmanship will incline the Arabs to accept a settlement which does not dispose once and for all of their fundamental grievance – the status of the Palestinian refugees. So long as that question remains unsettled, Hussein may fight a losing battle against Colonel Boumedienne. And if Boumedienne wins, there will be a fourth Arab–Israeli war. It will not be so short as the third; and there can be no assurance that this time Israel will win.

Notes

1. THE CONFLICT

1 Publication of the Sykes-Picot Agreement by the Bolsheviks after the October Revolution failed to stir Hussein, who expressed no opposition to Jewish settlement; Hussein's son, Feisal, even concluded an agreement on the Jewish National Home with the Zionist Chaim Weizmann. Their sentiments changed, however, when Feisal was turned out of Damascus in 1920, and the political ambitions of the Zionists began to be apparent.
2 The Mandate provided that 'the administration of Palestine, while ensuring that the rights and position of other sections of the population are not prejudiced, shall facilitate Jewish immigration under suitable conditions and shall encourage ... close settlement by Jews on the land' (Article 6). Jewish immigration during those years was as follows: 1923: 7,991; 1924: 13,553; 1925: 34,641; 1926: 13,910; 1927: 3,595; ... 1931: 5,533; 1932: 11,289; 1933: 31,977; 1934: 44,143; 1935: 64,147.
3 *Palestine: Statement of Policy*, May 1939, Cmd. 6019.
4 In order to secure agreement in the General Assembly, the Jewish Agency even accepted the transfer to the Arab State of a large area of Palestine along the Egyptian frontier.
5 These raids followed a terrorist attack by the Jews on a village near the Syrian border in December 1947.
6 Jon and David Kimche, *Both Sides of the Hill* (London, 1960).
7 Soon after the campaign began to link up the body of the State of Israel with the Negev pocket, Israeli forces drove the remaining elements of the Arab Liberation Army from the area north-west of Lake Tiberias.
8 Although Egypt was awarded provisional control over the Gaza Strip by the General Armistice Agreement, it remained part of Palestine. Egypt has observed this legal distinction, which has enabled her, unlike Jordan, to deny Egyptian citizenship to the Arab refugees.
9 Iraq and Saudi Arabia did not conclude Armistice Agreements with Israel, but gave separate undertakings that they would accept terms agreed upon by Palestine's Arab neighbours and the Arab League, respectively. Jordan assumed responsibility for all Iraqi forces in Palestine.

10 Like all statistics on the Arab refugees, these can only be rough approximations, since many refugees are not registered, some live in Iraq and Kuwait, and there is no systematic method for eliminating numbers of refugees who have died. There is also no indication here of the refugees' relative standard of living, which has been far higher in the Lebanon, for example, than in the Gaza Strip.

11 Following the 1948–49 war, Egypt contended that Israel had illegally occupied Eilat after their Armistice of 24 February. Israel replied that the southern Negev had not been contested by forces of Egypt and Israel. The movement of Israeli forces into Eilat was against nominal Jordanian opposition, and occurred the day before the Israel-Jordan truce.

12 Terence Prittie, *Israel* (London, 1967).

13 Egypt and Syria formed a Joint Military Command in October 1955. Jordan joined the command just before the 1956 war.

14 See Appendix 1.

15 Since the involvement of the Great Powers in the Middle East has been exhaustively dealt with elsewhere, little is said about them in this paper. The reader is referred particularly to the ISS publication, *Sources of Conflict in the Middle East*, Adelphi Paper No. 26, March 1966.

16 The Israeli Government now argues, perhaps partly to allay Arab fears, that diversion of sweet water from the Jordan will not permit large areas of the Negev to be brought under cultivation, chiefly because of a fall in the water table elsewhere in Israel and an increase in industrial demands for water. The future of the Negev will depend upon new desalination techniques.

17 See Appendix 2.

18 For most of the period since the Second World War, the United States has been the leading supplier of Egyptian imports, primarily in the form of foodstuffs sold for local currency. Relations between the United States and the UAR deteriorated during 1964, however, following the burning of the USIS library in Cairo; US aid was suspended. The two Governments managed to negotiate a $55-million aid agreement covering the first half of 1966, but this was not renewed, largely because of American concern over the Yemen war and Egyptian attacks on American policy in Vietnam.

19 Although the UAR was immediately concerned in the confrontation, she elected to contribute funds rather than receive them under this scheme.

20 Nasser accused Feisal of granting a military base to the British; this was perhaps a round about way of expressing his displeasure at the British agreement to supply Saudi Arabia with *Lightning* fighter aircraft.

21 Throughout her long confrontation with her Arab neighbours, Israel has chosen to meet provocation with stronger response – as in the reprisal raids before the wars of 1956 and 1967. This is a policy that has often served to escalate conflict. Her strategic vulnerability has also led her, in three wars, to believe her choice to be between 'death by a thousand cuts' and major military action.

22 The Armistice Demarcation Line between Israel and Syria was drawn between the Israeli Truce Line and the International Frontier, where the two were not the same. The area of Palestine between the Armistice Line and the Frontier was designated a demilitarized zone, of three sections, including areas on the eastern shores of Lake Tiberias and Lake Huleh that were on the Israeli side of the Armistice Line.

23 UNTSO was the successor of the Truce Commission established by the Security Council in April 1948. The Chief of Staff of UNTSO was made chairman of the four Mixed Armistice Commissions.

24 By October 1966, there were 66,085 complaints outstanding: 35,485 by Israel and 30,600 by Syria.

25 The Es Samu attack illustrated the strategic advantage which Syria held over

Jordan, *vis-à-vis* Israel. The nature of the terrain meant that Israel could mount reprisal attacks much more easily against Jordan than against Syria.
26 Between 25 January and 28 March, 1967, the Israeli-Syrian Mixed Armistice Commission received 790 formal Israeli complaints.

II. THE CRISIS

1 The date of Israel's Independence Day – 14–15 May 1948 – is reckoned by the Hebrew calendar; therefore by the Gregorian calendar it falls on a different date each year. In 1967 it again fell on 14–15 May.
2 According to *Al-Ahram* on 12 May, the Egyptian Government had barred units of the Sixth Fleet from visiting Egyptian ports. The ostensible reason appeared to stem from an interview given in April by Israel's Premier Eshkol to the magazine *US News and World Report*, in which he said: 'We ask the United States for arms and are told, "Don't spend your money. We are here. The Sixth Fleet is here" '.
3 'To your information, I gave my instructions to all UAR Armed Forces to be ready for action against Israel the moment it might carry out any aggressive action against any Arab country. Due to these instructions our troops are already concentrated in Sinai on our eastern borders. For the sake of complete secure [sic] of all UN troops which install OPs along our borders, I request that you issue your orders to withdraw all these troops immediately. I have given my instructions to our Commander of the eastern zone concerning this subject. Inform back the fulfillment of this request. Yours, Farik Awal (M. Fawzy), COS of UAR Armed Forces'.
4 On the afternoon of 17 May, U Thant handed two *aide-mémoires* to the UAR Permanent Representative. The first recapitulated the events of the previous twenty-four hours, and ended with a stern warning that UNEF 'cannot now be asked to stand aside in order to become a silent and helpless witness to an armed confrontation between the parties'. It either had to stay where it was, or depart entirely. U Thant added that the Chief of Staff of UNTSO had seen 'no recent indications of troop movements or concentrations along any of the lines which should give rise to undue concern'. The second *aide-mémoire* reviewed the 'Good Faith Agreement' of November 1956. See Appendix 1.
5 See Appendix 1.
6 *Ibid.*
7 The Yugoslav platoon at Sharm-el-Sheikh had withdrawn from the actual positions commanding the Straits of Tiran, at Ras Nasrani, on 19 May. The UAR probably could have imposed a blockade at any time from then on.
8 Unconfirmed reports from Israel after the war have indicated that David Ben-Gurion was considerably less willing to entertain military action than he had been eleven years earlier, as Prime Minister. He reportedly was concerned that Israel should have the support of at least one major Western power. Premier Eshkol, on the other hand, is reported to have been more inclined towards military action from the early stages of the crisis.
9 The previous evening the United States Government had also counselled the UAR to exercise restraint.
10 Mr Eshkol, in his reply on 1 June, stated that a settlement must be founded on 'the territorial independence and integrity of all States of the region; resistance to revanchism and attempts to change the situation by force; abstention from acts of hostility, including acts of sabotage carried out by infiltrators across the border and the imposition of a maritime blockade; and non-interference in the internal affairs of States'.
11 The rejection by President de Gaulle of Israel's bid for French support met with

strong opposition in France, both within the ruling Gaullist party and without. There have been recurrent reports that armaments shipments, including a few aircraft, continued to flow to Israel, until the French Government formally declared an arms embargo on the first day of the war. After that, according to widespread reports in Western capitals, some aid reached Israel through third countries.

12 The latter image was presented in two television interviews given by President Nasser to Messrs. Anthony Nutting and Christopher Mayhew, M.P., a few days before the war.

13 For a considerable segment of public opinion in Israel, this article was too accurate in analyzing Israel's position to permit further doubts that Nasser had calculated the consequences of closing the Straits of Tiran.

14 One division in the Gaza Strip was that of the Palestine Liberation Army, and cannot be accorded equal weight in the order of battle with the other Egyptian forces. This division was in position when the crisis began.

III. THE WAR

1 Israel time, which is an hour behind Cairo time.

2 Israel's *Sherman* tanks were relics of the 1940s, while the *Centurions* had long been obsolescent and the *Pattons* were cast-offs from the Bundeswehr. Their excellent performance in this war was unexpected, and was due almost entirely to the high maintenance and training standard of the Israeli Defence Forces.

3 These figures for armaments are those at present available to the Institute for Strategic Studies. A full presentation is given in Appendix 3. Their accuracy, particularly in relation to the Israeli forces, cannot be guaranteed. Israeli security is excellent, and the precise size of her armed forces remains one of her most closely guarded secrets.

4 The Israelis are reported to have held back no more than twelve operational aircraft for defensive operations over Israel.

5 The largest regular formation in the Israeli Army was the brigade. Larger formations were, like Army Corps in the British Army, created *ad hoc* of whatever combination was suitable to the task in hand. Thus General Tal's division contained a preponderance of armour; General Joffe's was entirely armoured; General Sharon's was a balanced force of infantry, armour, and parachute troops.

6 It was afterwards emphasized by General Hod that two-thirds of all sorties flown were 'taking part in the land battle', mostly in striking Egyptian armour and vehicles behind the battle zone. Israeli ground forces had been warned to expect little air co-operation in the earlier phases of operations. But aircraft which could not be used in the main air battle, such as the Fouga *Magister* trainers, were placed at General Gavish's disposal from the very beginning.

Appendixes

1. The United Nations Emergency Force

The United Nations Emergency Force (UNEF) was initially established by a series of three General Assembly Resolutions adopted between 4 and 7 November 1956. The first requested the Secretary-General to present 'a plan for the setting up, with the consent of the nations concerned, of an emergency international United Nations Force to secure and supervise the cessation of hostilities. In accordance with all the terms of the [cease-fire resolution, of 2 November]'.

Mr Hammarskjöld lost no time, and the following day the General Assembly accepted his recommendation to establish 'a United Nations Command for an emergency international Force', and authorized recruitment of officers. On 7 November the General Assembly accepted Hammarskjöld's final report and approved his plans. In addition it created an Advisory Committee of seven countries to assist the Secretary-General. He was required to consult this Committee on a number of matters, including regulations and instructions essential to the effective functioning of the Force. The Advisory Committee, in turn, had the right at any point to request a meeting of the General Assembly to consider any matter that in the Committee's opinion was of 'urgency and importance'. Nothing was said about the Security Council. Indeed, it had no standing with regard to the operation of UNEF other than its continuing mandate under the UN Charter to consider threats to the peace.

From the beginning, there were three interrelated questions to be answered. What were UNEF's functions? How long was it to remain in being? And what would happen if there were a disagreement between the United Nations and the host state over the answers to the first two questions?

Hammarskjöld's statement about the functions of UNEF (quoted in the text) seemed straight-forward enough. But there was a difference of opinion from the first. The three occupying powers wished the Force to be a means of pressuring Egypt to reach some political settlements. The Arab States, on the other hand, conceived the role of the Force to be the limited one of overseeing the cease-fire and withdrawal of British, French, and Israeli troops. The latter view prevailed within the General Assembly at the time, partly because of the need to gain Egypt's consent to the Force, and partly because neither the United States nor the Soviet Union was inclined to support the former view. The Russians argued then and later that the Assembly had no power to create an international peace force, but did not vote against the resolutions establishing it after Egypt agreed to Hammarskjöld's plan.

However, the Secretary-General had given certain assurances to Britain and France on 7 November to secure their agreement to a cease-fire; in particular, he agreed that the peace force 'would be competent to secure the objectives' of the General Assembly's cease-fire resolution of 2 November. Later, these assurances and the resolutions establishing UNEF formed the basis of a widely held view that UNEF's role properly went beyond the temporary one of supervising the cease-fire and troop withdrawls; in part, the cease-fire resolution had urged the parties to the Armistice Agreements 'to desist from raids across the armistice lines into neighbouring territory, and to observe scrupulously the provisions of the armistice agreements'. Did this mean that UNEF would remain on Egyptian soil until these injunctions were observed?

This provision gained its importance from subsequent developments. Immediately after the UN troops arrived in Egypt on 15 November, Hammarskjöld flew to Cairo to achieve an understanding with President

Nasser on the functioning of the Emergency Force. They concluded an *aide-mémoire* that included what has come to be known as the 'Good Faith Agreement': they agreed that with regard to UNEF, both the UN and the Egyptian Government would be guided, in good faith, by the General Assembly resolutions establishing the Force, and the Force would be maintained 'until its task is completed'.

But what did the phrase 'until its task is completed' mean? Since there was a difference of opinion concerning the nature of the roles originally assigned to UNEF, there was bound to be controversy over the meaning of the Good Faith Agreement as well. In a statement released on 19 June 1967, U Thant specifically endorsed the narrower view, although on 17 May he had recalled this Agreement to the attention of the Egyptian Government. The UAR was certainly not prepared to accept any but the most narrow view.

Whatever the relative merits of the different arguments in this dispute, the matter did not rest there. On 2 February 1957, the General Assembly adopted a further resolution with regard to the Emergency Force, formally broadening its functions. The resolution provided that, 'after full withdrawal of Israel from the Sharm-el-Sheikh and Gaza areas, the scrupulous maintenance of the Armistice Agreement requires the placing of the United Nations Emergency Force on the Egyptian-Israel armistice demarcation line and the implementation of other measures as proposed in the Secretary-General's report [of 1 February 1957]'. The 'other measures' were deliberately left ambiguous; they were later stretched to embrace the establishment of UNEF posts at Sharm-el-Sheikh and Ras Nasrani, controlling the Straits of Tiran.

This resolution provided the most widely accepted basis for the stationing of UNEF on Egyptian territory; significantly, the resolution came after the Good Faith Agreement and, it has been argued, was not subject to it.

These considerations touch on a central problem that was evident from the beginning: what would happen if Egypt asked UNEF to leave. She clearly had the right to do so: the Force was in Egypt on sufferance, since enforcement action could only be taken by the Security Council under Chapter VII of the UN Charter. At the very least, such an Egyptian request would have to come to the Secretary-General, since the Force had been established in Egypt under an agreement between Mr Hammarskjöld and President Nasser. And the Secretary-General, in turn, would have to consult the Advisory Committee, which, if it chose to do so, could ask for a meeting of the General Assembly. But should more be done than this?

During the crisis of May 1967, U Thant was criticized for ignoring a memorandum written by Hammarskjöld in August 1957, concerning the conditions under which UNEF was to remain in Egypt, which indicated that, in case of disagreement between the Secretary-General and the Government of Egypt, 'the matter would at once be brought before the General Assembly'. But U Thant correctly stated that this so-called 'Hammarskjöld Memorandum' had no standing because it was not an official UN document and had never been conveyed to the Egyptian Government.

But U Thant overlooked a more substantial interpretation by Hammarskjöld of the procedure to be followed, which was contained in his 1958 Summary Study of experience derived from the establishment and operation of the Force (A/3943). Hammarskjöld had not challenged the 'sovereign right of the host government' but he did lay down firmly that, 'were either side to act unilaterally in refusing continued presence or deciding on withdrawal, and were the other side to find that such action was contrary to a good-faith interpretation of the purposes of the operation, an exchange of views would be called for towards harmonizing the positions' (Para. 158). This interpretation went unchallenged, and may fairly be considered to have met with the approval of the principals involved.

In any event, the problems that would arise if and when Egypt asked UNEF to leave had not been ignored over the years; the issue was widely discussed in the standard texts on United Nations peace-keeping operations, and had been a central concern of the Israeli Government when deciding to withdraw its forces from Sharm-el-Sheikh.

In conclusion, it should be noted that considerable thought had also been given to the problems that could arise if one or more of the countries contributing forces to UNEF decided to withdraw them, as did Yugoslavia and India in 1967. There had been some difference of opinion on this issue, although the agreements between the participating States and the United Nations indicated that 'adequate prior notification' must be given. Hammarskjöld himself had been aware of the political risks inherent in becoming too dependent upon any single State's contribution to the Force, and had adopted a policy of balancing the relative sizes of different contingents.

2. The Jordan Waters

The Upper Jordan River is formed by the confluence of three principal rivers: the Dan, which has its source in Israel; the Hasbani (Lebanon); and the Baniyas (Syria). The average annual flow of these three sources was estimated in 1953 to be 258 million cubic metres a year (mcm/year) for the Dan, and 157 mcm/year for each of the other two rivers. Thus the Upper Jordan is a plentiful source of sweet water until it reaches Lake Tiberias, where salt springs increase the salinity of the water to the point at which it must be mixed with fresh water to be suitable for irrigation. But below Lake Tiberias, the Lower Jordan is joined by another fresh water source, the Yarmuk River (475 mcm/year), flowing into Israel from the east, where it forms part of the Syria-Jordan border. The Lower Jordan flows south into the Hashemite Kingdom, finally reaching the Dead Sea.

The Jordan Valley Unified Water Plan of 1955, negotiated by Ambassador Eric Johnston, proposed to divide these waters among the riparian States according to the use they could effectively make of them, in the following manner:

Jordan: 100 mcm/year from the Jordan; 377 mcm/year from the Yarmuk; and 243 mcm/year from side wadis of the Jordan.

Lebanon: 35 mcm/year from the Hasbani.

Syria: 22 mcm/year from the Jordan; 90 mcm/year from the Yarmuk; and 20 mcm/year from the Baniyas.

Israel: The balance of the Jordan waters after the other riparian States had satisfied their needs. This amount has been variously calculated to be between 400 and 490 mcm/year (about one-third of the total), including 25 mcm/year specifically allocated from the Yarmuk.

Among the Arab countries, Syria has been using about 68 mcm/year of water from the Yarmuk River, and a small amount from the Baniyas, while the Lebanon has made some use of the Hasbani. But it is Jordan that has been most enterprising in the use of water, and since 1958 has been developing plans to use the Yarmuk, beginning with irrigation of the East Ghor region just east of the Jordan. Although this diversion scheme will raise the salinity of the Lower Jordan, it has not been a serious point at issue between Jordan and Israel, because the latter accepts that under the Johnston Plan the great bulk of the Yarmuk waters was intended for use by Jordan.

For the same reason, one would not expect Israel to be unduly concerned about a limited diversion of the Baniyas and Hasbani Rivers before they reach the Israel frontier. Indeed, much of the annual flow of these two rivers is in the form of flash floods, and it is open to question whether the flood waters could be effectively dammed without an engineering feat far beyond what the Arabs have contemplated. But the Arab diversion schemes of 1964 were undertaken with a view to thwarting the development of Israel, and this must seem to the Israeli Government to be a serious challenge, whether or not it is likely that the Arabs could do Israel significant damage.

The dispute has been further complicated by evidence that there is less water available than was believed in 1953, and by inefficient use of the total water resources of the Jordan Valley system because of separate national development. As a result, the withdrawal of the Johnston Plan quotas by all the riparians is no longer possible, a factor destined to increase anxiety on both sides of the dispute.

Until June 1967, development of the Arab diversion projects had progressed only sporadically, since the Baniyas River works were repeatedly shelled by the Israel Defence Forces. The Lebanon was particularly reluctant to proceed without credible assurances that Israeli military action could be met in kind by forces of the Unified Arab Command.

Having occupied the Syrian Heights during the recent war, Israel now holds the Baniyas River, and is in a position to hold hostage the Jordanian projects on the Yarmuk River.

3. Armed forces of the belligerents (4 June 1967)*

Israel

ARMY

Total strength: 275,000 (fully mobilized).
8 armoured brigades (3,500 men each).
22 infantry brigades (4,500 men each).
1 parachute brigade (4,000 men).
800 tanks, including 250 *Centurions*, 200 *Super-Shermans*, 200 M-48 *Pattons*, and 150 AMX-13s.
250 SP guns, including 155mm howitzers on *Sherman* chassis and 105 mm howitzers on AMX chassis.
Anti-tank weapons included the 106mm recoilless rifle mounted on jeeps, and SS-10 and SS-11 missiles mounted on weapons carriers.
Separate regional defence units in the border areas.

NAVY

Total strength: 3,000 (regulars).
2 destroyers.
1 anti-aircraft frigate.
4 submarines.
1 patrol vessel.
3 landing craft.
14 patrol craft of less than 100 tons.

AIR FORCE

Total strength: 8,000 men; about 280 combat air-craft (including armed trainers).
25 *Vautour* light bombers.
72 *Mirage* III-C interceptor fighter-bombers.
20 *Super-Mystère* interceptors.
45 *Mystère* IV fighter-bombers.
50 *Ouragan* fighter-bombers (obsolescent).
60 *Magister* trainers (can be armed).
About 40 *Noratlas*, C-47, and *Stratocruiser* transports.
25 helicopters, including S-58 and *Alouettes*.
Some light aircraft, including *Piper Cubs*.
2 battalions of *Hawk* surface-to-air missiles.

United Arab Republic

ARMY

Total strength: 180,000 (including mobilized reservists).
2 armoured divisions (with 350 medium and heavy tanks each).
4 motorized rifle divisions (with about 150 medium tanks each).
1 parachute brigade.
12 artillery regiments.
About 1,200 tanks and assault guns, including 350 T-34, 50 PT-76, 500 T-54 and T-55, 60 JS-3, and 150 Su-100.
100 surface-to-surface missiles with ranges of between 200 and 450 miles were believed not to be operational.
Army reserves total a further 60,000. There was a para-military National Guard of about 60,000.
Forces in the Yemen were probably less than 50,000.
The Palestine Liberation Army (PLA) consisted of about 30,000 irregular troops trained by the Egyptians, a large proportion of whom (about 10,000) were stationed in the Gaza Strip.

NAVY

Total strength: 11,000.
8 destroyers (6 ex-Soviet *Skory*-class, 2 ex-British 'Z' type).
11 submarines (ex-Soviet 'W'-class).
6 escort vessels.
6 coastal escorts.
18 missile patrol boats (10 *Osa*-class, 8 *Komar*-class, both with *Styx* short-range cruise missiles).
10 minesweepers.
About 50 small patrol vessels.

AIR FORCE

Total strength: 20,000 men; 500 combat aircraft.
30 Tu-16 medium jet bombers.
40 Il-28 light jet bombers.
120 MiG-21 C/D jet interceptors.
80 MiG-19 all-weather fighters or fighter-bombers.
200 MiG-15, MiG-17, and Su-7 fighter-bombers.
About 60 transports, including Il-14 and An-12, and 60 helicopters, including 8 Mi-6 *Hook*.
Training aircraft, some of which could be armed, made up another 120 aircraft.

AIR DEFENCE was provided both by conventional anti-aircraft guns and by 150 SA-2 *Guideline* surface-to-air missiles deployed in 25 batteries of six launchers each. These missiles were supported by a recently installed radar network and by the six squadrons of MiG-21 interceptors.

Jordan

ARMY

Total strength: 55,000.
6 infantry brigades.
3 armoured brigades.
250 tanks, including 150 M-48 *Pattons*. Also some *Centurion* tanks and 155mm howitzers.

NAVY

A few patrol craft in the Dead Sea and Gulf of Aqaba.

AIR FORCE

Total strength: 2,000.
21 *Hunter* Mk. 6 fighters and fighter-bombers.
F-104s not operational.

Syria

ARMY

Total strength: 50,000.
2 armoured brigades.
2 mechanized brigades.
5 infantry brigades.
About 400 Soviet tanks, of which only 200 were operational
Soviet artillery up to 155mm.
10 SA-2 *Guideline* sites.

NAVY

Total strength: 1,500.
6 coastal escorts.
2 minesweepers.
4 missile patrol boats (*Komar*-class).

AIR FORCE

Total strength: 9,000 men; 120 combat aircraft.
6 Il-28 light bombers.
20 MiG-21 jet interceptors.
20 MiG-19 jet interceptors.
60 MiG-17 fighter-bombers.
Transports, trainers, and helicopters.

Iraq

ARMY

Total strength: 70,000.
1 armoured division.
4 infantry divisions.
About 600 tanks, of which 400 were operational: mostly T-54 and T-34 with some *Centurions*.

NAVY

Total strength: 2,000.
Small number of MTBs and patrol vessels.

AIR FORCE

Total strength: 10,000 men; 200 combat aircraft.
10 Il-28 jet bombers.
60 MiG-21 interceptors.
50 *Hunter* Mk. 9 ground-attack.
30 MiG-17 and MiG-19 jet fighters.
20 T-52 jet *Provost* light-strike.
2 *Wessex* helicopter squadrons.
About 40 Soviet and British medium transports.

Note

* The authors are indebted to Mr David Wood, of the ISS, for permission to quote these figures, which were released to the press on 6 and 7 June.

5 The Asian Balance of Power
A Comparison with European Precedents
Adelphi Paper 44, 1968

Coral Bell

I

The transfer of concepts or techniques derived from the history of one area to the prospective future of another is necessarily a dangerous and delicate task. In this case it might seem an academic or even a mischievous one if the indigenous diplomatic traditions of Asia already provided workable answers to the security problems of that area. But though an attempt to make them do so may be read into the doctrine of non-alignment, the effort cannot claim much success. In the twelve years since the most ambitious enunciation of the doctrine, at Bandung in 1955, the 'area of peace' that non-alignment was supposed to provide in Asia has in fact been the scene of more military activity than any other part of the world, whereas the area organized on classic balance-of-power principles into two tight military coalitions, Europe, has witnessed only one minor military encounter lasting a few days, Hungary in 1956.[1] On the evidence of these years, one might say that the amoral traditions of the balance of power have done better (at least in respect of peace) for those who have lived by them than the moral aspirations of non-alignment.

One Western security-concept has admittedly been tried in Asia, to some extent in competition with non-alignment, the concept of containment, and it might be judged to have cost more, in terms of pain and death as well as money, and to have had no better success in terms of security or stability than non-alignment. But containment, a strategy which has been mistaken for a policy, is based on American assumptions which differ substantially from the European assumptions of the balance of power.

This essay will attempt to consider how far the traditional European concepts and experience can be applied to contemporary Asian security problems. It will be an Australian view in the sense that the author, as an Australian, must be conscious that her own country's efforts to provide for its future security should include some assessment of the prospects for such a balance. Perhaps there is a certain appropriateness to an Australian examination of this question, since Australians are the only group of Westerners who must remain fully and inescapably vulnerable to the diplomatic stresses arising in Asia, on whose periphery they live or die. The intellectual concepts involved are theirs by direct inheritance, and the possibility of applying them to this particular environment is more directly to their interest than that of any other group of Westerners.

The phrase 'an Asian balance of power' might be construed to mean either a balance of power intended to restrain any overweening ambitions in Asia, or a balance of power confined to Asian states (with Australians considered honorary Asians by virtue of proximity). I will consider both these interpretations, looking first at the question of what kind of balance could operate in the area, and second at the question of whether it would remain viable if non-Asian powers opted out of it. The notion of an Asian region will be held to cover the area from Pakistan east and north to Japan and Soviet Asia. There may be much to be said for regarding the Middle East as Western Asia, and for believing that it will ultimately share some of the interests and dangers of Southern Asia and Eastern Asia, but in the time-span which it is at present possible to contemplate, roughly to the late 1970s, the smaller definition of Asia seems the more useful.

Reflecting on the security history of this Asia, which is essentially an arc round the periphery of China, one must be strongly conscious not only that the notion of a power-balance is a Western importation, but that even the notion of Asia is to some extent a Western construct. There is no indigenous historical tradition of Asia as a single system of independent sovereignties in the European manner, and very little sense (until recent times) of the concept of being Asian as against being Chinese, or Indian, or Thai, or Japanese. Even now Asia remains a preoccupation of Westerners and the Westernized elite. It is not the most relevant concept for the Chinese, who live in a world divided between the revolutionaries and those whose interest is to frustrate them, so that a Bolivian or Albanian peasant is much more a brother than a Thai or Singapore capitalist. Nor for the Japanese, who live in the Pacific and cast themselves as its prosperous industrial *avant garde*. Nor for the Indians, preoccupied with the world of poverty that stretches west and south as well as east. Almost the only thing one can say about Asians as a whole is that China is a great central enigma common to all their worlds.

This centrality of the Chinese position, in geographic and demographic reality as well as in the Chinese concept of world politics, is the prime obstacle to belief in a workable Asian balance of power. As Herbert Butterfield points out, the classic concept of the European balance system was 'a kind of terrestrial counterpart of the Newtonian system of astronomy. All the various bodies, the greater and the lesser powers, were poised against each other, each exercising a kind of gravitational pull on all the rest. When one of these bodies increased its mass, therefore – when for some reason France, for example, had an undue accession of strength – the rest could recover an equilibrium only by regrouping themselves, like sets of ballet-dancers making a necessary rectification in the distances, and producing new combinations'.[2]

If there is an astronomical metaphor that fitted the traditional place of

China in the Chinese world, it is the proverb 'There can be only one sun in the sky'. The Chinese proper, the Han people, were surrounded by a solar system of quasi-assimilated non-Han peoples, imperial dependencies and vassal states. The distinction between the inner and outer zones of this universe was a distinction of time rather than kind. The autonomy of the local rulers was not a negation of Chinese power, but a particular mode of exercising it, adapting it to local circumstances. The lesser sovereigns ruled, in theory, because legitimacy was conferred on them by the ruler of China. Within this periphery, no rule was legitimate which did not have the sanction of Chinese recognition. Where there were rival factions to the succession to power in these peripheral states, the Chinese might choose between them, as they now choose between two factions in Vietnam, two in Laos or Thailand, or between many in Burma. There are clear imperial precedents, for instance, for the *Peking Review* in recent months manifesting China's displeasure at President Ne Win, and its support for the rival leadership of Ba Thein Tin and the Burma Communist Party.

The only Western approximation of the process of growth of Chinese power and influence, from the original base on the Yellow River to a world-state co-extensive with its own world, would be the growth of the Roman world-state. Even this is not a very good parallel, for the Chinese world-state was much the more comprehensive and long-lasting, and the Romans remained well aware of rival Asian civilizations, some older than their own. Hume's argument that the growth of the Roman world-state might be ascribed to the failure of Rome's neighbours to operate a balance-of-power system against it seems readily applicable to the Chinese experience.[3]

It may of course be that consideration of the imperial past has not much relevance to consideration of the future of Chinese foreign policy. But China has been a very tenacious power: tenacious of its people (the descendant in the male line of a Chinese does not become non-Chinese, even in generations of residence abroad, unless China has signed a renunciatory treaty with his country of birth); tenacious, at least in intention, of territory acquired (an area won for civilization – that is for China – was not to be considered permanently lost, even if temporarily out of control); tenacious of old scores (recently the *Peking Review* has been using a slogan 'Blood debts must be paid in blood', and there is not much doubt that the present government of China believes, reasonably enough, that it has a good many such debts to collect).

It may seem excessively pessimistic to argue that the unfamiliarity of the concept to the power against whom the system would be directed for the foreseeable future (for China is at least at the moment the only Asian power in any position to develop overweening ambitions) is a serious obstacle to its workability. But one should not underrate the degree to which international politics runs on a system of expectations. Even in Europe, the balance of power worked because of a belief that it would work, and because of the will to work it. All the participants, even those against whom it was being operated, accepted it as part of the normal order of the world. In this matter

Russia was entirely European, and Stalin a full inheritor of the convention, much more so than Roosevelt. One might cite the well-known instance of his casual tick of acquiescence in Churchill's proposal on the division of influence in the Balkans, and his failure to resist British enforcement of this understanding in the action against the Greek insurgency of 1944. At a later stage he no doubt made efforts to tilt the balance rather more in Russia's favour, in Greece as elsewhere. But there was nothing incompatible with tradition in that, and he withdrew at all points where Western reaction was strong enough to indicate the possibility of an overturn of the system.

The centuries of Russian experience as a full participant in, and at times a considerable imperial beneficiary of, the European balance-of-power game was an underrated factor of great importance in the restoration of the post-war balance in Europe. One might certainly say that Soviet power approximated more and more to the traditional diplomacy of Russia as a great power, and contained less and less revolutionary fervour, from the time of Stalin's assumption of the role of chief decision-maker. Some of his decisions no doubt represented misjudgments of the balance of forces, for instance the Nazi-Soviet Pact in 1939 and the 1947–48 Soviet policies in Eastern Europe; but at least they were misjudgments within a convention familiar to the decision-maker, and accepted by him, on the level of operational policy if not on that of declaratory policy. It is only when one compares the difficulties that would be involved in constructing a balance *vis-à-vis* China with those operating in the balance *vis-à-vis* Russia that the importance of the other side's familiarity with the game becomes apparent.

As Butterfield points out, the European system depended on refined thought, careful contrivance and elaborate artifice.[4] It involved respect for the system of independent sovereignties *as such*, the belief that such a system represented in some way an order of justice in the world, and that it was in the long-term interest of all participants that it be preserved. One need hardly point out how dismally far these concepts are from the contemporary Chinese doctrine about the world-conflict, in which the present system of states is seen as an order of injustice, due to go into the ashcan of history within the foreseeable future. It is true that a similar view to the present Chinese one was associated with the early post-revolutionary period of Soviet foreign policy, but in the Chinese case the countervailing tradition of balance-of-power policy has been much thinner and less favourable. The Chinese were victims rather than beneficiaries of the system: the best one could say about it from the viewpoint of Chinese historic experience was that the balance of power among its European predators operated to some extent to inhibit their inroads on Chinese territory and sovereignty. And even at that, one would have to add that the inhibitions were not very firm or effective.

These arguments might lead one to conclude not only that it will be difficult to construct any kind of viable balance in Asia but that it will be impossible, since in the last analysis Chinese acceptance of the system is essential to its functioning. Certainly if there were any more promising horse to run in the security stakes, one would incline to enter it instead. But on recent historical experience the other candidates look even less promising. Moreover, there is one parallel case of an ingrained resistance to balance-of-power concepts which may be cited as evidence of the possibility of a change of historic attitudes. The case is that of the United States. If one contrasts the wholehearted repudiation of the concept by American statesmen in the early twentieth century (e.g. Woodrow Wilson) with its endorsement by some of the more candid Washington policy-makers at present, one is struck by the transformation which a few years' experience of the burdens of the dominant power can produce.[5]

This American change has to some extent been disguised by the confusions which exist between the notion of containment and that of a balance of power, and these confusions, like a good deal else about containment, originated in the American experience with Europe. That is to say, a misnaming or misunderstanding of what had been achieved in Europe was the basis of a mistake about what should be attempted in Asia. What was really achieved for Europe after 1949 was an overall balance of power which kept diplomatic relationships stable. But largely out of deference to historic American reservations about the notion of a balance of power, this achievement was tactfully called 'containment'. Insofar as the word 'containment' appeared to imply a military line which could realistically be construed as denying the adversary powers the prospect of advance, it was never a convincing description of the position. The force goals of NATO never were quite attained: they came to seem less relevant because of the growth of optimism about the stability of the balance. And this balance was not a true European one in the sense of being confined to the European powers or achieved entirely in the European theatre. It was a compote in which the overall ascendancy of American power more than compensated for the local deficiencies of NATO. Of course the local forces were important for various reasons, but it was not on them that, for instance, the security of Berlin or the general crystallization of the *status quo* depended.

The reasons why it was preferable, from the point of view of American policy-makers, to refer to this very substantial achievement as 'containment' rather than as 'an effective balance-of-power coalition committed (theoretically) to a forward defence-line' owe something no doubt to a humane tendency towards shorthand, as well as to the historic American distrust of balance-of-power arrangements. But it is ironic that a concept whose originator (George Kennan) came to dislike the way it was interpreted, and which was never quite an accurate description even of the situation in which its success was real though misdescribed, came to be the dominant concept in an area, Asia, to which it was far less appropriate.

II

It seems unnecessary to go over the reasons why containment was always a doubtful and prospectively expensive notion for Asia.[6] In view of the present deep division in America over the war in Vietnam, which by implication affects the whole future of American responsibilities and commitments in Asia, it may be more useful to examine the other side of the current American ambivalence: the factors making for involvement.

When one examines the decisions made in America's Asian policy over the rather more than a century in which she has concerned herself there, the policy choices often continue to seem baffling, even when one knows the acknowledged reasons for them, because of a sort of disproportion between causes and effects. That is, if one coldly considers the actual level of American economic interests or direct strategic interests in Asia at various times since the mid-nineteenth century, it is difficult to construe them as vital enough to warrant the actual historical record of America's readiness to become involved in Asia, as against her chariness about involvement in Europe or the Middle East or Africa. In each of the last three wars in which the United States has been engaged – Vietnam, Korea and World War II – the precipitating incident has been Asian. Only with regard to Latin America have American Administrations shown the same sort of readiness to act militarily. And this has also been true with regard to lesser kinds of diplomatic involvement; though for the whole period, except possibly a very few years at the peak point of Japanese power, it has been extremely difficult to believe that Asia contained any forces authentically dangerous to American security.

This is no longer true, and thus one must argue that the reasons for future commitments are much more real and powerful than those which produced past commitments. There may be two views about the wisdom of Mr McNamara speaking, as someone has said, as a sort of public relations officer for the Chinese nuclear missile, but his forecast of Chinese ability by the mid-1970s to strike a considerable number of American cities does represent an entirely new level of Asian power to 'hit America where it lives'. If the United States has involved herself so readily in the past against some rather shadowy threats, it is difficult to believe that she will cease to do so in the period when the threat has at last assumed substance.

Furthermore, it seems likely that Asia will provide a larger proportion of total American foreign-policy preoccupations in the future than in the past, because the area of contest to which it has often had to yield priority, Europe, seems unlikely to put in a competitive bid for so serious a diversion of resources – goods and attention – as it did in 1917 or 1939 or 1949. Latin America is always a potential competitor for American attention and resources, but, one would think, will not be able to outbid Asia within the next decade or two, since it contains no power of anything like China's potential capacity to be dangerous. The Middle East or Africa could conceivably be competitors, but only if the Soviet Union decides to abandon the advantages of the *détente* with the United States, which looks extremely unlikely at the moment. The caution of Russian policy in and after the Arab–Israeli war of June 1967 must be interpreted as determination to avoid any confrontation with the United States, even at the cost of renouncing some possible extra Soviet diplomatic gains in the Arab world. Thus the probability of the United States having her attention compulsorily wrenched away from Asia by Russian initiatives elsewhere seems comparatively low, and the claims of Asia on American attention are correspondingly more likely to remain dominant. The chief question mark over this assumption is the possibility of a major success for China's 'people's war' theory somewhere in Latin America or Africa.

Assuming the likelihood of continued American preoccupation with Asia, one may also have to assume that it will continue to prove difficult for American policy-makers to move from the intuitive sense that the national interest is involved in Asia to an adequate definition of the nature of that interest. The reason why America's Asian policy has presented a rather dishevelled and disoriented image, like the feathers of a bird caught in passing in a brisk game of shuttlecock, is that the forces between whom the Asian policy options are batted about in Washington have been unfortunately well matched in skill and moral zeal. They have been, on the one side, the spokesmen for the very strong American paternalist tradition with respect to the old China, who are still outraged by what happened in 1949–50 in China and Korea, and, on the other, the spokesmen for the equally strong American anti-colonialist liberal tradition in policy.

The liberal tradition has been, and will remain, forceful enough to prevent acceptance of an imperial role in the European manner, which means among other things refusal or evasion of the constructive aspects of imperialism, and this in turn tends to militate against the general effectiveness of American policy. In the case of Vietnam or Laos, for instance, economic aid without strings or controls was finely non-imperialist in theory. In practice, since it tended to prevent effective American action to combat local corruption and inflation, it was perhaps more damaging to the fabric of the local societies than straight imperial control; it increased rather than diminished social frictions, thereby preventing the societies concerned from reaching enough cohesion to be able to defend themselves effectively against the forces which look to Hanoi. Similarly, in the case of the 'pacification' policy in Vietnam, American inability to take over the full decision-making role of an imperial power has meant that most of the labour of those engaged in the effort has been lost through local political or administrative inadequacies.

The necessity of defining the American purpose in terms of the pieties of anti-colonial liberalism has imposed an undue faith in the forces of nationalism, or rather an oversimplified interpretation of its nature. The American conventional wisdom on Asia included the proposition that 'the nationalists' (as against the old European administrators) were natural 'bulwarks against the spread of Communism'. Bulwark is a word that produces a reassuringly solid and monolithic mental image. But 'the nationalists' are not much like that. No one can doubt the reality and persistence of Asian nationalism, but it is the persistence of a sandbank rather than of a bulwark. Its elements may be almost indestructible, but it will disperse, re-form, change shape, according to the governing currents. This adaptability is a source of strength to the nationalists themselves, but has not proved very convenient as a foundation for American efforts. China in the grip of the cultural revolution is perhaps demonstration enough that a Communist government not only can secure the adhesion of nationalist feeling; it can turn the utmost virulence of nationalism to its own political purposes. So the American assumption since 1954 that Western interests must be complementary to those of 'the nationalists' (as classified in Washington) has been a source of confusion in policy-making.

These difficulties in defining the American interest in Asia will probably persist, since the conflicting traditions which have prevented clarity of definition in the past will probably persist. A definition in terms of old-fashioned great-power responsibility is still not possible, because it would be a violation of the anti-colonial tradition. A definition in terms of 'helping free governments survive' tends to look rather unconvincing when the actual nature of the political situations concerned is examined. A definition in terms of power-bargaining and tacit agreement on spheres of influence is difficult, because of the American convention of diplomacy as a sphere of moral action. Even a definition in terms of the balance of power is somewhat at odds with the normal political vocabulary of most American leaders: it perhaps must still be reserved to the level of the Under-Secretary of State rather than the President.

Thus it may be that the objectives of policy will have to remain swaddled in a certain amount of protective verbal flannel. However, the strategies by which these objectives may be pursued must be discussed, since their respective costs are going to affect American domestic politics profoundly. I said earlier that containment was a strategy which had been mistaken for a policy. What I had in mind by this phrase is that to define a policy is to define an end; to define a strategy is to define a means. I am not implying that any rational American policy-maker really assumes that military containment at its present level of costs for the United States is an end in itself. But since (for the reasons mentioned earlier) the ends of American policy in Asia have not been susceptible of an agreed definition, the word containment has had to stand as a sort of all-purpose compendium, packing together ends and means in tactful imprecision. The prestige of the success in Europe of a policy which also was described as containment has helped to provide a vague, rosy, came-the-dawn prospect of an ultimate stability in Asia beyond the present struggle, and an ultimate mellowing of the adversary power, like that of the Soviet Union in Europe.[7]

These hopeful assumptions and analogies need some examination. Is containment on the present pattern 'cost-effective' as a strategy in Asia? What is its interaction with the strategy being operated on 'the other side of the hill'? On what conditions or with what adjuncts could it produce any kind of viable Asian balance of power? If such a balance were produced, could it remain viable without the proliferation of nuclear weapons among other Asian powers?

The first two of these questions may be considered together, since I would argue that containment considered as an American strategy *vis-à-vis* China not only emerges very badly from examination by the criterion of cost-effectiveness; it also offers 'the other side of the hill' the situation in which its own strategy becomes most cost-effective.

Looking first at the American side, one must of course concede that the financial element in costs is not of decisive importance to the American economy. The proportion of GNP now being devoted to the war in Vietnam is about 3.3 per cent, and despite some awkward difficulties of inflation and taxation, this could not in itself be politically crucial in an economy of the size and power of America's. The politically effective form of costs are the casualty figures and their domestic repercussions. These have only been really serious since President Johnson's decision on 'Koreanization' of the war in February 1965, and in that time have already done more damage to the electoral prospects of the President and the Democratic Party than anything since Truman's inability to wind up the Korean war. Incidentally, Truman was of course much closer to an armistice in Korea at the time the Democrats lost the 1952 election than Johnson is to an armistice or even a truce in Vietnam at present.

To these human and political costs for America one must add diplomatic costs of two sorts: first, costs in terms of the American alliance structure in Europe (which arise chiefly from the war not being within the moral consensus of the European allies), and, second, costs in terms of the *détente* with the Soviet Union. One may well feel that the *détente* is a growth of such weedlike sturdiness that even the American engagement in Vietnam has only slowed its development, not endangered its survival. But the Chinese charges against the Soviet Union of 'collusion' with the United States, which get their substance from the *détente*, are lent embarrassing emotional overtones in the Communist world by the fact of American hostilities against North Vietnam, and thus the development of the relationship becomes a very mixed blessing to Russian decision-makers.

Finally, one may add the domestic social costs to America in terms of the alienation of a considerable part of her electorate – mostly young middle-class voters or future voters – from the official image of their country's purposes in the world. This segment of the American electorate or potential electorate may not be numerically strong enough to affect the Presidential election result, but it is not therefore to be disregarded. It is never a light thing for a government to lose the confidence of young articulate opinion: European governments did so in the early 1930s, largely through their apparent wrong-headedness in handling the depression and the rise of fascism, and the consequences of that alienation or desertion are not altogether worked out even now. The United States suffers in the eyes of her European allies and those of many of her own people from what one may call the David and Goliath syndrome: she finds herself seen as Goliath, despite her own injured and to some extent well-founded assumption that her function is really that of a Samson holding up the pillars of the temple.

Whatever one's view of this moral alienation from American official purposes, it must be conceded that, all in all, containment on the present pattern has been a high-cost strategy, and that the full account is not yet rendered. The official Washington spokesmen for policy would tend to counter this charge by claiming that it is also a high-effectiveness strategy, but the arguments here seem to rest on some desperately unconvincing psychological judgments about the other side, rather than real calculations of military or political or diplomatic effects. The case, as presented for instance by President Johnson's chief adviser on international affairs, Mr Rostow, is that defeat in Vietnam will have a profoundly traumatic effect on the Chinese decision-makers, rather as the Cuba missile crisis did on Khrushchev, and will be seen as a conclusive defeat for the whole Chinese theory of people's war.[8] He has even implied that the war, if seen through to victory by the United States, could be 'the last war'. This somewhat millenarian view appears to owe rather more to faith than to such evidence as is available on Chinese attitudes. It is true that whereas Hanoi was very close to an actual military victory in February 1965, it cannot any longer hope for one in the same time-scale, now that its combat adversaries include the United States. It is also true that when a sufficient amount of American resources are poured into them, some unpromising Asian societies may be transformed into reasonably solid and defensible Western bridgeheads in Asia, as witness Taiwan and South Korea.

Conceding these points, one must still be reserved about reasoning from an effective defeat of the insurgency in South Vietnam (and even that is remote enough), or a North Vietnamese decision to quit (which is remoter still), to an effective defeat for the theory of people's war, and a consequent Chinese abandonment of hopes for the 'countryside of the world'. Surely, of all political decision-makers, those imbued with a guerrilla ethos (like the Chinese), and dedicated to maintaining it against their one-time friends (the Russians) as well as against their foes, are the least likely to assume that defeat in one campaign, or on one battle-field, means the loss of the struggle?

But the more important point is that the theory of people's war is for Chinese decision-makers essentially a theory about the *absorption of the adversary's resources*. They have said this with great clarity on several occasions, most recently for instance in the *Peking Review* of 8 September 1967, in an article which ascribes to the Vietnamese forces the pinning-down of 700,000 American troops, and describes this as 'a miracle in the annals of war'. The increasing scale of American effort is thus seen as an index of success in the long-range conflict, even if (improbably) it had to be construed as a portent of failure on this particular battlefield. In Lin Piao's words, 'The more successful the development of people's war in a given region, the larger the number of US forces that can be pinned down and defeated there'.[9] Thus, on a Maoist view, even a military stalemate in Vietnam, or a reduction of the insurgency to the first stage, need not be considered as a defeat, since the essential fact would remain that an insurgency based primarily on the resources of a peasant society of 17 million people (North Vietnam), supported by only moderate amounts of arms supplies from the USSR and China, had absorbed American resources to this spectacular level.

If one extrapolates from the Vietnam situation to other potential theatres of conflict on the same pattern, assuming a similar level of costs for the United States, it looks like a blueprint for Chinese victory by military proxy. This is of course the whole point of the phrase about 'destroying the enemy by drawing him in deeper to drown in the sea of people's war'. There is an old Chinese saying that the most successful strategist is the general who wins his battle without actually fighting it. The Maoist adaptation requires the battles to be fought elsewhere, by someone else, preferably at quite a distance from China. (Chinese enthusiasm for 'people's war' situations in Latin America or Africa is more visibly wholehearted than for those in Asia, a nice expansion of the other old Chinese maxim about using barbarians to control barbarians.)

Unfortunately, American policy, in casting the North Vietnamese as military proxies for China, by that very decision made them so, without any choice on their own part. The American decision preceded the Chinese doctrine by eleven years. It can be dated from Mr Dulles's assumption, after the Geneva Conference in 1954, that any extension of the area of Ho Chi Minh's control in Vietnam (even one achieved by the scheduled elections) would mean a dangerous enlargement of the area of China's effective power. To question this assumption is not to doubt the reality of Ho's Communism. But if Communists in China can fall into a frenzy of chauvinistic nationalism against a neighbour, the Soviet Union, against whom they have some historic grievances, what reason is there for doubting that Communists in North Vietnam could cherish similar nationalistic resentments against a neighbour, China, against whom they have more solid and longer-established national grievances? A military defeat for North Vietnam, achieved at the cost of investing more than half a million American troops for perhaps five years against the forces of a small peasant society (which is the *most* favourable outcome for America on the present concept) is the sort of American success which ought logically to inspire the Chinese to murmur 'Another such victory and they are undone'. The only end to the hostilities which would represent a diplomatic defeat for Peking (as against Hanoi) is one which provided for some detachment of North Vietnam from China. Thus, the American decision to fight on so unfavourable a battlefield as Vietnam has maximized the cost-effectiveness of the Chinese strategy: effectiveness on the Chinese theory being measurable by the scale of investment of military resources forced upon the United States, and costs in this case being diminished by the Soviet Union's need, for the sake of her standing in the Communist world, to supply the more sophisticated part of the North Vietnamese armoury.

III

These quibbles about past and irreparable decisions may seem academic. There is a school of thought which would say: perhaps this was an ill-chosen strategy, but the Americans are now well beyond the point of no return; perhaps Vietnam was an unfavourable battlefield, but once it was chosen (or rather accepted), no retreat was possible without enormous damage to the whole American position in the struggle for the world, and even some complementary damage to the Russian position, in the sense of conceding a victory to China.

Though this is the strongest of the arguments against any change of strategy, it is not necessarily conclusive. One may concede, as I would, that any retreat on the part of the United States from her present strategy will probably damage the American alliance structure in Asia, and yet hold that this loss or damage will be less than the prospective 'opportunity costs', diplomatic and otherwise, accruing from persistence in that strategy. This is particularly the case if one is thinking of containment as a means towards the end of constructing a balance of power.

A balance-of-power policy can be effectively pursued only if the leader of the alliance will agree to define the common interest in a fashion consonant with the other members' definitions of their respective national interests. Further, these definitions must take into account not only the estimated benefit to the national security of each country concerned, but the level of costs for this extra protection. It should also take into account, since national decisions, despite Mr McNamara, are not yet taken by cost-effectiveness analysis alone, a sort of international consensus on what is morally licit in relations between states.

The present American strategy does more or less meet these three criteria for a certain number of powers: Australia and New Zealand, Thailand, Philippines, South Korea. And apart from these governments which are in overt agreement with American policy and/or strategy, there is also, one must admit, a considerable amount of disguised or covert agreement among Asian decision-makers that their countries are in some sense 'fringe beneficiaries' of the American effort. But it is not possible for them to say so, for reasons of electoral tact or such. Decision-makers may be prepared to give a private, or some a public, assent to a policy such as inhibiting the further growth of Chinese influence in Southern Asia, but they cannot endorse the strategy through which it is pursued if, like the Vietnam war, it lies too far outside the moral consensus, or looks too costly an operation to become involved in. The way round this problem is not to abandon the policy, but to reframe the strategy so that it fits the moral consensus.

The other main argument used to resist any effort to divorce the hostilities in Vietnam from the theory of people's war is the argument that, in effect, all battlefields are equally unfavourable for the West, and that if there has to be a test case it might as well be Vietnam. The first of these assumptions is not only defeatist but so totally at odds with observed reality that once it is made explicit it seems hardly worth refuting. The 'third world' is not all of a piece: its constituent societies perhaps differ more radically from each other than developed societies do. Tolstoy once observed that happy families are all alike, but unhappy families are each unhappy in their own way. Something of the sort is true as regards developed and underdeveloped countries. Even such close Asian neighbours as Thailand, Laos, Cambodia and Vietnam differ profoundly from each other in the political and sociological conditions which affect the feasibility or level of prospective success of 'people's war'. The challenger has, of course, always some choice of battlefields and weapons, but to assume that one has to meet him on any battlefield he chooses is not necessarily the soundest mode of generalship.

Unfortunately one is also here involved with the chief distinction in moral feeling between the American doctrine of containment and the European doctrine of the balance of power. The territorial aspect of containment – the resolution to deny territory to the adversary power – may be justified to decision-makers as a strategic necessity: it is also presented at the level of public debate as a moral duty to the people whose country is being contested, and it is felt as such by many decision-makers. One may argue that such a moral judgment is simplistic, that to insist on a small power's right to remain a battlefield is a rather ambivalent form of loyalty to an ally, and that, as Senator Robert Kennedy has bravely pointed out, to choose someone else's country as a preferable battlefield to one's own, which is the cruder reasoning behind containment, takes some moral justifying.[10] Yet there is a difficult transition from such arguments to a decision to allow the most effective local political force to make good its ascendancy in Vietnam. The absence of any such debate in the traditional balance-of-power approach to small states was one aspect of its amorality: it was also one reason for its flexibility, and its success in mitigating conflicts between the major powers. Comparing the Asian situation with its European parallel, one must concede that the tacit understanding that people would have to compound as best they might with the dominant power in their diplomatic sphere was an unavowed condition of stabilization there. Moral sympathy in the West for Hungarians or East Germans who found it difficult to live with their respective regimes was real enough, but it was not allowed to disturb the dominant powers' accommodation with each other in 1956 or 1961.

However, it is no doubt political stamina in Hanoi and Washington, rather than moral feeling (though the two are not totally unconnected), which will be decisive. Truong Chinh once remarked, 'Time is our best strategist'. If his expectations are answered in the foreseeable future, one would assume that the road to settlement will run through Moscow and bypass Peking, but that the factors of change will be those of American political opinion in a Presidential election year, or just afterwards, so that 1968–69 may prove as important a turning point as 1952–53.

The aftermath of any settlement in Vietnam (other than an improbable degree of American military victory) will almost certainly include a strong American impulse to avoid further involvement on the Asian mainland, as was the case after Korea. One must anticipate a swing towards what is known as the offshore or peripheral strategy, which would base itself on sea- and air-power and a foothold on islands down the Asian coast. Indeed, American policy-makers have spoken in the past as if a winding-up of the engagement in Vietnam would enable them to quit the Asian mainland altogether, and though it is difficult to reconcile this forecast with, for instance, the development of the situation in Thailand, the strength and the persistence of the desire for disengagement cannot be denied. The impulse is naturally strongest while the memory of some traumatic Asian encounter is still vivid, as after the 1949 collapse in China (Acheson's incautious 1950 definition of the defence perimeter) or the initial policy formulations of the Eisenhower Administration in 1953–54 ('instant and massive retaliation at points of our own choosing').

So far this impulse has been constantly defeated by the fact that no one has ever produced a convincing demonstration – or even a convincing theory – of precisely how influence may be wielded over the sort of small-scale actions which actually change the pattern of power in Asia, by lurking near the coast in the Seventh Fleet or equipping the island chain with *Minuteman* missiles, and though local forces might in certain circumstances prove adequate, not much attention has so far been paid to the diplomatic preconditions necessary to make them so. The real problem on the mainland may be described as military-territorial attrition, a process whereby the fiat of an established government ceases to run in portions of the countryside, as is already the case in about half of South Vietnam and two-thirds of Laos, and which could conceivably become the case in north-eastern Thailand, and in much of Cambodia, Burma, Malaysia or even West Bengal. Once this process in rural areas has gone far enough, securing a change in the city-based political elite may require no more than the tap that breaks a beam hollowed out by dry rot. A declaratory policy based on peripheral strategic concepts was tried in the original 'massive retaliation' speech of early 1954 and in the original notion, as put by Mr Dulles in 1954, of the military sanctions behind SEATO. In neither case were the results encouraging.

So, though this certainly has the advantage of being a low-cost strategy, it must also on the evidence be regarded as a low-effectiveness strategy, if one remains concerned with inhibiting the extension of Chinese power. As a means of promoting a viable balance of power in Asia, it seems almost as unpromising as the present containment operation, though for the opposite reason, in that it offers too low a schedule of prospective effectiveness, as against the present strategy's too high schedule of costs.

There is, however, a third possible choice for the United States. I will call it the 'redoubt' concept, because though it has something in common with what is called the 'enclave' strategy in General Gavin's formulation,[11] it does not necessarily assume a territorial commitment in South Vietnam. The 'enclave' strategy offers a lower schedule of military and moral costs than the present American line, but it would not necessarily make a diplomatic accommodation with Hanoi easier, unless there is a very surprising change of heart in Ho's government. Thus it would not necessarily conduce to building a viable balance of power, since that objective requires an outcome in Vietnam which shows *both* that the American interest remains committed to the security of the small powers on the Asian mainland (which is the issue on which the peripheral strategy is unconvincing) *and* that the system can be maintained without too exorbitant a schedule of costs for those participating, including the United States (which is the issue on which the present strategy has become unconvincing).

The point of a redoubt is that if its area is well selected, it should provide the defender with favourable conditions for resisting further encroachment, diplomatically, politically and morally, as well as militarily. Western military effort in Asia will continue to look morally anomalous unless it is based on a reasonably clear consensus, in the local societies concerned, about the nature of the political system they prefer to live with.

Thailand and Malaysia-Singapore are in a different category from Vietnam in this respect. Their political elites have not suffered the same sort of fragmentation as in Vietnam. Such charismatic leadership as exists is on the Western side, whereas in Vietnam it has fallen to Ho Chi Minh. The societies concerned are a long way above the Asian level in rates of economic growth. They can be regarded as candidates, with any luck, for a Japanese-style progression towards approximations of Western prosperity, rather than as candidates for the Chinese road of revolutionary austerity. A central redoubt of these Western-oriented states, cushioned from actual contact with China by a neutral Burma and (hopefully) a neutralization system covering all three of the ex-Indo-China states, could have some political and diplomatic stability to it, though a considerable input of Western military resources would certainly remain necessary for a decade or more, and an American guarantee, like that to Japan, over an even longer period. Analogies from European diplomatic experience should not be pushed too far in the Asian context, but the role of Malaysia and Thailand in such a system would be somewhat akin to the role of the Low Countries in the traditional British balance-of-power approach to continental Europe.

One of the dilemmas of diplomatic timing is that an alliance constructed too soon may prove counterproductive, by setting up irritants, as SEATO did, whereas one constructed too late may be powerless to restrain a situation which has already gathered momentum towards disaster, as was the case with the British diplomatic efforts in Europe in March 1939. But occasionally decision-makers do manage to recognize the right moment to make a leap for it, as the European leaders did in 1948–49 in the formation of NATO. The traumatic effect of losing an area of contest can sometimes be very helpful in producing this moment of recognition. Conceivably there might emerge a close parallel between, on the one hand, the connection of Czechoslovakia in

1948 with the balance-of-power coalition formalized in NATO in 1949, and, on the other, possible events in Vietnam in 1968 and the moment for a similar sort of initiative in Asia.

From the point of view of the major Asian powers, opinion is now much more propitious for such a development than it was at the false start of 1954. The highwater mark of the Asian optimism according to which no power from within the Asian world offered any threat, and Westerners had no future diplomatic role in Asia, was at Bandung in 1955: it has been ebbing, though not steadily, ever since, and is beginning to be, for some leaders, no more than a nostalgic memory from their age of diplomatic innocence. The Prime Ministers of small states like Singapore are more able to be candid about this change than the leaders of larger states, but no one can be in doubt about the transformation that has overtaken Indian attitudes towards China since 1962, or Indonesian attitudes towards China since the *coup* in 1965. Even the ambivalences of the Japanese attitude have been tending towards resolution in a direction unfavourable to China since the full stresses of the cultural revolution began to make themselves apparent in 1967. Some of the manifestations of the cultural revolution appear to have shaken the faith even of such True Believers, originally, in the doctrine of redemption by non-alignment alone as Burma and Cambodia.

IV

The timing of the construction of a balance-of-power coalition is in the last analysis dependent on the adversary power contemplated: only *that* power can be an adequate architect of the consensus of alarm on which the coalition needs to be based. Thus Stalin in his 1947–48 policies created the essential consensus of alarm which formalized itself in NATO. Possibly Mao in the cultural revolution will prove to have at least dug the foundations for a similar consensus *vis-à-vis* China.

To assume that this pre-condition for constructing a balance may exist in Southern Asia by 1968–69 does not, however, mean assuming that Asian decision-makers will be as deft at taking the leap as the European governments were in 1948. The Europeans were reviving their own old tradition, with the help of some financial and military resuscitation techniques from the United States. The Asians would be borrowing a tradition which the European Left long told them they must regard with moral disdain, and the American idealists used to tell them they must view with alarm. There are, it is true, some analogous diplomatic devices in the traditions of a few Asian powers, especially India in the 'mandala' theory of Kautilya.[12] The Japanese in the early twentieth century also showed considerable interest in the notion of a power-balance in their part of the world.[13] But the only state more or less in the area which can be regarded in this respect as a full participant in the Western tradition (by inheritance from Britain) is Australia, which is not of sufficient diplomatic weight or leverage for the task of coalition-making. It can be a useful lieutenant, but not a principal.

When one contemplates the Asian powers who might be considered capable of making up an exclusively Asian balance *vis-à-vis* China if it were a matter only of material factors like population, economic development, size of armed forces, ability to construct advanced weapons and so on, one is brought up against the overriding importance of non-material factors like political will. India is populous, but one South-East Asian Prime Minister has described her, not unjustly, as 'a banyan tree which does not want to shelter anyone'. Japan is reaching levels of wealth and technological advancement which will in theory shortly make her the third power of the world, but she is still profoundly quietist in international politics, and should perhaps be allowed to remain so. Indonesia is a dangerous enigma. The small powers – Thailand, Malaysia, Singapore, Australia, the Philippines – may be useful cogs when larger powers have provided the main machinery, but they cannot themselves construct it. Pakistan, in the nature of the system, must see her interests lying in the continuance of the present tacit alliance with China, and this may be her most useful role. As I said earlier, the prime difficulty in believing in the viability of an Asian balance is the difficulty of believing in its acceptance even over the long term by China. But it may bring this distant prospect at least marginally closer if China is allotted some assets in the system, such as an ally, who might also help along the process of communication. Any member of the society of states needs to acquire some diplomatic investments it finds valuable before its activities can be inhibited by the threat of losing them.

But all in all one must concede that, unaided, the Asian powers must look like a rope of sand in relation to China for the next decade or so. There is between them no diplomatic cohesion, or joint political will, or tradition of alliance and military co-operation, or power to make joint decision, that can foreseeably be expected to match China's ability to make her own decisions. This disparity, sometimes called the 'decision gap', is quite normal in the relation between a single large power and a countervailing alliance, but it is particularly striking in this case because of the newness of Asian states to this line of diplomatic effort.[14]

The implication of this fact seems to me to be that the construction and initial operating of a balance of power *vis-à-vis* China would be too heavy a task for the Asian states alone. The prospect of success would depend on involving one of the powers of the central balance, probably the United States, though if the Soviet Union were inclined to the task she would have many advantages in undertaking it. Nor are incentives altogether lacking, for Chinese interests compete more directly with Soviet ones than with American, already in ideology and potentially in territory.

However, for the time being one must assume that the only probable outside sponsoring power is the United States, with possibly some minor help from Britain in the Indian Ocean area.[15] To revert again to the comparison with the process by which the balance of power coalition was built to cover the European situation, it must be noted that the Asian powers are in fact less competent militarily and diplomatically in relation to China than the West European powers were in relation to the Soviet Union in the initial period there, say 1949–55; that their consensus must be expected to be slower in making itself effective, since they have no similar tradition of alliance diplomacy; and that China is far more advanced in nuclear weaponry *vis-à-vis* Asia than the Soviet Union was then in similar weaponry *vis-à-vis* Europe (which already had one actual and one clear prospective nuclear power). On all the signs, therefore, one would have to suppose that the Asian members of the coalition would take longer in getting on to their own feet than the European ones did. In the European case the reassertion of independence might perhaps be dated at 1958, so that allowing a similar ten-year transition period, one would not expect a viable Asian balance before the end of the 1970s.

There remains the central question, of whether a balance of power *vis-à-vis* a nuclear-armed China can be kept viable by Asian participants alone, unless some of them are also nuclear powers. Ultimately one is faced by a choice between evils: either the costs and risks of the Western powers remaining in the Asian balance, at least as last-ditch nuclear guarantors, or else the costs and risks of nuclear proliferation in Asia, first to India and Japan, and later perhaps to other powers. To my mind the dangers of nuclear proliferation in Asia are far greater and less susceptible to control than the alternative dangers, and therefore the national interests of the powers of the central balance ought logically to require them to remain committed to that area, in the hope of reducing the possibilities of disaster. Unfortunately this is not a situation likely to be governed solely by the rational choice of lesser evils. As in Europe, nationalist feeling tends to incite the local powers concerned to acquire their own nuclear weapons, and weariness of the burden of involvement tends to lead the powers of the central balance to opt out.

Here again the deciding vote, in a sense, will belong to the adversary power. The assumption that the appropriate balance *vis-à-vis* China is a regional balance made up exclusively of Asian powers is based on an unconscious premise that China is, and is likely to remain, just a regional power with primarily Asian interests. This is a premise most readily adopted by Europe-oriented analysts who do not take China very seriously even now. But it was not the assumption that the Chinese made about China's place in the world, even in the days of her weakness under the Manchus and the Nationalists. Most certainly it is not the assumption they now make about the proper and natural status of China, and her revolutionary destiny. On the contrary, there could hardly be a more thorough-going claim to universality than that made for the thoughts of Mao Tse-tung.

The strategic doctrine of the 'countryside of the world' is not a doctrine for expanding China's power in Asia. It is a doctrine about how the 'cities of the world' – i.e. the industrialized states, including those of Western Europe as well as North America – may be subjugated or undermined by the subsistence peasantries of Asia and Africa and Latin America. It is a doctrine which looks to bringing down the entire present structure of the society of states, in the interests of a concept of revolutionary justice. Whatever one's views about the international division of labour, it hardly seems reasonable to suppose that the business of coping with so ambitious a project is a matter for a regional grouping. Thus if the reality of China's operational policy, when she moves beyond her present nominal nuclear status, bears any resemblance to her present view of her role in world politics, the dominant powers of the central balance will automatically find themselves involved.

Notes

1. Even this was not quite a military encounter in the conventional sense, but rather a military suppression of a city-based insurgency.
2. 'The Balance of Power', in Herbert Butterfield and Martin Wight, eds, *Diplomatic Investigations* (London: Allen & Unwin, 1966), p. 132.
3. 'Of the Balance of Power' in *Essays Moral, Political and Literary* (1752).
4. *Op. cit.*, p. 147.
5. See, for instance, a speech by the Under-Secretary of State for Political Affairs, Eugene V. Rostow, on 11 September 1967, in which he says not only that the United States shares with Europe responsibility for maintaining a balance of power in the world, but that the first task of those who want peace in Vietnam is to build and secure a reasonable balance of power.
6. For an admirable account, see David P. Mozingo, 'Containment in Asia Reconsidered', *World Politics*, April 1967; reprinted in *Survival*, July 1967.
7. See, for example, a lecture by Mr W. W. Rostow, President Johnson's chief adviser on international security affairs, reported in *The Times*, 24 February 1967.
8. *Ibid.*
9. *Long Live the Victory of the People's War!*, first published in September 1965, and since republished in various texts, including Samuel B. Griffith, *Peking and People's Wars* (London: Pall Mall, 1966), p. 102.
10. Speech reported in *The New York Times*, 27 November 1967.
11. See *The New York Times*, 4 February 1966.
12. See John W. Spellman, *Political Theory of Ancient India* (Oxford: Clarendon Press, 1964), pp. 149 *et seq.*
13. I. H. Nish, *The Anglo-Japanese Alliance: The Diplomacy of Two Island Empires, 1894–1907* (London: Athlone Press, 1966), pp. 379–81.
14. These judgments are of course tentative and impressionistic. To attempt to justify them would require another article, or several, and they may well be falsified by the development of events. For the case in favour of a purely Asian balance, see Alastair Buchan, 'An Asian Balance of Power?', in *Encounter*, December 1966.
15. I incline to the view that, given certain circumstances, the European powers may at some future date again see their national interests as affected by events in Asia, but the likelihood of their actively involving themselves in the 1970s seems rather low, and Britain's decision on exit from East of Suez militarily will reduce still further the prospect of her being able to give any useful transitional aid, unless the effort at construction can be got under way well before 1971. On the other hand, it is just possible that the knowledge of a British decision on departure, plus the 1968 American debate on disinvolvment from Asia, will prove useful catalysts in the Asian process of change.

6 Change and Security in Europe
Part II: In Search of a System
Adelphi Paper 49, 1968

Pierre Hassner

I. The Notion of a European Security System

One notion – three problems

The analysis in Part I of this study introduced us to the concept of a European security system and to some of its supports. The concern of the latter has as much to do with their respective political objectives as with system-building or even with security as such. But, in order to do justice to the concept, I shall consider it on its own merits by analysing the several components and by trying to specify the basic requirements it has to satisfy. This will lead to a variety of possible definitions influenced by various political situations and objectives, resulting in several alternative models, which I shall try to specify by indicating how the various existing nations and organizations might fit into each of them.

The only way of achieving reasonable clarity is by exposing some ambiguities. A useful starting point is with the three words – *European, security* and *system*. Their possible meanings give an indication of the various directions in which the quest for a European security system may lead us.

A. The term *European* can be taken in a more active or passive sense, which immediately gives us the two opposite answers to our problem; it can also lead to a variety of conflicting conclusions, according to the geographical scope of the definition.

The first distinction can be made clear by asking – as was done by one of the proponents of an 'Eastern Locarno', the Belgian Senator Henry Rolin, whether, when speaking of a 'European security system', we mean a 'European system of security' of a 'system of European security'. Is the method, the system, to be European, or only the result, the security? Are the Europeans to be security producers, or just consumers? Are we to aim at the security of the Europeans, by the Europeans, for the Europeans or is Europe's security to be provided basically by the two great powers, with or without the representation or the participation of the Europeans? This poses the problem of the relationship between the regional or continental balance and the global one.

But it also involves us in considering the meaning of the geographical term 'European'. This is most vividly illustrated by the Gaullist formula of 'Europe from the Atlantic to the Urals'. Obviously it has its roots in geography textbooks; but even more obviously this phrase has the political meaning of excluding America while including the USSR and leaving the status of Britain ambiguous. Similarly the Soviet-inspired formulae of 'Europe for the Europeans', 'a Monroe Doctrine for Europe', and indeed, a European security conference or system, while leaving room for American participation from a back seat, try to exploit the affinity between the normal geographical definition of continental Europe and a geo-political organization based on the exclusion of the maritime powers. Geography can be twisted to suit one's objective, to give Europe an extension based on the distinction drawn between the exclusively European nation-states and the two flanking world powers, or between continental Europe (including the USSR) and the United States, or between the Atlantic world (of which Europe would be a part as well as the source) and the Asian one or, on the other hand, to give Europe an extension founded on a more comprehensive conception including the two flanking powers and stretching from San Francisco to Vladivostok.

If, as several historians have argued, the *European States System* was implicitly in demise at the turn of the century, and had finally collapsed for all to see by 1945, not as a result of military occupation but from the necessity of historical evolution, then the *European Security System* which would be supposed to organize it obviously would have to follow this changed meaning of Europe and to become an *East–West Security System*.[1]

However, if the geographical concept of Europe and the political notions of a 'European Europe' or a 'Europe from the Atlantic to the Urals' are no longer obvious frameworks in which to find an answer to the security problem, they have not lost their meaning as indications of a specific aspect of this problem. The central fact is that the three main powers in Europe have, on the one hand, something inherently ambiguous, indefinite and unsettled in the character of their presence on the European scene and, on the other hand, an actual or potential dimension and power out of proportion to those of the more settled nation-states of Europe. These three countries are, of course, the United States, the Soviet Union and Germany. The first two share the characteristic of being, in different ways, both European and non-European, of having been established by their past, by the Second World War and by postwar developments as full members of the European System, although the manner in which they involve themselves in European affairs is not as consistent as is the case with the smaller continental states. This double status of the two great powers places the European balance in a close although variable relationship with the global balance, and hence with the local balance of other continents like Asia.

But, even if the Soviet Union and the United States could be disengaged from Europe, there remains the problem of Germany. Obviously the European problem and the German problem are seen from the security viewpoint as two aspects of the same question – what kind of Germany would fit into what kind of Europe so as to be neither too strong nor too weak for the European environment? The fact that a united Germany could be expected to dominate a continental Europe immediately brings into evidence both the essential role of the two great powers and the crucial role of Germany's domestic evolution: thus, a global and a national development appear to be the essential elements of Europe's security problem.

But if Europe appears to be this intermediate area whose security is directly affected by the triangular relationship between Germany, the Soviet Union and the United States, then it would seem that in following this definition some European states are more European than others. Some feel threatened by Germany, some by Russia, some by both, some by neither. In a military and even in a political sense the security problems of the Balkans, of Spain and Portugal, possibly of Northern Europe, are not the same as those of the centre of Europe, where, from Britain and France to Poland and Czechoslovakia, the German–Russian 'relationship of major tension' dominates the scene.

So the question arises whether a 'European Security System' would answer the varied problems of different areas of Europe, or whether, just as in some respects the framework has to be more than European, in others it does not have to be broken down into several subregional security systems. The south-eastern regions of NATO and of the Warsaw Pact respectively appear to constitute a unit of their own. At the opposite geographic pole, while Germany experiences the beginnings of a 'new Central European consciousness', on the other side the short-lived attempts at creating a solidarity of the so-called northern tier of the Warsaw Pact (Poland, Czechoslovakia and the DDR) while based on hostility to West Germany and to the idea of German reunification, did imply, nevertheless, a certain *de facto* 'solidarity of fate' which is also expressed in the various Eastern security plans, covering the two Germanies, Poland and Czechoslovakia.[2]

B. The same ambiguity applies to the concept of *security*. It embraces the question of structure; of the identity and pattern of states involved, *security of what against what?* and the question of content; of the nature of security itself, of the values it is supposed to preserve, of the threats it is directed against.

On the first question, assuming for the time being that one is concerned with the military security of states, this system can protect: (1) all the states against a threat external to their system; (2) all the states against one of them; (3) all the states against each other; (4) every state against every other; (5) all the states against accidents connected with the system itself. In the first case, the system is in fact one of collective defence – like an alliance. The second would also involve collective defence, but rather than holding a line against a menacing environment it would mean closing a circle around the most menacing member of the group. This could take either the flexible form of various powers rallying together against whichever of them threatens to become too strong; or the more rigid one of a peace settlement, trying to prevent a defeated candidate for hegemony from resuming his bid, by imposing binding limitations on him and commitments on his victors.

The third type constitutes collective security proper, which is distinguished by its stress on reciprocity and solidarity. Like the balance of power, it is not directed against a particular enemy or a particular threat defined in advance, but against any of the powers involved if they happen to commit aggression; like the 'peace settlement' type, however, it relies on the keeping of binding commitments (in this case reciprocal guarantees of common action against any aggressor) rather than on empirical power adjustments based on each state's individual reading of the situation and of its own interest.

The fourth type could be said to be the same in reverse: it also implies the rejection of partial alliances or defence arrangements which, by ensuring the security of some might appear to threaten that of others, or of flexible balances which might lead to unpredictability, and hence to insecurity. But it is based on every state ensuring its own security itself – against any individual aggressor or a coalition of them. Instead of 'all for each, each for all', it would be: 'everyone for himself'; instead of the complete centralization of collective defence or alliances, and of the *ad hoc* co-ordination of flexible balances, there would be complete decentralization.

Even if this atomistic structure were attainable, it would not be incompatible with some of the measures taken in the common interest under my fifth type – which would correspond, more or less, to arms control and crisis-management: measures taken not against aggression but against the consequences of the existence of military establishments and technologies and of the sheer multiplicity of states – against war breaking out by accident, misunderstanding or insubordination, or against its getting out of control if started.

The existence of these problems of war avoidance and war limitation shows, even before any political considerations are introduced, that the problem of security cannot be reduced to that of deterrence. Nor are the four models themselves which are roughly based upon bipolarity, the classical balance of power, collective security, and the 'unit veto system' determined simply by the numbers of actors involved: their more important characteristics, their differing degree of centralization, are deeply influenced by differing concepts of their function.[3]

A direct link is provided by the classical notions of generalization and localization of conflicts and wars. The more centralized, universal and reciprocal a security system is, the more it will tend to make for generalization. A common criticism of collective security has been that it tended to transform every dispute into a world war. While many qualifications have to be made when one comes to specific cases and to complex systems, it does remain true that the threat of generalization is basically meant to *deter* aggression, but that if war does break out, then attempts at *limiting* it seem to point towards localization.

This may no longer be the case if one takes a step backward, from the deterrence of war to the avoidance of conflict, and a step forward, from the limitation of war to the establishment of peace. It may be that local measures applied to specific problems are most conducive to security by preventing the situation where war has to be deterred by the threat of generalization, and it may also be true that only the intervention of a concert of the great powers or of the councils of an international organization could obtain (whether through mediation or through pressure) the termination of war and hence a framework for peace. Of course, the intervention of the great powers may be meant to ensure the localization of war; localization may come out of the fear of generalization and from its conscious avoidance. But the point is that through these two notions, considerations attached to security lead us from the military aspects of the deterrence and limitation of war, to the political question of the prevention and settlement of conflicts.

Here, though, it is much harder to be sure of what values one is trying to protect, against what threats and by what means. Whose security is one protecting? That of countries, of states, of regimes, of governments, of goods, of populations, of minorities, of individuals? Obviously the requirements will not be the same in every case. Many security systems seem aimed mainly at guaranteeing the security of unpopular governments against their citizens. This is what Holy Alliances – one classical and still very relevant form of security system – are about.

In its most general terms, the question is: does security mean security against revolution? Everybody would admit that security means the avoidance of war; almost nobody would admit (although many would feel) that security means the avoidance of change. But when it comes to domestic violence, to violence short of interstate war, the answers are much less clear. Since we live in an age where war and revolution, aggression and subversion, inter-state war and internal war, are hopelessly entangled, there arise serious political, legal and moral questions, and practical limitations are imposed on any international security system. It is arguable whether it is better to outlaw or deter war, to limit its cost by restraint or its duration by every effort aimed towards insulation. Both courses, however, seem much less promising when applied to revolution. And yet, recent events in Czechoslovakia and in France with the concern, the fear, the irritation or the hope they created in neighbouring countries reveal this as *the* most crucial problem for the stability and progress of Europe. If, then, the attempt to build a European Security System can neither ignore nor resolve this problem, the system appears rather as a consequence than a cause of an existing order based upon a given political, ideological, social, economic and technological balance.

C. The word *system*, then, appears as the most urgently in need of clarification among the three components of the phrase 'European Security System'. It has three connotations: complexity, construction and fixity. Since we speak of a system, we can mean neither an isolated measure nor an isolated feature of reality but a set of interdependent and coherent measures or features. Second, we seem to imply, although less certainly, a rational, intellectual or mechanical and deliberate construction as opposed to a natural, organic or historical product with all its possible confusions and hazards. And third, with this emphasis on reason rather than life, it is assumed that although systems may be flexible and responsive to change, they would cease to be systems if this flexibility was not meant to restore a given equilibrium against environmental disturbances or, at the very least, to keep a certain proportion or structure, and consequently a certain permanence in the midst of evolution.

It is very striking, however, if one looks at the existing specific proposals for a European Security System, and at the realities of the situation, that none of these characteristics seems to be universally and unambiguously present.

It is very hard to say how from one or several measures a security system is evolved, and when this system really implies a political settlement. Many current proposals – in particular the Eastern ones – include under the name of a European Security System a package of three or four declarations or agreements without explaining to what extent they constitute a system rather than an addition to existing measures. But what really constitutes a system? In 1925 or 1926, if it had been asked on what system the security of Europe was based, should mention have been made of the League of Nations, of the Locarno Agreement or of the pattern made up from the respective strengths of the different powers? Of course all of these played a part, as had other more classical and bilateral pacts signed by France: the regional pacts served to bridge the credibility gap between the universal guarantees of collective security and the material balance of forces.

But this raises the issue of coherence – which is becoming increasingly relevant in today's world where instead of one security system there may be a series of overlapping balances and commitments, some of them contradictory, some complementary, some unilateral, some reciprocal, some global, some regional, some stable, some flexible which, all together, in the way they affect the calculus of ambitions, risks and costs of the various states, produce at a given moment what would be more correctly called a security *situation* rather than a security *system* – or else, and this is the second and more important observation, 'system' would have to be taken in the sense of *pattern*, as in 'international system'.

When we talk of a tight bipolar international system or of a hegemonic one, we use the term not in the sense of a deliberate construction but simply in the sense of a given pattern of relationships among a set of units. These relationships cannot be deduced simply from the size and number of the units. Specific arrangements like alliances, pacts, guarantees, international institutions, all contribute to define these relationships and to compensate for the stark logic of size and numbers. But the fact remains that the basic reality on which these arrangements rely, even while they modify it, is the balance resulting from the strength and number of states and from their existing combinations and groupings. A security system then is nothing other than the international system seen from the point of view of security: it is another name for the balance of power, of hopes and fears which deter a potential disturber of peace and security. In this sense then, a security system does not have to be constructed: there is always one in being, to the extent that we do not have a permanent total war of all against all.

The question is the same as that for *laissez-faire* economics: does the necessary and beneficial character of the market or of the balance and the element of automatic adjustment in their operation mean that they do not have to be instituted and regulated, that conditions for their operation do not have to be created and maintained, that safeguards against their failing or collapse do not have to be prepared? This is the role of a visible hand operating a consciously managed system, in addition to the invisible hand operating an automatic one. At the very least, it means trying deliberately to institute or to maintain a balance, where circumstances have destroyed one or threaten to do so.

Hence, the two more fruitful meanings of the term *system* in 'European Security System', both of which would be intermediary between security *measures* and a security *situation* are, on the one hand, political-military agreements erected on the basis of existing realities, but planned in such a way as to maximize certain features like security, the *status quo* or the interests of a given power or set of powers: this is the sense in which we speak of 'the Bismarck System' or of the Atlantic System. On the other hand, a given political settlement or international order – also based on the manipulation of the balance in order to stabilize it, but attacking, so to speak, the non-security dimensions of security. In both cases, pacts, agreements, institutional arrangements are inseparable from power ratios: this is what alliances, protection and guarantees mean. There would then be, following the first meaning, a reordering of the European scene based on a given pattern of relationships manipulated in order to establish those unilateral, bilateral, multilateral or collective defence and security arrangements most conducive to security. Following the second meaning, one should remember that security is neither to be defined unambiguously nor to be obtained in isolation, that a new military balance can only be the obverse of a new political order, that if security is not to rely only on a 'balance of terror', then it must go even further than a 'balance of prudence': it must rest on a 'balance of satisfaction'.

This conceptual analysis would seem to confirm the empirical description I gave in Part I of this study.[4] Security in the narrow sense is to be found at the beginning and the end. Starting from a given security situation, a given military balance, the effort towards qualitative improvement must be based on the settlement of political conflicts and disputes; such a political settlement and peaceful order as might emerge would in turn have to be protected by a security system in the narrower sense. This, again, could range from a conscious attempt at stabilizing the balance on which the settlement is based, to a more centralized and institutionalized attempt at supplementing or superseding it by a permanent co-operation of the various states, or by the authority of an impartial organization, or one or more of the great powers.

This link, then, between the institutional, the political and the military aspects of international order would seem to question the very notion of a security *system*, or at least the possibility of considering it, much less of applying it, in isolation. To speak of a security system may be to say too much or too little: too much for security measures meant to improve or stabilize a given military balance and political order, too little for a settlement or peaceful order, which can offer security only if it goes beyond it and, in a certain sense, transcends it in favour of political solutions.

Of course, the questions: addition or substitution? consolidation or overcoming of the *status quo*? can be solved if the former is the means towards the latter. This would be the idea – not a very obvious one at first sight, although it is frequently expressed in the East and increasingly in the West, especially in Germany – that the best way towards all-European *rapprochement* is to consolidate the division of Europe, the best way towards the reunification of Germany is the recognition of two German states.

Naturally, the link is in the notion of security and in the distinction between various spheres: it is to the extent that clear borders are drawn on essential military, territorial, political and even, to a large extent, social and ideological matters, that exchanges, dialogues and co-operation can operate safely across these borders in the economic, the private or the cultural spheres. Even in the areas of the first type, some 'small steps' can be taken towards change and towards *rapprochement*, but only with the understanding that they will not lead to a fundamental questioning of the *status quo*.

It would seem that in this scheme the more serious element is the freeze, the division or the *status quo*, while the opposite dimension is brought in as a minor qualification or as a vague or distant sweetener. But the necessity of going through an acceptance of the *status quo* and a consolidation of the existing alliances to a modification of the *status quo* and an overcoming of the blocs can also be defended, while putting the accent on the evolutionary objective rather than on the conservative starting point.

Perhaps the chief lesson from a reflection on the term 'system' is to show, concerning *time*, how the same ambiguity arises in consideration of the term 'Europe' and of generalization and localization, as has been discovered concerning *space*. Just as a European Security System should be in one way insulated from, and in another way protected by, the global balance, so it should be both predictable and flexible, and should both prevent anarchy and encourage change. The two great powers have failed in their attempts to graft their group of European powers into a community with them. Consequently, a certain differentiation of their respective 'Europes' from them is both desirable and inevitable; but no solution is possible without their direct or, at least, their indirect participation, without their physical presence or, at the very least, their guarantees. Similarly, a European Security System has to be predictable enough to prevent violent conflict, but flexible enough to permit peaceful change. Take away one of these aspects and you achieve neither. The real question is whether the attempt to introduce an evolutionary process in the security arrangements proper (as was the case for instance, in the idea of the 'European clause' of the MLF) is, while welcome, not equally as difficult to apply as the contrary attempt to freeze the political *status quo* for all time.

This brings us back to the crucial and central duality between military security and political settlement, which emerges most clearly from my examination of the central term of *security*. A provisional conclusion (indicating three problems rather than three answers) of our discussion of the three concepts would then be that a European Security System should be neither essentially European, nor essentially a system, nor deal essentially with security. Or rather, put more positively, it should be European but linked to the global system; it should be a system but linked to a process of evolution; and it should deal with security but in connection with the political problems of a European settlement and of international order. Nobody has expressed this last point better than Henry Kissinger, when writing about the Congress of Vienna but in fact thinking of our own time. 'If an international order expresses the need for security and an equilibrium, it is constructed in the name of a legitimizing principle. Because a settlement transforms force into acceptance, it must attempt to translate the requirements of security into claims and individual demands into general advantage. While powers may appear to outsiders as factors in a security arrangement, they appear domestically as expressions of a historical existence. No power will submit to a settlement, however well-balanced and however "secure", which seems totally to deny its vision of itself. There exist two kinds of equilibrium then: a general equilibrium which makes it dangerous for one power or group of powers to attempt to impose their will on the remainder; and a particular equilibrium which defines the historical relation of certain powers towards each other. The former is the deterrent against a general war; the latter the condition of smooth co-operation.'[5]

Applied to the contemporary problem of a European Security System, this analysis shows that any examination of the various existing models must compare them in terms of their various answers both to the problem of balance (the regional and the global, and the relationship between the two) and to the problem of legitimacy (as general, ideological, traditional, legal or moral principles and as a variety of geographically and historically conditioned interpretations of the former). In substantive terms, most current proposals imply, in various forms and proportions, a balance based less immediately on the immediate confrontation of the two superpowers, and a legitimacy based less on ideology.

Whatever the solution, the basic problem appears as one of the link between the various dimensions of the security problem, applied to the particularly complex and ambiguous region of Europe. Geographically, the problem can be defined as that of the relationship between the military status and the security of Germany, of Europe and of the two superpowers. The link between the limitation of German and of other European armaments runs from the Versailles Conference to the various conferences of the 1950s. But it is obviously connected with the relationship between a political solution of the German problem, the political structure of Europe, and the nature of the international system, especially of the Soviet–American relationship. The real question is: what kind of Germany can be fitted into what kind of Europe and what kind of world?

Alternative frameworks

(a) Types of international systems

In order to examine the various possible answers to questions posed above, it might be best to start with a classification of international systems, which should be both politically relevant and logically complete. It could be based, for instance, on the number of the states which operate the system, and on the type of relationship (conflict or co-operation, *de facto* balance or institutional agreements) between them. The eight resulting models would then be: A. *unipolar* (1) empire or (2) federation; B. *bipolar* (3) confrontation or (4) co-operation; C. *multipolar* (5) balance or (6) concert; D. *universal* (7) unit veto system or (8) collective security.

Of these, the first two would presuppose a political transformation which would be both beyond the scope of this study and beyond that of international relations proper. The last two models 7, 'everyone for himself' and 8, 'all for each, each for all' cannot be dismissed so summarily but they, too, presuppose some kind of balance. A trend towards universal self-reliance or towards universal solidarity can hardly eliminate the need for more specific alignments or the existence of an international structure, which implies some protection and influence of some powers over others.

From the viewpoint of this power structure the four possible models (3, 4, 5 and 6) evolve around the criteria of the number of states and of the types of relationship: *bipolar* confrontation and condominium, *multipolar* balance and concert. But if we apply them in the case of America, the USSR and Europe, we see that these types represent only directions, the actual models being subdivisions or combinations. For instance bipolar co-operation can take the form of either condominium or division into spheres of influence – just as, conversely, bipolar balance can mean partition as well as confrontation; an increasingly co-operative partition may lead to a military thinning-out which can, in the end, reach the point of disengagement.

In this case, the structure and role of Europe become very important; combined with the bipolar relationship and commitment, they can go from a neutralized Europe which would be a military vacuum, through the balance or concert of a 'Europe of the States' representing an autonomous regional or continental equilibrium, to a unified Europe which, whether in a federation or under the domination of one country, would represent one pole of military power. The element of co-operation and institutionalization implicit in the notion of a European concert as opposed to a European balance will, if pushed to the extreme, lead precisely to an integrated Europe, but this could mean either an integrated Western Europe with Eastern Europe remaining divided and dependent on the Soviet Union or could encompass the whole Continent.

Similarly, in the case of the principles of legitimacy, an abstract analysis today would distinguish three types: *ideology* (in the sense of the principles on which bipolarity and the cold war are based – Communism and liberal democracy), *nationality* (the principle which wrecked both the Vienna and the Versailles settlements; the first because it rejected it, the second because it adopted it) and *prosperity* (the basis of a '*détente* American style', hoping for the modification of the *status quo* through depoliticization and economic convergence). To these, more specifically, might be added a fourth, the *Europeanist* idea, which contains elements of all three, since it appeals to a solidarity similar to the national one, but is oriented towards the creation of a community defined by commitment to liberal democracy and economic progress, as well as by geographical boundaries.

(b) Models for European security

If, following a simplified view, we limit ourselves to the criteria of Russian and American presence and of European autonomy and unity, we may distinguish from the point of view of the two great powers a European system (*a*) in which both the United States and the Soviet Union would be present (in varying degrees of competition and co-operation, of territorial division or of joint, symbolic or effective occupation); (*b*) in which only the United States would be present (an Atlantic community to which Eastern Europe would be attracted); (*c*) in which only the Soviet Union (Europe from the Atlantic to the Urals) would be present; and (*d*) one from which both would have disengaged (with or without guarantees).

From the point of view of Europe itself, a distinction can be drawn between (*a*) a Europe which, whether formally neutralized or denuclearized or keeping the nuclear and conventional forces it has, would basically remain an object of confrontation or protection rather than a pole of power and an element of balance; (*b*) a 'Europe of the States', relying exclusively, mainly or partly on its own balance; (*c*) an integrated Europe, which, militarily at least, would constitute one centre of power; and (*d*) a combination of the three last models, forming in turn a regionally differentiated, partially integrated or partially neutralized Europe.

Combining the two criteria, we can now see four models emerging, which correspond, for present-day Europe, to the two *bipolar* (confrontation and co-operation) and the two *multipolar* (balance and concert) types of international system. These are: (1) a modified *bipolarity* (or a more stable, less costly and more co-operative *status quo*); (2) *Disengagement* (replacing the two alliances by a system of guarantees centred on Germany, following the model of Locarno); (3) *Europeanization* following the pattern of a return to a 'Europe of the States' (based on the balance and concert between Gauls, Germans and

Slavs); (4) *Europeanization* under a form of *European integration* – centred on the existing communities but spreading eastwards and leading eventually towards a United States of Europe.

All four models represent a mixture of historical evolution and of deliberate planning, which might conceivably lead, if not to a fully fledged 'system', at least to some form of European balance and order, involving some kind of tacit agreement or explicit settlement of Europe's political problems. If, as has been argued, the problem of military security must be seen in connection with that of political stability, we must next turn to the political problem of a European settlement and to the various possible models for the political structure of Germany and Europe to which our security models would have to apply. These need to be examined from the more orthodox point of view of 'cost-effectiveness', of balance and military security proper, but this examination will be meaningful only if it is preceded by, and based on, an indication of the political requirements for a peaceful European order.

II. Germany and Europe: the political foundations of security

The former French Foreign Secretary, M. Couve de Murville, has pointed out that the 'problem of European security' as normally designated by East European governments was none other than the German problem. It is difficult to quarrel with his identification, yet it is possible to point out the ambiguity. For the Soviet Union, it means that the only potential threat to Europe's military security comes from the danger of a revived German power; to which Western (and some Eastern) critics would rejoin that the European balance has to be protected equally from Soviet military superiority. For the West, it means that the political problem of Germany's division is the main source of Europe's dissatisfaction and insecurity; to which the Russians would reply that the threat to security comes not from Germany's division but from the attempts made to overcome it. The only possible reconciliation of the two views, and the best definition of European security, is the search for a formula that would satisfy both the political aspirations of the German people, and the military requirements of the European balance.

A settlement for Germany?

We must, then, expect to become involved in the all too familiar yet tragic complexities of the 'German question'. But the relationship between this question and our own general problem, while inescapable, is far from clear.

It becomes increasingly apparent, however, that ways of overcoming or transforming the German question cannot be defined in the abstract, at a general or European level, but will be strongly influenced by the evolution of both the societies of, and the public opinions in, the two Germanies; indeed, the recent trend has been consistently away from the Four-Power responsibility, towards a search by the two Germanies for ways of opening a direct dialogue with each other. On the other hand, it seems no less clear that the great powers cannot simply negotiate a solution to the German problem among themselves and then dictate it to the respective Germanies, equally, they will not and, indeed, cannot leave it in entirely German hands; thus, they cannot find or impose a solution, but they can prevent one that does not meet their favour. The dislikes and objections of the various powers, some of them shared, some contradictory, some held by all or some of the Germans, and some directed against the Germans, tend towards the production of a cumulative pressure in favour of the *status quo*.

Perhaps the present-day German problem was best summarized by a British author writing in 1906: 'Suspicious of all sentimentalities in foreign affairs, we have always acknowledged that from the German point of view the aims of German foreign policy are entirely justified. The only objection to them is that in no point of the world can they be realized without threatening the security and independence of existing states or destroying their present order. That is not the fault of the German nation, it is its misfortune.'[6]

This problem of the discrepancy between the aims and interests of Germany and of Europe as a whole can be found at various stages and various levels. Germany could be said to be the nation which always arrives too late. Bismarck was the greatest master of classical cabinet diplomacy and warfare, but belonged to an age when national feelings and enthusiasms twisted certain aspects of his work and deprived some others (like the annexation of Alsace and Lorraine) of the legitimacy which would have made them acceptable in earlier times. Germany's bid for colonies came at a time when the great distribution had already taken place; her bid for hegemony in Europe followed the earlier attempts of Spain and France, but came at a time when the standards of behaviour and style were no longer favourable to open conquest, and when the growth of external powers had begun the transformation of the European system into a region of the planetary one. Today, Germany has both legality and morality on her side, when she invokes the principles of self-determination and of the right of nationhood, which provided the ideology both of Versailles and of decolonization; but in Europe their genuine application would be directly contrary to the existing balance, not to mention that in the case of the Polish territories they would come into collision with competing (more recent but no less valid) claims to *Heimatrecht*.

Consequently, the German case raises special difficulties for Europe under each aspect of the international system. From the viewpoint of structure and balance, it has often been said, from Kissinger to Kiesinger, that Germany has always been either, too weak, or too strong, for Europe. A. J. P. Taylor expressed the idea in the simplest terms by writing, 'What is wrong with Germany is that there is too much of it'. But he also gave warning that her division (including the separation of Austria) was no more natural than her unity, and that 'it is more practicable to make Germany's neighbours strong than to make Germany weak'.[7]

It is commonly said today, and with considerable justification, that a strong industrial power of 75 million people would not be regarded with favour by any of her neighbours and this would not be conducive to the stability of the Continent. But the forcible division into two states, created by the Soviet–American military presence and by Europe's division, is today the main factor in the perpetuation of these realities themselves. The currently fashionable notion of two German states accepting each other peacefully and cordially, and practising mutual *détente, entente* and co-operation as all other European states, ignores the fact that in Germany the process will tend never to go far enough for fear of its going too far. The two German states would have to be just sufficiently friendly not to be engaged in hostile competition for supremacy, but not so friendly as to fall into each other's arms; after all, Europe has two centuries' experience of competition between two German states, played upon by the other European powers, and by German irredentism.

The root of the problem, of course, is the ambiguity of Germany's national identity: hence the most widely accepted contemporary principle of legitimacy is also, in the case of Germany, a source of instability. The fact that Germany is the only major nation which has not unequivocally completed her national evolution makes her also the only one which, willy-nilly, has classical border problems with her neighbours. More fundamentally, Austria and even East Germany have sufficient reality and identity to throw doubt on the notion of an indivisible German nation, yet they lack just enough of it to make it doubtful that two, three or four Germanies could co-exist peacefully as friendly, neighbouring foreign states. Finally, the modern principles of legitimacy, ideology and prosperity also tend to exacerbate the problem: certainly both reunification, confederation and peaceful co-existence between the two German states would be easier if they were not built on opposing *raisons d'être*. Prosperity itself, while tending to create common interests and to transcend barriers, remains for the present a differentiating factor and a source of rivalry and envy. These being the difficulties of the problem, it would be even more absurd to try to produce a relevant plan for a settlement of the German question than it would be to produce models for European security. The only possible course is to draw some fairly obvious correlations between the various possible broad directions on the level of Germany and that of the system.

Four basic elements seem to be involved in any eventual settlement of Germany's situation: her borders (and hence her relations with her neighbours); her inner structure (unified, divided, confederate); her armament (disarmed, conventionally armed, nuclear); the international status or alignment (neutralized, free to choose her or their orientation, integrated in an alliance or a community) of the German state or states.

Of these, only the first one admits of a categorical and unequivocal answer. No one concerned primarily with European security would hesitate to recommend the acceptance of present borders, accompanied by the exchange of non-aggression or non-violence pledges and of agreements on the rights and status of minorities. The effect of the international system on this and all the other potential conflicts, concerning territorial and minority problems, would be roughly as follows: the bipolar *status quo*, by depriving the various states of their freedom of action is the safest guarantee against territorial conflicts erupting into violence, but while it may, to some extent, contribute to their disappearance by distracting attention when they involve two members of the same camp (like Germany and France), the two oppositions reinforce each other when the two parties belong to different camps (like Germany and Poland).

However, the most dangerous situation seems to be the return to a 'Europe of the States' system — which, being based on the independence of nation-states, encourages their self-assertion and its eventual utilization by the other powers in the making and unmaking of coalitions. Here more than on any other issue the only positive way towards resolving the conflicts, as distinct from avoiding their explosion, lies on the road to all-European integration. In a Federal Europe, boundary and minority problems would lose their relevance.

Without going as far as this, progress in the circulation of labour and goods and in the interdependence of societies as the Common Market foreshadows, would, along with any accompanying prosperity, contribute towards de-emphasizing the territorial issues in the East as it has already done in the West. In the long term, something in the manner of the 'northern triangle' in the East (Poland, Czechoslovakia, East Germany) which seems to have certain economic implications, might extend to West Germany and give some consistence to the idea of a Central Europe, provided that the persistence of Germany's Western ties and her partners' Eastern ties prevented such a grouping from becoming an instrument of German domination. Security proposals like the Rapacki plan, in the manner in which they apply to the same area, might have as their main value the emphasizing of this consciousness of *Schicksals-gemeinschaft* [solidarity of fate], and its channelling in a peaceful direction.

On the other three aspects of the German problem, each of the alternative answers (unification or partition; neutrality or alliance; disarmament or rearmament) can be and has been proposed with some justification and in a variety of forms.

The classical model of a negotiated solution for Germany, a Germany reunified and neutralized whether armed or disarmed, called for the former Anthony Eden's (Lord Avon) classical objection: if Germany is to be neutral and disarmed, who will keep her disarmed? If she is to be neutral and armed, who will keep her neutral?

The answer seems to be first, that Germany's neutrality is not really conceivable except as part of a larger belt of states and without a dissolution of the two alliances, leading to disengagement; and second, that given the uncertainties summarized by Eden, the two great powers would not trust mere legal guarantees or a continental balance. Thus, in the absence of an integrated Europe, only a combination of some form of disengagement with bipolar control would be compatible with such a solution of the German problem.

A Germany which was united but free to follow her orientation and enter an alliance would mean, whether she was armed or disarmed, a victory for one of the cold-war camps if she joined NATO or the Warsaw Pact. This is inconceivable in the case of an armed Germany and most unlikely, given the present balance, with a disarmed one. So following this, the only possibility would be that of Germany as part of a 'Europe of the States' system, with the risks of domination by herself or by the Soviet Union. If, on the other hand, she should join a European grouping, whether West, Central or all-European, the risks would probably be diminished, but much would depend on the degree of strength and cohesion of this grouping and, consequently, on whether it represented an indirect form of bipolar control, a 'Europe of the States' balance, or a genuinely different structure.

Two German states armed and free to choose their orientation in a 'Europe of the States' system would probably form the most unstable and dangerous combination of all. If the two alliances continued, two armed German states integrated in their respective alliances would mean continuation of the *status quo* unless their armament became nuclear. The total disarmament of the two German states would be incompatible with the requirements and nature of the two alliances; a reduction in their armament and the recognition of special military limitations (justified in particular by German signatures on the Non-Proliferation Treaty) might be a useful step which, while keeping the framework of the two alliances, might contribute to their *rapprochement*. The danger is that it could lead to the neutralization of a divided Germany. This is probably the goal of Soviet and possibly French policy: certainly it is the only formula for Germany which could be the logical corollary of a Franco–Soviet pact.[8] But a Germany both divided and neutralized can only be a dissatisfied one. One wonders which variant is the worst: to increase her dissatisfaction by keeping her disarmed, or her ability to challenge the *status quo* by allowing her (or rather them) to become armed. At any rate, to the disadvantage of German frustration would be added that of European imbalance in favour of the Soviet Union.

Fortunately, it would seem that none of these simple models has much plausibility, because the three relevant questions are unlikely to be answered in such terms as can easily be reduced to one of the three alternatives. Rather, these appear as the opposite and inaccessible ends of a spectrum within which the more realistic if less easily definable possibilities are included. We do not know what the structure, the armaments or the international situation of Germany will or should be, but we do know that the trend is towards a Germany which would have an intermediate status in our three requirements.

First, Germany can be neither truly reunified into one centralized sovereign state, nor completely divided into two hostile sovereign states.

Second, she should not be disarmed but will nevertheless have to accept qualitative and perhaps quantitative limits to her armaments.

Third, Germany can be neither left on her own in active non-alignment nor isolated in passive neutrality, nor completely integrated or paralysed in a centralized alliance or a supranational community.

Between these extremes, three positive observations are probably valid for whatever combination may emerge: first, the evolution has only begun, hence each of these scales must be seen in an evolutionary or dynamic perspective; second, the international framework should be flexible and tolerant enough to accommodate various intermediary alternatives, while remaining sufficiently rigid or constraining to preclude such extreme alternatives as might jeopardize the security of other European powers or the stability of the continent. The requirement, then, for the European system is that it, too, must be a mixed, intermediate and evolutionary one, moving in various possible forms between some maintenance of bipolar control, and some physical disengagement of the two great powers; and between a certain reassertion of the flexible game between European nation-states, and some limitation through new regional or all-European ties.

How many Germanies?

The range of possible types of relationship between West and East Germany is fairly well indicated by the present policy of the Bonn government, with its refusal simultaneously to ignore or isolate East Germany, or to recognize or treat her as a sovereign state. Relations between the two existing political regimes or 'realities' should be encouraged in every way, and must never be allowed to be registered as international relations between two foreign countries. This may well be a transitional compromise policy leading either to full recognition of East Germany or to a revival of the straight-forward demand for outright reunification. But it has a logic of its own.

Between the present 'little steps' policy and the long-range speculations of the West German Minister for All-German Affairs, Herr Herbert Wehner, about the conditions for a confederacy, and an economic community involving some kind of recognition of a liberalized East Germany, the link lies in the striving for an institutionalized co-existence between the two German regimes, a *geregeltes Nebeneinander*. Closer links and some convergence would make recognition possible, and would activate a certain acknowledgment of the division. This in turn would lead to some kind of confederation or community, since East Germany would have been made *konföderationsfähig* (acceptable as a confederation partner), provided the international environment permitted this.[9] The danger is, of course, that in the process West Germany might be led to make irreversible concessions to the two-states theory, without any real assurance that the responses from East Germany and the international environment, necessary to the success of the Wehner strategy, were forthcoming.[10]

The various attempts made at drawing up plans for a German and a European settlement stem, partly, from an attempt to link these various aspects into a process that should be both institutionalized and dynamic. The central and most controversial or ambiguous feature is the same as with the Wehner policy: to link some kind of recognition of East Germany with progress towards some form of reunification.

But how can we know that recognition will lead to reunification? To what extent would this recognition influence the nature and the structure of a reunified Germany? The orthodox Western answer since the Geneva Conference of 1959 is to keep the concept of a German state reunified by free elections as an ultimate goal, but also to recognize that East Germany cannot be disposed of overnight and is likely to retain some of her specific features, especially in the social field. Then, to try to resolve the dilemma by a provisional stage, followed after a given number of years by a referendum.

The most useful models, however, are probably once again, the intermediate ones. These would sacrifice one or two among the three components of the more ambitious ones – such as, the binding time-table, the ultimate reunification, or the principle of self-determination. Some would suggest a 'conditional recognition', coupled with the announcement of reunification or confederation as an ultimate goal, but ideas vary as to whether a time-table should be attached to the latter, and whether the former would be revocable if the promise was not fulfilled.

Similarly, others, abandoning the call for free elections in the DDR, would take over the old Eastern programme of confederation based on *de facto* or *de jure* recognition, followed by talks between the two German states or simply by convergent evolution, but based on the acceptance of the two different social orders and political regimes. Herr Wehner has, on the other hand, recently spelled out more officially and in greater detail than ever before, the priority of political and human freedom for the East Germans over national reunification for Germany. This would mean accepting for an indefinite future the so-called Austrian solution. There is of course a latent irony which may reduce the practical difference between the models, for if one considers the two existing regimes it is difficult to imagine that a confederation between a Communist and a non-Communist regime could go much beyond economic association.

Conversely, if East German citizens were free to choose their own regime, the likelihood would be that both they and West Germans, in spite of their desire to preserve their respective identities, would want to come together in some political combination.

Even within the middle road, then, one finds the basic dichotomy between the international requirements of a solution tending towards two German states, or towards a reunified Germany. Normalized relations between West Germany and a more humanized East Germany might lead, although with difficulty, to some far-reaching changes such as Herr Wehner's economic confederacy; but basically they would not challenge the existing structure of Europe. At best they would take place within the framework of a generalized *détente* and co-operation between the two existing alliances, and between the various nation-states of Europe.

If the confederation was to be a real one, involving at least in part a common defence and common foreign policy, then the system of European security would have to be very different. It would have to be compatible both with two German states and with a *de facto* reunification that might be decided between them, and would have to keep them both from any attempt at joint domination of Europe, and from fratricidal strife. This would require an institutionalized structure, and an all-European one.

Clearly, this would not be compatible with each Germany remaining in her own respective military alliance, at least in their present form. But it would be no less incompatible with straightforward great-power disengagement; for the Soviet Union and the United States cannot be expected not to wish for some method of influencing or controlling the evolution of a German confederation towards either greater centralization or disintegration. Indeed, the closer Germany comes to reunification, the more the old dual type of control through NATO and the Warsaw Pact becomes impracticable and the more *some* form of control becomes indispensable. The conclusion then seems inescapable that only some combination of Europeanization, and a more co-operative and indirect bipolar superpower control, is capable of squaring this particular circle.

How many arms?

This emerges even more clearly if one looks at the two other elements that have more directly to do with the international framework. Clearly, arms limitation and arms control must be a crucial element of Germany's status, for nobody, including most Germans, believes that a reunified Germany free to manufacture her own nuclear weapons is desirable for the future stability of Europe. However, in terms both of creating a stable balance, and of creating a legitimate order which should not be considered as unjust and discriminatory by the German people, such limitations must be linked to a more general structure of obligations and restraints, whether within an alliance or community, or an all-European system. This is the most precise *locus* for the inevitable link between the German and the European security issue. As with the one between recognition and reunification, this particular link can be seen at various levels and can point to various possibilities. Philip Windsor explicitly combines the relationships, the central link between them being the withdrawal of Soviet troops from Central Europe. This alone makes possible a basic change in East Germany and a subsequent reunification, but in turn, it could only be made possible by progress in arms control: 'The best approach to the whole problem seems therefore that of arms-control agreements between the two alliances. A detailed policy of linking arms control with recognition and disarmament with reunification – even many years ahead, but within a specified time-table – would offer the best hopes of putting an end to the indissoluble problems of Germany and the cold war.'[11]

Both aspects of this policy (which taken as a whole would probably require too much co-ordination and control to be feasible in the present state of the two alliances) are currently discussed or practised. The prevailing model is the linking of arms control with recognition, without much hope of reaching disarmament and reunification.

This means, of course, while keeping the link between military and political measures on which the West has always insisted, giving the Russians something for which they have been asking as against something they have always wanted, and abandoning as unrealistic the more ambitious aspects (withdrawal of Soviet troops and German reunification), always part of the West's traditional objectives. However, many in the West hope to re-establish at least a tacit *quid pro quo* at a lower level.

The trend in West Germany lies towards arms-control proposals and unilateral arms limitation (possibly including a reform of the Bundeswehr, destined to make it more exclusively and obviously defensive)[12] in the hope that these would encourage political evolution or, at least, contribute towards an improvement in the climate, which would be the necessary precondition. A more direct link is sought by certain diplomatic planners who would like to trade security measures on the Soviet agenda (such as non-aggression pledges) against improvements in communication between the two Germanies. They see this as one aspect of a bilateral German–Soviet deal in a collective or multilateral framework, that might be decided at a European security conference: the Soviet Union would obtain a legitimization of the strategic *status quo* against a modification in the political one, designed to make it more acceptable to Germany.

Again, in this perspective, the maintenance of the two alliances, in a more co-operative relationship, and of the existing military balance, albeit at a lower and less costly level, would be the obvious framework. Certainly, this type of negotiation is the only one which has any plausibility at all in the present-day context. On the other hand, it is a reasonable and, in my view, an essential requirement, that it should not be allowed to legitimize and solidify the *status quo* in such a way as to block the path towards the more far-reaching settlement, which unpredictable circumstances might one day make possible.

In such a changed context, the two issues of reunification and disarmament which constituted the 'disengagement debates' of the 1950s would together re-emerge. The link is the obvious one that for reunification, or for East German self-determination, one must have the withdrawal of Soviet troops, but that this withdrawal is only possible if they are not to be replaced by West German or NATO troops. To a certain extent, this has been recognized in the West. The 1959 plan of the Western powers already suggested that, while a reunified Germany would be free to join NATO, no troops of the alliance should be stationed in East Germany, and that for a transitional period Soviet troops could be maintained there after the political transformation. One 'Austrian' solution goes further than that, since it includes, in Herr Wehner's formulation as in Professor Kissinger's, the notion of a demilitarized, neutral East Germany. After reunification, Professor Kissinger envisages that foreign troops would withdraw within the Federal Republic to a distance roughly equivalent to the Elbe-Oder one.[13] Such suggestions may not be very practical, but they emphasize the crux of the problem, namely the disparity between the two Germanies. If West Germany keeps her NATO role and her American troops, while East Germany is demilitarized and neutralized, it means all-out defeat for the Russians. If West Germany is also neutralized and demilitarized, NATO is likely to be paralysed, especially after the defection of France.

Moreover, from the Russians' point of view, the real question is whether the removal of German participation in NATO increases or diminishes the guarantees of her arms limitations, and especially her nuclear abstinence. A Federal Republic which remains a full member of NATO gives the Soviet Union no supplementary guarantees, which would make it worthwhile for her to make concessions on East Germany. Conversely, a Germany which is no longer integrated in an organization is a Germany infinitely less predictable than today. From the point of view of integration as from that of troop deployment, then, the solution can only be as paradoxical as the problem, *viz.* Germany must be both within and without, she must be part of a larger whole, but in a special position.

This leads us to the three basic principles of the West's German policy, which have often been attacked as incompatible: organization, arms limitation, reunification.[14] As the French diplomat who reminds us of them points out, the first one, in its Atlantic (military) and European (economic and political) form, is the most important, as the basis and framework for the other two. But from the beginning, Germany has accepted specific limitations on her armaments (no manufacture of nuclear weapons) and freedom of action (as the only ally whose army is directly integrated in NATO). These limitations, in turn, have been officially linked to the problem and hope of reunification.

The time has now come to give a higher priority to the latter; this means both that Germany must probably accept a higher measure of discrimination and arms limitation, a more explicit and final renunciation of national control of nuclear weapons, perhaps a reduction in her troops level to be coupled with Soviet reductions, and that the military organization (NATO) and the political-economic one (EEC) have themselves to be transformed in the direction of an approach to the East. But a policy of limitation and discrimination for Germany without either integration or reunification would raise the question: can Germany accept this inferior status merely as a punishment for the war of another generation? Obviously, she can accept it only if she belongs to a wider organization, which is ruled by the same principles and yet takes into account the hopes on which her acceptance of a special position is based. Given geographic, strategic and political realities, this larger organization must be firmly based on existing West European institutions. But because of Germany, these institutions must of necessity be open towards the West and the East, through the participation of the US, the association of Eastern Europe and agreement with the Soviet Union.

How many ties?

Just as Berlin, while Germany is not completely reunified, must at the same time keep its institutional links with West Germany, find a place and a stable relationship within its Eastern environment, and enjoy the guarantee which it can get only from its Four-Power status, so the Federal Republic must remain part of Western Europe and increasingly acquire a specific position, taking into account the direction of her interests and perhaps of her associations, towards Central Europe; and she must also remain open to the supervision of the superpowers. The West European institutions themselves should be carried along by Germany in her increasingly Central European preoccupation and connections. Indeed, the European level, by the institution of all-European commissions in which the East Europeans could participate, or via the economic detour of East Germany's association with the Common Market as suggested by François Duchêne and Miriam Camps,[15] provides the right approach for Germany's contacts with the East, and for some form of reunion of the Germans or of reassociation of the German states.[16]

For a considerable length of time, however, Germany would remain in a distinctive but somewhat uncertain position as a member of the Western alliance looking towards the East. But in this contradiction lie precisely the seeds of the only promising institutional formula and political development.

This has been best expressed by the original proponent of an Eastern Locarno, Dr Georg Pfleiderer, whose ideas seem both more original, and more realistic, than the simple notion of Locarno as a reciprocal guarantee pact.

Far from presenting a new Locarno as an alternative to the alliance system, Pfleiderer saw in it an alternative to the neutralization of Germany: 'The best model which can be considered for mutual security and from which it is particularly desirable to start since it worked admirably for years, is the European Treaty System as it developed in 1925–26 out of the Locarno pact, the admission of Germany into the League of Nations and the German-Soviet Treaty of Berlin of 24 April, 1926. The meaning of that system was that Germany was, through Locarno and the League of Nations, clearly and unequivocally bound by treaty to the West, but that she settled her relationship with the East, i.e. the Soviet Union, according to her special position by her own arrangement, and this with the agreement of her Western partners.

'In the recognition by the West of Germany's particular situation, and in the correct handling of this particularity by Germany, an element of Soviet security and of world peace was contained.'[17]

Contrary to many of the ideas of the early 1950s, this way of posing the German problem becomes increasingly relevant. It does not lead back to 1945 or to the suppression of the organizations and institutions which have given Germany, and Europe, some security and stability; it responds to the need for a greater national freedom of action and a wider European framework than have been so far provided by existing Western institutions. The resulting direction consists of the addition of a new type of tie to the existing one, thus balancing and compensating the first by the second, rather than suppressing it. Here, for the first time, the German and the European roads meet. Germany's security and aspirations are not easy to fit into any kind of European structure, and her situation is bound to remain contradictory and ambiguous to a certain degree; but this is increasingly now the state of all European blocs, associations and communities.

Germany's specific problem, arising from her division and her size, makes it imperative that she should seek her national goals only in a collective framework. This combination of freedom and constraint is possible only if membership in several distinct systems gives her both some freedom of action in choosing the relative emphasis given to each of these communities at different times and on different problems, and some limitation to freedom of action, since one system of ties is loosened only to the advantage of one or several others.[18]

A structure for Europe?

What is true of Germany is also true of every European state, with the possible exception of the two superpowers: that the only way to increase independence without diminution of security lies neither in the adoption of a position of passive neutrality, nor of active non-alignment between two monolithic alliances, nor in the replacing of them altogether by a system of flexible balance of power and of shifting alignments, but in making the alignments within the existing groups less automatic and exclusive. And the only way to achieve this relativization of alignments is by multiplying them, by building up a network of overlapping and cross-cutting relationships of co-operation which in turn may produce new divisions, but from this very fact might undercut the old polarization.[19] The distinction between neutrals and allied powers tends to become blurred and to be replaced by an indefinite variety of alignments and conflicts within or without formal alliances. The position of each state and the general balance are defined by the pattern which emerges from the ordering of preferences between conflicting ties and loyalties.[20] Perhaps the most forceful statement of the basis for a peaceful European order was given forty years ago by a prophetic French author, who wrote that the Machiavelli of the future would have to 'seek equilibrium not any longer in the equality of oppositions but in the proportioning of associations'.[21]

Already, most European states, including those of Eastern Europe, see their chance both for gaining a greater immediate independence from their respective superpower, and for preparing a different system for tomorrow, in the creation of new sub-bloc or trans-bloc associations. Many writers from the smaller East European countries, especially Czechoslovakia, have emphasized the desirability of special ties between European states, particularly between small states irrespective of their social orientation and of their alliances, as the best way of advancing European security, and as an alternative to challenging or abandoning these alliances themselves.[22]

The creation, on Rumanian initiative, of the group of nine small European countries (three Western, three Eastern, three neutral) and its functioning in the framework of the UN Assembly is a promising step in this direction.

Other interesting cross-cutting developments are beginning to take place on a regional basis. The schemes for Balkan solidarity and co-operation, proposed mainly by Rumania but with some Bulgarian and Yugoslav support, and the more or less symmetric ones proposed by Hungary in the Danubian direction are straws in the wind as are, in a different way, the Finnish initiatives in the Nordic area and there, thus remains a vacant central space for a possible Central European 'peace zone'.[23]

Of course, all these initiatives have, for the time being, a strong component of diplomatic shadow-boxing or romantic nostalgia; moreover, the immediate political aims and results are ambiguous as regards relations both with the West and with the Soviet Union. They can mean *rapprochement* and they can also mean, and probably meant in the past, an attempt to create friction within the opposite grouping; this may still be in some cases their main consequence. By the same token, they may have been encouraged by the Soviet Union at one time and appeared to challenge her rule at another, just as intra-bloc special relationships, like the ephemeral 'Northern triangle' of the Warsaw Pact, were both an instrument of the Soviet attempt to check the influence of the Rumanian example, and a factor of Central-East European independence like the reviving 'Little Entente' of Czechoslovakia, Rumania and Yugoslavia. In the long run, whatever the immediate purposes and results, it seems likely that any progress in the establishing of special ties on a geographical basis, between two or more Warsaw Pact countries and, even more so, between these and other European countries, can only have a positive effect on the perspectives for a peaceful European order.

This effect is likely to be most important in the elusive yet decisive field of legitimacy and ideology: regional ties and the emergence of a European, or of a small- and middle-power point of view within existing groupings have the double virtue of both eroding the Communist and anti-Communist legitimacy which justifies Soviet domination, while showing an alternative road which is not the one of nationalistic self-assertion. If the erosion of Communist ideology and of Soviet rule is to lead to a Europe based on the national principle, there is already enough evidence of the persistence of old conflicts to enable us to predict a definite turn for the worse,[24] including the reappearance of such national claims as were encouraged in the past by Germany, whose proposed European order was, after all, the only one to follow the national principle to its logical conclusion by detaching Croatia or Slovakia from their multi-national states. If the Communist order is replaced or transformed under the influence of the movement towards European integration, then the so-far abortive projects for a Balkan-Danubian federation might have their first serious chance. They would provide the only satisfactory solution not only to minority conflicts within East European states, but to the collective weakness and division of these states themselves, and to their inability to balance either the Soviet Union or Western Europe. An 80 to 130 million strong federation would provide the missing fourth element in the structure sketched by Zbigniew Brzezinski as 'a future co-operative community, involving eventually four major units, America and Russia as the peripheral participants, and West Europe and East Europe as the two halves of the inner core (in time perhaps becoming still more closely linked).[25]

If the solution were to be found in building an abstract institutional model, the most satisfactory structure for Europe would be two federations of Western and Eastern Europe, constituting an all-European confederation with Germany or the two Germanies on the one hand, Poland and Czechoslovakia on the other, constituting a special Central European arms-control zone; and the Soviet Union and the United States being linked with each other and the European confederation through a mutual security treaty (involving for reasons of security which are presented below, 'multilateral hostages', especially in Berlin), economic association and common technological projects. One might even represent this structure in the form of three circles, two overlapping ones enclosed in a wider one.

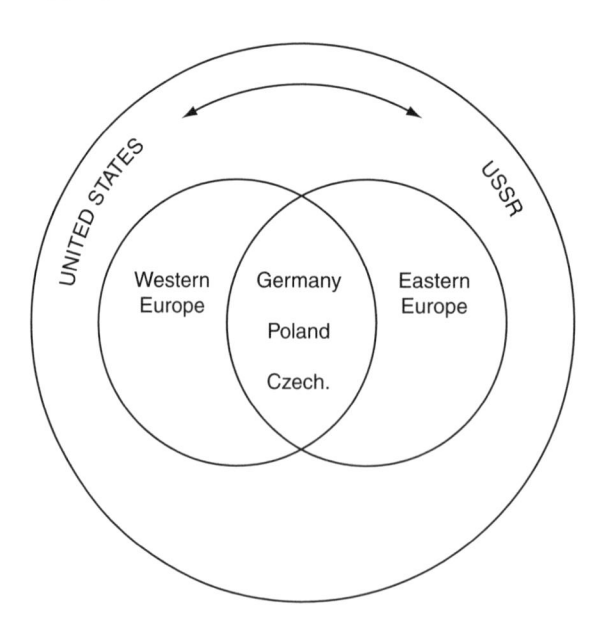

I purposely leave open the central question of whether Germany would constitute one or two states and, in the second case, of whether they would both belong to the West European Federation or one to the West, and the other to the East European one, in which case their special links would only amount to a special and stronger case within a framework of links between the two federations. The point about the threefold notion of a confederation made of two federations and a central overlapping arms-control zone, is that it could accommodate the various possible combinations of German unity and reduce the difference between them.[26]

But the main purpose of the exercise would be to show that institutional model-building is at best premature as a contribution to a European settlement. First, a fully fledged settlement of this kind, which would indeed represent a genuine political revolution, could only come at the end of a very long process of economic, social, cultural and ideological evolution, of which today we can only glimpse the barest beginnings. Second, it is in the very nature of a process that works at so many levels and is submitted to so many influences to be unpredictable not only in its course, but also in its results. Its relations with the future organization and balance of Europe are likely to be much more complex, and less intellectually satisfying, than is imagined either by those who rely on elaborate blueprints for a federal constitution or a security system, or by those who are content to put their hopes in a process which, by producing an interlocking of interests, would make war impossible (which it will never be) or unprofitable (which it has already been for quite some time).[27]

The problem of security, hence of balance, will always be there. But its political and military dimensions cannot be foreseen or speculated upon in isolation, since they will be decisively affected by the balances and imbalances which will result from different phases of technological and economic progress, and degrees of political and psychological presence and involvement.

These are bound to disturb the symmetrical structures that can be worked out on paper. The question is whether, with the help of political will and imagination, they can at some point produce a multi-dimensional 'balance of imbalances' which would provide the basis and the setting for the resolution of Europe's unsolved problems. For instance, Eastern Europe is likely to remain significantly weaker and more divided than Western Europe, being simultaneously more attracted towards the latter than *vice versa*, and more dependent on the Soviet Union than Western Europe is on the United States. This, however, gives all the more reason for favouring anything which may increase the imperfect degree of Eastern Europe's unity, of its ties with the West and of its autonomy *vis-à-vis* the Soviet Union. Similarly, it is likely that the United States will continue to be technologically and economically superior to the Soviet Union and Western Europe, while the Soviet Union may very well appear more directly present and concerned both politically and militarily than the United States. The two phenomena may well be put to good use for a renewed balance. However, this might mean the victory of present trends towards a Europe dominated economically by the United States and militarily by the Soviet Union, both (specially the latter) being able to turn their superiority into political hegemony, unless European political will and unity introduces a third factor without which the first two, in spite of their inevitable and in some ways beneficial aspects, would be oppressive and intolerable.

Again, nobody can say whether this European element will take the form of one or several federations or confederations, or what pattern of links and influences will emerge from such phenomena as the 'technological gap', West European co-operation, the Common Market's relations with East European states, Eastern Europe's willingness and ability to enter (with or without the Soviet Union) into multilateral enterprises with Western Europe or the United States.

But whatever actual balance and organization takes shape, it will have to be based more on the making and combining of ties, even contradictory ones, than on cutting them. By the same token, it will have to combine the three levels – the national (and particularly the inter-German one), the European (in the form both of West European institutions and of all-European co-operation) and the global East–West one (if only as an ultimate condition or guarantee).

Thus, for the present, the chief virtue of approaching European security as a 'system' may lie less in any particular scheme than in underscoring the daily need for a flexible yet indissoluble link between these three indispensable elements of policy – Germany's *Ostpolitik*, European integration and co-operation, and US–Soviet *détente* and arms-control negotiations.

III. The European and the global balance: the security requirements of stability

The conclusions of our search for the political conditions of a peaceful European order may be too general, and flexible, to impose any given framework from the viewpoint of security; but since they do pose certain requirements, for the articulation of national, regional and global levels, all these in turn serve as standards for the comparison between the two universal ('unit veto', and 'collective security') and the four regional (bipolarity, disengagement, 'Europe of the states' and 'integrated Europe') models of European security systems which I distinguished in the first chapter.

I shall start with a critical examination of self-defence and collective security, but only as a preface to the four basic systems which all involve a specific European and global balance.

A. *Two abstract solutions*

(i) *Everyone for himself?*

The 'unit veto system' as such is conceivable only in a possible future state of technology; even then it would hardly be favoured by any planner looking for a stable system. But already certain trends in its direction affect the present European political situation and military balance, and hence any future institutional arrangements. Politically, the trend is towards a 'renationalization of politics', in the words of Helmut Schmidt, and away from integrated blocs and alliances, which means not only that every state tends to want to make its own decisions but that some, including some small ones, take these positions in open defiance of one or both of the great powers, and without any tangible assurance of countervailing support (Rumania, Albania). Militarily, a medium state like France insists on its ability to deter any threat coming from anyone, and to rely ultimately on itself for its security; hence the traditional distinctions between small, medium and great powers tend to lose their clarity if not their meanings, almost as much as the distinctions between allies, neutrals and non-aligned.

However, if Switzerland can maintain her traditional neutrality, if today Albania can feel free to abuse every country under the sun except distant China, or if France can claim to protect not only herself but Western Europe more effectively than the United States, this is possible precisely because of the complexity of an international system, two of whose essential and most stable aspects are the balance of mutual deterrence between the United States and the Soviet Union, and the direct relevance of this central balance to the European situation through the great-power institutional commitment and the physical presence of their troops.[28] Given this situation, some states can choose armed neutrality, others can opt out of the military security effort altogether, some can rely on participation in an alliance, and others can put their military effort again at the service of their diplomacy, in order to throw doubts on the role of the present system and to indicate the possibility of an alternative one. Never have so many owed so much flexibility to the stability provided by so few. If either the central balance or its direct links with the European situation were removed, the ambiguity expressed in our inability to answer the question: 'Who owes how much security to whom?' might persist, but the stability associated with it would not. The differences in the power of states in relation to potential aggressors and in their links with potential protectors would assert themselves with a vengeance.

No wonder, then, that in the European case, nobody wishes Germany to rely for her own security on her ability to destroy every other power. Some multilateral framework, some collective arrangement committing stronger states to the protection and restraint of smaller ones must be an essential part of any European system.

(ii) Each for all, all for each?

But does this framework have to involve the notion of balance? Do these arrangements have in effect to be alliances? This is a problem raised by the second universal model, that of *collective security*, and it is a much more central one, since to dismiss it means to dismiss the basic alternative proposed from so many quarters to the confrontation of the two alliances in Europe.

Here again, the actual evolution of the political and security situation lends much weight to their claims. One which has been described is the increasingly multilateral, and reciprocal character of alignments and commitments. We tend to have, instead of two united military blocs unambiguously directed against each other, an increasingly complex system where not only alliances are instruments of unilateral control or of mutual influence and restraint between the leader and his lesser associates, but the leader of the opposite coalition actually sees an advantage in this control and this restraint.

In European terms, if the purpose of NATO, the Warsaw Pact, and American and Soviet troops is to prevent fighting not only between the United States and the Soviet Union or between Germany and Poland, but also between Greece and Turkey or between Rumania and Hungary; if what is to be prevented is not only Germany's conversion to Communism or capitalism but her emergence (be it in the form of civil war or of nuclear power) as a threat to the common peace and stability of the continent, should not the common function of these organizations, or of these troops, become the official basis of their existence, and should this not be done by bringing them under a common roof where their residual, mutually antagonistic tasks could appear as what they are, *viz.* the deterrence of one conceivable conflict or aggression among many others?

By no longer stressing a particular conflict, a particular enemy or even a particular potential aggressor, a single collective security system would encourage mutual co-operation instead of perpetuating mutual distrust and hostility. By ending the political division of the continent and of Germany in two institutionalized blocs or alliances, it would seem to be both a condition and a consequence of their eventual reunification. Whether at the beginning or at the end of the process, whether as the sanction of a territorial *status quo* which could only have lost its hostile and its provisional character, or as the sanction of a new settlement, the military presence of the United States and the Soviet Union, and also the military positions of European countries like Germany, could be adapted to what had become their real or at least their main function, rather than being maintained at a level and within a structure which is the relic of a fading confrontation.

In this case multilateralization or a de-emphasized long-range military posture would appear as positive ways of managing or regulating the military balance and political relationship of Germany, of the two Europes and the superpowers, rather than acting as a substitute for them.

Experience from the inter-war period shows that collective security was, at best, a framework for specific regional balances and political commitments, and that the burden of the peace rested on the stability of these balances and the strength of the commitments incurred. The specific character of the postwar and of the present European situation (the division of Europe and of Germany into two, perhaps converging but certainly different social systems, the essential yet ambiguous presence of the United States and the Soviet Union, the evolution of military technology) emphasize the more the impossibility of leaving the threat to peace simply anonymous, the reaction supposed to deter or punish it simply collective and the commitment to do so simply declaratory or legal. As in the inter-war period when, as Arnold Wolfers has shown, the French conception (shared by Winston Churchill) of the League and of collective security was one of an institutionalized great coalition against the 'German menace',[29] in the same way today's proponents of a collective security system can again be divided between genuine idealists or universalists, and those who think mainly in terms of security against a specific (named or unnamed) potential aggressor, which for the most part remains Germany. Thus, more especially from the Eastern side, two French inter-war distinctions between *garanties physiques* and *garanties supplémentaires*, and between 'general treaties' and 'special accords' would play a most important role. Collective security might be useful but only as a supplement or a framework for either direct guarantees resulting from physical presence and military readiness, or for regional agreements between two or more states who have security interests in common against one or more others (the bilateral pacts replacing the Warsaw Pact might be the equivalent of the French treaties with East European countries).

An intermediate solution would be of the Locarno variety; regional pacts – in this sense partial and relying on some implicit territorial balance and differentiation – yet reciprocal and singling out no one as a potential aggressor. The problem would be that if, as in the Locarno agreement, some countries would pledge not to attack each other and some external powers would reciprocally guarantee the signatories against each other from outside attack, the first category would then know who was the potential enemy and the second would have to know it to a certain extent, in order to make the guarantee credible. Whether one thinks in terms of deterrence, of defence, punitive sanctions or retaliation, it is very difficult to be serious about any form of security role without preparing in some way for its implementation. This is no easy matter and it becomes questionable if one can do any contingency-planning for crises without having some idea of the likely opponent. While to the theorist, reciprocity is more peaceful and co-operative, to the military planner and the statesman who tries to deter, what counts are actual preparations and demonstrations, which can hardly be either universal or impartial.[30]

This is even more true if one sees the same problem from the other side: not 'Who is to be deterred?' but 'Who is to deter?' Again, to say 'everyone together' as the collective security doctrine has it, runs against the universal experience that states will resort to war only when they feel directly threatened, and that even in a regional framework peace is not indivisible enough for a Scandinavian country to identify the security of a Balkan country with its own or *vice versa*. Second, if one thinks in terms of a pre-organized and institutionalized collective military force, all the familiar issues so often studied in the context of the UN (political authority, unity of command, composition of the force, strength and credibility as against a possible opponent) reappear.

Both a pledge of collective intervention against an aggressor, and the organization of a standing multi-national force, involve (if they are to retain any credibility) a requirement of military (or at least inter-staff) co-operation which would become paralysed by the possibility that one of those concerned might become the aggressor against whom the organization would have to be used. Since, presumably, the differences in military power would continue to exist, the question of whether collective security could function against one of the superpowers is obviously crucial; but when answered in the negative it still leaves open the question whether both superpowers, one of them, or neither, would take part in such a multi-national force, offer their explicit guarantee, or whether the system would be operated by the Europeans, the American and Soviet guarantee remaining separate or even implicit. Finally, this raises a crucial problem linked to the consequences of military technology. Historically, it would seem that both a flexible balance of power[31] and collective security[32] stand to benefit from a type of war which does not entail extensive peacetime military preparation and co-ordination, but which does involve slow and cumbersome mobilization during the first phase of hostilities. This gave a chance to the *status quo* coalition to organize itself and to bring its superior strength to bear, thus overcoming the aggressor's advantage of initiative and unity. The changes in technology, the danger of surprise attack, the stress on deterrence, on unity of decision, on advance planning and on forces in being, made this type of war seem obsolete, and encouraged the emergence of institutionalized multilateral peacetime alliances of the NATO type.

However, a new round seems to be emerging. The likelihood that a war in Europe would be a nuclear one, the fact that the essential nuclear balance is the strategic Soviet–American one, and the spectacular progress made in strategic mobility would seem to remove any incentive for a cumbersome integrated alliance based upon huge ground armies, and to clear the way for substituting the guarantee, the protection or commitment of the superpowers to intervene, for the actual physical presence of their troops. Hence, the military conditions of disengagement plus multilateral guarantees which did not exist in the 1950s may be fulfilled in the 1970s. But if guarantees are commitments to intervene, the crucial factor becomes the credibility of such commitments in the nuclear age, more especially in the present condition of the nuclear strategic balance.

At this point a glance at Vietnam, at the recent Middle East crisis, and the relative uncertainty about who guarantees whom, and to what extent in Asia as compared to Europe, confirms the prediction of strategic analysis. The strategic nuclear balance makes the two great powers determined to avoid fighting directly against each other, even with conventional weapons, and using nuclear weapons, even against lesser powers.

The result, as shown in the Middle East, is a relative freedom for local power relations to assert themselves, and for situations to be modified by the use of force, when the two great powers are not directly and physically involved. In some cases, both are relatively ambiguous in their support of their respective allies, beyond the restraint (by deterrence and conciliation) of the other superpower. In other cases, as in Vietnam, the first power to commit itself has a relatively free hand (as far as the direct intervention of the other great power is concerned), at least as long as the former does not use nuclear weapons.

In a situation of strategic balance, nuclear weapons would, then, seem to limit the chances of intervention, and hence the credibility of the guarantees of one nuclear superpower to a third country against an attack by the other superpower. To give credibility to the commitment, whether through symbolic identification or through submission to a certain risk of automatic escalation, nothing can then replace actual entanglement and no entanglement speaks more clearly than the actual physical presence of troops.[33]

When the global nuclear balance is characterized by mutual invulnerability, at least to the extent of a sufficient mutual level of assured destruction, the basis of security both for the superpowers and for third countries, according to the extent to which they depend on them, is to be found in 'hostages'. The modern equivalent of the Hobbesian: 'Covenants without swords are but words' might be 'guarantees without hostages are but mirages'.

This does not necessarily mean the condemnation of a European system based on collective security. It does mean, however, that the security of the present system in Europe has very largely owed its superiority, compared with that of other regions, precisely to the very factor which would be called into question if the present alliances were replaced by an American disengagement, even accompanied by guarantees.

Certainly in a system where two German states exist, the twin goals of guaranteeing their security and of restricting their freedom of action, of preventing them from being friendly to the point of reunification and hostile to the point of war, is achieved most satisfactorily by the presence of Soviet and American troops. Egypt and Israel have both more freedom of action, and less security, than the two German states. Why the rivalry of these states and their desire to reunify their whole country on their own terms has not led to war, as did the two-Korea and the two-Vietnam situations, can be answered in part as follows: because a war between the two Germanies would have automatically meant a war of the two superpowers. The same physical presence which creates the certainty of escalation also gives them the means of preventing it by controlling their allies.

One may be content with the residual value of guarantees without hostages, or dispense with them altogether, either if the balance of satisfaction and the demilitarization of politics has gone as far as to render the security problem obsolete, or if the emergence of a European pole has rendered the role of the global balance a supplement or a reinsurance to a purely local one. In both cases a collective security type of system is again possible only as an institutional arrangement based on a new balance or a new settlement.

An alternative but not contradictory direction would be the search for a substitute to military troops stationed on the front line of alliances as hostages, or to hostages as tokens of commitments. Soviet and American troops might stay in Europe, but in a more symbolic and co-operative fashion;

and various solutions – multilateralization, exchange of military hostages – could be envisaged. They all would have political implications, for or against such possibilities as a Soviet–American condominium, and would have less plausibility, if two or more powers were supposed to act together, than the protection of one leader.

As for substitutes to the permanent presence of troops, Osgood and Tucker rightly observe: 'The absence of a strictly military reason for institutionalized co-ordination may only mean that states will either have to find non-military reasons (such as military and political sharing) for maintaining these deterrent devices, or else invent alternative ways of demonstrating military solidarity (such as military exercises, exchange of military personnel, and the like).'[34]

States would become more self-reliant but would still need protection; alliances would become less entangling but would still require credibility. Can one find plausible ways of squaring these circles? This is perhaps the crux of the security problem in both Europe and the world at large. There seems to be some discrepancy between the political evolution of international relations towards a position of flexibility and renationalization, and the military-technological evolution requiring a real entanglement to make commitments stick.

The problem of a European security system, then, becomes how to make political realities more flexible – which seems to be required both by actual trends and for the possible settlement of conflicts – without military commitments becoming too flexible for safety. Since conciliation of conflicting requirements and contradictory trends is the essence of the matter, all the principles of order and security have to be combined in some way or other, the proportion varying according to the model used. No European state can rely completely either on itself or on the international community for its security, and hence the balance between groups of states linked by formal or informal relations of solidarity, protection or alliance must be the basis of European security; but the system must reflect the need for increased independence of states symbolized by the unit-veto system, and the need for reciprocal arrangements rather than bipolar hostility symbolized by collective security.

For political reasons one may choose to emphasize the reciprocal framework and have *de facto* groupings and balances within a formally all-European arrangement; or, for security reasons, to emphasize the specific commitments and have military alliances constitute the formal framework, while playing an essentially reciprocal and all-European role. This difference is important, but less so than the recognition that alliances can survive only if they are reoriented towards another role than that of preparing for war against each other; and that multilateral security arrangements can survive only if they rely on a more specific structure of balances, ties and commitments than the abstract and universal notion of collective security would allow for.

B. Four models for European security

What can this specific structure be? Here we must examine our four types of European models in order to confront their political objectives and their military requirements.

(1) Modified Bipolarity

The extent to which the problem of European Security is defined in the narrow sense, as the avoidance of war (the political implication being the desirability of keeping the *status quo*, or of allowing only for as much change as necessary for or compatible with the maintenance of the existing military balance) would seem to make clear that the most advantageous model is the modified bipolarity one. It combines the nearest approximation to a regional balance on the ground, in terms of numbers of men and unity of command, through the existence of the two alliances, and the closest link to the global strategic balance, through the physical presence of both American and Soviet troops. Moreover, the existence of multilateral alliances and the presence of their leaders also seems the best way of preventing the eruption of war out of national conflicts, as distinct from solving the conflicts themselves. As far as the German problem is concerned, the present system may prevent its solution but in the meantime it does constitute the best check against any explosion. The risks of escalation in an incident involving Berlin are certainly increased by the presence of Soviet and American troops, but here again, short of a political solution, these troops are also the best means of preventing escalation by controlling their respective allies and, last but not least, by what has been called the de-escalatory effect of the threat of escalation.

But there are certain objections to the present system. Looking at the East–West balance on the ground, the situation is from both a strictly military and arms-control viewpoint less stable than it would seem, given the low threshold for the use of nuclear weapons and the decreased space for land warfare since the defection of France.[35]

Regarding relations with the global balances, the presence of American and Soviet troops increases the difficulty of insulation, and so, as some would argue, increases the risk of Europe becoming involved in a conflict started, for instance, over Vietnam. Finally, as I have shown at length in Part I, economic, psychological and political considerations challenge the present level, and perhaps the existence, of the balance so that it may have to be changed to survive.

That is why the concept of modified bipolarity is relevant. This necessitates moving from confrontation to partition into spheres of influence, combined with a certain measure of co-operation between the two superpowers, of disengagement of their troops and of greater freedom of action for their allies. A lighter, more co-operative and more flexible system would result, if some of its requirements did not seem to diverge. To decrease the number of conventional troops, following political and financial trends, would mean increasing Western Europe's reliance on deterrence and on nuclear weapons and consequently on the United States, to say nothing of the disadvantages of the low nuclear threshold from the viewpoint of military stability.[36] The strategic evolution towards a more mobile, peripheric strategy relying on the possibility of 'Big Lift' type of operation rather than the permanent stationing of troops, might provide a solution by permitting a decrease in the number of troops without an increase in reliance on nuclear weapons. In addition, this would provide a more satisfactory relationship with other regional balances such as the Asian one, by giving the United States greater flexibility in the shifting of her forces from one theatre to the other, while slightly decreasing for the Europeans the risks of automatic involvement in Asian conflict. But anything which decreases the automatic dependability of the American involvement restores to the European scene a greater unpredictability which is the inevitable consequence of a larger and more flexible role for the European countries themselves. The relative strength of German troops and of the other allies on the central front, the potential conflicts between other allies in other areas, the greater difficulties of crisis-management, the psychological preponderance of the Soviet Union through geographical proximity and a demographic superiority which would be less visibly or tangibly – even if not less reliably – compensated by the American presence would be some of the consequences. All this would seem to indicate that if the thinning-out was supposed to go beyond a limited rationalization of the existing deployment, its destabilizing factors should be checked (to say nothing of its political opportunities being exploited) by institutional and reciprocal arrangements.

According to the extent of great-power military presence, the scope of their co-operation and the aspects they would choose to emphasize through their institutional agreements, the model of modified bipolarity would lean either towards the reciprocal stabilization of the existing alliances, or towards disengagement plus guarantees.

The first direction is what Karl Birnbaum has called the *direct* road to European security. To borrow the distinction stressed by Georg Bluhm, this road is supposed to lead to the *control* and *management* of conflict by modifying the military arrangements in Central Europe in such a way that is conducive to peace in contrast to the *indirect* road approach, which is concerned with the ultimate *resolution* of conflict by political evolution in Europe as a whole.[37] However, given the state of military stability and political instability, as has been described, and the possible interplay between the two, the difficulty is rather to find measures which should improve the atmosphere, while safeguarding a currently decaying political framework and modifying an at present satisfactory military situation. Yet, whatever measures are taken in this direction within the framework of the two alliances run the risk either of making a very marginal increase in safety, and consequently having a rather negligible political effect, or of throwing doubt on the stability of the two alliances by jeopardizing the military balance, or opening the way to a new political framework.

The way out of this dilemma would be based on two considerations. First, since the high level of military expenditure is now the main concern of the West European powers and the main threat to the existing system, to decrease the level of forces without decreasing the credibility of the global deterrence and the stability of the regional balance would go a long way towards succeeding in politics without really trying: reducing military forces and financial costs would *ipso facto* reduce political tensions at least within NATO.

However, assuming this feat is technically possible, it is politically conceivable only on one important condition, which is our second consideration: that it presupposes a much greater degree *both* of inter-alliance and of intra-alliance (or, more specifically, of US–Soviet and US–West European) trust and co-operation than Vietnam, French and probably Soviet policy permit today. Almost by definition, the distinctive feature of co-operative bipolarity, of the approach to *détente* through revived alliances and to alliances through a new birth of *détente*, is the combination of understanding and co-operation between alliances and among allies. Not only are these indispensable for fruitful negotiations and acceptable institutional arrangements, yet even more are unilateral arms-control measures apt to be made impossible or harmful by hostile political exploitation. As long as political goals diverge, the margin for arms-control measures in Europe, building on common interests between all concerned, is narrow, and to be effective they are likely to have to rely on and tend towards significant political changes connected with the 'indirect road to security', and with the resolution of existing conflicts.

The most obvious expression of the desire to stabilize the situation by co-operation would be in measures taken to eliminate even further the reciprocal fear of surprise attack, as well as the danger of accidental conflict and uncontrolled escalation, by an improvement in both trust and communications between the two alliances. These begin with the exchange of non-aggression pledges, through the mutual inspection of troop movements, eventually to improved communications and consultation (via a hot line between supreme commanders or via a standing East–West commission ready to discuss any emergency) between the two alliances in time of crisis. The difficulty, in each case, however, is to distinguish between the symbolic and the effective.

The non-aggression pledges could not even be expected to generate or diffuse good will; if they have any meaning and impact at all, it can only be as a symbol (probably dangerous today, possibly useful tomorrow in the perspective of co-operative bipolarity) of the symmetry between the two alliances and, at least implicitly, between the two Germanies.

Mutual troop inspection through fixed or mobile observers is the preference of anyone wishing to produce some positive arms-control measure: since the one thing that nobody fears is a massive surprise ground attack, and as the two sides already monitor the movements of each other's troops, a symbol of co-operation can be added, not affecting in any way the actual security relationship.

Zbigniew Brzezinski, outlining the perspective of security agreements between the two alliances, which from now on must concentrate on the promotion of peace, puts forward as his most specific suggestion concerning security the initiation of 'open-ended discussions of security in Central Europe between the two alliances', which 'could lead, perhaps by the early 1970s, to the creation of a European Security Commission, based on the two alliances', the actual purpose of which would be to monitor troop movements in Central Europe and make periodic inspections of troop deployments.[38]

In fact, apart from the symbolic value of creating an institutionalized expression of the inter-alliance approach to *détente*, such discussions and such a commission would have value mainly in the extent to which they would examine the more important, but also controversial, fields of control and resolution of conflict, of 'crisis-management' and of political settlement. This appears the more clearly in the case of more ambitious measures such as arms freezes and limitations, reciprocal reductions of troops or nuclear-free zones. In Part I, I have tried to describe the interplay of political and military problems created by troop reduction and the various possible ways it might affect both the intra- and the inter-alliance balances.[39] The nature and gravity of the problems will vary according to whether the reductions are unilateral or negotiated, and whether their scope takes in a given country or zone, the whole Central European front, the whole of Europe or the whole of the two alliances, including the forces of the two superpowers not directly assigned to the European Theatre.

At one extreme, *de facto* modifications and adjustments of the regional and of the global balance through unilateral reductions or increases, which are usually, but not automatically, matched by the other side, can and will occur, as they already have in the past. Yet, almost by definition, they cannot go far enough to affect the stability of the global balance or the certainty of the protection it extends to the regional one, without affecting the very maintenance of the existing alliance system.

At the other extreme, a negotiated agreement on the demilitarization or denuclearization of a group of countries, including Germany, is very unlikely to be achieved as an arms-control measure within the framework of the two alliances. Indeed, anything which could even be interpreted remotely as a reinforcement in Germany's special or 'discriminated' status, combined with a decrease in her security, can only occur in one of three ways: as a *de facto* measure, if strategic and economic evolution have made it possible and desirable, and if it can be divested of its political implications as well as of its military dangers; as a step in Germany's bilateral political exploration and dialogue with the Soviet Union; or as part of some kind of settlement of the German and European problem. This settlement may conceivably be reached (in a rather distant future) through the bipolar road of conversations between the two great powers and between the two alliances, but even if it did underwrite the continued presence of the former and the continued validity of the latter, it could not help involving a fundamental reordering of the relations between the two Germanies, the two Europes and the two superpowers.

Between these two extremes there is room for a relatively modest, progressive and flexible structure made of 'some East–West security relationships between the two existing but looser alliances'.[40] But the essential point, as soon as these relationships are seen as requiring negotiations to change the situation, rather than to sanction it, is the question of the multilateral or bilateral character of these contacts and negotiations. Both the crisis-management and the political dialogue cannot help having some features of a bilateral understanding between the two powers. This is precisely why Soviet–American co-operation of any value, leading to a transformation of their relationship, must, if the two alliances are to be safeguarded, be accompanied by a new institutional reaffirmation of American ties with her European allies, and by some progress in the unity of Western Europe and in her role in NATO.

The model of modified bipolarity leads then, if the modification is to be taken seriously, to at least some steps in the direction of the other models. A viable *de facto* system based on co-operation between the two alliances in an atmosphere of *détente* must allow the United States to fulfil her role with fewer men and less money (hence at least some military disengagement); and allow Germany to pursue her *rapprochement* with East Germany and her demonstration of peaceful intent (hence some diminution of her direct military role). The system must compensate for these two trends by forming new (possibly non-military) ways of tying both the United States and Germany to the rest of the alliance; consequently, it must involve both the reaffirmation of American-European interests and commitments (just as, by itself, the Non-Proliferation Treaty *should* in principle lead to tighter rather than looser links between the great powers and the nations who agree to give up nuclear self-protection) and an increase in European unity and autonomy. Modified bipolarity is less a model in itself than a first step in the direction of disengagement, or europeanization, or both.

(2) Disengagement plus guarantees

The important and sometimes overlooked point about this model is that it, too, represents a modified form of bipolarity. The basic balance would continue to be the global American–Soviet one. Only, instead of this strategic balance being closely linked by physical presence to the regional one, the latter is, for all practical purposes, suppressed or reduced to a balanced minimum of continental forces, while the link with the global balance, which will have to carry the whole burden of deterrence and stability, is provided by the guarantees of reciprocal agreement rather than by the troops of the two alliances.

It would then seem that from the point of view of military stability and security the result would risk being negative on every level: while the regional balance is suppressed in favour of a *de facto* Soviet superiority, the global balance is both more immediately essential and less immediately linked to the local situation. The withdrawal of American troops would decisively weaken the local balance by the termination of their military function of defence; it would greatly weaken the impact of the global balance by the suppression of their deterrent function as hostages. A weaker Western Europe would be protected by a weaker American commitment.

The counter-argument, from the security viewpoint, is that the binding force of legal instruments is no less great than arrangements for a hostage-type alliance. In the absence of a satisfactory settlement, a unilateral withdrawal of American troops, or even a mutual withdrawal, and a dissolution of the two alliances if accompanied by the maintenance of the Soviet Union's hegemony in the East and rights of re-entry into the DDR through the new system of bilateral pacts might mean, to use Löwenthal's expression, a 'Finlandization' of Western Europe. But this (so the argument runs) would no longer hold true if a really reciprocal and binding agreement was concluded; then the assurance that re-entry by one side would mean re-entry by the other and experience of past Russian practice of keeping this type of agreement once they have signed it, should be sufficient to ensure stability. The freedom of action of both the superpowers and the medium European powers would be diminished, but it is in this very freezing of the military situation, formalized by agreements on denuclearization and arms limitation, that the maintenance of the *status quo* would be guaranteed.

While this argument of the symbolic value of written agreements for constraining future Soviet and American conduct is not to be lightly dismissed, it still seems that both inescapable military realities and probable psychological reactions will tend to militate in the opposite direction. Militarily, the geographical proximity of Soviet troops would create a more serious imbalance than would be the case in a mutual thinning-out; distance may have lost much of its importance due to the possibility of 'Big Lift' operations but this presupposes the maintenance on the ground of troops, installations and equipment. The usefulness of peacetime training, or of wartime crisis-management or controlled escalation, would be borne home to the United States in the event of a Soviet surprise attack made possible by a local imbalance of forces; in this situation they would be presented with an all or nothing choice, the very thing they are most anxious to avoid. Both the credibility of deterrence and the possibility of defence would be gravely jeopardized.

It might be argued that since, having made the political choice of entering this agreement, the Russians have no intention of launching a surprise attack, then the practical aspects of defence count for very little and whatever residual deterrence is necessary can be safely left to the guarantee. But while this is probably accurate as far as Soviet intentions are concerned, it is almost certainly wrong if one tries to envisage the psychological expectations and likely political atmosphere and attitudes of the European countries. After all, the Russians would probably also not launch an attack if there was no explicit American guarantee, but only the remote possibility of intervention due to the existence of the strategic balance. However, this does not mean that degrees of certainty and degrees of deterrence do not matter. The Russians have probably no intention of repeating their 'Hungarian' intervention in Albania, Rumania, Czechoslovakia, Bulgaria or Finland; yet each of these countries adopts a different evaluation of their ability to resist Soviet 'suggestions' and risk Soviet displeasure, so the military factor must enter their calculations (as has been made painfully clear in the case of Czechoslovakia) in a way it does not for the countries of Western Europe.

This element of unpredictability which comes from the absence of a direct and visible American counterweight would create at least a certain risk of miscalculation, and hence of insecurity, which cannot help but affect the political *status quo* to the advantage of the Soviet Union. Such a change, so aptly described by the term 'Finlandization', could be reduced but not prevented if the Soviet Union renounced her bilateral treaties with Eastern Europe, or even if the United States and the Soviet Union maintained purely symbolic contingents in Berlin. While the European situation may seem calm enough not to make of a 'new Locarno' a recipe for doom, it must still be concluded from the point of view of security and balance that such a system would be decidedly inferior to the present one.

If the security of Europe is to continue to be primarily based on the Soviet–American bipolar balance and thus on the American commitment, then there is everything to be said for keeping American troops in Europe. The existence of a regional balance makes military protection a more serious proposition; and the existence of hostages does the same for the security commitment. Both considerations merge into the obvious one that the United States can be reasonably expected by both the Russians and West Europeans to make good her commitment only if she is involved from the beginning of a crisis, both in the passive sense of not being able to avoid being engaged, and in the active sense of being able to play a decisive role in the political and military management of the crisis.

On the other hand, if American disengagement is considered as inevitable or as desirable for political reasons, then this can only mean that, rightly or wrongly, the American guarantee and the Soviet–American global equilibrium are no longer the main bases of European security. Their diminishing relevance can in turn mean only some degree of Soviet hegemony in Europe, or the emergence of a European or Continental regional balance, which would act either as a substitute or a supplement to the American-based one. American disengagement can only then be the first step in a process of Sovietization (in its milder and more modern form of 'Finlandization'), or the last step in a process of Europeanization.

(3) Europe of the States

The Gaullist notion of a 'Europe of the States' 'from the Atlantic to the Urals' would be described by its critics as being subjectively aimed at 'Europeanization' and yet leading objectively to 'Finlandization'. It is all the more interesting, then, that the most subtle defender of De Gaulle's 'grand design', Prof. George Liska, who insisted in *Europe Ascendant*, on the first aspect, has recently spelled out the implications of a Franco-Soviet sponsored European Security Pact in terms of acceptance of a limited Soviet hegemony in Europe. Instead of aiming at a European balance, a world system of complementary imbalances should be sought, favouring the Soviet Union in Europe and the United States globally.

'The pact should be built around the Soviet Union as Europe's foremost power, implicitly aimed at West Germany, Europe's physical centre and psychological point of common concern, and in the last resort circumscribed by the strategic vigilance of the United States as the condition of Western Europe's self-confidence *vis-à-vis* Soviet Russia.' But, on the other hand, despite the vast disparity in military strength between France and Russia, the Soviets may well conclude that they need France to keep Western Europe quiet and any American action awkward or illegitimate, should good reasons arise for intervening militarily against a resurgent Germany about to go nuclear.'[41]

In its general implications, this three-tiered scheme does seem to correspond more closely than the simple concept of balance to the strategic relationship between the United States, the Soviet Union and Europe.

However, the putting into practice of any concept which leaves America content with global preponderance, and with abandoning Europe to the limited preponderance of the Soviet Union assisted by France as a junior partner, seems pretty implausible.

Even more obscure is the role of France, which appears to be limited to one of a legitimizing function for various aspects of Soviet control of both Eastern Europe and Germany. While this role may have a certain political plausibility in a period of change and manoeuvre, it becomes extremely difficult to envisage just how France would 'keep Western Europe quiet or any American action awkward or illegitimate' in the event of Soviet intervention against Germany. The balance of risks and interests within the political-military Soviet–German–American triangle would surely overwhelmingly outweigh, in any such apocalyptical situation, the moral or psychological approval or disapproval of France.

Last but not least, there is the problem of Germany. The overall weight of Germany as compared to France, and the other medium European states, constitutes the disruptive factor in any continental European system, and most strikingly so in such a system based on control by a Franco-Soviet concert. Again, the same dialectic is at work: if all that is wanted is preservation of the *status quo*, and especially the essential feature of the *status quo* as constituted by Germany's non-access to nuclear weapons, this is in America's interests as well as in France's. This can be secured either by Soviet–American agreement, or by Germany's integration into a larger Western whole, or by both, more effectively than by any threat of a bizarre scenario involving Soviet intervention protected by France against reaction from the United States. On the other hand, if one assumes America's withdrawal, the resulting European balance cannot help but be determined by the nature of the relationship between Germany and the Soviet Union.

If one considers the problem in terms of diplomatic and military combinations between European states, every possible solution is faced with the basic difficulties of both balancing a Soviet Union whose present power is known to be superior, and of controlling the evolution of a Germany whose future power is unknown.

If one thinks of the European system as one of balance between two alliances, West and East, in which the United States does not participate, two problems then become immediately apparent. Without Russia, Eastern Europe is too weak to balance Western Europe; with Russia, she is too strong. On the Western side, a similar problem arises with respect to Germany. If Western Europe is, according to de Gaulle's wishes, to have 'a defence which is her own defence', and if this defence is to be conceived of as the mere co-ordination of national contributions, then it would appear that it can do neither with nor without German participation. A mere addition to or co-ordination of the French and British nuclear forces would be incapable of both balancing and deterring the Soviet Union and of satisfying Germany's desire for equality and participation. On the other hand, the disappearance of NATO would have removed the integration of the Bundeswehr. If Germany participated on an equal footing in the West European alliance, the first two obstacles would be only partially overcome (Western Europe would still be weaker and possess a less credible deterrent, in terms of unity of control, than the Soviet Union, and Germany would not have satisfied all her national aspirations since she would still be divided). But the third one would assume dangerous proportions – if not in terms of what Germany might do – at least in terms of everyone else's fears and reactions, especially those of the Soviet Union, Poland and Czechoslovakia.

If one thinks of the opposite *alliance de revers* type of combination – that is of a *de facto* encirclement of Germany by her neighbours, one would have, regarding Germany's strength *vis-à-vis* that of Europe, problems similar to the Versailles settlement. To the extent that these would be alleviated by the different position of the Soviet Union and the United States, they in turn would raise the post-World War II dilemma of how to avoid replacing the risks of German by those of Soviet domination, without accepting some milder form of domination from the United States. Germany would have to be strong and sovereign enough to satisfy her own people. At the same time, she would have to be sufficiently weak or controllable not to be able to embark upon a course which could become a threat to the security of the continent.

Obviously, the nation-states of Western Europe (even including Britain) and Eastern Europe (excluding the Soviet Union) would be in an even less favourable position than they were after 1919 to keep this European balance and to prevent the natural weight and dynamism of German power from reasserting itself. The decrease in stature brought on Britain, France and Poland by World War II, which has made the presence of the Soviet Union and the United States both possible and necessary, would still be felt in relation to a renascent German power.

If the aim is to make the indispensable Soviet and American participation in the balance-and-control operation a less direct and physical one, Germany (or the two Germanies) would have to be cemented into a much more solid European framework, which would require that Western and Eastern Europe (albeit in differing proportions) become both stronger and more united, within their own region and with the other half, than they are now. Barring this eventuality, Russia's full and physical participation in the system leads to the risk of her exercising her hegemony over the continent, or at least being able to play with the various possible combinations either with or against Germany. For the small and middle countries of Europe, the only acceptable prospects are either an equilibrium which, to avoid domination by either Germany or Russia or a confrontation between them, must include the United States, or a radical and distant transformation of the situation through the creation in the West of a new political unit capable of resisting domination either by the United States, or the Soviet Union, or Germany, whose own weight would still be better balanced in an institutionalized framework than through diplomatic agreements and alignments. The combination of West European integration and all-European reunification could then lead from a bipolar system to a European one built, as geography requires, around Germany, but neither against nor under her.

Whether, then, one starts with any of the first three models envisaged – one is necessarily led to the fourth, as the only partial alternative to Soviet–American bipolarity and the necessary condition of Soviet–American disengagement and of a more 'continental' Europe whether within, between or beyond existing alliances. There can be no increase in the European role which does not imply a decrease in European security if it is not preceded or at least accompanied by an increase in European institutionalized co-operation.

(4) Integrated Europe

We are thus led, under the label of our fourth model – Europeanization through integration – to two different stages. The first one, based upon a bipolar balance, involves, to begin with, a strengthening of the West and East European element in the two alliances, and, further and more specially, the creation of some kind of West European defence community (the East European symmetric one being beyond the limits of realistic speculation). The second would involve an all-European confederal or federal system, on

Change and Security in Europe 257

the lines described above, to which the two great powers would be linked, but through looser institutional and military ties than those operating at the centre of the structure.

The essential point to grasp is the relationship between the two stages. True, they can be conceived separately; the first one can be pursued for its own sake if one believes in the permanence of the division between the two Europes and the two Germanies. But, if pursued exclusively or in isolation, it would almost certainly create a tension that would be harmful both to security and to the evolution towards an all-European system. Yet if one looks at the second stage, it appears that it must include at least some elements of the first: a united or uniting Europe from the Atlantic to the Bug or 'from Brest to Brest' must contain some regional differentiation and overall balance; both would seem to involve a pole of power and stability in Western Europe, based on special links between the present EEC or WEU countries. Indeed, and this is my third observation, if the all-European model were to come into being at all, it is difficult to see what could be a more important factor than precisely this progressive unity and attraction of Western Europe under the umbrella of the Soviet–American bipolar relationship. Only this process could create a sufficient stabilization of the continent to make the two great powers consider that a less direct presence would be compatible with their own security and that of Europe.[42]

The priority, then, would appear to be a strengthening of the specific and autonomous ties between the small and medium European members within the two alliances, in such a fashion as not to do irreparable damage to the other two dimensions: the creation of new ties with the nations of the other half, and the redefinition of their relation with their respective superpower. The third dimension, the disengagement or the permanent engagement of the great powers in a new form, should only be the last stage of the process.

In an evolutionary perspective then, it seems without doubt to be true that the single direction most likely to advance the cause of a future peaceful order in Europe is progress towards a West European military community. Yet the continuing importance of the East–West strategic balance, and more especially of the American commitment, and the increasing relevance of the East–West *détente*, and more specifically of the German problem, place this effort under severe limitations. The result is much more likely to be, at least for a very long time to come, a combination of our four models than a straightforward application of the fourth one.

If we start from a comparison between the two simplest basic balances, the Soviet–American and European one, we have already seen there were three dangers in that substitution of the latter for the former. A West European coalition lacks enough strength and enough cohesion to provide a credible system of deterrence against the Soviet Union and a binding framework for Germany, yet it risks jeopardizing the American presence and weakening the American commitment which, at present through NATO, functions satisfactorily. Hence, the justification for a European community effort within

NATO stems from the fact that greater unity is supposed to bring greater strength (through the pooling of efforts), greater credibility (by pointing to a possible solution to the control issue) and a tighter framework for Germany (through military integration and political community) without prematurely throwing doubt on America's role; contrary to the Gaullist method, the accent would be on building new ties rather than on scrapping old ones.

By the same token, the maintenance of the Atlantic Alliance and the addition of integrated European controls to it should mitigate the Eastern fears of Germany raised by any West European military effort. It is essential to see that these various advantages are parts of a whole. A concerted European military effort, especially a nuclear one, which would weaken the ties with the United States without being preceded by much progress in political unity, would be doubly dangerous, as far as the Russian and the German problems were concerned. An increase in the military strength and responsibility of the various West European nations without corresponding progress in their political integration, or of progress in the latter without a spill-over into the military field, could be positive ones, but only as long as they did not pose as alternatives to the American role in Europe. In military, as in political and economic affairs, the less united the West Europeans are, the more they will have to accept American predominance. But, conversely, is independence from the United States the main or the only goal of a European military effort? And to what extent, and through what stages, is it likely to be achieved?

The answer may be in the basic distinction, which has been elaborated, among others, by J. L. Richardson[43] and Neville Brown,[44] between two types of European deterrent – one designed to supplant and the other to supplement the American protection.

The first type would not only be costly, but would very likely have to be provided entirely from Europe's own resources; it would have to cover all the rungs of the escalation ladder from conventional forces to forces able to deliver selective and discriminating nuclear strikes. Alternatively, it would have to rely on an imperfect and partial deterrence, which would be all the more dangerous since its very existence would make the American presence less certain.

The second type would be much less costly, and could conceivably be accepted by the US in order to prevent the first.[45] At any rate its building and its strategy would be co-ordinated with, or fitted within, the framework of NATO and US strategy. Its function would be to serve as an insurance; to be 'held in trust' for the coming of a federal Europe and of a negotiated settlement, or to limit the damage in the case of a break-down of the alliance. More immediately, it would increase the uncertainty of the aggressor and the probability of escalation, or, more specifically, it might serve to offset the possible Russian calculation of intimidating the United States by holding Western Europe as hostage, or of waging 'limited general war by proxy'. For this, the possibility of strict and proportionate or reflex retaliation provided by the 100 or 200 missiles of the French and British forces would be sufficient. The main protection against most types of attack would still be the American one, and the European deterrent would only be a method of influencing its character and its timing, and would supplement it in the case of certain specific contingencies based on possible Soviet calculations.

It might be argued that, because of the difficulties of collective control and of the dangers of German participation, increase in tension with the East would be more certain than increase in security. This may well be so; and this is why the case for a West European deterrent would be a very weak one if it were to be based on considerations of short-range security. However the same factors (the multilateral character and the link with the US) may limit the dangers as well as the immediate utility of the enterprise. At any rate, there would be no reason for Germany to get nearer the nuclear trigger, especially if a special agreement or unilateral declaration specifically excluded this possibility.[46] East European reactions are still likely to be hostile, but this may be tempered, as in the American case, by the desire to influence the future orientation of the force away from a fully fledged independence (especially for Germany) and from a fully fledged arms race.

Indeed, the vital question is the evolutionary one. Three possibilities are likely to emerge from this 'junior deterrent' policy. The first that it should acquire a permanent character; the situation then would be that of a NATO in which the European pillar, although decidedly inferior to the American one, would have significantly more cohesion and more influence than at present. From the viewpoint of the general system, it would mean 'bipolarity plus European integration', probably the most favourable situation from the point of view of security. The second would be a break-up of the alliance and an American withdrawal, which would conceivably provide the incentive for the military effort, financial outlay and the political urgency — all of which today are lacking — which are essential for converting the junior deterrent into a fully fledged one, capable of some kind of (probably rather unstable) balance with the Soviet Union. The third would be some kind of general arms-control agreement, such as a limitation or reduction of nuclear or all weapons in Europe. In this eventuality, the existence of a small European deterrent capable of being significantly stepped up might act as a bargaining counter and induce the Soviet Union to include her 700 MRBMs in the arms-control negotiation, and conceivably to arrive at some kind of balance, stabilized at a lower level, in a pacified Europe.[47]

However, it would be wrong to work today directly towards these long-range perspectives, even though it is vital to do nothing, such as, for example, abandoning the European clause on the non-proliferation treaty, which would make them impossible to attain. I might dissent from Alastair Buchan on the difficulty or likelihood of arriving one day at a European nuclear force; but I can hardly fail to agree with him that this would be decidedly the wrong end from which now to start.[48] While, as he points out, the proposition that military integration can only follow the political one is not necessarily true, it certainly remains so where the nuclear level is involved, if only because any suspicion of German national participation in a nuclear enterprise would be very harmful to all, not least to the Germans themselves. Of the various formulae he suggests, a non-nuclear European Defence Commission would contribute most directly to a desirable system of European security. But the two others – a European Technological Community and an 'Advanced Projects Authority' would contribute indirectly to the kind of Europe which alone would make this system possible.

The character of this Europe, and consequently of the nature of the relationship between West European states, the United States and Eastern Europe, is likely to be determined less by the security issue proper, than by the proportion or combination that will emerge between the European states' desire for greater technological and economic independence from the United States, for an East–West settlement and for a solution to the German problem.

West European integration is probably the necessary pre-condition of both these objectives, and of any European security system whose stability could be even remotely comparable to the present one. But conversely, her own character will be determined by them. As Miriam Camps has remarked[49] European unification can no longer be considered as an obvious goal either in terms of prosperity or of security, but must stand or fall by the contribution made towards increasing Europe's role as compared to that of the United States, and towards promoting a settlement in Central Europe.[50]

More specifically, just as a European deterrent is justified less in terms of security than as a necessary ingredient of a united Europe, so European integration itself, while possibly counter-productive in terms of immediate East–West *détente*, might nevertheless be indispensable if the condition for what Marshall Shulman calls a 'second stage of *détente*', perhaps twenty years from now, is a European settlement,[50] and if such a settlement must involve the three interdependent goals of a less direct Soviet and American presence, of a Germany less divided and, between these two, of a European collective structure no less solid than today as a protection both for and against Germany itself. The need, in the meantime, is for interim policies, policies which are justified in their own terms but which also take their full meaning either as contributions, or as precautions, predicated on this long-range perspective. Mr Heath's notion of holding the British and the French deterrent 'in trust' for a future Europe; the idea of many Germans that Franco-German friendship must be maintained at all costs, not for its benefits today but its possible importance tomorrow, are (whatever their merits as far as the actual issues are concerned) good examples of this attitude.

It should even be possible to work both more positively and directly within the protective cocoon of today's alliance systems, for the growth of tomorrow's butterflies. What may appear today as a useless institutional machinery or as sterile and repetitive meetings, could prepare and foreshadow the future European settlement and structure. Such desirable forums could include a

West European caucus within NATO; certain institutional or informal ways for East European states to get together, tolerable to the Soviet Union, and finally East–West commissions and assemblies, as suggested independently by Jean Laloy and Zbigniew Brzezinski, designed to discuss, on an official or unofficial level, not only economic and technological co-operation, but the organization of *détente*, the management of possible crises, the preparation of possible settlements. Both for their practical effectiveness and for their symbolic or prophetic value, it is desirable that the discussions or institutions which touch directly on political and security matters should include either both the United States and the Soviet Union or neither.

More generally and perhaps more negatively, the two basic principles, as enunciated by Stanley Hoffmann, would be to act neither as if tomorrow was already here, nor as if it would never come.[51] A third principle is to be prepared to be both surprised and disappointed by the actual settlement, if and when our efforts succeed. For, as R. H. Tawney wrote in another context: 'It is the tragedy of a world where man must walk by sight that the discovery of the reconciling formula is always left to future generations, in which passion has cooled into curiosity, and the agonies of people have become the exercise in the schools. The devil who builds bridges does not span such chasms till much that is precious to mankind has vanished down them for ever.'[52]

Notes

1 See L. Dehio, 'The Passing of the European System', *Germany and World Politics in the Twentieth Century* (London: Chatto & Windus, 1960), p. 124, and C. Fisher, 'The Changing Dimensions of Europe', *Journal of Contemporary History*, July 1966, p. 3.

2 Richard Löwenthal, 'The Germans Feel like Germans Again', *The New York Times Magazine*, 6 March 1966, p. 42.

3 See M. Kaplan, *System and Process in International Politics* (New York: John Wiley, 1964), p. 50, and P. Gallois, *Stratégie de l'âge nucléaire* (Paris: Calmann-Lévy, 1960).

4 *Change and Security in Europe. Part I: The Background*, Adelphi Paper No. 45 (London: ISS), February 1968.

5 Henry Kissinger, *A World Restored* (London: Weidenfeld & Nicolson, 1957), pp. 145–47.

6 Article by J. L. Garvin in *Outlook*, 1906, quoted by Gerhard Ritter in *The German Problem* (Columbus: Ohio State University Press, 1965).

7 A. J. P. Taylor, 'German Unity', in *Europe, Grandeur and Decline* (London: Pelican, 1967), pp. 121–26.

8 See Proposal No. 7 in Herr Ulbricht's 31 December 1966 speech: 'The governments of both German states sign a treaty through which they pledge themselves to accept together and simultaneously a status of neutrality for both German states, guaranteed by the Powers', *Archivder Gegenwart*, I, 1967, p. 12896.

9 See 'Wehners Denkmodelle', *Die Zeit*, 10 February 1967, and Dietrich Schwarzkopf, 'Wehners Einladung zur Konföderation', *Die Welt*, 27 February 1967.

10 See what may well be a prophetic article by M. Croan, 'Party Politics and the Wall', *Survey*, October 1966.

11 Philip Windsor, 'Berlin', in Evan Luard, ed., *The Cold War* (London: Thames & Hudson, 1964), p. 138.
12 See Theo Sommer, 'Erst streichen, dann denken', *Die Zeit*, 14 July 1967, and 'Eine Armee für morgen', *Die Zeit*, 28 July 1967.
13 See Henry Kissinger, *The Troubled Partnership* (New York: McGraw-Hill, 1965), p. 220.
14 See 'Die deutsche Frage in 1967 – aus französischer Sicht', *Moderne Welt*, 2/67, pp. 146–49.
15 François Duchêne, 'Britain in a Harder World', *Journal of Common Market Studies*, July 1965, and Miriam Camps, *European Unification in the Sixties* (New York: McGraw-Hill, 1966), pp. 227–30.
16 See also the latest suggestions of Zbigniew Brzezinski, 'The Framework of East–West Reconciliation', *Foreign Affairs*, January 1968, p. 273.
17 'Denkschrift' of K. G. Pfleiderer, 'Treaty System and Eastern Policy', September 1952. *Wege nach Gesamteuropa*. (Dokumentation der Beziehungen zwischen West- und Osteuropa, 1943–1965, Cologne, 1966.)
18 Jean Laloy has recently sketched this model of Germany at the centre of several overlapping communities, in 'Prospects and Limits of East–West Relations', *Western and Eastern Europe: The Changing Relationship*, Adelphi Paper No. 33 (London: Institute for Strategic Studies, March 1967), p. 10.
19 The behaviour not only of France and Rumania but of other Western and Eastern allies within international organizations provides a precise illustration of these two points.
20 This point is developed in my *Les Alliances sont-elles dépassées?* (Paris: Fondation Nationale des Sciences Politiques, 1967).
21 Alfred Fabre-Luce, *Locarno sans rêves* (Paris: B. Grasset, 1927), p. 206.
22 See Antonin Snejdarek, 'Small Countries and European Security', Adelphi Paper No. 33, *op. cit.*, p. 41; A. Ort, 'La neutralité dans le cadre des relations entre pays socialistes et pays occidentaux', IPSA Meeting, Brussels, September 1967; and Ladislav Liska, 'On the Problem of European Security', *International Relations* (Prague), Vol. I, 1966, p. 19.
23 See J. Brown, 'Die ungarische Aussenpolitik im Schatten des Bundnisses mit der Sowjetunion', *Europa-Archiv*, Folge 15, 1967, pp. 541–50, and C. Andras, 'Neighbours on the Danube: New Variations on the Old Theme of Regional Co-operation', *R.F.E. Research*, December 1967.
24 André Fontaine, 'Personnalité nationale et réconciliation européenne', *Le Monde*, 17–18 September 1967.
25 Z. Brzezinski, *Alternative to Partition* (New York: McGraw-Hill, for The Council on Foreign Relations, 1965), p. 175, pp. 264–65.
26 For more detailed attempts at speculation along similar lines see Klaus Mehnert, *Der deutsche Standort* (Stuttgart, 1967), on the dimensions and structure of a united Europe, and Walter Schütze, 'Modèles de Sécurité Européenne', *Politique Etrangère* 6/1967, on an arms-control zone and a Central European union. The idea of an integrated and neutralized Central Europe to accommodate a united and neutralized Germany has recently been advocated by the Slovak historian Daniel Rapant, 'On Dualism', *Slovenske Pohlady*, November 1967.
27 See Georg Bluhm, *Détente and Military Relaxation in Europe: A German View*, Adelphi Paper No. 40 (London: Institute for Strategic Studies, September 1967), p. 9 *passim*.
28 See Georg Bluhm, *op.cit.*, p. 10.
29 Arnold Wolfers, 'Policies of Peace and Security After World War I', *Discord and Collaboration: Essays on International Politics* (Baltimore: Johns Hopkins Press, 1962).
30 See G. Hudson, 'Collective Security and Military Alliances', in Butterfield and

Wight, eds, *Diplomatic Investigations* (London: Allen & Unwin, 1966), pp. 176–180. These considerations would seem to show the alleged rationale for the French *défense tous azimuts*, namely the idea of a 'balance of alliances', or of preparations with one power against another power's threat and *vice versa*, is unrealistic from a military point of view. See, for the French view, General Ailleret, ' "Défense dirigée" ou "Défense tous azimuts" ', *Revue de Défense Nationale*, December 1967, translated in *Survival*, February 1968, and G. Chaffard, 'La Défense "tous azimuts" ', *Le Monde Diplomatique*, January 1968.
31 Robert E. Osgood and Robert W. Tucker, *Force, Order and Justice* (Baltimore: Johns Hopkins Press, 1967), p. 72.
32 Inis L. Claude, *Power and International Relations* (New York: Random House, 1962), p. 192.
33 See T. Schelling, *Arms and Influence* (New Haven: Yale University Press, 1966), p. 61. For the whole analysis of commitment and the manipulation of risk, see *Arms and Influence*, pp. 35–126 *passim*.
34 Osgood and Tucker, *op. cit.*, pp. 117–181.
35 See Philip Windsor, 'Nato and European Détente', *The World Today*, September 1967.
36 See Alastair Buchan, 'Nato – Krise und europäische Entspannung', *Europa-Archiv*, 10 May 1967, p. 310.
37 See Georg Bluhm, Adelphi Paper No. 40, *op. cit.*, p. 2, and Karl Birnbaum, 'The Western Alliance and European Security', a paper prepared for a Conference of the Atlantic Institute, 25–27 January 1968, reprinted in *Europa-Archiv*, Folge 7, 1968, and in *Survival*, June 1968.
38 Z. Brzezinski, 'The Framework of East–West Reconciliation', *Foreign Affairs*, January 1968, p. 272.
39 Adelphi Paper No. 45, *op. cit.*, pp. 8–9 and 21–22.
40 Brzezinski, *op. cit.*, p. 266.
41 See George Liska, *Imperial America: The International Politics of Primacy* (Baltimore: Johns Hopkins Press, 1967), pp. 61–80, and *Europe Ascendant: The International Politics of Unification* (Baltimore: Johns Hopkins Press, 1964).
42 See W. Cornides, 'German Unification and the Power Balance', *Survey*, January 1966, pp. 140–49.
43 J. L. Richardson, *Germany and The Atlantic Alliance* (Cambridge, Mass., and London: Harvard University Press and Oxford University Press, 1966), pp. 211–23.
44 Neville Brown, 'British Arms and the Shift Towards Europe', *International Affairs*, July 1967, and *Arms Without Empire*, Penguin Books, 1967, pp. 83–97. See also H. Kahn and W. Pfaff, 'Our Alternatives in Europe', *Foreign Affairs*, July 1966.
45 An American author whose main purpose is to show that in military as distinct from economic affairs there is no substitute for American leadership, indicates nevertheless that an integrated European nuclear force, with British participation, might be acceptable to the US as a second best or a lesser evil: Harold van B. Cleveland, *The Atlantic Idea and its European Rivals* (New York: McGraw-Hill, 1967), pp. 148–149.
46 Brzezinski, 'The Framework of East–West Reconciliation,' *op. cit.*, p. 210, recommends 'a special security arrangement precluding West German participation in a European nuclear strike force'. This would be acceptable or not, according to the meaning one gives to 'participation', and to 'European'. Certainly, any German physical control or ultimate decision in a multinational nuclear force should be excluded. Whether this exclusion should cover any form of German contribution to an integrated force, and whether in the distant case of a united Europe endowed with one political and military authority the access of German

members to the relevant supra-national bodies and functions should still be forbidden is more doubtful.
47 See Neville Brown, *Arms Without Empire, op. cit.*, pp. 86–87, and 97. The case for including the Soviet MRBMs in negotiations for European security is put by Elizabeth Young in 'Negotiating European Security', *The Guardian*, 15 May 1967.
48 Alastair Buchan, 'The Implications of a European System for Defence Technology', *Defence, Technology and the Western Alliance*, No. 6 (London: Institute for Strategic Studies, October 1967).
49 Miriam Camps, *European Unification in the Sixties*, London 1967, p. 227.
50 Marshall Shulman, 'Europe versus *détente*', *Foreign Affairs*, April 1967.
51 Stanley Hoffmann, *Gulliver's Troubles* (New York: McGraw-Hill, 1968), p. 515.
52 Quoted in *Encounter*, October 1967, p. 72.

7 Urban Guerrilla Warfare
Adelphi Paper 79, 1971

Robert Moss

The kidnapping of ambassadors, the hijacking of aircraft and the bombing of company offices are likely to continue to be familiar hazards of life in the 1970s. Such incidents attract headlines, but they are only part of the repertoire of urban guerrilla warfare, and not the most important part. On the face of it, the phrase 'urban guerrilla' is a nonsense. From the time of Clausewitz, it has been generally agreed that guerrilla warfare can only be carried on where insurgents can range widely over the countryside and dispose of irregular, difficult terrain as a base-area. Most theorists of guerrilla warfare agree with Fidel Castro that 'the city is a graveyard of revolutionaries and resources'.[1]

But there has been a recent upsurge of revolutionary violence in western industrial cities; in Latin America, the heirs of Che Guevara have made the city their target; and Maoist groups in India have launched a terrorist campaign in New Delhi and Calcutta. In cities like Montevideo or Guatemala City, urban terrorism is in some ways the precise counterpart of rural guerrilla warfare – just as riots can be seen as the urban equivalent of spontaneous peasant uprisings. In military terms, the terrorists and the guerrillas are waging a campaign of harassment and attrition against superior, conventional forces. Their basic target is not control of territory, but control of men's minds. They are essentially political partisans, for whom success or failure will hinge less on what happens on the battleground than on their capacity to get their message across, to erode the morale of the forces of order, and to induce a general 'climate of collapse'.

Terrorism as a political weapon

Terrorism could be defined as the systematic use of intimidation for political ends; Lenin put it tersely when he said that the purpose of terror is to terrorize. In the colonial situations, the goal of political terrorists was to persuade the occupying power that it had become too costly to hold on. This was the technique successfully applied by the Irgun and the Stern Gang in Palestine, and by the EOKA in Cyprus. The desire to win world publicity, in the hope of enlisting outside support and of provoking a political debate inside Britain, was a key element in this strategy. The 'Preparatory General Plan' drawn up by General Grivas in Athens before the start of the EOKA campaign, defined the political objective in the following terms: 'The British must be continuously harried and beset until they are obliged by international diplomacy exercised through the United Nations to examine the Cyprus problem and settle it in accordance with the desires of the Cypriot people and the whole Greek nation.'[2]

The strategy of the Irish Republican Army (the IRA) in Northern Ireland today has some similar features. The IRA, who see themselves as victims of a 'colonial' situation, are hoping that their campaign of selective terrorism against the British troops stationed in Ulster will lead, first, to a breakdown in army discipline and morale and, second, to a failure of the will in Westminster: the political decision to hand the province over to Dublin.

Within an independent state, the use of terror is more complex. It can be employed as a defensive or an offensive weapon, to preserve the *status quo* (the original *raison d'être* of the Ku Klux Klan, the Organisation de l'Armée Secrète (OAS) in Algeria or the *esquadrão da morte* in Brazil) or to overturn the existing system. It can be used to erode democratic institutions and clear the way for the seizure of power by an authoritarian movement (like the Nazis) as well as to resist an absolutist government or a foreign invader. The *Narodniks* in Tsarist Russia regarded assassination as a means of 'warning off' members of the official hierarchy who sought to abuse their powers. Unlike most present-day terrorists, the *Narodniks* were acutely conscious of the moral dilemmas involved in the systematic use of political violence. They argued that they had been forced to use terror because the Tsarist regime had closed all possibilities of peaceful reform. The leaders of the *Narodnaya Volya* organization even promised that, if they ever saw signs of even 'the possibility of an honest government' they would then 'oppose terrorism, as we are now opposed to it in free nations'.[3] Nothing could be farther removed from the spirit and tactics of contemporary terrorists, like the Weathermen or Uruguay's Tupamaros. Both those groups, with differing success, have set out to undermine their countries' democratic institutions and to create the conditions for civil war by bringing about a polarization of political forces.

Most terrorists in modern history have alienated public sympathy by adopting gangster-style techniques. A good example of that was the reaction of the crowd in an Istanbul street in June 1971 after the Turkish police had managed to rescue a fourteen-year-old girl from her kidnappers in a brilliantly executed operation. The guerrillas, members of the Turkish People's Liberation Army, shouted to the crowd 'We are doing this for you' as they exchanged fire with the police from an upstairs window. But the crowd in the street broke through police barricades in an attempt to lynch the single terrorist who finally emerged alive. That is a fairly extreme example of the circumstances under which terrorist actions are purely counter-productive. A schoolgirl who is taken hostage may be expected to arouse more popular sympathy than a middle-aged banker or a *gringo* diplomat who finds himself in the same situation. But the normal response to terrorism is revulsion. That is why the more successful urban guerrillas, in Latin America in particular, have gone to considerable pains to try to rationalize their crimes and have been very selective in choosing their targets. Terrorists can never win popular support unless they can explain their actions as something more than random criminal assaults or lunatic gestures.

The need to make converts also explains the exceptional importance of marksmanship for the urban guerrilla. There has to be some discrimination in the choice of targets. At least at the outset, the urban guerrilla is less concerned with intimidating the civil population than with proving that the government and the forces at its disposal are vulnerable to attack. It is only when a rebel movement has *already* established a secure grip on a significant part of the civil population that it can afford to use terror as a means of extorting aid and supplies, of conscripting new recruits and deterring potential defectors. The Viet Cong have perfected the system of 'repressive' terrorism since the late 1950s. Terrorism against neutral or anti-Communist elements in government-controlled areas has usually taken the form of preliminary warnings, followed by kidnapping or assassination. Over the four-year period between 1966 and 1969, American estimates place the total number of assassinations at 18,031. There were an estimated 25,907 kidnappings for indoctrination and other purposes. Terrorism in Communist-controlled areas has ranged from verbal intimidation through 'home surveillance' and 'thought reform' to execution.[4]

In Latin America, the terrorists have singled out individuals and installations that they can publicly identify with what they regard as an oppressive system. The Guatemalan terrorists, for example, have kidnapped an archbishop and a foreign minister as well as local businessmen and foreign envoys. The bombings in Montreal by the Front de Libération du Québec (FLQ) were primarily aimed at foreign enterprise and military installations. The IRA snipers in Ulster have made the British Army their prime target. Selective assaults on soldiers and policemen can bruise the morale of men who have to wear uniform (an essential precondition for any successful uprising) as well as eliminate enemies.

But indiscriminate terror also has a place in urban guerrilla warfare. The IRA bombing campaign in England that began in January 1939, was one of the most notorious examples. In the fifteen months that followed, bombs were, exploded in station buildings, electricity plants, letter-boxes, cinemas, post offices, public lavatories, shops and telephone boxes. The campaign may not originally have been intended to cause injuries, but the targets chosen and the extraordinary incompetence of those who manufactured and deposited the bombs made that inevitable. The worst incident came on 25 August 1939, when five people were killed in an explosion in Broadgate in Coventry. But the campaign was entirely counterproductive, coming at a time when the British Government was wholly preoccupied with Nazi expansion in Europe, and it only resulted in effective police action to curb the IRA.[5] In Algiers in 1955, Front de Libération Nationale (FLN) terrorism progressed from actions against men in uniform, to selective assaults on individual Europeans, to the depositing of bombs in public places where French Algerians were known to gather (cafés, restaurants and so on). The FLN used indiscriminate terror to dig an unbridgeable gap between the Arab and European populations and to provoke the kind of communal backlash that helped them to destroy their rivals for the Arab leadership – those they described as 'the party of the lukewarm'.[6] There was a period when the FLQ terrorists in Quebec went about the English-Canadian suburb of Westmount in Montreal dropping bombs into pillar-boxes. That was partly an attempt to intensify the feelings of distrust and mutual dislike between the English and French communities.

In the United States, the Weathermen and the radical 'bombers' set out to attack the entire capitalist system by a wave of assaults on property. There were 4,330 incendiary bombings in the fifteen months up to April 1970, and the targets included banks, company offices, high school buildings, and military installations. Attempts to rationalize the bombings were hardly designed to convert public opinion. A letter to *The San Francisco Chronicle* from a group calling itself 'The Volunteers of America', after the bombing of the Bank of America's Santa Barbara branch in June last year, likened the role of the bank to that of 'the German financiers during the rise of Hitler'. A letter from another group, 'Revolutionary Force 9' declared that companies like IBM and Mobil Oil are 'the enemies of all life', responsible not only for the prolongation of the Vietnam war but for such diffuse crimes as 'encouraging sexism and the degradation of employees'.

The American bombings are the work of a lunatic fringe, not a case of terrorism used rationally as a political weapon. But it is a central goal of all urban guerrillas to break down the existing social framework and encourage a general feeling of insecurity and disorientation. It has been argued that the first task of the rebel is to 'disrupt the inertial relationship between incumbents and the mass'.[7] This terminology cannot be applied to western pluralistic societies, where relations between government and people are complex and multi-faceted. But conditions of general insecurity favour extremists in any society. The government is discredited because it cannot protect the civil population, and the people will finally be forced to side with whatever group is in a position to apply coercion or guarantee protection.

The varieties of urban militancy

Terrorism is only one form of urban militancy. Unlike riots, political strikes, student demonstrations and ghetto revolts, terrorism is a minority technique, and the need to ensure security under urban conditions dictates a fairly standard form of organization: members of the terrorist group are divided into cells or 'firing groups' of from three to five men, with a link man in each. This clearly limits the possibility of betrayal or of police infiltration, but it also limits the possibility of political agitation.

The terrorist has a political tool; the urban guerrilla has a strategy for revolution (however utopian it may seem). The Brazilian guerrilla leader, Carlos Marighella – who was shot dead in a police ambush in São Paulo at the end of 1969 – outlined part of that strategy in his *Minimanual of the Urban Guerrilla*. Marighella wrote that 'It is necessary to turn political crisis into armed conflict by performing violent actions that will force those in power to transform the political situation of the country into a military situation. That will alienate the masses who, from then on, will revolt against the army and the police and thus blame them for this state of things.'[8] That is one scenario for civil war. It might be called the strategy of militarization. Marighella's thesis, that by inviting repression the urban guerrillas will pave the way for popular revolt, seems to be working out in one part of Latin America – Uruguay. But Uruguay is an isolated case. In the rest of the continent, the urban guerrillas are learning to their cost that, if the government is sufficiently ruthless and can present a united front, effective repression is more likely than a popular uprising. The same is almost certainly true of western societies. Modern techniques of police control rule out the possibility of a successful urban uprising unless a political crisis cripples the government or the loyalty of the security forces is in doubt.

It is dangerous to generalize about the causes of urban revolts. Clearly, the reasons why men revolt in Guatemala City or Belfast are different. It is possible to define three main contemporary forms of urban guerrilla warfare: (i) 'Technological terrorism' in the industrial cities; (ii) Ghetto revolts and separatist uprisings; and (iii) Urban violence in the pre-industrial cities (notably Latin America). It is striking that, in the industrial countries, the groups that have resorted to urban terrorism draw their support from marginal social elements: middle-class student radicals or cultural and ethnic minorities. The increased frequency of this kind of political violence in western societies is bound up both with a romantic or nihilistic disenchantment with existing systems and with a curious resurgence of sectional loyalties. The Basque extremists who kidnapped the West German Consul at San Sebastián in 1970, the Flemings who take to the streets to protest about the dominance of the French language in Brussels and the Quebec terrorists who claim to be combating Anglo-Saxon imperialism are similar in their origins and the roots of their complaints. In the age of what Marshall McLuhan calls 'the global village', there is a new insistence on the *patria chica*.

A hypothetical revolution in a western country would have to be city-based; but it has come as a surprise to some observers that, since about the time of Che Guevara's death in the Bolivian hills in October 1967, his successors in Latin America have made the city their target. The reasons are fairly simple. The first was the patent failure of peasant uprisings and rural guerrilla movements in Latin America in the decade of the 1960s. Between 1965 and 1968, the Peruvian Army mopped up the remains of Hugo Blanco's peasant revolt; the rebel movements in Colombia and Venezuela melted away into insignificant frontier bands; and the Guatemalan Army waged a ruthlessly efficient campaign (including extensive resettlement and also, according to some reports, the use of napalm and defoliants) against guerrilla forces in the eastern hills. Equipped and guided by the Americans, Latin American security forces displayed a vastly increased capacity to handle rural uprisings. At the same time, it became apparent that a provincial revolt was rarely a direct threat to the government in countries where wealth and power was gravitating towards a few enormous metropolitan centres. Secondly, the guerrillas realized that it is much easier to win headlines by kidnapping a foreign envoy than by gunning down country gendarmes. Urban operations have an obvious attraction for an isolated extremist group bent on winning publicity, and, by the end of the 1960s, most guerrilla organizations in Latin America were cut off not only from the Moscow-line Communist parties, but from Castro as well. Finally, the shift to the cities was an attempt to take advantage of the continent's phenomenal urban growth. Latin America's cities are growing faster than any in the world, but industrialization has lagged behind, creating vast and unpoliceable slums.[9]

It remains to be seen whether the special factors that have conditioned the rise of urban guerrilla warfare in Latin America will influence the future course of insurgency in Asia or Africa. It is surprising that there has so far been little urban terrorism in Asian cities, given the political instability of many of the countries in the region. The Tet offensive in South Vietnam in 1968 and the Gestapu affair in Indonesia in 1965 (when the Indonesian Communist Party, with the collusion of President Sukarno, tried to stage a *putsch* by assassinating army leaders) might be classed among the rare attempts at urban insurrections. The Maoist groups in India recently broadened their tactics to include urban guerrilla techniques. In May 1970, one of the main organs of the Communist Party of India (Marxist-Leninist) (CPI (M-L)) announced that 'While the main task of armed struggle would be in the villages, the party would not allow towns and cities to become strongholds of bourgeois terror'.[10] In the same month, the Naxalites (a terrorist movement that takes its name from the Naxalbari uprising in 1967) made their first appearance in New Delhi, handing out leaflets and painting slogans on walls. One of their spokesmen promised that 'The red terror activities in cities and towns have come to stay.'[11] By the end of the year, the Naxalites were reported to have made 50–60 active recruits at Delhi University, and to have built up a support group on the campus of about 200.[12]

These figures, insignificant in themselves, were a sign of an attempt to transfer terrorist operations to the towns from their original base in the rural areas of West Bengal and Andhra Pradesh. This tactic was at odds with the Maoist ideology of the groups responsible. For example, Charu Mazumdar, the leader of the CPI(M-L), has remained insistent that 'the path of India's liberation is the path of people's war' and that the first step along that path is to create 'small bases of armed struggle' all over the country.[13] He has also insisted that rural guerrilla warfare and agitation among the peasant poor is an essential apprenticeship for the young students and urban unemployed who have formed the backbone of the Maoist fighting squads.[14] A similar ideological rigidity has impeded the emergence of urban guerrilla warfare in other Asian countries.

The main thing that turned the Indian Maoists towards an urban campaign was a series of reverses in the countryside. The Naxalites, for example, were active for many years among the Girijan tribesmen, who occupy an area of some 500 square miles of hilly uplands in Srikakulum. It is good country for guerrillas, and the Naxalites also found a popular grievance to exploit. From the early 1960s, there was considerable unrest among the Girijans, stemming from the fact that merchants and money-lenders in the towns were acquiring tribal lands through usury. But government legislation to control the transfer of land placated the Girijans, the Naxalites were divided by personal jealousies and dissension, and, by mid-July 1970, the police were confident that they had eliminated all of the six original leaders in Srikakulum. As in Latin America, urban terrorism was employed by the Indian Maoists both in the attempt to offset their rural setbacks and as a means of tying up the security forces and adding to the political crisis. The Indian Minister of Home Affairs announced on 18 November 1970 that there had been 341 murders in West Bengal since March, of which 172 were political. He added that 25 policemen had been killed during 526 attacks on individual members of the force.

Events in East Pakistan, the influx of East Bengali refugees, and the presence of the Mukti Fauj (the East Bengali resistance movement) have opened new possibilities for India's Maoists. But there is also considerable scope for urban terrorist activity in other parts of Asia. In Thailand, the failure of the Thai Communist Party to develop urban guerrilla activity in Bangkok reflects the fact that the Thai insurgency is still largely bound up with the sectional grievances of ethnic minorities (encouraged, especially in the north-east, by the Chinese and North Vietnamese). But the Thai police have reported increasing activity by the Communists in Bangkok, and this could eventually lead to a campaign of selective terrorism. In Malaysia, the remnants of Chin Peng's Communist guerrillas are based in the wild country up around the Thai border, although early in 1971 there were signs of a more aggressive forward movement towards the tin-mining region around Ipoh. But the fact that a future insurgency in Malaysia would almost certainly be bound up with deteriorating race relations, and that the west coast cities are overwhelmingly Chinese, means that the possibility of a future urban guerrilla campaign cannot be lightly passed over. In Singapore, some of the extremist elements associated with the *Barisan Socialis* (the main opposition to the ruling People's Action Party) have been pressing for a campaign of street violence. The city-state is exceptionally well-policed, but its total dependence on trade and foreign investment might encourage extremists to try to precipitate an economic crisis through political violence.

It is possible to make three general observations about the patterns of political violence in both the industrial and the pre-industrial cities:

(i) *The disruptive effects of population movements.* Internal migration has had an unsettling effect in both North America and the third world, for rather different reasons. The cities of the third world are like sponges, sucking in the surplus rural populations faster than they can absorb them. The visible effect of this process has been the mushroom-like spread of slums and shanty-towns. Each city is encircled by its 'misery-belt' of huts patched together out of odd bits of cardboard, tin and timber. In Rio de Janeiro, the *favelas* climb higgledy-piggledy up the hillsides; in Mexico City, the squatters' encampments fan out from the suburban fringes across the dusty plain.

The process has gone farthest in Latin America. More than two-thirds of the populations of Argentina, Uruguay, Venezuela and Chile now live in towns. For Mexico, Brazil and Colombia, the figure is over 50 per cent. In southern Asia, by comparison, some 14 per cent of the population of the region live in towns. The figure for black Africa is slightly lower – about 13 per cent. But the static population spread matters less than the startling rate at which urbanization has been taking place. Third world cities are growing at a rate of between 3 and 8 per cent a year. That means that most of them are doubling in size every 10 or 15 years.[15] The reason for this is internal migration rather than natural population growth, since there is evidence to suggest that the birth-rate in most cities is below the national average.

There are many reasons why peasants are leaving the land. Overpopulation or land-hunger is probably the most important, and it has been accentuated in some areas by mechanization and the application of modern techniques that have caused extra redundancies. Better roads and communications between city and countryside have facilitated population movements, and the fact that more people are going to school or listening to radios has influenced job expectations and helped to give the city a glamorous image in the minds of young villagers. It must be added that political disturbances and natural disasters (like the droughts that send hordes of starving peasants, or *retirantes*, out of north-eastern Brazil towards the coastal cities every few years) have triggered off the most dramatic population shifts. South Vietnam's cities doubled in size between 1963 and 1968;[16] Phnom Penh was swamped by rural refugees in the months after the fall of Prince Sihanouk in March 1970; and Calcutta's crowded streets have been swollen to bursting by the influx of Bengalis who have fled the war across the border. In Guatemala, peasant unrest and a sustained campaign of political terrorism drove the *hacenderos* (wealthy land-owners) and the more affluent peasants, as well as the poor, to take the roads to the major towns in search of security in the course of the 1960s.[17]

Urbanization in the third world is often compared with the process of urban growth in Europe and North America in the nineteenth century, but it differs from that earlier model in two vital ways. Firstly, third world cities are growing faster. The average rate of urban growth in Europe between 1850 and 1900 was only about 2.1 per cent. Secondly, the rise of the European cities was related to industrialization. In most third world countries, the Urban Revolution was not preceded by an Industrial Revolution. To take one comparison, 12 per cent of India's population were living in towns in 1951, while 11 per cent of the total work force were employed in industry. Austria had reached the same stage of urbanization by 1870, but in that year 30 per cent of the Austrian work force were employed in industry.[18] Failing to find jobs in industry, most of the rural migrants in third world cities have had to scrape a living in the service sectors – a polite phrase that usually means nothing more than a daily round of boot-blacking, begging for odd jobs, or cleaning public buildings. Some 60 per cent of Chile's labour force are employed in jobs that do not produce goods. Whereas in England after the Industrial Revolution, factory-owners were crying out for manpower, it seems likely that in most third world countries the gap between the number of rural migrants looking for work and the number of new jobs being created by local industry will become bigger, not smaller.

This makes it impossible to apply the comfortable view of the link between urbanization and political violence derived on European experience to third world conditions. According to the popular view, the life cycle of civil violence in western societies passed through three phases in the course of urban growth and industrial development: an early phase, in which political violence was a response to the social disruption and disorientation resulting from the rise of urban industry; a transitional phase, in which a militant union movement emerged and briefly posed a serious threat to bourgeois society; and a 'mature' phase, in which the organized working class was peacefully integrated into the new social system. As recent historians have demonstrated, that view of the past is inaccurate and simplistic even for western societies.[19] It simply does not fit the very different circumstances of the third world, where the flight of peasants to the towns has created a whole new social class that the Brazilians call *marginais* (or 'marginal people') and that Marx, who had a notoriously low view of their revolutionary potential, called the *lumpenproletariat*. Friedrich Engels claimed that the members of this 'underclass' were 'absolutely venal and absolutely brazen', wholly concerned with the routine of eking a living by petty theft or by performing minor services.

In contrast, Frantz Fanon, the psychologist from Martinique who joined the Algerian revolution, saw them as the armies of future revolutions. He believed that this 'horde of starving men, uprooted from their tribe and from their clan, constitutes one of the most spontaneous and most radically revolutionary forces'.[20] Was he right? Are the people of the slums a potentially revolutionary force? It has been argued that recent migrants are too preoccupied with surviving from day to day to lend their support to a political movement; and that men who are always moving from one shack to the next without steady jobs are not easily organized by a party or a revolutionary group. It is certainly true that the 'bazaar system' in third world cities provides some kind of safety valve; unemployment is worse than under-employment, and the profusion of uneconomic service industries and petty retailing at least makes it possible for people to eat. Assuming that rural migrants have only modest expectations, the service industries are capable of absorbing new arrivals into what has been described as a 'system of shared poverty': a buffer-zone between the traditional and the modern economies.[21] But it seems doubtful whether this constitutes any long-term solution, both because of rising expectations and because eventually the parasitic service sector will be saturated. This means that a rising proportion of the population of third world cities will remain outside the modern economy and the present forms of social organization while becoming increasingly conscious of their plight.

Their political responses in the past are therefore no certain guide to the future. In Latin America, the slum-dwellers have been notoriously susceptible to the appeal of populist demagogues like Juan Perón in Argentina or Rojas Pinilla in Colombia. They have tended to vote for the man, not the party, and to be strongly influenced by promises of local improvements. A public opinion poll conducted among one slum community in Manila on the eve of the 1963 municipal elections showed that most of those interviewed wanted to re-elect the existing mayor because he had made a promise to them while a candidate four years previously to build cat-walks between their stilt shanties.

One fairly sophisticated analyst has argued that the slum-dwellers are 'basically conservative so long as life is barely livable' but 'catapult to revolution the moment that life is no longer seen as livable for whatever reason'.[22] The slum fringes of the third world cities contain a volatile mass that may explode during periods of rapid social transition or economic recession. And the urbanization process has had other political side-effects. In South-east Asia in particular, it has heightened racial tensions, usually at the expense of the Chinese who dominate local commerce. There have been anti-Chinese riots in several Asian cities, and it is worth noting that it was Malays who had migrated from the east coast who were responsible for the violent race riots in Kuala Lumpur in May 1969.[23] At the same time, the concentration of wealth and power in a few enormous cities means that, in Latin America in particular, a rebel movement cannot confine itself to the countryside if it hopes for success. Moises Moleiro, a former Venezuelan guerrilla leader, pointed out in a recent article: 'In Venezuela, it is just not possible to start a rural uprising that will end with the countryside encircling the town. The rural areas are marginal to the life of the country . . . A peasant revolt is impossible, in the last analysis, because we are not a peasant people.'[24] In the major Latin American countries, it seems that a peasant revolution is no more possible than in the industrialized west.

In the United States, internal population movements have added to social tension in subtler ways. Recent statistics from the American Census Bureau show that half of the country's negro population is now concentrated in 50 cities. Fifteen of those cities account for a third of the total. While black Americans have been moving into the city centres, middle-class whites have escaped to the suburbs, taking new industry with them. But this is not a one-way process. A recent study of the Cleveland riots of 1967 showed that negroes with steady incomes were also moving out of the ghettos, leaving behind those at the very bottom of the social scale.[25] The black ghetto in

Detroit or Chicago is not simply a racial enclave, but also an island of deepening poverty. And the fact that the ghettos are often located close to the traditional centres of commerce or command key services like railway lines or power stations makes racial unrest a threat to the normal functioning of the economy.

(ii) *The sense of relative deprivation.* Population movements in the Americas have sometimes added to the sense of relative deprivation. A negro left behind in the 'riot zones' of Chicago or Washington while a more enterprising neighbour moves out to a new factory job in the suburbs will feel a more acute sense of frustration and is more likely to join a rioting mob on a hot summer's night. Men do not rebel because they are deprived, but because they are conscious that they are deprived. De Tocqueville's celebrated argument that the French Revolution came about because things were getting better (so that people who had formerly accepted their lot became conscious of the possibility of changing it) works equally well in reverse. Uruguay is the one country in Latin America where armed revolution seems possible in the foreseeable future. Yet it has also been one of the most enlightened societies in Latin America, with a tradition of constitutional rule and much of the apparatus of a welfare state. Uruguay is a democracy that has come upon hard times. The economic crisis that began in the late 1950s has crippled public service salaries and led to cutbacks in social spending, while the activity of an exceptionally efficient guerrilla movement has forced the Government to resort to repressive measures. The reason why the Tupamaros have been able to count upon a substantial amount of middle-class support has been that people's expectations have been disappointed.

(iii) *The character of the terrorist.* But urban guerrilla warfare is essentially the work of a tiny self-styled revolutionary elite. That makes it important to consider whether there is not something in the apparent truism that 'it takes a rebel to rebel'.[26] The FLQ in Quebec, the National Liberation Action (ALN) in Rio, and the Weathermen in the United States draw their recruits from similar social sectors and share not only a certain range of guerrilla techniques, but a common faith in political violence and the theory of a global revolution. Frantz Fanon provided the most comprehensive version of the now-fashionable theory of violence as a liberating force. 'At the level of individuals,' according to Fanon, 'violence is a cleansing force. It frees the native from his inferiority complex and from his despair and inaction; it makes him fearless and restores his self-respect.'[27] The radical 'New Left' in western countries as well as the guevarists in Latin America have tended to talk in similar terms.

What Fanon completely failed to analyse was the corrupting effect of the systematic use of political violence, and its reinforcement of the totalitarian impulse. He also ignored the attraction of a terrorist organization for some criminal elements. It is no accident that the IRA Provisionals in Belfast have drawn support from petty criminals in the Catholic slums and have set up their own protection rackets for extorting 'party funds'. The British Army has reported cases where the Provisionals have broken a man's back with an iron bar or kicked a pregnant woman in the stomach in order to compel submission or the payment of regular contributions. The FLQ in Montreal has recruited drifters and corner pickpockets from the *hangars* (or gang-territories); and the Moslem FLN in Algiers enlisted the services of professional thugs like Ali-la-Pointe. The frequent confusion between criminal and political motives is bound to be accentuated when guerrilla groups rely upon 'fund-raising' devices like bank-robberies for their finance – and that is why Cuban leaders, as well as Russian, have criticized this kind of operation.

The irony is that the founding impetus of many urban guerrilla groups has come from young idealists: middle-class students and intellectuals who share a belief in a global revolution aimed primarily at the United States. The Tupamaros first signed their name to a manifesto protesting about the American involvement in Vietnam. The FLQ in Quebec wrote the slogan 'Long Live the Cuban Revolution!' on the bottom of a kidnap note; and Pierre Vallières, their spiritual leader, has a wild-eyed vision of a world-wide revolution that would take account of the 'cultural and ethnic origins' of workers as well as their 'proletarian character'.[28] With the American Weathermen, the idea of a global holocaust approaches sheer nihilism, an itch to tear down the class from which these middle-class rebels sprang and everything it stands for. The Weathermen are essentially derivative: they see themselves as the white auxiliaries of a revolution that would be made by coloured men through a great upheaval in the third world and an uprising by Black Power groups in the United States.

The theory of international solidarity, it must be added, has not been accompanied by much interchange of cadres or resources. The Cubans, the North Koreans and the Palestinians have all provided a certain amount of training for urban guerrilla groups. Some of the 70 Brazilian political prisoners who were freed in exchange for the life of the Swiss Ambassador in January 1971 had received training in Uruguay,[29] and there are signs that the Tupamaros have close links with guerrilla movements in Argentina and Bolivia as well. But the urban guerrillas are almost entirely self-reliant in terms of arms and supplies, and the form of co-operation that counts for most is the borrowing of ideas. The most dramatic example of that was the wildfire spread of diplomatic kidnapping as a political technique after the Brazilians used it to secure the release of 15 prisoners in 1969. But terrorist groups have also copied methods of 'armed propaganda'. For example, in October 1969, on the second anniversary of Che Guevara's death, the Tupamaros occupied the town of Pando and held it for about 15 minutes while commando groups raided the police barracks and the banks. It was a brilliant publicity technique, and probably a decisive turning-point in their campaign of political terror – although a rear-guard party of Tupamaros was intercepted by the Army on the way back to Pando and shot to pieces.[30] At any rate, the Argentine Revolutionary Armed Forces (FAR) were sufficiently impressed by the occupation of Pando to copy it in the following year, when they took over the town of Garín. In planning for the exercise, they even referred to Garín among themselves as 'Pandito' (or 'little Pando').

The arsenal of the urban guerrilla

There are four main urban guerrilla techniques that have been explored over the past few years, and largely explain the success of a group like the Tupamaros. They are (i) Armed propaganda; (ii) Political kidnapping; (iii) 'Stiffening' riots and strikes; and (iv) Subversion of the security forces. These will be briefly discussed in turn.

(i) *Armed propaganda* can be defined as the attempt to prove to the people, through successful military actions, that the government is weak and the guerrillas are strong. One of the central problems for all guerrilla movements is how to get their message across to the man in the street. As a Tupamaro mouthpiece put it, the problem is that 'for the urban guerrilla, discretion must take the place of the rural guerrilla's hideout in the jungle'.[31] Since the possibilities for normal political agitation are restricted (and since the urban guerrillas have normally held themselves aloof from the traditional political parties, including the Communists) 'armed propaganda' must take the place of polemics. A good example was the occupation of Pando by the Tupamaros, or their raid on the naval training barracks in Montevideo last year. In the face of official censorship, the Tupamaros have tried to construct 'counter-media', including a private radio transmitter and the use of electronics experts to break into normal broadcasts with special messages. They have also taken over public meeting-places like cinemas and workers' canteens to deliver impromptu harangues.

(ii) *Political kidnapping* has been used to capture publicity, to free political prisoners and to extract other concessions, and to provoke controversies within governments. The Government of President Pacheco Areco in Uruguay was so deeply divided after the wave of kidnappings in August 1970, for example, that he was on the point of handing in his resignation before the police captured several Tupamaro leaders in a lucky strike.[32] The Brazilian experience shows just how dangerous it is for governments to give in to kidnappers. It cost the Brazilian Government 15 political prisoners to free and American Ambassador, but later the price was 70 for a Swiss Ambassador – rampant inflation by anyone's standards, and a sign that for kidnappers, as for other mortals, the appetite grows with the eating. The game of bluff that is being played out between governments and guerrillas is not over. The Tupamaros held Geoffrey Jackson, the British Ambassador to Uruguay, for eight months after his capture in January 1971 in what they grandiosely called a 'people's prison'. They also held a number of prominent Uruguayans, including a close friend of the President and a former Minister of Agriculture. The Tupamaros, secure in the knowledge that they can outfox the police, did not let themselves be panicked into murdering another hostage as they murdered the

American Dan Mitrione last year. They learned that they could humiliate the Government and the police more effectively by playing a waiting game.

(iii) *'Stiffening' riots and strikes* is one way of establishing closer links between the terrorist organization and popular grievances. Recent experience of urban riots in Northern Ireland and the United States supports the idea that crowd disturbances can pass through several phases and can finally pass under the control of extremist organizers. Since mid-1970 for example, the rioting in Ulster has ceased to be a fairly spontaneous cycle of communal conflict and has assumed a more sinister character. The British troops, rather than members of the other religious community, became the prime targets for hostile mobs egged on and infiltrated by the IRA. Street violence was prolonged in Belfast and Londonderry for five or six nights on end. Members of the crowds were armed with fire-bombs and gelignite nail-bombs, snipers fired on the British troops from neighbouring buildings, and there was systematic arson and destruction of property. On the night of 27 June 1970, more than 100 fires were started in Belfast, and troops were fired on in Ballymacarett and the Crumlin Road by IRA snipers armed with machine-guns. The pattern of those riots was repeated in 1971. Similarly, in the United States, from early in 1968 there was evidence of much greater organization and increased sniping in negro riots, although many Black Power leaders were distrustful of the riot as a political weapon and the incidence of rioting fell away after 1968.

(iv) *Subversion of the security forces* was seen by Lenin as one of the essential preconditions for a successful urban uprising. 'Unless the revolution assumes a mass character and affects the troops, there can be no question of a serious struggle.'[33] All serious rebel movements have attempted to demoralize and subvert the army and the police and, historically, revolution has only been possible when (for internal or external reasons) this has already succeeded. Urban guerrillas are bound to be outgunned unless they can at least manage to neutralize a majority of the security forces, and one of the reasons for the Tupamaros' remarkable capacity for survival has been that they have shaken the confidence of the men in uniform by alternately circulating propaganda and practising selective assassination, while infiltrating their own agents at all levels. (It was the presence of a Tupamaro agent on the nightwatch at the naval training barracks that enabled the guerrillas to occupy it last year.) Terrorists have two apparently contradictory means of subverting the armed forces: one is to appeal to individual soldiers or policemen as 'fellow-workers'; the other is to issue threats and carry out selective terrorism or harassment.

The process has gone further than is sometimes realized in some western countries. Subversion in the American Army is obviously bound up with opposition to the Vietnam war and resistance to conscription; underground GI news sheets are primarily anti-*Vietnam* publications. Eldridge Cleaver, the man who is now contesting the leadership of the Black Panthers from his exile in Algiers, has said in his quasi-apocalyptic way that 'the stockades in Babylon are full of soldiers who refuse to fight. These men are going to become some of the most valuable guerrilla fighters.' Perhaps this need not be taken too seriously; but it does seem that disaffected conscripts have supplied the American underground with arms, instruction and trained recruits. The Deputy Attorney-General of California announced in April 1971, for example, that his office had recovered 55 grenades, 94 bricks of plastic explosives, 10 bazookas, 52 rifles and 65 revolvers stolen from local army bases. The racial factor has added to the dissension in the ranks. Fighting between black and white GIs has become commonplace in Vietnam, but there have been similar incidents among the American forces stationed in Germany, and rioting by black soldiers at bases in the United States, including Fort Hood and the riot control training centre in Kansas. One of the prime techniques used by radical activists in the American Army has been to try to pit conscripts against professional soldiers. One of the group responsible for the bombing of a military police station in San Francisco last year, for example, declared: 'We consider the GI to be a civilian, whereas we consider the lifers and the military structure to be a structure which is evolving to a more Gestapo-type experience.'[34] In other contexts, terrorists have tried to isolate the 'élite' units and those directly responsible for counter-insurgency operations from the armed forces as a whole.

The limits of urban violence

Are the urban guerrillas likely to achieve their goals? In western industrial societies, to ask this question is really to ask whether revolution is possible. In the third world, urban guerrilla warfare fits into pre-existing patterns of insurgency and political instability. The modern city is vulnerable to terrorist attack; but in the last analysis, success or failure hinges on the public reaction.

(i) *The vulnerability of the industrial city.* The complexity of the modern city makes it vulnerable to the forms of sabotage that might be called 'technological terrorism'. No extremist group has succeeded in causing serious disruption in transport and communications in a western society, although in the United States there has been a wave of assaults on property (and in Puerto Rico this has been part of a concerted drive by the Armed Liberation Commandos to scare off outside investors).[35] But the possibility of programmatic sabotage of essential services cannot be discounted, and plans for such a campaign in the United States have been elaborated by the Revolutionary Action Movement (RAM) – an organization of black extremists founded by Robert A. Williams. One of Williams' supporters has argued: 'What we must understand is that Charlie's system runs like an IBM machine. But an IBM machine has a weakness, and that weakness is complexity. Put something in the wrong place in an IBM machine and it's finished for a long time.'[36] Williams pointed out that it is possible to use primitive techniques to disrupt sophisticated institutions. He advocated a black revolutionary organization divided into three sections: armed self-defence groups operating legally; underground guerrilla squads to be employed against the police during riots; and a system of autonomous 'fire teams' who would be responsible for programmatic sabotage. They would pose as 'moderates' or 'patriots' in order to infiltrate high-security zones. Their first targets would be transport and communications in the major cities, followed by random attacks on corporation buildings and military installations. The saboteurs would try to create general panic and urban chaos by diverse means. For example, they might scatter tacks or boards with protruding nails on turnpikes and at major intersections during rush-hour traffic. And Williams took an unhinged arsonist's pleasure in the prospect of 'strategic fires' started across the countryside by teams of roving guerrillas. The fires would be used as a diversion and 'to elicit panic and a feeling of impending doom'.[37] Williams, unlike most other Black Power leaders, believes in the possibility of a minority revolution in the United States. His lunatic schemes for 'liberation zones' in the deep South or his idea that American middle-class society is so soft that it would fall apart as soon as economic production fell need not be taken seriously. But he pointed out that a marginal extremist group does have the *technical* power to cause enormous damage. The political consequences are a different matter.

(ii) *Terrorism and public opinion*. Herbert Marcuse was right to insist that the most violent political groups in western societies are composed of marginal social elements: ethnic and cultural minorities, and middle-class radicals. That is the source of their weakness. If they push the confrontation of political forces too far through the use of violence, they will eventually be swamped by the majority groups.

The advocates of 'student power' feel differently. They argue that the events of May 1968 in France demonstrated that radical students can provide the trigger for a broader movement of social unrest in an advanced industrial society. They point to the occupation of factories by French workers between 14 and 17 May and to the overnight formation of strike committees as examples of popular 'spontaneity'. They argue that orthodox Communists are wrong to insist that a 'vanguard party' is a pre-requisite for revolution. 'What we need,' according to Daniel Cohn-Bendit, 'is not an organization with a capital O, but a host of insurrectional cells, be they ideological groups, study groups – we can even use street gangs.'[38]

But in fact there has not been a follow-up to May 1968. The temporary alliance between students and workers that was achieved in France crumbled away once the Government made up its mind to grant some limited economic concessions (the highest wage-rise granted was about 14 per cent). While student theorists were talking of revolution, most of the workers who joined the rallies and participated in strikes were merely posing bread-and-butter demands that the system was able to satisfy. The decisive factor that helped to turn the tide in Paris was the hostility and distrust shown by the leaders of the French Communist Party and the trade unions towards the student movement. What made a real insurrection in France in 1968 impossible was the factor that the students had decided to neglect: the absence of a mass organization with a coherent strategy for the seizure of power. It was abundantly clear in May that the French Communists were not prepared to adopt this role. And the leaders of the Italian Communist Party (PCI) have swung towards an equally reformist position more recently.

Until the twelfth Party Congress in 1968, the Italian Communists had probably played a more militant part in political strikes and student protest than any other Moscow-line Communist party in Europe. In June 1969, the 'Manifesto' group (the left-wing extremists associated with the paper *Il Manifesto*) were excluded from the party on the grounds that they had acted as a divisive force and sapped the party's strength. The present tactical goal of the party leadership, according to Luis Magri, one of the 'Manifesto' rebels, 'is a convergence between the working class and the "advanced" wing of big capital, on a common economic programme for the elimination of parasitism and the development of social services, that will harmoniously reconcile the exigencies of productivity and the needs of the workers within the system'.[39] It remains to be seen whether the new orientation of the party executive (which is being encouraged by Aldo Moro and others within the Christian Democratic Party who have floated the idea of achieving an 'understanding' with the PCI) will turn out to be more than a tactical ruse. The 'Manifesto' group still hopes to inspire a revolt within the party ranks and argues that continuing labour unrest, student radicalism and the resurgence of extreme right-wing groups like the Italian Social Movement (MSI) are all leading towards the polarization of political forces, not to any lasting form of 'convergence' between capitalist and Communist.

The important thing to note is that, in the two European countries with the highest incidence of political violence, the Moscow-line Communist parties seem to have placed themselves *hors de combat* as far as student rebellion and insurrectionary tactics are concerned. Something similar has happened in Japan, where student militants have remained fairly isolated from unionized workers – apart from the few thousand who have joined the Youth Committees against the War, founded in 1965, and the radical railway workers who have joined in political strikes against the Japanese–American alliance. The nationalism and devotion to duty that are built into the Japanese social system have discouraged widespread protest movements, and the fragmented character of Japanese trade unions (each corporation has its trade union) has deterred attempts at nation-wide political strikes.

In the United States, student rebels are almost completely divorced from the union movement, although there was a strong faction inside the Students for a Democratic Society (SDS) group that argued that effective political action would only be possible through off-campus agitation. But that faction was outvoted by those who formed the Weathermen in 1969, and the SDS strategy was narrowed down to support for minority groups and third world revolutionaries through a campaign of terrorist violence. 'Winning state power,' according to the first important Weatherman manifesto, 'will occur as a result of the military forces of the US extending themselves around the world and being defeated piecemeal.'[40]

The student radicals have declined in political importance because events showed that they were incapable of cementing a broad front with workers or the traditional left-wing parties. The nature of New Left protest limits its popular appeal. It is partly a *qualitative* protest against the lifestyles of bourgeois society and the problems of living in an advanced industrial country (centralization, urbanization, pollution and so on); and partly a *vicarious* protest in sympathy with deprived minority groups of guerrillas and peasant rebels in the third world. It has rarely touched upon the everyday problems of the ordinary man. It is interesting to note that as student radicals have rediscovered their basic isolation as a political force, they have become more violent and more 'professional'. The way that Japanese student militants have organized themselves for street-fighting is a dramatic example of that. Since 1967, they have provided themselves with helmets and gloves and sometimes gas masks; the 'combat section' is armed with stones and Molotov cocktails, the 'defence section' with long bamboo poles. They have also adopted more sophisticated riot tactics. Since the major protest rallies in October–November 1969 (against Mr Sato's departure for the United States), commando squads of five or six youths have staged diversionary attacks – breaking windows, throwing fire-bombs and so on – while the big demonstration is held in another part of the city.[41] Similar rituals of violence have become familiar in Paris, where the mass demonstrations of 1968 have given way to gladiatorial skirmishes between disciplined student gangs and riot police who, in their turn, have become more professional and are now equipped with additional powers under the new anti-riot laws. The case of the Weathermen was the supreme example of how one radical student movement, failing to strike a responsive chord among the nation as a whole, took to underground violence.

It is tempting to judge these *groupuscules* and would-be guerrillas in the light of one of Lenin's more acute observations: 'Serious politics begins where millions of men and women are.' Popular attitudes about politics and violence in most western societies mean that most people will tend to view a terrorist group like the Weathermen with incomprehension or anger – although it is important to note that the attitudes of minority groups are sometimes different. The 'Angry Brigade' terrorists who bombed the flat of Mr John Davies, the British Secretary for Trade and Industry, on 31 July 1971 (supposedly in sympathy with Upper Clyde Shipyards workers threatened with redundancy) were not likely to win much of a hearing in a society where the legitimacy of the private use of political violence is not generally accepted. In the United States, a country with a record of much greater civil violence, the report of a recent national commission of violence was undoubtedly right when it said: 'The historical and contemporary evidence of the United States suggests that popular support tends to sanction violence in support of the *status quo*; the use of public violence to maintain public order; the use of private violence to maintain popular conceptions of social order when government cannot or will not.'[42] Put in cruder terms, this means that an increase in left-wing or revolutionary political violence is likely to mobilize the 'law and order' majority and drive the government to take progressively tougher measures.

In short, the failure to mobilize popular support is the weakness of most of the contemporary urban guerrilla movements. Where they can find this support they have a chance of success: where they can't, they fail. And failure is frequent. This stems partly from the fact that the movements are estranged from the major left-wing parties (Asia is an exception), but also from something more fundamental. The terrorist is a man who refuses to compromise, to explore the possibilities of peaceful change. It is part of his task to convince his potential supporters that there are no prospects for constitutional change or non-violent reform. Hence the dilemma of a group like the Chilean Movement of the Revolutionary Left (MIR), which advocates violent revolution, after a Marxist President, Dr Salvador Allende, was voted into power in September 1970. It is also the dilemma of armed extremists in the western democracies. Their common tactic is to try to erode public confidence in the constitutional system by creating disorder in the streets, economic chaos and a polarization of political forces around the 'law and order' issue. As Che Guevara observed, 'Where a government has come to power through some popular vote, fraudulent or not, the guerrilla outbreak cannot be promoted since the possibilities of peaceful struggle have not yet been exhausted.'[43]

That judgment might seem to have been partially invalidated by the rise of powerful urban guerrilla movements in Venezuela and Uruguay, two functioning democracies where a genuine change in society can be brought about via the ballot-box. But an election was instrumental in stealing the remnants of the terrorists' support in Caracas, and the same may still prove true in Uruguay.

(iii) *The problems of response.* Experience has shown that most modern governments can contain urban terrorism, so long as they can count on the loyalty of the security forces. The question is at what cost. Experience also leads to the sorry conclusion that police-states are the most efficient of all in suppressing terrorist groups. No one is anticipating a wave of urban guerrilla activity in the Soviet Union or in South Africa.

Venezuela and Brazil are good examples of strong handling. In Venezuela, this was combined with the use of an election to swing public opinion away from the guerrillas.[44] President Betancourt was very astute in handling the armed forces and in dealing out repression. By studiously cultivating his senior officers, Betancourt won back the support of the security forces (which had been notoriously faction-ridden) while crushing the 1962 mutinies ruthlessly. He took great pains to show his respect for the due legal process, and exceptional measures were applied only when moderate opinion was already convinced of the need for them. For example, a vicious attack by the National Liberation Front (FLN) on an excursion train in September 1963, provided the perfect justification for the tough measures and emergency laws that were applied immediately afterwards. Finally, by holding a free election (where 90 per cent of the voters turned out despite the FLN instruction to boycott the polls) Betancourt imposed a shattering political defeat on the rebels. After December 1963, the insurgents were hopelessly divided and the Communists returned to the theory of 'peaceful co-existence' that was formally reinstated as party policy in 1967. The Venezuelan insurgency is now confined to a few roaming guerrilla bands in the hills of Falcón province who have so far managed to survive but have no impact on the politics of the country as a whole.

The example of Venezuela is important, because the guerrillas came closer to realizing the conditions for a successful urban insurrection than any later movement has managed to come. Looking back on 1962, Teodoro Petkoff, a leader of the Venezuelan Communist Party, still insists that 'we could have won'.[45] Betancourt's formula for urban counter-insurgency may not be relevant to all contemporary situations. The Brazilians, operating within a very different political framework, have tried something cruder. The military response of the Brazilian Government to the urban offensive was to eliminate the terrorist bases in the cities and to force them to do battle in situations where they were bound to be outgunned. This tactic depended (as did the French operation in Algiers in the late 1950s) on the use of mass interrogation – including the frequent and often irresponsible use of torture – to track down the guerrillas. Operation *Bandeirantes*, the counter-guerrilla operation launched in São Paulo in 1969, was carried out by three columns of the Second Army, each of which was subdivided into sections responsible for interrogation, analysis of intelligence, and fighting operations.[46] In the last quarter of 1970, there were six street battles in Rio and São Paulo, from which the security forces emerged the clear victors. By the end of 1970, several urban guerrilla groups had been decisively crushed, including the Revolutionary Armed Vanguard-Palmares and the Revolutionary Communist Party of Brazil, and successive leaders of the National Liberation Action (ALN) had been captured or killed. Several attempts by the People's Revolutionary Vanguard (VPR) to found a rural base had been defeated by classic methods of encirclement, and urban terrorist operations in the first half of 1971 were confined to insignificant robberies and acts of random terrorism. In the course of the campaign, it became clear that the terrorists partly succeeded in their tactic of driving President Garrastazú Medici's Government towards more repressive measures, and there is no doubt that these served to alienate important sections of the Brazilian middle class as well as liberal opinion abroad. On the other hand, the cohesion of the Brazilian armed forces, the size and complexity of the country, and a period of sustained economic growth all helped the Government to overpower its local opposition.

But urban guerrillas can succeed in producing a polarization of political forces in such a way that the situation cannot easily be untangled, and this is precisely what extremists of both sides are counting on. Tom Hayden, one of the founders of the SDS, gave an American version of Marighella's strategy of militarization when he wrote: 'The coming of repression will speed up time, making a revolutionary situation more likely – We are creating an America where it is necessary for the government to rule behind barbed wire, for the President to speak only at military bases and, finally, where it will be necessary for the people to fight back.'[47]

It is in this sense that the urban terrorist in industrial societies should be seen as a political catalyst. It is arguable that, in most cases, urban guerrillas are dangerous less for what they do than for what they inspire: the erosion of the consensus, a hardening of the political battle lines, and a backlash that strikes back too hard and too indiscriminately. Terrorism and street violence were used by the Nazis to help break down the fabric of Weimar Germany; the assassination of leading moderate politicians was used by ultra-nationalist groups in inter-war Japan to swing government policy towards a programme of military expansion. What worked for the far right between the wars is likely to have rather different consequences for the far left today, although the tactic is similar. In the advanced industrial societies, political terrorists are unlikely to win support except in conditions of extreme social and economic crisis. On the other hand, as Mr Pierre Trudeau, the Prime Minister of Canada, observed after the Cross-Laporte kidnappings in October 1970: 'It only takes a few fanatics to show us just how vulnerable a democratic society can be when democracy is not ready to defend itself.'[48] The full logic of that statement seems to be working itself out in Uruguay.

The Uruguayan Government of President Pacheco Areco has faced a sustained offensive from the National Liberation Movement (Tupamaros) since 1968. (The organization was founded in 1963.) The security problem and the emergency measures that Pacheco applied to deal with it have deeply divided the Government and in June 1971 there was an unsuccessful attempt to impeach the President by Congress. The Tupamaros have shown signs of having infiltrated the armed forces, the police and the civil service. Although the relatively powerful Uruguayan Communist Party and the trade union leadership have refused to declare public support for the guerrillas, they may have to revise their attitude if the left wing *Frente Amplio* is defeated in the November 1971 presidential elections. The success of the Tupamaros in winning popular support has owed something to the country's continuing economic crisis (stemming from the drop in the world price of pastoral products) and to their very selective methods. Uruguay is a small and vulnerable democratic society that has come upon hard times – a welfare state that failed. But the most important factor was that the Government of President Pacheco Areco was weak and divided, while the security forces at his disposal were tiny and without experience of counter-guerrilla operations. There are only about 12,000 men in the Uruguayan armed forces and 22,000 in the police. At the same time, President Pacheco found his hands tied by public opinion when it came to dealing with the guerrillas. Congress resisted the requested re-introduction of emergency measures. The weightiest obstacle to a revolution is the possibility of military intervention by one of the giant neighbours, Brazil or Argentina.

The situation in Ulster is a special case, which might be defined as *quasi-colonial* in the sense that the IRA bases its hopes on the calculation that the British Government will eventually respond to the human and economic costs of maintaining order in the Province by pulling out altogether. The IRA has set out to undermine successive moderate Unionist governments in Stormont in order to provoke a right-wing Protestant backlash, or direct rule from Westminster (which has sometimes been regarded as a step towards the unification of Ireland). The IRA's strength in the current campaign has stemmed from the measure of support it can command from the Catholic part of the population rather than from any degree of military competence or ingenuity. The IRA's campaign of terror in 1970–71 had some success, helping to precipitate the fall of the Northern Ireland Prime Minister in March 1971, and then, in August 1971, leading to the introduction of internment. From its original role of keeping the peace between the Catholic and Protestant communities, the British Army moved over to an offensive intended to root out the IRA as a fighting force. Although the new tactics produced military results, they helped to polarize opinion in Ulster and enabled Catholic critics to represent the army as a repressive force. In this sense, IRA terrorism succeeded. It led to a situation where the British Army, which began as the referee between the two communities in Ulster, appeared as a party to the quarrel. The chaos it engendered helped to postpone the application of social reforms designed to get to the root of the problem and thus eroded Catholic faith in solutions within the existing framework.

Whatever their hopes of success, the tactics employed by the urban guerrillas pose a direct threat to the international order. The theory of global revolution that has been used in the attempt to rationalize crimes against diplomats and other foreign citizens is a flat rejection of the principles that have traditionally guided relations between sovereign states. The claim to a right to rebel under intolerable social and political conditions cannot be used to sanction this type of international crime. It is also clear that there is an indirect link between civil violence and the strategic balance.

In the United States, the immediate effect of mounting civil dissent (for which the common platform is opposition to the Vietnam war) has been to impose constraints on foreign policy. Dissent within the American armed forces has made it increasingly probable that the Army will have to dispense with the draft and 'to professionalize' – which will clearly limit the country's capacity to intervene in outside conflicts and will also make it difficult to maintain current troop levels in Europe. The likelihood that dissent will continue to take violent forms in the United States adds to the possibility that the Americans will enter a new isolationist phase in their attitude to the world. Although race relations and Black Power violence remain the most obvious threats to civil peace in America, these are unlikely to boil over into full-scale ghetto revolts. It is hard to imagine that any rational Black Power leader would expose his followers to the risks involved in an uprising in a limited area that could be easily encircled – or that any American government would fail to take vigorous action against it.

Terrorism may prove to have the most dangerous effects in western industrial societies. A revolution in Uruguay, after all, would hardly alter the strategic balance in any significant way. On the other hand, ghetto revolts in the United States could disrupt the most powerful economy in the world and impose severe constraint on America's capacity to act as a great power. A sustained campaign of urban terrorism in Europe might undermine popular faith in the democratic system and raise the prospect of a more repressive form of government. Terrorists, of course, rarely make revolutions. In Latin America, for example, the most radical social changes in recent years have been brought about by a reformist military junta, in Peru, and a freely elected Marxist government in Chile. These are likely to be the patterns for future bloodless revolutions. And the Chilean formula could apply to Italy, where the prospect of a governing coalition including Communists is much more immediate, and more serious, than a revolution of the streets. This leads to the conclusion that the urban guerrilla is a political catalyst whose actions can radicalize a society and bring about the kind of social and economic confusion that will lead to a decline in popular belief in peaceful solutions. The end results may be indirect and will often take forms that neither the guerrillas nor the government anticipated.

Notes

1 See Carl von Clausewitz, *On War*, trans. J. J. Graham (London: Routledge and Kegan Paul, 1956), Book VI, chapter 26; Peter Paret and John W. Shy, *Guerrillas in the 1960s* (New York: Praeger, 1962), pp. 11–15; Régis Debray, *Revolution in the Revolution?* (Harmondsworth: Penguin, 1968), p. 67.
2 Reprinted as Appendix I in *The Memoirs of General Grivas*, ed. Charles Foley (London: Longmans, 1964), p. 204.
3 See Feliks Gross, *The Seizure of Political Power* (New York: Philosophical Library, 1957), pp. 109–10; Gross, 'Political Violence and Terror in Nineteenth and Twentieth Century Russia and Eastern Europe' in *Assassination and Political Violence*: A Staff Report to the National Commission on the Causes and Prevention of Violence (New York, 1970), pp. 516–44; Stepniak, *Underground Russia* (New York: Scribners, 1892).
4 See Stephen T. Hosmer, *Viet Cong Repression and its Implications for the Future* (Lexington, Mass.: RAND Corporation, 1970), pp. 63–111.
5 See Tim Pat Coogan, *The IRA* (London: Pall Mall, 1970), pp. 150–73.
6 See, *inter alia*, Roland Gaucher, *Les terroristes* (Paris: Albin Michel, 1965), pp. 255–77, and Edgar O'Ballance, *The Algerian Insurrection* (London: Faber, 1967), pp. 53–54.
7 See Thomas Perry Thornton, 'Terror as a Weapon of Political Agitation' in Harry Eckstein (ed.), *Internal War* (New York: Free Press of Glencoe, 1964), p. 74.
8 See 'On Principles and Strategic Questions', reprinted in *Les Temps Modernes* (Paris) November 1969. See also Appendix.
9 See the author's *Urban Guerrillas in Latin America* (London: Institute for the Study of Conflict: Conflict Studies No. 8, 1970).
10 *Times of India*, 19 May 1970.

11 *Indian Express*, 13 May 1970.
12 *The Hindustan Times Weekly*, 17 January 1971.
13 *Forum* (Dacca), 7 November 1970.
14 *Times of India*, 19 May 1970.
15 See D. J. Dwyer, *Urbanization as a Factor in the Political Development of South-East Asia* (Discussion paper at Pacific Conference, Viña del Mar, Chile, 27 September-3 October 1970).
16 On Vietnam, see Samuel P. Huntington, 'The Bases of Accommodation' in *Foreign Affairs* (New York), 46, 1968, p. 648.
17 See Bryan Roberts, 'Migration and Population Growth in Guatemala City' in Roberts and Lowder, *Urban Population Growth and Migration in Latin America* (Liverpool: University of Liverpool Press, 1970).
18 B. F. Hoselitz, 'The Role of Urbanization in Economic Development' in Roy Turner (Ed), *India's Urban Future* (Berkeley: University of California Press, 1962), pp. 164–67.
19 See, for example, Charles Tilly, 'Collective Violence in European Perspective' in *Violence in America: Historical and Comparative Perspectives*: A Report to the National Commission on the Causes and Prevention of Violence (New York, 1969), esp. pp. 33–37.
20 Frantz Fanon, *The Wretched of the Earth*, trans. C. Farrington (Harmondsworth: Penguin, 1970), p. 103.
21 One of the more convincing arguments along these lines is T. G. McGee and W. R. Armstrong, 'Revolutionary Change and the Third World City' in *Civilisations* (Paris), Vol. XVIII, No. 3, 1968.
22 Martin Oppenheimer, *Urban Guerrilla* (Harmondsworth: Penguin, 1970), p. 42.
23 See, for example, John Slimming, *Malaysia: Death of a Democracy* (London: Murray, 1969), pp. 25–60, and T. G. McGee, *The Urbanization Process in the Third World* (London: Bell, 1971), pp. 64–89; 149–72.
24 Moises Moleiro, 'Las Enseñanzas de la Guerra Revolucionaria en Venezuela' in V. Bambirra *et al.*, *Diez Años de Insurrección en América Latina* (Santiago: Prensa Latino-Americana, 1971), Vol. 1, p. 173.
25 See Walter Williams, 'Cleveland's Crisis Ghetto' in Peter H. Rossi (ed.), *Ghetto Revolts* (New York: Trans-Action Books, 1970), pp. 13–30.
26 Brian Crozier, *The Rebels* (London: Chatto and Windus, 1960), p. 9.
27 Fanon, *op. cit.*, p. 74.
28 Pierre Vallières, *Nègres blancs d'Amérique* (Montréal: Editions Parti Pris, 1969), pp. 66–67.
29 See *O Jornal do Brasil*, 12 January 1971.
30 See Maria Esther Giglio, *La guerrilla tupamara* (Havana: Caso de las Américas, 1970), and *Revolución y Cultura* (Havana) No. 21, December 1970.
31 *Granma* (Havana), 8 October 1970.
32 *Latin America* (London), 26 February 1971; *Prensa Latina* (Havana), 7 April 1971.
33 Lenin, 'Lessons of the Moscow Uprising' in *Collected Works* (Moscow, 1967), Vol. II, p. 174.
34 Warren Hinckle, *Guerrilla War in the USA* (unpublished manuscript, New York, 1970), p. 151.
35 See 'Porto-Rico: Le Réveil en Armes' in *Africasia* (Paris), 26 April 1971; and interview with Alfonso Beal reprinted in John Gerassi (ed.), *Towards Revolution* (London: Weidenfeld and Nicolson, 1971), pp. 641–44.
36 Max Stanford, 'Black Guerrilla Warfare: Strategy and Tactics' in *The Black Scholar* (San Francisco), November 1970, p. 37.
37 Robert F. Williams, 'The Potential of a Minority Revolution: Part 2' in *The Crusader* (Havana), August 1965.
38 Daniel Cohn-Bendit, *Obsolete Communism: The Left-Wing Alternative*, trans.

A. Pomerans (Harmondsworth: Penguin, 1968), p. 256. See Daniel Singer, *Prelude to Revolution: France in May, 1968* (London: Cape, 1970) for an interesting attempt to use *les événements* as a basis for prediction.
39 See Lucio Magri, 'Italian Communism Today' in *New Left Review* (London), No. 66 March–April, 1971, p. 49.
40 See 'You Don't Need a Weatherman to Know Which Way the Wind Blows' in Harold Jacobs (Ed), *Weatherman* (New York: Ramparts, 1970), p. 53.
41 For a useful discussion of changing techniques, see Bernard Béraud, *La gauche révolutionnaire au Japon* (Paris: Editions du Seuil, 1970), pp. 131–37.
42 *Violence in America*, op. cit., pp. 813–14.
43 Che Guevara, *Guerrilla Warfare* (Harmondsworth: Penguin, 1969), p. 14.
44 This account largely follows Moises Moleiro, *El MIR de Venezuela* (Havana: Guaivas Instituto del Libon, 1967) and Richard Gott, *Guerrilla Movements in Latin America* (London: Nelson, 1970), pp. 93–165.
45 See interview with Petkoff in *World Marxist Review* (Moscow), April 1968.
46 See, *inter alia*, João Quartim, 'La guérilla urbaine au Brésil' in *Les Temps Modernes* (Paris), November 1970, pp. 838–74.
47 Tom Hayden, *Rebellion and Repression* (Cleveland, Ohio: Meridian, 1969), pp. 14 and 16.
48 *Le Monde* (Paris), 20 October 1970.

APPENDIX

Minimanual of the urban guerrilla

By Carlos Marighella

A definition of the urban guerrilla

The chronic structural crisis characteristic of Brazil today, and its resultant political instability, are what have brought about the upsurge of revolutionary war in the country. The revolutionary war manifests itself in the form of urban guerrilla warfare, psychological warfare, or rural guerrilla warfare. Urban guerrilla warfare or psychological warfare in the city depends on the urban guerrilla.

The urban guerrilla is a man who fights the military dictatorship with arms, using unconventional methods. A political revolutionary and an ardent patriot, he is a fighter for his country's liberation, a friend of the people and of freedom. The area in which the urban guerrilla acts is in the large Brazilian cities. There are also bandits, commonly known as outlaws, who work in the big cities. Many times assaults by outlaws are taken as actions by urban guerrillas.

The urban guerrilla, however, differs radically from the outlaw. The outlaw benefits personally from the action, and attacks indiscriminately without distinguishing between the exploited and the exploiters, which is why there are so many ordinary men and women among his victims. The urban guerrilla follows a political goal and only attacks the government, the big capitalists, and the foreign imperialists, particularly North Americans.

Another element just as prejudicial as the outlaw and also operating in the urban area is the right-wing counter-revolutionary who creates confusion, assaults banks, hurls bombs, kidnaps, assassinates, and commits the worst imaginable crimes against urban guerrillas, revolutionary priests, students, and citizens who oppose fascism and seek liberty.

The urban guerrilla is an implacable enemy of the government and systematically inflicts damage on the authorities and on the men who dominate the country and exercise power. The principal task of the urban guerrilla is to distract, to wear out, to demoralize the militarists, the military dictatorship and its repressive forces, and also to attack and destroy the wealth and property of the North Americans, the foreign managers, and the Brazilian upper class.

The urban guerrilla is not afraid of dismantling and destroying the present Brazilian economic, political, and social system, for his aim is to help the rural guerrilla and to collaborate in the creation of a totally new and revolutionary social and political structure, with the armed people in power.

The urban guerrilla must have a certain minimal political understanding. To gain that he must read certain printed or mimeographed works such as:

Guerrilla Warfare by Che Guevara
Memories of a Terrorist
Some Questions about the Brazilian Guerrillas
Guerrilla Operations and Tactics
On Strategic Problems and Principles
Certain Tactical Principles for Comrades Undertaking Guerrilla Operations
Organizational Questions
O Guerrilheiro, newspaper of the Brazilian revolutionary groups.

Personal qualities of the urban guerrilla and how he subsists

The urban guerrilla is characterized by his bravery and decisive nature. He must be a good tactician and a good shot. The urban guerrilla must be a person of great astuteness to compensate for the fact that he is not sufficiently strong in arms, ammunition, and equipment.

The career militarists or the government police have modern arms and transport, and can go about anywhere freely, using the force of their power. The urban guerrilla does not have such resources at his disposal and leads a clandestine existence. Sometimes he is a convicted person or is out on parole, and is obliged to use false documents.

Nevertheless, the urban guerrilla has a certain advantage over the conventional military or the police. It is that, while the military and the police act on behalf of the enemy, whom the people hate, the urban guerrilla defends a just cause, which is the people's cause.

The urban guerrilla's arms are inferior to the enemy's, but from a moral point of view, the urban guerrilla has an undeniable superiority.

This moral superiority is what sustains the urban guerrilla. Thanks to it, the urban guerrilla can accomplish his principal duty, which is to attack and to survive.

The urban guerrilla has to capture or divert arms from the enemy to be able to fight. Because his arms are not uniform, since what he has are expropriated or have fallen into his hands in different ways, the urban guerrilla faces the problem of a variety of arms and a shortage of ammunition. Moreover, he has no place to practise shooting and marksmanship.

These difficulties have to be surmounted, forcing the urban guerrilla to be imaginative and creative, qualities without which it would be impossible for him to carry out his role as a revolutionary.

The urban guerrilla must possess initiative, mobility, and flexibility, as well as versatility and a command of any situation. Initiative especially is an indispensable quality. It is not always possible to foresee everything, and the urban guerrilla cannot let himself become confused, or wait for orders. His duty is to act, to find adequate solutions for each problem he faces, and not to retreat. It is better to err acting than to do nothing for fear of erring. Without initiative there is no urban guerrilla warfare.

Other important qualities in the urban guerrilla are the following: to be a good walker, to be able to stand up against fatigue, hunger, rain, heat. To know how to hide and to be vigilant. To conquer the art of dissembling. Never to fear danger. To behave the same by day as by night. Not to act impetuously. To have unlimited patience. To remain calm and cool in the worst conditions and situations. Never to leave a track or trail. Not to get discouraged.

In the face of the almost insurmountable difficulties of urban warfare, sometimes comrades weaken, leave, give up the work.

The urban guerrilla is not a businessman in a commercial firm nor is he a character in a play. Urban guerrilla warfare, like rural guerrilla warfare, is a pledge the guerrilla makes to himself. When he cannot face the difficulties, or knows that he lacks the patience to wait, then it is better to relinquish his role before he betrays his pledge, for he clearly lacks the basic qualities necessary to be a guerrilla.

The urban guerrilla must know how to live among the people and must be careful not to appear strange and separated from ordinary city life.

He should not wear clothes that are different from those that other people wear. Elaborate and high fashion clothing for men or women may often be a handicap if the urban guerrilla's mission takes him into working-class neighbourhoods or sections where such dress is uncommon. The same care has to be taken if the urban guerrilla moves from the South to the North or *vice versa*.

The urban guerrilla must live by his work or professional activity. If he is known and sought by the police, if he is convicted or is on parole, he must go underground and sometimes must live hidden. Under such circumstances, the urban guerrilla cannot reveal his activity to anyone, since that is always and only the responsibility of the revolutionary organization in which he is participating.

The urban guerrilla must have a great capacity for observation, must be well informed about everything, principally about the enemy's movements, and must be very searching and knowledgeable about the area in which he lives, operates, or through which he moves.

But the fundamental and decisive characteristic of the urban guerrilla is that he is a man who fights with arms; given this condition, there is very little likelihood that he will be able to follow his normal profession for long without being identified. The role of expropriation thus looms as clear as high noon. It is impossible for the urban guerrilla to exist and survive without fighting to expropriate.

Thus, within the framework of the class struggle, as it inevitably and necessarily sharpens, the armed struggle of the urban guerrilla points toward two essential objectives:

(a) the physical liquidation of the chiefs and assistants of the armed forces and of the police;
(b) the expropriation of government resources and those belonging to the big capitalists, latifundists, and imperialists, with small expropriations used for the maintenance of individual urban guerrillas and large ones for the sustenance of the revolution itself.

It is clear that the armed struggle of the urban guerrilla also has other objectives. But here we are referring to the two basic objectives, above all expropriation. It is necessary for every urban guerrilla to keep in mind always that he can only maintain his existence if he is disposed to kill the police and those dedicated to repression, and if he is determined – truly determined – to expropriate the wealth of the big capitalists, the latifundists, and the imperialists.

One of the fundamental characteristics of the Brazilian revolution is that from the beginning it developed around the expropriation of the wealth of the major bourgeois, imperialist, and latifundist interests, without excluding the richest and most powerful commercial elements engaged in the import-export business.

And by expropriating the wealth of the principal enemies of the people, the Brazilian revolution was able to hit them at their vital centre, with preferential and systematic attacks on the banking network – that is to say, the most telling blows were levelled against capitalism's nerve system.

The bank robberies carried out by the Brazilian urban guerrillas hurt such big capitalists as Moreira Salles and others, the foreign firms which insure and reinsure the banking capital, the imperialist companies, the federal and state governments – all of them systematically expropriated as of now.

The fruit of these expropriations has been devoted to the work of learning and perfecting urban guerrilla techniques, the purchase, the production, and the transportation of arms and ammunition for the rural areas, the security apparatus of the revolutionaries, the daily maintenance of the fighters, of those who have been liberated from prison by armed force and those who are wounded or persecuted by the police, or to any kind of problem concerning comrades liberated from jail, or assassinated by the police and the military dictatorship.

The tremendous costs of the revolutionary war must fall on the big capitalists, on imperialism, and the latifundists and on the government too, both federal and state, since they are all exploiters and oppressors of the people.

Men of the government, agents of the dictatorship and of North American imperialism principally, must pay with their lives for the crimes committed against the Brazilian people.

In Brazil, the number of violent actions carried out by urban guerrillas, including deaths, explosions, seizures of arms, ammunition, and explosives, assaults on banks and prisons, etc., is significant enough to leave no room for doubt as to the actual aims of the revolutionaries. The execution of the CIA spy Charles Chandler, a member of the US Army who came from the war in Vietnam to infiltrate the Brazilian student movement, the military henchmen killed in bloody encounters with urban guerrillas, all are witness to the fact that we are in full revolutionary war and that the war can be waged only by violent means.

This is the reason why the urban guerrilla uses armed struggle and why he continues to concentrate his activity on the physical extermination of the agents of repression, and to dedicate twenty-four hours a day to expropriation from the people's exploiters.

Technical preparation of the urban guerrilla

No one can become an urban guerrilla without paying special attention to technical preparation.

The technical preparation of the urban guerrilla runs from the concern for his physical preparedness, to knowledge of and apprenticeship in professions and skills of all kinds, particularly manual skills.

The urban guerrilla can have strong physical resistance only if he trains systematically. He cannot be a good fighter if he has not learned the art of fighting. For that reason the urban guerrilla must learn and practise various kinds of fighting, of attack, and personal defence.

Other useful forms of physical preparation are hiking, camping, and practice in survival in the woods, mountain climbing, rowing, swimming, skin diving, training as a frogman, fishing, harpooning, and the hunting of birds, small and big game.

It is very important to learn how to drive, pilot a plane, handle a motor boat and a sail boat, understand mechanics, radio, telephone, electricity, and have some knowledge of electronic techniques.

It is also important to have a knowledge of topographical information, to be able to locate one's position by instruments or other available resources, to calculate distances, make maps and plans, draw to scale, make timings, work with an angle protractor, a compass, etc.

A knowledge of chemistry and of colour combination, of stamp-making, the domination of the technique of calligraphy and the copying of letters and other skills are part of the technical preparation of the urban guerrilla, who is obliged to falsify documents in order to live within a society that he seeks to destroy.

In the area of auxiliary medicine he has the special role of being a doctor or understanding medicine, nursing, pharmacology, drugs, elementary surgery, and emergency first aid.

The basic question in the technical preparation of the urban guerrilla is nevertheless to know how to handle arms such as the machine gun, revolver, automatic, FAL, various types of shotguns, carbines, mortars, bazookas, etc.

A knowledge of various types of ammunition and explosives is another aspect to consider. Among the explosives, dynamite must be well understood. The use of incendiary bombs, of smoke bombs, and other types are indispensable prior knowledge.

To know how to make and repair arms, prepare Molotov cocktails, grenades, mines, home-made destructive devices, how to blow up bridges, tear up and put out of service rails and sleepers, these are requisites in the technical preparation of the urban guerrilla that can never be considered unimportant.

The highest level of preparation for the urban guerrilla is the centre for technical training. But only the guerrilla who has already passed the preliminary examination can go on to this school – that is to say, one who has passed the proof of fire in revolutionary action, in actual combat against the enemy.

The urban guerrilla's arms

The urban guerrilla's arms are light arms, easily exchanged, usually captured from the enemy, purchased, or made on the spot.

Light arms have the advantage of fast handling and easy transport. In general, light arms are characterized as short barrelled. This includes many automatic arms.

Automatic and semi-automatic arms considerably increase the fighting power of the urban guerrilla. The disadvantage of this type of arm for us is the difficulty in controlling it, resulting in wasted rounds or in a prodigious use of ammunition, compensated for only by optimal aim and firing precision. Men who are poorly trained convert automatic weapons into an ammunition drain.

Experience has shown that the basic arm of the urban guerrilla is the light machine gun. This arm, in addition to being efficient and easy to shoot in an urban area, has the advantage of being greatly respected by the enemy. The guerrilla must know thoroughly how to handle the machine gun, now so popular and indispensable to the Brazilian urban guerrilla.

The ideal machine gun for the urban guerrilla is the Ina 45 calibre. Other types of machine guns of different calibres can be used – understanding, of course, the problem of ammunition. Thus it is preferable that the industrial potential of the urban guerrilla permits the production of a single machine gun so that the ammunition used can be standardized.

Each firing group of urban guerrillas must have a machine gun managed by a good marksman. The other components of the group must be armed with ·38 revolvers, our standard arm. The ·32 is also useful for those who want to participate. But the ·38 is preferable since its impact usually puts the enemy out of action.

Hand grenades and conventional smoke bombs can be considered light arms, with defensive power for cover and withdrawal.

Long barrel arms are more difficult for the urban guerrilla to transport and attract much attention because of their size. Among the long barrel arms are the FAL, the Mauser guns or rifles, hunting guns such as the Winchester, and others.

Shotguns can be useful if used at close range and point blank. They are useful even for a poor shot, especially at night when precision isn't much help. A pressure airgun can be useful for training in marksmanship. Bazookas and mortars can also be used in action but the conditions for using them have to be prepared and the people who use them must be trained.

The urban guerrilla should not try to base his actions on the use of heavy arms, which have major drawbacks in a type of fighting that demands lightweight weapons to insure mobility and speed.

Home-made weapons are often as efficient as the best arms produced in conventional factories, and even a cut-off shotgun is a good arm for the urban guerrilla.

The urban guerrilla's role as gunsmith has a fundamental importance. As gunsmith he takes care of the arms, knows how to repair them, and in many cases can set up a small shop for improvising and producing efficient small arms.

Work in metallurgy and on the mechanical lathe are basic skills the urban guerrilla should incorporate into his industrial planning, which is the construction of home-made weapons.

This construction and courses in explosives and sabotage must be organized. The primary materials for practice in these courses must be obtained ahead of time to prevent an incomplete apprenticeship – that is to say, so as to leave no room for experimentation.

Molotov cocktails, gasoline, home-made contrivances such as catapults and mortars for firing explosives, grenades made of tubes and cans, smoke bombs, mines, conventional explosives such as dynamite and potassium chloride, plastic explosives, gelatine capsules, ammunition of every kind are indispensable to the success of the urban guerrilla's mission.

The method of obtaining the necessary materials and munitions will be to buy them or to take them by force in expropriation actions especially planned and carried out.

The urban guerrilla will be careful not to keep explosives and materials that can cause accidents around for very long, but will try always to use them immediately on their destined targets.

The urban guerrilla's arms and his ability to maintain them constitute his fire power. By taking advantage of modern arms and introducing innovations in his fire power and in the use of certain arms, the urban guerrilla can change many of the tactics of city warfare. An example of this was the innovation made by the urban guerrillas in Brazil when they introduced the machine gun in their attacks on banks.

When the massive use of uniform machine guns becomes possible, there will be new changes in urban guerrilla warfare tactics. The firing group that utilizes uniform weapons and corresponding ammunition, with reasonable support for their maintenance, will reach a considerable level of efficiency. The urban guerrilla increases his efficiency as he improves his firing potential.

The shot: the urban guerrilla's reason for existence

The urban guerrilla's reason for existence, the basic condition in which he acts and survives, is to shoot. The urban guerrilla must know how to shoot well because it is required by his type of combat.

In conventional warfare, combat is generally at a distance with long-range arms. In unconventional warfare, in which urban guerrilla warfare is included, the combat is at close range, often very close. To prevent his own extinction, the urban guerrilla has to shoot first and he cannot err in his shot. He cannot waste his ammunition because he doesn't have large amounts, so he must save it. Nor can he replace his ammunition quickly, since he is part of a small group in which each guerrilla has to take care of himself. The urban guerrilla can lose no time and must be able to shoot at once.

One fundamental fact, which we want to emphasize fully and whose particular importance cannot be overestimated, is that the urban guerrilla must not fire continuously, using up his ammunition. It may be that the enemy is not responding to the fire precisely because he is waiting until the guerrilla's ammunition is used up. At such a moment, without having time to replace his ammunition, the urban guerrilla faces a rain of enemy fire and can be taken prisoner or be killed.

In spite of the value of the surprise factor which many times makes it unnecessary for the urban guerrilla to use his arms, he cannot be allowed the luxury of entering combat without knowing how to shoot. And face to face with the enemy, he must always be moving from one position to another, because to stay in one position makes him a fixed target and, as such, very vulnerable.

The urban guerrilla's life depends on shooting, on his ability to handle his arms well and to avoid being hit. When we speak of shooting, we speak of marksmanship as well. Shooting must be learned until it becomes a reflex action on the part of the urban guerrilla.

To learn how to shoot and to have good aim, the urban guerrilla must train himself systematically, utilizing every apprenticeship method, shooting at targets, even in amusement parks and at home.

Shooting and marksmanship are the urban guerrilla's water and air. His perfection of the art of shooting makes him a special type of urban guerrilla – that is, a sniper, a category of solitary combatant indispensable in isolated actions. The sniper knows how to shoot, at close range and at long range, and his arms are appropriate for either type of shooting.

The firing group

In order to function, the urban guerrillas must be organized in small groups. A group of no more than four or five is called *the firing group*.

A minimum of two firing groups, separated and sealed off from other firing groups, directed and coordinated by one or two persons, this is what makes a *firing team*.

Within the firing group there must be complete confidence among the comrades. The best shot and the one who best knows how to manage the machine gun is the person in charge of operations.

The firing group plans and executes urban guerrilla actions, obtains and guards arms, studies and corrects its own tactics.

When there are tasks planned by the strategic command, these tasks take preference. But there is no such thing as a firing group without its own initiative. For this reason it is essential to avoid any rigidity in the organization in order to permit the greatest possible initiative on the part of the firing group. The old-type hierarchy, the style of the traditional left doesn't exist in our organization.

This means that, except for the priority of objectives set by the strategic command, any firing group can decide to assault a bank, to kidnap or to execute an agent of the dictatorship, a figure identified with the reaction, or a North American spy, and can carry out any kind of propaganda or war of nerves against the enemy without the need to consult the general command.

No firing group can remain inactive waiting for orders from above. Its obligation is to act. Any single urban guerrilla who wants to establish a firing group and begin action can do so and thus become a part of the organization.

This method of action eliminates the need for knowing who is carrying out which actions, since there is free initiative and the only important point is to increase substantially the volume of urban guerrilla activity in order to wear out the government and force it onto the defensive.

The firing group is the instrument of organized action. Within it, guerrilla operations and tactics are planned, launched, and carried through to success.

The general command counts on the firing groups to carry out objectives of a strategic nature, and to do so in any part of the country. For its part, it helps the firing groups with their difficulties and their needs.

The organization is an indestructible network of firing groups, and of coordinations among them, that functions simply and practically with a general command that also participates in the attacks; an organization which exists for no purpose other than pure and simple revolutionary action.

The logistics of the urban guerrilla

Conventional logistics can be expressed by the formula CCEM:

C – food (*comida*)
C – fuel (*combustivel*)
E – equipment
M – ammunition (*munições*)

Conventional logistics refer to the maintenance problems for an army or a regular armed force, transported in vehicles with fixed bases and supply lines.

Urban guerrillas, on the contrary, are not an army but small armed groups, intentionally fragmented. They have no vehicles nor fixed bases. Their supply lines are precarious and insufficient, and have no established base except in the rudimentary sense of an arms factory within a house.

While the goal of conventional logistics is to supply the war needs of the gorillas to be used to repress urban and rural rebellion, urban guerrilla logistics aim at sustaining operations and tactics which have nothing in common with a conventional war and are directed against the military dictatorship and North American domination of the country.

For the urban guerrilla, who starts from nothing and has no support at the beginning, logistics are expressed by the formula MDAME, which is:

M – mechanization
D – money (*dinheiro*)
A – arms
M – ammunition (*munições*)
E – explosives

Revolutionary logistics takes mechanization as one of its bases. Nevertheless, mechanization is inseparable from the driver. The urban guerrilla driver is as important as the urban guerrilla machine gunner. Without either, the machines do not work, and as such the automobile like the machine gun becomes a dead thing. An experienced driver is not made in one day and the apprenticeship must begin early. Every good urban guerrilla must be a good driver. As to the vehicle, the urban guerrilla must expropriate what he needs.

When he already has resources, the urban guerrilla can combine the expropriation of vehicles with other methods of acquisition.

Money, arms, ammunition and explosives, and automobiles as well, must be expropriated. And the urban guerrilla must rob banks and armouries and seize explosives and ammunition wherever he finds them.

Urban Guerrilla Warfare 299

None of these operations is undertaken for just one purpose. Even when the assault is for money, the arms that the guards bear must also be taken.

Expropriation is the first step in the organization of our logistics, which itself assumes an armed and permanently mobile character.

The second step is to reinforce and extend logistics, resorting to ambushes and traps in which the enemy will be surprised and his arms, ammunition, vehicles, and other resources can be captured.

Once he has the arms, ammunition, and explosives, one of the most serious logistics problems the urban guerrilla faces at any time and in any situation, is a hiding place in which to leave the material and appropriate means for transporting it and assembling it where it is needed. This has to be accomplished even when the enemy is on the lookout and has the roads blocked.

The knowledge that the urban guerrilla has of the terrain, and the devices he uses or is capable of using, such as guides especially prepared and recruited for this mission, are the basic elements in the solution of the external logistics problem the revolutionary faces.

The technique of the urban guerrilla

In its most general sense, technique is the combination of methods man uses to carry out any activity. The activity of the urban guerrilla consists in waging guerrilla warfare and psychological warfare.

The urban guerrilla technique has five basic components:

(a) one part is related to the specific characteristics of the situation;
(b) one part is related to the requisites that match these characteristics, requisties represented by a series of initial advantages without which the urban guerrilla cannot achieve his objectives;
(c) one part concerns certain and definite objectives in the actions initiated by the urban guerrilla;
(d) one part is related to the types and characteristic modes of action for the urban guerrilla;
(e) one part is concerned with the urban guerrilla's method of carrying out his specific actions.

The technique of the urban guerrilla has the following characteristics:

(a) it is an aggressive technique, or in other words, it has an offensive character. As is well known, defensive action means death for us. Since we are inferior to the enemy in fire power and have neither his resources nor his power force, we cannot defend ourselves against an offensive or a concentrated attack by the gorillas. And that is the reason why our urban technique can never be permanent, can never defend a fixed base nor remain in any one spot waiting to repel the circle of reaction;
(b) it is a technique of attack and retreat by which we preserve our forces;

(c) it is a technique that aims at the development of urban guerrilla warfare, whose function will be to wear out, demoralize, and distract the enemy forces, permitting the emergence and survival of rural guerrilla warfare which is destined to play the decisive role in the revolutionary war.

The initial advantages of the urban guerrilla

The dynamics of urban guerrilla warfare lie in the urban guerrilla's violent clash with the military and police forces of the dictatorship. In this clash, the police have the superiority. The urban guerrilla has inferior forces. The paradox is that the urban guerrilla, although weaker, is nevertheless the attacker.

The military and police forces, for their part, respond to the attack by mobilizing and concentrating infinitely superior forces in the persecution and destruction of the urban guerrilla. He can only avoid defeat if he counts on the initial advantages he has and knows how to exploit them to the end to compensate for his weaknesses and lack of *matériel*.

The initial advantages are:

(a) he must take the enemy by surprise;
(b) he must know the terrain of the encounter better than the enemy;
(c) he must have greater mobility and speed than the police and the other repressive forces;
(d) his information service must be better than the enemy's;
(e) he must be in command of the situation and demonstrate a decisiveness so great that everyone on our side is inspired and never thinks of hesitating, while on the other side the enemy is stunned and incapable of responding.

Surprise

To compensate for his general weakness and shortage of arms compared to the enemy, the urban guerrilla uses surprise. The enemy has no way to fight surprise and becomes confused or is destroyed.

When urban guerrilla warfare broke out in Brazil, experience proved that surprise was essential to the success of any urban guerrilla operation.

The technique of surprise is based on four essential requisites:

(a) we know the situation of the enemy we are going to attack, usually by means of precise information and meticulous observation, while the enemy does not know he is going to be attacked and knows nothing about the attacker;
(b) we know the force of the enemy that is going to be attacked and the enemy knows nothing about our force;
(c) attacking by surprise, we save and conserve our forces, while the enemy is unable to do the same and is left at the mercy of events;

(d) we determine the hour and the place of the attack, fix its duration, and establish its objective. The enemy remains ignorant of all this.

Knowledge of the terrain

The urban guerrilla's best ally is the terrain and because this is so he must know it like the palm of his hand.

To have the terrain as an ally means to know how to use with intelligence its unevenness, its high and its low points, its turns, its irregularities, its regular and its secret passages, abandoned areas, its thickets, etc., taking maximum advantage of all this for the success of armed actions, escapes, retreats, cover, and hiding places.

Its impasses and narrow spots, its gorges, its streets under repair, police control points, military zones and closed-off streets, the entrances and exits of tunnels and those that the enemy can close off, viaducts to be crossed, corners controlled by the police or watched, its lights and signals, all this must be thoroughly known and studied in order to avoid fatal errors.

Our problem is to get through and to know where and how to hide, leaving the enemy bewildered in areas he doesn't know.

Familiar with the avenues, streets, alleys, ins and outs, and corners of the urban centres, its paths and shortcuts, its empty lots, its underground passages, its pipes and sewer system, the urban guerrilla safely crosses through the irregular and difficult terrain unfamiliar to the police, where they can be surprised in a fatal ambush or trapped at any moment.

Because he knows the terrain the guerrilla can go through it on foot, on bicycle, in automobile, jeep, or truck and never be trapped. Acting in small groups with only a few people, the guerrillas can reunite at an hour and place determined beforehand, following up the attack with new guerrilla operations, or evading the police circle and disorienting the enemy with their unprecedented audacity.

It is an insoluble problem for the police in the labyrinthian terrain of the urban guerrilla, to get someone they can't see, to repress someone they can't catch, to close in on someone they can't find.

Our experience is that the ideal urban guerrilla is one who operates in his own city and knows thoroughly its streets, its neighbourhoods, its transit problems, and other peculiarities.

The guerrilla outsider, who comes to a city whose corners are unfamiliar to him, is a weak spot and, if he is assigned certain operations, can endanger them. To avoid grave errors, it is necessary for him to get to know well the layout of the streets.

Mobility and speed

To insure a mobility and speed that the police cannot match, the urban guerrilla needs the following prerequisites:

(a) mechanization;
(b) knowledge of the terrain;
(c) a rupture or suspension of enemy communications and transport;
(d) light arms.

By carefully carrying through operations that last only a few moments, and leaving the site in mechanized vehicles, the urban guerrilla beats a rapid retreat, escaping persecution.

The urban guerrilla must know the way in detail and, in this sense, must go through the schedule ahead of time as a training to avoid entering alleyways that have no exit, or running into traffic jams, or becoming paralysed by the Transit Department's traffic signals.

The police pursue the urban guerrilla blindly without knowing which road he is using for his escape.

While the urban guerrilla quickly flees because he knows the terrain, the police lose the trail and give up the chase.

The urban guerrilla must launch his operations far from the logistics base of the police. An initial advantage of this method of operation is that it places us at a reasonable distance from the possibility of persecution, which facilitates the evasion.

In addition to this necessary precaution, the urban guerrilla must be concerned with the enemy's communications system. The telephone is the primary target in preventing the enemy from access to information by knocking out his communications system.

Even if he knows about the guerrilla operation, the enemy depends on modern transport for his logistics support, and his vehicles necessarily lose time carrying him through the heavy traffic of the large cities.

It is clear that the tangled and treacherous traffic is a disadvantage for the enemy, as it would be for us if we were not ahead of him.

If we want to have a safe margin of security and be certain to leave no tracks for the future, we can adopt the following methods:

(a) purposely intercept the police with other vehicles or by apparently casual inconveniences and damages; but in this case the vehicles in question should not be legal nor should they have real licence numbers;
(b) obstruct the road with fallen trees, rocks, ditches, false traffic signs, dead ends or detours, and other ingenious methods;
(c) place home-made mines in the way of the police, use gasoline, or throw Molotov cocktails to set their vehicles on fire;
(d) set off a burst of machine-gun fire or arms such as the FAL aimed at the motor and the tyres of the cars engaged in pursuit.

With the arrogance typical of the police and the military fascist authorities, the enemy will come to fight us with heavy guns and equipment and with elaborate manoeuvres by men armed to the teeth. The urban guerrilla must respond to this with light weapons easily transported, so he can always escape with maximum speed, without ever accepting open fighting. The urban guerrilla has no mission other than to attack and retreat.

We would leave ourselves open to the most stunning defeats if we burdened ourselves with heavy arms and with the tremendous weight of the ammunition necessary to fire them, at the same time losing our precious gift of mobility.

When the enemy fights against us with cavalry we are at no disadvantage as long as we are mechanized. The automobile goes faster than the horse. From within the car we also have the target of the mounted police, knocking him down with machine gun and revolver fire or with Molotov cocktails and grenades.

On the other hand, it is not so difficult for an urban guerrilla on foot to make a target of a policeman on horseback. Moreover, ropes across the streets, marbles, cork stoppers are very efficient methods of making them both fall. The great disadvantage of the mounted policeman is that he presents the urban guerrilla with two excellent targets: the horse and its rider.

Apart from being faster than the horseman, the helicopter has no better chance in persecution. If the horse is too slow compared to the urban guerrilla's automobile, the helicopter is too fast. Moving at 200 kilometres an hour it will never succeed in hitting from above a target lost among the crowds and the street vehicles, nor can it land in public streets in order to catch someone. At the same time, whenever it tries to fly low, it will be excessively vulnerable to the fire of the urban guerrilla.

Information

The possibilities that the government has for discovering and destroying the urban guerrillas lessen as the potential of the dictatorship's enemies becomes greater and more concentrated among the popular masses.

This concentration of opponents of the dictatorship plays a very important role in providing information as to moves on the part of the police and men in government, as well as in hiding our activities. The enemy can also be thrown off by false information, which is worse for him because it is a tremendous waste.

By whatever means, the sources of information at the disposal of the urban guerrilla are potentially better than those of the police. The enemy is observed by the people, but he does not know who among the people transmits information to the urban guerrilla. The military and the police are hated for the injustices and violence they commit against the people, and this facilitates obtaining information prejudicial to the activities of government agents.

The information, which is only a small area of popular support, represents an extraordinary potential in the hands of the urban guerrilla. The creation of an intelligence service with an organized structure is a basic need for us. The urban guerrilla has to have essential information about the plans and movements of the enemy, where they are, and how they move, the resources of the banking network, the means of communication, and the secret moves the enemy makes.

The trustworthy information passed along to the urban guerrilla represents a well-aimed blow at the dictatorship. It has no way to defend itself in the face of an important leak that jeopardizes its interests and facilitates our destructive attack.

The enemy also wants to know what steps we are taking so he can destroy us or prevent us from acting. In this sense the danger of betrayal is present and the enemy encourages betrayal or infiltrates spies into the organization. The urban guerrilla's technique against this enemy tactic is to denounce publicly the traitors, spies, informers, and *provocateurs*.

Since our struggle takes place among the masses and depends on their sympathy – while the government has a bad reputation because of its brutality, corruption, and incompetence – the informers, spies, traitors, and the police come to be enemies of the people without supporters, denounced to the urban guerrillas, and, in many cases, properly punished.

For his part the urban guerrilla must not evade the duty – once he knows who the spy or informer is – of wiping him out physically. This is the correct method, approved by the people, and it minimizes considerably the incidence of infiltration or enemy spying.

For the complete success of the battle against spies and informers, it is essential to organize a counter-espionage or counter-intelligence service. Nevertheless, as far as information is concerned, it cannot all be reduced to a question of knowing the enemy's moves and avoiding the infiltration of spies. Information must be broad, it must embrace everything, including the most insignificant matters. There is a technique of obtaining information and the urban guerrilla must master it. Following this technique, information is obtained naturally, as a part of the life of the people.

The urban guerrilla, living in the midst of the people and moving about among them, must be attentive to all types of conversations and human relations, learning how to disguise his interest with great skill and judgment.

In places where people work, study, live, it is easy to collect all kinds of information on payments, business, plans of all types, points of view, opinions, people's state of mind, trips, interiors of buildings, offices and rooms, operation centres, etc.

Observation, investigation, reconnaissance, and exploration of the terrain are also excellent sources of information. The urban guerrilla never goes anywhere absentmindedly and without revolutionary precaution, always on the lookout lest something occur. Eyes and ears open, senses alert, his memory engraved with everything necessary, now or in the future, to the uninterrupted activity of the fighter.

Careful reading of the press with particular attention to the organs of mass communication, the investigation of accumulated data, the transmission of news and everything of note, a persistence in being informed and in informing others, all this makes up the intricate and immensely complicated question of information which gives the urban guerrilla a decisive advantage.

Decision

It is not enough for the urban guerrilla to have in his favour surprise, speed, knowledge of the terrain, and information. He must also demonstrate his command of any situation and a capacity for decision without which all other advantages will prove useless.

It is impossible to carry out any action, however well planned, if the urban guerrilla turns out to be indecisive, uncertain, irresolute.

Even an action successfully begun can end in defeat if the command of the situation and the capacity for decision falter in the middle of the actual execution of the plan. When this command of the situation and a capacity for decision are absent, the void is filled with vacillation and terror. The enemy takes advantage of this failure and is able to liquidate us.

The secret for the success of any operation, simple or complicated, easy or difficult, is to rely on determined men. Strictly speaking, there are no easy operations. All must be carried out with the same care exercised in the case of the most difficult, beginning with the choice of the human element, which means relying on leadership and capacity for decision in every test.

One can see ahead of time whether an action will be successful or not by the way its participants act during the preparatory period. Those who are behind, who fail to make designated contacts, are easily confused, forget things, fail to complete the basic elements of the work, possibly are indecisive men and can be a danger. It is better not to include them.

Decision means to put into practice the plan that has been devised with determination, with audacity, and with an absolute firmness. It takes only one person who vacillates to lose all.

Objectives of the urban guerrilla's actions

With his technique developed and established, the urban guerrilla bases himself on models of action leading to attack and, in Brazil, with the following objectives:

(a) to threaten the triangle in which the Brazilian state system and North American domination are maintained in Brazil, a triangle whose points are Rio, São Paulo and Belo Horizonte and whose base is the axle Rio–São Paulo, where the giant industrial-financial-economic-political-cultural-military-police complex that holds the entire decisive power of the country is located;
(b) to weaken the local guards or the security system of the dictatorship, given the fact that we are attacking and the gorillas defending, which means catching the government in a defensive position with its troops

immobilized in defence of the entire complex of national maintenance, with its ever-present fears of an attack on its strategic nerve centres, and without ever knowing where, how, and when that attack will come;

(c) to attack on every side with many different armed groups, few in number, each self-contained and operating separately, to disperse the government forces in their pursuit of a thoroughly fragmented organization instead of offering the dictatorship the opportunity to concentrate its forces of repression on the destruction of one tightly organized system operating throughout the country;

(d) to give proof of its combativeness, decision, firmness, determination, and persistence in the attack on the military dictatorship in order to permit all malcontents to follow our example and fight with urban guerrilla tactics. Meanwhile, the government, with all its problems, incapable of halting guerrilla operations in the city, will lose time and suffer endless attrition and will finally be forced to pull back its repressive troops in order to mount guard over the banks, industries, armouries, military barracks, prisons, public offices, radio and television stations, North American firms, gas storage tanks, oil refineries, ships, aircraft, ports, airports, hospitals, health centres, blood banks, stores, garages, embassies, residences of outstanding members of the regime, such as ministers and generals, police stations, and official organizations, etc.;

(e) to increase urban guerrilla disturbances gradually in an endless ascendancy of unforeseen actions such that the government troops cannot leave the urban area to pursue the guerrillas in the interior without running the risk of abandoning the cities and permitting rebellion to increase on the coast as well as in the interior of the country;

(f) to oblige the army and the police, with the commanders and their assistants, to change the relative comfort and tranquillity of their barracks and their usual rest, for a state of alarm and growing tension in the expectation of attack or in search for tracks that vanish without a trace;

(g) to avoid open battle and decisive combat with the government, limiting the struggle to brief and rapid attacks with lightning results;

(h) to assure for the urban guerrilla a maximum freedom of manoeuvre and of action without ever relinquishing the use of armed violence, remaining firmly oriented towards helping the beginning of rural guerrilla warfare and supporting the construction of the revolutionary army for national liberation.

On the types and nature of action models for the urban guerrilla

In order to achieve the objectives previously enumerated, the urban guerrilla is obliged, in his technique, to follow an action whose nature is as different and as diversified as possible. The urban guerrilla does not arbitrarily choose this or that action model. Some actions are simple, others are complicated. The urban guerrilla without experience must be incorporated gradually into actions and operations that run from the simple to the complex. He begins with small missions and tasks until he becomes a completely experienced urban guerrilla.

Before any action, the urban guerrilla must think of the methods and the personnel at his disposal to carry out the action. Operations and actions that demand the urban guerrilla's technical preparation cannot be carried out by someone who lacks that technical skill. With these cautions, the action models which the urban guerrilla can carry out are the following:

(a) assaults;
(b) raids and penetrations;
(c) occupations;
(d) ambush;
(e) street tactics;
(f) strikes and work interruptions;
(g) desertions, diversions, seizures, expropriations of arms, ammunition, explosives;
(h) liberation of prisoners;
(i) executions;
(j) kidnappings;
(k) sabotage;
(l) terrorism;
(m) armed propaganda;
(n) war of nerves.

Assaults

Assault is the armed attack which we make to expropriate funds, liberate prisoners, capture explosives, machine guns, and other types of arms and ammunition.

Assaults can take place in broad daylight or at night.

Daytime assaults are made when the objective cannot be achieved at any other hour, as for example, the transport of money by the banks, which is not done at night.

Night assault is usually the most advantageous to the urban guerrilla. The ideal is for all assaults to take place at night when conditions for a surprise attack are most favourable and the darkness facilitates flight and hides the identity of the participants. The urban guerrilla must prepare himself, nevertheless, to act under all conditions, daytime as well as night-time.

The most vulnerable targets for assault are the following:

(a) credit establishments;
(b) commercial and industrial enterprises, including the production of arms and explosives;
(c) military establishments;

(d) commissaries and police stations;
(e) jails;
(f) government property;
(g) mass communication media;
(h) North American firms and properties;
(i) government vehicles, including military and police vehicles, trucks, armoured vehicles, money carriers, trains, ships, and planes.

The assaults on establishments are of the same nature because in every case the property and buildings represent a fixed target.

Assaults on buildings are conceived as guerrilla operations, varied according to whether they are against banks, a commercial enterprise, industries, military camps, commissaries, prisons, radio stations, warehouses for imperialist firms, etc.

The assaults on vehicles – money-carriers, armoured cars, trains, ships, aircraft – are of another nature since they are moving targets. The nature of the operations varies according to the situation and the possibility – that is, whether the target is stationary or moving.

Armoured cars, including military cars, are not immune to mines. Obstructed roads, traps, ruses, interception of other vehicles, Molotov cocktails, shooting with heavy arms, are efficient methods of assaulting vehicles.

Heavy vehicles, grounded planes, anchored ships can be seized and their crews and guards overcome. Aircraft in flight can be diverted from their course by guerrilla action or by one person.

Ships and trains in movement can be assaulted or taken by guerrilla operations in order to capture the arms and munitions or to prevent troop displacement.

The bank assault as popular model

The most popular assault model is the bank assault. In Brazil, the urban guerrilla has begun a type of organized assault on the banks as a guerrilla operation. Today this type of assault is widely used and has served as a sort of preliminary examination for the urban guerrilla in his apprenticeship for the techniques of revolutionary warfare.

Important innovations in the technique of assaulting banks have developed, guaranteeing flight, the withdrawal of money, and the anonymity of those involved. Among these innovations we cite shooting the tyres of cars to prevent pursuit; locking people in the bank bathroom, making them sit on the floor; immobilizing the bank guards and removing their arms, forcing someone to open the coffer or the strong box; using disguises.

Attempts to install bank alarms, to use guards or electronic detection devices of US origin, prove fruitless when the assault is political and is carried out according to urban guerrilla warfare technique. This technique tries to utilize new resources to meet the enemy's tactical changes, has access to a fire power that is growing every day, becomes increasingly astute and audacious, and uses a larger number of revolutionaries every time; all to guarantee the success of operations planned down to the last detail.

The bank assault is a typical expropriation. But, as is true in any kind of armed expropriatory action, the revolutionary is handicapped by a two-fold competition:

(a) competition from the outlaw;
(b) competition from the right-wing counter-revolutionary.

This competition produces confusion, which is reflected in the people's uncertainty. It is up to the urban guerrilla to prevent this from happening, and to accomplish this he must use two methods:

(a) he must avoid the outlaw's technique, which is one of unnecessary violence and appropriation of goods and possessions belonging to the people;
(b) he must use the assault for propaganda purposes, at the very moment it is taking place, and later distribute material, leaflets, every possible means of explaining the objectives and the principles of the urban guerrilla as expropriator of the government, the ruling classes, and imperialism.

Raids and penetration

Raids and penetrations are quick attacks on establishments located in neighbourhoods or even in the centre of the city, such as small military units, commissaries, hospitals, to cause trouble, seize arms, punish and terrorize the enemy, take reprisal, or rescue wounded prisoners, or those hospitalized under police vigilance.

Raids and penetrations are also made on garages and depots to destroy vehicles and damage installations, especially if they are North American firms and property.

When they take place on certain stretches of the highway or in certain distant neighbourhoods, the raids can serve to force the enemy to move great numbers of troops, a totally useless effort since he will find nobody there to fight.

When they are carried out in certain houses, offices, archives, or public offices, their purpose is to capture or search for secret papers and documents with which to denounce involvements, compromises, and the corruption of men in government, their dirty deals and criminal transactions with the North Americans.

Raids and penetrations are most effective if they are carried out at night.

Occupations

Occupations are a type of attack carried out when the urban guerrilla stations himself in specific establishments and locations for a temporary resistance against the enemy or for some propaganda purpose.

The occupation of factories and schools during strikes or at other times is a method of protest or of distracting the enemy's attention.

The occupation of radio stations is for propaganda purposes.

Occupation is a highly effective model for action but, in order to prevent losses and material damage to our ranks, it is always a good idea to count on the possibility of withdrawal. It must always be meticulously planned and carried out at the opportune moment.

Occupation always has a time limit and the faster it is completed, the better.

Ambush

Ambushes are attacks typified by surprise when the enemy is trapped across a road or when he makes a police net surrounding a house or an estate. A false message can bring the enemy to the spot where he falls into the trap.

The principal object of the ambush tactic is to capture enemy arms and punish him with death.

Ambushes to halt passenger trains are for propaganda purposes and, when they are troop trains, the object is to annihilate the enemy and seize his arms.

The urban guerrilla sniper is the kind of fighter especially suited for ambush because he can hide easily in the irregularities of the terrain, on the roofs and the tops of buildings and apartments under construction. From windows and dark places, he can take careful aim at his chosen target.

Ambush has devastating effects on the enemy, leaving him unnerved, insecure, and fearful.

Street tactics

Street tactics are used to fight the enemy in the streets, utilizing the participation of the masses against him.

In 1968 the Brazilian students used excellent street tactics against police troops, such as marching down streets against traffic, utilizing slings and marbles as arms against the mounted police.

Other street tactics consist in constructing barricades; pulling up paving blocks and hurling them at the police; throwing bottles, bricks, paperweights, and other projectiles from the top of apartment and office buildings against the police; using buildings under construction for flight, for hiding, and for supporting surprise attacks.

It is equally necessary to know how to respond to enemy tactics. When the police troops come protected with helmets to defend themselves against flying objects, we have to divide ourselves into two teams: one to attack the enemy from the front, the other to attack him in the rear, withdrawing one as the other goes into action to prevent the first from becoming a target for projectiles hurled by the second.

By the same token it is important to know how to respond to the police net. When the police designate certain of their men to go into the masses to arrest a demonstrator, a larger group of urban guerrillas must surround the police group, disarming and beating them and at the same time letting the prisoner escape. This urban guerrilla operation is called the *net within the net*.

When the police net is formed at a school building, a factory, a place where the masses assemble, or some other point, the urban guerrilla must not give up or allow himself to be taken by surprise. To make his net work the enemy is obliged to transport the police in vehicles and special cars to occupy strategic points in the streets in order to invade the building or chosen locale. The urban guerrilla, for his part, must never clear a building or an area and meet in it without first knowing its exits, the way to break the circle, the strategic points that the police might occupy, and the roads that inevitably lead into the net, and he must hold other strategic points from which to strike at the enemy.

The roads followed by the police vehicles must be mined at key points along the way and at forced stopping points. When the mines explode, the vehicles will fly into the air. The police will be caught in the trap and will suffer losses or will be victims of ambush. The net must be broken by escape routes unknown to the police. The rigorous planning of the retreat is the best way of frustrating any encircling effort on the part of the enemy.

When there is no possibility of a flight plan, the urban guerrilla must not hold meetings, assemblies, or do anything else since to do so will prevent him from breaking through the net the enemy will surely try to throw around him.

Street tactics have revealed a new type of urban guerrilla, the urban guerrilla who participates in mass demonstrations. This is the type we designate as the urban guerrilla demonstrator, who joins the ranks and participates in popular marches with specific and definite aims.

These aims consist of hurling stones and projectiles of every type, using gasoline to start fires, using the police as a target for their fire arms, capturing police arms, kidnapping agents of the enemy and *provocateurs*, shooting with careful aim at the henchmen torturers and the police chiefs who come in special cars with false plates in order not to attract attention.

The urban guerrilla demonstrator shows groups in the mass demonstration the flight route if that is necessary. He plants mines, throws Molotov cocktails, prepares ambushes and explosions.

The urban guerrilla demonstrator must also initiate the *net within the net*, going through government vehicles, official cars, and police vehicles before turning them over or setting them on fire, to see if any of them have money and arms.

Snipers are very good for mass demonstrations and, along with the urban guerrilla demonstrators, can play a valuable role.

Hidden at strategic points, the snipers have complete success, using shotguns, machine guns, etc. whose fire and recoil easily cause losses among the enemy.

Strikes and work interruptions

The strike is a model of action employed by the urban guerrilla in work centres and schools to damage the enemy by stopping work and study activities. Because it is one of the weapons most feared by the exploiters and oppressors, the enemy uses tremendous fighting power and incredible violence against it. The strikers are taken to prison, suffer beatings, and many of them wind up assassinated.

The urban guerrilla must prepare the strike in such a way as to leave no tracks or clues that identify the leaders of the action. A strike is successful when it is organized through the action of a small group, if it is carefully prepared in secret and by the most clandestine methods.

Arms, ammunition, Molotovs, home-made weapons of destruction and attack, all this must be supplied beforehand in order to meet the enemy. So that it can do the greatest possible damage, it is a good idea to study and put into effect a sabotage plan.

Work and study interruptions, although they are of brief duration, cause severe damage to the enemy. It is enough for them to crop up at different points and in different sections of the same area, disrupting daily life, occurring endlessly one after the other, in authentic guerrilla fashion.

In strikes or simple work interruptions, the urban guerrilla has recourse to occupation or penetration of the locale or can simply make a raid. In that case his objective is to take hostages, to capture prisoners or to kidnap enemy agents and propose an exchange for the arrested strikers.

In certain cases, strikes and brief work interruptions can offer an excellent opportunity for preparing ambushes or traps whose aim is the physical liquidation of the cruel, bloody police.

The basic fact is that the enemy suffers losses and material and moral damage, and is weakened by the action.

Desertions, diversions, seizures, expropriations of arms, ammunition, explosives

Desertion and the diversion of arms are actions effected in military camps, ships, military hospitals, etc. The urban guerrilla soldier, chief, sergeant, sub-official, and official must desert at the most opportune moment with modern arms and ammunition to hand them over for the use of the Brazilian revolution.

One of the opportune moments is when the military urban guerrilla is called upon to pursue and to fight his guerrilla comrades outside the military quarters. Instead of following the orders of the gorillas, the military urban guerrilla must join the revolutionaries by handing over the arms and ammunition he carries, or the military plane he pilots.

The advantage of this method is that the revolutionaries receive arms and ammunition from the army, the navy, and the air force, the military police, the civilian guard, or the firemen without any great work, since it reaches their hands by government transport.

Other opportunities may occur in the barracks, and the military urban guerrilla must always be alert to this. In case of carelessness on the part of the commanders or in other favourable conditions, such as bureaucratic attitudes and behaviour or relaxation of discipline on the part of sub-lieutenants and other internal personnel, the military urban guerrilla must no longer wait but must try to advise the organizations and desert alone or accompanied, but with as large a supply of arms as possible.

With information from and participation of the military urban guerrilla, raids on barracks and other military establishments for the purpose of capturing arms can be organized.

When there is no possibility of deserting and taking arms and ammunition, the military urban guerrilla must engage in sabotage, starting explosions and fires in munitions and gunpowder.

This technique of deserting with arms and ammunition, of raiding and sabotaging the military centres, is the best way of wearing out and demoralizing the gorillas and of leaving them confused.

The urban guerrilla's purpose in disarming an individual enemy is to capture his arms. These arms are usually in the hands of sentinels or others whose task is guard duty or repression.

The capture of arms may be accomplished by violent means or by astuteness and by tricks or traps. When the enemy is disarmed, he must be searched for arms other than those already taken from him. If we are careless, he can use the arms that were not seized to shoot the urban guerrilla.

The seizure of arms is an efficient method of acquiring machine guns, the urban guerrilla's most important arms.

When we carry out small operations or actions to seize arms and ammunition, the material captured may be for personal use or for armaments and supplies for the firing groups.

The necessity to provide firing power for the urban guerrilla is so great that, in order to take off from zero point, we often have to purchase one weapon, divert or capture a single arm. The basic point is to begin, and to begin with a great spirit of decisiveness and of boldness. The possession of a single arm multiplies our forces.

In a bank assault, we must be careful to seize the arm or arms of the bank guard. The remainder of the arms we find with the treasurer, the bank teller, or the manager must also be seized ahead of time.

The other method we can use to capture arms is the preparation of ambushes against the police and the cars they use to move around in.

Quite often we succeed in capturing arms in the police commissaries as a result of raids from outside.

The expropriation of arms, ammunition, and explosives is the urban guerrilla's goal in assaulting commercial houses, industries, and quarries.

Liberation of prisoners

The liberation of prisoners is an armed operation designed to free the jailed urban guerrilla. In daily struggle against the enemy, the urban guerrilla is subject to arrest and can be sentenced to unlimited years in jail. This does not mean that the revolutionary battle stops here. For the guerrilla, his experience is deepened by prison and continues even in the dungeons where he is held.

The imprisoned urban guerrilla views jail as a terrain he must dominate and understand in order to free himself by a guerrilla operation. There is no prison, either on an island, in a city penitentiary, or on a farm, that is impregnable to the slyness, the cleverness, and the firing potential of the revolutionaries.

The urban guerrilla who is free views the penal establishments of the enemy as the inevitable site of guerrilla action designed to liberate his ideological brothers from prison.

It is this combination of *the urban guerrilla in freedom and the urban guerrilla in jail* that results in the armed operations we refer to as the liberation of prisoners.

The guerrilla operations that can be used in liberating prisoners are the following:

(a) riots in penal establishments, in correctional colonies and islands, or on transport or prison ships;
(b) assaults on urban or rural penitentiaries, houses of detention, commissaries, prisoner depots, or any other permanent, occasional, or temporary place where prisoners are held;
(c) assaults on prisoner transport trains and cars;
(d) raids and penetrations of prisons;
(e) ambushing of guards who are moving prisoners.

Execution

Execution is the killing of a North American spy, of an agent of the dictatorship, of a police torturer, of a fascist personality in the government involved in crimes and persecutions against patriots, of a stool pigeon, informer, police agent, or police *provocateur*.

Those who go to the police of their own free will to make denunciations and accusations, who supply clues and information and finger people, must also be executed when they are caught by the urban guerrilla.

Execution is a secret action in which the least possible number of urban guerrillas are involved. In many cases, the execution can be carried out by one sniper, patiently, alone and unknown, and operating in absolute secrecy and in cold blood.

Kidnapping

Kidnapping is capturing and holding in a secret spot a police agent, a North American spy, a political personality, or a notorious and dangerous enemy of the revolutionary movement.

Kidnapping is used to exchange or liberate imprisoned revolutionary comrades, or to force suspension of torture in the jail cells of the military dictatorship.

The kidnapping of personalities who are known artists, sports figures, or are outstanding in some other field, but who have evidenced no political interest, can be a useful form of propaganda for the revolutionary and patriotic principles of the urban guerrilla provided it occurs under special circumstances, and the kidnapping is handled so that the public sympathizes with it and accepts it.

The kidnapping of North American residents or visitors in Brazil constitutes a form of protest against the penetration and domination of United States imperialism in our country.

Sabotage

Sabotage is a highly destructive type of attack using very few persons and sometimes requiring only one to accomplish the desired result. When the urban guerrilla uses sabotage the first phase is isolated sabotage. Then comes the phase of dispersed and generalized sabotage, carried out by the people.

Well-executed sabotage demands study, planning, and careful execution. A characteristic form of sabotage is explosion using dynamite, fire, and the placing of mines.

A little sand, a trickle of any kind of combustible, a poor lubrication, a screw removed, a short circuit, pieces of wood or of iron, can cause irreparable damage.

The objective of sabotage is to hurt, to damage, to make useless and to destroy vital enemy points such as the following:

(a) the economy of the country;
(b) agricultural or industrial production;
(c) transport and communications systems;
(d) the military and police systems and their establishments and deposits;
(e) the repressive military-police system;
(f) the firms and properties of North Americans in the country.

The urban guerrilla should endanger the economy of the country, particularly its economic and financial aspects, such as its domestic and foreign commercial network, its exchange and banking systems, its tax collection system, and others.

Public offices, centres of government services, government warehouses, are easy targets for sabotage.

Nor will it be easy to prevent the sabotage of agricultural and industrial production by the urban guerrilla, with his thorough knowledge of the local situation.

Industrial workers acting as urban guerrillas are excellent industrial saboteurs since they, better than anyone, understand the industry, the factory, the machine, or the part most likely to destroy an entire operation, doing far more damage than a poorly informed layman could do.

With respect to the enemy's transport and communications systems, beginning with railway traffic, it is necessary to attack them systematically with sabotage arms.

The only caution is against causing death and fatal injury to passengers, especially regular commuters on suburban and long-distance trains.

Attacks on freight trains, rolling or stationary stock, stoppage of military transport and communications systems, these are the major sabotage objectives in this area.

Sleepers can be damaged and pulled up, as can rails. A tunnel blocked by a barrier after an explosion, an obstruction by a derailed car, cause tremendous harm.

The derailment of a cargo train carrying fuel is of major damage to the enemy. So is dynamiting railway bridges. In a system where the weight and the size of the rolling equipment is enormous, it takes months for workers to repair or rebuild the destruction and damage.

As for highways, they can be obstructed by trees, stationary vehicles, ditches, dislocations of barriers by dynamite and bridges blown up by explosion.

Ships can be damaged at anchor in seaports and river ports or in the shipyards. Aircraft can be destroyed or sabotaged on the ground.

Telephonic and telegraphic lines can be systematically damaged, their towers blown up, and their lines made useless.

Transport and communications must be sabotaged at once because the revolutionary war has already begun in Brazil and it is essential to impede the enemy's movement of troops and munitions.

Oil lines, fuel plants, depots for bombs and ammunition, powder magazines and arsenals, military camps, commissaries must become targets *par excellence* in sabotage operations, while vehicles, army trucks, and other military and police cars must be destroyed wherever they are found.

The military and police repression centres and their specific and specialized organs, must also claim the attention of the urban guerrilla saboteur.

North American firms and properties in the country, for their part, must become such frequent targets of sabotage that the volume of actions directed against them surpasses the total of all other actions against vital enemy points.

Terrorism

Terrorism is an action, usually involving the placement of a bomb or fire explosion of great destructive power, which is capable of effecting irreparable loss against the enemy.

Terrorism requires that the urban guerrilla should have an adequate theoretical and practical knowledge of how to make explosives.

The terroristic act, apart from the apparent facility with which it can be carried out, is no different from other urban guerrilla acts and actions whose success depends on the planning and determination of the revolutionary organization. It is an action the urban guerrilla must execute with the greatest cold bloodedness, calmness, and decision.

Although terrorism generally involves an explosion, there are cases in which it may also be carried out by execution and the systematic burning of installations, properties, and North American depots, plantations, etc. It is essential to point out the importance of fires and the construction of incendiary bombs such as gasoline bombs in the technique of revolutionary terrorism. Another thing is the importance of the material the urban guerrilla can persuade the people to expropriate in moments of hunger and scarcity resulting from the greed of the big commerical interests.

Terrorism is an arm the revolutionary can never relinquish.

Armed propaganda

The co-ordination of urban guerrilla actions, including each armed action, is the principal way of making armed propaganda.

These actions, carried out with specific and determined objectives, inevitably become propaganda material for the mass communications system.

Bank assaults, ambushes, desertions and diverting of arms, the rescue of prisoners, executions, kidnappings, sabotage, terrorism, and the war of nerves, are all cases in point.

Aircraft diverted in flight by revolutionary action, moving ships and trains assaulted and seized by guerrillas, can also be solely for propaganda effects.

But the urban guerrilla must never fail to install a clandestine press and must be able to turn out mimeographed copies using alcohol or electric plates and other duplicating apparatus, expropriating what he cannot buy in order to produce small clandestine newspapers, pamphlets, flyers, and stamps for propaganda and agitation against the dictatorship.

The urban guerrilla engaged in clandestine printing facilitates enormously the incorporation of large numbers of people into the revolutionary struggle, by opening a permanent work front for those willing to carry on revolutionary propaganda, even when to do so means acting alone and risking their lives as revolutionaries.

With the existence of clandestine propaganda and agitational material, the inventive spirit of the urban guerrilla expands and creates catapults, artifacts, mortars, and other instruments with which to distribute the anti-government pamphlets at a distance.

Tape recordings, the occupation of radio stations, and the use of loudspeakers, drawings on walls and in other inaccessible places are other forms of propaganda.

In using them, the urban guerrilla should give them the character of armed operations.

A consistent propaganda by letters sent to specific addresses, explaining the meaning of the urban guerrillas' armed actions, produces considerable results and is one method of influencing certain segments of the population.

Even this influence exercised in the heart of the people by every possible propaganda device revolving around the activity of the urban guerrilla does not indicate that our forces have everyone's support.

It is enough to win the support of a part of the people and this can be done by popularizing the following slogan: 'Let he who does not wish to do anything for the revolutionaries, do nothing against them.'

The war of nerves

The war of nerves or psychological war is an aggressive technique, based on the direct or indirect use of mass means of communication and news transmitted orally in order to demoralize the government.

In psychological warfare, the government is always at a disadvantage since it imposes censorship on the mass media and winds up in a defensive position by not allowing anything against it to filter through.

At this point it becomes desperate, is involved in greater contradictions and loss of prestige, and loses time and energy in an exhausing effort at control which is subject to being broken at any moment.

The object of the war of nerves is to misinform, spreading lies among the authorities, in which everyone can participate, thus creating an air of nervousness, discredit, insecurity, uncertainty, and concern on the part of the government.

The best methods used by the urban guerrilla in the war of nerves are the following:

(a) using the telephone and the mail to announce false clues to the police and the government, including information on the planting of bombs and any other act of terrorism in public offices and other places, kidnapping and assassination plans, etc., to oblige the authorities to wear themselves out, following up the information fed them;
(b) letting false plans fall into the hands of the police to divert their attention;

(c) planting rumours to make the government uneasy;
(d) exploiting by every means possible the corruption, the errors, and the failures of the government and its representatives, forcing them into demoralizing explanations and justifications in the very mass communications media they maintain under censorship;
(e) presenting denunciations to foreign embassies, the United Nations, the papal nunciature, and the international judicial commissions defending human rights or freedom of the press, exposing each concrete violation and use of violence by the military dictatorship and making it known that the revolutionary war will continue its course with serious danger for the enemies of the people.

How to carry out the action

The urban guerrilla who correctly carries through his apprenticeship and training must give the greatest importance to his method of carrying out action, for in this he cannot commit the slightest error.

Any carelessness in the assimilation of the method and its use invites certain disaster, as experience teaches every day.

The outlaws commit errors frequently because of their methods, and this is one of the reasons why the urban guerrilla must be so insistently preoccupied with following the revolutionary technique and not the technique of the bandits.

And not only for that reason. There is no urban guerrilla worthy of the name who ignores the revolutionary method of action and fails to practise it rigorously in the planning and execution of his activity.

The giant is known by his toe. The same can be said of the urban guerrilla who is known from afar for his correct methods and his absolute fidelity to principles.

The revolutionary method of carrying out action is strongly and forcefully based on the knowledge and use of the following elements:

(a) investigation of information;
(b) observation or *paquera*[*];
(c) reconnaissance or exploration of the terrain;
(d) study and timing of routes;
(e) mapping;
(f) mechanization;
(g) selection of personnel and relief;
(h) selection of firing capacity;
(i) study and practice in completion;
(j) completion;
(k) cover;
(l) retreat;
(m) dispersal;

(n) liberation or transfer of prisoners;
(o) elimination of clues;
(p) rescue of wounded.

Some observations on the method

When there is no information, the point of departure for the planning of the action must be investigation, observation, or *paquera*. This method also has good results.

In any event, including when there is information, it is essential to take observations or *paquera*, to see that the information is not at odds with observation or *vice versa*.

Reconnaissance or exploration of the terrain, study and timing of routes are so important that to omit them is to make a stab in the dark.

Mechanization, in general, is an underestimated factor in the method of conducting the action. Frequently mechanization is left to the end, to the eve of the action, before anything is done about it.

This is an error. Mechanization must be considered seriously, must be undertaken with considerable foresight and according to careful planning, also based on information, observation, or *paquera*, and must be carried out with rigorous care and precision. The care, conservation, maintenance, and camouflaging of the vehicles expropriated are very important details of mechanization.

When transport fails, the principal action fails with serious moral and material consequences for the urban guerrilla activity.

The selection of personnel requires great care to avoid the inclusion of indecisive or vacillating personnel with the danger of contaminating the other participants, a difficulty that must be avoided.

The withdrawal is equally or more important than the operation itself, to the point that it must be rigorously planned, including the possibility of failure.

One must avoid rescue or transfer of prisoners with children present, or anything to attract the attention of people in casual transit through the area. The best thing is to make the rescue as natural as possible, always winding through, or using different routes or narrow streets that scarcely permit passage on foot, to avoid an encounter of two cars. The elimination of tracks is obligatory and demands the greatest caution in hiding fingerprints and any other sign that could give the enemy information. Lack of care in the elimination of tracks and clues is a factor that increases nervousness in our ranks and which the enemy often exploits.

Rescue of the wounded

The problem of the wounded in urban guerrilla warfare merits special attention. During guerrilla operations in the urban area it may happen that some comrade is accidentally wounded or shot by the police. When a guerrilla in the firing group has a knowledge of first aid he can do something for the wounded comrade on the spot. In no circumstances can the wounded urban guerrilla be abandoned at the site of the battle or left to the enemy's hands.

One of the precautions we must take is to set up nursing courses for men and women, courses in which the urban guerrilla can matriculate and learn the elementary techniques of first aid.

The urban guerrilla doctor, student of medicine, nurse, pharmacologist, or simply the person trained in first aid, is a necessity in modern revolutionary struggle.

A small manual of first aid for the urban guerrilla, printed on mimeographed sheets, can also be undertaken by anyone who has enough knowledge.

In planning and completing an armed action, the urban guerrilla cannot forget the organization of medical logistics. This will be accomplished by means of a mobile or motorized clinic. You can also set up a mobile first aid station. Another solution is to utilize the skills of a nursing comrade who waits with his bag of equipment in a designated house to which the wounded are brought.

The ideal would be to have our own well equipped clinic, but this is very costly unless we use expropriated materials.

When all else fails, it is often necessary to resort to legal clinics, using armed force if necessary to demand that the doctors attend to our wounded.

In the eventuality that we fall back on blood banks to buy blood or whole plasma, we must not use legal addresses and certainly not addresses where the wounded can really be found, since they are under our care and protection. Nor should we supply addresses of those involved in the organization's clandestine work to the hospitals and health centres where we take them. Such concerns are indispensable to cover any track or clue.

The houses in which the wounded stay cannot be known to anybody with the unique and exclusive exception of the small group of comrades responsible for their treatment and transport.

Sheets, bloody clothing, medicine, and any other indication of treatment of the comrades wounded in combat with the police, must be completely eliminated from any place they visit to receive medical treatment.

Guerrilla security

The urban guerrilla lives in constant danger of the possibility of being discovered or denounced. The chief security problem is to make certain that we are well hidden and well guarded, and that there are secure methods to keep the police from locating us or our whereabouts.

The worst enemy of the urban guerrilla and the major danger we run is infiltration into our organization by a spy or an informer.

The spy trapped within the organization will be punished with death. The same goes for those who desert and inform to the police.

A good security is the certainty that the enemy has no spies and agents infiltrated in our midst and can receive no information about us even by indirect or distant means. The fundamental way to insure this is to be cautious and strict in recruiting.

Nor is it permissible for everyone to know everyone and everything else. Each person should know only what relates to his work. This rule is a fundamental point in the ABC's of urban guerrilla security.

The battle that we are waging against the enemy is arduous and difficult because it is a class struggle. Every class struggle is a battle of life or death when the classes are antagonistic.

The enemy wants to annihilate us and fights relentlessly to find us and destroy us, so that our great weapon consists in hiding from him and attacking him by surprise.

The danger to the urban guerrilla is that he may reveal himself through imprudence or allow himself to be discovered through lack of class vigilance. It is inadmissible for the urban guerrilla to give out his own or any other clandestine address to the enemy or to talk too much. Annotations in the margins of newspapers, lost documents, calling cards, letters or notes, all these are clues that the police never underestimate.

Address and telephone books must be destroyed and one must not write or hold papers; it is necessary to avoid keeping archives of legal or illegal names, biographical information, maps, and plans. The points of contact should not be written down but simply committed to memory.

The urban guerrilla who violates these rules must be warned by the first one who notes his infraction and, if he repeats it, we must avoid working with him.

The need of the urban guerrilla to move about constantly and the relative proximity of the police, given the circumstances of the strategic police net which surrounds the city, forces him to adopt variable security methods depending on the enemy's movements.

For this reason it is necessary to maintain a service of daily news about what the enemy appears to be doing, where his police net is operating and what gorges and points of strangulation are being watched. The daily reading of police news in the newspapers is a great fountain of information in these cases.

The most important lesson for guerrilla security is never, under any circumstances, to permit the slightest sign of laxity in the maintenance of security measures and regulations within the organization.

Guerrilla security must be maintained also and principally in cases of arrest. The arrested guerrilla can reveal nothing to the police that will jeopardize the organization. He can say nothing that may lead, as a consequence, to the arrest of other comrades, the discovery of addresses and hiding places, the loss of arms and ammunition.

The seven sins of the urban guerrilla

Even when the urban guerrilla applies his revolutionary technique with precision and rigorously abides by security rules, he can still be vulnerable to errors. There is no perfect urban guerrilla. The most he can do is to make every effort to diminish the margin of error since he cannot be perfect.

One of the methods we should use to diminish the margin of error is to know thoroughly the seven sins of the urban guerrilla and try to fight them.

The first sin of the urban guerrilla is inexperience. The urban guerrilla, blinded by this sin, thinks the enemy is stupid, underestimates his intelligence, believes everything is easy and, as a result, leaves clues that can lead to his disaster.

Because of his inexperience, the urban guerrilla can also overestimate the forces of the enemy, believing them to be stronger than they really are. Allowing himself to be fooled by this presumption, the urban guerrilla becomes intimidated, and remains insecure and indecisive, paralysed and lacking in audacity.

The second sin of the urban guerrilla is to boast about the actions he has completed and broadcast them to the four winds.

The third sin of the urban guerrilla is vanity. The urban guerrilla who suffers from this sin tries to solve the problems of the revolution by actions erupting in the city, but without bothering about the beginnings and the survival of the guerrilla in rural areas. Blinded by success, he winds up organizing an action that he considers decisive and that puts into play all the forces and resources of the organization. Since the city is the area of the strategic circle which we cannot avoid or break while rural guerrilla warfare has not yet erupted and is not at the point of triumph, we always run the fatal error of permitting the enemy to attack us with decisive blows.

The fourth sin of the urban guerrilla is to exaggerate his strength and to undertake projects for which he lacks forces and, as yet, does not have the required infrastructure.

The fifth sin of the urban guerrilla is precipitous action. The urban guerrilla who commits this sin loses patience, suffers an attack of nerves, does not wait for anything, and impetuously throws himself into action, suffering untold reverses.

The sixth sin of the urban guerrilla is to attack the enemy when he is most angry.

The seventh sin of the urban guerrilla is to fail to plan things, and to act out of improvisation.

Popular support

One of the permanent concerns of the urban guerrilla is his identification with popular causes to win public support.

Where government actions become inept and corrupt, the urban guerrilla should not hesitate to step in to show that he opposes the government and to gain mass sympathy. The present government, for example, imposes heavy financial burdens and excessively high taxes on the people. It is up to the urban guerrilla to attack the dictatorship's tax collection system and to obstruct its financial activity, throwing all the weight of violent revolutionary action against it.

The urban guerrilla fights not only to upset the tax and collection system; the arm of revolutionary violence must also be directed against those government organs that raise prices and those who direct them, as well as against the wealthiest of the national and foreign profiteers and the important property owners; in short, against all those who accumulate huge fortunes out of the high cost of living, the wages of hunger, excessive prices and rents.

Foreign trusts, such as refrigeration and other North American plants that monopolize the market and the manufacture of general food supplies, must be systematically attacked by the urban guerrilla.

The rebellion of the urban guerrilla and his persistence in intervening in public questions is the best way of insuring public support of the cause we defend. We repeat and insist on repeating: *it is the best way of insuring public support*. As soon as a reasonable section of the population begins to take seriously the action of the urban guerrilla, his success is guaranteed.

The government has no alternative except to intensify repression. The police networks, house searches, arrests of innocent people and of suspects, closing off streets, make life in the city unbearable. The military dictatorship embarks on massive political persecution. Political assassinations and police terror become routine.

In spite of all this, the police systematically fail. The armed forces, the navy, and the air force are mobilized and undertake routine police functions. Even so they find no way to halt guerrilla operations, nor to wipe out the revolutionary organization with its fragmented groups that move around and operate throughout the national territory persistently and contagiously.

The people refuse to collaborate with the authorities, and the general sentiment is that the government is unjust, incapable of solving problems, and resorts purely and simply to the physical liquidation of its opponents.

The political situation in the country is transformed into a military situation in which the gorillas appear more and more to be the ones responsible for errors and violence, while the problems in the lives of the people become truly catastrophic.

When they see the militarists and the dictatorship on the brink of the abyss, and fearing the consequences of a revolutionary war which is already at a fairly advanced and irreversible level, the pacifiers, always to be found within the ruling classes, and the right-wing opportunists, partisans of non-violent struggle, join hands and circulate rumours behind the scenes, begging the hangmen for elections, 'redemocratization', constitutional reforms, and other tripe designed to fool the masses and make them stop the revolutionary rebellion in the cities and the rural areas of the country.

But, watching the revolutionaries, the people now understand that it is a farce to vote in elections which have as their sole objective, guaranteeing the continuation of the military dictatorship and covering up its crimes.

Attacking wholeheartedly this election farce and the so-called 'political solution' so appealing to the opportunists, the urban guerrilla must become more aggressive and violent, resorting without let-up to sabotage, terrorism, expropriations, assaults, kidnappings, executions, etc.

This answers any attempt to fool the masses with the opening of Congress and the reorganization of political parties – parties of the government and of the opposition it allows – when all the time the parliament and the so-called parties function thanks to the licence of the military dictatorship in a true spectacle of marionettes and dogs on a leash.

The role of the urban guerrilla, in order to win the support of the people, is to continue fighting, keeping in mind the interests of the masses and heightening the disastrous situation in which the government must act. These are the circumstances, disastrous for the dictatorship, which permit the revolutionaries to open rural guerrilla warfare in the midst of the uncontrollable expansion of urban rebellion.

The urban guerrilla is engaged in revolutionary action in favour of the people and with it seeks the participation of the masses in the struggle against the military dictatorship and for the liberation of the country from the yoke of the United States. Beginning with the city and with the support of the people, the rural guerrilla war develops rapidly, establishing its infrastructure carefully while the urban area continues the rebellion.

Urban guerrilla warfare, school for selecting the guerrilla

Revolution is a social phenomenon that depends on men, arms, and resources. Arms and resources exist in the country and can be taken and used, but to do this it is necessary to count on men. Without them, the arms and the resources have no use and no value. For their part, the men must have two basic and indispensable obligatory qualities:

(a) they must have a politico-revolutionary motivation;
(b) they must have the necessary technical-revolutionary preparation.

Men with a politico-revolutionary motivation are found among the vast and clearheaded contingents of enemies of the military dictatorship and of the domination of US imperialism.

Almost daily such men gravitate to urban guerrilla warfare, and it is for this reason that the reaction no longer announces that it has thwarted the revolutionaries and goes through the unpleasantness of seeing them rise up again out of their own ashes.

The men who are best trained, most experienced, and dedicated to urban guerrilla warfare and at the same time to rural guerrilla warfare, constitute the backbone of the revolutionary war and, therefore, of the Brazilian revolution. From this backbone will come the marrow of the revolutionary army of national liberation, rising out of guerrilla warfare.

This is the central nucleus, not the bureaucrats and opportunists hidden in the organizational structure, not the empty conferees, the clichéd writers of resolutions that remain on paper, but rather the men who fight. The men who from the very first have been determined and ready for anything, who personally participate in revolutionary actions, who do not waver or deceive.

This is the nucleus indoctrinated and disciplined with a long-range strategic and tactical vision consistent with the application of Marxist theory, of Leninism and of Castro-Guevara developments, applied to the specific conditions of the Brazilian situation. This is the nucleus that will lead the rebellion through its guerrilla phase.

From it will come men and women with politico-military development, one and indivisible, whose task will be that of future leaders after the triumph of the revolution, in the construction of the new Brazilian society.

As of now, the men and women chosen for urban guerrilla warfare are workers; peasants whom the city has attracted as a market for manpower and who return to the countryside indoctrinated and politically and technically prepared; students, intellectuals, priests. This is the material with which we are building – starting with urban guerrilla warfare – the armed alliance of workers and peasants, with students, intellectuals, priests.

Workers have infinite knowledge in the industrial sphere and are best for urban revolutionary tasks. The urban guerrilla worker participates in the struggle by constructing arms, sabotaging and preparing saboteurs and dynamiters, and personally participating in actions involving hand arms, or organizing strikes and partial paralysis with the characteristics of mass violence in factories, workshops, and other work centres.

The peasants have an extraordinary intuition for knowledge of the land, judgment in confronting the enemy, and the indispensable ability to communicate with the humble masses. The peasant guerrilla is already participating in our struggle and it is he who reaches the guerrilla core, establishes support points in the countryside, finds hiding places for individuals, arms, munitions, supplies, organizes the sowing and harvesting of grain for use in the guerrilla war, chooses the points of transport, cattle raising posts, and sources of meat supplies, trains the guides that show the rural guerrillas the road, and creates an information service in the countryside.

Students are noted for being politically crude and coarse and thus they break all the taboos. When they are integrated into urban guerrilla warfare, as is now occurring on a wide scale, they show a special talent for revolutionary violence and soon acquire a high level of political-technical-military skill. Students have plenty of free time on their hands because they are systematically separated, suspended, and expelled from school by the dictatorship and so they begin to spend their time advantageously, on behalf of the revolution.

The intellectuals constitute the vanguard of resistance to arbitrary acts, social injustice, and the terrible inhumanity of the dictatorship of the gorillas. They spread the revolutionary call and they have great influence on people. The urban guerrilla intellectual or artist is the most modern of the Brazilian revolution's adherents.

Churchmen – that is to say, those ministers or priests and religious men of various hierarchies and persuasions – represent a sector that has special ability to communicate with the people, particularly with workers, peasants, and the Brazilian woman. The priest who is an urban guerrilla is an active ingredient in the ongoing Brazilian revolutionary war, and constitutes a powerful arm in the struggle against military power and North American imperialism.

As for the Brazilian woman, her participation in the revolutionary war, and particularly in urban guerrilla warfare, has been marked by an unmatched fighting spirit and tenacity, and it is not by chance that so many women have been accused of participation in guerrilla actions against banks, quarries, military centres, etc., and that so many are in prison while others are sought by the police.

As a school for choosing the guerrilla, urban guerrilla warfare prepares and places at the same level of responsibility and efficiency the men and women who share the same dangers fighting, rounding up supplies, serving as messengers or runners, as drivers, sailors, or aircraft pilots, obtaining secret information, and helping with propaganda and the task of indoctrination.

Note

* In Brazil the expression *fazer a paquera* is used to designate the preparations for hunting paca, a mammal rodent of South American origin. By extension, the term *paquera* is used as a synonym for checking or vigilance.

8 Oil and Influence
The Oil Weapon Examined
Adelphi Paper 117, 1975

Hanns Maull

Introduction

> *Oil weapon*, as used in this Paper, signifies any manipulation of the price and/or supply of oil by exporting nations with the intention of changing the political behaviour of the consumer nations. For reasons given later, the political potential of the oil price is fairly restricted, so that in effect we are mainly concerned with supply interruptions.
>
> *Oil power* is the power which stems from the dependence of the consumer nations on oil. This forms the basis of any successful application of the oil weapon and includes all factors which allow the producers to influence and control the political behaviour of the consumers. The oil weapon, therefore, is one specific way of using oil power: other ways would be the threat to use the oil weapon, or simply the diplomatic exploitation of consumer dependence.

Two years after the hectic reactions to the first successful application of the oil weapon, the sense of emergency of the energy crisis has widely been replaced by complacency. A cursory glance might seem to justify this complacency: a world-wide recession and unusually mild winters have brought down oil consumption in the industrialized countries and forced the oil producers to reduce their production (and some of them even to lower the price of oil). Besides, the freezing of official oil price levels until September 1975 has meant an effective erosion of the purchasing power of producers' oil revenues, as a consequence of inflationary rises in the cost of imports from the consumer countries.

Yet this seeming return to equilibrium of the international oil system is deceptive. OPEC proved its cohesiveness under pressure, and there is little prospect that a further reduction in demand for oil could reach a level where the organization would come under serious strain and break apart. On the contrary, it looks as if the decrease in oil consumption will soon be replaced by a growing demand for OPEC oil, as the industrialized economies recover from the 1974/75 recession (oil conservation has so far been only marginally policy-induced). A consistent energy policy by the most important actor in the international oil market, the United States, has been blocked by the struggle between President and Congress, and this – together with the decline of American indigenous oil production – has meant that American dependence on Middle Eastern oil imports has not been reduced. The substance of producer power has, therefore, hardly been diminished. What must be even more worrying is the small amount of progress towards a settlement of the Israeli–Arab conflict – for, even though the energy crisis and the Middle East conflict are separate problems, they are strongly linked by the present political situation in the Middle East. Another oil embargo involving production cutbacks is, therefore, a distinct possibility, and has been hinted at repeatedly by Arab oil producers, including Saudi Arabia.

An analysis of the politics of oil and the potential and limitations of the oil weapon in some respects appears more timely now than a year ago, because of a widespread sense that the successful application of the oil weapon in 1973/74 was an event unique in international politics, and that its recurrence is unlikely. In fact, the oil weapon has become, and will continue to be, a force in the international system.

Oil is the raw material most intrinsically interwoven with politics, and oil embargoes and boycotts have repeatedly served as political tools. Even though the political leverage provided by the oil trade has not been used only by countries in the Middle East, this area has been exposed to the politics of oil three times within less than twenty years – each time in connection with Israeli–Arab wars. In 1956 the Suez Canal and the Iraq Petroleum Company pipeline from the Iraqi oilfields to the Mediterranean were closed, and about two-thirds of Middle East exports to Europe had to be re-routed or were cut off. The result was a moderate increase in the price of oil over a short period of time. Some European countries faced temporary shortages, certain industries were affected, but overall production in European countries belonging to the Organization for Economic Co-operation and Development (OECD) continued to grow. In 1967, the Suez Canal was again closed – this time for a long period. Kuwait, Libya, Iraq and Saudi Arabia stopped production after the outbreak of the war – partly as a result of government decisions (Kuwait, Iraq), partly as a result of strikes by oil workers (Libya, Saudi Arabia) – and this stoppage was then replaced by selective embargoes against Britain, the United States and West Germany. Again, the success of the 'oil weapon' was virtually nil and 'hurt the Arabs more than anyone else', in the words of a Saudi Arabian oil minister.[1]

Why did the oil weapon score such a remarkable success in 1973, when only six years earlier it had totally failed? And what exactly is the role the oil weapon will play in future international relations? The substance of the oil weapon and the various forms of its application, as well as the influence producers can derive from it without using it at all, are the main concern of this Paper. This restricts its scope to the political aspects of the international oil market, so that the economic aspects are not considered further than is absolutely necessary for this purpose.

The Paper will first try to establish the essence of oil power by analysing its preconditions on the basis of the 1973/74 crisis. Then it will consider the future development of oil power, with particular reference to the limitations and weaknesses of the oil weapon, as well as possible new dimensions of oil power. Finally, it looks into the politics of some key producer countries to speculate about what possible and probable intentions on the part of these Middle Eastern states could once again lead to the application of the oil weapon.

I. Oil power: a political reality

To find out why oil power has become a political reality since 1967 we have to look at the basis of this power: the trade relationship between producers and consumers. Around 1970 the international oil market was said to have turned from a buyers' to a sellers' market. This was a rather vague way of saying that a fundamental imbalance had developed in the trade relationship between producers and consumers, an imbalance by then no longer offset by outside factors such as political dependence or economic counterweights. This allowed the relationship to be used for political purposes.[2] The leverage inherent in such an imbalance stems from the capability to interrupt trade, and, the larger the difference between the damage the interruption causes to the consumer and that it causes to the supplier, the stronger the leverage.

The damage the target country actually experiences depends on the amount of impoverishment the stoppage or the reduction of supplies inflicts. A good indicator of this is the previous expansion of oil imports, which demonstrates oil's growing importance to the target. The damage experienced is also reflected in the length and costliness of the adjustment process which the supply interruption makes necessary.

One of the main characteristics of the international oil market in recent years has been its rapid expansion. Caused by the parallel boom in all major Western industrialized economies, demand for oil grew at a continuous, and even accelerating, pace to the 1973 peak. This unprecedented rise was the result not only of the 'natural' growth in demand accompanying expanding economies but also of the switch to oil as the predominant source of energy supply.[3] Nowhere in the Western world (apart from Canada) was indigenous production sufficient to satisfy the growing demand, so oil had to be imported to fill the gap between supply and demand. Table 1 shows clearly the absolute and relative growth of the significance of imported oil in the energy balance of the Western world. It also shows the strong position of the Arab countries as suppliers; attempts to diversify the sources of imports proved ineffective due to the unique position of the Arab world in terms of oil production (32.8 per cent of world production in 1973) and reserves.

The absolute growth of oil imports shows the increasing damage potential, and the relative growth shows the Arab producers' strong leverage *vis-à-vis* Europe, Japan and – to a lesser extent – the United States. In the case of the United States, dependence on Arab oil accelerated after indigenous production peaked out in 1970.[4]

Table 1 Oil import dependence – United States, Japan and Western Europe

	Western Europe			Japan			United States		
	1956	1967	1973	1956	1967	1973	1956	1967	1973
Oil imports (million tons)	121.5	443.6	736.2	12.4	116.8	282.5	57.3	116.5	300.7
Imports as % of energy supply	20.7	52.7	62.9	22.9	67.2	85.4	5.6	7.7	17.4
Arab oil imports as % of energy supply	13.4	36.0	45	12.8	33.4	33	1.3	0.6	5

Sources: BP *Statistical Review of the World Oil Industry, 1973;* UN *Statistical Papers,* Series J. (Due to difference in the two sources, figures for 1973 are not directly comparable with those of 1956 and 1967.)

Since energy is of overwhelming importance for the functioning of all aspects of industrialized economies and societies, the Arab producers' leverage was considerable – unless the consumer economies could adjust to interruptions in supply in such a way as to prevent major disturbances. While they had achieved adjustments at fairly low cost in 1956 and 1967, the situation in 1973 had changed fundamentally. The supply crises in 1956 and 1967 proved manageable because supplies were available from alternative sources, although admittedly at a somewhat higher price: Venezuela, the United States and Iran could step up their production by using excess capacity and divert some of it to European countries affected by the supply interruptions.[5] In 1973, no substantial stand-by capacity was available – certainly nowhere near enough to make up the reduction the Arab oil producers decided upon. Other producers in the Third World also showed no intention of increasing their production, since they, too, profited from the squeeze through its impact on oil prices. Existing stockpiles were hardly more than a temporary cushion against the impact of the Arab oil weapon, and the adjustment had to be achieved by savings in consumption and the limited possibilities of substituting other sources of primary energy for oil.

The European countries, Japan and even the United States, therefore, faced a situation in which the Arab oil producers provided them with a scarce and enormously important raw material for which there was no real substitute – an optimum precondition for the exertion of political pressure, provided there was no countervailing dependence by the producers on stable oil supplies and/or on imports from the consumer countries. We must ask: was the trade relationship between producers and consumers balanced? And, also, was it based upon mutual benefit?

Looking at the structure of trade between producer and consumer countries to establish the degree of balance or imbalance in the relationship, one has to consider two further points. Are oil producers sufficiently dependent on goods supplied by the oil consumers to provide realistic counter-leverage?

And are the producers so dependent on the continuation of oil exports that any interruption or reduction would also inflict heavy damage on them?

The Arab countries are indeed to a certain extent dependent on imports from the Western industrialized countries, especially food: for example, in 1972 they imported cereals and cereal products worth at least $297 million from eight industrialized countries (the United States, Canada, West Germany, France, Britain, Italy, the Netherlands and Switzerland).[6] Since the United States has an especially strong position in the world grain market, there appeared to be a possibility of exerting counter-pressure – and indeed this was hinted at by the then Vice-President Ford (8 January 1974). But it appears doubtful whether a counter-embargo could have been organized by Western grain producers; and, even if one assumes such an attempt would have succeeded, the Soviet Union might have derived considerable political advantage from stepping in to make up the shortfall (American grain exports to the Arab countries were about 2 million tons in 1972, while Soviet grain production in 1973 was a record-breaking 222.5 million tons). Some oil producers also possessed large foreign exchange holdings which gave them a good chance of weathering any prolonged trade war and so contributed to their low vulnerability.[7]

As for the other form of dependence mentioned there can be little doubt that the economies of the large-scale oil exporters in the Third World have been largely dependent on oil revenues and the indirect benefits derived from oil production.[8] However, for mutual dependence to exist between producers and consumers, there must be strong incentives for *both* sides to maintain the existing trade relationships. Some producers (the low absorbers) already had more revenue than they could spend, and world-wide inflation and currency devaluations were eroding its value – hence they had no incentive to meet the growing demand by increased oil production.

The loss of control

So far we have been dealing with imbalances inherent in the trade structure itself; but to arrive at a more complete picture of the problem, we must consider other aspects of the producer-consumer relationship as well. Though the imbalance of the trade structure was considerably aggravated after about 1970, it can be argued that it existed long before. But in the past, the asymmetries in the consumer-producer relationship enabled the consumer countries to control the behaviour of the producer states. This control had rested on two pillars: the major international oil companies, and Western (first British, then predominantly American) influence in the Middle East oil-producing countries. These allowed the consumers to bring the producers into a world economy working in favour of the industrialized countries (and their oil companies). However, they were gradually eroded by political factors inside and outside the area – most importantly the ascendancy of Arab nationalism and a growing Soviet influence challenging the West,

Oil and Influence 333

which, in Arab eyes, was compromised by its imperialist heritage and its support for Israel. While the oil producers asserted their independence and sovereignty and displayed greater confidence in voicing their grievances and demands, not only were the Western consumers simultaneously becoming increasingly dependent on these countries, they also continued to be politically involved in the Middle East area (e.g., through American support for Israel).

This situation made them vulnerable and exposed them to political demands by the oil producers. By 1970 the erosion of consumer bargaining power and the increase in the strength of the producers were well advanced, and the producers only needed to be aware of the full range of their new power. This constitutes another fundamental difference between 1967 and 1973: in 1973 the Arab producers were not only fully aware of their dramatically increased strength but were willing and able to use it.

The catalyst was the revolutionary *élan* of a new regime in Libya, which wanted to establish its nationalist and progressive credentials by taking the lead in the struggle against Western, imperialist influence in the Middle East. In 1970 it put pressure on the oil companies and, in doing so, clearly demonstrated the fundamental shift in bargaining power from the oil companies (which acted for the consumers as well as in their own interests) to the producers. By 1970 Libyan production had been raised to 3.3 million b/d to compensate for the closure of the Suez Canal in 1967, the production lost as a result of the Nigerian civil war of 1967–70 and the prolonged interruption to the supply of Saudi oil along the Trans-Arabian pipeline (sabotaged by guerillas in Syria in May 1970). Europe's increased dependence on Libyan oil (25 per cent) was skilfully exploited: one after the other, companies were forced to accept a large price increase and a revised tax structure. This demonstration of oil power led to a series of negotiations for improved terms for producer countries in the Mediterranean and the Gulf which came to a short-lived standstill with agreements between the oil companies and the producers, reached in Teheran and Tripoli in early 1971.

Higher prices suited the oil companies, which wanted to diversify their sources of supply by developing the reserves in Alaska and the North Sea and unconventional sources of oil, such as tar sands. All these alternatives implied high investment outlays (which had to be financed partly through profits) and higher production costs. But, since higher prices further reduced the incentive for the oil-rich low absorbers to sustain and increase the prevailing production levels, they strengthened the position of the producers even more. However, securing higher prices was not the producers' only strategy. Efforts to gain increased producer participation in, and ultimately total control over, oil production in their own countries dominated the year 1972. This, together with concern about conservation, which led to the introduction of production ceilings in Kuwait and Libya, may have met certain long- and short-term interests of the producers. But they certainly also worked as power-increasing strategies which strengthened the producer's control, increased the squeeze on the international oil market and made any threat involving supply interruptions much more credible than before.

Application of the oil weapon

The *intention* to apply the oil weapon in the Israeli-Arab context had long figured prominently in Arab thinking, and President Nasser had proclaimed oil as one of the three components of Arab power.[9] The closer the linkage between the Arab–Israeli conflict and Persian Gulf politics became (and the alignment between Saudi Arabia and Egypt had finally established such a close connection), the greater the temptation to trade stable and sufficient oil supplies against a change in the United States' Middle East policy. The general mood in the Arab world was definitely moving in this direction, and a clear sign of how far it had progressed came when the Saudi oil minister, Sheikh Yamani, declared on a visit to the United States that his country was prepared to supply the quantity of crude oil needed only if the United States created the right political atmosphere.[10] This clear warning, and subsequent confirmations by King Faisal himself, showed that a growing willingness to use economic pressure to force a change in the American attitude to the Israeli-Arab conflict had pervaded the decision-making level of a country considered one of America's staunchest allies, and whose king, less than a year earlier, has still advocated a policy of 'oil and politics don't mix'.

On 17 October 1973 the OAPEC conference in Kuwait (with the exception of Iraq which followed its own policy) decided to cut production by a minimum of five per cent of the September production levels, and thereafter each month by five per cent of the previous month's output.

The agreement was followed by immediate cuts of 10 per cent by Saudi Arabia and Qatar and 5 per cent by Libya, together with an embargo on oil exports to the United States by Libya and Abu Dhabi. Then, on 19 October, President Nixon asked Congress to agree to a $2.2 billion military aid programme for Israel. Saudi Arabia reacted by placing an embargo on all exports to the United States. This was eventually applied by all other Arab producers and was extended to cover other countries, primarily the Netherlands (a move which, whether intentionally or not, aimed at the heart of the European oil distribution system: the port of Rotterdam). Egypt, Syria and Tunisia did not announce any cuts, while Iraq embargoed supplies to the United States and the Netherlands but otherwise tried to restore her output, which had been affected by war damage at the Mediterranean oil terminals in Syria. Iraq dissociated herself from the oil weapon as designed by Saudi Arabia and followed her own line, nationalizing American and Dutch oil interests and urging other producers to break diplomatic and economic relations with the United States and withdraw funds invested there.

On 4 November the Arab oil ministers (again with the exception of Iraq) decided to standardize the level of production cutbacks at 25 per cent of September production; on 24 December production was increased to 85 per cent of the September figure. The OAPEC embargo on the United States was lifted on 18 March 1974 – though Syria and Libya dissociated themselves from this – and Saudi Arabia subsequently increased her production considerably. The embargo against the Netherlands was finally lifted on 10 July, the decision having been delayed by a reluctant Saudi Arabia.

Effectiveness of the oil weapon

The objective behind the Arab oil producers' decision of 17 October and the subsequent measures was to use economic pressure to change the consumer states' political attitude to the Israeli-Arab conflict. The system of measures and rules was carefully designed to provide maximum flexibility by means of a range of sanctions and rewards. The United States was, of course, the main target, and the Arab producers expected her to bring pressure to bear on Israel in order to achieve their objectives (return of all territories occupied in the 1967 war, including Jerusalem, and restoration of the legitimate rights of the Palestinians). In theory, the embargo should have been the main weapon, general cutbacks in production being necessary only to prevent its circumvention (even if most-favoured countries had received supplies on the prewar level, this still would hardly have been sufficient to meet their growing demands). In other words, solidarity was to be made painful for the consumers, who all found themselves with at best the bare minimum of necessary oil supplies and could hardly afford to re-export any of them. In addition, Arab oil ministers also threatened further sanctions against any country which displayed solidarity with an embargoed country.

This system, reportedly elaborated by a group of Arab oil experts long before the October war, was meant to create a shortage in the United States, leading to inconvenience for the final consumer and consequent political pressure on the administration to change its Middle East policy. Other Western consumer countries affected by the oil weapon, were also expected to exert influence on American policy through their governments.

However, even though the Arab oil producers managed to build up economic pressure, they were not totally successful. The embargo did not work properly for two reasons: firstly, some Arab oil evidently 'leaked' to the United States despite the embargo; and, secondly, the international oil distribution system was managed by oil companies in such a way as to spread the damage fairly evenly, by diverting Arab oil away from embargoed ports and replacing it with non-Arab oil. In the case of the United States, total imports of crude and products fell from about 6–6 million b/d in November (when the embargo was not yet effective, due to the time-lag involved in transporting the oil) to about 5.1 million b/d in January. They then increased to around 5.5 million b/d – as opposed to a projected import figure for the first quarter of 1974 of 7.8 million b/d. The shortfall against a projected total oil demand for the first quarter of 19.7 million b/d was thus somewhere between 11 and 14 per cent, not the 17 per cent predicted by the President.[11]

Arab oil still reached the United States, though on a small scale; Saudi Arabian imports, 18 million barrels in November, amounted to only 7 million in December, while in January the figure was down to 957,000 barrels and in February to 552,000.[12] Libyan oil also leaked through the embargo (though this cannot be confirmed from American statistics, which do not given the source of oil imports).

The case of the Netherlands was somewhat similar; there, the embargo caused a serious problem only for a short period in December. A good indicator for the Netherlands is re-exports from Rotterdam's refining centre, which fell to 39 per cent of their normal level in the first half of December but recovered to 90 per cent in January – the embargo had become 'almost irrelevant', as the *Petroleum Economist* said, due to the flexibility of the international distribution system. Comparison of the Dutch oil deficit during the last quarter of 1973 with that of other EEC countries and the United States shows that the shortfall was indeed spread fairly evenly, and definitely not in accordance with Arab categorizations of friendly, neutral and hostile. Deficits ranged from 9 per cent (Netherlands) to 25 per cent (Denmark), with the United States, Germany, France and Italy in the 11–14 per cent range.[13]

Approximately equal import deficits do not, however, imply equal damage to the economies concerned. Not only was the shortfall for the embargoed United States no higher than those of other, neutral or even friendly, countries – the United States also was in a favourable position because of her consumption patterns.

First of all, her high per capita energy consumption indicates a large saving potential. Secondly, the proportionate dependence of the various consumption sectors differed markedly from that of the other industrialized consumers in Europe and Japan. Since there is considerable flexibility in overall energy consumption (with the possibility of one form of energy being substituted for another), savings in energy can normally be translated into savings in oil, most conveniently and least harmfully in the transport and the commercial/residential sectors. Tables 2 and 3 show the United States' favourable position in this respect, and hence in respect of interruptions in oil supply.

Let us now attempt to assess how the economic pressure exerted on Western consumer countries (despite the apparent partial failure of the embargoes) was translated into political influence. Clearly, the attitudes of Western Europe,

Table 2 Main consumption sector requirements as % of total oil requirements (1971) United States, Japan and Western Europe

	Industry (incl. non-energy use)	Transport/residential/commercial use
United States	24.7	75.3
Japan	55.2	44.8
Western Europe	42.3	57.7

Source: OECD Observer, December 1973 p. 24.

Table 3 Consumers' energy saving capacity and energy consumption as % of indigenous production (1971)

Vulnerability	Countries	Saving Capacity indicator*	Indigenous oil production as % of consumption	Indigenous energy production as % of consumption
High	Japan, Italy, Belgium, France	0.6–0.8	0–6.0	11.0–22.0
Medium	Britain, Netherlands, West Germany	0.9–1.1	2.0–7.0	51.0–64.0
Low	USA, Canada	1.1–1.4	74.0–98.0	89.0–110.0

Note: * The saving capacity indicator calculated by OECD compares the abilities of consumer countries to absorb reductions in oil supplies. These very according to the different consumption structures.
Source: OECD Observer, December 1973, p. 35.

Japan and the United States towards the Israeli-Arab conflict have changed significantly since October 1973. However, it seems misleading to attribute these changes solely to the impact of the oil weapon. The most important of them was, of course, the shift in the United States' Middle East policy – but Washington had some very good reasons to put pressure on Israel so as to achieve some progress towards a Middle East settlement, quite apart from the pressure stemming from Arab oil embargoes and cutbacks. First, the Middle East was, and still is, a potential source of superpower conflict (as the events in October 1973 demonstrated) and hence a danger to her détente policy. Secondly, American success in bringing Israel to terms with her Arab neighbours' demands and achieving a stable settlement (or even a serious attempt to do so) would no doubt greatly enhance Washington's position in the Middle East, since the support for Israel constitutes its most important handicap in the Arab world.

On 6 November, the foreign ministers of the EEC agreed on a resolution which also marked a new approach to the Israeli-Arab conflict. The resolution called for Israel to withdraw to the lines she held at the time of the first ceasefire of 22 October (Egypt by that time wanted withdrawal to the same line) and full implementation of UN Security Council resolution 242 in an interpretation which did not differ from the Egyptian one. The inadmissibility of the acquisition of territory by force was set out as one of the principles of the envisaged settlement, and Israel was urged to end the occupation of the areas she had conquered in 1967. The resolution further called for respect for the territorial integrity, sovereignty and independence of all states in the area and their right to live in peace within secure and recognized boundaries, and stated that any full and lasting agreement would have to take into account the legitimate rights of the Palestinians.

This resolution was widely seen as favourable to the Arabs and provoked bitter criticism in Israel. But, again, it seems an over-simplification to ascribe its content solely to the effectiveness of the oil weapon. Rather, it can be argued that it constituted a new step towards the gradual development of a common Middle East position by the European Community and reflected a slow but clear shift by the British and even West German governments from a pro-Israeli to a more neutral stand. Of course, this shift took into account the Community's high dependence on Arab oil, but the use of the oil weapon speeded up and crystallized the EEC position, rather than fundamentally changing it.

Japan was the most vulnerable of all industrialized consumer countries and the shortfall in oil supplies seemed to affect economic production fairly directly and seriously. At the beginning of December, the Ministry of International Trade and Industry (MITI) calculated the reduction in oil supplies at 16 per cent and predicted the following consequences: steel production would be down by 8–11 per cent, paper and pulp production by 30 per cent, petrochemicals by 20 per cent, cement by 13 per cent, and aluminium by 14 per cent. Furthermore, MITI foresaw a considerable additional push for inflation caused by higher oil prices and shortages.[14] As a result, Japan's modification of her Middle East policy was most marked, even though she finally managed to achieve most-favoured nation status without actually breaking diplomatic relations with Israel. All the same, she had to give up her low-profile, business-first foreign policy, which had achieved neutrality towards the Middle East conflict mainly by being vague. As one official put it, 'our interpretation of the UN resolution 242 has been ambiguous in the past and we are simply modifying it'.[15] The modifications included an appeal to Israel to return to the May 1967 borders and then negotiate a security agreement with the Arab states. Japan also adopted the principle that no territorial gains by military force should be permitted, and the government further explained that it would interpret the Security Council resolution 242 in accordance with the Arab attitude. The Minister of International Trade and Industry, Mr Nakasone, explicitly stated that Japan no longer agreed with the principles of the United States' Middle East policy.

An effect of the oil weapon over and above shifting the policies of consumer governments towards the Israeli-Arab conflict was to produce splits and tensions in the Western alliance and within the EEC. These tensions reflected basic differences in interest between the consumer countries and also, it seems, some mismanagement in dealing with them.

The differences concern, first of all, actual dependence on Arab oil. As pointed out earlier, the United States found herself in a much better position than both Europe and Japan; but even within Western Europe there were marked differences in dependence and vulnerability (see Table 3).

Another fundamental difference involved diverging energy policies. Again, it was France which found herself in a markedly different position from her partners. First, her energy policy had for a long time been marked by the search for stable oil supplies, independent from the 'majors'. This had led to the creation of government-owned, or at least government-influenced, French oil companies which sometimes competed strongly with the majors, and to a large amount of state intervention in energy and oil policies. Secondly, her energy policy since de Gaulle had developed a strong pro-Arab tendency, since it was to the Arab world that France looked for her stable and independent oil supplies. Great Britain and the Netherlands, on the other hand, were both the home of major international oil companies, and therefore refused any kind of interventionist government policy – even more so on a Community level. West Germany, Belgium and Italy fell somewhere between these two poles, the first two leaning towards a liberal policy, the last, through her state company (ENI), following a line similar to France but allowing the international oil companies a greater role.

But the core of the disagreement in the Western alliance and the European community was the issue of security. During the Israeli-Arab war, the United States pursued a policy which took account of American concern for the global balance *vis-à-vis* the Soviet Union and aimed to prevent any shift in Moscow's favour. The European countries, however, were primarily concerned about their oil supplies, and were not prepared to see their economic security put at risk. Apart from Portugal, which allowed the United States to use an air base in the Azores for her airlift to Israel, European governments therefore preferred to take a neutral attitude and to appease the Arabs. Britain declared an embargo on deliveries of arms and spares to all combatant states; this hurt the Israelis more than the Arabs. West Germany protested (after the war was over) against the use of her ports for the transfer of American war material from Germany to Israel. Secretary of Defense Schlesinger's veiled threat that the United States might reconsider her military presence in Germany demonstrated, however, that Germany faced a dilemma: she did not want to antagonize either the Americans or the Arabs.

Within the European Community a basically nationalistic approach prevailed. The problem here was the embargo against the Netherlands. While the Dutch urged the other member countries to show solidarity and arrive at some form of oil-sharing, France and Britain, anxious not to lose their status as friendly countries in Arab eyes, opposed such a move. (Actually, the EEC had no contingency plans for sharing out the oil, since this had been left to the OECD; the OECD oil committee, reportedly under French and British influence, decided not to put its oil-sharing system into action.) Though this did little economic damage (since the oil was shared more or less equally by the companies), the political damage to the idea of European solidarity was considerable: the EEC had to face the hard truth that national interests still had priority over European solidarity.

The oil weapon created a situation where the consumer nations had to react – so that it was no longer possible to gloss over the differences within the Western alliance and the European Community. As problems of oil supply became interwoven with other issues (the essence and character of American-European relations, the size of the Community's Regional Fund), they became increasingly complex and difficult to resolve. This makes it unlikely that the splits and tensions within the West were foreseen and deliberately exploited by the Arab oil producers; it also appears questionable whether they actually served Arab interests. These tensions may have provided an extra incentive for the United States to settle the oil crisis by working for an Israeli-Arab settlement, and the use of the oil weapon did spur the EEC into adopting a united attitude to the Middle East conflict. Nonetheless, despite any independent and active role which the Arab producers may have expected Europe to play in the process of reaching a settlement, a solution to the conflict still had to be found within the context of superpower bipolarity.

To sum up, it is certainly true that the use of the oil weapon caused a change in the Middle East policies of the main consumer countries, but this change did not constitute a total reversal of previous policies and, at least in the case of the United States, stopped well short of full acceptance of Arab objectives. The fact that the oil weapon was sheathed again before any of the stated Arab objectives had been achieved underlines that its success was not unqualified.

II. Oil power: potential and limitations in the future

So far, we have been concerned primarily with the supply crisis of 1973–74. The scope of the analysis will now be expanded to take into account some 'guesstimates' about the development of oil power until 1985 – a period for which we possess at least some guidelines, derived from the last crisis, the present situation and factors which will evidently play a significant role over the coming period.

If we want to speculate about the future importance of the oil weapon in international relations, we must first attempt to assess the future development of oil power in terms of the degree of balance/imbalance in the trade relationship between producers and consumers. Have we already reached the peak of oil power, or is it to grow further?

Development of oil power

The strength of oil power depends on the development of the oil import gap of major industrialized countries, which in turn depends on assumptions about supply- and demand-price elasticities (i.e., the responsiveness of changes in quantities supplied or demanded to price changes) and any orchestrated measures taken towards consumer self-sufficiency. We shall use a set of estimates (see Table 4) based on these two factors and the following assumptions:

1 The price of oil (in constant US $) will be around $7 per barrel for Persian Gulf crude (which is below the present price level).
2 Energy demand will be 10 per cent below pre-October 1973 estimates in

Table 4 Estimated energy consumption and oil imports, 1980 and 1985

	Total energy consumption (million b/d^a)			Total oil imports (million b/d)			Oil imports as % of energy consumption		
	1973^b	1980	1985	1973^b	1980	1985	1973^b	1980	1985
Western Europe	23.4	33.4	41.9	14.7	17	18	63	51	43
Extrapolated targets^c		36.8			11.1				30
United States	35.2	44.9	54.7	6.0	2	3	17	4.5	5.5
Project Independence targets		42.3	50.0		5.9^d	0^d		14^d	0^d
Japan	6.6	10.7	14.4	5.6	7	9	85	65	62
Revised official targets		11.8	14.8		7.7	9.8		65	66

Notes:
a Oil equivalent.
b Actual figures.
c Using EEC Commission targets and assuming the 1973 ratio of EEC to total Western European consumption.
d Total energy imports.

Sources: Deutsche Gesellschaft für Auswärtige Politik, *Lösungsvorschläge für die Welt-Energieprobleme, Bericht einer Expertengruppe aus Ländern der Europäischen Gemeinschaft, Japan and Nordamerika* (Bonn: 1974), pp. 16, 18 (Arbeits-papiere zur Internationalen Politik); United States Atomic Energy Commission, Report to the President, *The Nations' Energy Future* (Washington, 1973); *Petroleum Economist* May 1974, p. 166, July 1974, p. 254, June 1974, p. 215.

areas apart from Western Europe (where it will be 5 per cent lower) and the Third World (where it will be 15 per cent lower). A comparison with preliminary government recalculations of their targets show that these assumptions are reasonable and in some cases even conservative.

3 In all consumer countries reductions in energy demand can be translated into oil savings.
4 In the United States and Western Europe there will be some substitution of oil by other sources of energy.

On the demand side, these estimates show a total oil import requirement for the three major consumer areas of 26 million b/d in 1980 and 30 million in 1985; world import demand is put at 30 million and 35 million b/d respectively. Let us now contrast these demand estimates with the production potential of the OPEC countries, particularly the high absorbers. So far these countries have shown a desire to maximize their production in order to fuel their ambitious development programmes and overcome their state of underdevelopment. Present production and future production potential of these producers are listed in Table 5.

Comparison of Tables 4 and 5 shows that the gap to be filled by

Table 5 High absorbers: present and potential output (million b/d)

	1973	1980	1985
Venezuela	3.5	3	3
Indonesia	1.3	2.5	3
Algeria	1.1	1.5	2
Nigeria	2.1	3	4
Iraq	2.0	3	5
Iran	5.9	9	9
Others	1.5	3	4
Price effect*	–	1.5	3
Total	17.4	26.5	33

Note: * Price effect: allowance for the impact of supply/price elasticity on production. This reflects the fact that higher prices allow more effective (though more costly) extraction techniques.

Sources: Deutsche Gesellschaft für Auswärtige Politik, *op. cit.*, p. 19; *BP Statistical Review of the World Oil Industry, 1973, op. cit.*, p. 6.

producers other than those considered as production maximizers is 3.5 million b/d in 1980 and 2 million b/d in 1985. Theoretically, the gap would have to be closed by some or all of the following (all low-absorbers): Libya, Kuwait, Saudi Arabia, the United Arab Emirates and Qatar. These countries would then play the role of marginal suppliers. Of course, such a development is highly unlikely, since it rests on assumptions which cannot all be taken for granted: a very effective energy policy on the part of the consumer nations, and a *laissez-faire* policy on the part of the producers (which would be in strong contradiction to their present cartel policies). The producers have a vested interest in high prices and a tight supply/demand situation, and are likely to resort to some measures of market control. Furthermore, the assumption that the high absorbers will continue to keep actual output near to the ceiling of production potential neglects the possibility of price maximization, rather than production maximization. It also ignores the possibility that – given successful industrialization – increased non-oil exports and the replacement of imports by home-produced goods might reduce reliance on oil for export earnings. Iran, Algeria, Venezuela and, possibly, Iraq might well be capable of achieving such an industrial base in the foreseeable future. On the other hand, the low absorbers might find it in their interest to keep production at a fairly high level so long as the present price prevails.

On the consumer side, the developments in the first year after the supply crisis are hardly encouraging. The fall in oil consumption appeared to be almost entirely due to the world-wide recession, and, because of the threat to employment, no energetic and lasting conservation efforts were undertaken. Disillusionment with certain alternative sources of energy (such as nuclear energy and shale oil), for environmental reasons and because of their uncertain profitability prospects, also raised doubts about whether

Oil and Influence 343

dependence on Middle East oil could be significantly reduced within the next ten years. Certainly it will be some years before efforts by international oil companies and consumer government to develop alternative sources of supply, so as to change the economic framework of producer power, show their impact.

The problem of precision: the international distribution system

The supply crisis of 1973–74 not only revealed the strength of the oil weapon but also exposed some of its weaknesses. Arguably the most important of these is its lack of precision. The producers' handling of the oil weapon, and the rules and regulations that accompanied its use confirm that they aimed at discrimination between the various consumer countries. However, the flexibility of the international oil market (which in terms of distribution, transport and processing is still by and large controlled by the international oil companies[16]) prevailed over attempts to direct the oil weapon only against certain consumers. The very core of the discriminatory strategy, the embargo, therefore failed – a fact which even the producers themselves admitted – so that the only effective sanction the Arab producers possessed was the general cut-back in production.

The flexibility of the international distribution system has two main aspects: the tanker (and pipeline) system and the refineries. The question of whether the flexibility of the international oil market can be upheld in these two areas is of paramount importance for the future of the oil weapon in international relations. If the producers succeeded in destroying this flexibility, they would be able to discriminate against a single consumer, and therefore apply considerably stronger pressure. The oil weapon would thus gain immensely in applicability and could be used for a much wider set of objectives.

The threat of precision: bilateral arrangements and power-increasing strategies

In the aftermath of the October 1973 to March 1974 supply crisis there was a rush by consumer governments to conclude bilateral deals with producers so as to secure oil supplies. For some time this posed the real threat of a fundamental change in the international oil market towards strong dependence by single consumers on particular producers. This possibility now appears remote, not least because of a certain reluctance on the part of producers such as Saudi Arabia to enter into agreements of this kind. To be sure there were quite a number of bilateral deals, but they concentrated on assistance by industrialized countries with the problems of economic development of the producer countries, which opened up possibilities for the consumers to offset part of their balance-of-payments deficits by increased exports. There is no evidence of the widespread inclusion of supply guarantees in such deals, even though the hope of achieving security of supplies was clearly among the consumers' motives for concluding them.

Even the present form of bilateral deal, however, appears not to be without political problems. It has been argued repeatedly and convincingly that a strictly nationalistic economic approach to solving the present problems of the consumer countries that centres around bilateral deals would lead to a scramble for markets and competition for the oil producers' revenue surplus. The result would undoubtedly be increased conflict between the consumer countries, and possibly also higher oil prices; the strongest economic powers would prevail, while the weakest would find their problems aggravated. The developing countries without indigenous energy resources would be hardest hit. They would not be able to increase their exports so as to pay their oil bills, and could not hope to attract large capital inflows from the oil producers. Above all they might find their other imports costing more as a consequence of world-wide inflation, due not least to rocketing oil prices.

These drawbacks and limitations would appear to provide strong incentives for finding international solutions to problems such as the orderly transfer of wealth to the producers, the recycling of oil revenue surpluses to consumer countries in need and co-operation in the development of sufficient sources of energy.

While a largely bilateral supply structure is unlikely in the near future, the adoption by some or all the producers of a deliberate power-increasing strategy for purely political reasons could pose a serious threat. Such a strategy could be followed in three ways: the producers could try to increase the dependence of consumer countries on energy under their control; they could attempt to destroy the flexibility of the distribution system by building up a large share in it; or they could simply strengthen their hold on the international oil companies (e.g., by building up large shareholdings).

At the time of writing, there are hardly any signs of such developments, but if they did come about they would clearly lead to a dangerous level of permanent confrontation between producer and consumer countries and/or detrimental economic implications for the producers themselves. For instance, to achieve higher dependence on oil the price would have to be lowered considerably, and even then memories of the last supply crisis would prevent consumers from again relying heavily on imported oil. The producers could also expand their control over energy sources by investing in coal, nuclear energy and conventional and unconventional oil sources outside their area, thereby gaining a substantial foothold in the world energy industries. This might be desirable for economic reasons, but it would hardly contribute to the producers' political power (which stems from the ability to interrupt supplies), since these investments would be outside their effective control and, because the threat of nationalization works both ways, might even serve as hostages in a future supply crisis. Economically, both producers and consumers could gain from such investments, but a necessary precondition would be to develop safeguards against their political use in any form (though most investments made initially for economic reasons would probably take a different form from those made for purely political, power-increasing purposes).

The same holds true for downstream investment by the producers. Expansion of their activities into the tanker and refinery business, and ultimately also into the consumer distribution networks, can be expected for sound economic reasons – indeed for the same reasons which turned the international oil companies into integrated enterprises. However, investments aiming at increased political power, so as to enable the oil weapon to be used in a discriminatory manner, would again take a different form. In essence, the problem appears to be one of thresholds: controlling 5 per cent of the world tanker fleet might not be politically dangerous, but controlling 20 per cent would be.

The oil producers certainly have the potential to acquire a politically dangerous share in the world tanker fleet. Several producers already possess tankers[17] and have ordered a considerable number of new carriers.[18] After the delivery of present orders (which will take until 1979) Kuwait and Iraq, with approximately 2 million and 1.5 million deadweight tons (dwt) respectively, will own the largest fleets among the Arab countries, while Iran has stated her intention to build up a fleet totalling 1 million dwt.[19] With the foundation of the Arab Maritime Petroleum Transport Company (a sub-organization of OAPEC) and its plan to spend $2,000 million over the next five years on tankers, product carriers and liquefied natural gas (LNG) carriers, and with the further expansion by other producers which can be expected, the combined Arab fleet might amount to some 20 million dwt in the early 1980s. For the journey from the Persian Gulf via the Cape route, the amount of oil which by then could be transported annually in producer-owned tankers would be about 100 million tons. However, compared with a world tanker fleet of 246 million dwt (including combined carriers) in 1974 and 221 million dwt on order,[20] these figures for new-built Arab tanker capacity are probably not important enough to pose a real threat to the flexibility of the international distribution system.

The tanker market is a purely competitive business, and although limited shipbuilding capacity may prevent the oil producers from gaining sufficient control by ordering new tankers, the present large tanker surplus could enable them to buy a large second-hand fleet. In a time of tanker surplus private owners might not be assured of full employment of their tankers, and could in any case only expect a low return, but producer governments could probably force employment of their fleets to transport their oil.[21] Costs would be no serious obstacle: if tanker capacity costs $150 per dwt, a fleet of, say, 50 million tons (about one-fifth of the present world tanker fleet) would cost $7.5 billion – a sum definitely within the reach of the oil producers.[22] Another possibility is that they could charter a substantial tanker capacity. This could hardly be done at very short notice, since the capacity available within days is minute, but every year about 14 per cent of the world tanker fleet enters the charter market.[23] In either case, however, the consumer governments would receive clear warning signals well in advance.

Another way for the oil producers to increase their power would be to attempt to gain control over the international oil companies. They could try to acquire large share holdings or, in any future application of the oil weapon, simply to attempt to force the companies to stop *all* deliveries to an embargoed country – not only deliveries of the producers' own oil. The first possibility poses the same kind of problems for the producers as all investments outside their direct territorial control; the second depends on the leverage they possess *vis-à-vis* the companies. This leverage rests on the investments and assets of the companies in the producer countries and their privileges in these countries (they pay lower oil prices than customers without production facilities there). Leverage on both counts has been gradually weakened through participation or nationalization, and, since the producers started to assert themselves and free themselves from the hegemony the companies had long exerted over these countries and their oil industry, the relationship between producers and companies has been moving towards co-existence based on mutual interests: the companies fulfil certain important functions for the producers, which for the time being, they cannot do without.

However, there must be doubts whether in any future supply crisis the oil companies will be as well placed to manage the international distribution system efficiently and share out available supplies as they were in 1973. Apart from the possibility of stronger producer interference, there also is the question of consumer government involvement: the companies have been heavily criticized for their management in the last crisis.

The emergency programme of the International Energy Agency[24] might help the companies to destroy the flexibility of the oil weapon once more by allocating available oil supplies fairly, since it provides them with the necessary governmental approval. Moreover, it would (if effective) provide another barrier to discriminatory application of the oil weapon, since the scheme obliges every member to maintain an emergency oil reserve of 60 (later 90) days' consumption and to have contingency plans for reducing oil consumption. If one or more member countries suffer a reduction in supplies of 7 per cent or more, or can be expected to experience such a shortfall, the affected countries will have to activate measures to save 7 per cent of oil consumption. If the shortfall exceeds 12 per cent of demand a 10 per cent saving will be required, the rest being made up by other members. If this cannot be done the available oil will be shared between member countries.

The scheme therefore provides an institutionalized device to prevent discriminatory application of the oil weapon against a single member of the IEA. Whether it stands the test of application or could be circumvented or invalidated by the producers remains to be seen. It is certainly true that the scheme depends on the oil companies' control over the international distribution system, since the companies will be in charge of the management of the allocation. Sufficient producer control over the international tanker fleet would therefore most likely invalidate the scheme, or at least require additional measures.

The ceiling of the oil weapon: world economic crisis and fundamental political change

If we assume that the future international oil market will retain its present flexibility and that discrimination will be impossible, then the damage caused by supply interruptions will be distributed more or less evenly, and it will be the most vulnerable consumers which suffer most.

In the last supply crisis, these were Japan and those developing countries with either little or no indigenous energy resources and/or heavy dependence on imported oil; next in vulnerability came some of the European consumers. The producers, therefore, faced a choice of either taking into consideration the impact of the oil weapon on the weaker consumers, or else pressing ahead in order to exert pressure on the main target, in that case the United States. If in future the producers take into account the situation of the weaker consumers, then this sets a fairly low ceiling for overall cutbacks, and it looks as if the oil weapon's lack of discriminatory capability actually gives any target a whole group of hostages – consumer countries weaker than itself. In applying the oil weapon, therefore, the producers not only risk political alienation of non-target countries but also turmoil and unpredictable developments in and around those countries. Once a major industrialized country was caught in a serious economic crisis triggered by shortage of oil supplies, a chain reaction throughout the world economy would probably be inevitable, the consequences of which would be unpredictable and uncontrollable and might backfire on the producers themselves. Economic crises in the consumer countries would lead to social tensions and political unrest, and dramatic changes could not be ruled out. New radical governments, in the face of tremendous domestic pressure, might decide to try solving the supply crisis by military force – desperate and irrational as such a move might be.

But the producers operate not only within the context of a rather sensitive world economy but also in an international political system, and they have to consider the impact of the oil weapon on this – and especially on the superpower balance. The conservative Arab oil producers cannot be interested in weakening the Western alliance, and more precisely the position of the United States, either on a global or a regional level. In the last crisis the United States was clearly given carrot and stick treatment; not only was she subjected to an embargo, she was also invited to play a more prominent role in the Middle East. In future, if a producer thinks an alignment with the United States desirable, he will probably not press too hard and will rely on rewards as well as sanctions, since in the long run an alignment has to be based on mutuality of interest and predictable behaviour by both sides. If the United States were antagonized she would try to reduce her dependence on the producers as quickly as possible and would look for other allies to pursue her interests; these allies might be found within the producer society (perhaps an opposition group which could be helped to power) or in the area. So long as rational behaviour prevails among producer governments, therefore, consideration for the regional and global political context, as well as for the functioning of the world economic system, sets a limit to the pressure which could be exerted through the oil weapon.

However, even within the limits of this pressure, the built-in time lag of the oil weapon appears to constitute another problem for the producers. There is a lag in the transport system which means that tankers loaded before the decision to interrupt supplies was taken will still be arriving in the consumer countries for some weeks afterwards – the exact time depending on the distance to the destination. This lag might be increased by the consumer countries' use of stocks and stand-by capacity, possibly within the framework of the IEA. All this means that the oil weapon is a somewhat awkward instrument of political coercion, with a tendency to draw out a crisis situation. On the one hand, this gives decision-makers time, reducing the psychological pressures of an acute crisis and consequently also some of the dangers of irrational behaviour. On the other hand, the time-lag inherent in supply interruptions might devalue the oil weapon in certain kinds of crises and could be used by consumers to decide on countermeasures or to try to respond in other areas: e.g., by threatening the producer's allies or shifting support to his regional rivals.

It appears, then, that the political and economic effects of using the oil weapon cannot be separated – indeed its power is derived from the economic damage it can inflict. But the economic consequences of a serious supply interruption stretch over years and are hardly controllable by the producers. Oil supply shortages cause fertilizer shortages, which in turn affect the grain harvests months after the oil weapon has been sheathed. Higher oil prices speed up inflation and trigger off a wage-price spiral. Insofar as the oil weapon aims at the basic functions of a society, the decision to apply it resembles the decision to go to war: once it is made, the exact course of events and the consequences might get out of control. This does not exclude the possibility of a further application of the oil weapon, but it is not going to be an instrument frequently used for exerting political pressure. The implication also might be that the producers will look for new ways and means to use their oil power.

The impact of applying the oil weapon

What has been the impact of the first successful application of the oil weapon? Will it enhance or reduce its power? There is some contradiction in the answers to these questions. Certainly, the future application of the oil weapon has now become more credible, since the Arab producers have actually shown the will to use it. On the other hand, it is to be hoped that the consumers will have learned from the 1973–74 crisis: the political risks of relying heavily on energy imported from producers who have little economic incentive to continue the prevailing level of production, and who could easily afford to reduce it, or even halt it for some time, has now become obvious. This awareness should trigger off a whole series of processes aimed at reducing this insecurity. In the longer run, these will probably result in a situation similar to that outlined in Table 8.4, with the consumer countries' dependence on imported oil significantly diminished. However, even in the shorter run the consumer countries could reduce the impact of the oil weapon. The 1973–74 crisis demonstrated that the shortfall of oil which can be absorbed without serious consequences is higher than expected, and that, as long as industrial production and vital transport functions can be upheld, the immediate effect of the oil weapon is limited. By preparing emergency allocation plans, increasing the flexibility of the internal distribution and refining systems and by co-ordinating consumer policies the impact of any future oil shortage could be reduced. This might partly be offset, however, by greater economy in the use of oil during the period between now and any future use of the oil weapon, due to attempts to reduce the impact of higher oil prices. Reductions in non-essential oil use and deliberate measures and contingency plans to improve the capacity to absorb shortages might thus have a roughly balancing effect. But, even so, the psychological climate has changed: consumer governments should now be less inclined to panic and resort to *sauve qui peut* policies. While in 1973 no government seemed to know exactly what the oil embargoes and cutbacks really meant for them, the oil weapon and its impact should now be a known quantity.

The net effect, it seems, is that the producers' freedom of manoeuvre will become more restricted. In order to bring substantial pressure to bear on consumers, they may have to resort to much higher initial pressure, bringing them dangerously near to the limits at which the oil weapon becomes counter-productive.

Producer solidarity

The solidarity of Arab oil producers proved their greatest strength in 1973–74, but at the same time the crisis revealed the fragility of this solidarity; differences of interest, mistrust and concern about the future balance within the Arab world soon created cracks. Producer solidarity will continue to be an important factor in the success of any future application of the oil weapon – and indeed might be the decisive factor.

One of the differences of interest that would have to be overcome is economic. Some of the oil producers urgently need every penny of their oil revenue to meet their expenditures and might suffer heavily from a substantial loss of revenues over a long period (though in 1973–74 the producers more than made up for the reduction in output by the increase in prices). This possibility did concern OAPEC states, as witness the introduction into the important resolutions of 17 October and 28 November of damage-limiting clauses which set a floor to production cutbacks. Indeed one country – Iraq – refrained from *any* general cutbacks, most likely for fear of just such losses of vital revenue. As a consequence of the prolonged struggle with the Iraq Petroleum Company, Iraq had never experienced the same degree of production expansion as the Gulf states. The leadership – already set on a course of rapid economic growth and fundamental social and economic change – therefore decided to adopt a different policy against the United States and the Netherlands: nationalizing their oil interests and declaring embargoes against them, but without reducing Iraq's overall production. Algeria and some of the small Gulf sheikhdoms also needed all the oil revenues they could get, and the Algerian Head of State, Houari Boumedienne, actually stressed in an interview with a Lebanese newspaper that his country suffered from the general production restrictions since it did not possess large foreign exchange reserves.[25] Algeria's position also reveals another difference of economic interest: as Boumedienne pointed out in his interview, the Algerian economy is closely linked with the European area and is bound to suffer from adverse developments there.

The first difference could be overcome by designing a production cut-back scheme according to each producer's degree of vulnerability to losses of revenue, rather than according to a general margin of production cutbacks for all producers (countries like Saudi Arabia, Kuwait, Abu Dhabi and Libya would then bear the main burden of reductions). For the second difference, which depends on the amount of integration into and sensitivity to, the industrialized economies, there is no simple solution.

Producer solidarity would always have to face the problem of a common political objective. Even Arab hostility to Israel in the last crisis did not produce a really unified position, for a rift within the Arab world and within the producer action group soon became evident. Egypt pressed for a political solution based on compromises and co-operation with the United States, while Libya and Iraq refused any kind of negotiated settlement in advance and protested against the conclusion of a cease-fire. Syria's leadership had decided to fight the war along Egyptian lines but faced constant pressure from more radical groups inside the power elite, especially the army, and the tactical moves necessary for President Assad to retain his position resulted in a Syrian course wavering between negotiation and obstruction. This rift between conservatives and progressives and between moderate and radical attitudes towards the Israeli-Arab conflict was bound to reappear over the question of how and when the oil restrictions were to be eased, if at all.

Political moves also indicated the growing dissension in the Arab oil producer group. Libya tried to bridge the rift between herself and Egypt and press for closer co-operation between the two countries, and it seems likely that this was meant as a move to counterbalance Saudi Arabian influence. The decision to lift the embargo against the United States was repeatedly postponed – allegedly because of opposing views about its desirability among the Arab producers. When the lifting was finally declared on 17 March, Libya and Syria did not join the Saudi-Egyptian leadership. Arab disunity was probably fostered by the Soviet Union, whose past success in the Middle East was largely due to the conservative-progressive confrontation and the conflict with Israel, and in a direct attack on Egypt, Moscow warned of any premature relaxation in the economic pressure on the United States. Similarly, the decision to lift the embargo against the Netherlands led to a split in OAPEC, with Saudi Arabia (reportedly influenced by the United States) delaying the lifting, and Algeria strongly advocating – and then unilaterally declaring – an end to the embargo.

III. Oil power: the wider context

If it is possible to draw any conclusions about oil power (and with the host of factors influencing the future development of oil power, they must be very tentative indeed), then they could be summed up as follows: oil power as the result of an imbalanced trade relationship will continue, but it may well have reached its peak and could lessen in the medium term. The only real qualitative increase which might come about in the future would be the possibility of being able to use the oil weapon selectively. This possibility cannot be ruled out but, even if it is realized, oil power is not unlimited except in the sense that it could trigger a vicious circle of growing and uncontrollable damage.

As long as rational behaviour prevails, there appear to be various restraints and ceilings on the amount of pressure which could be exerted. But, assuming that the producers do not want to cause uncontrollable and rapidly spreading damage to the world economy, they do nevertheless have some freedom of action and the ability to impose sanctions. They can exert disintegrative economic pressure on alliances and create conflict and tensions within and among industrialized nations. They could exacerbate the differences between developed and less-developed countries or mitigate them. They might be able to draw other states into regional conflicts, and even influence the global balance of power – although admittedly only indirectly and in a way which could hardly be called 'controlled'. It is unlikely that the producers could exert a direct influence on the strategic and security balance (even though the world-wide naval operations of the West, and probably also the Soviet Union, are to a limited extent dependent on Middle East oil for bunkering and are therefore somewhat vulnerable), since the backbone of the strategic balance, the nuclear deterrent, would not be affected; even serious restriction of the operational capacity of conventional forces seems unlikely, since stockpiling and a flexible supply system could probably cushion the impact of regional shortages. On balance, however, the oil weapon would seem to be a weapon of last resort. Its problems of control and precision, the inherent time-lag and the difficulty of organizing an action group sufficiently coherent to guarantee success make it unlikely to be frequently used for comparatively minor objectives. Producers might therefore try to substitute other forms of rewards

352 *Hanns Maull*

and sanctions derived from their oil power which would give them political influence and leverage. Before we turn to this problem, however, we have to consider briefly who will actually have the power to use the oil weapon.

Who could apply the oil weapon?

A precondition for using the oil weapon successfully would be the ability to cause real and serious damage to the consumer countries. This is the very essence of oil power, since leverage sufficient to cause only inconvenience would not be very effective. The 'more' in damage potential, even though it might never be used, is at the heart of real power.

There are four theoretical cases to consider: the application of the oil weapon by one producer against one consumer; by one producer against all consumers; by a group of producers against one consumer; and, finally, the application of the oil weapon by a group of producers against all consumers.

We already are in a situation of substantial production capacity surplus,[26] so the first possibility can largely be discounted, on the grounds that there would be sufficient stand-by capacity in other producing areas to make up the short-fall in deliveries from one producer to one consumer. The only single consumer with a demand so large as to pose a potential problem is Japan, and as long as she keeps her sources of supply sufficiently diversified, there is no real threat. Only if sources of supply were insufficiently diversified and all other producers were unable or unwilling to make up one producer's shortfall would there be a real political problem. Assuming that in 1985 Japan depended on a single producer for one-third of an import demand of 9 million b/d, the producer would have to cut production by 3 million b/d in order to exploit that dependence for political purposes. Such a cut would be feasible for countries such as Saudi Arabia or Iran but, in the absence of special arrangements among producers, it should be possible for Japan to make up the losses from other sources.

If the oil weapon could be directed against an individual target country separately, then the further possibility arises of its unilateral use by one producer against any country which is heavily dependent both on few sources of supply and on tankers owned by the producer in question. In the case of an embargo, surplus capacity from other areas might not reach such consumers because of lack of alternative tanker capacity. Apart from availability of surplus production and spare tanker capacity, a further key variable in such a situation would be the behaviour of other producers.

Looking now at the possibilities of a non-discriminatory use of the oil weapon by a single producer (the more likely case), we first have to make a tentative assessment of the damage threshold. If we assume a world net import demand of 30 million b/d in 1980 and 35 million b/d in 1985 (in line with the estimates put forward on p. 11) and postulate a 20 per cent shortfall as the damage threshold for the most dependent consumer countries, then this produces figures of 6 million b/d in 1980 and 7 million b/d in 1985.

Looking at the production potential of the producer countries (Table 5), we can conclude that Iran is one of the countries which could afford unilateral production cut-backs of this order, while Iraq, whose reserves are said to be potentially very large, might also be very nearly in a position to do so. But it is Saudi Arabia, a low absorber with a production potential of up to 20 million b/d, which is least vulnerable to losses of income even over a prolonged period. Saudi Arabia, then, if one considers her capabilities alone (without allowing for intentions) is by far the most likely to apply the oil weapon unilaterally.

The most dangerous case would be action by a group of producers against one consumer. This assumes that the flexibility of the international distribution system would be destroyed. Again, however, such action could only be successful if there were no stand-by capacity outside the action group and no consumer solidarity. Obviously, not all countries will be vulnerable even to a total embargo (this would be true, for example, of the United States if she faced an Arab action group), and it is difficult to see a target other than the United States, which could arouse a sufficient degree of hostility in several producer countries. However, if there were such a country, the political leverage producers could apply to it would be enormous.

The fourth possibility is co-ordinated producer action against all consumers. Given the political and economic differences in OPEC it is hard to imagine a general application of the oil weapon by that organization for political reasons. The greatest potential for producer solidarity no doubt exists, and will continue to exist, in the Middle East and North Africa, among Arab producers organized in OAPEC. Co-ordinated Arab action will continue to constitute the most real threat to consumer states. But solidarity is difficult to obtain and could be mobilized only in a limited number of cases – and solidarity inevitably makes the application of the oil weapon more complicated, since the producers' various policies have to be accommodated and combined into a single policy.

So long as a strong faction among the producers favours a course of moderation, therefore, a common application of the oil weapon will most likely be based on the mildest of the possible options. The various ceilings on the use of the oil weapon will doubtless also come into play, particularly as group action raises the level of potential damage. That potential would, however, be greatly enhanced by Saudi participation. Indeed, given Saudi Arabia's strong influence in Kuwait and the Persian Gulf sheikhdoms, any attempt to create an Arab oil action group without her would face considerable difficulties. Even if she did not attempt to make up the losses caused by the Arab producer group, her abstention would mean a considerable reduction in the damage the group could inflict, since the only other country with a strong bargaining position and low vulnerability would probably be Libya. Actual Saudi opposition would probably cause such a use of the oil weapon to fail – though, since this would imply an open clash between 'progressive' and 'conservative' Arab countries, oil supplies might be interrupted by sabotage and guerilla activity in the Persian Gulf.

Price as a weapon

In the definition of the term 'oil weapon' already given, it has been said that the weapon consists of the manipulation of oil supplies and/or price for political purposes, and it has been noted that both will most likely go together in any future interference with supplies. But could the price of oil alone also be used as a political tool?

Manipulating price does, of course, in principle offer the possibilities of both conferring rewards and inflicting sanctions. Some consumers might be sold oil on preferential terms (indeed this already has happened in the case of developing countries), and preferential prices and the threat of their withdrawal could constitute considerable leverage *vis-à-vis* weak consumer countries, and might be used to achieve political and economic influence. Apart from these limited possibilities, however, the price of oil can probably not be used as a negative sanction.

The producers having gradually become fully aware of their market bargaining power and raised prices accordingly, the price of oil is presumably now not too far off the ceiling imposed by the cost of developing other sources of oil and energy and by the vulnerability of the consumer states. For the future, it can be expected that OPEC will keep the price of crude near this ceiling for purely economic reasons. Price is the only interest common to all OPEC members, and those countries which are still concerned about securing maximum income will resist, and already have resisted, any attempts to bring prices down. There will therefore be little room for using higher prices as a lever for political purposes – quite apart from the fact that oil prices by themselves are probably very difficult to handle as a purely political weapon, since market factors and economic interests still play an important role in their formation. Prices will therefore probably only be important in connection with another attempt to use production cutbacks for political leverage; they might well shoot up again in such a situation of shortage, though this might be detrimental to the longer-term economic interests of the producers.

Oil revenues: the monetary dimension of oil power

The quadrupling of oil prices during 1973, combined with the continuing demand for oil, has brought forward a new form of oil power: enormous revenue surpluses. Estimates of the actual amount of future surplus in the longer-term vary but give an impression of the dimensions of the oil producers' financial power.[27] Table 6 gives some estimates of OPEC oil income in 1974.

The amount of revenue surplus in the more distant future depends on a variety of economic and political factors, such as the pace of economic

Table 6 Estimated production and revenues of OPEC countries (1974)

Country	Est. production (million b/d)[a]	Average export earnings per barrel ($)[b]	Est. oil revenues ($ million)
Saudi Arabia	8.643	9.25	29,181
Iran	6.128	9.30	20,801
Kuwait	2.843	8.93	9,267
Iraq	1.829	10.47	6,990
Abu Dhabi	1.750	9.82	6,272
Qatar	0.546	10.00	1,993
Oman	0.297	9.60	1,041
Dubai	0.232	9.17	766
Bahrain	0.068	9.08	225
SUBTOTAL	22.336		76,536
Libya	1.700	12.27	7,613
Algeria	0.889	12.26	3,978
Venezuela	3.025	9.50	10,489
Nigeria	2.300	10.71	8,991
Indonesia	1.457	9.10	4,839
Ecuador	0.232	8.77	743
TOTAL	31.939		113,189

Notes
Oil revenue estimates are based on the assumption that total production is exported. Due to indigenous consumption, and to fluctuation in prices, these figures give only an approximate impression of OPEC oil revenues.

a *Source: Oil and Gas Journal*, 30 December 1974.
b *Source: Middle East Economic Survey*, 31 May 1974.

development in the producer countries, the development of Arab politics[28] and the development of consumption and the terms of trade with the industrialized countries. But there will be vast surpluses for some time, and this money can and will be used politically.

One use would be to shift foreign exchange holdings from one currency into another.[29] However, unless the oil producers transfer their surplus into the Soviet Union or store it under their beds, they cannot avoid circulating it in the international monetary system. Within this system, provisions to avoid drastic fluctuations of exchange rates already exist in the form of swap arrangements among central banks, and, if necessary, these could be improved or new ones designed. If such measures failed there would still be the possibility of international agreements to control and restrict large currency movements and, as a last resort, the freezing of oil producers' assets. (Ironically, while the industrialized countries worry about the disruptive potential of Arab revenue surpluses, the Arab countries worry about their assets being frozen.[30]) The use of foreign exchange holdings as a weapon therefore does not appear very likely, since the consumer countries would have better methods of protecting themselves against this than against oil supply interruptions.

Other applications of the producers' financial power for political ends are much more likely. Most of the Arab producers are politically and militarily vulnerable, and so will be under strong pressure to buy their security by appeasing the Arab have-nots. If they are not seen to share at least some of their wealth with these have-nots, and to throw some of their weight behind them, the result could be a new confrontation in the Arab world. For this reason development assistance, grants, payment for arms and similar projects in the Arab world will swallow a large slice of the oil revenue surplus.

Similarly, money could be used to cement political alignments, so as to give the oil-producers greater influence in inter-Arab relations, and to weaken countries hostile to the producers by financing opposition groups and subversive movements or by bribing politicians and army officers. Rivalries and divisions among the producers themselves (such as those between Saudi Arabia and Libya) might even result in competition among producers for influence in other countries, with the accompanying beneficial effects for the target.

In a wider geographical context, oil money could be used as a reward for political ends, as well. Clearly, the attractiveness of large-scale Arab investment provides strong leverage on both developed and developing countries, but particularly on the latter, and the same goes for grants and cheap loans. Libya and Saudi Arabia have already used their wealth in this way: both of them offering credits and grants for African countries willing to break diplomatic relations with Israel, and Saudi Arabia attempting to offset Libyan influence in black Africa. Libya also is said to finance opposition groups and guerilla movements both inside and outside the Arab world.[31]

Spin-off of oil power

If the producers exploit their current position skilfully, they could become very influential indeed, because of the combination of their ability to manipulate the price and supply of oil with the ability to deploy their financial capacity for political ends. Saudi Arabia is well placed in both respects, while Iran, too, stands to gain diplomatically by virtue of both her oil production rate and the economic and military power which she can now develop rapidly.

Apart from the deliberate exploitation of oil power for specific purposes, however, the Arab producers and Iran will play a more important role in international relations in general – simply because they constitute a factor to be taken into account by foreign policy decision-makers throughout the world. This influence will be achieved without great effort simply because of the present and likely future state of the international oil market and the political implications which result from it. These implications, which give oil power a day-to-day pay-off aspect, are the following:

a   The oil-producing countries, or most of them, will command vast financial reserves and surpluses. In order to attract oil producers' investible funds, other countries will make considerable efforts and offer advantages. These will result, directly or indirectly, in even more oil power and political influence, because economic assistance and development will create new capabilities, and because political concessions can be expected to form part of any package offered to obtain a share in Arab wealth. It will be very difficult not to be on good terms with the oil-producing countries.

b   The predicted rise in oil demand has to be met by Arab oil production beyond a level which would result in full absorption of oil revenues by the producer country. Even if there were an arrangement which solved some of the problems of investing the revenue surpluses generated by extracting more oil, rather than leaving it in the ground, it still seems likely that the economic incentives to increase production will not be sufficient to ensure that the demand is met. This clearly brings in other forms of incentives – political incentives. These could be handed out both on a bilateral basis and internationally. The first would involve policies of appeasement: i.e., conceding the oil producers' demand and supporting their policies. The second would imply a general upgrading of the role of oil producers in international organizations and processes; this could apply above all to financial institutions, where the oil producers will be directly involved on a major scale, but it could also apply to political organizations, such as the United Nations.

c   Finally, and most importantly, the very possibility of application of the oil weapon can be politically exploited. Like military power, it does not actually have to be applied to provide political leverage. The rhetoric of the oil weapon, oil diplomacy (possibly including the use of symbolic stoppages and embargoes to show that the producers mean business) and accommodation of consumers' policies to producer objectives even before these have been formulated as demands – these will all be important aspects of future international politics, and almost certainly the most salient expression of oil power.

The daily pay-off of oil power, then, will constitute one of the ever-present factors in future international relations. So could the forms of power derived from oil power as such: economic and military power.

To the degree that the oil producers succeed in building and developing modern industrialized socities, some of them will become economic powers large enough to overshadow their regions. To be sure, the difficulties of leap-frogging modernization are enormous: shortage of skilled labour, technicians and administrators; lack of infrastructure; shortage of raw materials other than oil in many countries; divisions between rural and urban and between traditional and modern sectors and the consequent cultural lags in way of life and attitudes. Furthermore, there are also problems caused by the fact that the ability of underdeveloped countries to industrialize is constrained by the pre-existence of large-scale industries in the developed countries. The oil-producers do, however, have two advantages: capital and the power, exploiting consumer dependence on oil, to gain entrance into new markets for their industrial products and to secure themselves a privileged position in those markets. The real transformation of oil power into economic power, however, can probably only take place through the development of the internal markets. To achieve this, the producers must meet two preconditions: there must be a sufficiently large population, and the standard of living and spending power of all classes (not only the small upper and middle classes) must be increased. The latter in turn requires fundamental changes in the social (and ultimately also the political) structure, since the rural masses, which still largely live in poverty and caught in pre-industrial cultural patterns, must be enabled effectively to improve their lot. In the light of this, one could expect that Algeria, Iran, Venezuela and possibly Iraq might become economic powers of regional importance within the period under consideration. The other oil producers will probably still be struggling with the problems and difficulties of development, though some of them could use their financial power to acquire a share in industrial production abroad.

A second form of power derived from oil power is military strength, and the amount of military expenditure and of large-scale arms imports from industrialized countries has risen recently on an unprecedented scale, especially in the case of Arab producers and Iran.[32] The reasons for these huge deals are manifold – considerations of internal and external security, prestige and status, and interstate rivalries – but they have introduced, or are about to introduce, extremely sophisticated modern weapon systems (such as the F-14 or MiG-23 fighters, 'smart' bombs and missiles) to the Persian Gulf and the Israeli-Arab zone. Effectively, the gap in conventional military technology between the industrialized countries and this Third World area has been closed. Nonetheless, it seems doubtful whether this increase in hardware can be translated into an equivalent increase in military power. The vast amount of sophisticated weapons now pouring into these countries poses enormous problems of absorption in training, service and maintenance, and shortage of skilled personnel will mean both heavy dependence on foreign assistance and a considerable delay before fighting power increases to match the equipment inventory. The impact of these large purchases on the importers will also be considerable in economic and political terms. Manning the new systems will constitute a heavy drain on trained technicians and specialists in their societies, while the large military expenditures and the huge amounts of hardware will further strengthen the political influence of the army officers.

The main consideration appears to be whether the increased military power of the states involved leads to fundamental imbalances. Iran is striving for military superiority in the Persian Gulf and for an influential role beyond it, with the intention of stabilizing the *status quo*, and her growing power might indeed have such a stabilizing effect in the Indian subcontinent. In the Gulf itself, however, the Arab states (and especially Saudi Arabia and Iraq) seem unwilling to accept Iranian military hegemony and will try to increase their own military power to prevent it as far as possible. Given the now well-established link between the Persian Gulf and Israeli-Arab zone, this in turn could lead to a conventional imbalance in the latter area. Here, and possibly also in the Gulf, the result might be that some countries would look to nuclear weapons to reestablish the balance. Israel already at least possesses the capacity to build nuclear devices in a very short time, and other countries might follow. The spread of nuclear technology for peaceful purposes to Iran, Egypt, Libya and Saudi Arabia opens vast possibilities for nuclear proliferation.[33]

IV. Intentions behind the oil weapon

Having tentatively assessed the damage potential and the capabilities which the oil weapon provides and the limitations and preconditions for its successful application, we will now try to outline possible intentions and objectives, as well as situations which might lead one or more producers to use the oil weapon again.

It is assumed that intentions are shaped by two sets of factors: internal and external. Internal factors include the interests of the decision-makers and influences and pressures on them from within their society, including ideologies and perceptions. Ideologies are thought to correspond at least loosely with the interests of the political and economic elites and counter-elites but might develop their own momentum and are therefore worth separate consideration. Foreign policy factors include any producer's regional and global relationships and the alliances and foreign policy objectives of the other countries. It is also assumed that the behaviour of the producer states will not be guided by outside powers (at least not where this would interfere with the interests of the producer country or, more precisely, its leadership). It seems unlikely that the West will regain its previous degree of control over the oil producers (even though closer economic interaction might lead the producers into considerable dependence on the West and therefore restrict their freedom of action), and the hypothesis of 'Soviet hands on the tap' is highly improbable for the same reasons which apply to the West (strength of Arab nationalism, awareness of power, declining value of military force as a means of control) and because the Soviet Union faces certain additional weaknesses (her limited economic potential, the fact that Soviet goods and technology are often non-competitive with the West's, and the fact that the Soviet bloc cannot provide an alternative market for Middle East oil).

Let us first consider the internal and external setting of three producers – Iran, Iraq, and Saudi Arabia. These are the three countries which, during the period under consideration (or at least the latter half of it), might be able to cut back production sufficiently to cause considerable damage to consumers. They are also to a certain extent representative of the producers in general, since they cover two Arab regimes, one progressive and one conservative, and one non-Arab producer. Furthermore, all three states border on the Persian Gulf and are linked by a variety of coinciding and conflicting interests.

Iran

Iran is definitely the most powerful of the three states. Her population now numbers about 32 million people, during the last decade she has rapidly developed an industrial sector which is not dependent on oil, and the country contains rich natural resources apart from oil. She is also one of Asia's biggest importers and, last but not least, is a formidable military power with a modern army, navy and air force.

Iran's rapid development into a state of regional-power status during the last decade was the result of a process of determined reform (the White Revolution) initiated from the top, without any participation by the population in the political and economic decision making. The Shah is still the main, overwhelmingly important political factor, and he controls the political process by a variety of means. Political opposition is virtually eliminated by co-opting potential counter-elites into the present system and by suppression. In a broader perspective, the Shah's power rests on two pillars: the combined support of the old upper class, which his land reform programme turned from a feudal, land-based group into an industrially-based group, and the growing middle class in the cities; and, secondly, the loyalty of the armed forces (and specifically the officer corps). These groups also profited most from the White Revolution.

Political stability and economic progress are still closely interconnected. To assure the survival of his regime, the Shah has to accommodate the demands of his main supporters and also to defuse the potential for social conflict by substantially raising the living standard of hitherto neglected groups and classes. The pledge of further rapid economic growth and development is therefore based not only on economic but also on political reasons. Both are reflected in the main objectives of the new 1973–78 development plan, which aims for rapid economic growth, equitable distribution of income and wealth, a better socio-economic balance between rural and urban areas, administrative reform and stronger national defence, as well as expanded industrial output and international trade.

This programme clearly shows Iran's capacity to absorb even higher oil revenues to a large extent. Moreover, her comparatively limited oil reserves allow her to go for higher crude oil prices, since she does not have to be concerned about the eventual substitution of Middle East oil by other sources. By the time this substitution is reasonably advanced Iran can hope to have an economic base which will allow her to halt any crude exports and concentrate on goods produced with her own oil as a raw material and a source of cheap energy.

A large portion of future oil revenues will be absorbed by defence. The 1973–74 budget allocated slightly more than $2 billion for that purpose, and the defence budget is expected to run at 25 per cent or more of each national budget during the five-year period of the development plan.[34] Iranian defence expenditure helps to ensure the loyalty of the officer corps, which might be the only possible threat to the present political system, and strengthen the army, which has the potential to crush any internal opposition to the present order. But defence expenditure also serves various external functions – mainly, it seems, as an instrument of an ambitious foreign policy designed to increase Iran's influence in the region and to provide an integrative force, a common focus for nationalist sentiments of the whole Iranian people. The impressive arms build-up can therefore be expected to continue, and might also be reinforced by an indigenous arms industry.

Iran's foreign policy unfolds mainly in two spheres: global and regional. The global setting is dominated by Iran's long border with Russia, by past experience of Russian interference in Iran's internal affairs and by the Russian objective of securing access to warm-water ports in the Indian Ocean. The underlying pattern of Iran's relations with the superpowers is therefore clearly pro-Western – mistrust of Soviet intentions and reliance on the United States as the main ally – and a fundamental reversal of the pattern seems unlikely as long as the present regime remains in power. In the day-to-day aspects of diplomacy, however, Iran sets out formally to accord strictly equal treatment to both the United States and the Soviet Union; a state visit by the Shah to Washington is consequently balanced by one to Moscow. Iran has a wide range of trade and economic relations with the Soviet Union and has even bought some weapons there since 1967, when she concluded a small-arms deal worth some $110 million. She has recently also introduced China into this balancing act (Peking supports Iran's arms build-up and her claim that only littoral states should be responsible for the security in the Persian Gulf).

Iran justifies her concern about the Persian Gulf as a defensive precaution against possible encirclement by hostile, pro-Soviet states. Iraq has been her main source of anxiety, since the 1958 revolution there, because the progressive governments which followed the fall of the Hashemite monarchy have all proved more or less hostile to Iran. The main bone of contention has been the dispute over the Shatt el-Arab waterway. There have also been tensions between the two over alleged Iranian interference in the Kurdish problem in Iraq and over the expulsion of Iranians from Iraq; sporadic border incidents occurred, the last in 1974, and both sides tried to foster internal problems of the other country.

The Iraqi-Soviet treaty of friendship in 1972 and Soviet diplomatic progress in India and Afghanistan intensified Iranian fear of encirclement by Soviet allies, as did the danger to Persian Gulf stability posed by the South Yemen and by the Popular Front for the Liberation of Oman (PELO), a group supported mainly by the South Yemen, and probably also Iraq, which has been conducting a guerilla war in the Omani province of Dhofar.

Against this potential threat to her vital trade links in the Persian Gulf, Iran tried to establish her predominance there, using a combination of military superiority and diplomatic moves. She imposed a military solution on the dispute over the Tumb Islands with the Sheikhdoms of Sharjah and Ras al Khaimah by simply occupying the islands, and she gave military assistance to the Sultan of Oman in his fight against the rebellion in Dhofar. On the other hand the patronage she is exerting over the sheikhdoms on the west coast of the Gulf builds on close ties between the two Gulf coasts and on educational and health assistance Iran has made available for the United Arab Emirates. Iran also dropped her claim to Bahrain as a gesture of goodwill when Britain withdrew her presence in the Gulf, and it seems that she has effectively taken over from Britain the role of guaranteeing the *status quo* in the Gulf. The existence of the conservative sheikhdoms prevents closer co-operation by the radical forces in the Persian Gulf, although a fundamental change in one of them (as opposed to a palace revolt) might well trigger a similar development in others, eventually turning the whole west coast of the Gulf into a progressive, nationalistic and possibly united front, hostile to Iranian influence in the area.

To promote stability in the Persian Gulf and prevent an Arab-Iranian confrontation, Iran tried to improve her relations with the Arab world after the October war, using both economic assistance and diplomatic support. This strategy proved successful, and it reached its climax in the announcement in March 1975 of the outlines of an overall agreement with Iraq to settle all disputes between the two countries which traded Iraqi concessions in the Shatt el-Arab conflict for discontinuation of Iranian support for the Kurdish rebellion in Iraq. Whether this agreement will prove durable, remains to be seen.

In an attempt to secure Iran's trade interests and foster her importance in the wider region, the Shah directed his attention to the Indian Ocean. Again his main interest seemed to lie in preserving the *status quo*. After the Indo-Pakistani war Iran made it clear that she could not tolerate a further disintegration of Pakistan, but at the same time tried to achieve friendly relations with India. She also offered to mediate in the conflict between Pakistan and Afghanistan. Since Pakistan takes a growing interest in fostering her relations with the Arab world (the air forces of Abu Dhabi and Libya employ Pakistani pilots, and Pakistan would obviously be interested in forging close economic links with the Arab states), Iran can also hope to contribute indirectly to stability in the region by close co-operation with Pakistan. The same objective can also be assumed to underlie Iran's new interest in the Central Treaty Organization (CENTO) and in the Regional Co-operation for Development Programme with Turkey and Pakistan (which ultimately envisages a customs union comparable to the European Free Trade Association or the early European Community).

Here, another fundamental concern of Iranian foreign policy becomes visible. If Iran is to press on with her industrialization programmes her own domestic market might soon be insufficient to absorb the increased industrial production, and the country will look for new markets in the region. Indeed, it looks as if economic considerations might constitute a very important motive behind Iran's foreign policy — and probably also the only 'offensive' motive, the pursuit of which needs political stability and appears to be linked to the present *status quo* in the area.[35]

To sum up, one can make the following points about the Iranian attitudes towards the use of oil power and the oil weapon. Assuming internal political stability – and indeed as one prerequisite of such stability – Iran's oil revenues will be used largely for development and social change, economic growth and the diversification of oil power. Oil power and the economic strength and military influence derived from it will be used to secure the regional *status quo* in the Persian Gulf and the Indian Ocean, probably accompanied by an expansion of Iranian economic and political influence which would render the country a regional power centre. The use of the oil weapon seems highly unlikely and would probably only occur in a situation where Iran felt some fundamental interest was threatened in a way which it was beyond the scope of her other – considerable – capabilities to cope with.

Iraq

Like Iran, Iraq is a country with considerable potential for economic growth – mainly in the agricultural, but also to some extent in the industrial sector. She possesses a vast area of potentially fertile land and rich, if still not fully exploited, water resources. The population of about ten million includes many skilled and professional people. However, Iraq's overall performance in the economic field lagged behind Iran's; between 1964 and 1969 her annual average growth in Gross National Product only reached some 5.8 per cent. While the performance has improved since then, a comparison of her potential and actual achievements leads one to conclude that in the past Iraq has missed a chance of economic development.

The present government has therefore opted for an economic policy of rapid growth through effective exploitation of oil reserves. It is intended to create a diversified industrial base of a non-capitalist nature (i.e., a mixed economy heavily relying on the public sector) and to use agrarian reform as the chosen way to achieve social justice and more equal income distribution. As in the case of Iran, the military forms a strong pressure group which will have to be accommodated and controlled if the present regime is to survive, but it does also look as if survival will be possible in the long run only if the government succeeds in raising the standard of living throughout the country.

Between 1961 and 1970, the Kurdish revolt and the consequent almost continuous state of civil war in the north of the country contributed to the relatively poor performance of the Iraqi economy (according to one estimate, the war absorbed 90 per cent of annual oil revenues[36]). In 1970, it looked as if a settlement was finally in sight: Baghdad and the Kurdish leaders agreed on a 15-point programme for Kurdish autonomy to be implemented by 1974. However, relations between Baghdad and the Kurds gradually deteriorated, and in March 1974, after the central government's unilateral declaration of an 'autonomy law' unacceptable to the Kurds, renewed fighting broke out. The agreement with Iran in March 1975, which resulted in the withdrawal of

Iranian support (in hardware, logistics and troops), allowed Baghdad to launch a decisive military offensive which, in combination with strong Iranian pressure on the Kurdish leadership, succeeded in forcing the Pesh Merga (Kurdish irregulars) to leave Iraq or surrender. Whether this is the end of the long Kurdish fight for autonomy within Iraq remains to be seen, but for the time being another obstacle to rapid internal development and economic growth has been removed.

There can be no doubt that Iraq does desperately need a decisive new development effort, especially in the rural areas which hold the majority of the population. The country has a great deal of potentially fertile land, but in order to develop it a large and expensive system of drainage and irrigation is needed to bring down the high water table level and reverse the process of salinization which affects large areas. Current plans provide for the reclamation of no less than one million hectares at a cost of £2,000 million, but even this represents only one-fifth of the land which needs improvement. A system of dams and irrigation channels to control and utilize the rich water resources of the Euphrates and the Tigris needs huge investments – and so do the government's plans to transform agriculture into a largely mechanized sector based on co-operatives.

Industrialization is less urgent in Iraq than in other developing countries, since the country is basically agrarian, and her agriculture could probably accommodate twice her present population. But while the 1970–74 development plan gave high priority to agriculture, industrialization was also an important objective. Iraq already has a small industrial base (employing roughly 10 per cent of the labour force in 1971) which she plans to extend rapidly, and she is well off for raw materials other than oil (deposits of iron ore, chromite, copper, lead and zinc have been found in the north, and test drilling is now being carried out). The 1970–74 development plan envisaged a total investment of some $4,700 million, and the present plan (1974–79) has provisionally allocated $7,500 million, so that the greater part of any increased oil revenues could be absorbed. The government seems aware of the country's present opportunities and has decided to exploit them fully by expanding the oil sector as quickly as possible; production, currently running at 2.2 million b/d, is to increase to 6 million b/d in 1981.[37]

Iraq's foreign policy setting may be described on two levels: that of her relationships with the great powers, and that of her relationships with other countries in the region. With regard to the former, Iraq's close alliance with Moscow, formalized in the treaty of friendship in 1972, is the outstanding feature. The Baghdad regime's hostility to 'Imperialism' and 'Zionism', its socialist convictions and the need for assistance in the 'battle of endurance' against the Western oil companies made the government almost naturally turn to the Soviet Union, which became the main supplier of arms and economic assistance. Furthermore, the need for a powerful ally to balance Iran's overwhelming military power and Iraq's isolation in the Arab world further enhanced the need for outside support. This isolation was felt increasingly in

Baghdad as developments in other Arab countries turned in a conservative direction – for example with the ousting of the Ali Sabri group by President Sadat in Egypt and the abortive Sudanese *coup* by a left-wing coalition with strong Communist support (the short-lived government in Khartoum was immediately recognized by Baghdad). After the 1973 war, Iraq again diverged from the mainstream of Arab opinion concerning the Israeli-Arab conflict, rejecting any political solution and declaring full support for the Palestinians and later, when differences of opinion arose in the Palestinian Liberation Organization about the future approach towards the conflict, she stood by the hard-liners of the 'Palestinian Rejection Front'.

Internal reasons also favoured a closer link with Moscow: the Ba'th regime wanted to integrate the Communist Party into government and, while relaxation of earlier tough suppression of the Communists helped rapprochement with Moscow, the Soviet Union presumably also used her influence to achieve accommodation between Ba'thists and Iraqi Communists. Finally, Baghdad hoped to isolate the Kurds, who in the past received some support from the Soviet Union and from the Iraqi Communists.

Even though the Soviet Union is undoubtedly Baghdad's main ally, in recent times Iraq has repeatedly shown a desire to improve relations with the West.[38] This is probably because economic relations with the West are more profitable than support from the Soviet Union and her allies in Eastern Europe, and the Iraqi government was reportedly not very happy with the latter's economic assistance (a Czech refinery at Basrah, for instance, was not completed to schedule). Big contracts in the oil sector are now expected to go mostly to Western companies, and there is a clear desire to get on better terms with European countries. Iraq's short- and medium-term need for Western assistance and know-how as well as the need for long-term export markets for her vast potential oil production make such co-operation attractive for her.

On the regional level, Iraq's position is characterized by her isolation in the Arab world and her policy of opposing the *status quo* in the Gulf. Saudi Arabia and Iran, both allied to the United States and linked to the Western capitalist economy, are deeply suspicious of the radical government in Baghdad and its claim to a bigger say in Gulf politics. One of the bones of contention has repeatedly been Kuwait. In 1961 President Qasem claimed Iraqi sovereignty over this small but oil-rich state, but was thwarted by British and Arab military support to Kuwait. After Kuwait refused an Iraqi demand for a loan in December 1972 tensions and border clashes occurred. The underlying reasons for the dispute with Kuwait, however, are more complicated and reflect economic issues (Iraq's need for a new, large oil terminal in view of her small coastline and her dependence on access to the Gulf via the Shatt el-Arab, and disputes over the potentially very rich sea-bed in the north of the Gulf) as well as fear of Iran's predominance and the threat it posed to Iraqi sea communications through the Gulf. Iraq's 1973 demand for parts of Kuwait territory met with the opposition not only of Iran, but also Saudi Arabia; Iran's offer of military assistance to Kuwait was in fact turned down, but a later offer by Saudi Arabia was accepted, and Saudi troops moved into Kuwait to protect the border with Iraq.

An analysis of probable future intentions suggests that Iraq is much more likely to resort to the oil weapon than Iran. Internal factors tend to produce radical and revolutionary external policies, and the country is basically striving to change the present regional *status quo*. The leadership might therefore feel threatened by external forces and react aggressively against these – real or perceived – threats. Once involved in a regional conflict, however, Iraq might quickly find herself in a position of inferiority which could only be coped with either by relying on massive Soviet support or alternatively by using the oil weapon to influence the behaviour of her immediate opponents via pressure on their Western allies. On the other hand, one has to bear in mind that Iraq's capabilities are restricted, first because the oil weapon could probably only be applied effectively in the context of a producer action group, and secondly because she will need a large amount of her oil revenue to sustain and expand her programme of rapid economic growth and social change. Since economic success is probably also an important factor for the internal stability of the present order, this would work as a moderating influence on her foreign policy and reduce the incentive to use the oil weapon.

Iraq's foreign policy in the first months of 1975 did indeed show a marked swing towards more moderate policies and towards improving relations both with other Arab countries (except Syria) and with Iran. This would appear to reflect a concentration on domestic affairs and rapid internal development, and possibly also a desire not to become too dependent on the Soviet Union. The March 1975 outline agreement on settling all her disputes with Iran highlights this change in Iraqi foreign policy.

Saudi Arabia

In Saudi Arabia the present leadership must above all be concerned about the potential danger of a radical nationalist opposition at home. This would most likely stem from the officer corps, and unrest and attempts to overthrow the monarchy reported in 1969, followed by drastic purges in the air force, demonstrate that a Libyan-type *coup* is a distinct possibility within the rest of this decade. A fundamental change in the political system seems more likely in Saudi Arabia than in either of the other two countries discussed here. The survival of the regime probably depends on its capacity to avoid alienation of the officer corps and accommodate and integrate it. This group asks not only for material privileges (which will be easy to provide) but probably also for a gradual expansion of political participation and of consideration of the political mood within the army (which is likely to be more nationalist and moderate than the present leadership). A return to the previous regional isolation of the 1960s, therefore, seems improbable: Saudi Arabia will further try to play an important role in Arab affairs, designed to accommodate or isolate potential external adversaries. This trend is likely to gain momentum when the political elite is extended to include the army officers and the technocrats; these groups will become more important as the formerly direct relationship between ruler and ruled in the traditional structure is gradually eroded – a process which has already started. Should the present leadership succeed in satisfying these potential counter-elites and integrating them into the political and economic structure by giving them special privileges, more influence and some say in foreign policy, and should the monarchy effectively manage social and economic change without losing control over the side-effects of that process, there is probably a good chance for the survival of the present order.

As for superpower relations, the Soviet Union seems to be excluded as a potential ally under present circumstances for ideological as well as political reasons. If regional considerations allow (i.e., if the United States is acceptable within the Arab world as an ally), Saudi Arabia can be expected to continue to rely on American support but in a looser relationship than in the past. Economic links with Japan and Western Europe will be accompanied by political relations of greater importance, and the country will probably develop a rather diffuse foreign policy via involvement in various international organizations dealing with the recycling and investment of Saudi oil revenues and economic assistance to the Third World. This will probably also result in various bilateral agreements.

In the regional arena Saudi Arabia at the moment seems to be basically satisfied with the *status quo* in the Persian Gulf, though there is a certain amount of suspicion about Iranian intentions.[39] These are unlikely to lead to serious conflicts, however, and Saudi Arabia will probably concentrate on the task of spending her oil surplus.

Saudi Arabia's economic position is somewhat different from other oil producing states, since the sheer magnitude of her oil reserves places the country in a separate category: she may be able to produce crude oil well into the twenty-first century, and possibly even into the twenty-second (i.e., into a period when oil might have lost its importance). It also looks doubtful whether she will be able to build up, to a degree sufficient to sustain the country's standard of living, an industrial base capable of using all her oil to produce goods based on cheap oil both as a source of energy and as a raw material. Any further disruption of the international oil market, therefore, would increase the danger of making the Saudi oil worthless. For this reason the country cannot be interested in further disturbances of supplies and price increases; a stable relationship with consumer countries would serve her interest best. Undoubtedly Saudi Arabia will do a lot to create an economic base and diversify her sources of income, and there thus is some potential for oil revenue absorption. But the enormous revenues which have been predicted for her will to a considerable extent have to be directed into investments outside the country, and even outside the region – which again will probably contribute to a search for stable consumer-producer relations.

Capabilities mark Saudi Arabia as the country most likely to use the oil weapon. Given the present political order, however, an analysis of possible intentions seems to indicate that, while the decision-makers might be pressed into using their powerful leverage, they are not very likely to use it as an active instrument of their foreign policy. For various reasons, Saudi Arabia would probably prefer a stable producer-consumer relationship, and she seems satisfied with the present *status quo*. On the other hand, the Saudi government would appear to be more exposed to pressures both from inside and outside the country than Iraq. The present regime's vulnerability not only to internal challenges but also to radical Arab opposition from outside is considerable, and to accommodate these forces the government might have to adopt policies much more radical than it would like. The assassination of King Faisal and the smooth transition of power demonstrated the relative strength of the Saudi regime, which rests basically on the vast royal family and its omnipresent influence within society and politics. On the other hand, the loss of Faisal's unique position of strength both in Saudi Arabia and in the Arab world could well lead to the new regime being more strongly exposed to the various pressures from within and outside – pressures, which will often be contradictory, therefore complicating predictions about the future course of the policies of King Khalid and Crown Prince Fahd.

Other possibilities that might lead Saudi Arabia once more to unsheath her oil weapon could stem from a fundamental change in the present social and political order. This would create a new type of situation, or, as an intermediate possibility, might lead to a more adventurous foreign policy in the Persian Gulf designed to reduce the Iranian influence (which in itself would constitute a challenge to the *status quo*).

The role of ideology: nationalism and its future importance

Modern Arab nationalism played a significant part in the erosion of Western influence and control over the Arab world. It is made up of strong anti-Western sentiment, inclination towards various forms of socialism (public ownership of industry and the nationalization of foreign interests as a means to rapid social and economic modernization and greater equality) and, last but not least, fervent opposition to the state of Israel. It will be of some significance in the future, though most likely with considerable changes. Further successes by radical Arab nationalism will have to be achieved against conditions less favourable than during the last two decades. In the past this nationalism has been the ideology of a new class pressing for political power against a traditional order often marked by inefficiency, corruption and inability to fulfil the growing expectations of the peoples concerned. The vast oil revenues available to the oil-producing countries (which are largely governed by conservative regimes) might now reverse that precondition. There is a good chance that these regimes might not only succeed in maintaining the political and social *status quo* within their own societies against the background of social and economic change; they might even be able to reverse the swing of the 1960s towards the Left in the Arab world (indeed they have already started to do so).

The most important ideological factors of the future will probably be strong nationalism (mainly local but on some issues also pan-Arab – e.g., vis-à-vis Israel), independence from foreign interference and influence, and social justice (which, given the enormous resources of the oil-producers, could be achieved through a purely 'capitalist' approach). Arab nationalism could be conveniently married with Islamic tradition, which might as easily result in a radical as in a conservative orientation (cf. the different, but equally 'Islamic', ideologies of Saudi Arabia and Libya). Another trend, which could actually tend to erode the importance of ideologies, is a pragmatic and technocratic orientation towards solving the various problems accompanying social change. Such an approach will more and more replace the ideological approach, since social tensions and conflict will diminish as the oil wealth spreads throughout the Arab countries, and the problem changes from sharing scarce resources into effectively allocating and managing vast resources.

Overall, then, a gradual decline in the importance of ideology can be expected, though some relics will undoubtedly remain. Among them will be strong antagonism towards any attempt by outside powers to interfere with the sovereignty of the states in the area, and some degree of common opposition against Israel – the actual degree depending largely on the progress made towards an Israeli-Arab settlement.

Possible future application of the oil weapon

Like other weapons, the oil weapon has offensive and defensive capabilities. The threat and the application of the oil weapon for defensive purposes would aim at securing vital interests of an oil-producer country (or, more precisely, its incumbent regime). The offensive use would aim to increase power and influence and would involve a change in the *status quo*. In this section we shall briefly consider three possibilities: the defensive use of the oil weapon against consumer countries; defensive and offensive use of the oil weapon in a regional context, with the consumer countries being used as targets (but only to further the ultimate purpose of achieving objectives against other countries in the Middle East) and the offensive use of the oil weapon in a global context.

The most obvious contingency in which the oil weapon would be used is a threat to the sovereignty and integrity of a producer or one of its allies by a consumer state attempting to intervene militarily or by subversive means. The fundamental nature of the threat posed to a producer by such intervention would remove many of the restraints and limitations of the oil weapon discussed earlier. The supply interruption would probably take the form of destruction of oil installations, since immediate concern for the survival of the present regime in the producer country would override consideration of future consequences for consumers or even the producers themselves. (Such a situation is equivalent to a typical escalation process in warfare, which increases the damage for both sides.) Such an attack would also create considerable pressure for producer solidarity and vastly improve the chances of co-ordinated producer action. This contingency is therefore unlikely.

Oil power and the oil weapon could, of course, also be used in the defence of important economic interests of the producer countries: e.g., stability of the terms of trade (the ratio of oil price to the price of goods imported by producers), pursuit of economic development and modernization, and a stable return on foreign investments. The various forms of oil power could also be used to prevent erosion of the producers' present power by consumer co-operation in sharing out oil supplies in a crisis or by diversifying away from OPEC oil.

Looking at the regional setting, any future application of the oil weapon seems unlikely, except in two contexts: the Israeli-Arab conflict and a clash in the Persian Gulf. The Israeli-Arab conflict is the most likely contingency; should fighting break out again on a large scale, or the present negotiations for a settlement end in a stalemate without further prospect of at least some progress along the lines desired by the Arab states, then a new application of the oil weapon seems almost inevitable. This issue provides a framework for common action by Arab producers, and they would be under considerable pressure both from within and outside their own countries to repeat the past success in using the oil weapon; besides, the Arab producers have committed themselves to a solution of the Israeli-Arab conflict.

In the Persian Gulf, all the three states thought to be potential unilateral users of the oil weapon are littoral states and involved in the various actual or possible conflict constellations in the area, each involving a clash between two or more large producing countries: anti-*status quo* powers (Iraq, South Yemen) against *status quo* powers (Iran, Saudi Arabia); Iran against Saudi Arabia; and Iraq against Iran.

As for the first possibility (which could, but need not, involve South Yemen and other revolutionary forces, like the Popular Front for the Liberation of Oman), the basic intention and the driving force would be Iraq's desire for greater influence in the Persian Gulf. She might rely on other countries or groups in the Gulf for support and, even though such an alliance would not appear very stable, it might serve her purposes in the phase of common struggle against the *status quo*. She could also hope for Soviet support in such an attempt to expand her influence and change the balance of power in the Gulf. Various arguments seem to indicate, though, that the possibility of such a conflict is fairly remote. First, the overwhelming military superiority of Iran and (potentially) the even greater superiority of Iran and Saudi Arabia together would not allow Iraq openly to challenge those two states without Soviet support – but such support would inevitably lead to superpower conflict. Besides, the Soviet Union appears interested in good relations with Iran and could probably not be brought to take sides openly and exclusively. The same argument might even apply to China, which anyway would be unable to lend sufficient military support. The success of clandestine attempts to overthrow the regimes in Saudi Arabia and Iran will depend largely on the internal state of affairs in these countries, but the chances do not appear very promising. Still, open conflict between the groups espousing and attacking the *status quo* in the Gulf might result from an escalation process, without either side really intending to go to war, or from Iran just using a pretext to try to rid herself of the hostile regime in Baghdad.

Iraq might also try to confront the conservative powers separately. The success of an attempt against Saudi Arabia would depend partly on the state of the Iranian-Saudi relations, but even if Iran were not involved in the confrontation, Saudi Arabia would still be a formidable opponent. One bone of contention which could produce such a clash might be Iraq's claim to Kuwait, or parts of Kuwaiti territory; on this point Iraq could feel compelled, for internal reasons, to take risks rather than lose face and retreat. If Saudi Arabia were unable to cope with the Iraqi threat, Kuwait could expect some Arab support (military and/or political) and probably also Western assistance in the form of strong pressure on Moscow to restrain Iraq, or perhaps direct intervention with arms deliveries and even troops. Should the West be reluctant to give assistance Saudi Arabia and Kuwait might threaten to use their oil weapon in order to secure it. In such a conflict, and if there were a largely bilateral market structure, Iraq could use the leverage of her oil power against, say, France to force her to support Iraq politically and with arms deliveries, thereby creating a rift in the Western alliance.

The same issue of leadership and influence in the Gulf might also lead to a confrontation between Iraq and Iran, and Iraq might even be able to enlist the support of other Arab countries against Iran. There could be a danger of superpower confrontation arising out of an Iraqi-Iranian conflict, depending on what attitude Moscow took. Once again, the balance of power in the Gulf makes such a conflict unlikely – it would only be possible as 'accidental war', the consequence of hazardous brinkmanship. Nonetheless, if a conflict between Iraq and Saudi Arabia and/or Iran did occur, it would lead to serious disruption of oil supplies, since fighting would affect the trade routes in the Gulf.

At the moment, such a clash appears rather remote, given the recent improvement of relations between Iraq and the conservative states in the Gulf. However, a potential for conflict does exist, due not only to the already mentioned bones of contention between Iraq and Iran, but also to the ethnic differences and historical distrust between Arabs and Persians. Indeed the Iran-Iraq détente appears very vulnerable to any change in leadership, especially in Baghdad (Iraq's settlement with Iran has already come under severe attack from some Arab countries, especially Syria). In addition, a fall in demand for OPEC oil could be caused by consumers developing alternative sources of oil and energy supplies, and this could lead to a need to allocate production quotas among OPEC countries. Such a situation might find Iraq in an awkward position, since she has very good prospects of substantially raising production and also needs revenues urgently. She might then decide to adopt an aggressive export policy of undercutting, which would be mainly directed against Iran and Saudi Arabia.

Saudi Arabia and Iran could possibly clash if the United Arab Emirates and other small sheikhdoms on the west coast of the Gulf weakened and disintegrated. Both countries might then be tempted to establish their control over that area, since a *status quo* policy would no longer be possible. A similar development could result from an 'imperial' attitude by Saudi Arabia towards the sheikhdoms, possibly as a consequence of internal change in Saudi Arabia. It seems, however, that such a conflict would be counter-productive for both parties, so long as they intend to contain Iraqi and Soviet influence, and the incentive to reach agreement would be strong. Furthermore, the fact that the United States is the main supplier of arms and the principal ally of both countries would act as a restraint, as would the fact that war between them could not result in a decisive victory for either but might weaken both. The possibility of such a conflict appears remote; nevertheless, if it did occur disruption in the flow of oil would be likely. Besides the impact of military actions in the Gulf, supplies might be affected by the fact that Saudi Arabia, as the weaker side, would probably be tempted to resort to the oil weapon if she feared a decisive Iranian success.

A fundamentally new situation could result from a radical military *coup* in Saudi Arabia. If Iraq succeeded in engineering a Ba'thist-inspired *putsch* in Riyadh, a common front of Arab Gulf states against Iran could develop. But, given the potential for internal conflict and tension within such a grouping, it would probably not last for very long and would soon change into Saudi-Iraqi rivalry. The outcome might be the same if an independent military regime took power in Riyadh. Such a government would probably steer an independent course, opposed to Iran and her predominance in the Gulf (which it would definitely try to challenge, the bone of contention again being the small west-coast sheikhdoms), but also opposed to Iraq and her claim to leadership at least of the Arab side of the Gulf. Such a development in Saudi Arabia would almost certainly intensify the tripolarity in the Gulf and lead on to new possibilities for great-power confrontation. The Soviet Union would either be reluctant to take sides at all and would try to accommodate both parties in order to avoid conflict, or would vote for one side and (if the United States were not accepted for ideological reasons) leave the other without an ally. This might lead Iraq or Saudi Arabia to try to use China as a great-power ally. Alternatively, Europe or some European states could be drawn in as a balancing factor, again with serious consequences for great-power relations in other areas. The threat of the oil weapon would loom large, since a radical and ideologically dedicated Saudi government would possess enormous damage potential as long as the imbalance of bargaining power between this producer and the consumers prevails.

The possibilities discussed so far have concentrated on oil power being used mainly to involve consumers in regional conflicts to achieve producer objectives. Oil power and the oil weapon could also, in some circumstances, be used to minimize consumer involvement: the producers might try, by using the various sanctions and rewards oil power provides, to reduce consumer links with Israel and other countries considered hostile. A strategy of isolating Israel has been applied before, in Africa and with the economic boycott organized against companies investing in Israel. Japan, for instance, would find it difficult to resist sustained pressure to break diplomatic relations with Israel, and the only reason for the Arabs not to demand this is that such a development would have hardly any impact on the Israeli-Arab conflict.

Regional objectives or defence of vital interests are not the only possible motives for the application of oil power, however. The Arab producers might strive to become the leaders of the Third World. Some countries (Libya, Algeria) have indeed voiced such aspirations, but in practical terms oil power has not yet been used systematically for this purpose. Economically, only a limited part of Arab financial resources has been made available for the Third World, which has suffered most from higher oil prices. In principle, the oil producers could try to achieve the gradual redistribution of wealth on a global scale and the reversal of the trend towards consistently growing inequality between developed and less-developed countries. This would, however, require an extremely skilful application of all aspects of oil power and its derivatives – especially price and cash.

A starting point for such a strategy, which would aim at a controlled conflict between developed and less-developed countries, would be a two-tier price system for oil, giving developing countries a specially favourable price. This could be accompanied by a quota system favouring supplies to developing countries and keeping deliveries to developed countries scarce and expensive (withdrawal of the special status for Third World countries could block any attempts to re-export the cheap oil to developed countries). The vast oil reserve surplus which would probably prevail when the market was split into a large 'seller's' market and a small and artificial 'buyer's' market could be used as an additional means of encouraging industrialization and rapid development in the Third World. Not all the money would have to come from the oil producers, since they could use oil power to bring the developed countries to take an equal share in the institutions designed to finance the Third World development plans. The result of such a co-ordinated effort would be to impose low growth-rates on at least some consuming countries, while the economic development of the Third World would be speeded up. It would become very attractive for developed countries to invest 'upstream', where raw materials and cheap energy would provide favourable conditions and new large markets would be within reach, and one could imagine some consequent transfer of industrial production into the Third World. This would not necessarily be opposed to the long-term interest of the developed world, since it would defuse the potentially explosive aspects of the world class-structure, and the developed countries would probably still be in control of the world economy through their superior know-how, research and development capacity, and control of the world-wide communication and information systems.

The economic co-operation between the Arab states and the Third World countries would then have to be institutionalized politically. The first step might be an Organization of Raw Material Exporting Countries. Present institutions, like the United Nations and its affiliates, also could provide a framework for co-ordination, and no doubt the Arab states would have a very influential voice in any such institution. But they would have to be prepared not to seek dominance: they could only be successful if they stressed the basic unity of a Third World polarized against, but not in confrontation with, the developed countries.

Events in 1974–75 demonstrated that the OPEC countries will indeed strive for a leading role in the Third World. This became especially obvious in the discussion at the OPEC summit in Algiers and at the tripartite Paris meeting for the preparation of a producer/consumer conference. On both occasions OPEC states rallied behind the Algerian demand for a reform of the international economic order, which means above all a reorganization of the whole raw material trade between the Third World and the industrialized countries by means of producer cartels, so as to ensure stable returns for the producer countries. This would probably means some form of index-linking of raw material prices, as already suggested in the case of oil. OPEC's attempts to act as the *avant-garde* of the Third World would seem to be, at least in part, a power-increasing strategy adopted in the light of the United States' policy of non-cooperation in dealing with OPEC (though at the end of 1974 this policy changed somewhat towards a more co-operative approach). All the same, in 1974 the OPEC producers repeatedly managed to rally a substantial majority of Third World countries behind their policies, thereby asserting their intention of becoming a leading force in world politics as advocates of the less-developed countries.

The desirability of such a development could only be assessed after further detailed discussion, but it is unlikely to be realized fully. First, the degree of Arab unity required seems difficult to achieve. Since splits into various camps seem likely to continue (most notably a progressive-conservation division), various rivalries, on Third World strategies and on other matters, might emerge and partly offset each other (for instance, the competition between Libya and Saudi Arabia for political influence in certain African countries). Second, the Arab states seem to lack the capabilities required for leadership of the Third World. They do not have numbers of highly-educated people with specialist training, they do not have the planning and research capabilities for such a strategy of effectively assuming leadership in the manner outlined, and (considering the enormous amount of money needed to promote Third-World economic development) they might even lack the resources. The Arab states' oil wealth must be limited in duration, and they do not possess other resources sufficient to this task. They would also have to sacrifice some of their own interests (the reluctance to resort to a two-tier price system shows how difficult that is) and would probably have to increase production, so as to make sufficient amounts of oil available, without greatly increasing their revenues.

Finally, they would have to resist the temptation to create a clientele of dependent states which could also serve as markets for Arab products.

It seems more likely that certain aspects of this development will become reality, but in a different framework. The international system will be more differentiated. The developed states will be divided into the largely oil self-sufficient (possibly even oil-exporting) states, like the superpowers, Canada or Australia, and heavily dependent consumer states, like Japan and parts of Europe – and this would contradict predictions of various poles of more or less equal influence and importance. The developing countries will also be divided into the rich oil-exporting countries, a 'middle class' of countries with large raw material resources and some degree of self-sufficiency in oil, and, finally, the countries without significant natural resources of any kind. Simultaneously with this stratification of world society a network of linkages, based on various degrees of interdependence and imbalanced dependence will develop between various centres like the superpowers, Western Europe, Japan, China, the Arab countries and possibly other oil-producing countries, such as Iran or Venezuela. In particular, the Arab countries might function as a centre of the Islamic world or of parts of the African continent.

V. Conclusions

The picture emerging from our assessment of strength and weaknesses of the oil weapon is a complex one. Under present circumstances, its applicability would appear to be rather restricted; developments in the Israeli-Arab conflict still constitute the contingency most likely to lead the Arab oil producers once more to use the oil weapon, though open clashes in the Persian Gulf (which are in any case bound to lead to major supply interruptions) might also involve its deliberate application. Any analysis, however, cannot simply be based on present conditions, since oil power is derived from the state of the international oil market. This market is, in turn, subject to a wide range of influences, predominantly the strategies of major actors like producer and consumer governments and oil companies, and its dynamics are bound to influence strongly the ability of the producers to use their resource as a political instrument. The balance of power might swing back to the consumers of further towards the producers. In the short and medium term, the most essential and sensitive area appears to be the international distribution system; in the longer term, the geographical redistribution of supply-demand patterns might turn out to be the overriding element of change.

Should the producers acquire a sufficient share of the world tanker fleet to allow the discriminate application of the oil weapon, the range of this new factor in international relations could be expanded considerably. Under these circumstances it might be some developing countries which could be the most vulnerable consumers, for not only are they often dependent on one or two oil producers for substantial amounts of their energy supplies, but they might be the first to rely on rigid bilateral trade structures involving the tanker fleets of the oil producers. This vulnerability will no doubt be reflected in the foreign policies of such countries.

Leaving aside the possibility of such bilateral structures developing between oil producers and consumers, the result of our analysis might appear somewhat paradoxical. While the future possibilities for the application of the oil weapon seem very restricted, it will nonetheless be of very considerable importance in future international politics. This paradox is explained by the fact that the oil weapon, which is simply the ultimate sanction of oil power, is a sanction that will not be lightly resorted to but will nevertheless, by its very existence, constitute an omnipresent factor in international relations. Oil diplomacy will replace the actual use of the oil weapon because, while the latter is a relatively awkward and costly political instrument of last resort, oil diplomacy can make full use of all dimensions of oil power and the forms of power derived from it: threats, symbolic sanctions (embargoes without cutbacks, stoppages), wealth, military power and, finally, economic power. Already the influence of oil diplomacy can be felt in international organizations such as the United Nations, UNESCO, the IMF and the World Bank and in many areas of international economics, not to mention the Israeli-Arab conflict. Like other forms of power, oil power is diffuse and not quantifiable (it rather resembles credit-worthiness) and does not necessarily have to be congruent with the actual capabilities which back it: the oil producers are at the moment 'credited' with a power which could well exceed their actual capabilities.

The net result of the oil crisis in 1973–4 was a fundamental change in the international political system. A new group of actors has achieved prominence and begun to exert its influence in world politics. These powers will assume a mediating position between the highly developed countries and the majority of the Third World. They will in many aspects still be dependent on their great-power ally and their economic partners among developed countries, but their economic leverage will allow them to build a considerable and diversified power base, attracting surrounding states and areas which will then serve as raw material suppliers, markets and receivers of capital investment. The economic dependence and possible inferior military power of those countries would also open them to the political influence of the regional power.

Possible candidates for the regional power role are Iran (for parts of the Middle East and for the Indian sub-continent), Iraq (Arab world?), Saudi Arabia (Arab world, Africa), Algeria (Africa, Maghreb), Venezuela (Caribbean), Nigeria (West Africa), Indonesia (South-East Asia). The superpowers might use regional powers as substitutes for direct control and influence in certain areas of the Third World (as the United States has already been trying to do with Iran), but the regional powers will in the future probably strive for a higher degree of independence in which mutuality of interest will be paramount, and other forms of dependence will diminish in significance. This implies that regional powers might clash without their allies being able to prevent it (the foregoing discussion of Persian Gulf politics tried to speculate about such possibilities). Under the heading of mutuality of interest the consumer states will be asked to assist in the economic development of the oil-producing countries and in the building up of their power base by arms deliveries, technological assistance and political support. The producing governments might also want some help in the field of intelligence and counter-subversion capacities – in securing the internal order of their states against opposition groups.

One final point: our analysis of oil producers' possible intentions and the limited range of conflicts which might cause the oil weapon to be used again are largely based on the assumption of rational behaviour by the producer governments. While this assumption could be questioned, it would appear justified. First, the past behaviour of the oil producers has showed considerable skill and circumspection in their application of the oil weapon, and, second, successful application of the oil weapon requires co-operation between two or more producers to achieve sufficient damage potential (and potentially also sufficient control over the world tanker fleet). The assumption of irrationality would therefore demand joint irrationality by more than one producer government (this would even apply to Saudi Arabia, provided her production and her share of the international market do not increase significantly).

Nevertheless, a cataclysmic oil war cannot totally be ruled out. If the producers – or some of them – do not see any other option open to them and feel desperate enough to cause world-wide chaos, then 'total' oil war might break out. So long as the oil producers continue to supply the world with a vital share of its energy supply, the result would be a suicidal spiral of escalation and destruction on a world-wide scale.

Notes

1 Quoted in Walter Z. Laqueur, *The Struggle for the Middle East: The Soviet Union and the Middle East, 1958–1968* (Harmondsworth: Penguin, 1972), p. 153.
2 A. O. Hirschmann, *National Power and the Structure of Foreign Trade* (Berkeley and Los Angeles: University of California Press, 1945).
3 Cf. OECD Oil Committee, *Oil: the present situation and future prospects* (Paris, 1973), pp. 21–29. The United States, however, was an exception, since she had switched (although generally less impressively) from coal to gas, rather than to oil.
4 This is clearly demonstrated by comparing July 1972 and July 1973 supply patterns. During the intervening year indigenous production fell by 2.4 per cent, while crude oil imports increased by 62.5 per cent, residual fuel imports by 5.5 per cent and other oil product imports by 27.2 per cent, bringing the total import share to 6 million b/d out of a total supply of 17.5 million b/d (*Financial Times*, 14 September 1973). Between July and August 1973 alone, crude oil imports from the Arab states more than doubled, from 625,000 b/d to 1,285,000 b/d (*Arab Report and Record*, 16–31 October 1973, p. 484).
5 In 1967 Iran's production increased by 23 per cent while Iraq's fell by 11.5 per cent (Laqueur, p. 153); the United States increased production between May and August 1967 by about 1 million b/d (Sam H. Schurr *et al., Middle Eastern Oil and the Western World: Prospects and Problems*, New York: American Elsevier, 1971, p. 37).

6 *Neue Zürcher Zeitung*, 27 April 1974.
7 A comparison between foreign exchange holdings at the end of 1971 and figures for total import bills in the same year shows that Kuwait theoretically could pay for 5 years' imports, Libya for 3 years' and Saudi Arabia for 18 months'. See *Petroleum Press Service*, December 1973, p. 452; Charles Issawi, *Oil, The Middle East and The World* (Washington: Center for Strategic and International Studies, Georgetown University, 1972) Washington Papers No. 4, pp. 41–2.
8 In the late 1960s dependence on oil exports for gross foreign exchange earnings was around 75 per cent for Iraq, 85–90 per cent for Kuwait, Libya and Saudi Arabia, and close to 100 per cent for the sheikhdoms in the Persian Gulf. At the same time, the oil sector accounted for just under 20 per cent of GNP in Algeria and 33 per cent in Iraq; Saudi Arabia derived 55 per cent, Libya 60 per cent and Kuwait and the smaller sheikhdoms even higher percentages of GNP from the oil sector.
9 Gamal Abdel Nasser, *The Philosophy of the Revolution* (Cairo: Dar al-Kutub, 1955), pp. 67–69.
10 *Strategic Survey 1973* (London: IISS, 1974), p. 97.
11 European Community, 'The European Economy in 1973' (Brussels, 1974), p. 65; *Petroleum Economist*, April 1974, p. 175, June 1974, p. 24.
12 *Times*, 10 April 1974.
13 *Petroleum Economist*, March 1974, p. 98; European Commission, *Energy Balance of the Community* (Brussels, 1974).
14 *The Times*, 4 December 1973.
15 *The Times*, 23 November 1973.
16 The 'majors' control more than 60 per cent of the world tanker fleet, by ownership or long-term charter, and a similar proportion of world refinery capacity.
17 Total tonnage in mid-1974 was about 1.5 million dwt in crude, product, and liquefied natural gas (LNG) carriers (*Petroleum Economist*, August 1974, p. 305).
18 Arab orders amount to 4,783, 370 dwt. These orders include 714 million m^3 of LNG carriers for Kuwait and Algeria (*ibid.*, p. 307).
19 *Middle East Economic Digest*, 22 March 1974, p. 335.
20 *Petroleum Economist*, May 1974, p. 181.
21 Saudi Arabia has already indicated her intention to export 50 per cent of her oil in her own fleet by 1978.
22 M. A. Adelmann, *The World Petroleum Market* (Baltimore and London: Johns Hopkins U.P. 1972), p. 126, quotes prices between $100 and $138 per dwt for VLCC (very large crude carriers) from Japanese shipyards in early 1971.
23 *Ibid.*, pp. 104–60.
24 At the time of writing member countries are Belgium, Canada, Denmark, Germany, Ireland, Italy, Japan, Luxembourg, the Netherlands, New Zealand, Spain, Sweden, Switzerland, Turkey and Britain. Norway has a special associated status with the IEA.
25 Clyde H. Farnsworth, 'Mideast rivalries push oil prices', *International Herald Tribune*, 2 January 1974.
26 According to the report of a group of experts submitted to the Energy Co-ordinating Committee set up by the Washington Energy Conference, OPEC had unused capacity of 4.5 million b/d in April 1974. By the end of 1974 this surplus had reached over 6.2 million b/d.
27 An early 1975 World Bank estimate puts the accumulated OPEC surplus in 1980 at $460 billion at current prices ($248 billion at constant prices), of which Saudi Arabia, Kuwait, Qatar and the United Arab Emirates alone account for $335 billion. American government sources and estimates by the Chase Manhattan Bank project a lower figure for 1980.

28 Including the possibility of federations or alliances between producer and non-producer countries. Egypt alone will attract large sums simply because her political friendship is a key to influence in the Arab world as a whole.
29 The Arab countries have repeatedly threatened to use their revenue surpluses as a weapon, and after 1967 there was a shift of Arab money from Sterling into other currencies, mainly Francs. Libya also resorted to this method to punish Britain for her alleged complicity in the Iranian occupation of a few small islands in the Persian Gulf in November 1971. The Iraqi version, an appeal to withdraw all Arab funds from the United States, met with little approval. See Gerd Junne, 'Währungsspekulationen der Ölscheiche und Ölkonzerne', in H. Elsenhans (ed.), *Erdöl für Europa* (Hamburg: Hoffmann & Campe, 1974) pp. 277–302.
30 Kuwait, for example, keeps a large amount of her financial reserves as liquid as possible, to protect herself against such a measure (*The Economist*, 5 May 1973, p.44).
31 According to a report in *The Times*, (4 January 1974), Libya finances its own Palestinian underground movement and also contributes to Black September (£35 million), other Palestinian organizations (£20 million) and the Eritrean Liberation Front (£10 million), as well as opposition groups in Syria (£1.3 million), South Yemen (£1 million), Chad (£1.2 million) Morocco (£2 million), Tunisia (£1 million), Philippines (£2 million), Panama (£1.5 million), and Thailand (£300,000). See also *Arab Report and Record*, 5 January 1974, p.7.
32 For instance, Iran's recent purchase of 80 F-14 fighters from the United States, worth $1,800 million, far exceeds the total value of Iranian arms imports over the decade 1961–71. For further details on the arms trade, see Hanns Maull, 'The Arms Trade with the Middle East and North Africa', in *The Middle East and North Africa 1974/75* (London: Europa Publications, 1974), pp. 94–9.
33 Egypt might be provided with nuclear reactors and fuel by the United States and France, and Egyptian scientists are also working in Indian nuclear centres. Iran has its own Atomic Energy Commission, with an Argentinian adviser. She will receive two nuclear reactors and the necessary fuel from the United States (according to a provisional agreement) and two nuclear power stations are to be provided by France, which will also provide nuclear fuel and set up a nuclear research centre. Negotiations and agreements about nuclear co-operation exist between Iran and India, Canada, South Africa and possibly the Soviet Union. Saudi Arabia and Libya have also voiced interest in nuclear power plants. See *Middle East Economic Digest*, 5 July 1974, p. 764, 31 May 1974, p. 625; *Arab Report and Record*, 1–15 June 1974, p. 220.
34 Keith McLachlan, 'Strength through Growth: Iran on the March', *New Middle East*, June 1973, pp. 20–23
35 Iran has proposed a common market of the littoral states of the Indian Ocean which, according to an interview with the Shah in a Bombay weekly, should be built around a closer Indian-Iranian economic co-operation. Iran promised India considerable aid and arranged for oil deals at very favourable terms. Pakistan also will receive Iranian oil 'at a price we can afford', according to a Pakistani spokesman. Iran also negotiated large loans to, and economic co-operation projects with, Arab countries such as Egypt, Syria and Morocco. The agreement with Egypt provides *inter alia* for joint ventures in Egypt and Egyptian purchases of machinery, equipment and buses. See *Middle East Economic Digest*, 31 May 1974, p. 623; *The Economist*, 4 May 1974, p. 52.
36 Jean Gueyras, 'Les Dirigeants de Baghdad ont besoin de stabilité pour consolider leur succès dans le pays', *Le Monde Diplomatique*, July 1973, pp. 21, 28.
37 *The Middle East and North Africa 1972/3*, (London: Europa Publications, 1973), p.553; *Middle East Economic Digest*, 24 May 1974, p. 600.
38 See Gueyras, *op. cit.* and Robert Graham, 'Iraq: rising expectations', *Middle East*

International, October 1973, pp. 9–11. See also the interview with the Iraqi oil minister, Saadoun Hudammi, in *Le Monde*, 19 December 1973.
39 The immediacy of these conflicts has been considerably reduced in 1974/5, as highlighted by an agreement between Saudi Arabia and Abu Dhabi which settled the territorial disputes between the two countries: Saudi Arabia accepted Abu Dhabi's claim to the Buraimi oasis in exchange for a potentially oil-rich strip of land.

Appendix I: Terminology

Absorbers

Low absorbers are producer countries with small populations and high oil production, and consequently high per capita oil revenues (above $1,500 per year). Socio-economic restrictions limit the capacity of these countries to invest revenues productively at home or to spend them on imports. Low absorbers are Saudi Arabia, Kuwait, Abu Dhabi, Qatar, Libya.

High absorbers are producer countries with relatively large populations and per capita oil revenues under $1,500 per year. Depending on their degree of socio-economic development, these countries could invest a large share of their revenues on development and/or imports. High absorbers are Iran, Iraq, Algeria, possibly also Bahrain and Venezuela.

Oman, Nigeria and Indonesia are in a somewhat different position: in all three, infrastructural and socio-economic restrictions limit the speed with which oil revenues can be translated into development. Indonesia and Nigeria will nevertheless be able to absorb large investments and might even still depend on foreign financial assistance.

International Oil Companies

(*a*) The 'majors' or 'seven sisters': Exxon, Texaco, Gulf, Standard Oil of California, Mobil (all American); British Petroleum (British); and Royal Dutch/Shell (Dutch/British).

(*b*) Wholly or partly state-controlled: Compagnie Française des Petroles (40 per cent owned by the French government – often included with the 'majors'), ELF/ERAP (French), ENI (Italian).

(*c*) Other integrated companies ('independents'): Standard Indiana, Atlantic Richfield, Continental, Sun, Occidental, Phillips, Getty, Amerada Hess (all American).

(*d*) ARAMCO: The Arabian-American Oil Company, a consortium of American majors operating the bulk of Saudi Arabia's oil production.

OAPEC

The Organization of Arab Petroleum Exporting Countries, founded in 1968 by Libya, Saudi Arabia and Kuwait. Other members are: Abu Dhabi, Algeria, Bahrain, Egypt, Iraq, Qatar and Syria. Oman and Tunisia have applied for membership.

OPEC

The Organization of Petroleum Exporting Countries, founded in 1960 by Iran, Venezuela, Iraq, Saudi Arabia and Kuwait. Other members, with their year of entry, are: Qatar (1961), Libya and Indonesia (1962), Abu Dhabi (1967), Algeria (1969), Nigeria (1971), Ecuador (1973) and Gabon (1975).

Oil Production/Consumption

Levels are measured in *barrels* and *metric tons*, rates of production in barrels per day (b/d) and metric tons per year. Occasionally, b/d have been converted to t/year, using the approximate conversion rule of 1 million b/d = 50 million t/year. One barrel approximately equals 0.734 tons (the exact conversion depends on the specific gravity of the crude oil type); one ton approximately equals 7.33 barrels.

Persian Gulf

This term has been used throughout this Paper to include Iraq, Kuwait, Saudi Arabia, Bahrain, Qatar, the United Arab Emirates, and Oman.

Appendixes II and III: Statistical profile of main Middle Eastern and Third World oil exporters

Appendix II: Oil power 1974

	Published proven reserves (end-1974)		Production			
	million barrels	% of world total	million b/d	% of world total	Estimated revenues ($m)	Foreign exchange holdings ($m end-1974)
Saudi Arabia*	173,150	24.2	8.64	15.2	29,181	13,424
Iran	66,000	9.2	6.13	10.8	20,801	7,653
Kuwait*	81,450	11.4	2.84	5.0	9,262	933
Iraq	35,000	4.9	1.83	3.2	6,990	3,036
United Arab Emirates	33,920	4.7	2.03	3.6	7,200	n.a.
Qatar	6,000	0.8	0.55	1.0	1,993	n.a.
Oman	6,000	0.8	0.30	0.5	1,041	200
Bahrain	336	0.05	0.07	0.1	225	n.a.
Libya	26,600	3.7	1.70	3.0	7,613	3,504
Algeria	7,700	1.1	0.89	1.6	3,978	1,362
Venezuela	15,000	2.1	3.03	5.3	10,489	5,412
Nigeria	20,800	2.9	2.30	4.1	8,991	5,506
Indonesia	15,000	2.1	1.46	2.6	4,839	1,386

* Including share of Neutral Zone.

Appendix III: Absorption capacity 1974

	Imports ($m)	Estimated per capita oil revenue ($)	Estimated population	Development expenditure ($m)[a]
Saudi Arabia	3,473	5,305	5,500	DP 1975–80: 140,000
Iran	5,974	642	32,410	DP 1973–8: 42,800[b]
Kuwait	1,529	8,424	1,100	DB 1974–5: 340
Iraq	1,176[c]	651	10,740	DP 1974–9: 7,500
United Arab Emirates	800 (1973)	22,154	325	DP 1968–73: 740
Qatar	195 (1973)	22,144	90	DB 1974–5: 154
Oman	134 (1972)	1,407	740	n.a.
Bahrain	450	937	240	DB 1975: 100.9
Libya	3,140	3,399	2,240	DP 1972–5: 7,421
Algeria	3,715	243	16,350	DP 1974–7: 23,529
Venezuela	4,042	894	11,730	–
Nigeria	2,734	148	60,860	DP 1970–4: 2,371[b]
Indonesia	2,597[c]	38	126,780	DP 1974–9: 11,708

a DB – Development Budget; DP – Development Plan.
b Figures include only government expenditure as envisaged in Plan.
c First three quarters only.

9 The Spread of Nuclear Weapons
More May Be Better
Adelphi Paper 171, 1981

Kenneth N. Waltz

Introduction

What will the spread of nuclear weapons do to the world? I say 'spread' rather than 'proliferation' because so far nuclear weapons have proliferated only vertically as the major nuclear powers have added to their arsenals. Horizontally, they have spread slowly across countries, and the pace is not likely to change much. Short-term candidates for the nuclear club are not very numerous, and they are not likely to rush into the nuclear military business. Nuclear weapons will nevertheless spread, with a new member occasionally joining the club. Counting India and Israel, membership grew to seven in the first 35 years of the nuclear age. A doubling of membership in this decade would be surprising. Since rapid changes in international conditions can be unsettling, the slowness of the spread of nuclear weapons is fortunate.

Someday the world will be populated by ten or twelve or eighteen nuclear-weapon states (hereafter referred to as nuclear states). What the further spread of nuclear weapons will do to the world is therefore a compelling question.

Most people believe that the world will become a more dangerous one as nuclear weapons spread. The chances that nuclear weapons will be fired in anger or accidentally exploded in a way that prompts a nuclear exchange are finite, though unknown. Those chances increase as the number of nuclear states increase. More is therefore worse. Most people also believe that the chances that nuclear weapons will be used vary with the character of the new nuclear states – their sense of responsibility, inclination toward peace, devotion to the *status quo*, political stability, and administrative competence. If the supply of states of good character is limited, as is widely thought, then the larger the number of nuclear states, the greater the chances of nuclear war become. If nuclear weapons are acquired by countries whose governments totter and frequently fall, should we not worry more about the world's destruction than we do now? And if nuclear weapons are acquired by two states that are traditional and bitter rivals, should that not also foster our concern?

Predictions on grounds such as the above point less to likelihoods and more to dangers that we can all imagine. They identify some possibilities among many, and identifying more of the possibilities would not enable one to say how they are likely to unfold in a world made different by the slow spread of nuclear weapons. We want to know both the likelihood that new dangers will manifest themselves and what the possibilities of their mitigation may be. We want to be able to see the future world, so to speak, rather than merely imagining ways in which it may be a better or a worse one. How can we predict more surely? In two ways: by deducing expectations from the structure of the international political system and by inferring expectations from past events and patterns. With those two tasks accomplished in the first part of this paper, I shall ask in the second part whether increases in the number of nuclear states will introduce differences that are dangerous and destabilizing.

I. Deterrence in a bipolar world

The world has enjoyed more years of peace since 1945 than had been known in this century – if peace is defined as the absence of general war among the major states of the world. The Second World War followed the first one within twenty-one years. As of 1980, 35 years had elapsed since the Allies' victory over the Axis powers. Conflict marks all human affairs. In the past third of a century, conflict has generated hostility among states and has at times issued in violence among the weaker and smaller ones. Even though the more powerful states of the world have occasionally been direct participants, war has been confined geographically and limited militarily. Remarkably, general war has been avoided in a period of rapid and far-reaching changes – decolonization; the rapid economic growth of some states; the formation, tightening, and eventual loosening of blocs; the development of new technologies, and the emergence of new strategies for fighting guerrilla wars and deterring nuclear ones. The prevalence of peace, together with the fighting of circumscribed wars, indicates a high ability of the post-war international system to absorb changes and to contain conflicts and hostility.

Presumably features found in the post-war system that were not present earlier account for the world's recent good fortune. The biggest changes in the post-war world are the shift from multipolarity to bipolarity and the introduction of nuclear weapons.

The effects of bipolarity

Bipolarity has produced two outstandingly good effects. They are seen by contrasting multipolar and bipolar worlds. First, in a multipolar world there are too many powers to permit any of them to draw clear and fixed lines between allies and adversaries and too few to keep the effects of defection low. With three or more powers, flexibility of alliances keeps relations of friendship and enmity fluid and makes everyone's estimate of the present and future relation of forces uncertain. So long as the system is one of fairly small numbers, the actions of any of them may threaten the security of others.

There are too many to enable anyone to see for sure what is happening, and too few to make what is happening a matter of indifference.

In a bipolar world, the two great powers depend militarily mainly on themselves. This is almost entirely true at the strategic nuclear level, largely true at the tactical nuclear level, and partly true at the conventional level. In 1978, for example, the Soviet Union's military expenditures were over 90% of the total for the Warsaw Treaty Organization, and those of the United States were about 60% of the total for NATO.[1] With a GNP 30% as large as ours, West Germany's expenditures were 11.5% of the NATO total, and that is the second largest national contribution.[2] Not only do we carry the main military burden within the alliance because of our disproportionate resources but also because we contribute disproportionately from those resources. In fact if not in form, NATO consists of guarantees given by the United States to her European allies and to Canada. The United States, with a preponderance of nuclear weapons and as many men in uniform as the West European states combined, may be able to protect them; they cannot protect her.

Because of the vast differences in the capabilities of member states, the roughly equal sharing of burdens found in earlier alliance systems is no longer possible. The United States and the Soviet Union balance each other by 'internal' instead of 'external' means, relying on their own capabilities more than on the capabilities of allies. Internal balancing is more reliable and precise than external balancing. States are less likely to misjudge their relative strengths than they are to misjudge the strength and reliability of opposing coalitions. Rather than making states properly cautious and forwarding the chances of peace, uncertainty and miscalculation cause wars.[3] In a bipolar world, uncertainty lessens and calculations are easier to make. The military might of both great powers makes quick and easy conquest impossible for either, and this is clearly seen. To respond rapidly to find changes in the military balance is at once less important and more easily done.

Second, in the great-power politics of a multipolar world, who is a danger to whom, and who can be expected to deal with threats and problems, are matters of uncertainty. Dangers are diffused, responsibilities blurred, and definitions of vital interest easily obscured. Because who is a danger to whom is often unclear, the incentive to regard all disequilibrating changes with concern and respond to them with whatever effort may be required is weakened. To respond rapidly to fine changes is at once more difficult, because of blurred responsibilities, and more important, because states live on narrow margins. Interdependence of parties, diffusion of dangers, confusion of responses: These are the characteristics of great-power politics in a multipolar world.

In the great-power politics of a bipolar world, who is a danger to whom is never in doubt. Moreover, with only two powers capable of acting on a world scale, anything that happens anywhere is potentially of concern to both of them. Changes may affect each of the two powers differently, and this means all the more that few changes in the world at large or within each other's national realm are likely to be thought irrelevant. Self-dependence of parties, clarity of dangers, certainty about who has to face them: These are characteristics of great-power politics in a bipolar world. Because responsibility is clearly fixed, and because relative power is easier to estimate, a bipolar world tends to be more peaceful than a multipolar world.[4]

Will the spread of nuclear weapons complicate international life by turning the bipolar world into a multipolar one? The bipolar system has lasted more than three decades because no third state has developed capabilities comparable to those of the United States and the Soviet Union. The United States produces about a quarter of the world's goods, and the Soviet Union about half as much. Unless Europe unites, the United States will remain economically well ahead of other states. And although Japan's GNP is fast approaching the Soviet Union's, Japan is not able to compete militarily with the superpowers. A state becomes a great power not by military or economic capability alone but by combining political, social economic, military, and geographic assets in more effective ways than other states can.

In the old days weaker powers could improve their positions through alliance by adding the strength of foreign armies to their own. Cannot some of the middle states do together what they are unable to do alone? For two decisive reasons, the answer is 'no'. First, nuclear forces do not add up. The technology of warheads, of delivery vehicles, of detection and surveillance devices, of command and control systems, count more than the size of forces. Combining separate national forces is not much help. Second, to reach top technological levels would require full collaboration by, say, several European states. To achieve this has proved politically impossible. As de Gaulle often said, nuclear weapons make alliances obsolete. At the strategic level he was right.

States fear dividing their strategic labours fully – from research and development through production, planning, and deployment. This is less because one of them might in the future be at war with another, and more because anyone's decision to use the weapons against third parties might be fatal to all of them. Decisions to use nuclear weapons may be decisions to commit suicide. Only a national authority can be entrusted with the decision, again as de Gaulle always claimed. Only by merging and losing their political identities can middle states become great powers. The non-additivity of nuclear forces means that in our bipolar world efforts of lesser states cannot tilt the strategic balance.

Great powers are strong not simply because they have nuclear weapons but also because their immense resources enable them to generate and maintain power of all types, military and other, at strategic and tactical levels. Entering the great-power club was easier when great powers were larger in number and smaller in size. With fewer and bigger ones, barriers to entry have risen. The club will long remain the world's most exclusive one. We need not fear that the spread of nuclear weapons will turn the world into a multipolar one.

The effects of nuclear weapons

Nuclear weapons have been the second force working for peace in the post-war world. They make the cost of war seem frighteningly high and thus discourage states from starting any wars that might lead to the use of such weapons. Nuclear weapons have helped maintain peace between the great powers and have not led their few other possessors into military adventures.[5] Their further spread, however, causes widespread fear. Much of the writing about the spread of nuclear weapons has this unusual trait: It tells us that what did *not* happen in the past is likely to happen in the future, that tomorrow's nuclear states are likely to do to one another what today's nuclear states have not done. A happy nuclear past leads many to expect an unhappy nuclear future. This is odd, and the oddity leads me to believe that we should reconsider how weapons affect the situation of their possessors.

The military logic of self-help systems

States co-exist in a condition of anarchy. Self-help is the principle of action in an anarchic order, and the most important way in which states must help themselves is by providing for their own security. Therefore, in weighing the chances for peace, the first questions to ask are questions about the ends for which states use force and about the strategies and weapons they employ. The chances of peace rise if states can achieve their most important ends without actively using force. War becomes less likely as the costs of war rise in relation to possible gains. Strategies bring ends and means together. How nuclear weapons affect the chances for peace is seen by considering the possible strategies of states.

Force may be used for offence, for defence, for deterrence, and for coercion. Consider offence first. Germany and France before World War I provide a classic case of two adversaries each neglecting its defence and both planning to launch major attacks at the outset of war. France favoured offence over defence, because only by fighting an offensive war could Alsace-Lorraine be reclaimed. This illustrates one purpose of the offence: namely, conquest. Germany favoured offence over defence, believing offence to be the best defence, or even the only defence possible. Hemmed in by two adversaries, she could avoid fighting a two-front war only by concentrating her forces in the West and defeating France before Russia could mobilize and move effectively into battle. This is what the Schlieffen plan called for. The Plan illustrates another purpose of the offence: namely, security. Even if security had been Germany's only goal, an offensive strategy seemed to be the way to obtain it.[6]

The offence may have either or both of two aims: conquest and security. An offence may be conducted in either or in some combination of two ways: preventively or pre-emptively. If two countries are unequal in strength and the weaker is gaining, the stronger may be tempted to strike before its advantage is lost. Following this logic, a country with nuclear weapons may be tempted to destroy the nascent force of a hostile country. This would be preventive war, a war launched against a weak country before it can become disturbingly strong. The logic of pre-emption is different. Leaving aside the balance of forces, one country may strike another country's offensive forces to blunt an attack that it presumes is about to be made. If each of two countries can eliminate or drastically reduce the other's offensive forces in one surprise blow, then both of them are encouraged to mount sudden attacks, if only for fear that if one does not, the other will. Mutual vulnerability of forces leads to mutual fear of surprise attack by giving each power a strong incentive to strike first.

French and German plans for war against each other emphasized prevention over pre-emption – to strike before enemies can become fully ready to fight, but not to strike at their forces in order to destroy them before they can be used to strike back. Whether pre-emptive or preventive, an offensive first strike is a hard one, as military logic suggests and history confirms. Whoever strikes first does so to gain a decisive advantage. A pre-emptive strike is designed to eliminate or decisively reduce the opponent's ability to retaliate. A preventive strike is designed to defeat an adversary before he can develop and deploy his full potential might. Attacks, I should add, are not planned according to military logic alone. Political logic may lead a country another country to attack even in the absence of an expectation of military victory, as Egypt did in October of 1973.

How can one state dissuade another state from attacking? In either or in some combination of two ways. One way to counter an intended attack is to build fortifications and to muster forces that look forbiddingly strong. To build defences so patently strong that no one will try to destroy or overcome them would make international life perfectly tranquil. I call this the defensive ideal. The other way to inhibit a country's intended aggressive moves is to scare that country out of making them by threatening to visit unacceptable punishment upon it. 'To deter' literally means to stop someone from doing something by frightening him. In contrast to dissuasion by defence, dissuasion by deterrence operates by frightening a state out of attacking, not because of the difficulty of launching an attack and carrying it home, but because the expected reaction of the attacked will result in one's own severe punishment. Defence and deterrence are often confused. One frequently hears statements like this: 'A strong defence in Europe will deter a Russian attack'. What is meant is that a strong defence will dissuade Russia from attacking. Deterrence is achieved not through the ability to defend but through the ability to punish. Purely deterrent forces provide no defence. The message of a deterrent strategy is this: 'Although we are defenceless, if you attack we will punish you to an extent that more than cancels your gains'. Second-strike nuclear forces serve that kind of strategy. Purely defensive forces provide no deterrence. They offer no means of punishment. The message of a defensive strategy is this: 'Although we cannot strike back, you will find our defences so difficult to overcome that you will dash yourself to pieces against them'. The Maginot Line was to serve that kind of strategy.[7]

States may also use force for coercion. One state may threaten to harm another state not to deter it from taking a certain action but to compel one. Napoleon III threatened to bombard Tripoli if the Turks did not comply with his demands for Roman Catholic control of the Palestinian Holy Places. This is blackmail, which can now be backed by conventional and by nuclear threats.

Do nuclear weapons increase or decrease the chances of war? The answer depends on whether nuclear weapons permit and encourage states to deploy forces in ways that make the active use of force more or less likely and in ways that promise to be more or less destructive. If nuclear weapons make the offence more effective and the blackmailer's threat more compelling, then nuclear weapons increase the chances of war – the more so the more widely they spread. If defence and deterrence are made easier and more reliable by the spread of nuclear weapons, we may expect the opposite result. To maintain their security, states must rely on the means they can generate and the arrangements they can make for themselves. The quality of international life therefore varies with the ease or the difficulty states experience in making themselves secure.

Weapons and strategies change the situation of states in ways that make them more or less secure, as Robert Jervis has brilliantly shown.[8] If weapons are not well suited for conquest, neighbours have more peace of mind. According to the defensive-deterrent ideal, we should expect war to become less likely when weaponry is such as to make conquest more difficult, to discourage pre-emptive and preventive war, and to make coercive threats less credible. Do nuclear weapons have those effects? Some answers can be found by considering how nuclear deterrence and how nuclear defence may improve the prospects for peace.

First, wars can be fought in the face of deterrent threats, but the higher the stakes and the closer a country moves toward winning them, the more surely that country invites retaliation and risks its own destruction. States are not likely to run major risks for minor gains. Wars between nuclear states may escalate as the loser uses larger and larger warheads. Fearing that, states will want to draw back. Not escalation but de-escalation becomes likely. War remains possible, but victory in war is too dangerous to fight for. If states can score only small gains, because large ones risk retaliation, they have little incentive to fight.

Second, states act with less care if the expected costs of war are low and with more care if they are high. In 1853 and 1854, Britain and France expected to win an easy victory if they went to war against Russia. Prestige abroad and political popularity at home would be gained, if not much else. The vagueness of their plans was matched by the carelessness of their acts. In blundering into the Crimean War they acted hastily on scant information, pandered to their people's frenzy for war, showed more concern for an ally's whim than for the adversary's situation, failed to specify the changes in behaviour that threats were supposed to bring, and inclined towards testing strength first and bargaining second.[9] In sharp contrast, the presence of nuclear weapons makes states exceedingly cautious. Think of Kennedy and Kruschev in the Cuban missile crisis. Why fight if you can't win much and might lose everything?

Third, the question demands a negative answer all the more insistently when the deterrent deployment of nuclear weapons contributes more to a country's security than does conquest of territory. A country with a deterrent strategy does not need the extent of territory required by a country relying on a conventional defence in depth. A deterrent strategy makes it unnecessary for a country to fight for the sake of increasing its security, and this removes a major cause of war.[10]

Fourth, deterrent effect depends both on one's capabilities and on the will one has to use them. The will of the attacked, striving to preserve its own territory, can ordinarily be presumed stronger than the will of the attacker, striving to annex someone else's territory. Knowing this, the would-be attacker is further inhibited.[11]

Certainty about the relative strength of adversaries also improves the prospects for peace. From the late nineteenth century onwards the speed of technological innovation increased the difficulty of estimating relative strengths and predicting the course of campaigns. Since World War II, technology has advanced even faster, but short of an anti-ballistic missile (ABM) breakthrough, this does not matter very much. It does not disturb the American-Russian equilibrium because one side's missiles are not made obsolete by improvements in the other side's missiles. In 1906 the British *Dreadnought*, with the greater range and fire power of its guns, made older battleships obsolete. This does not happen to missiles. As Bernard Brodie put it: 'Weapons that do not have to fight their like do not become useless because of the advent of newer and superior types'.[12] They do have to survive their like, but that is a much simpler problem to solve (see discussion below).

Many wars might have been avoided had their outcomes been foreseen. 'To be sure,' Georg Simmel once said, 'the most effective presupposition for preventing struggle, the exact knowledge of the comparative strength of the two parties, is very often only to be obtained by the actual fighting out of the conflict'.[13] Miscalculation causes wars. One side expects victory at an affordable price, while the other side hopes to avoid defeat. Here the differences between conventional-multipolar and nuclear-bipolar worlds are fundamental. In the former, states are too often tempted to act on advantages that are wishfully discerned and narrowly calculated. In 1914, neither Germany nor France tried very hard to avoid a general war. Both hoped for victory even though they believed their forces to be quite evenly matched. In 1941, Japan, in attacking the United States, could hope for victory only if a series of events that were possible but not highly probable took place. Japan would grab resources sufficient for continuing the conquest of China and then dig in to defend a limited perimeter. Meanwhile, the United States and Britain would have to deal with Germany, which, having defeated the Soviet Union, would be supreme in Europe. Japan could then hope to fight a defensive war for a year or two until America, her purpose weakened, became willing to make a compromise peace in Asia.[14]

Countries more readily run the risks of war when defeat, if it comes, is distant and is expected to bring only limited damage. Given such expectations, leaders do not have to be insane to sound the trumpet and urge their people to be bold and courageous in the pursuit of victory. The outcome of battles and the course of campaigns are hard to foresee because so many things affect them, including the shifting allegiance and determination of alliance members. Predicting the result of conventional wars has proved difficult.

Uncertainty about outcomes does not work decisively against the fighting of wars in conventional worlds. Countries armed with conventional weapons go to war knowing that even in defeat their suffering will be limited. Calculations about nuclear war are differently made. Nuclear worlds call for and encourage a different kind of reasoning. If countries armed with nuclear weapons go to war, they do so knowing that their suffering may be unlimited. Of course, it also may not be. But that is not the kind of uncertainty that encourages anyone to use force. In a conventional world, one is uncertain about winning or losing. In a nuclear world, one is uncertain about surviving or being annihilated. If force is used and not kept within limits, catastrophe will result. That prediction is easy to make because it does not require close estimates of opposing forces. The number of one's cities that can be severely damaged is at least equal to the number of strategic warheads an adversary can deliver. Variations of number mean little within wide ranges. The expected effect of the deterrent achieves an easy clarity because wide margins of error in estimates of probable damage do not matter. Do we expect to lose one city or two, two cities or ten? When these are the pertinent questions, we stop thinking about running risks and start worrying about how to avoid them. In a conventional world, deterrent threats are ineffective because the damage threatened is distant, limited, and problematic. Nuclear weapons make military miscalculations difficult and politically pertinent prediction easy.

Dissuading a would-be attacker by throwing up a good-looking defence may be as effective as dissuading him through deterrence. Beginning with President Kennedy and Secretary of Defense McNamara in the early 1960s, we have asked how we can avoid, or at least postpone, using nuclear weapons rather than how we can mount the most effective defence. NATO's attempt to keep a defensive war conventional in its initial stage may guarantee that nuclear weapons, if used, will be used in a losing cause and in ways that multiply destruction without promising victory. Early use of very small warheads may stop escalation. Defensive deployment, if it should fail to dissuade, would bring small nuclear weapons into use before the physical, political and psychological environment had deteriorated. The chances of de-escalation are high if the use of nuclear weapons is carefully planned and their use is limited to the battlefield. We have rightly put strong emphasis on strategic deterrence, which makes large wars less likely, and wrongly slighted the question of whether nuclear weapons of low yield can effectively be used for defence, which would make any war at all less likely still.[15]

Lesser nuclear states, with choices tightly constrained by scarcity of resources, may be forced to make choices that NATO has avoided, to choose nuclear defence or nuclear deterrence rather than planning to fight a conventional war on a large scale and to use nuclear weapons only when conventional defences are breaking. Increased reliance on nuclear defence would decrease the credibility of nuclear deterrence. That would be acceptable if a nuclear defence were seen to be unassailable. An unassailable defence is fully dissuasive. Dissuasion is what is wanted whether by defence or by deterrence.

The likelihood of war decreases as deterrent and defensive capabilities increase. Whatever the number of nuclear states, a nuclear world is tolerable if those states are able to send convincing deterrent messages: It is useless to attempt to conquer because you will be severely punished. A nuclear world becomes even more tolerable if states are able to send convincing defensive messages: It is useless to attempt to conquer because you cannot. Nuclear weapons and an appropriate doctrine for their use may make it possible to approach the defensive-deterrent ideal, a condition that would cause the chances of war to dwindle. Concentrating attention on the destructive power of nuclear weapons has obscured the important benefits they promise to states trying to coexist in a self-help world.

Why nations want nuclear weapons

Nations want nuclear weapons for one or more of seven reasons. First, great powers always counter the weapons of other great powers, usually by imitating those who have introduced new weapons. It was not surprising that the Soviet Union developed atomic and hydrogen bombs, but rather that we thought the Baruch-Lilienthal plan might persuade her not to.

Second, a state may want nuclear weapons for fear that its great-power ally will not retaliate if the other great-power attacks. Although Britain when she became a nuclear power thought of herself as being a great one, her reasons for deciding later to maintain a nuclear force arose from doubts that the United States could be counted on to retaliate in response to an attack by the Soviet Union on Europe and from Britain's consequent desire to place a finger on our nuclear trigger. As soon as the Soviet Union was capable of making nuclear strikes at American cities, West Europeans began to worry that America's nuclear umbrella no longer ensured that her allies would stay dry if it rained. Hugh Gaitskell, as Leader of the Opposition, could say what Harold Macmillan, as Prime Minister, dared not: 'I do not believe that when we speak of our having to have nuclear weapons of our own it is because we must make a contribution to the deterrent of the West'. As he indicated, no contribution of consequence was made. Instead, he remarked, the desire for a nuclear force derives in large part 'from doubts about the readiness of the United States Government and the American citizens to risk the destruction of their cities on behalf of Europe'.[16] Similar doubts provided the strongest stimulus for France to become a nuclear power.

Third, a country without nuclear allies will want nuclear weapons all the more if some of its adversaries have them. So China and then India became nuclear powers, and Pakistan will probably follow.

Fourth, a country may want nuclear weapons because it lives in fear of its adversaries' present or future conventional strength. This is reason enough for Israel's nuclear weapons, which most authorities assume she either has at hand or can quickly assemble.

Fifth, some countries may find nuclear weapons a cheaper and safer alternative to running economically ruinous and militarily dangerous conventional arms races. Nuclear weapons may promise increased security and independence at an affordable price.

Sixth, countries may want nuclear weapons for offensive purposes. This, however, is an unlikely motivation for reasons given below.

Finally, by building nuclear weapons a country may hope to enhance its international standing. This is thought to be both a reason for and a consequence of developing nuclear weapons. One may enjoy the prestige that comes with nuclear weapons, and indeed a yearning for glory was not absent from de Gaulle's soul. But the nuclear military business is a serious one, and we may expect that deeper motives than desire for prestige lie behind the decision to enter it.

Mainly for reasons two through five, new members will occasionally enter the nuclear club. Nuclear weapons will spread from one country to another in the future for the same reasons they have spread in the past. What effects may we expect?

Relations among nuclear nations

In one important way nuclear weapons do change the relations of nations. Adversary states that acquire them are thereby made more cautious in their dealings with each other. For the most part, however, the relations of nations display continuity through their transition from non-nuclear to nuclear status.

Relations between the United States and the new nuclear states were much the same before and after they exploded atomic devices, as Michael Nacht points out.[17] Because America's relations with other nations are based on complex historical, economic, political, and military considerations, they are not likely to change much when lesser parties decide to build nuclear forces. This continuity of relations suggests a certain ambivalence. The spread of nuclear weapons, though dreaded, prompts only mild reactions when it happens. Our 'special relationship' with Britain led us to help her acquire and maintain nuclear forces. The distance tinged with distrust that marks our relations with France led us to oppose France's similar endeavours. China's nuclear forces neither prevented American-Chinese rapprochement earlier nor prompted it later. American-Indian relations worsened when America 'tilted' toward Pakistan during the India-Pakistan War of 1971. India's nuclear explosion in 1974 neither improved nor worsened relations with the United States in the long term. Unlike Canada, we did not deny India access to our nuclear supplies.[18] Again in 1980, President Carter approved shipment of nuclear fuel to India despite her refusal to accept safeguards on all of her nuclear facilities, as required by the Nuclear Non-Proliferation Act of 1978, a provision that the President can waive under certain circumstances. In asking Congress not to oppose his waiving the requirement, the President said this: 'We must do all we reasonably can to promote stability in the area and to bolster our relations with states there, particularly those that can play a role in checking Soviet expansionism'.[19] Nor did Pakistan's refusal to promise not to conduct nuclear tests prevent the United States from proposing to provide military aid after the Soviet Union's invasion of Afghanistan in December of 1979.

Stopping the spread of nuclear weapons has had a high priority for American governments, but clearly not the highest. In practice, other interests have proved to be more pressing. This is evident in our relations with every country that has developed nuclear weapons, or appeared to be on the verge of doing so, from Britain onwards. One may expect that relations of friendship and enmity, that inclinations to help and to hinder, will carry over from the pre- to the post-nuclear relations of nations.

What holds for the United States almost surely holds for the Soviet Union. The Soviet Union has strongly supported efforts to stop the spread of nuclear weapons. She has good reasons to do so. Many potential nuclear states are both nearby and hostile, from West Germany through Pakistan to South Korea. Others, like Iraq and India, are nearby and friendly. In international politics, however, friendliness and hostility are transient qualities. No doubt the Soviet Union would prefer conventional to nuclear neighbours whatever their present leanings may be. But also, after the discredit earned in occupying Afghanistan, the Soviet Union would like to repair relations with third-world countries. If we had refused to supply nuclear fuel to India, would the Soviet Union have done so? Secretary of State Edmund Muskie and others thought so.[20] For the Soviet Union, as for the United States, other interests may weigh more heavily than her interest in halting the spread of nuclear weapons.

One may wonder, however, whether the quality of relations changes within alliances as some of their members become nuclear powers. Alliances relate nations to one another in specific and well defined ways. By acquiring nuclear weapons a country is said to erode, and perhaps to wreck, the alliance to which it belongs. In part this statement mistakes effects for causes. Alliances are weakened by the doubts of some countries that another country will risk committing national suicide through retaliation against a nuclear power that attacks an ally. Such doubts caused Britain to remain a nuclear power and France to become one, but it did not destroy NATO. The Alliance holds together because even its nuclear members continue to depend on the United States. They gain strength from their nuclear weapons but remain weak in conventional arms and continue to be vulnerable economically. In an unbalanced world, when the weak feel threatened, they seek aid and protection from the strong. The nuclear forces of Britain and France have their effects on the Alliance without ending dependence on the United States.

Nuclear weapons were maintained by Britain and acquired by France at least in part as triggers for America's strategic deterrent. Given a sense of uncertainty combined with dependence, Europeans understandably strive to fashion their forces so as to ensure our commitment. They also wish to determine the form the commitment takes and the manner of its execution. After all, an American choice about how to respond to threats in Europe is a choice that affects the lives of Europeans and may bring their deaths. Europeans want a large voice in American policies that may determine their destiny. By mounting nuclear weapons, Britain and France hope to decide when we will retaliate against the Soviet Union for acts committed in Europe. Since retaliation risks our destruction, we resist surrendering the decision.

Alliances gain strength through a division of military labour. Within NATO, however, British and French duplication of American strategic nuclear weaponry on a minor scale adds little to the strength of NATO. The most striking division of labour is seen in the different ways European countries seek to influence American policy. Whether or not they are nuclear, lesser powers feeling threatened will turn to, or remain associated with, one or another of the great powers. So long as West European countries fail to increase and concert their efforts, they remain weak and feel threatened. Countries that are weak and threatened will continue to rely on the support of more powerful ones and to hope that the latter will bear a disproportionate share of the burden. West European states have become accustomed to depending on the United States. Relations of dependency are hardest to break where dependent states cannot shift from reliance on one great power to reliance on another. Under those circumstances, alliances endure even as nuclear weapons spread among their members.

From NATO's experience we may conclude that alliances are not wrecked by the spread of nuclear weapons among their members. NATO accommodates both nuclear and conventional states in ways that continue to evolve. Past evidence does not support the fear that alliances, which have contributed an element of order to an anarchic world, are threatened by the spread of nuclear weapons. The Soviet Union won't permit the East European countries to become nuclear powers and the United States has accommodated two of her allies doing so, though uneasily in the case of France. The spread of nuclear weapons among members of an alliance changes relations among them without breaking alliances apart.

II. The further spread of nuclear weapons

Contemplating the nuclear past gives grounds for hoping that the world will survive if further nuclear powers join today's six or seven. This tentative conclusion is called into question by the widespread belief that the infirmities of some nuclear states and the delicacy of their nuclear forces will work against the preservation of peace and for the fighting of nuclear wars. The likelihood of avoiding destruction as more states become members of the nuclear club is often coupled with the question of *who* those states will be. What are the likely differences in situation and behaviour of new as compared to old nuclear powers?

Nuclear weapons and domestic stability

What are the principal worries? Because of the importance of controlling nuclear weapons – of keeping them firmly in the hands of reliable officials – rulers of nuclear states may become more authoritarian and ever more given to secrecy. Moreover, some potential nuclear states are not politically strong and stable enough to ensure control of the weapons and of the decision to use them. If neighbouring, hostile, unstable states are armed with nuclear weapons, each will fear attack by the other. Feelings of insecurity may lead to arms races that subordinate civil needs to military necessities. Fears are compounded by the danger of internal coups in which the control of nuclear weapons may be the main object of the struggle and the key to political power. Under these fearful circumstances, to maintain governmental authority and civil order may be impossible. The legitimacy of the state and the loyalty of its citizenry may dissolve because the state is no longer thought to be capable of maintaining external security and internal order. The first fear is that states become tyrannical; the second, that they lose control. Both these fears may be realized, either in different states or, indeed, in the same state at different times.[21]

What can one say? Four things primarily. First, possession of nuclear weapons may slow arms races down, rather than speed them up, a possibility considered later. Second, for less developed countries to build nuclear arsenals requires a long lead time. Nuclear power and nuclear weapons programmes, like population policies, require administrative and technical teams able to formulate and sustain programmes of considerable cost that pay off only in the long run. The more unstable a government, the shorter becomes the attention span of its leaders. They have to deal with today's problems and hope for the best tomorrow.[22] In countries where political control is most difficult to maintain, governments are least likely to initiate nuclear-weapons programmes. In such states, soldiers help to maintain leaders in power or try to overthrow them. For those purposes nuclear weapons are not useful. Soldiers who have political clout, or want it, are less interested in nuclear weapons than they are in more immediately useful instruments of political control. They are not scientists and technicians. They like to command troops and squadrons. Their vested interests are in the military's traditional trappings.

Third, although highly unstable states are unlikely to initiate nuclear projects, such projects, begun in stable times, may continue through periods of political turmoil and succeed in producing nuclear weapons. A nuclear state may be unstable or may become so. But what is hard to comprehend is why, in an internal struggle for power, any of the contenders should start using nuclear weapons. Who would they aim at? How would they use them as instruments for maintaining or gaining control? I see little more reason to fear that one faction or another in some less developed country will fire atomic weapons in a struggle for political power than that they will be used in a crisis of succession in the Soviet Union or China. One or another nuclear state will experience uncertainty of succession, fierce struggles for power, and instability of regime. Those who fear the worst have not shown with any plausibility how those expected events may lead to the use of nuclear weapons.

Fourth, the possibility of one side in a civil war firing a nuclear warhead at its opponent's stronghold nevertheless remains. Such an act would produce a national tragedy, not an international one. This question then arises: Once the weapon is fired, what happens next? The domestic use of nuclear weapons is, of all the uses imaginable, least likely to lead to escalation and to threaten the stability of the central balance. The United States and the Soviet Union, and other countries as well, would have the strongest reasons to issue warnings and to assert control.

Nuclear weapons and regional stability

Nuclear weapons are not likely to be used at home. Are they likely to be used abroad? As nuclear weapons spread, what new causes may bring effects different from and worse than those known earlier in the nuclear age? This section considers five ways in which the new world is expected to differ from the old and then examines the prospects for, and the consequences of, new nuclear states using their weapons for blackmail or for fighting an offensive war.

In what ways the actions and interactions of new nuclear states differ from those of old nuclear powers? First, new nuclear states may come in hostile pairs and share a common border. Where states are bitter enemies one may fear that they will be unable to resist using their nuclear weapons against each other. This is a worry about the future that the past does not disclose. The Soviet Union and the United States, and the Soviet Union and China, are hostile enough; and the latter pair share a long border. Nuclear weapons have caused China and the Soviet Union to deal cautiously with each other. But bitterness among some potential nuclear states, so it is said, exceeds that experienced by the old ones. Playing down the bitterness sometimes felt by the United States, the Soviet Union, and China requires a creative reading of history. Moreover, those who believe that bitterness causes wars assume a close association that is seldom found between bitterness among nations and their willingness to run high risks.

Second, some new nuclear states may have governments and societies that are not well rooted. If a country is a loose collection of hostile tribes, if its leaders from a thin veneer atop a people partly nomadic and with an authoritarian history, its rulers may be freer of constraints than, and have different values from, those who rule older and more fully developed polities. Idi Amin and Muammar el-Qaddafi fit into these categories, and they are favourite examples of the kinds of rulers who supposedly cannot be trusted to manage nuclear weapons responsibly. Despite wild rhetoric aimed at foreigners, however, both of these 'irrational' rulers became cautious and modest when punitive actions against them might have threatened their ability to rule. Even though Amin lustily slaughtered members of tribes he disliked, he quickly stopped goading Britain once the sending of her troops appeared to be a possibility. Qaddafi has shown similar restraint. He and Anwar Sadat have been openly hostile since 1973. In July of 1977 both sides launched commando attacks and air raids, including two large air strikes by Egypt on Libya's el Adem airbase. Neither side let the attacks get out of hand. Qaddafi showed himself to be forbearing and amenable to mediation by other Arab leaders. Shai Feldman uses these and other examples to argue that Arab leaders are deterred from taking inordinate risks not because they engage in intricate rational calculations but simply because they, like other rulers, are 'sensitive to costs'.[23]

Many Westerners who write fearfully about a future in which third-world countries have nuclear weapons seem to view their people in the once familiar imperial manner as 'lesser breeds without the law'. As is usual with ethnocentric views, speculation takes the place of evidence. How do we know, someone has asked, that a nuclear-armed and newly hostile Egypt or a nuclear-armed and still hostile Syria would not strike to destroy Israel at the risk of Israeli bombs falling on some of their cities? More than a quarter of Egypt's people live in four cities: Cairo, Alexandria, Giza, and Aswan. More than a quarter of Syria's live in three: Damascus, Aleppo, and Homs.[24] What government would risk sudden losses of such proportion or indeed of much lesser proportion? Rulers want to have a country that they can continue to rule. Some Arab country might wish that some other Arab country would risk its own destruction for the sake of destroying Israel, but there is no reason to think that any Arab country would do so. One may be impressed that, despite ample bitterness, Israelis and Arabs have limited their wars and accepted constraints placed on them by others. Arabs did not marshal their resources and make an all-out effort to destroy Israel in the years before Israel could strike back with nuclear warheads. We cannot expect countries to risk more in the presence of nuclear weapons than they have in their absence.

Third, many fear that states that are radical at home will recklessly use their nuclear weapons in pursuit of revolutionary ends abroad. States that are radical at home, however, may not be radical abroad. Few states have been radical in the conduct of their foreign policy, and fewer have remained so for long. Think of the Soviet Union and the People's Republic of China. States co-exist in a competitive arena. The pressures of competition cause them to behave in ways that make the threats they face manageable, in ways that enable them to get along. States can remain radical in foreign policy only if they are overwhelmingly strong – as none of the new nuclear states will be – or if their radical acts fall short of damaging vital interests of nuclear powers. States that acquire nuclear weapons will not be regarded with indifference. States that want to be freewheelers have to stay out of the nuclear business. A nuclear Libya, for example, would have to show caution, even in rhetoric, lest she suffer retaliation in response to someone else's anonymous attack on a third state. That state, ignorant of who attacked, might claim that its intelligence agents had identified Libya as the culprit and take the opportunity to silence her by striking a conventional or nuclear blow. Nuclear weapons induce caution, especially in weak states.

Fourth, while some worry about nuclear states coming in hostile pairs, others worry that the bipolar pattern will not be reproduced regionally in a world populated by larger numbers of nuclear states. The simplicity of relations that obtains when one party has to concentrate its worry on only one other, and the ease of calculating forces and estimating the dangers they pose, may be lost. The structure of international politics, however, will remain bipolar so long as no third state is able to compete militarily with the great powers. Whatever the structure, the relations of states run in various directions. This applied to relations of deterrence as soon as Britain gained nuclear capabilities. It has not weakened deterrence at the centre and need not do so regionally. The Soviet Union now has to worry lest a move made in Europe cause France and Britain to retaliate, thus possibly setting off American forces. She also has to worry about China's forces. Such worries at once complicate calculations and strengthen deterrence.

Fifth, in some of the new nuclear states civil control of the military may be shaky. Nuclear weapons may fall into the hands of military officers more inclined than civilians to put them to offensive use. This again is an old worry. I can see no reason to think that civil control of the military is secure in the Soviet Union, given the occasional presence of serving officers in the Politburo and some known and some surmised instances of military intervention in civil affairs at critical times.[25] And in the People's Republic of China military and civil branches of government have been not separated but fused. Although one may prefer civil control, preventing a highly destructive war does not require it. What is required is that decisions be made that keep destruction within bounds, whether decisions are made by civilians or soldiers. Soldiers may be more cautious than civilians.[26] Generals and admirals do not like uncertainty, and they do not lack patriotism. They do not like to fight conventional wars under unfamiliar conditions. The offensive use of nuclear weapons multiplies uncertainties. Nobody knows what a nuclear battlefield would look like, and nobody knows what happens after the first city is hit. *Uncertainty* about the course that a nuclear war might follow, along with the *certainty* that destruction can be immense, strongly inhibits the first use of nuclear weapons.

Examining the supposedly unfortunate characteristics of new nuclear states removes some of one's worries. One wonders why their civil and military leaders should be less interested in avoiding self-destruction than leaders of other states have been. Nuclear weapons have never been used in a world in which two or more states possessed them. Still, one's feeling that something awful will happen as new nuclear powers are added to the present group is not easily quieted. The fear remains that one state or another will fire its weapons in a coolly calculated pre-emptive strike, or fire them in a moment of panic, or use them to launch a preventive war. These possibilities are examined in the next section. Nuclear weapons may also back a policy of blackmail, or be set off anonymously, or be used in a combined conventional-nuclear attack.

Consider blackmail first. Two conditions make for the success of nuclear blackmail. First, when only one country had nuclear weapons, threats to use them had more effect. Thus, President Truman's nuclear threats may have levered the Soviet Union's troops out of Azerbaijan in 1946. Second, if a country has invested troops and suffered losses in a conventional war, its nuclear blackmail may work. In 1953, Eisenhower and Dulles may have convinced Russia and China that they would widen the Korean War and intensify it by using nuclear weapons if a settlement were not reached. In Korea, we had gone so far that the threat to go further was plausible. The blackmailer's nuclear threat is not a cheap way of working one's will. The threat is simply incredible unless a considerable investment has already been made. Dulles's speech of 12 January 1954 seemed to threaten, massive retaliation in response to mildly bothersome actions by others. The successful seige of Dien Bien Phu in the spring of that year showed the limitations of such threats. Capabilities foster policies that employ them. But monstrous capabilities foster monstrous policies, which when contemplated are seen to be too horrible to carry through. Imagine an Arab state threatening to strike Tel Aviv if the West Bank is not evacuated by Israelis. No state can make the threat with credibility because no state can expect to execute the threat without danger to themselves.

Some have feared that nuclear weapons may be fired anonymously – by radical Arab states, for example, to attack an Israeli city so as to block a peace settlement.[27] But the state exploding the warhead could not be sure of remaining unidentified. Even if a country's leaders persuade themselves that chances of retaliation are low, who would run the risk? Once two or more countries have nuclear weapons, the response to nuclear threats, even against non-nuclear states, becomes unpredictable.

Although nuclear weapons are poor instruments for blackmail, would they not provide a cheap and decisive offensive force when used against a conventionally armed enemy? Some people think that South Korea wants, and that earlier the Shah's Iran had wanted, nuclear weapons for offensive use. Yet one cannot say why South Korea would use nuclear weapons against fellow Koreans while trying to reunite them nor how she could use nuclear weapons against the North, knowing that China and Russia might retaliate. And what goals could a conventionally strong Iran have entertained that would have tempted her to risk using nuclear weapons? A country that takes the nuclear offensive has to fear an appropriately punishing strike by someone. Far from lowering the expected cost of aggression, a nuclear offence even against a non-nuclear state raises the possible costs of aggression to incalculable heights because the aggressor cannot be sure of the reaction of other nuclear powers.

Nuclear weapons do not make nuclear war a likely prospect, as history has so far shown. The point made when discussing the domestic use of nuclear weapons, however, bears repeating. No one can say that nuclear weapons will never be used. Their use, although unlikely, is always possible. In asking what the spread of nuclear weapons will do to the world, we are asking about the effects to be expected as a larger number of relatively weak states get nuclear weapons. If such states use nuclear weapons, the world will not end. And the use of nuclear weapons by lesser powers would hardly trigger them elsewhere, with the US and the USSR becoming involved in ways that might shake the central balance.

Deterrence with small nuclear forces

A number of problems are thought to attend the efforts of minor powers to use nuclear weapons for deterrence. In this section, I ask how hard these problems are for new nuclear states to solve.

The forces required for deterrence

In considering the physical requirements of deterrent forces, we should recall the difference between prevention and pre-emption. A preventive war is launched by a stronger state against a weaker one that is thought to be gaining strength. A pre-emptive strike is launched by one state to blunt an attack that another state is presumably preparing to launch.

The first danger posed by the spread of nuclear weapons would seem to be that each new nuclear state may tempt an old one to strike preventively in order to destroy an embryonic nuclear capability before it can become militarily effective. Because of America's nuclear arsenal, the Soviet Union could hardly have destroyed the budding forces of Britain and France; but the United States could have struck the Soviet Union's early nuclear facilities, and the United States and the Soviet Union could have struck China's. Such preventive strikes have been treated as more than abstract possibilities. When Francis P. Matthews was President Truman's Secretary of the Navy, he made a speech that seemed to favour our waging a preventive war. The United States, he urged, should be willing to pay 'even the price of instituting a war to compel co-operation for peace'.[28]

The United States and the Soviet Union considered making preventive strikes against China early in her nuclear career. Preventive strikes against nuclear installations can also be made by non-nuclear states and have sometimes been threatened. Thus President Nasser warned Israel in 1960 that Egypt would attack if she were sure that Israel was building a bomb. 'It is inevitable', he said, 'that we should attack the base of aggression, even if we have to mobilize four million to destroy it'.[29]

The uneven development of the forces of potential and of new nuclear states creates occasions that seem to permit preventive strikes and may seem to invite them. Two stages of nuclear development should be distinguished. First, a country may be in an early stage of nuclear development and be obviously unable to make nuclear weapons. Second, a country may be in an advanced stage of nuclear development, and whether or not it has some nuclear weapons may not be surely known. All of the present nuclear countries went through both stages, yet until Israel struck Iraq's nuclear facility in June of 1981 no one had launched a preventive strike. A number of reasons combined may account for the reluctance of states to strike in order to prevent adversaries from developing nuclear forces. A preventive strike would seem to be most promising during the first stage of nuclear development. A state could strike without fearing that the country it attacked would return a nuclear blow. But would one strike so hard as to destroy the very potential for future nuclear development? If not, the country struck could simply resume its nuclear career. If the blow struck is less than devastating, one must be prepared to repeat it or to occupy and control the country. To do either would be difficult and costly.

In striking Iraq, Israel showed that a preventive strike can be made, something that was not in doubt. Israel's act and its consequences, however, make clear that the likelihood of useful accomplishment is low. Israel's strike increased the determination of Arabs to produce nuclear weapons. Arab states that may attempt to do so will now be all the more secretive and circumspect. Israel's strike, far from foreclosing Iraq's nuclear future, gained her the support of some other Arab states in pursuing it. And despite Prime Minister Begin's vow to strike as often as need be, the risks in doing so would rise with each occasion.

A preventive strike during the second stage of nuclear development is even less promising than a preventive strike during the first stage. As more countries acquire nuclear weapons, and as more countries gain nuclear competence through power projects, the difficulties and dangers of making preventive strikes increase. To know for sure that the country attacked has not already produced or otherwise acquired some deliverable warheads becomes increasingly difficult. If the country attacked has even a rudimentary nuclear capability, one's own severe punishment becomes possible. Fission bombs may work even though they have not been tested, as was the case with the bomb dropped on Hiroshima. Israel has apparently not tested weapons, yet Egypt cannot know whether Israel has zero, ten, or twenty warheads. And if the number is zero and Egypt can be sure of that, she would still not know how many days are required for assembling components that may be on hand.

Preventive strikes against states that have, or may have, nuclear weapons are hard to imagine, but what about pre-emptive ones? The new worry in a world in which nuclear weapons have spread is that states of limited and roughly similar capabilities will use them against one another. They do not want to risk nuclear devastation anymore than we do. Pre-emptive strikes nevertheless seem likely because we assume that their forces will be 'delicate'. With delicate forces, states are tempted to launch disarming strikes before their own forces can be struck and destroyed.

To be effective a deterrent force must meet three requirements. First, a part of the force must appear to be able to survive an attack and launch one of its own. Second, survival of the force must not require early firing in response to what may be false alarms. Third, weapons must not be susceptible to accidental and unauthorized use. Nobody wants vulnerable, hair-trigger, accident-prone forces. Will new nuclear states find ways to hide their weapons, to deliver them, and to control them? Will they be able to deploy and manage nuclear weapons in ways that meet the physical requirements of deterrent forces?

The United States even today worries about the vulnerability of its vast and varied arsenal. Will not new nuclear states, slightly and crudely armed, be all the more worried about the survival of their forces? In recent years, we have exaggerated the difficulty of deterrence by shifting attention from situations to weaponry and from weapons systems to their components. Some Americans are concerned about the vulnerability of our strategic system because its land-based component can be struck and perhaps largely destroyed by the Soviet Union in the middle 1980s. If the Soviet Union tried that, we would still have thousands of warheads at sea and thousands of bombs in the air. The Soviet Union could not be sure that we would fail to launch on warning or fail to retaliate later. Uncertainly deters, and there would be plenty of uncertainty about our response in the minds of the Soviet Union's leaders.

In McNamara's day and earlier the term 'counterforce' had a clear and precise meaning. Country A was said to have a counterforce capability if by striking first it could reduce country B's missiles and bombers to such small numbers that country A would be reluctantly willing to accept the full force of B's retaliation. In this respect, as in others, strategic discourse now lacks the clarity and precision it once had. Whether in a conventional or a nuclear world, one cannot usefully compare some components of a nation's military forces without taking account of what other components can do. Both the United States and the Soviet Union have strategic nuclear weapons that can destroy some of the other side's strategic nuclear weapons. Neither the United States nor the Soviet Union can reduce the other side's strategic forces to the point where it no longer retains an immense capability for striking at cities and a considerable capability for striking at military targets as well. That we have ten thousand warheads to the Soviet Union's six thousand makes us no worse and no better off than we were when the ratio was even more favourable. That the throw-weight of the Soviet Union's missiles exceeds ours by several times makes us no better and no worse off than it would be were the ratio to be reversed.[30]

Deterrent forces are seldom delicate because no state wants delicate forces and nuclear forces can easily be made sturdy. Nuclear weapons are fairly small and light. They are easy to hide and to move. Early in the nuclear age, people worried about atomic bombs being concealed in packing boxes and placed in the holds of ships to be exploded when a signal was given. Now more than ever people worry about terrorists stealing nuclear warheads because various states have so many of them. Everybody seems to believe that terrorists are capable of hiding bombs.[31] Why should states be unable to do what terrorist gangs are thought to be capable of?

It is sometimes claimed that the few bombs of a new nuclear state create a greater danger of nuclear war than additional thousands for the United States and the Soviet Union. Such statements assume that pre-emption of a small force is easy. It is so only if the would-be attacker knows that the intended victim's warheads are few in number, knows their exact number and locations, and knows that they will not be moved or fired before they are struck. To know all of these things, and to know that you know them for sure, is exceedingly difficult. How can military advisers promise the full success of a disarming first strike when the penalty for slight error may be so heavy? In 1962, Tactical Air Command promised that an American strike against Soviet missiles in Cuba would certainly destroy 90% of them but would not guarantee 100%.[32] In the best case a first strike destroys all of a country's deliverable weapons. In the worst case, some survive and can still be delivered.

If the survival of nuclear weapons requires their dispersal and concealment, do not problems of command and control become harder to solve? Americans think so because we think in terms of large nuclear arsenals. Small nuclear powers will neither have them nor need them. Lesser nuclear states might deploy, say, ten real weapons and ten dummies, while permitting other countries to infer that the numbers are larger. The adversary need only believe that some warheads may survive his attack and be visited on him. That belief should not be hard to create without making command and control unreliable. All nuclear countries must live through a time when their forces are crudely designed. All countries have so far been able to control them. Relations between the United States and the Soviet Union, and later among the United States, the Soviet Union, and China, were at their bitterest just when their nuclear forces were in early stages of development, were unbalanced, were crude and presumably hard to control. Why should we expect new nuclear states to experience greater difficulties than the old ones were able to cope with? Moreover, although some of the new nuclear states may be economically and technically backward, they will either have an expert and highly trained group of scientists and engineers or they will not produce nuclear weapons. Even if they buy the weapons, they will have to hire technicians to maintain and control them. We do not have to wonder whether they will take good care of their weapons. They have every incentive to do so. They will not want to risk retaliation because one or more of their warheads accidentally strikes another country.

Hiding nuclear weapons and keeping them under control are tasks for which the ingenuity of numerous states is adequate. Nor are means of delivery difficult to devise or procure. Bombs can be driven in by trucks from neighbouring countries. Ports can be torpedoed by small boats lying off shore. Moreover, a thriving arms trade in ever more sophisticated military equipment provides ready access to what may be wanted, including planes and missiles suited nuclear warhead delivery

Lesser nuclear states can pursue deterrent strategies effectively. Deterrence requires the ability to inflict unacceptable damage on another country. 'Unacceptable damage' to the Soviet Union was variously defined by Robert McNamara as requiring the ability to destroy a fifth to a fourth of her population and a half to two-thirds of her industrial capacity. American estimates of what is required for deterrence have been absurdly high. To deter, a country need not appear to be able to destroy a fourth or a half of another country, although in some cases that might be easily done. Would Libya try to destroy Israel's nuclear weapons at the risk of two bombs surviving to fall on Tripoli and Bengazi? And what would be left of Israel if Tel Aviv and Haifa were destroyed?

The weak can deter one another. But can the weak deter the strong? Raising the question of China's ability to deter the Soviet Union highlights the issue. The population and industry of most states concentrate in a relatively small number of centres. This is true of the Soviet Union. A major attack on the top ten cities of the Soviet Union would get 25% of its industrial capacity and 25% of its urban population. Geoffrey Kemp in 1974 concluded that China would probably be able to strike on that scale.[33] And, I emphasize again, China need only appear to be able to do it. A low probability of carrying a highly destructive attack home is sufficient for deterrence. A force of an imprecisely specifiable minimum capability is nevertheless needed.

In a 1979 study, Justin Galen (pseud.) wonders whether the Chinese have a force physically capable of deterring the Soviet Union. He estimates that China has 60 to 80 medium-range and 60 to 80 intermediate-range missiles of doubtful reliability and accuracy and 80 obsolete bombers. He rightly points out that the missiles may miss their targets even if fired at cities and that the bombers may not get through the Soviet Union's defences. Moreover, the Russians may be able to pre-empt, having almost certainly 'located virtually every Chinese missile, aircraft, weapons storage area and production facility'.[34] But surely Russian leaders reason the other way around. To locate virtually all missiles and aircraft is not good enough. Despite inaccuracies, a few Chinese missiles *may* hit Russian cities, and some bombers *may* get through. Not much is required to deter. What political-military objective is worth risking Vladivostock, Novosibirsk, and Tomsk, with no way of being sure that Moscow will not go as well?

Prevention and pre-emption are difficult games because the costs are so high if the games are not perfectly played. Inhibitions against using nuclear forces for such attacks are strong, although one cannot say they are absolute. Some of the inhibitions are simply human. Can country A find justification for a preventive or pre-emptive strike against B if B, in acquiring nuclear weapons, is imitating A? The leader of a country that launches a preventive or pre-emptive strike courts condemnation by his own people, by the world's people, and by history. Awesome acts are hard to perform. Some of the inhibitions are political. As Bernard Brodie tirelessly and wisely said, war has to find a political objective that is commensurate with its cost. Clausewitz's central tenet remains valid in the nuclear age.[35] Ultimately, the inhibitions lie in the impossibility of knowing for sure that a disarming strike will totally destroy an opposing force and in the immense destruction even a few warheads can wreak.

The credibility of small deterrent forces

The credibility of weaker countries' deterrent threats has two faces. The first is physical. Will such countries be able to construct and protect a deliverable force? We have found that they can readily do so. The second is psychological. Will an adversary believe that retaliation threatened will be carried out?

Deterrent threats backed by second-strike nuclear forces raise the expected costs of war to such heights that war becomes unlikely. But deterrent threats may not be credible. In a world where two or more countries can make them, the prospect of *mutual* devastation makes it difficult, or irrational, to execute threats should the occasion for doing so arise. Would it not be senseless to risk suffering further destruction once a deterrent force had failed to deter? Believing that it would be, an adversary may attack counting on the attacked country's unwillingness to risk initiating a devasting exchange by its own retaliation. Why retaliate once a threat to do so has failed? If one's policy is to rely on forces designed to deter, then an attack that is nevertheless made shows that one's reliance was misplaced. The course of wisdom may be to pose a new question: What is the best policy once deterrence has failed? One gains nothing by destroying an enemy's cities. Instead, in retaliating, one may prompt the enemy to unleash more warheads. A ruthless aggressor may strike believing that the leaders of the attacked country are capable of following such a 'rational' line of thought. To carry out the threat that was 'rationally' made may be 'irrational'. This old worry achieved new prominence as the strategic capabilities of the Soviet Union approached those of the United States in the middle 1970s. The Soviet Union, some feared, might believe that the United States would be self-deterred.[36]

Much of the literature on deterrence emphasizes the problem of achieving the credibility on which deterrence depends and the danger of relying on a deterrent of uncertain credibility. One earlier solution to the problem was found in Thomas Schelling's notion of 'the threat that leaves something to chance'. No state can know for sure that another state will refrain from retaliating even when retaliation would be irrational. No state can bet heavily on another state's rationality. Bernard Brodie put the thought more directly, while avoiding the slippery notion of rationality. Rather than ask what it may be rational or irrational for governments to do, the question he asked, and repeated in various ways over the years, was this: How do governments behave in the presence of awesome dangers? His answer was 'very carefully'.

To ask why a country should carry out its deterrent threat once deterrence has failed is to ask the wrong question. The question suggests that an aggressor may attack believing that the attacked country may not retaliate. This invokes the conventional logic that analysts find so hard to forsake. In a conventional world, a country can sensibly attack if it believes that success is probable. In a nuclear world, a country cannot sensibly attack unless it believes that success is assured. An attacker is deterred even if he believes only that the attacked *may* retaliate. Uncertainty of response, not certainty, is required for deterrence because, if retaliation occurs, one risks losing all. In a nuclear world, we should look less at the retaliator's conceivable inhibitions and more at the challenger's obvious risks.

One may nevertheless wonder, as Americans recently have, whether retaliatory threats remain credible if the strategic forces of the attacker are superior to those of the attacked. Will an unsuccessful defender in a conventional war have the courage to unleash its deterrent force, using nuclear weapons first against a country having superior strategic forces? Once more this asks the wrong question. The previous paragraph urged the importance of shifting attention from the defender's possible inhibitions to the aggressor's unwillingness to run extreme risks. This paragraph urges the importance of shifting attention from the defender's courage to the different valuations that defenders and attackers place on the stakes. An attacked country will ordinarily value keeping its own territory more highly than an attacker will value gaining some portion of it. Given second-strike capabilities, it is not the balance of forces but the courage to use them that counts. The balance or imbalance of strategic forces affects neither the calculation of danger nor the question of whose will is the stronger. Second-strike forces have to be seen in absolute terms. The question of whose interests are paramount will then determine whose will is perceived as being the stronger.

Emphasizing the importance of the 'balance of resolve', to use Glenn Snyder's apt phrase, raises questions about what a deterrent force covers and what it does not.[37] In answering these questions, we can learn something from the experience of the last three decades. The United States and the Soviet Union have limited and modulated their provocative acts, the more carefully so when major values for one side or the other were at issue. This can be seen both in what they have and in what they have not done. Whatever support the Soviet Union gave to North Korea's initial attack on the South was given after Secretary of State Acheson, the Joint Chiefs of Staff, General MacArthur, and the Chairman of the Senate Foreign Relations Committee all explicitly excluded both South Korea and Taiwan from America's defence perimeter. The United States, to take another example, could fight for years on a large scale in South-east Asia because neither success nor failure mattered much internationally. Victory would not have made the world one of American hegemony. Defeat would not have made the world one of Russian hegemony. No vital interest of either great power was at stake, as both Kissinger and Brezhnev made clear at the time.[38] One can fight without fearing escalation only where little is at stake. And that is where the deterrent does not deter.

Actions at the periphery can safely be bolder than actions at the centre. In contrast, where much is at stake for one side, the other side moves with care. Trying to win where winning would bring the central balance into question threatens escalation and becomes too risky to contemplate. The United States is circumspect when East European crises impend. Thus Secretary of State Dulles assured the Soviet Union when Hungarians rebelled in October of 1956 that we would not interfere with efforts to suppress them. And the Soviet Union's moves in the centre of Europe are carefully controlled. Thus her probes in Berlin have been tentative, reversible, and ineffective. Strikingly, the long border between East and West Europe – drawn where borders earlier proved unstable – has been free even of skirmishes in all of the years since the Second World War.

Both of the nuclear great powers become watchful and wary when events occur that may get out of control The strikes by Polish workers that began in August of 1980 provide the most recent illustration of this. The Soviet Union, her diplomats privately said, was 'determined to find a peaceful solution'. And a senior Carter Administration specialist on the Soviet Union was quoted as follows: 'It is a very explosive situation. Everyone is aware of it, and they are all reluctant to strike a match.'[39] Even though many steps would intervene between workers' strikes and the beginning of any fighting at all in the centre of Europe, both the Soviet Union and the United States showed great caution from the outset. By political and military logic, we can understand why nuclear weapons induce great caution, and we can confirm that they do by observing the differences of behaviour between great powers in nuclear and great powers in conventional worlds.

Contemplating American and Russian post-war behaviour, and interpreting it in terms of nuclear logic, suggests that deterrence extends to vital interests beyond the homeland more easily than many have thought. The United States cares more about Western Europe than the Soviet Union does. The Soviet Union cares more about Eastern Europe than the United States does. Communicating the weight of one side's concern as compared to the other side's has been easily enough done when the matters at hand affect the United States and the Soviet Union directly. For this reason, Western Europe's anxiety over the coverage it gets from American strategic forces, while understandable, is exaggerated. The United States might well retaliate should the Soviet Union make a major military move against a NATO country, and that is enough to deter.

The problem of extended deterrence

How far from the homeland does deterrence extend? One answers that question by defining the conditions that must obtain if deterrent threats are to be credited. First, the would-be attacker must be made to see that the deterrer considers the interests at stake to be vital ones. One cannot assume that countries will instantly agree on the question of whose interests are vital. Nuclear weapons, however, strongly incline them to grope for *de facto* agreement on the answer rather than to fight over it.

Second, political stability must prevail in the area that the deterrent is intended to cover. If the threat to a regime is in good part from internal factions, then an outside power may risk supporting one of them even in the face of deterrent threats. The credibility of a deterrent force requires both that interests be seen to be vital and that it is the attack from outside that threatens them. Given these conditions, the would-be attacker provides both the reason to retaliate and the target for retaliation. Deterrence gains in credibility the more highly valued the interests covered appear to be.

The problem of stretching a deterrent, which has so agitated the western alliance, is not a problem for lesser nuclear states. Their problem is to protect not others but themselves. Many have feared that lesser nuclear states would be the first to break the nuclear taboo and that they would use their weapons irresponsibly. I expect just the opposite. Weak states find it easier than strong states to establish their credibility. Not only will they not be trying to stretch their deterrent forces to cover others but also their vulnerability to conventional attack lends credence to their nuclear threats. Because in a conventional war they can lose so much so fast, it is easy to believe that they will unleash a deterrent force even at the risk of receiving a nuclear blow in return. With deterrent forces, the party that is absolutely threatened prevails.[40] Use of nuclear weapons by lesser states will come only if survival is at stake. And this should be called not irresponsible but responsible use.

An opponent who attacks what is unambiguously mine risks suffering great distress if I have second-strike forces. This statement has important implications for both the deterrer and the deterred. Where territorial claims are shadowy and disputed, deterrent writs do not run. As Steven J. Rosen has said: 'It is difficult to imagine Israel committing national suicide to hold on to Abu Rudeis or Hebron or Mount Hermon'.[41] Attacks on Israel's occupied lands would be imaginable even if she admitted having nuclear weapons. Establishing the credibility of a deterrent force requires moderation of territorial claims on the part of the would-be deterrer. For modest states, weapons whose very existence works strongly against their use are just what is wanted.

In a nuclear world, conservative would-be attackers will be prudent, but will all would-be attackers be conservative? A new Hitler is not unimaginable. Would the presence of nuclear weapons have moderated Hitler's behaviour? Hitler did not start World War II in order to destroy the Third Reich. Indeed, he was surprised and dismayed by the British and French declaration of war on Poland's behalf. After all, the western democracies had not come to the aid of a geographically defensible and militarily strong Czechoslovakia. Why then should they have declared war on behalf of a less defensible Poland and against a Germany made stronger by the incorporation of Czechoslovakia's armour? From the occupation of the Rhineland in 1936 to the invasion of Poland in 1939, Hitler's calculations were realistically made. In those years, Hitler would almost surely have been deterred from acting in ways that immediately threatened massive death and widespread destruction in Germany. And, if Hitler had not been deterred, would his generals have obeyed his commands? In a nuclear world, to act in blatantly offensive ways is madness. Under the circumstances, how many generals would obey the commands of a madman? One man alone does not make war.

To believe that nuclear deterrence would have worked against Germany in 1939 is easy. It is also easy to believe that in 1945, given the ability to do so, Hitler and some few around him would have fired nuclear warheads at the United States, Great Britain, and the Soviet Union as their armies advanced, whatever the consequences for Germany. Two considerations, however, work against this possibility. When defeat is seen to be inevitable, a ruler's authority may vanish. Early in 1945 Hitler apparently ordered the initiation of gas warfare, but no one responded.[42] The first consideration applies in a conventional world; the second in a nuclear world. In the latter, no country will press another to the point of decisive defeat. In the desperation of defeat desperate measures may be taken, but the last thing anyone wants to do is to make a nuclear nation feel desperate. The unconditional surrender of a nuclear nation cannot be demanded.

Dreaming up situations in which someone may have 'good reason' to strike first has plagued strategic thought ever since Herman Kahn began writing scenarios. Considering one such scenario is worthwhile because it has achieved some popularity among those who believe that deterrence is difficult.[43] Albert Wohlstetter imagines a situation in which the Soviet Union might strike first. Her leaders might decide to do so in a desperate effort to save a sinking regime. The desperation could be produced, Wohlstetter thinks, by 'disastrous defeat in peripheral war', by 'loss of key satellites', by the 'danger of revolt spreading – possibly to Russia itself', or by 'fear of an attack by ourselves'. Under such circumstances, the risk of *not* striking might 'appear very great to the Soviets'.[44] Imagination places the Soviet Union in a situation where striking first is bad, but presumably not striking first is even worse.

One common characteristic of scenarios is that they are compounded of odd elements. How can the Soviet Union suffer disastrous defeat in a peripheral war? If the war is peripheral, defeat may be embarrassing, but hardly disastrous. Another common characteristic of scenarios is the failure to say how the imagined act will accomplish the end in view. Some rulers will do anything to save themselves and their regimes. That is the assumption. But how a regime can hope to save itself by making a nuclear strike at a superior adversary, or at any adversary having a second-strike force, is not explained. Why is not striking first even worse than doing so, and in what way does it entail a smaller risk? We are not told. The most important common characteristic of scenarios, and often their fatal flaw, is also present in this one. The scenarist imagines a state in the midst of a terrible crisis in which the alternatives are so bad that launching a first strike supposedly makes some sense, but he does not say how this situation might come about. How could the Soviet Union get into such a mess, and what would other states be doing in the meantime? Scenarios often feature just one player, keeping others in the background even though two or more states are necessarily involved in making and in preventing wars. To think that the Soviet Union would strike the United States because of incipient revolt within her borders is silly. To think that the Soviet Union would strike first believing that we were about to do so is not. One must then ask how the US would behave if the USSR were seen to be in a perilous condition. It is sometimes surprisingly difficult for strategists to think of the actions and interactions of two or more states at the same time. No country will goad a nuclear adversary that finds itself in sad straits.

When vital interests are at stake, all of the parties involved are strongly constrained to be moderate because one's immoderate behaviour makes the nuclear threats of others credible. No one would want to provoke an already desperate country if that country had strategic nuclear weapons. Equally, a regime in crisis would desperately want to avoid calling nuclear warheads down upon itself. What scenarists imagine seldom has much to do with how governments behave. The bizarre qualities of various scenarios that depict a failure of deterrence strengthens one's confidence in it.

Three confusions mark many discussions of deterrence. First, that nuclear weapons affect the deterrer as well as the deterred is often overlooked. The many who fear that a country will foolishly launch missiles in a moment of panic overlook the care other countries will take in order not to make a nuclear country excessively nervous. Second, those who are sceptical of deterrence easily slip back from nuclear logic, by which slight risk of great damage deters, to conventional logic, by which states may somewhat sensibly risk war on narrowly calculated advantages. Thus some Americans fear that the Soviet Union will strike first – destroying most of our land-based warheads, planes on the ground, submarines in port, and much else besides. The strike would be made on the chance that we would not strike back with some of our thousands of remaining warheads. But states do not risk immense losses unless the odds on succeeding are overwhelmingly high. No one can say what the odds might be. Third, the quality of states' external behaviour is commonly inferred from their internal characteristics. Thus many emphasize the importance of *who* the new nuclear states will be and dwell on the question of whether their rulers will be 'rational'. They have failed to notice that radical states usually show caution in their foreign policies and to notice that nuclear weapons further moderate the behaviour of such states when vital interests are at issue. Nuclear peace depends not on rulers and those around them being rational but on their aversion to running catastrophic risks.

Arms races among new nuclear states

One may easily believe that American and Russian military doctrines have set the pattern that new nuclear states will follow. One may then also believe that they will suffer the fate of the United States and the Soviet Union, that they will compete in building larger and larger nuclear arsenals while continuing to accumulate conventional weapons. These are doubtful beliefs. One can infer the future from the past only insofar as future situations may be like present ones for the actors involved. For four main reasons, new nuclear states are likely to decrease rather than to increase their military spending.

First, nuclear weapons alter the dynamics of arms races. In a competition of two or more parties, it may be hard to say who is pushing and who is being pushed, who is leading and who is following. If one party seeks to increase its capabilities, it may seem that the other(s) must too. The dynamic may be built into the competition and may unfold despite a mutual wish to resist it. But need this be the case in a strategic competition between nuclear countries? It need not be if the conditions of competition make deterrent logic dominant. Deterrent logic dominates if the conditions of competition make it nearly impossible for any of the competing parties to achieve a first-strike capability. Early in the nuclear age, the implications of deterrent strategy were clearly seen. 'When dealing with the absolute weapon', as William T. R. Fox put it, 'arguments based on relative advantage lose their point'.[45] The United States has sometimes designed her forces according to that logic. Donald A. Quarles argued when he was Eisenhower's Secretary of the Air Force that 'sufficiency of air power' is determined by 'the force required to accomplish the mission assigned'. Avoidance of total war then does not depend on the '*relative* strength of the two opposed forces'. Instead, it depends on the '*absolute* power in the hands of each, and in the substantial invulnerability of this power to interdiction'.[46] To repeat: If no state can launch a disarming attack with high confidence, force comparisons are irrelevant. Strategic arms races are then pointless. Deterrent strategies offer this great advantage: Within wide ranges neither side need respond to increases in the other side's military capabilities.

Those who foresee nuclear arms racing among new nuclear states fail to make the distinction between war-fighting and war-deterring capabilities. War-fighting forces, because they threaten the forces of others, have to be compared. Superior forces may bring victory to one country; inferior forces may bring defeat to another. Force requirements vary with strategies and not just with the characteristics of weapons. With war-fighting strategies, arms races become difficult, if not impossible, to avoid. Forces designed for deterring war need not be compared. As Harold Brown said when he was Secretary of Defense, purely deterrent forces 'can be relatively modest, and their size can perhaps be made substantially, though not completely, insensitive to changes in the posture of an opponent'.[47] With deterrent strategies, arms races make sense only if a first-strike capability is within reach. Because thwarting a first strike is easy, deterrent forces are quite cheap to build and maintain. With deterrent forces, the question is not whether one country has more than another but whether it has the capability of inflicting 'unacceptable damage' on another, with unacceptable damage sensibly defined. Once that capability is assured, additional strategic weapons are useless. More is not better if less is enough.

Deterrent balances are also inherently stable. If one can say how much is enough, then within wide limits a country can be insensitive to changes in its adversaries' forces. This is the way French leaders have thought. France, as former President Giscard d'Estaing said, 'fixes its security at the level required to maintain, regardless of the way the strategic situation develops in the world, the credibility – in other words, the effectiveness – of its deterrent force'.[48] With deterrent forces securely established, no military need presses one side to try to surpass the other. Human error and folly may lead some parties involved in deterrent balances to spend more on armaments than is needed, but other parties need not increase their armaments in response, because such excess spending does not threaten them. The logic of deterrence eliminates incentives for strategic arms racing. This should be easier for lesser nuclear states to understand than it has been for the US and the USSR. Because most of them are economically hard pressed, they will not want to have more than enough.

Allowing for their particular circumstances, lesser nuclear states confirm these statements in their policies. Britain and France are relatively rich countries, and they tend to overspend. Their strategic forces are nevertheless modest enough when one considers that their purpose is to deter the Soviet Union rather than states with capabilities comparable to their own. China of course faces the same task. These three countries show no inclination to engage in nuclear arms races with anyone. India appears content to have a nuclear military capability that may or may not have produced deliverable warheads, and Israel maintains her ambiguous status. New nuclear states are likely to conform to these patterns and aim for a modest sufficiency rather than vie with each for a meaningless superiority.

Second, because strategic nuclear arms races among lesser powers are unlikely, the interesting question is not whether they will be run but whether countries having strategic nuclear weapons can avoid running conventional races. No more than the United States and the Soviet Union will lesser nuclear states want to rely on the deterrent threat that risks all. And will not their vulnerability to conventional attack induce them to continue their conventional efforts?

American policy as it has developed since the early 1960s again teaches lessons that mislead. For almost two decades, we have emphasized the importance of having a continuum of forces that would enable the United States and her allies to fight at any level from irregular to strategic nuclear warfare. A policy that decreases reliance on deterrence increases the chances that wars will be fought. This was well appreciated in Europe when we began to place less emphasis on deterrence and more on defence. The worries of many Europeans were well expressed by a senior British general in the following words: 'McNamara is practically telling the Soviets that the worst they need to expect from an attack on West Germany is a conventional counterattack'.[49] Why risk one's own destruction if one is able to fight on the ground and forgo the use of strategic weapons?

The policy of flexible response lessened reliance on strategic deterrence and increased the chances of fighting a war. New nuclear states are not likely to experience this problem. The expense of mounting conventional defences, and the difficulties and dangers of fighting conventional wars, will keep most new nuclear states from trying to combine large war-fighting forces with deterrent forces. Disjunction within their forces will enhance the value of deterrence.

Israeli policy seems to contradict these propositions. From 1971 through 1978, both Israel and Egypt spent from 20% to 40% of their GNPs on arms. Israel's spending on conventional arms remains high, although it has decreased since 1978. The decrease followed from the making of peace with Egypt and not from increased reliance on nuclear weapons. The seeming contradiction in fact bears out deterrent logic. So long as Israel holds the West Bank and the Gaza Strip she has to be prepared to fight for them. Since they are by no means unambiguously hers, deterrent threats, whether implicit or explicit, will not cover them. Moreover, while America's large subsidies continue, economic constraints will not drive Israel to the territorial settlement that would shrink her borders sufficiently to make a deterrent policy credible.

From previous points it follows that nuclear weapons are likely to decrease arms racing and reduce military costs for lesser nuclear states in two ways. Conventional arms races will wither if countries shift emphasis from conventional defence to nuclear deterrence. For Pakistan, for example, acquiring nuclear weapons is an alternative to running a ruinous conventional race with India.[50] And deterrent strategies make nuclear arms races pointless.

Finally, arms races in their ultimate form – the fighting of offensive wars designed to increase national security – also become pointless. The success of a deterrent strategy does not depend on the extent of territory a state holds, a point made earlier. It merits repeating because of its unusual importance for states whose geographic limits lead them to obsessive concern for their security in a world of ever more destructive conventional weapons.

The frequency and intensity of war

The presence of nuclear weapons makes wars less likely. One may nevertheless oppose the spread of nuclear weapons on the ground that they would make war, however unlikely, unbearably intense should it occur. Nuclear weapons have not been fired in anger in a world in which more than one country has them. We have enjoyed three decades of nuclear peace and may enjoy many more. But we can never have a guarantee. We may be grateful for decades of nuclear peace and for the discouragement of conventional war among those who have nuclear weapons. Yet the fear is widespread, and naturally so, that if they ever go off, we may all die. People as varied as the scholar Richard Smoke, the arms controller Paul Warnke, and former Defense Secretary Harold Brown all believe that if any nuclear weapons go off, many will. Although this seems the least likely of all the unlikely possibilities, it is not impossible. What makes it so unlikely is that, even if deterrence should fail, the prospects for rapid de-escalation are good.

McNamara asked himself what fractions of the Soviet Union's population and industry the United States should be able to destroy in order to deter her. For military, although not for budgetary, strategy this was the wrong question. States are not deterred because they expect to suffer a certain amount of damage but because they cannot know how much damage they will suffer. Near the dawn of the nuclear age Bernard Brodie put the matter simply: 'The prediction is more important than the fact.'[51] The prediction, that is, that attacking the vital interests of a country having nuclear weapons may bring the attacker untold losses. As Patrick Morgan more recently put it: 'To attempt to "compute" the cost of a nuclear war is to miss the point.'[52]

States are deterred by the prospect of suffering severe damage and by their physical inability to do much to limit it. Debate over the Soviet Union's civil defence efforts calls attention to this inability. Defensive measures can reduce casualties, but they would still be immense were either of the great powers to launch a determined attack. Moreover, civil defence cannot save the Soviet Union's heavily concentrated industries. Warheads numbered in the hundreds can destroy the United States and the Soviet Union as viable societies no matter what defensive measures they take. Deterrence works because nuclear weapons enable one state to punish another state severely without first defeating it. 'Victory', in Thomas Schelling's words, 'is no longer a prerequisite for hurting the enemy'.[53] Countries armed only with conventional weapons can hope that their military forces will be able to limit the damage an attacker can do. Among countries armed with strategic nuclear forces, the hope of avoiding heavy damage depends mainly on the attacker's restraint and little on one's own efforts. Those who compare expected deaths through strategic exchanges of nuclear warheads with casualties suffered by the Soviet Union in World War II overlook this fundamental difference between conventional and nuclear worlds.

Deterrence rests on what countries *can* do to each other with strategic nuclear weapons. From this statement, one easily leaps to the wrong conclusion: that deterrent strategies, if they have to be carried through, will produce a catastrophe. That countries are able to annihilate each other means neither that deterrence depends on their threatening to do so nor that they will do so if deterrence fails. Because countries heavily armed with strategic nuclear weapons can carry war to its ultimate intensity, the control of force, in wartime as in peacetime, becomes the primary objective. If deterrence fails, leaders will have the strongest incentives to keep force under control and limit damage rather than launching genocidal attacks. If the Soviet Union should attack Western Europe, NATO's objectives would be to halt the attack and end the war. The United States has long had the ability to place hundreds of warheads precisely on targets in the Soviet Union. Surely we would strike military targets before striking industrial targets and industrial targets before striking cities. The intent to do so is sometimes confused with a war-fighting strategy, which it is not. It would not significantly reduce the Soviet Union's ability to hurt us. It is a deterrent strategy, resting initially on the threat to punish. The threat, if it fails to deter, is appropriately followed not by spasms of violence but by punishment administered in ways that convey threats to make the punishment more severe.

For several reasons, then, deterrent strategies promise less damage than war-fighting strategies. First, deterrent strategies induce caution all around and thus reduce the incidence of war. Second, wars fought in the face of strategic nuclear weapons must be carefully limited because a country having them may retaliate if its vital interests are threatened. Third, prospective punishment need only be proportionate to an adversary's expected gains in war after those gains are discounted for the many uncertainties of war. Fourth, should deterrence fail, a few judiciously delivered warheads are likely to produce sobriety in the leaders of all of the countries involved and thus bring rapid de-escalation.

A deterrent strategy promises less damage, should deterrence fail, than does the Schlesinger-Brown 'countervailing' strategy, a strategy which contemplates fighting a limited, strategic nuclear war. War-fighting strategies offer no clear place to stop short of victory for some and defeat for others. Deterrent strategies do, and that place is where one country threatens another's vital interests. Deterrent strategies lower the probability that wars will be fought. If wars are nevertheless fought, deterrent strategies lower the probability that they will become wars of high intensity.

A war between the United States and the Soviet Union that did get out of control would be catastrophic. If they set out to destroy each other, they would greatly reduce the world's store of developed resources while killing millions outside of their own borders through fallout. Even while destroying themselves, states with few weapons would do less damage to others. As ever, the biggest international dangers come from the strongest states. Fearing the world's destruction, one may prefer a world of conventional great powers having a higher probability of fighting less destructive wars to a world of nuclear great powers having a lower probability of fighting more destructive wars. But that choice effectively disappeared with the production of atomic bombs by the United States during World War II. Since the great powers are unlikely to be drawn into the nuclear wars of others, the added global dangers posed by the spread of nuclear weapons are small.

The spread of nuclear weapons threatens to make wars more intense at the local and not at the global level, where wars of the highest intensity have been possible for a number of years. If their national existence should be threatened, weaker countries, unable to defend at lesser levels of violence, may destroy themselves through resorting to nuclear weapons. Lesser nuclear states will live in fear of this possibility. But this is not different from the fear under which the United States and the Soviet Union have lived for years. Small nuclear states may experience a keener sense of desperation because of extreme vulnerability to conventional as well as to nuclear attack, but, again, in desperate situations what all parties become most desperate to avoid is the use of strategic nuclear weapons. Still, however improbable the event, lesser states may one day fire some of their weapons. Are minor nuclear states more or less likely to do so than major ones? The answer to this question is vitally important because the existence of some states would be at stake even if the damage done were regionally confined.

Looking at the situation of weaker nuclear states and at the statements of stronger nuclear states, one suspects that weak states are less likely to use nuclear weapons first than are strong ones. Many have worried about conventional wars between minor nuclear states becoming nuclear wars as one side loses. It is NATO, however, that plans to use nuclear weapons in battle if conventional troops cannot hold. Moreover, after the Soviet Union invaded Afghanistan in December of 1979, American officials considered using nuclear weapons in the Middle East if need be. At various times, some Americans have thought of reasons for making limited counterforce strikes – firing a few missiles at the Soviet Union to show our determination – an idea revived by James R. Schlesinger when he was Secretary of Defense. Among others, Generals Earle G. Wheeler and George Brown, former chairmen of the Joint Chiefs of Staff, have talked of our emerging from a nuclear war with a 'relative advantage' over the Soviet Union by targeting their 'war recovery capabilities'.[54] Presidential Directive 59, signed by President Carter in July of 1980, contemplates fighting a limited nuclear war, perhaps a prolonged one, if deterrence should fail. And some of the Soviet Union's military leaders have publicly discussed using nuclear weapons to win wars.

The United States and the Soviet Union have more readily contemplated the use of nuclear weapons than lesser nuclear states have done or are likely to do. But planning is distinct from deciding to act. Planners think they should offer Presidents a range of choices and a variety of nuclear weapons to carry them through. In the event, Presidents, like Party Chairmen, will shy away from using nuclear weapons and will act with extreme care in dealing with situations that might get out of control, as they have done in the past. New nuclear states are likely to be even more mindful of dangers and more concerned for their safety than some of the old ones have been. Ordinarily, weak states calculate more fearfully and move more cautiously than strong ones. The thought that fear and caution may lead insecure countries to launch preventive or preemptive strikes has amplified anxieties about the instability of regions populated by lesser nuclear powers and about the extent of destruction their weapons may bring. Such worries rest on inferences drawn from the behaviour of conventional states and do not apply to nuclear ones, for reasons already discussed.

Nuclear weapons lessen the intensity as well as the frequency of war among their possessors. For fear of escalation, nuclear states do not want to fight long or hard over important interests – indeed, they do not want to fight at all. Minor nuclear states have even better reasons than major ones to accommodate one another peacefully and to avoid any fighting. Worries about the intensity of war among nuclear states have to be viewed in this context and against a world in which conventional weapons become ever costlier and more destructive.

The roles and reactions of the great powers

Should a great power help a lesser one improve its force once it has shown the will and the ability to build one? Will great powers be drawn into the nuclear confrontations of lesser ones, or will they draw away from them to avoid involvement? Will small nuclear powers cut themselves adrift from the great powers and follow independent policies? Will small countries' nuclear forces trigger an arms race between the great powers? These questions suggest four ways in which big and small nuclear powers may interact.

Small and crude forces tempt pre-emption, so it is thought, and may be used in reckless and unintended ways because of inadequate command and control. These dangers can be removed by great powers assisting lesser ones in building and managing their forces. Nevertheless, neither the United States nor the Soviet Union will want to help much, lest countries come to believe that they can build insufficient and unreliable forces and rely on one of the great powers to turn them into something substantial. Such hindrance is unfortunate, if improving others' forces serves wider interests. Is help required, not just for the sake of the recipient, but also to avoid nuclear imbalances between states that might prompt wars and to reduce the chances of accidents that might set them off? We saw earlier that these are minor worries. Because they are minor, the United States and the Soviet Union are not likely to be tempted to give technical help to countries entering the nuclear military business.

Nuclear weapons in the hands of six or seven states have lessened wars and limited conflicts. The further spread of nuclear weapons can be expected to widen those effects. Should the United States then promote the spread of nuclear weapons for the sake of peace, even though we need not for the sake of stability? To do so would replace one extreme policy with another. Present policy works hard to prevent additional states from acquiring nuclear weapons. My examination of the effects of nuclear weapons leads to the conclusion that our policy is wrong without supporting the proposition that true proliferation – the rapid spread of nuclear weaponry – is desirable. Rapid change may be destabilizing. The slow spread of nuclear weapons gives states time to learn to live with them, to appreciate their virtues, and to understand the limits they place on behaviour.

Will the United States and the Soviet Union be drawn into the struggles of lesser nuclear states? This question loses much of its urgency given the aversion of states to crises that raise the spectre of nuclear war and the care they take in crises that do so. Will they then draw away from other states' crises rather than being drawn in? The United States and the Soviet Union will continue to have interests in various parts of the world for all of the old political, economic, and military reasons. In a region where nuclear powers are locked in dispute, the great powers will move cautiously in attempting to tend to their separate and to their common interests. We can hardly expect the United States or the Soviet Union to risk more in other people's crises than they have risked in their own. Neither the United States nor the Soviet Union want a regional nuclear confrontation to become a global one. If that risk hangs over them, their strong mutual interest is to withdraw.

Will lesser nuclear powers want to edge away from their great-power patrons in order to be able to choose their policies more freely? To do so would be risky. A nuclear Israel, for example, may threaten to fire missiles at her attackers' cities if ever their victory in war seems likely. In the face of possible Russian opposition, signs of American acquiescence in Israel's policy would help to make the prospect of retaliation credible. Any lesser power contemplating the use of nuclear weapons even for deterrent or defensive purposes will expect opposition from at least one of the great powers. An alliance or some other kind of connection with one of them may stay the hand of the other. This is another way of saying that even with nuclear weapons weaker states continue to depend on stronger states in various ways.

By acquiring nuclear weapons a state changes one variable in a complex equation of forces. That variable is the most important one. Nuclear weapons increase the ability of states to fend for themselves when the integrity of their legitimate boundaries is at stake. Thus an Israeli deterrent force would enable Israel to maintain her legitimate boundaries while reducing her extreme dependence on the United States. In recent years our aid has amounted to a seventh or an eighth of Israel's GNP yearly. Such dependence will substantially lessen only if military security becomes less of a concern or can be more cheaply provided. Nuclear weapons and strategies, however, do not cover all of the military problems of new nuclear states nor are military problems the whole of their concerns. Israeli dependence on the United States will not disappear so long as she remains a small country in a hostile world. Similarly, the deterrent effect of China's nuclear weapons makes her less dependent on others militarily, without much reducing her need for economic and technical assistance. Nuclear weapons are useful against threats to a state's territorial integrity, but most of the doings of states fall far short of this extreme. Independent nuclear forces reduce dependency by lesser powers on others without eliminating it.

Will the nuclear arms of lesser powers stimulate the great powers to further exertion? And will arms control and disarmament agreements be harder to reach? Consider arms racing first. A faster race between the great powers may come about in the following way, and to some extent already has. The United States or the Soviet Union builds more missiles and more defences against missiles as she perceives a growing threat from China. The increased effort of one of the great powers prompts the other to try harder, and the effects become reciprocating causes. Action, reaction, and over-reaction by the United States and the Soviet Union have formed a pattern too familiar to disregard. The pattern is likely to repeat itself, but it need not.

Consider a historical case. In 1967, McNamara half-heartedly proposed deploying a cheap ($5-billion) ABM system designed to handle an attack by China even though, as he said, we had 'the power not only to destroy completely her entire nuclear offensive forces, but to devastate her society as well'. Whatever his political and bureaucratic reasons, he publicly argued that a light ABM system offered four advantages:

(1) China might miscalculate.
(2) America would be showing Asian states that she would not let China blackmail them and would thus dampen their desires to have their own nuclear weapons.
(3) America would gain marginal protection for *Minuteman* sites against an attack by the Soviet Union.
(4) America would be safe against accidental launchings.[55]

Had the United States persisted in building a 'Chinese' system, this might have prompted further efforts by the Soviet Union. The United States and the Soviet Union can react to third countries' nuclear forces in ways that stimulate their own competition in arms, but they need not do so, as is shown by examining McNamara's four reasons. His fourth reason applies to any and all nuclear countries. It raises the question of the value of taking out an ABM insurance policy against accidental firings whether by third countries, by the Soviet Union, or by the United States. His third reason applies explicitly to the Soviet Union and not to third nuclear countries. His second reason rests on a false belief about the feasibility of nuclear blackmail. Only the first of McNamara's reasons applies specifically to the forces of China or of any lesser nuclear country. It raises this question: Under any imaginable circumstances, might a lesser nuclear country's miscalculation lead it to launch an attack on the United States? The miscalculation would have to be monumental. Building missile defences against China would imply that great powers can deter each other but cannot deter minor ones. The weakness of the proposition is apparent.

Nor need more missiles be added to either great power's arsenal in order to deter lesser nuclear powers, even should the great powers fail to deter each other. In 1978, the United States had about 2,150 warheads on land-based launchers, about 5,120 on sea-based launchers, and about 2,580 in bombers.[56] These numbers had changed little by 1980. One study estimates that the Soviet Union's best attack, launched in the mid-1980s and coming at the worst time for us with our forces only on normal day-to-day alert, would leave us with about 6,400 warheads and about 1,800 equivalent megatons. After such an attack, the Soviet Union would have about 6,000 warheads left and 6,000 equivalent megatons. We would still have more than we need since 1,000 *Poseidon* warheads (the force loading of some six submarines) can 'destroy about 75 percent of the Soviet industrial targets'. With our present force we can absorb a first strike and still destroy the Soviet Union as 'a modern industrial society', and do so with missiles to spare for counterforce attacks.[57] And we and they would have more than enough left over to deter third countries. This plenitude of deliverable warheads is sometimes referred to as 'sufficiency'. The great powers scarcely need get into an arms race because of what lesser powers do.

Still, the United States and the Soviet Union do race from time to time, and the racing has been fuelled in part by what third countries have done. The Soviet Union, for example, argues that many of her intermediate and medium-range ballistic missiles are needed because of the threat posed by China. Some of the NATO countries then conclude that because these missiles threaten Western Europe, cruise issiles and *Pershing* IIs must be deployed there. This then further worries the Soviet Union. No one doubts these effects.

Strategic arms races between the United States and the Soviet Union, however, are produced mainly by the strategies they follow and by the kinds of forces they build. In their strategies, dissuasion by deterrence has always been alloyed with defensive and war-fighting policies and capabilities. The number of Russian cities worth striking is finite and indeed quite low. We have long had more survivable warheads than Russian cities to strike. If only cities were aimed at, many warheads would lack targets. The quantity of warheads on hand and their increased accuracy constitute arguments for a counterforce strategy. In the last two decades, the balance between deterrent strategy and war-fighting strategy has tilted towards the latter. Available weapons affect the strategy a country adopts, and the strategy that is fashioned in turn calls for the further development of weapons. If each side views the other's strategic forces as designed for fighting wars as much as, or more than, for deterring them, then arms races become very difficult to avoid. Such perceptions vary with changes in the strategies and forces of the great powers, not of the lesser ones. Great powers engage in arms races mainly because of what other great powers do. That was true in a multipolar, conventional world; it remains true in a bipolar, nuclear world.

Conclusion

The conclusion is in two parts. After saying what follows for American policy from my analysis, I briefly state the main reasons for believing that the slow spread of nuclear weapons will promote peace and reinforce international stability.

Implications for American policy

I have argued that the gradual spread of nuclear weapons is better than no spread and better than rapid spread. We do not face a set of happy choices. We may prefer that countries have conventional weapons only, do not run arms races, and do not fight. Yet the alternative to nuclear weapons for some countries may be ruinous arms races with high risk of their becoming engaged in debilitating conventional wars.

Countries have to care for their security with or without the help of others. If a country feels highly insecure and believes that nuclear weapons will make it more secure, America's policy of opposing the spread of nuclear weapons will not easily determine theirs. Any slight chance of bringing the spread of nuclear weapons to a full stop exists only if the United States and the Soviet Union constantly and strenuously try to achieve that end. To do so carries costs measured in terms of their other interests. The strongest means by which the United States can persuade a country to forgo nuclear weapons is a guarantee of its security, especially if the guarantee is made credible by the presence of American troops. But how many commitments do we want to make, and how many countries do we want to garrison? We are wisely reluctant to give guarantees, but we then should not expect to decide how other countries are to provide for their security. As a neighbour of China, India no doubt feels more secure, and can behave more reasonably, with a nuclear-weapons capability than without it. The thought applies as well to Pakistan as India's neighbour. We damage our relations with such countries by badgering them about nuclear weapons while being unwilling to guarantee their security. Under such circumstances they, not we, should decide what their national interests require.

If the United States and the Soviet Union lessen their opposition to the spread of nuclear weapons, will not many states jump on the nuclear bandwagon? Some have feared that weakening opposition to the spread of nuclear weapons will lead numerous states to make them because it may seem that 'everyone is doing it'.[58]

Why should we think that if the United States relaxes, numerous states will begin to make nuclear weapons? Both the United States and the Soviet Union were more relaxed in the past, and these effects did not follow. The Soviet Union initially furthered China's nuclear development. The United States continues to help Britain maintain her deterrent forces. By 1968 the CIA had informed President Johnson of the existence of Israeli nuclear weapons, and in July of 1970 Richard Helms, Director of the CIA, gave this information to the Senate Foreign Relations Committee. These and later disclosures were not followed by censure of Israel or by reductions of assistance to her.[59] And in September of 1980 the Executive Branch, against the will of the House of Representatives but with the approval of the Senate, continued to do nuclear business with India despite her explosion of a nuclear device and despite her unwillingness to sign the Nuclear Non-Proliferation Treaty.

Assisting some countries in the development of nuclear weapons and failing to oppose others has not caused a nuclear stampede. Is the more recent leniency towards India likely to? One reason to think so is that more countries now have the ability to make their own nuclear weapons, more than forty of them according to Joseph Nye.[60]

Many more countries can than do. One can believe that American opposition to nuclear arming stays the deluge only by overlooking the complications of international life. Any state has to examine many conditions before deciding whether or not to develop nuclear weapons. Our opposition is only one factor and is not likely to be the decisive one. Many countries feel fairly secure living with their neighbours. Why should they want nuclear weapons? Some countries, feeling threatened, have found security through their own strenuous efforts and through arrangements made with others. South Korea is an outstanding example. Many South Korean officials believe that South Korea would lose more in terms of American support if she acquired nuclear weapons than she would gain by having them.[61] Further, on occasion we might slow the spread of nuclear weapons by *not* opposing the nuclear-weapons programmes of some countries. When we oppose Pakistan's nuclear programme, we are saying that we disapprove of countries developing nuclear weapons no matter what their neighbours do. Failing to oppose Pakistan's efforts also sends a signal to potential nuclear states, suggesting that if a country develops nuclear weapons, a regional rival may do so as well and may do so without opposition from us. This message may give pause to some of the countries that are tempted to acquire nuclear weapons. After all, Argentina is to Brazil as Pakistan is to India.

Neither the gradual spread of nuclear weapons nor American and Russian acquiescence in this has opened the nuclear floodgates. Nations attend to their security in ways they think best. The fact that so many more countries can make nuclear weapons than do make them says more about the hesitation of countries to enter the nuclear military business than about the effectiveness of American policy. We can sensibly suit our policy to individual cases, sometimes bringing pressure against a country moving towards nuclear-weapons capability and sometimes quietly acquiescing. No one policy is right for all countries. We should ask what our interests in regional peace and stability require in particular instances. We should also ask what the interests of other countries require before putting pressure on them. Some countries are likely to suffer more in cost and pain if they remain conventional states than if they become nuclear ones. The measured and selective spread of nuclear weapons does not run against our interests and can increase the security of some states at a price they can afford to pay.

It is not likely that nuclear weapons will spread with a speed that exceeds the ability of their new owners to adjust to them. The spread of nuclear weapons is something that we have worried too much about and tried too hard to stop.

The nuclear future

What will a world populated by a larger number of nuclear states look like? I have drawn a picture of such a world that accords with experience throughout the nuclear age. Those who dread a world with more nuclear states do little more than assert that more is worse and claim without substantiation that new nuclear states will be less responsible and less capable of self-control than the old ones have been. They express fears that many felt when they imagined how a nuclear China would behave. Such fears have proved unfounded as nuclear weapons have slowly spread. I have found many reasons for believing that with more nuclear states the world will have a promising future. I have reached this unusual conclusion for six main reasons.

First, international politics is a self-help system, and in such systems the principal parties do most to determine their own fate, the fate of other parties, and the fate of the system. This will continue to be so, with the United States and the Soviet Union filling their customary roles. For the United States and the Soviet Union to achieve nuclear maturity and to show this by behaving sensibly is more important than preventing the spread of nuclear weapons.

Second, given the massive numbers of American and Russian warheads, and given the impossibility of one side destroying enough of the other side's missiles to make a retaliatory strike bearable, the balance of terror is indestructible. What can lesser states do to disrupt the nuclear equilibrium if even the mighty efforts of the United States and the Soviet Union cannot shake it? The international equilibrium will endure.

Third, at the strategic level each of the great powers has to gauge the strength only of itself in relation to the other. They do not have to make guesses about the strengths of opposing coalitions, guesses that involve such imponderables as the coherence of diverse parties and their ability to concert their efforts. Estimating effective forces is thus made easier. Wars come most often by miscalculation. Miscalculation will not come from carelessness and inattention in a bipolar world as it may in a multipolar one.

Fourth, nuclear weaponry makes miscalculation difficult because it is hard not to be aware of how much damage a small number of warheads can do. Early in this century Norman Angell argued that wars could not occur because they would not pay.[62] But conventional wars have brought political gains to some countries at the expense of others. Germans founded a state by fighting three short wars, in the last of which France lost Alsace-Lorraine.

Among nuclear countries, possible losses in war overwhelm possible gains. In the nuclear age Angell's dictum, broadly interpreted, becomes persuasive. When the active use of force threatens to bring great losses, wars become less likely. This proposition is widely accepted but, insufficiently emphasized. Nuclear weapons have reduced the chances of war between the United States and the Soviet Union and between the Soviet Union and China. One may expect them to have similar effects elsewhere. Where nuclear weapons threaten to make the cost of wars immense, who will dare to start them? Nuclear weapons make it possible to approach the deterrent ideal.

Fifth, nuclear weapons can be used for defence as well as for deterrence. Some have argued that an apparently impregnable nuclear defence can be mounted. The Maginot Line has given defence a bad name. It nevertheless remains true that the incidence of wars decreases as the perceived difficulty of winning them increases. No one attacks a defence believed to be impregnable. Nuclear weapons may make it possible to approach the defensive ideal. If so, the spread of nuclear weapons will further help to maintain peace.

Sixth, new nuclear states will confront the possibilities and feel the constraints that present nuclear states have experienced. New nuclear states will be more concerned for their safety and more mindful of dangers than some of the old ones have been. Until recently, only the great and some of the major powers have had nuclear weapons. While nuclear weapons have spread, conventional weapons have proliferated. Under these circumstances, wars have been fought not at the centre but at the periphery of international politics. The likelihood of war decreases as deterrent and defensive capabilities increase. Nuclear weapons, responsibly used, make wars hard to start. Nations that have nuclear weapons have strong incentives to use them responsibly. These statements hold for small as for big nuclear powers. Because they do, the measured spread of nuclear weapons is more to be welcomed than feared.

Notes

1 Unless otherwise specified, data are from *The Military Balance* (London: IISS), yearly volumes.
2 Federal Minister of Defence, *White Paper: The Security of the Federal Republic of Germany and the Development of the Federal Armed Forces* (Bonn, 1979), p. 276.
3 Geoffrey Blainey, *The Causes of War* (London: Macmillan, 1970), pp. 108–19.
4 Cf. Kenneth N. Waltz, *Theory of International Politics* (Reading, Mass.: Addison-Wesley, 1979), ch. 8, parts II and III.
5 Cf. John J. Weltman, 'Nuclear Devolution and World Order', *World Politics*, vol. 32, January 1980, pp. 172–4.
6 Cf. Robert J. Art and Kenneth N. Waltz, 'Technology, Strategy, and the Uses of Force', *The Use of Force* (Boston: Little, Brown, 1971), pp. 6–11.
7 Cf. *ibid*. For the different implications of defence and deterrence, see Glenn H. Snyder, *Deterrence and Defense* (Princeton: Princeton University Press, 1961).
8 Robert Jervis, 'Cooperation under the Security Dilemma', *World Politics*, vol. 30, January 1978. Cf. Malcolm W. Hoag, 'On Stability in Deterrent Races', *World*

Politics, vol. 13, July 1961; Stephen Van Evera, 'Nuclear Weapons, Nuclear Proliferation, and the Causes of War', (unpublished paper, 1978).
9   See Richard Smoke, *War: Controlling Escalation* (Cambridge, Mass.: Harvard University Press, 1977), pp. 175–88.
10 Glenn H. Snyder, *op. cit.* in note 7, p. 44; Stephen Van Evera, 'The Effects of Nuclear Proliferation' (unpublished paper, 1976).
11 See Snyder, *op. cit.* in note 7, pp. 37, 49, 79–82; Bernard Brodie, *Escalation and the Nuclear Option* (Princeton: Princeton University Press, 1966), pp. 74–8; Robert Jervis, 'Deterrence Theory Revisited', *World Politics*, vol. 31, January 1979; and Shai Feldman, *Israeli Nuclear Deterrence: A Strategy for the 1980s?* (Berkeley, Calif.: Ph.D. dissertation, 1980), *passim*.
12 Bernard Brodie, *War and Politics* (New York: Macmillan, 1973), p. 321.
13 Georg Simmel, 'The Sociology of Conflict, I', *American Journal of Sociology*, vol. 9, January 1904, p. 501.
14 George Sansom, 'Japan's Fatal Blunder', *International Affairs*, October 1948 (in Art and Waltz, *op. cit.* in note 6), pp. 208–9.
15 I shall concentrate on nuclear deterrence and slight nuclear defence. A defensive nuclear doctrine, although it has not been welcomed in American or NATO military circles, was at times supported by Bernard Brodie and has been persuasively expounded by Sandoval, Shreffler, and a few others. See, for example, R. R. Sandoval, 'Consider the Porcupine: Another View of Nuclear Proliferation', *Bulletin of the Atomic Scientists*, vol. 32, May 1976; R. Shreffler and R.R. Sandoval, *Nuclear Weapons, Their Role in U.S. Political and Military Posture, and an Example* (Los Alamos Scientific Laboratory, September 1975); and R. Shreffler, 'The New Nuclear Force', in *Tactical Nuclear Weapons: European Perspectives* (Stockholm: International Peace Research Institute Yearbook, 1978).
16 *Hansard*, 1 March 1960, cols 1136–8.
17 Michael Nacht, 'The United States in a World of Nuclear Powers', in Joseph I. Coffey (ed.), *Nuclear Proliferation: Prospects, Problems, and Proposals* (Philadelphia: The Annals of the American Academy of Political Science, 1977), pp. 163–4.
18 Ashok Kapur, 'Nth Powers of the Future', in Coffey, *op. cit.* in note 17, p. 94.
19 *New York Times*, 20 June 1980, p. A3, 'U.S. Says Decision on Atom Fuel for India is Tied to Afghan Crisis'.
20 Richard Burt, 'Russia Shares Dilemma over Nuclear Spread', *New York Times*, 20 July 1980, p. E5.
21 Cf. Lewis A. Dunn, 'Nuclear Proliferation and World Politics', in Coffey, *op. cit.* in note 17, pp. 102–7.
22 Stephen Van Evera, *op. cit.* in note 10.
23 Shai Feldman, *op. cit.* in note 11, ch. 4.
24 *Ibid.*, Table 1.
25 For brief accounts, see S. E. Finer, *The Man on Horseback* (London: Pall Mall Press, 1962), pp. 106–8; and Roy Medvedev, 'Soviet Policy Reported Reversed by SALT ll', *Washington Star*, 7 July 1979, p. 1.
26 Kenneth N. Waltz, 'America's European Policy Viewed in Global Perspectives', in Wolfram F. Hanrieder (ed.), *The United States and Western Europe* (Cambridge, Mass.: Winthrop, 1974), p. 31; Richard K. Betts, *Soldiers, Statesmen, and Cold War Crises* (Cambridge, Mass.: Harvard University Press, 1977), App.A.
27 Cf. Lewis A. Dunn, *op. cit.* in note 21, p. 101.
28 Quoted in Walter H. Waggoner, 'U.S. Disowns Matthews Talk of Waging War to Get Peace', *New York Times*, 27 August 1950, p. 1.
29 Quoted in William B. Bader, *The United States and the Spread of Nuclear Weapons* (New York: Pegasus, 1968), p. 96.
30 Robert Jervis, 'Why Nuclear Superiority Doesn't Matter', *Political Science Quarterly*, vol. 94, Winter 1979–80.

31 For example, David M. Rosenbaum, 'Nuclear Terror', *International Security*, vol. 1, Winter 1977.
32 Graham T. Allison, *Essence of Decision* (Boston: Little, Brown, 1971), p. 126.
33 Geoffrey Kemp, *Nuclear Forces for Medium Powers*, Adelphi Papers Nos. 106 and 107 (London: IISS, 1974).
34 Justin Galen (pseud.), 'US' Toughest Message to the USSR', *Armed Forces Journal International*, February 1979.
35 See, for example, Bernard Brodie, 'The Development of Nuclear Strategy'. *International Security*, vol. 2. Spring 1978, p. 12.
36 James R. Schlesinger, 'U.S.-U.S.S.R. Strategic Policies', Hearing before the Subcommittee on Arms Control, International Law and Organizations of the Committee on Foreign Relations, U.S. Senate, 93rd Congress, 2nd Session, 4 March 1974; in Robert J. Pranger and Roger P. Labrie (eds.), *Nuclear Strategy and National Security: Points of View* (Washington DC: American Enterprise Institute, 1977), p. 105; Paul H. Nitze, 'Assuring Strategic Stability in an Era of Detente', *Foreign Affairs*, vol. 54, January 1976; and Colin S. Gray, 'Nuclear Strategy: A Case for a Theory of Victory', *International Security*, vol. 4. Summer 1979, pp. 67–72.
37 Glenn H. Snyder, 'Crisis Bargaining', in C.F. Hermann (ed.), *International Crises: Insights from Behavioral Research* (New York: Free Press, 1972), p. 232.
38 John G. Stoessinger, *Henry Kissinger: The Anguish of Power* (New York: W.W. Norton, 1976), ch. 8.
39 Murrey Marder, 'Saving Poland without a Nuclear War', *Washington Post*, 24 August 1980, p. 16.
40 Shai Feldman, *op. cit.* in note 11, ch. 1.
41 Steven J. Rosen, 'Nuclearization and Stability in the Middle East', in Onkar Marwah and Ann Schulz (eds.), *Nuclear Proliferation and the Near-Nuclear Countries* (Cambridge, Mass.: Ballinger, 1975), p. 173.
42 Frederic J. Brown, *Chemical Warfare: A Study in Restraints*, excerpted in Art and Waltz, *op. cit.* in n.6, p.183.
43 Albert Wohlstetter, 'The Delicate Balance of Terror', *Foreign Affairs*, vol.37, January 1959; Morton A. Kaplan, 'Strategy and Morality', in Kaplan (ed.), *Strategic Thinking and Its Moral Implications* (New York: Macmillan, 1973), p.26; Richard Rosecrance, *Strategic Deterrence Reconsidered*, Adelphi Paper No. 116 (London: IISS, 1975), p.34.
44 Albert Wohlstetter, *op. cit.* in note 43, p.46.
45 William T.R. Fox, 'International Control of Atomic Weapons', in Bernard Brodie (ed.), *The Absolute Weapon* (New York: Harcourt, Brace, 1946), p. 181.
46 Donald A. Quarles, 'How Much is Enough', *Air Force*, vol. 49, September 1956, pp. 51–2.
47 Department of Defense, FY 1980, *Annual Report* (Washington DC), pp. 75–6.
48 Valéry Giscard D'Estaing, 'Part II of the press conference by Valéry Giscard D'Estaing, President of the French Republic' (New York: French Embassy, Press and Information Division, 15 February 1979), p. 6.
49 Quoted in Eldon Griffiths, 'The Revolt of Europe', *Saturday Evening Post*, vol. 263, 9 March 1963, p. 19.
50 Richard K. Betts, 'Paranoids, Pygmies, Pariahs, and Nonproliferation', *Foreign Policy* no. 26, Spring 1977, pp. 161–2.
51 Bernard Brodie, *op. cit.* in note 45, p. 74.
52 Patrick Morgan, *Deterrence: A Conceptual Analysis* (Beverly Hills: Sage, 1977), p. 116.
53 Thomas Schelling, *Arms and Influence* (New Haven: Yale University Press, 1966), p. 22.
54 Bernard Brodie, *op. cit.* in note 12, p. 423; *op.cit.* in note 35, p.21.

55 Robert S. McNamara, 'Excerpts from a Speech Delivered before the Editors of United Press International, San Francisco, California', 18 September 1967, in Art and Waltz, *op. cit.* in note 6, pp. 509–13.
56 Congress of the United States, Congressional Budget Office, *Counterforce Issues for the U.S. Strategic Nuclear Forces, Background Paper* (Washington DC: USGPO, January 1978), Table 2, p. 18.
57 *Ibid.*, pp. 27–8.
58 Joseph S. Nye, 'Maintaining a Nonproliferation Regime', unpublished paper, June 1980.
59 Shai Feldman, *op.cit.* in note 11, ch. 5.
60 Joseph S. Nye, *op.cit.* in note 58.
61 Interviews conducted by the author, December 1978.
62 Norman Angell, *The Great Illusion* (London: Heinemann, 1914).

10 Intervention and Regional Security
Adelphi Paper 196, 1985

Neil Macfarlane

Introduction

This study is an examination of a number of recent cases of intervention in third-world conflict. It seeks to determine what their sources and consequences were and what patterns they display, if any. The topic is a timely one for a number of reasons.

First, the USSR has in the past decade rapidly increased her capacity to project force throughout the Third World.[1] The Soviet government has shown its willingness to use these enhanced capabilities in order to influence political outcomes in its favour in Angola, Ethiopia and, most recently, in Afghanistan. This in turn has been one of several causes of the dramatic deterioration in Soviet-American relations, one aspect of which is the return to power politics and global activism in word, if not yet in deed, on the part of the US. The apparently increasing probability that the US government will be more willing than it has been since the Vietnam War to use force in the Third World in defence of perceived US interests, and to link internal conflicts and regional disputes to the superpower balance, is an additional reason for an examination of intervention at this time.

Morever, there is evident in the evolution of world politics in the last two decades a diffusion of economic and military power throughout the international system. This trend has been facilitated by massive transfers of arms to third-world states and has been reflected in the growing confidence and assertiveness of these new actors in world politics. One aspect of this phenomenon has been a growing incidence of intervention by third-world states in the affairs of their neighbours (e.g. India in East Pakistan, Syria in Lebanon, Vietnam in Kampuchea, Zaire and South Africa in Angola, Tanzania in Uganda, Libya in Chad, Somalia in Ethiopia, and so on). Another is the reduced capability of the superpowers to control the course and outcome of third-world conflicts.

Finally, the last two decades have witnessed a growing dependence in the Western world on resources found in Asia, Africa, and Latin America. This involves not only energy, but also rare metals vital to high-technology industry and defence production. It raises the prospect of intervention in order to secure access to these materials in situations where regional instability threatens the continuity of supply.

These developments raise a number of important questions for both scholars and policy-makers. Is it likely that Soviet activism will persist? Is American bellicosity mere rhetoric or will it be backed up by action? Is there occurring in the Third World an erosion of the accepted norms of international conduct concerning forceful intrusion into the internal affairs of other states? What implications do the answers to these questions have for regional security in the rest of the 1980s? The developments also draw our attention to a number of broader issues. Is intervention on balance pernicious in its systemic and regional effects? If so, what means are available to regulate intervention, and what are the prospects for the success of such efforts?

In approaching these issues, it is necessary first of all to define the concept of intervention. The classical definition, an act of coercive interference in the internal affairs of a state, is a useful beginning for two reasons. By emphasizing intrusion into internal conflict, it allows us to distinguish intervention from actions which are designed to affect a state's external behaviour but not its domestic politics. Furthermore, the stress on coercion makes it possible to distinguish between acts of intervention and non-coercive types of power projection (e.g. the installation of a base by mutual agreement between the external actor and the host country).

However, such a definition is inadequate without further precision. Left as it is, it includes not only military actions but also such non-military forms of coercion as trade and credit sanctions. Focusing on the coerciveness of an action without attention to the means used makes it impossible to distinguish intervention from a plethora of other activities the intent or impact of which is to affect internal political outcomes.[2] As such, the utility of intervention as a category of analysis becomes questionable. For this reason, the discussion here is limited to the use of military force to interfere in the internal affairs of other states. Such a limitation is consistent with the manner in which the word is commonly used with reference to events in international politics.

A further problem is that such a definition leaves unclear the boundary between military assistance and intervention. It may well be that there is no clear-cut distinction to be made between military assistance which is used internally and coercively (arms supply, training, the provision of advisers and logistical support) and intervention itself. However, in common usage, intervention usually carries the connotation of a more direct military involvement than these forms of assistance. Cases generally referred to as intervention share one characteristic: the involvement in combat roles of either the regular military forces of the external power or of irregulars acting in the interests and at the behest of the intervening power.

The most important implication of defining intervention as a coercive military intrusion into the internal affairs of another state is that the definition does not distinguish between action on behalf of governments, action against governments, and action in instances where no clear governmental authority exists. This lack of distinction is deliberate. The word intervention carries with it a negative moral and legal connotation in a world ostensibly devoted to the concepts of sovereignty and self-determination. There is a large body of international opinion which maintains that intervention is wrong and inadmissible as a form of state behaviour, as well as being illegal.[3] In order to avoid opprobrium, therefore, there is a temptation on the part of those actors who do interfere in the internal affairs of other states to define intervention selectively. Governments using the term tend to apply it to actions taken by their adversaries and to deny its applicability to their own actions. American spokesmen decry Soviet action in Angola, Ethiopia and Afghanistan as intervention, while denying that US actions in El Salvador and elsewhere should be so characterized. Soviet commentators deny that Soviet actions in the above-named countries were interventions, while using the term to blacken American involvement in Central America.

In other words, both sides in the global rivalry attempt to define the scope of the concept in such a way as to reflect and further their own political interests. They justify such selectivity in terms of the legitimacy of aid to established governments or peoples attempting to exert their right of national self-determination, or, more abstractly, they assert their commitment to the defence of freedom against Communism or to the cause of proletarian internationalism.

Beneath these self-interested and somewhat disingenuous attempts to limit the applicability of the concept, there does exist a genuine and profound moral divide. This concerns the concept of legitimacy and the attempt to link it to the definition of intervention. The negative connotation inherent in the word intervention is reflected in the tendency to limit its use to situations in which an intrusion is deemed illegitimate. The legitimacy of an intrusion is usually judged in terms of the perceived legitimacy of the internal beneficiary of the assistance. Unfortunately, there is deep disagreement on what the sources of a group's or a regime's legitimacy are, on how legitimacy should be judged, and on who should do the judging.

In the Soviet context, a legitimate or just cause is one which furthers the progress of mankind towards socialism. Hence, movements which espouse the socialist cause, as the latter is understood by Soviet analysts and policymakers, are legitimate, whether or not there is any broad popular support for them. Accordingly, assistance to these groups is also legitimate. It is not the people concerned who determine legitimacy, but those who interpret the revealed truth of Marxism-Leninism. In liberal democratic theory, by contrast, it is popular approval and consent, frequently expressed, which confer legitimacy and which are the criteria by which the legitimacy of a regime should be judged.

This is not to say that such standards are always followed when states espousing such ideologies choose to support one side or another in an internal conflict. The point is that where there is no agreement within the international community on what legitimacy is and on how it is adduced, the concept itself is not useful in defining intervention. The lack of distinction in the definition employed here is an attempt to avoid the unwarranted value judgments inherent in any attempt to link intervention with legitimacy. For the purpose of this Paper, the important factor is intrusion into the domestic political process, and not the side on which this intrusion occurs or the manner in which it is justified.

A second implication concerns actors. Intervention as defined above may be undertaken not only by military units of the intervening power but also by irregular units organized, financed or given sanctuary by the intervening state, or by some combination of the two. Along these lines, for instance, Zaire and South Africa have intervened in the Angolan political process, not only by committing units of their own armed forces but also by arming, training, harbouring and delivering units of the *Frente Nacional de Libertação de Angola* (FNLA) and the *União Nacional para a Independência Total de Angola* (UNITA).

Third, intervention may be overt, as in the case of Soviet-Cuban activities in Angola and Ethiopia, or covert, as in the case of US Central Intelligence Agency (CIA) activity in Angola. While the covert dimension is not excluded, the focus of this Paper is on the overt. Overt cases are easier to deal with, as more information is available. In addition, given that overt interventions usually take place on a much larger scale than covert ones, and have historically had a much greater impact on regional balances of power and perceptions of threat, as well as on the conduct of relations between the superpowers, it is probable that as a rule they are of greater import.

In applying the definition of intervention as a coercive military intrusion into an internal political conflict to recent events in the Third World, several instances quickly come to mind: the case of Zairean, South African and (Soviet-backed) Cuban actions in Angola; that of Somali, South Yemeni, Soviet and Cuban intrusion in Ethiopia; the Shaba affairs in Zaire; the Tanzanian invasion of Uganda; action by Libyan, French and Organization of African Unity (OAU) forces in Chad; and the Soviet incursion in Afghanistan. A number of other developments which some have referred to as instances of intervention cannot be so characterized in terms of the definition used here. American activities in El Salvador, for instance, do not (as yet) qualify as intervention, for no combat units have been deployed, the American presence being limited to some fifty advisers in training roles.

The situations of intervention which this Paper focuses on are those of Angola (1975–6), the Horn of Africa (1977–8), Chad (1980–82) and Afghanistan (1979 to the present). All four were of great regional and international significance. The Angolan situation and, in particular, the Soviet-Cuban intervention in that country had serious repercussions on the process of detente, many Americans reaching the conclusion that Soviet policy-makers viewed detente as a means of drawing unilateral advantage from third-world conflicts. The coming to power in Angola of a group highly dependent on support from the USSR and her allies also placed the latter in a position to take advantage of further regional instability.

Soviet-Cuban intervention in the 1977 conflict between Ethiopia and Somalia put another nail in the coffin of detente. It prevented the dismemberment of Ethiopia and permitted the USSR to replace the US as the preponderant superpower in this most populous and potentially powerful state in the region. Both the Angolan and Ethiopian involvements underlined the USSR's status as a power with global military reach.

The conflict in Chad brought humiliation to France, previously the principal external actor in Chadian politics, and called into question the wisdom and viability of French military interventionism in Africa. It also displayed graphically the substantial new military power of Libya, and the revisionist character of its regional aspirations, while revealing in a rather depressing way the limitations affecting regional organizations – in this case the OAU – in their attempts to resolve internal conflicts.

Finally, the Soviet intervention in Afghanistan was particularly disturbing, since it was the first time since World War II that the USSR had committed substantial units of her own armed forces in an internal conflict in a third-world country. Soviet actions raised serious doubts about the security of Western interests in the Gulf and stimulated President Carter to enunciate the strategic doctrine that bears his name, besides making it virtually certain that American plans for a rapid deployment force would bear fruit. Moreover, it also provoked a substantial deterioration in Soviet-West European relations and hardened the commitment of NATO members to higher defence spending and to the modernization of conventional and nuclear forces in the European theatre.

Beyond their obvious regional and global importance, these cases as a group possess a number of characteristics which lend themselves to the purposes of this analysis. They provide a great diversity of interveners, from the superpowers, via a European power and major and minor regional powers, to, finally, an inter-governmental organization. This is complemented by wide variety in means and levels of commitment. The cases also display a broad spectrum of motives for intervention: narrow national security concerns; irredentism; the quest for oil; the desire to secure influence or deny it to an adversary; the defence of an individual power's credibility with allies; and the establishment of its status as a world power. They vary in choice of targets, some being undertaken in defence of established governments, some against them, and some in situations where no clear governmental authority existed. They span two of the three continents of the Third World. For all these reasons, one can be reasonably confident that, if these cases yield any general conclusions about the conditions, consequences and regulation of intervention, those conclusions hold currently for the phenomenon of intervention in third-world civil conflict as a whole.

It might, of course, be true that it is a waste of time to generalize at this level, given the diversity between the countries of Asia, Africa and Latin America. Certainly it would be rash to ignore the historical, cultural, economic and political differences among this group of states in any attempt to isolate patterns which hold true for the Third World as a whole. It may be that there are no such patterns. That would itself be a useful conclusion; however, it is one which should be established by analysis, rather than asserted *a priori*.

There are numerous well-researched chronological and historical accounts of the cases considered here.[4] For this reason, the Paper does not include any extensive narrative account of them. Instead, it is organized thematically. The themes are illustrated with reference to the cases. The first theme to be discussed is that of the conditions under which intervention occurs.

I. The sources of military intervention

Western accounts of intervention in the Third World tend to focus on the interests and decision-making of the external actor in the attempt to explain why these events occur. Hence, Soviet intervention in Angola is explained in terms of the USSR's quest for influence in Southern Africa, her global rivalry with the US, her desire to gain a strangle-hold over the Cape Route or to deny Western access to sources of 'strategic minerals'. France's intervention in her African ex-colonies is ascribed to her desire to maintain a sphere of influence in Africa, both for economic reasons and to satisfy a perhaps atavistic hankering for great-power status. American action in Central America is put down to considerations of national security in the context of a threat of Soviet-Cuban expansion into what has been a region dominated by American power. There is no question that this perspective is important, but it is incomplete. It fails to explain what made action appear necessary or desirable at a given historical moment and why intervention, rather than some other form of involvement, was chosen.

In order to account for intervention, it is necessary to examine not only the incentives of the intervening power but also the characteristics of the international system, of the target state and of the region which conduce to intervention. Moreover, at all three levels – that of the international system, that of the intervening actor, and that of the target environment – a set of factors is operating which constrains interventionist behaviour. Finally, the decision to intervene is a response to catalytic factors specific to particular crises in third-world politics. Acts of intervention are the result of a complex and dynamic interaction among factors internal to both target and intervening states and matters relating to the position of both *vis-à-vis* the rest of the international system. The discussion in this chapter of the conditions of military intervention therefore falls into three main parts. First, broad factors which are conducive to intervention are examined – those in the target environment, in the motivation of external actors, and springing from the nature of the international system. Second, factors constraining intervention are examined; and, finally, immediate triggering factors leading to intervention are discussed.

FACTORS CONDUCIVE TO INTERVENTION

The target environment

The four cases considered in this Paper point to several generalizations about the character of the target environment which are pertinent to the discussion of the sources of intervention. First, while it may be somewhat tautological to say that deep internal divisions are a precondition of intervention, given that this Paper focuses on intervention in internal war, it is none-the-less significant. Societies which ultimately experience military intervention are generally lacking in political integration and chronically unstable, and their populations have little if any commitment to central political authority. This lack of integration often reflects deep-seated ethnic and class conflicts between groups comprising the society in question. It sets the scene for the armed conflict within the population that in turn provokes military intervention. Moreover, intervention is usually a new stage in a long-standing involvement on the part of an external actor in an internal conflict on the side of a party to that conflict.

Angola

Angola, for instance, is divided into three major ethnic groups: the Ovimbundu (approximately 1,700,000 in number) the Mbundu (around 1,053,000), and the Bakongo (621,000).[1] These are themselves in some respects artificial categories, since each is subdivided into numerous clans and kinship groupings, and it is at this lower level that the sense of group identity has been strongest. The struggle for independence, to the extent that it fostered indentification with broader groupings, did so at the tribal level. Despite the efforts of the *Movimento Popular para a Libertação de Angola* (MPLA) in particular to overcome ethnic barriers and to construct a truly national movement, each of the three liberation movements active in the war for independence from Portuguese rule drew the bulk of its support from one of the three ethnic groupings – the MPLA from the Mbundu, the FNLA from the Bakongo, and UNITA from the Ovimbundu. Before the collapse of the Portuguese, the movements fought as much against each other as against colonial rule.[2] In the same manner, in the aftermath of the Portuguese collapse, the civil war was fought along ethnic lines.

Beyond these divisions within the black population, there have been, and are, important racial cleavages within the country. While many of the leading cadres of the MPLA were white or mulatto, the FNLA in particular eschewed collaboration with non-blacks throughout much of its history. The FNLA's animosity to whites and mulattos was evident in its conduct in Northern Angola during its 1961 uprising, which took on the character of a race war against non-blacks. Elements within the MPLA have also on occasion exhibited a strong anti-white, anti-mulatto racism. It has been suggested that such sentiments motivated the 1977 attempted coup by disaffected black leaders within the movement.[3]

Complementing these ethnic and racial cleavages were significant ideological differences between the three liberation movements which later became the major contestants in the civil war. While the MPLA quite clearly favoured a radical socialist outcome in Angola from very early in its history, the FNLA tended to avoid questions of ideology and was clearly suspicious of the social and economic policies favoured by the MPLA. This is perhaps not surprising for a movement which found itself comfortable with the politics of Zaire's President Mobutu Sese Seko.

The fission of the liberation movement along ethnic, racial, and ideological lines, and the viciousness of rivalries within it, contrast sharply with the history of anti-colonial struggle elsewhere in Portuguese Africa. This is of fundamental importance in explaining why intervention occurred in Angola and not in Guinea-Bissau or Mozambique.

Chad

This picture of fragmentation and resultant instability and conflict is applicable in the case of Chad as well. There the ethnic fragmentation is even more far-reaching and is complicated by religious divisions which in part coincide with and in part cut across ethnic lines. The largest ethnic group is the mainly sedentary Sara (some 800,000 people, or 24% of the population), occupying the southern part of the country. It – like Angolan ethnic groups – is subdivided into clans and, beyond this, into extended family units. Again, these were the principal foci of group identity in the pre-colonial period. Throughout the centre of the country there are also a large number of nomadic and semi-nomadic Arab tribes and clans the Djoheina, the Hassauna, the Awlad Sulayman and the Tunjur – totalling 460,000, or 14% of the population. The third major grouping (in political if not in numerical terms) is the Toubou, occupying the Borkou–Ennedi–saTibesti (BET) region (200,000 in 1965). They are in turn divided into two major clans (Teda and Daza) and several minor clans. Beyond this, there are innumerable smaller groups scattered throughout the country.

The religious composition of the population is also complex. Muslims make up approximately 50% of the population, followers of various traditional religions 43% and Christians 7%. There are again important divisions in these categories, making it difficult for each group to function as a single unit in Chadian politics. Both Protestant and Catholic missions have been active in Chad, while the Muslim population is divided into Tijaniyya, Qadiriyya and Sanusiyya *sufi* orders (the first being the largest) each historically viewing the others as converts.

A number of these ethnic and religious groupings have close affinities with like groups in neighbouring countries. The Sanusiyya order, for instance, entered Chad from Libya, while a number of Arab clans in the east of the country have close ties to communities in western Sudan.[4]

Internal conflict in Chad has tended to define itself along ethnic and religious lines. These conflicts have a long history; Arabs raided Sara settlements for several centuries in order to take slaves, while Toubou tribesmen attacked Arab trans-Saharan caravans in order to exact tribute. The uneven impact of the colonial experience served to reinforce ethnic animosities. The Sara adapted most easily to French rule, and benefited most from it in terms of educational and employment opportunities and infrastructural and agricultural development. As a result they dominated the Chadian government and civil service in the aftermath of independence. For the Arabs, in particular, this was a difficult pill to swallow, for they had traditionally viewed the Sara as an inferior people. Arab (and Toubou) resentment of the central government was deepened when the Southerners used their control of government to exploit groups in the east and north. The tax revolt at Mangalmé in 1965 was provoked by illegal tax increases imposed by insensitive and corrupt officials appointed by the central government.[5] Likewise, the rebellion of the Toubou in the mid-1960s was in part the direct result of the public humiliation of the Derde – their traditional leader – by southern soldiers garrisoned in the BET after the withdrawal of the French. The weakness of national consciousness in Chad, the cross-border ethnic affiliations of several principal groups and the welter of internecine conflicts that beset the population make the country one of the least convincing legacies of the colonial division of Africa.

Ethiopia

Ethiopia, by contrast, has often been perceived as a country with a strong historically-based national identity and consciousness. This impression – assiduously cultivated by the Amhara elite of the imperial regime – was, however, a myth masking long-standing ethnically based exploitation and disaffection within the country. Ethiopia is not a long-standing national entity, despite the longevity of the Amhara-Tegray Christian imperial tradition, but, like most of the other countries in Africa, is a legacy of the colonial division of Africa. The difference is that Ethiopia is in large part the result of colonial expansion by an African people, the Amhara, who, with the related Tegray, comprise about 35% of the total population. In the nineteenth century, particularly in the 1890s under Menelik II, this group expanded southward, westward and south-eastward at the expense of the Oromo, Afar and Somali peoples. This process drew to its close in the aftermath of World War II with northward expansion when Eritrea was first federated with, and then absorbed into, the unitary Ethiopian state. The expansion into non-Amhara areas was, on the whole, not accompanied by sustained attempts to improve the welfare of their populations or to integrate them into the broader framework of an Ethiopian nation. Instead, the imperial regime under Haile

Selassie emphasized the extraction of wealth from, and the control of, what were clearly considered to be subject peoples.[6]

The Oromo peoples (approximately 7 million) make up by far the largest ethnic grouping in the Ethiopian population, inhabiting the southern and central parts of the country (Bale, Arusi, and Wollo provinces among others). While some of the Oromo elite were 'Amharized' in the seventeenth and eighteenth centuries (when Oromo expansion constituted a severe threat to the Amhara), the bulk of this group were the victims of the outward expansion of the Amhara, their lands being granted to Menelik's and Haile Selassie's officers or being taken up by the imperial family. The Oromo peasantry became tenants. While historically the Oromo have lacked a national consciousness of their own, by the 1960s and 1970s the shared experience of exploitation and alienation from power combined to foster what might be called an 'Oromo nationalism', a movement of protest against Amhara domination which expressed itself in rebellions in Bale, in particular, in the mid-1960s and again in the mid-1970s.[7]

The Somali minority also caused problems for the central government. The incursions of Somalia into the Ogaden in 1964 and again in 1977 were both responses to and attempts to profit from the discontent of ethnic Somalis in that region.

Perhaps the most persistent problem of this sort has been that of Eritrea. While the population of Eritrea is by no means ethnically homogeneous, the fact that the region has been historically far more exposed than the rest of the country to external influences, that it was under Italian rule for some seventy years, and that between World War II and its absorption by Ethiopia its political life was relatively free under a British military administration, gave it an identity distinct from that of the rest of the Ethiopian empire. Its separateness was reinforced by its far higher level of economic development and greater urbanization. The central government's dismantling of the separate political institutions granted to Eritrea under the 1952 federation, and the manifest discrimination against Eritrea in its policies of economic and particularly industrial development only accentuated the Eritreans' sense of distinctness and reinforced their resentment at having been joined to Ethiopia in the first place.

As in Chad, Ethiopia's complexity is not simply ethnic, for the population is heterogeneous in religious terms as well. While Coptic Christianity was the official religion of imperial Ethiopia, State and Church being organically linked, Muslims make up approximately half the population, and there are also numerous followers of traditional religions. Internal conflict thus also follows religious lines, for the Christian population has traditionally viewed itself as surrounded and assailed by a Muslim threat, while the imperial government treated Muslims as second-class citizens for generations.

In addition to these ethnic and religious divisions, Ethiopia was fraught with economic conflicts in the period before the 1974 Revolution. In the agricultural sector, the burden of various 'feudal' tithes on the peasantry had resulted in repeated peasant revolts in the centre and south of the country. These class grievances often coincided with ethnic ones, as in the case of Oromo peasants revolting against Amhara landowners. In addition, the 1960s saw the beginnings of capitalist agriculture in certain parts of rural Ethiopia, such as the Awash Valley.[8] This resulted in the displacement of large numbers of tenants and also of nomads accustomed to using the land in question, bringing further unrest between landowners and peasants. The situation deteriorated further with the droughts of the early 1970s. The extent of rural discontent was indicated by the fact that in 1974 peasants in the south, in particular, spontaneously mounted attacks on landlords and redistributed land in the aftermath of the September Revolution. The military government found it necessary to curb these *jacqueries* before bringing into effect its own land reform.

In urban areas a fairly rapid process of industrialization in the 1960s had created a small working class and a well-organized but largely apolitical trade union movement. The prospect of employment drew large numbers from the countryside. The economic stagnation of the early 1970s and the effect of the drought in stimulating further migration to the cities combined to result in significant urban unemployment. The situation of the urban lower classes was exacerbated by the crop failures, because a reduced supply of basic foodstuffs contributed to inflation. The rise in prices was also fuelled at this time (1972–4) by rapid expansion of the money supply, the result of vastly increased foreign exchange earnings associated with a rise in both the world price and Ethiopian production of coffee. The economic hardship of inflation and food shortages was also felt intensely by lower-grade civil servants, such as teachers and clerks, and this burden was particularly onerous in the light of the conspicuous consumption of those benefiting from higher coffee revenues. These grievances led to large-scale strikes and demonstrations in the capital in early 1974. More seriously from the point of view of the regime, the economic pressure was felt especially strongly by junior officers and enlisted men in the armed forces. The mutinies of February–March 1974, which started the process of revolution, were protests over pay and working conditions and were not, on the whole, politically motivated.[9]

The last source of social conflict within Ethiopian society which should be mentioned here also concerns what might, in Marxist terms, be called the petty bourgeoisie. The intelligentsia (teachers, civil servants and students), while becoming increasingly politically conscious, were denied any effective participation in the political process. Power was monopolized by a coterie of aristocrats and favourites of Emperor Haile Selassie. Moreover, as the number of graduates outstripped the number of positions available for them, serious unemployment developed among intellectuals. The resulting frustration, coupled with an awareness of the government's incapacity to deal with the country's more pressing problems (such as the famine of 1973–4 in Wollo), found its expression in radical opposition to the regime.[10] Haile Selassie fell because his regime lacked the dynamism, creativity and popular support to meet these challenges.

His successors faced the same set of problems – though they were now perhaps even more pressing – as expectations on the part of ethnic minorities and disadvantaged classes were raised, and as opposition groups both at the centre (the trade unions and the Marxist opposition) and on the periphery (the Eritreans, the Oromo, and the Somalis) attempted to take advantage of the general political disarray to further their particular interests, often through armed struggle. The *Dergue* (the ruling military committee) also faced a number of new problems. Its programme of land reform met substantial opposition on the part of landowners and local officials in a number of provinces, and elements of the elite closely associated with the *ancien régime* formed opposition movements, such as the Ethiopian Democratic Union (EDU), and posed an additional military challenge to the military regime.

Afghanistan

The last case is that of Afghanistan. Here, too, the population is fragmented into a number of disparate ethnic groups: the Pashtun (40% of the population), the Tadzhiks (35%), the Hazaras (10–12%), the Nuristanis (3%), and a number of others (Baluchis, Uzbeks, Turkmen, Khirghiz, and so on).[11] A number of these are split between Afghanistan and neighbouring countries. Large groups of Pashtun live in Pakistan, the majority of Tadzhiks, Khirgiz and Uzbeks reside in the USSR, the Turkmen are divided between Afghanistan, Iran and the USSR, and the Baluchs between Afghanistan, Iran and Pakistan. Here too, ethnic differences are complemented by religious ones, the Tadzhiks and Hazaras being predominantly Shi'a Muslim, while the Pashtun are Sunni Muslim.

The central government has historically been Pashtun-dominated. Other groups have not only been denied access to power but have been denied means of cultural expression in their own languages. Structures of central authority have traditionally been weak, which has made it difficult for any government to control the country as a whole.

It has also impeded the development of a united resistance to the USSR. Philippe Roger characterized the resistance to the Soviet presence as: 'Unanimous and disunited. For no clan, no village renounces its particularism, its style, its prejudices, even in the name of a fight waged against a common enemy.'[12] The result is a movement split into at least six major factions and numerous smaller ones, divided along clan, tribal, linguistic and religious lines.

Once again, these ethnic and religious divisions are supplemented by economic and social ones (class, rural/urban, traditional/modern). The limited expansion of the industrial sector, mainly in Kabul, produced a small working class. The growth of the state sector resulted in the development of a bureaucratic middle class composed principally of civil servants, teachers and army officers. The monopoly of power held by the royal clan and traditional elites blocked whatever political aspirations the new urban classes might have entertained. This favoured their radicalization, and so it was among these groups that the Marxist-Leninist People's Democratic Party (PDP) had its greatest impact. The government's resistance to political pluralism and the frustrations this induced were a fundamental cause of the 1973 coup and the 1978 Revolution.

The limited modernization occurring in urban Afghanistan contrasted starkly with relative stagnation in the economy and social institutions of rural areas. The power of the royal government rested to some extent on the support of rural elites opposed to political and social development. The Daud regime was also dependent on the acquiescence, if not the support, of these groups and hence avoided any challenge to their interests. By contrast, when the PDP took power in 1978, it set out deliberately to challenge not only the tribal and clan structures of power, but also the traditional values on which they were based.

The new regime sought, in particular, to change land tenure patterns and to improve the situation of women. In any attempt to enumerate the immediate causes of the insurgency, land reform, the elimination of the dowry, the effort to force women in rural areas to attend literacy classes, and the resentment which all these things awakened among the traditionalist rural population would have to occupy a major position.[13] Underlying this, however, it was the lack of any tradition of acceptance of central authority, and the focusing of loyalties instead on the clan and tribe, which rendered resistance inevitable in the face of any attempt by the central government to alter profoundly the rural way of life.

It bears mention here that the party that took power in 1978 was in many respects a microcosm of the society as a whole, for it, too, was divided into factions – *Parcham* and *Khalq* – vying for power and capable of extreme ruthlessness towards their ostensible comrades. Since 1978 there have been repeated reports of assassinations of Parchamis by Khalqis and *vice versa*, and of pitched battles in the streets of Kabul between partisans of the two groups. When Hafizullah Amin took power in September 1979 he filled the prisons with Parchamis, having many of them tortured and executed. Since Babrak Karmal came to power there have been reliable reports of Khalqi contacts and co-operation with the *Mujaheddin*, and of further infighting in government circles.[14]

Internal fragmentation

All four of these countries, then, are fragmented along ethnic, religious, class and ideological lines. These divisions have fostered political instability, and all four countries have experienced conflict along these 'fault lines' in their societies. But one might well ask why this is important. After all, most societies are fragmented in one way or another, and this does not bring intervention. However, these cases are further distinguished by weakness of central authority and of group loyalties to that centre. In most cases pluralism within a society is balanced by a general recognition of the legitimacy and coercive power of the state, and this limits the extent to which pluralism manifests itself as a force in society. In addition, a general recognition of the importance of national identity inhibits the resort to external support. In the cases under discussion, by contrast, many of the groups involved showed little awareness of national concerns, little acceptance of the legitimacy of the state and little respect for its coercive power; there had been insufficient time, capacity and will to nurture these sentiments. Since the national government was usually the preserve of a single ethnic group, this lack of national commitment on the part of others is not surprising; nor, for that matter, was their willingness to seek help abroad.

In each case, these internal conflicts led eventually to the use of force. The resort to violence, to insurgency and civil war creates new needs, which in general can only be satisfied by external actors. The parties to the internal conflict, having chosen the military option, are driven to seek elsewhere the means to pursue it. This invites external involvement. It will be seen below that foreign intervention came as a response to the needs of a local client in a situation of crisis. It was, for example, a request for assistance from the MPLA which precipitated Cuban-Soviet involvement in Angola. In Ethiopia, it was an invitation from the *Dergue*, hard pressed from all sides, which opened the door to Soviet and Cuban involvement. In Afghanistan, the initial large-scale Soviet involvement was again an attempt to meet the needs of a local client faced with a serious problem of insurgency and incapable of staffing and running the central and provincial administrations. Finally, French military involvement in Chad, in 1968, 1975 and 1983 was at the request of the incumbent government, which found itself incapable of holding its own against insurgents. Libyan involvement began as a response to the needs of the *Front de Libération Nationale Tchadienne* (FROLINAT), and Libya intervened in 1980 at the request of FROLINAT's leader Goukouni Oueddei. Nigeria's head of state, Gen. Obasanjo was not far off the mark, when he averred, with reference to intervention in Africa, that:

> We the African leaders must also realize that we cannot ask outside powers to leave us alone while, in most cases, it is our own actions which provide them with the excuse to interfere with our affairs.

He went on explicitly to point out the link between internal instability and intervention by arguing that the best defence against external forces was a government that treated all of its citizens 'fairly and decently', and which attempted to secure the support of the majority of the population for the policies it pursued.[15]

It is not, of course, being argued here that internal political and social disintegration are *necessary* conditions for intervention. It is quite possible in the abstract to conceive of an intervention taking place in societies without serious internal political conflicts. In practice, however, interventions seem generally to occur on behalf of a local actor engaged in an internal conflict, and at his request. It is through a local agent that the external actor pursues his interests.

Motivation of external actors

As stated earlier, it is not being argued that local conflict and lack of integration are *necessary* conditions for intervention. No more are they *sufficient* ones; external actors must have some reason of their own for becoming involved in an internal conflict in another country. In addition to having reasons, they also face constraints on their actions. Both motives and constraints may be constant over time and space, or they may be variable in content and strength with respect to specific historical and geographical realities.

In discussing motives, it must be stressed that the analysis is highly speculative. Even when the relevant documents are available, motives for a specific policy are often obscure, since the written word may not reflect the thinking of those involved. The task is even more intractable when, as in the case of more recent events, such sources are seldom available at all. One is forced in such instances to induce a rationale for action from the events themselves, viewed in the context of the overall behaviour and historical and cultural traditions of the power in question.

The problem is further complicated by the fact that the intervening actor is not a monolithic entity, but is complex, being composed of various competing and co-operating groups, each with its own set of motives which may coincide with, complement or contradict those of other groups. Policy is generally just as much the result of bargains struck among these groups as it is of the decision of a single determining personality. While this pluralism in policy-making is perhaps best documented in the American case, there is every reason to assume that comparable bargaining processes take place in such polities as the USSR as well – albeit in a rather more muted and limited manner, given the greater centralization of power in that system. In this kind of policy-making context, different decision-makers may support an action for different reasons. Hence, it is improbable that one can account for policies in terms of single motives, or maintain with certainty that a single motive is the determining one.

There are a number of basic motivations which may underlie involvement in the affairs of other states: ideological commitment; the quest for influence; considerations of status and prestige; strategic and security concerns; and economic gain. All are probably relevant to the cases considered here.

Ideology

Oran Young made the point some years ago that 'the coexistence of competing conceptions of appropriate forms of political order will tend to heighten incentives for intervention'.[16] Along these lines, Soviet support for a leftist national liberation movement in Angola, for an Ethiopian regime which had embraced 'scientific socialism' and embarked on a series of reforms of anti-capitalist orientation and for an avowedly Marxist-Leninist regime in Afghanistan were consistent with the USSR's conception of desirable political evolution in the Third World.

Analogously, initial Chinese involvement in Angolan affairs in the late 1950s and early 1960s may be accounted for partly in terms of an ideological commitment to anti-colonial armed struggle. Moreover, the dispute between the USSR and China which set the scene for their competitive interference in southern African affairs in the 1970s was partially ideological in origin, the two having parted company on such issues as the inevitability of war, the desirability of peaceful co-existence, the significance of the Third World in the world revolutionary process, and the possibility of non-violent revolution.

Ideological incentives are also important in accounting for the behaviour of Cuba, the third Communist protagonist in the cases considered here. While Cuban involvement in Angola and Ethiopia results from a variety of factors, there is little reason to doubt that the Cuban leadership is genuinely committed to its conception of the 'world socialist revolution', and that this commitment was a motivating factor in its decision to provide support to Angola's MPLA in particular.

Ideological incentives for intervention are not characteristic of the Communist powers alone. Robin Hallett, in his discussion of the sources of South African intervention in Angola, cautions that the Afrikaner preoccupation with 'the Communist menace' should not be belittled.[17] Zaire's President Mobutu displays a similar aversion to Communism, and an important (though by no means the only) factor in accounting for Zairean intervention, as well as for Zairean support for South African involvement, was his discomfort at the prospect of being bordered by leftist, if not Marxist, regimes on both north and south.

Ideological incentives for intervention in the four cases considered here go beyond the Communist–anti-Communist confrontation. In the case of Somalian intervention in Ethiopian affairs, for instance, a convincing case can be made that the dominant factor underlying the decision was pan-Somali nationalism, the desire to make the Somalian state coterminous with the Somali nation. Somalian irredentism has caused persistent difficulties not only in Somalian-Ethiopian relations, but also in Franco-Somalian relations over the fate of Somali-related groups in Djibouti, and in Somalian-Kenyan relations over the status of the Somali population of north-eastern frontier districts of Kenya. In the case of Chad, it is plausible (and is certainly claimed by Libyan propaganda organs[18]) that Libya entered the Chadian conflict to help Arab and Islamic groups against their ethnic and religious adversaries.

Influence, status and prestige

Of the other political motivations for intervention in the cases considered here, the most significant are the quest for power and influence and that for status and prestige. The boundary between considerations of ideology and political interest as incentives for intervention is, however, cloudy.

In the first place, perceived interest is to a degree defined by ideology. Hence, the apparent Soviet preoccupation with undermining Western positions in the Third World is partly the result of the ideological presumption that there exists between capitalist and socialist states an ineradicable conflict of values and interests. Likewise, the United State's perceived interest in containing, if not rolling back, the USSR is the result not only of the bipolar structure of the international system but also of American fear and dislike of Communism.

Secondly, power and influence may serve ideological ends. As such, the dichotomy between ideology and power politics is in part a false one. This is also true because ideology, as a mobilizing and legitimizing device, is a source of power. In this case, ideological competition is a contest for power. In this context it is often noted that the legitimacy of the Soviet leadership's claim to rule, both in the USSR and in the international Communist movement, is based on the credibility of its commitment to world revolution. Support for liberation movements, such as the MPLA, or for 'progressive' regimes, such as that of Ethiopia, strengthens the credibility of this commitment. Questioning the sincerity of the commitment – or, for that matter, the correctness of Soviet doctrine – is therefore a threat to the legitimacy of the Communist Party of the Soviet Union (CPSU) and; at one remove, to Soviet rule. Hence the doctrinal challenging of the CPSU by the Chinese Communist Party is, by intention and in its consequences, an attempt to weaken the USSR. Sensitivity to Chinese attempts to use ideological criticism to undermine Soviet influence in the Third World during a period of detente with the US goes a long way towards accounting for Soviet involvement in Angola.[19]

Despite the interweaving of considerations of power and ideology, it is clear that, in the cases considered here, the pursuit of power and influence has been an important determinant of interventionist behaviour. It would be as naïve to account for this pursuit solely in terms of ideology as it would be rash to deny the significance of ideology completely. It is quite plausible, for instance, that the Soviet–American conflict would exist without the ideological dispute. The gap in potential and actual power which separates the two superpowers from other states makes them, to some extent, natural rivals (see below) and sets the scene for the competition for influence which was, undoubtedly, a major factor underlying Soviet and American actions in Angola as well as Soviet intervention in Ethiopia.

Similarly, while there is an ideological component to the Sino-Soviet dispute, it is also a product of the geographical fact of contiguity and the historical evolution of relations between the two powers. Ideological conflict is complemented by, and perhaps to some extent results from, geographically and historically derived conflicts of interest. This was reflected in their competitive behaviour in the Angolan crisis.

Considerations of status and prestige too, must be taken into the reckoning in accounting for Soviet interventions in the Angolan and Ethiopian conflicts. In the early 1970s it was frequently affirmed by Soviet statesmen – among them Leonid Brezhnev, Dimitri Ustinov, and Andrei Gromyko[20] – that the USSR was now a power of global reach and that, consequently, she had a right to involvement in the resolution of any international dispute, no matter how small or how far removed from the borders of the USSR. Perhaps the most effective means to bring this claim to the attention of other powers was actually to project force into regional disputes. By her involvement in Angola and Ethiopia, the USSR established her status as a world power willing and able to undertake and sustain distant commitments, lending credibility to her assertion that she should be treated as such.

In the case of Cuba, questions of power and influence were important but in a different way, since Cuba, through her military intrusions in Angolan and Ethiopian affairs, was seeking not to best an adversary, but to maintain and enhance her status in the eyes of a generous and long-suffering benefactor, the USSR. Cuban assistance in the implementation of Soviet policy not only reduced Cuba's perceived dependence on the USSR but also served to assure further Soviet generosity by underlining the mutuality of benefit from the relationship.

As with the USSR, Cuban actions in Angola and Ethiopia also reflect a concern with status and prestige. By underlining its commitment to revolutionary causes in the Third World, the Cuban regime was strengthening its claim to leadership of progressive forces in the Third World. Moreover, Castro may have hoped that success abroad, by adding to Cuba's international visibility and prestige, might compensate at home for the economic failures of his government and its continuing intolerance of dissent.

In the Chadian case, pan-Islamic and pan-Arab motivations must be linked with the territorial aspirations of Libya's nationalist elite in accounting for Libyan behaviour. Chad was the only contiguous area in which Col. Gaddafi could exercise these aspirations without colliding directly with formidable regional actors (Algeria and Egypt) or running a high risk of military reaction by France (Niger, Tunisia). Moreover, there is perhaps some justice to the Nigerian claim[21] that Libya did indeed view Chad as a springboard from which it would be possible for her to play a much more active role in sub-Saharan regional politics.

Finally, the French involvement in Chad cannot be explained solely in terms of France's continuing sense of responsibility. It is also a result of her fear of the potential impact on French credibility elsewhere in Francophone Africa of abandoning first President Tombalbaye, then President Malloum, and now President Habré. Moreover, one can explain France's commitment to the concept of *Francophonie* and to a special political, cultural, economic and military relationship with her former colonies partly in terms of her desire to continue to be recognized as a power of global significance. Ironically, a socialist government is in all likelihood more sensitive to these concerns, given its potential susceptibility to criticism from the right for softness in foreign policy.

Strategic motivations

Just as aspirations for power and influence blend at the margin with more basic ideological considerations, so strategic motivations are in large part derived from conceptions of political interest. Hence, the USSR's self-image as a power with global political interests leads logically to a concern with the acquisition of support facilities for worldwide force projection. It follows, for instance, that Soviet involvement in Angola and the Horn of Africa may be explained in part in terms of a desire for port and landing facilities in order to make naval deployments and surveillance of Western naval and other military activities in the Indian Ocean and the South Atlantic easier. Also in the event of war between NATO and the Warsaw Pact such facilities would indeed facilitate the interdiction of important Western economic lifelines – most notably the flow of oil to Western Europe around the Cape of Good Hope and through the Red Sea and the Suez Canal – although in such an eventuality it is probable that rapid escalation to nuclear warfare would render such activities irrelevant. Moreover, tanker traffic or oil production could be halted more easily either by attacks on the oil fields themselves or by interdiction in the Persian Gulf and the Straits of Hormuz.

It might also be argued that in a confrontation short of war, Soviet force projection capabilities could be used to impede tanker traffic so as to apply pressure on the Western Alliance. This too lacks plausibility, however, as it is difficult to envisage how any sustained attempt to constrict oil flows could avoid involving an unacceptable (from the Soviet perspective) risk of escalation.

That said, the USSR's requests to her clients for bases in Angola and Ethiopia suggest that strategic considerations did play a role in her decision-making. Of course, such demands could be evidence not so much of motive as of a Soviet propensity to seek whatever advantages could be gained, once the decision to intervene had been made.

It has been argued that strategic considerations lay behind the Soviet decision to invade Afghanistan as well – again largely with oil in mind. According to this thesis, the Soviet position in Afghanistan allows more effective air interdiction of the Straits of Hormuz than would be possible from air bases in the Caucasus. Moreover, it eases any Soviet attempt to take advantage of internal disorder or regime collapse in Iran. Reports from the autumn of 1982 in the *New York Times* and other newspapers pointed to the construction or improvement of military airfields in Western and Southern Afghanistan as evidence of Soviet thinking along these lines. Subsequent State Department statements, however, asserted that this construction was intended primarily to allow more efficient counter-insurgency operations within Afghanistan. The time interval between the Soviet intervention and this infrastructural improvement lends credence to this view. That is not to deny, of course, that these facilities could be useful in force projection in the Persian Gulf or in a naval engagement in the Bay of Bengal.

It is probable that the Soviet invasion of Afghanistan stemmed from broader security considerations. Growing instability along the USSR's southern fringe, and the Islamic fundamentalism which was in part its cause, provoked concern in Moscow. This was aggravated by the ethnic and religious affinities between the population in Afghanistan and the inhabitants of Soviet Central Asia, and by longer-term demographic shifts in the USSR itself. These factors encouraged a demonstration of resolve to defend Soviet interests in the region. Action was also favoured by the fear that allowing an allied socialist regime in a contiguous country to fall prey to indigenous discontent would set a destabilizing precedent for Soviet satellites in Eastern Europe. Hence, considerations of both internal and – if one accepts that the Soviet government perceives the security of its Western frontier to be linked to control of those countries on its European fringe – external security favoured intervention.

Strategic incentives may have had some role in Soviet decisions to become involved in Angola, Ethiopia and Afghanistan. Equally, the desire to deny strategic gains to the USSR may have influenced initial moves by the US and her allies in Angola, not only for the reasons discussed above but also from concern to ensure access to southern African sources of strategic minerals in the face of growing regional instability. There is ample reason to question whether such considerations should be taken seriously by American policy-makers and whether, if taken seriously, they should be implemented through support for South Africa and opposition to indigenous radical movements and governments.[22] Nonetheless, discussion of the problem of resource access in the American strategic studies literature suggests that important elements of the defence community view the US as being seriously vulnerable to denial of access to these resources and assume that this vulnerability dictates the policy mentioned above.

Narrow security concerns are of greater importance in accounting for South African involvement in Angola. South African policy-makers could be reasonably certain that an MPLA regime in Luanda would give the guerrillas of the South West Africa People's Organization (SWAPO) sanctuary in Angola, whence raids could be mounted against military and civilian installations in Namibia and, perhaps ultimately, against South Africa itself. This potentially entailed a substantial deterioration in Namibian internal security and the prospect of counter-insurgency operations becoming much more costly (in men and materiel), as well as rendering any unilateral South African solution to the Namibia question far less likely to succeed.

It may be surmised that similar considerations weighed in Zairean decision-making. Relations between the MPLA and successive Zairean governments had been little short of homicidal since 1963, when the Kinshasa regime evicted the MPLA from Zaire and threw in its lot with the FNLA. Mobutu could therefore be reasonably certain that the MPLA, if it took power in Angola, would tolerate the activities of Zairean dissidents on Angolan soil. The likelihood of this prospect was considerably enhanced when the guerrillas of the *Fédération Nationale de Libération Congolaise* (FNLC) – the group subsequently responsible for the Shaba incursions in 1977 and 1978 – declared their support for the MPLA in Angola's civil war.

Economic considerations

The mention above of 'strategic' minerals shows how strategic and security considerations shade into economic ones, the final category of incentive to be discussed here. It is difficult to separate the notions of security and economic interest, because in a number of ways the viability of national defence rests upon access to resources found in other countries. The clearest case of this is perhaps Western dependence upon oil from the Persian Gulf. However, the linkage between resources and security is not the only 'economic incentive' for intervention. In a number of the cases considered here the decision-making of intervening powers may have been influenced by economic interest with no immediate connection to security

In the case of Angola, a concern to safeguard the investment of South African interests in the minerals and energy sectors of the Angolan economy provided a further rationale for South African intervention.[23] Moreover, it is plausible to view Zaire's invasion of Cabinda in November 1975 as a grab for the Angolan enclave's oil resources.

French interventions in Africa may also be tied to economic interests. The obvious economic advantages gleaned by France through her special relationship with her former colonies – sources of raw materials, markets for French goods and expertise and preferential treatment of French investment – favour a forward diplomatic and military posture in Africa. French economic interests in Chad are negligible – the country's markets for imports being insignificant, cotton production in the south unimportant when compared to French investments in the Ivory Coast, Gabon, and elsewhere, and Chad's mineral wealth largely unsurveyed and therefore unknown. However, the security of France's economic stake elsewhere in Africa rests in part on the perception of elites in Francophone Africa as a whole of French willingness to defend them. Hence, the economic argument favours intervention, even in areas where the stake is not large.

In Afghanistan, Soviet intervention was quickly followed by agreements between Kabul and Moscow which radically increased the level of natural gas exports from Afghanistan to the Soviet Union, and which tied the Afghan economy even more tightly to COMECON. This might be construed as evidence of an economic incentive for intervention.[24] However, despite the probable importance of Afghan gas to Soviet Central Asia (given the curtailment of Iranian gas exports), the disproportion between the gain to the Soviet economy from reducing Afghanistan to an economic satellite and the scale of Soviet action, and the risks inherent in it, suggests that economic incentives were not important in Soviet decision-making. Instead, as with Soviet lobbying for bases in Angola and Ethiopia, these economic measures suggest a *post facto* attempt to maximize gains from a policy adopted for other reasons.

Proneness to intervention

The above discussion of incentives for intervention deals in the main with the perspective of decision-makers in the intervening state – with what motivations might be relevant when bureaucrats and politicians discuss how to respond to internal and regional disputes in the Third World. But the analysis of what stimulates intervention can be taken to a more profound level by asking whether certain kinds of states are intrinsically more prone to intervention than others. Six general points should be made here.

First, it is probable that regimes which are not the product of popular consent are more likely to undertake intervention than ones which enjoy a broad measure of domestic support. This is because they seek through foreign policy to gain the public acceptance which they feel that they cannot obtain through internal reform and the decentralization of power. In other words, dictatorial regimes are, in the abstract and all other things being equal, more likely interveners than democratic ones. This is also true because, over the short term, in totalitarian states public opposition is less likely to operate as a constraint on foreign policy (see below). Of course it is true that popularly elected regimes have also been frequent interveners, but they do not suffer from the same structurally determined impetus towards activism abroad.

The second point is related to the first. States which for a variety of reasons (under-development or structural rigidities) are not capable of meeting the economic and social aspirations of their publics are more probable interveners. They seek to divert or avert domestic dissatisfaction through foreign success.

Third, some states lack resources of foreign policy other than military instruments (perhaps again because of economic problems or because of a lack of historical, cultural, and economic links with the Third World). Such states are more likely to use force in pursuit of their objectives than states which possess a wider array of diplomatic resources.

Fourth, states with a long-standing martial tradition and in which the military establishment has an important, if not dominant, role in policy-making are more likely to choose military instruments in foreign policy.[25]

Fifth, powers which are new and unsated – whether at regional or global level – are more interventionist than are established ones. It is by a process of assertion and response that they define their niche in world politics and that the system adjusts to them.

Finally, states which seriously propound universalist ideologies – and in particular revolutionary states – are committed to proselytization. This encourages intervention in order to spread the faith. (The 1960s and 1970s saw frequent assertions either that ideology was becoming unimportant as a determinant of foreign policy, or, more strongly, that it was losing its importance as a political variable in general. Soviet interventionism in the mid-1970s, and the coming to power of a viscerally anti-Communist Executive in the US drew this line of argument into question. The emergence of universalist Islamic fundamentalism also justifies scepticism. In fact, it might be argued that the late 1970s and early 1980s have witnessed a 're-ideologization' of international politics.)

Applying these generalizations in specific instances, all six apply in varying degrees to the USSR. It is therefore not surprising that, in the cases considered here, she is the most frequent intervener. The first, second, third and sixth (and perhaps the fifth) apply to Cuba. This suggests that there are important factors, separate from Soviet influence, which favour Cuban interventionism. Point six explains in part Libyan interventionism and suggests that proselytizing Islamic states, such as Iran, are important potential interveners. Point five raises alarming prospects for the foreign policies of a whole array of newly powerful regional actors from Vietnam in south-east Asia to newly rich Iraq and Iran, to Libya and Nigeria, and, in Latin America, to Brazil. It should be emphasized that none of these points alone, nor any combination of them, determines absolutely that states will adopt interventionist foreign policies. The behaviour of states depends not only on profound forces, but also on a host of mitigating or exacerbating factors of varying force and intensity.

In concluding this discussion of incentives for intervention and forces impinging upon the intervening actor which favour it, the indeterminate character of the analysis must be stressed yet again. It is difficult, if not impossible, to know with any certainty why individuals, let alone states, act as they do. It is possible, as we have been seen, to explain these instances of intervention in terms of a number of different motives. The conclusions drawn about the extent to which such behaviour is threatening to one's own interests or to international order depend to a large extent on which of these basic motivations one chooses to emphasize. Hence, in the case of Soviet intervention in Afghanistan, one's assessment of its implications for the West is coloured significantly by whether one believes Soviet action to have been based on a narrowly defined conception of the security of the USSR and the potential threat which instability in Afghanistan and in south-west Asia posed to control of Soviet Central Asia, or whether one sees it as the first step in a Soviet strategy to obtain a warm water port in the Indian Ocean or to threaten Western access to Persian Gulf oil. Unfortunately, Soviet behaviour is consistent with either interpretation, and there is no way of knowing which is correct, or whether in fact both may not be valid.

The international system

The preceding discussion of factors conducive to interventionism suggests at least two characteristics of the international system which also favour intervention. In the first place, international systems encompassing large numbers of states which suffer from high levels of internal instability are likely to have a high incidence of intervention. Similarly, systems characterized by ideological divisions and competition are prone to military interference by states in the affairs of their neighbours.[26] However, these are not the only systemic factors stimulating intervention.

A third is asymmetry in the distribution of power. More or less equal states have the capacity to resist each other's attempts to intervene in their internal affairs. In such systems, the incidence of intervention will be low. By contrast, systems in which power is unevenly distributed will be intervention-prone.[27] It is no accident that in all four of the cases considered here, there have existed substantial perceived or actual asymmetries in power between the intervener and his target.

In this sense, the dispersion of power throughout the system which was alluded to in the Introduction should bring with it a decline in interventionism. This will be discussed further below. Two caveats should, however, be included here. The first is that, despite this diffusion, there remains a massive gap between the military capabilities of the superpowers and those of regional powers in the Third World and (if the Anglo-Argentinian war over the Falkland Islands is any indication) a substantial disparity between the European industrial powers and the newly-powerful in Asia, Africa and Latin America. Second, this dispersion of power is not uniform, but has benefited most of all a small number of regionally significant states. This has created even greater regional imbalances than existed previously, facilitating intervention by local actors, as is evident in South African actions in Angola, Somalian actions in Ethiopia, and Libyan actions in Chad. The diffusion of power towards the Third World has caused a multiplication of asymmetries within it.

This is related to a final systemic point. It is not only the degree of distribution of power through the system which is important, but also the structure of that distribution, be it unipolar, bipolar or multipolar. Relations between states since World War II have been strongly conditioned by military bipolarity. The effect of bipolarity on the incidence of intervention is ambiguous. On the one hand, the more rigidly divided a system, and the more confrontational that division, the more a potential shift of alliances by committed states will seem damaging to other states' interests.[28] This encourages intervention in the affairs of allies to prevent such eventualities. The post-war history of Eastern Europe is studded with interventions of this type, and the Soviet invasion of Afghanistan may also be explained partially in these terms, as was intimated above.[29] Moreover, the bipolarity of the system and the adversarial relations between the poles encourages competition for influence in areas where the lines are not clearly drawn, as we have seen from the discussion of political motives for intervention.

On the other hand, however, the dangers inherent in bipolar tension may lead each side to avoid situations where direct confrontation is possible (see the section below on constraints). Furthermore, inherent in the existence of more than one major power in a system is the ability of smaller states to forestall intervention by playing one major power off against the other.[30] In the middle and late 1950s, for instance, Egypt saw value in cementing her ties with the USSR, so as to forestall threats from the West. Federal Nigeria, in her civil war with secessionist Biafra used the threat of closer ties with the USSR to deter Western governments from becoming involved on the side of Biafra, and putting pressure on the Federal Government to make undesirable compromises.[31] This leads to the discussion of constraints on intervention.

FACTORS CONSTRAINING INTERVENTION

Any power considering an act of intervention is faced with a number of constraints on its ability to do so. These must be weighed against those factors which favour intervention in any decision about whether and to what extent to become embroiled in a conflict inside another state. They are material (economic and military), political and normative, and they originate in the international system as a whole, the intervening state, and the target environment.

The target environment

At the level of the target state, two factors have an especially important effect on the possibility of intervention from outside. The first is the degree of internal cohesion in the society in question. It was shown above that all four of the cases considered here involved societies beset by chronic internal conflict and in which popular identification with the state was weak. The converse of this is that states which are not affected by such instability and internal division provide few internal hooks on which to hang an intervention.

This is related to a second point: that potential intervention is constrained by internal opposition to external involvement in a country's domestic affairs. If such nationalist sentiment exists to the degree that groups involved in internal disputes will bury the hatchet in the face of intrusion from outside, and if the strength of this sentiment is perceived by outsiders, it will operate to deter intervention. It is commonly asserted that the growth of third-world nationalism in the last three decades has rendered intervention by non-third-world actors a far more costly and hence unattractive option of policy. To take a specific example, the failure of the Nasser regime in Egypt to crumble when faced with Anglo-French intervention, and the intensity of popular Egyptian opposition to the foreign presence, made the operation far more difficult than anticipated and, ultimately, rendered it unsustainable.

Regional opposition can also operate to constrain intervention by extra-regional actors. One of the most important factors deterring American involvement in the Somalian-Ethiopian dispute was the wide-spread support for the Ethiopian position by African states apprehensive about Somalian infringement of OAU norms concerning the inviolability of frontiers established during the colonial partition of Africa. A similar constraint may have influenced the Libyan decision in late 1981 to withdraw from Chad. Libya's intervention and the subsequent merger agreement between the two countries aroused widespread indignation in Africa. There is reason to assume that this reaction was one factor among many contributing to the Libyan withdrawal – a factor which had added weight at the time since Gaddafi was then in line for the chairmanship of the Organization of African Unity. (This element of the Libyan calculus lost much of its weight, however, when Gaddafi lost his opportunity to head the OAU, and the weakening of this constraint may in part explain Libya's renewed intervention on behalf of Goukouni Oueddei in 1983.)

Intervening states face similar pressures at the level of the third-world as a whole. Overwhelming support by Asian, African and Latin American countries for UN General Assembly resolutions prohibiting military intervention confirms a profound aversion to such intrusions on the part of third-world states as a whole, particularly when the intrusions originate in the developed world. States valuing their image in the 'South' and their relations with specific states in Asia, Africa and Latin America must think twice about the implications of their military activities there. The intensity and near-unanimity of the third-world response to the Soviet invasion of Afghanistan is a recent reminder of the strength of this sentiment.

It should be stressed, however, that these constraints operate selectively. In the target state, intervention against widely popular groups is more likely to provoke internal hostility than is assistance to such groups, for the one constitutes a denial and the other an affirmation of self-determination. Regional opposition to intervention is liable to be far less strong when the intrusion is, or can be credibly construed as, a defence of self-determination or of regional norms. Hence, Soviet/Cuban assistance to Ethiopia met little African criticism, being widely viewed as a defence of a state's territorial integrity against an attempt by another external actor to dismember it. Likewise, in the Angolan case, much of the disapproval within the region of Soviet/Cuban involvement on behalf of the MPLA, and in violation of an OAU prohibition on involvement in the conflict, evaporated once the extent of South African involvement became clear. Nigeria, for instance, in recognizing the MPLA regime, stated categorically that she took this step as a result of South African involvement against the MPLA. Soviet/Cuban involvement was again seen as a defence of a regional norm, namely opposition to apartheid.

Influences on intervening states

The attitude of adversaries

Moving beyond the target environment, potential interveners face a number of constraints, both internally and in their relations with other states. Of greatest importance in the latter context is the attitude of adversaries. For example, the expectation by one superpower that the other will react vigorously to an act of intervention, and the risks of escalation attendant upon such a confrontation, inhibit military interference in the affairs of other states.

While direct evidence of this effect is sparse, the very fact that there has been no case since World War II in which the military forces of the two superpowers have confronted each other on the territory of a third-world state is indicative of its strength. So, too, is the fact that neither superpower has tended to intervene in areas where both sides have made clear that they perceive their vital interests to be at stake. In this context, it is significant that, despite the persistence of conflict in the Middle East and the repeated opportunities for intervention which this has fostered, neither power (with the possible and marginal exception of US actions against Syrian forces in Lebanon) has become directly involved in offensive military operations against the clients of the other.

This effect tends to limit intervention by either superpower, first, to those regions in which it enjoys an overwhelming military superiority or which are tacitly or explicitly recognized as being within its sphere of influence and, second, to areas perceived to be less central to the interests of both. In the case of Soviet intervention, Afghanistan falls into the first category, and Ethiopia and Angola into the second. This constraint may also explain the preference of both superpowers for employing the military effectives of proxies or of countries sharing their objectives (e.g. Cubans, South Africans and Zaireans in Angola). The strength of this constraint is to some extent dependent on the credibility of the adversary. Hence, the USSR may have acted as she did in Angola, Ethiopia and Afghanistan in part because she perceived the US, in the aftermath of Watergate and in the confusion of the Carter period, to be unwilling or unable to respond resolutely to Soviet initiatives.

Regional actors, too, must take into account the position of unfriendly superpowers in contemplating intervention. The possibility of counter-intervention not only by the superpowers, but also by other powerful extra-regional actors is an important factor shaping a local intervener's prospects for success. Failure accurately to assess this constraint was a critical factor in the failure of interventions by Zaire and South Africa in Angola and by Somalia in Ethiopia. It is plausible that anticipated extra-regional opposition explains in part why it was in Chad rather than in Niger that Libya chose to exercise her aspirations. Moreover, it is clear that Libya's policy towards Tunisia has been constrained by French support for the latter.

Wariness of extra-regional actors may also be inferred from the limited character of recent South African intrusions in Angola. Some of these have been quite substantial by regional standards and have evoked not only SWAPO and Angolan, but also some Cuban resistance. But they have never been of a magnitude and geographical scope sufficient to threaten the MPLA government directly. This would have risked substantial Cuban involvement and involved the possibility of more direct Soviet involvement.

However, it is not only potential opposition from outside the region which constrains regional actors. A government contemplating intervention in a neighbouring state must also take account of the likely response of other regional actors in assessing his prospects for success, for assistance by other states in the region to those opposing the intervention may alter significantly the internal balance of forces faced by the intervening power. In this context, it is probable that one determinant of the Libyan decision to withdraw from Chad in 1981 was the assistance rendered by Sudan and Egypt to Hissène Habré's *Forces Armées du Nord* (FAN). The limited character of Libyan pressure on Sudan – despite the weakness of the latter and the remarkable hostility between the two – may be explained largely in terms of the strong commitment of Egypt to the survival of the Nimeiri regime in Sudan. In the Central American context, doubts about the character of American and Latin American reactions are probably an important factor in Cuban deliberations concerning broader involvement in Nicaragua, El Salvador, and Guatemala.

The attitudes of friends

Regional states contemplating intervention must consider not only the position of adversaries, but also that of friends. Their actions may be severely constrained, for instance, by the attitude of those powers on whom they depend for arms. A patron's failure to resupply his client could leave the latter dangerously overextended. Eloquent testimony to this problem was provided by Somalia, which, in the midst of her incursion into the Ogaden, found herself cut off by the USSR, her previous supplier, and – owing to the clearly aggressive character of her actions – was unable to line up a new source of materiel.

In the case of the middle powers, intervention may be rendered difficult, if not unsustainable, by the disapproval of major allies. The case of Suez illustrates the difficulty for Western European powers of initiating major military action in the face of active American opposition. (The Suez example may, of course, be less instructive in a period where American hegemony in the West is less obvious.) On a more technical level, such powers may lack the transport capability necessary for the projection of force in situations where they are contemplating military action, and hence may be dependent for logistical support on one of the super-powers. French intervention in Shaba, for instance, would have been far more difficult had the US not provided long-range air transport. Similarly, the Cuban interventions in Angola and Ethiopia would have been far less effective, if not impossible, without the Soviet airlift, because success in each case depended on the rapid delivery of large numbers of troops and substantial quantities of equipment. This Cuba could not have achieved alone.

Military constraints

The mention of logistical limitations brings us to the consideration of constraints which originate *within* the state contemplating intervention. In the first place, the propensity of a state to intervene is strongly affected by the existence or absence of the military force necessary to undertake the operation. As Adam Yarmolinsky put it:

> In fact, the availability of military force may be the principal practical determinant of a decision to intervene. Of course military force isn't always used just because it's there, but if it isn't there, it can't be used.[32]

It is a commonplace that the infrequency of Soviet military activity in the Third World in the 1950s and 1960s was largely stemmed from the absence of the capability to project and sustain force. Where this was tried, as in the Congo in 1960 and in Cuba in 1962, it rapidly became clear that the USSR was massively outclassed; the result was humiliating retreat. A major permissive condition of greater Soviet activism in the 1970s and early 1980s was the development of just such capabilities. However, the USSR remains constrained by the clear inferiority *vis-à-vis* the US of her long-range air transport, her naval air and fighter cover, and her amphibious capabilities in situations carrying a significant risk of American counter-intervention.[33]

It is evident that the country least affected by military constraints on intervention in non-contiguous areas is the United States. As the development of the US Rapid Deployment Force proceeds, this is likely to be increasingly true. The military constraint is most compelling for regional actors, most of whom lack substantial integrated intervention capabilities and significant indigenous armaments industries (the latter shortcoming entailing the dependence on foreign suppliers mentioned above). Moreover, they generally lack the professional skills to use such capabilities effectively, though some of the regional powers active in the cases considered here (South Africa, Somalia and Libya) have displayed considerable proficiency in their operations.

Economic constraints

The military constraint is closely linked to the economic one. Intervention, like any other military activity, is a costly business. Any decision to embark upon it that results from an attempt to weigh costs and benefits must take into account the likely effect on other branches of the military and on the economic condition of the country as a whole. Moreover, sudden changes in economic conditions can prejudice the outcome of actions taken in better times. A run on sterling in 1956, coupled with US unwillingness to assist

Britain in beating it off, made it impossible, in the opinion of the Eden Cabinet, to continue the Suez operation. Likewise, it is plausible that the softness of world oil prices as a result of deflated demand, and the consequent short-fall in Libyan oil revenues, was one further factor accounting for the Libyan withdrawal from Chad in 1981. Nigeria's sudden loss of enthusiasm for the OAU force in Chad may be attributed in part to this same cause, particularly in the light of the escalating cost and open-ended character of this commitment and the failure to find anybody else to share the cost.

The strength of the economic constraint varies with the type of action undertaken and its duration, as well as with the resources of the intervener. Put simply, large interventions cost more than small ones, long ones more than short ones, and the wealthy are more capable than the poor of mounting an intervention. The crippling effect on Tanzania's economy of intervention in Uganda illustrates the potential impact on a poor country of costly military activity abroad. Even the most powerful can feel its bite, however, if the action is sufficiently large or if economic conditions are poor. By the end of the 1960s, the US intervention in Vietnam was a significant drain on the American economy. Also, it is quite possible that worsening conditions in the Soviet economy will render the USSR far more reluctant to undertake large-scale interventions than she was in the mid-1970s.

Domestic constraints

The economic constraint is closely linked to domestic political limitations on interventionism, for the sentiment that scarce resources could be better used in different ways can fuel popular opposition to military adventures abroad. However, it is more usually disagreement with the foreign-policy objectives being pursued, or a belief that the value of these objectives is insufficient to justify the risks to fellow nationals and the cost in lives of the operation, which is of greatest significance in stimulating popular resistance to interventionism – as the experience of American opposition to the war in Vietnam suggests.

Government sensitivity to public opinion naturally varies from state to state. Of the interveners in the cases discussed here, it is the US which is most strongly affected by this constraint. The last seven years have shown how difficult it has been for her to develop a national consensus, or (more modestly) a consensus within the US Government, on a policy of intervention. This is largely the result of the *dénouement* of American involvement in Vietnam. Popular and Congressional opposition to military adventures in third-world countries rendered it impossible for the Ford Administration to pursue its chosen policy in Angola in 1975. One might have expected the 'Vietnam syndrome' to have lost some of its strength with time and the resurrection of the Cold War in American consciousness, but its remaining vigour is evident in the widespread opposition to any use of American troops in El Salvador. This dislike of involving American units in third-world conflicts is shared by important elements of the defence establishment, judging from the Pentagon's conspicuous lack of enthusiasm for intervention in Central America.

This essentially political constraint has brought with it a number of legal ones. Both during and after the Vietnam War Congress severely restricted the Administration's ability to use force without Congressional approval, as well as prohibiting American involvement in specific conflicts (as in Angola, South-east Asia, and Western Sahara). In other areas (such as El Salvador) it established rather stringent conditions for the continuation of American assistance.

The French government has also, though to a lesser degree, felt the constraint of public opinion on intervention in certain African contexts. The involvement in Chad met with significant popular disapproval, the press repeatedly voicing the fear that Chad would turn out to be France's Vietnam. The degree of public dislike of the Chadian connection was perhaps best indicated by the fact that, when French forces responded to President Malloum's appeal for assistance in early 1978, the operation was conducted with great secrecy. The full scale and extent of French intervention were concealed from the public until after the spring 1978 elections, lest the chances of government candidates be severely prejudiced.

Authoritarian regimes are clearly less susceptible to this kind of domestic pressure than democratic ones. Just as Soviet defence policy-making is unhampered by the existence of an independent and vocal peace movement, so the USSR is free of any significant publicly-expressed opposition to intervention. Nonetheless, substantial and costly involvements are likely to be unpopular, both within government circles and with the public at large. Sensitivity to this problem perhaps explains why the Soviet press has taken great pains initially to play down the size of the Afghan conflict and latterly to justify Soviet involvement. The recent banning of public funerals for servicemen in Lithuania indicates official concern about opposition to the war. Evidence of opposition elsewhere in the USSR may be drawn from reports that Afghan students in Tashkent have been subjected to beatings and other forms of harassment by Soviet Central Asians. Posters and leaflets criticizing Soviet involvement in Afghanistan have appeared in the Central Asian cities of Samarkand and Tashkent, the Baltic Republics, Kiev, Moscow and Leningrad.[34] In an earlier period, it was in part elite dissatisfaction with Khruschev's forward policy in the Third World which led to his downfall in 1964.

Factors in the international system

Legal constraints

Beyond these military, economic and political constraints upon potential interveners, certain aspects of the structure of the international system inhibit military interference in a state's internal affairs. The most obvious is international law.

The evolution of the present system of states was accompanied by the growth of a body of customary and treaty laws pertaining to state behaviour. One element of this process was the recognition that intervention, since it violated another state's sovereignty, was in principle contrary to international law.[35] More recently, the UN has played an active role in the definition of legal norms concerning intervention. The UN Charter states more or less unequivocally that the aggressive use of force by one state against another is illegal. This implies a prohibition on intervention not requested by a recognized government.

The UN General Assembly has on a number of occasion endorsed a general prohibition on 'armed intervention' in internal conflicts.[36] But General Assembly resolutions on the subject do not explicitly prohibit assistance to established governments. In this sense, they uphold what remains the predominant principle of international law; that 'the incumbent government is entitled to assistance from other states while rebels are not – at least until they have been accorded the status of belligerents'.[37] Mainstream legal thinking on intervention is, therefore, selective in inhibiting interventionist behaviour: to the extent that states take it seriously, it constrains intervention against established regimes while permitting it in their support.

Several qualifications are necessary here. First, the General Assembly has to some extent weakened the traditional prohibition on assistance to insurgent groups by calling upon member governments to assist national liberation movements and by maintaining that their struggles are matters of international rather than domestic jurisdiction. This is an extension of a justification of intervention in terms of the right of self-determination which is of much longer standing. The General Assembly has failed to define precisely what disputes fall into the category of wars of national liberation, but, judging from the body of its resolutions on the subject and from the legal literature surrounding them,[38] three kinds of insurgent movements may be included: struggles against colonial rule (Angola prior to April 1974, for example); those against apartheid; and those against 'foreign occupation' (the General Assembly views Namibia and also Palestine in these terms). In addition to calling upon states to support, materially and morally, movements involved in these struggles, the General Assembly has attempted to prohibit assistance to governments which are the target of wars of liberation.[39] While the status of General Assembly resolutions as law remains a matter of considerable dispute, states such as the USSR have justified interference in what they consider to be wars of national liberation as a response to the dictates of international law, citing the relevant General Assembly resolutions. It is plausible, therefore, that this set of developments has weakened the already selective legal constraint on intervention.

Second, and perhaps more importantly, the effectiveness of the international legal constraint is greatly limited by the failure of international lawyers to arrive at a generally accepted definition of intervention. Lawyers suffer the same problems as political scientists in 'drawing precise boundary lines between the pressures that are constantly exercised by individual states or groups of states against others, on the one hand, and forms and degrees of pressures that are forbidden by international law on the other hand'.[40] Moreover, the legal debate is enmeshed in the East–West ideological conflict evidenced by conflicting Soviet and American views on whether and in what ways involvement in struggles for national liberation constitutes intervention. This had led some writers to argue that, because of conflicting world views, analytical approaches and value commitments, precise definition is impossible.

The effectiveness of international law in constraining intervention is further limited by the elasticity of a number of associated concepts which are used to justify intervention. It is widely accepted, for instance, that states may intervene to protect the lives of nationals abroad. But the degree of threat sufficient to legitimize military intrusion is a matter of debate. Likewise, many scholars accept that gross violations of human rights constitute a sufficient justification of 'humanitarian intervention', but there is no commonly accepted definition of human rights or of the threshold of violation which renders intervention permissible.

Finally, it is often argued that assistance to insurgent groups becomes lawful when a state of belligerency is established. Alternatively, some argue that, once a civil conflict reaches this level, neutrality in the conflict is to be preferred, whereas assistance to the incumbent government is permissible before the establishment of belligerency. But both of these positions assume that the status of belligerency is easily determinable. In theory, such a state exists when a government has lost control of a significant portion of its territory to insurgents, or when each side in a conflict recognizes the other as a belligerent. However what constitutes 'a significant portion' or the granting of recognition are politically contentious. The incumbent government will resist admitting that the first criterion is met and will refuse to concede the latter one, in order to restrict as far as possible both the insurgents' access to international assistance and, more generally, external involvement in a conflict which it wishes to keep 'in the family'. By contrast, the opposition seeks to internationalize the dispute as quickly as possible. The issue of belligerency cannot therefore be left to the parties to the conflict or to their supporters, yet there exists no supranational authority recognized by parties to the conflict as competent to judge it.

For all these reasons, international law as a constraint on intervention is a weak reed. Nonetheless, since states do not as a rule like to be perceived as contravening norms of law, in cases where the balance between perceived benefits and costs of intrusion is unclear, law may have a marginal role in constraining intervention.

Moreover, international law concerning non-interference in the internal affairs of other states is an institutional manifestation of a more basic and generally accepted rule of conduct in inter-state relations: the mutual recognition of equal sovereignty. Coercive behaviour in international politics is frequent enough to make one wonder whether this norm is not more honoured in the breach than in the observance. Even so, there is good cause to believe that intervention would be far less exceptional if this understanding did not exist and if it did not form a reasonably reliable basis on which to predict the behaviour of others. Its strength rests on a shared interest in being able to govern without continual intrusion from outside, and from the awareness that any substantial erosion of the principle would greatly reduce whatever predictability there is in inter-state relations.

TRIGGERING INTERVENTION

While conditions in the target environment, the structure of the international system, the motivations of external actors, and the constraints under which all the actors must operate are all important in establishing the context in which a decision to intervene is taken, they are not sufficient to explain why an act of intervention takes place at a specific time and why this particular instrument of policy is chosen, rather than some other less extreme one.

Judging from the four cases considered here, the decision to intervene is a reactive one. It is a response to catalytic events in the target state, to sudden changes in the fortunes of local allies or adversaries and in the type and level of involvement by other external actors. These events radically alter the trade-off of costs and benefits faced by the intervening power in such a way as to make the option of intervention appear either irresistible or unavoidable. Intervention is, in short, the product of crisis.

Angola

In the case of Angola, the decisions of the several external actors to intervene were made partly as a result of sudden changes in the internal situation and partly in response to the decision of other actors to enter.

Perhaps the first change to be stressed was the collapse of the Portuguese metropolitan government in April 1974. While the USSR, China, the US, South Africa and Zaire had all long been involved in Angolan affairs, this event created a fundamentally new situation – a political vacuum which would be filled by one or more of the contending liberation movements. This dramatically altered the prospects for external actors gaining influence in what was a rapidly changing region, as well as creating new dangers for regional actors, such as Zaire and South Africa, whose security would be to some extent affected by the outcome of the transition to independence in Angola. It is in this context that the decision of Zaire, the first power to intervene militarily in Angola, should be explained.

Zairean units crossed the frontier with FNLA guerrillas in February 1975, a month after arrangements for the Portugese withdrawal and the transfer of power had been finalized by Lisbon in conjunction with the three liberation movements. The Zairean government may have been encouraged in its action by the American decision in January to resume support for the FNLA (this decision, too, should be seen as a response to the situation of flux created by the imminent Portuguese departure).

Soviet interest was also spurred by the April 1974 coup in Portugal. While the USSR had cut her assistance to the MPLA and redirected it from Agostinho Neto's faction to that of Daniel Chipenda in 1973, the Lisbon coup caused a reassessment of her policy. This was encouraged by the Portuguese Communist Party, which, unlike the USSR, had steadfastly maintained its commitment to Neto. Soviet interest was further heightened by the growing Chinese association with the FNLA, evident in June 1974, when Chinese instructors arrived in Zaire to train that organization's guerrillas, and in September, when they were followed by 450 tons of arms. Small amounts of Soviet arms were provided to the MPLA late in 1974.[41] The first evidence of significant Soviet involvement appeared in March and April 1975, when cargo ships carrying consignments of Soviet arms destined for the MPLA appeared in Luanda and Pointe Noire.

The chronology would suggest that this increase in Soviet assistance was in the immediate sense a reaction to Zairean and American actions. The USSR's local client, the MPLA, was just emerging from a series of severely debilitating factional disputes which had weakened the movement considerably. It was already inferior, in numbers if not in organization, to the FNLA, which was receiving substantial quantities of assistance from external patrons. The FNLA's actions suggested that it was attempting to achieve a military preponderance which would allow it either to eliminate its opponents or to secure a dominant position in the transition to independence. This was paralleled by a breakdown of the fragile truce between the rival movements and the return to armed conflict in Luanda and elsewhere. Soviet policy-makers, and Cuban ones as well, were faced with the choice of letting the FNLA win the day or of providing the MPLA with the means to resist.

Soviet material assistance, and Cuba's provision of some 230 advisers in the late spring tilted the balance of forces in favour of the MPLA. It began to win the war against the FNLA in the north and centre and, in the summer of 1975, successfully challenged UNITA in the cities of central Angola.

The boot was now on the other foot. Zaire, the US and South Africa were faced with the apparent choice of increasing their own commitment or seeing their allies bested by a movement whose ideology and ties to the Soviet bloc were noxious to them. The three decided to attempt to reverse the fortunes of the opposition to the MPLA. They all substantially increased their assistance to the FNLA. The United States and South Africa also began to assist UNITA. In August, South African troops entered Angola and in October began to move rapidly northwards, in conjunction with FNLA and mercenary forces. In September Zaire added a further two battalions of paratroops to her contingent in Angola. By the end of October, Luanda was again being threatened, this time from both north and south. The tables had been turned again.

The Soviet and Cuban governments once more faced a choice. They could abandon the MPLA, or they could substantially increase their commitment to it. The situation closely paralleled that faced in February and March, but at a substantially higher level of conflict. In addition, Soviet and Cuban prestige was now on the line to a far greater degree, given their earlier decision to back the MPLA; backing down now would call into question the credibility of their commitments to clients as well as encouraging the Western powers to challenge them elsewhere. A decision to bail out the MPLA necessitated the use of troops from outside, for the MPLA lacked personnel trained in the use of weapons to be provided. Furthermore, that organization could not field sufficient numbers of reliable troops to deal with the threats from both north and south. The USSR and Cuba undertook this commitment and the massive escalation which it involved.

The chain of action and reaction was broken by the US Congress in December 1975, when it denied the Ford Administration the resources necessary to continue the conflict.

The Angolan conflict would thus support the view that intervention was in the immediate sense a response to catalytic factors, to discrete historical events specific to the Angolan situation: the Lisbon coup, the Alvor Accords of January 1975 (under which a transitional government was established to share power between the three independence movements and the Portuguese until full independence in November 1975), the shifting fortunes of local clients, and the moves of other external actors.

Ethiopia

Similarly, certain catalytic events are of great significance in accounting for intervention in Ethiopia. The first was the 1974 Revolution itself, which created a situation of flux and opportunity for the USSR in a country that had previously been a closed preserve of the US. Moreover, it initiated a collapse of central control over the outlying regions of the country. By 1977, persistent factionalism within the *Dergue* and repeated purges within the officer corps were combined with chronic violence in the capital and insurgencies of varying seriousness in Eritrea, the Ogaden, Wollo, Tigré and Gondar provinces.

This collapse was one factor contributing to Somalia's decision to intervene in the Ogaden in 1977: she acted on the assumption that Ethiopia was incapable of mounting an effective response. Somalian action was also favoured by the termination of the military assistance agreement between the US and Ethiopia in April 1977. Ethiopia had lost her major source of external support and had not yet found a new one. Speed was necessary, for it was evident that relations between Cuba and the USSR, on the one hand, and Ethiopia, on the other, were already improving; it would be but a matter of time, therefore, before Somalia's 'window of opportunity' was closed. Somalia accordingly probed in force in May and June of 1977 and struck with the bulk of her forces in August. She chose military action, rather than some other instrument of policy, because it was the only one which could achieve her policy objective, namely the detachment from Ethiopia of the Somali-inhabited areas of the Ogaden.

Soviet and Cuban relations with Ethiopia had been improving steadily in the meantime. In April 1976 the *Dergue* announced Ethiopia's adherence to 'scientific socialism'. In June 1976 the USSR and Ethiopia signed a cultural agreement, while in the previous month it had been reported that Ethiopia had received substantial amounts of Yugoslav and Czech light weapons. The *Dergue's* move leftwards continued during the summer of 1976, when an Ethiopian delegation visited Moscow, and a secret visit by Col. Mengistu Haile Mariam to the USSR followed in December, during which an agreement was signed for the sale to Ethiopia of approximately $100 million worth of outmoded Soviet armour.[42] The February 1977 coup, in which Gen. Teferi Bante and a number of other moderate officers lost their lives, further accelerated the radicalization of Ethiopian domestic and foreign policies. Communist approval of this turn of events was signalled by a visit to Addis Ababa by Fidel Castro in March.

The rupture of the Ethiopian-American military relationship in April also accelerated Soviet and Cuban involvement. The very survival of the Ethiopian regime depended on obtaining large deliveries of arms and ammunition to deal with the insurgencies in Eritrea and Tigré and the growing unrest in the Ogaden. The fact that the US was insufficiently forthcoming over this was a major cause of the deterioration in relations between the two countries in 1975–7, and of Ethiopia's attempt to diversify her sources of support abroad. The severing of the military link between the two countries in April 1977, the final stage in this process, made the search for new sources of supply all the more urgent, and it is probably no coincidence that Mengistu left for further talks in Moscow at the beginning of May, only a few days after the formal breach with the US.

From the Soviet perspective, the break with the US confirmed the genuineness of the opportunity in Ethiopia, as well as removing the USSR's major opponent from the field. In the aftermath of Mengistu's May visit to the USSR, the delivery of Soviet arms to Ethiopia accelerated, and the first 200 advisers arrived to train Ethiopian troops.[43]

The actual military intervention by the USSR and Cuba, however, can be accounted for only in terms of Somalian actions. Before the Somalian invasion, Soviet policy had been to cultivate Ethiopia, while maintaining good relations with Somalia. But the latter's intrusion into the Ogaden in July and August rendered this policy no longer viable and presented the USSR with a choice. She was forced to opt for one side or the other and to do so quickly, given the rapid advance of Somalian forces and the deterioration of the situation within Ethiopia. That she chose Ethiopia had much to do with that country's greater intrinsic importance. In addition, the Somalian President's alarming proclivity for independent action made it likely that a weak Ethiopian regime would be more dependent on the USSR than Somalia, and hence more susceptible to penetration and influence. In any case, the Somalian incursion into

Ethiopia faced the Soviet Union with the embarrassing prospect of supporting and arming a state which was attempting to dis-member its neighbour – which would have done her relations with the rest of Africa no good at all, for reasons discussed above. She chose the military instrument largely because it was the only response which was likely to forestall a Somalian victory, the Ethiopian army clearly being in no condition to handle both the Ogaden invasion and the growing insurgent pressure in Eritrea.

Here too, then, intervention was in the most direct sense a reaction to specific events in the target state (the Revolution, the rupture in the US-Ethiopian military relationship, and the rapid deterioration of the internal security situation) and to changes in the behaviour of other external actors (the US and Somalia).

Afghanistan

The period after the 1978 coup in Afghanistan witnessed a rapid increase in Soviet involvement in Afghan domestic affairs. Hundreds of Soviet civilian advisers were seconded to ministries depleted by the voluntary departure and subsequent purges of Afghan officials, and the growing insurgency broadened the role of Soviet personnel in the Afghan Armed Forces. By early December 1979 it was reliably reported that there were approximately 4,000 Soviet military advisers in the country.[44] The Soviet commitment to the People's Democratic Party (PDP) regime was large, expensive and public, but by this time the situation in Afghanistan had deteriorated to the point where the USSR could see only two options open to her: withdrawing and letting events take their course; or massively increasing the scale of both military commitment and political involvement. The former would probably have involved the fall of the PDP and either a long period of anarchy or the emergence of a radical Islamic regime.[45] Neither of these outcomes would be particularly appealing from the Soviet perspective, and either would certainly imply losing the investment of men, money and material placed in Afghanistan since 1973 (and particularly since 1978), besides involving a loss of political credibility with both allies and adversaries. In this sense, the entire train of events militated in favour of the second option: intervention.

That it took the form it did (i.e. intervention against the ruling government) and occurred when it did had much to do with Hafizullah Amin's successful coup in September 1979. There were two reasons for this. First, Amin was a far less pliable instrument than his predecessor Nur Muhammad Taraki, and resisted the accretion of Soviet influence. (He illustrated his autonomy by demanding the recall of Soviet Ambassador Puzanov, whom he believed to have been involved in Taraki's attempt in September to have him removed as Prime Minister.) This independence rendered it unlikely that he would accept the degree of Soviet involvement which the Soviet Union's leaders believed was necessary to stablize the situation. Another manifestation of Amin's unwillingness to take Soviet instructions was his refusal to moderate the social policies which had provoked the insurgency in the first place. Such an attempt to defuse opposition to the regime might have made the internal situation controllable at a much lower level of Soviet involvement than eventually occurred. Amin's refusal to compromise, and his ruthless persecution of the opposition therefore only strengthened the insurgency, imperilling the Soviet position even more.

Jiri Valenta is probably close to the mark in maintaining that in Soviet eyes, Amin was both a loser and a traitor.[46] He had to be removed if Soviet interests in Afghanistan were to be preserved. The opposition to Amin within the regime lacked the power and the will to do this, so the USSR had to do it, and – given the character of the action to be taken against Amin, the nature of the threat to PDP rule and the Soviet presence, and the Afghan forces' inability to quell that threat on their own – military intervention was the only course of action which held out some prospect of success. Soviet policy-makers either had to redefine their objectives in Afghanistan or to order their troops in.

In this case too, intervention was, in its timing and its form, a reaction to a relatively rapid deterioration in the target state's internal situation and to discrete historical events forcing the intervener to choose between withdrawal and escalation.

Chad

Turning finally to Chad, this discussion focuses on the French interventions of 1968, 1978 and 1983 and on the Libyan incursions of 1980 and 1983. It is clear that in the three French cases, intervention was a response to sudden deteriorations in the fortunes of a local client, the Chadian government. The basic reasons for France's commitment to the Tombalbaye, Malloum and Habré regimes were discussed above. However, the timing of her actions clearly reflects their reactive character.

In 1968, FROLINAT forces were rapidly consolidating their hold on the North and East, the area under the control of the central government was shrinking, and it appeared to external observers that the collapse of the Tombalbaye regime was certain unless it received external military assistance. Tombalbaye himself recognized this when he urgently requested French intervention. The dispatch of French forces was a natural response, given France's perception of her own interests and commitments, and given her history of intervention in situations where governments of her ex-colonies were threatened by internal unrest.

A similar situation prevailed in 1978. Goukouni Oueddei's FROLINAT forces, in conjunction with those of Acyl Ahmat, had quickly taken control of the Borkou-Ennedi-Tibesti area and much of Biltine Prefecture and were sweeping south and west towards the capital. Malloum's hold on power appeared to be weakening, and outside observers were predicting the military collapse of the central government. The French response to Malloum's request for assistance was rapid and decisive, and the rebel offensive was checked. In both of these cases, armed forces were used, rather than some other instrument, because of the urgency of the situation and the military character of the threat. Aid packages or rhetorical expressions of support were insufficient for the purpose which France had in mind. The apparent choice she faced in both cases was military involvement or the acceptance of a very high probability that the regime (and the French position in Chad) would be destroyed – a motivation hardly any different from that which obtained in 1983.

In 1983 France responded to the fairly rapid deterioration of the Chadian government position in the north-east (and particularly to the Libyan-supplied and logistically supported drive on the strategic oasis of Faya-Largeau) by stepping up deliveries of military supplies to the Ndjaména regime in late June and early July. When this proved insufficient to stem the rebel tide, and when the extent of the involvement of Libyan mechanized and air force units became clear, the French government dispatched some 2,000 paratroopers to man a line of defence running through the centre of the country, along with *Jaguar* and *Mirage* jets to provide air cover. This, too, took place in conditions where, in the absence of intervention, the survival of the government was questionable and in response to frantic appeals from that government for French intervention.

Several specific events may have influenced Libya's choice of intervention and the timing of her initiative in late 1980. Her military involvement in Chadian affairs predates the 1980 intervention by many years. She had been assisting FROLINAT rebels for some years before the fall of King Idris in 1969, and throughout the 1970s, she had been intimately involved in factional strife within FROLINAT as part of her attempt to consolidate her hold over the Aouzou Strip (which she had annexed in 1973). Libya had provided Goukouni Oueddei (the Toubou leader of FROLINAT's principal military forces) with substantial numbers of advisers during his 1977 and 1978 thrust southward and eastward, and her troops moved in behind his advance, strengthening her position in northern Chad. The Libyan army intervened in factional warfare between Goukouni's forces and those of Acyl Ahmat (a Chadian Arab leader of FROLINAT's eastern faction) in northern Chad in 1978. In the same year, Libya sponsored a series of peace conferences at Sebha, Benghazi, and Tripoli in an attempt to secure her position in Chad and a role for her clients, Goukouni and Acyl, in the central government.

In 1979 her role was less prominent. The French-sponsored Malloum regime collapsed, the remnants of the Chadian army withdrew to the south under Lieutenant Colonel Kamougué (a Sara lieutenant of Malloum), and Oueddei's forces entered Ndjaména, establishing an interim administration in conjunction with units loyal to Hissène Habré (at one time a rival of Goukouni for control of FROLINAT and subsequently a minister in Malloum's government). Libya's peace-keeping role was eclipsed by the OAU and by Nigeria, which sponsored a series of conferences in Kano and Lagos in an attempt to achieve a broadly-based resolution of Chadian problems. These culminated in the Lagos Accords of August 1979, providing for the withdrawal of French forces and laying the basis for a transitional government of national unity (GUNT) which included all the major disputing parties, with Goukouni as President, Kamougué as Prime Minister, and Habré as Minister of Defence. The Accords also called for the dispatch of an OAU peace-keeping force, only one contingent of which – the Congolese – ever arrived.

Libya was not inactive during this period. She began delivery of arms to Kamougué's forces in April 1980 – in all likelihood to forestall the emergence of a central government powerful enough to challenge her presence in northern Chad. In June she attempted to take advantage of the preoccupation of all the Chadian factions with political affairs in the capital by expanding her area of direct control and mounted a major military operation out of the Aouzou Strip. This incursion was successfully resisted by units loyal to Goukouni, Libya's former *protégé*. The scope of Libyan activities was circumscribed by the continued presence of French forces in the capital and by Libya's unwillingness to be obviously responsible for the failure of the OAU initiative.

Events in 1980 evolved rapidly, however, in a direction which favoured large-scale Libyan intervention. France completed her withdrawal from Chad in the spring, but the OAU force never materialized. Meanwhile, the transitional government broke down in hostilities which began in January and lasted through the year. These pitted forces loyal to Goukouni (*Forces Armées Populaires* (FAP)), Acyl Ahmat, and Kamougué against Habré's *Forces Armées du Nord* (FAN). The first three enjoyed Libya's backing, and in June 1980 a representative of Goukouni signed a treaty of friendship with Libya, Article 1 of which committed both parties to mutual defence against aggression. It was this document which was later cited by Libya as a legal justification for her massive intervention in Chadian internal affairs in the autumn.

In short, French withdrawal relieved Libya of the need to worry about direct confrontation with French forces. The failure of an OAU replacement force to emerge meant that Gaddafi did not need to fear running foul of OAU peace-keeping efforts. In fact he could argue that he was fulfilling a task that the OAU had taken upon itself but had found itself incapable of completing. Moreover, those factions within the GUNT with whom Libya at the time retained reasonably close relations formed the core of the transitional government – Habré having left it, and Kamougué's *Forces Armées Tchadiennes* (FAT) participating only diffidently in the government's affairs and in the new outbreak of civil war which racked the capital in the late spring and summer of 1980. This allowed Libya to claim that her intervention was on behalf of a legally-constituted government and at its request, rather than being in support of rebel groups, as had previously been the case. These factors go some way towards explaining why late 1980 was an auspicious moment for Libyan intervention.

However, one crucial factor should not be ignored. Habré had been the most vehemently and consistently anti-Libyan personality in Chadian politics. As a leading member of FROLINAT in the mid-1970s, he had strongly resisted that organization's acceptance of Libya's annexation of the Aouzou Strip, and this was a major cause of his split with Goukouni in 1976. By the autumn of 1980 it was becoming apparent that Goukouni's coalition was losing ground to Habré both in Ndjaména and in the countryside, and it was apparent that for Gaddafi the situation had come to a head. Libya could intervene, or she could reconcile herself to the likelihood that Habré would become the dominant force in Chadian politics; the latter eventuality would constitute a collapse of her policy in Chad, as well as endangering, politically if not militarily, her position in the Aouzou Strip. It was in this context that Gaddafi chose to intervene.[47] The constraints on direct action had weakened, while the dangers of inaction had grown.

In 1983, the timing of Libyan intervention was influenced by a number of factors. In 1982, benefiting from Egyptian and probably American assistance, Habré succeeded in pushing Goukouni's forces out of Ndjamena and establishing his own government. Libya responded by re-establishing Goukouni in northern Chad, but Gaddafi's continuing quest for the chairmanship of the OAU restrained her from any highly visible attempt to reverse the course of events in Chad. However, this constraint largely disappeared in mid-1983, when Mengistu Haile Mariam was named OAU chairman, and it is probably not coincidental that Goukouni's challenge to Habré, and the Libyan involvement in Chad, escalated dramatically in a matter of weeks after the Addis Ababa OAU summit at the beginning of June. The constraint of possible French counter-intervention may also have been weakened in Gaddafi's eyes by the fact that the French Socialist Party – which, in the past, had been lukewarm, if not actively opposed, to French interventionism in Africa – held the presidency.

The cases compared

What do these cases tell us, then, about the nature of catalytic factors producing military intervention? First, it is often true that intervention occurs in response to an urgent request by a client whose survival is at stake. Second, in such cases, and in a number of others (such as Soviet intervention in Afghanistan) where no invitation was issued, the evolution of the internal political situation is such as to put seriously at risk the policy and interests of the external actor. This often, though by no means necessarily, results from involvement of another outsider on the other side of an internal dispute. In such situations, the decision-maker is faced with the choice of doing nothing and accepting a high probability of defeat, or attempting to reduce that probability by escalating his country's involvement. Defeat often carries with it repercussions beyond the borders of the target state, affecting the credibility of the external actor's commitments elsewhere. In these situations intervention is an attempt to salvage the situation or to put it on a new footing.

Alternatively, intervention may be a response to the emergence of new opportunities, such as the withdrawal of other external actors and the resultant weakening of the constraints on the power contemplating intervention (as with Libya in Chad), or the apparent collapse of the central authority in the target state (as in Ethiopia before the Somalian invasion).

It may well be that in specific situations both kinds of catalytic factor are present. The decline in the fortunes of a local client may coincide with, or follow upon, the weakening or withdrawal of constraints on intervention (as in the case of Libyan intervention in Chad).

In general, therefore, intervention comes as a reaction to specific historical events in the target state, though it occurs in the broader context of instability and conflict in the target state, basic interest (and consequent involvement) in the target state by the external actor, and the structure of constraints faced by the latter.

It remains to address the question of why military instruments are chosen rather than some other tool of policy. From the cases considered above, one can conclude that military intervention is chosen largely because, in the specific historical situation, it is perceived to be the *only* course of action which offers a reasonable prospect of success in achieving the external actor's short-term objectives. The situations discussed above on the whole demanded immediate and decisive action to deal with military threats. Diplomatic solutions are seldom immediate and seldom decisive, particularly in situations where the international community is split on the issue under consideration, and in a situation where the other side in such a conflict already has the advantage.

CONCLUSION

It was maintained in the introductory section of this Chapter that acts of intervention could not be adequately explained in a one-dimensional manner, but that they were the result of interaction between a number of dimensions bearing upon the decision-making of the intervening actor.

The political environment in the target state is an essential aspect of the explanation, in that it determines the permissive conditions in which intervention takes place. Deep-seated internal conflicts, often culminating in a state of internal war, create in internal actors needs which can only be satisfied by recourse to external sources of support. This creates openings which outsiders can exploit.

However, external actors must have reasons of their own for wishing to become involved. Hence, any account of intervention must examine the basic motives and structural characteristics of external actors. But any treatment of the motives for intervention must also be balanced by a consideration of the constraints under which the intervener must operate, an assessment of the objective capabilities at his disposal. The intervener must ask not only what he is likely to gain but also what he risks losing and, more basically, whether what he is contemplating can physically be done. It is only in considering these constraints that one can discover why intervention does not occur in some cases where the permissive conditions are present and where basic motivations for it are strong, whereas in others it does.

Even this, however, is insufficient as a characterization of the conditions of intervention. While these factors can explain why states involve themselves in the affairs of other states, they do not fully account for timing or the choice of military means. The choice of this instrument of policy at a specific point in time must be explained in terms of catalytic events: the sudden emergence of opportunities in the target environment or of threats to the position of an external actor's clients and, by extension, to the perceived interests of the external actor himself. These events and their implications alter the balance of costs and benefits upon which the external actor's policy-making is based.

To summarize, the conditions of intervention comprehend the basic characteristics of the target society and polity; the character, fundamental interests and purposes of external actors; the constraints under which the latter must operate; and the development of the political situation in the target environment in question. Intervention, as a historical phenomenon, like imperial expansion in the nineteenth century, is both active and reactive and is explicable in terms of causative factors in both metropolitan and peripheral environments, as well as in the structure of the international system as a whole.

II. Outcomes of intervention

The principle that intervention should be discouraged or prevented rests on two premises. The first is that, if no action is taken to discourage or prevent it, states will continue in specific circumstances to view intervention as necessary and as offering a reasonable prospect of success. The second is that the international system and its member states would be better off without intervention – that, rather than being a solution to problems of international security, intervention is itself one of those problems. These assertions are by no means self-evident. Accordingly, this Chapter examines the outcomes of intervention in Angola, Chad, Ethiopia and Afghanistan, in order to determine in the first place whether intervention is on balance a successful option of policy. Second, it considers whether, and in what respects, intervention constitutes a problem of regional security.

RECORD OF THE INTERVENERS

The question of whether an intervention has been successful or not is a difficult one. In the first place, it requires that the objectives of the action be defined, a task which, as noted in Chapter I, is rather speculative. Second, even where objectives can be defined with a reasonable degree of certainty, they are usually multiple – some short-term, some long-term, some primary, others secondary, some optimal, some 'second-best'. When some are met completely, others partially, and some not at all, it is not clear how the overall success of an operation is to be judged. As a basis for discussion, it is postulated here that an intervention is successful in the short term when its military and immediate political objectives are satisfied. Its success in the longer term must be judged in terms of the durability of the political solution which has resulted, the degree to which the internal forces against whom the intervention was aimed remain active, the nature of the political and strategic advantages accruing to the intervener, and the extent to which intervention has resulted in long-term and costly commitments of the intervener's military forces and other resources.

Short-term results

Looking initially at the short term, it could be argued that intervention was successful in four of the cases considered here: the USSR and Cuba in Angola, and again in Ethiopia; the USSR in Afghanistan; and Libya and France in Chad. In the case of Angola, perhaps the major Soviet and Cuban short-term objective was to assure the victory of the MPLA in the civil war. This was accomplished by introducing into the conflict a quantity of men and material which was sufficient to determine the outcome of the conflict. When the MPLA then formed a government which excluded representatives of the other movements, there was established at a stroke a regime in Angola which adopted a 'socialist orientation', over which both Cuba and the USSR enjoyed a substantial amount of influence in foreign policy, and which agreed to provide sanctuary for (and Soviet and Cuban access to) SWAPO guerrillas, allowing these external actors to increase their involvement in and influence over the southern African liberation struggle. Moreover, both countries gained a substantial amount of prestige in radical third-world circles and in Black Africa for their defence of the MPLA against South Africa. The returns to both the USSR and Cuba were, therefore, considerable.

In the case of Ethiopia, the two countries' short-term objective was to save the regime from defeat by Somalia and to give it the means to survive in the face of internal ethnic and political dissent. Again they succeeded, gaining thereby a substantial degree of influence in Ethiopian affairs and displacing the US. In a more concrete sense, the USSR also obtained a limited degree of access to Ethiopian port facilities at Assab and Massawa and in the Dahlak Islands, establishing Soviet forces on both sides of the Straits of Bab el Mandeb.

In Afghanistan, the Soviet Union sought most urgently to replace the unreliable and intransigent Amin with a more pliable and obedient personality, as well as to forestall the total collapse of the PDP regime in Kabul. These objectives were attained, and the USSR also managed to consolidate her military and political control over Afghanistan, while securing airfields which placed Soviet bombers in a far more favourable position to interdict the Straits of Hormuz.

Finally, in the case of Chad, all three of France's interventions sought to prevent the total collapse of her client regime. This they did, halting the southward advance of elements of FROLINAT towards the capital in 1968 and 1978 and Goukouni's Libyan-backed offensive in 1983. Likewise, Libya's 1980 intervention succeeded in eliminating the immediate military threat to

Goukouni's rump government by destroying Habré's units in Ndjaména, and that in early and mid-1983 prevented a complete victory for Habré and made Goukouni once again a force to be reckoned with in any eventual resolution of the conflict in Chad.

Long-term results

Angola

However, looking beyond immediate objectives and towards the longer term, the results are less clear. Cuban and Soviet military assistance has never completely solved Angola's internal security problem. Government control is still effectively contested in the South and centre of the country (Moxico, Cuanda Cubango, Cunene and Bié provinces) by UNITA, which, with South African support, continues to mount an effective insurgent challenge. Reports also indicate that FNLA insurgency in the northern provinces along Zaire's frontier is causing increasing problems for the Luanda regime.[1] South African forces attack SWAPO and Angolan military installations in Southern Angola with impunity, as well as terrorizing the civilian population of the area. It must be said, therefore, that the MPLA's hold on Angola remains shaky.

The solution to the problem of insurgency presumably lies in some sort of political accommodation and power sharing between UNITA and the MPLA. This has, however, been consistently rejected by the MPLA, whose survival must instead be guaranteed by the continuing presence of some 15–20,000 Cuban military personnel. But this presence, and the extensive Soviet military assistance programme, are financed largely out of Angolan oil revenues, which is holding back the country's economic development.

There is also the problem of factionalism and disunity within the MPLA itself, the extent of which was shown by the attempted coup in 1977. That episode also graphically displayed what seems to be the most important function of the Cuban forces in Angola: to forestall internal challenges to the MPLA leadership. (Despite loud assertions that they are there to protect Angola from South Africa, these forces have avoided contact with South African intruders in the southern part of the country.)

While it is true that intervention has bought Cuba and the USSR a fair degree of influence with the Angolan regime, their control is by no means absolute or assured. A number of important personalities in the MPLA have resisted the accretion of Soviet influence, among them the late President Agostinho Neto and his successor, Eduardo dos Santos. The dominance of pro-Soviet elements (such as Iko Carreira, the ex-Minister of Defence, and, with some qualification, Lucio Lara, the MPLA Secretary General) within the party and government is continually under challenge, not only from the 'nationalists' mentioned above but also from a group which might be styled 'pragmatist' (which would include Lopo do Nascimento, the Planning Minister). This group, whose concern is above all to accelerate the development of

Angola's economy, is well aware both of the limitations on Soviet ability to help with this and of the benefits of economic co-operation with the West.

On specific issues the Luanda government has shown itself quite capable of taking independent positions on issues where Soviet preference conflicts with its perception of Angola's national interest. For example, it has refused to grant base rights to the USSR and, despite Soviet opposition, has co-operated closely with the Western powers on the latter's initiative for a settlement of the Namibian question.[2] Furthermore, it has sought and developed close ties with a number of American multinational companies which provide Angola with the bulk of her foreign exchange. It is not unreasonable to suggest, in fact, that the main stumbling block to improved relations between the US and Angola, and to a greater Western role in that country which might balance that of the Eastern Bloc, is the refusal of successive American Administrations to come to grips with the fact of the MPLA victory.[3] To argue, as many analysts have done, that Angola is to all intents and purposes a Soviet satellite is a ridiculous oversimplification, as well as an abdication of initiative in policy-making. There appears to be some recognition of this in recent American diplomacy in the region, and Assistant Secretary of State Crocker has been actively soliciting Angolan co-operation in an American-sponsored regional settlement. In this context, the United States appears finally to be moving towards formal recognition of the Luanda regime.

In any attempt to determine whether intervention in Angola was worthwhile from the Soviet perspective, the obvious short-term Soviet and Cuban success must be balanced against the continuing security problem (and consequent need for a substantial Cuban presence and Soviet assistance programme), the ambiguities in MPLA and popular Angolan attitudes towards their external benefactors, and the clear limits on Soviet influence over the Angolan regime. Any such evaluation must also take into account the wider perspective of Soviet foreign policy, and in particular the effects of the Soviet-Cuban adventure in Angola on the process of detente between the USSR and the US. In sum, it is by no means clear that in the longer term the Angolan operation should be viewed as a success for either the USSR or Cuba.

Ethiopia

Similar problems must be faced in assessing the Soviet and Cuban involvement in Ethiopia. The intervention, while it removed a number of immediate threats to the *Dergue*, by no means solved the Ogaden problem. Border skirmishes between Somalia and Ethiopia have continued, and each country provides sanctuary and logistic support to dissident elements from the other. The conflict in Eritrea also continues, Ethiopian forces showing themselves to be incapable of eliminating the insurgency in the highland areas of the province. This in turn has meant a substantial long-term commitment of Cuban troops in Ethiopia, mainly in the Ogaden,[4] as well as an extensive programme of Soviet military assistance. These are more expensive to the external actors than in the case of Angola, because Ethiopia has little if any foreign exchange to defray the costs, and it is probable that the USSR is carrying the bulk of the financial burden. Again, the solution to the internal and border security problems which necessitate this level of foreign military involvement presumably lies in a compromise involving regional autonomy for both Eritrea and the Ogaden, and some kind of cosmetic border adjustment with Somalia. However, as neither the Ethiopian government nor the Eritreans nor the Somalian government appears in any way inclined to negotiate seriously, there is no end to the conflicts in sight, and the drain on Soviet and Cuban resources is likely to persist.

As in Angola, while Soviet and Eastern bloc influence with the Ethiopian regime is substantial, it is nonetheless limited. Where the Ethiopian regime perceives its interests to depart from the recommendations or desires of its benefactors, it has shown itself to be perfectly willing to go its own way. For example, the leading faction in the *Dergue* has persistently resisted any arrangement which might dilute government authority in outlying regions, rejecting the idea that some measure of autonomy be granted to Eritrea, and rejecting also Castro's March 1977 proposal that the disputes of the Horn should be resolved by establishing a federation among the states of the region in which all ethnic groups would receive regional autonomy. Ethiopia also displayed her independence by taking advantage of the perceived instability of the Barre regime and mounting military incursions into Somalia in the summer and autumn of 1982. It is hard to believe that this conduct met with Soviet approval, as such actions could be construed as infringements of Somalia's sovereignty, with attendant effects on OAU opinion. Moreover, the incursions could (and did) stimulate a more assertive American role in the region. American visitors to Addis Ababa have recently reported considerable Ethiopian interest in improving relations with the US, while the Cuban troop presence has been reduced substantially. It has also been reported that Ethiopia has expelled some Soviet diplomatic personnel, though the circumstances underlying this action remain obscure.

Finally, the regime has been very slow in taking up Soviet and Cuban recommendations concerning the creation of a vanguard party which would eventually replace military rule.[5] The leaders, having spilt so much blood in consolidating their power, are apparently loath to contemplate its dilution.

Looking beyond the Ethiopian context to regional and world politics, the Soviet gain in Ethiopia was to some extent offset by the loss in Somalia. It has been argued above that, in terms of population and resources, Ethiopia is of greater regional importance than Somalia. Nonetheless, tilting towards Ethiopia cost the USSR the extensive naval and air facilities at Berbera, and the port rights in Eritrea and the privileges in the Dahlak Islands granted by Ethiopia are by no means equivalent in quality and extent. As David and Marina Ottaway have pointed out, nowhere else in Africa have friends or allies of the USSR granted her military facilities comparable to those in Somalia.[6] At the international level, Soviet and Cuban involvement in Ethiopia caused a further deterioration in Soviet-American relations and, specifically, the suspension of Indian Ocean force limitation talks. Brzezinski's remark that detente lies buried in the sands of the Ogaden is surely hyperbole, but it does indicate the impact on leading American policy-makers of Soviet involvement in that conflict.

Soviet and Cuban successes in the short term were thus once again balanced by the strategic losses associated with the break in relations between the USSR and Somalia, by failure to resolve the fundamental problems which caused the intervention (and which have necessitated what appeared until recently to be a permanent Soviet/Cuban presence and substantial outlays of military aid to Ethiopia), by the clear limits on the Soviet capacity to control events in the Horn, and by the effects of the involvement on Soviet-American relations.

Afghanistan

In Afghanistan, the short-term benefits must be weighed against the severe military and political problems which the USSR continues to face there. On the positive side, Soviet control of the Afghan regime is far more complete than in the previous two cases. The regime is still totally dependent on Soviet assistance and protection for its existence and operation. It seems to have no capacity for taking independent initiatives in policy-making, and is, in short, the creature of the USSR. One less attractive aspect of this dependency and incapacity is that the regime is unviable. Babrak Karmal's efforts to broaden his base of support have failed, and, as a result, a large and permanent Soviet presence is needed, not only to keep the administrative machinery running but also to hold at bay the undiminished rebel threat to the Kabul government. Despite the deployment of some 105,000 Soviet troops in Afghanistan, there has been little progress in reducing the area under rebel control, while Soviet casualties have been substantial (according to various estimates, between 11,000 and 15,000), as has the overall cost of the operation.

But the military costs are perhaps less important than the political ones. The Soviet intervention in Afghanistan alienated many third-world states in a way that the Angolan and Ethiopian interventions had not. The USSR was now seen not as a defender of a third-world state's territorial integrity or a staunch friend of the national liberation movement in its struggle against imperialism and apartheid, but as an imperialist power in its own right, using force in the attempt to swallow up a small, internally divided and largely defenceless neighbour. It also caused further problems in Soviet-American and Soviet-West European relations, causing nations such as France and West Germany to take a long and hard look at their relations with the USSR and giving political impetus to the conventional and nuclear rearmament of Europe. This intervention made the image of an expansionist and militarily threatening USSR more credible not only in the eyes of politicians of the Western Alliance but, perhaps more importantly, in the eyes of the publics before whom they had to justify defence spending.

478 *Neil Macfarlane*

At the strategic level, Soviet intervention in Afghanistan accelerated efforts by the US to expand her own capabilities to project force (through the Rapid Deployment Force), provoked President Carter to enunciate a clear commitment to the security of moderate states and oil supplies in the Persian Gulf (the Carter Doctrine), and ensured that American force levels in the Indian Ocean and Persian Gulf would remain high.

Chad

Of Chad, it is sufficient to note that, with both French and Libyan interventions, short-term success (in 1978 for France and in 1980 for Libya) was followed by withdrawal and the eventual victory of the forces against whom the interventions had been directed. The French failure called into question the credibility of French guarantees to other allies in Africa, and France's prolonged and costly involvement in Chad's affairs did much to render French interventionism unpopular in Africa as a whole. Libya lost substantial numbers of men[7] and equipment, suffered a considerable blow to her prestige and provoked suspicion and animosity in sub-Saharan West Africa. Moreover, Libyan involvement in Chad was one factor among several leading to increased American military assistance to Sudan. The present round of intervention and counter-intervention appears to have resulted in a stalemate with little immediate prospect of settlement.

An overview

It is difficult to find, in the cases covered in this Paper, an unambiguously successful intervention. Even in the minority of cases where interveners came close to meeting their immediate objectives, they found themselves bogged down in long-term involvements and paying substantial political costs in other areas of their foreign policies. One might well ask why, if this is the case, intervention recurs with such depressing regularity. But the perspective of the student of history or politics is not identical to that of a decision-maker. The latter is faced with important constraints on the amount of information available to him and the time which he has to seek it out. He is usually facing a situation of crisis in which it is unlikely that historical analysis will appear to him a productive use of the few hours he has available.

Furthermore, even if the 'lessons of history' are taken into account, pressures of the moment might appear sufficiently compelling to override them. For instance, it is plausible that, even had Soviet policy-makers been able to predict accurately the degree of internal resistance and intensity of international reaction to their intervention in Afghanistan, they would still have chosen to invade. That said, it is equally possible that in situations where the reasons for intervention are less compelling, past experience of high cost, low return and high risk of failure might swing the balance in favour of restraint in future.

It should be stressed here that this analysis applies principally to intervention in situations characterized by chronic violent instability or, more strongly, internal war. Its conclusions about success and failure do not, therefore, apply to what might be called 'surgical intervention' – the insertion of small numbers of troops in support of a government faced by a limited and temporary threat. Particularly where the opposition is poorly armed and lacks political organization, roots in the population and sources of external support, where the majority of the population supports or is apathetic towards the government, and where the political elite is not alienated from it, such intrusions have a much higher probability of success. In numerous interventions of this type short-term objectives have been achieved with very limited applications of force and without long-term costs or entanglements. Examples are British involvement in Kenya and Tanganyika in the early 1960s, Brunei in the mid-1960s and Oman in the 1960s, and the repeated French interventions in Africa in the 1960s and 1970s, culminating in the joint operations in Shaba in 1977 and 1978.

Criteria for success

The failure or ambiguous results of intervention in the cases considered here, and its success in others, leads naturally to the question of what criteria contribute to success. Is it possible to develop a recipe for successful intervention?

Success or failure depends, first of all, on a number of characteristics of the target environment. The extent of social cohesion is significant, as is the degree of popular support enjoyed by a government. In a cohesive society with a popular government, intervention on behalf of the latter carries a higher probability of success, all other things being equal, than intervention on behalf of opposition groups (one could cite in this context the British intervention in Tanganyika). By contrast, chronic instability and prolonged internal conflict resulting from, and in turn exacerbating, a lack of social cohesion reduce the probability of success in the long term, since it is difficult in such circumstances for external actors to impose a lasting solution to the problems which occasion intervention. This is evident in all four cases.

Also important is the organizational and military competence of the local client, as the experiences of the various interveners in the Angolan War indicate. Despite the MPLA's history of factional disputes, its political and military infrastructure was then clearly superior to that of its rivals, and the ideological commitment of its cadres to the cause clearly greater. This facilitated its victory.

Second, the probability of success depends to a degree on the objectives and nature of the intervener. With respect to objectives, the broader they are, the less likely they are to be achieved. The South African intervention in Angola suggests that it is easier to harass and destabilize a regime through limited military intrusions and sponsorship of opposition guerrilla groups than to impose a government of one's choice. More broadly, Max Beloff was probably right when, in comparing Soviet and Western interventions, he asserted that it is easier to use intervention to destroy a regime and impose a totalitarian replacement than to foster a 'self-sustaining democratic form of government' by the same means.[8] The Soviet experience in Angola, Ethiopia and Afghanistan would indicate, further, that establishing or sustaining a totalitarian regime through intervention is easier than establishing a 'self-sustaining' Marxist-Leninist social and political order.

With respect to the nature of the intervener, success is affected by the capacity and willingness of the intervening state to project into the target state a level of force sufficient to determine the outcome of the conflict in its favour, and to sustain its commitment until victory is achieved. In the early 1960s the USSR had the will to undertake military intervention in Africa (as in the Congo crisis) but lacked the capacity to achieve her objectives. By the mid-1970s, her capacity to project force had expanded to the point that, where she was not faced with a forceful American response, she could mount substantial military operations throughout the Third World with a reasonable prospect of success. Moreover, the relative insulation of the Soviet decision-making process from popular opposition makes it possible in domestic political terms for the USSR to sustain these operations indefinitely and at substantial cost.

The United States, by contrast, has possessed the capacity for massive intervention throughout the Third World since World War II. However, after the Korean War, and again after the Vietnam War, her willingness to do so was severely constrained by popular opposition to military involvement in local wars, and also by serious doubts within the military itself about the wisdom of such commitments. Such opposition had an important role in limiting the American response to Soviet escalation in Angola. Public opinion has not only affected the willingness of the United States to become involved but also her ability to stay the course when the costs are high. The case of Vietnam is again illustrative.

Finally, the probability of success is conditioned by the international context in which intervention occurs and, more specifically, by the degree of involvement in the target state of other actors or the degree to which competitive involvement is likely to ensue. An external actor's involvement is far more likely to succeed if its client's adversaries are not closely linked to foreign powers and also if its intervention does not provoke others to intervene. The latter condition depends in turn on the extent to which the interests of other external actors are at stake, on the degree to which their forces are already committed elsewhere, and on the domestic constraints they face in contemplating counter-intervention.

It is possible from the above to sketch out a recipe for successful intervention. Intervention is most likely to succeed:

– if the target society is well integrated, and is not suffering from serious internal conflict;

- if the client enjoys wide popular support and is well organized and comparatively proficient in military matters, while his adversary is isolated from the people, has no external backers, and is poorly organized;
- if the intervening actor is militarily powerful and proficient, his will is strong, he is not susceptible to popular pressure if and when the going gets rough, and his objectives are limited;
- and if intervention is unlikely to induce other powers to intervene in turn.

It is also possible to sketch a scenario in which the objectives of an intervener have a very low probability of being successfully attained. Failure is probable:

- in unintegrated societies where there are deep and lasting animosities between different communities and where the different groups contending for power have long-standing ties to, and commitments from, external actors;
- where the external actor's client is actively opposed by large sections of the population and is poorly organized and militarily incompetent;
- where the military resources of the external actor are limited, his resolve weak, domestic opposition to the intervention significant and the influence of public opinion upon the policy-making process high;
- and, finally, where intervention is likely to provoke counter-intervention by other external actors.

In the case of the comparatively successful British and French interventions mentioned above, the groups against which intervention was directed generally lacked political organization, widespread support among the population and the capacity to organize and sustain military operations. They had little access to external support of any significance. The population either remained aloof from the conflict or supported the group on whose behalf the intervention was taking place. Furthermore, internal conflict was at a low level and was generally concentrated in a specific geographical area, either in the capital or in a single region of the country. In such conditions the intervening state was able with a fairly small deployment of well-trained and well-armed troops to impose a solution in favour of its local client, which was generally the government of the country concerned.

The cases covered in this Paper are much less promising, involving wide-ranging internal armed conflicts in which substantial elements of the population are either engaged or perceive their interests to be at stake, where more than one faction has links to external sources of support and is capable of mounting reasonably effective and sustained military operations, and where more than one external power is involved.

These criteria are of course a matter of common sense, but it is evident that, in contemplating intervention, external actors frequently do not approach these issues in a systematic way, or else lack enough information to be able to make such an evaluation. In this context, it is perhaps not surprising that it is the ex-colonial powers – Britain and France – which have been more clearly successful. They were better placed to evaluate the prospects for success and the risks involved in operations of this type in their ex-colonies, at least in the period immediately following decolonization.

From the cases considered here and from the more general discussion of the criteria affecting the prospects for success of an intervention, it is clear that the prerequisites for success in an intrusion into an internal conflict of substantial scale are rather narrow, and the possiblities for failure or long-term high-cost involvement quite broad. As such, intervention in such situations does not seem to be a particularly promising option of policy.

CONSEQUENCES OF INTERVENTION

Many people, including those responsible for the US Rapid Deployment Force, as well as those in previous French administrations who favoured the use of French military forces in Africa, have clearly seen intervention as a means of solving problems, not as a problem in itself (except where it is a tactic used by an adversary to impinge upon their own country's interests). Hence, in the US it is Soviet, Cuban or Libyan intervention which is the problem; in the USSR it is American and French intervention which threatens peace and security. To Africans, the principal problem is extra-African intervention in the continent's affairs and not intervention by African states in the affairs of their neighbours.

There is no doubt some merit in the view that, objectively speaking, the use of force to interfere in other states' internal affairs has on occasion brought significant gains both to the target state and region, to the intervener and to the international system as a whole.[9] This must be borne in mind in any attempt to assess if and in what ways intervention constitutes a problem of international security.

However, to draw an analogy from American domestic politics, although possessing and using a gun may in specific circumstances protect one from harm as well as contributing to the social good, that does not mean that widespread personal ownership of lethal weapons is constructive or contributes to social order. The fact that in certain instances individual states may use intervention successfully to prevent developments which they consider pernicious, or even that intervention may in specific circumstances contribute to international peace and security (goals to which the bulk of the international community might subscribe), has little bearing on whether intervention is, in a general sense, a problem of international security.

There are, in fact, good reasons for seeing intervention as a problem at the broadest level of the structure of the international system, at the level of the target region, and at that of the state in which it occurs. In the first place, intervention erodes the basic organizational structure of the society of states. As noted above, this society is based on the general recognition of the principle of equal sovereignty: states recognize that other states possess both internal sovereignty (a monopoly of authority over affairs within its borders) and external sovereignty (non-subordination to a higher authority). The purpose of this norm is to minimize international conflict by separating domestic and international issues. It is reasonable to assume that conflict would be far more frequent if states did not *as a rule* follow the principle that the preservation or pursuit of their own interests through armed interference in the internal affairs of other states was an unacceptable form of behaviour. Intervention which occurs without the sanction of the legally-constituted government of the target state not only violates this norm but also undermines it in a wider sense. In the absence of a supra-national coercive authority, states' compliance with the norm of non-interference is predicated on the belief that most other states share an interest in the norm and are therefore willing to accept the obligation of non-intervention which it entails. The greater the incidence of intervention, the more this belief is drawn into question.

The superpower level

It was noted above that the contest between the two superpowers over Angola, and the essentially unopposed but much resented Soviet involvement in Ethiopia and Afghanistan, did much to exacerbate relations between them and slow, if not reverse, the process of detente. Assuming that good relations between the superpowers are conducive to international security, while bad relations between them increase the danger of general war, attempts by either to steal a march on the other through intervention in third-world disputes are best avoided. In a more concrete sense, as intervention by one or the other superpower risks counter-intervention by the other (or by its proxies), such events must carry with them the possibility, however small, of confrontation and escalation. Moreover, in this connection, a number of American analysts have mooted the idea of 'horizontal escalation': if the USSR intervened in a part of the Third World where she enjoyed a military edge, the response of the US should be to intervene in another part of the world in which she possessed a similar advantage. One should perhaps not take this kind of thinking too seriously, given the domestic constraints on all intervention in the US – although the American political system is less successful than many at weeding out the kinds of people to whom such a simplistic and irresponsible approach to international relations might appeal. In any case, this idea illustrates the possibility that intervention can lead to a widening of conflict by provoking counter-intervention in other states and regions.

The regional level

Defence expenditure

Intervention has led to significant increases in the defence spending of regional actors as part of a sustained effort to develop the capacity to meet what are perceived to be new external threats. It is significant that South Africa's defence budget doubled and then doubled again in the aftermath of the Angolan affair.[10] This was due in part to the collapse of the Portuguese buffer in Angola and Mozambique and the gradual erosion of the position of the white regime in Rhodesia, but it is reasonable to assume that it was also a response to the deployment in southern Africa of well-armed and well-trained units from Cuba.

Likewise, Nigeria responded to Libyan intervention in Chad by allocating $6.4 billion to defence expenditure in her fourth five-year development plan, and by increasing her defence budget by 33% from $1.7 billion in 1980–81 to $2.06 billion in 1981–2.[11] The Sudanese government responded in a similar fashion, though its procurement was largely financed by the US. Kenya's response to the Somalian-Ethiopian imbroglio was also to place greater emphasis on defence and to seek external sources of support. Her defence expenditure rose from $113 million in 1977 to $255 million in 1979 (from 2.4% to 4.8% of GNP).[12]

Outside Africa, the present modernization of Pakistan's defences, again largely financed by the US, is mainly in response to the Soviet intervention in Afghanistan. While defence spending in 1978 was $1.05 billion and in 1979 $1.18 billion, an increase roughly matching inflation, in 1980 it jumped to $1.54 billion and in 1981 to $1.89 billion. In both cases these increases were substantially in excess of the national inflation rate.[13] Ishaq Khan, Pakistan's Defence Minister, attributed the 1979–80 rise directly to the Afghan crisis.

In other words, at the regional level intervention seems to provoke a diversion of resources into military spending, and this in countries which can on the whole ill afford it. In addition, it induces regional actors to search for external support in the form of security guarantees and military assistance. This further complicates matters by engaging the interests of other external actors in the region.

One could argue, then, that intervention detracts from security at the regional level by creating precedents for the use of force in resolving disputes, enhancing the perceptions of threat among other regional actors, favouring increased outlays on arms and (if the increased availability of the means to use force heightens the probability that force will be used) increasing the likelihood of conflict in the region in question. In short, it is potentially, if not actually, destabilizing.

Refugees

In addition to the military dimension, conflicts in which intervention plays a role place significant burdens on other states in the region by producing large numbers of refugees. Zaire estimated in 1977–8 that she was sheltering approximately 470,000 Angolans, to which fresh upheavals in early 1978 added some 60,000. The Angolan War also resulted in the exodus to Portugal, South Africa and Rhodesia of several hundred thousand whites. As late as

1981 the UN High Commission for Refugees (UNHCR) estimated that 215,000 Angolan refugees remained in Zaire and 28,000 in Zambia.

In the case of Ethiopia, the years since 1977 have witnessed what the UNHCR has termed a 'massive exodus' associated with the Ogaden War and the continuing insurgencies in Eritrea and Tigré. The neighbouring countries of Djibouti, Somalia and Sudan estimate the numbers of Ethiopian refugees which they are harbouring respectively at 45,000, 1.5 million, and well over 400,000.

Turning to Afghanistan, the Pakistan government had registered 2,375,325 Afghan refugees by December 1981. These arrived for the most part after the Soviet intervention (the level of registration in December 1979 being only 400,000). To them should be added a substantial but indeterminate number of Afghan refugees in Iran. The numbers of refugees in both countries have since risen.

Finally, in the case of Chad, at the peak of fighting involving the Libyans some 250,000 Chadians had sought refuge abroad.[14]

Much of the cost of supporting refugees is met by international agencies, but contributions by host states are in many cases substantial, and again constitute an unproductive drain on scarce resources.[15] Moreover, the presence of refugees, particularly when they continue political activities, or when they ally themselves with their ethnic counterparts resident in the country, can create substantial political and security problems for the country sheltering them. Violence in refugee camps in Cameroon, problems in Sudanese-Ethiopian relations, Libyan attacks on Sudanese border villages in 1981, and Soviet/Afghan hot pursuit into Pakistan's Northwest Frontier Province and support of Kabul-based Pakistani opposition groups all illustrate the difficulties which large and politically active refugee groups can create for host governments.

It might be argued that these conflicts would have generated substantial numbers of refugees in any case, and that it is therefore wrong to attribute the refugee problem to intervention. There is some truth to this view; for instance, the presence of substantial numbers of Angolan refugees in Zaire dates back to 1961 at least. However, it stands to reason that intervention, by enhancing the military capabilities of its internal beneficiary, increases the scale of the problem by making life that much more difficult for civilians associated with opposition groups. This is clearly the case with Somali refugees from the Ogaden, Eritreans in Sudan, and Afghans in Pakistan.

The fact that intervention greatly enhances the military capabilities of those involved in internal conflicts and the military intensity of hostilities is also significant in judging the effects of such intrusions on the target state.

Casualties and internal displacement

Casualty figures are difficult to obtain in such conflicts and are generally unreliable. Furthermore, without knowing what would have happened if intervention had not occurred, it is impossible to be certain about how, over the course of a conflict, intervention affected numbers of dead and wounded. In particular, it is quite possible to argue that intervention may reduce casualties in cases where it decisively tips the scale in favour of one internal party, thereby ending a conflict which might otherwise have been indefinitely protracted. Nonetheless, in situations where intervention greatly increases the fire-power available to internal parties without providing a solution to the conflict, it is reasonable to suggest that the involvement of external actors, by increasing the intensity of the conflict, considerably increases the numbers of casualties among both combatants and non-combatants. In Afghanistan, for instance, it is unquestionable that Soviet intervention has resulted in a far higher rate of casualties among the Afghan population than there had been before the invasion.

Intervention for similar reasons impinges upon the domestic counterpart of the regional refugee problem, internal displacement of the population. The Angolan government, for example, has claimed that South African military incursions into southern Angola have resulted in the internal displacement of over 130,000 people. In Ethiopia, the Military Governor of Harar Province estimated that approximately 1,000,000 inhabitants of the province were displaced by the Ogaden War.[16]

Economic costs

The problem of displaced persons is closely related to the economic effects of intervention. Though reliable statistics are hard to come by, it is probable that in all the four cases examined in this Paper there was severe dislocation of economic activity in regions affected by internal conflict. Table 1 below, for example, shows trends in output of key commodities in Angola before, during and after intervention.

It would be highly questionable to attribute the severe reductions in economic activity solely to foreign intervention, for in all the cases considered here disruptive internal armed conflict predated intrusion from outside. In some (Chad, for instance) it is reasonably clear that this earlier conflict has more to do with the economic decline than intervention. In the case of Angola, it is probable that economic collapse was the result of the departure

Table 1 Output of key commodities in Angola, 1973–9

	1973	1974	1975	1976	1977	1978	1979
Coffee (000 tonnes)	210	224	180	67	67	50	60
Oil (000 tonnes)	n.a.	n.a.	7,791	7,564	7,062	7,277	n.a.
Diamonds (000 carats)	1,594	1,470	743	255	265	300	n.a.
Maize (000 tonnes)	430	400	450	450	350	400	300
Iron (000 tonnes)	3,752	3,328	1,664	n.a.	n.a.	n.a.	n.a.

Source: *UN Statistical Yearbook (1979–80)* (N.Y.: UN, 1982), pp. 109, 134, 201, 208, 230.

of the bulk of the Portuguese population and their removal or destruction of property essential to the operation of the economy. On the other hand, though, it is probable that the magnitude of this exodus was in part due to the intensity of the conflict, and to dislike of the prospect of a Marxist solution carried in on Cuban bayonets.

In some instances, however, one is tempted to go beyond the argument that intervention was not the principal cause of economic decline and to assert that it actually prevented or retarded the collapse of production. The fact that Angolan oil production was maintained throughout much of the conflict is largely due to the protection afforded by Cuban troops to the oil facilities operated by the Gulf Oil Company in Cabinda.

Despite these qualifications, it is again reasonable to suggest that, insofar as intervention widens a conflict and introduces weapons of greater destructive effect, it results in losses of production and damage to a country's economic base which are greater than would otherwise have been the case. In Angola, for example, the fighting in the south and centre of the country resulted in the destruction of most of the bridges in the region, severely hampering the revival of commerce; continued South African incursions in southern Angola have prevented the reopening of the iron-ore extraction projects at Kassinga; and South African logistical support for UNITA has greatly aided the latter's repeated closure of the Benguela railway, which has denied the Angolan Government significant transit revenues. In the case of Afghanistan, it is reasonably clear that deliberate Soviet bombing of crops in insurgent areas has severely disrupted agriculture in much of the country.[17] Soviet depredations in the countryside have also affected production by causing a significant portion of the rural population to flee to neighbouring countries or into the cities. Sabotage of transport links and industrial projects by groups opposed to the Soviet presence also hobbles the economy.

The point that as a rule intervention is damaging to the economy of the target state is merely a variant of the general point that war is itself economically disruptive in the areas in which the battles are fought. While conflict usually predates intervention, the latter usually increases the damage.

Intervention and political stability

The last issue to be dealt with here is that of the relationship between intervention and political stability in the target state. Once again, the subject defies easy generalization. In the first place, stability is itself difficult to define. When we speak of stability, we are usually referring in the narrowest sense to the freedom of a government or a constitutional system from violent domestic challenge or the danger of overthrow. This may be dependent in a superficial sense, and in the short term, on a government's capacity to muster a sufficient amount of force to deter or suppress challenges to its rule. In a deeper sense, however, stability rests upon the capacity of a government to acquire legitimacy, broaden its popular appeal, meet the needs of its people (or at least to make some semblance of trying to do so) and achieve political solutions to internal conflicts before they come to threaten the survival of the state or the incumbent regime. There is no real basis for claiming that stability is in itself to be valued, and this is not being claimed here. In conditions where a stable regime is conspicuously oppressive, incompetent and irresponsible, its stability, far from being desirable, is unfortunate. However, it is the case that stable political conditions are on the whole conducive to economic growth and social welfare. They provide an environment in which people may live and go about their business with a minimum of fear. Political instability, by contrast, often carries with it personal insecurity and disruption of economic life.

It should also be noted that there is no contradiction between the concept of stability and that of change. Indeed, consideration of the factors contributing to stability which were listed above leads to the conclusion that political stability assumes a capacity to adapt to change, rather than to stifle it.[18] Regimes which fail to meet (or consciously set their faces against) new demands which emerge from their internal political environments court instability by allowing frustration in the population to build into challenges to their rule.

Several conclusions about the relationship between intervention and the political stability of the target state follow from this. Intervention can be destabilizing or stabilizing in intent. States can interfere in the internal affairs of other states to prop up the ruling order, or to help to pull it down. For that matter, the intent of an intervention may have little to do with the question of stability. The French interventions in Chad in 1968, 1975 and 1983, and the Soviet interventions in Ethiopia and Afghanistan, were clearly intended to stabilize incumbent regimes or political systems in the face of internal and external threats. Libyan interventions in Chad before 1980 and in 1983 and South African intervention in Angola since 1976 set out to destabilize the recognized governments of those countries. And Soviet, Cuban, Zairean, American and South African interventions in Angola before 1976 occurred when there was no clearly established government to stabilize or destabilize. The intent of Somalian intervention in Ethiopia was related to stability only tangentially, its primary objective being not to affect the established government but to detach a portion of Ethiopian territory.

But intent is perhaps less important than consequences in considering the relationship between intervention and stability. The flat assertion that intervention is destabilizing at the national level, though perhaps appealing to those of liberal persuasion, is not tenable. It is quite conceivable, in the abstract, that where a basically competent, legitimate and popular government is faced with, for instance, a military mutiny or an externally-inspired insurgency, intervention may maintain or enhance its political stability by giving it protection without which it would in all likelihood not survive. Historical examples are not difficult to find – among them British intervention in Tanganyika and Oman, and French intervention in Gabon.

However, in situations where the roots of the internal conflict which induces intervention are deeper, and its scope wider, it would appear that intervention is less likely to lead to political stability. It is clear from the cases cited that intervention can operate in the short term to shore up a client regime, physically preventing its demise. In this limited sense, it is possible to speak, for instance, of Soviet/Cuban intervention in Angola enhancing political stability by helping the MPLA to emerge as Angola's government and forestalling or deterring sustained challenges to its rule. Likewise, Cuban and Soviet assistance to Ethiopia and Afghanistan probably prevented the collapse of the incumbent regimes. French and Libyan pro-government interventions in Chad had similar short-term results for the regimes of Tombalbaye, Malloum, Goukouni and Habré. In many of these cases, intervention also restored a modicum of order to previously chaotic internal conditions.

Yet in all these cases, intervention was insufficient to guarantee stability beyond the short term without a sustained commitment of external forces, because it failed to address the political problems which called forth intervention in the first place. Military victory is not enough when the conditions fostering further challenges to the regime remain. More specifically, the regime needs to make itself politically acceptable to those elements of the population in conflict with it – through broadening the government (as in the case of Angola); through constitutional or legislative change to meet the aspirations of disaffected groups (as in Ethiopia and Afghanistan); through the elimination or reduction of obvious discrimination and oppression; and through the redistribution of scarce resources to the benefit of particularly disadvantaged minorities (as in Chad). Unless it does so, the internal conflicts which are the sources of instability will persist, and military intervention will remain at best a temporary and imperfect solution (and one fraught with dangers of entanglement and escalation or of humiliating withdrawal). As Waltz has put it: 'Abiding solutions to most of a country's political problems have to be found by its citizens; foreigners can seldom be of much help.'[19]

Besides failing to address the political roots of instability, military intervention to prop up a government may, despite its military success, render the situation even less stable. In the first place, it may convince the client government, or strengthen its existing conviction, that political negotiation to solve internal problems is unnecessary and that a military solution is feasible. As a result, the government becomes more inflexible in the face of demands made upon it by alienated groups. For example, one effect of Soviet-Cuban assistance to the MPLA has been to strengthen its determination not to share political power with groups such as UNITA. In Ethiopia – despite Soviet and Cuban advice to the *Dergue* to compromise with the Eritreans – military intervention has made it possible for the regime to survive without compromise and to pursue indefinitely its military campaign against insurgents in Eritrea and elsewhere. In this sense, intervention may have rendered a political solution to this chronically destabilizing internal conflict even less likely than it would otherwise have been. In Chad, likewise, French intervention on behalf of Tombalbaye in 1968–9 made it possible for him, despite French pressure to meet the basic demands of disaffected Arab and Toubou minorities, to continue his oppression and exploitation of the northern and central tribes. Again, this rendered impossible a political compromise which might have softened some of the basic political and socio-ethnic contradictions which were tearing the country apart. Equally, Libyan, and subsequently OAU, intervention on behalf of the GUNT apparently convinced Goukouni that he could consolidate his control in Chad without any attempt to achieve a political solution in his conflict with Habre's FAN. This, coupled with the growing ineffectuality of external forces in Chad, left Habré with no choice but to reconstitute his forces and continue the military challenge.

Furthermore, the attempt to solve political problems by military means (of which intervention is an aspect) may harden the lines of internal conflict. The use of force embitters those on whom it is used, and it then becomes more difficult to achieve the political compromises necessary to remove the sources of political instability.

Finally, intervention on behalf of an established government may discredit that government in the eyes of its people, who come to see it as an instrument of a foreign power and as betraying the nation which it purports to serve. In other words, intervention may further undermine the legitimacy upon which the stability of a government ultimately rests.[20] Many sources have stated that the Cuban and Soviet presence in Angola has evoked a nationalist response among elements within the MPLA and in the population at large, and this resentment has to a degree extended to the government which brought them in. In Chad, Goukouni's resort to massive Libyan support, coupled with the manifest absence of any attempt by Libyan forces to win popularity, worked in Habré's favour, and he came to be seen by a significant portion of the population as the repository of Chadian aspirations to independence in the face of Libyan depredations. In Afghanistan, the PDP regime never enjoyed broadly based popular support, but after the overthrow of Amin and the arrival in force of the Soviet army an ever-widening portion of the people came to see it not only as a threat to deeply-held traditional values but also as the betrayer of Afghan independence to foreign infidels. The result was the alienation of elements of the urban elite and of the *Khalq* faction who, while they might have sympathized with the regime's social orientation, were unwilling to countenance the swallowing up of Afghanistan by the Soviet Union. Here again, therefore, Soviet intervention may have bought time for the PDP but made it more difficult for the government to establish the kind of political base necessary to render it stable in the longer term.

To sum up, then, there are good reasons for arguing that intervention, while in the short term it might have a stabilizing influence in the target state, in the longer term renders it more difficult to establish the base of popular acceptance upon which stability must ultimately rest. The case that intervention in the Third World generally has a negative impact on the level of the international system as a whole, on relations between East and West, and on the target region and state, is a compelling one. This in turn suggests that the international community should work towards minimizing its incidence and, in cases where it is an optimal solution to a specific problem, towards structuring it in such a way as to minimize associated risks and costs.

III. The regulation of intervention

Efforts to regulate intervention fall into two categories: attempts to prevent it in the first place; and attempts to end it, or prevent wider internationalization of an internal conflict, once some intervention has occurred. That this Chapter dwells more on the second category than on the first is inevitable, given that the cases covered here are cases of intervention. This concentration on responses to, rather than the prevention of, intervention does not constitute a denial of the importance of the latter. In many instances of internal conflict in which external actors have a stake in the outcome, intervention does not occur. This suggests not only that these actors face domestic political, economic and military constraints, but also that they are to some extent swayed by the attempts of the international community to regulate military interference in the internal affairs of other states through diplomacy or the construction of a legal framework restricting intervention. It probably also reflects the effectiveness of implicit or explicit deterrent threats by other interested external actors.

Attempts to regulate intevention may in theory be aimed at altering any of the conditions favouring intervention discussed earlier in this Paper. They may be directed at the basic characteristics of the political situation in the target state or at elements of the structure of the international system conducive to intervention. Alternatively, they may be aimed at affecting the balance of costs and benefits faced by the potential intervener, both with reference to a specific situation of intervention and to future situations in which the external actor might be tempted to intervene. In this sense, while responses to acts of intervention may have little immediate impact, they may contribute to the deterrence of similar acts in other locales. They may also involve the development of mechanisms for crisis avoidance or management which prevent situations developing in which external actors are faced with the stark choice of intervention or a significant political defeat, or where they perceive dramatic and irresistible opportunities which can be realized only through military interference.

In practice, in the cases considered here, there have been two foci of regulatory effort. The first has been on attempts to resolve internal conflicts either before intervention has occurred, in order to preclude it, or while it is taking place, in order to create the preconditions for the withdrawal of foreign forces. The other, and more important, focus has been on attempts to influence the external actor and to keep others out through exhortation, the threat of punishment or the offer of rewards.

In addition to this functional classification, attempts at regulation may also be divided according to the level at which they are undertaken: multilateral (by international or regional organizations, or by informal groups of states united in opposition to the behaviour of another); bilateral (involving agreement among the superpowers); or unilateral. The more prominent attempts to regulate intervention in the cases covered here were undertaken by regional organizations and groups of like-minded states, or unilaterally. The UN, however, played some role in the Afghan crisis, while the superpowers, in their attempt to 'codify' detente in the early 1970s, made what was interpreted by some as a bilateral attempt to regulate intervention.

Angola

Perhaps the most significant effort at prevention and regulation of intervention in Angola was that of the Organization of African Unity. The OAU chairman for 1974–5, Jomo Kenyatta, attempted to resolve the internal conflict and deal with the growing crisis when, at the beginning of 1975, he persuaded the three contending movements to accept the idea of a joint transitional government. This, it was hoped, would prepare the way for a peaceful transfer of sovereignty. When relations between the movements worsened in the spring, Kenyatta brought them together again in June at Nakuru, and produced another agreement on the cessation of hostilities and co-operation in government.

When the Kampala OAU summit was held at the end of July, the problem of foreign intervention in Angola had not attained its full dimensions. There was no indication as yet of significant South African action, the largest single intervener was an OAU member (Zaire), and Soviet and Cuban assistance to the MPLA was supported by a large number of radical African states. It was not surprising, therefore, that the summit did not produce a resolution condemning intervention. Instead, the resolutions concerning Angola called for an end to hostilities and put forward the possibility (never pursued) of an African force to keep the peace there. The Kampala summit marked the end of effective and impartial personal diplomacy on the part of the OAU chairman, for Kenyatta was replaced by Idi Amin, whose personal deficiencies were supplemented by a tendency, in conjunction with Zaire's President Mobutu, to take the part of the FNLA. After the summit, the OAU dispatched a Conciliation Commission to Angola to bring about an agreement between the MPLA, the FNLA, and UNITA. This failed dismally in the face of the determination of the first two to settle the dispute by force.

The next OAU initiative was the extraordinary summit conference on Angola in January 1976, where the organization attempted to address directly the problem of foreign intervention. This, too, was a failure, revealing just how deeply the OAU was divided on the legitimacy of intervention in the Angolan context and on the claims of the various contenders within Angola. Opposing resolutions were tabled by 'moderate' and 'radical' groups. The former called for a blanket condemnation of all foreign intervention and the establishment of a government which included all the movements. The latter sought the condemnation only of South African and 'imperialist' intervention, and the recognition of the MPLA as the legitimate government of Angola. The vote on admission of the MPLA government was deadlocked at 22 to 22, with Uganda (the chair) and Ethiopia (the host state) abstaining, and the meeting adjourned without adopting any resolution on the matter. When the OAU recognized the MPLA government in February, this was the result not of any 'African consensus' but of a change of mind by three states, which gave those in favour of the People's Republic of Angola's admission to the OAU a clear majority. More African states recognized Angola over the following months and years, though this reflected not so much their recognition of the legitimacy of Soviet-Cuban intervention as the fact that MPLA had established a government and control over much of the country, and that the contenders for power were discredited and in disarray.

In Angola, therefore, the OAU failed to prevent intervention by resolving the internal conflict and the crisis which it produced. It also failed to limit the scope of intervention. There is no indication, except perhaps in the case of China, that regional opinion played a major role in deterring external actors from intervening or in inducing them to withdraw. Those who withdrew did so largely because they were losing and were unwilling to bear the costs of redressing the balance of forces in Angola.

Limited bilateral attempts were also made, particularly by the American government, to influence Soviet and Cuban behaviour, both *vis-à-vis* Angola and in the wider context of Soviet activism in the Third World. In December 1975 President Ford met Anatoly Dobrynin, the Soviet Ambassador to the US, to warn him that, in the American view, Soviet involvement in Angola was linked to overall *détente* between the USSR and the US, and consequently that Soviet support for the MPLA was doing serious damage to Soviet-American relations at the global level. Secretary Kissinger, among others, maintains that this meeting resulted in the halt in the Soviet arms airlift between 9 and 25 December. The airlift resumed, in the Administration's view, after the US Congress, by banning American involvement in Angola, removed any serious risk of American reprisal.[1]

This view of the reason for the temporary halt to the airlift may be questioned.[2] Moreover, Kissinger drew a somewhat disingenuous picture in this statement and in press conferences in early 1976 – portraying the US as favouring mutual restraint by the super-powers so that Africans could solve their own problems unmolested by external pressures, and showing the USSR as a renegade committed to forceful expansion and bent on denying Africans the right to determine their own affairs. It ignores most notably the involvement of the US Central Intelligence Agency in the Angolan conflict, and also the American failure to propose mutual restraint to Moscow until the MPLA was clearly winning, the USSR and Cuba were massively committed, and it was evident that Washington's covert involvement in Angola was liable to be terminated by Congress. Nonetheless it is true that the Senate action damaged US credibility in a general sense by confirming the Soviet perception of

American irresolution, and this undermined Kissinger's belated attempt to convince the USSR that her Angolan intervention, and like actions elsewhere, were not tolerable.

This brings us to the wider issue of American involvement in Angola acting as a deterrent to Soviet activism in the Third World as a whole. According to John Stockwell, the point of American intervention in Angola was not to place Holden Roberto and the FNLA in power or deny victory to the MPLA but to increase the cost of victory to the USSR.[3] This, it was hoped, would convey the message that gains in the Third World were likely to be costly, and hence would discourage further Soviet adventurism. As it was, the scale of the American involvement apparently never sufficed to make the USSR and Cuba reconsider their policy. Furthermore, the American unwillingness to stay the course (particularly when taken in conjunction with the failure to bail out South Vietnam earlier in 1975) in all likelihood conveyed a message that was the opposite of the one intended. A logical conclusion for the USSR to draw from the American performance in Angola was that further Soviet interventions would also meet with an ineffectual, vacillating and half-hearted American response.

Ethiopia

At the multilateral level, the OAU played a far less active role in the case of intervention in Ethiopia. There was little inclination on the part of its member states to condemn Soviet and Cuban assistance to Ethiopia, because the generally recognized Ethiopian government had requested this help. Furthermore, in coming to the aid of the Ethiopian government the USSR and Cuba were defending one of the OAU's cardinal principles – that African states should not attempt unilaterally to alter boundaries on the continent through the use of force.

Where regional consensus did play a part was in limiting the internationalization of the conflict by discouraging external assistance to Somalia. It is generally accepted that a major reason for the American failure to help Somalia during the Ogaden War was the fear of alienating OAU opinion. The most specific expression of OAU attitudes to wider external participation in the conflict occurred when Iran made known her intention to assist Somalia if she were invaded by Ethiopia. The OAU secretariat responded that Iran would do better to help in finding a peaceful solution, and that Iranian attempts to 'extend her sphere of influence of Africa' were unwelcome.[4] The failure of the United States and her allies to respond to pleas for help from Somalia would suggest that where a broad regional consensus does exist, it may be effective in deterring intervention by external actors. This was reinforced by the adamant opposition of Kenya, the principal Western sympathizer in the region, to any security assistance to Somalia.

In addition to its limited role in preventing a widening of the Ogaden war, the OAU made a rather half-hearted attempt to mediate between Ethiopia and Somalia. The OAU Conciliation Commission summoned both sides to Libreville in June 1977 and called upon them to resolve their differences. There was, however, no common ground between the two, the OAU lacked the authority to impose a solution, and its exhortations were ignored.

The US went further than the OAU by openly opposing the Soviet and Cuban presence in Ethiopia and again took a number of unilateral steps to raise the costs of the venture to the USSR and Cuba. The most notable of these was the suspension of the Indian Ocean force limitation discussions. These were not, of course, a very high priority item on the American foreign-policy agenda, nor were they a cause which enjoyed much support in the American government of the day. (Events in the Horn probably shifted the balance of bureaucratic politics even further against the small group favouring these talks, as well as providing a convenient excuse for pulling out of the negotiations.) One is struck by the contrast between the abundance of American rhetoric about the Soviet intervention in the Horn and the absence of any significant policy response to it. It is probable that this had much to do with American unwillingness to jeopardize the Strategic Arms Limitation Talks (SALT) and with the apparent fact that, despite the abundance of geopolitical analysis, the Horn was not of fundamental importance to the architects of American foreign policy. Again, however, this could only have led the Soviet Union to conclude that the United States' bark was worse than her bite. The widely-aired accounts of disagreement within the Executive Branch over Indian Ocean policy could only have contributed to the impression of ineffectuality and disarray.

Chad

In the case of Chad, it was the regional dimension which was most prominent in attempts to terminate unilateral intervention, resolve the crisis which provoked it and get to grips with the endemic internal conflict which had produced that crisis. As in the Horn, the region succeeded in achieving a substantial degree of consensus on the undesirability of foreign intervention. The OAU also went further than it had in previous cases, intervening directly in the conflict both to replace the Libyan presence and to establish the modicum of internal security which it saw as a prerequisite for a political settlement. But because the OAU commitment was deeper, its failure was more wounding. For this reason, the organization's attempt to influence the outcome of the political process in Chad is particularly instructive.

The OAU was closely involved in Chad's affairs from 1978 onwards. In that year, as we have seen, Libya took the lead in sponsoring a peace conference, apparently intended to produce a cease-fire and internal settlement. This failed to produce a durable solution, and Libya was followed by Sudan and Nigeria in the effort to put an end to Chad's chronic internal instability. The long series of conferences in Kano and Lagos in 1979 culminated in the formation of a very broadly-based transitional government under Goukouni Oueddei in

November. That year also saw two abortive attempts to deploy peace-keeping forces in Chad. The Kano Accord of March 1979 stipulated that Nigeria should provide the troop complement, and Nigerian units were deployed in Ndjamena in April. They were withdrawn in June, as it became clear that their presence did not allow Nigeria to control Chad's politics (it would be fair to say that, for Nigeria, their presence was intended as much to further her own interests as to keep the peace). In August, the Lagos Accords stipulated that the agreed cease-fire should be monitored by an independent commission headed by the OAU Secretary General or his representatives. The commission was also to oversee a neutral force consisting of military units from countries not bordering on Chad (it was ultimately agreed that these should come from Guinea, Benin and the Congo). This stipulation was presumably intended to exclude those having the greatest interest in influencing the internal political outcome. Only the Congo actually sent troops, and these were withdrawn in March 1980, with the resumption of civil war.

The other notable aspect of the conferences held in Nigeria at this time was the repeated insistence on the withdrawal of French troops from Chad. France complied with these stipulations, pulling out completely by April 1980. However, this withdrawal was probably due less to African pressure than to France's growing realization that her presence was bringing no rewards and was irrelevant to the course of Chadian politics while subjecting French personnel to increasing risks.

The next OAU attempt to address Chad's problems was prompted by the Libyan intervention in November–December 1980. In January 1981 the OAU member states (other than Libya) most closely associated with the problem in Chad condemned Libya's action, despite the fact that her forces had been invited by a government recognized by the OAU. What created a consensus on the matter was apparently the announcement at the beginning of January of an agreement between Chad and Libya that the two countries should merge. This was widely interpreted as a Libyan attempt to alter by force frontiers established at the time of decolonization. On a more practical level, this proposed institutionalization of Libyan influence in Chad was unacceptable to those states in the area which feared Libyan expansionist ambitions in the Sahara and Sahel, notably conservative Francophone states such as Senegal and the Ivory Coast, as well as Nigeria.

The OAU attempted to end Libyan intervention by providing an alternative basis for Chad's internal security. Negotiations leading to the establishment of the inter-African peace force took place largely within the Franco-African rather than the OAU context. Nonetheless, it was largely the OAU *ad hoc* committee on Chad which shouldered the responsibility for peace-keeping, and the financing of the force was nominally an OAU responsibility. While originally troops were to have been supplied by Nigeria, Senegal, Togo, Benin and Zaire, several countries again did not meet their commitments, and the force turned out to be a Nigerian-Zairean-Senegalese affair, with the lion's share of the 3,500–3,700 troops provided by Nigeria.

This ambitious OAU venture also failed. It might be argued that OAU pressure was to some extent effective in prevailing upon Goukouni to ask for the Libyan forces to be withdrawn, and in inducing Libya to withdraw them. However, Goukouni had ample reasons of his own for wanting those forces to go, and it was French, rather than African, assurances of support which were the more telling. Moreover, Col. Gaddafi also had a number of good reasons for pulling out (the continuing and growing internal challenge to the Libyan presence, the over-extension of his armed forces, declining oil revenues, and his desire to be chairman of the OAU). Hence, as in the case of the French withdrawal, the role of regional pressure should not be overestimated.

With reference to Chad's internal politics, the OAU peace force failed to stabilize the situation or to halt the renewed outbreak of civil war. Its arrival was delayed, and the interval between Libya's withdrawal and the deployment of the OAU force was used by Habré to expand his area of control at the expense of the central government. The force's mandate was never clear, and its units quickly showed their unwillingness to take the offensive against Habré, to defend the central government or to attempt to enforce a cease-fire. In fact, it stayed on the sidelines.

The OAU also lacked sufficient resources to sustain the force, which, by February 1982 was facing serious financial difficulties. Nigeria, the country apparently bearing most of the burden, was in the throes of a fiscal crisis brought on by falling oil revenues, and extra-African sources of funding, such as the UN and the US, proved unwilling to take up the slack. As a result, the OAU started looking actively for ways to pull out. The mechanism selected in February was yet another peace plan which set a number of arbitrary and unrealistic deadlines for a cease-fire, political negotiations leading to elections and finally a withdrawal of OAU forces in June 1982. These arrangements were blithely ignored by Habré and rejected by Goukouni. Faced with this lack of co-operation, the Nigerian government began to threaten a unilateral withdrawal, which began in May.

Habré's victory over Goukouni in early June now provided the OAU with a way out of its expensive and embarrassing predicament, and official withdrawal of the force began in mid-June. The manner of its departure, however, only served to underline the irrelevance of the OAU presence.

In the Chadian case, therefore, it is fair to say – with some qualification concerning Libyan and French withdrawal – that OAU efforts were of little significance in prompting withdrawal by external actors. Nor is it probable that it prevented further internationalization of the conflict, since there was little apparent desire by other external actors to enter militarily. Finally OAU efforts at conflict resolution within Chad also failed. To the extent that Chad's internal conflict was temporarily resolved, this came about through Habré's military victory over his previous colleagues in the GUNT, Acyl Ahmat's fatal encounter with an aircraft propellor and the subsequent collapse of his faction, and the disintegration in internecine squabbles of Kamougué's southern forces.

The renewal of the civil war in 1983 demonstrates how little impact multilateral conflict regulation had on Chad's internal disputes. It is ironic that, while the OAU was of little consequence in determing the course of events in Chad, these events may have been instrumental in the near collapse of the OAU, whose November 1982 summit was cancelled because of a dispute over whether to recognize Habré's or Goukouni's delegation.

On the unilateral level, and with regard to Libyan intervention, the French and American governments in particular made some attempts to exert pressure on Libya. However, these should be understood not only in the Chadian context, but also in the broader one of Libyan subversion of regimes friendly to the West and (later in the period) of Sadat's assassination and consequent American concern about regime stability in Egypt and Sudan. While military pressure on Libya's eastern frontier (Operation Bright Star) may have played some role in persuading Gaddafi to trim his military commitments, on the whole both the French and American governments lacked the leverage to apply intense pressure on Libya even if they had desired to do so. In the case of the French government, even the desire was somewhat lacking, given Libya's economic importance to France both as a supplier of oil and as a market for finished products, including arms.

Afghanistan

Turning finally to Afghanistan, the seriousness of rivalries within south Asia and India's close relations with the USSR precluded a regional response to intervention. The most prominent multilateral responses took place in other contexts – in the UN, the EEC and NATO, the Islamic Conference, the Non-Aligned Movement, and the informal grouping of states which decided to boycott the 1980 Olympic Games.

A number of nations attempted to push through the UN Security Council a resolution condemning Soviet intervention and demanding an immediate withdrawal. Its fate of the Resolution displayed graphically the UN's weakness in any attempt to deal with issues where the vital interests of any permanent member of the Security Council are at stake: the resolution was passed by 13 votes to 2, but the Soviet negative vote constituted a veto. Stymied in the Security Council, those members opposing Soviet intervention succeeded in transferring the matter to the General Assembly, where a resolution calling for a Soviet withdrawal was adopted by 104 votes to 18, with 18 abstentions and 11 states absent. However, given the limitations on the General Assembly's legislative and executive powers, the UN role was limited to the expression of disapproval and exhortation to the effect that the USSR should pull out of Afghanistan.

The EEC adopted a declaration similar to the UN Resolution, took steps to ensure that EEC countries would not make up Soviet shortages of grain caused by the American grain embargo, suspended export credits on a number of agricultural products, and ceased to export surplus butter to the USSR. This rather unimpressive array of measures suggests that while EEC members felt compelled to do something, they were unwilling to back up their expressions of outrage with any significant attempt to increase the costs to the USSR of her intervention in substantive terms.

The Islamic Conference agreed unanimously (Syria and South Yemen being absent) to condemn the Soviet intervention, but again little emerged of a substantive nature that might have caused the USSR to reconsider her actions. The conference of Foreign Ministers of members of the Non-Aligned Movement, held in February 1981, was marked by a serious split on the question of Afghanistan – with Cuba and India, in particular, opposing outright condemnation of the Soviet action. Nonetheless, the conference managed to agree on a resolution which called in a restrained manner for the withdrawal of foreign troops and respect for Afghan independence. The USSR was not explicitly cited, however, and again the response to intervention remained on the level of exhortation rather than action.

Perhaps the widest and most deeply felt multilateral sanction on Soviet behaviour was the Olympic boycott. The success of the 1980 summer Olympic Games meant a great deal to the Soviet leadership, which hoped that they would add considerably to the regime's internal prestige as well as providing a showcase for the display to the world of the achievements of Soviet society. Sixty-two countries and territories did not participate (some, however, cited economic rather than political reasons for staying away), while 81 sent teams; the absentees included a number of the more significant sporting nations, such as the US, Japan and West Germany. The boycott significantly altered the character of the Games and, by extension, reduced the benefits which Soviet leaders had hoped for. Again, however, its cost to the USSR was insignificant in comparison to her growing stake in Afghanistan, and it was very improbable that the boycott could have played a role in modifying Soviet behaviour. It was, in fact, unlikely that this was seriously intended. Like many of the other multilateral steps mentioned above, it seemed to be motivated more by a desire to express disapproval and avoid giving an impression of complete acquiescence in Soviet misbehaviour than by a serious intention to alter Soviet policy.

The same would appear to be true of the unilateral steps taken by the US in response to the Soviet intervention. In addition to boycotting the Olympic Games and pressuring other states to do likewise, President Carter announced an embargo on grain exports in excess of amounts agreed in the Soviet-American grain agreement and on high technology (most importantly computers and oil-drilling equipment). The American government also suspended the process of ratification of the SALT II Treaty which was to have begun in late January 1980. Given the uncertain outcome of this process, and the embarrassment which would have accompanied the Treaty's possible rejection, one wonders whether the excuse of Afghanistan was not greeted with a sigh of relief by Carter's advisers. In fact, Soviet awareness of the likelihood that SALT II would not be ratified may in any case have significantly weakened the position of those in the Politburo who opposed intervention in Afghanistan.

Beyond these economic and political reprisals, a number of military steps were taken as well. In early January 1980, the US announced her intention to maintain a permanent naval presence in the Indian Ocean, and dispatched the aircraft carrier *Nimitz* to the area to join two other carriers stationed off Iran in connection with the hostage crisis. The decision to keep naval units in the area on a permanent basis was motivated to a large extent by a desire to deter further Soviet activity in the Gulf and south-west Asian areas, as well as to reassure local allies of American resolve. Similar motives may be attributed to American acceleration of the development of the Rapid Deployment Force.

The fact that all of these multilateral and unilateral responses to the Soviet intervention were on the whole rather insubstantial, and had little apparent effect on Soviet policy towards Afghanistan, suggests that as attempts to regulate intervention they were insufficient. It is unclear, however, just what could have been done to force the USSR to withdraw, short of counter-intervention in highly unfavourable circumstances and with attendant risks of escalation. Since this was not acceptable, doing something – however inadequate that something might be – was obviously preferable to passivity. A total lack of response would only have encouraged further Soviet interventions.

As it was, the political and military responses to the intervention, while not enough to affect the USSR's behaviour in Afghanistan, did make it clear to her that such behaviour was very widely perceived as unacceptable and incurred penalties (including loss of prestige and the loss of other objectives of Soviet policy). International reaction in the other two cases involving the USSR had not had this effect. It also encouraged the adversaries of the USSR to improve their capacity to respond militarily to intervention by Soviet or allied forces. If Soviet policy-making involves some attempt to weigh benefits and costs, these responses to the intervention may therefore help to deter Soviet intervention in situations where its benefits (or the costs of non-intervention) are less telling than they were in Afghanistan.

Balance sheet

The UN is remarkable in these four cases for its lack of a significant role in regulating or responding to intervention. In the African cases, it was constrained by the desire of the African community to keep it out (though one may conjecture that since these African cases divided the USSR and the US, the UN would have been incapable of effective action to resolve the internal conflict or restrain external actors even if it had been involved). The Afghan case shows that the UN Security Council cannot act in disputes where the interests of the superpowers are opposed, though in theory it has the power to do so The General Assembly, while capable of passing resolutions, does not have the power to implement them.

The wide divergence of interests within the UN, as well as its constitutional incapacity to reconcile or overrule them in crisis situations, explains why that organization has played so small a role, not only in the cases of intervention considered here, but also in the entire history of intervention since the Congo crisis. Its ineffectuality is also assured by its lack of a permanent enforcement mechanism and, consequently, by the *ad hoc* character of its responses in crises where it finds itself capable of assuming a role. As for addressing the internal conditions provoking crises, the UN is constrained by the restrictions its Charter imposes on involvement in the internal affairs of states and by the jealousy with which sovereignty is guarded by the new states.

Many similar limitations are shared by regional organizations' attempts to respond to and limit intervention. The African experience would suggest that internal conflict is as likely to split states within a region as it is to divide the international community as a whole. This is not surprising, since it is regional actors whose interests are most directly affected by internal conflicts within the region (as with Nigeria and Libya in Chad). Moreover, governments within regions show no less of a tendency towards ideological disagreement than does the international system as a whole – Pan-Arabism, Pan-Africanism, and Latin American solidarity notwithstanding. The African cases show clearly the problems which divergent interests and ideological divisions pose for attempts to reach an agreed regional response to intervention.[5] (They would seem to suggest that in fact intervention by local actors is more common than regional co-operative attempts to regulate intervention.) They also illustrate the difficulties these characteristics create for any regional attempt to resolve the internal conflicts which are one of the basic conditions of intervention. Regional actors are as likely to be involved in exacerbating civil conflicts or trying to draw unilateral advantage from internal crises as they are to be preoccupied with achieving a stable and equitable resolution of them.

The African experience would also suggest that regional organizations may lack the financial discipline and resources to respond effectively to situations where intervention is probable (or indeed has taken place), even if some measure of agreement is possible. OAU members have constantly failed to contribute sufficient funds to cover the budgets which they themselves have adopted. It was recently reported, for instance, that only $4 million of the total 1981–2 budget of $19 million had been paid in by June 1981, and the writer of the report concluded that the OAU was in effect bankrupt and subsisting on bank overdrafts.[6] This renders it unlikely that the OAU could meet the extraordinary expenses associated with peace-keeping. The experience in Chad – where the OAU, unable to meet the cost of its commitment, was in effect forced to bail out – shows the problems that this can create for the regulation of intervention.

Financial constraints also lay behind the numerous failures of members to provide troops for the OAU force. In such circumstances, it is the larger states, or those most directly interested in the affairs of the target state, which dominate the peace-keeping effort (Nigeria's preponderance in the peace-keeping force in Chad is a case in point). At the extreme, regional peace-keeping may in this way become a fig-leaf for intervention by a regional actor which wants to expand or maintain its own influence or reduce that of a regional rival (as with Nigeria in Chad, or Syria in Lebanon).

The structural limitations on multilateral responses to intervention are supplemented by an asymmetry of commitment between the internal and external actors already involved in a conflict within a state and those attempting to limit or to end it from outside. The ill-feeling separating the indigenous parties, profound to begin with, deepens with the passage of time and the shedding of blood; and as involvement by external actors grows, so too do their losses and their commitment of prestige. It is therefore difficult for either the internal actors or their external allies to respond with equanimity to disinterested appeals for compromise and withdrawal. On the other hand, those states and bodies not directly involved in the conflict have little at stake, and they are in general unenthusiastic about assuming the costs and risks which would be entailed by a response sufficient to bring an end to the intervention or hostilities. In short, those participating in an internal war are resistant to pleas for moderation, while those not involved are insufficiently motivated to back up their rhetoric with substance. In such circumstances, it is not surprising that the record of multilateral initiatives in the cases cited here is not particularly encouraging.

The same asymmetry of interests applies to unilateral responses to intervention. The very decision to intervene is indicative of the intensity of an external actor's interest in an internal conflict, and such a level of interest is unlikely to be shared by other states concerned at the intervention. In such a situation, efforts to modify the intervener's behaviour are liable to fail unless the other states can, at little cost to themselves, inflict substantial penalties on the malefactor. The case of Afghanistan illustrates this. While the US and her European allies were unquestionably upset about Soviet behaviour, they were unwilling or unable to take counter-measures of sufficient impact to override the considerations which induced the USSR to intervene and then subsequently keep her troops in Afghanistan.

The analysis above indicates that trying from outside to improve the internal conditions which may provoke intervention is unlikely to be successful. The same is true of attempts to induce interveners to withdraw once they have committed themselves.

This is not to say that attempts to regulate intervention are a waste of time. They may not be effective in the circumstances which provoked them, but hostile responses to intervention may assist in deterring similar actions elsewhere. This brings up a final point. Soviet actions in Angola, Ethiopia and Afghanistan all occurred in periods of disarray and indecision in American foreign policy, and the Soviet government acted as it did partly because it could be reasonably assured of American inaction. There was an asymmetry in the willingness of the two superpowers to deploy force in the Third World in pursuit of national objectives. This would suggest that a perceived willingness and capacity to use force to counter-intervene or to intervene pre-emptively is important in deterring intervention by adversaries in third-world countries. Paradoxically, comparative freedom from intervention by the superpowers and their proxies in third-world countries may be promoted if both sides are ready and willing to intervene against the other in order to prevent unilateral gains. In this context, notions such as that of the Rapid Deployment Force have a certain merit. This line of argument is merely a specific variant of the more general principle that, in the absence of a supreme law-giving and law-enforcing entity, security for the system as a whole is best assured by a balance in the capacity and will to use force.

IV. Conclusion and prospects

Summary of inferences

It is clear from Chapters I and II that the cases of intervention display a number of patterns in the conditions which give rise to military interference and the consequences which follow from it. It has been suggested that acts of intervention stem from political instability and conflict in the target state which create pressures upon internal actors that induce them to seek external support. Intervention does not, as a rule, occur without a prior relationship between an internal and an external actor, and it is usually a new stage in a long-standing relationship between the two.

The political and economic interests and ideological commitments of external actors, balanced against the various normative and objective constraints to which they are subject, determine their attitude to internal conflicts in other states. Intervention is in this sense the product not only of conditions of instability in the target state, but also of the intervener assessment of potential benefits and costs and of his capability for intervention.

Several aspects of the structure of the international system are also relevant in considering the conditions of intervention. Systems in which power is distributed asymmetrically, which are tightly organized into alliance systems, and in which states embracing competitive universalist ideologies coexist, are more prone to intervention than systems which do not exhibit these attributes. Bipolarity encourages intervention in 'grey zones', since every gain for one pole is a loss for the other. On the other hand, and particularly in the nuclear age, the possibility of superpower confrontation and escalation encourages caution in any direct challenge to the other superpower's interests.

The character of the political situation in the target state, the balance of costs and benefits faced by the external actor, the objective (military and economic) constraints upon him, and the nature of the international system provide the basis for explaining specific acts of intervention. But they are not sufficient to explain why intervention occurs at a specific time and place, or why an external actor chooses to use force, rather than some other instrument of policy, in the pursuit of his objectives. In this most immediate sense intervention is a product of crisis and rapid change in political conditions in the target state. This faces the external actor with the choice of defeat – bringing with it the loss of prior investment, humiliating withdrawal, loss of prestige, and gains to rivals – or else decisive escalation. Alternatively, it may present the potential intervener with a dramatic and ephemeral opportunity to realize long-standing and fundamental political ends. Perhaps the most important characteristic of these crises is the speed with which events occur and fortunes change. It is this which militates against the employment of other instruments – which generally take longer to have an effect and are in any case often inappropriate for affecting the outcome of an armed civil conflict.

With respect to consequences or outcomes, the analysis of the cases covered in this Paper indicates that intervention may bring the intervening power short-term political gains (influence and prestige, the weakening of adversaries) and military gains (access to bases), but that even in the short term it is a highly risky undertaking with significant chances of failure. The Angolan, Ethiopian and Afghan cases each suggest that the probability of success is enhanced where the external actor is willing and able to deploy forces in quantity and quality sufficient to determine the outcome, where the local client is politically viable (well-organized, flexible and popular) but the opposition is divided, unpopular and ineffectual, and where no counter-intervention occurs.

In the longer term, the record would suggest that intervention is likely to be unrewarding. The military instrument may perhaps buy time, but it is too blunt to resolve the political and social conflicts which provoked the intrusion. In fact, in that it may encourage local clients to believe that they need not address the grievances and aspirations of their rivals, it may impede the target state's political integration. Furthermore, even where intervention succeeds in establishing a local client in power or perpetuating his rule, the cases of Angola and Ethiopia suggest that the influence gained thereby is by no means absolute and permanent. The local actor's debt to his external benefactor does not prevent him from pursuing policies inimical to the latter. In general, the strength of nationalism throughout the Third World suggests that influence, however gained, is likely to be circumscribed and short-lived, particularly where the external actor attempts to exercise it in a manner inconsistent with his client's aspirations.

This assumes that the objectives of the external actor are relatively ambitious: installing a client in power, ensuring the stability of his rule, and consequently acquiring substantial influence over the affairs of the target state. But, as noted in Chapter II, interveners may be aiming somewhat lower than this – seeking instead merely to harass and to sow chaos, so as to destabilize an undesirable incumbent regime and prevent it from consolidating its hold over the country. The prospects of success here are somewhat better. It is easier to exacerbate civil conflicts than to resolve them, and easier to undermine a tottering regime than to shore it up.

From the perspective of the international system as a whole, intervention as a general phenomenon is damaging to international order, not only because the widespread use of force is corrosive in itself but also because intervention in many cases constitutes a challenge to one of the basic principles of international society – that of sovereignty, with its corollary of non-interference in the internal affairs of other states. At a less abstract level, superpower intervention in Angola, the Horn of Africa and Afghanistan has severely damaged relations between the US and the USSR, poisoning the process of *détente* and contributing substantially to the return to Cold War, not least by prompting the election of a Republican Administration committed to confrontation rather than co-operation.

It is, however, at the regional and national level that the consequences of intervention are most telling. In the first instance, intervention brings with it the militarization of regional politics, which in turn consumes scarce resources. It also encourages other states in the region to look for external support, further embroiling the region in extra-regional rivalries and conflicts. By increasing the scale of civil conflict it can also create problems for contiguous states, since it leads to substantial flows of refugees. This not only increases the economic burden upon states in the region but also creates security problems both for the state in which the intervention occurs and for its neighbours. Refugee populations frequently contain elements determined to wage a cross-frontier armed struggle, and this invites reprisal against the host country.

Finally, intervention can widen existing conflicts within the target state and increase the destructive capacities of internal actors, which leads to higher levels of civilian and military casualties and greater destruction of that state's economic and social base than would otherwise have been the case. In addition, it was noted above that intervention may inhibit a return to internal political stability by further embittering the participants in civil conflict, by evoking a nationalist response in the target population, and by encouraging the beneficiary of external support to believe that he need not negotiate.

The discussion in Chapter III of attempts to regulate or prevent intervention suggested the great difficulty of securing the withdrawal of an external actor by multilateral or unilateral pressure, once his forces had been committed. It also indicated that the attempt from outside to prevent intervention, or limit its extent, by dealing with the internal conditions provoking it was unpromising. This leaves the question of how the problem should best be addressed.

In the discussion of constraints on intervention and in that on unilateral attempts at regulation, it was suggested that at the level of the super-powers and their allies credible conventional deterrent capabilities may be effective in restraining intervention. Also, with regard to military interference by third-world actors, their continuing dependence on external sources for arms indicates that a general regime of restraint in conventional arms transfers could limit the incidence of intervention.

There are a number of difficulties with such an approach. First, it might be argued that this would be closing the stable door after the horse had bolted. Levels of armaments in the Third World are now so high that it is legitimate to question whether such restraints would have much effect, particularly when the possibility of re-transfer exists. Nonetheless, there are few countries in the Third World which could sustain a military operation of significant scale for any length of time without access to external sources of supply. This suggests that a supplier agreement could have a restraining effect.

The second problem is that limitation of arms transfers may stimulate indigenous arms production — as it clearly has in the case of South Africa. Thus the attempt to exercise control in the short term might in the longer term result in a loss of leverage and an inherently less controllable situation. This may be so, but the difficulties encountered by those third-world countries which have attempted to develop their own arms industries indicate that to change to indigenous production on any scale would be a very long, costly and painful process.

The third, and more telling, problem is the near impossibility of arriving at a relatively broad supplier agreement in present political and economic conditions. On the political side, the intense competition between the superpowers encourages both to supply clients with relative abandon. This does not create an atmosphere conducive to meaningful negotiations on limiting conventional arms transfers or on more broadly-based restraint in regional crises. In the economic sphere, both the superpowers and the major European suppliers use arms sales as a means to lengthen production runs and thus reduce unit costs for their own forces. For the smaller suppliers, arms sales enable them to maintain independence in the production of major weapons systems at less than prohibitive cost. In addition, the depressed state of the economies of major Western suppliers makes their governments resistant to policies which would cause the contraction of arms industries which are perceived to be important sources of employment. In short, the time is not propitious for multilateral restraint on the part of the major suppliers.

It is also true, however, that in situations of crisis unilateral restraint over transfers to clients by major suppliers can significantly affect the course of events, encouraging restraint on the part of potential interveners or frustrating the designs of those who have intervened. The Soviet refusal to resupply Somalia in late 1977, and the unwillingness of other powers to pick up the slack, was one important determinant of Somalia's forced withdrawal from Ethiopia. The problem here is that such decisions usually result from a calculation of interest on the part of the supplier, rather than from a spirit of restraint in crisis.

Finally, it has been argued here that intervention is in part a product of political instability in third-world states which is itself a result of scarcity of resources and insufficient political integration in target states. This would suggest that the ultimate solution to the problem of intervention lies in bringing those states to a level of political and economic development which permits the creation and perpetuation of stable and legitimate political institutions. Just how to do this is a matter of some dispute in academic and diplomatic circles. Even if a method were agreed upon, the ensuing transition would itself be destabilizing.[1] Moreover, it is fairly obvious that it would necessitate a far greater redistribution of global resources and a far higher level of multilateral cooperation in development and trade than has been achieved so far. This seems improbable because of the prominence of East–West conflict in the consciousness of governments of the 'North' and because these governments are increasingly pressed by domestic economic problems. This leaves little room for ambitious efforts at social reform on a global scale.

What has changed?

The cases covered here suggest that interventions in the 1970s and early 1980s are different from earlier interventionism in at least three ways. The first was the quiescence of the US: in only one case did she play a direct interventionist role, and that was short-lived and minor in scale. This contrasts rather starkly with the 1960s, and in particular with the American role in Vietnam and the Dominican Republic. That quiescence may be ascribed above all to the experience in Vietnam and its legacy of domestic opposition to American involvement in internal conflicts in the Third World. Most recent evidence, however, suggests that the US may have reverted to a much more active policy of third-world intervention under the Reagan Administration: witness Lebanon, Grenada and Central America. As Vietnam recedes into history, and as perceived Soviet expansionism in the Third World weighs more heavily in domestic American politics, interventionism is again becoming respectable.

The second difference is Soviet activism since the mid-1970s. Three of the four cases studied have involved intervention by the USSR or by Soviet allies benefiting substantially from Soviet logistical and material assistance. The intervention in Afghanistan was the first massive use of Soviet forces outside the boundaries of the Soviet sphere established during and in the immediate aftermath of World War II. Since it followed a period of relative introversion and caution in the mid-1960s, and of radical improvement in East–West relations in the early 1970s, it was particularly surprising. This change in Soviet behaviour may be ascribed to the development of the USSR's capacity to project force, the achievement of strategic parity with the US, and the new confidence which the Soviet leadership drew from these factors. It also stemmed from the desire to acquire a status as a world power commensurate with this growth in strength. Finally, it is highly plausible that it derived from a Soviet perception of American weakness and irresolution, brought on by the Vietnam debacle and strengthened by the American retreat in Angola. Again, this may be changing as the Soviet Union contemplates both a more assertive United States and the cost of her own earlier interventions.

The third significant change is the growing incidence of intervention by third-world actors. In three of the four cases – Angola, Ethiopia and Chad – regional actors intervened in the affairs of their neighbours. It is not difficult to find other recent examples – Tanzania in Uganda, Libya in Tunisia, Syria and Israel in Lebanon, Vietnam in Kampuchea and Laos and (somewhat earlier) India in East Pakistan. While the phenomenon is by no means new, there is little question that it is becoming increasingly frequent, for a number of reasons. First, many of these interveners are new states which have had little opportunity to assert themselves, and their regional politics remain to be defined, the colonial legacy being artificial and ambiguous. It takes a certain amount of time for regional balances and hierarchies to work themselves out and for a given state of affairs to attain general recognition, but one way for these relationships to define themselves and for an order to emerge is through armed conflict. Second, the rapid diffusion of weapons throughout the Third World in the past decade has provided the means for states there to use force in pursuit of their objectives. Finally, as regimes come to realize the intractability of their domestic problems and are pressured by the high and unfulfillable expectations of their peoples, they are tempted to engage in foreign adventures in order to divert popular attention from internal grievances.

One last difference from past intervention is a geographical one. While the first years after the independence of many African states in the early 1960s saw a number of small interventions, principally by the colonial powers, the last decade has seen Africa being drawn into the global rivalry between East and West and the increasing military activism there by the USSR in particular. This, coupled with the growing use of force by regional actors mentioned above and the specific problem of apartheid in southern Africa, has made that continent especially prone to intervention.

What of the future?

With reference to the USSR, the Angolan and Ethiopian ventures imposed no significant military and economic burdens and few political costs on her. In each case, the situation was stabilized and hostilities reduced to a relatively low level fairly rapidly. Limited involvement of Soviet military personnel meant few casualties.

The Afghan experience, by contrast, has involved large numbers of Soviet military personnel in combat roles, and the not insignificant levels of casualties have resulted in a limited amount of internal discontent. The conflict, and the Soviet involvement in it, continues five years after the initial Soviet intervention, with no improvement in the position of the USSR and her allies. The cost in material and the economic burden of sustaining Afghanistan's crippled economy are substantial, there is no end in sight for Soviet planners and policy-makers. Moreover, while Soviet actions in Angola and Ethiopia did little to alienate third-world opinion, the invasion of Afghanistan met with wide disapproval among Islamic states and in the Non-Aligned Movement. Repeated UN General Assembly Resolutions condemning the Soviet presence there have constituted a substantial blow to Soviet prestige and are a clear indication of growing Soviet unpopularity in the Third World. In the Western countries, the intervention in Afghanistan served as a reminder of the 'Soviet threat', strengthening those in Europe and the US who oppose the continuation of detente and favour conventional, and also theatre and strategic, nuclear re-armament.

If assessments of cost and benefit associated with potential future commitments are based in part on recent experiences, the consequences of the Angolan and Ethiopian actions in all likelihood encouraged further Soviet interventionism, but it is plausible that the Afghan imbroglio will have the opposite effect. While this will perhaps not be sufficient to hold back the USSR where the case for military interference is truly compelling, it may be of significance in discouraging such behaviour in more marginal circumstances.

Beyond Afghanistan, several other factors in the international situation would seem to favour caution on the part of the USSR. First among these is the more assertive anti-Sovietism and the unpredictability of the present American Administration. Second is the American conventional military build-up which is accompanying this posture. Third are events in Poland. While the USSR faces serious challenges within her European sphere of influence, she is less likely to allow her energies to be dispersed in adventures further afield.

Developments in Sino-Soviet relations may also favour less active military involvement in third-world conflicts. The intensity of competition between the two powers for influence in the Third World was no doubt of significance in accounting for Soviet involvement in Angola. But this diminished in the middle and late 1970s, as China concentrated less on her role in the Third World and more on relations with the US, Japan and Western Europe, and as she focused more narrowly on the development of her own economy. The past two years have seen a deterioration in Sino-American relations and some evidence of a renewal of China's emphasis on her role in the Third World, but it would seem unlikely that this will result in the re-emergence of intense Sino-Soviet rivalry there. In fact, the record of the last six months indicates that both China and the USSR are at least interested in, if not committed to, some improvement in their relations. This would militate against competitive involvement in third-world conflicts.

The USSR also faces serious economic difficulties in the next half decade. Such conditions do not favour the further extension of military commitments which would draw scarce resources from other sectors of the economy. Furthermore, Soviet intervention elsewhere strengthens the case of those in the West who seek to exacerbate these difficulties through selective embargoes on exports to the USSR and through credit restrictions. These economic problems are supplemented by the political ones associated with the process of succession within the Soviet leadership.

Finally, it may be that the Soviet assessment of medium- and long-range gains from the involvements in Angola and Ethiopia raises doubts about the overall value of such operations, despite their initial success.[2] This, too, may lead to the conclusion that Soviet resources are better directed elsewhere. In short, there is a convincing case to be made for the view that the USSR will be more cautious about military involvement in internal and regional conflicts in areas where immediate and vital Soviet interests are not at stake. This is of course not an argument for relaxation by the West, for it is in large part a more assertive posture on the part of the US in particular which has led to this result.

Many of these arguments also apply to Cuban interventionism, for, while it would be an oversimplification to say that Cuba was the creature of the Soviet Union in a narrow sense, the USSR provided, and continues to provide, the logistic support and the military equipment without which Cuban adventurism in Africa in particular would be next to impossible. Moreover, the Soviet Union pays the bills for some of these Cuban activities. In a period when she is herself experiencing hardship, she may come to see support for Cuban force projection, and indeed the scale of her overall commitment to Cuba (which now costs the USSR some $8 million a day),[3] as a luxury to be curtailed. There are historical precedents for Soviet changes in course with respect to third-world regimes with whom she has enjoyed close relations. In 1964–5, for instance, the USSR, facing internal economic problems, and having growing doubts about the tangible returns on her foreign assistance programmes, drastically curtailed the scale of her assistance to radical third-world regimes, and there are signs that her commitment to Cuba is at present less strong than it was in the mid-1970s. This may be one factor underlying recent Cuban interest in improved relations with the US.

Another reason to anticipate change in Cuban policy is Cuba's disillusionment with the USSR. This stems from two sources. The first is the inability, despite massive Soviet assistance, to resolve Cuban economic problems through industrialization and diversification away from sugar production. The second is the embarassment which the tight relationship with the USSR causes for Cuba in the Third World, particularly since the Soviet intervention in Afghanistan. The apparent desire for improved relations with the US and the more moderate states in the Caribbean Basin also favours restraint, but the significance of this factor depends to some extent on the Western response to Cuban initiatives. If Cuba meets with a steadfast US refusal to improve the bilateral relationship, she might reasonably conclude that there was nothing to be gained by restraint. The clear unwillingness of the present American Administration to contemplate any improvement in relations with Cuba goes far to explain her recent escalation of anti-American rhetoric and her less restrained support for Nicaragua's *Sandinistas*, particularly when this US hostility towards Cuba is coupled with intense military and covert pressure on Cuban allies in the region (viz. Nicaragua and Grenada).

Turning to the US, the failure to rescue the South Vietnamese regime in the spring of 1975 stemmed from a number of military, political and structural factors operating to constrain intervention, among them serious doubts among military about the merits of American involvement in limited wars in the Third World, the attempt by Congress to limit the Executive's discretion in foreign policy, and the distaste with which important sections of public opinion viewed the commitment of American forces in combat roles in the Third World. These all had significant repercussions on the Ford Administration's role in the Angolan conflict. Their continued strength is evident in constraints on the Reagan Administration's Central American policy.

It is clear that many in the Reagan Administration (among them former Secretary of State Haig, and former Under-Secretary of State Enders) have favoured a more substantial American involvement in El Salvador, but the lingering fear of entanglement by a large proportion of the American public, the refusal of many Congressmen and Senators to countenance any American commitment of troops in El Salvador, and the lack of substantial Pentagon support for expanding the US military role have severely circumscribed the Administration's capacity to pursue its favoured policy. Moreover, Congress has acted specifically to limit Executive discretion in its policy towards El Salvador and prohibit the involvement of American personnel in attempts to destabilize the *Sandinista* regime in Nicaragua. It has also severely circumscribed the Administration's capacity to become more closely involved in the Western Saharan conflict.

This would suggest that, while the United States' military capacity to project force throughout the Third World is growing, and is likely to continue to grow, there remain important domestic constraints on her ability to use this capacity. For this reason, it is difficult, despite the bellicose rhetoric from Washington, to envisage a significantly more interventionist American foreign policy in the Third World in general.

But do the instances of force projection in Lebanon and Grenada not suggest the contrary? In the case of the first US deployment in Lebanon, in spite of attendant risks, the objectives were clearly defined, their scope limited, and their substance almost universally accepted. Moreover, participation in combat was not envisaged; American forces were part of a broader multilateral effort, in which responsibility was shared with France and Italy; and American involvement was accepted by the various conflicting parties. The deployment was linked in the public mind with the peace process rather than the pursuit of specific American interests. For all these reasons, the initiative met with widespread approval and little opposition.

The second Lebanese deployment, despite its less clearly-defined objectives, scale and duration, was also multilateral, humanitarian in intent, and clearly linked to the peace process. As such, it too was initially relatively immune to liberal criticism. However, as American forces began to take the side of the Gemayel government against Syria and her Druse allies, domestic opposition grew and began to limit severely the Reagan Administration's freedom of action. More importantly, as American forces began to take significant casualties, and as their vulnerability to terrorist attack became increasingly evident, public pressure for withdrawal – particularly telling as elections approached – grew to the point where the Administration cut its losses, withdrawing the marine contingent in Beirut. This, too, underlines the significance of domestic constraints. The fact that the mission is generally perceived to have failed, and to have damaged US prestige in the region, suggests that the Lebanese experience is unlikely to serve as an encouragement for further force projection.

With regard to Grenada, it suffices to stress the uniqueness of the circumstances surrounding the intervention. Grenada is a minuscule country with a minuscule army incapable of mounting an effective resistance to a massively superior adversary. It lies, isolated, in a region which is overwhelmingly dominated by American conventional power, with little possibility of re-supply from, or, for forces opposing American action sanctuary in contiguous friendly countries. American intervention was supported by a significant number of neighbouring states. In such circumstances, it was possible for the United States to bring sufficient power to bear to present the American public and the world with a *fait accompli*. Moreover, she could do so with little risk of substantial political and diplomatic costs. The combination of these factors distinguishes Grenada in significant ways from other potential venues for American intervention, so there would seem to be little justification for generalizing from the Grenadan experience in assessing prospects for American intervention.

It has been suggested that one factor that might favour increasing recourse to intervention, not only by the US but also by other industrial powers, is a growing scarcity of raw materials and the concentration of remaining supplies in unstable parts of the Third World. The increasing sensitivity of Western economies to interruptions in the supply of oil and 'strategic minerals' might lead to intervention, either to prevent changes in regimes which might make interruption likely or to terminate such interruptions where they occur. While this prospect is not entirely beyond the realm of possibility – particularly in the longer term, when competition for access to a shrinking global resource base may grow increasingly intense – the line of argument is questionable on empirical grounds with respect to both consumer and supplier behaviour.

Firstly, the one major interruption in the supply of an essential commodity in the past decade – the 1973 oil embargo – did not result in intervention. Instead, it brought rationing as an immediate response. In the longer term, it brought an attempt by a number of those countries most dependent on Arab oil to distance themselves from Israel and from American policy in the Middle East and to improve their relations with major producers. It also resulted in a sustained effort by a number of major consumers to stockpile oil in sufficient quantities to ensure that short-lived interruptions would not result in serious dislocation and to reach agreements on the sharing of supplies in a crisis. Those who could, supplemented this with accelerated development of domestic petroleum reserves. The combination of the oil embargo and higher prices also favoured a diversification away from dependence on oil as the principal source of energy.

Secondly, this kind of argument suggests that security of access is jeopardized by the accession to power of radical regimes. This has been argued with respect to both the Middle East and Southern Africa. However, it ignores the facts that moderate Arab regimes were prominent in the oil embargo (and hence that moderation is no guarantee of access) and that left-wing or radical regimes are on the whole as eager to sell their goods in international commerce as moderate or right-wing ones.[4] The Angolan case illustrates the latter point. The MPLA government has eagerly sought the participation of foreign firms in the development of the Angolan economy, and its relations with corporate investors have been exemplary. The same is true on the whole of Gaddafi's Libya. In essence, for third-world states, radical or moderate, which seek to improve their lot, there is at present and for the foreseeable future no alternative to participation in the international capitalist economy. On the whole, therefore, the ideological complexion of a regime has little to do with the security or otherwise of access to raw materials. The frequency with which it is argued that such a connection does exist leads one to the conclusion that what is at issue here is not so much the question of access to resources as a visceral distrust of, and aversion to, leftist governments. It is perhaps not surprising that such arguments are particularly common in conservative and South African literature.

Third, it is as well to remember that oil in 1973 was an exceptional commodity in the degree to which production was concentrated, in the comparative cultural homogeneity of key producers, in the vulnerability of consumers to sudden interruptions of supply (given the importance of energy in most economic activity), and in the costs associated with attempts to convert quickly to other sources of energy. It was thus in many respects an ideal area for cartelization or the manipulation of access for political reasons. By contrast, most resources for which Western economies are dependent on third-world suppliers (such as copper, bauxite, iron ore, tin, etc.) are far less concentrated, far less central to economic activity, and far more easily and cheaply substitutable. It is for these reasons that the copper and bauxite producers, for instance, have had so little success in trying to form an effective cartel. It is for the same reasons that intervention to secure access to the broader range of third-world resources is improbable.

The exceptions, as has been argued *ad nauseam*, are the 'strategic minerals': chromium, platinum, vanadium, titanium and, to a lesser extent, manganese. These are essential in defence and high-technology industries, difficult to substitute, and their sources of supply are highly concentrated geographically, in southern Africa in particular. Here, however, stockpiling and the sharing of supplies are both feasible and considerably less risky than intervention.

Apart from the superpowers, the only major industrial power to have pursued a substantial policy of intervention in the past decade has been France. There are good reasons in this case too for expecting a reduced incidence of intervention. In the first place, whereas the bulk of France's interventions in Africa in the 1960s and 1970s were on balance successful, that in Chad was inconclusive, costly, embarrassing and damaging to French credibility. Such an experience may well lead France to give much more careful consideration to the potential hazards of involvement in internal wars in future. The Chad affair also awakened French public opinion to the perils of France's policy of intervention, strengthening the domestic political constraint on such activities. Moreover, the present socialist government may, in principle, be less prone to the use of force as an instrument of French foreign policy in Africa, and appeared initially to favour multilateral African solutions rather than unilateral French ones.

However, recent French behaviour in Chad demonstrates how difficult it is for *any* French government to resist appeals for assistance from client or allied regimes in Francophone Africa, particularly when these governments face *external* challenges. Failure to act in such circumstances calls French credibility – and the utility of close ties with France – into question and, moreover, violates France's self-image as the benevolent protector of her former colonies, which has important domestic political consequences. As suggested earlier, a left-wing government, concerned to show its determination to defend the national interest and fulfil the nation's mission, may be particularly susceptible to such pressures.

All this would suggest that the present French government may be more reluctant than its predecessors to use force, and more likely to search out alternatives, but that when the chips are down and the stakes sufficiently high it will fall into the more or less traditional pattern of French behaviour towards Francophone Africa. This is particularly true when the threat is commonly perceived to be external rather than internal.

In addition to these factors specific to intervening states, there are two characteristics of the present international system which are likely to discourage intervention. The first is ideological. One of the most significant problems for Libya in Chad and the USSR in Afghanistan was the intensely nationalistic response which their presence provoked and which redounded to the advantage of their clients' adversaries. Nationalism in the Third World is by no means new, but its potential impact on the prospects for successful intervention has clearly not been fully appreciated by a number of the interveners discussed in this Paper, including the USSR. As its significance is more fully digested, this too should operate in a general sense to discourage intervention.

The second factor is more practical. At several points in this Paper, it has been noted that the past decade has seen a massive proliferation of conventional armaments throughout the Third World. Access by both government and non-state actors to large quantities of quite sophisticated weapons makes internal conflicts far less susceptible to external control than was the case when interveners were dealing with essentially unarmed populations and under-armed local military establishments.

All of these factors suggest that the next decade is likely to be one in which military interference in internal conflicts will be rarer than it has been in the recent past. Nonetheless, two caveats must be entered. First of all, the basic permissive conditions of intervention stressed in Chapter I – the lack of political and social integration in target states and their consequent internal instability and conflict – are likely to remain endemic throughout much of the Third World, and the participants in these conflicts will continue to seek external assistance. Responses to such requests, however limited, will continue to engender commitments, and situations of crisis in which these commitments must either be forsaken or considerably broadened will continue to arise. None of this has changed or will change in the near future. But the structure of motivation and constraint affecting interveners has changed, and in such a way as to reduce the probability that those external actors considered above will opt for intervention in such situations.

The second qualification is that this particular analysis has so far ignored one category of intervener that has figured prominently elsewhere in this Paper, that of third-world states intervening in the affairs of their neighbours. There is every reason to assume that this form of intervention will persist and increase as regional actors continue to enhance their military capabilities. This is primarily because the character of post-colonial regional balances remains illdefined, and many countries continue to entertain ethnic, territorial and hegemonic aspirations that can be realized only by force and at the expense of other regional actors. In addition, regimes are likely to persist in trying to divert attention away from intractable internal problems and endeavouring to build a national consciousness by pursuing an active and forward foreign policy.

The stabilization of regional politics is likely to be achieved through a protracted process of role definition, with individual states testing and probing their neighbours, asserting themselves and resisting the assertions of others. Part of this process will be the attempt to influence political developments in neighbouring states by military and other means. Intervention has for many years been primarily a third-world phenomenon in terms of targets. To an increasing degree, it is likely to become so in terms of actors as well.

Notes

Introduction
1 For a balanced account of the expansion in Soviet force projection capabilities, see R. Menon, 'Military Power, Intervention, and Soviet Policy in the Third World', in R. Kanet (ed.), *Soviet Foreign Policy in the 1980s*, (New York: Praeger, 1982).
2 See J. Rosenau, 'Intervention as a Scientific Concept', *Journal of Conflict Resolution*, xiii, 2 (1969), p. 153.
3 For formal manifestations of such views, see 'Declaration on the Inadmissibility of Intervention' (United Nations General Assembly Resolution 2131–XX, 1965) and the 'Declaration on Friendly Relations' (United Nations General Assembly Resolution 2625–XXV, 1970).

4 In the case of Angola, see J. Marcum, *The Angolan Revolution, Vol. 2, Exile Politics and Guerrilla Warfare* (Cambridge, Mass: MIT Press, 1978); C. Ebinger, 'External Intervention in Internal War: the Politics and Diplomacy of the Angolan Civil War', *Orbis*, xx, 3 (1976); and R. Hallett, 'The South African Intervention in Angola, 1975–1976', *African Affairs*, lxxvii, 308 (1978), pp. 347–86. For Ethiopia, see C. Legum and W. Lee, *Conflict in the Horn of Africa* (London: Rex Collings, 1977); T. Farer, *War Clouds on the Horn of Africa: A Crisis for Detente* (New York: Carnegie Endowment, 1976). For Chad, see R. Lemarchand, 'Chad: The Roots of Chaos', *Current History*, lxxx (1981); V. Thompson and R. Adloff *Conflict in Chad* (London: Hurst, 1981). For Afghanistan, see H. Negaran, 'The Afghan Coup of April 1978: Revolution and International Security', *Orbis*, xxiii, 1 (1979); Z. Khalilzad, 'The Struggle for Afghanistan', *Survey*, xxv, 2 (1980); J. Valenta, 'The Soviet Invasion of Afghanistan: The Difficulty of Knowing Where to Stop', *Orbis*, xxiv, 2 (1980).

I. The sources of military intervention
1 R. Pelissier, 'Angola: Physical and Social Geography', in *Africa South of the Sahara* (London: Europa, 1982) p. 135.
2 Cf. Marcum (*op. cit.* in Introduction, note 4), *passim*.
3 J. Marcum, 'Angola', in G. Carter and P. O'Meara (eds), *Southern Africa: the Continuing Crisis* (Bloomington: Indiana UP, 1979), p. 194.
4 For extensive discussion of the ethnic and religious composition of Chad's population, see S. Decalo, *A Historical Dictionary of Chad* (London: Scarecrow Press, 1977).
5 S. Decalo, 'Chad: The Roots of Centre-Periphery Strife', *African Affairs*, lxxix, 317 (1980), p. 500.
6 See E. Keller, 'Ethiopia: Revolution, Class and the National Question', *African Affairs*, lxxx, 321 (1981), pp. 524–9; P. Gilkes, *The Dying Lion: Feudalism and Modernization in Ethiopia* (New York: St. Martin's, 1975); D. and M. Ottaway, *Ethiopia: Empire in Revolution* (New York: Africana, 1978); Farer (*op. cit.* in Introduction, note 4).
7 See P. Baxter, 'Ethiopia's Unacknowledged Problem: the Oromo', *African Affairs*, lxxvii, 308 (1978), pp. 283–96.
8 M. Ottaway, 'Social Classes and Corporate Interests in the Ethiopian Revolution', *Journal of Modern African Studies* xiv, 3, (1976), pp. 471–2.
9 Keller, (*op. cit.* in note 6), pp. 543–4; R. Love, 'Economic Change in Pre-revolutionary Ethiopia', *African Affairs*, lxxix, 312 (1979).
10 The Ottaways estimate that in 1973–4 more than 100,000 people died in the famine. See D. and M. Ottaway, *Afro-Communism* (London: Africana, 1981), p. 151.
11 G. Chaliand, *The Times*, 15 June 1980. For further information on Afghan ethnicity, see E. Naby, 'The Ethnic Factor in Soviet-Afghan Relations', *Asian Survey*, xx, 3 (1980), pp. 239–52.
12 P. Roger, *Le Monde*, 12 September 1980.
13 Chaliand (*op. cit.* in note 11). For an account of the reforms, see L. Dupree, 'Afghanistan under the Khalq', *Problems of Communism*, xxviii, 4 (1979), pp. 42–3.
14 On those points, see 'Crisis over Afghanistan', *Strategic Survey 1979*, (London: IISS, 1980), pp. 48–52; K. Wafadar, 'Afghanistan in 1981: The Struggle Intensifies', *Asian Survey*, xxii, 2 (1982), p. 148.
15 Speech of Gen. O. Obasanjo at the OAU Summit in Khartoum, 27 July 1978. Reprinted in *Survival*, xx, 6 (1978).
16 O. Young, 'Intervention and International Systems', *Journal of International Affairs*, xii, (1968), p. 183.
17 Hallett (*op. cit.* in Introduction, note 4), p. 363.

18 See *Al-Zahaf Al-Akhdar*, 26 December 1981, pp. 3–4.
19 On the Chinese factor in Soviet decision-making, see C. Legum, 'The Soviet Union, China, and the West in Southern Africa', *Foreign Affairs*, liv, 4 (1976), pp. 750–53; Ebinger (*op. cit.* in Introduction, note 4), pp. 686–8; J. Marcum, 'Lessons of Angola', *Foreign Affairs*, liv, 3 (1976), pp. 413–14.
20 See Brezhnev, cited in R. Kolkowicz, 'The Military and Soviet Foreign Policy', in Kanet (*op. cit.* in Introduction, note 1), p. 17; and A. Gromyko, cited in V. Aspaturian, 'Soviet Global Power and the Correlation of Forces', *Problems of Communism*, xxix, 3 (1980), p. 1.
21 *Keesing's Contemporary Archives* (1981), p. 31159.
22 L. Bowman, 'The Strategic Importance of South Africa to the United States: an Appraisal and Policy Analysis', *African Affairs*, lxxxi, 323 (1982), pp. 161–5.
23 Hallett (*op. cit.* in Introduction, note 4), p. 349.
24 On this point, see Z. Khalilzad, 'Soviet-Occupied Afghanistan', *Problems of Communism*, xxix, 6 (1980), pp. 29–30.
25 On the prominence of the military instrument in Soviet foreign policy, see S. Bialer, *Stalin's Successors*, (Cambridge: Cambridge UP, 1980), p. 264. See also W. Zartmann, 'The USSR in the Third World', *Problems of Communism*, xxxi, 5 (1982), pp. 76–80. On the military role in Soviet policy-making, see Kolkowicz (*op. cit.* in note 20), p. 31.
26 Young (*op. cit.* in note 16), p. 183; Rosenau (*op. cit.* in Introduction, note 2), p. 168.
27 Young (*op. cit.* in note 16), p. 180.
28 Rosenau (*op. cit.* in Introduction, note 2), p. 168.
29 With reference to Afghanistan and to the possible development of the Iranian Revolution, Rubinstein notes what he believes to be a Soviet propensity to intervene in order to institutionalize Communist rule in situations where leftist allies in contiguous countries are threatened with 'destabilization and counter-revolution' (A. Rubinstein 'Afghanistan: Embraced by the Bear', *Orbis*, xxvi, 1 (1982), p. 151).
30 Young (*op. cit.* in Introduction, note 2,), p. 181.
31 John Stremlau, *The International Politics of the Nigerian Civil War* (Princeton: Princeton UP 1979), p. 80.
32 A. Yarmolinsky, 'American Foreign Policy and the Decision to Intervene', *Journal of International Affairs*, xxii (1968), p. 233. See also K. Waltz, 'A Strategy for the Rapid Deployment Force', *International Security* V (1981), no. 4, pp.49–72.
33 Menon (*op. cit.* in Introduction, note 1), pp. 268–72.
34 B. Nahaylo, "Bring Our Boys Home' – but is Andropov ready to listen yet?', *The Times* (London), 27 June 1982, p. 12.
35 W. Friedmann, 'Intervention and International Law', in L. Jaquet (ed.), *Intervention in International Politics*, (The Hague: Netherlands Institute of International Affairs, 1971), pp. 40, 62.
36 See UN Resolution 2131–xx (1965); Resolution 2160–xxi (1966); and Resolution 2625–xxv (1970).
37 Friedmann, (*op. cit.* in note 35), p. 44.
38 See R. Higgins, 'Internal War and International Law', in C. Black and R. Falk (eds), *The Future of the International Legal Order* (Princeton: Princeton UP, 1971); J. Moore, *Law and Civil War in the Modern World* (Baltimore: Johns Hopkins UP, 1974); A. Cassese (ed.), *Current Problems of International Law* (Milan: Giuffré, 1975); A. Cassese (ed.), *The New Humanitarian Law of Armed Conflict*, (Naples: Editoriale Scientifica, 1975); N. Ronzitti, 'Wars of National Liberation – A Legal Definition', *Italian Yearbook of International Law*, (Naples: ditoriale Scientifica, 1975).
39 *Ibid.*, p. 193.

40 Friedmann (*op. cit.* in note 35), p. 41.
41 Ebinger (*op. cit.* in note 17), p. 688.
42 See D. Ottaway's articles in the *International Herald Tribune*, 18 April 1977, and the *Middle East Economic Digest*, 22 April 1977.
43 *Ibid.*
44 J. Valenta, 'From Prague to Kabul', *International Security*, v, 2 (1980), p. 116; Rubinstein (*op. cit.* in note 29), p. 144.
45 Valenta suggests that upon his return from a fact-finding mission to Kabul in October 1979, Gen. Pavlovskii gave Soviet leaders an extremely pessimistic account of the prospects for the PDP regime in the absence of decisive Soviet action (Valenta (*op. cit.* in note 44), p. 206).
46 J. Valenta (*op. cit.* in Introduction, note 4), p. 206. In this vein, some Soviet commentators have equated Amin with Anwar Sadat. See V. Sidenko, 'Neob'yavlennaya Voina protiv Afganistana', *Pravda*, 5 February 1980.
47 R. Buitjenhuijs, 'Le FROLINAT, la Libye et la France: there is some system in their madness', provisional paper presented at a summer 1982 conference at the School of Oriental and African Studies, University of London.

II. Outcomes of intervention

1 J. Regan Kerney, 'FNLA is still fighting a forgotten war in Angola', *International Herald Tribune*, 24–25 December 1981.
2 C. Legum, 'International Rivalries in the Southern African Conflict', in Carter and O'Meara (*op. cit.* in Ch. I, note 3), pp. 4–5; O. Ogunbadejo, 'Angola: Ideology and Pragmatism in Foreign Policy', *International Affairs*, lvii, 2 (1981), p. 267.
3 G. Bender, 'Angola: Left, Right, and Wrong', *Foreign Policy*, 43 (1981), pp. 66–7; Ogunbadejo (*op. cit.* in note 2), p. 259.
4 Estimates of the present Cuban deployment range as high as 16,500. M. Robbins, 'The Soviet-Cuban Relationship', in Kanet (*op. cit.* in Introduction, note 1), p. 164.
5 P. Henze, 'Communism and Ethiopia', *Problems of Communism*, xxx, 3 (1981), pp. 63–4.
6 D. and M. Ottaway (*op. cit.* in Ch. 1, note 10), pp. 182, 183.
7 *The Economist*, 27 November-3 December 1982, p. 53, estimates Libyan dead at more than 1,000. 'Matchet's Diary' in *West Africa*, 6 December 1982, cites Tunisian sources which claim Libyan losses of 5,000.
8 M. Beloff, 'Reflections on Intervention', *Journal of International Affairs*, xxii (1968), p. 204.
9 Rosenau (*op. cit.* in Introduction, note 2), p. 151.
10 In 1972–3 South Africa's defence expenditure was 335,336,000 Rand (11.8% of state expenditure, and 2.1% of GNP); 1979–80, figures were 1,964,800,000 Rand (16.6% and 4.5%). *South African Yearbook, 1980–81* (Johannesburg: Dept. of Information, n.d.), p. 286.
11 *The Military Balance 1981–1982* (London: IISS, 1981), p. 63; J. de Onis, *International Herald Tribune*, 16 January 1981. It is unclear just how much of this projected increase has actually been spent, given Nigeria's current revenue problems. The increase is substantially above Nigeria's rate of inflation.
12 *World Military Expenditure and Arms Transfers, 1970–1974*, (Washington DC: ACDA, 1982). Figures are in 1978 constant dollars.
13 *The Military Balance 1979–1980* (London: IISS, 1979), p. 70; *(1980–81)*, p. 73; *(1981–82)*, p. 86; *(1982–83)*, p. 91.
14 These figures are drawn from a 1981 UNHCR report entitled *Study on Human Rights and Massive Exoduses* E/CN.4/1503 (New York: UN Economic and Social Council, 1981), Annexes I and II.
15 The cost to the Pakistan Government of assistance to Afghan refugees was estimated by Islamabad to be $160 million in 1981 (*Ibid.*, Annex II, p. 7).

16 *Ibid.*, p. 12.
17 Khalilzad (*op. cit.* in Ch. I, note 24), p. 30.
18 Samuel Huntington, in a recent article, goes so far as to argue that political stability 'can be most meaningfully conceived of in terms of historical patterns of change peculiar to individual societies'. S. Huntington, 'Remarks on the Meaning of Stability in the Modern Era', in S. Bialer, *Radicalism in the Contemporary Age*, Volume 3, (Boulder, Colo.: Westview, 1977), p. 282.
19 Waltz (*op. cit.* in Ch. I, note 32), p. 55.
20 With reference to the effect of American involvement on the legitimacy of the Saigon regime, see M. Walzer, *Just and Unjust Wars* (New York: Basic Books, 1977), p. 100.

III. The regulation of intervention
1 H. Kissinger, 'The Implications of Angola for Future US Foreign Policy', *Department of State Bulletin* lxxiv, 1912 (1976), p. 178.
2 L. Silverman, 'Third World Conflict and East–West Rivalry', paper presented at the Arms Control Association/IISS Conference on *The Utility of Force in International Security* at Bellagio, Italy, in July 1982, p. 23.
3 J. Stockwell, *In Search of Enemies* (New York: Norton, 1978), pp. 45–6.
4 Z. Cervenka, 'OAU's Year of Disunity', *Africa Contemporary Record, 1977–78 (New York: Africana, 1978), pp. A62–A63.
5 Linda Miller pointed to similar problems in 'Regional Organization and the Regulation of Internal Conflict', *World Politics*, xix (1967), pp. 590–91.
6 *Weekly Review* (Nairobi), 19 November 1982.

IV. Conclusion and prospects
1 Shahram Chubin has noted that the single most destabilizing factor in Persian Gulf regional security is the process of modernization. See S. Chubin, 'Gains for Soviet Policy in the Middle East', *International Security*, vi, 6 (1982), p. 123.
2 Seweryn Bialer has noted that Soviet experts have expressed considerable scepticism with respect to the degree of control which the USSR could exercise in these two countries and about the length of time which even this limited influence could be expected to last. Bialer (*op. cit.* in Ch. I, note 25), p. 229.
3 Robbins (*op. cit.* in Ch. II, note 4), p. 163.
4 On this point and Libya's and Iraq's violation of the 1973 oil embargo, see Waltz (*op. cit.* in Ch. I, note 32), p. 55.

11 Humanitarian Action in War
Aid, Protection and Impartiality in a Policy Vacuum

Adelphi Paper 305, 1996

Adam Roberts

Introduction

Humanitarian action as a response to war, and to violent crises within states, has been tried in the 1990s as never before. It would be easy to dismiss these efforts as failures. In Somalia, an international humanitarian involvement ended in 1995 in humiliating retreat. In Bosnia, the United Nations (UN) emphasis on humanitarian responses was mired in controversy and largely discredited by the fall of Srebrenica in 1995, which led to a significant change of Western policy. In Liberia, humanitarian agencies decided in June 1996 not to renew major operations because extensive looting resulted in their activities contributing to the war economy. The northern Iraq 'safe haven' concept was left in tatters by military actions there in September and October 1996. In Rwanda and Zaire, the record of the international community in protecting victims of genocide in 1994, and refugees in camps in 1996, has been pitiful. The litany of setbacks encompasses other conflicts, including those in the former Soviet Union.

The pendulum that swung so far towards humanitarian action in the first half of the 1990s has since then been moving in the opposite direction: such action has been in decline since a peak around 1993. Many countries are showing signs of reluctance to become deeply involved in war-torn countries and regions, even in a humanitarian role. Yet the demand for action continues. Operations are still launched, as in Zaire in November 1996. There remains an urgent need to appreciate what humanitarian action can and cannot achieve. The key issue is not whether there is a place for humanitarian action in international politics, but what that place is, and what forms such action can usefully take.

The humanitarian action that became a major part of the international community's response to the wars, civil wars and other crises of the 1990s took many forms – provision of food and shelter for refugees; airlifts of supplies to besieged populations; proclamations of 'safe areas'; attempts to ensure implementation of the laws of war; monitoring of detention conditions; the use of outside armed forces for 'humanitarian intervention' in situations of chaos, warlordism, massive atrocities and tyrannical government;

mine-clearance; and post-war (even sometimes intra-war) reconstruction. Non-governmental organisations (NGOs), governments, and international bodies (especially the UN) have been deeply involved in such action.

The increase in humanitarian efforts in the 1990s contained many elements of idealism, not least a hope that it was part of a larger process whereby the sovereignty of states would take second place to the human rights of citizens. Yet governmental involvement in humanitarian action owed much to political considerations that were often tinged with an element of *realpolitik*. Most states – lacking a strong interest in the civil wars raging around the world and no longer seeing them as part of a global confrontation in which they had a stake – were nervous about any deep or enduring military involvement. They were also reluctant to accept more than a token number of refugees from these conflicts. Yet in an age of global communications the public in many democratic states demanded some positive action. All this contributed to pressures for humanitarian action on a multilateral basis, and in particular for action to assist and protect people in their own country before they became refugees, as well as to assist the repatriation of those who had left. It required new forms of humanitarian action, such as establishing safe areas and protecting aid convoys, which required a significant military role.

Yet the question of defining exactly what the military role should be and how great a commitment it required proved to be difficult and controversial. There was and remains wide agreement among governments, many non-governmental aid organisations and international agencies that external armed forces can have legitimate roles in humanitarian action – for example in protecting the delivery of relief supplies, in providing security in refugee camps, and in enforcing ceasefires so that humanitarian organisations can perform their tasks. The idea that humanitarian organisations should always operate entirely independently of armed forces has had to be modified in many cases. However, there has been remarkably little serious thinking about military protection; and the record of outside military involvement supporting humanitarian action is full of instances of vacillation and retreat, poor coordination, a reluctance to make serious commitments and take serious risks, and achieving at best only temporary results.

Overall, the experience of humanitarian action in wars has raised many difficult questions and exposed controversies concerning its purposes, effects, modes of operation, and legitimate boundaries. Does such action save lives, or prolong wars? Can it stop the killing as well as the dying? Does it imply reluctant acceptance of forcible population movements? What is the role of the military in humanitarian assistance, and does that role risk dragging states into distant conflicts? Is there a right of 'humanitarian intervention' by outside armed forces? Should safety zones be created in conflict-torn areas, and if so, how should they be protected? Does participation in humanitarian assistance by peacekeeping forces blur their impartiality and expose them to danger? Do NGOs risk losing their autonomy or impartiality when they are part of a large coordinated international response? Has the increased emphasis of governments on humanitarian action been an abdication from serious policy-making?

There is a dearth of, and a need for, objective and intellectually tough case-by-case evaluations of humanitarian action tackling questions such as these. This paper, no substitute for such studies, is a contribution towards the broader reappraisal of this subject. It reflects a dissatisfaction with that intellectual tradition (of which many soldiers, policy-makers and humanitarian workers have been part) that sees humanitarian action and tough power-political or interest-based calculation as complete opposites, and seeks to show some of the numerous points of intersection between these two approaches.

The fact remains that alongside the growth of humanitarian action there has been a policy vacuum. Major powers and international organisations have lacked long-term policies addressing the substantive issues raised by the conflicts of the 1990s. This vacuum increases the demand for humanitarian responses but reduces their effectiveness.

The central argument of this paper is that a failure to develop serious policies regarding the security of humanitarian action, and of affected peoples and areas, has been the principal cause of the setbacks of humanitarian action in the 1990s. Such security issues, the inherent difficulties of which are undeniable, have been handled repeatedly in a short-term and half-hearted manner, often with elements of dishonesty and buck-passing. A particular difficulty in discussing the question of protection is that, in some legal parlance which is reflected in that of many aid organisations, 'protection' refers not to the provision of physical security, but to efforts (for example, by Red Cross personnel) to establish and maintain a special legal status for protected persons, such as civilians and prisoners of war (POWs). Constructive thinking about security is also not assisted by the tradition, in itself honourable, of associating humanitarian action with impartiality and neutrality: sometimes the provision of security may necessitate departures from these principles. The leading Western powers, which are the ones that have been principally involved in humanitarian action, have a particular obligation to develop coherent and defensible policies regarding humanitarian crises, which will not disappear just because responding to them has created difficulties.

I. The changing context of humanitarian action

The types of disaster that led to a growth in humanitarian action since the mid-1970s are not new. War, civil war, dictatorship, earthquake, famine and refugee flows have been familiar phenomena throughout recorded history. In the past, they rarely led to large-scale international efforts such as in the early 1990s. Clearly there were some new factors at work.

The 'complex emergencies' of the 1990s

One necessary condition for increased attention to humanitarian issues is the existence of disasters, especially those leading to the displacement of large numbers of people. There were many such disasters in the 1970s and 1980s, and even more in the post-Cold War world. Several totally different types of disaster have been involved:

- war (often involving civil war, general collapse of state institutions, and/or massive population displacement);
- dictatorial government (especially when in a virtual state of war with part of its own population);
- massive economic disruption and unemployment; and
- natural disasters.

The practice of states cooperating in response to some types of disaster – especially natural disasters such as earthquakes, floods and famines – is of long standing, and shows that states can sometimes take humanitarian action that is of a more or less disinterested nature, and do so effectively. In addition, man-made technological disasters, such as those at Bhopal in 1984 and Chernobyl in 1986, show the need for international humanitarian assistance. In these cases, the expertise and resources required for effective countermeasures may only be available internationally.

Wars, however, present a more complex problem. They have been the main cause of most humanitarian disasters in the 1990s, including in Afghanistan, northern Iraq, Rwanda, Somalia, southern Sudan, former Yugoslavia and some of the successor states of the former Soviet Union. In these and many other wars there has been extensive humanitarian action by states, international institutions and NGOs. The belligerent forces have often been prepared to accept humanitarian assistance from outside, or at least have been vulnerable to pressure to do so.

Most post-Cold War conflicts have been civil wars; indeed, a high proportion of wars since 1945 have been internationalised civil wars. The civil war aspect presents some especially difficult problems for international intervention of any kind, including humanitarian action. Civil wars are notoriously bitter and difficult to control. Some of the conflicts of the 1990s, including in Burundi, Liberia, Sierra Leone and former Yugoslavia, have been characterised by a pattern of assaults on defenceless civilians and an avoidance of direct combat between adversary forces. The blurring of distinctions between combatants and civilians creates special difficulties for humanitarian action.

The term 'complex emergencies' is increasingly used to describe those humanitarian disasters of the 1990s that involve internal conflict and have elicited a multi-faceted international response. As an official United States' government publication has stated:

Complex emergencies combine internal conflicts with large-scale displacements of people, mass famine, and fragile or failing economic, political, and social institutions. Some complex emergencies are exacerbated by natural disasters and severely inadequate transport networks.[1]

The use of the term 'complex emergencies' and various synonyms ('complex crises', 'complex humanitarian disasters') does usefully describe a reality of the late twentieth century, but is also open to objection. Giving a new label to old problems does not make them any easier to solve. The term fits, perhaps too easily, the ambition of some within the UN system to tackle simultaneously and in a coordinated manner different military, political and humanitarian roles – restoring peace, assisting refugees and war victims, encouraging respect for human rights and promoting socio-economic development. Whether this is really possible is doubtful. War is the violent expression of a complex set of opposing interests and aspirations. While it may be true that complicated questions rarely have simple answers, one cannot conclude that multi-faceted answers – as the term 'complex emergencies' often implies – are necessarily right.

While this concept always implies the existence of conflict, it may not be the result of war in any simple or classical sense. Dictatorial governments acting within their own territory have been another cause of humanitarian crises. Repressive action by government may occur in the aftermath of war, as in Cambodia in the late 1970s and Iraq in the 1990s, but sometimes, as in Haiti in 1991–94, it occurs in the absence of open war. When the problem is essentially one of an over-powerful government, humanitarian agencies often find it particularly difficult to act within the country concerned, and the UN Security Council has frequently been unable to take action. The responses and non-responses of the international community to the crises in Cambodia during the years of the Khmer Rouge regime (1975–79) and in Myanmar (Burma) in more recent years illustrate some of the limitations and difficulties of humanitarian action in facing extreme dictatorship.

More refugees, less asylum

The steady increase of refugee flows since the mid-1970s, and of the annual expenditure for this by the UN High Commissioner for Refugees (UNHCR), is shown in Table 1.

Refugee flows involve core issues in national and international politics. They can affect the stability of the states of origin and of resettlement, and they can constitute a trigger, or excuse, for military intervention. As Gil Loescher wrote in a 1992 study on the implications of refugee movements for international security:

> ... it is no longer sufficient to discuss the subject of refugees within a narrow national context or as a strictly humanitarian problem requiring

Table 1 Refugee numbers, and UNHCR expenditures, from 1975[2]

Year	Refugees (millions)	UNHCR Expenditure (US$ millions)
1975	2.4	69.0
1977	2.8	111.4
1979	4.6	269.9
1981	8.2	474.2
1983	10.4	397.6
1985	10.5	457.8
1987	12.4	460.3
1989	14.8	570.3
1991	17.2	862.5
1993	18.2	1,307.0
1995	14.5	1,140.0

Notes: The figures for the number of refugees are for 1 January each year, and refer only to people who have crossed an international border and have been granted asylum in another state. The figures do not include Palestinians assisted by the UN Relief and Works Agency for Palestine Refugees in the Near East (UNRWA), who numbered 2.8 million in 1995.

From 1993 onwards, the refugee figures could be supplemented by an additional category, 'other persons of concern to UNHCR'. These were as follows in 1995: internally displaced people, who have fled for similar reasons as refugees but have not crossed into another country (5.4 million), certain former refugees who have returned to their own homeland (4.0m), and war-affected populations and other groups benefiting from UNHCR's protection and assistance activities (3.5m). If these are added to the 1995 figure, the total is 27.4m.[3]

humanitarian solutions. Too often refugees are perceived as a matter for international charity organisations, and not as a political and security problem.[4]

Loescher advocated that Western governments, particularly West European states, should 'expand existing immigration programmes, guest worker agreements and migration quotas to relieve pressures on already overburdened asylum systems'.[5] This has not happened. The increase in refugee flows has coincided with a growing reluctance of states to grant asylum. In the past, many states recognised an obligation, derived from their own experiences and buttressed by international agreements, to accept refugees. Western states also had a political-strategic interest in those refugees whose presence was proof of the failures of communist systems. In the 1990s, states have not generally reacted to crises, as they often did in the past, by accepting large numbers of refugees. This fateful change in attitudes has had important consequences.

Wars and civil wars have been the main causes of increased refugee flows. The International Committee of the Red Cross (ICRC) has gone to extremes, stating that 'with the exception of displacements caused by natural or technological disasters, the prevention of population movements corresponds essentially to the prevention of armed conflict and the prevention of abuses during armed conflict'.[6] While this statement neglects the catastrophes caused by dictatorial government, it does indicate the key role of war, and the importance of preventing war if refugee flows are to be reduced. Yet there is a reluctance on the part of states to extend the formal definition of 'refugee' to encompass those fleeing from war, anarchy, destitution and famine, as distinct from persecution. There is also a tendency not to view the 'internally displaced' – those whose flight does not involve crossing international borders – as refugees entitled to asylum.

The work of UNHCR has had to adjust to changes in the character of refugee flows and the attitudes of states towards them. In accordance with its statute, UNHCR was traditionally involved mainly in assisting refugees who had left their own countries. Over the years, in response to a series of practical imperatives, UNHCR has come to concern itself substantially with internally displaced persons; and with temporary arrangements for refugees pending their return to their homes. UNHCR and other bodies are under increasing pressure to help prevent huge influxes to other countries, to try to feed and protect threatened people in or near their own countries, and to get those who have fled to return home.[7]

The hardening of attitudes towards refugee influxes has important political and military consequences. It causes feelings of guilt, especially in countries with traditionally liberal immigration policies, and strengthens the desire to take some other form of action, including financing assistance work; it also contributes to political pressure to tackle refugee issues in or near the country of origin, for example by creating safe areas and semi-permanent camps.

Large numbers of refugees kept in camps just outside their own country can help perpetuate old conflicts and even trigger new ones. They are more likely to take military action against the regime that has caused them to flee than are those who settle into the life of another society, especially if far from the conflict. Also, such concentrations of refugees may be perceived locally as a threat, particularly if there is an armed and activist political/military leadership among them, as in the cases of the Palestinian guerrilla movements in Jordan in 1970, and Interahamwe militias among the Hutu refugees in Zaire in 1994–96. All this potential for conflict has two major consequences. First, the maintenance of security in refugee camps is a serious issue with broad policy ramifications. Second, the return of refugees to their country of origin becomes a key regional and international interest, which is likely to be reflected in the terms of peace treaties and in other pressure to go home, whether or not it is safe to do so.

Attempting to tackle crises leading to human displacement at or near the source involves, or at least should involve, addressing the question of the security of vulnerable populations, whether in their own country or in emergency camps abroad. This question was not so difficult in an earlier era when most refugees settled within a foreign country and were protected by its legal and governmental system. In the crises of the 1990s there have been many *ad hoc* answers to this problem, often devised or implemented under UN auspices. Some of these answers have proved unsatisfactory.

Changes in UN security council practice

In the 1990s, the increased willingness of UN Security Council (UNSC) members to agree on common approaches, at least when not excessively burdensome, contributed to bringing humanitarian action to the fore of international politics. A small but significant measure of the increased capacity for agreement on the Security Council since the end of the Cold War is the number of resolutions passed. From 1945 to 1988 the average number of resolutions passed each year was about 15, and of vetoes cast, about five. Subsequent figures are given in Table 2.

Numerous Security Council resolutions since 1989 have addressed humanitarian issues arising from armed conflicts. Indeed, the word 'humanitarian' occurred with unprecedented frequency in the resolutions of 1990–95. On this basis, many actions by peacekeeping and other bodies operating under Security Council resolutions have been directly concerned with humanitarian efforts during or in the immediate aftermath of war.

One reason for the UNSC's astonishing attention to humanitarian issues is that, in a 15-member body, it is easier to reach agreement on the lowest common denominator of humanitarianism than on more partisan or risky policies. When dealing with complex conflicts and civil wars, it may be genuinely difficult to reach a decision on a definite political line, such as supporting one side or imposing a settlement by force; it is much easier to arrive at international agreement on more modest and apparently less risky action, aimed not at the use of force but rather at the alleviation of suffering combined with efforts to induce the parties to reach a settlement. Within the framework of a large multilateral institution such as the UN there is an inevitable tendency to respond to crises by operating in humanitarian mode.

Yet there is a sting in the tail of the Security Council's preoccupation with humanitarian issues. In the end, humanitarian policies often lead to deeper involvement. It is inherently difficult for major powers to proclaim humanitarian principles and policies in relation to a conflict, and then do nothing to protect the victims and/or punish their tormentors when atrocities occur. Thus an initial humanitarian involvement can lead to a more military one – a

Table 2 UN Security Council resolutions passed, and vetoed, 1990–95

Year	Resolutions passed	vetoed	Subject of vetoed resolutions
1990	37	2 (US)	Panama; Israeli-occupied territories
1991	42	0	
1992	74	0	
1993	93	1 (Russia)	Peacekeeping costs in Cyprus
1994	77	1 (Russia)	Former Yugoslavia
1995	66	1 (US)	Israeli-occupied territories

process involving awkward changes of direction. Further, it is inherently difficult to preach humanitarianism in one crisis and then not do so in the next, however unpromising the situation and however slim the interests of outside powers. These 'ratchet' effects of humanitarian policies in the Security Council have, for better or for worse, brought humanitarianism and strategy into a curious and fateful union.

There have been many remarkable innovations in the Security Council's practice in this area. New ground has been broken, and huge numbers of lives saved. However, this has been mixed with bitter experience. The UN's humanitarian approaches are frequently criticised. Initial hopes that the UN could be the central player in limiting and ending a wide range of conflicts have yielded to more modest appraisals.

Other factors contributing to humanitarian action

Other factors have contributed to the increase of humanitarian action.

- Extensive news coverage of wars and crises, especially on television, has led to strong public pressure on outside governments to act.
- There has been a hope that, regardless of political and national differences, humanitarian action could constitute a basis for united and effective responses to a wide range of crises, and could even point the way to a new order which transcends some of the limits of the system of sovereign states.
- Some peace agreements (e.g., in Mozambique and former Yugoslavia) have contained provisions to repatriate refugees and rebuild social and economic institutions – tasks which in many cases involve assistance from humanitarian organisations.

Some other factors may be involved. The very success of efforts to control the problem of international war may also have contributed to the growth of humanitarian action. Populations of secure states, who have little direct experience of war and who seem reluctant to wage war on someone else's behalf, may be particularly inclined to react to incomprehensible conflicts elsewhere by supporting impartial humanitarian efforts in the country concerned.

The increased emphasis on humanitarian action does appear to be mainly a Western phenomenon. As Minear and Weiss have observed:

> The concept of humanitarianism is most fully developed in the cultures and jurisprudence of Judeo-Christian nations. Reflecting those roots, the origin and constituencies of many of the better-known humanitarian organisations are Western . . . The dominant ideologies and styles of such agencies sometimes alienate non-Western countries and populations in which major disasters have occurred.[8]

In Western states, which provide the main sources of funding humanitarian action, social developments may also have played a part in its growth. As long ago as 1970, Ali Mazrui wrote:

> The growth of individualism in the West has curiously enough resulted both in reduced collective responsibility within the immediate society and increased capacity to empathise with man much further away, even in other lands altogether. The western individualist would be reluctant to contribute to the support of a distant cousin who finds himself in dire financial difficulties; and yet that same western individualist would be capable of rising to the occasion when news of a natural catastrophe in Pakistan or Chile reached him.[9]

Humanitarian budgets

The activities and budgets of the international agencies and NGOs concerned with humanitarian action in situations of war and internal conflict reached an unprecedentedly high level in the early 1990s. In many cases there was a peak in 1993, followed by a slight decline. The overall budget of UNHCR reached US $1,307m in 1993, dropping to $1,166m in 1994 and $1,140m in 1995. Similarly, the overall budget of ICRC increased from under 400m Swiss francs (SFr) in each of the years 1986–88 to SFr811m in 1993; since then it has declined to SFr749m in 1994, and SFr641m in 1995. To give an idea of the overall scale of humanitarian action at its height in 1993–94, a very rough indication of a few of the major international agencies' expenditures on emergency relief and rehabilitation is given in Table 3.

The overall global funding of emergency humanitarian assistance in 1994 has been estimated at US$7,200m, of which $1,200m came from private contributions. Virtually all the rest came from the Organisation for Economic Cooperation and Development (OECD) governments, as follows: US $1,700m, European Community Humanitarian Office (ECHO) $900m; all

Table 3 Expenditure of selected humanitarian agencies in 1993–94[10]

Organisation/Agency	Approx. expenditure for 1993 or 1994 (US$m)
Office of UNHCR	1,307
World Food Programme (WFP)	
– the food aid arm of the UN	1,200
European Community Humanitarian Office (ECHO)	900
International Committee of the Red Cross (ICRC)	519
International Federation of Red Cross and	
Red Crescent Societies (IFRC)	273
United Nations Children's Fund (UNICEF)	138
Oxfam UK and Ireland	115
UN Department of Humanitarian Affairs (DHA)	72

other OECD governments $3,400m – the nine largest donors (in order of the size of their contributions) being Germany, Sweden, the Netherlands, the UK, Canada, Norway, Austria, France and Italy. In 1995, the figures may have levelled off or even declined, suggesting an element of 'donor fatigue'.[11]

Governments have channelled a large proportion of their contributions to humanitarian assistance through international agencies such as UNHCR, as well as significant amounts through NGOs. Oxfam UK and Ireland is a case in point: of its overall budget of £103m (its highest ever) in 1994–95, £15m came from the UK government and £7m from the European Commission.[12] In yet other cases, governments have practically created NGOs (sometimes called GONGOs, or governmentally organised NGOs) to assist in one or another humanitarian project. For the most part, the tendency to act through non-governmental bodies reflects a respect for their expertise – a recognition that humanitarian assistance does properly have a large element of international and people-to-people contact – and perhaps also an anxiety not to attach the donor government's reputation too directly to actions which may go terribly wrong.

II. Humanitarian intervention

Whether or not humanitarian intervention is a legal right has been discussed for centuries by international lawyers. This issue has been revived in the 1990s in international diplomacy but with some new and unexpected elements. It has become a central issue in contemporary debates on the role of humanitarian action in international relations. American writers, often keen to see the old-fashioned and reprehensible international system transformed, have seen the UN-based interventionism of the 1990s as potentially creating part of a new international order.[1] British writers have generally been more cautious.[2]

'Humanitarian intervention', in its classical sense, may be defined as military intervention in a state without the approval of its authorities, and with the purpose of preventing widespread suffering or death among the inhabitants.[3] Confusingly, the term has come to be used with a much broader and less precise meaning – major humanitarian action in an emergency situation, not necessarily involving use of armed force, and not necessarily against the will of the government. Some writers have used it in both senses.[4] The following discussion sticks to the first, classical, meaning of the term. Both of these concepts of 'humanitarian intervention' overlap with, but are not identical to, that of 'safety zones', which have been established in many different forms in conflicts of the 1990s, and are discussed further in Section III of this study.

Humanitarian intervention versus non-intervention

The idea of humanitarian intervention in its classical sense involves a violation, albeit in exceptional circumstances, of the principle of non-intervention. This rule – the prohibition of military incursions into states without the consent of the government – is often criticised as a principle based more on order than on justice, but it does have a serious moral basis. It provides clear guidelines for limiting the uses of armed force and reducing the risk of war between armies of different states. It involves respect for different societies with varying religions, cultures, economic systems and political arrangements. It acts as a brake on the crusading, territorial and imperial ambitions of states.

The actual observance of this rule has been imperfect. States have circumvented or violated it on many occasions and for many reasons, including the protection of nationals, support for opposition groups, the prevention of shifts in the balance of power and counter-intervention in response to another state which is deemed to have intervened first. Yet the principle survives, evidence, perhaps, that a robust rule can outlive its occasional violation. It has not served badly as an ordering mechanism of international relations in the post-1945 era.

Because non-intervention is such an important principle, it is not surprising that the idea of 'humanitarian intervention' has never been formally accepted in any general legal instrument. Yet even the stoutest defender of non-intervention must concede a weakness. Can that rule really apply when the situation is so serious that the moral conscience of mankind is affronted? What is the ethical or logical foundation of the rule that makes it so rigid, so uncomprehending of misery, that it cannot allow for exceptions? One might even say that if a coherent philosophy of humanitarian intervention were developed, it could have the potential to save the non-intervention rule from its own logical absurdities and occasional inhumanities.

The sheer force of circumstance which brought about the new practice, and doctrine, of humanitarian intervention can not be disputed. The age-old problem of whether forcible military intervention in another state to protect the lives of its inhabitants can ever be justified became politically sensitive when harrowing situations, extensively reported on television, led to calls for action, and when the UN Security Council, no longer hamstrung by East–West disagreement, was able to reach authoritative decisions, giving a degree of legitimacy to interventions which might otherwise have been hotly contested. Also, the dangers experienced by many humanitarian workers in the field have led to strong calls for intervention. As two leading NGOs have stated:

> The principle of sovereignty should not block the protection of the basic rights of women, men and children (including the right to emergency relief and safety) which we believe all governments are obliged to protect through the UN.[5]

Developing a coherent notion of humanitarian intervention involves questions about authorisation. The possibility that the society of states, acting through regional or global bodies, might in some way authorise particular acts of intervention significantly weakens the traditional objection to humanitarian intervention. A main foundation of the non-intervention rule has been a concern about states acting unilaterally, pursuing their own interests, dominating other societies and getting into clashes and wars with each other. If an intervention is authorised by an international body and has specific stated purposes, this concern begins to dissolve. Hedley Bull noted in 1984 that an era characterised by increased attention to human rights and focus on the UN was bound to see doctrines of humanitarian intervention revived.

> Ultimately, we have a rule of non-intervention because unilateral intervention threatens the harmony and concord of the society of sovereign states. If, however, an intervention itself expresses the collective will of the society of states, it may be carried out without bringing that harmony and concord into jeopardy.[6]

Since the Second World War there has been a strong tendency for military interventions to be conducted on a multilateral basis, or at least with multilateral fig-leaves, hence the frequent use of regional organisations to sanctify such interventions as those of the Soviet Union in Czechoslovakia, of Syria in Lebanon, or of the United States in Grenada. In these and other cases 'humanitarian intervention' was often part of the justification made by those intervening.

Security Council decisions since 1991

Since the end of the Cold War, the UN Security Council has emerged as the main body authorising interventions, including those on humanitarian grounds, and for enunciating their purposes. In this matter the UN has obvious advantages over bodies with more limited membership. If the UN Security Council authorises an intervention, the risks of competitive chaos and insecurity and of pursuit of unilateral advantage may be greatly reduced.

The role of the UN, especially the Security Council, has given a degree of international legitimacy to uses of force that might otherwise have been open to extensive criticism. Resolutions regarding former Yugoslavia, Somalia, Rwanda and Haiti have all put great emphasis on humanitarian issues as justifications for the use of outside forces.

However, none of these five cases was a purely humanitarian intervention. The principal departure from the textbook definition was over the question of consent of the state in which the intervention takes place. In theory the absence of consent is virtually a defining feature of humanitarian intervention. In all these cases in which the UN Security Council used humanitarian justification for military involvement, the whole question of consent proved to be far more subtle in fact than it ever was in legal theory.

In northern Iraq, the UN required, in the Delphic terms of Resolution 688 of 5 April 1991, that 'Iraq allow immediate access by international humanitarian organisations to all those in need of assistance in all parts of Iraq', which was less than a formal authorisation of intervention, but was nevertheless of considerable help to the US and its coalition partners. The military operation within northern Iraq which began on 17 April 1991 must be seen partly in the special context of post-war actions by victors in the territory of defeated adversaries. Further, there was Iraqi consent to the subsequent presence of the UN Guards Contingent in Iraq.

In former Yugoslavia, the Security Council resolution authorising the UN Protection Force (UNPROFOR)'s initial deployment in February 1992 was phrased to suggest that, although there was consent on that occasion, the Council might actually require the parties involved to accept the continued presence of peacekeeping forces with a humanitarian role whether they wanted them or not.[7] Subsequent resolutions on Bosnia-Herzegovina suggested that if UNPROFOR and its humanitarian activities were obstructed, further measures not based on the consent of the parties might be taken to ensure delivery of humanitarian assistance.[8] However, UNPROFOR operated for the most part on the basis of consent. Thus, although its actions in Bosnia were a clear case of humanitarian action in war, they were not a clear case of humanitarian intervention.

In Somalia, the US-led invasion of 9 December 1992 had the full blessing of UN Resolution 794 – the first to authorise explicitly a massive military intervention by member-states within a country without an invitation from the government. However, there was no Somali government to give or refuse consent, so the intervention by the Unified Task Force (UNITAF) in December 1992, and its continuation by the United Nations Operation in Somalia (UNOSOM II) in May 1993, was hardly a classic case of humanitarian intervention. Further, its actual conduct raised questions about the label 'humanitarian intervention'.

With regard to Rwanda, the initial deployment of the UN Assistance Mission for Rwanda (UNAMIR) in November 1993 was by consent of both the government of Rwanda and the Rwandan Patriotic Front (RPF). However, subsequent revisions of UNAMIR's mandate, in a series of Security Council resolutions from April 1994, gave it additional roles. Although Rwanda was a member of the UN Security Council from 1 January 1994, these new roles were not based explicitly on the consent of the government, because it was the government of Rwanda that was instigating or tolerating the mass killings. Resolution 918 of 17 May 1994 expressed concern over 'a humanitarian crisis of enormous proportions' and decided to expand UNAMIR's mandate – to contribute to the security and protection of displaced persons, refugees and civilians at risk in Rwanda, including establishing and maintaining, where feasible, secure humanitarian areas; another clause calls for providing security and support for the distribution of relief supplies and humanitarian relief operations.

This mandate was repeated and reaffirmed in Resolution 925 of 8 June 1994, which referred to 'reports indicating that acts of genocide have occurred in Rwanda', and underscored that 'the internal displacement of some 1.5 million Rwandans facing starvation and disease and the massive exodus of refugees to neighbouring countries constitute a humanitarian crisis of enormous proportions'. Great difficulties arose in gathering forces to carry out the mandate. In a further decision, Resolution 929 of 22 June 1994, the Security Council accepted an offer from France and other member-states to establish a temporary operation there under French command and control. The Council stated that in doing so it was acting under Chapter VII of the UN Charter, and it authorised France to use 'all necessary means to achieve the humanitarian objectives' set out in Resolution 925 (and also in Resolution 918 as mentioned above). This was the prelude to the French-led *Opération Turquoise* in western Rwanda in summer 1994.

There was much controversy about the French action, as indeed there was about the entire UN role, based mainly on the view that there should have been earlier, larger and more decisive humanitarian intervention. In particular, it is charged that in April 1994 no option for handling the war against civilians was presented promptly to the Security Council, which persisted for too long in seeing the problem in the familiar terms of implementing a ceasefire. Such criticisms were directed mainly at UN Security Council Resolution (UNSCR) 912 of 21 April 1994, in which, at the height of the crisis within Rwanda, the Council had actually decided to reduce the size of UNAMIR from 1,700 to 270 personnel – a decision that was never fully implemented.[9]

The crisis in Haiti following the September 1991 *coup d'état* which toppled President Jean-Bertrand Aristide led to numerous UN Security Council resolutions imposing economic sanctions and expressing concern about the humanitarian situation. The General Assembly, too, expressed its concern, for example in its Resolution 47/20 of 22 March 1993, which urged members 'to increase their humanitarian assistance to the Haitian people'. Abortive attempts to secure a negotiated transfer of power led to the passing of UNSCR 940 on 31 July 1994 authorising the use of 'all necessary means to facilitate the departure from Haiti of the military leadership ... and to establish and maintain a secure and stable environment'. This resolution is remarkable for its unequivocal call for action to topple an existing regime. It did so partly on the basis of humanitarian considerations. Following this, a US-led force intervened in Haiti in September 1994, but only after a last-minute agreement providing a basis for a US military role in Haiti, signed in Port-au-Prince by former US President Jimmy Carter and Haiti's military-installed President, Emile Jonassaint. Thus even in this case, where the UN Security Council was operating in enforcement mode, there was some hesitation in using force: some element of consent from the government in place was sought and obtained.

Questions about consistency of UN decisions

While none of the five cases outlined above was purely textbook, all contained some elements of humanitarian intervention. The situation in Rwanda perhaps corresponded most closely to the picture of an utterly oppressive regime slaughtering its own people. Yet the actual intervention that followed was even more hesitant and equivocal than in the other cases. All of these uses of armed force with a humanitarian rationale raise questions about the consistency and seriousness of UN practice.

The first question has to do with the terms of the UN Charter. There is the general concern that humanitarian intervention is obviously in conflict with Article 2(1): 'The Organisation is based on the principle of the sovereign equality of all its members.' There is also a more specific concern. It is sometimes suggested that the Security Council is a structurally flawed body on matters of humanitarian intervention, because under the Charter and its own past practices it cannot authorise a military action purely on the grounds of grave human-rights violations. In order to act under Chapter VII of the Charter, as it did in each of these cases, the Security Council's action must be premised on a formal determination of the existence of a threat to international peace and security. The contrast between the legal and the real grounds of action is clearest in Resolution 794 of 3 December 1992 on Somalia. It mentions 'a threat to international peace and security' once, as if to clear a necessary legal hurdle; however, the word 'humanitarian' is mentioned no less than 18 times – a dismal record for a UN Security Council resolution, but an indication of the reasoning and intentions behind the authorisation to intervene. Once a consensus has emerged that action is warranted (whether on humanitarian or other grounds), this requirement has not proved a major obstacle, but many states have been uneasy about an emerging UN practice that might one day threaten their own sovereignty.

In cases of genocide there is another possible basis for Security Council action. The 1948 Genocide Convention, Article VIII, specifies that any contracting state 'may call upon the competent organs of the United Nations to take such action under the Charter of the United Nations as they consider appropriate for the prevention and suppression of acts of genocide'.[10]

Another basis for doubt about UN practice in the 1990s has to do with selectivity and so-called 'double standards'. Undoubtedly, the conscience of mankind was shocked by the plight of Iraqi Kurds, the vicious fighting and sieges in former Yugoslavia, the starvation in Somalia and the genocide in Rwanda, but there have been other perhaps equally shocking situations in the past few decades. That genocide in Cambodia, mass shootings in Beijing, ruthless dictatorship in Myanmar or catastrophe in Sudan did not lead to humanitarian interventions suggests that other factors are involved. Such intervention seems for the most part to be confined to cases of which there has been extensive television coverage or some particular interest in intervention, and which is not likely to provoke dissent by a great power or massive military opposition. In short, it may largely be confined to highly publicised situations of war, chaos and disintegration – Somalia and Yugoslavia being prime examples – or to interventions in small states not capable of offering serious military opposition, such as Haiti. It is not an answer to the often more serious problem of the over-powerful and brutal state. True, the operation in northern Iraq in 1991 was an intervention in a state with an all-too-powerful government, but that was an exceptional circumstance: it had recently been defeated in war, and the victors felt an unusually high degree of responsibility for the plight of the inhabitants, because of US encouragement to engage in an ill-starred and brutally suppressed rebellion.

Overall, the practice of the Security Council does suggest a high degree of selectivity about situations in which humanitarian intervention might be authorised, and this selectivity involves many factors other than the plight of the people whom an intervention might be intended to assist. This parallels the Security Council's familiar selectivity in certain other spheres, such as in the question of which invaded states it assists with forceful measures. The same unheroic defence can be made of Security Council practice in both cases – prudence is not a bad guide to action, some degree of selectivity is inevitable, and it is better to uphold basic principles selectively than not at all.

A third problem with this UN practice is that it is extremely hard to divine anything like a doctrine from such a varied set of cases and approaches. Security Council resolutions have moved the matter forward inch by inch, in a thoroughly pragmatic way. The authorising resolutions offer no general defence of humanitarian intervention. Rather, they are dotted with references to the wholly exceptional circumstances of the particular case at hand. Thus UNSCR 794 of 3 December 1992 authorising *Operation Restore Hope* in Somalia contains the following wording in the preamble at the express wish of African states: 'Recognising the unique character of the present situation in Somalia and mindful of its deteriorating, complex and extraordinary nature, requiring an immediate and exceptional response.' In other words, they did not want the invasion of Somalia to be viewed as a precedent for invasions of other sovereign states.

This reluctance to define a doctrine of 'humanitarian intervention' may stem from a sense that to give explicit legal approval to the principle may be to open a door that is better kept closed. If the door must sometimes be opened, there should be an awareness before passing through it that the other side is legally questionable territory.

Purposes and results of 'humanitarian interventions'

The greatest difficulties arising from this contemporary practice of interventions with a humanitarian rationale have to do with their uncertainty of purpose, their inadequate means, and their questionable consequences. In interventions, what does the word 'humanitarian' mean, and does it accurately describe anything beyond the original motive? How can this translate into actual policies to transform a situation? Does it make sense to call an intervention 'humanitarian' when the troops involved may have to fight and kill those who, for whatever reasons, seek to obstruct them? Or when the troops involved fail to provide what the inhabitants most desperately need – including security?

In many instances of 'humanitarian intervention' since 1990, the repeated emphasis on the word 'humanitarian' has gone hand-in-hand with the absence of a serious long-term policy with respect to the target country, except in the limited matters of providing food and medical aid, and trying to get rival factions to reach a peace accord. Some of the emphasis on humanitarianism is vulnerable to the criticism that it reflects the natural desire to do *something* in the face of disaster, and a tendency to forget that in all these cases the disaster has been man-made, and requires changes in policies, institutions and possibly even in the structure of states and their boundaries.

The vagueness and incompleteness of the aims in some of these interventions is striking. In northern Iraq, the extent to which Kurdish autonomy was or was not supported was unclear. In former Yugoslavia, the mandates of UNPROFOR varied from place to place and from time to time, but were widely viewed by the inhabitants as inadequate. In Somalia, the mandates of the forces intervening under UN auspices were never clear on the key issues of who was in charge of the country's administration, and what was to be done about the weapons and warfare of the clans and warlords. In Rwanda, many critics have asserted that the UN should have had a more forceful policy, and should perhaps have sided with the RPF forces. In all these cases, there are reasons for the vagueness of goals: more precision would have implied a willingness to impose a pre-determined outcome, would have been open to the accusation of dictatorial interference, and would in any case probably have split the Security Council.

The results of the post-1990 cases of intervention have been, at best, mixed. In northern Iraq, there was a temporary improvement in the situation in the Kurdish areas; yet even there, the modest security that was achieved for the Kurds in 1991 remained under constant threat. The original intervening forces, led by the US, were not willing to stay, nor to stop the strife between different Kurdish factions which always threatened to drag in the neighbouring powers of Turkey, Iran and of course, Iraq. The US Central Intelligence Agency (CIA)'s efforts to influence political developments in the area, far from offering protection, made the Kurdish individuals involved vulnerable to reprisals in September 1996 when Iraqi forces re-entered some cities in the Kurdish region.

In the absence of a clear policy and a strong governmental force in the area, the original US-led intervention proved to be a step onto a slippery slope, helping to create the conditions for further interventions. From August 1991, Turkish forces launched attacks in northern Iraq against their foes in the Kurdish Workers Party (PKK); a Turkish military operation in March 1995 was particularly extensive, involving some 35,000 troops; and in 1996 there were further major Turkish military campaigns against PKK bases in northern Iraq. Iranian forces actively supported the Patriotic Union of Kurdistan (PUK). Throughout, there was much nervousness about whether Saddam Hussein's government and armed forces could be kept indefinitely from re-entering the region and wreaking vengeance on their adversaries, which is what eventually happened by invitation from the Kurdish Democratic Party (KDP) in September 1996. Many lives were saved by establishing the 'safe haven', especially in 1991. Inasmuch as the 'safe haven' has continued in some form, it is because it reflects not only a humanitarian involvement, but also a US strategic interest in keeping Iraq down. It constitutes a warning of what can go wrong with humanitarian intervention.

In former Yugoslavia, UNPROFOR did fulfil some humanitarian purposes. It assisted with the delivery of food and other supplies to Sarajevo. However, both in Bosnia and in the Serb-held areas of Croatia, it failed conspicuously to protect the inhabitants from their adversaries. To the modest extent that UN involvement in Yugoslavia can be considered a case of humanitarian intervention, it is one which exposes certain limitations to the idea, at least when there is no real willingness to provide protection.

In Somalia, the follow-up to *Operation Restore Hope* of December 1992 was sadly reminiscent of colonial policing. The words of the UN military spokesman in Mogadishu on 10 September 1993, the day after yet another incident in which UN troops killed a number of civilians, are an appropriate epitaph for short-sighted optimism. 'Everyone on the ground in that vicinity was a combatant, because they meant to do us harm.' The UNOSOM II peacekeeping operation left the country in March 1995 having saved many who would otherwise have starved, but without having achieved a major change in the chaotic clan warfare that had led to the UN's initial involvement in 1992.

In Rwanda, despite ample early warning, the interventions under UN auspices within the country were limited in size, in duration and in goals. This sad experience illustrates the reluctance of states to take decisive and enduring action in a situation of great danger, especially where they have few direct interests.

The operation in Haiti had an unusually clear stated purpose – the restoration of a democratically elected government. There was also a strong motive for intervention as a means of stopping refugee flows to neighbouring states, including the US. Here intervention seems to have been successful, partly because the US was committed to change. However, any optimism must be tempered by awareness of the very limited long-term results of previous US interventions: huge difficulties were encountered earlier in the twentieth century when trying to eradicate violence and dictatorship from Haitian politics.

The results of international intervention in internal conflicts since 1991 have been, at best, mixed. As Lori Fisler Damrosch has written, 'In the eyes of many, collective institutions have done little to restrain internal conflicts: rather, it is the institutions themselves that seem under restraint'.[11]

Problems with the 'humanitarian intervention' concept

The 1990s practice of humanitarian intervention has resulted from real and urgent crises. It has also introduced innovative features, the most significant of which is the emphasis on the UN Security Council as the authorising body, and it has undoubtedly saved many lives. However, five serious problems have been exposed.

- The term 'humanitarian intervention' is a misnomer, a justification which should be viewed sceptically. It carries the implication that military intervention in another country can be humanitarian in four respects – in its original motives, in its stated purposes, in its methods of operation and in its actual results. There are doubts as to whether such action can really be humanitarian in any, let alone all, of these ways. In particular, an intervention force in a crisis-torn country, in order to bring an end to the conflict that caused its dispatch there, may need to take tough action, or even to take sides, in ways that go well beyond the normal meaning of 'humanitarian intervention'.
- The claim that an intervention by one's own forces is 'humanitarian' – the provision of assistance to unfortunate peoples incapable of providing for themselves – appeals too easily to ethnocentric tendencies. An operation armed with moral rectitude but potentially weakened by contempt for local forces can easily degenerate into arrogance, anger, bathos and despair.
- Any intervention is liable, sooner or later, to provoke local opposition. Even humanitarian assistance can rouse strong local resentment, especially if the very necessity for its presence cruelly exposes failings in the target society, or if the forces involved are substantially ignorant of, or arrogant towards, local forces and customs with which they have no long-term relationship. Thus what begins as humanitarian intervention risks ending in humiliating exit.
- A multilateral intervention, authorised by the Security Council, is especially at risk due to certain inevitable features of the way the UN goes about its collective business – compromise, inertia, formal impartiality and (sometimes) avoidance of difficult issues. There may be a lack of clear strategic direction in any operation, a lack of knowledge of the country and its languages, a lack of any deep commitment or sense of responsibility on the part of troop-contributing states, and a lack of willingness to take on governmental functions.
- There are structural causes for the commonly encountered tension between armed forces engaging in humanitarian intervention and the humanitarian organisations whose work they assist. Such organisations value their independence and/or impartiality. If they cooperate in armed interventions for humanitarian purposes, they may end up acting as humanitarian auxiliaries of armed forces, and perceived as accomplices in any excesses.[12]

There is absolutely no possibility of securing general agreement among states about the legitimacy of humanitarian intervention. The many interesting attempts to devise formal criteria for intervention are not likely to win the approval of more than a handful of states.[13] Humanitarian intervention will, and perhaps should, remain in a legal penumbra, as something which may occasionally be approved by the Security Council or by other bodies, may reluctantly be tolerated by states, but cannot be given any generic advance legitimation. Such legitimation is unattainable not only because intervention involves breaking a valued norm, but also because it is impossible to spell out in advance the circumstances in which such interventions might conceivably be justified. The fear of such action getting out of hand is not unreasonable. In too many states there are living memories of external domination, and real fears that outsiders, in the name of humanitarianism, could find more or less plausible grounds for intervention. To reopen the door to external interventions in any general way would be deeply unpopular in many states, often for very good reasons. In addition, power political calculations of several kinds necessarily enter into considerations of whether a particular intervention should be initiated or supported, and provide a further bulwark against the emergence of a doctrine of humanitarian intervention.

Despite the frequency of cases since 1991 involving strong elements of humanitarian intervention, the twin principles of sovereignty and non-intervention remain fundamentally important in the international system. These principles may be modified through a wide variety of transnational developments and international institutions, but only in very extreme cases, and with a wide range of procedural and substantive safeguards, can they be directly overridden by overt cases of humanitarian intervention. This is one reason why, in many situations, the Security Council has in the end preferred action that is more modest than full-scale humanitarian intervention. In actual practice, it has often ended up seeking to protect inhabitants with such devices as 'safe areas' and other forms of safety zones, often with the consent of the states in which they are situated.

III. Forms of humanitarian action

The rise of humanitarian considerations as part of the conduct of international relations in the early 1990s was by no means limited to the extreme case of 'humanitarian intervention'. Several other distinct forms of humanitarian action were implemented in the midst of ongoing wars, including the delivery of relief supplies, the use of UN peacekeeping forces for humanitarian purposes, and the establishment of safety zones. There were also attempts to develop international administrative roles, and to punish violations of the laws of war. All these approaches achieved some results, but also had problems and involved controversy. Sometimes different actions taken for different humanitarian purposes conflicted with each other.

Delivery of humanitarian relief during wars

Debates about the delivery of food and other supplies to beleaguered populations during wars has a long history. Early in the First World War, the US government considered a plan for supplying food to Germany, which was badly affected by the Allied blockade. It did so partly because it was alarmed by the conduct of both the UK and Germany towards neutral shipping, and especially by a war-zone plan proposed by Germany which would have had a particularly adverse effect on US trade. The US Secretary of State reported to President Wilson, 'I am led to believe from Conversations with the German and Austrian Ambassadors that there would be a chance of securing the withdrawal of the military zone order in return for favorable action on the food question.'[1] He then went on to propose an agreement covering four points, of which the first was food:

> Food sent to Germany for the use of non-combatants, to be consigned to American agents and by American agents delivered to retail dealers licensed for that purpose by the German Government – the license specifying that the food so furnished was to be sold to non-combatants and not to be subject to requisition. Any violation of the terms of the license could work a forfeiture of the right of such dealers to receive food for this purpose.[2]

This plan was deeply resented, especially in the UK, where it was deemed a German blackmail proposition and interpreted to mean 'free food to Germans after they have done their best by mines and torpedoes to cut off England's food'.[3] It was not in the end implemented, but many other programmes were, especially in 1917–18.[4] It is, however, a useful illustration of how easily humanitarian aid can become entangled with other issues, and how assertions that food aid will benefit only non-combatants can seem unconvincing.

Although there have been many such failures, war has also been the midwife of modern humanitarianism, leading to the birth of major organisations dedicated to humanitarian relief. Many have acquired important roles in peace as well as war. What is now ICRC was founded after the Battle of Solferino in 1859. The First World War led to the creation of the Save the Children Fund in the UK and the American Relief Association in the US. Oxfam was founded in 1942 out of concern about delivering food in the Balkans. *Médecins sans Frontières* was formed in 1971 following the Biafran war. In all these cases the perception that these bodies did not represent states, especially belligerent states, was crucial to their credibility. ICRC, in particular, maintained its reputation for impartiality by avoiding partisan statements, and by maintaining confidentiality in such humanitarian activities as visits to POW and internment camps.

Delivery of humanitarian aid during war provokes awkward questions about the consequences of such action. It is often asserted that:

- A proportion of humanitarian aid ends up in the hands of belligerent forces. This can happen for many reasons. Aid may be commandeered at gunpoint, an aid agency may build a working relationship with one particular party, and even the best distribution system may not be able to prevent supplies from getting through to armed forces.
- Even if delivered solely to civilians, aid can still favour one side more than the other, for example, if the aid is delivered directly to a city which is the capital of a country at war (such as Sarajevo), or if the aid enables locally produced supplies to be directed to the armed forces.
- By propping up one or both belligerents, and postponing the onset of war-weariness, aid may actually have the perverse effect of prolonging wars, and ultimately increasing the death, destruction and suffering which they cause.
- There are frequently powerful pressures on agencies to give more aid to one side than another, or even to withhold aid altogether from some parties in the hope that this will induce them to make political compromises.
- Some humanitarian deliveries, especially if conducted by a state rather than an international organisation, may contain or be accompanied by supplies of arms.

Accusations that aid can have some of these effects were frequently made with respect to former Yugoslavia in 1991–95; it is a fact (though one which can be justified in several ways) that international aid organisations and NGOs were far more heavily involved in Bosnian government-held areas than in the Serb-held ones, and that some aid did find its way to the armies involved. Sometimes, indeed, aid may be given deliberately to assist one side in a conflict. This was the case with aid to the Cambodian refugee camps on the Thai border in the early 1980s.

In many recent wars, humanitarian organisations involved in aid delivery have had genuine difficulty asserting their autonomy and immunity. The delivery of aid has resulted in threats to the humanitarian workers involved and widespread seizure and looting of aid shipments. In Liberia in June 1996, such problems led Oxfam and 12 other humanitarian agencies, including ICRC, to decide not to renew major operations. Subsequently, the UK and US governments, and the European Union, followed a similar policy. As David Bryer, Director of Oxfam, has stated:

> The Liberian warlords had looted more than four hundred aid vehicles and millions of dollars of equipment and relief goods, and those thefts had directly supported the war, and caused civilian deaths and suffering. The vehicles and radio equipment had been used for military purposes, and sold, along with diamond and gold deposits which the different factions control, to purchase arms . . . In this case, I do think that more lives are likely to be saved by preventing such looting than by providing

humanitarian aid ... protection from violence is more vital than humanitarian relief ... What I don't accept is that such abuse of aid necessarily means that we should not do it. The question to ask is whether such abuse means that the *net* impact of that aid helps civilians fulfil their rights to material necessities and protection from violence. In Liberia and, looking back, in Somalia, I think the answer is on one side. In Bosnia and in Zaire, I think it is on the other, and that we have been right to stay.[5]

The concept of 'humanitarian space' has been advanced in order to invoke the idea that aid operations, even in the midst of war, should be free from interference of various kinds.[6] However, the concept remains ill-defined and ineffective. The weaknesses, evasions and ambiguities that surround it are evidence of the difficulty that some international and humanitarian organisations have in coming to terms with the critical importance of physical security, both of humanitarian operations themselves, and of the people they are supposed to assist.

Use of UN peacekeeping forces for humanitarian purposes

In the post-Cold War world, and to an unprecedented extent, forces operating under a UN mandate have become involved in a wide range of humanitarian tasks. These have taken the following main forms:

- Protecting humanitarian relief workers, such as those representing international agencies and NGOs, from attacks by belligerents and generally from the dangers of war.
- Directly engaging in humanitarian action, for example delivering humanitarian relief supplies, maintaining essential services and reconstructing damaged buildings.
- Facilitating contacts between adversaries over such matters as resettlement of refugees and visits to grave sites.
- Establishing certain designated areas ('safety zones') where a high degree of protection is intended for the inhabitants from the threat or use of force.

Such tasks were a key part of the UN's effort in several war situations, including in former Yugoslavia, Somalia and Rwanda. Peacekeeping forces have been deeply involved in such activities, sometimes as an almost complete substitution for traditional peacekeeping activities, such as manning cease-fire lines, since in these conflicts there was often little or no peace to keep. Other forces and agencies operating in association with the UN have also been involved in these various humanitarian tasks. For an international organisation such as the UN to attempt this in the midst of ongoing wars is historically unprecedented. The tasks are by nature extremely difficult, and also controversial.

This change in practice has not always been reflected in general statements about the purpose and character of peacekeeping.[7] Within the UN, against a background of multiple and difficult commitments of peacekeeping forces, humanitarian issues have not loomed large in attempts to establish criteria that should be considered before new tasks are undertaken. A UN Security Council Presidential Statement on Peacekeeping, issued on 3 May 1994, listed six factors which must be taken into account when a new operation is under consideration. These are the existence of a threat to international peace and security, whether regional bodies are ready to assist, the existence of a cease-fire, a clear political goal which can be reflected in the mandate, a precise mandate and reasonable assurances about the safety of UN personnel.[8] This list contained no reference to humanitarian operations in the midst of continuing hostilities, and indeed suggested a natural desire to return to something more like normal peacekeeping. Two days later, on 5 May 1994, the Clinton administration's long-planned Presidential Decision Directive 25, on 'multilateral peace operations', did suggest that one relevant consideration for the US when voting on a military operation proposal under UN auspices would be whether there was an 'urgent humanitarian disaster coupled with violence'. There would also have to be consideration of 'the political, economic and humanitarian consequences of inaction by the international community'.[9]

There have been some remarkable successes in using UN peacekeeping forces for humanitarian purposes in situations of war, civil war and breakdown of government. Many lives have been saved and refugee flows limited by some of these humanitarian actions. Sarajevo, where a population of well over 350,000 was at risk during the siege, is a case in point. Despite the many failures and interruptions, the maintenance of supplies – gas, water and electricity, as well as food and materiel brought in by land convoys and air – did effectively mitigate many of the extreme cruelties of siege warfare.

This achievement would have been impossible without UN peacekeeping forces. The figures for supplies brought in by the UNHCR airlift are impressive. The longest-running humanitarian air-bridge in history, it lasted from 30 June 1992 to 5 January 1996. Although there were many periods when, due to Serb threats, it was not possible for aircraft to fly to Sarajevo at all, during the three-and-a-half years of the airlift there were 12,951 sorties delivering 160,677 tonnes, of which 144,827 were food and the rest non-food items (such as shelter materials and medical supplies).[10] In other words, an average of about 125 tonnes a day was delivered. During many months of the war the airlift provided more than 85% of all assistance reaching Sarajevo. In addition, over 1,000 patients were medically evacuated by air, plus over 1,400 of their relatives.[11] While the Sarajevo airlift was remarkable in the hostile circumstances, the overall tonnage delivered in three and a half years was about the same as the average delivered each month in the Berlin airlift of 1948–49.[12]

The special problems attendant upon humanitarian efforts by peacekeeping forces in situations of great violence have been well publicised. They fall under the following headings:

- Humanitarian action often involves compromises with belligerents, making impartiality difficult to maintain. Any action in the midst of an ongoing conflict requires consent of the parties on the ground. Convoys cannot move, aircraft cannot fly and hospitals cannot operate if there is no such consent. Thus peacekeepers inevitably find themselves dealing closely with one belligerent or another.
- Humanitarian action often favours one side more than the other, further straining the credibility of the peacekeepers' impartiality. Relief supplies are often, and for good reasons, provided more to one side than to another; so is the protection afforded by the establishment and maintenance of specially designated safety zones.
- While the peacekeepers' impartiality is often considered essential during an ongoing conflict, it is particularly hard to maintain while conducting or authorising military actions that are seen as partial to one side – such as enforcing economic sanctions and 'no-fly zones', punishing infractions of cease-fire agreements, or pressing a recalcitrant party to accept a particular approach to a settlement.
- Personnel carrying out humanitarian work in the midst of ongoing conflict usually have to be dispersed to many parts of a war zone, making them exceptionally vulnerable to reprisals and hostage-taking by belligerents. When the personnel involved are troops supplied for a peacekeeping operation, their vulnerability can inhibit powers from taking forceful military action even when this seems to be required.
- It can be very difficult to recruit and maintain troops with the necessary training and discipline to carry out peacekeeping/humanitarian tasks in a war zone, and generally to mobilise political, diplomatic and financial support in a long war if major powers do not see that their interests are directly affected.
- The heavy demands of running peacekeeping/humanitarian missions in a large number of conflicts simultaneously has exposed certain limits to the UN's capacity to manage operations, and (even more dramatically) the political and resource limits within which the UN has to operate. Many states have been unwilling to provide all the forces, materiel and finance required for such operations. Consequently there has been pressure to handle more problems on a regional basis.

These problems proved exceptionally debilitating in both Somalia and Bosnia. The sense that humanitarian issues were among the factors that made it harder to stick to tried-and-tested notions of peacekeeping was evident in UN Secretary-General Boutros Boutros-Ghali's January 1995 report, *Supplement to an Agenda for Peace*. In the passage below he seemed to hold the humanitarian cart responsible for running over the peacekeeping horse:

> There are three aspects of recent mandates that, in particular, have led peace-keeping operations to forfeit the consent of the parties, to behave

in a way that was perceived to be partial and/or to use force other than in self-defence. These have been the tasks of protecting humanitarian operations during continuing warfare, protecting civilian populations in designated safe areas and pressing the parties to achieve national reconciliation at a pace faster than they were ready to accept. The cases of Somalia and Bosnia and Herzegovina are instructive in this respect.[13]

Boutros-Ghali went on to indicate that 'additional mandates that required the use of force . . . could not be combined with existing mandates requiring the consent of the parties, impartiality and the non-use of force. It was also not possible for them to be executed without much stronger military capabilities than had been made available'.[14] This is a classic reflection of the view, drawn largely from Somalia, that it was disastrous for UN forces to cease to be impartial and to use too much force. This is not the only possible interpretation of the causes of failure in Somalia, but it prevailed, leading many in the UN and elsewhere to be extremely cautious in Bosnia.

Events in Bosnia in 1992–95 suggested that the relationship between humanitarian and peacekeeping roles, while extraordinarily complex, can have positive aspects. Despite all the disappointments, the presence of UN peacekeeping forces, whose mission was largely to support humanitarian action, may have reduced at least slightly the incidence of extreme atrocities, helped prevent a process of creeping unilateral interventions in the war and may even have prepared the way for a peace settlement by demonstrating the readiness of the international community to assist and monitor such an outcome.

In the months leading up to the General Framework Agreement for Peace in Bosnia and Herzegovina agreed at Dayton, Ohio in November 1995, the relationship between humanitarian action and a peace settlement was especially complex and paradoxical. The Security Council repeatedly asserted that there was such a connection: 'the provision of humanitarian assistance in Bosnia and Herzegovina is an important element in the Council's effort to restore international peace and security in the area'.[15] This may in the end have been true, but with a qualification. It was not so much the attempt to provide humanitarian assistance itself, but rather the Serb rejection of that attempt in the first half of 1995, which created the conditions for the serious effort of August–November 1995 to restore peace and security in the area. A more robust policy of decisive enforcement action only became possible in Bosnia after the humanitarian aid programme had practically stopped in mid-1995 due to Bosnian Serb actions. Once UNPROFOR no longer had personnel widely spread out and hence vulnerable to Serb retaliation, it was more able to act, and once the Bosnian Serbs had shown contempt for humanitarian efforts, for the 'safe areas' and for the Security Council, there was more reason to act. Thus the Western powers, and the UNPROFOR commanders, became less cautious about authorising a major use of force by NATO, as they eventually did in *Operation Deliberate Force* in August 1995. In short, a humanitarian involvement, especially in the 'safe areas', had a 'ratchet' effect, leading eventually to a major NATO military campaign.

Safety zones

'We don't need food. We need safety'. A placard with these words was carried by a refugee child in Safwan, in the demilitarised zone in southern Iraq, in April 1991.[16] Agencies are frequently concerned primarily about the delivery of food, blankets and medical supplies, when in many wars what is needed above all is security. Sadako Ogata, the UN High Commissioner for Refugees, has recognised the problem with admirable frankness. 'Humanitarian assistance is much more than relief and logistics. It is essentially and above all about protection – protection of victims of human rights and humanitarian violations'.[17] However, providing security frequently stretches the limits of humanitarian efforts and challenges the idea of impartiality.

One approach to the provision of security is safety zones. The idea that certain areas should enjoy special protection, even in the midst of ongoing war, has long been reflected in provisions of the laws of war. For example, the 1907 Hague Convention IV, Article 27, states:

> In sieges and bombardments all necessary steps must be taken to spare, as far as possible, buildings dedicated to religion, art, science, or charitable purposes, historic monuments, hospitals, and places where the sick and wounded are collected, provided they are not being used at the time for military purposes. It is the duty of the besieged to indicate the presence of such buildings or places by distinctive and visible signs, which shall be notified to the enemy beforehand.

The 1949 Geneva Conventions provided for the establishment of 'hospital zones and localities', which would normally involve prior agreement between the belligerents, to protect wounded, sick and aged persons, children under 15 years of age, expectant mothers and mothers of children under seven.[18] They also provided for the establishment, by agreement between the belligerents, of 'neutralised zones' to shelter wounded and sick combatants or non-combatants, as well as civilians who take no part in hostilities.[19] The 1977 Geneva Protocol I added a provision for 'demilitarised zones' by agreement between the belligerents.[20] All these arrangements have obvious limitations. They are based on the assumptions that the security zone is a very limited area, that all combatants and mobile military equipment have been withdrawn and that no acts of hostility would be committed by the authorities or the population. They require consent, in most cases formal, between belligerents; they depend on complete demilitarisation of the area, which is hard to achieve in practice; and they do not specify arrangements for defending the areas or for deterring attacks on them.

The post-Cold War period has seen significant variations on these arrangements.[21] There have been several attempts to create areas of special protection, in which the victims of a conflict and the humanitarian bodies that assist them can have a degree of safety. Such areas have been variously called 'corridors of tranquillity', 'humanitarian corridors', 'neutral zones', 'open relief centres', 'protected areas', 'safe areas', 'safe havens', 'secure humanitarian areas', 'security corridors' and 'security zones'. The Security Council has been active in promoting such zones, and has itself used at least five of these terms for them.[22] The UNHCR has also had a significant role in promoting these concepts, and indeed itself established on the basis of consent two 'open relief centres' (ORCs) in Sri Lanka, where local inhabitants could take refuge when threatened by the conflict between government forces and Tamil rebels.[23] The variety of terminology is a reflection of the wide range that such areas can assume, and the absence of a standard legal concept.

Five features of most of the areas of special protection as actually established have been as follows:

- different nomenclature from that specified in the conventions has been used;
- areas of special protection have generally been proclaimed or supported by outside states and international bodies, especially the UN Security Council, rather than by the belligerents themselves;
- outside military forces have in all cases except Sri Lanka had responsibilities for protecting these areas;
- a central concern has been with the safety of refugees, and the prevention of massive new refugee flows; and
- military activity of one kind or another by local belligerents has sometimes continued within the areas of special protection.

The major area of special protection in the post-Cold War era, which contributed to the development of the concept elsewhere, was northern Iraq in the immediate aftermath of the 1991 Gulf War. Following a failed uprising which the Western powers helped to incite, huge numbers of people, mainly in northern and southern Iraq, fled their homes, many ending up on the Iranian and Turkish borders. Starting on 17 April 1991, a military operation by US, UK and French forces helped to establish a 'safe haven' in part of Iraq north of the 36th parallel. This was to enable some 400,000 mainly Kurdish refugees on the Turkish border to return to a degree of safety in northern Iraq. UN Secretary-General Javier Pérez de Cuéllar initially expressed doubts about this move, saying that it posed a legal problem 'even if there is no difficulty from the moral and humanitarian point of view'.[24]

On 18 April, as a result of extended negotiations with the Iraqi government, UN officials secured an agreement to allow humanitarian aid workers and relief supplies access to Iraq's entire population, including Kurds and Shi'a refugees. On 21 April, the Iraqi government requested that the UN Secretary-General assume responsibility, within the framework of the 18

April agreement, for the transit centres at Zakho in northern Iraq. Following this request, UNHCR assumed responsibility for humanitarian assistance in the coalition's security zone by mid-June 1991. This was the framework within which the coalition troops were replaced by a 500-strong United Nations Guards Contingent in Iraq (UNGCI). This contingent was drawn from the UN Guards, whose role is essentially that of doormen at UN premises, and it was given a unique status, being neither a peacekeeping force nor an enforcement body. Its formal task was to protect all staff, equipment and supplies of the Inter-Agency Humanitarian Programme in Iraq. It was presented to Baghdad as direct and limited support to the humanitarian operation, and to the Kurds (especially through a massive leaflet campaign) as a real safeguard which would allow them to return. Many Kurds thus repatriated voluntarily, but their decision to do so was in part based on false assumptions.

With the deployment of UNGCI, the main military back-up for the 'safe haven' in northern Iraq became an external one – the ominously entitled *Operation Poised Hammer* in Turkey, by which the coalition, even after its troops had withdrawn from northern Iraq, threatened Iraq with air attack if it did not comply with the various terms imposed on it. Having been initially established without the consent of the Iraqi government, the 'safe haven' in northern Iraq was not just an unusual safety zone, but also an unorthodox case of 'humanitarian intervention'. Its special features included the fact that it was established by the forces of three or four powers with only a limited degree of authority from UN Security Council resolutions, and that there was no chance of completely disarming the area, as it was inhabited by Kurds for whom bearing arms and internecine warfare is a way of life. It has endured for five years, which is longer than any other contemporary safety zone, but the protection offered is increasingly eroded. Its central limitation – that there was neither the capacity nor the will either to stop or significantly influence local military activities – was its undoing; military forces from Turkey, Iran and eventually Iraq itself went in, or were invited in, to support factions they viewed as friendly and to fight those which they saw as a threat.

The 'safe areas' in Bosnia and Herzegovina in 1993–95 also ran into problems largely because of the inherent difficulty of controlling military activities within the safe area as well as activities against it. Established during war, with the consent of the host government, they were designed to protect the inhabitants of six towns (including large numbers of refugees who had fled to them) from Bosnian Serb forces who were in a position to besiege them, and were militarily predominant. This was bound to be a particularly difficult task.

The language of the resolutions establishing the 'safe areas' in Bosnia suggests that humanitarian considerations loomed large in the Security Council. The initial resolution of April 1993 demanding 'that all parties and others concerned treat Srebrenica and its surroundings as a safe area which should be free from any armed attack or any other hostile act' used the word 'humanitarian' eight times, including three condemnations of violations of international humanitarian law.[25] These concerns were also reflected in the resolution of May 1993 extending the concept of 'safe area' to five additional threatened areas: Sarajevo, Tuzla, Zepa, Gorazde and Bihac. This declared that the concept of 'safe area' involved 'full respect by all parties of the rights of UNPROFOR and the international humanitarian agencies to free and unimpeded access to all safe areas in the Republic of Bosnia and Herzegovina and full respect for the safety of the personnel engaged in these operations'.[26] The geographical limits of most of the safe areas were never defined.

The events in and around the 'safe areas' in 1993–95 provided poignant proof that the proclamation of humanitarian goals still leaves a host of questions to be addressed. The most difficult one was how the UN, or NATO, was going to protect these areas. A June 1993 resolution provided a dual framework for the use of force in aid of the safe areas. On the one hand, UNPROFOR was authorised to 'deter attacks against the safe areas', and also, 'acting in self-defence', to take action dealing with bombardments against, and armed incursions into, them. On the other hand, 'UN Member States, acting nationally or through regional organisations or arrangements' (a clear reference to NATO) were authorised to take, in coordination with the UN Secretary-General and UNPROFOR, 'all necessary measures, through the use of air power, in and around the safe areas in the Republic of Bosnia and Herzegovina, to support UNPROFOR in the performance of its mandate'.[27] This tortuous language reflected equivocation among the leading members of the Security Council about the extent to which they were prepared to become directly involved in the conflict.

For the UN and NATO, the problem of protecting the six 'safe areas' was compounded by the fact that these were not neutral zones, but areas in which, and from which, Bosnian forces operated. The Serbs complained continuously that the so-called 'safe areas' were being used by the Bosnians to launch attacks against them, as was conspicuously the case with the Bosnian offensive launched from Bihac in November 1994. The Bosnian government cannot be blamed for its desire to maintain armed forces in the 'safe areas'; it naturally saw these forces as having a role both defending the areas, and in military operations aimed at ending their encirclement.

A further problem for the UN and NATO was the high degree of uncertainty about when and how forces was to be used. Should it be used whenever the safe areas were attacked or humanitarian convoys stopped, even if the Bosnian armed forces had been engaged in attacks launched from the safe areas? And should the use of force be confined to the smoking guns directly implicated in attacks on the 'safe areas', or be directed more generally at Bosnian Serb military assets? These questions were especially hard to answer since any use of force required the agreement both of NATO and of Boutros-Ghali's representative in former Yugoslavia, Yasushi Akashi. The latter's extreme caution regarding the use of force seemed to be unhappily vindicated when such uses of force as did take place led to Serb retaliation in the form of taking UNPROFOR personnel hostage. During 1994 and the first half of

1995, despite some successes, such as the establishment of the heavy weapons exclusion zone around Sarajevo, no convincing answers were found. From the outset of the 'safe areas' concept, there were concerns (already articulated by Under-Secretary-General Kofi Annan on 4 June 1993 in a message seeking clarification of UNSCR 836) that the use of air-power would have serious security implications for personnel engaged in humanitarian assistance.

In mid-1995, Bosnian Serb arrogance made possible the emergence of an effective policy. By virtually stopping UN operations in Serb-held areas, including humanitarian aid to the safe areas, the Serbs effectively reduced UNPROFOR's vulnerability to reprisals. Then, by committing appalling atrocities in connection with the conquest of Srebrenica and Zepa in July 1995, they exposed the bankruptcy of existing Western and UN policies. Responding to what was both a humanitarian disaster and an affront to their credibility, the UN and NATO had to move towards decisive military action against the Serbs.

Overall, the experience of special protection areas suggests that preventing military activity within them is extremely difficult. In refugee camps there has often been coercive pressure on inmates from armed groups, whether inside or outside the camp. Areas of special protection may be used by one party as a springboard for military attacks, as in Bosnia-Herzegovina in 1993–95.

Sometimes the outside bodies which have designated certain areas as safe may have to take military action to make them so. In such cases, humanitarian considerations may point to the need to take sides in the conflict, at least to the extent of punishing and deterring those who violate safe areas. Humanitarian concerns can thus be part of the ratchet-like process whereby large international bodies are slowly goaded from the sidelines of conflicts, until they end up as active participants.

Trusteeship and other administrative roles

A logical consequence of the international community's increased emphasis on humanitarian action might well be the establishment of temporary trustee-type administrations in areas undergoing social and political breakdown. Such administrations might be established with the consent of local parties, or in a framework of coercive 'humanitarian intervention'.

In countries where the UN has become involved in peacekeeping and humanitarian activities because of a general breakdown of government, the organisation and its leading members have been reluctant to assume responsibility for government. For the most part such UN roles in government have been confined to administrative assistance, civil affairs programmes, training, helping to hold or monitor elections, and generally giving advice.

Former Yugoslavia is a clear case in point. The UN Secretariat was consistently reluctant to adopt any of the various plans advanced for administering Sarajevo even after a proper peace agreement was reached. This view was reinforced by the problems encountered by the EU Administrator for Mostar, who assumed his difficult responsibilities on 23 July 1994, in the wake of the US-brokered peace agreement between the Bosnian government and Bosnian Croats of February–March.

In some countries where government scarcely exists, or is itself part of the problem, limited roles of the type that the UN has assumed in recent operations may be inadequate. The absence of direct administrative responsibility may sometimes restrict the options available to UN forces to primarily military ones.

A major difficulty is that the historical record of various forms of mandate, trusteeship and international administration has been mixed. Iraq and Rwanda, both of which were under trusteeship for substantial periods in the first half of this century, serve as reminders that trusteeship is no simple cure-all. However, proposals for such arrangements have continued to appear in international diplomacy, and the concept certainly merits reconsideration.[28]

There is no sign of any new formal system of trusteeship. In some respects an imperial situation exists today, but who are the imperialists? Except in cases of regional hegemony, old-fashioned direct exercise of dominance is out of fashion. The UN Trusteeship Council, by ending the special status of Palau, has completed its last remaining task. While there may in some circumstances be good reasons to establish a temporary externally based administrative system, especially when such a proposal has the active support of all parties in a dispute, the probability is that, if this is done at all, it will be done indirectly, by the accretion of functions to various UN or other agencies and forces in a particular country and not by the proclamation of a new general system of trusteeship.

Implementing the laws of war

One branch of humanitarian consideration that has come into sharp focus in recent conflicts is the laws of war. This body of law – also known as the 'rules of war' (a term often used within armed forces), and as 'international humanitarian law' (a term generally taken to encompass a wide range of human-rights instruments) – is intended to guide the conduct of belligerents and occupying powers, and to ensure particularly that certain basic rules are observed, including helping the wounded, proper treatment of prisoners, respect for inhabitants of occupied territories, and non-use of prohibited means and methods of warfare. It also deals with such enduring issues as the rights and duties of neutral powers.

Many formal provisions in the laws of war covering implementation and enforcement have been little used. For example, there have been relatively few cases of belligerents appointing protecting powers, which are supposed to perform such tasks as looking after the interests of civilians in occupied territories and facilitating the establishment of hospital zones. The provisions in the four 1949 Geneva Conventions for trial or extradition of offenders have scarcely been invoked, and no use at all has so far been made of the International Humanitarian Fact Finding Commission, set up in 1991 in accord with the terms of the 1977 Geneva Protocol I. All this does not mean the Conventions have not been implemented, but rather that implementation has often assumed different forms from what was originally envisaged.[29]

In the main conventions there is extensive provision for ICRC and other bodies to carry out a wide range of humanitarian and monitoring tasks, and in most conflicts it has been ICRC representatives who have done so, especially visiting places of detention and assisting with exchanges of prisoners. Belligerents are willing to entrust ICRC with such tasks partly because it is recognised as an independent and neutral intermediary. The combined emphasis on confidentiality and on host government consent which governs much of ICRC's work has been a strength as well as a weakness – a strength, because it allowed access to places where others could not go; but a weakness, because in the many cases where it was aware of infractions of the conventions, it could do relatively little. Over the past two or three decades ICRC has increasingly reminded belligerents of their obligations under the conventions and has issued public protests at particularly outrageous actions. In former Yugoslavia, ICRC publicly denounced ill-treatment of detainees and civilians on 23 August 1992, when ICRC was denied access to the Manjaca and Omarska camps, and on 7 September 1994, after the belligerents, despite repeated appeals from ICRC, continued to disregard the security of civilians.[30] In summary, ICRC can help implementation of the conventions, but it does not have (and indeed has never sought) a capacity to enforce them; that remains the responsibility of states.[31]

Since the mid-1980s, the UN has become more involved in enforcing provisions of international humanitarian law. Evidence of this growing role includes the following:

- In the **Iran–Iraq War**, the UN Secretary-General, acting on his own behalf, dispatched a mission to the area in January 1985 to investigate the conditions under which POWs were being held.

  On 21 March 1986, a UN Security Council statement for the first time criticised Iraq by name for using gas.[32] On 26 August 1988, the Security Council unanimously adopted Resolution 620 condemning 'the use of chemical weapons in the conflict between Iran and Iraq'.

- In the **Iraq–Kuwait conflict,** from August 1990 onwards, several UN Security Council resolutions criticised Iraqi violations of international humanitarian law, including seizure of hostages, in occupied Kuwait.

  UNSCR 674 of 29 October 1990 invited states to collect information on grave breaches by Iraq and make it available to the Security Council.

  After the suspension of hostilities on 28 February 1991 the Security Council took no further action on this front. However, its Resolution 686 of 2 March 1991 did require Iraq to accept liability for loss, damage or injury arising from its invasion and occupation of Kuwait.

- In the **wars in former Yugoslavia**, UNSCR 764 of 13 July 1992 reaffirmed that all parties are bound to comply with their obligations under international humanitarian law, and that persons who commit or order the commission of grave breaches are individually responsible.

  UNSCR 771 of 13 August 1992 called on states to collate substantiated information on violations of humanitarian law, and also said that if the parties failed to comply the Council would take 'further measures'.

  UNSCR 780 of 6 October 1992 asked the Secretary-General to establish an impartial Commission of Experts, which was done that same month.

  UNSCR 808 of 22 February 1993 established an international tribunal regarding violations of international humanitarian law in former Yugoslavia since 1991.

  UNSCR 827 of 25 May 1993 approved the Statute of the International Tribunal for the Prosecution of Persons Responsible for Serious Violations of International Humanitarian Law Committed in the Territory of the Former Yugoslavia Since 1991, which was subsequently established in The Hague.

- In **Somalia**, UNSCR 794 of 3 December 1992 made several references to international humanitarian law, deploring widespread violations and stating that it 'strongly condemns all violations of international humanitarian law occurring in Somalia, including in particular the deliberate impeding of the delivery of food and medical supplies essential for the survival of the civilian population, and affirms that those who commit or order the commission of such acts will be held individually responsible'. This was the resolution that authorised the US-led UNITAF to intervene in Somalia; citing violations of international humanitarian law as part of the justification for intervention was unusual.

- Over **Rwanda**, UNSCR 918 of 17 May 1994 requested the Secretary-General 'to present a report as soon as possible on the investigation of serious violations of international humanitarian law committed in Rwanda during the conflict.'

  UNSCR 955 of 8 November 1994 approved the Statute of the International Tribunal for Rwanda.

Apart from the UN Security Council, other international bodies have been increasingly preoccupied with issues relating to the implementation, or failure to implement, international humanitarian law. This was an important aspect of two cases taken to the International Court of Justice. The first was *Nicaragua v. USA*, on which judgment was given on 27 June 1986. This case concerned the legitimacy of planting mines in Nicaraguan waters, but also involved a number of other issues of the laws of war. The second was the case brought by Bosnia and Herzegovina against the Federal Republic of Yugoslavia (FRY), *Case Concerning the Application of the Convention on the Prevention and Punishment of the Crime of Genocide*.

One call for more effective implementation of international humanitarian law was the International Conference on the Protection of War Victims, held in Geneva from 30 August to 1 September 1993. Representatives of 160 states attended. Like the 1989 Paris Conference on Chemical Weapons, this tried to restore the sanctity of battered norms. Virtually all the recommendations in the declaration agreed at the conference were aimed at increasing the number of formal adherents to the existing rules of international humanitarian law and improving the dissemination and practical implementation of those rules.

Thus, since the mid-1980s there has been an exceptional amount of high-level activity designed to improve the implementation of the laws of war. In particular, the UN Security Council has acquired a greater role than was foreseen in the conventions themselves. This has proved extremely problematical. It has required the UN to uphold standards in circumstances where it cannot ensure their application.

Several conflicts, especially in former Yugoslavia and Rwanda, have compelled UN peacekeeping forces and international humanitarian agencies to confront the issue of how to act when they have evidence of massive violations of the most basic humanitarian rules by belligerents. Inasmuch as an answer has emerged, it appears to be that information on violations may be recorded and passed on, at least by some national contingents through their own national authorities, and through humanitarian workers. However, in some cases there have been understandings that such information would not be used or be the basis for formal evidence without further consultation.

In former Yugoslavia, despite the establishment of the International Criminal Tribunal in 1993, UN peacekeepers were not given a formal mandate to arrest suspected war criminals and hold them for possible trial, nor did they actually do so. Indeed, many UNPROFOR reports played down the war crimes issue. Clearly there would be some built-in problems for peacekeepers if they were expected to negotiate with belligerents on a wide range of matters (such as allowing the transit of relief convoys and helping arrange a peace settlement), while at the same time they were asked to arrest the same belligerents on war crimes charges. The Dayton Agreement of November-December 1995 contained specific commitments about the prosecution of war crimes. The establishment of the NATO-led Implementation Force (IFOR) in Bosnia in December raised hopes that suspected war criminals would be arrested. Yet IFOR was not given orders to pursue this matter actively. Maintaining a precarious peace between belligerents seemed to have priority over forceful implementation of humanitarian norms. IFOR inherited UNPROFOR's dilemmas.

The issue of punishment of war crimes exposes the continuing tension between the power of states and non-state entities on the one hand, and ideas of an over-arching international order on the other. For most of the time the laws of war, like other parts of international law, must be implemented through national mechanisms of various kinds – national laws, manuals of military law, government-established commissions of inquiry, and courts and courts-martial. The weaknesses of relying on national implementation are notorious, and the record of non-state entities in applying the laws of war is even more problematic. Yet the point has not been reached where implementation on a supra-national level is proven. The establishment of the international tribunals for Yugoslavia and Rwanda is a significant step in that direction.

Concern about implementing international humanitarian law is a driving force behind proposals for the establishment of a permanent international criminal court, which is the subject of ongoing negotiations under UN auspices. There is no disagreement that this international court would be involved in trying three 'core crimes' – war crimes, crimes against humanity and genocide. However, there are numerous issues yet to be resolved about jurisdiction over other crimes, and the extent to which the prosecutor might have an independent investigatory role. Whether or not the champions of this proposal overcome the concerns of states about independent supra-national investigations into their security activities, the demand for effective implementation of the laws of war is likely to remain very strong, and to be difficult to translate into effective policies of international enforcement against recalcitrant states.

IV. Key issues

Attempts to carry out humanitarian missions in war situations have repeatedly highlighted certain inter-connected issues – impartiality, reconciling humanitarianism and human rights, possible prolongation of wars, accountability of humanitarian organisations, humanitarian problems of international economic sanctions, humanitarian assistance and development assistance as rivals, armed protection of humanitarian workers, and legal protection for peacekeeping forces and humanitarian workers.

Impartiality and neutrality of humanitarian work

The concepts of impartiality and neutrality have for over a century been central to most approaches to humanitarian action in war. ICRC exemplifies this tradition. In its definition, the principle of impartiality means that the Red Cross 'makes no discrimination as to nationality, race, religious beliefs, class or political opinions. It endeavours to relieve the suffering of individuals, being guided solely by their needs, and to give priority to the most urgent cases of distress'. The principle of neutrality is defined thus: 'In order to continue to enjoy the confidence of all, the Red Cross may not take sides in hostilities or engage at any time in controversies of a political, racial, religious or ideological nature.'[1]

Impartiality and neutrality have also, for over a century, been the foundation of the international legal protection of humanitarian action in war. As the 1977 Geneva Protocol I states, 'relief actions which are humanitarian and impartial in character and conducted without any adverse distinction shall be undertaken, subject to the agreement of the Parties concerned in such relief actions. Offers of such relief shall not be regarded as interference in the armed conflict or as unfriendly acts'.[2]

For ICRC in particular, a reputation for impartiality, independence and neutrality is essential if it is to act in war zones, and to perform such delicate tasks as visiting people under internment, negotiating the release of POWs, and organising medical transport. The same is true, if to a slightly lesser degree, of many other humanitarian organisations.

Yet the idea of impartiality and neutrality has been under particular threat in the 1990s. Some of the problems are familiar. In wartime, humanitarian action, whether organised on its own or in conjunction with other measures, may seem impartial and disinterested to the outsiders engaging in it, but can be viewed differently by the local forces. History suggests that such efforts can seldom be perceived as impartial for any length of time. There are particular problems when, as so often happens in war, one party perceives the other not just as an aggressor, but as a ruthless or even genocidal power seeking to prevent humanitarian assistance reaching the victims of aggression. In such circumstances, one party may view another as simply not entitled to humanitarian assistance, and may act accordingly.

In civil wars, which have been the main form of conflict since 1945, the difficulties confronting a relief operation are especially great. Combatants' perceptions of neutrality become the practical measure of neutrality. Since rival communities are often very close physically and may aim at uprooting civilians, each community may be particularly aware of, and hostile to, any aid or protection accorded to its enemies.[3] An international relief presence often puts money into the hands of warlords, involves a degree of recognition of them as 'the authorities' in a particular area, and may act as a deterrent to air strikes against them.

The involvement of governments and major international political organisations in humanitarian action has added to the problems of maintaining impartiality and neutrality. NGOs working in conflict situations are often the channel by which governments, international organisations and major foundations distribute their humanitarian aid. Many such NGOs naturally fear that there may be political pressure on them to act in a way that would weaken their impartiality, or that mere association with a particular source of funding could be damaging.

The sheer scale of humanitarian action, and the involvement of governments and international organisations in financing it, have led it to be used as a means of achieving political objectives. This accusation was made regarding the situation in Georgia up to 1995:

> To date, efforts to use humanitarian instruments to facilitate normalisation have been dysfunctional. Attempts to achieve the rapid return of the internally displaced populations before conditions were conducive

jeopardised their security and set back the peace process. Denial of assistance to insurgent regions by UN and other aid agencies has had serious negative consequences for their populations while doing little to push Abkhaz and Osset leaders to compromise in the political negotiations. In short, politicisation of humanitarian action – itself a departure from humanitarian principles – has undercut the attainment of humanitarian objectives.[4]

The need to secure some form of physical protection in war zones for aid workers, their activities and those they seek to assist presents a major challenge to impartiality and neutrality. The importance of such protection has been increasingly recognised by many involved in humanitarian work. Yet it is impossible to obtain such protection and maintain traditional views of this work as being above, or at least outside, the fray. Such protection – whether from local, external, multinational or even UN-authorised forces – jeopardises the impartiality and neutrality of aid efforts. Even if the forces involved are multinational and under UN auspices, they may be seen as favouring one side, especially if the UN is simultaneously involved in such political issues as enforcing sanctions, or trying to resolve the conflict.

A further, closely related challenge to impartiality and neutrality derives from the fact that many aid workers, as in Rwanda and Bosnia, may come to take a partisan view about the causes of a conflict, may protest publicly about atrocities, and may develop strong sympathies or antipathies to the parties. They may be particularly inclined to do so if outside states and international organisations have themselves offered no more than a humanitarian response. In the 1990s, international humanitarian agencies and NGOs have sometimes advocated major shifts in public policies, including even military intervention by outside powers or the creation of a new administration in a country. It is natural for them to want the international community to devote major human, military and financial resources to such purposes. In Bosnia and Rwanda, for example, many aid workers argued that there should have been a much more forceful UN role against the main groups engaged in mass killings – the Serbs in the former, the Hutu governmental forces in the latter.

Articulating policy in this way is inevitably controversial. Relief organisations have been criticised for making 'extraordinarily bold calls, apparently unimpeded by limits on their mandate and expertise, or by accountability'.[5] However, bold policy articulation represents, to some, an escape from a straitjacket. The requirements of impartiality and neutrality have often led humanitarian organisations (and those in charge of peacekeeping operations) to describe conflicts in excessively bland or even misleading terms. Equally, when dependent on the cooperation of the predominant force in an area, humanitarian organisations have sometimes avoided systematic criticism of its crimes or failures. In Ethiopia in the late 1980s, for example, despite the evidence that repeated humanitarian crises were caused largely by disastrous government policies, ongoing civil war, and the absence of institutions through which changes could be introduced, 'a political emergency was redefined as a natural disaster'.[6] There is also pressure on humanitarian organisations to present the recipients of their assistance as 'deserving poor', worthy of their donors' generosity. Hence there can be a tendency to underestimate the extent to which, for example, certain refugee camps are filled by criminals or dominated by armed gangs.

Another reason why aid workers have become increasingly outspoken is the failure of major powers to develop clear and coherent policies themselves. Indeed, the very retreat of major powers into the bland language of humanitarianism has forced aid workers to advocate policy. David Bryer has wryly said of humanitarian organisations operating in Bosnia, 'by filling a policy vacuum, we have been elevated into political actors ourselves ... While NGOs have taken on some functions which were previously the ambit of states or inter-governmental bodies, the humanitarian response has often been the only meaningful expression of governments' concern'.[7] He has added a more general explanation of why NGOs sometimes advocate controversial policy positions:

> Is it not that the 'complex emergencies' of this decade have held up a critical mirror to the previous professional compartments of emergency aid, development, security, human rights and international relations? They have shown us that it is impossible either to understand or to relieve such suffering without placing emergency aid – however 'impartial' – into a wider strategy, which *inter alia* enables the recipients of such aid to have protection. It is not the task of aid agencies to provide that protection, beyond cooperating with official and NGO human rights bodies when they have evidence of abuses, but it is incumbent on them to articulate what other actors could do to provide that protection. To take extreme examples, if NGOs come to advocate any use of military forces, it is only as a last resort, but it is not outside the interest in political and security issues which they now see as relevant. The greater recognition that providing aid can do harm as well as good makes many NGOs judge that they should not give that aid if they do not also press those who can reduce or prevent its abuse.[8]

The need for 'governments to address the policy vacuum' was emphasised by the International Federation of the Red Cross and Red Crescent Societies at its 1995 International Conference. However, the movement seemed to envisage that the function of governmental action is 'to underpin humanitarian assistance whose independence and impartiality is respected and guaranteed', and to provide 'humanitarian space'.[9] In reality, humanitarian action itself often involves elements of partiality; and for governments to address policy vacuums often involves forging alliances between local parties, supporting one side or opposing another, and encouraging temporary or permanent withdrawals of exposed humanitarian workers.

The fact that some humanitarian actions have involved departures from traditional principles of non-partisanship has had one obvious consequence; it has led those organisations most anxious to retain a reputation for impartiality and neutrality to be circumspect in their relations with their more outspoken or engaged counterparts. ICRC has exemplified most clearly the concern that associating its work with that of others may undermine its impartiality. It has vigorously objected to the abuse of the Red Cross symbol by other humanitarian organisations. It has also pointed out that humanitarian work with political organisations, even as universal as the UN, contains pitfalls for the unwary. As the President of ICRC said in an address to the UN General Assembly in November 1992:

> ... humanitarian endeavour and political action must go their separate ways if the neutrality and impartiality of humanitarian work is not to be jeopardised ... it is dangerous to link humanitarian activities aimed at meeting the needs of victims of a conflict with political measures designed to bring about the settlement of the dispute between the parties.[10]

It is undeniably difficult for the UN, and for agencies within the UN system, to maintain impartiality when the system is by nature involved in a wide range of political decision-making, and when its security responsibilities may lead it to advocate enforcement measures against a particular party. This consideration, as well as the complex and cumbersome character of UN structures, has led some to conclude that the UN should not be in the humanitarian relief business at all. As James Ingram, Executive Director of WFP from 1982 to 1992, has stated:

> The question arises whether humanitarian goals may not be better achieved under a new and different regime. I believe they would. The United Nations should confine its role to political functions associated with the resolution of disputes, the prevention of conflict and coercive interventions to end it. Reaching and succouring the victims of conflict and coordinating the relief efforts of the international community should cease to be a United Nations responsibility.[11]

Ingram proposes instead that the humanitarian goal of saving lives should be performed by an enlarged and internationalised ICRC, or else by a new organisation established by governments, preferably outside the UN framework. These proposals are not likely to be implemented. The political pressures in the UN system militate in favour of its involvement in this field, and despite all the difficulties some UN agencies have developed impressive skills and reputations. However, these proposals do usefully focus attention on the unavoidable conflicts between the UN's political and impartial humanitarian roles.

Can the principles of impartiality and neutrality stand up to the weight of the manifold challenges? These principles have had strong reaffirmation in the Red Cross movement's 1994 Code of Conduct for relief workers (discussed further below), and also in the Madrid Declaration of representatives of prominent humanitarian agencies and donors, drawn up at a 'humanitarian summit' on 14 December 1995. The Madrid Declaration did state bluntly that 'humanitarian assistance is neither a solution nor a panacea for crises which are essentially manmade'. It also reaffirmed a commitment 'to protect and feed the victims'. However, neither of these statements explored how protection was to be achieved. They avoided a simple truth, namely that if the provision of physical protection within conflict zones is seen as a necessary part of humanitarian action, then sometimes it may be necessary to have alliances with powers and even with local parties. The failure to bite this bullet may at times involve humanitarian workers betraying and abandoning those whom they seek to assist.

Tension between humanitarianism and human rights

One point of concern in many instances of humanitarian action has been the apparent clash with human rights. Because it is deemed to require impartiality humanitarian activity has frequently avoided political issues, even in cases involving fundamental human rights. The dichotomy between humanitarianism and human rights, always problematic, has been challenged in the post-Cold War era. Some NGOs concerned with human rights have made trenchant criticisms of the even-handedness, tentativeness and ineffectual character of many UN peacekeeping and humanitarian activities. Human Rights Watch, a US-based organisation, said in a 1993 report:

> While severe human rights abuses often play a critical part in fueling armed conflict and aggravating humanitarian crisis, they have been given a low priority by the officials who oversee UN field operations. This lost agenda handicaps the UN in its new and ambitious undertakings, as it sells short one of the central ideals on which the UN was founded.[12]

Similarly, in a striking and occasionally strident critique of the role of humanitarian bodies in the conflicts of the 1990s, London-based African Rights has identified what it terms 'the basic dilemma':

> During the Cold War, a small and sharply-circumscribed space was labelled 'humanitarian'. The space was defined by Western governments and host governments, in ways that suited their political interests. Currently, there is a sharpened awareness of the problems of operating relief programmes under authorities (governments, rebel armies and militias) that are abusing human rights. These are old problems, but now there is the possibility to talk openly about them, and perhaps even to change

operating practices. The central dilemma is whether it is possible to supply humanitarian assistance, under the auspices of a governing authority that abuses human rights, without also giving undue assistance to that authority, and hence doing a disservice to the people one is aiming to help.[13]

This publication, 'Humanitarianism Unbound?', itemises various ways in which relief has become intimately involved in insurgency and counter-insurgency warfare, the struggle for state power, and warlordism: material assistance to the combatants; providing strategic protection, for example by keeping roads open for both humanitarian and military traffic; and providing legitimacy to the controlling authority in any of a wide variety of ways, including, for example, disguising forced relocation to protected sites as a humanitarian relief operation. Humanitarian operations can also let governments off the hook from their own responsibilities for looking after the populations under their control. Humanitarian agencies are specifically accused of denying a case of forced resettlement in Ethiopia in 1988, despite the fact that their own staffs witnessed it.[14]

Sometimes humanitarian relief is seen as a weak substitute for human rights. In the 1990s, relief aid has been directed towards countries undergoing civil war in order to contain the outflow of refugees. In the process, norms have shifted from the right to asylum, and the right to leave one's country, to far more nebulous concepts such as 'in-country protection'. Providing relief can easily become a substitute for protecting persecuted people.

There is undeniably some tension between humanitarian and human-rights approaches, which seem to call for different and apparently incompatible policies – the first, for impartial delivery of relief, and the second, for robust opposition to those who violate human-rights norms. Yet there is no point in 'a fruitless theoretical argument about whether rights to humanitarian assistance or protection from violence are more important'.[15] Practice has shown that there is some scope for overlap. The UN has incorporated a human-rights element into some of its peacekeeping operations, especially its contributions to post-war reconstruction after the long civil wars in Cambodia and El Salvador. UNHCR has tried to combine its humanitarian action with a human-rights dimension, especially in drawing attention to gross violations in former Yugoslavia; its right to do so has not been questioned.[16] The process of bringing human rights, especially protection from violence, into humanitarian activities reinforces the conclusion that in practice humanitarian and political activities cannot be completely separated.

Possible prolongation of wars

Does the provision of humanitarian assistance during a war actually prolong it? This accusation has been made with particular frequency in connection with the wars in Ethiopia in the 1980s, and Somalia, Bosnia, Liberia and

Sierra Leone in the 1990s. Of Ethiopia, for example, African Rights has said, 'There is little doubt that aid to the government side prolonged the war'.[17]

It is a truth not denied by any of the major humanitarian agencies involved in these conflicts that, despite serious efforts to prevent such an outcome, a proportion of aid does end up in the hands of the warring parties. Some may be taken at established checkpoints, as dues paid to ensure its onward passage; some may be stolen at gunpoint. Even if what is safely delivered is given only to civilians, some of them may pass it on to soldiers; the net effect in any case may be to release food, fuel or other supplies for use by the armed forces.

Thus humanitarian aid may provide a cushion which enables armies to carry on fighting; it may also enable losing sides to avoid admitting defeat, since they are protected from the pain and loss of life which might cause them to sue for peace. A dependency culture could emerge, in which a society relied heavily on aid, saw its own agriculture and industry weakened by an influx of foreign aid that undermined local market mechanisms, and was unable to end the fighting that had originally created the need for aid.

Actual cases frequently reveal quite different patterns. Since, in most conflicts, armies are the last groups to suffer starvation, the importance of food aid seeping through to them is often marginal. Frequently the provision of humanitarian assistance is merely neutral, enabling non-combatants to survive, but not fundamentally affecting the duration let alone the outcome of a war.

It may be impossible to know how long a war would have continued in the absence of such an effort, but even if aid were to prolong a war, that would not in itself prove that the effect of the aid was entirely negative. For example, in Bosnia and Herzegovina the humanitarian aid could conceivably have helped belligerents, and in particular the Bosnian government forces, to soldier on. Yet coupled with peacekeeping efforts, it also assisted in substantially reducing war-related deaths in Bosnia, especially in 1993 and 1994. Thus the war may have lasted longer but been less costly. In addition, the aid may have helped stave off what could otherwise have been a Bosnian defeat in the face of Serb offensives and harsh winters under siege. Finally, it helped to keep Bosnia in international focus, and contributed to the emergence in 1995 of a more active Western policy towards the conflict.

If humanitarian aid may on occasion prolong wars, the refusal to provide aid may provoke them. The spectacle of those who have the capacity to assist choosing not to do so can have huge emotional power. It is the humanitarian equivalent of the Red Army camped on the east bank of Vistula while the 1944 Warsaw uprising was brutally suppressed by the Germans.[18] The UK's fanatical adherence to *laissez-faire* during the 'great famine' in Ireland in 1845–49, and its refusal to take administrative or humanitarian measures to save lives, left an enduring legacy of bitterness.[19] This is still contributing to violence and distrust over a century later. The international community can hardly wish the twenty-first century to witness any repetition of this dismal experience on a global scale.

Accountability and codes of conduct

Many of the NGOs and relief agencies involved in humanitarian action make decisions about the fates of thousands of people, provide a flow of information about crisis situations and, increasingly, engage in policy advocacy. Yet they are not always fully accountable for their actions. Also, the codes of conduct under which they operate are proving problematic.

In the country where operations take place there is often an absence of formal controls. In failing or failed states, for example, there may be no functioning ministries to regulate programmes, no labour legislation to constrain hiring and firing policies, and no structures to enforce demands for local financial accountability. 'In this case, the power relations between host and NGO are dramatically tilted in favour of the latter – and the hosts sometimes resort to the power of the gun to reassert their influence, in a malign way'.[20]

Furthermore, there is often a lack of serious, publicly available professional analysis of the impact of humanitarian action. Those engaged in relief actions know of cases in which the wrong types of goods were sent, distribution was woefully mismanaged, or grain supplies arrived late but just in time to destroy the market in local produce, thus exacerbating problems of dependency. The proliferation of new NGOs with little or no professional expertise has been a particular concern.

The major players do train their personnel and do have procedures for assessing the needs of victims and the impact of their action. However, there remains a case for developing higher professional standards, fuller accountability, and more open public debate about the roles of international agencies and NGOs. The distribution of humanitarian relief must be viewed as an activity that requires professional management and evaluation.

A ten-point Code of Conduct for relief workers, drawn up in 1994 and unanimously approved by representatives of 142 governments in December 1995, and also endorsed by over 70 NGOs, sought to address problems of ethics and accountability. 'Aid is given regardless of race, creed or nationality of the recipients ... Aid priorities are calculated on the basis of need alone. We shall endeavour not to act as instruments of government foreign policy. We hold ourselves accountable to both those we seek to assist and those from whom we accept resources'.[21] Not one of the ten points addressed in any way the critical issue of how to protect vulnerable populations and aid activities, nor how impartial relief work could be combined with human-rights advocacy, sanctions or other coercive measures. Governments and NGOs appeared to be addressing humanitarian issues in a pious and abstract manner far removed from the harsh dilemmas resulting from wars. The December 1995 Madrid Declaration was another reflection of this tendency.

It is easy to agree on such principles as accountability, but much harder to act on them. One critical account of humanitarian action in war is the five-volume Joint Evaluation of Emergency Assistance to Rwanda issued in 1996. This interesting exercise in accountability resulted from a multinational, multi-donor research effort, whose main objective was 'to draw lessons from the Rwanda experience relevant for future complex emergencies as well as for current operations in Rwanda and the region, such as early warning and conflict management, preparation for and provision of emergency assistance, and the transition from relief to rehabilitation and development'. The volume on humanitarian aid concluded unambiguously that 'humanitarian action cannot serve as a substitute for political, diplomatic and, where necessary, military action. The onus of responsibility must, first and foremost, be upon the political and diplomatic domain to address complex emergencies'. It also called on the UN Security Council to establish a Humanitarian Sub-Committee to 'inform fully the Security Council of developments and concerns regarding the humanitarian dimensions of complex emergencies'.[22] Its conclusions may be flawed – the discussion of protection is weak, and one more UN committee does not seem likely to transform the landscape – but the study is a welcome recognition that humanitarian action needs to be subject to thorough evaluation and accountability. As was stated in the study's conclusions, 'A tendency by some official agencies and NGOs to emphasise or inflate positive accomplishments and play down or ignore problems resulted in distorted reporting. Even basic data on staff, finances and activities were difficult or impossible to obtain from a number of NGOs'.[23]

Humanitarian problems of international economic sanctions

International economic sanctions are often viewed in a favourable light because they constitute a form of international pressure that falls short of war. UN-authorised impositions of sanctions, rare until 1990, have increased greatly since. The main cases of UN sanctions since 1945 (with the principal authorising resolution in brackets) are listed in Table 4.

While the humanitarian or other rationales for using sanctions as distinct from other forms of pressure are often persuasive, the experience of some of these cases suggests that there are conflicts between sanctions and humanitarianism. Frequently (as in the cases of Iraq in 1991 and Haiti in 1994) sanctions are preludes to measures involving the use of armed force. Further, ordinary citizens of the target state, especially the poor and the vulnerable, normally suffer the adverse effects of sanctions more than the government and its armed forces. Any sanctions based on the idea that domestic suffering will make people rise up against their government clearly conflict with humanitarian priorities. Finally, sanctions can, as in the case of Haiti, contribute to migration out of the sanctioned state.

In two of the major cases of general economic sanctions in the post-Cold War period – Iraq, and Serbia/Montenegro – the UN Security Council has made provision for exceptions on humanitarian grounds, for example, when there is a demonstrated need for food or medicine for vulnerable sections of the population. The imperatives that led to provision for possible exceptions were obviously overwhelming, yet the experience has left questions in the

Table 4 Cases of UN sanctions since 1945

Year	Location Type of sanction (Authorising resolution)
1966–79	**Rhodesia** General economic sanctions, following its unilateral declaration of independence. (UNSCR 232 of 16 December 1966.)
1977–94	**South Africa** Embargo on the supply of arms on the grounds that their acquisition by South Africa constitutes a threat to international peace and security. (UNSCR 418 of 4 November 1977.)
1990–	**Iraq** General economic sanctions, following its invasion of Kuwait. (UNSCR 661 of 6 August 1990.)
1991–96	**Yugoslavia (and its successor states)** Arms embargo, following the outbreak of fighting. (UNSCR 713 of 25 September 1991.)
1992–	**Somalia** Arms embargo following outbreak of internal conflict. (UNSCR 733 of 23 January 1992.)
1992–	**Libya** Arms and air traffic embargo, following demands on Libya to renounce support for terrorism. More general sanctions were imposed in November 1993. (UNSCR 748 of 31 March 1992 and 883 of 11 November 1993.)
1992–96	**Federal Republic of Yugoslavia (Serbia and Montenegro)** General economic sanctions, following the FRY's military involvement in Bosnia and Herzegovina. (UNSCR 757 of 30 May 1992.)
1992–	**Liberia** Arms embargo, following cease-fire violations. (UNSCR 788 of 19 November 1992.)
1992–	**Khmer Rouge-held areas of Cambodia** Petroleum sanctions following failure of the Party of Democratic Kampuchea to comply with its obligations under the 1991 Paris agreements. (UNSCR 792 of 30 November 1992.)
1993–94	**Haiti** Arms embargo and petroleum sanctions, owing to the refugee flows from Haiti, and the failure of the regime to restore the legitimate government. (UNSCR 841 of 16 June 1993.)
1993–	*União Nacional para a Independência Total de Angola* **(UNITA) rebel movement in Angola** Arms embargo and petroleum sanctions following its failure to accept the results of elections and to observe a cease-fire. (UNSCR 864 of 15 September 1993.)
1994–	**Rwanda** Arms embargo, following the continuing and systematic violence within the country. (UNSCR 918 of 17 May 1994.)
1996–	**Sudan** Restrictions on Sudanese officials abroad and on aircraft movements following an assassination attempt against President Hosni Mubarak of Egypt. (UNSCR 1070 of 16 August 1996.)

minds of those involved in managing such policies. If such humanitarian exceptions are permitted, they could reduce the suffering caused by the sanctions, and so weaken their already uncertain effects. A different and probably more serious concern is that the existence of humanitarian assistance is assumed by the Security Council to mean that there is a safety net under the vulnerable, when in fact humanitarian exceptions do not work well. The target state, as in the case of Iraq, may simply reject them, at the cost of huge suffering.[24] It may be difficult to justify humanitarian aid while simultaneously imposing sanctions, especially in view of the rhetoric of humanitarianism, which abhors political distinctions and asserts the impartiality of assistance efforts. The UNHCR Chief of Mission in Serbia and Montenegro, Judith Kumin, referred to 'a fundamental contradiction – trying to implement a humanitarian programme in a sanctions environment'.[25] If this contradiction was more widely understood, the Security Council, when imposing sanctions, would at least be making an informed decision reflecting the reality that humanitarian exceptions are likely to be limited and controversial, and the vulnerable will still suffer most.

Humanitarian assistance versus development assistance

Economic and administrative failure can take as heavy a human toll as war. Poor nutrition, contaminated water supplies, inadequate health facilities and high unemployment can all cause massive human suffering and loss of life. They can also contribute to the breakdown of states and the outbreak of war. More lives might be saved by addressing these enduring problems in many countries than by concentrating so many resources on a limited number of war-torn countries. No-one disputes the truism that, where war is concerned, prevention is better than cure.

Humanitarian aid and development aid are sometimes seen as rival claimants for limited funds. In 1980, funding by governments for emergency humanitarian relief constituted less than 1.5% of total official development assistance (ODA) spending world-wide; in 1993 and 1994, it was about 10%. This is still a small part of the total, but has been enough to reinforce concern that there is increasing willingness to use humanitarian assistance as a foreign-policy tool, often in isolation from any long-term strategy.[26] There is often more than a suspicion that aid is channelled in a humanitarian direction because a particular war has caught the public's attention, rather than because of any well-considered plan for usefully spending funds. Aid for the developing countries of the 'South' has declined in the 1990s, being squeezed not only by the flow of funds to emergency humanitarian relief, but also by the demands of the post-communist countries for capital and assistance. Furthermore, the belief that effective economic development comes first from within societies themselves and that many externally supported development programmes, especially in some Cold War client states, have failed, is growing increasingly prevalent.

The rivalry between these two approaches is exacerbated by the fact that they have separate and to some extent rival organisational bases in the UN system. Also, humanitarian aid under UN auspices is sometimes associated with supranational interventionism, whereas economic development projects are generally conducted in close association with recipient governments. In addition, some humanitarian aid is criticised as a panic response to contain flows of refugees.

Despite these tensions, humanitarian assistance and development assistance need not be seen as rivals. Many organisations, from ICRC to Oxfam, do not limit their action to emergency assistance. Both organisations distribute seed and agricultural tools to enable people to recover a measure of self-sufficiency, and rehabilitation programmes make up a large part of their relief activities. In short, there is a continuum between emergency action and rehabilitation/development programmes.

Armed protection

The role of military forces is now the most important single issue to address; there has been too little sustained discussion of this issue. Military assistance for humanitarian workers and military protection of vulnerable populations has expanded in the 1990s, and has taken many forms – not just full-scale humanitarian intervention or establishing safety zones, but also the armed protection of convoys, and the maintenance of order in refugee camps. Those providing the armed protection have included not only UN peacekeeping forces, but also those of individual countries, and locally raised forces of an *ad hoc* character.

Some observers have seen a general pattern of military involvement in humanitarian action as natural, perhaps inevitable. Richard Connaughton, writing from a military perspective, has gone so far as to say:

> In a conflict environment, humanitarian organisations will increasingly look to the military, certainly in the early stages, for those capabilities which they themselves do not possess. These capabilities include the provision of security, protection, resources including transportation, the capacity to control and the provision of information.[27]

In practice, most international humanitarian organisations with conflict experience seek to distance themselves from 'the military', whether local or foreign, for as long as they can, and want a degree of control over the type of military support provided for their activities. Although in some situations many of them do have to rely on armed forces for assistance, the relationship with their protectors can be among the most problematic aspects of humanitarian action in war.[28] It can be open or covert, can involve favours and bribery, and often threatens the impartiality of humanitarian work. Some organisations, including ICRC, have come to see occasional recourse to armed escorts as a necessary stop-gap measure, which has its limitations and contradictions. It is no substitute for the hoped-for restoration of respect for the Red Cross emblem. They argue, persuasively, that as long as armed escorts are needed to protect their activities, there can be no realistic hope that belligerents will show respect for defenceless civilians and prisoners. However, in many conflicts the issue of protecting humanitarian workers and vulnerable populations is likely to require not only a hope that the belligerents will observe the rules of restraint, but also a preparedness to take action to encourage them to do so.

One key issue is the protection of the humanitarian workers themselves. The crises of the post-Cold War era have led to many proposals for providing armed protection to humanitarian workers, whether working for UN or for other agencies. The situation of such workers in Somalia before UNITAF's intervention in December 1992 was among the many frustrating and tragic experiences leading to such demands. The proposal received high-level support, including from UN Under-Secretary-General Jan Eliasson in February 1993:

> Additional measures for respect of humanitarian aid and for protection of relief personnel are now necessary. The blue ensign of the United Nations and the symbols of the International Red Cross and Red Crescent, and of other relief agencies, no longer provide sufficient protection.[29]

Citing such concerns, Childers and Urquhart suggested setting up 'a separate and distinctive United Nations Humanitarian Security Police'.[30] Humanitarian personnel, they argued, might need protection before there is a UN military intervention, and might also need to keep some visible distance from UN military forces.

Some UN reports have suggested that some proposed national volunteer corps known in the organisation as 'white helmets' might not only support 'humanitarian relief' rehabilitation and technical cooperation for development activities', but also (at least potentially) provide 'with their presence a deterrent and a symbolic protective cover in their working relationship with humanitarian operators.' They are envisaged as having 'a reassuring effect' and becoming 'a component of security and safety in the rehabilitation stage of emergency operations'.[31]

Such a protective role would go far beyond that of the existing UN volunteers, with which the proposed 'white helmets' are often, confusingly, associated. The UN volunteers, established in 1970, offer professional expertise, not protection. They operate under the UN Development Programme, and by 1994 numbered about 4,000. Increasingly since the 1980s, they have played a humanitarian assistance role, including in areas of conflict, and sometimes in conjunction with UN peacekeeping operations.[32] The UN General Assembly has passed resolutions in favour of the 'white helmets', but these have referred to their role in activities like those of the UN volunteers (humanitarian relief, rehabilitation, technical cooperation), not to their possible protective or deterrent function.[33]

The various proposals for a dedicated UN force to protect humanitarian operations have not moved towards a detailed operational plan. There are six considerations against such a force.

- The sheer scale and difficulty of the protection problem suggests the need for a much larger and more professional force than anything that has been envisaged to date.
- Since there are already precedents of UN peacekeepers and UN-authorised enforcement bodies specifically assisting humanitarian workers, it is not obvious that a new force would add much.
- In the major case where UN peacekeepers/enforcers were not acceptable – northern Iraq since 1991 – it was never likely that any other UN force (apart from the harmless UN Guards) would have been any more acceptable to Baghdad.
- The creation of a new force might complicate yet further the already Byzantine complexity of UN force structures in the field, especially if it was not under the authority of the Security Council.
- It could cause resentment in many host countries, either because it was considered unnecessary, or because the protection was provided only for the humanitarian workers, not for those they were there to help.
- Many humanitarian workers and organisations, both inside and outside the UN system, do not want this particular kind of protection, which they view as unrealistic.

In the absence of any single model or organisational basis of protection, there was a marked trend in the early 1990s towards more, and more varied forms of, protection. The elements of failure in the armed protection of humanitarian work in Somalia in 1992–93 did not stop this trend.

Rwanda represents an extreme case of physical protection of threatened people (as distinct from, say, food aid) as the critical issue. In the Rwanda crisis of 1994 three military operations supported and protected humanitarian assistance, and also protected threatened populations – the UN peacekeeping operation UNAMIR, the French *Opération Turquoise*, and the US *Operation Support Hope* in the camps in eastern Zaire. These three operations, each with very different basic mandates, represent an evolution from UN-based multilateral force, the control of which was heavily criticised, to an operation led by a single country. *Operation Support Hope* was deliberately presented as entirely distinct from UN peacekeeping: 'This is not peacekeeping, it is an humanitarian operation.'[34]

Analyses of Rwanda by those involved in humanitarian aid have not always discussed the matter of protection consistently. The volume on aid in the Joint Evaluation of Emergency Assistance to Rwanda stated clearly in the main body of the text that 'the critical need was for security and physical protection', yet the 'Findings and Recommendations' failed to pick up this theme or to explore its implications. Instead, much attention was given to the intellectually easier, but arguably less important, question of whether delivery of aid by the military is more expensive than delivery by civilian aid organisations.[35]

Legal protection for peacekeepers and humanitarian workers

The idea that certain classes of people, such as those performing particular humanitarian services, should have a privileged position has always had a place in the laws of war. Treaties currently in force contain numerous provisions for the protection of religious and medical personnel, agents of relief societies, journalists and civil defence workers; and for respect for the Red Cross and UN emblems.[36]

UN peacekeeping troops, and also humanitarian workers, were in obvious danger in the conflicts of the early 1990s, and the number of casualties was higher than in earlier operations. Between 1948 and 1990 there were 398 fatalities in peacekeeping missions; between 1991 and August 1995 there were 456.[37] The worst year was 1993, largely because of events in Somalia. There was also an increase in ICRC fatalities – less than ten per annum in each of the years 1985–91, 18 in 1992, and 23 in 1993. However, there were none in 1994 and 1995.

When UN peacekeeping forces are involved in hostilities, are they to be regarded (at least for the purposes of the laws of armed conflict) simply as belligerents, on an equal footing with other parties? Or are they in some way in a superior position?[38] It is natural to want to give UN forces, and humanitarian workers, a privileged status. Many Security Council resolutions have already sought to secure respect for both peacekeeping personnel and humanitarian workers. In former Yugoslavia, a resolution in June 1992 demanded 'that all parties and others concerned cooperate fully with UNPROFOR and international humanitarian agencies and take all necessary steps to ensure the safety of their personnel'.[39] In Rwanda, a resolution in June 1994 demanded 'that all parties in Rwanda strictly respect the persons and premises of the United Nations and other organisations serving in Rwanda, and refrain from any acts of intimidation or violence against personnel engaged in humanitarian and peace-keeping work'.[40]

In December 1994, the UN General Assembly approved the text of the Convention on the Safety of UN and Associated Personnel. It was a response to the many cases of attacks on, and hostage-taking of, UN peacekeepers and those working for humanitarian organisations, and followed the many Security Council resolutions condemning such attacks and calling on parties to ensure the safety of such personnel. During the negotiating phase, humanitarian organisations expressed concern that the Convention would protect only those personnel who are formally participating in a UN operation, as distinct from all humanitarian workers who may be assisting such an operation, or such workers in conflicts where there is no UN operation. However, the final text includes not only peacekeeping troops, but also humanitarian workers with, for example, an NGO or a specialised agency, provided they are part of an operation under UN authority and control.[41]

Can the new Convention on the Safety of UN Personnel be implemented, or is it another case of the UN willing the end but not the means? Article 11, echoing the 1949 Geneva Conventions, requires states parties to follow an 'extradite or prosecute' rule regarding alleged offenders – that is, those suspected of attacks on UN and associated personnel. Thus, like so many treaties, the Convention relies heavily on states being willing and able to take action against their own nationals. If this does not work, what happens? The Delphic terms of Article 7(3) appear to leave the matter to states. 'States Parties shall cooperate with the United Nations and other States Parties, as appropriate, in the implementation of this Convention, particularly in any case where the host State is unable itself to take the required measures.' The Convention does not directly address the possibility that UN peacekeeping forces might themselves take action against alleged offenders; if they were to do so, UN forces could find themselves parties to an armed conflict, in which case the convention would probably cease to apply at that point, being replaced by the law of international armed conflict.[42] This would imply an important transition of the status of a peacekeeping operation, with broad policy ramifications.

The critically important issue of protecting peacekeepers and humanitarian workers is becoming part of international law. (There are also provisions for their protection in the Protocol on mines agreed in 1996, outlined below.) Yet there are risks in stressing their special legal status. The humanitarian worker might end up involuntarily assuming the role sometimes played by the missionary in the nineteenth century – when attacked, providing a basis or at least an excuse for external military action. There are also risks, all too obvious after the events in Mogadishu in 1993, in calling those who oppose or threaten UN personnel 'outlaws'. Special protection of peacekeepers and humanitarian workers, if not implemented with considerable caution and skill, could be associated with a new kind of colonial mentality.

Anti-personnel land-mines

Anti-personnel land-mines have rightly become a focus for much humanitarian agitation and action. There are about 100m land-mines scattered throughout 64 countries which are killing on average 30 people a day and injuring over 35, many of the casualties being children. They have necessitated huge and expensive efforts to de-mine affected areas, and to assist the many people maimed by mines.[43] The UN General Assembly has repeatedly called for states to adopt moratoria on the export of anti-personnel land-mines, and to agree to new prohibitions and restrictions on the use of such weapons.[44]

Within some major armies there has been extensive reconsideration of anti-personnel mine use. Prominent figures including General Norman Schwarzkopf have said that they serve no useful military purpose. A group of military experts convened by ICRC in February 1996 stated that the military value of land-mines as used in the past 55 years had received little attention in published military studies. They noted that establishing extensive minefields is time-consuming, expensive and dangerous, and that although anti-tank mines are militarily useful, anti-personnel mines are much less so.[45]

Anti-personnel land-mines are classic subjects for prohibitions under the laws of war, both because they are indiscriminate, and because they continue to cause damage after wars have ended. Protocol II of the 1981 Convention on Specific Conventional Weapons placed some limits on their use, but its effect has been minuscule, and it was not formally applicable in non-international armed conflicts. In May 1996 a review conference of parties to the 1981 Convention agreed to an 'Amended Protocol II', applying to internal as well as international conflicts, prohibiting the use of undetectable anti-personnel mines, placing restrictions on the use of other mines, and seeking to establish special protection for a wide range of UN, ICRC and other humanitarian missions.[46] Campaigners for the complete abolition of anti-personnel mines were disappointed that these gains were so limited.

On 5 October 1996, at a diplomatic conference in Ottawa, 50 countries (including the US, the UK, France, Japan, Germany and Iran) agreed to a declaration calling for a global ban on anti-personnel land-mines. Controlling this problem would be a major contribution to the cause of humanity in warfare. A complete prohibition of the production, sale and use of such weapons, although hard to enforce in many conflicts, would reduce the huge number of non-combatant and post-war casualties. International collaboration on mine removal is already developing, and should also be a priority of governments and armed forces.

V. Coordinating humanitarian action

The problem of coordinating the manifold and often competing actions of humanitarian organisations is not new. Even when few organisations are involved the coordination problems are daunting. These are especially difficult in civil wars: the number of belligerent parties, the disputes as to their status, the general social disorder, and the fast-moving character of events all create problems for humanitarian operations, and at the same time reinforce the need for coordination.

The UN has long had a practice whereby the Secretary-General designated in a particular country a specific UN agency as the 'lead agency' with overall responsibilities for humanitarian relief operations. In Cambodia, the lead agency was the United Nations Children's Emergency Fund (UNICEF). In former Yugoslavia (where the operation began shortly before Department of Humanitarian Affairs [DHA] was set up) it was, and remained, UNHCR.

This 'lead agency' system has been challenged in the 1990s, including in several countries at war.

The wide range of official and unofficial organisations

Many different organisations are involved in humanitarian work; each has its own special skills and capabilities, and the situations in which they act are different. They include local governmental bodies, aid and disaster relief agencies of individual foreign countries, and international organisations under UN or other auspices. They sometimes also include certain military formations, especially some UN peacekeeping or UN-authorised forces.

Beyond such official bodies there are literally thousands of relief agencies with very different structures, functions, and capacities, including local NGOs (which are commonly neglected elements of humanitarian relief efforts), and also NGOs operating internationally. Many NGOs are proud of their independence, and of their ability to act quickly. For example, the willingness of *Médecins sans Frontières* to act anywhere, without waiting for formal political agreement, has evoked much support, even though this group has had to withdraw from some impossibly dangerous situations, as in Somalia after the UN-backed UNITAF military intervention.

The large number of NGOs involved in humanitarian action in 'complex emergencies' can sometimes be a problem. In Bosnia, in the words of the Director of Oxfam, 'although the duplication of NGO activities in Bosnia has been kept to a minimum by the UNHCR taking a clear coordinating role, by December 1995 there were 279 international NGOs operating ... a figure which represents an almost fourfold increase over two years'.[1] In the Rwanda crisis in 1994, at least 200 NGOs were involved as well as many other international bodies; efforts at coordination were themselves numerous, varied and largely unsuccessful.[2]

It has been suggested that, within the UN system, the different and overlapping mandates of various agencies make effective responses impossible, that there is a need for overall strategic direction, for a clearer division of labour, or for greater coordination between them. Some have even said that their numbers should simply be reduced. As Gareth Evans has explained:

> There are widely acknowledged inadequacies in the present UN international system, and structural reasons lie at the heart of them. In the first place, the post-Second World War relief system evolved from a structure created for different purposes. Apart from UNHCR and UNICEF, all the main agencies now involved in emergencies – i.e., WFP, UNDP [UN Development Programme], FAO [Food and Agriculture Organisation] and WHO [World Health Organisation] – acquired that role as a secondary function, the main role being seen as the promotion of economic and social development. Notwithstanding the dramatic

upsurge in their humanitarian relief work in the 1980s, the organisation of the agencies underwent no fundamental change.[3]

The picture of a large number of agencies, within and beyond the UN system, designed for one set of problems and having trouble adapting to another set, is not altogether fair. Many agencies have moved gradually beyond their original purposes and have tackled other problems than those they were originally set up to address.

There have been several proposals to remedy this. These have included proposals for establishing a single consolidated UN body, for which various titles have been suggested, including UN Relief Agency, or UN Disaster Response Agency. This idea carries with it two main risks. First, all UN agencies go through periods of poor performance, so having all eggs in a single basket is unwise. Second, consolidating everything under one roof might only exacerbate the divide between humanitarian relief and economic development. In the end the UN has established the DHA with a modest coordinating role.

For UNHCR in particular, there are risks in being subordinated to a single consolidated UN body. UNHCR's core responsibilities are unique in that they are imposed by events outside the control of the its Executive Committee, the UN General Assembly and the Security Council. Whatever the financial and political climate, more refugees mean more work. Moreover, this responsibility is discharged on behalf of those who by definition have no government to which they can turn. In a single UN humanitarian agency these unique responsibilities, which at times require opposition to the wishes of governments, would inevitably be diluted at the refugees' expense.

Because the UN system has been so obviously over-stretched in a wide variety of humanitarian and peacekeeping roles, it might be logical to look to regional organisations of one kind or another to fill the gap. Such organisations very enormously. Some, such as the European Union, have substantial resources and are developing expertise, for example through the European Community Humanitarian Office (ECHO). Other regional organisations (including the Commonwealth) are better suited to the taks of mediation and conflict prevention than emergency humanitarian action.

The UN Department of Humanitarian Affairs

The UN has addressed the problem of a confusion of humanitarian activities by attempting to coordinate, not consolidate within a single agency. This effort is centred on the DHA, based in New York and Geneva. The DHA, set up in March 1992, was intended to have a key role within the UN system by providing early warnings of humanitarian disasters and coordinating action in the field. It has modest funds, including a Central Emergency Revolving Fund (CERF) to provide reimbursable advances to pay for emergency humanitarian action.[4]

The response to DHA has been mixed. Elements of coordination have developed. Under the DHA, an Inter-Agency Standing Committee (IASC) meets quarterly, with representation from the heads of key UN agencies, ICRC and the Federation of Red Cross Societies, and from three groups of NGOs. For particular countries in crisis there are now single-needs assessments. There are also the UN Consolidated Inter-Agency Humanitarian Assistance Appeals, though only one (that for former Yugoslavia) has been adequately funded since these appeals were introduced in 1992.[5]

Within some war-torn countries DHA coordination has made a difference. In Angola, where DHA was asked to provide a coordinating role in March 1993, 'almost every organisation involved in humanitarian assistance wanted coordination, albeit "light and not bureaucratic" '. At the same time, however, DHA had 'to distance itself from the UN's political activities because Angolans, the government, and UNITA, perceived them as a failure'.[6] In several countries (for example Mozambique, Rwanda and Somalia), the DHA has appointed a Humanitarian Coordinator with overall responsibility for relief efforts. This is intended to replace the previous system of the 'lead agency'. Sometimes this has worked. As two NGOs have said:

> Our experience of working with UN agencies in emergencies is varied, but one thing we have learnt is that it is vital for the in-country UN authority to build a consensus among the various relief agencies and NGOs involved. In Mozambique, the Humanitarian Coordinator, whose authority is delegated from the Special Representative, has on the whole been able to do this.[7]

Inevitably, within the new system there are still many problems. The system of coordination is not fundamentally different from one instituted 20 years earlier, on the basis of General Assembly Resolution 2816 calling on the Secretary-General to appoint a Disaster Relief Coordinator. The DHA has few resources compared to the other agencies it is intended to coordinate. It has itself suffered from problems of coordination and continuity, due partly to being split between two sites (New York and Geneva), and having had no less than three directors in its four years of existence. It has no executive power to direct aid in a particular crisis. The idea of coordination does not itself address the wider problem of overlapping mandates of different agencies. Pressures for centralised and coordinated decision-making can reduce operational effectiveness and flexibility in the field. The role of individual states, especially donors (whether of finance or services), has not diminished, and adds a layer of complexity. It is significant that a key UN Secretariat decision in the humanitarian field – to evacuate UN personnel from the camps in eastern Zaire following the outbreak of fighting there in late October 1996 – was taken by the UN Security Coordinator in the Department of Administration and Management, in consultation with various officials and agencies, and not by DHA.

The emphasis on coordination within a country under a Humanitarian Coordinator does not itself solve the problem of crises which, as frequently happens, spill over frontiers and involve the territory of several states, nor does it solve the problem of relations with special envoys to a region, appointed by the UN Secretary-General. Somalia and Rwanda, baptisms of fire for the system, served as reminders that when problems on the ground are extremely difficult and the political responses to them are flawed, to expect a coordination system to achieve success is to expect miracles. In many conflicts in the former Soviet Union, too, the DHA has been unable to assume the central coordinating role that was originally envisaged. Indeed, where there are significant refugee flows and a major UNHCR presence, it is not realistic to expect that representatives of UNHCR with its substantial budgets and responsibilities, and a strong tradition of being a 'lead agency', will accept 'coordination' from a much less powerful and less experienced body such as DHA. There remains, as there was before, an element of personal chemistry and happenstance in whether the different aspects of a relief effort do or do not meld into an effective whole in a particular crisis.

A practical and political problem of the new system is the division of responsibilities in the field between the UNDP, concerned primarily with long-term development projects, and the DHA, concerned with emergency relief. There are genuine uncertainties about where their respective responsibilities end; the area of rehabilitation lies uneasily between development and relief. Also, many governments, especially in the Group of 77 (developing countries), are critical of the idea of a Humanitarian Coordinator for a particular country. They fear that this might involve meddling in their internal affairs. The fact that the appointment of a Humanitarian Coordinator is not subject to the *agrément* of the country concerned has strengthened such fears, reinforcing as it does the notion that humanitarian action and humanitarian intervention are intimately linked. There has been similar concern over the post of Emergency Relief Coordinator.[8]

Attempts to coordinate, including those taking place under DHA auspices, naturally receive a mixed response from some non-UN bodies, which could reasonably fear some loss of identity or capacity to act independently. ICRC, which is of course a special case, has participated in various DHA initiatives, but in that context has had to reiterate its independence and impartiality. ICRC has also been concerned that the UN, by concentrating on humanitarian action, risks abandoning its purportedly proper role in the international division of labour, which is to work on politico-military responses to conflicts.

Strengthening the coordination of humanitarian activities is politically sensitive and inherently difficult. In UN General Assembly debates on the matter on 23 and 25 November 1994, many Group of 77 states expressed reservations about the direction in which coordination had been moving. However, those involved in UN humanitarian operations in the field generally take the view that the most worrying problem is not coordination, but actual capacity. The inadequacy of resources, which reflects the limited character of states' commitment to humanitarian relief, remains the largest constraint on effective action. It is doubtful whether DHA is an improvement on the 'lead agency' approach, and whether it can endure in its present form.

Early warning

A key element in any organisation's response to challenges is early warning. Such warning may be valuable if it can assist efforts to prevent crises, for example through diplomatic initiatives; indeed early warning is quite often considered a part of 'preventive diplomacy'.[9] However, early warning also has a role in the prompt and efficient delivery of humanitarian relief. Furthermore, an efficient system of warning has a crucial role to play in the perceived fairness of any system of relief.

If governments and international agencies simply react to the latest television reports, certain crises will be favoured and others ignored, much as the continuing tragedy in Afghanistan has largely been ignored in the West in the post-Cold War period. There is clearly a need for a more systematic form of situation assessment. There is also a need for the media covering humanitarian disasters to encourage more thoughtful and judicious discussion of possible responses, rather than simply implying, as they sometimes do, that external military intervention is the main mode of response and is relatively unproblematic.

Within many parts of the UN system there are means of gathering information and issuing warnings about impending disasters. Leading figures in such UN bodies as UNHCR and DHA, and also in non-UN bodies such as ICRC, can point to the stream of reports, press releases and memoranda they have issued, and which have not been followed by action. Partly this may be the problem of 'clutter', which is familiar to students of intelligence agencies. There are so many warnings of so many impending crises that it is hard for governments or UN bodies to know which ones really matter. As Gareth Evans has noted:

> While there is little doubt that it is important for the UN to have good sources of information about the whole range of emerging threats, disputes, conflicts and other security crises, the problem is not only the lack of information, but also the system's ability to absorb the enormous amount of incoming information, analyse and apply it in a meaningful way.[10]

The problem of early warning is sometimes in reality a problem of will and capacity. Information is received but not acted upon. Governments and international bodies can suffer from 'compassion fatigue' every bit as much as individuals; and also from the all-too-human tendency to put off problems till tomorrow. They may only be stirred from inactivity by the actual advent of disaster, or by powerful media campaigns.

Not surprisingly, the idea that a particular body should be charged with amassing relevant information and issuing a formal warning of impending disaster has gained strength. To an extent, DHA has this function, which could be further extended in crisis areas.[11] There are practical snags in proposals for a system of formal early warning. Some countries would vehemently object to being named publicly as the location of incipient catastrophe, and many UN officials sympathise with this. If, for example, Algeria was declared to be on the brink of civil war, a huge diplomatic earthquake would follow, and any advantage would be minimal.

Some have suggested that ICRC, being impartial and independent, should have a role as an independent issuer of warnings. The political constraints on making public pronouncements have decreased with the passing of the Cold War, but they have not disappeared. ICRC is reluctant to go beyond its current range of carefully modulated whistle-blowing. When ICRC issues a warning, it is to help the victims; on occasion, though, it may think twice, and act only confidentially.

The increasing recognition of the importance of early warning and prevention has led to a large number of new initiatives, one of which was the establishment in 1994–95 of the International Crisis Group (ICG), a private, non-profit corporation established partly on the basis of work at the Carnegie Endowment for International Peace in Washington DC. ICG aims to alert governments and the world community when it believes the time is right for mediation or other diplomatic efforts to avert incipient disasters and their huge humanitarian ramifications. As its prospectus says, 'ICG will set out to demonstrate that timely expenditure on preventive measures is not simply a moral necessity, but also an economic one'.[12]

An early warning system is only relevant if there is also an early action system. Yet in the experience of humanitarian organisations, early action is triggered not only by humanitarian concern, but by political pressure and by state interests. The central problem remains the world's will and capacity to respond.

Conclusions

The major increase in international humanitarian action in wars and other crises is the result not only of the end of the Cold War, but also of factors that have emerged over a long period and are likely to endure into the next century – the prevalence of civil wars and failed states, the anxiety of many countries to forestall refugee influxes by supporting humanitarian action in or near the country of origin, and the desire of the relatively secure (especially in Western democratic states) to do something about widely reported disasters. Frequently, when populations are threatened with starvation, eviction and death, it is impossible for outside bodies to do nothing. Not to act when there is the capacity to do so is itself likely to be a source of future recrimination and hostility. Even if humanitarian action goes through cycles of decline it will not disappear; it reflects interests as well as altruism. Decision-makers need to plan for such action, offer assistance, and be aware of its merits and weaknesses.

Humanitarian efforts have achieved some important results since 1991, especially in saving lives. It enabled Kurds stranded in the mountains in 1991 to return home to relative, albeit temporary, safety. It averted the worst consequences of famine in Somalia in 1992–93. It subsequently prevented or mitigated at least two widely predicted disasters – mass starvation in Sarajevo in the three winters starting in 1992–93, and the uncontrolled spread of the extensive outbreaks of cholera and dysentery in the camps on the borders of Rwanda in 1994.

Yet the overall record of humanitarian action in the wars of the 1990s has been flawed. An underlying problem has been the inability to ensure security. The lack of protection for aid convoys and activities has contributed, in some cases, to the war economy. The lack of protection for vulnerable populations, including in supposedly protected areas from Srebrenica to Sulaimaniya, has been shameful. This has caused disillusion and a feeling that in some instances such endeavours may actually prolong wars. What lessons are to be learnt from these failures?

An attempt must be made both to build on the substantial achievements of the humanitarian efforts of the post-Cold War era and to overcome the no less substantial failures. It is now widely agreed that such an attempt must involve a far higher level of accountability of organisations involved in such efforts; there has not been nearly enough clear, complete, truthful and timely reporting of what has and has not been achieved. Such an attempt requires a capacity to think in both strategic and humanitarian terms simultaneously, and to temper idealism with some tough realism about what net benefits can actually be achieved. In responding to the wars and crises of the present era, there are no tried and tested answers.

An exploration of the failures of humanitarian action in the security field has to begin by recognising a harsh truth. The adoption by states and international bodies of the banner of humanitarian action was associated with a policy vacuum, former Yugoslavia and Rwanda being the prime examples. The existence of such vacuums is not surprising. Faced with complex conflicts on which they have different perspectives and limited interests, individual states and international organisations will continue to find it easier to agree on humanitarian action than on definite political prescriptions. The unavoidable inhibitions against outside powers deciding the outcome of a local or civil war reinforces the likelihood of ending up with policies that are even-handed and bland. Humanitarian action may continue, sadly, to be a substitute for long-term policies and difficult strategic decisions.

Four critical questions are raised by the vastly increased international diplomatic and military involvement in humanitarian action. Can it be made more effective through more coordination? When humanitarian priorities are in conflict with each other, or with important policy considerations, what is to be done? Does humanitarian action, by its nature, have to be neutral, impartial and independent, or can it be associated with the use of armed forces, and support for a particular side in a conflict? Can the poor performance regarding the protection of aid activities and vulnerable populations be remedied in any way?

Effectiveness through coordination?

There has long been a school of thought that a major cause of the troubles faced by charitable efforts has been a lack of coordination. The sheer number of organisations involved, their duplication of activities, their competition for attention, and their herd instinct to rush to the same crisis while ignoring others, all add to the persuasiveness of this diagnosis, and have resulted in calls for better coordination.

The practice so far of coordination, especially among different UN agencies, has yielded ambiguous results. The attempt by DHA to coordinate the activities of different agencies and outside bodies is gaining some support, and has reaped significant benefits, especially in countries where it has a strong and respected local representative. However, there are limits to what can be achieved. These result partly from the unique identity and mission of each agency, and the sensitivities of UN member-states. Some Group of 77 members are nervous about the potential power of the DHA to coordinate activities in particular countries. There is also a potential clash of priorities between the agencies associated with development on the one hand and humanitarian relief on the other. Above all, the DHA still lacks the financial strength, stable leadership and professional expertise of some other agencies.

The current emphasis on coordination could lead to illusions about what it could achieve. Some aspects of humanitarian work, such as ICRC's treaty-defined roles, may be best done independently. Furthermore, if the main coordinating body is a UN one, its actions may be considered tainted by some belligerents because of the UN's other simultaneous activities. Moreover, the main problems facing these efforts are not lack of coordination, but a lack of resources, a lack of political will to act and a lack of convincing answers to the security dilemmas of conducting humanitarian action in situations of war and conflict.

Above all, the call for coordination is of limited relevance if the scope for humanitarian action is restricted, as it necessarily is in some situations. Professionals in humanitarian organisations are acutely aware of the limits of what such action can achieve. Many of them subscribe fully to the view that it is not a substitute for political, diplomatic and military actions needed to address and end conflicts. The primary preoccupation of the UN and many national governments with humanitarian action can easily seem to be a betrayal of their larger responsibilities, and leads some people involved to view such action critically, even dismissively.

Tension between humanitarian priorities

One objective problem that has contributed to coordination difficulties is the tension that often exists between different humanitarian priorities, as well as between them and other policies. All good things do not come together. The implementation of international humanitarian law, or of human-rights law, may require action to be taken against one side, jeopardising the impartial distribution of relief. Similarly, if a peace agreement is reached at the end of a long war, those implementing its terms often have to choose between the key requirement of maintaining peace (which may involve, most basically, monitoring cease-fire lines between belligerents) and the further requirement of implementing the more detailed provisions of a peace accord on such matters as conducting elections, cooperation in joint institutions, and the arrest of individuals for violations of the peace agreement itself or of general international humanitarian norms. Such dilemmas were faced by UN forces in Cambodia in 1992–93, and IFOR in Bosnia in 1995–96. Often in such cases, for better or for worse, outside forces put the fundamental requirement of maintaining the cease-fire first, and other considerations (including humanitarian ones) second.

The hideous issue of enforced population movements and so-called 'ethnic cleansing' exposes a brutally clear clash between humanitarian and hard-nosed realist approaches to managing conflict. No humanitarian approach can accept that populations can be terrorised out of their homes by nationalist zealots and never afforded the chance to return. Peace negotiations in the Arab–Israeli conflict, Cyprus, Bosnia and elsewhere have involved persuasive demands that a right to return should be accepted and implemented. Yet a lesson of many conflicts with an ethnic dimension is that where two peoples are divided by extreme mutual fears, they may need to remain apart, even in separate states, long enough to let the bitterness subside. UNHCR has reluctantly assisted in some population movements whose effects it deplores. In a world in which humanitarian norms are widely supported but *realpolitik* has not lost its power, there is a large gap between words and actions. The Dayton Agreement proclaims a right to return home, but IFOR assigns that a low priority because it can do so little to stop continuing terror against minorities.

The lesson of such difficulties is that the pursuit of humanitarian objectives itself requires the continuous exercise of judgement. Yet judgement in political decision-making is not facilitated by the circumstances in which it currently takes place – the Cable News Network (CNN) factor leading to pressure for action, the tendency of politicians to talk in soundbites, the pressure to think short-term rather than long-term, and the need to resort to the lowest-common-denominator language of multilateralism.

Impartiality and the ethos of humanitarian work

Fuller recognition of the central importance of security to humanitarian action has serious consequences for some of the most cherished ideas underlying humanitarian work. The concepts of impartiality and neutrality, widely seen as key requirements of humanitarian action in war, need to be critically re-examined. Many humanitarian workers adhere to these ideas, not because they are unaware of their defects, but because the alternatives appear worse. ICRC, for example, is right to assert that vital services, such as visiting detainees, could not be carried out at all if the organisation was perceived as *parti-pris* in a conflict. Clearly for ICRC, as for most UN peacekeeping forces, impartiality is a priceless asset which is not to be lightly compromised or quickly abandoned.

However, some humanitarian organisations and activities are associated more with one side than another anyway. National Red Cross societies are often very close to their own political authorities, sometimes notoriously so, yet they may carry out useful actions within their own sphere. Completely independent aid agencies often develop sympathy for one side in a conflict, and may act as a means of raising international support for it. Moreover, in many conflicts in the 1990s humanitarian aid has not been seen as impartial by those whose opinions count, namely the belligerents. This (as well as the perception that outside powers are not serious about backing up their words with action) helps to explain why parties to conflicts have often blocked and even attacked humanitarian operations.

If impartiality has value, as it undoubtedly does, it also has defects. It may be hard to square with other policies being pursued simultaneously. If sanctions are imposed on a state because of its violations of humanitarian law, then the impartial distribution of aid to inhabitants of that state risks becoming a bad joke. If the UN Security Council or a regional alliance were to conclude that the best way to end a war is to give material support to one side, that may again involve in practice denying help to that side's adversaries, and even going so far as to turn a blind eye to certain violations of humanitarian norms by the side being assisted or its co-belligerents. If one side consistently violates a ceasefire agreement or refuses to accept an election result as part of a peace agreement, then to continue with certain aid programmes in its territory in the name of impartiality and neutrality may be a mistake.

The result of these pressures is that in actual practice the concept of impartiality often bursts at the seams. Still notionally supported, as with the arms embargo on all parties to the wars in former Yugoslavia, it may be covertly flouted in undercover diplomacy, secret arms shipments, and other activities of diplomats, armed forces and intelligence agencies.

The principle of impartiality, as a basis for humanitarian action in war, cannot and should not be abandoned, especially by those organisations whose daily work requires the cooperation of all belligerents. The reiteration of the principle in the Red Cross movement's 1994 Code of Conduct for relief workers is understandable. However, the Code's avoidance of all difficult issues, including security, renders it of limited value, and its endorsement by over 140 governments only confirms the impression that they do not always take humanitarian issues seriously. Similar problems arose with the December 1995 Madrid Declaration of representatives of prominent humanitarian agencies. In fact, many in such bodies as ICRC and UNHCR who have to work at the sharp end, being well aware of the limits of impartiality, do not advocate it as a general policy for states and intergovernmental organisations, which should properly view it as one starting point, not as a policy strait-jacket. With respect to many conflicts, fairness in exercising judgement (including humanitarian action) may be a better guide to policy than impartiality, and may point in different directions.

Security as a key aspect of humanitarian action

If the practice of the 1990s has proved anything it is that humanitarian assistance cannot realistically be considered in isolation from security issues. The cost of failing to address the protection issue is high, not just for those being assisted, and not just for humanitarian agencies and NGOs, but also for outside powers. The pattern of half-hearted guarantees and post-disaster evasions has reflected badly on the credibility of the UN Security Council, and also on that of major states for whom a reputation for dependability is an important asset.

The argument that no humanitarian effort can afford to be associated with particular external powers or uses of force does not stand up. The armed forces of individual countries, as well as those under UN auspices, have frequently been involved in humanitarian action. Some specialist technical tasks often have to be entrusted to armed forces, for example, dropping emergency food supplies to some besieged communities and de-mining. Some basic security and logistical tasks may be best performed by external military forces, as happened in the camps on Rwanda's borders in 1994.

There are several circumstances in which humanitarian action may need to be associated with threats and uses of force. The most obvious is when those being assisted need security above all else. Unless they can be rescued and taken far from the scene of the conflict, their security can seldom be ensured by neutral and impartial non-military action alone, least of all in bitter civil wars. If safety zones are to be proclaimed, there will normally have to be a will and capacity to deter attacks on them and to defend them. Force in some form may also be needed to maintain discipline among those being assisted, for example when a refugee camp contains armed bands, or when rioters threaten aid depots.

Implementing the laws of war – international humanitarian law – can also be an important aspect of protection, and can require some uses of force. To stop genocide, to prevent the slaughter of innocent civilians in a 'safe area', to ensure observance of rules about delivering aid, and to arrest those charged with war crimes may at times require a degree of coercive power and a willingness to get involved in a conflict. ICRC has repeatedly recognised that it is states that have the primary responsibility for ensuring implementation of the Geneva Conventions. A corollary is that states may sometimes have to use force in implementing them. In the nature of things they will do so with mixed motives, multiple purposes and questionable co-belligerents. NATO's *Operation Deliberate Force*, starting in August 1995 following Bosnian Serb atrocities at Srebrenica and Sarajevo, is a case in point. An incidental consequence of this reasonably tough line against the Bosnian Serb forces was that the performance of the humanitarian supply operation improved substantially in subsequent weeks.

Action by states to prevent atrocities and random killing can take other forms. If the international community's countless expressions of concern about the human disasters of contemporary wars are to mean anything the issue of anti-personnel land-mines, which are killing about 200 people a week, must be tackled more effectively. The contemporary uses, and indeed fundamental characteristics, of these weapons violate basic principles of the laws of war. A universal prohibition of their manufacture, sale and use will be hard to achieve, not least because some states are reluctant to agree to it. However, a prohibition, even if incompletely supported, could help limit the huge and pointless carnage they cause.

The revival of the idea of humanitarian intervention – of multilateral military involvements which do not have the consent of the country concerned – has represented a major means of linking humanitarian action and the use of force. While important results have been achieved, the varied experiences of northern Iraq, Somalia, former Yugoslavia, Rwanda and Haiti suggest that this approach may be flawed in practice, as well as much contested in theory. There have been certain important new elements, especially authorisation from the UN Security Council. However, there is no general agreement in the international community on the legitimacy of humanitarian intervention, still less on any agreed definition of the circumstances in which it might be justified. The recent cases confirm that powers are reluctant to take part in interventions where the costs are high, which of course includes situations of major ongoing war. Even when countries are willing to act, there is often a lack of clarity about commitments and goals. There is room for doubt as to whether 'humanitarian intervention' is an appropriate generic term to describe all aspects of such actions. The principle of non-intervention retains its importance, and only in the most exceptional cases is the international community likely to tolerate 'humanitarian intervention'. The UN-based interventionism of recent years seems to be ebbing.

The varied experience of attempts to protect vulnerable populations in war points to a central contradiction. On the one hand, it is clearly an illusion to suppose that force and humanitarianism exist in two separate and entirely distinct spheres. Protection is properly seen not as an occasional add-on to humanitarian relief supplies, but as a key aspect of the international community's response to wars and crises. On the other hand, in most conflicts it is far from obvious what kind of protection can be offered, and who is to provide it.

The difficulty of providing protection for vulnerable groups in the midst of ongoing conflicts is huge. Outside powers, whether under UN, NATO or any other auspices, may lack the political will to deploy forces on the spot and keep them there. Hence the tendencies of the Western powers to rely on airpower, with all its limitations, to protect safety zones, as in northern Iraq and the Bosnian 'safe areas', and to commit ground forces only for a limited period, as in Somalia. These tendencies are unlikely to change suddenly.

This explains why the answer to the question of what kind of protection is provided, and by whom, has frequently been UN peacekeeping. In some circumstances, for example post-war reconstruction, this can work effectively. However, experiments in the 1990s with deploying UN peacekeepers in situations of ongoing conflict to assist humanitarian relief efforts have not on the whole been successful: in Somalia, Rwanda and Bosnia such deployments repeatedly led to demands for new forces to be introduced with tougher mandates, and not under UN control. In each case this was done, albeit only temporarily. The evidence appears to be that multilateral peacekeeping forces under UN command and attached to the idea of impartiality are not normally able to act with the degree of commitment and decisiveness that the fast-changing and bloody situations of contemporary wars require.

The question of securing protection for vulnerable populations in their own countries – whether through the actions of states or of UN forces – cannot be permanently separated from the larger question of defining a policy in relation to ongoing conflicts. Security has to come from a local balance, and sometimes local parties and armed forces, with all their faults, may represent the best means of achieving a settlement.

The most promising approach to the role of the military in relation to humanitarian efforts is likely to be a pragmatic one. While not denying a role for UN peacekeeping forces, or for full-scale 'humanitarian intervention' in cases of extreme emergency, such an approach also stresses the importance of other forms of military protection and assistance, not all of which will necessarily be mandated by the UN Security Council or run under UN control. Local forces, host-country governments, outside powers, regional organisations and alliances may all have a role in providing such help. Sometimes the fact that the forces involved are those of a major power, which is not likely to tolerate their humiliation, may assist this role and have a deterrent function. Sometimes, too, a local power with a real interest in the outcome, and the determination to stay for as long as it takes, may achieve more results than a disinterested distant state whose public, or government, has a short attention span.

Above all, future attempts to protect populations in areas of conflict need to avoid the elements of ambiguity, verging on dishonesty, that have characterised many such efforts in the post-Cold War period. Such protection, for example through 'safety zones', requires clarity about the nature of the zones and the question of the legitimacy of military activity in them; it also requires major and sometimes long-term military commitments. It should only be extended when there is serious political support.

There are obvious risks in approaches that emphasise military support as a natural corollary of humanitarian action. The military could too easily see themselves as God's gift to humanitarian workers, whose proper concern with impartiality and independence make them prickly customers. A general perception that humanitarian action was but a harbinger of military involvement would exacerbate concern in target countries, and could be deeply damaging to humanitarian organisations. Further, there is always the possibility that what starts as military protection of humanitarian action may end as direct, unintended and unconstructive military involvement in a distant conflict. These risks are bound to lead to parsimony in the use of force, but should not deter states from providing military support for humanitarian purposes where it is genuinely needed, properly thought out, and has a prospect of achieving worthwhile results. The bland statements, half-promises and betrayals of the 1990s cannot be repeated without doing great harm, not just to those in need of assistance, but also to those states and organisations that seek to help them.

Notes

I. The changing context of humanitarian action

1 *Global Humanitarian Emergencies, 1995* (New York: US Mission to the UN, January 1995), p. 1. A subsequent edition of this report was published in February 1996.
2 UN High Commissioner for Refugees (UNHCR), *The State of the World's Refugees 1995* (Oxford: Oxford University Press, 1995), pp. 19–20, 36, 248 and 255. The 1995 figure was supplied directly by UNHCR. See also the note of scholarly caution about the problem of refugee statistics, pp. 244–46.
3 *Ibid.*, p. 247.
4 Gil Loescher, *Refugee Movements and International Security*, Adelphi Paper 268 (London: Brassey's for the IISS, 1992), p. 5.
5 *Ibid.*, p. 68.
6 Yves Sandoz, 'Internally Displaced Persons', paper presented at UNHCR Sub-committee on International Protection, Geneva 18 May 1994.
7 The expanded function was frankly recognised in a UNHCR document, 'Protection Aspects of UNHCR Activities on Behalf of Internally Displaced Persons', EC/1994/SCP/CRP.2, 4 May 1994. See also the useful discussion in *The State of the World's Refugees 1995*, pp. 19–55.
8 Larry Minear and Thomas G. Weiss, *Mercy Under Fire: War and the Global Humanitarian Community* (Boulder, CO: Westview, 1995), pp. 21–22.
9 Ali Mazrui, address at the Regional Institute of the League of Red Cross Societies, Dar-es-Salaam, 23 November 1970, quoted in David P. Forsythe, *Humanitarian Politics: The International Committee of the Red Cross* (Baltimore, MD: The Johns Hopkins University Press, 1977), p. 241.
10 *Global Humanitarian Emergencies, 1995*, pp. 35–36, supplemented from the 1996 edition, and from other sources. Some of these expenditures are not war-related. In several cases the figure in the right-hand column is only that part of the

agency's overall budget that is classified as related to humanitarian relief, emergency assistance, etc.
11 *Ibid.*, 1996 edition, p. 22. Also, *Development Cooperation: Efforts and Policies of the Members of the Development Assistance Committee, Report 1995* (Paris: Organisation for Economic Cooperation and Development [OECD], 1996), p. 95.
12 All Oxfam budget figures supplied directly by Ed Cairns of Oxfam, August 1996.

II. Humanitarian intervention

1 US surveys reflecting the preoccupation with this theme have included Lori Fisler Damrosch (ed.), *Enforcing Restraint: Collective Intervention in Internal Conflicts* (New York: Council on Foreign Relations Press, 1993). This book was written when enthusiasm for collective intervention was widespread. Despite its title and optimistic theme, its analysis of particular cases is sober. For latter-day attempts at a more transformational view see Gene M. Lyons and Michael Mastanduno (eds), *Beyond Westphalia? State Sovereignty and International Intervention* (Baltimore, MD: The Johns Hopkins University Press, 1995).
2 See Ian Forbes and Mark Hoffman (eds), *Political Theory, International Relations and the Ethics of Intervention* (London: Macmillan, 1993), and James Mayall (ed.), *The New Interventionism 1991–1994: United Nations Experience in Cambodia, Former Yugoslavia and Somalia* (Cambridge: Cambridge University Press, 1996).
3 For a succinct and sceptical survey of the history of 'humanitarian intervention' in international legal debate over the centuries, see Ian Brownlie, *International Law and the Use of Force by States* (Oxford: Clarendon Press, 1963), pp. 338–42.
4 'Humanitarian intervention' is viewed in both these senses in John Harriss (ed.), *The Politics of Humanitarian Intervention* (London: Pinter for the Save the Children Fund, 1995), pp. xi, 2–3, 8–9, etc.
5 'United Nations Interventions in Conflict Situations', a submission from Community Aid Abroad Australia, and Oxfam UK and Ireland, to Ambassador Richard Butler, Chair of the UN Preparatory Committee for the Fiftieth Anniversary (Oxford: Oxfam, February 1994), p. 10.
6 'Conclusion', in Hedley Bull (ed.), *Intervention in World Politics* (Oxford: Oxford University Press, 1984), p. 195. See also his remarks on p. 193 about the impact of 'the growing legal and moral recognition of human rights on a world-wide scale' on the question of humanitarian intervention.
7 United Nations Security Council Resolution (UNSCR) 743, 21 February 1992, establishing UNPROFOR, not only specified that the Security Council was carrying out its responsibility 'for the maintenance of international peace and security' (i.e., it was acting under Chapter VII of the UN Charter), but also recalled the provisions of Article 25 (which requires UN member-states 'to accept and carry out the decisions of the Security Council in accordance with the present Charter').
8 See UNSCR 758, 8 June 1992; UNSCR 761, 29 June 1992; and UNSCR 770, 13 August 1992.
9 On the Rwanda catastrophe in 1994, and the humanitarian actions in relation to them, see especially *The International Response to Conflict and Genocide: Lessons from the Rwanda Experience* (Copenhagen: Steering Committee of the Joint Evaluation of Emergency Assistance to Rwanda, 5 vols, March 1996). For a critical account of the UN Security Council's role, see Study 2, *Early Warning and Conflict Management*, pp. 41–57. The discussion of security issues in this study is weak. The account of the response of the UN headquarters in New York to the crisis omits reference to some key documents. Further, there is no systematic exploration of what kind of military intervention might have protected the inhabitants, and how troops could have been found for it.
10 For a critical view of the provisions and working of the 1948 Genocide Convention

see Leo Kuper, *Genocide: Its Political Use in the Twentieth Century* (New Haven, CT: Yale University Press, 1982), pp. 36–39 and 174–85.
11 Damrosch (ed.), *Enforcing Restraint*, p. 1.
12 See the sceptical view on armed interventions for humanitarian purposes expressed by Yves Sandoz of the International Committee of the Red Cross (ICRC) in *International Review of the Red Cross*, no. 288, May–June 1992, p. 222.
13 Gareth Evans, Australian Foreign Minister at the time, enumerated a comprehensive list of conditions that would need to be satisfied in any case of intervention, and which were seen as a necessity if a 'right of humanitarian intervention' was to be recognised. Gareth Evans, *Cooperating for Peace: The Global Agenda for the 1990s and Beyond* (St Leonards, New South Wales: Allen & Unwin, 1993), p. 156.

III. Forms of humanitarian action

1 W. J. Bryan, US Secretary of State, to President Woodrow Wilson, 15 February 1915, in *Foreign Relations of the United States: The Lansing Papers 1914–1920* (Washington DC: US Government Printing Office [GPO], 1939), vol. I, p. 353.
2 Bryan to Wilson, 18 February 1915, *ibid.*, p. 362. The (principally German) *quid pro quo* was to have been in three areas: certain limitations on the use of naval mines; submarines not to attack commercial vessels; belligerents not to use neutral flags on merchant vessels.
3 Walter H. Page, US Ambassador to the UK, to the US Secretary of State, 27 February 1915. *Ibid.*, pp. 364–65.
4 For documents on US involvement in relief operations in numerous countries in the latter stages of the First World War, see especially *Papers Relating to the Foreign Relations of the United States, 1918*, Supplement 2, *The World War* (Washington DC: GPO, 1933), pp. 459–647.
5 David Bryer, 'Providing Humanitarian Assistance During Internal Conflicts', address to International Peace Academy Conference, Vienna, 23 July 1996, p. 3.
6 Boutros Boutros-Ghali has said that safeguarding the concept and reality of 'humanitarian space' is 'one of the most significant challenges facing the humanitarian community'. *Confronting New Challenges: Annual Report on the Work of the Organization 1995* (New York: United Nations, 1995), p. 172. The concept was discussed with particular reference to Central America in Minear and Weiss, *Mercy Under Fire*, pp. 38–45.
7 For an analysis which does not dwell on the possible conflicts between humanitarianism, human rights and peacekeeping, see the UN Joint Inspection Unit report by Francesco Mezzalama, 'Investigation of the Relationship Between Humanitarian Assistance and Peace-Keeping Operations', distributed to the General Assembly as UN document A/50/572, 24 October 1995.
8 Statement by the President of the Security Council, UN document S/PRST/1994/22 of 3 May 1994, p. 2, discussing the Secretary-General's report, 'Improving the Capacity of the United Nations for Peace-keeping', UN document S/26450, 14 March 1994.
9 *The Clinton Administration's Policy on Reforming Multilateral Peace Operations* (Washington DC: US Department of State Publication 10161, May 1994), 15 pp. This is virtually the text of Presidential Decision Directive 25, less some appendices. The two factors cited are both on p. 4.
10 Figures supplied by UNHCR, Geneva, 12 February 1996.
11 UNHCR, *The State of the World's Refugees 1995*, p. 126.
12 The Berlin blockade lasted from 24 June 1948 to 12 May 1949. Figures for monthly tonnages delivered varied from 70,241 (June-July 1948) to 235,377 (April 1949), delivered by 14,036 and 26,025 sorties respectively. The airlift continued until September 1949, because of a railway strike and continued traffic

12. restrictions, with even higher tonnages delivered. Robert Jackson, *The Berlin Airlift* (Wellingborough, Northants: Patrick Stephens, 1988), p. 146.
13. 'Supplement to An Agenda for Peace: Position Paper of the Secretary-General on the Occasion of the Fiftieth Anniversary of the United Nations', UN document A/50/60, 3 January 1995, paragraph 34.
14. *Ibid.*, paragraph 35.
15. UNSCR 770, 13 August 1992. This point was reaffirmed in UNSCR 787, 16 November 1992.
16. Photograph in *The Times*, 18 April 1991, p. 3.
17. From remarks by Ogata at a conference on 'Conflict and Humanitarian Action', Princeton, NJ, 22–23 October 1993, quoted in Minear and Weiss, *Mercy Under Fire*, p. 21.
18. 1949 Geneva Convention I, Article 23; and 1949 Geneva Convention IV, Article 14.
19. 1949 Geneva Convention IV, Article 15.
20. 1977 Geneva Protocol I, Article 60. See also Article 59, on 'Non-defended localities'.
21. For a useful general survey, see Karin Landgren, 'Safety Zones and International Protection: A Dark Grey Area', *International Journal of Refugee Law*, vol. 7, no. 3, July 1995, pp. 436–58.
22. The following is a selection of terms which have appeared in UN Security Council resolutions: 'security zone' (UNSCR 757, 30 May 1992, Sarajevo and its airport); 'United Nations protected areas (UNSCR 762, 30 June 1992, Croatia); 'safe area' (UNSCR 819, 16 April 1993, Srebrenica); 'neutral zone' (UNSCR 918, 17 May 1994, Kigali airport); and 'secure humanitarian areas' (UNSCR 925, 8 June 1994, Rwanda).
23. The UNHCR stated in 1995 that there had not been a single death in an ORC in Sri Lanka as a result of military action. 'Safe Areas: A Substitute for Asylum?', *The State of the World's Refugees 1995*, p. 128. Between 1994 and mid-1996, thousands of people in the ORCs had returned home.
24. Reports in *The Times*, 18 April 1991, pp. 1 and 3.
25. UNSCR 819, 16 April 1993.
26. UNSCR 824, 6 May 1993.
27. UNSCR 836, 4 June 1993.
28. See Gerald B. Helman and Steven R. Ratner, 'Saving Failed States', *Foreign Policy*, no. 89, Winter 1992–93, pp. 3–20; and Peter Lyon, 'The Rise and Fall and Possible Revival of International Trusteeship', *Journal of Commonwealth and Comparative Politics*, no. 31, March 1993, pp. 96–110.
29. Explored further in Adam Roberts, 'The Laws of War: Problems of Implementation in Contemporary Conflicts', in European Commission, *Law in Humanitarian Crises*, vol. I, *How Can International Humanitarian Law be Made Effective in Armed Conflicts?* (Luxembourg: Office for Official Publications of the European Communities, 1995), pp. 13–82.
30. ICRC special brochure, *Saving Lives: The ICRC's Mandate to Protect Civilians and Detainees in Bosnia-Herzegovina* (Geneva: ICRC, April 1995), pp. 3 and 9. This also gives impressive figures regarding ICRC visits to detainees (p. 13), and releases of detainees under ICRC auspices. The circumstances in which ICRC was prepared to make public statements about violations had been outlined in 'Action by the International Committee of the Red Cross in the Event of Breaches of International Humanitarian Law', *International Review of the Red Cross*, no. 221, March–April 1981.
31. For a useful survey of ICRC's role from 1945 to 1975, see Forsythe, *Humanitarian Politics*.
32. UN Security Council Statement S/PV.2667, 21 March 1986.

IV. Key issues
1 From 'Fundamental Principles of the Red Cross', proclaimed by the XXth International Conference of the Red Cross, Vienna, 1965.
2 1977 Geneva Protocol I, Article 70.
3 Points made with particular clarity by Nicholas Morris of UNHCR in a note on 'Humanitarian Aid and Neutrality', 16 February 1995.
4 S. Neil MacFarlane, Larry Minear and Stephen D. Shenfield, *Armed Conflict in Georgia: A Case Study in Humanitarian Action and Peacekeeping* (Providence, RI: Thomas J. Watson Institute, 1996), occasional paper 21, p. x. This report was based on fieldwork in Georgia up to March 1995. Subsequently, and following the development of a more tolerant attitude on the part of the Georgian government, UNHCR and DHA have displayed greater sensitivity to humanitarian needs in their own right in Abkhazia and South Ossetia.
5 'Humanitarianism Unbound? Current Dilemmas Facing Multi-Mandate Relief Operations in Political Emergencies' (London: African Rights, Discussion Paper no. 5, November 1994), p. 2.
6 *Ibid.*, p. 11.
7 David Bryer, 'Lessons from Bosnia: The Role of NGOs', seminar paper at All Souls College, Oxford, 1 March 1996, pp. 2 and 5. See also the chapter 'A World at War' in *The Oxfam Poverty Report 1995* (Oxford: Oxfam, June 1996), pp. 42–70.
8 David Bryer, letter to the author, 2 April 1996.
9 International Federation of Red Cross and Red Crescent Societies, *World Disasters Report 1996* (Oxford: Oxford University Press, 1996), pp. 7 and 142.
10 Cornelio Sommaruga, President of ICRC, at the UN General Assembly, 20 November 1992. *International Review of the Red Cross*, no. 292, January-February 1993, pp. 52 and 53.
11 James C. Ingram, 'The Politics of Human Suffering', *The National Interest*, no. 33, Fall 1993, p. 60. Adapted from his chapter in Thomas G. Weiss and Larry Minear (eds), *Humanitarianism Across Borders* (Boulder, CO: Lynne Rienner, 1994).
12 *The Lost Agenda: Human Rights and UN Field Operations* (New York: Human Rights Watch, 1993), p. 1. See also the similar arguments in *Peace-keeping and Human Rights* (London: Amnesty International, January 1994).
13 'Humanitarianism Unbound?', p. 4.
14 *Ibid.*, pp. 4–5 and 11.
15 Bryer, 'Providing Humanitarian Assistance During Internal Conflicts', p. 3.
16 Personal communication from Nicholas Morris, UNHCR, 27 March 1995. See also the judicious discussion, 'Increased Emphasis on Human Rights', in *State of the World's Refugees 1995*, pp. 40–42.
17 'Humanitarianism Unbound?', p. 11.
18 Described by a participant who later became Professor of International Relations, J.K. Zawodny, *Nothing But Honour: The Story of the Warsaw Uprising, 1944* (London: Macmillan, 1978), especially pp. 69–78.
19 Cecil Woodham-Smith, *The Great Hunger: Ireland 1845–49* (London: Hamish Hamilton, 1962), especially pp. 410–11.
20 'Humanitarianism Unbound?', p. 7.
21 Points 2, 4 and 9 of 'Code of Conduct for the International Red Cross and Red Crescent Movement and NGOs in Disaster Relief'. For more on this agreement, its background, and the NGOs subscribing to it, see *World Disasters Report 1996*, pp. 145–49. See also the general discussion of accountability, including a proposal for 'a new humanitarian watchdog', in Minear and Weiss, *Mercy Under Fire*, pp. 77–84 and 211.
22 *The International Response to Conflict and Genocide*, Study 1, *Historical Perspective: Some Explanatory Factors*, p. 6; and Study 3, *Humanitarian Aid and Effects*, pp. 6 and 157.

23 *The International Response to Conflict and Genocide – Synthesis Report*, p. 60.
24 On Iraq's rejection of resources available to relieve suffering, see 'Situation of Human Rights in Iraq: Note by the Secretary-General', UN Document A/50/734, 8 November 1995, pp. 12–16.
25 Quoted in Minear and Weiss, *Mercy Under Fire*, p. 69.
26 Figures for emergency funding and overall ODA funding, and ample evidence of the concern of development assistance specialists about the rise in spending on emergency relief, can be found in *Development Cooperation Report 1994* (OECD), pp. 80–84; and *Development Cooperation Report 1995*, p.95. This concern is also noted in *World Disasters Report 1996*, p. 62.
27 R.M. Connaughton, *Military Support and Protection for Humanitarian Assistance: Rwanda April–December 1994* (Camberley, Surrey: Strategic and Combat Studies Institute, occasional paper no. 18, 1996), p. 4.
28 For a sensitive exploration, highlighting elements of convergence between the attitudes of military and civilian groups, see Hugo Slim, 'The Stretcher and the Drum: Civil-Military Relations in Peace Support Operations', *International Peacekeeping*, vol. 3, no. 2, Summer 1996.
29 Speech by Jan Eliasson in Atlanta, Georgia, 17 February 1993. Cited in Erskine Childers and Brian Urquhart, *Renewing the United Nations System* (Uppsala: Dag Hammarskjöld Foundation, 1994), p. 118.
30 *Ibid.*, pp. 118 and 204.
31 Joint Inspection Unit report, *Investigation of the Relationship Between Humanitarian Assistance and Peace-Keeping Operations*, October 1995, pp. ix and 28.
32 The actual work of the UN volunteers in conflict and post-conflict situations is well described by participants in *Volunteers Against Conflict* (Tokyo: United Nations University Press, 1996).
33 See UN General Assembly Resolution (UNGAR) A/49/139, 20 December 1994, and UNGAR 50/19 of 28 November 1995, both entitled 'Participation of Volunteers, "White Helmets", in Activities of the United Nations in the Field of Humanitarian Relief, Rehabilitation and Technical Cooperation for Development'.
34 Quoted in Connaughton, *Military Support*, p. 18.
35 *The International Response to Conflict and Genocide*, Study 3, *Humanitarian Aid and Effects*, pp. 11 and 156–66. The volume entitled *Synthesis Report*, in discussing the protection of victims and the role of military contingents (pp. 48–49, 56 and 60), advocates that UN peacekeeping forces be given a clear mandate to protect civilians when large numbers are threatened by violence, but does not discuss the implications for the impartiality of UN forces.
36 For example, 1907 Hague Convention IV, Regulations, Articles 21, 23 and 27; 1949 Geneva Convention IV, Articles 11 and 14–26; 1977 Geneva Protocol I, Articles 8–31, 37(1)(d), 38, 61–71 and 79.
37 Boutros Boutros-Ghali, *Confronting New Challenges*, p. 229.
38 For earlier discussions, see the 1971 Zagreb Resolution of the Institute of International Law on 'Conditions of Application of Humanitarian Rules of Armed Conflict to Hostilities in which United Nations Forces May Be Engaged', reprinted in Adam Roberts and Richard Guelff (eds), *Documents on the Laws of War* (Oxford: Oxford University Press, 2nd edition, 1989), pp. 371–75.
39 UNSCR 758, 8 June 1992. Similar demands for the safety of UN and humanitarian personnel can be found in many subsequent resolutions on former Yugoslavia, including UNSCR 761, 29 June 1992; UNSCR 764, 13 July 1992; UNSCR 770, 13 August 1992; and UNSCR 802, 25 January 1993.
40 UNSCR 925, 8 June 1994.
41 Convention on the Safety of United Nations and Associated Personnel, approved

by UNGAR 49/59, 9 December 1994, Article 1. Full text in UN document A/RES/49/59, 17 February 1995.
42 Article 2(2), on scope of application, says: 'This Convention shall not apply to a United Nations operation authorised by the Security Council as an enforcement action under Chapter VII of the Charter of the United Nations in which any of the personnel are engaged as combatants against organised armed forces and to which the law of international armed conflict applies.'
43 These figures, based on UN and US official sources, are mainly from ICRC, *Anti-personnel Landmines: Friend or Foe? – A Study of the Military Use and Effectiveness of Anti-personnel Mines* (Geneva: ICRC, March 1996), p. 9.
44 See UNGAR 50/70 (O), and UNGAR 50/74, both adopted without a vote on 12 December 1995.
45 ICRC, *Anti-personnel Landmines: Friend or Foe?*, pp. 71–73.
46 Amended Protocol II to the 1981 UN Convention on Specific Conventional Weapons, Articles 1(2) and 3–12.

V. Coordinating humanitarian action

1 David Bryer, 'Lessons from Bosnia: The Role of NGOs', p. 8.
2 *The International Response to Conflict and Genocide*, Study 3, *Humanitarian Aid and Effects*, pp. 10, 122–36. On the coordination lessons, see also the *Synthesis Report*, pp. 57–59.
3 Evans, *Cooperating for Peace*, pp. 158–59.
4 DHA was established following UNGAR 46/182, 19 December 1991. For a survey of UN coordination efforts under the DHA, including details of the Central Emergency Revolving Fund, see 'Strengthening of the Coordination of Emergency Humanitarian Assistance of the United Nations: Report of the Secretary-General', UN document A/49/177/Add.1, 1 November 1994.
5 For figures on the actual income received by the UN Consolidated Inter-Agency Humanitarian Assistance Appeals, 1992–95, see Boutros-Ghali, *Confronting New Challenges*, p. 174.
6 Toby Lanzer, *The UN Department of Humanitarian Affairs in Angola: A Model for the Coordination of Humanitarian Assistance?* (Uppsala: Nordiska Afrikainstitutet, Studies on Emergencies and Disaster Relief, no. 5), pp. 8, 10.
7 'United Nations Interventions in Conflict Situations', submission from Community Aid Abroad Australia, and Oxfam UK and Ireland, p. 14.
8 This post was also established on the basis of UNGAR 46/182. For a brief account, see Tom J. Farer and Felice Gaer, 'The UN and Human Rights: At the End of the Beginning', in Roberts and Kingsbury (eds), *United Nations, Divided World* (Oxford: Oxford University Press, 2nd edition, 1993), p. 256.
9 Early warning is discussed as a subcategory of preventive diplomacy in Boutros Boutros-Ghali, *An Agenda for Peace* (New York: United Nations June 1992), paragraphs 26 and 27.
10 Evans, *Cooperating for Peace*, p. 70.
11 In a country where emergency operations have commenced, an 'integrated early warning cell should be established within the DHA field coordination office'. Conclusion 6 of *The International Response to Conflict and Genocide*, Study 3, *Humanitarian Aid and Effects*, p. 158.
12 International Crisis Group, 'General Prospectus' (London: October 1995), p. 2.

Glossary

CERF	Central Emergency Revolving Fund (DHA)
CIA	Central Intelligence Agency
CNN	Cable News Network
DHA	Department of Humanitarian Affairs (UN)
ECHO	European Community Humanitarian Office
FAO	Food and Agriculture Organisation (UN)
FRY	Federal Republic of Yugoslavia (Serbia and Montenegro)
GONGO	Governmentally-organised non-governmental organisation
GPO	Government Printing Office (US)
IASC	Inter-Agency Standing Committee (DHA-based)
ICG	International Crisis Group
ICRC	International Committee of the Red Cross
IFOR	Implementation Force (NATO)
IFRC	International Federation of Red Cross and Red Crescent Societies
KDP	Kurdish Democratic Party
NGOs	Non-governmental organisations
ODA	Official development assistance
OECD	Organisation for Economic Cooperation and Development
ORC	Open relief centres
PKK	Kurdish Workers Party
POW	Prisoner of war
PUK	Patriotic Union of Kurdistan
RPF	Rwandan Patriotic Front
SFr	Swiss francs
UNDP	United Nations Development Programme
UNAMIR	United Nations Assistance Mission for Rwanda
UNGAR	United Nations General Assembly Resolution
UNGCI	United Nations Guards Contingent in Iraq
UNHCR	United Nations High Commissioner for Refugees
UNICEF	United Nations Children's Fund
UNITA	*União Nacional para a Independência Total de Angola*
UNITAF	Unified Task Force
UNOSOM	United Nations Operation in Somalia
UNPROFOR	United Nations Protection Force
UNRWA	United Nations Relief and Works Agency for Palestine Refugees in the Near East
UNSC	United Nations Security Council
UNSCR	United Nations Security Council Resolution
WFP	World Food Programme (UN)
WHO	World Health Organisation (UN)

12 The Transformation of Strategic Affairs
Adelphi Paper 379, 2006

Lawrence Freedman

Introduction

A recurrent theme in much contemporary writing on strategy is that war in its classical form, involving set-piece battles between regular armies, does not have much of a future.[1] This issue is particularly important for the United States. Its international role relies on an ability to take on all comers in all circumstances. It has superior capabilities for nuclear exchanges and conventional battle, but capabilities at the level upon which most contemporary conflict takes place have been found wanting when recently put to the test. After Vietnam, the US armed forces demonstrated a marked aversion to counter-insurgency operations and dismissed peacekeeping as an inappropriate use of capabilities geared to high-intensity combat. They acknowledged a lack of comparative advantage in low-intensity operations, as they prepared for bigger things, but they also took comfort in the apparent lack of any strategic imperative that would oblige them to engage in distant civil wars. On occasion, as in Somalia, the US government chose to engage, but the military leadership left little doubt that as far as it was concerned this was a bad choice, and, at least in this case, experience seemed to prove it right. Afghanistan and Iraq, however, have created new strategic imperatives and so engagement has become unavoidable, continuous and vexatious. The US would not be the first apparently unbeatable military power to find itself undone by an inability to take seriously or even to comprehend enemies that rely on their ability to emerge out of the shadows of civil society, preferring minor skirmish to major battle, accepting no possibility for decisive victory but instead aiming to unsettle, harass, demoralise, humiliate and eventually to wear down their opponents. This was, after all, the basis of many successful 'wars of national liberation' against colonial powers. Meanwhile, the strategic imperatives that would justify the large-scale investments in nuclear and conventional capabilities that dominate the Pentagon's budget are no longer self-evident.

This paper does not argue that major regular wars will not occur in the future or that it is pointless to prepare for them. There have been many predictions of the obsolescence of major war that turned out almost immediately to be wrong.[2] These predictions were often quite correct on the irrationality of warfare but wrong on their assumptions that rationality would prevail, or at least in terms of appreciating the short-term conditions that might lead countries to act so decisively against their long-term interests. While the impulse to acquire colonies or to secure markets through conquest may never again reach nineteenth-century proportions, different impulses towards interstate war may arise, perhaps as a result of conflicts over scarce resources or in the wake of great environmental upheavals. Perhaps the current consensus on the irrationality of major war depends more than is appreciated on a calculation of the prevailing balance of power; if guards should be lowered or offensive capabilities suddenly increased, then these calculations may start to look quite different. Given these possibilities, some expenditure on nuclear and conventional forces might be prudent to deter great power confrontations (although this sort of claim is impossible to prove). The capacity for regular war is not confined to the major powers and it would not be surprising if one of the many territorial disputes among minor powers reached such a critical point that resort to arms seemed to be the only way to achieve a resolution. These uncertainties mean that it is highly likely that governments will continue to make provisions for regular war and to train their armed forces accordingly. Even while they may accept that a full-blown capacity for regular war may never be used, there are aspects of contemporary conflict which still involve high-intensity operations and can take advantage of the most advanced weapons systems.

Nor is it necessarily the case that the recent pattern of Western engagement in irregular warfare will continue, even though they now have experiences at home in an extreme, if only sporadic, form. In the conflicts that now demand immediate attention it is suicide bombers who appear to be most threatening. As agents of terror they might turn up almost anywhere, including in city centres, with a strategic purpose that appears little more than an expression of a generalised sense of global grievance; alternatively they act as the shock troops of more localised but intensely vicious insurgencies. If this represents a trend in how to express personality disorders then it may last for some time. If it is, however, strategic in inspiration then it may prosper or fizzle out depending on whether it is setting back or advancing the causes that it is supposed to serve.[3]

There is an argument that the risks of having to cope with acts of indiscriminate ferocity could be reduced if states were to refrain from future engagement with the more troubled parts of the world. During the 1990s it seemed reasonable to suppose that Western countries would have to engage in distant conflicts – even when their interests were at most indirectly involved – to protect vulnerable populations at risk from internal repression or intercommunal disorder. During the present decade it has become evident that Western interests could be more directly at stake but also that they are not so easy to secure through the use of force. It is quite possible that in response to events in Iraq there will be an attempt to wind down existing Western commitments and a reluctance to take on more. If the real need is to prevent terrorist acts within Western countries then that may depend more on the quality of work by intelligence agencies and the police than the use of armed forces in expeditionary roles.

Nonetheless, this paper assumes that, for the moment, the most perplexing problems of security policy surround irregular rather than regular war. It is, of course, a matter of enormous relief that these wars lack the sense of ultimate, existential danger posed by the major wars of the past, but that is also the reason why they are so perplexing. When the security of the state is threatened by a large and self-evidently hostile enemy then all social and economic resources can be mobilised in response. When, by contrast, there is a debate to be had about the nature of the threat and whether matters are made better or worse by direct action, military operations appear to be more discretionary and national mobilisation on even a modest scale becomes more difficult. Describing and quantifying the risks becomes harder, complicating the terrible calculus of costs and benefits that policy-makers face when embarking on any military operation, whereby collections of lives are weighed against one another, or the tangibles of human and physical destruction are set against the intangibles of high principle and even reputation. Even when military action is chosen, operations undertaken in politically complex settings can be full of surprises and lead to new missions and new rationales. The surprises often result from a failure to understand the strategic cultures and agendas of both friends and enemies, and the mixtures of motives and attitudes that influence their behaviour. Coping with these new conditions presents a substantial challenge to strategists.

The experience of Iraq since 2003 can and will be taken to reinforce the principled and prudential reasons to challenge the very idea that war might be used as a means of achieving supposedly liberal goals. It may be that this will encourage Western countries to leave the weak and failed states of the world well alone. It is not the purpose of this paper to identify contingencies for future military action. For a variety of reasons I believe that, over the medium and long term, non-intervention will be a difficult position to sustain although in the short term it may be a tempting one to try. Current exigencies may well draw Western governments into events around the globe, particularly as they affect Muslim countries. Even those aspects of contemporary conflict best handled by the police and intelligence services raise questions of strategy and the legitimacy of action.

This sets the context for the four core themes of this paper. The first is the difficulty the US armed forces face in shifting their focus from preparing for regular wars, in which combat is separated from civil society, to irregular wars, in which combat is integrated with civil society. Second, the political context of contemporary irregular wars requires that the purpose and practice of Western forces be governed by liberal values. This is also the case with regular wars, to the extent that they occur, but it is the integration with civil society that makes the application of liberal values so challenging. Third, the paper argues that this challenge becomes easier to meet when military operations are understood to contribute to the development of a compelling narrative about the likely course and consequence of a conflict, in which these values are shown to be respected. Fourth, while it is vital that the employment of armed force remains sensitive at all times to the underlying political context and to the role of narratives in shaping this context, a key test of success will always be the defeat of the opposing forces. The application of this test in regular war remains straightforward; this is not the case in irregular war, which can be of long duration and contain frequent shifts in tempo and focus. These themes raise issues that go beyond those connected with the 'war on terror', although this has undoubtedly highlighted their main features and associated dilemmas. Together they set the terms for contemporary strategic thinking.

Strategy

The concept of strategy that underpins this paper is closely related to the concept of power, understood as the ability to produce intended effects. Power is often discussed simply as capacity, normally based on military or economic strength, but in the face of certain challenges or in the pursuit of particular objectives much of this capacity may be useless. It takes strategy to unleash the power inherent in this capacity and to direct it towards specific purposes. Strategy is about choice. It depends on the ability to understand situations and to appreciate the dangers and opportunities they contain. The most talented strategists are able to look forward, to imagine quite different and more benign situations from those that currently obtain and what must be done to reach them, as well as more malign situations and how they might best be prevented. In so doing they will always be thinking about the choices available to others and how their own endeavours might be thwarted, frustrated or even reinforced. It is this interdependence of choice that provides the essence of strategy and diverts it from being mere long-term planning or the mechanical connection of available means to set ends. To focus on strategy is to emphasise the importance of choice and the extent to which the development of the international system will be much more than a function of impersonal trends or structural logic. In this respect, the transformation of strategy refers to the changing conditions in which choices must be made. While strategic discourse has now moved well beyond its etymological roots in the art of generals, and is notably prominent in organisational and business theory, this paper sticks close to the classical usage. This requires consideration of the changing character of armed forces, in terms of the development of military capabilities and the prevalent forms of conflict that shape their distribution and application.

The link with other forms of power comes at the level of grand strategy, at which the military instrument must be assessed in relation to all the other instruments available to states – economic, social and political. This is evident, for example, in the debate over the relative merits of 'hard' versus 'soft' power and the claim that in the contemporary international environment influence is as likely to flow through cultural and economic relationships as military ones. Even when it comes to military affairs, wider socio-economic and technological changes have a major impact. Indeed discussions about changes in military affairs are as likely to focus on these factors as much as the changing nature of conflict.

Strategy has traditionally been concerned with attempts by states to influence both their position within the international system and the structure of the system itself. Over past decades, changes in the international system have resulted in important developments in thinking about military strategy, for example the rise and fall of wars of decolonisation, the fixation with nuclear deterrence and the revival of interest in conventional warfare. The reasons for suggesting that a transformation of strategy is now underway reflect the demilitarisation of inter-state relations, particularly among the great powers, and the expansion of the state system as a result of decolonisation, which has resulted in many new states that are also internally unstable. Often this instability leads to violence and brings irregular forces into being. Foreign governments must then decide whether to become involved in helping to restabilise the situation or to mitigate the consequences of failing to do so. These are difficult choices and the way that they have been made and implemented has also contributed to the transformation of strategy. A further twist has been added by the arrival of super-terrorism as a major security threat and the campaign led by the Bush administration to deal directly with those responsible for past acts of terrorism and potentially for future acts. The 'war on terror', and also the more altruistic humanitarian interventions, require the separation of militants from their potential sources of support, which means understanding and, if possible, influencing the civil societies from whence they come.

Transformation

I addressed these issues in a 1998 *Adelphi Paper* entitled *The Revolution in Strategic Affairs*.[4] In it I challenged the view that a technology-driven revolution in military affairs (RMA) was underway. Although some important changes had taken place in the way that the armed forces were able to go about their business, largely the result of advances in information and communication technologies, their impact on the actual conduct of war depended on the interatction of these developments with changes of a quite different type – in political affairs – which pointed away from the decisive clash between great powers. The RMA focused on major wars like those of the past, involving regular armed forces that would benefit from technological enhancements. This paid insufficient attention to the wars that might actually have to be fought, which were more likely to be asymmetrical and irregular. This was because there was a revolution in political affairs underway that was at least as important as a revolution in military affairs. Together they could (if this language were to be employed) constitute a revolution in strategic affairs.

In some respects events since 1998 have vindicated this analysis, but there are others in which it needs to be brought up to date, notably with regard to the 'global war on terror' and the experiences of Kosovo, Afghanistan and Iraq. This *Adelphi Paper*, picking up on the themes of its predecessor, argues for thinking about the role of armed force in the light of changing political conditions and not just the new configurations made possible by the latest technological advances and organisational concepts.

I. Networks, culture and narratives

Since Carl von Clausewitz borrowed the concept of the 'centre of gravity' from Newtonian physics, referring to the point in a body about which it will balance, it has served as a metaphor for ways in which a well-aimed offensive thrust might knock the enemy sideways.[1] Clausewitz, considering regular war, wondered not only about the centre of gravity of an army in battle but of a whole nation. He could claim that if a nation depends on its army for protection, then the army is the nation's centre of gravity. But what if the nation were as dependent upon an alliance or on suppressing insurrectionists? Might these not also be centres of gravity? Clausewitz thought that indeed they could be and so extended the metaphor to the point where it became critically misleading and far too mechanically applied – especially by his later imitators. The term has now become used as a synonym for any potentially decisive vulnerability. Because every body must have a centre of gravity so then, it is assumed, must every army or every society. All that has to be done is to identify and to attack this centre.

In the 1980s air forces were taken up with the metaphor and spent much time discussing where the centre might be found and how it could then be targeted accurately, as if the centre of gravity of a state, and even a whole society, might be found in a collection of buildings or key facilities. Since then the vital centre has come to be identified in terms of information networks and, more recently, culture. This chapter first describes the recent development of official American strategic thinking and then considers the influence of ideas of 'network-centric' and 'culture-centric' warfare. It concludes by identifying the concept of a strategic narrative as an analytical device.

The revolution in military affairs

To understand the transformation that has taken place in military thinking a useful starting point is the 1991 Gulf War. This appeared to be a classic of manoeuvre warfare, confirming the validity of military preferences by being fought successfully along wholly conventional lines. The enemy was disoriented by means of highly mobile firepower, made possible by technical superiority and skilful orchestration of professional forces. It reflected ideas that had been under development since the late 1970s, marked in 1982 by the adoption of the doctrine of AirLand Battle, in preparation for the great confrontation between the Warsaw Pact and NATO. The renewed emphasis on manoeuvre was an explicit criticism of what was said to have been an excessive prior preoccupation with attrition. Reviving the operational arts also meant reviving ideas, going back to the aftermath of First World War, of how warfare might be rescued from the terrible consequences of attrition, in which victory required staying power above all else, as the opposing forces slogged it out, with casualties accumulating, treasury reserves depleted, industry pushed to full stretch and society becoming more fragile. The new approach was to consider the battlefield in the round. The critical attributes of successful operations were stressed as 'initiative, depth, agility and sychronization'.[2]

In 1991 the coalition, led by the United States, and including strong British and some French participation, fought along NATO lines against an opponent that had been prepared, though not very well, to fight along Warsaw Pact lines. The success of *Operation Desert Storm* convinced the military that they were thinking along the right lines. Indeed, up to this point the operational possibilities of improvements in sensors, smart weapons and systems integration were untested hypotheses. There had been talk of a renaissance in conventional strategy in the early 1970s when these new technologies first made themselves felt and this continued until the last years of the Cold War as strategies were sought that could reduce dependence on nuclear deterrence. It remained hard to imagine the scenarios, however, in which the efficacy of these strategies could be proven. Under Cold War conditions, there would always be the possibility, if a conventional battle were being lost, of escalation to nuclear exchange. Little in American military practice, up to 1991, gave cause for great confidence. The best arguments seemed to be with the sceptics, who warned of how the most conceptually brilliant systems would be brought down low by their own exceedingly complex designs, inept maintenance, incompetent operators or simply employment in climactic or topographical settings for which they were not intended. The pre-*Desert Storm* debate in the US featured many worries about the effects of sand and desert sun on equipment, predictions of high casualties in 'blue-on-blue' attacks and malfunctioning indicators leading coalition units to inflict as much damage on each other as on the enemy. These negative expectations, which may well have encouraged Saddam Hussein to risk a war with the United States, underestimated the seriousness with which the American military leadership had addressed the deficiencies exhibited in Vietnam and the promise offered by the new technologies.

First and foremost, therefore, the revolution resulting from the Gulf War was one of expectations. Up to 1991, the Americans seemed to have lost their grip on the art of warfare; after *Desert Storm* they appeared to be unbeatable – at least when fighting on their own terms. For this reason, one of the most impressive aspects of *Desert Storm* was that sufficient equipment worked as advertised to bamboozle Iraqi forces. There were compelling demonstrations of precision guidance – most dramatically in the images of 'smart' bombs entering command centres or of the *Tomahawk* cruise missile, fired from an old battleship converted for the purpose 1,000 kilometres away, navigating its way through the streets of Baghdad, entering its target by the front door and then exploding. Targets were, generally, chosen with care and, generally, attacked with confidence and minimal civilian casualties.[3]

Because the Gulf War was so one-sided, it displayed the potential of modern military systems in a most flattering light. It was as if Saddam Hussein had been asked to organise his forces in such a way as to offer coalition countries the opportunity to show off their own forces to their best advantage. A battle plan unfolded that followed the essential principles of Western military practice against a totally out-classed and out-gunned enemy who had conceded command of the air. There were no chronic deficiencies in either resources or logistics – only some unseasonable weather. The result, as noted in the *Gulf War Air Power Survey*, was not 'merely . . . a conducive environment for the successful application of Western-style air power' but 'circumstances . . . so ideal as to approach being the best that could be reasonably hoped for in any future conflict'.[4] This limited the extent to which formal doctrines, staff training, procurement policies and so on were truly validated, though not the extent to which they were deemed to have been so.

Proposals for future force structure built on what had worked well in ejecting Iraqi forces from Kuwait in 1991. This was the origin of the RMA, which had a number of influential proponents in the Pentagon. This assumed a technological dynamic that promised the eventual domination of the 'information environment' and thereby the 'battlespace', a term upgraded from the earlier 'battlefield' to capture the idea of combat in three dimensions. The RMA would involve a marriage of information and communications systems with those that apply military force. The potential fruits of this marriage would reflect the quality of the information that it was increasingly possible to collect, assess and transmit virtually instantaneously. The resulting combination of speed and accuracy with which force could then be applied, was described as the 'system of systems', making it possible to attack discrete though distant targets with ever greater care and precision under ever more reliable command and control.[5] While enemy commanders were still attempting to mobilise their resources and to develop their plans, they would be rudely interrupted by decisive and lethal blows inflicted by American forces for whom time and space were no longer serious constraints, leaving the enemy shocked and disabled. There was thus a move away from the crude elimination of enemy forces to more subtle notions of putting them in a position where resistance would be futile, by being able to act more quickly and to move more deftly.

The promise was particularly great for land forces. While navies and air forces had long shown how they could operate in this way, armies had traditionally sought to occupy territory and not just to eliminate items upon it.

For those concerned about casualties and long-term commitments, however, ground forces are key. Infantrymen make up around 80% of US combat deaths in recent conflicts, even though they account for just 4% of the total force.[6] For some time, US military thinking has been devoted to finding ways of prevailing on land without excessive risk. RMA advocacy argued that as they took ground, the armies could manage without having their own firepower beside them, even when on the defensive, and instead rely on artillery and aircraft deployed well to their rear. Relieved of the need to travel accompanied by heavy armour and artillery, they should then be far lighter and more mobile and able to dispense with a long logistic tail. With more manpower kept to the rear, less would be at risk. In this way, warfare would move away from mass slaughter to something more contained and discriminate, geared towards disabling an enemy's military establishment with the minimum necessary force. No more resources should be expended, assets ruined or blood be shed than absolutely necessary to achieve specified political goals.

Transformation and the QDR

During the administration of President George W. Bush the theme of revolution was displaced by that of 'transformation', with Secretary of Defense Donald Rumsfeld acting as its champion. Rumsfeld's conviction that the armed forces had become too cumbersome, geared to fighting an enemy that was unlikely to materialise while increasingly unsuited to fighting those who might, came to be reflected more in operational than budgetary terms. The wars in Afghanistan and Iraq provided an opportunity to demonstrate what could be achieved by relatively small and light forces enjoying air superiority. Given the prevailing balance of forces it was possible for American commanders to fight somewhat ad hoc campaigns, taking advantage of opportunities for breakthroughs as they arose. The ease with which the conventional stages of the battle were passed reinforced Rumsfeld's view that speed and flexibility were key to effective combat. Unfortunately, however, this method worked far less well with the next stage of bringing security to the country and defeating the various forms of resistance to the occupying powers that soon emerged.

The impact of both bureaucratic inertia and operational experience on transformation efforts is evident in the February 2006 *Quadrennial Defense Review Report* (QDR).[7] It has become a common complaint that the term 'transformation' describes a process rather than a destination and that the QDR's meditations on the implications of an age of uncertainty and surprises and calls for flexibility and adaptability indeed suggest disorientation more than a strategy. A further complaint is that despite Rumsfeld's own bold talk of major structural changes in the defence budget (now coming in at $500 billion), more than a decade of discussion of a less platform-centred approach to warfare, and a stress on lighter forces more appropriate to contemporary conditions, the US defence budget is still dominated by platforms. Rumsfeld has been no more successful than his predecessors in turning the armed services away from the 'big ticket' systems of aircraft, warships and armoured vehicles that would only really be necessary in the event of a major war against a far more substantial enemy than can currently be identified. Recognition of new strategic challenges is indicated in the pledges to 'beef up' Special Forces, to increase by a third the number of personnel specialising in psychological operations and civil affairs and to spend more on Unmanned Aerial Vehicles (UAVs).

Nonetheless, the 2006 QDR demonstrates considerable movement in US thinking since 2001. While no mistakes are acknowledged, there is an implicit recognition that the US military, and particularly the army, must make a greater effort to come to terms with irregular warfare, especially in the face of 'dispersed, global terrorist networks that exploit Islam to advance radical political aims'. The talk now is of a 'long war'.[8] The thrust of the QDR is the extent of the transformation required of US forces in response to the new strategic environment. Instead of worrying about a single, predictable and therefore deterrable state it is now necessary to address complex and unpredictable challenges, some of the most dangerous emanating from non-state actors who may well be found, and thus engaged, within countries with which the US is not actually at war. The QDR presumes the need to act before rather than after situations have reached crisis point and with 'a wartime sense of urgency'. So the option of pre-emption, highlighted so boldly in the president's 2002 *National Security Strategy*,[9] is still implied but there is now less confidence in the idea that a developing threat can be eliminated in anticipation by a bold stroke. Instead the talk is of the need of a surge capacity to meet the different types of threat as they arise.

The QDR describes four categories of problems and suggests that they require distinctive types of forces. Defeating terrorist networks thus demands Special Forces; defending the homeland in depth involves better forms of detection and protection; shaping the choices of countries at strategic crossroads will be helped by traditional mixes of conventional and nuclear forces to remind them of the wisdom of avoiding the path of confrontation; and preventing hostile states and non-state actors from acquiring or using weapons of mass destruction may require complex packages of military and non-military capabilities. The underlying theme of the document, however, is less a matter of gearing capabilities to specific problems but a fundamental shift in attitude. Planning cannot be a leisurely process geared to possible threats, but must instead be fast moving and adaptive, geared to real threats. Forces can no longer be allowed simply to reflect the distinctive institutional preferences of the single services and be maintained in a static, hollow form, only to be filled should a need arise. Instead they should be complete, integrated and ready to move, but also flexible and tailored to the crisis at hand, with powerful operational teeth and the shortest possible logistical tail. Instead of a dominant focus on major conventional combat operations it is now necessary to prepare for 'multiple irregular, asymmetric operations'. Although one might not guess from the actual budgetary commitments, these require less of an 'emphasis on ships, guns, tanks and planes' and less concern about amassing forces to engage in set-piece manoeuvres, judged by their kinetic impact. There must be more of an emphasis on 'massing effects', drawing more on 'information, knowledge and timely, actionable intelligence'.

War: 'network-centred' or 'culture-centred'?

Arguably the most important single proposition influencing contemporary American strategic thought in both official and unofficial circles is the identification of information as the key factor in military operations. It derives from a conviction that a new stage in some historically defined, and often technologically determined, sequence has been reached. The information age has been identified as the successor to the agricultural and industrial ages, bringing with it fundamental charges in the organisation of all human affairs, including the use of purposive violence.[10]

Information, once in electronic form, is unlike any other commodity: it is easy to generate, to transmit, to collect and to store. Incalculable amounts are now pumped out daily on to the internet to a near-infinite number of potential recipients with no expectation of payment and only occasional requests for user registration. 'Blogs', message boards and email contacts bring together individuals with at least one thing in common, despite many other differences. The problems this creates are those of superfluity and overload, of sorting information, identifying what is needed and distinguishing the important from the trivial and the background noise.

The tradition of worrying about information as a scarce commodity led strategists to address its growing wider importance in similar terms to other vital commodities, such as fuel and food. If information of high quality can be acquired and protected it is possible to stay ahead of opponents and competitors. Such information might include intellectual property, sensitive financial data and the plans and capabilities of government agencies and private corporations. Considerable effort goes into protecting this information from disruption or tampering and assuring its integrity. The concern lies with attack by viruses, worms, trojan horses or logic bombs,[11] often launched from distant servers for no obvious purpose but sometimes with a clear and malign intent. Criminals would be after sensitive personal details to help them to steal identities or to misappropriate funds.

Much of the early discussion on information warfare concerned these privileged information stores and flows, and the new targets being offered to wily opponents.[12] In a culture that had assumed that the best military strategies were those that caused the minimum casualties, the thought that an enemy would aim for the support systems of modern societies was both comforting and alarming at the same time.[13] The direct hurt would be slight while the indirect hurt – as transport, banking and public health systems began to break down – could be substantial. The threat gained credibility as the frequency with which companies and even high-profile networks, such as that of the US military, were attacked by a variety of hackers grew. The fear was that an enemy able to mobilise an army of software wizards could subvert an advanced society using the most insidious electronic means. But much of this was 'hacktivism', a way of making political or cultural points rather than of threatening the economy or social cohesion. Even if more determined adversaries were prepared to mount more substantial attacks the result would be likely to be 'mass disruption' rather than 'mass destruction', with inconvenience and disorientation more evident than terror and collapse.[14] These remain serious issues and considerable sums are now spent on ways of protecting and managing privileged information flows. Those involved consider themselves to be in constant battle with sophisticated foes who are persistently probing for the weakest links in networks.

A similar tendency in thinking can be observed when considering the consequences of the information age for military operations. As already remarked, the impact of the new information technologies was a key theme underlying the proclamation of the RMA. In this context the focus was on how the new technologies would affect classical forms of military operation. Its influence was evident in the 1998 paper *Joint Doctrine for Information Operations*, where information superiority was defined in largely warfighting terms, as 'the capability to collect, process, and disseminate an uninterrupted flow of information while exploiting or denying an adversary's ability to do the same'.[15] If information superiority were lost in the midst of operations the military could find air defence systems disabled, missiles sent off course, local commanders left in the dark and senior commanders confused as their screens went blank.

This view of information operations was soon challenged from two directions. It was firstly pointed out that the model for future war being proposed was one that played entirely to American strengths, including in the most advanced technologies, and for that very reason was unlikely to be embraced by the country's enemies who would be bound to look for strategies that played to American weaknesses, such as its impatience and intolerance of casualties. Such strategies came to be described as 'asymmetric', an adjective that appears regularly in the most recent QDR. This speaks to concerns that the optimum strategies for those unable to match America's conventional military capabilities (in other words, almost everyone) will be to encourage either the quagmires of irregular warfare or escalation into weapons of mass destruction. The second source of dissent came from elements in the military establishment who were dubious about the claims being made about the declining role of massed firepower and the possibility that 'information superiority' could dispel the 'fog of war'. Marine Corps Lieutenant General Paul Van Riper observed: 'Never saw and don't believe bytes of information kill enemy soldiers.' Van Riper acknowledged that improved information was helpful in supporting commanders, although he added that when this arrived as a mass of data it was of limited value.[16] The 1999 Kosovo campaign demonstrated that even with apparently complete information superiority, the fog of war had not lifted and that there were severe problems in acquiring accurate information and disseminating it effectively.[17] It was in this context that the notion of 'transformation' appeared a less ambitious and institutionally threatening concept.

The influence of the information environment then came to be seen in the ability to communicate across horizontal lines, thereby facilitating less hierarchical and flatter forms of command and control. This idea has been picked up in the notion of 'network-centred warfare'. As initially developed by Vice Admiral Arthur K. Cebrowski, US Navy, and John J. Garstka, this is geared to making battles more efficient in the same way that the application of information technology by businesses was making economies more efficient.[18] By means of 'excellent sensors, fast and powerful networks, display technology, and sophisticated modeling and simulation capabilities', information superiority could be achieved. This would mean that the force would have 'a dramatically better awareness or understanding of the battlespace rather than simply more raw data'. This could make up for deficiencies in numbers, technology or position and speed up command processes. Forces could be organised 'from the bottom up – or to self-synchronize – to meet the commander's intent'. This would lead to 'the rapid foreclosure of enemy courses of action and the shock of closely coupled events'. There would be no time for the enemy to follow the famous 'Observe-Orient-Decide-Act Loop'.[19] Even as the battle develops, situational awareness could be maintained.

Although in discussing the move from 'platform-centered' to 'network-centered' warfare, the Pentagon largely followed this formulation (Garstka was one of the authors), it also recognised that, following the physical and information domains, there was a 'cognitive domain', that of:

> the mind of the warfighter and the warfighter's supporting populace. Many battles and wars are won or lost in the cognitive domain. The intangibles of leadership, morale, unit cohesion, level of training and experience, situational awareness, and public opinion are elements of this domain. This is the domain where commander's intent, doctrine, tactics, techniques, and procedures reside.[20]

The shift to a focus on irregular warfare has had consequences for thinking about the role of information and, in particular, the cognitive domain. If the aim is to achieve a decisive victory in a regular war then information superiority will play a supplementary role, as an 'enabler', making superiority possible in the physical environment in which force is applied. In irregular warfare, superiority in the physical environment is of little value unless it can be translated into an advantage in the information environment. A sense of security, for example, is a matter of perception as much as physical fact. It has been argued that as this is the 'chosen battlespace' of its foes, the US must learn to conceptualise its victories in terms of shaping perceptions over time.[21] This fits in with the broader vision of the influence of the information age as explored by two RAND analysts, David Ronfeldt and John Arquilla. They developed the concept of 'netwars' as 'an emerging mode of conflict (and crime) at societal levels, short of traditional military warfare, in which the protagonists use network forms of organization and related doctrines, strategies, and technologies attuned to the information age'. In contrast to the large, hierarchical, stand-alone organisations that have become well established over the years and conduct police and military operations, and which extremists have often mimicked, the protagonists of netwar are 'likely to consist of dispersed organizations, small groups, and individuals who communicate, coordinate, and conduct their campaigns in an internetted manner, often without a central command'.[22]

One school of thought which draws on these insights is bound up with the view that fourth-generation warfare (4GW) has now begun. This was first developed by William Lind with a number of military colleagues.[23] According to their scheme, the first three generations had developed in response to each other (line and column, massed firepower and blitzkrieg). Into the fourth generation was carried an increasingly dispersed battlefield, reducing the importance of centralised logistics and mass (either men or firepower), and a tendency for victory to come through the implosion of the enemy rather than its physical destruction. The essence of 4GW lies in the blurring of boundaries – between war and peace, between civilian and military, between tactics and strategy, between order and chaos. Such war cannot be contained in either time or space. According to Thomas X. Hammes, such war spans the 'spectrum of human activity':

> In sum, 4GW is politically, socially (rather than technically) networked and protracted in duration. It is the anti-thesis of the high-technology, short war the Pentagon is preparing to fight.[24]

Here, the cognitive domain takes on growing importance and is influenced by far more than the speed and accuracy of information flows. There is the basis for a greater appreciation of the role of established belief systems and embedded views of the world, which helps to guide the interpretation of incoming information.

Unfortunately, whereas the RMA points to a singular form of regular warfare, which because it so suits the US is unlikely to be fought, 4GW points to almost everything else. It certainly takes in the sort of warfare in which the US is currently engaged and its influence can be seen in current views on how this should be addressed. The fact that 4GW is based on poor history, and does scant justice to the forms both regular and irregular warfare can take, is not in itself a reason for neglecting its prescriptive aspects. It is, however, important to note that the new 4GW is not usefully understood as an evolution from previous generations of warfare, as the first to third generations describe tendencies in thinking about regular battle.

The methods that are classified as 4GW are those used by the weak against the strong. Those fighting a conventionally superior capability wish to avoid direct battle in order to survive over the long term. They must find ways to demoralise the enemy while building up political support, until a tipping point is reached and the balance of power shifts decisively. This is the approach of guerrillas, resisters, partisans, insurgents, subversives, insurrectionists, revolutionaries, secessionists and terrorists and it has a long history. The methods employed by such groups are not a progression from forms of regular war, but instead constitute a parallel development. The category of 4GW is a broad one, and includes not only activities far removed from regular war but also strategies that intersect with it, either because they are complementary (for example, work with partisan groups during the Second World War) or merge into it. As the movements grow in military strength they come to embrace the methods of regular war. The generality of contemporary unconventional conflict is difficult to capture in a single category, for this is bound to miss its diversity and complex interaction with more conventional forms of warfare.

Part of the influence of 4GW theory, bolstered by recent experience, lies in the identification of 'culture' as a strategic factor in its own right as a critical influence on the cognitive dimension. Instead of the rigid empiricism of 'network-centric' warfare in its first guise, there has been an almost post-modernist embrace of pre-rational and embedded patterns of thought that allow individuals, and broad social groups, to be caught up in a particular view of the world that helps them to make sense of unfolding events, even to the point of being highly resistant to inconvenient facts. In a particularly extreme formulation, such as Lind's, culture has become the weakest strategic link, a point which the enemy can work upon to fracture American security.[25]

Major-General Robert H. Scales, Jr, in seeking to explain the contrast between the failure of Islamic armies when fighting conventional battles, Western-style, but their far greater success in unconventional war, has developed the concept of 'culture-centric warfare'.[26] In facing an enemy that 'uses guile, subterfuge, and terror mixed with patience and a willingness to die', he argues, too much has been spent attempting to gain 'a few additional meters of precision, knots of speed, or bits of bandwidth' and too little to create a 'parallel transformation based on cognition and cultural awareness'. Winning wars requires:

> creating alliances, leveraging nonmilitary advantages, reading intentions, building trust, converting opinions, and managing perceptions – all tasks that demand an exceptional ability to understand people, their culture, and their motivation. . . .
>
> Sensors, computer power, and bandwidth count for little against a dispersed enemy who communicates by word of mouth and back-alley messengers and fights using simple weapons that do not require networks or sophisticated technological integration to be effective.

Care is needed here. In practice, culture is less of a fixed and known quality but more an amalgam of language, tradition, religious practices and social structures, and political values. The key question is the degree to which the culture, or some element within it, has become politicised, differentiating groups from each other. It is one thing to support a national soccer team; another to feel patriotic pride at a military display; another still to be consumed with hatred of all those with an alien culture. Culture, and the cognition which it influences, is rarely fixed but in a process of development and adaptation, shaped by the encounter between received beliefs and everyday experience, and by the competing analyses and explanations provided by the print, broadcasting and web-based media.

Strategic narratives

It is in this context that the concept of narratives – compelling story lines which can explain events convincingly and from which inferences can be drawn – becomes relevant. Narratives are designed or nurtured with the intention of structuring the responses of others to developing events. They are strategic because they do not arise spontaneously but are deliberately constructed or reinforced out of the ideas and thoughts that are already current. According to Ronfeldt and Arquilla,[27] networks are held together by narratives. They emphasise that narratives go beyond rhetoric 'scripted for manipulative ends', but instead 'provide a grounded expression of people's experiences, interests, and values'. Stories both 'express a sense of identity and belonging', and 'communicate a sense of cause, purpose, and mission'. This helps a dispersed group to cohere and guides its strategy. Individuals know the sort of action expected of them and the message to be conveyed.

Narratives are about the ways that issues are framed and responses suggested. They are not necessarily analytical and, when not grounded in evidence or experience, may rely on appeals to emotion, or on suspect metaphors and dubious historical analogies. A successful narrative will link certain events while disentangling others, distinguish good news from bad tidings, and explain who is winning and who is losing. This usage reflects the idea that stories play an extremely important role in communication, including the ways that organisations talk about themselves. The notion of the narrative is already well established among strategies working in the domestic political arena, for example in guiding the activity popularly known as 'spin'. Ideas about 'controlling the agenda', keeping some big ideas to the fore and not allowing them to be crowded out by trivialities, inserting the right 'soundbites' into news bulletins, ensuring party members stay 'on message' and influencing the 'story line' reflect the view that opinions are shaped not so much by the information received but the constructs through which that information is interpreted and understood. The concept is therefore now central to the study of journalism.[28] Convincing the public that the economy is really doing well when the latest data suggest the opposite, or that the murky past of a candidate for high office is irrelevant, requires a keen sense of how the media works, from timing news announcements, both positive and negative, briefing key journalists and keeping an eye on internet 'blogs'. An effective narrative will work not only because it appeals to the values, interests and prejudices of the intended audience but also because it is not going to be exposed by later information and events.

There is nothing new in the concept that worthy causes or quality products can fail because of ineffectual communication. Intellectuals through the ages have been animated by the conviction that language and the construction of ideas matter. Contemporary interest in the matter is fuelled by the intensity and complexity of the media environment but also by an anxiety on the part of commentators that spin diminishes public discourse, assuming limited attention spans, fascination with process rather than substance, with who is up or down rather than what is right or wrong. The ability of single-issue pressure groups to convince people that anything genetically modified is dangerous or that the theory of evolution is bunkum can be seen as testament to the inability of those with cautious, moderate, analytical viewpoints to shape debates while challenged by the dramatic and sensational.

The ability to market political ideas, policies and even individual candidates should not be exaggerated. Although some stories can be sustained as matters of faith, in many cases if they are not grounded in some sort of reality they are likely to fail eventually, and those that have promulgated them will suffer a resultant loss of credibility. The more overt the spinning, the less trustworthy the source. The growing public awareness of the constancy of spin means that it has reduced underlying levels of trust in governments, despite the increased recruitment of communication specialists.

This point is particularly important when the narratives concern war. When territory is lost or armies surrender no amount of clever talk can hide the defeats. The importance of morale, at the front and to the rear, has long demanded that narratives be deployed with sensitivity, even if that term has not been used. Military strategists are grasping at it whenever they wonder how to fight the 'propaganda war' (or more euphemistically these days the 'information war') and it is implied with every reference to a battle for 'hearts and minds'. At times of major war, whole government departments are devoted to psychological warfare or what might now be called 'public affairs'. Winston Churchill's great gift as a war leader was said to be in mobilising the English language as a weapon of war, to inspire and to reassure the British people.[29] There are a number of reasons why this question of narrative has moved to the centre-stage of strategy at this time, and these reasons differ somewhat from those of the past. This is largely a function of the same media environment that is affecting domestic political life, but which is taken to extremes when armed forces are engaged in combat.

The discretionary and often controversial nature of contemporary conflicts means that they interesect in crucial ways with the domestic political debate. The 2003 Iraq War helps to explain the growing interest in the concept of the narrative in mainstream strategic studies. For the first time since Vietnam the conduct of a protracted conflict has become a major issue in American politics. Prior to the 2003 war with Iraq, the US government made assertions which were recognised at the time as being overstated and were shown later to have been quite wrong with respect to such matters as nuclear programmes and the links between Saddam Hussein and al-Qaeda.[30] As the rationale moved towards the delivery of freedom and democracy to a post-Saddam Iraq, the ability to provide a convincing narrative that explained the ferocity of the insurgency and the difficulties of nation-building became critical to the debate about whether the war had been worth the pain and cost. Within Iraq itself, the question of whether the insurgents could ever be overcome affected not only morale but also basic political decisions on how to relate to the American-backed government. The issue of Iraq in the rhetoric of US and coalition governments was couched within the terminology of the 'war on terror' – itself the subject of rigorous debate as critics argued that such language encouraged attempts at military solutions to an essentially political problem – and poorly specified the problem as being about an objectionable tactic rather than an ideology.

An important part of the narrative is the way that issues come to be framed. A common complaint of critics of war (and sometimes just those eager for a different perspective) is that the experts used by the media to explain the course of conflict tend to be a certain sort of specialist, thinking within an established framework who can only throw light on what might be considered their professional précis of why troops are being deployed in a particular way, or the capabilities of weapons systems. Jay Rosen, for example, has described his failed attempts during the 1991 Gulf War to interest TV stations in another angle. He chose the concept of a just war, how it might look from different ethical and religious perspectives, and how it might be applied in this case. No such discussion was aired. This, according to Rosen, illustrates how the media's ability to decide what to include is a choice about which concerns and voices matter. 'To put it another way, journalists make casting decisions. They decide whom to cast in what roles in the drama of public life.'[31]

One should not expect mainstream strategists to get too upset about this. After all, it is their expertise that will be deemed most relevant and they will make the media appearances. When a nation's security and prestige is at stake it is not surprising that the question of whether the war can be won looms larger than that of whether the war is just. Perhaps media discussions reinforce established views, but there can also be dangers if these same discussions give undue prominence to perspectives that are held only by a minority, or turn off readers and viewers because they cannot engage their interests. The point can also be made that when the 2003 war came along, questions of legitimacy were much more to the fore, certainly before it started, albeit more in the European than the American media. Once the war is underway the 'who is winning and how' questions become more salient again, but the truly tricky period comes afterwards. During a regular conflict, strategists can talk about the things they understand, such as logistics, firepower and manoeuvre. But just like a regular army, they can all of a sudden appear to be out of their depth as a conflict takes on a more irregular form. To know who is winning and who is losing, different questions need to be asked. Who is the enemy? What are they fighting for? How do these people fit into the local political structure? What sort of support do they enjoy? How do we know? What is it about 'our side' that allows them to have such a constituency? What does 'victory' mean in this context? To answer these questions requires different sorts of expertise.

For regular forces trying to cope with swarms of irregulars this raises the question of whether the narrative can provide a special focus for their efforts to disrupt the enemy. It has been argued that:

> A grand counter-terrorism strategy would benefit from a comprehensive consideration of the stories terrorists tell; understanding the narratives which influence the genesis, growth, maturation and transformation of terrorist organizations will enable us to better fashion a strategy for undermining the efficacy of those narratives so as to deter, disrupt and defeat terrorist groups.[32]

The idea of the narrative therefore opens up another possibility of military operations. Instead of being geared to eliminating the assets of the enemy, they might need to be focused on undermining those narratives on which that enemy bases its appeal and which animates and guides its activists.

II. The transformation of grand strategy

Liberalism is the most important expression of the political aspects of Western culture. It must therefore provide the foundation for any compelling strategic narratives, although liberalism contains a number of inherent tensions which affect the way these narratives develop. It is these tensions which provide the substance of internal Western debate over the rights and wrongs of military operations. But before discussing these tensions, it is necessary to consider the changes in the international system which have not only highlighted the importance of irregular warfare but also raised new questions about liberal values and the use of force.

Grand strategy

In traditional 'realist' views of the international system, power appears as both ends and means, measured in terms of the more blatant indicators of military and economic strength, deriving its main purpose from its own accumulation and its only validation through comparison with others. The only test of a regime claiming sovereignty over a particular territory would be that it was sovereign in practice: that it could maintain an internal order and survive war. This did not allow for challenges to a regime according to higher claims of justice or righteousness. The only challenge which mattered would be one based on power. The answer to the apparent problem that if effective power were the basis of legitimacy then superior power would always be more legitimate lay in the understanding that an unregulated anarchy would be disastrous and that therefore a form of self-regulation was necessary. Realism thus encourages the view that in vital respects the contemporary international system is not so different from that of two centuries ago and that the key changes can be charted largely with reference to those in the material foundations of power. Those at the top of the hierarchy are assumed to acquire a natural affection for the status quo and are therefore inherently conservative. They are prepared to defend their privileged position against the malcontent revisionists who want to restructure the system to give themselves pride of place.

This is a view that is easy to caricature but not to disregard. If states believe that the international system works in a particular way, and act accordingly, then this view will be constantly reinforced. Furthermore, at certain critical junctures, raw military power matters and can make all the difference. States that neglect this factor may suffer. This 'realist' view, however, remains vulnerable to the charge of being too cynical in assuming that power is all that matters, that domestic politics are irrelevant and that the individual units only relate to each other on the basis of a straightforward calculus of relative strength, varied by means of alliances and the occasional war.

In this realist tradition, grand strategy is concerned with the use by states of all available means – social, economic, political as well as military – to position themselves within the international system. Since the evaporation of the threat posed by the Soviet bloc at the end of the 1980s this has not seemed problematic: the United States and its allies have enjoyed unprecedented levels of security. It could almost be said that the problem of major war has been solved. During the early stages of the development of the state system, it was taken for granted that the natural vocation of great powers was to expand, which meant that war was likely to result from the vulnerability of small powers in the face of neighbouring predators and the constant risk of great powers colliding with each other. By the end of the twentieth century, however, all parts of the world were spoken for, with no territory up for grabs. Having disposed of their empires, the old imperial powers had little interest in taking on subject populations. This did not mean that all thoughts of mergers and acquisitions had been banished, especially in the more unsettled regions, but there were no longer competitive drives for colonies or attempts to refashion boundaries into more convenient shapes that might be easier to defend or contain more lucrative assets. Western governments were also no longer in thrall to mercantilism. Once they might have contemplated a world full of 'vital interests', in terms of colonies or trade and supply routes, but such a perspective was now outdated. Market factors became far more important than the political in determining patterns of trade and access to raw materials and in a global economic system.

The Cold War had pitted liberalism and socialism, two traditions that had emerged out of the European Enlightenment, against each other. It ended the way it did because people living under the dead hand of European communism were increasingly looking to the West for political and economic guidance. When that struggle was over, liberalism emerged triumphant. There was now not only one dominant power but also one dominant ideology, which would, in principle, result in a more manageable global order. With state socialism discredited there was no real alternative model for other states to adopt. Asian countries still claiming to be Marxist, notably China but also Vietnam, sought access to international markets.

Globalisation

Colonialism, which provided a vehicle for great power rivalry, was also profoundly illiberal in its underlying presumption. The continental empires of Eurasia – the Austro-Hungarian and the Ottoman – lacked any ideological basis for justifying their particular configuration. The Ottoman Empire had Islam, but this provided no basis for holding on to Christian provinces. They were both vulnerable to liberal sentiment elsewhere, particularly in Britian, objecting to the suppression of nationalist aspirations. It took, of course, some time before non-Europeans were also allowed to share these aspirations. In Africa and Asia, liberal colonisers had an extraordinary capacity to convince themselves that the subject peoples were more than happy to merge their destinies with the metropolis, or at least that they would if they had the capacity to think these destinies through for themselves.

It took the upheavals associated with the Second World War to create the conditions for full-scale decolonisation outside Europe and the Americas. The forces of nationalism made themselves felt in the 'third world' (the first two being the capitalist and socialist worlds). Initially these forces were resisted but gradually they were accommodated. The processes of decolonisation and the conduct of the Cold War became increasingly intertwined. In some ways they could be said to have concluded at the same time with the implosion of European communism. This resulted in the end of satellite status for central and eastern European states and the creation of 15 new states out of the Soviet Union. The fragmentation continued in Europe, with five new states emerging violently out of the former Yugoslavia and two more peacefully out of the former Czechoslovakia. At the end of the Second World War, the UN was formed with 51 member states; there are now 191. While the end of the Cold War created the potential for a more orderly world, decolonisation had left it more disorderly.

The legacy of the decolonisation process was contradictory: it simultaneously enhanced both the significance of sovereignty and the moral force of the principle of self-determination. This would not have been problematic if states were all organised on the basis of coherent, homogenous nations. Unfortunately, the concept of the 'nation-state' is often wishful thinking. Nations are created through bonds of language, religion, ethnicity and culture. States require loyalty to institutions and laws. These inherent tensions, which many states have learned to manage through a variety of constitutional devices to the point where shared identities and loyalties have been forged that transcend national differences, have often been aggravated by the deficient processes of decolonisation. Many states contain more than one nation while nations are often to be found in more than one state. A key source of contemporary global disorder in a nutshell is that people give their loyalties to nations but they are governed by states.

To the speed with which new states came into being, the lack of prior preparation for self-government and the fragile nature of the civil societies upon which they were based could often be added undeveloped economies and poverty. Undeveloped institutional structures meant that the new states were often unable to contain and channel the inevitable political tensions. Endemic instability in many new states recast the problem of order. For most of the twentieth century it was bound up with inter-state relations and particularly the challenge of persuading a number of competing great powers to co-exist without war. Now it was the result of the proliferation of states, many of which were failing in the key test of statehood by being unable to monopolise violence within their own borders.

These failures and inabilities were viewed with some concern in the West, but the inclination was not to get involved. At first, after the collapse of communism, the expectation was that liberal capitalism would advance through seduction rather than rape. Countries seeking to integrate into the global marketplace would accept the political consequences. In central and eastern Europe, for example, the prospect of membership of the European Union was the single most important factor encouraging and guiding the economic and political reforms in the post-communist states. Not only were capital, goods and services moving around the world with extraordinary speed and efficiency, but so too were the concepts and practices of the dominant actors. Gaining access to Western markets and credits required conceding ground to Western information and ideas. On this basis, the problems of world order could be resolved without effort. Market forces would bring about new types of cooperative relationships which states dare not ignore and would be wise to embrace. They would produce greater prosperity and the steady embrace of democracy, which would in turn encourage a disinclination to war.

The 1990s were certainly good economic years for Western consumers but there was no simple, single explanation for this prosperity. What was presented as a systemic shift could also be interpreted as a rather fortuitous conjunction of disparate factors. Low commodity (particularly oil) prices helped. The beneficiaries were also thinly spread: many parts of the world – notably sub-Saharan Africa – were completely excluded and instead caught in cycles of poverty and despair. The 'trickle-down effect' from the good times in the West on the rest of the world was tangible but modest. Meanwhile, the numbers afflicted by HIV/AIDS rose, as did concerns about global warming. There was evidence of remorseless demographic pressures, with populations increasingly dominated by the young, urban and unemployed. The world's population increased from 2.5 billion in 1950 to 6 billion in 2000. Within another 50 years, 60% of the world's population will live in cities. The demands on agriculture were becoming intense, aggravated by environmental degradation and the scarcity of fresh water. Under these conditions, market-based remedies were not always appropriate or sufficiently radical.

There was nothing inevitable about globalisation in the form of economic interdependence leading to more peace.[1] Countries plugged into the Western economic system did not necessarily conform to Western political values and practices. In Asia and the Middle East, the alternatives to authoritarianism and repression often presented themselves more in anarchic or totalitarian forms than as democracy (and that was certainly the view of many of the regimes in question). Western hegemony was treated with suspicion. While much commercial and financial activity was conducted by entities which enjoyed significant autonomy and were not beholden even to those states which hosted their headquarters, they were largely and unmistakably Western in character. However diverse and pluralistic the world seemed to Western eyes, and however irrelevant twentieth-century concerns about great power struggles appeared, to non-Western eyes the world was being shaped by a group of victorious great powers seeking to impose an ideological hegemony of their own, which demonstrated a low tolerance of any opposition. Because the attempted ideological hegemony was liberal in both economic and political terms, it was neither as repressive nor aggressive as the attempted Nazi or communist hegemonies it defeated, and could make a more impressive empirical case that it was underpinned by convincing economic and social theory. Nonetheless, it could still appear threatening to those whose local order had more illiberal roots and who were culturally resistant to what was considered in the West to be political and economic 'best practice'.

In the West, an opportunity for restricting the role of the state (but maintaining its capacity to regulate the private sector for the collective good) could, if applied in less developed countries, lead to the growth in power of the shadowy and unaccountable, from groups with bizarre ideologies to those settling ethnic scores, from warlords to organised crime. Without an effectively functioning state, political freedoms may start to appear to be meaningless: economic power can become one sided to the point where individuals feel bereft of real choice and attempts to express the collective will are readily subverted through corrupt practices. In all societies, ultimate power depends on the control of the means of organised violence – the police and the armed forces. Here there are limits to any re-balancing of the relationship between the state, individuals and other socio-political groups. It remains the case that the most fundamental challenge a state can face – internally as well as externally – is to its monopoly of organised violence, reflected in gang warfare or civil war as much as external war, and the acquisition of military capabilities by illegitimate groups at home as well as hostile powers abroad. The most important challenges for international order come from places where this capacity for internal order has been lost.

Weakness and failure in the non-Western world have consequences for Western states: sudden population movements; environmental disasters; local conflicts being exported through expatriate communities. Even before the emergence of jihadist terrorism as the top priority for Western security agencies in 2001, there were links between the degree of disorder in particular countries and the quality of Western life. This could manifest itself in the production and distribution of hard drugs for Western markets or refugees from conflicts adding to the strain on local communities when they turned up as asylum seekers. International criminal organisations grew in power and influence as a direct consequence of economic and trade liberalisation and the opportunities provided by modern telecommunications and information systems. Those trafficking in people, drugs, arms and precious goods became much more sophisticated in their manipulation of the financial system, taking opportunities for political corruption and fuelling conflicts. Gangsters shaped not only criminal networks but almost parallel political systems, sometimes with their own armed forces. This activity was not always necessarily of a disorderly nature. Such arrangements could involve clear lines of authority and enforced rules – it was just that there was only a scant relationship to formal governmental structures. In many countries, in combination with fragile state structures, crime as big business became a political as well as an economic force to be reckoned with. Moreover, politically extreme groups with a propensity for violent action often interacted naturally with criminal networks. New, shadowy centres of power emerged requiring as much attention as radical and delinquent states.

This is not to argue for the proclamation of a systemic shift in a more malign direction, instead of more positive notions of globalisation. It is probably best to avoid the simplistic drawing of trend lines in either optimistic or pessimistic directions. The more persuasive conclusion is that Western governments have difficult choices to make about how they look after their own people and act beyond their borders.

American grand strategy

With the end of the Cold War not only was the US confirmed at the top of the hierarchy but so also was its ideology. This was first evident in great power relations. There were no longer ideological struggles fuelling great power competition. According to the accepted nostrums of realist international theory, the first priority of its security policy must be to hold on to that position. The leaked *Defense Planning Guidance* of 1992 described the first objective of the United States as 'to prevent the re-emergence of a new rival, either on the territory of the former Soviet Union or elsewhere, that poses a threat on the order of that posed formerly by the Soviet Union'. This carried through to a determination to prevent any 'hostile power from dominating a region whose resources would, under consolidated control, be sufficient to generate global power'.[2]

Realist scholars searched for potential revisionists, with the candidates not always confined to the overtly hostile: a united Germany was identified, as was the economically dynamic Japan.[3] In the event both countries, having made the case during previous decades for the possibility of international strength based largely on economic rather than military power, entered a period of stagnation and fell back in the power stakes. Even if they had not it was by no means obvious on what basis they would mount an overt challenge to American primacy, from which they had both benefited over the previous four decades. Thereafter, China came to be written about in terms similar to those once reserved for Japan, with an expectation that its fast-growing economic strength would continue unabated (despite developing environmental, social and political problems) and would soon be translated into military capacity to be followed by increasingly aggressive political demands.[4]

Official America has been careful when it comes to identifying major countries, with whom it is attempting to have cooperative relations, as potential threats. The 2006 QDR refers to a category of states (including China but also Middle Eastern countries) at a 'strategic crossroads'. They are to be encouraged to think of the most positive route to follow by having their attention drawn to the substantial US military strength that they might have to confront should they choose the most negative. Whether or not these countries really consider themselves to be at a strategic crossroads, facing definitive choices about their future international alignments and aspirations, this formulation at least acknowledges that they are not yet set in their ways.

At the same time, American power, and the political, economic and cultural hegemony that can flow from it, inevitably generates anxiety and various forms of resistance around the world. The problem for those who might want to act as a counterweight to it is that they lack the raw strength, certainly individually but also collectively, to do so. In addition, they are not invariably in opposition to the generality of American foreign policy. The most thorough study of the problem of why American primacy makes other states anxious and how they respond to it demonstrates that real constraints on American foreign policy can emerge from these responses, but also the diversity of forms they can take, from sullen resistance to active accommodation as well as conscious balancing.[5] In traditional, inter-state terms, attempts to organise countervailing power have been somewhat half-hearted. For example, those who intended to provide a counterweight to American policy around the time of the 2003 Iraq War foundered on the varying agendas of the members (Russia, China, France and occasionally Germany) and their lack of fundamental differences with the United States.

In fact the diplomatic rows, in particular in the run-up to the 2003 war, were intense largely because the experience from the end of the Cold War up to this point had suggested that there was a sufficient consensus among the great powers, and in particular the five permanent members of the UN Security Council, to enable the UN to function. A big boost had occurred to the organisation's standing in 1990–91 when it served as the focal point for international opposition to Iraq's occupation of Kuwait and was asked to give its blessing to military action. This was a case of a lesser, though still substantial, state challenging the status quo through a clear act of aggression. Soviet support was achieved by working through the Security Council. President George H.W. Bush hailed this approach as evidence of a 'new world order', although actually it was more a revived old order. The new understanding between Moscow and Washington allowed the UN Security Council to work at last as originally intended.[6] The justifications for Kuwait's forceful liberation derived less from liberal values than from traditional concepts of security and order. Iraq had challenged a basic principle of international order – non-aggression. Building the coalition to liberate Kuwait required honouring the other core norm of non-interference in internal affairs.

Yet while this fitted in with their self-perception as upholders of the international status quo, the new configurations of power meant that the erstwhile status quo powers of the West found themselves occupying the position of the radicals, subverting disagreeable regimes and demanding changes in inefficient economic practices. This hegemony, however, could not be an effortless development, as the enthusiasts for globalisation hoped, as events moved inexorably in their direction simply because of the proven superiority of their political and economic structures. If they could only feel adequately secure through the construction of a global liberal order they were going to find it hard work. Instead of yesterday's 'troublespots' progressively turning into today's 'emerging markets', it soon became apparent that a more likely prospect was of a patchy and controversial process whereby the leading Western states combined to bring a modicum of stability to areas of conflict, often on an emergency basis, using economic and military means. So the spread of the Western model was as likely to depend on deliberate and determined political action as much as on osmosis or market forces. Meanwhile, a substantial proportion of the world's population would continue to live in a distressed state for some time to come and this distress could be aggravated by political disorder or result in such disorder.

Liberal wars

All societies expect to fight their wars according to the core values upon which they are based. In the case of Western countries this must mean liberal values, though the term 'liberal' can have a number of potential meanings, not all of them helpful. It can, for example, imply support from only one part of the political spectrum and not necessarily the most important part. In the United States the term is often used as a synonym for 'leftist' or even 'socialist'. In Europe, where the term has different ideological implications, the lack of liberalism in contemporary America is often criticised. In practice, however, as I have demonstrated elsewhere, political debate on both sides of the Atlantic draws on classical liberal values.[7] These values provide the philosophical underpinnings of all Western states, defining the essence of a good society with their focus on individualism, civil and political liberties, the rule of law, the consent of the governed and opposition to arbitrary authority. These values have survived challenges from totalitarian and authoritarian regimes and movements of many complexions. Liberal ideology inspired the transatlantic states in two world wars and the Cold War. Its victories in these confrontations explains why these states do not now experience serious forms of existential threat from other great powers. Those states that might challenge their ascendancy in economic or political terms, for example China, lack the basis for an inter-nationalist ideological appeal. Liberalism remains a potent force because it does have such appeal. When Western governments deviate from these principles they can expect heavy domestic criticism in response. So they will always seek to demonstrate that their actions are perfectly compatible with them. It may be that future political developments will divert Western countries away from these principles, influenced perhaps by religious fundamentalism, racism or extreme nationalism but, although tendencies exhibiting these alternative philosophies are evident, they are far from likely to refashion Western political life.

There are two different types of difficulty with the term 'liberal' that are much more serious. The first points to a familiar tension in the liberal tradition, between upholding the core values of individualism and liberty, even when they are disruptive and inconvenient, and a yearning for the conditions of relative calm and order in which liberal values are more likely to thrive. The second points to the very idea of a liberal war as oxymoronic: war has an inherently illiberal quality. Wars are arbitrary and unpredictable in their effects, ruining and cutting short many lives and imposing great sacrifices on others. They require the suppression of individuality and the qualification of civil liberties in pursuit of the collective good. They invoke, in prospect and practice, the rawest human emotions, almost always including fear and chronic insecurity, as well as greed and protectiveness toward others, heroism and cruelty. Plans may be hatched by the cool and the calculating, but they are likely to be implemented by the passionate and the unpredictable. Because Western liberal societies recoil at these inherent characteristics of war, they have recoiled at war itself, and when it appears to be unavoidable they have sought to render it more rational and controllable.

Historically, liberalism has been associated internationally with the attempt to find an answer to the problem of war by encouraging benign socio-economic developments that undermine nationalism, enlightened dispute settlement and strong international institutions. Yet it has also developed as a response to the problem of injustice and the denial of political rights. The tension between the strand of liberalism that is anti-militarist and anxious to find peaceful forms of dispute resolution and the strand that abhors injustice and repression is captured by the norm of non-interference in internal affairs, which can be presented both as a vital principle of international order and a charter for domestic repression, and is thrown into relief when challenges arise from illiberal ideologies that show scant respect for either human rights or international law and institutions. The tension between the two strands of liberalism as they tried to solve the problems of war and injustice together was well described by Michael Howard in *War and the Liberal Conscience*. It is worth quoting his conclusion at length. The liberal tradition, he wrote:

> has certainly been a tradition often marred by naiveté, by intellectual arrogance, by ignorance, by confused thinking and sometimes, alas, by sheer hypocrisy. But how can one fail to share the aspirations of those who carried on in this tradition, or deny credit to their achievements? It is thanks to the patient work, over nearly two centuries, of the men and women who have been inspired by the liberal conscience that so much progress has been made in the creation of a global community of nations; that values are today asserted as universal to which all states without exception pay at least lip service; that it is recognised even if only in principle that states have communal obligations and duties within a freely-accepted framework of international society. The danger lies in forgetting that each actor in this society of states, including those who have not yet achieved statehood, embodies distinct cultural perceptions and values; that it is ultimately concerned quite inevitably and properly with its own survival; and that it is unwilling, whatever declarations may be made to the contrary, totally to rely on the power and the will of the international community as a whole to protect it.[8]

In international relations theory, liberalism is still associated with an optimistic view of the possibilities of taming the international system's anarchic and unruly character by encouraging economic interdependence, reliance on reason and goodwill in managing crises and conflicts and institutional innovation at the supranational level. It seeks to encourage states to rely less on 'hard' military power and more on 'soft' forms,[9] including cultural appeal, diplomatic clout, positions in international organisations and the capacity to dole out economic and technical assistance. One consequence of this preoccupation with the problem of war has been to encourage measures, such as disarmament or respect for the fragile claims of international law, that reduce the capacity to implement purely national strategies in response to international challenges.

Accepting that the dangers inherent in the international system can be mitigated by insisting that all states respect each other's sovereignty can also mean accepting the potentially illiberal subordination of the rights of individuals and groups to those of states. In this respect, an anxiety to prevent war can mean playing down ideological differences, for example with suggestions that the sources of conflict are likely to be found in misperceptions and miscalculations, often aggravated through arms races. For these reasons, internationalist approaches are likely to work best when there is not so much wishful thinking but genuinely a greater underlying consensus and a readiness to avoid bringing conflicts to a head. The effort to avoid war while ensuring respect for the sovereignty of all states tends to be more manageable when there is a common ideological basis for the exercise of power within individual states. The original Treaty of Westphalia of 1648, which established the primacy of sovereignty and non-interference in internal affairs, was about preventing future clashes between Protestant and Catholic countries over the composition of each other's regimes. After the Napoleonic Wars, the victorious powers sought to manage the system through a set of rules which essentially conservative states should have had no difficulty in following when regulating their relations. They were wary of any revolutionary ideology which provided not only a catalyst for the accumulation of power and territory but also contested their own legitimacy. Such gatherings as the Congress of Vienna in 1815, the League of Nations in 1919 and the United Nations in 1945 followed the defeat of threatening ideologies – in turn revolutionary republicanism, anti-democratic authoritarianism and racist nationalism. Each time, the hope was that a new consensus could be based on a set of shared principles. They failed when new ideological fault-lines opened up.[10]

Attempts to establish the rule of international law, and even to move towards world government, assumed that these could be founded upon the core principles of liberalism, depending upon the right to liberty at the individual level and self-determination at the national. So long as there was mutual respect for these rights then there was no problem. The challenge for international order, as with domestic order, was to ensure that the community as a whole protected these rights against those who sought to deny them. This carried two difficulties. First, liberalism, taken seriously, is subversive and thus inherently disorderly. Second, it must include a basic freedom to ignore the problems of others and this makes it difficult to develop a theory of political obligation, which is essential if great powers are to take responsibility for international order. Liberalism provides no rationale for interfering with the attempts of self-defining political units to create their destinies just so long as they do not interfere unduly with the destinies of others.

Defensive and offensive liberal wars

The pressures to get involved and to address developments within states that pose a challenge to the liberal conscience, can be described as a move from *defensive* to *offensive* liberal wars. The defensive types are undertaken in the face of threats to liberal values. On this basis, the two world wars and the Cold War of the last century were liberal wars, at least for the transatlantic powers. So, in some respects, is the 'war on terror'.[11] In these cases, liberalism defines the ideological stakes involved in these conflicts, what it is the Western democracies believe they are fighting for. Such wars are wholly consistent with the principle of non-interference in internal affairs, especially as it is liberal affairs that are the target of the interference. *Offensive* liberal wars, by contrast, challenge this principle. These are designed to bring liberal values to parts of the world where they are not yet in evidence. For that reason they tend to focus on the balance of power within states rather than between states and reflect the growing importance of the norms of human and minority rights. This means that almost by definition they challenge the norm of non-interference in internal affairs.

The possible existence of a category of military operations that involved working within other states rather than against them became evident in the immediate aftermath of the 1991 Gulf War. When the Kurds to the north and the Shi'ites to the south rebelled against the Iraqi regime they were ruthlessly suppressed. The coalition did nothing. As fleeing Kurds were caught on the borders between Iraq and Turkey (which would not let them enter), and with the international media, still in the area after the war, reporting on the terrible hardships they suffered, the coalition countries accepted that perhaps the internal affairs of Iraq had become their business. UN Security Council Resolution 688 of April 1991 deplored the repression and, while it did not authorise any action at all, the sentiment it expressed was taken as a form of authority for the establishment of a safe haven in northern Iraq, initially protected by coalition forces. This set a precedent for future humanitarian interventions. The most important events in terms of forcing governments to address the problems of humanitarian intervention were the wars of the Yugoslav dissolution. After the short but barely contested secession of Slovenia in June 1991, the other wars were vicious and marked by the forcible eviction of populations – so-called ethnic cleansing – to redraw political borders. Croatia, Bosnia and Kosovo set the developing terms for intervention in the internal affairs of states behaving badly. Out of this came the new dispensation that, in exceptional circumstances, major powers could ignore the norm of non-interference.

The 'international community', to the extent that its views were expressed through the UN Security Council, increasingly expected its members to uphold the basic rights of individuals and minorities. A high-level group of academics and former practitioners produced a report, called *The Responsibility to Protect*, deliberately over-turning the old presumption of a responsibility to stay out.[12] This reflected a growing reluctance to turn a blind eye to crude forms of repression and persecution for the sake of a quiet life. 'Human security' emerged as a set of requirements to be set against those of national and international security. This was connected to evidence of repression, social breakdown and the manifold deprivations and depravities associated with civil war. There were other more self-interested reasons for getting involved: because expatriate communities were at risk or pernicious and repressive ideologies were taking root; because, left unregulated, such conflicts could encourage crime and various forms of trafficking in drugs, arms or people; or else because they might spread, so that a whole region might be dragged down, resulting in refugee flows, interrupted trade and general mayhem. The nearer to home the greater these dangers, which is why neighbouring powers were more likely to intervene in regional conflicts (Russia in its 'near abroad', the US in Haiti, West Europeans in the former Yugoslavia, Australia in East Timor). These factors also help to explain why, except where there were historic links (as with Britain in Sierra Leone), intervention in Africa proved to be so problematic.

Furthermore, interventions created new interests. The reputations of the intervening countries and the sponsoring multilateral organisation (if any) would be affected by their performance in the conflict and their ability to get results. It took most of the 1990s, for example, for the idea of an active European foreign policy to recover from the dismal failure of the first attempts to forge one in the context of the break-up of Yugoslavia early in the decade. At the same time, non-intervention could also have an effect on reputation and encourage others subsequently to disregard the non-intervener's concerns when pursuing their own particular quarrels. Nonetheless, the impact of a decision to admit failure and to withdraw was always likely to be far more significant than holding back in the first place.[13]

This trend was not without its critics in the West. Jurists were anxious about the challenge posed to the principle of non-interference while governments saw dangers of being pressed into costly and hazardous interventions. Media pressure was often blamed, as if by highlighting human distress and political abuses it could move governments to take action in areas where prudence might otherwise have held them back. When moral imperatives drive foreign policy there are risks of double standards and unintended consequences. Once the rights of states do not take precedence then all demands for self-determination must be taken seriously, even where groups are not suffering evident persecution and denial of political opportunities, or where it is hard to see how they could realistically lead to viable statehood, or where the satisfaction of one group would inevitably raise exactly the same demands from others who might fear becoming disadvantaged minorities within the new states. Russia and China, as the most important states on the edges of the Western system and willing participants in the international economy, were concerned that they were the ultimate targets of efforts to relax the previous norm of non-interference in internal affairs in order to complete the Western hegemonic project. This encouraged them to uphold the norm with greater conviction. Western governments would therefore be taking risks in wider political relations by commenting actively on events in Chechnya or human rights in China.

The distinction between defensive and offensive wars fits in with the distinction between wars of necessity and wars of choice.[14] Wars of necessity are prompted by direct threats to the survival of the state. With wars of choice there is no direct threat to primary interests: secondary interests may be at stake but the state will survive if no action is taken. In this context, the wars of necessity involve the defence of liberal values and those of choice involve their promotion. Wars of necessity are likely to be prompted by the rise of strong states – great powers – with the capacity to challenge the status quo. They are also likely to be fought between regular forces. Wars of choice, however, tend to reflect the problems of weak states and tend to involve irregular forces. Casualties in a war of necessity, to protect core values, to spare one's homeland from devastation or occupation by an alien power, might be unavoidable; casualties for more marginal political purposes, especially if these appear impossible to achieve, are much harder to justify.

Because Western liberal societies recoil at the inherent characteristics of war, they have recoiled at war itself, but when war is unavoidable they have sought to adapt it to render it more rational and controllable. The tension between waging wars for avowedly liberal ends but not always with evidently liberal means may be easier to manage in the case of defensive wars than offensive. Operations undertaken with the expressed aim of promoting liberal values but conducted with scant respect for individual life or dignity are likely to be futile and counter-productive in their consequences. In recent years there has been optimism about the developing possibilities for discrimination and precision in the application of force, thus making it possible to keep casualties on both sides down to the minimum and mitigating, if not eliminating, the most illiberal aspects of war. This helps to explain the tendency to seize on new technologies, as a means of turning war against its own nature.

The management of this tension between liberal ends and illiberal means is at the heart of many of the problems of contemporary strategy. All strategy is concerned with the relationship between ends and means, but military strategy is also about the relationship between two or more opposing forces. The ability to contain the effects of war depends not only on one's own strategic choices but also those of the opposing side. To the extent that attempts are being made to design strategies appropriate to liberal values, it may suit opponents to design strategies that thwart such attempts. For this reason, one of the core dilemmas identified by Western strategists is the tendency for asymmetry, whereby an attempt by one side to keep the fight focused on combatants and to spare civil society from damage, that is to render wars as regular as possible, might be countered by an opponent determined to push the conflict into civil society.

By the start of the twenty-first century, it seemed that it was only with some difficulty that Western states were edging towards a grand strategy appropriate for the new conditions. While events had cast them in the role of radicals, able to use their military and economic power to promote their ideology and change the behaviour of states reluctant to accept the values and practices of liberal capitalism, in other respects they were still conservative in nature. They hoped that the logic of the new situation would encourage others to embrace their values (which is what did happen in much of post-communist Europe), but when this did not happen their enthusiasm for radical initiatives was contained. It was hard to present the challenge ahead as a single campaign, into which a variety of types of activity might be integrated. Instead, particular events presented themselves as individual crises to which responses were often ad hoc, without an obvious pattern. Sometimes, therefore, governments were prepared to commit resources, to ask for sacrifices, to address public misgivings and to form international coalitions; sometimes they were not.

Rather than a coherent grand strategy specifying the role for armed force, the tendency instead was to produce tests that allowed the various relevant principles to be weighed against each other in the light of the features of a particular case. Two sets illustrate the possibilities of this approach. The first is connected with a cautious approach to interventions in third world conflicts and the second a more activist. After the 1982–4 debacle in Beirut, US Secretary of Defense Caspar Weinberger set down restrictive criteria for assessing future proposals for military interventions. The first test was that the US 'should not commit forces to combat overseas unless the particular engagement or occasion is deemed vital to our national interest or that of our allies'. The other tests referred to the need, once a commitment had been made:

> to do so wholeheartedly and with the clear intention of winning, with clearly defined political and military objectives, continually reassessing the relationship between our objectives and the forces committed, with the support of the American people and their elected representatives in Congress, and as a last resort.[15]

The logic of this position was that armed forces should be kept for the big occasions and that their use would be inappropriate when national interests were not at stake. There were two large political assumptions behind Weinberger's analysis. The first was dependence on the continuing support of public opinion, which in turn was dependent upon avoiding wars that were apt to become protracted, complex, indecisive and costly in casualties, without serving any vital interest. The second was that such wars were possible to avoid by focusing on aggressive states challenging the status quo while staying clear of conflicts underway within states.

By way of contrast, in a much-publicised speech in Chicago in April 1999, at a delicate period in the Kosovo campaign, British Prime Minister Tony Blair pondered the 'circumstances in which we should get actively involved in other peoples' conflicts'. At the time the British had framed defence policy in terms of an essentially altruistic foreign policy. The British *Strategic Defence Review* of 1998, for example, spoke of the military as a 'force for good'.[16] In his speech, Blair argued, on the one hand, for the need to qualify the principle of non-interference in the affairs of other states in the face of acts of genocide and oppression and when regimes are so narrowly based as to lack legitimacy. Yet, on the other, he accepted that it would be impossible to take on all undemocratic regimes engaged in acts of barbarity. He therefore suggested five tests as justification for intervention: a sure case; the exhaustion of all diplomatic options; the feasibility of sensible and prudent military operations; preparedness for a long-term commitment; and the involvement of some national interests.[17] The big difference was in the readiness even to contemplate interventions on matters in which the most vital interests were not engaged. After that, Blair's criteria were not notably more permissive than Weinberger's.

The 'global war on terror'

It was only with the terrorist attacks on the United States of 11 September 2001 that a unifying theme for Western grand strategy emerged. These attacks now appear as a turning point in international affairs as significant as the end of the Second World War in 1945 and the Cold War in 1989. They marked the end of the more optimistic years of the 1990s and set in motion a series of events that has transformed the foreign policy of the United States. From the start, President George W. Bush insisted that his country was at war. While the militants of al-Qaeda and its associates were described as challenging all civilised nations, the audacity and tragedy of the strikes against the Pentagon and the World Trade Center underscored the view that the United States was facing a unique threat and entitled to respond accordingly.

At the time of writing, this campaign can be said to have succeeded in one fundamental sense. Despite rumours and alarms, thus far there have been no further terrorist attacks of any size on American soil. Occasional, often quite deadly, attacks have taken place against allied and friendly countries although in no case have the militants been able to turn these into a state-threatening campaign (with the somewhat ironic exception of Iraq). The continuing sense of emergency, both nationally and internationally, including constant precautionary checks on people as they go about their daily business, and a reluctance to allow those who might be aiding, abetting, plotting or conducting acts of terror the normal protections of the law, has led to a presumption of apparently indefinite insecurity and accusations that this is being fostered for unconnected political, generally repressive purposes. The botched occupation of Iraq has made its own contribution, as has the damage done to both alliance relations and confidence in multilateral organisations. These are bad-tempered times.

From the start, the designation 'global war on terror' created anxiety among those who saw this as encouraging tendencies towards a militarised foreign policy or even a militarised society. A more benign explanation was that this was a war only as a rhetorical device along the lines of other wars, also proclaimed by presidents, against poverty, cancer or drugs. The best argument that 'war' is a wholly appropriate description of the struggle in which the United States is engaged is that its opponents also claim that they are engaged in a war. These claims had been made throughout the 1990s. There are good reasons to deny such groups the dignity of full-blooded enemy status. At some point, however, they become hard to dismiss as little more than a nuisance, as bands of fantasists and mischief-makers without significant support, and require extraordinary measures to prevent them from inflicting real harm. In this respect, the war did not start on 11 September 2001 but had begun, at least in jihadist eyes, much earlier. The jihadists believed themselves to be responding to a series of events, many of which had long faded from Western memories and were at any rate perceived as being quite disconnected, but which, to them, came together as part of a generalised Western war against Islam. Moreover, the jihadists had already mounted a number of attacks, with varying degrees of success, against American targets. The significance of the declaration of war by the US government was that it could no longer deny the existence of a struggle that was already underway.

But with whom were the Americans struggling? A general 'war on terror' lacks political context. Terrorism may be a state of mind but it is not a state, nor even a political movement. The use of terror, especially when it takes the form of random, vicious attacks against defenceless and innocent civilians, may reveal many of a group's values and ultimate objectives but it is still essentially a tactic and might be discarded for other tactics without the group itself believing much has changed. The tactic is one traditionally favoured by insurgents and insurrectionists because they lack the direct means of challenging the armed forces of the state. By itself it is normally a poor tactic as it has rarely served by itself to mobilise popular support against the state, and when that popular support already exists then alternative methods to terrorism are often possible. Because the term is pejorative, normally used to smear opponents, few groups actually proclaim themselves to be terrorists. To understand those who do resort to terroristic tactics it is helpful to consider their ideology and political programme as a whole. It then becomes apparent that many quite distinctive groups have indulged in terrorism, which is why analysts tend to distinguish between religious, nationalist, leftist, rightist and cultist types. In principle, therefore, a war on terror can take in campaigns against a large range of groups with very little else in common beyond their chosen tactics. At one point, the White House mooted 'Struggle Against Violent Extremism' (SAVE) as a preferable slogan to the 'Global War on Terror', but this never really caught on, and the president found that it lacked the immediate impact of the slogan that had first come to mind. If SAVE had been adopted this would potentially have broadened the campaign even more and brought no new clarity to the situation. The references in the 2006 QDR to the 'long war' say something sobering about duration though nothing about content.

In this respect, one objective could be to establish a new norm of international politics, to the effect that terrorist methods are illegitimate in all circumstances, so almost any cause might be invalidated by their adoption. This could follow the attempt to create a norm of humanitarian intervention.

Indeed there are important links between the acts which prompt humanitarian intervention and those which prompt a war on terrorism. In both cases the victims are most likely to be defenceless civilians. The moral objection lies in the use of violent means against non-combatants for political objectives. In both cases, taking action is likely to mean ignoring inhibitions against interfering in the internal affairs of other states.

In another sense, however, there is an important difference. Vicious domestic persecution or ethnic cleansing are weapons used by the strong against the weak, so that the weak can only find redress if those who are attacking them are in turn attacked by even stronger powers, which is why this becomes a test for a contemporary form of internationalism. Terrorism, by contrast, is a weapon habitually used by the weak against the strong. It is a form of response that does not rely on taking on the enemy at its strongest point but instead looking for vulnerabilities in its social structure. So while the victims of ethnic cleansing and other human rights abuses have by definition already been marginalised, the victims of terrorism are more likely to be found in the cities of the strong. This is why it is more likely to prompt a response by the strong and why a war to ease humanitarian distress may well be against the established regime, yet a war against terrorism may well be in its support.

There is evidence that revulsion at a particular sort of political violence as used by one group delegitimises it for others and that can have important political consequences. For example, the Provisional Irish Republican Army soon realised in late 2001 that the American people were going to be less inclined to see the romance in their 'military operations' against the British state and more likely to see the menace. At the same time, the origins and character of political violence can be so various that blanket denunciations may soon lead to awkward associations with states using subtler or at least more covert forms of oppression, or fine judgements in situations where many groups are engaged in violence against each other, all claiming it to be for self-defence.

The alternative is to accept that the war is with a political group, but here different problems arise because there are no single words to describe a complex phenomenon. All descriptions are loaded. It is clearly much more than al-Qaeda, because that label does not speak for all the relevant jihadist activists and is now a rather capacious umbrella under which many groups find cover. To agree that this is a global struggle linking many conflicts across many regions, all involving Muslim populations but otherwise quite disparate, is to concede a lot. From the Western perspective, Kashmir, Afghanistan, Indonesia, Iraq, Palestine, Chechnya, Uzbekistan, Bosnia and Kosovo, and many more countries, all seem to be quite different in many respects, including in their impact on Western sympathies. If they are all of a piece for many activists who travel from one to the other on the assumption that they are moving to different fronts of the same war, then the strategic challenge may be to undermine rather than to reinforce that assumption. The fact that they act in the name of Islam does not mean that a certain sort of austere literalism in belief and behaviour leads inexorably to approval for violence against civilian unbelievers or apostates. Furthermore, this highly politicised version of Islam with quasi-clerical leadership is challenged by those who believe that the clergy should confine themselves to spiritual matters. In general, the terms 'jihadist', which has a more warrior-like connotation (although 'jihad' can be used in a moderate form and not necessarily just as 'holy war' involving armed struggle), and al-Qaeda, accepting that this includes a number of loosely affiliated groups, are used here.

The philosophy animating these groups contains common elements. They see Western countries as threatening both because of the values they represent (secular and liberal) and their past role in supporting oppressive and corrupt regimes. Their long-term objectives are to re-establish the old caliphate and to insist on the full application of sharia law. More immediately, their aim is to persuade Western states to disengage from conflicts and countries involving Muslim populations and to desist from supporting regimes which crack down on popular Islamic movements. There are, in addition, often more apocalyptical notions swirling around the writings and speeches of the leaders of these groups, claiming vengeance for past wrongs and offering uncompromising visions of the struggle. These groups are profoundly illiberal in their instinct for theocracy, their intolerance of diversity and dissent, and their homophobia and misogyny. Yet at the same time they can play on themes which liberals recognise, including anti-imperialism and the sense of outrage and grievance among the poor and dispossessed, as well as distaste for many of the regimes which the West has backed in the past, and in some cases still backs.

Whether or not the terminology is appropriate, the 'global war on terror' has undoubtedly brought to a head all the tensions inherent in a liberal grand strategy. The enemy poses a direct challenge to liberal values, in terms of both narrow and broad definitions, and is by the same token vulnerable to the spread of these values. Jihadism is unlikely to prosper in functioning liberal democracies and efficient market economies. Yet, in other respects, it is a product of globalisation. The underlying vision is internationalist, with little respect for state boundaries. It is able to take full advantage of modern forms of communication and the ease with which money can be moved. In this regard, there is often an overlap with criminal organisations, which take advantage of the same facilities. It therefore adds to the pressure to monitor and regulate these facilities. In addition, many of the regimes fighting terrorism are illiberal and even liberal regimes have made cases for illiberal measures, albeit on an emergency basis.

President Bush framed the response to 9/11 in terms of national security and it was on this basis that Afghanistan and Iraq were occupied. Within this framework it was accepted that the insidious nature of the threat required measures that could not be guaranteed to accord at all times with liberal values. In light of its experience since 2003 the Bush administration might wish it had handled matters differently. In particular, this experience has pointed to the perils of ignoring questions of legitimacy in the conduct of military operations.

III. Asymmetric war

The 2006 QDR discusses the special challenges posed by terrorist networks in the context of the wider problem of asymmetric threats. This problem is a natural consequence of US superiority in conventional capabilities. In the past, in conflicts between advanced states it was presumed that while variations between individual weapons types might make a difference, there would be broad symmetries between the belligerents, thus placing an even greater premium on numbers, training and tactics. In practice, the United States has pulled ahead technologically from even its closest allies and certainly its old enemies. It now accounts for half of all world military expenditure and other Western countries for about another third. It has prepared itself for a game that only it can play in a league in which it is the sole participant. Even if China were to challenge the United States, the most likely trigger for a major clash of this sort would be Taiwan and that would be, at least in the first instance, as much a naval as a land battle. It is hard to imagine contingencies in which the United States would seek to defeat the army of another major power, or indeed circumstances in which another major power would knowingly try to defeat the United States in conventional battle. This does not mean that future inter-state wars are impossible, with or without the United States, or that they might not take on the form of classical conventional warfare. It does, nonetheless, put a large question mark against the notion of a true revolution in military affairs because of the unlikelihood that all serious powers as well as aspirants will structure their armed forces in similar ways to prepare for some rather standardised encounters.

The issue is not simply one of a basic power imbalance. The strategic choices apparently mandated by the RMA do not so much slavishly follow a line of technological development, but rather a line of political expectation and of ethical thinking in Western societies, based on the Christian just war tradition and liberal values, with questions of discrimination and proportionality in warfare to the fore.[1] It assumes the following elements:

- Professionalism of armed forces. High-quality weaponry reduces the relative importance of numbers, although it also puts a premium on high-quality troops.
- Decisive force directed to clear political ends. The military expect to be set well-defined objectives by their political masters, which it is their job to meet, preferably without further political interference.
- Intolerance of casualties. Even with professional forces there is an expectation that strategies should be designed to keep casualties to a minimum.
- Intolerance of collateral damage. If war is the responsibility of governments and armed forces but not the population at large then all civilians

must be deemed innocent unless proven guilty. This argues for targeting military assets rather than people.

There is, therefore, a connecting theme of separating the military from the civil, of combatants from non-combatants, of fire from society, of organised violence from everyday life. So long as armed forces are organised around the belief in victory through decisive battle, this should be achieved as quickly and as painlessly as possible, with the minimum of damage to civilian life and property. For a war to be fought along these lines not only must the belligerents have acquired comparable substantial and advanced military capabilities but they must also inhabit the same moral and political universe.

If they do, of course, then the narrative surrounding the conflict can be confusing. By and large it is politically convenient to be able to portray enemies as inhabiting a quite different and invariably disagreeable moral universe that provides them with rationalisations for terrible deeds. It thus helped the British government in the 1982 Falklands War that it was facing a military junta, just as it helped in 1991 that Saddam Hussein was an established mass-murderer and serial aggressor. So an enemy committed to fighting on Western terms would be problematic in its own way. One that spared civil society, minimalised casualties all round, allowed civilians their sanctuaries, honoured the Geneva Conventions and generally targeted systems rather than people would not suggest a propensity for barbarism. However, enemies that prefer to use brains rather than brawn and do not want to cause too much hurt are not only hard to find but might also be expected to be prepared to resolve differences without resort to arms. The vast literature on the circumstances in which democracies go to war makes it clear that at the very least it is more likely against enemies whose political structures and methods are objectionable from the start.

At any rate, given that it is now even harder to find enemies who are capable of fighting on Western terms even if they wanted to, those that actually do exist will adopt strategies that give them a fighting chance, even though they are unconventional and deeply unpleasant. Until quite recently, the members of NATO were, at least in principle, prepared to threaten nuclear attacks to deter aggression. The risk of having to implement that threat was extremely small, though large enough to have the requisite deterrent effect, but the fact remains that reliance upon the most complete of all threats to civil society was until very recently a centrepiece of Western strategy. It was not because of an increased moral maturity that nuclear deterrence ceased to be the centrepiece of western strategy for dealing with conventional threats but because it was possible to deal effectively with such threats on their own terms, without escalation. The incentives for escalation now lie with the adversaries.

The obvious point, found in much of the commentary on the RMA, is that those who are almost bound to lose wars fought on Western terms have every incentive to adopt alternative strategies that play to their advantages. These could be found in geography (short supply lines and opportunities for urban warfare), a threshold of pain (a readiness to accept casualties), patience (leading to frustration in Western capitals) and even a relative lack of humanitarian scruples (allowing the war to extend into civil society). These are now described as asymmetric strategies. If the promise of precision warfare lies in keeping casualties and economic damage down on both sides and confining them largely to the military sphere, the same logic might lead those seeking to discourage Western military action to adopt tactics and weapons that have exactly the opposite effects. While precision warfare allows for strategies designed to limit the damage on all sides, it does not preclude strategies based on alternative assumptions. New options are also emerging for those anxious to maximise the human cost of war. Though there may be less excuse for crude and indiscriminate modes of war-fighting with the systems associated with the RMA, they do provide opportunities for those who deliberately seek to target civil society. One side may boast that the accuracy of its weapons allows it to avoid nuclear power plants, hospitals and apartment blocks. Another may be pleased to use the same accuracy to score direct hits on these targets so as to maximise rather than minimise human suffering.

In addition, the technological breakthroughs of the middle of the last century, represented by nuclear weapons and long-range missiles, are still with us. They expanded the means of destruction and extended the range through which they could be applied. Attempts to mitigate their effects, for example through improving anti-missile defences, have been far less impressive. The capability to destroy hundreds of thousands of human beings in a nuclear flash therefore remains part of our everyday reality and, despite the cumulative efforts of the abolitionists, is likely to be so for the foreseeable future.[2] Chemical weapons first made their presence felt during the First World War. There may, of course, be other technologies that are still in their infancy but which might have startling effects. The biotechnologies, for example, have so far been less conspicuous in their conventional military applications than electronics. They appear more in predictions of grotesque and malign type of weapons.[3] If the main business of warfare is to eliminate or paralyse the opponent's military capacity then these forms of destruction appear as unnecessarily cruel and ruinous. But if the main business is to intimidate, to coerce, or simply to wreak vengeance then it makes a sort of sense to target civil society. Just as NATO was prepared to adopt policies of nuclear deterrence when it felt conventionally inferior, when the old balance of conventional power was reversed Russia adopted a similar posture.

The idea of asymmetric conflict has been around since the 1970s, as a reflection of the Vietnam experience.[4] The first explicit mention of the concept in a Pentagon document was in the 1995 *Joint Doctrine*,[5] in a reference to engagements between dissimilar forces. In this context asymmetry could work to the advantage of the US in line with its comparative advantages. Thus USAF General Ronald R. Fogelman spoke in 1996 of a 'new American way of war':

America has not only the opportunity but the obligation to transition from a concept of annihilation and attrition warfare that places thousands of young Americans at risk in brute, force-on-force conflicts to a concept that leverages our sophisticated military capabilities to achieve US objectives by applying what I like to refer to as an 'asymmetric force' strategy.[6]

As it became apparent that it would suit the US to fight symmetrically, on its terms, asymmetry acquired more negative implications. The 1997 QDR observed that: 'US dominance in the conventional military arena may encourage adversaries to use . . . asymmetric means to attack our interests overseas and Americans at home'.[7] The basic frustration with this approach was summed up in a 1998 report from the National Defense University which characterised asymmetry as not 'fighting fair'.[8] As the concept moved into the wider policy debate, the inclination was to develop a generic concept. Thus the 1999 *Joint Strategy Review*[9] defined asymmetric approaches as those that attempted 'to circumvent or undermine US strengths while exploiting US weaknesses using methods that differ significantly from the United States' expected method of operations'. These could be applied 'at all levels of warfare – strategic, operational, land tactical – and across the spectrum of military operations'. Put this way the approach becomes synonymous with any sound strategy for fighting the United States and loses any specificity. Moreover, this generic depiction of asymmetric warfare encourages the analysis to start with an appreciation of US vulnerabilities which is likely to reflect the concerns of the moment (information warfare against critical infrastructure, weapons of mass destruction) rather than the opponent's mind-set. Thus the critical planning document released in 2000, *Joint Vision 2020*, unlike its 1995 predecessor, *Joint Vision 2010*,[10] did address the problem, but used as a key example the threat of long-range ballistic missiles. This, of course, was against the background policy debate of the moment, which was whether the United States should opt to develop a new missile-defence system.

At the end of September 2001, as Washington was still mulling over how best to deal with al-Qaeda, the Pentagon published its new QDR, which included a reference to the necessity to 'degrade an aggressor's ability to coerce others through conventional or asymmetric means, including CBRNE [chemical, biological, radiological, nuclear and enhanced high explosive] weapons'. So while references to asymmetric warfare were plentiful, the concept was still largely linked to proper war, serving as an argument for missile defences. It was not linked to 'small-scale contingencies' which would best be undertaken in concert with allies and friends and by specialised units.[11] Even studies which, after 11 September 2001, could claim to have been prescient in their warnings about the hazards of 'super-terrorism', tended to discourage a focus on al-Qaeda. Thus the Hart-Rudman Commission, which had identified 'unannounced attacks on American cities' as the gravest threat, also suggested that 'terrorism will appeal to many weak states as an attractive, asymmetric option to blunt the influence of major powers. Hence, state-sponsored terrorist attacks are at least as likely, if not more so, than attacks by independent, unaffiliated terrorist groups.'[12] North Korea and Iraq once again appeared as likely culprits, so that this threat also could be seen as having its most credible form in a derivative of the standard scenarios. In the 2006 QDR the asymetric problem is taken to refer to both irregular warfare and WMD.

In retrospect, the notion of asymmetric war turned out to be less helpful than at first assumed. To observe that an enemy unable to fight on one's own terms is likely to fight differently is banal. Listing the potential sources of difference can involve mentioning all aspects of warfare, including political factors such as motivation and alliances, or geographical factors, such as familiarity with terrain and occupation of high ground, as well as capabilities and strategic preferences. A more serious problem was that a reference to asymmetric warfare turned into a strong proposition that the natural incentive for those facing the conventional superiority of the United States and its allies was to opt for WMD as the natural means of playing on the West's preference for more people-friendly forms of warfare. The shock of 9/11 reinforced this view, encouraging a focus on a particularly dire scenario in which terrorist groups had possession of the most deadly weapons. The United States had taken on board the notion of asymmetric war but had geared it to the dominant scenarios guiding all American force planning. These still pointed to proper wars between the armed forces of major powers, with far less attention being given to those lesser, irregular types.

Irregular warfare

Up to this point the problem of irregular warfare had come to be associated with humanitarian interventions. The key feature of these interventions was that they sought to influence the character and course of a developing conflict which was neither taking place upon nor directly threatening national territory and did not relate to any specific obligations to allies. Thus they involved intervention in conflicts that were already underway and lacked any overriding strategic imperative. Beyond that, this category encompassed a wide range of possibilities. The conflict could be developing within one particular state or involve a number of states; its stage of development could be early or quite mature; and it could range from sporadic skirmishing to significant battles. Interventions could take a range of forms: from enforcing a blockade to clearing the skies of aircraft engaged in prohibited activities; from providing humanitarian relief to taking and defending territory. They also had an unavoidably discretionary aspect. At any given time there were numerous conflicts underway, many of a long-standing and murderous consistency. It would simply be beyond the capacity of willing interveners and international organisations to deal with all but a few of these at any given time.

The United States had not been a willing intervener. This was because of three aspects of these sorts of interventions which were likely to make them unpopular with the military and with the public: the tendency of 'mission creep'; the likelihood of casualties when no vital interests were at stake; and the distraction from preparations for proper war.

Mission creep

Military officers yearn for a precise definition of aim against which they can plan and judge success, and that, crucially, tells them when they and their troops are allowed to go home. Yet interventions in civil wars were unlikely to have clear-cut, let alone happy, endings. 'Mission creep' entered the strategic lexicon during the 1990s to describe the irritating tendency of interventions to move out of whatever boundaries had been originally set for them. One reason for this was the tendency to set forces at a level proportionate to the interests at stake. This could lead to token contributions, which was likely to lead to futility. It is as difficult to intervene marginally as it is to be slightly pregnant. The mere act of using military force symbolises resolve and deep concern and so can convey determination. However, symbols without substance, for example deployments well away from the area of any likely hostilities and with extremely restricted rules of engagement, are most likely to convey a lack of resolve. It may be true in international politics as in plays, as Chekhov once observed, that if a gun appears on the wall in Act One you can be sure that it will have been used by Act Three. Governments might agree to operations with quite limited liabilities, but once engagement has begun, and little is being achieved, then there will be pressure to increase force contributions and activity levels. Disengagement involves severe reputational risks. The internal dynamics of these conflicts can shift alarmingly, often to the point that common decency requires additional effort by outside forces to prevent some calamity. If force levels and tactics are set solely in relation to the interests at stake they may have little relation to those of the opponents: limited means are not necessarily sufficient to support limited interests. Extra forces, however, do not guarantee speedy solutions. Because their origins lie in inter-communal conflict these interventions are hard to bring to an end. In addition, the military find that civilian agencies assume that they have infinite resources to solve problems well beyond their traditional role, from feeding refugees to basic police duties.

It was Bosnia that encouraged the notion of 'mission creep', as UN troops with a peacekeeping mandate were told to protect Muslim safe areas from Serb aggression without being properly prepared for this new task. If they took their role seriously then they were at severe risk; if they failed to do so, then tragedy and disillusion could result. Richard Cheney (as a former secretary of defense) observed in 1993:

> I don't think that advocates of U.S. military force to end the bloodshed in Bosnia have properly considered what would be entailed . . . You need an

objective that you can define in military terms ... If you say, 'Go in and stop the bloodshed in Bosnia,' that's not sufficiently clear to build a mission around. Does that mean you're going to put a U.S. soldier between every Bosnian Serb and Bosnian Muslim? You also need to know what constitutes victory. How would you define it? How would you know when you achieved it?[13]

Richard Holbrooke, the American negotiator of the Dayton accords, later complained in his book *To End a War*, that the military used 'mission creep' as 'a powerful pejorative'. It conjured up 'images of quagmire', he noted, without ever being clearly defined. It was always used in a negative sense to kill a proposal.[14]

The military's desire for a clear task it can execute according to its best professional judgement is understandable. In serious combat with enemy armed forces they expect to be spared from constant political interference once the basic rules of engagement have been set. It is also the case that forces becoming involved in civil wars are unlikely to have a simple straightforward mission. External intervention normally involves a number of interweaving civilian and military strands and disparate national and international agencies in conditions which can change quite rapidly. But in these complex civil-military conflicts the military's role is always likely to evolve. Whether the mission is to contain the conflict, to set rules for its conduct, to ease suffering or to broker a settlement, there is bound to be a dynamic interaction with the interests of the local parties. Thus intervention has to be recognised not as being directed against a specific end, but as being part of a process, though undoubtedly a process with defined stages. Military action alone can never be sufficient: at best it can create conditions for a more favourable political outcome. Only once the fragility of local institutions, infrastructure and economic activity is addressed will it be safe to leave. By definition, a country which can only be stabilised by outside intervention is no longer fully self-governing.

The very fact that military measures have had to be employed means that some parties whose consent may be essential to the viability of a political solution feel bitter and cheated. By the time military action has become necessary it must be assumed that satisfactory solutions based on harmony, justice and consensus are no longer possible, at least not in the short term. The uncertain political support for these operations, especially after the Somalia debacle, led the Americans to insist on an 'exit strategy' even as they entered a conflict. In Bosnia a firm timetable (geared to the 1996 presidential election in the US) had to be abandoned as it became apparent that early withdrawal would result in instability. Insisting on an 'exit strategy' at the point of entry was something of a giveaway, encouraging the opponent to threaten an interminable conflict, in which the fighting would be long term and bitter, even if also spasmodic and at a low level.

Casualty aversion

Since the later stages of the Vietnam War it has been taken for granted that there is low popular tolerance for high casualty rates in any conflict falling short of an existential struggle for national survival. Some were prepared to see this as a secular trend, the consequences of a post-heroic age,[15] although past ages were not always that heroic, except in an involuntary sense. There was a presumption that there would be increasing reluctance to put the young generation at risk in war, even with all-volunteer forces. Yet, in the 1991 Gulf War, Western countries were prepared to accept substantial casualties in order to reverse aggression. Few anticipated the modest scale of casualties resulting directly from *Desert Storm*. Equally, and in part because of this, few anticipated the heavy casualties, over time, suffered in the 2003 Iraq War, which resulted in a build-up of political opposition clearly linked to the lack of commensurate political gain. In his work on Vietnam, John Mueller argued that there was a direct link between support for the war and the level of casualties.[16] Later work has questioned the suggested automaticity of more casualties and less support. In Vietnam, the key was the growing sense of the pointlessness of the sacrifice and its lack of proportion to the real interests at stake in the conflict. More recent analysis has stressed the relevance of the objective of the military mission and the resulting success or failure. This means that support for intervening in civil wars is low, multilateral support matters and that there is a preference for less risky options such as air strikes.[17] A study carried out in 1999 by the Triangle Institute of Security Studies, which demonstrated that even in a case where it would be assumed that casualty tolerance would be close to zero (action to stabilise a democratic government in the Congo), the public was not only prepared to accept quite high levels of combat deaths, but that these levels were significantly higher than those accepted by the civilian elite, and even more so than the military elite. This led to the bizarre conclusion (pre-Iraq) that senior military officers had become more casualty averse than the average American citizen.[18] The notion of casualty intolerance had become so internalised that military and political leaders had become loath to put it to the test.

The strength of the presumption of casualty intolerance was illustrated in the US Army's 1993 *Field Manual 100–5: Operations*. 'The American people expect decisive victory and abhor unnecessary casualties. They prefer quick resolution of conflicts and reserve the right to reconsider their support should any of these conditions not be met.'[19] This led to what Jeffrey Record described as 'Force-Protection Fetishism'. The result of this fetish was that lack of loss – not mission accomplishment – becomes the standard for judging an operational success.[20] The 1999 Kosovo War demonstrated the impact of this concern and, despite the consequences it had for mission accomplishment in terms of relieving the developing humanitarian catastrophe, it was considered to have been validated. When Secretary of Defense William S. Cohen and Chairman of the Joint Chiefs of Staff General Henry H. Shelton identified the 'paramount lesson learned from Operation Allied Force' it was that 'the wellbeing of our people must remain our first priority'.[21] As a US Army brigade moved into Kosovo as part of the force intended to bring some calm to the country after the war, its mission statement listed as its first priority 'self-protection' with the 'peacekeeping tasks' secondary. US troops stayed, separated from the society which they were supposed to help calm, in a guarded and well-appointed compound, while the troops of allies intermingled with the local population.

When the risk of the combination of casualties and futility appears high, governments have been quick to extricate themselves. The withdrawals in response to the 241 marines lost in the October 1983 attack on their barracks in Beirut and the loss of 18 rangers in Somalia a decade later suggested that there were some causes that were not worth a substantial loss of life. This was despite explanations for withdrawal other than the absolute level of casualties. Notably, most European countries have been less affected by casualty aversion than the United States. France took casualties in Lebanon and Bosnia regularly without evidently flinching, while Britain, with years of steady losses in Northern Ireland, made the case for taking the risk of a ground offensive in Kosovo. The idea that casualty intolerance was a particularly American vulnerability had strategic consequences and gave ideas to the opponents of the United States. Osama bin Laden, for example, in an interview prior to 9/11 made specific mention of the rush to get out of Somalia. He remarked on how his comrades who had fought in Somalia had been surprised by the 'low spiritual morale' of the Americans. He noted how 'the largest power on earth' left 'after some resistance from powerless, poor, unarmed people'.[22]

Lesser contingencies

Humanitarian interventions were also resented as a distraction from the main business of preparing for a major war. This assumed, as the 1997 National Defense Panel put it, that the relatively calm, international environment of the 1990s was no more than an 'interlude'. Eventually a serious 'peer competitor' would emerge, ready to challenge the benign hegemony of the United States. The penalties could be severe if investment for this moment was neglected because of a distracting preoccupation with 'recent trends in civil disturbance',[23] leading to a chase after minor irritants.

Colin Powell, who rose to high office working closely with Weinberger under President Ronald Reagan and then became chairman of the Joint Chiefs of Staff under George H.W. Bush and Bill Clinton, was very much of the view that American military power was best employed in an overwhelming manner to achieve clearly defined objectives with both speed and minimum casualties.[24] He was particularly dismissive of the idea of using American forces on such inappropriate tasks as 'constabulary duties'.[25] Out of this came the critical distinction between real 'war', defined in terms of 'large-scale combat operations', and 'operations other than war', which included shows of force, operations for the purposes of peace enforcement and peacekeeping, and counter-terrorism and counter-insurgency. These latter types of operations were much more discretionary and, it was clearly implied, best avoided.[26] The sort of improper war the military had in mind was the earlier stages of the Vietnam War which had been conducted as a counter-insurgency campaign against Viet Cong guerrillas. So while the military expected few political restraints on how they might go about war-fighting they sought to establish restraints on the wars that should be fought.[27] The US military establishment became so reluctant to engage in small wars that it failed to prepare for them.[28] By 1986, even *Field Manual 90–8: Counterguerrilla Operations*, dealing with action directed against armed anti-government forces, was claiming that the 'basic concept of AirLand Battle doctrine can be applied to Counterguerrilla operations'.[29]

Throughout the 1990s, the US military remained wary of irregular wars and refused to make major changes in doctrine and training to accommodate them, insisting that forces optimised for large-scale conventional war would be able to accomplish other, supposedly less demanding, tasks. General Wesley K. Clark's account of the management of the Kosovo War, from his vantage point as Supreme Allied Commander Europe, makes clear that – as far as the Pentagon was concerned – the demands of this campaign should not be allowed to reduce preparedness for the planning priorities of Iraq and North Korea.[30] *Joint Vision 2010* sought to build on the country's 'core strengths of high quality people and information-age technological advances' by developing four operational concepts: 'dominant maneuver, precision engagement, full dimensional protection, and focused logistics'. It claimed that the application of these concepts would provide 'Full Spectrum Dominance', a capability 'to dominate an opponent across the range of military operations'.[31] Priority was nonetheless given to preparations for major war, on the off-chance that there might be a very large-scale contingency at some point in the future, effectively dismissing the relatively small-scale contingencies that became common in the 1990s as secondary and residual.[32] Once they were viewed as 'lesser-included cases', the special demands, in terms of equipment mixes, training and rules of engagement, made by these smaller-scale contingencies, were not accorded the same priority as the major contingencies.[33]

All these factors influenced the incoming Bush administration in 2001, which was therefore expected to share this reluctance to address lesser contingencies. The prospective national security advisor, Condoleezza Rice, observed that:

> The president must remember that the military is a special instrument. It is lethal, and it is meant to be. It is not a civilian peace force. It is not a political referee. And it is most certainly not designed to build a civilian society. Military force is best used to support clear political goals, whether limited, such as expelling Saddam from Kuwait, or comprehensive, such

as demanding the unconditional surrender of Japan and Germany during World War II.

From this she drew the conclusions that US intervention in 'humanitarian' crises would be at best 'exceedingly rare'. The criteria for becoming involved were familiar: the president should ask 'whether decisive force is possible and is likely to be effective and must know how and when to get out'. Humanitarian interventions were thus largely jobs for allies.[34]

IV. The transformation of military strategy

During the 1990s, the United States adopted not only a concept of proper and largely regular war, for which it could develop a formidable strategy, but also a concept of improper and largely irregular wars, for which it could not. One response by its enemies might be to draw it into an irregular war on the ground. This could be avoided by staying clear of contingencies which were likely to involve irregular combat.

The temptation of air power

Proper war has had a clear operational sequence. This was followed meticulously in the 1991 Gulf War: first, remove the enemy air defences and then go for strategic targets. These ranged from the obviously military, including command and control bunkers, to the militarily relevant, for example energy and transport, and on to the more effectively civilian, such as the so-called 'leadership targets'. The next phase involved the preparation of the battlefield prior to the land battle, with the evident hope that strategic airpower would prove decisive before this point was reached. Since then, as a result of the growing air superiority of the US, these stages have been contracted. It is no longer necessary to spend so long on air defences. In the campaigns against Iraq in 1991 and Yugoslavia later in the decade, air defences were a serious issue as they were based on the equipment and systems adopted by Warsaw Pact countries. The Iraqi system in particular was extraordinarily extensive, built up as a result of the war with Iran and the Israeli attack on the Osiraq nuclear reactor in 1981. Much of it was destroyed during the first weeks of the 1991 war. Attempts to reconstruct the defences were constantly thwarted during the various spats between the US and the Iraqis, resulting from the coalition's constant air patrols, so that by the 2003 war Iraq could do little.

It was clear from the 1991 Gulf War onwards that it was impossible to conduct a conventional ground war while having conceded command of the air. The allies could always fight in three dimensions while Iraq was confined to only two. Without air protection, a dug-in army is doomed over time, while one on the move is highly vulnerable as soon as it is spotted. Meanwhile, an offensive enjoying air superiority can move very quickly indeed. The advantage in land war was not with the defence or the offence but the side with air superiority. With air power, a modest margin of superiority in capability tends to translate into a decisive margin in battle. This was not the same, however, as arguing that it could be used strategically, independently of land forces and also without devastating enemy society. Regardless, the evident comparative advantage of the West in airpower means that it appears as a virtually risk-free military option. If air power were an area of undisputed superiority and land operations carried the risk of severe casualties then the optimum strategy would rely on air power alone. This option became extremely tempting when some involvement in improper wars became unavoidable, because it meant that US forces could keep clear of one of their most hazardous aspects, taking on irregular forces on the ground.

Air – or cruise missile – strikes were often invoked as the first tough measures to be taken after diplomatic isolation and economic sanctions were perceived to have failed. It is almost the military equivalent of breaking diplomatic relations – something that is relatively painless for the instigator to do though it may not actually be very helpful. Air defences became targets of choice not because they were essential to securing air superiority but because they had notional military value and rarely involved casualties, and so might make some coercive point without causing a political storm. The claim that airpower could defeat a determined enemy on its own depended on the 'centres of gravity' approach.[1] This involved a crude political theory, which worked on the assumptions that a society can be understood as a closed interdependent system in which damage to a few critical components can bring everything else to a grinding halt and also that this can be achieved from the air. It was always likely that attempts to break an enemy state through air raids would involve inflicting real pain on the enemy's society. The lesson from the old debate on strategic bombardment – that attacks on an enemy population cannot by themselves break the will of the enemy government – did not lead to the corollary that the fate of the enemy population is somehow irrelevant and that the government's standing can readily be broken by other means. Inevitably, and despite self-denying ordinances about attacking civilian targets, it was the targets that were relevant to both civilian and military affairs that were chosen. Some caused more hurt. Attacks on energy supplies might not cause too many casualties, but, as it was discovered after the 1991 Gulf War, the long-term effect on a society could be disastrous, especially if water supplies were harmed. The basic problem remained that very few political objectives could be met directly by air attack alone. Its use can influence the victim's calculations, but it cannot achieve the physical control of enemy decision-making that is always at least a theoretical possibility following a land offensive.

The idea that air power might work on its own, at least as a coercive instrument, gained support during the 1990s through a selective reading of the critical events. Slowly but surely during the Bosnian conflict, those involved, including NATO and the UN, realised that they were moving a long way from traditional peacekeeping involving collections of lightly armed, indifferently trained troops. At best, such forces alleviated local distress and diverted the fighting elsewhere; at worst they created a vulnerability that would argue against a more robust stand at a later date. There were still occasions when minimal force would be needed, but it had become apparent that external interventions designed to ease and overcome conflicts could require active and often robust military operations.[2] Establishing 'no-fly' zones, as was done over Bosnia as well as Iraq, could only have a limited effect on the main struggle for power going on below where there had been less success in establishing 'no-artillery' zones and 'no-ethnic cleansing' zones.

Demands for a more robust approach always pointed to an increased use of airpower. When this came in Bosnia, with *Operation Deliberate Force* in 1995,[3] preceding the Dayton settlement, this was considered a great success. It was described in 1997 'as the prime modern example of how judicious use of airpower, coupled with hard-nosed diplomacy, can stop a ground force in its tracks and bring the worst of enemies to the bargaining table'.[4] The basis of this claim is that, while it was underway, Ambassador Richard Holbrooke, then US Assistant Secretary of State for European and Canadian Affairs, was busy negotiating with the Bosnian Serb leadership on behalf of the contact group which led to the Dayton conference and eventually to a settlement.[5] Yet in *Deliberate Force* the bombing was not initiated to influence the peace process. It was represented officially as an effort to protect the safe areas and, in particular, Sarajevo. Nor was it graduated according to the requirements of diplomacy. It may have sapped the Serbs' will to fight but their basic problem was that the ground war had turned. The Croatian army had pushed Serbs out of western Slavonia and Krajina and within Bosnia the Serb hold on territory had dropped from 70% to about 50% as a result of Croat and Muslim offensives. In addition, the UN forces had moved into more defensive positions, while elements of NATO's rapid reaction force deployed into the Sarajevo area from mid-June shelled Serb forces at the start of the air campaign. From this experience, the West concluded correctly that diplomacy in the Balkans had to be backed by credible force, but, less reliably, that this could be provided through the severe but measured application of air power.

Led by President Bill Clinton, NATO decided that it could repeat this misinterpreted experience in 1999 in order to persuade the Serb leadership to call off its ethnic cleansing of Kosovo and to withdraw its forces. During the Kosovo air campaign, NATO was caught out by the unrealistic expectations it had perpetuated about avoiding collateral damage. Great attention was paid by the media to 'blunders'. Once exacting standards for precision are set, the routine tragedies of past wars can appear as outrages that threaten to invalidate the whole purpose of a modern war. As appropriate targets may well lie in the grey area between the strictly military and the civil, Western countries will inevitably fall short of these standards. Public opinion often appeared uncomfortable with the results of NATO's bombing but still recognised that terrible things happen in war by accident as well as by design and, critically, took the view that those who initiate violence should not be surprised if it comes to engulf their societies.

The air threat posed to Serbia and its armed forces up to late March 1999 was large enough to signal an interest but insufficient to compel the target to change its behaviour. It was reasonable for the Serbs to assume that they would have to face little more than four days of raids on air defence sites and command centres. Once its bluff was called, NATO had to implement this inadequate threat with initially inadequate results. The level of air strikes was raised in a hurry, increasing the risk not so much of casualties but of blunders and moving to what was by necessity in practice, a punitive campaign. The evidence of Kosovo suggests that it was the impact on the civilian sphere that made the most difference, as the quality of life in Serbia steadily deteriorated under the impact of NATO's air bombardment. Attempts to target Serb military capabilities, especially those engaged in ethnic cleansing, were hampered by the use of concealment, camouflage and dummy equipment. Increased Kosovo Liberation Army (KLA) activity made a difference, especially when this forced Serb units out into the open where they could be more readily targeted by NATO aircraft. The damage to the Serb economic – as much as military – infrastructure probably contributed to Belgrade's decision to agree to terms. The fact that this campaign eventually helped to compel a change in Belgrade's policy was later taken as some sort of vindication of air power acting alone.[6]

Yet the war in Kosovo was partly won on the ground – but not by NATO. The hints that NATO was contemplating an eventual land invasion may well have been instrumental in persuading Belgrade to withdraw, but the growing strength of the KLA was probably more important. The whole objective of the Serb campaign was to defeat the KLA and to deprive it of the population base required for sustained operations. But the ability of the KLA to grow in strength and confidence must have indicated to President Slobodan Milosevic that in the end he would lose Kosovo and that there was little point in taking even more pain from NATO air power. The unwillingness or inability to commit NATO troops had two important political consequences. First, it gave the Serbs the time and the space for ethnic cleansing, which was largely carried out by units barely inhibited by NATO airpower. Second, as NATO forces effectively followed it into Kosovo, the KLA acquired far more political clout and prestige than was commensurate with the alliance's pre-war Western political goals. This added to the demands on the post-war peacekeeping force, which soon looked to be set for a long stay.

Fighting the 'war on terror'

As the ultimate source of the 9/11 attacks, the choice of Afghanistan as a target was straightforward and relatively uncontroversial. Al-Qaeda had developed a symbiotic relationship with the Taliban regime and used the country as a headquarters and for training. The move to dislodge them in October 2001 began in a standard American pattern, with a strategic air campaign. This bore similarities to that in Bosnia in 1995 as well as Kosovo in 1999, with a focus on air defences, command networks and arms dumps, and occasional 'leadership' targets. But the infrastructure of Afghanistan was so wretched and primitive that there were few suitable targets to be attacked. What was the point of aiming for power plants in a country where only 6% of the population had electricity? Excessive bombing would risk doing no more than 'rearranging the sand', which was said to have been the main result of the cruise missile strikes against a supposed al-Qaeda conclave in Afghanistan in August 1998 after the attacks on the US embassies in East Africa. Unlike in the case of Kosovo, there was no optimism that such a campaign could by itself achieve the strategic objective, which went beyond the coercive demands on Milosevic. There was still the same problem of meeting pre-war promises to avoid civilian casualties. It soon became apparent after one, largely unsuccessful, commando-type raid that such operations required far better logistics and intelligence than were available and that the air raids, after striking the few genuinely important targets, were doing more harm than good. The Afghan people were angry with the Americans because of civilian deaths, while the Taliban fighters were feeling even more confident because they had largely survived unscathed. If American troops came, as 'creatures of comfort', they would prove no match for fighters who had seen off much tougher Soviet soldiers.[7]

In late October, the US resorted to a lower-risk military strategy although this potentially carried greater political risks. Though relying on air power in isolation was not going to bring results, the United States was still not ready to commit substantial ground forces of its own to the campaign. Instead there was to be close cooperation with the anti-Taliban Northern Alliance. This involved putting to one side misgivings about the Alliance's combat capability as well as the narrowness of its political base. The Northern Alliance took on the crucial infantry role, playing a more substantial and explicit part than the KLA played in Kosovo, but with the same risks of awkward political associations. Now the air campaign had land operations to serve as a focus. As B-52s dropped 'dumb' bombs on the Taliban's forward positions the results were impressive. Almost as soon as the northern city of Mazar-e-Sharif fell, the fighting spirit of the Taliban appeared to evaporate, and a series of sharp advances backed by betrayals and defections did the rest. Soon Kabul fell and effectively the Taliban was defeated. Although, prior to the start of the air strikes, there had been many indications that the Pentagon understood that this time substantial ground forces might be required, in the event there was clear relief that they had not been necessary and that the US could chalk up, at least in its initial stages, another war virtually free of combat casualties.

After the cities had fallen, attention moved to the Tora Bora caves where a network of hiding places and passages had been prepared for sturdy defence. Here operations were far less successful. This was not territory in which the Northern Alliance was of much value and the coalition lacked the troops and local knowledge to hunt down the enemy. Osama bin Laden and his key lieutenants escaped into Pakistan. In December 2001, before the frustrations at Tora Bora, President George W. Bush suggested that a lesson of more general application had been learned. He spoke enthusiastically about the combination of 'real-time intelligence, local allied forces, special forces, and precision air power' that had produced a victory in the first round of the war, adding that this conflict 'has taught us more about the future of our military than a decade of blue ribbon panels and think tank symposiums'.[8] There were apparently few enemies that could not be battered into submission through the application of carefully targeted but also overwhelming air power, even while acknowledging that it worked best when used in conjunction with ground forces (preferably someone else's), which would oblige the enemy to occupy open positions, help to identify targets and to follow through after the bombing.

There was nothing exceptional in the combination of the post- and the premodern. The most effective irregular forces have always proved to be adept at borrowing the more advanced technologies when it suited them: witness the Mujahideen's use of *Stinger* anti-aircraft missiles to blunt Soviet air power in Afghanistan; or Hizbollah's ability to provide videos of their ambushes of Israeli units in Lebanon to the news media; or for that matter al-Qaeda's ability in September 2001 to mount an audacious attack by turning Western technology against itself, with knives acting as the force multiplier at the critical moment as aircraft were hijacked. Moreover, in practice an important factor in the swift success of the ground campaign was a tried and tested Afghan way of warfare, depending on coercive diplomacy, with protracted sparring to see who had superior power, before the hard bargaining began on the terms of surrender or, as likely, defection. US special forces may have had sophisticated new equipment to help them to operate in unfamiliar terrain, and the role played by UAVs in finding and even attacking targets was impressive, but a critical item in their armoury was large wads of dollars which could provide a formidable inducement to waverers. For those with the sense not to fight to the bitter end, defeat became rather like insolvency, with the faction in question soon trading under another name. Trading was often the operative word, for with territorial control came the ability to take a share of all economic activity, including trafficking in guns and drugs. Surrender was conditional: remarkably few Taliban fighters were disarmed and many appeared to have drifted back, still armed, to their villages or into banditry. So, while the Americans were relieved by the speed of the Taliban surrender, they did not always appreciate its conditional quality.

Also in late 2001, Deputy Secretary of Defense Paul Wolfowitz explained that 'one of the lessons of Afghanistan's history, which we've tried to apply in this campaign, is if you're a foreigner, try not to go in. If you do go in, don't stay too long, because they don't tend to like any foreigners who stay too long.'[9] In practice, an early departure was impossible. Despite itself, the United States soon learned that it had little choice but to get involved in nation-building. Initially it considered this a job for others, organised into an international force to help the new government to secure Kabul at least, while a separate force under its own command carried on hunting guerrillas and terrorists, even at the cost of undermining the stabilisation project. Eventually, more sensible and extensive arrangements were introduced, although valuable time had been lost.

The defeat of the Taliban regime and its al-Qaeda allies, in return for attacks launched from Afghanistan in the past, was followed by the defeat of Saddam Hussein's regime in 2003 for what might be launched from Iraq in the future. The move against Iraq was far more controversial. It was also described as a war of necessity and as part of the 'war on terror'. In building the domestic case, direct links between Saddam Hussein's regime and al-Qaeda, and even with the 9/11 attacks, were constantly asserted, although the evidence was flimsy. The international case was based on Iraqi non-compliance with a series of UN resolutions requiring the elimination of all WMD. The evidence here was stronger but still in vital respects overstated. The humanitarian advantage of getting rid of an evil regime was also cited, but not as the prime purpose. Only after the regime was overthrown and neither WMD nor real evidence of links with al-Qaeda had been found, did this humanitarian rationale come to the fore.

The initial 2003 Iraqi campaign was different from that of Afghanistan. There was no longer seen to be a need for an extended strategic air campaign. Nor was there a sufficiently strong local force to take on the Iraqis (other than the Kurds in their semi-autonomous northern territories). In consequence, coalition armies were engaged from the start. During the years since 1991, when strategy had been cautious, the gap between US and Iraqi forces had widened even further. It had then been assumed that intensive preparation of the battlefield was vital, by destroying from the air as many tanks and artillery pieces as possible, while scaring the ordinary troops into desertion and demoralisation. This was before coalition ground forces advanced. The speed with which Iraqi resistance crumbled in 1991 reduced the expectations for 2003. That war demonstrated just how overwhelming the air superiority of the US conventional forces had become. In 2003, initial progress was halting and gave some clues as to what was to come: no massive popular enthusiasm for the occupying forces, the use of guerrilla tactics by the coalition's opponents. Nevertheless, the combination of rapid manoeuvre and deadly air strikes soon proved irresistible and the regime's resistance crumbled. Any troop concentrations offered easy targets against which there was no reliable form of defence. Even acknowledging the enfeebled state of Iraqi forces, to occupy a country this size with only three divisions was remarkable. Soon, Saddam Hussein was in hiding. His sons were killed in an ambush and by the end of the year he had been dragged from a hole in the ground. The ruthless efficiency of the initial occupation was impressive and confirmed the complete superiority of the United States in conventional warfare.

The contrast with what followed was stark. While the major combat operations proved to be relatively undemanding, dealing with the insurgency that followed turned out to be both demanding and deadly, threatening to stretch out almost indefinitely. The Ba'ath regime may not ever have expected to be able to mount much conventional resistance prior to the war and always planned guerrilla warfare. This did not materialise in the fights for the major cities, including Baghdad, where a degree of urban warfare had been anticipated. It was only later, as the US mismanaged the post-war occupation, that the insurgency began to make itself felt. The qualitative superiority that allowed the US to defeat with ease the larger, although generally third-rate, Iraqi army meant that it lacked the numbers on the ground to establish its presence and to assert local authority after the war. Having begun with a legitimacy deficit, in terms of both domestic and international support for a war which was widely seen to have a contrived rationale, the US-led coalition struggled against an enemy as vicious as it was determined.

Just as Washington had overstated the threat posed by pre-war Iraq it had understated the problems of post-war Iraq.[10] The experience of Afghanistan at least encouraged some recognition that issues of reconstruction and nation-building could not be ducked, yet there was a degree of wishful thinking about the ease with which this deeply divided and brutalised society could settle on a new form of government. Even more seriously, the transition from an invading force to an occupying administration was poorly handled. In part, this was because preparations had been made to cope with the expected problem of hundreds of thousands of refugees, in flight from urban fighting, instead of the actual problem of a breakdown of law and order in the cities. More critically, there were simply too few troops. Secretary of Defense Donald Rumsfeld had made a point of demonstrating just how much could be achieved in modern warfare with remarkably few troops on the ground, but this meant ignoring all pre-war calculations that suggested that numbers in the region of 500,000 would be needed, rather than the 135,000 actually available. After Army Chief of Staff General Eric K. Shinseki advised that hundreds of thousands of troops might be needed, Wolfowitz observed that he found it 'hard to conceive that it would take more forces to provide stability in a post-Saddam Iraq than it would take to conduct the war itself and to secure the surrender of Saddam's security forces and his army'.[11]

This problem was exacerbated by the failure to hold the Iraqi army together (admittedly difficult as so many had deserted and the barracks had been destroyed). The process of building up competent Iraqi forces for internal security was thereafter slow and difficult. Lastly, those US troops available were not well trained for a post-war setting. They remained in 'force protection' mode and killed too many ordinary Iraqis. The point was made eloquently by a marine serving in central Iraq: 'If anyone gets too close to us we . . . waste them. It's kind of a shame, because it means we've killed a lot of innocent people.'[12] US troops became alienated from the Iraqi people, thereby helping their enemies to acquire recruits and local sanctuaries. This problem grew with the insurgency, in which the armed opposition was able to blend in with civilians and so undermine any hopes of developing trust between the Americans and the local population, especially in Sunni areas. The British, in the relatively more hospitable Shi'te south and with more experience of this sort of situation, had fewer problems although they were unable to exercise much influence on local power struggles.

Immediately after 9/11, the US promised a new type of war as it sought to respond to a new type of threat. Yet have the campaigns in Afghanistan and Iraq really marked the anticipated break with the past? The attitude of the United States was certainly different. It was in an uncompromising mood, ready to take the military initiative, mobilising massive forces to do so and (at least rhetorically) accepting the sacrifices that the new campaigns might require. The wars were not presented as discretionary nor, initially, as humanitarian in purpose. They reflected the strategic imperatives of the new age of jihadist terror and so their legitimacy was derived from the demands of national security. The argument went that as the security of all civilised people was at risk from groups such as al-Qaeda, then all should join the campaign. At the same time, this was a matter of self-defence and there was no absolute requirement to find a sponsoring organisation. At most, the UN could take over occupied countries once the offending regimes had been overthrown. Not even NATO, however, could expect to influence the command and control of the military campaign. The war would be conducted by a coalition of the willing (mainly drawn from the 'Anglosphere' of the US, the UK and Australia) and on American terms.

Yet, although the 'war on terror' at first involved military operations of a somewhat old-fashioned variety, invading and occupying other countries against the wishes and resistance of the regimes in power, in other respects these operations could be seen as reinforcing the underlying trend. US forces found themselves having to cope with an enemy that intermingled with civil society, in wars that could not end with decisive battles but only with the collapse of political will. As the US 'will' had broken first in a number of relatively recent conflicts (Vietnam, Lebanon and Somalia), it was not unreasonable for its enemies (and potential friends) to suppose that this might break again.

Once the old order had been overthrown, the problems of establishing a new order led to demands on armed forces similar to those resulting from humanitarian interventions and, in particular, the need to create conditions for economic and political reconstruction by maintaining security against those who wished to disrupt this process. Moreover, the situations in Afghanistan and Iraq required the United States to take operations of this type seriously. In this respect, the 'war on terror' provided more and better reasons to become involved in the problems of distant parts of the third world. If these problems were ignored, these distant countries could well turn into breeding grounds for terrorism and sanctuaries for those plotting further attacks on the US and its allies. What may turn out to be more important than the content of new strategic priorities of the current decade is the mixed experience of their pursuit. The consequences of the invasion and occupation of Iraq in particular have raised major questions about military methodology and the legitimacy of the use of force.

Out of this experience comes a growing sense of the ideological as well as the operational aspects of contemporary conflict. These ideological aspects appear in many forms: as questions about the relationship between civil liberties and terrorist threats; the importance of 'hearts and minds' in a counter-insurgency campaign; how to engage with the different religious and political strands within the Islamic world; and whether censorious international opinion or disappointed allies really matter. One of the 'lessons learned' has been to recognise the importance and impact not only of ideas, but also of images. Some of these images, including the collapse of the Twin Towers in New York, the abuse of prisoners at Abu Ghraib, the long beard of Osama bin Laden and a haggard Saddam Hussein emerging from a hole in the ground, have developed an iconography all of their own. This suggests that a focus on the kinetic aspects of war must miss some of the more intriguing, difficult and significant features of contemporary conflict.

V. Strategic communications

The information environment

The ability to turn potentially hostile public opinion in one's favour, but also to retain the support of a home population, can be a vital strategic attribute. When efforts to this end fail it is tempting to blame the media for neglecting to draw salient facts to the public's attention, for passing on enemy propaganda and for deliberately misleading in pursuit of their own agendas. The importance of the media has increased because of our growing ability to collect and transmit images and words across continents. Governments and armed forces find that they must take this into account in their plans and practices, developing some sensitivity as to how past boasts might return to haunt them or casual cruelty might be broadcast around the world. The public disillusionment over Vietnam was often credited to the influence of the harsh portrayals of combat in the media, which picked up on the contradictions between official claims and the realities of the war on the ground. The sceptical attitude of journalists and broadcasters was a change from those of the previous generation who had accepted their role as a patriotic extension of the war effort. After Vietnam, policy-makers knew that they could never assume a respectful hearing, especially when events were taking a turn for the worse. In terms of the communication between the combat zone, the 'home front' and on to the wider international audience, the media's role was crucial.

Over the past two decades changing technology has recast the role of the media. In the Falklands in 1982, the British government was able to control reporting from the journalists with the Task Force, largely for logistical reasons. This has proved to be progressively more difficult in subsequent wars, as direct satellite links allow for more freelance operations by journalists. The military have had to learn to live with the consequences of the increasing openness of information, rather than developing a capacity for its denial. One day, they may successfully demonstrate their determination to ensure pin-point accuracy by showing videos of smart attacks on command centres. The next day, they may be responding to television footage of the human cost of another missile taking a wrong turning. The same television stations carry the claims of all sides in a conflict and, as a matter of course, now seem to show military operations from the perspective of both those launching them and those on the receiving end. Against this backdrop, governments and military commanders are bound to put considerable effort into describing, explaining and justifying operations. The ground might be prepared by feeding snippets of information, and operations may be timed with television schedules in mind. Spokespersons will need to avoid appearing unaware of blunders by their own side or risk being caught out in self-contradiction. A charismatic commander will be encouraged to help to convince a sceptical public as much as to boost the morale of front-line troops. And so military operations have come to be understood in terms of the stories they tell as much as their direct impact on the enemy's physical capacity. The broadcasting media will transmit 'breaking news' far faster than most government systems and so operational secrecy in modern limited wars now requires their active connivance. Even a sudden news blackout from a particular base or aircraft carrier can be extraordinarily telling, a sure indication that something significant is underway. Aspects of this would have been intolerable to previous generations of military commanders – especially those who considered themselves at risk of defeat, allowing for no margin of error. If commanders can feel relaxed about this new situation, it is because they are working within comfortable margins. The superiority of Western forces in regular war means that they can allow the media much more latitude and, indeed, given them even more facilities because images of overwhelming and irresistible power will add to the coercive effect of their capabilities. When it comes to irregular warfare, the opportunities that the diffusion of the technologies for collecting and distributing information give to small groups of highly motivated individuals have created a different set of problems.

As the modern media have become increasingly competitive and dispersed, an additional twist has been added by the rise of the internet. High-quality material on almost anything can be found on the internet using free search engines. For a low price it is possible to get the sort of satellite images and navigational guidance that would once have been available only to the armed forces. Easy and uncontrollable forms of global and instantaneous communication have exponentially increased the number of actors able to shape the narrative. Pictures and videos of important events are as likely to be taken by passers-by or by people involved in the action on mobile phone cameras, as by commissioned professionals. This provides a major opportunity for pressure groups and political activists to shape perceptions by providing the media with images of their activities or those they wish to expose.

This new information environment has had important political effects and created new strategic options. In theory, taken as a whole, the information revolution ought to work more to the detriment of closed than open societies, just as when information was scarce and controllable it could be used for elitist purposes. Many of the early advances in communications, such as the radio, were seen as natural instruments of totalitarianism. Radio released individuals from dependence upon local sources of knowledge, thereby diminishing at a stroke traditional sources of authority and creating a 'mass society', reliant on externally generated news which could be controlled by a central authority. The masses need hear only one voice and this voice would be inescapable. This same central authority would be able to monitor loose talk and subversive action. This was the grim vision of George Orwell's *1984*, in which Big Brother controlled the information environment. It did not work out that way because no country could ever be sealed off from external influences. In the end, the most vulnerable points of the Soviet system turned out to be its inability to block broadcasts of the BBC World Service and the Voice of America or to prevent the intrusion into Soviet and East European homes of Western television programmes that undermined the official line simply by demonstrating an alternative. This did not require any overt political message.

The opportunities for political subversion through information flows that are hard to detect and prevent have grown with each technological innovation. Thus audio tapes were employed during the 1978 overthrow of the Shah of Iran, videotapes in the Philippine 'People Power' revolution of 1986 and fax machines in the campaign against Panama's General Manuel Noriega in the late 1970s.[1] It is now harder than ever before to keep society sealed off from external influences, although governments continue to try. When the Mexican government moved against the Zapatistas in 1994, the rebels used laptops to issue commands and the internet to publicise allegations of government atrocities to gain support from international organisations. Increasingly, no special effort is required to transmit video and audio material through the internet. Yet authoritarian governments have not all buckled under this weight. The contest between the free-flow of information and authoritarian regimes is currently at its most intense in China, which has developed the world's most sophisticated internet filtering system, seeking to prevent access to pornography, religious material and political dissent. This effort is bolstered by both legal regulation and technical control, involving thousands of personnel censoring communications including web pages, online discussion forums and email messages. Cybercafés are required by law to track internet usage by their customers and to keep records.[2] Even the search engines which symbolise the promise of democratic access to information, such as Yahoo and Google, have compromised their principles in order to secure market access to China. The Chinese system is generally considered to be successful and a model for those who wish to maintain a monopoly of political power. How successful this effort can be in the longer term, especially as China engages intensely with the international economy and its citizens travel the world, remains to be seen. The answer, as is normally the case, probably depends on the extent of the social and political stresses and strains developing in society for other reasons. This is an issue of demand as much as supply, of a hunger for news and ideas that can explain unfolding events and suggest effective ways forward, and a readiness to take risks and to affront the authorities in the search for this material.

In the more open societies of the West, the new means of communication are a formidable weapon in the hands of the disaffected and alienated. They facilitate the development and spread of alternative world-views that are able to challenge what are presented to be malign, incredible and, therefore, mendacious mainstream views. One of the striking things about al-Qaeda is its combination of a fundamentalist theology, which pits itself against modernity (its ally the Taliban banned television), and a readiness to exploit the possibilities of the revolution in communications technology to the full. Bin Laden's group was among the first to use commercial satellite telephones and to produce propaganda videos with hand-held cameras. Their fighters were reported to be retreating from Afghanistan carrying laptops as well as Kalashnikovs. At first, al-Qaeda, with its followers, associates and imitators, used the internet to build, indoctrinate and inspire support. Eventually it came to be used for more activist purposes. Young militants are as likely to be found in anonymous cybercafés as in training camps abroad, following message boards, taking instruction in bomb-making, sniping and how to move across international borders, or even watching snuff videos from Iraq. Teenagers in the cities of northern England can be inspired by the hardened veterans of campaigns in Chechnya and Kashmir. Just like enthusiasts for eccentric hobbies and unusual sports, they can meet like-minded individuals through the internet and agree to work together. In their plans at least they are no longer constrained by time and space. Their communications can be encrypted, carried in numerous languages or just lost in the billions of everyday communications beyond the scope of monitoring agencies. At the time of the 9/11 attacks one source had identified 12 jihadist websites; four years later the figure was 4,500 sites, representing a virtual 'community of belief' or 'one big *madrassa*'. Discussions of strategy and plans, and even technical instruction, can take place in sanctuary conditions.[3] The internet allows pressure groups and individuals to reach mass audiences far more directly than before without the mediating influence of the mass media. A starting point of engagement can be described and interpreted through extensive networks of activists and sympathisers. Once the raw material is present in this network, a political critical mass can be created at the press of an 'enter' key.

Media battles

The ability to take advantage of this new information environment is now considered to be an essential attribute in contemporary conflicts. Jean Seaton observed with regard to Kosovo that the 'media and public opinion are the territory in which the battle for intervention is fought'.[4] As one commentator on the role of narratives in US domestic politics observed that, as a result of Iraq 'foreign policy and even warfare itself has moved its central locality from the battlefield to the narrative on the airwaves and internet'. Matt Stoller argues that although previous conflicts were media-driven, 'the battlefield dictated the spin'. Now, he claims, the spin drives the conflict, whether targeted at Iraqis, Americans or Europeans.[5] Perhaps the most eloquent testimony to the importance of these issues came in the rather pained July 2005 letter purported to come from Osama bin Laden's lieutenant, Ayman al-Zawahiri, to Abu Musab al-Zarqawi, the Jordanian leader of the Iraqi insurgency. In this letter, Zawahiri stresses the importance of public support in the Muslim world, and notes how it might be turned off by attacks on mosques, even though they are Shi'ite rather than Sunni, and by video beheadings of kidnapped Westerners:

> I say to you: that we are in a battle, and that more than half of this battle is taking place in the battlefield of the media. And that we are in a media battle in a race for the hearts and minds of our Umma.[6]

If a regular battle is won then the results can be measured in casualties and territory. Measuring the results of a narrative or media battle is much more difficult. The media often declares a victor on the basis of what are essentially media values – slick presentation, fluency, a steady diet of new stories, avoiding getting caught in embarrassing contradictions. Such evaluations may be more about how the message is packaged rather than the message itself. It would be unwise to dismiss the importance of packaging, but many audiences may be more forgiving of an amateurish approach if that gives them greater confidence in the integrity of the message. More seriously, audiences are likely to test the message by reference to their own experience and established belief systems. Indeed, success in a narrative battle lies in changing these belief systems so that significant sections of the population start to see the developing conflict in a different light. Given the resilience of belief systems this may be no small matter. Even if this is achieved, then there still have to be consequences. People have to act differently and these actions must have consequences in turn.

For example, the possibility that Western governments might be moved by the suffering of the victims of aggression has influenced the strategies of those seeking to draw Western states into conflicts from which they might normally have expected to steer clear, and also of those seeking to keep them out. Those who have the upper hand will want to persuade outsiders not to meddle; those losing out will be searching for ways to suck outsiders in. There is nothing novel about belligerents conducting their affairs with one eye on the possibilities of others joining in, seeking alliances on the one hand, and declarations of neutrality on the other. For those encouraging intervention, the key message to communicate would be that they could not cope on their own and risked being overwhelmed by a ruthless enemy careless of human life. The advantage of a victim strategy was illustrated early in the wars of the former Yugoslavia. In August 1991, Serb forces began a three-month siege of the Croatian town of Vukovar, with 45,000 inhabitants, which eventually took the lives of more than 2,000 people and reduced the city to rubble. While this was underway, Serb forces took a third of Croatia's territory, even though Serbs represented just over 12% of the population. The international media soon picked up on the images of distressed people being shelled out of their homes. In these circumstances, 'media manipulation became not so much a complement for military engagement as a substitute for it'.[7] The government in Zagreb made no attempt to defend Vukovar, sending minimal material support. The strategy worked: mounting indignation, not least in Germany, meant that international pressure was put on the Serbs and Croatian independence was recognised. Although the Bosnian government did not initially follow a victim strategy, eventually it had few options. As the conflict deepened, along with the human tragedy it engendered, Sarajevo worked to shame the international community into sorting out the mess, or at least into giving the Bosnian government the wherewithal to do it itself. It was alleged that incidents were staged in order to stimulate Western interest in the Bosnian Muslims' plight.[8]

Governments which are minded to do so can resist such media-reliant campaigns. It is only when they are uncertain about what policy line to take or start to have doubts about the direction policy has taken that they will allow themselves to be influenced strongly by mainstream media, let alone internet campaigns. As the late Peter Jennings of ABC Television insisted: 'political leadership trumps good television every time'.[9] The readiness of the American and British governments to persevere in Iraq, despite a lack of international support and a decline in domestic support, indicates the limits of both a hostile media and disenchanted public opinion. There is always the argument that the ballot box is the place where public support should be tested and both these governments won elections post-Iraq.

Nonetheless, assumptions about the impact of the media become part of the narrative itself: governments start to factor into their thinking the possibility that images revealing large-scale suffering may push them into 'doing something', while images exposing the cost of that 'something' may impede action. And governmental resolve is not always so firm. As wars of choice, the humanitarian interventions of the 1990s always appeared dependent on fragile public support that might applaud an operation to relieve suffering but then could be turned by bad news or doubts about where operations were leading. The idea of the 'CNN effect' conveyed concerns that viewers might be so touched by images of desperate humanity that they would demand action, even in quite inappropriate circumstances. This was said to be relevant to the American intervention in Somalia in December 1992. 'How can ifs and buts compete', wrote one columnist, 'with the image of a mother and child dying before our eyes?'[10] The novelty, observed British Foreign Secretary Douglas Hurd, lay not in 'mass rape, the shooting of civilians, in war crimes, in ethnic cleansing, in the burning of towns and villages', but 'that a selection of these tragedies is now visible within hours to people around the world. People reject and resent what is going on because they know it more visibly than before.'[11] However, that the idea that strong images or descriptions of suffering could be of sufficient eloquence to generate policy is not supported by the evidence. Attempts to pin down the CNN effect have yet to prove its existence.[12] The example of the gassing of Kurds in the city of Halabjah by Iraqi forces in 1988, as part of a vicious campaign being waged by Saddam Hussein. This was well reported at the time, but Western governments were then attempting to develop a policy of constructive engagement with Iraq and so chose not to make a fuss. In other circumstances, when the objective was to encourage action, this atrocity would have been highlighted by every official spokesman. This illustrates the extent to which governments are not just the recipients of strong story lines developed in the media, but work hard to insert their own constructions on events into public debate in order to garner support for policies.

Although the decisions of democratically elected governments can claim a natural legitimacy, they prefer to be working with public opinion and are apt to become nervous if they have failed to persuade international opinion. The legitimacy of a military operation is a subjective attribute, related to questions of legality and morality as well as security. Because it is subjective this is an area where the inability to develop persuasive narratives about the whys and wherefores of a controversial policy will make itself felt. An operation's legitimacy will be hard to obtain and sustain if it is not in accord with the prevailing political culture, and in the West, that means with liberal values. Western forces should not engage in gratuitous cruelty; military actions must be clearly linked to a realisable political purpose. The wider international community will judge the application of force by high standards and expects that every effort would be made to keep both civilian and military casualties to a minimum. For any operational move there will be a number of different audiences beyond the immediate combatants. The course of the fighting will be followed closely by those who have a stake in its outcome, including international organisations, and as the fighting becomes intense and difficult it will become a matter of intense speculation, agitating and exciting the international media and internet bloggers alike.

There will always be an argument that military actions that might make Western opinion uncomfortable might still be vital if the enemy is to be defeated. For though any use of violent methods is bound to lead to unease, if the cause is adopted as just, then these methods might be tolerated as unavoidable. Against this claim that desperate times require desperate measures, it will be argued that such measures directed at civilians, such as air raids, or rough and ready forms of interrogation, are not only ethically dubious but militarily pointless or even counter-productive. It is normally claimed, for example, that civilian populations are hard to coerce through strategic bombing or that little information of any reliability emerges through torture. This may well be true, although there will still be exceptions, where threats to populations or to individuals will result in their wills breaking. The only real test of restraint as a matter of principle in these areas is in those cases where there might be reason to suppose that real benefits could result from extreme coercive measures. Even so, they will still be damaging because revelations of such behaviour will undermine confidence in and respect for the values and conduct of Western countries. A strategy based on a commitment to liberal values may well involve operational penalties: against these must be put the advantages of being able to avoid divisive debates about extreme tactics and to draw upon broader sources of support.

Hearts and minds

The reason why these battles are assumed to make a difference in irregular war is that the conduct of such wars depends on the attitudes of ordinary civilians for the provision of recruits, sustenance and shelter, and these attitudes might well be subject to private change. In regular war, the morale of ordinary soldiers can be a target, but they will be subject to military discipline and so any major changes in attitudes will take time before they have an effect.

Few phrases sum up the target of this battle more than 'hearts and minds'. It has been part of common parlance since it was first used extensively in Vietnam.[13] It is referred to whenever questioning harsh methods used by one's own side and whenever there is a need to persuade people, through good works and sensitivity to their concerns, that the government and the security forces are really on their side. It sums up the idea of wars being won in the cognitive rather than the physical domain. It supports an essential counter-insurgency, and counter-terrorism, strategy by suggesting a way of winning over a population that might otherwise be hostile (and which subjected to brute force almost certainly will be), thereby depriving militant opponents of their potential sources of backing.

It may be possible, as Israel has demonstrated, to box in and hold down a hostile population. It has coped with the second intifada by setting barriers to movement and engaging in selective assassination. But while such tactics may work to contain the anger of people under occupation, they cannot be the basis for governing them. Tough action is more likely, at least in the short term, to forge links between the militants and the wider population than to break the resistance, although it is often rationalised on the assumption that reliably punitive retaliation will encourage the relatively uncommitted segments of the population to back off. Such coercive strategies tend to be favoured when much political ground has already been lost, along with local hearts and minds. An example of this turn came in April 2004, when the deliberately provocative murder of four American contractors in the Iraqi city of Fallujah by Sunni militants led to a tough American urban offensive. By way of symbolising the change of attitude, Robert D. Kaplan reports meeting up with US marines prior to the Fallujah battle and finding them sporting moustaches to identify with the local population; when they prepared for the battle, angry at recent events, they shaved them off.[14] According to British Army Brigadier Nigel Aylwin-Foster, the insurgent action was designed to create a disproportionate response and in this it was successful. The American anger led to a 'kinetic' rather than a strategic response, which, in the event, was not followed through to its logical conclusion because of the evident political backlash that resulted. Aylwin-Foster suggests that the inclination to intimidate opponents rather than to win over waverers has been a feature of pacification operations in Iraq. One analysis that he cites of operations conducted from 2003 to 2005 notes that most were 'reactive to insurgent activity – seeking to hunt down insurgents. Only 6% of ops were directed specifically to create a secure environment for the population.' Unfortunately the damaging political consequences of these actions were not always appreciated. Because the cause was just, it was assumed that the actions would be understood even when they resulted in tragic errors.[15]

The strategy of search and destroy (or 'cordon and sweep' in Iraq) reflects the familiar military view that ultimately physical force is all that matters in war, that the basic objective is to hold territory and to kill the enemy, gaining respect if not love. This approach did not, however, fare that well in Vietnam either: it was always easier to destroy than to search, and the indiscriminate nature of the destruction served to antagonise the local population and so to add to the stock of militants. Military operations are judged only by their presumed military effects and not their political ones. It is, of course, much harder to train soldiers to withhold fire, not to rise to provocations and to reach out to a wary local population when this might put them in danger. When nerves are frayed it does not take much to turn a tense encounter into a vicious fire-fight with profound political consequences.

Montgomery McFate, with the unusual status of a cultural anthropologist working for the Pentagon, has identified three examples of mistakes in Iraq that resulted from a lack of appreciation of Iraqi culture. First was a failure to grasp that the civilian apparatus of the country would not survive the loss of the regime as power would revert to the tribes; second, there was a presumption that key communications would flow through the broadcast media rather than coffee-shop rumours (and US force protection doctrine meant that coffee shops were out of bounds); third, an Iraqi propensity to get physically close to those they were addressing was found threatening by American troops, while the hand gestures for stop were reversed in the American and Iraqi cultures, leading to tragic misunderstandings at road blocks.[16] Yet, in other respects, common sense as much as deep cultural awareness is required. In his trenchant critique of US Army counter-insurgency operations, Aylwin-Foster described the requirements of successful operations, different from those required for conventional warfighting, as the ability to 'see issues and actions from the perspective of the domestic population' and 'how easily excessive force, even when apparently justified, can undermine popular support'.[17]

The difficulties faced in Iraq have led to soul-searching within the US Army. Whereas after Vietnam the army recovered through a rediscovery of the operational art of major war, that option is not available now. The commitments in Afghanistan and Iraq cannot be readily abandoned and those officers coming through their tours of duty have been made painfully aware of the inadequacy of prior preparations for these conflicts and the need to do better next time. They realise that they have been trained to shoot, but less well how to cope with crowds, to maintain contact with local dignitaries and to distribute food. At the Army's Command and General Staff College all students are being instructed in counter-insurgency. At the 'elite School of Advanced Military Studies . . . 31 of 78 student monographs this year were devoted to counterinsurgency or "stability operations", compared with "only a couple" two years ago'. A new manual on counter-insurgency operations is being written, with input from the British army. One officer has been quoted as saying: 'We used to say that if you could do the war fighting, the other stuff was a lesser included case. What we've learned the hard way is that the other stuff is much more difficult.'[18] Major-General Robert H. Scales, Jr, in developing his theme of culture-centric warfare, has argued the need for 'a cadre of global scouts, well educated, with a penchant for languages and a comfort with strange and distant places. These soldiers should be given time to absorb a single culture and to establish trust with those willing to trust them.'[19]

When conducting counter-insurgency operations, heightened cultural awareness is not essential to realise that arbitrary arrests, displays of brute force, rudeness and disrespectful behaviour are likely to generate alienation and hostility. Reactions to being treated harshly and disdainfully for no good reason, especially by uninvited foreign troops, are not likely to vary greatly among otherwise diverse cultures. In the aftermath of such behaviour, repairing the damage and putting a positive 'spin' on events requires more than a keen and well-resourced public affairs outfit but rather evidence that policies have been changed and more appropriate behaviour is now in place.

A simple switch to a hearts and minds strategy approach may not, however, be the answer. This is because while it is clear what it does not involve, in terms of avoiding provocative military action, its more active features are less clear. In fact the term itself requires some unpacking. Just as search and destroy are not always in harmony, nor are hearts and minds. In other contexts, heart and mind are often pitted against each other – strong emotions versus cool calculation, appeals to values and symbols versus appeals to the intellect. In strategic discourse, much hearts and minds theory seems very hearts oriented, as if by showing a human face with a ready smile, with desperately needed goods and services being brought by Sergeant Bountiful backed up by Major Reassurance, a thankful but hitherto sullen populace can be won over. Such activities can undoubtedly have substantial payoffs, but only in favourable conditions. This points to two important limitations of the approach.

First, they must address the real concerns and grievances of the local people. The failure of the hearts and minds approach in Vietnam (some say it was never really given a chance before it was discarded) was because its purposes were subverted to serve the needs of the South Vietnamese regime rather than the people. That is, to succeed it has to be passingly democratic and this may well upset local power structures. In part it may be a matter of civic action, repairing roads and building schools, or making securing power and sanitation infrastructures, but at some point issues of official repression, land reform or ethnic mix may become germane. Daniel Byman observes how, in the war against terror, the allies of the US:

> are often the source of the problem as well as the heart of any solution ... The nature of regimes and of societies feeds an insurgency, but the United States is often hostage to its narrow goals with regard to counterinsurgency and thus becomes complicit in the host-nation's self-defeating behavior.[20]

If the sources of discontent are to be found in the local power structure, an effective strategy may require acting as a radical, even subversive local force. This can be a difficult manoeuvre when continued presence depends on the support of the local elites. Alternatively, as the British have found in southern Iraq, where there is something of a political vacuum, non-provocative action can mean conceding the political initiative to local gangs and militias.

Second, there is a chicken-and-egg problem, because these strategies can be too dangerous to follow without local security, until local security is established they cannot be followed. Without security, foreign troops and local people will be unable to interact closely and to develop mutual trust. Security is not just a matter of immediate safety: it also requires a look forward, assessing the likely future power structure that will emerge as the conflict develops and will probably be in place when the foreign troops leave. In this respect, a more minds-oriented approach must establish trust by addressing questions about who is likely to prevail in the continuing political and military struggle and the nature of the long-term political agendas of all involved. The insurgent can sow doubts as to the trustworthiness of the local population, about what is real and what is fake, as to who is truly on one's side and who is pretending. As the insurgents and counter-insurgents play mind games to gain local support, they may be as anxious to create impressions of strength as of kindness, to demonstrate a likely victory, as well as largesse.

Strategic communication

These problems are faced at the macro- as well as the micro-level. Embedded beliefs are difficult to dislodge and doing so is more than a matter of presentation. Even before the Iraq War of 2003, opinion polls were recording highly unfavourable views of the United States, including in supposedly allied countries such as Saudi Arabia and Kuwait. After the war, around the world, support for American policies was at an all-time low. Since then, and despite efforts to turn the tide, matters have barely improved.[21] After years of playing down the importance of public diplomacy and strategic communications, the US government has recently shown increased interest in them. 'Public diplomacy' is now defined as 'government-sponsored programs intended to inform or influence public opinion in other countries'. This is in contrast to normal diplomacy which is government-to-government and often kept as confidential as possible.[22] Byman warns that 'al-Qaeda is winning the battle of ideas'. Accordingly: 'Public diplomacy should try to offer a competing narrative, one that plays up the friendlier side of U.S. foreign policy and justifies less popular aspects.'[23]

In an article in the *Wall Street Journal* in July 2005, Donald Rumsfeld described how the Pentagon was working to adapt to the new realities of the information age. As successes, he cited the embedding of hundreds of reporters in US military units in *Operation Iraqi Freedom*, with few restrictions on what they could broadcast or publish, and the increasing amounts of information posted on the department's web pages, including material relevant to allegations of detainee abuse. The challenge of conveying accurate and complete information was multiplied, he noted, 'when it comes to the battle of perceptions beyond our borders'.[24] In February 2006 he complained to the Council on Foreign Relations that:

> Our enemies have skillfully adapted to fighting wars in today's media age, but for the most part we, our country, our government, has not adapted. Consider that the violent extremists have established media relations committees – these are terrorists and they have media relations committees that meet and talk about strategy, not with bullets but with words. They've proven to be highly successful at manipulating the opinion elites of the world. They plan and design their headline-grabbing attacks using every means of communication to intimidate and break the collective will of free people.
>
> They know that communications transcend borders and that a single news story handled skillfully can be as damaging to our cause and helpful to theirs as any other method of military attack. And they're doing it. They're able to act quickly. They have relatively few people. They have modest resources compared to the vast and expensive bureaucracies of Western governments.
>
> Our federal government is really only beginning to adapt our operations

to the 21st century. For the most part, the U.S. government still functions as a five and dime store in an eBay world. Today we're engaged in the first war in history – unconventional and irregular as it may be – in an era of e-mails, blogs, cell phones, Blackberrys, Instant Messaging, digital cameras, a global Internet with no inhibitions, cell phones, hand-held video cameras, talk radio, 24-hour news broadcasts, satellite television. There's never been a war fought in this environment before.[25]

The difficulty the US exhibits when dealing with this situation is evident in the search for an appropriate language to describe the conflict. William Safire has noted how uncomfortable the Bush administration has appeared with the word 'insurgents' because of its connotation of 'admirable "underdogs" in a struggle against the established order or entrenched leadership', rather than enemies of a legitimate government, and also because it suggests that the disparate elements engaged in Iraq are more unified than is the case. Thus Bush, in preference to a single term, has referred to 'a combination of rejectionists, Saddamists and terrorists'. The previous category of 'Saddam loyalists' had been shortened to remove reference to an attribute – loyalty – that might be seen as positive by resentful Sunnis.[26] Another example of efforts at finding the language to build a compelling narrative came with the attempt to fill a gap by describing a strategy for Iraq. Contrary to what might have been expected, this was not the result of full discussions with local commanders. The aim was rather to explain matters to the American people to ensure that they did not come to favour a precipitate withdrawal. After Peter Feaver of Duke University presented an analysis which suggested that US public opinion would support the Iraq war, despite mounting casualties, if they believed it would ultimately succeed, he was recruited to work in the White House. Feaver was credited with drafting the administration's *Our National Strategy for Victory in Iraq*, released in December 2005. Hence the constant repetition of the word 'victory' in the president's speech launching the document.[27]

A far more serious challenge was in Iraq itself. There are now some 200 Iraqi-owned newspapers and 15 to 17 Iraqi-owned television stations. In Afghanistan there are some 350 magazines and newspapers and 68 television and radio stations. Some of these are supported financially by the US (often quite openly to encourage democracy). In other cases, inducements have been given to encourage various outlets to take stories that have been written under official US guidance but are published without attribution. Whatever the accuracy of such stories, they are almost bound to have a positive and upbeat theme and it may not require great insight to guess their provenance. When covert, propagandistic activities, involving large sums of money, are eventually disclosed in the US press, then the net effect is not only to discredit the 'news' stories that have been planted, but also the government for attempting to manipulate the media.[28] The pictures of torture at Abu Ghraib were undoubtedly a public relations disaster for the United States, because they provided vivid portrayals of matters which had previously been alluded to in print. It soon became evident that the behaviour they were portraying was real, widespread and a consequence, even if unintended, of high-level decisions. Because they were in stark contrast to the claims the US had made about itself, and the contrast it was trying to draw with the old Iraqi regime, the images were not easy to explain away. This case demonstrated how difficult it is for a government, especially one viewed with such suspicion as America is, to find ways of turning the tide of foreign opinion. Where it has been done, marginally, is where the US has demonstrated that it can act effectively in response to a humanitarian crisis, as in the cases of the 26 December 2004 tsunami and the October 2005 Pakistan earthquake.

Networks and hierarchies

The other role that might be played by a strategic narrative relates less to persuading a wavering opinion but in providing guidance for those already committed. This relates to the claim that information technology allows for an extremely dense communication net, thereby supporting networking types of organisation while making life difficult for other more hierarchical forms. In this context, a strategic narrative that helps with the appreciation of a situation and suggests courses of action can act almost as a substitute for normal command and control. So long as the core norms and values are internalised, and a particular analysis accepted, then there is no need to issue orders. This is then said (for example by the 'fourth-generation school', as discussed in chapter one) to create new possibilities for irregular warfare, as it helps dispersed, perhaps quite small, groups to coordinate their activities even without any formal organisation. The lack of central leadership means that a 'decapitation' attack is impossible. This can also be turned into an argument for flatter organisational structures in Western armed forces.

These claims need to be treated with some care. Fighting networks rather than hierarchies has been compared to playing the Chinese game of 'Go' rather than chess. Terrorists, insurgents or even non-violent radical groups do not need to rely on frontal assaults and hierarchical command chains but can 'swarm', advancing in small groups from many different directions and using different methods, in a network held together by mobile phones and the web. Such swarming certainly makes it difficult for governments to know quite what the arguments they are trying to contest are and renders them vulnerable to media ambush or, in the case of guerrilla warfare and terrorism, real ambush. The novelty of such tactics and their inherent advantages should not be overstated. It is quite natural for radical groups, especially during their early stages, to be based on loose networks of individuals. To the extent that they risk attracting the attention of the authorities they find it safer to operate as semi-independent cells, communicating with each other and their shared leadership as little as possible. To be sure, the internet and other forms of digitised communication make it easier to keep in touch, but the number of security breaches attributed to mobile phones must make them hesitant about talking too openly or too specifically. At any rate, in the past, even when the key forms of communication were pamphlets and public meetings, 'communities of belief' often developed, as demonstrated by religious sects and radical movements. In this respect, Marxism was a fabulous example of a strategic narrative that sustained countless political groups, from successful revolutionary parties to fringe 'groupscules'. Radical Islam can perform a similar function, with a basic message that is widely shared and capable of being disseminated by a variety of means.

Such narratives enable these groups to hold together; they help them to gather new adherents and to unnerve opponents. Indeed, without the narratives they would be pointless and there would be no purpose to the association. A more critical question, however, is whether they can enable these groups to move beyond the cellular form. When numerically weak and outgunned, it helps to be dispersed and to operate in quite small cells. In this form they can score occasional tactical successes. If one cell goes down, then another can still continue with the struggle. When prominent targets and themes present themselves they can swarm around them, adding to the security concerns of governments and picking up on the unpopularity of certain policies. But if they never move beyond that point then they cannot progress politically. The great theorists of guerrilla warfare, such as Mao Zedong, were always clear that their objective was to create the conditions for a more decisive clash, in the demoralisation of the enemy and the desertion of its troops, and in the growing confidence and consciousness of the movement's supporters.

This was because the aim was to seize control of the state, the formal structures of power and in particular the means of organised violence. This required the sort of leadership that could see and then seize the opportunities to mobilise sufficient force to strike the decisive blows. Successful guerrilla groups are those that are able to turn themselves into conventional forces capable of occupying capital cities and installing governments. Even with chaotic revolutionary processes at play, at some point an assertive leadership would set the revolution on its new course. Thus Lenin made his push for power months after the fall of the Tsar, while the Ayatollah Khomeini was not really able to turn Iran into an Islamic Republic after the Shah's departure until he could see off the competing claims of liberal constitutionalists and sundry leftists. It is difficult to move beyond being a nuisance and harassing the enemy to seizing control without an authoritative point of decision.

If, as argued in the introduction to this paper, strategy is about the creation of power, then at some point it is also bound to be hierarchical. Many organisations could usefully work with flatter hierarchies: few can cope if they are totally flat. Priorities will still have to be set, resources allocated and an overview of a developing situation established. The information that allows for the horizontal integration of disparate groups and activities can also reinforce vertical integration, and this will enable the successful strategist to develop and communicate a coherent set of policies, to allocate resources in the most effective manner, to shift the weight of activity from one front to another and to choose measures most appropriate to the task in hand. In practice, political leaders and military commanders who are most effective and less reliant on formal chains of command are those with a natural authority and a message that is understood and readily communicated without having to be spelled out in detail to subordinates. It is inherent in irregular warfare that vital decisions, potentially with huge strategic consequences, have to be taken at a unit or even individual level. By their very nature, however, especially when risks are being taken with the lives of troops or apparently innocent civilians, these decisions are likely to draw in senior commanders and central government. Calming local demonstrations, taking prisoners, attacking supposed terrorist hideouts can all have major repercussions if poorly handled. Again, this reinforces the requirement for forms of communication down the lines of command that go beyond rules of engagement and specific orders and encourage a clear understanding of the stakes in the conflict and the expectations this creates for individual behaviour.

The role of strategic narratives in irregular warfare is therefore to provide a framework of understanding that can bind a fighting force together. By providing a strategic context it should guide tactical decisions. If this is the case then the challenge for counter-insurgency and counter-terrorism operations is to seek to unbind the enemy force by undermining the strategic narratives. This requires playing on the natural fault-lines within the political movements that spawn terrorist groups in order to aggravate their differences. Such an approach is helped by the familiar tendency of radical movements to fragment into competing factions. These movements are not inherently pragmatic. They deal in ultimate ends and so small divisions over political programmes or current tactics can quickly be magnified into fundamental differences of principle. Those of a certain political generation will recall endless, pointless debates among competing socialist factions, often quite tiny, about obscure questions of Marxist-Leninist theory. Such an approach can consider itself successful so long as the insurgents or terrorists are prevented from moving beyond their networked, cellular form. If the enemy is not making progress it is apt to get frustrated with intense, internal strategic debates, with some arguing for more dramatic military actions to attract more attention and recruits, while others will argue the need for patient political work to develop a constituency. These disagreements may be personalised and factionalised and it could happen that these schisms reach such an intensity that the factions begin to fight.

There are numerous indications that such arguments are already raging among al-Qaeda and its affiliates. These debates are about both internal rivalries and strategic directions. They concern questions such as: is this movement engaged in a series of national campaigns which need to be won on their own terms or must the focus remain at all times on the global struggle? Are there not dangers in a sectarian stance when there might be opportunities to reach out to all strands of Islam? Are there innocents in this struggle or is anybody, however young or infirm, a legitimate casualty? Would it not be wiser to concentrate on the enemy elite and those who help them to stay in power? These debates are evident in the intercepted letter, already cited on p. 655, from al-Zawahiri to al-Zarqawi. The old guard can also see al-Zarqawi taking over their leadership role. His methods may inspire fear and a sort of respect, but might even lead to some soul-searching among those jihadists who train to take up the fight against crusaders and Zionists and then find themselves blowing up mosques and wedding parties. Doubts in the ranks lead to operational problems and even intelligence windfalls for the authorities. Once it is known that a group has informers in its midst and has been compromised, internal suspicions grow and capabilities are further reduced. It would, of course, be unwise to rely on such processes causing jihadist groups to implode. But it would be equally unwise to ignore the basic point that terrorists believe that they are acting strategically, and that attacks on their strategies, demonstrating their ultimate futility as well as their obnoxious morality, can undermine both their confidence and capabilities.

Contemporary circumstances give insurgents and terrorists tactical opportunities that they would have lacked in previous eras. They can plot and act on a global scale, and when they do so successfully they can cause the enormous dislocation of whole societies. The costs involved in mounting operations can be met from an individual's budget, while the economic costs inflicted can reach billions of dollars. Suicidal methods have an alarming multiplier effect on the likelihood of attacks succeeding and the resulting casualties. Participation in such atrocities holds an appeal for a substantial number of people and many more may cheer them on. For all these reasons, preventing terrorist attacks and mitigating their consequences should they occur has become a high priority for governments. Yet the strategic achievements of this activity have been meagre. A number of attacks have been thwarted and where they have succeeded the political effects have either been marginal or counter-productive to their cause.

Only in Iraq itself has an effective campaign been developed. In the chaos following the overthrow of Saddam's regime, opportunities were created for the insurgents and a critical mass of activists came into being. There are divisions among the various groups on both objectives and methods. As the most extreme base themselves narrowly on the Sunni community there are limits to their size and prospects. They cannot 'win' although they can cause a lot of death and destruction. If other countries succumb, it will only be because the militants have found ways of exploiting social and political divisions that are already well established. These methods are never sufficient to kick-start campaigns: they only work to move them into more confrontational stages.

To what extent can it be said that there has been a transformation of strategic affairs? The international system has certainly been transformed. The most important, and welcome, change has been the decline in inter-state wars and of great power confrontation in general. This is part of a broader, and also positive, drift downwards in the incidence and impact of wars of all types. The Canadian Human Security Centre reports that the world is tangibly becoming more peaceful: the number of armed conflicts has declined by more than 40% since 1992. There are now fewer international crises and military coups than ever before. Wars are less deadly and less money is spent on arms. Only international terrorism is increasing.[29] Western armed forces face a narrowing of the range of contingencies for which their use might be contemplated. They cannot be sure which contingencies will prompt a decision by their governments to intervene, but they can assume that if they are asked to engage this will be in a conflict that is already underway and tending towards irregular warfare.

Regular warfare cannot be ruled out and, arguably, remains unlikely only because of the deterrent effect of continuing to make substantial provision for it. Some recent conflicts have involved operations that resemble past battles in pitting conventionally organised forces against each other. Preparing for such battles has long been the main business of the military. Thinking about regular warfare offers strategists a sort of comfort zone, where conflict will be governed by familiar principles and sets understood requirements for the development of capabilities, doctrine and training. Irregular warfare, by contrast, is unfamiliar and perplexing, lacking obvious boundaries. The range of forms it can take is disorienting, taking in guerrilla struggle, warlord rivalries and gangsterism, inter-communal violence and mass-casualty terrorism. The standards of victory can be equally confusing, especially when (as is usually the case) no culminating point is reached. These conflicts often either peter out or are marginalised by political developments, with the militants neither seizing power nor surrendering. Unlike regular warfare, irregular conflicts are unlikely to turn on having the most advanced technology or the imposition of overwhelming force. The military role may be quite limited, with key tasks in the hands of intelligence agencies and the police, and with even political leaders and intellectuals who frame and describe the core issues at the heart of the struggle. Whoever takes the lead, success will depend on how a particular irregular war's purpose, course and conduct is viewed by public opinion at home as well as within the theatre of operations. Success in such warfare depends on an understanding of behaviour and attitudes, and so science and engineering may provide fewer clues about its future than sociological and anthropological assessments of questions of identity and social cohesion.

As always, some history might also be helpful. Though irregular war requires a shift in focus, the issues raised are hardly novel. Those who served in the anti-colonial wars of the twentieth century would recognise many of the dilemmas faced by their contemporary counterparts as they try to think of ways to win over sullen populations by offering current security and hope for the future, acquiring reliable intelligence, setting traps while avoiding obvious ambushes, flushing out militants and turning some into informers, building up credible local leadership while catching or discrediting those of the enemy, and dividing and ruling through judicious use of amnesties and political initiatives. They might be shocked by the media gaze that ensures that these efforts are watched and evaluated constantly and globally, so that every mistake and false move is broadcast immediately, and constant difficulty is experienced in distinguishing minor tactical success from major strategic advances. But they might also conclude that this reinforces the lessons of past conflicts, that acquiring or retaining the trust and confidence of populations requires sensitivity to their concerns and treating them with respect. This can then be the basis of a compelling strategic narrative. This is not simply a matter of presentational skills, to be handed over to a public affairs unit. In this regard, developing a narrative is not a strategy in itself. If a convincing narrative can be constructed, that will normally be because the underlying strategy is sound and because it speaks to established belief systems, which in the case of the US and its allies, must mean to liberal values.

Notes

Introduction
1 John Keegan, *A History of Warfare* (New York: Knopf, 1993); Martin van Creveled, *The Transformation of War* (New York: Free Press, 1991); General Sir Rupert Smith, *The Utility Of Force: The Art of War in the Modern World* (London: Allen Lane, 2005).
2 Norman Angell, *The Great Illusion* (London: William Heinemann, 1914); Walter Millis, *An End to Arms* (New York: Atheneum Press, 1964). See also van Creveld (fn 1).
3 On the argument that suicide bombing can be understood in strategic terms see Robert A. Pape, *Dying to Win: The Strategic Logic of Suicide Terrorism* (New York: Random House, 2005).
4 Lawrence Freedman, *Adelphi Paper 318. The Revolution in Strategic Affairs.* (Oxford: Oxford University Press, 1998).

I. Networks, culture and narratives
1 Actually, if you want to knock a body off balance the worst place to aim for is the centre of gravity.
2 US Department of Defense, *Field Manual 100-5: Operations* (Washington DC: Department of the Army, 1982), vol. 2–1.
3 Anthony H. Cordesman and Abraham R. Wagner, *The Lessons of Modern War, Vol. IV: The Gulf War* (Boulder, CO: Westview, 1996).
4 Barry D. Watts, 'Effects and Effectiveness', in Eliot A. Cohen, ed., *Gulf War Air Power Survey, Vol. 2: Operations and Effects and Effectiveness* (Washington DC: GPO, 1993), p. 363.
5 Important articles in defining the RMA were Andrew F. Krepinevich, 'Cavalry to Computer: The Pattern of Military Revolutions', *The National Interest*, no. 37, Fall 1994; William A. Owens, 'The Emerging System of Systems', *US Naval Institute Proceedings*, May 1995, pp. 36–39; and Eliot A. Cohen, 'A Revolution in Warfare', *Foreign Affairs*, vol. 75, no. 2, March/April 1996. For an analysis of the various theories see Colin S. Gray, *Strategy for Chaos: Revolutions in Military Affairs and the Evidence of History* (London: Frank Cass, 2002).

6 Robert H. Scales, *Yellow Smoke: The Future of Land Warfare for America's Military* (Lanham, MD: Rowman & Littlefield, 2003).
7 US Department of Defense, *Quadrennial Defense Review Report* (Washington DC: Department of Defense, February 2006). The full text is available to download from: http://www.dod.gov/qdr/report/Report20060203.pdf.
8 Even compared with the *National Defense Strategy* document of March 2005, which set its foundations, there is a sharper focus on dealing with the new threats and less emphasis on conventional military operations. US Department of Defense, *National Defense Strategy* (Washington DC: Department of Defense, March 2005). The full text is available to download from: http://www.defenselink.mil/news/Mar2005/d20050318nds1.pdf. For a critique of the QDR see Michèle A. Flournoy, 'Did the Pentagon Get the Quadrennial Defense Review Right?', *The Washington Quarterly*, vol. 29, no. 2, Spring 2006, pp. 67–84.
9 The White House, *The National Security Strategy of the United States of America* (Washington DC: The White House, September 2002). The full text is available to download from: http://www.white-house.gov/nsc/nss.pdf.
10 An influential book in this regard was Alvin Toffler and Heidi Toffler, *War and Anti-War: Survival at the Dawn of the 21st Century* (New York: Little, Brown & Co., 1993).
11 Steven Metz, *Armed Conflict in the 21st Century: the Information Revolution and Post-Modern Warfare* (Carlisle, PA: Strategic Studies Institute, 2000).
12 'Information technology might provide a politically usable way to damage an enemy's national or commercial infrastructure badly enough to attain victory without having to first defeat fielded military forces'. *Ibid*.
13 John Arquilla and David Ronfeldt, 'The Advent of Netwar: Analytic Background', *Studies in Conflict and Terrorism*, vol. 22, no. 3, July–September 1999.
14 Jerrold M. Post, Keven G. Ruby and Eric D. Shaw, 'From Car Bombs to Logic Bombs: The Growing Threat from Information Terrorism', *Terrorism and Political Violence*, vol. 12, no. 2, Summer 2000, pp. 102–3.
15 US Joint Chiefs of Staff, *Joint Publication 3–13: Joint Doctrine for Information Operations* (Washington DC: GPO, October 1998), p. GL-7.
16 William M. Arkin, 'Spiraling ahead: With the loss of its greatest champion, what's to become of transformation?', *Armed Forces Journal*, February 2006. For a full statement of Van Riper's views see 'Information Superiority': Statement before the Procurement Subcommittee and Research and Development Subcommittee of the House National Security Committee in Congress on 20 March 1998: http://www.comw.org/rma/fulltext/infosup.html.
17 Timothy L. Thomas, 'Kosovo and the Current Myth of Information Superiority', *Parameters*, vol. 30, no. 1, Spring 2000, pp. 13–29.
18 'At the structural level, network-centric warfare requires an operational architecture with three critical elements: sensor grids and transaction (or engagement) grids hosted by a high-quality information backplane. They are supported by value-adding command-and-control processes, many of which must be automated to get required speed.' Cebrowski and Garstka, 'Network-Centric Warfare: Its Origin and Future', *US Naval Institute Proceedings*, January 1998.
19 As developed by John Boyd. See Robert Coram, *Boyd: The Fighter Pilot Who Changed the Art of War* (New York: Little, Brown & Co., 2002).
20 US Department of Defense Report to Congress, *Network Centric Warfare* (Washington DC: Department of Defense, July 2001), p. iv.
21 Major Norman Emery, US Army, Major Jason Werchan, US Air Force and Major Donald G. Mowles, US Air Force, 'Fighting Terrorism and Insurgency: Shaping the Information Environment', *Military Review*, January-February 2005, pp. 32–38.
22 Arquilla and Ronfeldt, eds, *Networks and Netwars: The Future of Terror, Crime, and*

Militancy (Santa Monica, CA: RAND, 2001). The full text is available at: www.rand.org/publications/MR/MR1382/. For a summary of their arguments, see Ronfeldt and Arquilla 'Networks, Netwars, and the Fight for the Future', *First Monday*, vol. 6, no. 10, October 2001: http://firstmonday.org/issues/issue6_10/ronfeldt/index.html.

23 William S. Lind, Colonel Keith Nightengale, Captain John F. Schmitt, Colonel Joseph W. Sutton and Lieutenant Colonel Gary I. Wilson, 'The Changing Face of War: Into the Fourth Generation', *Marine Corps Gazette*, October 1989, pp. 22–26; Lind, 'Understanding Fourth Generation War', *Military Review*, September–October 2004, pp. 12–16. This reports the findings of a study group which he convened at his house.

24 Hammes, 'War Evolves into the Fourth Generation', *Contemporary Security Policy*, vol. 26, no. 2, August 2005. This issue contains a number of critiques of the idea of fourth-generation warfare, including one by the author. For a full account of Hammes's ideas see *The Sling And the Stone: On War in the 21st Century* (St Paul, MN: Zenith Press, 2004).

25 Lind presents anything corrosive of the cultural foundations of a society as part of such a war. Cultural damage appeared as the product of deliberate and hostile moves by enemies, aided and abetted by naïve and wrong-thinking elements at home, rather than of broader and more diffuse social trends or economic imperatives. See Bill Berkowitz, 'A mighty Lind', September 2003. http://www.workingforchange.com/article.cfm?ItemID=15659.

26 Scales, 'Culture-Centric Warfare', *US Naval Institute Proceedings*, October 2004.

27 Arquilla and Ronfeldt (eds), *Networks and Netwars*.

28 See for example Robert Fulford, *The Triumph of Narrative: Storytelling in the Age of Mass Culture* (Toronto: Anansi, 1999); Jay Rosen, 'PressThink Basics: The Master Narrative in Journalism', September 2003. http://journalism.nyu.edu/pubzone/weblogs/pressthink/2003/09/08/basics_master.html.

29 Cohen, *Supreme Command: Soldiers, Statesmen, and Leadership in Wartime* (New York: The Free Press, 2002).

30 Freedman, 'War in Iraq: Selling the Threat', *Survival*, vol. 46, no. 2, Summer 2004, pp. 7–50.

31 Jay Rosen, 'Theoretical Foundations: Public Journalism as a Democratic Art', July 2002, http://www.imdp.org/artman/publish/printer_23.shtml.

32 William D. Casebeer and James A. Russell, 'Storytelling and Terrorism: Towards a Comprehensive "Counter-Narrative Strategy" ', *Strategic Insights*, vol. IV, no. 3, March 2005.

II. The transformation of grand strategy

1 A recent article claims that globalisation had some responsibility for the First World War. See David M. Rowe, 'The Tragedy of Liberalism: How Globalization Caused the First World War', *Security Studies*, vol. 14, no. 3, Spring 2005, pp. 407–447.

2 The leaked draft of the Department of Defense's *Defense Planning Guidance for the Fiscal Years 1994–1999* of 18 February 1992 was published in the *New York Times* on 8 March 1992.

3 John J. Mearsheimer, 'Back to the Future: Instability in Europe After the Cold War', *International Security*, Vol. 15, No. 1, Summer 1990, pp. 5–56. See also Mearsheimer, *The Tragedy of Great Power Politics* (New York: W.W. Norton & Company, 2001).

4 For a sceptical view see Gerald Segal, 'Does China Matter?', *Foreign Affairs*, vol. 78, no. 5, September/October 1999. Segal's views were assessed in Barry Buzan and Rosemary Foot, eds, *Does China Matter? A Reassessment* (Abingdon: Routledge, 2004). For a more recent assessment of Chinese thinking see Avery Goldstein,

Rising to the Challenge: China's Grand Strategy and International Security (Palo Alto, CA: Stanford University Press, 2005).

5 Stephen M. Walt, *Taming American Power: The Global Response to US Primacy* (New York: W.W. Norton, 2005).
6 Freedman, 'The Gulf war and the new world order', *Survival*, vol. 33, no. 3, May/June 1991.
7 Freedman, 'The age of liberal wars', *Review of International Studies*, forthcoming 2006.
8 Michael Howard, *War and the Liberal Conscience: The George Trevelyan Lectures in the University of Cambridge, 1977* (London: Maurice Temple Smith, 1978), pp. 134–5.
9 Joseph S. Nye, *Soft Power: The Means to Success in World Politics* (New York: PublicAffairs, 2004).
10 The constructivist literature in international relations has shown more interest in ideas about the meaning of great power and the nature of the international system, and their influence on foreign policy, than the role of ideologies. Jeffrey W. Legro's, *Rethinking the World: Great Power Strategies and International Order* (Ithaca, NY: Cornell University Press, 2005) is a good example of this although it deals with both the Soviet Union and China.
11 For an analysis of the problem of self-defence in similar terms see James Gow, *Defending the West* (Cambridge: Polity Press, 2005).
12 Report of the International Commission on Intervention and State Sovereignty, *The Responsibility To Protect* (Ottawa: International Development Research Centre, December 2001). The full text is available to download from: http://www.iciss.ca/pdf/Commission-Report.pdf.
13 Objectives could be set for military intervention as a result of exaggerated expectations for non-military forms of coercion. The European Union and the UN made demands on the former Yugoslavia which could not be enforced via trade embargoes and diplomatic isolation. Either they had to abandon their initial position (with a consequent loss of authority) or consider escalation. The prudent military planner, therefore, would start work as soon as an explicit international commitment to a particular outcome for a particular conflict had been made, even though the possibility of military enforcement was being excluded at the time.
14 This distinction is developed further in Freedman, *Adelphi Paper 318. The Revolution in Strategic Affairs*.
15 Weinberger, *Fighting for Peace: Seven Critical Years in the Pentagon* (New York: Warner Books, 1990), pp. 453–4. See Kenneth Campbell, 'Once Burned, Twice Cautious: Explaining the Weinberger-Powell Doctrine', *Armed Forces and Society*, vol. 24, no. 3, Spring 1998. It has been noted that application of the Weinberger tests in 1965 would probably have permitted entry into the Vietnam War.
16 White Paper presented to the UK parliament by the Secretary of State for Defence, *Strategic Defence Review*, July 1998: http://www.mod.uk/issues/sdr/wp_contents.htm.
17 'Doctrine of the International Community', speech by Tony Blair to the Economic Club, Chicago, 24 April 1999: http://www.number-10.gov.uk/output/Page1297.asp.

III. Asymmetric war
1 See James Turner Johnson, *Morality and Contemporary Warfare* (New Haven, CT: Yale University Press, 1999).
2 The various views on the future role of nuclear weapons can be found in the contributions to John Baylis and Robert O'Neill, eds, *Alternative Nuclear Futures: The Role of Nuclear Weapons in the Post-Cold War World* (Oxford: Oxford University Press, 1999).

3 President Clinton was apparently persuaded of the potential risks of biotechnological warfare by the novel *The Cobra Event* by Richard Preston, in which a terrorist releases an engineered virus in New York, causing auto-cannibalism.
4 Andrew Mack, 'Why Big Nations Lose Small Wars: The Politics of Asymmetric Conflict', *World Politics*, vol. 27, no. 2, January 1975, pp. 175–200.
5 'Asymmetric engagements are battles between dissimilar forces'. US Joint Chiefs of Staff, *Joint Publication 1: Joint Warfare of the Armed Forces of the United States* (Washington DC: GPO, January 1995), p. iv.
6 Cited in John T. Correll, 'Casualties', *Air Force Magazine*, June 2003, p. 49.
7 Secretary of Defense William S. Cohen, *Report of the Quadrennial Defense Review* (Washington DC: Department of Defense, May 1997), Section II.
8 US Joint Chiefs of Staff, *Joint Vision 2020* (Washington DC: GPO, 2000), p. 5. The full text is available to download from: http://www.dtic.mil/jointvision/jvpub2.htm. The following paragraph draws heavily on Metz and Douglas V. Johnson, *Asymmetry and U.S. Military Strategy: Definition, Background, and Strategic Concepts* (Carlisle, PA: Strategic Studies Institute, 2001).
9 US Joint Chiefs of Staff, *Joint Strategy Review 1999* (Washington DC: GPO, 1999), p. 2.
10 US Joint Chiefs of Staff, *Joint Vision 2010* (Washington DC: GPO, 2000). The full text is available to download from: http://www.dtic.mil/jv2010/jv2010.pdf.
11 *Report of the Quadrennial Defense Review* (Washington DC: Department of Defense, September 2001), p. 21, http://www.defenselink.mil/pubs/qdr2001.pdf. A former Secretary of Defense, William J. Perry, also gave the impression that the most important policy response to the terrorist attacks would be in the area of missile defence, in 'Preparing for the Next Attack', *Foreign Affairs*, vol. 80, no. 6, November/December 2001, pp. 31–45.
12 The United States Commission on National Security/21st Century, *New World Coming: American Security in the 21st Century* (Washington DC: Department of Defense, 1999), p. 48. For a similar emphasis see also National Commission on Terrorism, *Countering the Changing Threat of International Terrorism: Pursuant to Public Law 277, 105th Congress* (Washington DC: US Congress, 2000). This also focused on a state-sponsored, mass casualty, catastrophic attack and implied that US policy might be too heavily focused on Osama bin Laden. Similarly, a major study by the Center for Strategic and International Studies (CSIS), with many thoughtful recommendations to improve homeland defence, made national missile defence the priority issue, and focused on chemical, biological, nuclear and radiological weapons and cyber-terrorism. Frank Cilluffo *et al.*, *Defending America in the 21st Century: New Challenges, New Organizations, and New Policies: Executive Summary of Four CSIS Working Group Reports on Homeland Defense* (Washington DC: CSIS, 2000).
13 Interview by Andrew Herson, *Policy Review*, Summer 1993, p. 145, cited in Richard Eichenberg, 'Victory Has Many Friends: U.S. Public Opinion and the Use of Military Force, 1981–2005', *International Security*, vol. 30, no. 1, Summer 2005, pp. 140–77.
14 Richard Holbrooke, *To End a War* (New York: Random House, 1999).
15 Edward N. Luttwak, 'Toward Post-Heroic Warfare', *Foreign Affairs*, vol. 74, no. 3, May/June 1995, pp. 109–22.
16 John Mueller, *War, Presidents and Public Opinion* (New York: Wiley, 1973).
17 Eichenberg, 'Victory Has Many Friends'. See also James Burk, 'Public Support for Peacekeeping in Lebanon and Somalia: Assessing the Casualties Hypothesis', *Political Science Quarterly*, vol. 114, no. 1, Spring 1999, pp. 53–78; Eric V. Larson, *Casualties and Consensus: The Historical Role of Casualties in Domestic Support for U.S. Military Operations* (Santa Monica, CA: RAND, 1996); Steven Kull and Clay Ramsay, 'The Myth of the Reactive Public: American Public Attitudes on

Military Fatalities in the Post-Cold War Period', in Philip Everts and Pierangelo Isernia, eds, *Public Opinion and the International Use of Force* (London: Routledge, 2001), pp. 205–28. A recent literature review concludes 'there is no convincing evidence that casualty aversion has become the dominant factor in determining the use or non-use of force by democracies'. Hugh Smith, 'What Costs will Democracies Bear? A Review of Popular Theories of Casualty Aversion', *Armed Forces & Society*, vol. 31, no. 4, Summer 2005, p. 508.

18 In other contingencies involving Taiwan and Iraq the acceptable levels were much higher but the ordering of tolerance, with the public most relaxed, remained the same. The results were reported by Peter D. Feaver and Christopher Gelpi, *Choosing Your Battles: American Civil-Military Relations and the Use of Force* (Princeton, NJ: Princeton University Press, 2003). For a discussion of all relevant findings see Charles Hyde, 'Casualty Aversion: Implications for Policy Makers and Senior Military Officers', *Aerospace Power Journal*, vol. 14, no. 2, Summer 2000, pp. 17–27.

19 Cited in Andrew Erdmann, 'The U.S. Presumption of Quick, Costless Wars', *Orbis*, vol. 43, no. 3, Summer 1999, pp. 363–81.

20 Jeffrey Record, 'Force-Protection Fetishism: Sources, Consequences, and (?) Solutions', *Aerospace Power Journal*, vol. 14, no. 2, Summer 2000, p. 5.

21 Prepared joint statement on the Kosovo After Action Review presented by Secretary of Defense William S. Cohen and General Henry H. Shelton, Chairman of the Joint Chiefs of Staff, before the Senate Armed Services Committee, October 14, 1999, http://www.defenselink.mil/news/Oct1999/b10141999_bt478-99.html.

22 Interview with CNN's Peter Arnett, 11 May 1997.

23 Report of the National Defense Panel, *Transforming Defense: National Security in the 21st Century* (Washington DC: Department of Defense, December 1997), p. 1. The report is available to download from: http://www.dtic.mil/ndp/FullDoc2.pdf. Douglas A. MacGregor, *Breaking the Phalanx: A New Design for Landpower in the 21st Century* (Westport, CT: Praeger, 1997).

24 Colin Powell and Joseph Persico, *My American Journey: An Autobiography* (New York: Random House, 1995). See also Charles Stevenson, 'The Evolving Clinton Doctrine on the Use of Force', *Armed Forces and Society*, vol. 22, no. 4, Summer 1996, pp. 511–35.

25 Colin Powell, 'U.S. Forces: Challenges Ahead', vol. 71, no. 5, *Foreign Affairs*, Winter 1992/93, pp. 32–45.

26 The distinction was developed under Powell's guidance in the US Department of Defense, *Joint Pub 3-0: Doctrine for Joint Operations* (Washington DC: Joint Chiefs of Staff, 1993). See Stevenson, 'The Evolving Clinton Doctrine', p. 517.

27 Andrew J. Bacevich, *The New American Militarism: How Americans are Seduced by War* (New York: Oxford University Press, 2005).

28 Cohen, 'Constraints on America's Conduct of Small Wars', *International Security*, vol. 9, no. 2, Fall 1984, pp. 151–81.

29 Cited in Larry Cable, 'Reinventing the Round Wheel: Insurgency, Counter-Insurgency, and Peacekeeping Post Cold War', *Small Wars and Insurgencies*, vol. 4, no. 2, Autumn 1993, pp. 228–62.

30 Clark, *Waging Modern War: Bosnia, Kosovo and the Future of Conflict* (New York: PublicAffairs, 2001).

31 Joint Chiefs of Staff, *Joint Vision 2010*, p. 1.

32 Douglas Lovelace, Jr, *The Evolution of Military Affairs: Shaping the Future U.S. Armed Forces* (Carlisle, PA: Strategic Studies Institute, 1997).

33 Jennifer M. Taw and Alan Vick, 'From Sideshow to Center Stage: The Role of the Army and Air Force in Military Operations Other Than War', in Zalmay M.

Khalilzad and David A. Ochmanek, eds, *Strategy and Defense Planning for the 21st Century* (Santa Monica, CA: RAND & US Air Force, 1997), pp. 208–209.
34 Condoleezza Rice, 'Campaign 2000: Promoting the National Interest', *Foreign Affairs*, vol. 79, no. 1, January/February 2000, p. 53.

IV. The transformation of military strategy
1 See above, p. 600. Colonel J. Warden, USAF, *The Air Campaign: Planning for Combat* (Washington DC: NDU, 1988).
2 *Report of the Panel on United Nations Peace Operations* (Brahimi Report), United Nations, August 2000, http://www.un.org/peace/reports/peace_operations/.
3 Robert C. Owen, 'The Balkans Air Campaign Study: Part Two', *Airpower Journal*, vol. 11, no. 3, Fall 1997, pp. 6–26.
4 John A. Tirpak, 'Deliberate Force' *Air Force Magazine*, vol. 80, no. 10, October 1997, pp. 36–43.
5 See Holbrooke, *To End a War*.
6 John Keegan, 'So the Bomber Got Through After All', *Daily Telegraph*, 4 June 1999. For a sceptical view see E.H. Tilford, 'Operation Allied Force and the Role of Air Power', *Parameters*, vol. 29, no.4, Winter 1999–2000, pp.6–26. For assessments of the war, see Tim Judah, *Kosovo: War and Revenge* (New Haven, CT: Yale University Press, 2000); and Albrecht Schnabel and Ramesh Thakur, eds, *Kosovo and the Challenge of Humanitarian Intervention: Selective Indignation, Collective Action, and International Citizenship* (Tokyo: United Nations University Press, 2000). On the issue of humanitarian intervention, see Adam Roberts, 'NATO's "Humanitarian War" over Kosovo', *Survival*, vol. 41, no. 3, Autumn 1999, pp. 102–23.
7 Edward Cody, 'Taliban's Hide-and-Wait Tactics Tied to U.S. Aversion to Casualties', *International Herald Tribune*, 22 October 2001.
8 Remarks by the President at the Citadel, Charleston, South Carolina, 11 December 2001.
9 Interview broadcast on CBS 'Face the Nation', 18 November 2001. A transcript is available at http://www.defenselink.mil/transcripts/2001/t11182001_t1118wol.html.
10 George Packer, *The Assassin's Gate: America in Iraq* (New York: Farrar, Straus and Giroux, 2005).
11 Hearings, *Department Of Defense Budget Priorities For Fiscal Year 2004*, Committee on the Budget One Hundred Eighth Congress: First Session, 27 February 2003.
12 'American Army Tactics in Iraq', *The Economist*, 29 December 2004.

V. Strategic communications
1 Gladys Ganley, 'Power to the People via Personal Electronic Media', *The Washington Quarterly*, vol. 14, no. 2, Spring 1991, pp. 5–26.
2 *Internet Filtering in China in 2004–2005: A Country Study*, http://www.opennetinitiative.net/studies/china/.
3 Steve Coll and Susan B. Glasser, 'Terrorists Turn to the Web as Base of Operations', *Washington Post*, 7 August 2005. See also Timothy L. Thomas, 'Al Qaeda and the Internet: The Danger of "Cyberplanning"', *Parameters*, Spring 2003, pp. 112–23.
4 Jean Seaton, 'Why Do We Think The Serbs Do It? The New "Ethnic" Wars and the Media', *Political Quarterly*, vol. 70, no. 3, July–September 1999, p. 261.
5 Matt Stoller, 'The Narrative as Battlefield', 14 December 2003, http://www.bopnews.com/archives/000084.html.
6 The text of the letter is available in English from the Office of the Director of National Intelligence: http://www.dni.gov/release_letter_101105.html.
7 James Gow and James Tilsey, 'The Strategic Imperative for Media Management'

in James Gow, Richard Paterson and Alison Preston, eds, *Bosnia by Television* (London: British Film Institute, 1996), p. 107.
8 Gow and Tilsey, Ibid., pp. 109–10. For an analysis of the same episode, as part of a general critique on the loss of journalistic objectivity during the conflict see John Burns, 'The Media as Impartial Observers or Protagonists' in *Bosnia by Television*, pp. 96–7. For those in charge of the international organisations operating on the ground, including the United Nations Protection Force, this eroded sympathy for people who, they felt, were constantly playing with the truth in order to influence world opinion. It encouraged the perception that 'they are all as bad each other' and mutual irritation as local UN commanders were obliged to challenge the accounts of their local interlocutors. This is reflected in the memoir of General Sir Michael Rose, *Fighting for Peace: Bosnia, 1994* (London: The Harvill Press, 1998). For a critique see Michael Williams, 'Perceptions of the war in Bosnia', *International Affairs*, vol. 75, no. 2, April 1999, pp. 377–382.
9 In Philip Seib, *Headline Diplomacy: How News Coverage Affects Foreign Policy* (Boulder, CO: Praeger, 1997), p. 135.
10 Walter Goodman, cited in Miles Hudson and John Stanier, *War and the Media*, revised edn (Stroud: Sutton Publishing, 1999), p. 256.
11 *The Times*, 18 August 1992, cited in Martin Bell, *In Harm's Way* (London: Hamish Hamilton, 1995), p. 137.
12 Piers Robinson, 'The CNN effect: can the news media drive foreign policy?, *Review of International Studies*, vol. 25, no. 2, April 1999, pp. 301–09. The original CNN effect, it might be noted, referred to the ubiquity of the channel (so that all sides were using the same information source) as much as to the particulars of its effects. The term itself originated during the Gulf War and was naturally promoted by CNN's owner, Ted Turner. See Thomas B. Allen, F. Clifton Berry and Norman Polmar, *CNN: War in the Gulf* (Atlanta, GA: Turner Broadcasting, 1991).
13 The origins go back to a letter from John Adams to Thomas Jefferson of 19 April 1817. The American Revolution, he observed, 'was effected before the war commenced. The Revolution was in the minds and hearts of the people; a change in their religious sentiments, of their duties and obligations . . . This radical change in the principles, opinions, sentiments, and affections of the people was the real American Revolution'.
14 Kaplan, *Imperial Grunts: The American Military on the Ground*, (New York: Random House, 2005).
15 Cited Aylwin-Foster, 'Changing the Army for Counterinsurgency Operations', *Military Review*, November–December 2005, p. 5.
16 Montgonery McFate, 'The Military Utility of Understanding Adversary Culture', *Joint Forces Quarterly*, no. 38, July 2005, p. 44.
17 Aylwin-Foster, 'Changing the Army for Counterinsurgency Operations', p. 4.
18 Thomas E. Ricks, 'Lessons Learned in Iraq Show Up in Army Classes: Culture Shifts to Counterinsurgency', *Washington Post*, 21 January 2006.
19 Scales, *Culture-Centric Warfare*. It is instructive to compare these proposals with remarkably similar ideas that were propounded in the late 1950s as the Americans were encouraged to pay more attention to the third world. See in particular William J. Lederer and Eugene Burdick, *The Ugly American* (New York: Fawcett House, 1958).
20 Daniel Byman, *Going To War With The Allies You Have: Allies, Counterinsurgency, And The War On Terrorism* (Carlisle, PA: Strategic Studies Institute, November 2005).
21 Pew Global Attitudes Project, 'U.S. Image Up Slightly, But Still Negative: American Character Gets Mixed Reviews', 23 June 2005: http://pewglobal.org/reports/display.php?PageID=800.

22 The term 'public diplomacy' was first used in 1965 by Edmund Gullion, a career foreign service diplomat and subsequently dean of the Fletcher School of Law and Diplomacy at Tufts University, in connection with the establishment at the Fletcher School of the Edward R. Murrow Center for Public Diplomacy. Charles Wolf, Jr and Brian Rosen, 'Public Diplomacy: Lessons from King and Mandela', *Policy Review*, no. 33, October/November 2005.
23 Byman, 'Al-Qaeda as an Adversary: Do we understand our enemy?', *World Politics*, vol. 56, no. 1, October 2003, pp. 162–3.
24 Rumsfeld, 'War of the Words', *Wall Street Journal*, 18 July 2005. The Pentagon website is www.defenselink.mil.
25 Rumsfeld, 'New Realities in the Media Age', speech delivered at the Council on Foreign Relations, New York, 17 February 2006: http://www.cfr.org/publication/9900/. A few days later his British counterpart, Dr John Reid, made similar points in a speech to the War Studies Department at King's College London. 'One observer, with one videophone, or today even one mobile phone, standing in one square metre of a vast and hugely complex theatre of operations can convey an oversimplified and sometimes misleading picture with an impact that is incalculable.' http://www.mod.uk/DefenceInternet/DefenceNews/DefencePolicyAndBusiness/WeMustBeslowerToCondemnQuickerToUnderstandTheForcesJohnReid.htm.
26 Safire, 'Insurgent irresponsiveness', *International Herald Tribune*, 16 January 2006. In developing his theme of how in wartime words are weapons, Safire notes how the Israelis lost the battle in attempting to call the land west of the Jordan River by the biblical Judea and Samaria, or even 'administered territories'.
27 Scott Shane, 'Bush's Iraq speech echoes a new voice', *International Herald Tribune*, 4 December 2005.
28 Jeff Gerth, 'Military's Information War Is Vast and Often Secretive', *New York Times*, 12 December 2005.
29 Human Security Centre, *Human Security Report 2005: War and Peace in the 21st Century* (New York: Oxford University Press, 2006). The full report can be downloaded from: http://www.humansecurityreport.info/.

Index

A
Abdullah, King 127, 130, 131
ABM systems 114–15, 420
Abu Aweiqila 172–3
Abu Ghraib 663–4
accountability 564–5
Acheson, D. 73
active constraints on the manufacture of nuclear weapons 90–93, 101, 104–6, 117–18
Acyl Ahmat 468, 469, 497
Adelphi Papers series 1–2; choice of name 1; regional analyses 12
administration: as form of humanitarian intervention 551–2
Advanced Projects Authority 260
adversaries: attitude of 455–6; relative strength of 390
Afghanistan: political stability 490; refugees 485; Soviet Union intervention 20–21, 433, 442, 466–7, 473, 477–8, 498–500, 507, 508–9; 'war on terror' 23, 25, 645–8
Africa 44–5, 108, 118–19, 356, 508; *see also under individual countries*
African Rights 561, 563
aid: during war 541–3; humanitarian vs development aid 567–8; *see also* humanitarian action in war
air power 25, 642–5
aircraft 94, 161
AirLand Battle 25, 601
Akashi, Y. 550
al-Qaeda 15, 612, 628, 630–31; internal debates 666–7; and internet 654; 'war on terror' 645–51
Alastair Buchan Lecture 5
Algeria 146, 167, 266, 350
alienation of the electorate 203
Allende, S. 283
alliances: and Germany 228–30, 235–6; networks of alliances and structure for Europe 236–40, 248–51, 260–61; nuclear sharing within 99–100; nuclear states and spread of nuclear weapons 394–5; reciprocal stabilisation of existing alliances 248–51; timing and formation 209–10; *see also* NATO, Warsaw Pact
allies, attitudes of 456–7
Allon, Y. 141, 159
Alvor Accords 464
ambushes 310
Amer, A.A. 138
American Assembly of Columbia University 85
American Relief Association 541
Amin, H. 441, 466–7, 473
Amin, I. 398, 492
ammunition: diversions and seizures 312–14
Andersen, H.C. 106
Angell, N. 424–5
Angola 20, 45–6, 432, 435–6, 442, 513; economic effects of intervention 486–7; political stability 489, 490; refugees 484–5; regulation of intervention 492–4; results of intervention 473, 474–5; triggers for intervention 462–4
Angry Brigade 282
anonymous firing of nuclear weapons 400
Antarctica 119
anti-colonialism 37–8
anti-personnel land-mines 572–3, 585
Arab–Israeli conflict 10–12, 108, 121–94; historical and political perspective 122–43; immediate origins of Six-Day War 143–60; oil weapon and 16–18, 156, 165–6, 329, 334, 336–8, 350, 370; Six-Day War *see* Six-Day War
Arab League 127, 131, 146
Arab Liberation Army 127
Arab Maritime Petroleum Transport Company 345
Arab nationalism 124, 126–7, 368–9

Arab refugees 131
Arab Unified High Command 137, 138
Archidamus, King of Sparta 6, 76
Argentine Revolutionary Armed Forces (FAR) 276–7
Aristide, J-B. 534
Armed Conflict Database 20
armed forces, professionalism of 632
armed propaganda 16, 276–7, 277, 317–18
armed protection of humanitarian workers 568–71
Armistice Agreements 129, 130
arms/weapons: capture of 313–14; diversions of 312–13; Germany and armament 228–30, 232–4; nuclear *see* nuclear weapons; spin-off from oil power 358; urban guerrillas 294–6
arms control 217; European arms-control zone 238–9, 250–51; Germany 232–4; NATO and 43–4, 53
arms races 412–14, 421
arms transfers, restraint in 505–6
Aron, R. 3, 38
Arquilla, J. 608, 610
arsenals, nuclear 421
Asia 270–71, 274; balance of power 13, 195–213; *see also under individual countries*
assassinations 267
asylum 524–6
asymmetric war 626, 632–42; *see also* irregular warfare
asymmetry in distribution of power 452
Atassi, President Al 140
Atoms for Peace Programme 88
attrition 601
Australia 195–6, 206, 210–11
Austria 227
Austrian solution 231
Austro-Hungarian Empire 615
authorisation of humanitarian intervention 531–2
Aylwin-Foster, N. 659, 660

B
Ba Thein Tin 197
Ba'athist Party 136, 365
balance of power 113–14, 115, 216–17; Asia 13–14, 195–213; between NATO and Soviet Union 35–6, 50–51; Europe 196, 197–8, 199, 210, 211–12
Balfour Declaration 10, 124
Balkan federation 237–8
Baniyas River 137, 189–90
bank assaults 308–9
bargaining 82–3
Baruch plan 99

battlespace 602
Begin, M. 152, 160
Belgium 40, 44, 45
Bell, C. 13. *See also* Chapter 5.
Beloff, M. 479–80
Ben-Ari, Colonel 169
Ben-Gurion, D. 128, 133, 152, 159
Berlin Crisis 3, 32, 35, 42, 46
Betancourt, President 283–4
Bevin, E. 126
Biafra 453
Bihac 550
bilateral agreements 56; oil 343–4, 375–6
Bin Laden, Osama 647, 651, 654
bipolarity 216–17, 223–4, 399; deterrence in a bipolar world 384–95; effects of 384–6; European security system 224, 247–51; and intervention 452–3
Birnbaum, K. 248
Bismarck, O. von 226
Black Power 278, 286–7
blackmail 389, 400
Blair, T. 627–8
Bluhm, G. 248
bombs 317
borrowing of ideas 276–7
borders 227–8
Bosnia 22, 520, 542, 563, 585; administration 551–2; air power 643–5; IFOR 555; mission creep 637–8; NGOs 574; safety zones 549–51; UNPROFOR 533, 537, 538, 546, 550–51, 555; use of UN peacekeeping forces for humanitarian purposes 545–7; victim strategy 656; war crimes 555
Boumedienne, H. 182, 350
Bourguiba, President 139, 146
Boutros-Ghali, B. 545–6
Bradwell nuclear power station 91
Brazil 284, 292, 293, 305
Brezhnev, L. 446
Britain *see* United Kingdom
Brodie, B. 390, 406, 407, 415
Brown, G. (British Foreign Secretary) 153, 155
Brown, General G. 417
Brown, H. 413, 415
Brown, N. 258
Bryer, D. 542, 559
Brzezinski, Z. 238, 250, 261, 263–4, 477
Buchan, A.F. 2–6, 25, 259–60. *See also* Chapter 1.
Buchan, J. 2
budgets, humanitarian 529–30
Bull, H. 20, 532
Burma 197

Bush, G.H.W. 620
Bush, G.W. 628, 631, 647, 663; administration of 24, 26, 603
Butterfield, H. 196, 198
Buzzard, A. 3
Byman, D. 661, 662

C

Camps, M. 235, 260
Canada 9, 40, 41, 117–18; and Arab–Israeli conflict 148–9, 153–4; Front de Libération du Québec (FLQ) 267, 268, 275, 276; Japan–Canada Agreement 118
Canadian Human Security Centre 668
Canadian Institute of International Affairs 85
capacity, as dimension of power 598
capture of arms 313–14
Carnegie Endowment for International Peace 85
Carter, J. 394, 433
Carter Doctrine 478
Castro, F. 265, 446, 476
casualties 485–6; intolerance of 632, 639–40
CCEM logistics formula 298
Cebrowski, A.K. 607
central and eastern Europe 108, 216, 237–8, 615, 616; *see also under individual countries*
Central European arms-control zone 238–9, 250–51
Central Intelligence Agency (CIA) 537
Central Treaty Organization (CENTO) 362
Chad 20, 433, 436–7, 442, 454, 514; political stability 488–9; refugees 485; regulation of intervention 495–8; results of intervention 473–4, 479; triggers for intervention 467–70
Chalfont, Lord 85
challenge, verification by 9, 103
Chandler, C. 293
Cheney, R. 637
Childers, E. 569
Chile 287
China 420, 619, 625; Asian balance of power 13, 196–7, 199, 200, 202, 205, 210–13; control of nuclear proliferation 98, 99, 114, 119; internet filtering system 653–4; motivations for intervention 444, 445; Sino-Soviet relations and Soviet interventionism 509; theory of 'people's war' 204–5
choice 24, 598; wars of 625–6
Churchill, W.S. 611
cities: no-cities strategy 7, 74–5, 76–9, 81–2; urban guerrilla warfare *see* urban guerrilla warfare; vulnerability of industrial cities 279–80

civil control of military 399–400
civil wars 523, 558–9
Clark, W.K. 641
'classical' approach to non-proliferation 98, 98–101
Clausewitz, C. von 406, 600
Clausewitzian principle of political context 11, 178
Cleaver, E. 278
CNN effect 656–7
Code of Conduct for relief workers 561, 564, 583–4
codes of conduct 564–5
cognitive domain 607
Cohen, W.S. 639–40
Cohn-Bendit, D. 280
Cold War 1, 11, 21, 109, 113–14, 615
collateral damage 632–3
collective defence 216–17
collective security 217, 223; and European security system 241–6
colonialism 615
combined conventional–nuclear attack 400
communications 25, 651–69; conflict driven by media 655–7; hearts and minds 25, 658–61; information environment 651–3; networks and hierarchies 664–6; strategic communication 662–4
communism: collapse in Europe 616; and structure of European security system 236
Communist Party of India (Marxist–Leninist) (CPI (M–L)) 270
communities of belief 665
complex emergencies 22–3, 522–4; *see also* humanitarian action in war
confederations: European 238–9; Germany 230–32
Congo 44
Congress of Vienna (1815) 222, 623
Connaughton, R. 568
consent 532–3
constraints: on intervention 453–62, 505–7; on manufacture of nuclear weapons 90–94, 101, 104–6, 117–18
containment 195, 199, 207; doubtful possibility for Asia 199–205
contractors, murder of 659
control: and *controle* 66–7; loss of and oil power 332–4
controlled response 5, 73–84, 414
Convention on the Safety of UN and Associated Personnel 571–2
Convention on Specific Conventional Weapons 573

coordination of humanitarian action 573–80; effectiveness through 581
cost: of developing nuclear weapons 95–6; of intervention 486–7; and spread of nuclear technology 89–90; and technological evolution 87–8
cost-effectiveness: and containment 202–4
counterforce strategy 6, 74–5, 76–80, 403–4
counter-insurgency 660–61
counter-revolutionaries 290
'countervailing' strategy 416
'countryside of the world' 204, 212–13
Couve de Murville, M. 225
covert intervention 432
credibility of small deterrent forces 406–9
crime: international 618; war crimes 556–7
Crimean War 389–90
Croatia 656
Crocker, C. 475
Cuba 451; disillusionment with Soviet Union 510; future of interventionism 510; intervention in Angola 432, 463, 473, 474–5; intervention in Ethiopia 433, 465–6, 473, 475–7; motivations for intervention 444, 446
Cuban missile crisis 4, 45, 114, 390
Cultural Revolution 210
culture: mistakes made by US army in Iraq due to ignorance of culture 659–60; networks, narratives and 24–5, 600–13
culture-centred war 605–10
cut-off agreements 92–3, 95, 101, 104–6, 117–18
Cyprus 80, 265–6
Czechoslovakia 218, 237

D
Damrosch, L.F. 538
Danubian federation 237–8
Davies, J. 282
Dayan, M. 133, 152, 159, 160, 169
Dayton Agreement 546, 555, 582, 644
De Gaulle, C. 40, 69, 70, 386
'decision gap' 211
decolonisation 615–16
defence expenditure 360–61; and intervention 483–4; *see also* military expenditures
defensive liberal wars 623–8
defensive weapons 113; nuclear weapons as 388–9, 392, 425; oil weapon as 369–70
Deir Yassin massacre 131
delivery systems for nuclear weapons 94
Demilitarized Zone (Israeli–Syrian border) 140, 141

democracy 16
demonstrations, mass 311–12
Denmark 154
denuclearised zones 9, 107–9, 118–19
Department of Humanitarian Affairs, UN (DHA) 575, 575–8, 578, 579, 581
dependence, oil power and 17–18, 330–2
deprivation, relative 16, 275
Desert Storm, Operation 601–2
desertions 312–13
détente 114, 200, 203
deterrence: in a bipolar world 384–95; credibility of small deterrent forces 406–9; extended 409–12; forces required for 401–6; with small nuclear forces 401–18
developing countries 111–12, 356; aversion to intervention 454; Group of 77 577, 581; intervention by 507–8, 515; interventions in 20–22, 429–519; possible future application of oil weapon 373–5; urbanisation 272–4
development aid 111; humanitarian aid vs 567–8
dictatorial governments 524
diplomats 46–7
disarmament 8–9, 97, 101, 110–12; Germany 228–30; NATO and 43–4; nuclear-free zones 9, 107–9, 118–19
disengagement with guarantees 224, 244–5, 251–3
'disimperialism' 35, 37–8
dissemination of nuclear technology 85–6, 90
diversions of arms 312–13
Dobrynin, A. 493
domestic politics: imposing constraints on intervention 458–9; strategic narratives 610–13
domestic stability 396–7; intervention and 487–91
donor fatigue 529–30
Dos Santos, E. 474
Duchêne, F. 235
Dulles, J.F. 73, 205, 208, 400, 408

E
Earle, E.M. 2
early warning 578–9
East Germany *see* German Democratic Republic
Eastern European defence community 238–9, 250–51, 256
Eban, A. 152, 155, 158, 160, 174, 175
economy: as a constraint on intervention 457–8; effects of intervention on 486–7; economic motivations for intervention 449–50

economic sanctions 565–7; and Arab–Israeli conflict 131–2, 133
Eden, A. 228
education 89–90
Egypt 350, 453; armed forces 161, 192–3; Armistice Agreement 129, 130; creation of Jewish state and 126–7; defence pact with Jordan 158; forces moved into Sinai 158; hostility with Libya 398; mobilisation in response to expected Israeli attack on Syria 145–6; Six-Day War 161, 163–7, 170–74, 175; Straits of Tiran 132, 133, 151–7, 181; Suez crisis 9, 17, 131–3, 329; UNEF 133–4, 147–50, 180–81, 186–9; *see also* Arab–Israeli conflict, Nasser
Eighteen-Nation Disarmament Conference (ENDC) 97, 116
Eilat 132–3
Eisenhower, D.D. 134; administration of 64
El Fatah ('Conquest') raids 140, 143
El Kony, M. 148, 154
El Salvador 432, 458, 510
Elazar, Brigadier-General 170, 173, 176
ElBaradei, M. 5
Eliasson, J. 569
Emergency Relief Coordinator 577
emerging economies 18, 357–8, 376
enclave strategy 208–9
enforced population movements 582
Engels, F. 273
enriched uranium 105
EOKA 265–6
equal sovereignty, mutual recognition of 461–2, 482–3, 531–2, 540, 622–3
Eritrea 437, 438, 475, 476
Eshed Kinrot pumping station 136–7
Eshkol, L. 142–3, 144, 152, 159, 167
Ethiopia 427–30, 433, 437–40, 442, 454; political instability 489; refugees 485; regulation of intervention 494–5; results of intervention 473, 475–7; triggers for intervention 464–6
Ethiopian Democratic Union 440
ethnic cleansing 582, 630, 645
Europe 3–5, 214–16; balance of power 196, 197–8, 199, 210, 211–12; change and security in *see* European security system; changes in scope of European NATO members' interests and influences 39–40; NATO and reconsideration of defence of Europe 48–53; oil import dependence 17, 330–31; regionalism and nuclear-free zones 108–9; risks of war receding 109; security 116–17; structure of 236–40; tension between Europe and US in NATO over US strategic nuclear weapons 63–9; US and containment 199; US relationship to European NATO allies 3–5, 36–9
'Europe of the States' 224–5, 228, 254–6
European Community Humanitarian Office (ECHO) 575
European Defence Commission 260
European Economic Community (EEC) 40–41; oil weapon and conflict 337–40; regulation of intervention 498–9
European integration 14, 224, 225, 256–61
European Security Commission 250
European Security Pact 254
European security system 14, 214–64; abstract solutions 240–46; alternative frameworks 223–5; four models for 224–5, 247–61; Germany and 215–16, 221, 225–40, 241, 242, 250–51, 254–6; notion of and problems 214–23; structure 236–40
European Technological Community 260
European Union (EU) 616
Europeanism 224
Evans, G. 574–5, 578
executions 314–15
'exit strategy' 638
explosives 312–14
extended deterrence 409–12

F
factionalism 666
Faisal (or Feisal), King 139, 146, 334, 368
Fallujah, murders of contractors in 659
Fanon, F. 273, 275
Fawzy, M. 145, 147, 158
Feaver, P. 663
Fedayeen raids 133, 134
Fédération Nationale de Libération Congolaise (FNLC) 449
Fedorenko, N. 154, 162–3, 174–5
Feisal (or Faisal), King 139, 146, 334, 368
Feldman, S. 398
finance 89–90
Finlandisation 253, 254
Finletter, T. 47
firing groups (cells) 268, 297–8
First World War 390, 541
fissile materials, and cut-off agreements 90–93, 95, 101, 104–6, 117–18
'flexible response' 6–7, 73–84, 414
Fogelman, R.R. 634–5
food aid 541
force-projection facilities 447–8
force-protection fetishism 639
Forces Armées du Nord (FAN) 456, 469

Forces Armées Populaires (FAP) 469
Forces Armées Tchadiennes (FAT) 469
Ford, G. 493
Ford Foundation 10
former Yugoslavia 554, 624, 656;
  see also Bosnia
fourth-generation warfare (4GW) 25,
  608–9
Fox, W.T.R. 412
France 218, 482; and Arab–Israeli conflict
  153–4; domestic constraints on
  intervention 459; and European security
  system 254; future of interventionism
  513–14; intervention in Rwanda 534,
  570; interventions in Chad 433, 467–8,
  469, 473, 478, 496, 514; motivations for
  intervention 446–7, 449; and NATO 37,
  38, 39–40, 62, 64–5, 69, 70; nuclear
  deterrent 38, 64–5, 66, 69, 83–4, 98, 99,
  393, 395; oil 338–9; regulation of Libya's
  intervention in Chad 498; and student
  revolt 280–81, 282; and Suez crisis 133
Freedman, L. 24–5. *See also* Chapter 12.
Frente Nacional de Libertação de Angola
  (FNLA) 432, 435–6, 463, 474, 492
Front de Libération Nationale (FLN)
  (Algiers) 267–8, 276, 283–4
Front de Libération Nationale Tchadienne
  (FROLINAT) 442, 467, 468, 473
Front de Libération du Québec (FLQ) 267,
  268, 275, 276
'Full Spectrum Dominance' 641

G
Gadhafi, M. (Gaddafi, el-Qaddafi) 398, 454,
  469, 470, 497
Gaitskell, H. 392
Galen, J. (pseud.) 405
gang warfare 80, 81
Garstka, J.J. 607
gas 88
Gavin, General 208
Gavish, General 146, 171, 172
'general war' 74
generalisation, of conflicts and war 217–18
Geneva Conventions (1949) 547, 552–3
Geneva Disarmament Conferences 97, 113
Geneva Protocol I (1977) 547, 556–7
genocide 535
Georgia 557–8
German Democratic Republic (East
  Germany) 227, 230–32, 233–4, 235
German Federal Republic (West Germany)
  230–32, 233–4, 235
Germany 99–100, 619; arms limitation and
  control 232–4; and European security
system 215–16, 221, 225–40, 241, 242,
  250–51, 254–6; and NATO 37, 40, 65, 70;
  neutrality vs alliances 228–30, 235–6; and
  oil weapon 339; reunification 228–30,
  230–32, 233–4; settlement for 225–30;
  Treaty of Berlin 235; US wartime relief
  supply plan 541
ghetto revolts 15–16, 269
Girijan tribesmen 271
global economic crisis 347–8
global revolution 275–6, 286
'global war on terror' 23, 628–32, 645–51
globalisation 9, 615–18, 631
Gomulka plan 108
Good Faith Agreement 188
Goukouni Oueddei 442, 467, 468, 469, 470,
  473–4, 490, 495–6, 497
government: intervention on behalf of
  489–90; response to urban guerrilla
  warfare 283–6
'graduated deterrence' 6–8, 73–84, 414
grain 332
grand strategy 598–9, 613–32; American
  618–20; 'global war on terror' 628–32;
  and globalisation 615–18; liberal wars
  620–28
Great Britain *see* United Kingdom
great powers *see* Soviet Union, super-powers,
  United States of America (USA)
Greece 40
Grenada 512
Gromyko, A. 446
'Gromyko umbrella' 110
ground forces 602–3
Group of 77 577, 581
guarantees 243; disengagement with 224,
  244–5, 251–3
guerrilla warfare 182, 665; urban *see* urban
  guerrilla warfare
Guevara, C. 269, 283
guidance systems 94–5
Gulf of Aqaba 132–4, 151–7, 174
Gulf War of 1991 25, 600–02, 620, 639,
  642

H
Habré, H. 446, 468, 469–70, 474, 490,
  497
Haganah 125, 129
Hague Convention (1907) 547
Haile Selassie 437–8, 439
Haiti 534, 538
Hallett, R. 444
Halperin, M. 5
Hammarskjöld, D. 134, 187, 188
Hammes, T.X. 608

Hart-Rudman Commission 635–6
Hasanein Haikal, M. Mohammed 157
Hasbani River 137, 189–90
Hassner, P. 14–15. *See also* Chapter 6.
Hayden, T. 284–5
Healey, D. 6, 73
hearts and minds 25, 658–61
Heath, E. 260
Helms, R. 423
hierarchies, networks and 664–9
Hitler, A. 410
Ho Chi Minh 205, 209
Hod, M. 165, 166, 167
Hoffmann, S. 14, 261
Holbrooke, R. 638, 644
horizontal escalation 483
Horn of Africa *see* Ethiopia
hostages 245–6
Howard, M. 2, 3, 10–12, 622. *See also* Chapter 4.
human rights 461; humanitarianism and 561–2
Human Rights Watch 561
humanitarian action in war 22–3, 520–93; changing context 522–30; coordination of 573–9, 581; forms of 540–56; global expenditures on 529–30; impartiality and neutrality 545, 556–61, 583–4; key issues 556–73; legal protection for peacekeepers and humanitarian workers 571–2; security as a key aspect of 584–7; tension with human rights 561–2; tension between humanitarian priorities 582
humanitarian aid: delivery during wars 541–3; vs development aid 567–8
humanitarian budgets 529–30
Humanitarian Coordinator 576, 577
humanitarian intervention 22–3, 530–40, 585, 624, 629–30, 636–42; vs non-intervention 530–32; problems with concept 539–40; purposes and results of 536–8; questions about consistency of UN decisions on 535–6; Security Council decisions since 1991 532–4
humanitarian space 543
humanitarian workers: armed protection 568–71; legal protection 571–2; policy articulation 558–9
Hume, D. 197
Hungary 195, 408
Hunter, R. 10–12. *See also* Chapter 4.
Hurd, D. 657
Hussein, King 131, 141, 142, 158, 165, 167, 183; PLO 138; rapprochement with Nasser 158
Hussein, S. 612, 633, 648, 651, 657

I
ideology 224, 227, 445; motivation for intervention 443–4; role in relation to oil weapon 368–9
images 651
impartiality 545, 556–61; and the ethos of humanitarian work 583–4
imperialism 179
Implementation Force (IFOR) 555
imports: dependence on 329–30, 330–31; oil import dependence 330–31
India 117, 149, 394; and Asian balance of power 210, 211; and urban guerrilla warfare 15, 265, 270–71
Indian Ocean 500
indigenous arms production 506
individualism 529
Indo-China 45
Indonesia 211
industrial cities, vulnerability of 279–80
industrialisation 87, 272–3; and Iraq 364
influence, pursuit of as motivation for intervention 445–7
information: environment and strategic communications 651–4; key factor in warfare 605–10; *see also* intelligence
Ingram, J. 560
inspection: control of proliferation 93, 105; mutual troop inspection 249–50
'instrumental' approach to non-proliferation 98, 101–6
insurgency 13, 80–81, 658–61; Iraq after 2003 war 649–50, 659–60, 667
integration, European 14, 225, 256–61
intellectuals 326–7
intelligence 164; and urban guerrilla warfare 301, 303–4
interdependence 9, 44–5
internal conflict 435–43, 453
internal displacement 16, 272–5, 486, 525–6
International Assembly on Nuclear Weapons 85
International Atomic Energy Agency (IAEA) 86, 91, 96, 104, 118
International Committee of the Red Cross (ICRC) 525, 541, 568, 568–9, 577, 578; budget 529; early warning 579; fatalities 571; impartiality 556, 557, 560, 583; implementation of conventions 553, 585
International Conference on the Protection of War Victims 555
International Court of Justice 554
international criminal court 556
International Crisis Group (ICG) 579

international economic sanctions 131–2, 565–7
International Energy Agency (IEA) emergency programme 346–7
International Federation of the Red Cross and Red Crescent Societies 559
International Humanitarian Fact Finding Commission 553
International Institute for Strategic Studies (IISS) (formerly Institute for Strategic Studies) 1, 2, 3, 10–11, 26; Alastair Buchan Lecture 5; Armed Conflict Database 20; contribution of French intellectuals 14; International Assembly on Nuclear Weapons 85
international law 459–62, 623; humanitarian 552–6, 584–5
international oil companies, oil producers' control over 346
international order 220–21, 222
international system 667–8; changes in 599, 613–18; factors conducive to intervention 452–3; factors constraining intervention 459–62; factors likely to discourage future intervention 514; oil crisis and 347–8, 356–9, 376; stratification 375; types of 223–4
international tribunals 554, 556
internet 652–4
intervening states: influences on 455–9; motivations for intervention 21–2, 443–50; nature of 480; objectives 479–80; proneness to intervene 450–51
intervention 20–22, 429–519; changes 507–8; consequences of 482–91; criteria for success 479–82; definition 430–32; factors conducive to 435–53, 503–4; factors constraining 453–62, 505–7; future of 508–15; humanitarian *see* humanitarian intervention; long-term results of 474–8; outcomes of 472–91, 504–5; and political stability 487–91; prospects of 503–15; regulation of 491–503, 505; short-term results of 473–4; sources of military intervention 434–72; target environment 435–43, 453–4; tests to justify intervention 627–8; triggering 462–71
Iran 494, 538; and Iraq 361, 362, 363–4, 365; oil weapon 353, 358–9, 359, 360–63, 370–72
Iran–Iraq War 553
Iraq: and Arab–Israeli conflict 146, 158, 167, 194, 350; Gulf War of 1991 25, 600–02, 620, 639, 642; humanitarian action in war 520, 533, 536, 537–8, 548–9; insurgency 649–50, 659–60, 667; Iran and 361, 362, 363–4, 365; Iraq–Kuwait conflict 365–6, 371, 553; Israel's attack on nuclear facility 19, 402; mistakes made by US army due to ignorance of Iraqi culture 659–60; oil weapon 350, 353, 359, 363–6, 370–72; overthrow of Nuri-es-Said's government 135; Six-Day War 165, 167; Suez crisis 134; suppression of Kurds 363–4, 537–8, 624, 657; UNGCI 533, 549; war of 2003 and occupation 5, 22, 24, 26, 611–12, 619–20, 639, 648–51
Iraq Petroleum Company 17, 329, 359
Ireland: Great Famine 563; Northern Ireland 266, 278, 286
Irish Republican Army (IRA) 266, 267, 275–6, 278, 286
'irrational' leaders 398
irregular warfare 24–6, 596–7, 604, 607, 609, 636–42, 647, 666, 668–9; *see also* terrorism
Iska, Colonel 173
Islam 630–31, 665
Islamic alliance 151
Islamic Conference 498–9
Israel 190, 373, 414; Arab–Israeli conflict *see* Arab–Israeli conflict, Six-Day War; armed forces 128, 161–3, 191; attack on Iraq's nuclear facility 19, 402; celebration of founding of the state of Israel 143–4; dependence on US 419; nuclear weapons 393
Israeli army, civilianisation of 163
Italian Communist Party (PCI) 281
Italy 40

J

Jackson, G. 277
Japan 386, 619; Asian balance of power 210, 211; Japan–Canada Agreement 118; oil import dependence 17, 330–31; and oil weapon 338, 352; and urban guerrilla warfare 281, 282
Jennings, P. 656
Jerusalem 126, 127, 143; Six-Day War 169, 175
Jervis, R. 389
Jewish immigration to Palestine 125–6
Jewish State 126–9; *see also* Arab–Israeli conflict, Israel
jihadists 629, 630–31, 667; jihadist websites 654
Joffe, Brigadier-General 171, 172, 173
Johnson, L.B. 6, 11, 115–16, 117, 153, 203
Johnston Plan 137, 189–90
joint Arab command 158

Joint Evaluation of Emergency Assistance to Rwanda 564–5, 570–71
Jordan 146, 189; Anglo-Jordanian Treaty 134; armed forces 161, 193; Armistice Agreement 129, 130; assassination of Abdullah 131; defence pact with Egypt 158; diplomatic relations with Syria broken off 151; partition of Palestine 126–8; Samu raid 141; Six-Day War 160, 165, 167, 175
Jordan Valley Unified Water Plan 189
junior deterrent policy 259

K
Kamougué, Lieutenant Colonel 468, 469
Kano Accord 496
Kaplan, R.D. 659
Karmal, B. 441, 477
Kekkonen plan 108
Kemp, G. 405
Kennan, G. 199
Kennedy, J.F. 6, 35, 40, 49, 50, 63, 67; administration of 4, 38, 39, 57; and controlled response 73
Kennedy, R. 207
Kenya 484
Kenyatta, J. 492
Khan, I. 484
Khomeini, Ayatollah 665
Khrushchev, N. 34, 35, 50–51
kidnapping: as analogy 7, 81; urban guerrilla warfare 267, 276, 277–9, 315
Kissinger, H. 5, 50, 222, 233–4, 493–4
knowledge of terrain 182, 199, 301–02
Korea, South 206, 423
Korean War 203, 400
Kosovo 639–40, 644–5
Kosovo Liberation Army (KLA) 645
Kosygin, A.N. 116, 117, 140, 166
Kumin, J. 567
Kurdish Workers Party (PKK) 537–8
Kurds 363–5, 537–8, 548–9, 580, 624, 657
Kuwait: and Arab–Israeli conflict 146, 166, 167; and conflict with Iraq 365–6, 371, 553

L
Lagos Accords 468–9, 496
Laloy, J. 261
land-mines 572–3, 585
language, and strategic communication 662
Laos 201; crisis of 1961 35
Latin America 44–5, 107, 118, 200; urban guerrilla warfare 15–16, 265, 267, 269–70, 272, 274, 287; *see also under individual countries*

laws of war 552–6, 571, 573, 584–5
lead agency system 573–4
League of Nations 219, 235, 623
Lebanon 190; Arab–Israeli conflict 135, 146, 166, 167; Armistice Agreement 130–2; US intervention 511–12
legal constraints on intervention 459–62
legal protection of humanitarian workers and peacekeepers 571–2
legitimacy 222, 224; Germany 227; and intervention 431–2
Lenin, V.I. 265, 278, 282, 665
'lesser contingencies' 640–42
liberal wars 620–3; defensive and offensive 623–8
liberalism 26, 201, 615
liberation of prisoners 314
Liberia 520, 542–3
liberty, right to 623
Libya: Arab–Israeli conflict 146, 350; and Egypt 398; interventions in Chad 433, 442, 454, 456, 468–70, 473–4, 478, 496–7, 498; motivations for intervention 444–6; and oil weapon 334, 349–51, 357
light arms 294–5
limited war 75, 511, 652
Lin Piao 204
Lind, W. 608
Lisbon coup 463
Liska, G. 254
local security 661
localisation 217–18
Locarno Pact 219, 235, 243
Loescher, G. 524–5
logistics 298–9
long-range missiles 634

M
Macfarlane, N. 20–21. *See also* Chapter 10.
machine guns 129, 176, 294–6
Madrid Declaration 561, 564, 584
Maginot Line 389, 425
Magri, L. 281
Malaysia 209, 211, 271
Malloum, President 446, 459, 467–8
'Manifesto' group 281
Mao Zedong 665
Marcuse, H. 280
marginais ('marginal people') 273–4
Marighella, C. 15, 269; *Minimanual of the Urban Guerrilla* 15, 269, 289–327
Maritime Declaration 155–6
market development 358
Marxism 665
mass demonstrations 311–12

'massive retaliation' 64, 73, 74, 81, 82
Matthews, F.P. 401
Maull, H. 16–18. *See also* Chapter 8.
Mazrui, A. 529
Mazumdar, C. 270–71
McFate, M. 659
McNamara, R. 6, 73, 74–6, 200, 405, 415, 420
MDAME logistics formula 298–9
Médecins sans Frontières 541, 574
media 612, 669; conflict driven by 655–8; information environment 651–4
Mengistu Haile Mariam 465, 470
Mexico 653
Middle East 108, 244; *see also* Arab–Israeli conflict, Six-Day War
migration: enforced 582; internal displacement 16, 272–5, 486, 525–6; Jewish immigration to Palestine 124–5
militarisation strategy 269
military, role of and humanitarian action 22–23, 584–7
military assistance and intervention 430
military competence 479
military constraints on intervention 457
military expenditures 112, 385; *see also* defence expenditure
military intervention *see* intervention
military planning 59–61
military power, as spin-off from oil power 356–9
military security 216–18, 222
military strategy, transformation of 642–51
military–territorial attrition 208
Milosevic, S. 645
Minear, L. 528
Ministers of Defence 56
miscalculation 420–21, 424
missiles 94–5; long-range 634
mission creep 637–8
Mitla Pass 173
Mitrione, D. 278
mobility 300, 301–3
Mobutu Sese Seko 436, 444, 449, 492
modified bipolarity 224, 247–51
Moleiro, M. 274
Morgan, P. 415
Morocco 167
Moss, R. 15–16. *See also* Chapter 7.
motivations: of intervening actors 21, 443–50; of urban guerrillas 325–6
Movement of the Revolutionary Left (MIR) 283
Movimento Popular para a Libertação de Angola (MPLA) 435–6, 449, 463–4, 473, 474, 479, 489, 490, 492, 493, 513
Mueller, J. 639
multipolarity 384–5
mutual troop inspection 249–50
Myrdal, A. 7, 8–9. *See also* Chapter 3.

N
Nablus 170
Nacht, M. 393
Nakasone, Y. 338
Napoleon III 389
Narkiss, Brigadier-General 169, 172–3
Narodniks 266
narratives, strategic 24–5, 610–13, 669; hearts and minds 25, 658–61; networks and hierarchies 664–9
Nasser, G.A. 10, 131, 135–6, 142, 150–51, 165, 402; Arab revolution 136, 151; Arab unity 136, 137, 139–40; Good Faith Agreement 187–8; Israeli forces on Syrian border 144; rapprochement with King Hussein 158; Straits of Tiran 10, 156–7, 179–81; Suez Crisis 132, 133; UNEF 147–50, 180–81
nation, state and 615–16
national interest 113, 119
National Liberation Action (ALN) 275, 284
nationalism 514; Arab nationalism 124, 368–9; Asia 201–2; and oil weapon 368–9; and opposition to external intervention 453
NATO 2–5, 31–72, 100, 109, 199, 209, 210, 216, 385, 633; Bosnia 550–51, 555, 585, 644–5; changes in context and function 33–6; Chief of Staff of NATO 59, 60–61; Deputy Secretaries-General 58–9, 60; development of new relationship between political institutions and strategic weapons and planning 43, 53–7; enhancement of political institutions' authority 42–8; and European security system 257–8; Military Committee 55, 59; radical overhaul of institutions and machinery of 57–63; reconsideration of defence of Europe 48–53; reunification of Germany and participation in 233–4; Secretariat 42, 43, 58, 61, 62–3, 66–7; Secretary-General 42, 58, 60; and spread of nuclear weapons 395; Standing Group 55, 59; Supreme Commander Europe (SACEUR) 55, 59, 61; trends in internal relationships 36–41; US strategic nuclear weapons as source of tension 63–9
NATO Council 42–3, 45–6, 55, 66–7, 69;

proposal for reform 57–8, 59, 60, 62–3; status of members 46–8, 58
NATO deterrent 65–6
natural disasters 523–4
Naxalites 270, 271
Ne Win 197
necessity, wars of 625–6
Negev Desert 127, 129–30, 132, 136–7
nerves, war of 318–19
'net within the net' (urban guerrilla operation) 311
Netherlands, the 40; oil weapon 334, 335, 336, 339, 351
Neto, A. 474
'netwars' 608
network-centred war 605–10
networks: culture, narratives and 25, 600–13; and hierarchies 664–9
neutrality: Germany 228–30; and humanitarian action 545, 556–61, 583–4
New Zealand 206
Nigeria 453, 454, 468, 484, 496, 497
Nixon, R. 334
'no-cities' strategy 74–5, 76–9
non-aggression pledges 249
Non-Aligned Movement 498–9
non-alignment doctrine 195
non-dissemination 99–100, 101–2
non-governmental organisations (NGOs) 530, 557, 574; accountability and codes of conduct 564–5; policy advocacy 559
non-intervention principle 461–2, 530–32, 540, 597, 622–3, 625
non-proliferation 97–106
Non-Proliferation Treaty 7, 96, 97–101, 106, 118
Norstad, General 55
Northern Alliance 646
Northern Ireland 266, 278, 286, 640
Norway 40
nuclear development, stages of 402–3
nuclear energy 7–8, 86–96, 105–6
nuclear-free zones 9, 97, 118–19, 250
nuclear reactors 89
nuclear sharing, multilateral 116–17
nuclear states: arms races among 412–14; relations among 393–5; why nations want nuclear weapons 392–3
nuclear status 92
nuclear testing 93, 100–01; ban 92–3, 101–4, 118
nuclear verification 118
nuclear weapons 634; active constraints on manufacture 90–93, 101, 104–6, 117–18; and Asian balance of power 212; control of proliferation 7–9, 85–120; deterrence with small nuclear forces 401–18; and domestic stability 396–7; effects of 387–95; and European security system 244–5, 258–60; 'flexible response' 6–8, 73–84, 414; 'massive retaliation' 64, 73, 74, 81, 82; and NATO and defence of Europe 48–53; nuclear future 424–5; political aspects of proliferation 97–112; positive aspects of measured spread of 383–425; proliferation of 18–19, 112–19; and regional stability 397–401; roles and reactions of great powers 418–21; shorter-range nuclear weapons 52, 54, 70; Soviet–US parity 48–9; technological aspects of proliferation 85–96; US strategic nuclear weapons as source of tension in NATO 63–9; why nations want nuclear weapons 392–3
Nuri-es-Said 135
Nye, J. 423

O
Obasanjo, General 442
objectives: of intervening actors 479–80; of urban guerrilla warfare 305–6
occupation: Iraq 648–50; urban guerrilla warfare 277, 310
offensive liberal wars 623–8
offensive weapons 113; oil weapon as 370–75
officers 162–3
Ogaden 438, 464–5, 475, 476
Ogata, S. 547
oil 88; access to and intervention 512–13; dependence on oil imports 17, 330–31; exporters 380, 381; price 354, 373; producer solidarity 349–51, 353–4; production cutbacks 334–5, 350; revenues 349–50, 354–6; as a weapon *see* oil power, oil weapon
oil consumption 336, 337, 341–3
oil distribution system 343, 344–7
oil diplomacy 376
oil power 17, 328, 380; development of 340–43; monetary dimension 354–6; potential and limitations in the future 340–51; wider context of 351–9
oil weapon 16–18, 328–82, 512–13; application of 334–5; and Arab–Israeli conflict 17–18, 156, 329, 334, 337–8, 350, 370; ceiling of 347; effectiveness of 335–40; impact of applying 348–9; intentions behind 359–75; possible future application of 369–75; precision of 343–7; who could apply it 352–4

Olympic Games boycott 499
Organisation of African Unity (OAU) 501–2; Angola 492–4; Chad 468, 469, 470, 495–8; Ethiopia 494–5
Organisation of American States 41
Organisation of Arab Petroleum Exporting Countries (OAPEC) 334–5, 349–50, 351, 353, 380–81
Organisation for Economic Co-operation and Development (OECD) 33; humanitarian budgets 529–30
Organisation of Petroleum Exporting Countries (OPEC) 328, 353, 354, 374; production and revenues 354, 355
Organization of Raw Material Exporting Countries 374
Oromo nationalism 438
Orwell, G., *1984* 653
Osgood, R.E. 246
Ottaway, D. 476
Ottaway, M. 476
Ottoman Empire 615
outlaws 289, 319
Oxfam 529, 530, 541, 542, 568

P

Pacheco Areco, President 285
Pakistan 211, 362, 394, 414, 423, 485; defence expenditure 484
Palestine 124–31; British Mandate 125, 127, 128, 182; Jewish immigration to 125–6; partition 126, 127; *see also* Arab–Israeli conflict, Six-Day War
Palestine 'Entity' 138
Palestine Liberation Organisation (PLO) 138, 147, 365
Palestine Rejection Front 365
Palestinian refugees 131
Pando, occupation of 276–7, 277
Partial Nuclear Test Ban 114
partition: Germany 228–30, 230–32; Palestine 125, 127
passive constraints on the spread of nuclear technology 89–90
Patriotic Union of Kurdistan (PUK) 538
Pearson, L.B. 7, 9, 134. *See also* Chapter 3.
peasants 326
Peel Commission 125
People's Democratic Party (PDP) 441, 466
People's Revolutionary Vanguard (VPR) 284
people's war, theory of 204–5
Pérez de Cuéllar, J. 548
Pericles 81
peripheral strategy 208

Perón, J. 274
Persian Gulf 358–9, 361–2, 370–72; Gulf War of 1991 25, 600–02, 624, 639, 642
Peru 287
Petkoff, T. 284
Pfleiderer, G. 235
Philippines 206, 211
Pinilla, R. 274
planning 44–5, 61–2; political institutions in NATO and 43, 53–7
plutonium 89, 91, 105
Poland 108, 238; workers' strikes 408
Polaris submarines 67
policy articulation 558–9
policy vacuums 559
political context, Clausewitzian principle of 11, 178
political kidnappings 276, 277–8, 315
political–military agreements 220–21
politics: political aspects of non-proliferation 97–112; spin 610–11
Popular Front for the Liberation of Oman (PFLO) 361
population movements *see* migration
populist demagogues 274
Portugal 40, 45–6, 462, 463
Powell, C. 640
power 613–14; asymmetric distribution of and intervention 452; oil power *see* oil power; strategy and 598–9
precision guidance 602
pre-emption 163–5, 387–9, 401, 403–6, 604
pre-industrial cities, urban violence in 15–16, 269
preventive strikes 387–8, 401–3, 406
priests 327
prisoners, liberation of 314
proliferation of nuclear weapons *see* nuclear weapons
Proliferation Security Initiative (PSI) 9
prolongation of wars 562–3
propaganda, armed 16, 276–7, 277, 317–18
prosperity 224, 227
protection: armed protection of humanitarian workers 568–71; key aspect of humanitarian action 584–7; legal protection of humanitarian workers and peacekeepers 571–2
Provisional IRA 275–6, 630
Prussia 163
psychological warfare 611
public diplomacy 662–4
public opinion: media and 655–8; and terrorism 266–7, 280–83, 323–5

Q

Qaddafi, M. el- *see* Gadhafi
Quadrennial Defense Review Report (QDR) 603–4, 606, 619, 632, 635
Quarles, D.A. 412

R

Rabin, General 143, 144, 169
radical foreign policy 398–9
radical movements 666
radical regimes (leftist regimes) 513
radio 653
Rafi party 142, 159
raids 309
Rapacki plan 108, 228
Rapid Deployment Force 457, 478, 500
rationality 377, 407
raw materials, access to 512–13
'real war' 640–41
realism, international 613–14
reciprocal stabilisation of existing alliances 248–51
Record, J. 639
redoubt strategy 208–10
refugee camps 526
refugees 131, 484–5, 524–6
regional actors: consequences of intervention on 483–91; as constraints on intervention 455–6
Regional Co-operation for Development Programme 362
regional security, intervention and 20–21, 429–519
regional stability 397–401
regionalism: opposition to intervention 454; political and military problems and non-proliferation 106–9; regional pacts within European security system 243; within NATO 40–41
'regular warfare' 25, 129, 668
regulation of intervention 491–503, 505
relative deprivation 16, 275
relative strength of adversaries 390–91
relief supplies during war 541–3
resources, absorption of adversary's 204–5
reunification of Germany 228–30, 230–32, 233–4
revolution 218
revolution in military affairs (RMA) 23–4, 599, 600–03, 606, 632–4
Revolutionary Action Movement (RAM) 279–80
Revolutionary Force 268
Riad, General 158
Rice, C. 641–2
Richardson, J.L. 258

right to bear arms 21
Rikhye, Major-General 147, 148
riots 278
Roberts, A. 22–3. *See also* Chapter 11.
Robles, A.G. 9
Roger, P. 440
Rolin, H. 214
Ronfeldt, D. 608, 610
Rosen, J. 612
Rosen, S.J. 409
Rostow, W. 204
Rumsfeld, D. 603–4, 649, 662–3
Rusk, D. 155, 174
Russia 266, 625; *see also* Soviet Union
Rwanda 520, 535, 538, 554, 574, 580; Joint Evaluation of Emergency Assistance to 564–5, 570–71; UNAMIR 533–4, 570

S

sabotage 315–17
Sadat, A. 398
Saddam Hussein *see* Hussein, S.
safeguards (nuclear) 90–3, 95, 101, 104–6, 117–18
safety zones 530, 547–51, 586–7
Safire, W. 663
SALT II Treaty 499
Samu raid 141
sanctions, economic 131–2, 134, 565–6
Saphire, J. 160
Sarajevo 544, 550, 551, 580, 644
Saudi Arabia: and Arab–Israeli conflict 127, 139, 146, 167; and oil weapon 353, 356, 359, 365–6, 366–8, 370–2
Save the Children Fund 541
Scales, R.H., Jr 609, 660
Scandinavia 108
Schelling, T.C. 5–7, 407, 415. *See also* Chapter 2.
Schelling Point 7
Schlesinger, J.R. 339, 417
Schlieffen Plan 387
Schmidt, H. 3, 240
Schwarzkopf, N. 573
search and destroy strategy 659
Seaton, J. 655
Second World War 126, 200, 390, 410
security: ambiguity of concept 216–18; European security system *see* European security system; as a key aspect of humanitarian action 584–7; local security and hearts and minds strategy 661; as motivation for intervention 448–9; offensive force and 387; oil weapon and

339–40; safety zones 530, 547–51, 586–7; and urban guerrillas 321–2
security assurances 117
security research institutions 10
seizures, arms 312–14
selectivity 535–6
self-defence 216–17, 223, 240–41
self-determination, right to 623
self-help systems 387–92
separatist uprisings 15, 269
September 11 terrorist attacks 23, 628, 636, 648
Serbia 645
SHAPE 44, 55, 57, 59
Sharm-el-Sheikh 10, 147–8, 150–51
Sharon, Brigadier-General 171, 172, 173–4
Shatt el-Arab waterway 361, 362
Shelton, H.H. 639–40
Shi'ites 548, 624
Shinseki, E.K. 649
shooting 296–7
short-range nuclear weapons 70
Shukeiry, A. 138
Shulman, M. 260
Simmel, G. 390
Sinai 158, 170, 175
Singapore 209, 211, 271
Six-Day War 11–12, 121–94, 199–200; armed forces 161–3, 191–4; course of the war 160–78; immediate origins 143–60; oil weapon 16–18, 328
Slessor, J. 3
slum-dwellers 274
small deterrent forces 401–18; credibility 406–9
small nuclear powers 404; great powers and 418–21
Smoke, R. 415
Snyder, G. 407
social cohesion 479
socialism 615
Somalia: humanitarian action 22, 520, 533, 536, 538, 545–6, 554, 580; intervention in Ethiopia 444, 456, 464–5, 475, 476, 506; OAU and regulation of intervention 494–5; Soviet loss of facilities in 476; UNITAF 533; UNOSOM II 533, 538
South Africa 432, 444, 448, 449, 463, 484
South Korea 206, 423
South West Africa People's Organization (SWAPO) 448
Southeast Asia Treaty Organisation (SEATO) 208, 209
sovereignty, principle of 461–2, 482–3, 531–2, 540, 622–3

Soviet Union 74, 87, 89, 351, 507; and Arab–Israeli conflict 135, 140–42, 144, 153, 166, 174–5, 180, 200–01; and Asian balance of power 200–01, 203; balance of power between NATO and 35–6, 52–3; bipolarity see bipolarity; challenges to the West and function of NATO 34–6; collapse of communism in eastern Europe 615; commitment to world revolution 445; constraints on intervention 457–9; co-operation with US 251; cut-off of fissile materials for military purposes 105; and European balance of power 197–8; and European security system 214–16, 221–2, 232, 236, 239, 240, 246, 251, 252–3, 254, 255–6; future of interventionism of 480, 508–10; and German reunification and arms control 232–3; intervention in Afghanistan 20–21, 433, 442, 467, 473, 477–8, 498–500, 507, 508–9; intervention in Angola 432, 463–4, 473, 474–5; intervention in Ethiopia 433, 465–6, 473, 475–7; Iran and 361; Iraq and 364–5; motivations for intervention 443–4, 445–6, 447–8, 449–50; NATO and evaluation of policy 44; nuclear parity with US 48–9; power balance with US 114; and relations among nuclear nations 393; and spread of nuclear weapons 418–21, 422; Treaty of Berlin 235; and Western radio 653
spin 610–11
Srebrenica 549–50, 551
stability: domestic 396–7; intervention and 487–91; regional 397–401
Stalin, J. 198, 210
state, nation and 615–16
steam power 86
Stevenson, A. 47
'stiffening' riots and strikes, as urban guerrilla tactic 278
Stockholm International Peace Research Institute (SIPRI) 8
stockpiles 105; reduction of 92–3
Stockwell, J. 494
Stoller, M. 655
Straits of Tiran 10, 132–4, 151–7, 174, 180–1
strategic communications see communications
strategic minerals 513
strategic motivations 447–9
strategic narratives see narratives
strategy, power and 598–9

stratification of the international system 375
Strauss, F.J. 52
street tactics 310–12
strikes 278, 312
'Struggle Against Violent Extremism' (SAVE) 629
students 280–82, 326
Students for a Democratic Society (SDS) 281
sub-bloc associations 236–9
submarines 67
subversion of security forces 16, 277–9
Sudan 146, 166, 167, 484
Suez crisis 9, 17, 132–5, 329
suicide bombers 596
superpowers: attitude of adversaries and intervention 455; capacity and will to use force and regulation of intervention 502–3; and intervention 455, 483; roles and reactions and spread of nuclear weapons 418–21; *see also* Soviet Union, United States of America (USA)
'surgical' interventions 479
surprise 300–01
Survival 1
swarming 664
Sweden 108
Sykes-Picot agreement 124
Syria 190, 350; armed forces 161, 193–4; Armistice Agreement 129, 130; Ba'athist Party 136; Demilitarized Zone 140–41; diplomatic relations with Jordan broken off 151; El Fatah raids 140, 143; MiG fighter aircraft shot down 141–2; military coup of 1961 136; and partition of Palestine 127; rumours of Israeli attack on 144–5, 180; Six-Day War 166, 167–71, 175–7

T
Tal, Brigadier-General 171–4
Taliban regime 645–8
tankers 345
tanks 161, 170–74
Taraki, N.M. 466
Tawney, R.H. 261
Taylor, A.J.P. 226
technical aid 89–90
technical preparation 293–4, 325–6
technological advance 86–8, 390, 601–2, 634, 653
technological terrorism 15, 269, 279–80
technology: nuclear 85–96, of violence 81
teleseismological detection 102
terrain, knowledge of 162, 300, 301

terrorism 317, 667; character of terrorist 16, 275–7; 'global war on terror' 23, 628–32, 645–51; as political weapon 265–8; and public opinion 266–7, 280–83, 323–5; September 11 attacks 23, 628, 636, 648; state-sponsored 635–6; technological terrorism 15, 269, 279–80; *see also* urban guerrilla warfare, al-Qaeda
test ban treaty 92–3, 102–06, 118
Thailand 206, 209, 211, 271
Thomson, G. 153
Thucydides 6, 76
Tiberias, Lake 136–7, 144
time lag, and oil weapon 348
Tiran, Straits of 10, 132–4, 147, 151–8, 174, 178–9, 185–8
Tocqueville, A. de 275
Tombalbaye, President 446, 467, 489–90
Tora Bora caves 646–7
training 164; urban guerrilla 293–4, 325–6
transformation of strategic affairs 24–6, 595–677; asymmetric war 626, 632–42; grand strategy 598–9, 613–32; military strategy 642–51; networks, culture and narratives 25, 600–13; strategic communications 25, 651–69
treaty approach to non-proliferation 97–101, 106
Treaty of Berlin 235
Treaty of Westphalia 623
Triangle Institute of Security Studies 639
troop inspection, mutual 249–50
troops, physical presence of 245–6
Trudeau, P. 285
Truman, H.S. 203
Truong Chinh 207
trusteeship 551–2
Tucker, R.W. 246
Tunisia 146, 167
Tupamaros (National Liberation Movement of Uruguay) 266, 275, 276, 277–8, 285
Turkey 40, 537–8
Turkish People's Liberation Army 266

U
U Thant 148–9, 154, 156, 188–9
Ulster 266, 278, 286
uncertainty 391
underclass 273–4
underground testing 93, 100–01; ban on 92–3, 101–4, 118
União Nacional para a Independência Total de Angola (UNITA) 432, 435, 463, 474, 492
Unified Task Force (UNITAF) 533
unilateral application of oil weapon 352–4

unipolarity 223
unit veto system 216–17, 223, 240–41
United Kingdom 89, 482, 650; accession to EEC and special relationship with USA 40–41; and Arab–Israeli conflict 10, 124–6, 129, 133, 134, 152–3, 154–5, 165–6, 174, 180; IRA terrorism 266, 267, 275–6, 278, 286; and Jewish immigration to Palestine 126; and NATO 37, 38, 39–40, 46, 56, 64–5, 68–9, 70–71; and nuclear deterrent 64–5, 66, 68–9, 392–3, 395; Palestine Mandate 125, 127, 129, 183; Suez Crisis 132–5
United Nations 9, 35, 44, 61, 615, 623, 650; administration and trusteeship 551–2; Charter 460, 501, 535; coordination of humanitarian action 573–4, 574–5, 578–9; dedicated force to protect humanitarian operations 569–70; role of in disarmament 111; economic sanctions 565–7; impartiality 560; lead agency system 573–4; regulation of intervention 500–01; Special Committee on Palestine 127; Suez crisis 132
United Nations Assistance Mission for Rwanda (UNAMIR) 533–4, 570
United Nations Consolidated Inter-Agency Humanitarian Assistance Appeals 576
United Nations Department of Humanitarian Affairs (DHA) 575, 575–8, 578, 579, 581
United Nations Development Programme (UNDP) 569, 577
United Nations Emergency Force (UNEF) 134, 147–50, 180–81, 186–9
United Nations General Assembly 117, 133, 498, 500, 534; and Arab–Israeli conflict 134; and international law 460; and Palestinian refugees 131
United Nations Guards Contingent in Iraq (UNGCI) 533, 549
United Nations High Commissioner for Refugees (UNHCR) 526, 562, 575, 577, 578, 582; budget 529; expenditure 524, 525; safety zones 548; Sarajevo airlift 544
United Nations Humanitarian Security Police 569
United Nations Operation in Somalia (UNOSOM II) 533, 538
United Nations peacekeeping forces 562, 586; legal protection 571–2; use for humanitarian purposes 543–7; *see also under individual names*
United Nations Protection Force (UNPROFOR) 533, 537, 538, 546, 550–51, 555

United Nations Security Council (UNSC) 498, 500, 548, 555, 571, 584, 620; Arab–Israeli conflict 153–4, 166, 174–5; changes in practice and humanitarian issues 526–8; decisions since 1991 532–4; humanitarian intervention 531, 539, 540, 585; Humanitarian Sub-Committee 565; implementation of international humanitarian law 553–4; Presidential Statement on Peacekeeping 544; questions about consistency of decisions 535–6; sanctions 565–7
United Nations Truce Supervision Organisation (UNTSO) 141, 144, 167
United Nations volunteers 569–70
United States of America (USA) 3–4, 34, 71, 89, 595; Angola's relations with 475; and Arab–Israeli conflict 10, 135–6, 152–3, 155, 160, 165–6, 174, 175, 180; and Asian balance of power 13–14, 199–210; bipolarity *see* bipolarity; changing attitude to interventionism 507; containment and Asia 199–205; containment and Europe 199; controlled response 73–4, 74–6; co-operation with Soviet Union 251; cut-off of fissile materials for military purposes 105; dependence on oil imports 17, 330–31; development of official strategic thinking 600–05; domestic constraints on intervention 458–9, 480; and European security system 215–16, 224, 232, 238, 239, 241, 247–8, 251, 253, 256, 258–9; and French nuclear deterrent 83; future of interventionism 510–12; grand strategy 618–20; Gulf War of 1991 25, 600–02, 620, 639, 642; and humanitarian action 541, 544; impact of Soviet intervention in Afghanistan 478; influence of American policy on NATO planning 53–7; intervention in Angola 462–3, 464, 494; intervention in Rwanda 570; intervention in Somalia 22, 533; Iran and 361; Iraq war of 2003 and occupation 5, 21, 24, 26, 611–12, 619–20, 639, 648–51; military assistance to Ethiopia terminated 464, 465; mistakes in Iraq due to ignorance of Iraqi culture 659–60; NATO and defence of Europe 50–52; oil weapon 334–5, 335–6, 337, 347–8, 350–51, 353; policy process 67–8; population movements in 274–5; power balance with Soviet Union 113–14; QDR 603–5, 606, 619, 632, 635; quotas on Jewish immigration 126; Rapid Deployment Force 457, 478, 500; regulation of intervention 493–4, 495,

498, 499–500; relations with other nuclear nations 393–4; relationship with Cuba 510; relationship with European NATO allies 5–6, 36–9; right to bear arms 21; Soviet–US nuclear parity 48–9; and spread of nuclear weapons 418–21, 422–3; strategic communication 662–4; strategic nuclear weapons as source of tension in NATO 63–9; transformation of strategic affairs 24–6, 595–677; urban guerrilla warfare 268, 278–9, 279–80, 281–2, 282–3, 286–7; Vietnam War *see* Vietnam War; violence between settlers and Native Americans 80; 'war on terror' 24, 628–32, 645–51; wartime relief supply plan for Germany 541
unofficial organisations 574–5
uranium-235 91
urban guerrilla warfare 15–16, 265–327; 'action models' 306–19; arms 294–6; common errors of urban guerrillas 323; definition of urban guerrilla 289–90; initial advantages of urban guerrillas 300–05; limits of urban violence 279–87; logistics 298–9; method for carrying out action 319–20; *Minimanual of the Urban Guerrilla* 269, 289–327; objectives 305–6; patterns 271–7; personal qualities and subsistence of urban guerrillas 290–93; popular support 266–7, 280–83, 323–5; selection of guerrillas 325–7; shooting 296–7; technical preparation 293–4, 325–6; technique 299–300; varieties of urban militancy 268–77
urban violence in pre-industrial cities 15, 269
urbanisation 272–4
Urquhart, B. 569
Uruguay 269, 275, 283, 285
USS *Liberty* 175
Ustinov, D. 446

V
Valenta, J. 467
Vallières, P. 276
Van Riper, P. 606
Venezuela 283, 283–4
verification (nuclear) 118
verification by challenge 9, 102
'victim strategy' 655–6
Viet Cong 267
Vietnam 201
Vietnam War 13–14, 199–200, 206, 207–8, 244–5, 459, 507; and casualty aversion 639; costs of to USA 203–5; gang warfare 81; media and public disillusionment 651
Volunteers of America 268
Vukovar 656
vulnerability: of industrial cities 279–80; of personnel involved in humanitarian action 545

W
Waltz, K.N. 18–19, 489. *See also* Chapter 9.
war: complex emergencies 22–3, 522–4; controlled response and strategic warfare 5–7, 73–84; decline in incidence 668; humanitarian action *see* humanitarian action in war; laws of 552–6, 584–5; liberal wars 620–28; network-centred or culture-centred 605–10; nuclear weapons and frequency and intensity of 415–18; obsolescence incorrectly predicted 595–6; possible prolongation by humanitarian action 562–3; slow-mobilisation type of warfare 244
war crimes 555–6
war-deterring capabilities 412–13
war-fighting capabilities 412–13, 416, 421
'war of nerves' 318–19
'war on terror' 23, 628–32; transformation of military strategy 645–51
warning, early 578–9
Warnke, P. 415
Warsaw Pact 109, 216
Warsaw Uprising 563
water diversion schemes 137–8, 189–90
weak states 20–21
weapons/arms: capture of 313–14; diversions of 312–13; Germany and armament 228–30, 232–4; nuclear *see* nuclear weapons; spin-off from oil power 358; and urban guerrillas 294–6
weapons of mass destruction (WMD) 636, 648
Weathermen 266, 268, 275, 276, 281–2
Wehner, H. 230, 231
Weinberger, C. 627
Weiss, T.G. 528
Weizmann, E. 165–6
West Bank 170
West Germany *see* German Federal Republic
Western European defence community 238–9, 250–51, 256–8
Western hegemony 617
Wheeler, E.G. 417
'white helmets' 569–70
White Revolution 360
Wiesner Committee report 103

Williams, R.A. 279–80
Wilson, H. 153
Windsor, P. 232
Wohlstetter, A. 3, 49, 63, 410
Wolfers, A. 242–3
Wolfowitz, P. 647, 649
women 326–7
work interruptions 312
workers 326

Y
Yamani, Sheikh 334
Yarmolinsky, A. 457
Yarmuk River 137, 189–90

Yemen 167
Young, O. 443
Yugoslavia 237; former Yugoslavia 554, 625, 656; *see also* Bosnia

Z
Zaire 484, 520; intervention in Angola 432, 444, 448–9, 449, 462–3
Zapatistas 653
Zarqawi, Abu M. al- 655, 667
Zawahiri, A. al- 655, 667
Zepa 550, 551
Zionist Organisation 124
Zuckerman, S. 7–8, 18. *See also* Chapter 3.